TREATISE

ON THE

LAW OF PRIVATE CORPORATIONS

AGGREGATE.

BY

JOSEPH K. ANGELL AND SAMUEL AMES.

SEVENTH EDITION.

REVISED, CORRECTED, AND ENLARGED,

BY

JOHN LATHROP,
OF THE BOSTON BAR.

THE LAWBOOK EXCHANGE, LTD.
Clark, New Jersey

ISBN 978-1-58477-473-0

Lawbook Exchange edition 2005, 2020

The quality of this reprint is equivalent to the quality of the original work.

The Lawbook Exchange, Ltd.
33 Terminal Avenue
Clark, New Jersey 07066-1321

Please see our website for a selection of our other publications and fine facsimile reprints of classic works of legal history:
www.lawbookexchange.com

Library of Congress Cataloging-in-Publication Data

Angell, Joseph Kinnicut, 1794-1857.
Treatise of the law of private corporations aggregate / by Joseph K. Angell and Samuel Ames.— 7th ed., rev., corr., and enl. / by John Lathrop.
p. cm.
Originally published: 7th ed., rev., corr., and enl. / by John Lathrop. Boston: Little, Brown & Co., 1861.
Includes bibliographical references and index.
ISBN 1-58477-473-8 (cloth: alk. paper)
1. Corporation law—United States. I. Title: Law of private corporations. II. Ames, Samuel, 1806-1865.
III. Lathrop, John, 1835-1910. IV. Title.

KF1414.A752004
346.73 '0668—dc22
2004048662

Printed in the United States of America on acid-free paper

TREATISE

ON THE

LAW OF PRIVATE CORPORATIONS

AGGREGATE.

BY

JOSEPH K. ANGELL AND SAMUEL AMES.

SEVENTH EDITION.

REVISED, CORRECTED, AND ENLARGED,

BY

JOHN LATHROP,
OF THE BOSTON BAR.

BOSTON:
LITTLE, BROWN AND COMPANY.
1861.

CAMBRIDGE:
Allen and Farnham, Printers.

PREFACE

TO THE FIRST EDITION.

The reader does not require to be told, that we have in our country an almost infinite number of corporations aggregate, which have no concern whatever (other than as artificial inhabitants) with affairs of a municipal nature. These associations we not only find scattered throughout every cultivated part of the United States, but so engaged are they in all the varieties of useful pursuit, that we see them directing the concentration of mind and capital to the advancement of religion and morals; to the diffusion of literature, science, and the arts; to the prosecution of plans of internal communication and improvement; and to the encouragement and extension of the great interests of commerce, agriculture, and manufactures. There is a great difference, in this respect, between our own country and the country from which we have derived a great portion of our laws. What is done in England by combination, unless it be the management of municipal concerns, is most generally done by a combination of individuals, established by mere articles of agreement. On the other hand, what is done here by the coöperation of several persons, and by the combination of their capital, industry, and skill, is, in the greater number of instances, the result of a consolidation effected by an express act or charter of incorporation. Hence, as has been remarked by a learned judge,[1] the quantity of that kind of business, which may be brought into our courts, will be much greater than that which comes before the English courts. It is true, that there are cited in the following treatise a great number of English decisions; but they are, in general, cases of municipal corporations, and which have been referred to for the purpose of illustrating principles which govern bodies politic, whether public or private.

While, therefore, the reason is plain why so little attention has been devoted by English authors to the law of private corporations, we cannot but be impressed with a deep sense of the importance of this law in our own country. Indeed, the inconvenience experienced from the want of a work of reference upon the legal rights and obligations, which grow out of the relations between a body corporate and the public, and between a body corporate and its members, has hitherto in this country long been a subject of complaint. The design of the authors, in undertaking their arduous and uninviting task, was to supply this deficiency in our *bibliotheca legum*, as far as their qualifications would permit.

The first English work, which has professed to be exclusively and systematically devoted to corporation law, is that of Mr. Kyd, published in London, in 1793. The author just named assumed to treat generally of the law of corporations; but his work, for the reason adverted to, is chiefly made up of authorities and precedents that relate to municipal institutions; and yet, by reporting adjudged cases at length, he has swelled his work into two considerable octavo volumes. The production of Mr. Kyd is very far from meeting the wants of the profession in America at this day; *first*, because it is confined principally to municipal corpora-

---

[1] The late C. J. Tilghman, of Pennsylvania, in Commonwealth *v.* Arrison, 15 S. & R. 131.

tions; *secondly*, because corporation law had not attained its present perfection in England, when Mr. Kyd wrote; and, *thirdly*, because important changes, both silent and declaratory, have been made in this country, as regards the law of private corporations. It has long been the aim of our courts to apply the old principles of the common law upon the subject of corporations, with such modifications as are suited to the views of an enlightened age. "With the multiplication of corporations," says one of the judges of a sister State, "which has, and is, taking place to an almost indefinite extent, there has been a corresponding change in the law respecting them;" and he adds, that "this change of law has arisen from that silent legislation by the people themselves, which is continually going on in a country such as ours, the more wholesome, because it is gradual, and wisely adapted to the peculiar situation, wants, and habits of our citizens."[1]

Mr. Kyd's work remained for a long time the only English work upon the subject. In 1827, appeared the treatise of Mr. Willcock, which is more limited in its plan than the former; it is not only confined to municipal corporations, but the author avows, that he does not pretend to consider the power of a corporation to take, hold, and transmit property, make contracts, &c. As far as the treatise of Mr. Willcock goes, it is very faithfully prepared; and we cannot, in justice, refrain from conceding the obligations we owe him for references to English authorities upon the subjects of mandamus and quo warranto, the disfranchisement and amotion of members and officers, and the concurrence, required to do corporate acts.

PROVIDENCE, R. I., Nov. 11, 1831.

---

[1] Rogers, J., in Bushel *v.* Commonwealth Insurance Co. 15 S. & R. 176, 177.

CONTENTS.

[The references are made to the sections.]

INTRODUCTION.

CHAPTER I.

MEANING, SEVERAL KINDS, AND HISTORY OF PRIVATE CORPORATIONS.

CHAPTER II.

IN WHAT MANNER AND BY WHOM PRIVATE CORPORATIONS MAY BE CREATED.

CHAPTER III.

HOW THE BODY CORPORATE IS CONSTITUTED; AND OF ITS NAME, PLACE, MODE OF ACTION, POWERS, &C.

CHAPTER IV.

OF THE ADMISSION AND ELECTION OF MEMBERS AND OFFICERS.

CHAPTER V.

OF THE POWER OF A CORPORATION TO TAKE, HOLD, TRANSMIT IN SUCCESSION, AND ALIENATE PROPERTY.

CHAPTER VI.

OF PROPRIETORS OF COMMON AND UNDIVIDED LANDS.

CHAPTER VII.

OF THE COMMON SEAL AND OF THE DEEDS OF A CORPORATION.

CHAPTER VIII.

OF THE MODE IN WHICH A CORPORATION MAY CONTRACT, AND WHAT CONTRACTS IT MAY MAKE.

CHAPTER IX.

OF AGENTS OF CORPORATIONS, THEIR MODE OF APPOINTMENT, AND POWER.

CHAPTER X.

OF THE BY-LAWS OF CORPORATIONS.

CHAPTER XI.

OF THE POWER TO SUE AND THE LIABILITY TO BE SUED.

CHAPTER XII.

OF DISFRANCHISEMENT AND AMOTION OF MEMBERS AND OFFICERS.

CHAPTER XIII.

OF THE BURDENS TO WHICH THE BODY CORPORATE IS SUBJECT AND OF ITS LIABILITY TO BE TAXED.

CHAPTER XIV.

OF THE CORPORATE MEETINGS, AND OF THE CONCURRENCE NECESSARY TO DO CORPORATE ACTS.

CHAPTER XV.

OF SUBSCRIPTIONS FOR, AND ASSESSMENTS UPON, SHARES IN JOINT-STOCK CORPORATIONS.

CHAPTER XVI.

OF THE NATURE AND TRANSFER OF STOCK IN JOINT INCORPORATED COMPANIES.

CHAPTER XVII.

OF THE PERSONAL LIABILITY OF THE MEMBERS OF JOINT-STOCK INCORPORATED COMPANIES FOR THE DEBTS OF THE CORPORATION.

CHAPTER XVIII.

OF THE PROCESS, PLEADINGS, AND EVIDENCE, IN SUITS BY AND AGAINST CORPORATIONS, AT LAW AND IN EQUITY.

CHAPTER XIX.

OF THE VISITATORIAL POWER.

CHAPTER XX.

OF THE WRIT OF MANDAMUS.

CHAPTER XXI.

OF INFORMATIONS IN THE NATURE OF QUO WARRANTO.

CHAPTER XXII.

OF THE DISSOLUTION AND REVIVAL OF A CORPORATION.

TABLE OF CASES

CITED AND REFERRED TO IN THE FOLLOWING TREATISE.

[The references are to the sections.]

AMERICAN CASES.

A.

D.

E.

F.

G.

H.

I.

N.

O.

P.

Q.

R.

ENGLISH CASES.

INTRODUCTION.

§ 1. The Meaning and Properties of a Corporation. A corporation is a body, created by law, composed of individuals united under a common name, the members of which succeed each other, so that the body continues the same, notwithstanding the change of the individuals who compose it, and is, for certain purposes, considered as a natural person.[1]

§ 2. The definition, which Mr. Kyd has offered of the meaning of a corporation, is more descriptive: "A corporation, or a body politic, or body incorporate, is a collection of many individuals united in one body, under a *special denomination*, having perpetual succession under an artificial form, and vested by the policy of the law with the capacity of acting, in several respects, as an individual, particularly of taking and granting property, of contracting obligations, and of suing and being sued; of enjoying privileges and immunities *in common*, and of exercising a variety of political rights, more or less extensive, according to the design of its institution, or the powers conferred upon it, either at the time of its creation, or at any subsequent period of its existence."[2]

§ 3. The following, yet more extended description of a corporation, is given by Chief Justice Marshall, in the celebrated case of Dartmouth College *v.* Woodward:[3] "A corporation," says the Chief Justice, "is an artificial being, invisible, intangible, and existing only in contemplation of law. Being the mere creature of law, it possesses only those

---

[1] Browne's Civil Law, 99; Civil Code of Louisiana, tit. 10, ch. 1, art. 418; 2 Kent, Com. 215.

[2] 1 Kyd on Corp. 13.

[3] 4 Wheat. 636.

properties, which the charter of its creation confers upon it, either expressly, or as incidental to its very existence. These are such as are supposed best calculated to effect the object for which it was created. Among the most important are *immortality*, and, if the expression may be allowed, *individuality;* properties, by which a perpetual succession of many persons are considered as the same, and may act as a single individual. They enable a corporation to manage its own affairs, and to hold property without the perplexing intricacies, the hazardous and endless necessity of perpetual conveyances for the purpose of transmitting it from hand to hand. It is chiefly for the purpose of clothing bodies of men in succession, with these qualities and capacities, that corporations were invented, and are in use. By these means a perpetual succession of individuals are capable of acting for the promotion of the particular object, like one immortal being. But this being does not share in the civil government of the country, unless that be the purpose for which it was created. Its immortality no more confers on it political power, or a political character, than immortality would confer such a power or character on a natural person. It is no more a State instrument, than a natural person, exercising the same powers, would be." In a subsequent case, the same learned Judge says: "The great object of an incorporation is to bestow the character and properties of individuality on a collective and changing body of men."[1]

§ 4. Blackstone defines a corporation to be a *franchise*, "and each individual of the corporation," he says, "is also said to have a franchise, or *freedom*." The word "franchise," in its most extensive sense, is expressive of great political rights, as the right of being tried by a jury, the right a man may have to an office, and the right of suffrage. It is in this sense that the word is applied by Blackstone, when defining a corporation, and not in the less general and more appropriate sense of the exclusive exercise of some right, or the sole enjoyment of some profit, as the right to wrecks, or the privilege of a fair, or a market. "A corporation," says Mr. Kyd, "is a political person, capable, like a natural person, of enjoying a variety of franchises; it is to a franchise as the substance to its attribute; it is something to which many attributes belong, but is itself something distinct from those attributes."[2] "Franchises are special privileges conferred by government on individu-

---

[1] Providence Bank *v.* Billings, 4 Pet. 562.
[2] Bl. Com. 37; 1 Kyd, 15.

als, and which do not belong to the citizens of the country generally of common right; and, in this country, no franchise can be held, which is not derived from the law of the State."[1]

§ 5. The words *corporation* and *incorporation* are frequently confounded, particularly in the old books. The distinction between them is, however, obvious; the one is a political institution; the other only the *act* by which that institution is created.

§ 6. When a corporation is said to be a *person*, it is understood to be so only in certain respects, and for certain purposes, for it is strictly a *political* institution. The construction is, that when "persons" are mentioned in a statute, corporations are included if they fall within the general reason and design of the statute.[2] It is governed by the existing laws, in force at the time of its creation, in reference to ownership of property and the contracting of obligations, in the same manner as natural persons, except in so far as such laws are modified and changed by its charter.[3] Therefore, a corporation has been deemed a person within the meaning of the attachment laws of Alabama.[4] The same relation of debtor and creditor, in fact, subsists (unless otherwise specially restrained by the charter, or by a statute) between them, where a corporation is either the one or the other, as between individuals. A corporation, for instance, may, in insolvent circumstances, assign its property to trustees for the benefit of creditors, as well as a natural person.[5] But a trading corporation is not a person within the meaning of

---

[1] Bank of Augusta *v.* Earle, 13 Pet. 519.

[2] Generally, it seems, the term will be confined to natural persons, unless from the context, or other parts of the act, it appear that corporations were intended. School Directors *v.* Carlisle Bank, 8 Watts, 291; Blair *v.* Worley, 1 Scam. 178.

[3] See *post*, Chap. III.

[4] Planters, &c. Bank *v.* Andrews, 8 Port. Ala. 404. So in Illinois, Mineral Point R. Co. *v.* Keep, 22 Ill. 9.

[5] See State of Maryland *v.* Bank of Maryland, 6 Gill & J. 205. Where there is a capacity to contract, with a liability to pay, there is generally power to arbitrate; and the fact that one of the parties is a corporation makes no difference. Brady *v.* Mayor of Brooklyn, 1 Barb. 584. A fictitious body, composed of natural persons considered as a mere citizen, is within the meaning of the authority to exercise the power of eminent domain. Bellona Company's case, 3 Bland, Ch. 442. It is specially provided, in the Revised Statutes of some of the States, that "the word *person* may extend, and be applied to bodies politic and corporate, as well as to individuals." Thus, in the general provisions in the Revised Statutes of Massachusetts (ch. 2, s. 6). Undoubtedly, the language of a statute may indicate that the word "person" was used in a more limited sense.

the Act of Congress requiring priority of payment to be made to the United States when any *person* indebted to them shall become insolvent, &c., as persons who may die or abscond, are alone mentioned in the statutes of 1792 and 1797.[1] It appears that a corporation may be considered in a twofold respect, — in the *abstract*, and in the *concrete*. In the *abstract*, it is not a person, nor an animated body, but is only a kind of feigned or intellectual body, or the representation of a body animated. In the *concrete*, it is taken for the particular members of such corporation.[2] The latter may die, but the body corporate does not.

§ 7. But a corporation being a *political* institution merely, although, as above explained, it is regarded as a *person*, yet it has no other capacities than such as are necessary to effect the purposes of its creation. It cannot be deemed a moral agent, subject to moral obligation; nor can it, like a natural person, be subject to personal suffering. This principle explains many of the incapacities ascribed to a corporation, and without, as Mr Kyd says, having recourse to the quaint observation, common in the old books, "that it exists merely in idea, and has neither soul nor body."[3] It is reported by Lord Coke, that Chief Baron Manwood demonstrated that corporations have no soul by the following curious syllogism: "None can create souls but God; but a corporation is created by the king; therefore, a corporation can have no soul." It is in this view that a corporation cannot be guilty of a crime, as treason or felony.[4]

§ 8. The *immortality* of a corporation means only its capacity to take, in perpetual succession, as long as the corporation exists; so far is it from being literally true that a corporation is immortal, many corporations of recent creation are limited in their duration to a certain number of years. A corporation may not only be limited, as to duration, in its commencement, but, without limitation, may be dissolved, and consequently cease to exist, for want of members; also by voluntary surrender of franchises, forfeiture by misuser, &c.[5] When it is said,

---

[1] Commonwealth *v.* Phœnix Bank, 11 Met. 129.

[2] Ayliffe, 196.

[3] 10 Co. 32 b.; 1 Kyd, 71. It also explains the whole meaning of the term *mystical*, as used by Ayliffe, in his "Civil Law," in defining a Corporation.

[4] 1 Kyd, 71; 2 Bulst. 233.

[5] See 2 Kent, Com. 215.

therefore, that a corporation is immortal, it must be understood *theoretically;* and we can understand nothing more than that it *may* exist for an indefinite duration. The authorities which have been cited, if intended to prove its immortality in any other sense, do not warrant the conclusion drawn from them.[1]

§ 9. Upon the application of the epithet *invisibility* to corporations, which is often met with in the books, Mr. Kyd has afforded the following exposition: "That a body framed by the policy of man, a body whose parts and members are mortal, should in its own nature be immortal; or that a body, composed of many bulky, *visible* bodies, should be *invisible*, in the common acceptation of the word, seems beyond the reach of common understandings. A corporation is as visible a body as an army; for, though the commission or authority be not seen by every one, yet the body, united by that authority, is seen by all but the blind. When, therefore, a corporation is said to be invisible, that expression must be understood of the *right* in many persons collectively, to act as a corporation, and then it is as visible, in the eye of the law, as any other right whatever, of which natural persons are capable; it is a right of such a nature, that every member, *separately* considered, has a freehold in it, and all, *jointly* considered, have an inheritance which may go in succession."[2]

§ 10. The same writer denies his assent to the phrase *intangible*, as applied to a corporation; and it seems, he says, equally impossible to comprehend why a number of bulky persons may not be *touched*, as well as be seen. In one sense, however, a corporation is intangible, and that is, if an execution issue against it, there is no corporate body which can be arrested; and although the officer may both perceive and touch the bodies of the individual members, yet he may not take the body of either of them by virtue of the execution against the corporate body.[3] It was held, as long since as the reign of Edward IV. that a corporation could not be imprisoned; and it would be singular if that position should not now be recognized.[4]

---

[1] 1 Kyd, 17. The passage, cited from Grotius (b. 3, ch. 9, § 3), in support of the idea of the immortality of corporations, is so far from justifying the conclusion drawn from it, that it proceeds on the supposition that they may cease to exist. Ibid.

[2] 1 Kyd, 15, 16.

[3] Nichols *v.* Thomas, 4 Mass. 232.

[4] Proprietors of Merrimack River, &c., 7 Mass. 186. See *post*, 394–397.

§ 11. Object and Use of Corporations, &c. The purpose of endowing companies and societies with the functions peculiar to a corporation, is alluded to in the definition we have offered of Chief Justice Marshall, of the meaning of a corporation. The purpose is, indeed, at once apparent, when we contemplate an association of natural persons, without such functions. A common union of individuals by simple articles of association, it is very plain, is deficient in the coercive authority which is required to render their rules and regulations obligatory. Should the privileges and immunities of such an association become the subject of controversy, there exists no ability of making any defence; and when the members who compose it are dispersed by death, or otherwise, it has not the power to transfer the privileges given to it to other persons. With regard to the power of holding property, — if, for example, a grant of land should be made to twenty individuals not incorporated, the right to the land cannot be assured to their successors, without the inconvenience of making frequent and numerous conveyances. When, on the other hand, any number of persons are consolidated and united into a corporation, they are then considered as *one person*, which has but one will, — that will being ascertained by a majority of votes. The privileges and immunities, the estates and possessions of a corporation, when once vested, are vested forever, or, until the end of the period which may be prescribed for its duration; and this desirable object is effected without any new transfer to succeeding members. Persons, who are disposed to make appropriations for any useful purpose, can never fully obtain their object without an incorporating act of the government; and accordingly it has been generally the policy and the custom (especially in the United States) to incorporate all associations, which tend to the public advantage, in relation to municipal government, commerce, literature, charity, and religion.

§ 12. Unlike natural persons, corporations can be endued by the legislature with an immunity from death commensurate with the business the corporation is designed to undertake; hence it can safely contract for the payment of perpetual annuities, and the execution of protracted trusts. Its body is exempt, also, from change of residence, and its youth and vigor are perpetuated by a succession of fresh managers; while its funds can neither become legally diverted from its business, nor be withdrawn by personal gratification or necessity.[1]

---

[1] See Hunt's Merchants' Magazine, for December, 1850, p. 626. See *post*, Chap. V.

§ 13. The *public benefit* is deemed a sufficient consideration of a grant of corporate privileges; and hence, when a grant of such privileges is made (being in the nature of an executed contract), it cannot, in case of a private corporation, which involves private rights, be revoked.[1] The object in creating a corporation is, in fact, to gain the union, contribution, and assistance of several persons for the successful promotion of some design of general utility, though the corporation may, at the same time, be established for the advantage of those who are members of it. The principle is, and has been so laid down by Domat, that the design of a corporation is to provide for some good that is useful to the public.[2] "With respect to acts of incorporation," says one of the Judges of the Court of Appeals of Virginia, "they ought never to be passed, but in consideration of services to be rendered to the public."[3]

§ 14. There are various kinds of corporations, which are distinguished by their degrees of power and the object and purpose of their creation; and the members of some corporations are subject to certain liabilities which do not attach to the members of others. It is, therefore, proper, after having explained the meaning and general object of a body corporate, to clear the way to *private* corporations, and perhaps at the same time gratify the curiosity of some readers, by a preliminary notice of corporations of a higher kind. The word *corporation* is, we know, oftentimes significant of a community clothed with extensive civil authority; and a community of that kind is sometimes called a *political*, sometimes a *municipal*, and sometimes a *public* corporation. It is generally called *public*, when it has for its object the government of a portion of the State; and although in such a case it involves some private interests, yet, as it is endowed with a portion of political power, the term *public* has been deemed appropriate.[4] Another class of public corporations are those which are founded for public, though not for political or municipal purposes, and the *whole* interest in which belongs to the government. The Bank of the United States, for example, if the stock belonged *exclusively* to the government, would be a public corporation; but inasmuch as

---

[1] See Bl. Com. vol. 1, p. 467; Dartmouth College *v.* Woodward, 4 Wheat. 637. Also *post*, Chap. I.

[2] 2 Domat, Civil Law, 452.

[3] Per Roane, J., in Currie *v.* Mutual Ins. Society, 4 Hen. & M. 347. The principle of the public good is the principle on which charters of incorporation are granted in England. 1 Bl. Com. 467.

[4] See Tinsman *v.* Belvidere & Del. R. Co. 2 Dutch. 148.

there are other and private owners of the stock, it is a *private* corporation.[1] The distinction between public and *private* corporations will be somewhat more fully explained, in the commencement of the treatise. All *municipal* corporations are clearly bodies public and political.

§ 15. The analogy between the creation, constitution, mode of government, &c., between *municipalities* and private corporations is so great, and the effects of the former upon the destinies of mankind have been of so much importance, that we should hardly be excused in passing them over, without, at least, some attention to their rise and progress. The origin of *municipal* corporations may be referred to the earliest institution of civil police; or, in other words, to the first collection of individuals united for the purpose of a common government. Nations, or States, are denominated by publicists bodies politic; and are said to have their affairs and interests, and to deliberate and resolve in common. They thus become as moral persons, having an understanding and will peculiar to themselves, and are susceptible of obligations and laws.[2] In this extensive sense, the *United States* may be termed a corporation; they are a collective invisible body, which can act and be seen only in the acts of those who administer the affairs of the government, and also their agents duly appointed.[3] It may be so said of each State singly.[4] So the king of England is a corporation; and so is parliament.[5] The plan of forming or incorporating inferior and subordinate communities, *imperia in imperio*, such as cities and towns, may be referred to a period nearly as remote. "The same cause," says Domat, "which has linked men together in society, for supplying the wants of every one by the concourse and assistance of many others, has produced the first societies of villages, of boroughs, and of towns."[6] We read,

---

[1] Dartmouth College *v.* Woodward, 4 Wheat. 668; 2 Kent, Com. 222. The first kind of corporations, we have mentioned, are denominated by the Civil Code of Louisiana *political* corporations. Tit. 10, ch. 1, art. 420. See *post*, Ch. I. §§ 30–35.

[2] Vattel, 49.

[3] United States *v.* Hillegas, 3 Wash. C. C. 73.

[4] In various instances, where it becomes necessary to make the State a party to litigation, it is represented by its Attorney-General; in which cases the Court merely allows that he should be attended with a copy of the bill; but he cannot be forced to answer in any manner whatever; and, therefore, if the bill cannot be taken *pro confesso* against the State, the further progress of the suit must await his good pleasure. Per Bland, Ch. in McKim *v.* Odom, 3 Bland, Ch. 407.

[5] 10 Co. 29 b.; 1 Sheppard's Abr. 431.

[6] 2 Domat, Civil Law, 457. The word *corpus* denotes any corporation which is gov-

too, in the sacred writings, of salt being thrown on the ground where cities *had* stood;[1] and Pausanias has described the form of founding cities among the Greeks.[2]

§ 16. When the Roman arms had achieved the conquest of any foreign country, a colony was established by the authority of the parent State; and it was an imperative duty of those persons who proceeded to their place of destination, to found a colony, to arrange for the foundation and erection of a city (an *urbs*). Such cities were called *municipia*. Some of these *municipia* possessed all the rights of Roman citizens, except such as could not be enjoyed without residing in the city of Rome. Others enjoyed only the privilege of serving in the Roman legion, but had not the right of electing civil officers. They used their own laws and customs, which were called *Leges Municipales*, nor did they receive any Roman laws unless by their own free consent — *nisi fundi fieri vellent.*[3] When a city was to be built in a newly established colony, the founder, dressed in a Gabinian garb, marked out its compass by a furrow made with a plough, leaving a space wherever it was intended to erect a gate or *porta;* which operation was attended with certain imposing ceremonies, that are supposed to have been borrowed from the Etrurians.[4] Sylla, to reward his military officers, first introduced the custom of settling *military* colonies, which was imitated by Julius Cæsar, Augustus, and others. To these colonies whole legions were sent, with their officers, their tribunes, and centurions.[5] The colonies, it is said, differed from the free towns in this, that they used the laws prescribed by the Romans, but they were governed by similar magistrates. Their two chief magistrates were called *Duumviri;* and their senators *Decuriones*, the latter deriving their name from the circumstance, that when a colony was settled, every *tenth* man was made a senator.[6] Sir James Mackintosh, in describing the government of Britain, when subject to Roman power, tells us, that thirty-three town-

---

erned by particular laws given thereunto; but a *community* is a more general term, and may comprehend the whole state of the country, as well as of a city, town, or ville. Ayliffe, 197.

[1] Judges, ix. 45.

[2] Adam's Rom. Antiq. 73.

[3] Ibid. 71.

[4] Adam's Rom. Antiq. 72, 73; Liv. viii. 16; i. 44; Virg. Æneid, v. 755.

[5] But this custom afterwards fell into disuse. Tacit. Annals, xiv. 72.

[6] Adam's Roman Antiquities, 73, 74.

ships were established in that island from Winchester to Inverness, with various constitutions, to the magistrates of which was given the local police, and also a certain share of judicial power. The inhabitants of those townships, it is true, though they had the privileges of Roman citizens, could only exercise them within the walls of Rome, "which," says the same elegant writer, "was the sole remaining dignity which seems at last to have distinguished the conquering city from the enslaved world."[1] It is a fact as worthy of observation, as it has been rendered clear by the acuteness and erudition of modern antiquaries, that the municipal corporations, which the policy of the Romans created in Britain, formed the only shadow of government for the half century which ensued the abdication of the government of that country by the Romans.

§ 17. Soon after the year of our Lord 69, Gallic cities reared altars to Augustus at the angle of the Saone and the Rhine. But upon the evacuation of Gaul by the Romans, their municipal organization and magistracy would have terminated, had it not been for the influence of the Church. The Roman title of *defensor civitatis*, in every city devolved upon the bishops. "The imperial universality," says our authority,[2] "is destroyed, but there appears the catholic universality." This explains why the foundation of a number of French municipalities of distinction in modern France, may be traced back to a period anterior to the Christian era. Rheims had its foundation in the Druidical territory of the Carnuti, which was under the suzerains of the Remi;[3] and in the traditions of that town, as well as of others in France, down to a late period, the memory of the municipal institutions of the Roman Empire was retained. For this reason, when, in the 16th century, the special municipal jurisdiction of French towns was abolished by the edict of Moulins, Rheims was exempted from its operation, as a respect due to the high antiquity of its municipal privileges.[4] It is not to be

---

[1] History of England, by Sir James Mackintosh, vol. i. p. 30.

[2] Mitchelet, Professeur, &c. vol. i. p. 61.

[3] Ibid.

[4] Savigny, Rom. Law, &c. On this subject the work of Savigny referred to, abounds with proofs and illustrations. Among the direct proofs, is a letter of Pope John the Eighth, of the year 882, addressed to the Lombard city of Valva. Also, the *Codex Utinensis*, a modification of the *Visigothic Breviary*, adapting the system of the laws of that *Breviary*, to the existing wants and circumstances of the Romans in the Lombard Kingdoms.

doubted, that the remembrance and remains of the Roman municipia contributed to the formation of those elective governments of towns, which were the foundation of liberty among modern nations.[1]

§ 18. The establishment of towns, says Kent,[2] with corporate powers as local republics, was the original policy throughout New England, and it had a durable and benign effect upon the institutions and moral and social character of the people. M. De Tocqueville, in his *De la Démocratie en Amérique*,[3] appears to have been very much struck with the institutions of New England towns. He considered them as small independent republics, in all matters of local concerns, and as forming the principle of the life of American liberty, existing to this day.[4] They are allowed to assume upon themselves some of the duties of the State, in a partial or detailed form; but having neither property nor power for the purposes of personal aggrandizement, they can be considered in no other light than as the auxiliaries of the government, and as the secondary and deputy trustees and servants of the people.[5] In all the countries which had been provinces of the Roman empire, the municipal establishments of the Romans retained some vestiges of those elective forms, and of that local administration, which had been bestowed on them by the civilizing policy of those renowned conquerors, and which characterize the towns and cities of the present day. These remains of Roman government, though they were not sufficiently striking to attract the observation of the petty tyrants in whose territory they were situated,

---

[1] History of England, by Sir James Mackintosh, vol. i. pp. 31, 32. Savigny's Hist. of Roman Law, translated by Cathcart, vol. i.

[2] 2 Kent, Com. 4th edit. 274, n. c.

[3] Tome i. 64, 96. The judicial reports in this country, and especially in the New England States, abound with cases of suits against towns, in their corporate capacity, for debts and breaches of duty, for which they were responsible. 2 Kent, sup. 275, n. a.

[4] See *post*, Chap. VI. of Proprietors of Common and Undivided Lands. The charter of the city of St. Mary's in Maryland, when it was a *province* from the lord proprietary, affords an example of what, in England, are called *close* corporations; that is, where the major part of the persons to whom the corporate powers have been granted, on the happening of vacancies among them, have the right of themselves to appoint others to fill such vacancies, without allowing to the corporators, or the inhabitants in general, any vote in the election of such new officers. An *open* corporation of a city, &c. is where all the citizens or corporators have a vote in the election of the officers. At present there are in that State no *close* corporations. See note to p. 416 of 3 Bland, Ch.

[5] McKim *v.* Odom, 3 Bland, Ch. 417. Hence, funds in the hands of a city register, but due as wages to the city officers, cannot be attached by the creditors of such officers. Mayor & C. C. of Baltimore *v.* Root, 8 Md. 95.

yet, beyond doubt, they contributed to prepare the people for more valuable privileges in better times.[1]

§ 19. When feudal tyranny, exerted in the way of levying contributions for the prosecution of feudal wars, became insupportable, and the rights of the denizens of cities, which men esteem to be the most valuable in social life, were denied, the commercial cities of Italy were incited to throw off their feudal fetters, and to demand a government approximating in a much greater degree, to the freedom and independence of the Roman municipia; and this laudable and manly spirit was fortunately encouraged by the feeble and imperfect jurisdiction of the German emperors, their distance from Italy, and their engagement in papal controversies. Those cities, accordingly, in the eleventh century, boldly assumed new privileges, and formed themselves into bodies politic, under laws made by their own consent. In some instances sums of money were paid for certain immunities; and in others, they were conferred gratuitously. The passion for liberty had in fact become so general in Italy, before the termination of the last crusade, that every city had extorted, or purchased, or received from the generosity of the prince upon whom it had been dependent, a grant of very extensive and important corporate privileges.[2]

§ 20. The example, afforded by Italy, of innovation upon the principles of feudal government, was soon followed in France. The policy of conferring new privileges on the towns within his domains was adopted by Louis le Gros,[3] with the view of curbing the turbulence of his potent vassals. The privileges he bestowed were denominated "charters of community," — charters which had the effect of enfranchising the inhabitants — abolishing every indication of their servitude — and of forming them into corporations to be governed by ordinances passed by

---

[1] Sir James Mackintosh, *supra*, p. 204.

[2] 1 Rob. Charles V. ch. v. 25, 26. Otto Frisigensis, who is cited by Robertson, thus describes the state of Italy, under Fred. I.: "The cities so much affect, and are so solicitous to avoid the insolence of power, that almost all of them have thrown off every other authority, and are governed by their own magistrates; insomuch, that all the country is now filled with free cities, most of which have compelled the bishops to reside within their walls; and there is scarcely any nobleman, how great soever his power may be, who is not subject to the laws and government of some city."

[3] According to Robertson; but according to Sir James Mackintosh, the exemption of French towns from feudal rapacity was *extorted* from Louis le Gros. Hist. of England, vol. i. p. 205.

a council of their own nomination. The conduct of the monarch was imitated by the principal subordinate barons, who granted similar immunities to the towns within their own territories. These charters of liberty, owing to the necessity there was of procuring money to defray the expenses attending the expeditions to the Holy Land, were the subjects of bargain and sale; and thus, the consequences of the institution of independent corporate communities, which were repugnant to the maxims of feudal policy, and equally adverse to the sway of feudal power, were disregarded in the eagerness to obtain the "sinews of war."[1] The same practice was soon afterwards adopted in Spain, England, and the rest of the feudal countries; and by this means, as Kent in his Commentaries, observes,—"order and security, industry, trade, and the arts, revived in Italy, France, Germany, Flanders, and England."[2]

---

[1] The right of sovereignty, however, remained in the king, or baron, within whose territories the respective cities were located, and from whom they received their charters. See Rob. Charles V. 26, 207.

[2] 2 Kent, Com. 270, 271. To the institution of corporations, says that author, may be attributed, in some considerable degree, the introduction of regular government and stable protection, after Europe had for many years been deprived, by the inundation of the barbarians, of all the civilization and science which had accompanied the Roman power.

Mr. Wilcock, in his historical sketch of Municipalities, which prefaces his treatise on "Municipal Corporations," observes, that the establishment of those corporations "was the effect of that spirit of liberty which had gone abroad, and a considerable degree of power and independence already existing in the cities and towns to which charters were granted. They were already become influential and wealthy associations. Their traffic not only brought them riches, but gave them a maritime power not inconsiderable in those times. Their increasing wealth and commerce established among the burgher watch and ward, and voluntary associations for the protection of property, not efficient at all times against the rapacity of marauding barons, but capable of repelling those bands of outlaws and disciplined robbers, with whose predatory excursions the annals of European history are frequently stained. The dangers to which their property was exposed taught them the necessity, and they soon learned the power of union. While the barons were wasting their revenues and retainers in wild wars, and weakening each other with mutual conflicts, the towns were gradually and silently accumulating wealth, population, and power. At a very early period of our history, they were defended by walls. With Italian merchandise they imported the institutes of Venice and Genoa; and commerce with the Hanse Towns, then also in their infancy, introduced a similarity of internal arrangement. The grants of privileges contained in the charters were in fact confirmations of privileges already existing. This sanction gave confidence and firmness to the municipalities, with little loss or concession of the lords. It requires no historical documents to convince us, that had they not been already powerful, they would not have been equally favored by the barons and princes, each desiring the assistance of allies in the struggle between prerogative and privilege. The statesmen of those times had little idea of calling new powers into existence; the utmost extent of their policy was to avail themselves of those which they found at hand."—*Wilcock on Municipal Corporations*, 2.

§ 21. In the reign of Henry the First, of England, who was a contemporary of Louis le Gros, the inhabitants of London had begun to farm their tolls and duties, and they obtained a royal charter for that purpose. The example of London was soon followed by the other trading towns, and from this time forward the existence of the municipal corporations, called "boroughs," became more and more conspicuous.[1] The arrangement just mentioned, in relation to tolls and duties, seems to have suggested the first idea of a *borough*, considered as a *corporation*. Some of the principal inhabitants of a town undertook to pay the yearly rent, which was due to the superior, and in consideration of which they were permitted to levy the old duties, and become responsible for the funds committed to their care. As managers of the community, therefore, they were bound to fulfil its obligations to the superior; and by a very natural extension of the same principle, it was finally understood, that they might be prosecuted for all its debts; as they had, of course, a right of prosecuting all its debtors. The society was thus viewed in the light of a body politic, or fictitious *person*, capable of legal acts, and executing every kind of transaction by means of trustees. This alteration in the state of English towns was accompanied by many other improvements; they were placed in a condition that enabled them to dispense with the protection of their superior; and took upon themselves to provide a defence against foreign invaders, and to secure their internal tranquillity. In this manner they ultimately became completely invested with the government of the place.[2] There are many instances in England of grants by charter to the inhabitants of a town, "that their town shall be a free borough," and that they may enjoy a variety of privileges and exemptions without any *direct* clause of incorporation; and yet by virtue of such charter such towns have been considered as incorporated.[3]

§ 22. Such was the grand effect of the enlightened civil policy of Rome upon the civilization of the modern world, as it has been developed by the institution of municipal communities, who are invested with the privilege of managing their own local interests, under the protection

---

[1] Miller's Hist. Views of Eng. Gov. 340. The free cities of Germany had acquired, in the thirteenth century, such opulence as enabled them to form the famous Hanseatic League, which rendered them so formidable to the military powers in their vicinity.

[2] See 1 Kyd, 43.

[3] Ibid. 63, and Madox, Hist of Exch. 402.

of the parent state. From the conception of such an institution, too, grew the idea of private, civil, eleemosynary, and ecclesiastical corporate bodies, which are now more or less densely diffused throughout the regions of civilization and Christianity, with such powers and immunities annexed to them by law, as will enable them to effect the design and object of their creation. The love of commercial adventure induced the Roman people to combine their skill, labor, and capital for a common purpose ; and thus the matter was afforded for establishing general rules of partnership, and the various guilds and companies and colleges which existed at Rome, led to the determination of the exact notion of private corporate bodies, and to established rules of law applicable to such artificial or fictitious persons.[1]

§ 23. Both towns and other political divisions, as counties, hundreds, &c., which are established without an express charter of incorporation, are denominated *quasi* corporations. In the same class of corporate bodies are included Overseers of the Poor, Supervisors of a County and of a Town, Loan Officers of a County, &c., who are invested with corporate powers *sub modo*, and for a few specified purposes only.[2] The boards of Commissioners of Roads in South Carolina, are deemed *quasi* corporations.[3] So, also, are Trustees of the School Fund, in Mississippi,[4] and the Trustees of the Poor in the same State.[5] And the decisions have been, that the successors of such officers may sue for a debt or duty due their predecessors in their official capacity ; and also where the same officers contract a debt, by which they become liable to another and afterwards go out of office, they cannot be sued as *late* overseers, &c., but the action must be against their successors.[6] A legislative act which authorizes the judges of a particular Court to take bonds to themselves in their official capacity, confers on them, *as to such bonds*, a corporate character.[7]

---

1 See Long's Disc. at the Middle Temple, No. II. ; 1 Browne, Civil Law, 142.

2 2 Kent, Com. 221 ; North Hempstead *v.* Hempstead, 2 Wend. 109; Jansen *v.* Ostrander, 1 Cowen, 670. The superintendents of the poor in New York may sue for the conversion of personal property belonging to the county, either in their corporate name, or in their individual names, with the addition of their name of office. Keuren *v.* Johnston, 3 Denio, 183.

3 Com. Roads *v.* McPherson, 1 Speer, 218.

4 Carmichal *v.* Trustees, &c., 3 How. Miss. 84. So the Trustees of Schools in Illinois, Trustees of Schools *v.* Tatman, 13 Ill. 27.

5 Governor *v.* Gridley, Walk. Miss. 328.

6 Jackson *v.* Hartwell, 18 Johns. 422; and see 1 Kyd, 29, 30, 31.

7 Justices of Cumberland *v.* Armstrong, 3 Dev. 284.

§ 24. In the same class of corporations are also included School districts.[1] Thus, in the Supreme Court of Massachusetts, it was expressly decided, that a school district may sue as a corporation, by its corporate name.[2] The following extract from the opinion of the late learned Chief Justice Parker, in the case just referred to, places in a clear light what is meant by a *quasi* corporation; and shows that the extent of its powers is limited by the object of its creation: "That they" (school districts) "are not bodies politic and corporate, with the general powers of corporations, must be admitted; and the reasoning, advanced to show their defect of power, is conclusive. The same may be said of towns and other municipal societies; which, although recognized by various statutes and by immemorial usage, as persons, or aggregate corporations, with precise duties which may be enforced, and privileges which may be maintained, by suits at law, yet are deficient in many of the powers incident to the general character of corporations. They may be considered, under our institutions, as *quasi* corporations, with limited powers, coextensive with the duties imposed upon them by statute or usage; but restrained from a general use of the authority, which belongs to these metaphysical persons by the Common Law. The same may be said of all the numerous corporations, which have been, from time to time, created by various acts of the legislature; all of them enjoying the power which is expressly bestowed upon them, and perhaps, in all instances, where the act is silent, possessing, by necessary implication, the authority which is requisite to execute the purposes of their creation.[3] They differ in character, also, from those corporations which exist at common law, in some particulars. It is not necessary that our municipal corporations should act under seal, in order to bind themselves or obligate others to them.[4] A vote of the body is sufficient for this purpose; and this mode has prevailed with the proprietors of common and undivided land, even in the disposition of their real property, contrary to the gen-

---

1 Grant *v.* Fancher, 5 Cowen, 309, and authorities there cited. See also, Todd *v.* Birdsall, 1 Cowen, 258, and the authorities of different States there cited in the reporter's note. City of Lexington *v.* McQuillan, 9 Dana, 519; School District No. 3 *v.* Macloon, 4 Wisc. 79; Clarke *v.* School District No. 7, 3 R. I. 199; Horton *v.* Garrison, 23 Barb. 176. In actions against towns, each inhabitant is liable. Adams *v.* Wiscasset Bank, 1 Greenl. 361.

2 The Inhabitants of 4th School District *v.* Wood, 13 Mass. 192.

3 See Jackson *v.* Hartwell, 18 Johns. 422.

4 The doctrine is now well settled, that any corporation may become obligated without the common seal. See *post*, chapters relative to common seal, and the power to make contracts.

eral provision of law respecting the transfer of real estate.[1] It will not do, therefore, to apply the strict principles of law respecting corporations, in all cases, to these aggregate bodies, which are created by statute in this commonwealth. By the several statutes which have been passed respecting school districts, it is manifest, that the legislature has supposed that a division of towns, for the purpose of maintaining schools, will promote the important object of general education; and this valuable object of legislative care seems to require, in construing their acts, that a liberal view should be had to the end to be effected."[2]

§ 25. There may be, also, *private* corporations, created with powers *sub modo*, and for a few specified purposes only, and which are properly *quasi* corporations. The joint-stock banks in England of modern creation, called into existence by the act of 7 Geo. IV., are considered *quasi* corporations, as that Act provides for a continuance of the partnership, notwithstanding a change of partners. In this case the partnership has the corporate attribute of *succession*.[3] And a mining joint-stock company was deemed a *quasi* corporation, because a suit for a demand against the company might, by virtue of an act of parliament, be brought against the directors.[4] Here is attached the corporate liability of *being sued*, without the names of each individual partner composing the company. The General Assembly of the Presbyterian Church, in Pennsylvania, is not a *quasi* corporation; because it has not the capacity to sue and be sued as an artificial person; and a *quasi* corporation is also established by law, but that assembly is not. Neither does that assembly bear the same relation to the corporation of the trustees to the assembly, as the shareholders do to a bank or joint-stock company; for the latter are an integral part of the corporation. The assembly is a segregated association, which, though it is the reproductive organ of corporate succession, is not itself a member of the body.[5]

§ 26. Before proceeding to treat of *private aggregate* corporations, it

---

[1] See *post*, Ch. VI. *Of Proprietors of Common and Undivided Lands.*

[2] See Bank of United States *v.* Dandridge, 12 Wheat. 76; School Commissioners *v.* Dean, 2 Stew. & P. 110; City of Lexington *v.* McQuillan, 9 Dana, 516.

[3] Harrison *v.* Timmins, 4 M. & W. 510.

[4] Wordsworth on Joint Stock Companies, 41, 175.

[5] Commonwealth *v.* Green, 4 Whart. 531. A Congregational church in Massachusetts is neither a corporation nor a *quasi* corporation. Weld *v.* May, 9 Cush. 181; Jefts *v.* York, 10 Ibid. 392.

is proper to mention another general division of corporations, which has relation to the number of persons of which the corporation is composed; and that is, *sole* and *aggregate*. A *sole* corporation, as its name imports, consists only of *one* person, to whom and his successors belongs that legal perpetuity, the enjoyment of which is denied to all natural persons.[1] Corporations of this kind were not known to the civil law, the maxim of the Roman lawyers, being, "*tres faciunt collegium.*" Yet, even among the Romans, if a corporation *originally consisting* of three persons was reduced to one (*si universitas ad unum redit*), it could still subsist as a corporation, "*et stet nomen universitatis.*"[2] The King of England is an example of a sole corporation, and so also, it is considered, is a bishop and a vicar in that country. Thus, the parish minister of a church in England, is said to be seised, during his incumbency, of the freehold of the land, with which his church is endowed, as *persona ecclesiæ;* and he is deemed capable, as a sole corporation, of transmitting the land to his successors.[3] Fitzherbert and Brooke both say, upon the authority of the Year Books (11 Hen. IV.) that if a grant be made to the church of such a place, it shall be a fee in the parson and his *successors*.[4] It is stated by Kyd, that, in England, there are two kinds of sole corporations: the one when the person has the corporate capacity for his own benefit; the other when he acts only for the benefit of others as trustee. Of the former kind are, the king, a bishop, a parson, &c. Of the other, says he, the most familiar is the *chamberlain* of the city of London, who may take a recognizance to himself and his successors, in trust for the orphans.[5]

§ 27. Sole corporations, it is believed, are not common in the United States. In those States, however, where the religious establishment of the Church of England was adopted, when they were colonies, together with the common law on that subject, the minister of the parish was seised of the freehold, as *persona ecclesiæ*, in the same manner as in

---

1 1 Bl. Com. 469. 2 Ibid.

3 Baron Gilbert, in his Treatise on Tenures, says, that anciently abbots and prelates were supposed to be married to the Church, inasmuch as the right of property was vested in the Church, and the possession in the abbot or bishop. *Gilb. Ten.* 110.

4 Fitz. Feofft. pl. 42; Bro. Estate, pl. 49; cited by Mr. Justice Story, in Town of Pawlet *v.* Clark, 9 Cranch, 328.

5 1 Kyd, 29 to 32; Cro. Eliz. 464. For distinction between one who has a corporate capacity for his own benefit, and when he acts in trust for another, see Jansen *v.* Ostrander, 1 Cowen, 670.

England; and the right of his successors to the freehold, being thus established, was not destroyed by the abolition of the regal government, nor can it be divested even by an act of the State legislature. This was held by Mr. J. Story, in giving the opinion of the Supreme Court of the United States, in the case just referred to in that Court. In Massachusetts, it has been held that a minister seised of parsonage lands, in the right of the parish, is also a sole corporation for this purpose, and holds the same to himself and his successors.[1] "We are not aware," says Mr. Chief Justice Shaw of Massachusetts, "that there is any instance of a sole corporation in this Commonwealth, except that of a person, who may be seised of parsonage lands, to hold to him and his successors in the same office, in right of his parish." He adds: "There are some instances in which certain public officers are empowered by statute to maintain actions as successors, such as judges of probate, county and town treasurers; but it is only where it is expressly provided by statute."[2] A supervisor of a town in the State of New York is a *quasi* sole corporation, and his succcessor in office, who has taken a collector's bond, may sue upon it in his own name.[3] The governor of a state, as the head of the executive department, is also a *quasi* corporation sole, and bonds made payable to him which are appropriate to the execution of the laws, may be sued on in his name, for the benefit of those interested.[4] There are very few points of corporation law applicable to sole corporations; and those of a private nature cannot, at least as a general rule, take *personal* property in succession; and their corporate capacity of taking property is confined altogether to real estate.[5] It has been held that an individual banker, carrying on business under the general banking law of New York of 1838, is not a corporation.[6]

§ 28. The grant of corporate powers to *one* person, and his *associates*, does not require of such person that he should take associates before the act can take effect, or corporate powers be exercised; but virtually confers on him alone the right to exercise all the corporate

---

1 Brunswick *v.* Dunning, 7 Mass. 447; Weston *v.* Hunt, 2 Mass. 501.
2 Overseers, &c. *v.* Sears, 22 Pick. 125.
3 Jansen *v.* Ostrander, 1 Cowen, 670.
4 The Governor *v.* Allen, 8 Humph. 176.
5 Terret *v.* Taylor, 9 Cranch, 43.
6 Codd *v.* Rathbone, 19 N. Y. 37.

powers thereby granted.[1] It cannot properly, however, be said that one person, in such a case, is *created* a sole corporation, because, if so, he could not of himself make it aggregate. The act under which he derives his authority to act alone, has in view an aggregate corporation, for it expressly provides for *associates*.

§ 29. An *aggregate* corporation, as its name will readily suggest, consists of *several* persons, who are united in one society, which is continued by a succession of members. Of this kind are the mayor and commonalty of a city, the heads and fellows of a college, the members of trading companies, &c.[2] This distinction between aggregate and sole corporations was unknown to the Romans; all their corporations were aggregate. It was considered by them, that, where the major part of the body corporate acts, the act was the act of every particular member; but the major part must consist of two parts in three, and therefore, three in number are requisite to make a corporation.[3]

---

[1] Penobscot B. Corporation *v.* Lamson, 16 Me. 224. Hughes *v.* Parker, 19 N. H. 181, 20 N. H. 58.

[2] 1 Kyd, 76; 2 Kent, Com. 221.

[3] Wood, Civil Law, 134; Ayliffe, 197; 1 Browne, Civil Law, 142.

A TREATISE

ON

PRIVATE CORPORATIONS.

CHAPTER I.

MEANING, SEVERAL KINDS, AND HISTORY OF PRIVATE CORPORATIONS.

§ 30. According to the several definitions we have in our introduction offered of a corporation, it means an intellectual body, composed of individuals, and created by law; a body which is united under a common name, and the members of which are so capable of succeeding each other, that the body (like a river) continues always the same, notwithstanding the change of the parts that compose it. Within this definition, we have seen, are included *private* as well as *public* corporations. The latter have been already explained in our introduction; in which it has been shown to what extent private corporations may be deemed "persons;" and, also, that there may be private, as well as public, *quasi* corporations.

§ 31. The main distinction between public and private corporations is, that over the former, the legislature, as the trustee or guardian of the public interests, has the exclusive and unrestrained control; and acting as such, as it may create, so it may modify or destroy, as public exigency requires or recommends, or the public interest will be best subserved. The right to establish, alter, or abolish such corporations, seems to be a principle inherent in the very nature of the institutions themselves; since all mere municipal regulations must, from the nature of things, be subject to the absolute control of the government. Such institutions are the auxiliaries of the government in the important business of municipal rule, and cannot have the least pretension to sustain their privileges or their existence upon any thing like a *contract* between them and the legislature; because there can be no reciprocity of stipulation; and because their objects and duties are incompatible with every thing of the nature of compact.[1] And a municipal corporation may be abolished, although it is the trustee of a public charity.[2] But it is said that in respect to the right to make contracts, a municipal corporation stands on the same footing as a private corporation.[3] Private corporations, on the other hand, are created by an act of the legislature, which, in connection with its acceptance, is regarded as a *compact*, and one which, so long as the body corporate faithfully observes, the legislature is constitutionally restrained from impairing, by annexing new terms and conditions, onerous in their operation, or inconsistent with a reasonable construction of the compact.[4] Thus, it has been expressly held, that the legislature has no power to direct that any portion of the debts due a bank shall be received in any thing but gold or silver, as it impairs the contract created by the act of incorporation.[5] Private corporations are indisputably the creatures of public policy, and in the popular

---

[1] McKim *v.* Odom, 3 Bland, Ch. 417. Thus a town is organized by the act of incorporation simply, without any acceptance of it by a town meeting. Berlin *v.* Gorham, 34 N. H. 266. The power of a State to ordain police regulations for a city was considered at length in Mayor, &c. of Baltimore *v.* The State, 15 Md. 376.

[2] Montpelier *v.* East Montpelier, 29 Vt. 12.

[3] Atkins *v.* Randolph, 31 Vt. 226.

[4] Dartmouth College *v.* Woodward, 4 Wheat. 636. The legislature may incorporate a town either with or without the consent of a majority of its citizens. Cheaney *v.* Hooser, 9 B. Mon. 330, 334. The legislature has absolute control over municipal corporations, to create, modify, or to destroy them at pleasure. Robertson *v.* Rockford, 21 Ill. 451; The People *v.* Wren, 4 Scam. 273; Sloane *v.* The State, 8 Blackf. 361; City of St. Louis *v.* Russell, 9 Mo. 507; Rundle *v.* Delaware & Raritan Canal, 1 Wallace, C. C. 275; State *v.* New Orleans Gas Co., 2 Rob. La. 529; Paterson *v.* Society U. M., 4 N. J. 385; but not over corporations created for private advantage and emolument. Bailey *v.* Mayor, &c. of New York, 3 Hill, 531; State of Ohio *v.* Library Co., 11 Ohio, 96; Marietta *v.* Fearing, 4 Ohio, 427; Washington Bridge Co. *v.* The State, 18 Conn. 53; Young *v.* Harrison, 6 Ga. 130; County of Richmond *v.* County of Lawrence, 12 Ill. 1; President, &c. of Fort Gibson, 13 Smedes & M. 130; Hope *v.* Deadrick, 8 Humph. 1. As to the doctrine to the contrary in Bank of Toledo *v.* Toledo, 1 Ohio, State, 622, *quære*. See further, Central Bridge Corporation *v.* City of Lowell, 4 Gray, 474, and cases there cited. Shorter *v.* Smith, 9 Ga. 517; Collins *v.* Sherman, 31 Missis. 679. A clause in a charter of incorporation, reserving the right of altering, amending, or repealing it, does not authorize the legislature to displace the original corporators, or to add new ones to their number. Sage *v.* Dillard, 15 B. Mon. 340.

[5] Bush *v.* Shipman, 4 Scam. 190; and see M'Kim *v.* Odom, 3 Bland, Ch. 417.

meaning of the term, may be called public; but yet, if the whole interest does not belong to the government (as if the corporation is created for the administration of civil or municipal power), the corporation is private. A *bank*, for instance, may be created by the government for its own uses; but, if the stock is owned by private persons, it is a private corporation, although it is erected by the sanction of public authority, and its objects and operations partake of a public nature.[1] Railroads are private corporations,[2] and, "Generally speaking," say the court, in the case of Bonaparte *v.* Camden, &c. Railroad Company, "public corporations are towns, cities, counties, parishes, existing for public purposes; private corporations are for banks, insurance, roads, canals, bridges, &c., where the stock is owned by individuals, but their use may be public."[3] In all the last named, and other like corporations, the acts done by them are done with a view to their own interest, and if thereby they incidentally promote that of the public, it cannot reasonably be supposed they do it from any spirit of liberality they have beyond that of their fellow-citizens. Both the property and the sole object of every such corporation are essentially private, and from them the individuals composing the company corporate are to devive profit.[4]

§ 32. Nor does it make any difference that the State has an interest as one of the corporators, for it does not by such participation identify itself with the corporation. Says Marshall, C. J.: "The Planters' Bank of Georgia, is not the State of Georgia, although the State holds an interest in it." "And," says he, "it is a sound principle of law, that when a government becomes a partner in a trading company, it divests itself, so far as concerns the transactions of that company, of its sovereign character, and takes that of a private citizen."[5] A turnpike company, in which the State holds stock has been deemed likewise, in Pennsylvania, not to be such a public corporation as is exempt from the operation of a legislative act giving jurisdiction to the courts, upon the application of a creditor, to sequester the profits and tolls of the corpora-

---

1 Bank of U. S. *v.* Planters' Bank of Georgia, 9 Wheat. 907; Miners' Bank *v.* United States, 1 Greene, Iowa, 553.

2 Bonaparte *v.* Camden & Amboy R. Co., 1 Bald. C. C. 205; Alabama & Tennessee Rivers R. Co. *v.* Kidd, 29 Ala. 221.

3 Bonaparte *v.* Camden & Amboy Railroad Co., 1 Bald. C. C. 223.

4 Ten Eyck *v.* Delaware and Raritan Canal Co., 3 Harrison, 200; R. & G. Railroad Co. *v.* Davis, 2 Dev. & B. 451.

5 Case of Planters' Bank of Georgia, *sup.*

tion, for the payment of its debts.[1] And, although a State cannot be sued, yet, if it becomes interested as a stockholder in a corporation, such interest will not protect the corporation against a suit and all its incidents.[2] In the case of the State Bank of South Carolina *v.* Gibbs,[3] the State owned not only a portion, but the whole of the interests in the bank, and the court considered, notwithstanding, that the case was not distinguishable from that of the Planters' Bank of Georgia, and that it might with truth be said, that "the Bank of South Carolina is not the State of South Carolina," that the State did not transfer any portion of its sovereignty to that corporation, and did not communicate to it any of its privileges or prerogatives, but placed it upon the same level as other corporate bodies; and the same principle by which the case of the Planters' Bank of Georgia was governed, was applicable.[4] The "Bank of the State of Alabama" is a mere private corporation, and is invested with none of the incidents of sovereignty, and is therefore, as a plaintiff in a suit, liable to be barred by the statute of limitations.[5] The Federal Government may in like manner be a stockholder in a bank, without identifying itself with the corporation; and though the United States is a stockholder in the Bank of the United States, and is so far a party, in all suits to which the bank is a party, the doctrine of *nullum tempus occurrit regi* does not apply, to exempt the bank from the operation of the statute of limitations.[6] It is, in short, as before stated, a settled princi-

---

[1] Turnpike Co. *v.* Wallace, 8 Watts, 316.

[2] Seymour *v.* Turnpike Co., 10 Ohio, 476; Moore *v.* Trustees of W. & E. Canal, 7 Ind. 462.

[3] State Bank of South Carolina *v.* Gibbs, 3 McCord, 377.

[4] This case decided, that a debt due to the bank in question, was not a debt due to the public, and could claim no priority on that ground. Bank of Tennessee *v.* Dibrell, 3 Sneed, 379. In State Bank of North Carolina *v.* Clark, 1 Hawks, 36, the books of the bank were held inadmissible to show that the defendants had overdrawn, because the bank is only a private corporation. (Per Taylor, C. J., in delivering the opinion of the court.) It does not appear by the report of the case, whether the bank owned the whole of the stock or not, nor what portion of it, nor what control it had over the institution. According to the decision in the case of the Bank of South Carolina *v.* Gibbs, the State Bank of Arkansas is a private corporation. There are in the act creating it, no express words incorporating any particular persons, but the fund is placed under a given number of directors, to be elected by the legislature, with the usual banking powers conferred upon them; and powers were conferred also which could not exist, unless the persons who were to compose the directory were by implication incorporated. Mahoney *v.* Bank of Arkansas, 4 Ark. 620.

[5] Bank of the State of Alabama *v.* Gibson, 6 Ala. 814.

[6] Bank of United States *v.* McKensie, 2 Brock. C. C. 393.

ple, that when the sovereign becomes a member of a joint-stock corporation, the right of sovereignty, with respect to the transactions of the company, is devested, and the character is assumed of a private citizen. But where a corporation is composed exclusively of officers of the government having no personal interest in it, or with its concerns, and only acting as the organs of the State in effecting a great public improvement, it is a public corporation.[1]

§ 33. Public and municipal corporations may stand, in respect to grants made to them by the State on the same footing as would any individual or private corporation, upon whom like special franchise may have been conferred. In Bailey *v.* Mayor, &c. of New York,[2] the defendants were sued for injuries done by the city water commissioners in raising a dam upon the Croton River; and one of the grounds against the action was, that admitting the commissioners to be the agents of the defendants, they were not liable, inasmuch as they were acting solely for the State in prosecuting the work of supplying the city with water. But this view, the court declared, could not be maintained. The powers conferred by the several acts of the legislature authorizing the execution of the work, were not, strictly and legally speaking, conferred for the public benefit, and the grant was a special private franchise, made as well for the private advantage of the city, as for the public good. In its sovereign character the State owned no part of the work, and had no interest in it. The case was different from the case of powers granted exclusively for public purposes to counties, cities, and towns, where the corporations have no private estate or interest in the grant. If the powers conferred be granted for public purposes exclusively, they belong to the corporate body, in its public and municipal character; but if for purposes of private advantage and emolument, though the public may derive a common benefit therefrom, the corporation, *quoad hoc*, is to be regarded as a private company.[3]

§ 34. A *hospital* founded by private benefaction, is, in point of law,

---

[1] Sayre *v.* Northwestern Turnpike Co. 10 Leigh, 454.

[2] Bailey *v.* Mayor, &c. of New York, 3 Hill, 531.

[3] It is, as was observed by Nelson, C. J., upon the like distinction, that municipal corporations, in their private character, as owners and occupiers of houses and lands, are regarded in the same light, and dealt with accordingly. See Moodalay *v.* East India Company, 1 Brown, Ch. 469.

a private corporation, though dedicated by its charter to public charity. And a *college*, founded and endowed in the same manner, though for the general promotion of learning, is private.[1] A college, merely because it receives a charter from the government, if founded by private benefactors, it has been held, is not thereby constituted a public corporation, controllable by the government; nor does it make any difference, that the funds have been generally derived from the bounty of the government itself.[2] The trustees of the University of Alabama were held to be a public corporation, because the State had the *whole* interest in the institution, without being under any obligation of contract with any one.[3]

§ 35. A private corporation is also distinguishable from a municipal corporate body, by having a corporate fund from which a judgment can be satisfied; and by the irresponsibility of the members for the corporate debts beyond the amount of their interest in the fund; for towns, &c. being established only for political and civil purposes, each member of the same is liable in his person and private estate to the execution.[4] Private corporations are liable for misfeasance, and nonfeasance; but that a corporation established as a part of the government, is liable for losses by an omission to observe a law of its own in which no penalty is provided, is a principle for which there is no precedent.[5]

---

[1] Dartmouth College *v.* Woodward, 4 Wheat. 668. The case of St. Mary's Church, 7 S. & R. 559. 2 Kent, Com. 222.

[2] Allen *v.* McKeen, 1 Sumner, 276. An incorporated academy is a private corporation, although it may derive part of its support from the government. Cleaveland *v.* Stewart, 3 Ga. 283.

[3] Trustees, &c. *v.* Winston, 5 Stew. & P. 17. In City of Louisville *v.* Pres. & Trus. of University, 15 B. Mon. 642, the original charter of the University of Louisville, an institution founded and endowed by the city of Louisville, had been essentially changed, if not completely abrogated by an act of the legislature of Kentucky of 1851. The President and trustees of the University insisted that this act was unconstitutional and therefore void, as being an infringement of the rights of a private corporation. The question being carried up to the Court of Appeals, the conclusions of a majority of the court are thus declared by the chief justice: "We are of opinion, therefore, upon the ground of authority, as well as of reason, that the original charter of the University of Louisville creates a private corporation, which is protected by that clause of the constitution of the United States which prohibits the enactment of laws impairing the obligation of contracts; and that so much of the amended charter of the city of Louisville, of 1851, as relates to the preëxisting corporation and charter of the University, and vests or professes to vest in a new corporation or in new trustees, the property and privileges of the original corporation, is in violation of that constitutional prohibition, and consequently void."

[4] Merchants Bank *v.* Cook, 4 Pick. 414.

[5] Per Marshall, C. J., in Towle *v.* Common Council of Alexandria, 3 Pet. 409.

§ 36. Private corporations are of several kinds, and are known by certain appellations, according to the objects for which they are created. The first division is into *ecclesiastical* and *lay*. *Ecclesiastical* corporations are such as are composed of members who take a lively interest in the advancement of religion, and who are associated and incorporated for that object. They may be either sole, as a bishop, or parson, or aggregate, as in former times were the abbot and monks.[1] Before the reformation and the dissolution of monasteries, ecclesiastical corporations were of three kinds. The first consisted of those who were called the secular clergy, that is, a clergy composed of persons having communion with the world, like the modern clergy of England, and the clergy of the United States. The second were composed of monks, who were bound by a solemn vow entirely to renounce all intercourse with the world, and to spend their days in common together, under the direction of superiors, and according to regulations prescribed by the founder. The third were religious communities, the members of which, without any vow to relinquish intercourse with the laity, lived together in common, in order to serve the interests and objects of the church; and such were those, who, under the authority of the bishop, were employed as religious missionaries.[2]

§ 37. The Church of England, in its aggregate description, is not by the common law a corporation, and cannot receive a donation *eo nomine;* but a grant to a church of a particular place, vests the fee in the parson and his successors, by the common law.[3] The ecclesiastical establishment of England was adopted by the colony of Virginia, together with the common law in respect to it, so far as applicable to the circumstances of the colony. In Turpin *v.* Locket, in that State,[4] the question was, whether when the colony became a State, the legislature had the power to order the glebe lands to be sold, and the money applied to the use of the poor; and the decision of Chancellor Wythe, sustaining the validity of the acts of Assembly dissolving the vestries and providing for the sale of the glebe lands of the Protestant Episcopal Church, was

---

1 Terrett *v.* Taylor, 9 Cranch, 43. The first sort of corporation, says Ayliffe, in his Treatise on the Civil Law, has a respect unto such persons, whose principal business regards religion, as chapters of cathedral, or collegiate churches, monasteries, and the like; and these are styled *ecclesiastical* corporations. Ayliffe, Civil Law, 196.

2 2 Domat, Civil Law, 452.

3 Pawlet *v.* Clark, 9 Cranch, 294.

4 Turpin *v.* Locket, 6 Call, 113.

affirmed by an equal division of the judges of the Court of Appeals, and was subsequently maintained in a case in the same court.[1] Ecclesiastical corporations of all denominations have been created, to a greater or less extent, since the Revolution, in almost every State of the Union. They are commonly called, in the United States, *religious* corporations; and that description is given to them in the act of the State of New York, providing generally for the incorporation of religious societies, in an easy and popular manner, and for the purpose of managing with more facility and advantage, the temporalities belonging to the church or congregation.[2] The act of that State, of 1784, for the incorporation of such societies, recognized three distinct classes or bodies as existing in the incorporation of a Christian church, namely: the church or spiritual body, consisting of its office-bearers and other communicants; the congregation or electors, embracing all the stated hearers or attendants on divine worship; and the trustees, who were to have the control of the temporalities of the society for the benefit of the stated hearers and the communicants.[3] In the Reformed Dutch Church, under the statute of New Jersey, incorporating religious societies, the civil office of trustee grows out of the ecclesiastical office of minister, elder, or deacon.[4]

§ 38. In this country, it is not only obvious, but it has been so expressly held, that no ecclesiastical body has any temporal power to enforce its decisions and ordinances. Its jurisdiction is only advisory, or over the conscience of those who have voluntarily subjected themselves to a spiritual sway. Where a civil right depends upon an ecclesiastical matter, it is the civil tribunal, and not the ecclesiastical, which is to decide. Therefore, where, as well from the testimony as from the terms of a charter incorporating a church, it is apparent that it was in full connection with a synodical body, and not independent of it, as a con-

---

[1] Selden *v.* Overseers of the Poor, 11 Leigh, 127.

[2] 2 Kent, Com. 221, 222.

[3] Sawyer *v.* Cipperly, 7 Paige, 281. Under this general act, the members of a religious society, and not its trustees, are incorporated. Parish of Bellport *v.* Tooker, 29 Barb. 256; Robertson *v.* Bullions, 1 Kern. 243. See Wheaton *v.* Gales, 18 N. Y. 395. And a person who makes a contract with the trustees *de facto* of a religious corporation, who are in possession of all the church property, without knowledge of any illegality in their election, may enforce his claim on the contract, though the election should afterwards be adjudged illegal. Ebaugh *v.* German Ref. Ch., 3 E. D. Smith, 60.

[4] Doremus *v.* Dutch Reformed Church, 2 Green, N. J., Ch. 332. A deed of land to trustees *de facto* of an incorporated society conveys no title to the society. Bundy *v.* Birdsall, 29 Barb. 31.

gregation, if a portion of it secede, the rest, however small in number, secure their corporate existence, and are entitled to all the privileges and property of the corporation.[1]

§ 39. *Lay* corporations are divided into *eleemosynary* and *civil*. *Eleemosynary* corporations are such as are instituted upon a principle of *charity;* their object being the perpetual distribution of the bounty of the founder of them, to such persons as he has directed. Of this kind are hospitals for the relief of the impotent, indigent, and sick, or deaf and dumb.[2] And of this kind, also, are all colleges and academies which are founded where assistance is given to the members thereof, in order to enable them to prosecute their studies, or devotion, with ease and assiduity. The reason why the institutions of Oxford and Cambridge are not considered as eleemosynary is, that the stipends, which are annexed to particular magistrates and professors, are *pro opera et labore*, and are not merely charitable donations, since every stipend is preceded by service and duty.[3] Dartmouth College, in New Hampshire, on the other hand, is an eleemosynary corporation, because it was

---

[1] Per Johnston, Ch., in Harmon *v.* Dreher, 1 Speers, Eq. 87. See also, Keyser *v.* Stanisfer, 6 Ohio, 363; German Reformed Church *v.* Commonwealth, 3 Barr, 282; Den d. Am. Prim. Soc. *v.* Pilling, 4 N. J. 653; Robertson *v.* Bullions, *supra*. It is held, in Massachusetts, that the body of communicants gathered into church order, according to established usage, in any town or parish, established according to law, and actually connected and associated therewith, for religious purposes, for the time being, is to be regarded as the church of such society, as to all questions of property depending on that relation; and that an adhering minority of the church, and not a seceding majority, constitutes the church. Baker *v.* Fales, 16 Mass. 503; Stebbins *v.* Jennings, 10 Pick. 172, and many cases therein cited. That those who adhere to the original doctrines of the church corporation are entitled to the temporalities of the church, &c., see Gable *v.* Miller, 10 Paige, 627. The legal tribunals of the State have no jurisdiction over the church, or the members thereof, as such; and the ecclesiastical judicatories are not authorized to interfere with the temporalities of a religious society incorporated. Per Walworth, Ch., in Baptist Church *v.* Hartford, 3 Paige, 296; Sawyer *v.* Cipperly, 7 Paige, 281. Where there is a *trust*, however, a court of equity is bound to see it executed according to the intention of the original founders of the charity. Attorney-General *v.* Pearson, 3 Meriv. 264; and see *post*, Ch. on Power of Corporations to take and hold property. As to the doctrine that the nature of a trust for religious purposes may be inferred from parol evidence of the religious tenets of the creator of the fund, see Robertson *v.* Bullions, 1 Kern. 243.

[2] 1 Kyd, 26; American Asylum at Hartford *v.* Phœnix Bank, 4 Conn. 272. Infancy, insanity, infirmity, and helpless poverty have an undoubted claim upon the protecting care of the legislature; and bodies politic of this class, and having the care and relief of persons subjected to such deprivation in view, are hospitals, &c. Montesq. Sp. Laws, b. 23, c. 29; McKim *v.* Odom, 3 Bland, Ch. 407.

[3] 1 Bl. Com. 472.

founded by private benefactors for the distribution of private contributions.[1] And the corporation of Dartmouth College would not be an ecclesiastical corporation, even if it was composed entirely of ecclesiastical persons, because the object of it is not entirely ecclesiastical.[2]

§ 40. *Civil* corporations include not only those which are public, as cities and towns, but private corporations created for an infinite variety of temporal purposes. They comprehend institutions of learning, and it has been long established, that the universities of Oxford and Cambridge, in England, notwithstanding their subjection to the influence of the church, are civil corporations; though anciently they were deemed ecclesiastical.[3] But the most numerous, and, in a secular and commercial point of view, the most important class of private civil corporations, and which are very often called "companies," consists, at the present day, of banking, insurance, manufacturing, and extensive trading corporations; and likewise of turnpike, bridge, canal, and railroad corporations.[4] The latter kind have a concern with some of the expensive duties of the State, the trouble and charge of which are undertaken and defrayed by them in consideration of a certain emolument allowed to their members; and in cases of this sort there are the most unquestionable features of a contract, and manifestly a *quid pro quo*.[5] These joint-stock corporations, by a combination of capital and skilfully directed labor, have wonderfully contributed to the commercial prosperity of our country, and at no former period were they ever more rapidly increasing numerically than at the present. It is deemed proper, therefore, to consider them with some attention, as distinguished from common partnership associations and simple joint-stock companies, and in connection with the restricted and limited powers with which they are often created, and by which they are to be governed. A trading association may be but a mere partnership; or it may have corporate powers to a small extent, and *sub modo;* or it may be invested with corporate functions to a considerable and yet limited extent; or it may exist

---

[1] Dartmouth College *v.* Woodward, 4 Wheat. 681.

[2] Dartmouth College *v.* Woodward, 4 Wheat. 681; and 4 Bl. Com. 471.

[3] 1 Bl. Com. 471.

[4] The second sort of communities, says Ayliffe, in his Civil Law, extends itself to those persons who have to do with temporal affairs only, as the colleges, and the corporations of merchants, tradesmen, and artificers, usually called "companies." These he calls *secular.*

[5] McKim *v.* Odom, 3 Bland, Ch. 407. See *ante*, § 31.

with all the incidental functions and peculiar privileges which a grant of *unconditional* corporate power confers.

§ 41. The difference between a company established for private hazard and profit by an act or charter of incorporation, and an ordinary copartnership, is obvious and striking. The latter is simply a voluntary contract,[1] or the result of such a contract,[2] whereby two or more persons agree to combine their property or labor, or both, for the purpose of a common undertaking and the acquisition of a common profit; and the gain or loss is to be proportionally shared between them. But this definition greatly falls short of a company established as a body corporate, which, though originating in a voluntary contract, is the result not only of that, but of its confirmation by special legislative authority. This confirmation is indispensable to enable the parties to the compact to sue and be sued, as a company, by a general name, to act by a common seal, and to transmit their property in succession. One, if not the principal and main inducement, in procuring an act of incorporation, is to limit the risk of the partners, and to render definite the extent of their hazard; for it is a perfectly well-settled rule of law, that each member of a common partnership whether active, nominal, or dormant, is the accredited agent of the others, and, as such, has authority to bind them, to the extent of their private property, by any simple contract he may make, either respecting the goods or business of the concern, or by negotiable instruments in its behalf, to any person dealing *bonâ fide*.[3] This personal responsibility of stockholders is inconsistent with a perfect body corporate;[4] and, therefore, where an execution issued against a corporation by the name of the "President, Directors, and Company," with special instruction to the officer to take their bodies, for want of estate, no authority was communicated to him thus to do.[5] And the stock-

---

1 Gow on Part.

2 Smith on Mercantile Law.

3 See the above authorities, and Hess *v.* Werts, 1 S. & R. 350. See *post*, Chap. XVII.

4 As per Tilghman, C. J., in Myers *v.* Irwin, 2 S. & R. 731; Hurger *v.* McCullough, 2 Denio, 77; Van Sandau *v.* Moore, 1 Russ. Ch. 458. One of the greatest distinctions, in contemplation of law, between partnership and corporate companies, is that, in the first, the law looks to the individuals of whom the partnership is composed, and knows the partnership no otherwise than as being such a number of individuals; while in the second, it sees only the creature of the charter, the body corporate, and knows not the individuals. George's View of the existing (English) Law, 29.

5 Per Parsons, C. J., in Nicholas *v.* Thomas, 4 Mass. 232. See also, Man *v.* Chandler, 9 Ibid. 335; Commonwealth *v.* Blue Hill Turn. Cor., 5 id. 420; Marcy *v.* Clark, 17 id.

holders of a corporation do not become liable as partners, on notes given by the treasurer of the corporation, merely because after organizing under the act of incorporation, no corporate business is transacted, or because the notes were given for debts beyond the corporate authority of the company.[1]

§ 42. With the view of encouraging persons to an active and useful employment of their capital, a species of partnership has been introduced, in different parts of the world, with a restricted personal responsibility, and it, on that account, may be called a *quasi* corporation, and therefore is entitled to attention in treating of private, civil, and commercial corporations. Though the English law does not admit of partnerships with a restricted responsibility, they have been established in different parts of the continent, and in this country. In France, by the celebrated ordinance of 1673, *la Société en commandite*, or a limited partnership, was introduced for promoting the interests of the mercantile community and the benefit of the public, by which one or more persons were associated with one or more sleeping partners, who furnished a certain proportion of capital, and were liable only to the extent of the funds furnished.[2] This peculiar kind of partnership has been continued by the new commercial code of France.[3] It has been introduced into the civil code of Louisiana, under the title of Partnership *in Commendam*.[4] On account of its tendency to invite dormant capital into active and useful employment, it has obtained a very considerable extent of favor throughout the United States, and accordingly, it has been authorized by a legislative enactment in the States of New York, Massachusetts, Rhode Island, Connecticut, Vermont, New Jersey, Pennsylvania, Maryland, South Carolina, Georgia, Alabama, Florida, Mississippi, Indiana, and Michigan. The provisions of the New York act having been taken, in most of the essential points, from the French ordinance and code above named; and

---

333; Brewer *v.* Glocester, 14 id. 216; Merchants Bank *v.* Cook, 4 Pick. 414; Andrews *v.* Cullender, 13 id. 484; Atwater *v.* Woodbridge, 6 Conn. 223; Adams *v.* Wiscasset Bank, 1 Greenl. 361.

[1] Trowbridge *v.* Scudder, 11 Cush. 83.

[2] Lord Loughborough, in Coope *v.* Eyre, 1 H. Bl. 48, says: "In many parts of Europe, limited partnerships are admitted, provided they be entered on a register; but the law of England is otherwise, the rule being, that, if a partner shares in advantages, he also shares in the disadvantages."

[3] *Répertoire de Jurisprudence, par Merlin*, tit. *Société*, art. 2, *Code de Commerce*, b. 1, tit. 3, § 1.

[4] Civil Code of Louisiana, art. 2810.

the provision for limited partnerships in the other States (and which were subsequent in point of time to that of New York) is essentially the same.[1] It is the first instance, says Kent, in the history of the legislation of New York, that the statute law of any other country than Great Britain has been closely imitated and adopted.[2]

§ 43. In France, the contribution of a shareholder in a limited partnership, or *commandite* association, may consist of secrets of arts and manufactures, but their adoption must not in any way be accompanied by *acts of management*. This prohibition does not, however, extend to transactions between a shareholder acting in his individual capacity, on the one part, and the association acting by its managing partners, on the other; and this, though it is an essential condition of this species of trading association, that the non-responsible stockholder (*Commanditaire*) take no part in the management. Thus, C, a merchant, may be a shareholder in a *commandite* association, of which A and B are the responsible managing partners. A and B acting for the association, may buy from, or sell to, C, without in any way affecting the rights or immunities of the latter, as a non-responsible shareholder. Moreover, as a shareholder may sell goods to, and so become the creditor of, the *commandite* association to which he belongs, so, also, may he lend money thereto.[3]

§ 44. As an instrument for the aggregation of small capitals, and, therefore, rendering them immediately productive, a limited partnership, or *commandite* association, is highly efficient. Those persons who are indisposed to incur a liability to an uncertain extent in an ordinary copartnership, cannot fail to perceive the additional inducement to do so, which the responsibility of the managing partners of the *commandite* association furnishes. So, also, is the security of the public much greater in the case of a limited partnership, than in that of private traders. In the case of a private trading association, third parties have no security that there is a single dollar of capital. They have nothing but the reputation or credit of the parties, which, it is well known, has been in many cases unmerited. In the case of limited partnerships, the public have all the security which a common partnership affords, in respect to the credit and reputation of the managing partners, with the additional

---

[1] See 3 Kent, Com. 5th ed. 35.

[2] Ibid.

[3] Wordsworth on Joint-stock Companies, Appendix, 4.

guaranty furnished by a statement of the capital furnished by the shareholders. Then, there is the care which individuals would naturally take previous to becoming shareholders, to satisfy themselves of the qualifications of the managing partners. Then, again, there is the security afforded by the interest of the managing partners.[1]

§ 45. The statutes referred to of the above-mentioned States, in general, provide that *limited partnerships* may consist of one or more persons, who shall be called *general* partners, and who shall be, jointly and severally, liable as general partners; and of one or more persons, who shall contribute to the common stock a specific sum, in actual cash payment, as capital, who shall be called *special* partners, and who shall not be personally liable for any of the debts of the partnership. It is commonly prescribed, that the persons, forming such partnerships, shall severally subscribe a certificate, containing the names under which the partnership is to be conducted, the names and residences both of all the general and special partners, distinguishing who are general and who are special, the amount of capital which each special partner has contributed to the common stock, the general nature of the business to be transacted, &c. Such certificate is to be acknowledged and *registered* in the public records of the town or county in which the principal business of the partnership is situated, for the purpose of public inspection and notice; and notice of the partnership must, moreover, be given in newspapers. It has, in many cases, been the policy not to extend these partnerships to banking and insurance; and these are specially excepted in the acts of New York, New Jersey, Pennsylvania, Maryland, South Carolina, Alabama, Mississippi, Connecticut, Vermont, and Florida.[2] These partnerships may be said to be *quasi* corporations, on account of the exemption of some of the partners from personal responsibility, and their being placed, in this respect, upon a similar footing as the members of a perfect corporation.

§ 46. The invention of private corporations has been attributed by Sir William Blackstone, to Numa Pompilius.[3] That Numa adopted the policy of subdividing the Roman and Sabine parties into different classes, according to the trades and the manual occupations of the citi-

---

[1] Wordsworth on Joint-stock Companies Appendix.
[2] 3 Kent, Com. 35.
[3] 1 Bl. Com. 468.

zens composing those turbulent factions, is a fact very well authenticated.[1] The formation of such collective bodies by public authority may, however, be traced to the Greeks.[2] It appears, from a passage in the Pandects, that private corporations were borrowed from the laws of Solon, which licensed the institution of private companies, subject to the restriction of paying obedience to the laws of the State.[3] The Romans, it seems, were more jealous of authorizing private associations than were the Greeks, and hence were more formal in their mode of creating them. They denounced, as *illicit*, every society that had not been constituted by an express decree of the senate or of the emperor.[4] And there are many laws, from the time of the twelve tables down to the times of the emperors, which were passed against all illicit or unauthorized corporations.[5] The appellations given by the Romans to the companies of tradesmen, religious societies, &c., which they established, were *universitates*, as constituting one whole out of many individuals; and *collegia*, from being collected together. And here we may perceive the origin of the names of the literary seminaries, at which youth are at this day sent to complete their education, and to be instructed in the liberal sciences.

§ 47. As before intimated, the Romans were strict in requiring the express consent of government to authorize an association with the powers and privileges of a corporate body; and also in dissolving every combination not thus constituted. It is gathered from Suetonius,[6] that, in the age of Augustus, certain associations had become nurseries of faction and disorder, and that the emperor interposed, as Julius Cæsar had done before him, and dissolved all but the ancient and legal corporations — *cuncta collegia, præter antiquitus constituta, distraxit.*[7] The corporations destroyed by this imperial decree would seem to bear a resemblance to the trading combinations in England, that existed in London in the year 1180, and which are noticed by Madox as having been

---

1 Plutarch's Life of Numa.

2 See Ayliffe's Treatise on the Civil Law, p. 197.

3 Digest, 47, 22, 4, cited in 2 Kent, Com. 216. As the Romans were great borrowers from the Greeks, in literature, philosophy, and the fine arts, so were they in jurisprudence, and, indeed, in every thing, excepting the art of conquering the world.

4 See 2 Kent, Com. 216.

5 Taylor's Civil Law, 567, 570; Ayliffe, 196.

6 Ad. Aug. 32.

7 Suet. J. Cæsar, 42, cited in 2 Kent, Com. 217.

"set up without warrant from the king," and thus distinguished from warranted, or lawful companies.[1] A striking instance of Roman jealousy, in relation to combinations of individuals not expressly sanctioned by the government, is related by the younger Pliny,[2] and is thus mentioned by Kent: "A destructive fire in Nicomedia induced Pliny to recommend to the Emperor Trajan the institution, for that city, of a *fire company* of 150 men (*collegium fabrorum*), with an assurance that none but those of that business should be admitted into it, and that the privileges granted them should not be extended to any other purpose. But the Emperor refused to grant it, and observed that societies of that sort had greatly disturbed the peace of the cities; and he observed, that whatever name he gave them, and for whatever purpose they might be instituted, they would not fail to be mischievous." [3]

§ 48. It is evident that the capacities and incapacities of corporations, under our law, bear a strong resemblance to those under the Civil Law; and that the principles of law applicable to corporations, under the former, were borrowed, if not chiefly, in a great measure, from the latter.[4] It has been considered that the corporations of our own time, which more nearly resemble those of the Romans, are those which have been created in different parts of the United States by charters, that impose upon each member a personal responsibility for the company debts, and in that respect, resemble an ordinary copartnership.[5] Wood, it is true, on the authority of the *Digest*, b. 3, t. 4, l. 7, lays it down, that the debts of the whole body are not chargeable on the particular persons composing it.[6] But that rule, we apprehend, only held in case the corporation was *solvent;* as it is expressly laid down by Ayliffe, that if a corporation be *insolvent*, the persons who constitute it are obliged, by the Civil Law to contribute their private fortunes; and he refers to the first book of the *Code*, tit. 3.[7]

§ 49. By the Roman, as well as by the English system of jurisprudence, the division of corporations was into ecclesiastical and lay, civil

---

[1] Anderson, Hist. Commerce, and 1 Kyd, 44.
[2] Epist. B. 10, Letters 42, 48.
[3] See 2 Kent, Com. 217.
[4] Ibid.
[5] Penniman *v.* Briggs, 1 Hopk. Ch. 300.
[6] Wood's Civil Law, 134.
[7] Ayliffe, 200.

and eleemosynary. The restraints imposed upon them, also, bear a striking resemblance to the mortmain and disabling statutes, passed at an early period in England, and since received in the State of Pennsylvania, as the law of that State, — by the force of which, corporations are precluded from purchasing or receiving donations of land, without a license, and also from alienating, without just cause. They were not empowered to act otherwise than by attorney; the whole were bound by the act of the majority; and the modes of dissolution were the same as those now recognized, namely, *death*, *surrender*, *or forfeiture.*[1]

§ 50. Corporations for the advancement of learning, however (or what *we* denominate colleges), were entirely unknown to the antients, and are, says Kent, the fruits of modern invention. But, continues the same author, in the time of the latter emperors, the professors in the different sciences began to be allowed regular salaries from the government, and to become objects of public regulation and discipline. By the close of the third century, these literary establishments, says he, began to assume the appearance of public institutions;[2] and privileges and honors were bestowed upon the professors and students, who were subjected to visitation and inspection, by the civil and ecclesiastical powers. It was not, however, until at least the thirteenth century that colleges and universities began to *confer degrees*, and to attain the authority and influence they now enjoy.[3] It is true, there were numerous students at Oxford, and professors who read lectures in grammar, rhetoric, divinity, astronomy, philosophy, &c.; but still that seminary, like others, was usually called a school, and was not furnished with the power of granting public distinctions, like degrees. The University of Paris was the first which assumed the form of our modern colleges.[4]

§ 51. It would be unjust, in noticing the origin of the above institutions for the promotion of learning, to withhold a passing tribute to the Civil Law for its merit in the advancement and encouragement of literary and scientific seminaries; for to the honorable passion which univer-

---

[1] 1 Browne, Civil and Adm. Law, 142; 8 Wood, Inst. of the Civil Law, 134; 2 Kent, Com. 217.

[2] Particularly the schools at Rome, Constantinople, Alexandria, and Berytus. 2 Kent. Com. 270.

[3] Ibid.

[4] Browne, Civil Law, 112.

sally prevailed, after the discovery of the Pandects at Amalfi, for the study of the Civil Law, is to be ascribed the fact of the resort of such immense numbers to the universities, wherein it was taught, such as Bologna, Oxford, &c. The objects of study in these universities were divided into four branches; divinity, law, and physic, composed three, and the arts and sciences, cemented under one head, formed a fourth.[1]

§ 52. The practice of incorporating persons composing particular trades, after the manner of Solon and Numa, prevailed at a very early period in England. A charter is now extant which was conferred by Henry II. to the "Weavers' Company," which granted to them their guild, with all the freedom they had in his grandfather's (Hen. I.) days. A charter was given to "The Goldsmiths," in 1327; and another to "The Mercers," in 1393. "The Haberdashers" were incorporated in 1407; "The Fishmongers," in 1433; "The Vintners," in 1437; and "The Merchant Tailors," in 1466.[2]

§ 53. Among the secular corporations of the Roman Law were included companies composed of merchants, &c. which embarked in commercial adventures.[3] The spirit of commercial enterprise, which gave rise to the establishment, or perhaps more properly to the resuscitation of independent towns and cities in modern Europe, led also the way to commercial corporations of a less political character, and which principally consisted of mercantile and other adventurers. To such companies, which had in view their own private emolument, great privileges and monopolies were given, in order to induce them to hazard a considerable portion of their fortunes in the accomplishment of designs of private emolument, which would, it was supposed, at the same time, be beneficial to the government and the nation; and which, without charters of incorporation, would not have been prosecuted. As early as the year 1248, a company of Burgundians received an act of incorporation, in order to induce them to employ their capital for the promotion of ob-

---

[1] Ibid. The power of faculty of teaching the arts and sciences was bestowed by the State to the seminary; by the seminary to the individual; and hence, in process of time, these branches of learning came to be called *faculties;* and the criterion or essential difference of an university was the power and license of teaching the four branches, the supposed compass of *university* knowledge; and accordingly, the college of Dublin is properly an university; and so is that of Glasgow. Ibid.

[2] 1 And. Hist. Commerce, 250; Hume, Hist. of Eng. (reign of King John).

[3] Ayliffe, 196.

jects, the tendency of which was to the public benefit.[1] This company was afterwards translated to England, and there confirmed by Edward I., and received, in the reign of Henry VI., the name of the "Merchant Adventurers."[2] The revolutions which happened in the Low Countries towards the end of the sixteenth century, and which laid the foundation of the Republic of Holland, having prevented the company from continuing commerce with their ancient freedom, they were compelled to turn it almost wholly to the side of Hamburg, and the cities on the German Ocean; from which the name was changed to that of Hamburg Company, though the ancient title of Merchant Adventurers is retained in all their writings.[3] The Russian Company was first projected towards the end of the reign of Edward VI., and executed in the first and second years of Philip and Mary; but had not its perfection till its charter was confirmed by act of parliament, under Queen Elizabeth, in 1566. The charter of the Eastland Company, incorporated by Queen Elizabeth, is dated in the year 1579. The Turkey or Levant Company, had its rise under the same queen, in 1581; and so did the celebrated East India Company, in 1600. The charter of the Hudson's Bay Company, is dated in the year 1670; and the South Sea Company grew out of the long war between England and France, in the reign of Queen Anne.

§ 54. The Italian States were engaged in commerce as early as the age of Charlemagne, and in the tenth century the Venetians had even opened a trade with Alexandria, in Egypt.[4] The first establishment of banking in a regular and systematic form originated with that opulent and enterprising people about the middle of the twelfth century. A "Chamber of Loans" was instituted for the management of the fund, which was raised to relieve the State finances from the embarrassment occasioned by the expensive wars with the empire of the west; and this institution gradually improving in its plan was at length formed into the more perfect institution of the "Bank of Venice."[5] This celebrated

---

[1] Molloy, Marit. Law.

[2] And. Hist. of Commerce, 542.

[3] 1 Greg. Dict.

[4] 3 Rob. Hist. Charles V. 273, 274.

[5] 3 Edin. Encycloped. 217. The term *bank*, in reference to commerce, implies a place of deposit of money. Banks, like most commercial institutions, originated in Italy; where, in the infancy of European commerce, the Jews were wont to assemble in the market-places of the principal towns, seated on benches, ready to lend money; and the

bank served as a model to similar establishments, which, in succeeding ages, were founded by the governments of the different States and kingdoms of Europe.

§ 55. The Bank of Genoa commenced in 1407; though previous to this time, the republic borrowed large sums of money from the citizens, assigning certain branches of the public revenue for the payment of the interest, under the management of a board. The Genoese have been led from this circumstance to assume the merit of establishing a bank as early as the Venetians. In process of time the Genoese saw the expediency of consolidating the public loan into one capital stock, to be managed by a bank, called "The Chamber of St. George," to be governed by eight directors, annually elected by the stockholders and creditors. In the year 1444, to prevent the inconvenience of an annual election of directors, eight new governors for the management of the bank were chosen, two only of whom were to go out every year.[1] It was no small number of years before any other banks than those mentioned were established in Europe; it not having been until the year 1609, that the example of Venice and Genoa was followed by the great commercial city of Amsterdam. On the thirty-first of January, in that year, the Bank of Amsterdam was established, by a declaration of the magistrates of the city, under the authority of the States, that they were the perpetual cashiers of the inhabitants, and that all payments above 600 guilders (but afterwards reduced to 300), and bills of exchange, should be made in the bank. The beneficial effects of this establishment by the Dutch were soon perceived, and bank money immediately bore a premium.[2]

---

term *bank* is derived from the Italian word *banco* (bench). Banks are of three kinds, of *deposit*, of *discount*, and of *circulation*. In some cases, all these functions are exercised by the same establishment; sometimes two of them; and in other instances only one. 1. A bank of deposit receives money to keep for the depositor, until he draws it out. This is the first and most obvious purpose of these institutions. The goldsmiths of London were formerly bankers of this description; they took the money, bullion, plate, &c., of depositors, merely for safe keeping. 2. Another branch of banking business is the discounting of promissory notes and bills of exchange, or loaning money upon mortgage, pawn, or other security. 3. A bank of circulation issues bills or notes of its own, intended to be the circulating currency or medium of exchanges, instead of gold and silver. The Bank of England, the Bank of the United States, and the State banks in this country, are all of them banks of deposit, discount, and circulation. See Encyclopedia Americana, vol. i. art. *Bank*.

[1] 3 Edin. Encycloped. 217.

[2] Or *agio*, which is a term to denote the difference of price between the money of the bank and the coin of the country. 3 Edin. Encycloped. 217.

§ 56. In the year 1694, the charter of *incorporation* was granted by William and Mary to the "Bank of England," which, for opulence and the extent of its circulation, is now one of the most considerable in the world. The projector of the bank (William Patterson, a Scotchman), it is said, took for a model the Bank of St. George, in Genoa. The charter was granted for the term of twelve years; and the corporation was determinable on a year's notice. A governor, deputy-governor, and twenty directors, are annually elected from the proprietors, but not above two thirds of the directors for the preceding year can be chosen. There was a renewal of the charter of the Bank of England in the fortieth year of the reign of George III., when, on certain conditions, it was continued to the first of August, 1833. By the act which originally constituted this bank, as well as by the various subsequent statutes, numerous privileges are conferred on the governor and company; and salutary restrictions interposed for the protection and welfare of the institution. They are authorized to purchase and hold lands, with all the powers incident to other corporations. The stock is accounted as personal, and not as real estate, and goes to the executor, and not the heirs. All contracts, or agreements for buying or selling stock, must be registered on the books of the bank, within seven days, and the stock transferred within fourteen, after such contracts have been entered into.[1]

§ 57. It has never been the policy, in England, as in this country, to adopt, as a practice, the conferring of full and unqualified corporate privileges upon a body of men associated for the purposes of trade. Corporations have been occasionally permitted, in England, to engross some business to the exclusion of natural persons, as formerly the trade to China by the East India Company; and all the ancient charters for commercial purposes were intended, either to create monopoly, or to force capital into channels in which naturally it would not have flowed.[2] A report was once made to the king[3] on a proposed charter to a corpo-

[1] Ibid. 219. The Bank of England was first established by the 5 & 6 Wm. & Mary, c. 20, which, by sect. 19, gave power to their majesties, by letters-patent, to incorporate the subscribers and contributors to the sum of money therein mentioned, by the name of the "Governor and Company of the Bank of England." For a history of the various acts passed at different periods, in relation to this great moneyed corporate institution, the reader is referred to the case of the Bank of England *v.* Anderson, 3 Bing. N. R. 589. See *post*, Chap. XVI.

[2] See Art. II. Lond. Law Mag. vol. 38.

[3] Signed March 12, 1717, by Northey and Thompson.

rate body for marine insurance. Those who petitioned for it, represented, that merchants frequently sustained great loss for the want of an incorporated company of insurers, with a joint-stock, to make good all such total and partial losses of ships, and merchandise, at sea, as should be by them insured; and that a company for that purpose, with corporate powers and privileges, would be an encouragement to trade. The advantages usually supposed, in this country, to be derived from an act of incorporation are there set forth. The opinions of eminent merchants were obtained, which differed; and the weight of opinion was against the policy of an incorporated insurance company.[1]

§ 58. A parliamentary act of Geo. I. of 1719, it seems, however, was entitled an act for better securing certain powers and privileges *intended* to be granted by his majesty, by two charters of assurance of ships and merchandise at sea, and for lending money upon bottomry, as well as for "restraining several extravagant and unwarrantable practices therein mentioned." The first seventeen sections relate to the two assurance companies, the "Royal Exchange," and the "London," for assuring ships, to which charters were granted under this act. It having been clearly ascertained, in the course of time, that the number of members of a *partnership* and the extent of the transactions in which it engages, render it difficult to carry it on under the general rules provided by law for the government of partnerships, it became usual to have recourse to the legislature for its assistance in supplying the powers, without which it was impossible to conduct a proposed enterprise advantageously. The act in such cases, usually enables the company to sue and be sued in the name of its secretary, or some one member to be appointed for that purpose, thereby obviating the technical objections that might arise in consequence of the non-joinder of some among a great number of partners.[2] It thereby, so far, makes a joint-stock company a *quasi* corporation, though the act provides, that nothing therein shall extend to incorporate the partnership.

§ 59. When these large copartnerships were first thought of in England, it appears wonderful how little attention was paid to their constitution. At first they were formed by a mere deed,[3] though composed

---

[1] "Opinions of Eminent Lawyers," London, 1814, p. 308.

[2] See *post*, commencement of Chap. XVII.; and *ante*, § 24.

[3] Smith's Mercantile Law, 61.

of a number of persons too great to be brought into court. Afterwards they were in the habit of applying to the legislature for its sanction; and Lord Redesdale, after some experience of their effects, took care to prevent any acts from being passed, giving a legal existence to such bodies, unless there were contained in them stipulations that a memorial should be registered of the different individuals who were partners in the concern. But though the memorial told who the persons were with whom one had to deal, it gave such a legion of names that it was to no purpose to attempt to sue them all. The right of a creditor of the company to sue it was of no avail, for as soon as he declared on his contract, he was met by a plea in abatement, setting out the names and addresses of all the members of the company as co-defendants. Another mischief was, that the name, which was in the memorial to-day, ceased to be in it before six months had expired; and those who had claims on the body, had no means of enforcing their remedies as against a person so withdrawing from the association. Then came the improvement of permitting the secretary or treasurer of these partnerships to sue and be sued on behalf of the body. Unfortunately, however, it turned out, that the secretary, who sued individuals, obtained payment from them; while, on the other hand, individuals who sued the secretary, got verdicts and judgments, and nothing more. This led to a further change, which made every individual liable to execution, in consequence of a judgment recovered against the secretary. There was still one thing which had been totally overlooked. Though the secretary could sue and be sued by an individual, not a member of the company, there had not been devised any means by which an individual, a member of the body, suing as an individual member, the other members, could proceed. It was only in the year 1825 that the defect was removed.[1]

§ 60. With respect to joint-stock *banks* of issue, at a distance of more than sixty-five miles from London, they were governed by law of their own (Stat. 7, Geo. VI.) which not only *allowed*, but *compelled* them to appoint public officers, in whose names they were to sue and be sued. The attention of parliament was at length drawn to the extreme

---

[1] See the observations of Lord Chancellor Eldon, on the legal history of joint-stock companies, and on the provisions which have been introduced into acts of parliament, to the year 1826, creating or regulating such companies, in order to give effect to legal proceedings, to which they are parties, in the case of Van Sandau *v.* Moore, 1 Russ. Ch. 441.

inconvenience endured by other companies, and it was thought expedient to empower the crown to grant joint-stock companies such powers as were likely to be most useful to them without conferring upon them all the incidents of corporate existence. The first attempt made by the legislature to effect the object was by 6 Geo. IV. which enacted, that in any charter of incorporation thereafter to be granted, it should be lawful for the crown to provide, that the members of such corporation should be individually liable in their persons for the debts of the corporation, to such extent, and subject to such regulations and restrictions, as by the crown might be deemed useful and proper. The next instance of such interposition was the statute of 4 and 5 William IV., by which the crown was empowered to increase the privileges of companies, and to place them nearer to the level of corporations. For this purpose was the crown empowered to grant to joint-stock companies, by letters-patent, the privilege of bringing and defending actions in the name of any of their officers, upon certain conditions.[1] The provisions of this statute, however, not being found sufficiently extensive, and the subject having been much investigated and discussed, in consequence of the prodigious number of railroads, banking, gas, steam, mining, and other joint-stock companies, still another attempt was made. The next in relation to the subject was made by the statute of 1 Victoria, c. 73, entitled, "An Act to enable her majesty to confer certain powers and immunities on trading and other companies, by which the powers of the crown to confer peculiar privileges upon joint-stock companies became regulated." The first section of this statute recites, "that divers associations may be formed for trading and other purposes, some of which it would be inexpedient to incorporate, though it would be expedient to confer upon them some of the privileges of corporations, and also to confer upon them other powers and privileges;" and after reciting that the statutes of 6 Geo. IV. and 4 and 5 William IV. have not been found effectual for the purpose thereby intended, repeals the same. It has, among other less important provisions, the following: The crown may grant to any company, their heirs, &c., any privilege it might grant by charter of incorporation. In any such grant it may be provided, that all suits and proceedings *by or on behalf* of the company, shall be carried on in the names of two of its officers appointed to sue and be sued, in the name of the company; and that all suits *against* the company shall be carried on against such officer, or if there be none such, against any

---

[1] Smith on Mercantile Law. See *post*, Chap. XVII.

member of the company, provided that any member may be joined with such officer for the purpose of discovery, or in case of fraud. The liability of members of the company for its debts and engagements, may be limited in such grants, to such extent per share, as shall be therein declared. By this statute was introduced in England a completely new system; and one somewhat resembling that of the limited partnerships in our country, is created, to which companies receiving charters are subjected, which partakes in some degree of the nature of a corporation, though in other respects the members will be governed by the general law of partnership.[1]

§ 61. It seems, that under the above-mentioned act, very few applications for charters were made; and the rapid increase in the number of joint-stock associations rendered some *general* enactment, the operation of which should not be dependent upon their option, necessary. The statute of 7 & 8 Vict. c. 110, was therefore passed, which created a uniform system with reference to companies established after the first day of November, 1844. The provisions of this statute are so minute and numerous, that it is impossible to furnish an abridgment which can convey accurate information as to its provisions. Its object, speaking generally, may be said to be twofold, corresponding to the two classes of evils which it was designed to remedy. First, it aims to protect society from those mischiefs which arise incidentally, yet necessarily, from the establishment and the operation of powerful moneyed associations; and secondly, it aims to place the associations themselves, in such circumstances, entrust them with such powers, and endow them with such immunities, as shall fit them most appropriately for securing the objects proposed, and furthering the public welfare. It is provided, by section sixty-sixth, that every judgment, decree, or order obtained in a court of law or equity, against any company completely registered under this act, except such as are incorporated by act of parliament or charter, or companies the liability of the members of which is restricted by letters-patent, may be enforced against every member thereof, and execution issued against the property of any *former* or *existing* shareholder, if due diligence shall have been previously used to obtain satisfaction out of the effects of the company; but no execution can be issued against any

---

[1] Gow on Part. 3; Van Sandau *v.* Moore, 1 Russ. Ch. 458, *et seq.;* Wills *v.* Sutherland, 4 Exch. 211. See *ante,* § 42-46.

former shareholder, unless he were such at the time when the contract or engagement was entered into, for which the judgment was obtained, or become so while the contract was unexecuted, or was so at the time of the judgment being obtained; nor against any person who shall have ceased to be a shareholder for three years.[1]

§ 62. A sense of the public utility of the existence of trading companies, at length induced the British parliament to require that the condition and modes of their existence and operation should be so ordered as to produce the most benefits with the fewest evils; for there are obstacles, both to the formation and to the easy and beneficial operation of companies which the legislative power only can remove; and certain capacities essential to the interests both of the public and the company, which cannot be possessed without legislative interference; and legislative sanction and assistance have been found requisite in England, to enable the public to reap the full measure of those advantages which the carrying out of the principle of *association* is fitted to produce.[2]

§ 63. It would be a task much more easy to enumerate the corporations of the aggregate, and not of the municipal kind, now existing in Europe, than it would be to enumerate those now established in the United States. An absence of great wealth was common to the inhabitants of the United States at the commencement of the national independence, and such a condition of society came soon to be deemed preservative of our republican institutions; and it was this consideration which induced the abolishment of entailments, the suppression of the right of primogeniture, and protracted fiduciary accumulations. By the operation of such legislation, a state would have accomplished but little in the way of banking and insurance, and in turnpike and railroads, had not the absence of great capitalists been remedied by corporate associations, which aggregate the resources of many persons, and thereby yield the advantage of great capitals without the supposed disadvantages

---

[1] Art. II. Lond. Law Mag. vol. 33, and Art. I. of the same work, vol. 34.

[2] Ibid.; Smith, Mer. Law, 104. Lord Goderich, in a speech in parliament, when speaking upon the subject of the individual responsibility of joint-stock companies, said, that the surest way to keep open, not only the trade with North America, but with other countries, is *not* to give special privileges to a company; which, by the aid of these privileges, would rapidly succeed in driving all other competitors out of the trade. *From the London Shipping and Mercantile Gazette of December* 10, 1852. See *ante*, § 35, *et seq.*

of great private fortunes.[1] "It is remarkable," says Chancellor Bland, of Maryland, "that there is no instance of the creation of any body politic of this description (private) under the provincial government; but since the establishment of the Republic, they have increased and multiplied to a very large and still rapidly growing family; and the examples of this class of corporations are, the insurance companies, the freemason societies, the banks, the manufacturing companies, the library companies, &c."[2] In no country, indeed, have corporations been multiplied to so great an extent, as in our own; and the extent to which their institution has here been carried, may very properly be pronounced "astonishing."[3] The increase of corporations in the United States, has, in fact, kept pace in every part of it, with the increase of wealth and improvement. There is scarcely an individual of respectable character in our community, who is not a member of at least one private company or society which is incorporated. The number of banking companies, insurance companies, canal companies, turnpike companies, railroad companies, manufacturing companies, &c., and the number of literary, religious, and charitable associations, that are diffused throughout these United States, and amply invested with corporate privileges, must excite the surprise of Europeans, especially when they call to mind, that not much more than two centuries have elapsed since civilized man first found the country a wilderness, wherein the unlettered savage roamed in unmolested freedom.

§ 64. "The New York Convention, in the year 1821, attempted," says Kent, "to check the improvident increase of corporations, by requiring the assent of two thirds of the members elected to each branch of the legislature to every bill for creating, continuing, altering, or renewing any body politic or corporate." Even this provision, as we are told by the same author, "failed to mitigate the supposed evil;" and he refers the reader, for an instance of the failure, to the session of the New York legislature of 1823, that is, the first session after the operation of the check just mentioned. At that session, *thirty-nine* new private temporal corporations were instituted;[4] and, in 1838, a law was enacted by the legislature of that State, by which banks could be instituted by voluntary associations, under certain specified general forms

---

1 See Hunt's Merch. Mag. for December, 1850, p. 626.
2 McKim *v.* Odom, 3 Bland, Ch. 407.
3 2 Kent, Com. 219.
4 Ibid.

and regulations. It is true, that the legislature was unable to accord to the associations a perfect corporate organization, by reason that the constitution had been construed as prohibiting the creation of more than a single corporation in any one bill. The associations were, however, essentially corporations, though not endued with the usually prescribed machinery of a corporate seal, &c. The legislature of Massachusetts, in 1837, incorporated upwards of seventy manufacturing associations; and made, perhaps, forty other corporations relating to insurance, roads, bridges, academies, and religious objects.[1] The new constitution of New York, of 1848, interdicts special grants of corporate powers, and permits, under general laws, every person to obtain a corporate organization who desires the facility; and this has been viewed as a consummation of the greatest triumph that our American experiment of equal rights has ever achieved in practical results.[2]

§ 65. Kent truly observes, "that the multiplication of corporations in the United States, and the avidity with which they are sought, have arisen in consequence of the power which a large and consolidated capital gives them over business of every kind; and the facility which the incorporation gives to the management of that capital, and the security which it affords to the persons of the members, and to their property not vested in the corporate stock."[3] And the remark made by Mr. J. Duncan, of Pennsylvania, namely, that that State "was an extensive manufacturer of home-made corporations,"[4] will apply, at the present period more especially, as our readers well know, to every State in the Union.

---

[1] See note to 2 Kent, Com. 272.

[2] See Art. III. in Hunt's Merch. Mag. for December, 1850, entitled, "The Legislative History of Corporations in the State of New York," p. 610.

[3] 2 Kent, Com. 219.

[4] Bushell *v.* Commonwealth Ins. Co. 15 S. & R. 186.

CHAPTER II.

IN WHAT MANNER AND BY WHOM PRIVATE CORPORATIONS MAY BE CREATED.

§ 66. By the Civil Law no corporation could be created without the express approbation of the *sovereign*, after a satisfactory representation of their usefulness and tendency to promote the public good. In the words of Domat, "Communities, ecclesiastical and secular, are assemblies of many persons, united into one body, that is formed with the prince's consent, without which these kinds of assemblies would be unlawful." [1] It has, however, been laid down as the reader will probably recollect, by Blackstone, that corporations *seem* to have been erected by the Civil Law, by the mere act and voluntary association of the members, provided such convention was not contrary to law; and it does not appear, he says, that the prince's consent was necessary. Blackstone is doubtless correct as to temporary societies, or mercantile partnerships, formed for the interests of particular persons, and to continue during their lives; but as to corporate communities, intended to be permanent like the corporations of the present day, the rule of the Civil Law was, that they could not exist unless confirmed by the sovereign power.[2]

---

[1] 1 Domat, Civil Law, Prel. Book, tit. ii. sec. ii., xv. Mandatis principalibus præcipitur præsidibus provinciarum, ne patiantur esse (collegia), sodalitia neve milites collegia in castris habeant, *l.* 1, *ff. de colleg. et corp.* Neque societas, neque collegium, neque hujusmodi corpus passim omnibus haberi conceditur. Nam et legibus et senatus-consultis, et principalibus constitutionibus ea res coercetur. Paucis admodum in causis concessa sunt hujusmodi corpora; ut ecce vectigalium publicorum sociis permissum est corpus habere; vel aurifodinarum, vel argentifodinarum, et salinarum. Item collegia Romæ certa sunt quorum corpus senatus-consultis atque constitutionibus principalibus confirmatum est; veluti pistorum et quorundam aliorum et naviculariorum, *l.* 1, *ff. quod* cujus univ. nom. And see also Civil Code of Louisiana, Tit. Corporations.

[2] See 1 Browne, Civil Law, 101, 102; The Digest, 47, Lib. 22, 23, says expressly, that every corporation is illegal, *nisi ea vel Senatus Consulti auctoritate vel Cæsaris coierit.* Dr.

§ 67. In England, it is true, during the latter part of the Saxon period of its history, and for some time after the Conquest, the power of conferring corporate privileges was exercised by the nobles, within their respective demesnes. And there are many instances of towns within the territorial limits of the feudal barons, which had enjoyed such privileges by charters from their immediate lords; which privileges, having come to the crown by escheat were confirmed.[1] That the king, however, very soon after the conquest, was understood to possess the exclusive prerogative of creating *guilds*, appears from the circumstance, that many companies of a commercial character were suppressed about that period, as *adulterine* guilds; that is corporations set up without the royal or government warrant and authority.[2] In the time of Bracton, who lived in the reign of Henry III. and Edward I., the king's prerogative, as to the exclusive privilege of granting liberties and franchises in general, seems to have been fully established;[3] and the absolute necessity of the king's assent to the institution of any corporation was held, in the reign of Edward III. to have been previously settled as clear law.[4] The method by which the king's assent is expressly given, is either by *act of parliament* (of which the royal assent is a necessary ingredient), or by *charter*. The power of erecting a university was, on the continent, exercised by the prince or pope;[5] but the pope was never competent to create a corporation in England. At the time of the Reformation, in consequence of the statute 1 Edw. VI. which gave the colleges, therein described, to the king, it generally became a question whether the house claimed was a lawful college; the determination of which depended upon the authority by which it was established.[6] In the case of Greystock College, it appeared that Pope Urban, at the request of Ralph, Baron of Greystock, founded a college of a master and six priests, resident at Greystock, and assigned to each of the priests five marks per annum, besides their bed and chamber, and to their master forty pounds per annum; and it was certified, in the book of the first fruits and tenths, that this college was in being within five years before

---

Browne, in the work just referred to, is bold in differing from Blackstone, that corporations, by the Roman Law, were erected by the mere act of voluntary association of the members; and maintains that they were formed by a decree of the Senate, or by the Imperial Constitutions. See also Wood, Inst. of the Imp. Civil Law, 134, which refers to D. 3, 4, 1 & 2; Ayliffe, 196.

[1] 1 Kyd, 42; Miller on Eng. Gov. 149.

[2] 1 Kyd, 44.

[3] Bract. 1, 2, ch. 24, f. 55, 56.

[4] Bro. Corpor. 15; 10 R. 33.

[5] Ayliffe, 210.

[6] 1 Kyd, 44.

the making of the statute; and it was resolved by the justices, that this *reputative* college was not given to the king by that statute, because it wanted a *lawful beginning*, and the countenance also of a lawful commencement, for that the pope could not found or incorporate a college within the realm, nor assign, nor license others to assign temporal living to it; but that it ought to be done by the king himself, and by no others.[1]

§ 68. In England, the king or queen alone, when a corporation is intended with privileges, which, by the principles of the English Law, may be granted by the king, is qualified to create a corporation by his or her sole charter. Thus the city of Annapolis, in Maryland, was incorporated by a charter from Queen Anne, when she held the government of the Province.[2] When, on the other hand, it is intended to establish a corporation vested with powers which the king cannot of himself grant, recourse must be had to an act of parliament; as if it be intended, for example, to grant the power of imprisonment, as in the case of the College of Physicians; or to confer a monopoly, as in the case of the East India Company;[3] or when a court is erected, with a power to proceed in a manner contrary to the rules of the Common Law.[4] Until late years, most of the parliamentary acts creating corporations, confirm such as were before created by the king alone, without authority, as in the case of the College of Physicians, constituted by Henry VIII.[5]

§ 69. All the corporations, which are said in the English books to have been created by the *Common Law* and by *prescription*, imply the

---

1 Dyer, 81, pl. 64; 4 R. 109.

2 See note to p. 416 of 3 Bland, Ch.

3 Mr. Burke, in his speech on the India Bill, in considering that objection, which was made to the bill on the ground of its being an attack on "the *chartered* rights of men," observed, that that phrase was unusual in the discussion of privileges conferred by a charter like that of the East India Company. If the *natural* rights of men, he said, are clearly defined by express covenants, and secured against power and chicane, it is a formal recognition, by the sovereign power, of an original right in the subject; and that the charters, which by distinction are called *great*, are public instruments of this nature, as, for instance, the charters of King John and King Henry III. But there may be, and are, charters of a different nature. *Magna Charta* is a charter to *restrain* power; but the East India charter and other charters, which have been granted, are to *create* power. Burke's Speech on the India Bill.

4 1 Kyd, 61; Cro. Car. 73, 87.

5 8 Co. R. 114.

sanction of government. The corporations, existing in England by virtue of the Common Law, are supposed to have been warranted by the concurrence of former governments; Common Law being, in fact, nothing more than custom arising from an universal assent. The tenure of the king, and of all bishops, parsons, &c. to their respective offices, is founded on the principle just stated.[1] So, also, in the case of corporations, which are said to exist by *prescription*, such, for example, as the corporation of the City of London, and others which have enjoyed and exercised corporate privileges from time immemorial; they are in the eye of the law well founded; for though no legal charter can be shown, yet the legal presumption is, there once was a charter, which, owing to the accidents of time, is lost or destroyed.[2] A corporation by prescription, has been said to be a corporation which has existed from time immemorial, and of which it is impossible to show the commencement by any particular charter or act of parliament, the law presuming that such charter or act of parliament once existed, but that it has been lost by such accidents as length of time may produce.[3]

§ 70. There is no doubt, says Kent, that corporations, as well as other private rights and franchises, may exist in this country by *prescription*.[4] Indeed, the *Common Law*, so far as it relates to churches in this country, of the Episcopal persuasion, — the right to present to such churches, — and the corporate capacity of the parsons thereof to take in succession, has been expressly recognized by the highest authority.[5] The church entitled, must be a church recognized in law for this particular purpose. Whenever, therefore, previous to the Revolution, an Episcopal Church was duly erected by the crown, the parson thereof regularly inducted, had a right to the glebe in perpetual succession. Where no such church was duly erected by the crown, the glebe remained as an *hæreditas jacens*, and the State which succeeded to the rights of the crown, might, with the assent of the town, aliene or encumber it; or might erect an Episcopal Church therein, and collate either directly, or through the vote of the town, indirectly, its parson, who would thereby become seised of the glebe *jure ecclesiæ*, and be a

---

[1] 1 Bl. Com. 472; 1 Kyd, 39; Town of Pawlet *v.* Clark, 9 Cranch, 292.
[2] Ibid.; 2 Inst. 330.
[3] 1 Kyd, 14.
[4] 2 Kent, Com. 277.
[5] Town of Pawlet *v.* Clark, 9 Cranch, 294.

corporation capable of transmitting the inheritance. Such were the rights and privileges of the Episcopal Churches of New Hampshire, and the legal principles applicable to the glebes reserved in the various townships of that State, previous to the Revolution. Without, indeed, an adoption of some of the Common Law, it seems difficult to support the royal grants and commissions, or to uphold that ecclesiastical policy, which the crown had a right to patronize, and to which it so explicitly avowed its attachment.[1]

It may be considered well settled, that a corporation may exist in this country by *presumptive evidence*. In Massachusetts, where no act of incorporation could be found of a parish, which had existed more than forty years, evidence was admitted, to prove its incorporation by reputation.[2] And in another case in the same State, parol proof, tending to show the existence of an act incorporating a town with the ordinary powers and privileges, was deemed admissible at the expiration of thirty years; though in general, a record is to be proved by inspection, or a properly authenticated copy.[3] And an act of incorporation does not raise a conclusive presumption that the town was not incorporated before, but such incorporation may be shown by reputation.[4] Evidence of the destruction of part of the public records is admissible towards accounting for the loss of a charter.[5] It may, indeed, be safely relied on as a sound proposition, that, when an association of persons have for a long time acted as a private corporation, have been uniformly recognized as such, and rights have been acquired under them as a corporation, the law will countenance every presumption in favor of its legal corporate existence;[6] at least, unless against the sovereign.

§ 71. Although corporations may, as above mentioned, exist in this country by Common Law, and by reputation (the latter being presumptive evidence in favor that the body corporate has been legally consti-

---

[1] Ibid. See also, Terrett *v.* Taylor, 9 Cranch, 43. See *ante*, § 36.

[2] Dillingham *v.* Snow, 7 Mass. 547.

[3] Stockbridge *v.* West Stockbridge, 12 Mass. 400.

[4] Bow *v.* Allenstown, 34 N. H. 351.

[5] Bow *v.* Allenstown, 34 N. H. 351.

[6] Hagerstown Turn. Co. *v.* Creeger, 5 Harris & J. 122; Shrewsbury *v.* Hart, 1 Car. & P. 113. By virtue of usage, a corporation may have more than one corporate name. Ibid. All Saints Church *v.* Lovett, 1 Hall, 141; Trott *v.* Warren, 2 Fairf. 227; Dutchess Cotton Man. Co. *v.* Davis, 14 Johns. 238; Middlesex Husbandmen, &c. *v.* Davis, 3 Met. 133.

tuted against all but the sovereign), yet there are, comparatively, but few cases where a legislative act or charter cannot be shown. The State legislatures, in the United States, have for many years past, in very numerous instances, exercised the right of granting corporate privileges both to public and to private companies. The competency of the legislative power of a State to create corporations, with powers which are not repugnant to the constitution of the United States and the acts of Congress, and which do not conflict with the powers of the general government, nor with the constitution of the State, is so clear, so generally admitted, and has been so long and so often claimed and exercised, that it is unnecessary to offer any arguments or authorities to establish it. As is observed by the Supreme Court of the United States, in the case of M'Culloch *v.* State of Maryland, "a corporation must be considered not less usual, not of higher dignity, not more requiring a particular specification, than other means. If we look to the origin of corporations, to the manner in which they have been framed in that government from which we have derived most of our legal principles and ideas, or to the uses to which they have been applied, we find no reason to suppose that a constitution, omitting, and wisely omitting, to enumerate all the means for carrying into execution the great powers vested in government, ought to have specified this."[1] This reasoning, though it was applied to the government and constitution of the United States, will, obviously, as forcibly apply to a State government and constitution. It was held, in the State of Tennessee, that the incorporation of banking institutions, not being within any prohibition of the constitution of that State, remained to be exercised by the legislature, as one of its incidental powers.[2] By the constitution of Michigan, it is provided, that the legislature shall pass no act of incorporation, unless with the assent of at least two thirds of each house. It was held, by the Circuit Court of the United States, that this provision did not restrict the legislature from creating more than one corporation in the same act; and the act being passed by a constitutional majority, being within the restriction; the act of the legislature of Michigan, entitled, "an act to organize and regulate banking associations," under which the "Detroit Bank" was incorporated, was constitutional.[3] The Supreme Court of the State of Michigan, on the other hand, subsequently determined that the framers

---

[1] M'Culloch *v.* State of Maryland, 4 Wheat. 421.

[2] Bell *v.* Bank of Nashville, Peck, Tenn. 269.

[3] Per McLean, J., in Falconer *v.* Campbell, 2 McLean, C. C. 195.

of the constitution of that State intended that the legislature should be *directly* responsible to the people for *each and every act of incorporation* they might in their discretion pass, and maintained, in an elaborate opinion, that the rule that the reason and intention of the lawgiver will control the strict letter of the law, when the latter would lead to palpable injustice and absurdity, was decisive of the question before them.[1]

§ 72. The question, whether the Congress of the United States can create a corporation, has received the grave consideration of some of our most eminent statesmen and learned judges. The reply of Mr. Hamilton, when Secretary of the Treasury, to the objections of the Secretary of State and the Attorney-General, to the establishment of a national bank, which objections were founded on a general denial of the authority of Congress to erect corporations, is clear, able, and worthy of attention. Mr. Hamilton commenced his argument, by advancing the broad principle, that every power vested in a government, is, in its nature, SOVEREIGN, and includes, by *force* of the *term*, a right to employ all the means requisite, and fairly applicable to the attainment of the ends of such power, and which are not precluded by restrictions and exceptions specified in the constitution; or not immoral, or not contrary to the essential ends of political society. This principle, in its application to government in general, he doubted not, would be admitted as an axiom; and, therefore, he considered it incumbent on those who might incline to deny it, to prove a distinction, and to show that a rule, which, in the general system of things, is essential to the preservation of the social order, is inapplicable to the United States. The circumstance that the powers of sovereignty are, in this country, divided between the National and State governments, did not afford the distinction required; and it did not follow, he contended, from this circumstance, that each of the portions of power, delegated to the one or the other, is not sovereign with regard to its proper objects. It would only follow from it, that each has sovereign power as to *certain* things, and not as to *other* things. To deny, he said, that the government of the United States has a sovereign power as to its declared purposes and trusts, because its power does not extend to all laws, would be equally to deny that the State gov-

---

[1] Green *v.* Graves, 1 Doug. Mich. 351. The general banking law of Michigan being thus unconstitutional, in so far as it relates to corporate powers, no foreclosure can be maintained upon a mortgage executed to a bank, organized under its provisions. Hurlburt *v.* Britain, 2 Doug. Mich. 191.

ernments have sovereign power in *any* case, because their power does not extend to *every* case. But if it was deemed necessary to bring proof to a proposition, so clear as that which affirms that the powers of the federal government, as to its objects, are sovereign, the clause in the constitution would be decisive; the clause which declares that the constitution and laws of the United States made in pursuance of it, shall be the *supreme law of the land.* The power, then, he argued, which would create the supreme law of the land, in any case, was doubtless sovereign as to such case; and that this general and indisputable principle at once put an end to the question, whether the United States have power to create a corporation. For it is unquestionably incident to sovereign power to create corporations; and consequently, to the sovereign power of the United States in relation to the *objects entrusted to the management of the government.*[1]

§ 73. The above reasoning of Mr. Hamilton was subsequently sustained by a decision of the United States Supreme Court. That court held that the power of Congress to carry into execution the powers which belong to it, by the creation of a corporation, was within the scope of the constitution; that, whenever, in fact, the end of a State or of the general government, is legitimate, *all the means* which are appropriate and plainly adapted to the end (and are not expressly prohibited, and are consistent with the letter and spirit of the constitution), are clearly allowable; and that any law, which is not denied to Congress, and which is really calculated to effect any of the objects entrusted to Congress (as, for instance, the incorporation of a national bank), is in pursuance of the constitution.[2] That Mr. Madison entertained no doubt of the constitutionality of a national bank, would seem from his message of December, 1815.[3]

---

[1] For a continuance of this luminous and forcible argument of Mr. Hamilton, see the reasons submitted by him, according to the order of the President, in favor of the constitutionality of a National Bank. 1 Hamilton's Works, iii.

[2] M'Culloch *v.* State of Maryland, 4 Wheat. 424.

[3] Presidents' Speeches, p. 329. Mr. Madison, it is true, opposed the charter of the old bank, in 1791, as unconstitutional; yet he acknowledged himself bound, as President, to yield his opinion to the exposition of precedents. When he returned the United States Bank Bill, on the 30th of January, 1815, with his reasons (on account of its inexpediency), for not signing it, he says: "Waiving the question of the constitutional authority of the legislature to establish an incorporated bank, as being precluded in my judgment by *repeated* recognitions, under varied circumstances, of the validity of such an institution, in acts of the *legislative, executive,* and *judicial* branches of the government, accompanied by

§ 74. It was formerly asserted, that in England the act of incorporation must be the *immediate* act of the king himself, and that he could not grant a license to another to create a corporation.[1] But the law has since been well settled to the contrary; and the king may not only grant a license to a subject to erect a particular corporation, but give a general power by charter to erect corporations indefinitely.[2] This is on the principle that *qui facit per alium facit per se;* and the persons, to whom the power of establishing corporations is delegated, are only an instrument in the hands of the government.[3] In this manner the chancellor of the University of Oxford is authorized to grant corporate privileges, and has, by virtue of such authority, created several matriculated companies of tradesmen.[4] Under the provincial government of Maryland, municipal corporations were framed and called into existence by or with the immediate sanction of the lord proprietary or the monarch.[5] Before the Revolution, charters of incorporation

---

indications in different modes of the concurrence of the general will of the nation," &c. (Senate Journal, 3d Session, 13th Congress, p. 309). And see notes to the speech of Mr. Grimke, of South Carolina, delivered in December, 1828, on the constitutionality of the tariff, and on the true nature of State sovereignty. This speech was delivered in the senate of South Carolina. It may not be improper to recall the reader's recollection to the *origin* of the Bank of the United States. In May, 1781, the superintendent of finance laid before the Congress a plan of a bank; and on the 26th of that month, the resolutions concerning it were passed by Congress. The Congress resolved, that they approved of the plan of a bank submitted to their consideration by Mr. Robert Morris: That the subscribers to the bank shall be incorporated under the name of "The President, Directors, and Company of the Bank of North America;" That it be recommended to the several States, to provide that no other bank shall be established or permitted within the States, during the war: That the notes thereafter to be issued by the bank, payable on demand, should be receivable in payment of all taxes, duties, and debts payable to the United States: That Congress will recommend to the legislatures of the States, to pass laws, making it felony for any person to counterfeit bank-notes, or to pass them, &c. Under these resolutions, a subscription was opened for the national bank, and before the end of December, 1781, the subscription was filled, from an expectation of a charter of incorporation from Congress. The charter was granted by Congress, with a recommendation to the legislatures of each State, to pass such laws as they might judge necessary for giving its ordinance full operation. This recommendation was complied with by Pennsylvania, on the 18th of March, 1782; by Rhode Island, in January, 1782; and by Massachusetts, in January, 1782. See Lectures of Hon. James Wilson, one of the judges of the United States Supreme Court, and professor of law in the College of Philadelphia (vol. iii. p. 397).

1 10 Co. R. 27.

2 1 Kyd, 50.

3 1 Bl. Com. 473.

4 Ibid.

5 McKim *v.* Odom, 3 Bland, Ch. 416.

were likewise granted by the proprietaries of Pennsylvania, under a derivative authority from the crown; and those charters have been recognized since the Revolution.[1] A similar power has been delegated, by the legislature of Pennsylvania, with regard to churches.[2] The acts of the instrument, in these cases, become the acts of the mover, under the familiar maxim above mentioned.

§ 75. By virtue of the above maxim, a *Territory* of the United States may establish corporations; such power falling within the general legislative powers conferred by Congress. Accordingly, it has been held, that Missouri, when a Territory, might incorporate *towns*. The right reserved by Congress to disapprove, and thereby revoke, any act passed by the territorial legislature, the court, in this case considered, did not render the power of such legislature less sovereign in relation to one subject of legislation, more than another.[3] The Farmers and Mechanics Bank of Indiana, at the commencement of the State government, was recognized by the constitution as an existing corporate body, according to the charter granted to the bank by the legislature of the Indiana Territory.[4]

§ 76. No precise form of words is necessary in the creation of a corporation.[5] And if the words "found," "erect," "establish," or "incorporate," are wanting, it is not material;[6] for the assent of the government may be given constructively or presumptively without such words. It was held, in ancient times, if the king granted to a vill *gildam mercatoriam*, it was by such grant incorporated.[7] So, if the

---

[1] 3 Wils. Lect. 409.

[2] 3 Penn. Laws, 40; Case of St. Mary's Church, 7 S. & R. 517.

[3] Riddick *v.* Amelin, 1 Misso. 5, per Cook, J.

[4] Vance *v.* Farmers and Mechanics Bank of Indiana, 1 Blackf. 80. So of the Bank of Vincennes, id. 270. The territory of Michigan was organized, by act of Congress, in 1805, and a *territorial* government erected therein, that continued until her admission into the Union, in 1837. In 1835, the people adopted a State constitution, and elected a legislative body under it, which passed an act to incorporate the "Manhattan Bank," in March, 1836. The Supreme Court of Ohio held that the village of Manhattan, where the bank was located, was never, *de facto*, under the jurisdiction of the State of Michigan; that if the bank had been incorporated and authorized to do a banking business while it remained under the jurisdiction of Michigan, such authority would not have continued after it came under the jurisdiction of Ohio. Myers *v.* Manhattan Bank, 20 Ohio, 283.

[5] Rex *v.* Amery, 1 T. R. 575.

[6] 10 Co. 40 b.

[7] 1 Rol. 513.

king granted to a vill to be quit of toll, it was, for that purpose, incorporated. Or, if he granted lands to them, he gave them a corporate capacity to take, if a rent was reserved.[1] And, in England, there are many instances of grants by charter to the inhabitants of a town, "that their town shall be a *free borough*," and that they shall enjoy various privileges and exemptions, without any direct clause of incorporation; and yet, by virtue of such charter, such towns have been uniformly considered as incorporated.[2] The joint-stock banks in England, which are of modern creation, and called into existence by the act of 7 George IV., are considered as *quasi* corporations, as the act provides for the continuance of the partnership, notwithstanding the change of partners.[3] And a mining joint-stock unincorporated company was deemed a *quasi* corporation, because a suit for demands against the company, might, under an act of parliament be brought against the directors.[4] The legislature have power to permit one person or his successor to exercise all the corporate powers, and to make his acts, when acting upon the subject-matter of the corporation, and within its sphere of action and grant of powers, the acts of the corporation. The grant of corporate powers to one person, and his *associates* and *successors*, does not require of such person that he should take associates, before the act can take effect, or corporate powers be exercised, but virtually confers on him alone, the right to exercise all the corporate powers thereby granted.[5]

§ 77. The act of the State of Arkansas, creating a State Bank, simply declares that a bank shall be established, designated by name. There are in it, no express words incorporating any particular persons, but the fund is placed under the management and control of a given number of directory, who are required to be elected by the legislature, and the usual powers of banking conferred upon them. Though the court pronounced the act exceedingly vague and ambiguous, yet said it

---

[1] 4 Com. Dig. tit. *Franchises* (F. 6).

[2] Ibid. The grant of *gilda mercatoria*, it seems, however, did not invest the grantees with the local government of the place; for a *gilda mercatoria* established in a town, might be distinct from the general corporation of the town. 1 Kyd, 64. And in most of the royal boroughs in Scotland, there are several incorporated companies of trades, and a gildry, which is also an incorporated company, but distinct from the others; and the magistracy of the town is composed of members partly taken from the gildry, and partly from the traders. 1 Kyd, 65.

[3] Harrison *v.* Timmins, 4 M. & W. 510.

[4] Ibid.; and Wordsworth on Joint-Stock Companies, 41, 275.

[5] See *ante*, § 27.

was nevertheless capable of being defined and understood; and, taking all its parts together, and considering it as an entire whole, they thought no doubt could be entertained that it was the intention of the legislature to incorporate the directory, and that all the affairs of the corporation were put under their government. The directory, say the court, it is true, are not declared in express words to be incorporated, but still, the powers and authority conferred upon them, in regard to banking, cannot exist, unless they are incorporated. In the understanding of the court, all the authorities show, that a corporation may be established by necessary implication, as well as by express grant.[1] These authorities go to establish, that, whenever the language manifests the intention of the government to confer corporate privileges, they may be conferred without the adoption of any particular technical phraseology, or minutely descriptive language.[2]

§ 78. It is, indeed, a principle of law which has been often acted on, that where rights, privileges, and powers are granted by law to an association of persons, by a collective name, and there is no mode by which such rights can be enjoyed, or such powers exercised, without acting in a corporate capacity, such associations are, by implication, a corporation so far as to enable them to exercise the rights and powers granted.[3] The assent of government, in other words, to corporate organization, may, as before stated, be given constructively or presumptively, and without the use of the word "incorporate."[4]

§ 79. But the *intention* of the legislature in the enactment of a law concerning associations of persons, to establish them under corporate organization more or less extensive, must appear plain.[5] It was supposed that the Farmers Bank of Lancaster, in Pennsylvania, was virtually incorporated by an "Act relating to the association of individuals for the

---

[1] Mahoney *v.* Bank of Arkansas, 4 Ark. 620 — Opinion by Lacy, J.; Murphey *v.* Same, 2 Eng. 57; Woodruff *v.* Attorney-General, 3 Eng. 236.

[2] 1 Kyd, 63; see Intr. as to *quasi* corporations. Falconer *v.* Campbell, 2 McLean, C. C. 195.

[3] See *ante*, §§ 23, 24; Stebbins *v.* Jennings, 18 Pick. 187. New Boston *v.* Dunbarton, 15 N. H. 201.

[4] Tone Conservators *v.* Ash, 10 B. & C. 349.

[5] Phillips *v.* Pearce, 5 B. & C. 423; Lawrence *v.* Fletcher, 8 Met. 153; Medical Institution *v.* Patterson, 1 Denio, 618, 5 id. 618; Jackson *v.* Bank of Marietta, 9 Leigh, 240.

purpose of banking;" by which it was enacted that if any association of citizens should thereafter be formed for the purposes of banking, every member thereof should be individually and personally liable for the debts of the association. The court said, that such provision could not be construed into an implied incorporation of the company under the above name, or of any other company; and were of opinion, that the most that could be inferred from it was, that the act in question was an acknowledgment that such associations were lawful until prohibited by the legislature. The act was intended to prevent associations that were about to be formed, the members whereof endeavored to shield themselves from personal responsibility, by publishing to the world that they undertook to transact business on the express condition of being exempt from such responsibility.[1] Again, the Supreme Court of that State were empowered by the legislature, to certify that they confer on certain associations the powers and immunities of corporations; but that tribunal refuses to do so where the constitution of an association confers powers not specified in the act. Therefore, where by the terms of the constitution of a medical college, which was submitted to the court, authority was given to the college to confer degrees in medicine upon students and others, the court declined certifying in favor of the application.[2]

§ 80. Whenever it appears, that a charter has been granted to certain individuals to act as a corporation, who are actually in possession and enjoyment of the corporate rights granted, they have been held rightfully in such possession and enjoyment, against all wrong-doers, and all others who have acted or treated with them in their corporate character; that is, when it is shown, that the charter was granted on a *precedent condition*, for, as against all but the sovereign, the precedent condition shall be taken to be performed.[3] On the other hand, if the acts and proceedings of any company or association of long standing, consists only of such acts and proceedings as might be performed without an incorporating act, a grant of such an act cannot be inferred; and this is not only agreeable to the general rules and analogies of the law, but it has moreover been expressly so held by the Supreme Court of

---

[1] Myers *v.* Irvin, 2 S. & R. 368.

[2] Medical College case, 3 Whart. 445.

[3] Tar River Navigation Co. *v.* Neal, 3 Hawks, 520; Same *v.* Elizabeth City Academy, 6 Ired. 476; Rathburn *v.* Tioga New Co. 2 Watts & S. 74.

Connecticut.[1] In Ernst *v.* Bartle,[2] it was assigned as cause of demurrer, that the defendants were a corporation, and the agreement was made with them in their corporate capacity as trustees of a church; and that the covenant on which the suit was brought, was not shown to be under the corporate seal of the defendants as trustees. The court said, that, with regard to these objections, "it does not appear from the declaration, nor is it shown by the pleadings, that the defendants are a corporation, or capable of being such. The names and additions by which they are described, are a mere *descriptio personarum*, and they remain liable only in their private capacities."

§ 81. Private corporations, — turnpike and railroad companies, banks, &c. — are created by a charter or act of incorporation from the government, which is in the nature of a *contract*,[3] and, therefore, in order to complete their creation, something more than the mere *grant* of a charter is required; that is, in order to give to the charter the full force and effect of an executed contract, it must be *accepted;* as the government cannot incorporate persons for their benefit, in consideration of the benefit to accrue to the government, or to the public, without the consent of such persons.[4] The intention of such a grant of incorporation is to confer some advantage upon the grantees; but as the grant may be counterbalanced by the conditions which accompany it, the grant must be accepted by a *majority*, at least, of those who are intended to be incorporated. Mr. Justice Wilmot said, in the case of Rex *v.* Vice-Chancellor of Cambridge:[5] "It is the *concurrence* and acceptance of the university that gives the *force* to the charter of the crown." It is clear that government cannot enforce the acceptance of a charter upon a private corporation without consent; as "no corporator shall be subject to the inconveniences of it, without accepting of it and assenting to it."[6] It was held by the Supreme Court of Pennsylvania, that, before a charter can be considered as accepted by, or binding upon, a religious society, it must appear that they were notified of it, and that they duly met together to consult and deliberate upon it, and

---

[1] Green *v.* Dennis, 6 Conn. 302.

[2] Ernst *v.* Bartle, 1 Johns. Cas. 319.

[3] See *ante*, §§ 31-36.

[4] See *ante*, § 31, *et seq.;* Falconer *v.* Campbell, 2 McLean, C. C. 196.

[5] Rex *v.* V. Chan. Cambridge, 3 Burr. 1661.

[6] King *v.* Passmore, 3 T. R. 240; Bailey *v.* Mayor, &c. of New York, 3 Hill, 531.

that they accepted it in their associated capacity.[1] The same principle has been recognized by the Supreme Court of Massachusetts, in a case where the court say: "That a man may refuse a grant, whether from the government or an individual, seems to be a principle too clear to require the support of authorities."[2]

§ 82. The terms offered by the government may, therefore, be acceded to or refused by the intended body corporate, and if not acceded to, they have no binding effect.[3] It, of course, can have no binding effect on one party unless the other is bound. The proprietors of a toll bridge authorized by law, several years after the bridge was built, were incorporated. There was no distinct evidence that they had accepted the charter, but there was evidence of some of their own proceedings declining it; and in a *quo warranto* against them, for assuming to act as a body politic, they had traversed the allegation, and the attorney-general had, thereupon, entered a judgment of preclusion. It was held, that these facts proved that they had not accepted the charter, and were conclusive on the point that they did not become a body cor-

---

[1] Shortz *v.* Unangst, 2 Watts & S. 45.

[2] Ellis *v.* Marshall, 2 Mass. 279. An act, amending a charter of incorporation and providing that it shall not take effect until accepted by a majority in interest of the stockholders, will not be binding on dissentient stockholders, though accepted by such majority. New Orleans, Jackson & Great Northern R. R. Co. *v.* Harris, 27 Missis. 517.

[3] Dartmouth College *v.* Woodward, 4 Wheat. 518; and see also Lincoln and Ken. Bank *v.* Richardson, 1 Greenl. 79; Fire Department *v.* Kip, 10 Wend. 266; Haslett *v.* Witherspoon, 1 Strob. Eq. 209. In the words of McLean, J., "The organization being completed, existence is given to the artificial being, and its agency commences. It is now *in esse*, but before this, it was not. Vitality is given to it by the voluntary association and organization of its members. Had they remained passive, the law would have had no effect." Falconer *v.* Higgins, 2 McLean, C. C. 196. There is a difference, however, between a charter granted in general terms to incorporate the inhabitants of a city, and a charter which creates distinct parts of the corporate body, fills up some of the offices by name, and leaves it open to them to elect a number of freemen. As, where the king appointed a certain number of aldermen and common councilmen, by charter, who were the immediate grantees; and afterwards gave them power to swear freemen upon their request, they first taking the oaths; the freemen are not *ipso facto*, and without their assent, members of the corporation, though entitled to be admitted if they choose. Rex *v.* Amery, 1 T. R. 575. In the case of the College of Physicians, the charter was granted to six persons by name, and all others of the faculty of and in the city of London. By virtue of this charter, it was held, that all the practising physicians in London were not members of the corporation; and that the corporation were only bound to admit every person, whom they, on examination, thought fit to be admitted. Rex *v.* Askew, 4 Burr. 2199.

porate.[1] A statute relating to a corporation which required an acceptance of the act to be filed, or else to be void, was never accepted; and it was held, that the corporation could derive no advantage from the passage of the act; and at most, the act, during the time for accepting, could only be deemed a recognition of the lawful existence of the corporation as it was previously. The act became void by its non-acceptance.[2]

§ 83. It appearing that an acceptance of the charter is necessary, we next proceed to show what will amount to an acceptance, and how it may be proved. The question, whether a charter has been accepted, will of course, in a measure, depend upon the circumstance under which it was granted. If a peculiar charter is applied for, and it is given, there can be no reasonable ground to doubt of its immediate acceptance. It has, indeed, been held that grants beneficial to corporations, may be presumed to have been accepted, and an express acceptance is not necessary.[3] A corporation created by statute, which *requires* certain acts to be done before it can be considered *in esse*, must show such acts to have been done to establish its existence; but this rule does not apply to corporations declared such by the act of incorporation.[4] If a charter is granted to persons who have not applied for it, the grant is said to be *in fieri*, until there has been an acceptance expressed.[5] It may, for a time, remain optional with the persons intended to be incorporated, whether they will take the benefit of the act of incorporation; yet if they execute the powers, and claim the privileges granted, the duties imposed on them by the act, will then attach, from which they cannot discharge themselves.[6] The books of a corporation are the regular evidence of its doings, and the acceptance of the charter, should be proved by them. But if books have not been kept, or have been lost or destroyed, or are not accessible to the party upon whom the affirmative lies, then the acceptance may be proved by implication from the acts of the members of the alleged corporation.[7] It is not indispensable to show a written instrument, or even a vote of acceptance; and there may be

---

[1] Thompson *v.* New York and Harlem Railroad Co. 3 Sandf. Ch. 625.
[2] Green *v.* Seymour, 3 Sandf. Ch. 285.
[3] Charles River Bridge *v.* Warren Bridge, 7 Pick. 344.
[4] Fire Department *v.* Kip, 10 Wend. 266.
[5] Dartmouth College *v.* Woodward, 4 Wheat. 688.
[6] Riddle *v.* Pro. of Locks, &c. on Merrimack River, 7 Mass. 187.
[7] Hudson *v.* Carman, 41 Me. 84.

many instances in which an acceptance can be inferred.[1] An acceptance of charter, at least, for some purposes, may always be inferred from the exercise of corporate powers under it.[2] Where it appeared that the persons named in an act of incorporation, had *held meetings* under it, *adopted by-laws*, *elected officers*, and done *other* corporate acts, it was held to be sufficient evidence of the existence of a company capable of taking and holding property, though there was no legal record of the first meeting, and no formal acceptance of the charter.[3]

§ 84. The stockholders of a bank may be bound by an acceptance, or any conduct amounting to an acceptance, on the part of the directors.[4] But this rule is founded upon the consideration that certain persons have been invested with sufficient power to bind the whole body by their acceptance; were it otherwise, the charter must then be accepted, at least by implication, by a *majority* of the whole number of the com-

---

[1] Bank of U. States *v.* Dandridge, 12 Wheat. 71. It is not essential to the taking effect of the charter, that it should appear upon the corporate records. Russell *v.* M'Clellan, 14 Pick. 53. But parol evidence is inadmissible to prove acceptance, where the records of a corporate existence can be shown. Coffins *v.* Collins, 17 Maine, 440.

[2] Penobscot B. Corporaiton *v.* Lamson, 16 Me. 224; Middlesex Husbandmen, &c. *v.* Davis, 3 Met. 133; Way *v.* Billings, 2 Mich. 397.

[3] Trott *v.* Warren, 2 Fairf. 227; and see to the same effect All Saints Church *v.* Lovett, 1 Hall, 191; Dutchess Cott. Man. Co. *v.* Davis, 14 Johns. 238; Trustees of Vernon Society *v.* Hills, 6 Cowen, 23; Eaton *v.* Aspinwall, 19 N. Y. 119; Sampson *v.* Bowdoinham S. M. Corporation, 36 Me. 78; Eastern P. R. Co. *v.* Vaughan, 20 Barb. 155; W. & M. R. R. Co. *v.* Saunders, 3 Jones, N. C. 126. The production of a charter with proof of acts of user under it, is sufficient to establish corporate existence, where the charter confers corporate capacity and powers *in præsenti* and unconditionally, and does not make the right to their exercise depend upon any thing to be done *in futuro*. Crump *v.* United States Mining Co. 7 Gratt. 352; Commonwealth *v.* Claghorn, 13 Penn. State, 133; Cahill *v.* Kalamazoo Mutual Insurance Co. 2 Doug. Mich. 124. The production of an act of incorporation, and the actual use of the powers and privileges given by such act, furnish, in the absence of an authenticated record of organization, sufficient ground to justify all further inferences of other compliances with the proper requisites for a legal organization of the corporation. Narragansett Bank *v.* Atlantic Silk Co. 3 Met. 282; Farmers & Mechanics Bank *v.* Jenks, 7 id. 592; and see id. 133; Dedham Bank *v.* Chickering, 3 Pick. 335; Worcester Med. Inst. *v.* Harding, 11 Cush. 285; West Winsted Sav. Bank *v.* Ford, 27 Conn. 282; People's Sav. Bk. *v.* Collins, 27 Conn. 142; People *v.* Beigler, Hill & Denio, 133; Abbott *v.* Aspinwall, 26 Barb. 202. The books of a corporation, containing entries in accordance with its charter, when identified, are admissible to prove the organization and existence of the corporation. Buncombe Turn. Co. *v.* McCarson, 1 Dev. & B. 306. But see further, on this subject, Chapter IV. on the Admission and Election of Members and Officers.

[4] Lin. & Ken. Bank *v.* Richardson, 1 Greenl. 70.

pany. There is an authority for this distinction, in Pennsylvania, in a case where a minority of the persons, in whom a trust for a school fund was vested, procured a charter of incorpòration, under the act of 1791. It was held, that no rights could be acquired in opposition to the will of the majority.[1] If a charter be given to a company, and certain persons are nominated to admit others, the charter needs only be accepted by the majority of nominees; for they alone constitute the original corporation, and those who are afterwards admitted, manifest their assent by becoming members.[2] And even if their be but *one* nominee, his acceptance is sufficient.[3]

§ 85. A charter must be accepted as it is offered, and without *condition;* neither can there be a *partial* acceptance, any more than there can be an acceptance by part of the persons intended to be incorporated.[4] But if a new charter be given to a corporation already created, there may be a partial acceptance of the second charter; and the body corporate may act partly under the one and partly under the other. On a contest for the office of high steward of the University of Cambridge, it was held by the court, that the crown could not take away from the university any rights that had formerly subsisted in them under old charters or prescriptive usage; that the validity of these *new* charters must depend on the *acceptance* of the university; that when the crown gave the new statutes, the University of Cambridge was of ancient establishment, and had former charters of very old date, and there was no intention to alter or overturn their ancient constitution; that the new statutes undoubtedly meant to leave the ancient constitution of the university, in a great measure, as it was, without repealing their established rights and privileges; and that the university could not mean to accept them on any other terms; that it was not intended, by the new statutes, to alter the mode of election, unless the university chose so to do; that it was the *concurrence* and *acceptance* of the university that gave force to the charter of the crown; that they might accept the body of statutes *separately* and *distinctly*, and were not bound to accept all, or *leave* all; and

---

[1] Commonwealth *v.* Huston, 7 S. & R. 460; and see Dartmouth College *v.* Woodward, 4 Wheat. 688.

[2] Rex *v.* Amery, 1 T. R. 575.

[3] Penobscot B. Corporation *v.* Lamson, 16 Me. 224; Day *v.* Stetson, 8 Greenl. 865. See *ante,* § 28.

[4] Wilcox on Mun. Corpor. 30; Green *v.* Seymour, 3 Sandf. Ch. 285; Rex *v.* Passmore, 3 T. R. 240; Rex *v.* Amery, 1 T. R. 589; Rex *v.* Cambridge, 3 Burr. 1656.

that, in the present case, it appeared there was, in fact, a *partial* acceptance.[1]

§ 86. Sometimes, a particular subscriber to a joint-stock corporation may not be bound by an acceptance of the charter by the others. In an action, by a corporation, to recover from a subscriber to the stock the amount of his subscription, it appeared that the charter had been obtained in consequence of fictitious subscriptions to a part of the stock. Although it was held by the Supreme Court of Pennsylvania,[2] that, the defendant having accepted the charter, and acted under it, he was liable to pay; yet it was afterwards held, in the same case, again removed to the Supreme Court, by writ of error, that if the subscribers were ignorant of the fact of fictitious subscriptions having been made, their acceptance of the charter did not bind them.[3] But where there is no fraud, or undue concealment, it is otherwise. Thus, a member of an incorporated insurance company was held to be bound by a statute, which varied the terms of the original act of incorporation, such act being passed at the instance of a legal meeting of the company, though he was not present.[4] In such case, the member may, perhaps, be said to be bound by implication, as he may be under an original act of incorporation. Consenting by implication, under a special statute of incorporation, precludes the member from afterwards denying his liability to the lawful exactions of the corporation, on the ground that he did not solicit the privilege.[5]

§ 87. It has been stated, that the charter can be accepted neither conditionally nor partially; it is equally well established, that it cannot be accepted for a limited time. And if it has once been received, though but for an hour, or even a moment, it is conclusive and obligatory.[6]

§ 88. By a statute of New York, of 1811, manufacturing corporations may be created by the mere association of five or more persons,

---

[1] Rex *v.* Cambridge, 3 Bnrr. 1656–1661.
[2] Centre Turn. Co. *v.* M'Conahy, 16 S. & R. 140.
[3] M'Conahy *v.* Centre Turn. Co. 1 Penn. 426.
[4] Currie *v.* Mutual Ins. Co. 1 Hen. & M. 315.
[5] Ellis *v.* Marshall, 2 Mass. 269. See *post*, Chap. XV.
[6] Rex *v.* Bazey, 4 M. & S. 255.

filing a certificate designating their names, object, and location.[1] The numerous decisions which have been made in New York, in reference to banking institutions, have established beyond a doubt, that the companies formed under the act of 1838, are corporations. When the question was before the Court of Errors, there was no doubt as to the extent of the powers possessed by banking associations; the only question was, as to which class of legal existences bodies corporate with such powers properly belonged. The court decided they were corporations; that is, that which the legislature intended to create, and did create, was, according to the correct, *legal construction*, a corporation.[2] Persons intending to institute an association under this law, authorizing the business of banking, after subscribing articles of association, proceeded to elect a president and directors. The directors signed and recorded a certificate of its organization, made in the form prescribed, and proceeded to transact business. This certificate, not being signed by the stockholders, was not in compliance with the law, and consequently they had no corporate capacity.[3]

§ 89. The State of New York, in 1849, effected two important assimilations of natural persons to corporations. It enabled every voluntary joint-stock company, when composed of seven or more persons, to sue and be sued in the name of its president or treasurer, and guarded against the abatement of the suit by removal from office or the death of the officers or any of the associates. The general banking law, and the general laws for the formation of manufacturing establishments, insurance companies, plank, turnpike, and rail roads, go far, also, to enable any natural person to transact business for himself, under a corporate organization.[4]

§ 90. In Michigan, by "an act to organize and regulate banking associations," it is provided, that application is to be made, in writing, to

---

[1] 2 Kent, Com. 272 (note).

[2] See the opinion of the court, by Edwards, J., in Leavitt *v.* Blatchford, 5 Barb. 9. But see s. c. on appeal, 17 N. Y. 521, where several of the previous decisions are in part overruled, and where it is held that they are not subject to the "regulations to prevent the insolvency of moneyed corporations" (1 R. S. 588), except so far as they have been incorporated in the general banking law of 1838, or expressly applied by subsequent statutes.

[3] Valk *v.* Crandall, 1 Sandf. Ch. 179.

[4] Hunt's Merch. Mag. for December, 1850, p. 626. See *ante*, § 84.

the treasurer and clerk of the county, where the business is to be carried on, stating the amount of capital proposed. Of this application, public notice is required to be given. Bond, in the sum of 30,000 dollars, to be approved of by the treasurer and clerk, must be entered into. The capital stock is limited, and the subscriptions are to be received and apportioned, &c. Ten per cent. on the shares subscribed, is required to be paid. Then, on notice being given to the stockholders, they are authorized to meet and elect nine directors, a majority of whom are authorized to manage the affairs of the association. They are required to elect one of their number president; and it is provided, that "all such persons as shall become stockholders in any such association, shall, on compliance with the provisions of this act, constitute a body corporate and politic, in fact, in name, and by such name as they shall designate and assume to themselves, &c.; and by such name, they and their successors shall and may have continued succession, and shall, in their corporate capacity, be capable of suing and being sued," &c. The act not only gives in terms all the requisites to form a corporation, but the body, when formed, is technically designated by it as such. "Could the legislature," says Mr. J. McLean, "in language more clear and forcible, have created a corporation? Not a *quasi* corporation; not a joint-stock company, or a limited partnership, but, substantially and technically, a corporation." [1]

§ 91. The laws of Massachusetts have given as great facility to the institution of corporations. When any lands, wharves, or other real estate are held in common by five or more proprietors, they may form themselves into a corporation.[2] By subsequent statutes, three or more persons, who shall have associated themselves by articles of agreement, in writing, for the purpose of cutting, storing and selling ice, or of carrying on any mechanical, mining, quarrying, or manufacturing business, except that of distilling or manufacturing liquors, are constituted a corporation.[3] Ten or more may organize as a corporation for the purpose of making and selling gas, as a light in a city or town; [4] or for the business of banking; [5] and seven or more proprietors of a library may form

---

[1] Falconer *v.* Campbell, 2 McLean, C. C. 196. See, as to the construction of the general banking law of Michigan, *ante*, § 71.

[2] Rev. St. of 1835, part 1, tit. 13, c. 33, s. 1; Gen. Stats. c. 379.

[3] Stat. 1851, c. 133; 1852, c. 9; Gen. Stats. c. 61.

[4] Stat. 1855, c. 146; 1857, c. 276; Gen. Stats. c. 61, § 15.

[5] Stat. 1851, c. 267; 1852, c. 236; Gen. Stats. c. 57, § 110.

themselves into a corporation.[1] In 1838, the legislature of Indiana authorized any twenty or more citizens of any county, on giving three weeks' previous public notice, to organize themselves and become an agricultural society, with corporate powers; and the inhabitants of any town or village may incorporate themselves for the institution and management of a public library.[2] In Pennsylvania, the Courts of Quarter Sessions, "*with the concurrence of the grand jury of the county*, may incorporate towns and villages;"[3] and, also, literary, charitable, or religious associations, and fire companies may be incorporated under the sanction of the Supreme Court.[4]

§ 92. Where several individuals signed articles of association for such purposes as were contemplated by the statutes of the State of Vermont, of 1797 and 1814, and the form adopted was substantially in conformity to the one prescribed, and provided for the election of trustees, &c.; and no words were used, indicating an intention not to form themselves into a body corporate; it was held, that they became a corporation, under those statutes, notwithstanding they did not describe themselves as inhabitants of any town, and made no reference, in their articles of association, to the first section of the statute of 1797.[5]

§ 93. Land was conveyed by deed to the members of an incorporated religious society, who had entered into an agreement to build a meeting-house for them and their heirs and assigns. The grantees organized themselves as proprietors, according to the provision of the statute in Massachusetts; and the associates caused a meeting-house to be built. The legal estate in the house was held to be in the incorporated proprietors, and not in the religious society.[6]

§ 94. If there has been a user of a corporate franchise, by an association of persons, their existence as a corporation can only be inquired into by the government.[7] A person doing business with a bank, as a

---

1 Stat. 1851, c. 305; Gen. Stats. c. 33, § 10.

2 2 Kent, Com. 272 (note).

3 Purd. Dig. 130.

4 Ibid. 168, 172.

5 Rogers *v.* Danvers Universalist Society, 19 Vt. 187.

6 Howard *v.* Hayward, 10 Met. 304.

7 Thompson *v.* New York and Harlem Railroad Co., 3 Sandf. 625; Methodist Episcopal Church *v.* Pickett, 19 N. Y. 482; Elizabeth City Academy *v.* Lindsay, 6 Ired. 476;

corporation, cannot deny its existence;[1] and the execution of a note to company, payable to them as a corporation, is an admission of their existence as such.[2] The omission of trustees, by the act of incorporation of an insurance company, to organize it, could not be objected to by a contracting party, and any valid objection to the requisite organization could only be available in behalf of the government.[3]

CHAPTER III.

HOW THE BODY CORPORATE IS CONSTITUTED; AND OF ITS NAME, PLACE, MODE OF ACTION, POWERS, ETC.

§ 95. A CORPORATION is usually composed of natural persons merely in their natural capacity;[4] but it may also be composed of persons in their political capacity of members of other corporations.[5] Thus, by a charter of Edward VI., the mayor, citizens, and commonalty of London, are appointed Governors of Christ's Hospital of Bridewell, and incorporated by the name of the Governors of the possessions, revenues, and goods of the Hospital of Edward VI., King of England, of Christ Bridewell.[6] So the government of the country may be, and often is, one of the members of a private corporation; as in the case of the Bank of the United States, the Planters Bank of Georgia,[7] and the Bank of the State of South Carolina.[8] And a man, who forms a component part of a corporation aggregate, may have, to some purposes, a distinct corpo-

---

Grand Gulf Bank *v.* Archer, 8 Smedes & M. 151; Duke *v.* Cahawba New Co. 10 Ala. 82; and see *post*, Chap. XXI.

[1] Bank of Circleville *v.* Remick, 15 Ohio, 222.

[2] Jones *v.* Bank of Tennessee, 8 B. Mon. 122.

[3] Brouwer *v.* Appleby, 1 Sandf. 158; and see 4 Denio, 392; 9 Wend. 351.

[4] See *ante*, § 7. A corporation may consist of both men and women, provided its institution is not repugnant to the condition and modesty of women. Ayliffe, Civil Law, 204.

[5] 1 Kyd, 32.

[6] 10 Co. 31 b.

[7] 9 Wheat. 907.

[8] 3 McCord, 377; and see *ante*, §§ 31, 32, 33.

rate capacity, as, in England, a dean and a chapter form one corporation aggregate, but in many cases, both dean and prebendaries have distinct rights as corporations *sole;* each may have peculiar revenues appropriated to him and his successors in his political capacity; and the prebendaries alone, without the dean, may also form one aggregate corporation, distinct from that of dean and chapter.[1] That the same body of individuals should possess two distinct capacities, having certain rights, duties, and obligations in each, is no anomaly in the law.[2]

§ 96. So, also, several distinct and independent corporations may form the component parts of one general corporate body. For instance, in Shrewsbury, in England, there are several distinct and independent companies of carpenters, bricklayers, &c., and these all united form one great corporation under the name of the "Company of Carpenters, Bricklayers, &c., of Shrewsbury." There are some towns, also, in England, in which there are several incorporated companies of trades, which have so far a connection with the general corporation of the town, that no man can be a freeman of the town at large, and consequently a member of the general corporation, without being previously a freeman of some one of these companies; and of this description is the corporation of the city of London. The general corporate bodies of the English Universities are constituted nearly in the same manner; for every member of the general corporation must be a member of some one of the colleges or halls within the University.[3] There are technical difficulties in

---

[1] Something similar to this obtained, with respect to abbeys and priories, before the dissolution of the monasteries; of the former, there was but one kind; every house being independent; but of the latter there were two kinds; first, those where the prior was chief governor, as fully as any abbot in his abbey, and was chosen by the convent; secondly, those where the priory was a cell, subordinate to some great abbey, and the prior was placed and displaced at the will of the abbot. But there was a considerable difference between some of these cells; for some were altogether subject to their respective abbeys, who sent them what officers and monks they pleased, and took their revenues into the common stock of the abbeys; but others consisted of a stated number of monks, who had a prior sent them from the abbey, and paid a pension yearly, as an acknowledgment of their subjection, but acted in other matters as an independent body, and had the rest of the revenues for their own use. Burns, Eccles. Law, tit. *Monasteries*, § 7; 1 Kyd, 33, 34.

[2] Stebbins *v.* Jennings, 10 Pick. 171.

[3] 1 Kyd, 36. There are, also, several corporate companies of trades, without reference to any general corporation of the town in which they are, and indeed where there is no incorporation of the town at all. The Bank, the East India Company, the College of Physicians, and other scientific companies, have no reference to the general corporation of the city of London. Ibid. In Massachusetts, the North Parish in Harwich was incorporated

considering several corporations as *copartners*, or as having blended their powers and interests together, so that whatever should have been done by one should be binding on the others; and yet, if they are all composed of the same individuals, using several corporate powers for the same end and purpose, with nothing but the form of a record to distinguish them, equity would seem to require that they should not be allowed to sever to the prejudice of any persons with whom either might contract.[1]

§ 97. Many aggregate corporations are composed of distinct parts, which are called integral parts, without any one of which the corporation would not be complete, although none of them are by themselves a corporation. Thus, where a corporation consists of a mayor, aldermen, and commonalty, the mayor, the aldermen, and the commonalty are three integral parts; but neither of them has any corporate capacity, distinct from the other two, and, therefore, the mayor cannot, in his political character of mayor, take in succession any thing as a sole corporation; nor the aldermen, as a select body, take any thing to them and their successors as an aggregate corporation. In many aggregate corporations there is one particular person, who is called the head, and who forms one of the integral parts; such is the mayor of a city corporation, and the chancellor in the general corporations of the English Universities.[2] The corporation of St. Mary's Church, in the city of Philadelphia, consisting of three *clerical* and eight *lay* members, was considered by the court to be a corporation, composed of two distinct classes or integral parts.[3]

---

into a town by the name of Brewster, and having continued to act as a parish, it was contended, that it ceased to exist in that capacity upon its incorporation into a town; but it was decided that the parish still continued to exist. It was also settled as law, that the inhabitants of a town are not necessarily, and of course, members of a parish included within it; but that those who are exempted on account of their religious scruples and opinions, though members of the town, are not members of the parish, comprehended by the same boundaries. Dillingham *v.* Snow, 3 Mass. 276, 5 Mass. 547. And see Inhabitants of Milford *v.* Godfrey, 1 Pick. 98.

[1] Per Parker, C. J., in Proprietors of Canal Bridge *v.* Gordon, 1 Pick. 305.

[2] 1 Kyd, 36. But there may be a corporation aggregate of many persons, capable, without a head, as a chapter without a dean, or a commonalty without a mayor; thus, the collegiate church of Southwell, in Nottinghamshire, consists of prebendaries only, without a dean; and the governors of Sutton's Hospital, commonly called the Charter House, have no president or superior, but are all of equal authority; and at first the greater number of corporations were without a head. Ibid. 37.

[3] Corporation of St. Mary's Church, 7 S. & R. 517.

§ 98. As it has been stated by Kyd,[1] there are *three* different kinds of assemblies in corporations, which he styles *legislative*, *electoral*, and *administrative*. 1. The *legislative* assembly possesses the power of making laws; such as the court of common council, in London, the court of proprietors of the Bank of England, and of the East India and South Sea Companies.[2] And in this division of corporate assemblies, it is obvious, may be included any part of the body corporate in which is vested the authority of prescribing rules of conduct for the body at large. 2. The *electoral* assembly is that which is authorized to elect officers; such are, in general, the proprietors of stock companies; and the body at large of every corporation, when the power of election has not been vested in a minor body. 3. The *administrative* have the management of *particular affairs*, such as the courts of assistants in the city companies of Europe; the court of directors of a bank and other stock companies. The same body of men may, therefore, and frequently do possess, distinct powers; as, for instance, the *comitia majora* of the college of physicians, in the city of London, who possess the legislative, the electoral, and the administrative powers; so all the three powers are possessed by the congregation in the University of Cambridge, in England. In private corporations (which, to some extent, may be said to be towns in miniature), the electoral power is generally in the body at large, though it may be vested in a body selected solely to make elections, or in the legislative or administrative assembly. The qualification of persons to exercise the above powers, must, of course, depend upon the charter and the by-laws.[3] By the constitution of the railway companies in England, the proper organs through which they may act, are threefold: 1st, the general assembly of the company; 2dly, the board of directors; and, 3dly, a duly constituted agent.[4]

§ 98 *a*. The question in respect to the principle which seems to have been settled in England, that a corporation is dissolved when an integral part is gone, and the remaining parts are incapable of restoring it, or of doing any corporate act, seems chiefly to have arisen in *municipal*

---

[1] 1 Kyd, 399.

[2] So are the legislative courts of the different London companies of tradesmen; the *comitia majora* of the College of Physicians, the convocation in the University of Oxford, and the congregation or senate in the University of Cambridge. Ibid.

[3] 1 Kyd, 400. See *post*, chap. on By-Laws.

[4] See Walf. on Railways, 70.

corporations composed of mayor, aldermen, and burgesses, instituted for the government of towns, in their judicial concerns, police, or trade. Private corporations in this country (e. g. turnpike companies) bear little resemblance to English municipal corporations, either in design or constitution. A turnpike company, in the State of Pennsylvania, like many of the corporations there for civil purposes, existing either by special act of assembly, or under the act of 1791, is not a corporation composed of several integral parts; the stockholders constitute the company, and the managers and officers are their agents, necessary for the conduct and management of the affairs of the company, but not essential to its existence as such, nor forming an integral part. The corporation exists *per se*, so far as is requisite to the maintenance of perpetual succession, and holding its franchises; the non-existence of the managers not implying the non-existence of the corporation. The corporate functions may be suspended for want of the means of action, but the capacity to restore its functionaries, by means of elections, remains.[1]

§ 99. Every corporation should have a *name*,[2] by which it may be known as a grantor and grantee, and to sue and be sued, and do all legal acts. Such name is the very being of its constitution, the "knot of its combination," without which it could not perform its corporate functions.[3] The name of incorporation, says Sir Edward Coke, is a proper name, or name of baptism; and, therefore, when a private founder gives his college or hospital a name, he does it only as a god-father; and by that same name the king baptizes the corporation.[4] But though the name of a corporate body is compared to the Christian name of a natural person, yet the comparison is not, in all respects, perfectly correct. A Christian name consists, in general, but of a single word, as Oliver,

---

[1] Per Sergeant, J., in delivering the opinion of the court in Rose *v.* Turnpike Company, 3 Watts, 48. And see, too, Phillips *v.* Wickham, 1 Paige, 599, in which case it was decided, that a *quasi* corporation of the owners of certain drowned lands, created by act of the legislature, was not extinguished by the omission to elect their commissioners, who were annual officers, at the time designated by the act, but that, at the period of the next annual election, they might meet and choose commissioners for the ensuing year. The same principle is settled in Lehigh Bridge Company *v.* Lehigh Navigation Company, 4 Rawle, 9. See *post*, § 771, and *ante*, § 3.

[2] Com. Dig. tit. *Franchise* (F. 9), 10 R. 29 b.

[3] Smith, Mer. Law, 133.

[4] 10 R. 28.

or Robert, in which the alteration or omission of a single letter may make a material alteration in the name. In all grants *by* or *to* a corporation, though expressed to show that there is such an artificial being, and to distinguish it from all others, the body is well named, though there is a variation in words and syllables.[1] The name of a corporation frequently consists of several words, and an omission or alteration of some of them is not material.[2] The Supreme Court of New Hampshire say, that there is this difference between the alteration of a letter, or the transposition of a word, between naming a natural person and naming a corporate body: It makes entirely another name of the person in the one case, while the name of a corporation frequently consists of several *descriptive* words, and the transposition of them, or an interpolation, or omission of some of them, may make no essential difference in their sense.[3] The rule has been stated to be, that in grants and conveyances the name must be the same, in *substance*, as the true name; but need not be the same in words and syllables.[4] In a devise to a corporation, if the words (though the name be entirely mistaken) show, that the testator could only mean a particular corporation, it is sufficient; as, for instance, a devise to John, Bishop of Norwich, when his name is George.[5] So, it was held in Massachusetts, that a devise to "The Inhabitants of the *South* Parish," may be enjoyed by "The Inhabitants of the *First* Parish."[6] For a corporation to attempt to set aside its own grant, by reason of its misnomer, was severely censured, and in a great measure repressed, as early as the time of Lord Coke;[7] and where the name of a corporate *grantor* is mistaken, as where John, Ab-

---

1 10 Rep. 135. See Bac. Abridg. tit. *Corp.*

2 See 1 Kyd, 227.

3 Newport Mechanics Man. Co. *v.* Spirbird, 10 N. H. 123.

4 Per Parke, J., in Rex *v.* Haughley, 4 B. & Ad. 655.

5 Hob. 33.

6 First Parish in Sutton *v.* Cole, 3 Pick. 232. See also, Dauphin Turnpike Co. *v.* Myers, 6 S. & R. 12. See also, Medway Cott. Man. Co. *v.* Adams, 10 Mass. 360. Held, in New Hampshire, that where a promissory note was given to the *president, directors,* and *company* of, instead of to the Newport Mechanics Man. Co., which was the true name of the corporation to which the note was designed to be given; that the variance was not such as to preclude a recovery, in the name of said corporation. Newport Mechanics Man. Co. *v.* Spirbird, 10 N. H. 123. So also a joint-stock copartnership, whose proper title is "The Union Bank of Calcutta," is sufficiently described in a promissory note under the name of "The Proprietors of the Union Bank of Calcutta." Forbes *v.* Marshall, 11 Exch. 166, 32 Eng. L. & Eq. 589.

7 10 Co. 126 a. And see 2 Kent, Com. 2d ed. 292. Also, African Society *v.* Mutual R. Society, 13 Johns. 38.

bot of N. granted common of pasture to J. S. by the name of William, Abbot of N., the grant is still good.[1]

§ 100. A corporation may have one name, by which it may take and grant, and another by which it may plead and be impleaded. Thus it may purchase and grant by the name of "Master, Wardens, and Brothers," and be empowered to plead and be impleaded by the name of "Wardens" alone.[2] But in this respect, a distinction has been made between the case of a corporation by *prescription*, and that of a corporation by *charter;* the former may have several names to the same purpose; and *scire facias* will lie in one of the names on a judgment obtained in the other.[3] But a corporation by charter, it is said, though it may, either by charter, or by act of parliament, be empowered to act and purchase by one name, and sue and be sued by another, yet cannot have two names to the same purpose.[4] Mr. Kyd says: "This may be true with respect to a grant by *charter*," but adds, "There seems to be no reason why an *act of parliament* might not empower a corporation by charter, to use two names to the same purpose."[5] It has been held in Massachusetts, that a *parish* may be known by several corporate names; and the court say: "We know not why a corporation may not be known in its public proceedings by several names, as well as individuals."[6] A corporation which has been dissolved (or, more correctly, suspended) by the loss of the governing members, may be revived either by the old, or by a name different from that by which it was formerly known, still preserving its identity and ancient rights.[7] A corporation may also acquire a name by usage.[8]

---

[1] So, if the name be expressed by words which are synonymous, it is sufficient; as where a college was instituted by the name of *Guardianus et Scholares*, and they made a lease by the name of *Custos et Scholares*, it was adjudged good. Ibid. And so, if J. S. Abbot, of B., makes a lease by the name of J. S. Clericus, of B., 11 R. 21. And where the "Dean and Chapter of the Cathedral Church in Oxford," made a lease by the name of "The Dean and Chapter of the Cathedral Church in the University of Oxford," it was adjudged good, as the place of situation was well and sufficiently shown. Poph. 57.

[2] Bro. Corpor. 95; 1 Kyd, 229; Willcock on Mun. Corpor. 34.

[3] 1 Kyd, 229.

[4] 3 Salk. 102; Lutw. 108; Hard. 504.

[5] 1 Kyd, 230. A corporation by prescription may have more names than one. Willcock on Mun. Corpor. 34.

[6] Minot *v.* Curtis, 7 Mass. 441.

[7] 1 Kyd, 232; Willcock on Mun. Corpor. 36; Episcopal Charitable Society *v.* Episcopal Church, 1 Pick. 372.

[8] Smith *v.* Plank Road Co. 30 Ala. 650.

§ 101. For the purpose of preserving regularity in legal proceedings, a slighter variation of name may be sufficient to sustain a plea in abatement, than that which would be held necessary for the purpose of allowing a grant or other act to be avoided by the party, who would derive advantage from setting it aside, after having probably received a good consideration. The courts are more strict in compelling the exact insertion of the name, in actions brought by corporations, than in deeds executed by them; for in the former case a mistake may be remedied, but not so in the latter;[1] and they allow a variance to be taken advantage of in a plea of abatement, which they will not admit as sufficient ground for a nonsuit.[2]

§ 102. Though partnerships and simply joint-stock trading companies may be at liberty to change their name or style, yet, after a company has been *incorporated* by a name set forth in the act of incorporation, such incorporated company has not the right nor the power to change its name. The identity of name is the principal means for effecting that perpetuity of succession with members frequently changing, which is an important purpose of incorporation, and the corporate name can be changed only by the same power by which the corporate body has been created. It is obvious, likewise, that the title to shares and the right to assets would be likely to be brought into confusion if the name was subject to change.[3] The legislature may, however, change the name of a corporation, but if its identity appear, a mere change does not affect third persons.[4]

---

[1] Smith, Mer. Law, 133. The corporation must sue and be sued by its name, unless the act or charter of incorporation enables it to come into court in the name of a natural person, as its president, cashier, &c. Mannay *v.* Motz, 4 Ired. 195. As to process against corporations, see Regina *v.* Western Railway Co. 5 A. & E. 597; and *post*, Chap. XVIII.

[2] Willcock on Mun. Corpor. 37; and see also Minot *v.* Curtis, 7 Mass. 441. It was held, that using the name of Mayor and Burgesses of the "borough of S." where the charter incorporated the place by the name of the Mayor and Burgesses of the "borough of S. *in the county of S.*" to be called the Mayor and Burgesses of the "borough of S. in the county of S.," might be taken advantage of on a plea in abatement; but that a corporation, averring that it was incorporated by the former name, would not be subject to a nonsuit, though the latter appeared to be the true name, upon showing the charter; for this is an error in addition, and not in substance, and the defendant cannot say there was no such corporation. Lyme Regis, 10 R. 126; Strafford *v.* Balton, 1 B. & P. 41; Ipswich *v.* Johnson, 2 Barnard. 120; 1 Kyd, 258.

[3] Regina *v.* Registrar, &c. 10 Q. B. 839.

[4] Rosenthal *v.* Madison P. R. Co. 10 Ind. 359.

§ 103. A corporation, it is said, should be constituted of some *place*.[1] And though the place be not, in reality, in the country subject to the dominion of the government creating the corporation, the corporation should be mentioned as of that country; as the "corporation of St. John of Jerusalem, in England."[2] It is sufficient if the corporation is named of any place, though it may not have any lands or possessions there.[3]

§ 104. A private corporation, whose charter has been granted by one State, cannot hold meetings, pass votes, and exercise powers in another State. It can have no legal existence out of the boundaries of the sovereignty by which it is created, must dwell in the place of its creation, and cannot migrate to another sovereignty.[4] The case of McCall *v.* Byram Manufacturing Company, in Connecticut,[5] has been regarded as deciding, that corporations whose charters were granted by one State, could hold meetings, pass votes, and exercise powers in another State. The question presented in the case was, whether the secretary of a corporation was legally appointed by the directors, at a meeting held by them in the city of New York, the charter having been granted by the State of Connecticut; and the decision was in the affirmative. But the directors of a corporation are not a corporate body, when acting as a board, though they are competent to act as agents beyond the bounds where the corporation exists. It did, indeed, appear in the case, that all the meetings of the stockholders, and of the directors, were holden in the city of New York, but the capacity of the stockholders to act there, does not appear to have been discussed. A corporation duly organized, and acting within the limits of the State granting the charter, may by vote transmitted elsewhere, or by an agent duly constituted, act and contract beyond the limits of the State. But an authority given in a charter, in general terms, to certain persons to call the first meeting of the corporators, does not authorize them to call such meeting at any place without the limits of the State.[6]

---

1 1 R. 123; Potter *v.* Bank of Ithaca, 7 Hill, 530.

2 10 R. 32 b.

3 Com. Dig. tit. *Fran.* (F. 8).

4 Bank of Augusta *v.* Earle, 13 Pet. 519; Miller *v.* Ewer, 27 Me. 509; Farnum *v.* Blackstone Canal Co. 1 Sumner, 47; Runyan *v.* Coster, 14 Pet. 129; Day *v.* Newark India Rubber Co. 1 Blatchf. C. C. 628.

5 McCall *v.* Byram Manuf. Co. 6 Conn. 458.

6 Miller *v.* Ewer, 27 Me. 509, which explains the apparently contradictory decision in

§ 105. It is sufficient, if the corporation is named of any place, though it may not have any lands or possessions there; and as in the case of a natural person, it is not necessary that the corporation should actually exist within the limits of the sovereignty, in which a contract is made. But this rule is of course subject to the qualification, that if a corporation would exercise the powers with which it is endowed, in another State, it must be with regard to the laws of such other State. In the case of Runyan *v.* Coster, the legislature of the State of New York incorporated the New York and Schuylkill Company, by an act conferring the usual powers of a body corporate, the object of which was, to obtain coal from the mines of Pennsylvania. The company, in its corporate name and capacity, secured by purchase, valuable and extensive coal lands in Pennsylvania, under the power conferred by the legislature of New York, to purchase and hold land in the attainment of their object. It was adjudged by the Supreme Court of the United States, that the right to the land so purchased depended on the assent or permission, express or implied, of the State of Pennsylvania, and that the law of Pennsylvania, as to the right of purchasing and holding land by a corporation, must govern in a case where land within the limits of Pennsylvania had been purchased by a corporation created by the legislature of New York.[1]

§ 106. A college founded and established by the regents of a university in a particular place, has not the power to establish a school as a branch of such college, in a place different from that in which the college is located; and it was accordingly held that the establishment by Geneva College, located in Ontario County, in the State of New York, of a medical school in the city of New York, and the appointment of professors, to take charge of the same, was the usurpation of a franchise.[2]

Copp *v.* Lamb, 3 Fairf. 314. The legislature of one State cannot create a corporation so as to authorize it to build a bridge, extending within the limits of another State, and so as to empower such corporation to collect toll of one who passes only upon that part of the bridge within the limits of the other State. Middle Bridge Corp. *v.* Marks, 26 Me. 326. Where two corporations are created by adjacent States, with the same name, to construct a canal, to extend through a portion of each State, and afterwards their interests are united by subsequent acts of each State, this does not merge the separate corporate existence of such corporations. In such case a unity of stock and interest only is created. Farnum *v.* Blackstone Canal Co. 1 Sumner, 47.

[1] Runyan *v.* Coster, 14 Pet. 122. The case of Fairfax *v.* Hunter, 7 Cranch, 621, was cited by the court. And see *post*, Ch. V. § 2, as to power of corporations of one State to take and hold lands in another.

[2] People *v.* Trustees of Geneva College, 5 Wend. 211.

§ 107. A private trading corporation must be held *to reside* in the *town* where its principal office is, as a local inhabitant. Its residence depends not on the habitation of the stockholders in interest, but on the official exhibition of legal and local existence.[1] By the Revised Statutes of Maine, every private corporation may bring an action in any county in which such corporation shall have a place of business. It was held under this provision, that where a railroad passes over two counties, the railroad corporation may maintain an action of assumpsit in that county wherein they have an office, which is made "the depositary of the books and records of the company, by a vote of the directors, and a place where a large share of the business is transacted," although the company may at the same time have another office in the other county, where the residue of their business is transacted, and in which the treasurer and clerk reside.[2] In New York, companies organizing under the general act, are required to file a certificate setting forth the name of the city or town where the principal office is, and this certificate is conclusive in their favor as well as against them.[3]

§ 108. A corporation is a subject of the government of the country in which it is created, although the members composing it may be foreigners. A corporation incorporated by the law of Rhode Island, and

---

1 Bank *v.* McKenzie, 2 Brock. C. C. 392; Cromwell *v.* Ins. Co. 2 Rich. 512; Railroad Co. *v.* Stetson, 2 How. 497; Conn. & P. R. Co. *v.* Cooper, 30 Vt. 476; Thorn *v.* Central R. Co. 2 Dutch. 121; Edwards *v.* Union Bank, 1 Fla. 136; Taylor *v.* Crowland Gas and Coke Co., 11 Exch. 1, 29 Eng. L. & Eq. 516. See as to allegations of citizenship by a corporation in a United States court, N. Y. & E. R. R. *v.* Shepard, 5 McLean, C. C. 455; Lafayette Ins. Co. *v.* French, 18 How. 404. See *post*, Chap. XI. § 407.

2 Androscoggin, &c. Railroad Co. *v.* Stevens, 17 Me. 434. So the Baltimore and Ohio Railroad Company, though its principal office is in Maryland, may be sued in Virginia upon contracts there made. Balt. & Ohio R. R. Co. *v.* Gallahue, 12 Gratt. 655. See also, Bristol *v.* Chicago & Aurora R. R. Co. 15 Ill. 436; Indiana M. F. Ins. Co. *v.* Routledge, 7 Ind. 25; Moulin *v.* Insurance Co. 4 N. J. 222, 1 Dutch. 57. In the case of King *v.* Gardner, Cowp. 70, a corporation was decided by the Court of King's Bench, to come within the description of occupiers or inhabitants. In U. S. Bank *v.* Devaux, 5 Cranch, 84, it is said of a corporation, "this ideal existence is considered as an inhabitant, when the general spirit and purposes of the law require it." A corporation may have a constructive residence, so as to subject it, like a natural person, to be charged with taxes, and be submitted to a special jurisdiction. Cromwell *v.* Insurance & Trust Co. 2 Rich. 512; Glazio *v.* S. Carolina Railroad Co. 1 Strob. 70. But it has been held in Connecticut, that bank-stock belonging to a corporation having no local limits, but required by its charter to keep its office in the town of Hartford, is not taxable in the town of H. within *the meaning of the statute* of Connecticut, providing for the collection of taxes. Hartford Fire Insurance Co. *v.* Hartford, 3 Conn. 15.

3 Western Transp. Co. *v.* Schew, 19 N. Y. 408.

which is authorized by a statute of Massachusetts to hold real estate in that State, is considered in Massachusetts as a foreign corporation.[1]

§ 109. In Regina *v.* Arnaud,[2] a mandamus was directed to the collector and comptroller of the customs in and for the port of Liverpool, the object of which was, to compel them to register a vessel, the property of the Pacific Steam Navigation Company, a corporate body created by charter, for the purpose of providing vessels and employing them in the Pacific Ocean. It was admitted by the defendants, that the company, as a British corporation, might be the *owners* of British built vessels, and *primâ facia* would be, as such corporation, entitled to register them under the provisions of the law applicable to the registry of vessels by corporations. But it was said, that some of the members of the corporation in question were not British subjects, but foreigners, and consequently, that the vessel did not *wholly* belong to her Majesty's subjects, as required by the fifth section of the act, and was within the prohibition contained in the twelfth section of the act, against foreigners being entitled to be owners, in whole or in part, directly or indirectly, of any vessel requiring to be registered. "Now," said the court, by Lord Denman, C. J., "it appears to us, that the British corporation is, as such, the *sole owner* of the ship, and a British subject, within the meaning of the fifth section, so far as such term can be applicable to a corporation, notwithstanding some foreigners may individually have shares in the company, and that such individual members of the corporation are not entitled, in whole or in part, directly or indirectly, to be *owners* of the vessel. The individual members of the corporation, are, no doubt, interested, in one sense, in the property of the corporation, as they may derive individual benefit from its increase, or loss from its destruction; but in no *legal sense* are the individual members the owners. If all the individuals of the corporation were duly qualified British subjects, they could not register the vessel in their individual names, *as owners*, but must register it as belonging wholly to the corporation as owner." In reply to what was urged, that such might defeat the object and policy of the navigation laws in this respect, the learned judge said: "The individual members of the British corporation might, either originally or by transfer, be all foreigners. Such does not appear to be contemplated or provided by the act in question.

[1] Blackstone Manuf. Co. *v.* Blackstone, 13 Gray, 488.
[2] Regina *v.* Arnaud, 9 Q. B. 806.

If it be *casus omissus*, and evil consequences arise, they may be remedied by the interference of the legislature." [1]

§ 110. We have seen that in constituting a body corporate, a legal or artificial person is substituted for a natural person; and that where a number of natural persons are concerned, there is given to them the property of individuality. The Common Law of every State or country annexes to this local or artificial person, when created, certain incidents and attributes; and, both by the laws of England and the United States, there are several powers and capacities which tacitly, and without any express provision, are considered inseparable from every corporation. Kyd enumerates five of these as necessarily and inseparably belonging to *every* corporation. 1. To have perpetual succession, and hence, all *aggregate* corporations have a power, necessarily implied of admitting members in the room of such as are removed by death or otherwise. 2. To sue and be sued, implead and be impleaded, grant and receive by its corporate name, and do all other acts as *natural* persons may. 3. To purchase lands and hold them for the benefit of themselves and their successors. 4. To have a common seal; and, 5. To make by-laws, which are considered as private statutes for the government of the corporate body.[2] To these ordinary incidents of an incorporated company, Kent, in his commentaries, has added, as a sixth,—the power of amotion or removal of members; and in the power to purchase and hold property, he includes chattels as well as land.[3] And, he adds, that, "some of these powers are to be taken, in many instances, with much modification and restriction; and the essence of a corporation consists only of a capacity to have perpetual succession, under a special denomination, and an artificial form, and to take and grant property, contract obligations, and sue and be sued by its corporate name, and to receive and enjoy, in common, grants of privileges and immunities." [4] Kyd likewise remarks, " that to form the complete idea of a cor-

---

[1] See, "The Merchant Shipping Act," of Great Britain, 17 & 18 Vict. ch. 104, § 18.

[2] 1 Kyd, 69.

[3] 2 Kent, Com. 224.

[4] Ibid. According to Lord Holt, neither the actual possession of property, nor the actual enjoyment of franchises, are of the essence of a corporation. The King *v.* City of London, Skin. 310. To have a common seal, and to make by-laws, it is admitted, are very unnecessary to a corporation sole, though they may be practised by it; and that the last is not so inseparably incident to a corporation *aggregate*, that it cannot subsist without it; for there are some corporations aggregate, to which rules may be prescribed, and which they are bound to obey. See 1 Kyd, 69, and 1 Bl. Com. 475, 476.

poration aggregate, it is sufficient to suppose it vested with the three following capacities. 1. To have perpetual succession under a *special* denomination, and under an artificial form. 2. To take and grant property, to contract obligations, and to sue and be sued by its corporate name, in the same manner as an individual. 3. To receive grants of privileges and immunities, and to enjoy them in *common*."[1] A joint-stock corporation, *e. g.* a railroad corporation, may be regarded in three principal points of view; in regard, 1st, of its external relations, which have been mentioned; 2dly, of its internal relations (making of by-laws, &c.); and 3dly, of its *capital stock*.[2]

§ 111. Each of the above-mentioned incidental powers and capacities, of course, may be regulated and limited by the act or charter of incorporation; and when they are not in any degree restricted or curtailed, they can only be exercised to effect the purposes for which they were conferred by the government. Private corporations when originating according to the rules of the Common Law, must be governed by it, in their mode of organization, in the manner of exercising their powers, and in the use of the capacities conferred. But where a corporation relies upon a grant of power from the legislature for authority to do an act, it is as much restricted to the *mode* prescribed by the statute or charter for its exercise, as to the thing allowed to be done.[3] The legislature may create a corporation, not only without conforming to the rules of the Common Law, but in disregard of them; and when a corporation is thus created, its existence, powers, capacities, and mode of exercising them, must depend upon the law of its creation, and upon its objects.[4] The general practice in the United States, is, to specify the powers with which it is intended to endow the society or company incorporated; and

---

[1] 1 Kyd, 70.

[2] See Walf. on Railways. And see *post*, ch. in relation to the Nature, &c. of Stock.

[3] Farmers Loan & Trust Co. *v.* Carroll, 5 Barb. 613.

[4] Penobscot B. Corporation *v.* Lamson, 16 Me. 224; Com. of Roads *v.* M'Pherson, 1 Speers, 218. Where there are various alternative modes of exercising corporate powers, authorized by a charter without limitation of time, that subject each of them to be changed at the will of the corporation, no experimental trial of one of the modes, will amount to a forfeiture of a right to resort to either of the other modes, during the continuance of the charter. Baltimore & Ohio Railroad Co. *v.* Ches. & Ohio Canal Co. 4 Gill. & J. 1. But where the line of a railroad between given points was left to the discretion of the corporation, it was held, that, after having once made a selection and located the road, they could not vary it. Little Miami Railroad Co. *v.* Naylor, 2 Ohio State, 235; Louisville & Nashville B. T. Co. *v.* Nashville & Kentucky T. Co. 2 Swan, 282.

these powers will be found to be given in reference to the object in view in creating the corporation. If the object of the corporation is to *insure property*, for instance, it cannot exercise the power of acting as a *banking* institution. We shall have occasion to go at large into the subject of the inability of corporations to engage in any particular trade or business foreign to its institution, under the head of their power to make contracts; but here it may be proper to lay down what is the general and well-settled principle, that a corporation has no other powers than such as are specifically granted; or, such as are necessary for the purpose of carrying into effect the powers expressly granted. In other words, the general powers of a corporate body must be restricted by the nature and object of its institution. As has been said by the Supreme Court of the United States, "the exercise of the corporate franchise, being restrictive of individual rights, cannot be extended beyond the letter and spirit of the act of incorporation."[1] It is true there may be implied powers with the incidental, and whenever it is clearly so, those powers are as much beyond the control of subsequent legislation, as those expressly granted.[2] The case of the *Utica Insurance Company*, in New York, affords an illustration of what, as we shall by and by show more fully, is the well settled and general rule in this country, namely, that a corporation is confined to the sphere of action limited by the terms and intention of the charter. In that case it was held, that the company (not being authorized by charter to become proprietors of any *bank*, or fund for the purpose of issuing notes, receiving deposits, &c., which incorporated banks are allowed to do), was not authorized, under the restraining act, to discount notes and loan money; and that notes discounted, and securities for money loaned were void.[3] It was held in Ohio, that the stockholders of a canal company were holden, in their *individual capacity*, for notes issued by the company, intended to circulate as money; that they could only escape from pecuniary responsibility, by taking refuge behind their franchises, when pursuing the legitimate object for which those franchises

---

[1] Beaty *v.* Knowler, 4 Pet. 162. See *post*, Ch. VIII. and Jansen *v.* Ostrander, 1 Cowen, 686. See further as to the construction of charters of incorporation, Auburn & Cato P. R. Co. *v.* Douglass, 5 Seld. 444; Pennsylvania Railroad Co. *v.* Canal Commissioners, 21 Penn. State, 9; Commonwealth *v.* Erie & N. E. Railroad Co. 27 id. 339; Railroad Co. *v.* Payne, 8 Rich. 177.

[2] People *v.* Manhattan Co. 9 Wend. 351; People *v.* Marshall, 1 Gilman, 672.

[3] Utica Ins. Co. *v.* Scott, 19 Johns. 1. The lending of money by the company was not, however, declared void; it was held, that the money might be recovered, though the security was void.

were granted.[1] A striking illustration is, that a charter creating a Library Company a corporation, and giving it a capacity of suing and being sued, a power to make by-laws, and even the power *to make contracts, and to dispose of any real or personal estate, in any mode* the corporation may deem most proper, confers no authority to exercise the franchise of banking.[2] The modern language of the English courts is to the same effect.[3] If a corporation is created for purposes of trade, it results necessarily, that it must have power to accept bills and issue notes; but if a company be incorporated, not for the purposes of trade, but to supply water, or any purpose so disconnected with trade, no implication can arise, that it has power to issue notes and bills; and there must be express authority to enable the body corporate so to do.[4] But "the dealings of a corporation, which, on their face, or according to their ap-

---

[1] Lawler *v.* Walker, 18 Ohio, 151; and see Johnson *v.* Bently, 16 id. 97.

[2] State of Ohio *v.* Washington Library Co. 11 Ohio, 96; and see Knowles *v.* Beaty, 1 McLean, C. C. 43. See also, People *v.* Utica Ins. Co. 15 Johns. 358; Korn *v.* Mutual Ins. Society, 6 Cranch, 192; New York Fire Ins. Co. *v.* Ely, 5 Conn. 560; Gozzler *v.* Corporation of Georgetown, 6 Wheat. 593; Bank of Utica *v.* Smedes, 6 Cowen, 684; M'Mullen *v.* City Council, 1 Bay, 46; American Jurist, No. VIII. p. 306; Mayor, &c. *v.* McKee, 2 Yerg. 167; Webb *v.* Manchester, &c. 4 Mylne & C. 116; Pearce *v.* New Orleans Building Co. 9 La. 395; id. 461; Beaty *v.* Knowler, 4 Pet. 152; Stewart *v.* Stebbins, 1 Stew. 299; State *v.* Mayor, &c. of Mobile, 5 Port. Ala. 279; Betts *v.* Menard, 1 Breese, 10; Jackson *v.* Brown, 5 Wend. 590; Ohio Life & Trust Co. *v.* Merchants Ins. & Trust Co. 11 Humph. 1; President, &c. of Jacksonville *v.* McConnel, 12 Ill. 138; Sumner *v.* Marcy, 3 Woodb. & M., C. C. 105; Bangor Boom Corp. *v.* Whiting, 29 Me. 123; Perrine *v.* Chesapeake & Delaware Canal Co. 9 How. 172; Blanchard's Gun-Stock Turning Co. *v.* Warner, 1 Blatchf. C. C. 258; Trustees *v.* Peaslee, 15 N. H. 317; Wright *v.* Scott, H. L. 1855, 34 Eng. L. & Eq. 1; Chicago, Burlington & Quincy R. R. Co. *v.* Wilson, 17 Ill. 123; Curtis *v.* Leavitt, 15 N. Y. 9. So with public corporations. The licensing of an individual to occupy a part of a public street exclusively for his own use and benefit, by erecting and using a railroad for the transportation of stone and gravel, is not among the powers granted to the city of Portland, by any section of its charter. Green *v.* Portland, 32 Me. 431, and see Reynolds *v.* Mayor, &c. of Albany, 8 Barb. 59. There was an elaborate review of the authorities, on this subject, by the court, in the case of Barry *v.* Merchants Exchange Co., in which it is laid down, that the general powers incident to bodies corporate, are restricted by the nature and object of the institution of each; and every such corporation has power to make all contracts that are necessary and usual in the course of the business it transacts, as means to enable it to effect such object, unless expressly prohibited by law, or the provisions of its charter. With this limitation it may deal precisely as if it were a natural person, to attain its legitimate objects. Barry *v.* Merchants Exchange Co. 1 Sandf. Ch. 80, and cases therein cited; Brady *v.* Mayor of Brooklyn, 1 Barb. 584.

[3] Dublin Corporation *v.* Attorney-General, 9 Bligh, N. S. 395.

[4] Broughton *v.* Manchester Waterworks Co. 3 B. & Ald. 1. See also, 2 Kent, Com. 5th ed. 300.

parent import, are within its charter, are not to be regarded as illegal or unauthorized without some evidence to show that they are of such a character. In the absence of proof there is no legal presumption that the law has been violated. On the contrary," it has been said, "these artificial bodies, like natural persons, are entitled to the benefit of the rule which imputes innocence rather than wrong to the conduct of men."[1] And if a municipality is authorized "to establish and regulate markets," it may purchase lands upon which to erect a market building;[2] and may employ an architect to prepare plans, specifications, &c., for such a building.[3] If however there is a city ordinance on the subject of the letting of contracts and the issuing of proposals for estimates, where work is to be done for the city, a contract in violation of its terms would, it seems, be void.[4] A charter of incorporation so far requires by implication that the body corporate shall perform the business for which it was instituted, that a substantial suspension of the same is a violation of its charter.[5]

§ 112. The mode, by which corporations manifest their assent, make contracts, &c., is by their *common seal*, or, as it is sometimes expressed, *by deed;* or by *a vote of the company;* or by the contracts or agreements of their authorized *agents*. But though such are the usual modes in which corporations act, and though, as a general rule, the doings and declarations of individual members, not sanctioned by the body, are not binding upon it, yet the rules of law have, by modern decisions, been made so flexible, as to allow inferences to be drawn from corporate acts which tend to prove a contract or promise, as in cases of natural persons.[6] The powers, capacities, and capabilities peculiar to a corporation, and the modes in which it may act, and the interests of subscribers to joint-stock corporations, in regard to their stock, will be much more fully exhibited in the following chapters.

---

1 Chautauque County Bank *v.* Risley, 19 N. Y. 369, 381.

2 Ketchum *v.* City of Buffalo, 14 N. Y. 356.

3 Peterson *v.* Mayor of N.Y., 17 N. Y. 449.

4 Christopher *v.* Mayor of N. Y. 13 Barb. 567. In Peterson *v.* Mayor of N. Y., the ordinance was not given in evidence, and the court said that they would express no opinion upon its effect if it should be given in evidence at another trial, nor upon the correctness of the decision in Christopher *v.* Mayor of N. Y.

5 Jackson Marine Ins. Co., Matter of, 4 Sandf. Ch. 559.

6 See *post,* chapters relative to Common Seal, Contracts, and Agents.

CHAPTER IV.

OF THE ADMISSION AND ELECTION OF MEMBERS AND OFFICERS.

§ 113. IN respect to the power of admitting members, reference must often be had to the provisions and spirit of the charter; and when the charter is silent, we must look to the rules of the Common Law, and to the particular nature and purpose of the corporation. In certain corporations (such, for example, as religious and literary) the number of members is often limited by charter; and whenever there is a vacancy, it is usually filled by a *vote* of the company. The number of members who must *concur* in voting both for the admission of members and election of officers, is a subject we have reserved for a subsequent chapter, in which we shall treat of the concurrence necessary to do all corporate acts. As regards trading and joint-stock corporations, no vote of admission is requisite; for any person who owns stock therein, either by original subscription, or by conveyance, is, in general, entitled to, and cannot be refused, the rights and privileges of a member.[1] In a mutual insurance company, it is well known, that a person may become a member by insuring his property, paying the premium and deposit money, and rendering himself liable to be assessed according to the rules of the corporation.[2] In the important case of Overseers of the Poor *v.* Sears, SHAW, C. J., in delivering the opinion of the court, says: "In all bridge, railroad, and turnpike companies, in all banks, insurance companies, manufacturing companies, and, generally, in corporations having a capital stock, and looking to profits, membership is constituted by a

---

[1] Gilbert *v.* Manchester Iron Co. 11 Wend. 627; Sargent *v.* Franklin Ins. Co. 8 Pick. 90. A subscriber to the stock of an incorporated company, *whose subscription is received by the directors,* and regular certificates thereof issued, is a *bonâ fide* stockholder, entitled to vote at elections, although he has paid nothing for his stock. Downing *v.* Potts, 3 N. J. 66. And see *post,* Chapters XV. and XVI.; Gray *v.* Portland Bank, 3 Mass. 364; Rex *v.* Bank of England, 2 Doug. 524. A mandamus will be granted to a canal company to enter upon their books the probate of a will of a deceased shareholder. The King *v.* Worcester Canal Company, 1 Man. & R. 529.

[2] Sullivan *v.* Massachusetts Mutual Fire Ins. Co. 2 Mass. 315.

transfer of shares, according to the by-laws, without any election on the part of the corporation itself."[1] But it seems, that, although the party taking a conveyance of shares is entitled to membership, yet at an election, as for directors, his right to vote must be determined by the transfer-book of the company, the inspectors not being authorized to look beyond it;[2] he may have all the rights and be liable to all the duties of a member, without a certificate.[3] In general, a party can no otherwise become a member of a joint-stock trading corporate body, than by himself subscribing to the undertaking, or stepping into the place of an original subscriber; and it is the peculiarity of what is thus made the title of admission to the company, and the provision it affords for the succession of fresh members, that constitutes one of the main features of these companies, and mainly distinguishes them from ordinary corporations.[4] But the subscription for, and nature of, stock, its incidents and capability of transfer, are made the particular subjects of subsequent chapters.[5]

§ 114. The power of admitting new members, being incident, as has been before observed, to every corporation aggregate, it is not necessary that such power should be expressly conferred by the charter. A right as a corporator in a religious society, is obtained by stated attendance on divine worship, and contributing to its support by renting a pew or by some other mode usual in the congregation.[6]

§ 115. As to the power of electing officers, if the power is not expressly lodged in other hands (as, for instance, in a body of directors), it must be exercised by the company at large.[7] On this account, if an election is relied upon by any select body in pleading, it need not be shown by what authority and in what form such body is constituted; for

---

1 22 Pick. 122. And see Philadelphia Savings Institution, 1 Whart. 461; In the matter of Long Island Railroad Co. 19 Wend. 37.

2 Matter of Long Island Railroad Co. 19 Wend. 37; *Ex parte* Holmes, 5 Cowen, 426. And see *Ex parte* Desviolty, 1 Wend. 98.

3 Agricultural Bank *v.* Burr, 24 Me. 256; Chester Glass Man. Co. *v.* Dewey, 16 Mass. 19.

4 See Walf. on Railways, 252; Mann *v.* Currie, 2 Barb. Ch. 294.

5 See Chapters XV. and XVI.

6 Cammeyer *v.* United German Lutheran Churches, 2 Sandf. Ch. 186; Hamilton & Dearville Plank Road Co. *v.* Rice, 7 Barb. 157; Commonwealth *v.* Claghorn, 13 Penn. State, 133.

7 See State *v.* Ancker, 2 Rich. 244; Commonwealth *v.* Bousall, 3 Whart. 560.

a general allegation of election implies an election by the whole body in the exercise of their incidental power. The power may, by the charter or by a general statute, be taken from the body at large, and reposed in a body of directors, or any other select body.[1] In these, as in all other cases, the terms of the charter or act of incorporation, are overruling. A statute incorporated certain persons named, and others thereafter becoming members, to receive deposits of money, and pay interests to the depositors; and directed that, for the security of the depositors, a certain capital should be raised, to be divided into transferable shares. The statute also provided for yearly meetings of the members, and for the election of directors from among the members, and authorized the directors to provide for the admission of members, and directed them to appoint, from among the members, a committee of examination; and likewise, to make a dividend of profits, and pay the same to the stockholders or their representatives. It was held, that stockholders, as such, were not members of the corporation, and, of course, that the assignee of a stockholder did not, by the assignment, become a member; and that the original members continued to be members, although they never had any stock, or had disposed of it.[2]

§ 116. Where an act of incorporation provides that there shall be "three directors, *out of whom* a president shall be chosen," it is sufficient if the president be elected by a legally constituted meeting, at the same time with the other directors; without having been *previously* appointed a director. There is no real utility in requiring a circuity of action; and, as a *previous* election, as director, was not required by the act, there is no objection to the appointment of a president and director (both of which characters are to *combine* in the same person) at one ballot.[3]

§ 117. In the State of New Jersey, in all the acts incorporating banks, commissioners are appointed to open books and receive subscriptions for the capital stock; and as soon as lawful notice is given of a meeting of the subscribers, for the choice of officers, the subscribers acquire rights under it. It has been decided, that when the first elec-

---

[1] 1 Rol. Abr. 513, 1, 50; Philips *v.* Bury, Parl. Ca. 45; Willcock on Mun. Corpor. 201; Commonwealth *v.* Gill, 4 Whart. 228.

[2] Philadelphia Savings Institution, 1 Whart. 461.

[3] Currie *v.* Mutual Insurance Co. 4 Hen. & M. 315.

tion is authorized to be held, upon a call made by commissioners, it is not essential that the call should be the result of any formal order of the commissioners; if the original notice is in the handwriting of the secretary of the commissioners, he being one of them, and the names of the other commissioners are signed by him, and the notice is in no way disavowed by the commissioners, it will be deemed their act.[1]

§ 118. The corporation at large, may, if not inconsistent with the charter, make a *by-law* creating a select body, to whom they may delegate the power of electing officers and members.[2] Thus it was held, in the case of The Commonwealth *v.* Woelper, that the corporation might, by a by-law, give to the *president* the power of appointing inspectors of the corporate elections; and might, also, define by by-laws, the nature of the tickets to be used, and the manner of voting.[3] And it was decided, in Newling *v.* Francis, that when the mode of electing corporate officers was not regulated by charter or prescription, the corporation might make by-laws to regulate the election, provided they did not infringe the charter.[4] But this power must be exercised with caution and with no sinister design.[5]

---

[1] Hardenburgh *v.* Farmers & Mechanics Bank, 2 Green, Ch. 68.

[2] *Ex parte* Wilcocks, 7 Cowen, 402; Anonymous, 12 Mod. 225. It has been said that when the right of election was originally vested in the corporation at large, it could not be transferred to a select body by a new charter; but denied by Holt, C. J., Rex *v.* Larwood, Skin. 573; Rex *v.* Wymre, 2 Barnard. 391. There is certainly no good reason for maintaining that it cannot be so altered, unless we maintain that the franchise of being a corporation cannot be surrendered; but if we support the latter position, we can hardly admit so fundamental an alteration in the constitution. This alteration is not to be contended for on the same ground that a by-law, altering the manner of election, may be supported; that is, common assent; for, in the acceptance of the charter, the grantees assent not only for themselves, but their successors, also, forever; whereas, in making a by-law the assent binds (or is presumed to bind) only themselves and their successors, *until* the majority choose to change their will and repeal the ordinance. The cases which have been determined, on the presumption that the right of election may be restricted by a new charter, are so numerous, that the question seems to be no longer controvertible. Willcock on Mun. Corpor. 202.

[3] Commonwealth *v.* Woelper, 3 S. & R. 29.

[4] Newling *v.* Francis, 3 T. R. 189. The power of election must be exercised under the modifications of the charter or statute, of which the corporation is the mere creature, and which usually prescribes the time and manner of corporate elections, and defines the qualifications of the electors. If this be not done, it is in the power of the corporation

[5] St. Luke's Church *v.* Mathews, 4 Desaus. Ch. 578. And see *post*, chap. on *By-laws*.

§ 119. An article in the by-laws of a religious corporation, provided as follows: The president "shall convene the board of trustees at least once in every month, and may call extra meetings whenever, in his opinion, or in the opinion of three members of that body, it shall be deemed necessary for the interest or welfare of the congregation." Another article provided, that a majority of the board might admit new members. The president, on application of four members of the board, refused to call a meeting thereof; after which, a majority of the board convened without such call, after giving the president notice of the time and place of their intended meeting. It was held, that the board thus convened, had no power to elect new members of the corporation, and that all their acts were illegal and void.[1]

§ 120. In the case of Commonwealth *v.* Gill, in Pennsylvania, a question as to the regularity and validity of an election, was determined, which arose both under the act of incorporation and under a by-law. One section of the act provided, that there should be a meeting of the members, annually, for the choice of directors from among the members. A following section provided, that the directors should have power to provide for the admission of members. By a subsequent legislative act it was declared that stockholders (in a savings bank) should have a right of voting for directors, and that they should be eligible for directors. A *by-law* was passed, by the directors elected in pursuance of this last act, providing, that every person holding one share of the stock, should be a member of the institution; and that, upon a transfer of his stock, such person should cease to be a member. It was held, 1st. That the directors had not the power to elect members, but merely to provide for their admission; and 2d. That, if they had the power, the by-law was an unreasonable exercise of it, and inconsistent with the design of the charter, and therefore invalid.[2]

§ 121. By-laws for the good of the corporation, have been held to be valid, although they reduced the number of *electors* to narrower bounds than were prescribed by the charter. A leading case on this subject, is

---

itself, by its by-laws, to regulate the manner of election. 2 Kent, Com. 294. If neither the charter nor the by-laws prescribe the mode of election, the courts may give to the long-continued usage of the corporators the force of express provision. Juker *v.* Commonwealth, 20 Penn. State, 484.

[1] State *v.* Ancker, 2 Rich. 245.

[2] Commonwealth *v.* Gill, 3 Whart. 228. See *post*, chap. on *By-laws*.

the "case of corporations."[1] Several towns had been incorporated by charter, which directed the election of mayor, bailiff, alderman, &c., to be by the commonalty or burgesses, *generally*, but, by long continued usage those elections had been made by a select number of the principal persons of the commonalty, and not by the commonalty or burgesses at large. It was decided, after great deliberation and conference among all the judges, that the said elections were well warranted by the charters and by-laws, because the regulation under which they were made, tended to prevent disorder and confusion, and was, therefore, for the good of the corporation. That decision has ever since been held to be the law of England, and was recognized and applied in Pennsylvania, in the case of The Commonwealth *v.* Cain,[2] wherein it was held, that, where the charter of a church authorized the making of by-laws for its good government, and directed that the elections of ministers, &c., should be conducted agreeably to certain rules, one of which was, that no person was to have a vote except those who had been regularly admitted, and should have been members for twelve months preceding the election, — a by-law enacting that no member of the church, whose pew-rent was in arrear for a longer time than two years, should be entitled to vote for officers, was valid. By this decision no person was excluded from voting unless he was in default, in a matter essential to the support of the church, and he was not precluded from reinstating himself in his privilege, by paying his debt; and nothing was more manifestly for the good of the church than the by-law in question.[3]

§ 122. The power of election reposed in a select body, may be only of certain officers; and one class of officers may be made eligible by one select body, and another class by a different. And if it is declared by the charter, by whom some officers may be elected, and no provision is made for the election of others, the others must be chosen, of course, by the body at large, by virtue of their incidental authority.[4]

---

[1] 40 & 41 Eliz.; 4 Co. R. 78.

[2] Commonwealth *v.* Cain, 5 S. & R. 510. That the decision in this case could be supported on principle and without having recourse to the "case of corporations," and for comments on that case, see *post*, Chap. X. *Of the By-laws of Corporations.*

[3] Rex *v.* Maidstone, 3 Burr. 1837; 4 Burr. 2209; Rex *v.* Head, 4 Burr. 2521; Hoblyn *v.* Regem, 6 Bro. P. C. 519; Newling *v.* Francis, 3 T. R. 189; Rex *v.* Bird, 13 East, 385; Rex *v.* Westwood, 4 B. & C. 800.

[4] Rex *v.* Miller, 2 T. R. 280; Rex *v.* Varlo, Cowp. 250.

§ 123. It is said, that one cannot be elected to a corporate office in reversion; and, therefore, it is essential to a valid election, that there be a vacancy of the office at the time of the election. Indeed, if it had been customary to elect a person who shall succeed into the first vacancy, the corporation may, on the occurring of the vacancy, elect another, and set aside the officer elect.[1] So if A be illegally amoved, and B elected in his stead, and A afterwards is restored in obedience to the writ of mandamus, the election of B is void; for the restoration puts in A as of his ancient title, and has relation back to the moment of his amotion, from which he continues to have been a legal officer, as though he had never been amoved. And the validity of B's election depending entirely upon the legality of A's removal, B is not entitled to fill another vacancy, if one should happen in the same body, after the restoration of A; but he is returned to the same situation as though A had never been amoved and he never elected.[2]

§ 124. A *particular day* is generally appointed by the constitution of a corporation for the election of the principal officers. This is usually styled the "charter day," and is usually fixed with so much certainty that no doubt can arise. Where the trustees of a religious corporation were required, by statute, to be divided into three classes, and the seats of one class were to be vacated at the expiration of every year, so that one third should be "annually chosen," and the time of the annual election was required to be at least six days before the vacancies should happen; it was adjudged that an election on *Pinxter* Monday (*i. e.* the Monday after *Whitsunday*), in each year, though a movable holiday, and not a day certain, was valid. The court observed, that the church having fixed upon a yearly religious epoch, it would be revolting to hold the corporation dissolved, from the very first time that the elections were so held, and that all its subsequent elections and acts were void, merely because the holiday selected for the election, did not correspond with the solar year; and that they must give the statute a liberal and reasonable construction, for the benefit of the churches; and that there

---

[1] Willcock on Mun. Corpor. 207; 2 Kyd, 5.

[2] Ibid.; Colt *v.* Bishop of Coventry, Hob. 150; Owen *v.* Stainoe, Skin. 45; Shuttleworth *v.* Lincoln, 2 Bulst. 122. So, if, under the supposition that the place of A, an alderman, is vacant, while that of B, who is also an alderman, is really vacant, C be elected into the supposed vacant office of A, his election is void, and cannot be referred to the actual vacancy of B's office. Rex *v.* Smith, 2 M. & S. 407.

were many decisions in the books, showing that the election in such cases is valid, if made after the year, and especially if an integral part of the corporation remains.[1]

§ 125. Whenever the usual *place* of meeting has been changed, an election of an officer at the old place is invalid.[2] It has been held that the words, "between the hours of ten in the morning, and two in the afternoon," are not imperative, but merely directory, and an election may be well begun at any other reasonable time of the day.[3] The charters of private incorporated companies, in this country, are, in general, sufficiently free to allow an election of the necessary officers to be made when the occasion requires it. It is not necessary that the person elected be present at the assembly, if he is within such a distance that he can in due time enter upon the duties and exercise of his office.[4]

§ 126. If there is no form prescribed for the election, every candidate must be proposed singly, whether the election is by the whole body or by a definite class; and if the names of more than one be set down in a list, and the election proposed to be made of the whole by a single vote, such election is altogether void, although the names have been repeatedly read over, and an offer made to strike out any to which an objection should be made, and notwithstanding the election was by the unanimous consent of the entire body. For, it may be presumed that, instead of using his judgment as to the propriety of admitting any individual (which would be the case where they are separately proposed), each elector, desirous to obtain the admission of some one in particular, may compromise his opinion as to the others, and thus, persons may be introduced who would otherwise have been rejected.[5] Where a majority protest against the election of a proposed candidate, and do not propose any *other* candidate, the *minority* may elect the candidate proposed.[6]

---

1 People *v.* Runkel, 9 Johns. 147. And see Hicks *v.* Town of Launceston, 1 Roll. Abr. 512; Foot *v.* Mayor of Truro, Stra. 625.

2 Miller *v.* English, 1 N. J. 317; Den d. Am. Prim. Soc. *v.* Pilling, 4 id. 653.

3 Rex *v.* Poole, 7 Mod. 195. If the elective assembly be held on the charter day, it may be adjourned to a reasonable hour of the following day, without reference to the hours of ten and twelve. Ibid.

4 Rex *v.* Courtenay, 9 East, 261.

5 Rex *v.* Monday, Cowp. 539; Willcock on Mun. Corp. 215.

6 2 Kyd, 12; Oldknow *v.* Wainright, 2 Burr. 1017.

§ 127. After an election has been properly proposed, whoever has a majority of those who vote, the assembly being sufficient, is elected, although the majority of the entire assembly altogether abstain from voting; because their presence suffices to constitute the elective body, and if they neglect to vote, it is their own fault, and shall not invalidate the act of the others, but be construed an assent to the determination of the majority of those who do vote. And such an election is valid, though the majority of those whose presence is necessary to the assembly, protest against any election at that time, or even the election of the individual who has a majority of votes; the only manner in which they can effectually prevent his election, is by voting for some other qualified person.[1]

§ 128. The right of voting at an election of an incorporated company *by proxy* is not a general right, and the party who claims it, must show a special authority for that purpose. The only case in which it is allowable, at the Common Law, is by the peers of England, and that is said to be in virtue of a special permission of the king.[2] Chancellor Walworth, of New York, thought it possible that the right of voting by proxy might be delegated, in some cases, by the by-laws of a corporation, where express authority was given to make such by-laws, regulating the manner of voting. He was not aware of any case, other than the one before him, where the right was ever claimed; and the express power which is generally given to the stockholders of moneyed and other private corporations, was opposed to the claim, where there is no express or implied power contained in the act.[3]

---

[1] Ibid.; Rex *v.* Foxcroft, 2 Burr. 1020; Crawford *v.* Powell, 2 Burr. 1016, 1 W. Bl. 229. See Booker *v.* Young, 12 Gratt. 303; State *v.* Lehre, 7 Rich. 234. If the assembly be duly convened, and the majority vote for an unqualified person, after notice that he is not qualified, their votes are thrown away, and the person having the next majority, and not appearing to be disqualified, is duly elected. Claridge *v.* Evelyn, 5 B. & Ald. 86; Rex *v.* Parry, 14 East, 561. Where an officer of a corporation is required to be chosen by ballot, and the record of his election does not specify the mode, the legal presumption is, that he was chosen by ballot. Blanchard *v.* Dow, 32 Me. 557. So, where the statute requires the presiding officers at a meeting to be nominated by a majority of the members present, and the certificate of incorporation states them to have been elected by a plurality of votes, it will be presumed, in the absence of proof to the contrary, that the statute was complied with. Meth. Epis. Union Church *v.* Picket, 23 Barb. 436. See s. c. 19 N. Y. 482. See *post*, Chap. XIV. on Corporation Meetings.

[2] Phillips *v.* Wickham, 1 Paige, 590.

[3] 1 Paige, 590.

§ 129. In the case of the State *v.* Tudor, in Connecticut,[1] there was no clause in the act of incorporation, empowering the members of the company to vote by proxy; but a by-law passed by the company, provided that the shareholders might so vote. It was urged, on the one side, that it was incident to every corporation, the object of which is the acquisition of property, that votes might be given by proxy; and, at any rate, after the by-law before-mentioned, there could be no doubt as to such right. On the other side, it was said, that no such common-law right existed; that it was a fundamental principle, in corporations of every kind, that votes should be given in person, and not by proxy; that this being the Common Law, was the law of Connecticut; and that no by-law authorizing votes to be given by proxy could be valid, the same being contrary to the laws of Connecticut. The opinion of the court was, that the vote given by the attorney for his principal ought to have been received; and though the court deemed it unnecessary to say how the point would have been determined had no by-law been made, yet they expressed the opinion, that incorporated societies, whose object is the acquisition of property, stood on a different ground, as to this question, from those of every other kind. That is to say, it is not so clear that every vote given in a corporation of the former kind must be personal, as it is that it must be so in one of the latter. Ingersoll, who gave the opinion of the court, went on to observe: "I agree most fully, that, by the Common Law, every vote given in a corporation instituted for the public good, either the good of the whole State, or of a particular town or society, must be personally given. So, also, every vote given by a freeman for his representative, must be given by him in person. There is no deviation from this rule; the authorities on this subject are uniform. Neither can a vote be given, in a town or society meeting, merely on the ground of owning property within the limits of such town or society. But from the very nature of a moneyed institution, the mere owning of shares in the stock of the corporation, seems, of course, to give a right of voting. But, whatever right might have been the result of reasoning on the nature of moneyed institutions, still, since the passing of the by-law above-mentioned, I am very clear that the votes for the officers of this corporation, as well as all other votes relative to it, may be given by proxy."

---

[1] State *v.* Tudor, 5 Day, 329.

§ 130. In Taylor *v.* Griswold,[1] in the Supreme Court of New Jersey, after a full and learned discussion, it was held to be a principle of the Common Law, that where an election depended upon the exercise of judgment, the right could not be disputed; and that it required legislative sanction before any corporate body could make a by-law authorizing members to vote by proxy. The authority of the case of the State *v.* Tudor may, therefore, says Kent, in his Commentaries, be considered as essentially shaken.[2] An alien stockholder, it is very clear, cannot vote by proxy, where, by the terms of incorporation, the right so to vote is given to each stockholder being a citizen.[3]

§ 131. A mere tenant for years, or one who has taken the property on shares, and has no *substantial* interest therein, cannot exercise the right of voting for officers, without the concurrence of the real owner.[4] In the case of *Ex parte* Holmes, in the Supreme Court of New York,[5] a rule was moved for to establish the election of L. R. and twenty-four others, who, as was claimed, had been chosen directors of the Tradesmen's Insurance Company, in the city of New York. The act to facilitate proceedings against incorporated companies, upon which this motion was made, provides, "that in all cases where the right of voting upon any share or shares of the stock of any incorporated company shall be questioned, it shall be the duty of the inspectors of the elections to require the transfer books of said company, as evidence of stock held in the said company; and all such shares as may appear standing thereon, in the name of any person or persons, shall be voted on by such person or persons directly by themselves, or by proxy, subject to the provision of the act of incorporation." There was nothing in the act of incorporation which interfered to prevent the application of this provision. The court said, that the provision was broad enough *literally* to include all stockholders, whether in their own right, or as mere *trustees* for others; and then proceeded to observe: "But the question remains, whether the latter are to be deemed stockholders, within the spirit of the act. True, the stock on which they voted, in this case, stands in their name;

---

1 Taylor *v.* Griswold, 2 Green, N. J. 223.

2 2 Kent, Com. 4th ed. 294, note.

3 *Ex parte* Barker, rel. to Merc. Ins. Co. 6 Wend. 509.

4 Phillips *v.* Wickham, 1 Paige, 590.

5 *Ex parte* Holmes, 5 Cowen, 426.

but on the face of the entry they are declared to be mere nominal holders. The real owner of the stock should vote, especially where his name is truly expressed in the books; though it might be otherwise, if he chose to have the entry simply in the name of another, without expressing any trust. Now, these three persons, a majority of whom claim a right to vote, are mere trustees; and they are trustees, not for the directors, but the company, the corporation itself. If there could be a vote at all upon such stock, one would suppose that it must be by each stockholder of the company, in proportion to his interest in it. This brings us to the important difficulty in the case, which is, whether "stock, thus held, can vote at all. And we think it is not to be considered as stock held by any one for the purpose of being voted upon. No doubt the company may, from necessity, as in this case, take their own stock in pledge or payment; and keep it outstanding in trustees, to prevent its merger, and convert it to their security. But it is not stock to be voted upon, within the meaning of the charter, or the general act upon which we are proceeding. It is not to be tolerated, that a company should procure stock, in any shape, which its officers may wield to the purposes of an election; thus securing themselves against the possibility of removal." But a trustee holding stock in that character, for the benefit of others, may vote.[1]

§ 132. In the case of *Ex parte* Willcocks, in the State of New York,[2] the court say: "We do not hesitate to say, that, in a clear case of hypothecation, the *pledger* may vote. The possession may well continue with him, consistently with the nature of the contract; and the stock remains in his name. Till enforced and the title made absolute in the pledgee, and the name changed on the books, he should be received to vote. It is a question between him and the pledgee, with which the corporation have nothing to do."[3] In a subsequent case, in the same State, it was held, that hypothecated stock may be voted upon by the pledger, in corporations created before the first of January, 1828.[4] In a case in the Supreme Court of Massachusetts, it was held,

---

[1] Barker, *ex parte,* rel. to Merc. Ins. Co. 6 Wend. 509.

[2] *Ex parte* Willcocks, 7 Cowen, 402.

[3] The case of *Ex parte* Holmes (*supra*) was relied on as governing this case, but there the shares stood in the names of the persons who were trustees for the corporation. And it was not intended, by the decision in that case, to open an inquiry into every case of hypothecation.

[4] Barker, *ex parte,* rel. to Merc. Ins. Co. 6 Wend. 509.

that, if a stockholder of a bank transfers his shares by a writing, absolute in form, and surrenders his certificate of stock, and leaves with the cashier an agreement, in which (after reciting that he had transferred the shares, as collateral security for the payment of a note to the bank) he covenants, that, if the note shall not be duly paid, the bank may sell the shares, and apply the proceeds to the payment of the note, and hold the surplus to his use, — that he was still entitled to the rights of membership. The stockholder, in this case, paid interest from time to time, upon the note, after it had fallen due; but he continued to receive the dividends upon the shares.[1]

§ 133. There is a case, in which one of the reasons assigned, on a motion for a new trial, was, that *aliens* were not entitled to vote for vestrymen and churchwardens, in the corporation called "The Ministers, Vestrymen, and Churchwardens of the German Lutheran Congregation in and near the city of Philadelphia." The decision, however, was, that aliens, otherwise qualified, are entitled to vote. Yeates, J., made a distinction between *political* and *private* corporations, as to this right of aliens, and was unable to perceive any sound objection against aliens being included, in grants, with natural born subjects, merely for religious purposes. He observed: "Foreigners come to our shores, ignorant of our laws and customs, with all their different prepossessions for a particular system of polity. Should they think it expedient, they may distract, perplex, and thwart the public measures of the country. The sovereign power would naturally guard against such events, and prevent these new-comers from participating in all the rights of natural-born subjects, until they become seasoned to the soil, and familiarized with the new government and its legal institutions. The same dangers are not to be apprehended from foreigners desirous of being incorporated with others, merely for the exercise of religious duties." Tilghman, C. J., who considered the point somewhat elaborately, remarked: "The point turns on the charter; there the qualification is fixed; and there is no mention of citizen or subject, either in the charter itself, or in the fundamental articles to which it refers. I do not conceive that we have any right to insert it."[2] Aliens may even be elected trustees in a religious society.[3]

---

[1] Merchants Bank *v.* Cook, 4 Pick. 405.

[2] Commonwealth *v.* Woelper, 3 S. & R. 29; and see Stewart *v.* Foster, 2 Binney, 120; and *Ex parte* Barker, *ut sup.*

[3] Cammeyer *v.* United German Lutheran Churches, 2 Sandf. Ch. 186.

§ 134. Where the charter of a religious congregation conferred the right to vote on "the contributing members, being communicants of the said congregation," and by an act of assembly confirming the charter, it was provided, that no person should be entitled to vote who was *under the age of eighteen years*, it was held, that it was unnecessary that a member should have taken the sacrament after eighteen, to entitle him to vote. In the same case, it was held that a person may lose his membership, and consequently his right to vote, by uniting himself to another church professing an opposite creed.[1]

§ 135. If the right of election be reposed by charter in a select class, consisting of a definite number (twelve, for example), and the company have undertaken to increase the number, the elections of all persons, chosen after the number of twelve is complete, are a mere nullity; and if such persons give their vote as members of that class, they may be rejected as illegal.[2] But the election of a certain number of persons to fill a certain office, if the number chosen by the body at large is less than that prescribed by the charter, is valid. The charter of a company provided that its affairs shall be managed and conducted by *twenty-three* directors, of whom the major part shall constitute the board. On the charter day, an election was regularly held for an election of a new board of directors, when twenty-*two* individuals received the requisite number of votes. It was held that they were duly elected.[3]

§ 136. The mere circumstance that improper votes are received at an election, will not vitiate it. The fact should be affimatively shown, that a sufficient number of improper votes were received for the successful ticket, to reduce it to a minority, if they had been rejected; or, otherwise, the election must stand.[4] In *Ex parte* Murphy and others, at an annual election of St. Peter's Church, in the city of New York,

---

[1] Weckerley *v.* Geyer, 11 S. & R. 35. The association between a religious corporation and its corporators, being voluntary on the part of the latter, is dissolved by their withdrawing from attendance on its worship, and in uniting in the establishment of another like corporation. Cammeyer *v.* United German Lutheran Churches, 2 Sandf. Ch. 186.

[2] Rex *v.* Hearle, Stra. 625, 3 Bro. P. C. 178, Cowp. 567.

[3] In the matter of the Union Ins. Co. 22 Wend. 591; and see People *v.* Jones, 17 id. 81. In the former case, when the old board, conceiving that under such circumstances the election had wholly failed, ordered a second at which twenty-*three* directors were chosen, the court, under a special authority in such cases, ordered a new election to supply the vacancy of the *one* wanting at the first election.

[4] Rex *v.* Jefferson, 2 Nev. & M. 437; Rex *v.* Winchester, 2 Nev. & P. 274.

holden for the choice of *four* trustees, *eight* persons were voted for, *four* of whom had 102 votes, and *four* 100. The voting was by ballot. The inspectors having certified that the four having 102 votes were duly elected, a motion was made for leave to file an information, in nature of a *quo warranto*, against them, as unduly elected. One ground of the motion was, that two ballots were put into the box in the names of two persons who were formerly voters, but who had died some weeks before the day of election. This fact was not discovered until after the inspectors had given their certificate; nor did it at the trial appear for whom the two improper votes were given. The court held, that "the motion must be denied. For aught that appears, the spurious ballots were for the ticket which was in the minority. To warrant setting aside the election, it must appear affirmatively, that the successful ticket received a number of improper votes, which if rejected, would have brought it down to a minority. The mere circumstance that improper votes are received will not vitiate an election.[1] If this were otherwise, hardly an election in the State could be sustained."[2] The following are two modern English decisions: To impeach the election of a party, returned as elected, it is not sufficient to allege that many votes were bad and fictitious, without showing that some other candidate had a majority of legal votes.[3] But in a case where parties were declared to be elected town councillors, by the mayor, and they accepted the office and made the declaration requisite, a *mandamus* to admit other candidates on the ground of improper votes having been received, was refused.[4] In a late case in Missouri, a branch bank was authorized to choose three directors. Some of the stockholders being of the opinion that five was the number, voted a ticket having on it the name of five persons. There was also another ticket with the names of three persons. This latter ticket received a less number of votes than the other, but it was held that the persons whose names were upon it were rightfully elected.[5]

§ 137. If the charter declare that in default of certain acts, the election shall be void, no formality is required to annul it, but the place is

---

[1] At least, unless they were challenged. Chenango Mutual Ins. Co., Matter of, 19 Wend. 635; State *v.* Lehre, 7 Rich. 234.

[2] *Ex parte* Murphy, 7 Cowen, 153.

[3] Rex *v.* Jefferson, 3 Nev. & M. 487.

[4] Rex *v.* Winchester Mayor, &c. 2 Nev. & P. 274.

[5] State *v.* Thompson, 27 Misso. 365.

as vacant as though no election had ever taken place, and is not merely voidable. Another, therefore, may be elected into the office, without the necessity of resorting to an information in *quò warranto*, to oust the officer elect.[1] But if the charter do not so declare, an irregular election, as in case of the election of an unqualified person, is voidable only, and not actually void;[2] and hence, the acts of trustees of a religious corporation, irregularly elected, yet in *colore officii*, will be valid, until such trustees are ousted by judgment at the suit of the people.[3] Where votes were given for a candidate rendered ineligible, but of whose disqualification no express notice was given to the voters, it was held, that a party, having a minority of the votes, was not duly elected, and having accepted the office, a *quo warranto* was directed to issue.[4]

§ 138. If no particular form is prescribed for the election of officers, and the election has been conducted in good faith, it will not be set aside;[5] and where the legality of an election is disputed, evidence may be given of transactions previous to the election.[6] But no usage adduced in explanation, can sustain a corporate act, done in a manner plainly contrary to that prescribed by the charter. And yet, if the meaning of the words of the charter is doubtful, usage for a great length of time might be considered as explanatory of the intention of the government.[7] Where votes, rejected by inspectors at an election of directors, would, if received, have elected a certain ticket, and are adjudged to have been erroneously rejected, the only remedy is to set aside the election. The court, in such a case, has not the power to declare the ticket successful for which the votes would have been cast had they been received.[8] But it was held that the election will not be set aside on a summary application for that purpose, on the ground that the inspectors were not sworn in the form prescribed by a statute. And it seems that the election would not be set aside on such application, although no oath

---

[1] Rex *v.* Sanchar, 2 Show. 67.

[2] Rex *v.* Bridge, 1 M. & S. 76; Crawford *v.* Powell, 2 Burr. 1016. See Regina *v.* Chester, Q. B. 1855, 34 Eng. L. & Eq. 59.

[3] Trustees of Vernon Society *v.* Hills, 6 Cowen, 23. See also, Partridge *v.* Badger, 25 Barb. 146; Hughes *v.* Parker, 20 N. H. 58.

[4] Reg. *v.* Hiorns, 3 Nev. & P. 149.

[5] Rex *v.* Thetford, 8 East, 271; Rex *v.* Sparrow, 2 Stra. 1123.

[6] Phillips *v.* Wickham, 1 Paige, Ch. 590.

[7] Commonwealth *v.* Woelper, &c. 3 S. & R. 29.

[8] Long Island Railroad Co., Matter of, 19 Wend. 37.

whatever was administered to the inspectors, if no objection was interposed at the time of the election; and that it is enough that the inspectors were duly appointed and entered on the discharge of their official duties. That is, they are inspectors *de facto*.[1] The inspectors are not bound to close the polls at the end of an hour, notwithstanding, by a resolution of the board, from which they derive their authority, the election is limited to that time; for they are entitled to exercise a reasonable discretion in the matter.[2] If no time be limited, the poll may be adjourned from day to day.[3]

§ 139. In the case of the Bank of the United States *v.* Dandridge, Mr. Justice Story, in giving the opinion of the court, observes: "Persons acting publicly as officers of the corporation, are to be presumed rightfully in office." And again: "If officers of the corporation openly exercise a power which presupposes a delegated authority for the purpose, and other corporate acts show that the corporation must have contemplated the legal existence of such authority, the acts of such officers will be deemed rightful, and the delegated authority will be presumed. If a person acts notoriously as the cashier of a bank, and is recognized by the directors, or by the corporation, as an existing officer, a regular appointment will be presumed; and his acts as cashier will *bind the corporation*, although no written proof is, or can be, adduced of his appointment."[4] If the trustees of a religious corporation institute an action *colore officii*, the defendant cannot object to their right of recovery, upon the ground that they are not trustees, without showing that proceedings have been commenced against them by the government, and carried on to a judgment of ouster.[5] So inspectors of a corporate election, who act without an administering of the oath, if no objection was interposed at the time of the election, it is enough that they were duly appointed, and entered upon the discharge of their duties; they becoming thus inspectors *de facto*.[6] And it has also been

---

[1] Mohawk & Hudson Railroad Co., Matter of, 19 Wend. 135; Chenango Mutual Ins. Co. 19 id. 635.

[2] Mohawk & Hudson Railroad Co. *ut sup.*; and Chenango Mutual Ins. Co. *ut sup.*

[3] Ibid.

[4] Bank of United States *v.* Dandridge, 12 Wheat. 79. See also, Burgess *v.* Pue, 2 Gill, 254; McCullough *v.* Annapolis and Elkridge Railroad Co. 4 Gill, 58.

[5] All Saints Church *v.* Lovett, 1 Hill, 191; Doremus *v.* Dutch Reformed Church, 2 Green, N. J. Ch. 332; Smith *v.* Erb, 4 Gill, 437.

[6] Mohawk & Hudson Railroad Co., Matter of, 19 Wend. 135; Chenango Mutual Ins. Co. id. 635.

expressly held, in the State of Pennsylvania, that one who is elected to an office in a corporation, by the body in which the power to elect is vested, but by a less number of that body than the charter authorizes, is an officer *de facto*, and his acts, at least as they respect third persons, are binding on the corporation.[1] In this case, the company (bank) was governed by thirteen directors, five of whom were a quorum for the business of ordinary discounts, but a majority of the whole number was required for all business. At a meeting, when five only were present, the directors elected G. B. to fill a vacancy in the board; and, at another meeting, when eight were present, including G. B., agreed by a vote of six to one (one having retired before the vote was taken), to accept the real estate of a debtor, in satisfaction of a debt due to the bank, — G. B. voting in favor of the acceptance. It was held, that G. B. having come into the direction under color of right, was an officer *de facto*, and consequently, that the contract was binding on the bank.

§ 140. Even a Court of Equity will not interfere to restrain persons, claiming to be the rightful trustees of a corporation, from acting as such, on the ground that they have not been duly elected; the summary remedy of the corporators to contest the validity of the election of such trustees, is, in New York, by an application to the Supreme Court.[2] Neither will a Court of Equity entertain a bill by shareholders in an incorporated joint-stock company, seeking merely to restrain the directors *de facto* from acting as such, on the sole ground of the alleged invalidity of their title to their office. Whether the parties claiming to be directors, do or do not lawfully fill that character, depends upon a pure question of law; a preliminary question which must be decided before a Court of Equity can make any decree.[3]

---

1 Baird *v.* Bank of Washington, 11 S. & R. 411; Blandford *v.* School District, 2 Cush. 39; Delaware & Hudson Canal Co. *v.* Penn. Coal Co. 21 Penn. State, 131; Sampson *v.* Bowdoinham S. M. Corporation, 36 Me. 78; Penobscot & Kennebec Railroad Co. *v.* Dunn, 39 id. 587. See *post*, chapter on *Agents;* and see Fairfield Turnp. Co. *v.* Thorp, 13 Conn. 173; and Trustees of Vernon Society *v.* Hills, *ut sup.* A member elect of the legislature is permitted to retain his seat, although it is disputed; and is permitted to vote, so long as he retains his seat; and by his single vote, measures of great importance may be carried or defeated. It may afterwards be decided, that although a member *de facto*, he was not *de jure;* yet all the acts and votes of the former, until he was legally ousted, are as valid as they would have been if his seat could not be contested. Per Magruder, J., in delivering the judgment of the court in Smith *v.* Erb, 4 Gill, 437.

2 Mickles *v.* Rochester City Bank, 11 Paige, Ch. 118.

3 Mozley *v.* Alston, 1 Phillips, Ch. 790; Doremus *v.* Dutch Reformed Church, 2 Green, N. J. Ch. 332; and see *post*, Chap. XX. *Of the Writ of Mandamus.*

§ 141. In the case of *Ex parte* Wilcocks,[1] it was inquired by the counsel, whether it would be considered lawful for the *inspectors* of a corporate election to be candidates for the direction of the Utica Insurance Company. The answer given by the court was in the affirmative. The majority of the judges of the Supreme Court of Pennsylvania were of the same opinion, in the case of Commonwealth *v.* Woelper, &c.[2] In this case, it was objected, that one of the inspectors could not be voted for, because he was a *judge* of the election. He was viewed, however, by all the judges, except Gibson, as a *ministerial* officer; and the chief justice (Tilghman) understood it to have been a very common thing, in corporate elections, and in State elections, to vote for inspectors. Yeates, J., also held, that the acceptance of the office of judge of an election could not impair the freedom of choice in the corporators; and the practice of returning an inspector, he thought, was strikingly exemplified by what occurred at the election of common councilmen for the city of Philadelphia, in 1816. But Gibson, J., was unable to concur with the rest of the court; and he considered the judge of an election as a judicial, and not as a ministerial officer. If one who is the judge of an election, he thought, is at the same time a candidate, he has a direct interest in the event, and cannot be viewed in any other light than as judging in his own cause. The ground taken by Mr. J. Gibson is, at least, worthy of attention; though the weight of authority is against him.

Where an act of incorporation provides that a president shall be chosen "out of three directors," it is sufficient if the president be elected by a legally constituted meeting, and at the same time with the other directors, without having been *previously* appointed a *director*. It was considered in this case, that the president was appointed a director, *eodem flatu*, that he was made president; and that there could be no real utility in requiring an unnecessary circuity of proceeding.[3]

§ 142. It was said, by Chancellor Walworth, that he was not aware of any general principle of the Common Law, which authorizes all civil, or corporate officers, to hold over after the expiration of the time for which they were elected, until their places are supplied by others; and that the numerous statutes, both here and in England, giving such

---

[1] *Ex parte* Wilcocks, 7 Cowen, 402.

[2] Commonwealth *v.* Woelper, &c. 3 S. & R. 29.

[3] Currie *v.* Mutual Assurance Society, 4 Hen. & M. 315.

authority in express terms, seemed wholly inconsistent with any such common-law principle. But the case before him did not require the expression of a decisive opinion on the point.[1] In the case of The People *v.* Runkin, however, it was conceded by the Supreme Court of New York, that the trustees of a religious society, who go out of office at the end of the year, hold over until others are appointed. The question there was, whether an election, after the day of election, was good. The court said, "perhaps the language of the statute is too peremptory, that the seats of one third are to be vacated at the expiration of every year; but the corporation is not thereby dissolved; for two thirds of the trustees continue in office." The Court, in this case, also said, that trustees, elected after the election day, would be in by color of office; that the election would not be void; that their acts would be good; that the corporation would still remain; and the irregularity, if any, *would cure itself in a subsequent year.*[2]

§ 143. Without doubt, a statute or by-law, or even an appointment, may be so restrictive as to terminate an annual office at the end of the year; but an election to office, *for a year*, has never been considered as one of this description.[3] A clause in a charter, which directed that aldermen should be chosen annually, was held to be only directory, and not to determine the office at the end of the year after election; but that the person legally elected and sworn into office, should continue until removal.[4] In the State of Kentucky, old officers retain their powers

---

[1] Phillips *v.* Wickham, 1 Paige, Ch. 595. In the case of the Corporation of Tregony, 8 Mod. 127, the mayor was to be elected annually, but there was an express provision in the charter, that he should hold over until another was duly elected. But in the Banbury case (10 Mod. 340), where there could be no election without the presence of the old mayor, who was not authorized by the charter to hold over, and the day prescribed was permitted to pass without an election, the corporation was held to be dissolved. There are, undoubtedly, some common-law officers, who are to be elected or appointed periodically, but who, from the necessity of the case, continue to exercise their functions until others are elected or appointed to fill their places. In the Anonymous case, 12 Mod. 256, it is said, a constable is not discharged until his successor is appointed and sworn in; because the parish cannot be without an officer. But all these cases the Chancellor of New York, in the case above cited, apprehended, were dependent upon the peculiar provisions of their respective charters, and not upon any general principles of the Common Law.

[2] People *v.* Runkin, 9 Johns. 147. See also, Trustees of Vernon Society *v.* Hills, 6 Cowen, 23.

[3] McCall *v.* Byram Man. Co. 6 Conn. 428, in which is cited Kelly *v.* Wright, 1 Root, 83, and Foot *v.* Prowse, 1 Stra. 625; and see 2 Kent, Com. 238.

[4] Prowse *v.* Foot, 2 Brown, P. C. 289; Pender *v.* Rex, id. 294.

in case of a failure to elect on the day appointed, and may act until superseded by a new appointment.[1]

§ 144. Baron Comyn says: "If a corporation refuses to continue the election of officers till all die who could make an election, the corporation is dissolved."[2] But where the corporators, without the presence of any officers, or any act to be done on their part, possess the power to assemble and choose officers, to carry into effect the objects of the act of incorporation, a neglect to choose officers at the appointed time, will not work a dissolution; but will merely suspend the exercise of the powers of the corporation, until proper officers are chosen.[3] So, in case of an omission to continue certain officers who constitute an integral part of its body, if the bodies be supplied with officers *de facto*, it is sufficient to sustain the corporate existence as to strangers, and to enable the body corporate to maintain a suit.[4] The power to fill vacancies in a corporation, and elect officers, is a corporate incident, but this power does not attach to the board of officers, to fill vacancies in their own board.[5]

CHAPTER V.

OF THE POWER TO TAKE, HOLD, TRANSMIT IN SUCCESSION, AND ALIENATE PROPERTY.

§ 145. To enable it to answer the purposes of its creation, every corporation aggregate has, incidentally, at common law, a right to take, hold, and transmit in succession, property, real and personal, to an un-

---

[1] Wier *v.* Bush, 4 Littell, 433.

[2] 4 Com. Dig. 233, tit. Franchise, c. 4.

[3] Trustees of Vernon Society *v.* Hills, 6 Cowen, 33.

[4] Lehigh Bridge Co. *v.* Lehigh Coal and Navigation Co. 4 Rawle, 9. That a corporation is not dissolved by a failure to elect officers, Cahill *v.* Kalamazoo Mutual Insurance Co. 2 Doug. Mich. 124; and see *post*, Chap. XXII., wherein the subject of dissolution and revival of corporations is largely considered.

[5] Kearney *v.* Andrews, 2 Stock. Ch. 70.

limited extent or amount.[1] Accordingly, as the incident supposes the principal, it has been held that a grant of lands from the sovereign authority to the inhabitants of a county, town, or hundred, rendering rent, would create them a corporation for that single intent, or confer upon them a capacity to take and hold the lands in a corporate character, without saying to them and their successors.[2] And where it was evident from the different clauses of several local acts of parliament, that conservators of a river navigation were to take and transmit lands by succession, although they were not created a corporation by express words, they were considered from the possession of this incident to be incorporated by implication; so that they were entitled to sue, in their corporate name, for an injury done to their real estate, and in that character to receive their tolls.[3] After the issuing of letters-patent by the governor, in compliance with the requisition of an act of the general assembly creating a corporation, a deed to convey land to the company is good and effectual in Pennsylvania, for that purpose, although they may not have been so far organized as to have elected their officers; and their assent to it will be presumed.[4]

§ 146. The principal benefit of incorporation is, that by it the combined funds of a body of men may, through a long course of time, be steadily applied to the attainment of objects of public convenience or private utility, notwithstanding the changes, which, through the accidents of life, must be constantly going on among the members of the corporation.[5] As a matter of general law, the amount so to be held and applied, must, necessarily, be indefinite; since no rule could be laid

---

[1] Littleton, 49, 112, 114; Co. Litt. 44 a, 300 b; 1 Syd. 161 w; 10 Co. 30 b; 1 Kyd on Corp. 76, 78, 104; Com. Dig. tit. Franchise, F. 11, 15, 16, 17; Dy. 48 a; 4 Co. 65 a; 1 Bl. Com. 478; 2 Kent, Com. 227; M'Cartee *v.* Orph. As. Soc. 9 Cowen, 437; The Banks *v.* Poitiaux, 3 Rand. Va. 141; Reynolds *v.* Commissioners of Stark County, 5 Ohio, 205; Lathrop *v.* Comm. Bank of Scioto, 8 Dana, 119; Binney's case, 2 Bland, 142; Overseers of Poor of Boston *v.* Sears, 22 Pick. 122; Blanchard's Gun-stock Turning Factory, 1 Blatchf. C. C. 258. A corporation whose term of existence is limited to a number of years, may, nevertheless, purchase and hold land in fee-simple. Rives *v.* Dudley, 3 Jones, Eq. 126.

[2] Dyer, 100 a, pl. 70, cited as good law by Lord Kenyon, 2 T. R. 672; 2 Kent, Com. 225; North Hempstead *v.* Hempstead, 2 Wend. 109; Stebbins *v.* Jennings, 10 Pick. 188; Soc. for Prop. Gospel *v.* Town of Pawlet, 4 Pet. 480.

[3] Tone Conservators *v.* Ash, 10 B. & C. 349; Bridgewater Canal Co. *v.* Bluett, id. 393.

[4] Rathbone *v.* Tioga Navigation Co. 2 Watts & S. 74.

[5] Dartmouth College *v.* Woodward, 4 Wheat. 518.

down, ascertaining the means essential to effect the various purposes of incorporated companies. This amount, therefore, is sometimes fixed by the legislature, in the act or charter of incorporation, with special reference to the purposes of the particular grant. As sound policy requires that the property of a corporation should be restricted within reasonable limits, so it is easy to see that to enable the company to answer the purpose of its incorporation, it may also require that its capital stock shall amount to such a sum as would make it efficient for that purpose. And hence it is not uncommon for the charter or act of incorporation to provide that the capital stock, or a certain amount of it, shall be subscribed or paid in, before the company shall be at liberty to act under their charter.[1] Where, however, a bank is incorporated with the privilege of creating a stock not less than one sum nor greater than another, it may commence business with the smaller capital, and afterwards increase it to the larger.[2] And though a bank charter provided that the capital stock "*may* consist" of a certain amount, divided into shares of a certain amount each, and "*shall* be paid" in the following manner, &c., one dollar on each share in sixty, and one in ninety days after subscription, "*the remainder to be called for as the president and directors may deem proper, &c.*," and there was no clause expressly restricting the operation of the bank, until a certain amount of the stock was subscribed, the word "*may*" was construed in its ordinary sense, and not by the common rule as synonymous with the word "*must*," so that it was decided that a *bonâ fide* subscription of the capital stock prescribed by the charter, was not a condition precedent to the corporate existence or legal operation of the bank.[3] Even if the charter does contain a clause restrictive of the operation of a bank until a certain amount of its stock is subscribed, it would be difficult to maintain that a collusive subscription got up between the original subscribers and the commissioners, for the purpose of evading such a clause, could be permitted to be set up to the injury of the subsequent purchasers of the stock, who became *bonâ fide* holders, without participation in or notice of the fraud.[4] Indeed, if the subscription were fraudulent,

---

[1] Bend *v.* Susquehannah Bridge, &c. 6 Harris & J. 128.

[2] Gray *v.* Portland Bank, 3 Mass. 364.

[3] Minor *v.* Mechanics Bank of Alexandria, 1 Pet. 46. See Mitchell *v.* Rome R. R. Co. 17 Ga. 574.

[4] Per Story, J., id. See Walker *v.* Devereux, 4 Paige, 229; Johnston *v.* S. W. R. R. Bank, 3 Strobh. Eq. 263.

although the subscribers would not be permitted to avail themselves of the same, yet their subscription would not be a nullity; but the law would hold the parties bound to their subscription, and compellable to comply with all the terms and responsibilities imposed upon them thereby in the same manner as if they were *bonâ fide* subscribers.[1] If, by charter or act of incorporation, the stock of the company is divided into a certain number of shares, that number cannot be changed by the company.[2] Nor, if the charter requires that a certain number of shares be subscribed for before an assessment be laid, can an assessment be laid, until that number is subscribed for.[3] In such case, a subscription by one man for another, without authority, for the purpose of completing the requisite number of shares, will avail nothing in favor of the assessment;[4] and if any subscription were conditional, it must be shown that the condition was satisfied or waived.[5] And if part of the price conditionally subscribed for is paid before the performance of the condition, the subscriber may, upon a final breach, recover back the amount so paid.[6] But if there is an absolute contract in writing to take stock, it is not competent to prove by parol that the agreement was conditional, and that the condition has not been complied with.[7] If the charter declares that the capital stock of a corporation shall not be less than a certain number nor more than a certain other number, and provides that when the less number have been sub-

---

[1] Ibid.; and Walker *v.* Devereux, 3 Paige, 229; and see Selma and Tennessee Railroad Co. *v.* Tipton, 5 Ala. 787; Wayne *v.* Beauchamp, 5 Smedes & M. 515; White Mountain Railroad *v.* Eastman, 34 N. H. 124; Graff *v.* Pittsburg & Steubenville R. Co. 31 Penn. State, 489; Robinson *v.* Pittsburgh & C. R. Co. 32 Penn. State, 334.

[2] Salem Mill Dam Corporation *v.* Ropes, 6 Pick. 23; Oldtown and Lincoln R. R. Co. *v.* Veazie, 39 Me. 571.

[3] Ibid.; and Central Turnp. Corp. *v.* Valentine, 10 Pick. 142; N. H. Central R. R. *v.* Johnson, 10 Foster, 390; Stoneham Branch R. R. *v.* Gould, 2 Gray, 277; C. V. R. R. *v.* Barker, 32 N. H. 363.

[4] Salem Mill Dam Corporation *v.* Ropes, 9 Pick. 187.

[5] Penobscot & Kenebec R. R. *v.* Dunn, 39 Me. 587; Philadelphia & West Chester R. R. Co. *v.* Hickman, 28 Penn. State, 318; Berry *v.* Yates, 24 Barb. 199; Evansville R. Co. *v.* Shearer, 10 Ind. 244; Jewett *v.* Lawrenceburgh R. Co. id. 539. Where it was stipulated in the subscription paper signed by the defendant, that the capital of the proposed company should be $1,500,000, this condition was held not to be waived by the defendant's acceptance of his shares and payment of an assessment after the amount of capital stock had been reduced to $1,350,000. Atlantic Cotton Mills *v.* Abbott, 9 Cush. 423; Macedon & Bristol P. R. Co. *v.* Lapham, 18 Barb. 312. See City Hotel *v.* Dickinson, 6 Gray, 586.

[6] Jewett *v.* Lawrenceburgh R. Co. 10 Ind. 539.

[7] North Carolina R. Co. *v.* Leach, 4 Jones, 340.

scribed, the directors may make assessments thereon, the amount of the capital stock need not be fixed before assessments are laid.[1]

§ 147. In the case of banks, it is held in Mississippi, that the payment of their capital stock, *in specie*, is an essential requisite to their existence; a general law requiring the capital of all banks to be thus paid in. And where, in that State, the charter of a banking company enacted that the subscribers should pay at the time of subscription, twenty dollars on each share taken, *in specie*, or in the notes of specie paying banks, and was silent as to how or when the residue of the stock should be paid, but conferred all the usual rights, powers, and privileges, of banking, which were exercised by other banks in the State, the court decided that the residue of the capital stock was payable by the stockholders in specie only.[2]

§ 148. In England, the common-law right of corporations whether sole or aggregate, ecclesiastical or lay, to take and hold lands and tenements, has been restrained by a variety of statutes, from Magna Charta, 9 Hen. III. ch. 36, to 9 Geo. II. ch. 36, called statutes of *mortmain*, which were passed in conformity to a policy prevailing in that country, from a period somewhat anterior to the Norman conquest.[3] This system of laws appears to have originated in a desire to repress the grasping spirit of the Romish Church, which, by absorbing in perpetuity the best lands in the kingdom, prevented their transmission from man to man, withdrew them from those feudal services that were ordained for common defence, and curtailed the lords of the fruits of their signiories, their escheats, wardships, reliefs, and the like.[4] They were called statutes of mortmain, according to the better opinion, because designed to prevent the holding of lands by the *dead clutch* of ecclesiastical corporations, which in early times were composed of members dead in law, and in whose possession property was forever dead and unproductive to the feudal superior and the public.[5] Though the statute of 15 R. II. ch. 5, extended this system of restraint to civil or lay corporations, as within the mischief and prohibition, the name still remained; and in England,

---

1 White Mountains R. Co. *v.* Eastman, 34 N. H. 124.

2 King *v.* Elliot, 5 Smedes & M. 428.

3 Co. Lit. 2 b; 1 Bl. Com. 479; 2 Bl. Com. 268 to 274.

4 Co. Lit. 2 b; 2 Bl. Com. 269, 270; 2 Kent, Com. 228.

5 Co. Lit. 2 b; 1 Bl. Com. 479.

lands purchased by corporations are liable to forfeiture, unless a license in mortmain from the king, as ultimate lord of every fee, be first obtained. According to Blackstone, even this is not in all cases sufficient.[1] The statutes of mortmain make no mention of personal property; and hence, in England, the power of corporations aggregate to take such property remains, in general, unlimited, unless restrained by the charters or acts of parliament establishing them.[2] In some of these States, similar statutes restrain the right of corporations to the amount of personal property they shall hold; in which cases they are wholly territorial in their operation, and can therefore have no application to the right of a foreign corporation to hold personal property.[3]

§ 149. The English statutes of mortmain have been held by the Supreme Court of Pennsylvania to be the law of that State, so far as applicable to its political condition; and "all conveyances by deed or will, of lands, tenements, or hereditaments, made to a body corporate, or for the use of a body corporate, are void, unless sanctioned by charter or act of assembly."[4] They are, however, understood to apply, in that State, only so far as they prohibit dedications of property to superstitious uses or grants to corporations without a statutory license.[5] "In other States," says Kent, "it is understood that the statutes of mortmain have not been reënacted or practised upon."[6] It may be inferred, from the special power given to various corporations, by acts of the State legislatures, to hold real estate to a certain limited extent, that statute corporations, created for specific objects, would not have the power to take and hold real estate, for purposes wholly foreign to those objects.[7]

§ 150. The civil law in this particular, corresponded with the system established by the statutes of mortmain, since, according to it, a corpora-

---

1 Co. Lit. 2 b; 1 Bl. Com. 479.

2 1 Kyd on Corp. 104.

3 Vanseat *v.* Roberts, 3 Md. Ch. 119.

4 3 Binney, App. p. 626.

5 Methodist Church *v.* Remington, 1 Watts, 218.

6 2 Kent, Com. 229; M'Cartee *v.* Orp. As. Soc. 9 Cowen, 452; Lathrop *v.* Com. Bank of Scioto, 8 Dana, 119.

7 Ibid.; First Parish in Sutton *v.* Cole, 3 Pick. 239, 240, per Parker, C. J.; State *v.* Commissioners of Mansfield, 3 N. J. 500; State *v.* Newark, 1 Dutcher, 315; Riley *v.* City of Rochester, 5 Seld. 64.

tion could not purchase or receive donations of lands without license. *Collegium, si nullo speciali privilegio subnixum sit, hæreditatem capere non posse dubium non est.*[1] Though it be true, therefore, that the English statutes of mortmain owed their origin to the principles of the feudal system, it is evident that their policy was known and acted upon long anterior to the existence of that system as recognized by the common law.

§ 151. As a corporation may be deprived or restrained of its common-law right, of purchasing or receiving lands or other property, by general statutes applicable to all corporations, so the same right may be taken away or limited by its charter or act of incorporation; — a law peculiar to itself.[2] To prevent monopolies, and to confine the action of incorporated companies strictly within their proper sphere, the acts incorporating them almost invariably limit not only the amount of property they shall hold, but frequently prescribe in what it shall consist, the purposes for which it shall alone be purchased and held, and the mode in which it shall be applied to effect those purposes. The amount of the capital stock of a corporation is not *per se* a limitation of the amount of property, real or personal, which it may own, or by implication of the amount of its liabilities or outstanding obligations: but is rather regarded as the sum upon which calls may be made upon subscribers, and dividends are to be paid to stockholders. Accordingly, it was held, that where the capital stock of a building corporation was one million of dollars, this did not restrict the company from expending in their buildings two millions of dollars, and from incurring debts on bonds and mortgages for the excess of cost beyond their capital — their power to take and hold real estate being, in other respects, unlimited by the terms of their charter.[3] And where a church corporation is limited by charter as to the amount of income which it can receive from lands, such limit cannot apply to the accidental increase of income from the rise in value of these lands, in a long course of years, so as to divest their title to their estates, or to any portion of them; and even in case of a purchase of lands affording a greater income than that limited, this is a matter between the corporation and sovereign power only, with which individuals have no

---

[1] Browne's Civil Law, 145; Lib. 8 Cod. de hæred. instituen.; Salem Mill Dam Corporation *v.* Ropes, 6 Pick. 23.

[2] 2 Kent, Com. 228; 1 Kyd on Corp. 104.

[3] Barry *v.* Merchants Exchange Company, 1 Sandf. Ch. 280.

concern, and of which they cannot avail themselves in any mode against the corporation.[1]

§ 152. There can be no doubt that, if a corporation be forbidden, by its charter to *purchase* or *take* lands, a deed made to it would be void, as its capacity may be determined from the instrument which gives it existence.[2] There is, however, a broad distinction between a prohibition to *purchase* or *take*, and a prohibition to *hold;* and where the act incorporating a bank made it capable "to have, hold, purchase, receive, possess, enjoy, and retain lands, rents, tenements, goods, chattels, and effects of whatever kind, nature, or quality, to the amount of two millions of dollars, and no more; Provided, nevertheless, that such lands and tenements, which the said corporation are hereby enabled *to purchase and hold*, shall only extend to such lot and lots of ground, and convenient buildings and improvements thereon erected, or to be erected, which they may find necessary and proper for carrying on the business of the said bank, and shall actually occupy for that purpose;" it was decided, by the Supreme Court of Pennsylvania, that the bank might *purchase*, absolutely, lands in a distant country which they did not occupy, though they, or the third person to whom they might convey, would *hold* them by a title defeasible by the Commonwealth and the Commonwealth alone, as is the case with the title of aliens.[3]

§ 153. To a bill by certain banks, for the specific performance of a contract for the purchase of lands made by an individual with them, the defence set up was, that the charters of the banks, after authorizing them to purchase, hold, and enjoy lands and tenements, goods and chattels, to a specified value, to sell and dispose of them, provided, that the lands it should be lawful for them to *hold* should be only such as were for their immediate accommodation, &c., or acquired in satisfaction of debts, &c.; — that the lands in question did not fall within either of these descriptions, and that therefore the banks could not acquire or convey any title to a purchaser of them. The Court of Appeals of Virginia decided, that though, if in purchasing the land in question, the

---

1 Humbert *v.* Trinity Church, 24 Wend. 587; Harpending *v.* The Dutch Church, 16 Pet. 492, 493; Bogardus *v.* Trinity Church, 4 Sandf. Ch. 758, 759.

2 Leazure *v.* Hillegas, 7 S. & R. 319, per Tilghman, C. J.

3 Ibid.; Baird *v.* The Bank of Washington, 11 S. & R. 418; Goundie *v.* Northampton Water Co. 7 Barr, 239, 240; People *v.* Munroe, 5 Denio, 400, 401; McIndoe *v.* St. Louis, 10 Misso. 576.

banks violated their charters, they might, for that cause, be dissolved by a proceeding at the suit of the Commonwealth, yet that any conveyance made before dissolution would pass an indefeasible title to the purchaser; — that the charters did not prohibit the *purchase* of real property by the banks, but only limited the extent to which they should be allowed to *hold* such property; — and that the question, whether they had exceeded their limits or not, was not fit to be tried in the suit before them, or at the instance of the party before them.[1] On the other hand, in a late case in Michigan, it was deemed a good defence to a bill for specific performance, brought by a bank to enforce a contract by which it had purchased lands for the purpose of selling them again, that its charter made it lawful for the bank *to hold* such real estate only as was required for its accommodation in the transaction of its business, or such as might have been mortgaged to it *bonâ fide* by way of security, or conveyed to it in satisfaction of debts previously contracted in the course of its dealings, or purchased at sales upon judgments which might have been obtained for such debts; on the ground that such a contract was against the spirit, if not the terms of the charter, and that a court of equity will not lend its aid to enforce a contract of such a character.[2] A good defence to a bill for specific performance may be a very bad ground for a bill to set aside an executed contract; and where a corporation, vested with power to take and hold real estate for specified purposes, purchased and took a conveyance of land, and afterwards used the land for other purposes than the charter permitted, this abuse of power was deemed to be no ground for setting aside the deed at the instance of the vendor.[3] A railroad corporation may maintain a bill in equity for the specific performance of a contract to purchase of them lands which they have purchased for the purpose of having gravel dug therefrom, and transported, at a certain rate of freight, over their road, to be delivered to, and used by a third party.[4]

§ 154. Where by its act of incorporation, a bank was empowered to hold "such lands as were *bonâ fide* mortgaged, or conveyed to it, in

---

[1] The Banks *v.* Poitiaux, 3 Rand. Va. 136. See Silver Lake Bank *v.* North, 4 Johns. Ch. 370.

[2] Bank of Michigan *v.* Niles, 1 Doug. Mich. 401, affirming decree in s. c. 1 Walker, Mich. 99.

[3] Barrow *v.* Nashville and Charlotte Turnpike Co. 9 Humph. 304.

[4] Old Colony R. Co. *v.* Evans, 6 Gray, 25.

satisfaction of debts *previously contracted in the course of its dealings*," the Supreme Court of Pennsylvania adjudged, that it had a general power to commute debts *really* due for real estate; and that this power did not depend upon, whether, in the opinion of the jury, the debt was in danger, and prudence required that the real estate should be taken in satisfaction of it.[1] It was considered by the court, in this case, that a conveyance in trust to permit a corporation, which could not accept of the legal title, to receive the rents and profits, or a conveyance that in any shape would entitle the corporation to be put in possession, would be as much a violation of the law, as a direct conveyance of the legal title; but that a conveyance, made with a view not to permanent ownership by the corporation, but of raising money by the sale of the property, would be neither within the letter nor the spirit of the prohibition implied above.[2] An academy incorporated "to promote morality, piety, and religion, and for the instruction of youth in the learned languages, and in such arts and sciences as are usually taught in other academies," and authorized to hold and apply property within a certain limit to these purposes, was considered authorized to raise and hold a fund for the education of pious indigent young men, with a sole view to the Christian ministry.[3] A railroad company authorized to build a bridge across a stream, may undoubtedly buy one already built, and which answers the purpose of their grant;[4] or a company incorporated for the purpose of raising and smelting lead, the smelting works which had previously performed that part of the corporate business by contract.[5] An early charter in New York gave the city of Albany the right to establish, direct, &c. all ferries in the city. An act of 1826, declared that the charter should "be so construed, as to vest in the said mayor, aldermen and commonalty, the sole and exclusive right of establishing, licensing, and regulating all ferries on each side of the Hudson river between Albany and Greenbush." The Western Railroad corporation was at first authorized to make its western termination at a point opposite Albany. By a subsequent act it was authorized to construct a depot in

---

1 Baird *v.* The Bank of Washington, 11 S. & R. 411. But see Chautauque County Bank *v.* Risley, 19 N. Y. 369, overruling s. c. 4 Denio, 487, 488. Russell *v.* Topping, 5 McLean, 194; Ingraham *v.* Speed, 30 Missis. 410.

2 Ibid.

3 Amherst Academy *v.* Cowls, 6 Pick. 427.

4 Thompson *v.* New York & Harlem R. Co. 3 Sandf. Ch. 554, 555.

5 Moss *v.* McCullough, 7 Barb. 279.

Albany, and "to connect the same with its railroad by a single or double track;" but it was declared that the act should not be so construed as to authorize the company to construct a bridge across the Hudson river, or in any manner to obstruct its navigation. The railroad company ran their own ferryboats across, and in addition to the passengers brought by their cars, took over other passengers and teams gratuitously. The Supreme Court held that they did not infringe the rights of the person who ran another ferry under a license from the city of Albany, on the ground that a ferry meant the right to take goods or passengers across for hire.[1] This decision was reversed by the Court of appeals, on the ground that it made no difference that no toll was demanded. It was also held that a ferry, though a part of a railroad, did not cease to be a ferry; and that the defendants were only entitled to carry over their own servants and agents, and passengers and freight, brought over their road.[2]

§ 155. As corporations, unless restrained by their charters, have an indefinite right of purchase, where the restraint is imposed by a *proviso*, — as, "provided the lands be necessary for manufacturing purposes," — it is incumbent on the party objecting to the purchase, to bring the case, by proof, within the proviso.[3]

§ 156. A corporation may take a mortgage upon land by way of security for loans, made in the regular course of its lawful business, or in satisfaction of debts previously contracted in its dealings. Such acts are generally provided for in charters incorporating a certain class of corporations, such as banks, insurance companies, and the like; and, without such special authority, it would seem to be implied in the reason and spirit of the grant, if the debt was *bonâ fide* created in the regular course of business.[4] And, though a clause in the charter of a

---

[1] 30 Barb. 305.

[2] Aiken *v.* Western R. Co. 20 N. Y. 370.

[3] *Ex parte* Peru Iron Co. 7 Cowen, 540; Dockery *v.* Miller, 9 Humph. 731.

[4] Silver Lake Bank *v.* North, 4 Johns. Ch. 370; Baird *v.* Bank of Washington, 11 S. & R. 411; The People *v.* Utica Ins. Co. 15 Johns. 358; Utica Ins. Co. *v.* Scott, 8 Cowen, 709; The Farmers Loan & Trust Co. *v.* Clowes, 3 Comst. 470; Leazure *v.* Hillegas, 7 S. & R. 319; Susquehannah Bridge & Banking Co. *v.* General Ins. Co. 3 Md. Ch. Dec. 418; The Banks *v.* Poitiaux, 3 Rand. Va. 136; Mann *v.* Eckford, 15 Wend. 502; Thomaston Bank *v.* Stimpson, 21 Me. 195; Lagou *v.* Badollet, 1 Blackf. 418, 419; 2 Kent, Com. 282, 3d edit.

bank forbids it "to deal or trade, directly or indirectly, in any thing except bills of exchange, promissory notes, gold or silver bullion, or on sale of goods, the produce of its lands," it may nevertheless receive and hold bonds and mortgages, as securities for its debts; and, in the absence of proof to the contrary, such bonds and mortgages will be presumed to have come into the hands of the bank lawfully and within the scope of its corporate powers; the clause being designed merely to restrain the bank to its proper business of banking.[1] The capital stock of an insurance company may be invested in bonds and mortgages, executed directly to the corporation, or obtained by assignment, where the charter does not expressly prescribe the mode of investment, even though it impliedly give the power to invest in stocks.[2] And even where an act incorporating a company for the purpose of insuring lives, granting annuities, and loaning money in bond and mortgage, contained a provision by which the latter power was to cease at the expiration of fifteen years, the company were sustained in loaning money on bond and mortgage after the fifteen years had expired, on the ground, that the two first powers continuing, made it necessary for the corporation to invest their funds in order to carry on their business; the distinction being between the power thus to loan money as a principal business, or as a means of investment auxiliary to the other business of the corporation.[3] The securities taken by an insurance company are not affected by the fact, that they are taken at a different place from that at which by necessary intendment, its proper business should be transacted; provided there be no proof that the business, in which the securities were taken, was unauthorized, though it be shown that the company has an office for the transaction of business at the place where the securities were taken.[4]

§ 157. Where, by its charter, a bank was authorized to take mortgages in security for debts previously contracted, it was adjudged by Chancellor Kent, that, if the loan and mortgage were *concurrent* acts, and intended so to be, it was not a case within the reason and spirit of the restraining clause of the statute, which only meant to prohibit the banking company from investing their capital in real property and

---

1 Trenton Banking Company *v.* Woodruff, 1 Green, N. J. Ch. 117.
2 Mann *v.* Eckford, 15 Wend. 502.
3 Farmers Loan & Trust Co. *v.* Clowes, 4 Edw. Ch. 575.
4 Mann *v.* Eckford, 15 Wend. 502.

engaging in land speculations. "A mortgage taken to secure a loan, advanced *bonâ fide* as a loan, in the course, and according to the usage, of banking operations, was not, surely," says he, "within the prohibition."[1] This decision, in New York, was upon the construction of a clause in the charter of a Pennsylvania bank; and, in the subsequent case of Baird *v.* The Bank of Washington,[2] the Supreme Court of Pennsylvania viewed with the same liberality of construction, a similar clause in the charter of another bank in that State. The clause seems to have been introduced to prevent the bank from indirectly getting real estate into its hands, ostensibly in payment of a debt, but, in truth and fact, by a transaction which, in its origin, was a purchase. "The intention was," says Gibson, J., "to restrict the right to cases where the loan should be real, and not merely colorable; but I cannot think it was intended to narrow it further, or it would have been so expressed."[3] An act incorporating an insurance and loan company, provided, "that, in all cases where the said corporation have become the purchasers of any real estate, on which they have made loans, the mortgagors shall have the right of redemption of any such property on payment of the principal, interests, and costs, so long as it remains in the hands of the corporation unsold;" and, by virtue of it, a mortgagor's right of redemption was adjudged to continue, notwithstanding a contract for the sale of the mortgaged premises had been entered into and duly executed by the company, one third of the purchase-money paid, and possession taken by making surveys, &c.; the right of redemption, under such a clause, being extinguished only by the execution and delivery of a deed of conveyance to the purchaser, who must be deemed to have contracted with notice of the rights of mortgagor.[4] In such a case a purchase by an agent of the company does not bar the right of redemption, it being a purchase by the company within the meaning of the act.[5] A corporation, authorized to invest its capital *only* on bond and mortgage, cannot recover money lent by the corporation, except a bond and mortgage be taken as security for its repayment; every other security, as well as the contract itself, being void.[6] Sometimes the charter

---

1 Silver Lake Bank *v.* North, 4 Johns. Ch. 370.

2 11 S. & R. 411.

3 11 S. & R. 417.

4 Edwards *v.* Farmers' Fire Ins. Co. 21 Wend. 467.

5 Ibid.

6 Life and Fire Ins. Co. *v.* Mechanics Fire Ins. Co. 7 Wend. 31. See also, North

of such a company prescribes the time on which its mortgages shall be taken; and where the charter of a loan company provided that the mortgages taken by it should not be payable in a shorter time than one year, and that the interest thereon should be payable annually, and a mortgage taken in July by the corporation bore date eighteen days before the money was advanced, with interest to be paid yearly *on the first day of November in each year*, the court, to uphold the mortgage, decided that the mortgage could not be collected in less than a year from the date of the loan, that being the delivery, and so *the date* of the mortgage, and as to the interest, rejected the words, "the first day of November," as surplusage.[1]

§ 158. There are large classes of corporations which may and do rightfully invest their capital or funds in the stock of other corporations, for the purpose of secure and profitable investment; such, for instance, as religious and charitable corporations, and corporations for literary and scientific purposes. Insurance companies, unless expressly or impliedly restrained by their charters, or the general law, may rightfully invest their capital in the stock of other corporations, such as banks, railroads, and the like.[2] The specification, in the charter, of certain modes of investing the corporate funds would preclude all other modes of investment.[3] In what stocks it would be proper for them, in the absence of special restriction, to make such investments, must depend much upon the custom or usage of investment in the place and country. All corporations have power to take the stock of other corporations as incidental to the power of collecting a debt or making a sale. In such case, they would take it to sell or turn into money, and would not hold it as a permanent investment.[4] The power to take and hold depends greatly in such cases upon the purpose, whether within or beyond the legitimate sphere of the corporate action. And where a corporation, created to carry on the business of vending lumber and manufactures from wood,

---

River Ins. Co. *v.* Lawrence, 3 Wend. 482; New York Fire Ins. Co. *v.* Ely, 2 Cowen, 678; Mott *v.* United States Trust Co. 19 Barb. 568; United States Trust Co. *v.* Brady, 20 id. 119.

[1] The Farmers Loan and Trust Company *v.* Clowes, 3 Sandf. Ch. 339, 3 Comst. 470.

[2] Hodges *v.* New Eng. Screw Co. 1 R. I. 347, per Greene, C. J.

[3] Per McCoun, V. C., Scott *v.* Depeyster, 1 Edw. Ch. 513; and see Smith *v.* Alabama Life Ins. & Trust Co. 4 Ala. 558.

[4] Hodges *v.* New Eng. Screw Co. 1 R. I. 347, per Greene, C. J.; and Sumner *v.* Marcy, 3 Woodb. & M. 112.

issued promissory notes, for more than the amount of its authorized capital, in the purchase of the stock of a bank, for the avowed purpose of getting the virtual control of it, and of being better enabled to effect loans with it, this was held to be a clearly unauthorized transaction.[1] We have seen that an insurance company, impliedly authorized to invest *in stocks*, may nevertheless, without express authority, invest its capital stock in bonds and mortgages.[2] Where such a company was by charter restricted from dealing "*in the purchase or sale of any stock or funded debt whatever, created or to be created, by or under any act of the United States, or of any particular State*," the restriction was construed not to apply to investments in the stock of the *Bank* of the United States, or in the stock of the *banks*, or *money corporations* of any particular State.[3] The discounting by a bank, of bills of exchange, secured by a deposit of cotton to be shipped by the bank, and the proceeds credited to the borrower, was held not to be "*a dealing in goods, wares, and merchandise*," within the prohibition of a fundamental law of the bank, prohibiting such dealing.[4]

§ 159. An insurance company, restricted by charter from discounting notes, though authorized to take and hold securities *bonâ fide* pledged to them to secure debts due to them, cannot lend money on the hypothecation of stock and the taking of a note as collateral security for the payment of the loan.[5] A banking association adopted certain articles as the basis of their union, by which it was agreed, that the subscribers to the bank should be permitted to pay one tenth of their subscriptions in the stocks of certain incorporated companies, and the remainder in money. The articles of association authorized the immediate commencement of business, and provided for and contemplated an application to Congress for a charter, which was, some time after they had carried on business as an association, obtained, and provided *that the whole capital stock of the bank should be paid in money*. Upon a bill by one of the subscribers to have an account of the profits of the stock by him subscribed, and payment for the same, it was decided, that the stock subscribed and paid in had become consolidated with the other part of the capital of the association, having been received as so much money; that neither the sub-

---

1 Sumner *v.* Marcy, 3 Woodb. & M. 105.

2 Mann *v.* Eckford, 15 Wend. 502.

3 Verplanck *v.* Mercantile Ins. Co. 1 Edw. Ch. 84.

4 Bates *v.* The Bank of the State of Alabama, 2 Ala. 465 to 475.

5 North River Ins. Co. *v.* Lawrence, 3 Wend. 482.

scribers nor their assignees were entitled to have a specific return or an account of the same, and that the charter of incorporation produced no change in this respect.[1] A bank, or manufacturing corporation, may, it seems, buy its own stock, unless forbidden by charter, and the directors may dispose of stock so purchased; nor upon the resale, have the stockholders any right of preëmption.[2] A corporation owning its own stock, cannot, however, authorize its directors, or even the trustees of the stock held by them for its own use, to vote upon it; it not being permitted to a company to procure stock, which its officers may wield to the purposes of an election.[3] During the period that it is owned by the corporation it is deemed to be merged, though capable of being reissued.[4] In application to railway companies, the English courts hold, and with great reason, that the employment of the funds of the company in the purchase of its shares in the market, is a breach of trust in the managing body, for which the members of it may be made accountable; since it tends to destroy the very object for which the funds are put into the hands of the directors.[5] Sometimes, however, the deed of settlement provides, that in certain events the directors shall purchase shares in the stock of the company with its funds; and in such a case, a court of equity held the transaction binding upon the company, though by its neglect and irregularity in keeping a transfer-book, the forms of transfer pointed at by the deed, were not observed.[6]

§ 160. It should be observed however, with regard to the rights of a corporation over its property, that these are not always to be measured by the same standard as the rights of an individual over his property. You cannot, for instance, place the right of a canal company to demand toll, upon the ground that the company is the absolute owner of the works and the land it occupies, and may, therefore, like any other owner, demand compensation from any person passing over its property.

---

1 Holbrook *v.* Union Bank of Alexandria, 7 Wheat. 533.

2 Hartridge *v.* Rockwell, R. M. Charlt. 250. Williams *v.* Savage Manufacturing Co. 3 Md. Ch. Dec. 418.

3 *Ex parte* Holmes, 5 Cowen, 426; *Ex parte* Desdoity, 1 Wend. 98; Campbell *v.* Poultney, 6 Gill & J. 94.

4 Williams *v.* Savage Manufacturing Co. 3 Md. Ch. Dec. 418.

5 *In re* London, Birmingham, &c. R. Co. *Ex parte* Carpenter, 5 De G. & S. 402, 13 Eng. L. & Eq. 201, 303. See Barton *v.* Port Jackson and Union Falls P. R. Co. 17 Barb. 397.

6 *In re* The Northern Coal Mining Co. 13 Beav. 472, 4 Eng. L. & Eq. 72, 78, 79.

The corporation can exercise no power over the property it holds except that with which the charter has expressly or impliedly clothed it. It holds its property only for the purposes for which it was permitted to acquire it; and whether it may lawfully demand compensation from a person whom it permits to pass over its property, must depend upon the language of its charter, and not upon the mere common-law rights of property. A canal company, therefore, cannot, without express words, claim a right to demand toll, *to an unlimited extent* from every person passing through its canal, whether in the form of a direct tax levied on the passenger, or through a demand made upon the owner of a boat engaged in the transportation of passengers. Such an unlimited power to levy contributions should not be inferred where the slightest doubt could arise, and the words are capable of any other construction. Still less can such a power be inferred in a charter where the toll granted upon goods and merchandise of every kind, is carefully specified and fixed, and the act is altogether silent in relation to a toll upon passengers.[1] Nor has such a company power to refuse permission to passengers to pass through their canal. On the contrary, any one has a right to navigate the canal for the transportation of passengers, with passenger boats, without paying any toll on the passengers on board, upon his paying or offering to pay the toll prescribed by law upon the commodities on board, or the toll prescribed by law on a boat when empty of commodities.[2]

§ 161. A corporation can have no legal existence out of the sovereignty by which it is created, as it exists only in contemplation of law and by force of law; and when that law ceases to operate, and is no longer obligatory, the corporation can have no existence. It must dwell in the place of its creation and cannot migrate to another sovereignty. But although it may live and have its being in that State only, yet it does not follow that its existence there will not be recognized in other places; and its residence in one State creates no insuperable objection to its power of contracting in another. The corporation must show that the law of its creation gave it authority to make such contracts as those it seeks to enforce. Yet, as in case of a natural person, it is not necessary that it should actually exist in the sovereignty in which the

---

[1] Perrine *v.* Chesapeake & Delaware Canal Co. 9 How. 172. See, too, Camden and Amboy Railroad Co. *v.* Briggs, 2 N. J. 623.

[2] Ibid.

contract is made. It is sufficient that its existence, as an artificial person, in the State of its creation, is acknowledged and recognized by the State or nation where the dealing takes place, and that it is permitted by the laws of that place, to exercise the powers with which it is endowed.[1] Thus, a steamboat company incorporated in one State may take a lease of an office, as a place of business, in another State.[2] Every power which a corporation exercises in another State, depends for its validity upon the laws of sovereignty in which it is exercised; and a corporation can make no valid contract without the sanction, express, or implied, of such sovereignty, unless a case should be presented in which a right claimed by the corporation should appear to be secured by the Constitution of the United States.[3] Accordingly, where a coal company, incorporated by the State of New York for the purpose of supplying the city of New York and its vicinity with coal, purchased coal lands in Pennsylvania, the recitals in the act of incorporation, which gave the power to purchase and hold lands, showing that this power was granted with special reference to the purchase of lands in the State of Pennsylvania, it was held by the Supreme Court of the United States, that the right to hold the lands so purchased depended upon the assent, express or implied, of the State of Pennsylvania; and the Supreme court of Pennsylvania, having decided that a corporation of that State, or of any other State, has, without special license, a right to purchase, hold, and convey land, until some act is done by the government, according to its own laws, to vest the estate in itself, it was decided, that the lands purchased should remain in the corporation purchasing them, until divested by a proceeding instituted by the commonwealth of Pennsylvania for that purpose, as forfeited to its own use.[4] Indeed, in those States where there are no general statutes or settled policy restricting them in this respect, corporations of other States may purchase and hold lands *ad libitum*, provided their charters give them the competent power.[5] The burden

---

[1] The Commercial & Railroad Bank of Vicksburgh *v.* Slocomb, 14 Pet. 60; Irvine *v.* Lowry, 14 Pet. 293. And see Bank of Augusta *v.* Earle, 13 Pet. 584. As to place of a corporation, see *ante*, Ch. III.

[2] Steamboat Co. *v.* McCutcheon, 13 Penn. State, 133.

[3] Ibid.

[4] Runyan *v.* Coster, 14 Pet. 122.

[5] Silver Lake Bank *v.* North, 4 Johns. Ch. 370; Lumbard *v.* Aldrich, 8 N. H. 34; Lathrop *v.* Commercial Bank of Scioto, 8 Dana, 119; Bank of Washtenaw *v.* Montgommery, 2 Scam. 428; 2 Kent, Com. 284, 285; New York Dry Dock *v.* Hicks, 5 McLean, 111; Farmers Loan & Trust Co. *v.* McKinney, 6 id. 1.

is, however, upon the corporation, or those claiming under it, to show that by its charter, it is a body politic authorized to take or convey lands.[1]

§ 163. It is obvious that the real estate of a corporation can be dealt with only by the judicial authority of the State in which it lies; this holds, even though the corporation is created by the concurrent acts of several governments.[2] Nor is the applicability of this general principle affected by the fact, that the charter directs that the real property of the corporation shall be considered as personal estate; such a clause is merely a declaration, that by the municipal regulations of the State where it lies, such property shall be treated as personal and not as real estate; but by no means varies the international rule, that real estate, as part of the habitation of the nation, is to be governed by local law.[3] So, too, it has been held that it is for the courts of the State where the land lies, to construe the charter of a corporation and to determine whether the corporation is authorized thereby to take or hold such real estate, and that an adjudication upon the question of its corporate capacity, by a court of the State creating it, can have no further effect or authority than the reasoning, upon which it may have been founded, gives it.[4]

§ 164. Where two corporations are created by adjacent States with the same name, for the purpose of constructing a canal extending through a portion of both States, the interests of which are united by subsequent acts of the States, as the legislature of neither State can authorize an act — such as the raising of a dam — in the other, each act of incorporation must be construed as limited in its operation to the territorial limits of the State granting it.[5]

§ 165. The capacity of corporations created by the British crown in this country or Great Britain, to hold their lands or other property in this country, was not affected by the revolution; the dismemberment of empire not involving with it the destruction of civil rights.[6] The prop-

---

[1] Lumbard *v.* Aldrich, 8 N. H. 34.

[2] Binney's case, 2 Bland, Ch. 142.

[3] Binney's case, 2 Bland, Ch. 142.

[4] Boyce *v.* City of St. Louis, 29 Barb. 650.

[5] Farnam *v.* Blackstone Canal Corp. 1 Sumner, 46.

[6] Terrett *v.* Taylor, 9 Cranch, 43; Dartmouth College *v.* Woodward, 4 Wheat.

erty of such corporations in this country is also protected from forfeiture for the cause of alienage, by the sixth article of the treaty of peace of 1783, in the same manner as the property of natural persons; and the title thus protected is confirmed by the ninth article of the treaty of 1794.[1] It should be further observed that these treaties, so far as they stipulate for such permanent rights of property and general arrangements, and profess to aim at perpetuity, and to deal with the case of war as well as of peace, do not cease on the occurrence of war between Great Britain and this country, but are, at most, only suspended while it lasts; and unless they are waived by the parties, or new and repugnant stipulations are made, they revive in their operation at the return of peace.[2]

§ 166. It is laid down by several eminent writers, that a corporation cannot be seised of lands to the use of another, and that it is incapable of any use or trust.[3] It is certain, however, that many corporations are made trustees for charitable purposes, and are compelled to perform their trusts; which may, says Mr. Kyd, be reconciled to the rule, in this way; the trust is not vested in the corporation; but the natural persons of whom it is composed are created trustees, and their description, as constituent parts of a corporation, operates only as a more certain designation of their persons; this explanation appears more reasonable from what is said of a sole corporation on the same subject; "that a man who is a corporation sole, cannot be seised to use in his corporate capacity, nor by his corporate name alone, without his *natural* name, and then the addition of his corporate name must be considered only as a fuller description of his person."[4] However plausible this may have appeared, it is very clear that *corporations*, and not the members of whom they are composed, are made trustees for charitable purposes, and are compelled to execute their trusts.[5] One reason given for the inca-

---

518; Society, &c. *v.* New Haven, 8 Wheat. 464. See Dawson *v.* Godfrey, 4 Cranch, 323.

[1] Society, &c. *v.* New Haven, 8 Wheat. 464. See Orr *v.* Hodgson, 4 Wheat. 453.

[2] Ibid.

[3] Bro. Abr. Uses, pl. 10; Bacon on Uses, 57; Gilbert on Uses, by Sugden, 7 n; 1 Kyd on Corp. 72; Plowd. 102; 1 Cru. Dig. tit. 11, Use, ch. 2, § 15.

[4] 1 Kyd on Corp. 72, 73; 2 Leon. 122.

[5] Green *v.* Rutherforth, 1 Ves. 468, 470, 475; Attorney-General *v.* Lauderfield, 9 Mod. 287; Attorney-General *v.* Utica Ins. Co. 2 Johns. Ch. 384, 389; 2 Kent, Com. 226; Attorney-General *v.* Skinners Co. 5 Madd. 173; S. C. 1 Jacob, 629.

pacity of corporations to be trustees, is, that they cannot be compellable by subpœna to execute the possession to the use, because if they disobeyed they could not be enforced by imprisonment.[1] This reasoning proceeds upon the very erroneous supposition, that the only mode by which a Court of Chancery can enforce the execution of its process is by imprisonment, whereas by far the most effectual means of compulsion employed by equity, may be used against corporations, as, distringas,[2] sequestration,[3] injunction,[4] or in case of misapplication of the trust fund, by directing it to be conveyed to suitable trustees.[5] It has been said also, that the persons who compose a corporation might, in their *natural* capacities, have been seised to the use of another; and that it would be nugatory to allow them to do that in their *corporate* capacity, which they had the power to do in their *natural*, as the sole purpose of incorporating them, was to confer powers upon them, which they could not otherwise have.[6] Without adverting to the many rights which corporations enjoy in common with individuals, exclusive of their *privileges*, these bodies, on account of their peculiar structure and perpetual succession, seem, in the language of Kent, "to be proper and safe depositaries of trusts."[7] Accordingly, "among the almost infinite variety of purposes for which corporations are created at the present day, we find them," says he, "authorized to receive and take by deed or devise, in their corporate capacity, any property real and personal in trust, and to assume and execute any trust so created."[8] They "are also created with trust powers of another kind; as for the purpose of loaning money on a deposit of goods and chattels, by way of pledge or security.[9] Indeed, it is a sufficient reply to the reason just stated, that although individuals might get along with the business as trustees, and possibly execute the intent of the trust; yet by having corporate powers given them, that intent may be more effectually carried into execution."[10]

---

1 Gilb. Uses and Trusts, 5, 170; Jenk. 195; Plowd. Com. 102, 538; 1 Kyd on Corp. 72.

2 Newl. Harr. 149, 150; 2 Madd. 209, 210.

3 Ibid.; Mayor of Coventry *v.* Attorney-General, 2 Bro. P. C. 235.

4 Ibid.

5 Mayor of Coventry *v.* Attorney-General, 2 Bro. P. C. 235; 2 Madd. Chan. 77.

6 1 Kyd on Corp. 72; Gilb. Uses and Trusts, 5, 170.

7 2 Kent, Com. 226.

8 Ibid. See Farmers Fire Ins. and Loan Company, Laws of N. York, 17th April, 1822, ch. 240.

9 The New York Lombard Association, Laws of New York, 8th April, 1824, ch. 240.

10 Trustees of Phillips Academy *v.* King, 12 Mass. 555, per Thacher, J.

The last reason given for the incapacity of a corporation to stand seised of lands to the use of another, is, that such seisin is foreign to the purpose of its creation.[1] It is evident, however, that this is a mere begging of the question; since the execution of the trust may not only be in consistency with, but even in furtherance of the design for which the corporation was instituted.[2]

§ 167. At the time of passing the Statute of Uses, it was unsettled, whether a corporation could take to any other use than its own.[3] Brooke, in the 14th H. 8, inclined to the opinion that such a body might be enfeoffed to an express use,[4] though he subsequently states it as being the better opinion that it could not.[5] In the case of Sir Thomas Holland,[6] a distinction is taken between the capacity of a corporation to be enfeoffed originally to another's use, and its capacity to stand seised to an use, by limiting it out of, or charging it upon, its own possessions. Upon this case, Lord Chief Baron Comyn concludes that a corporation may make a deed of bargain and sale, since they may give a use, though they cannot stand seised to a use;[7] and this conclusion, Rowe says, is now generally received. Mr. Cruise, in his valuable Digest, objects to the case of Sir Thomas Holland, as of doubtful authority, inasmuch as the only principle upon which it can be supported, namely, that lands may be charged with an use, was utterly rejected in Chudleigh's case,[8] and states that it is now generally admitted that a corporation cannot stand seised to an use;[9] and in the case, Trustees of Phillips Academy *v.* King,[10] Mr. Justice Thacher informs us, "that if it (the case of Sir Thomas Holland) amounts to any thing, it is, that a corporation may be seised to the use of another." According to later authorities, it is said,[11] that a corporate body may be a trustee, not merely

---

1 1 Kyd on Corp. 72.

2 Trustees of Phillips Academy *v.* King, 12 Mass. 555, per Thacher, J.

3 Bacon on Uses, Rowe's 113th n.

4 Bro. Abr. tit. Feoff. al. Uses, pl. 10.

5 Ibid. pl. 40; Dy. 8 b.

6 3 Leon. 175.

7 Com. Dig. tit. Bargain and Sale, B. 3. See also, 2 Preston on Convey. 247, 254, 257, 263.

8 1 Co. R. 127 *a.*

9 4 Cru. Dig. tit. 32, ch. 9, § 16.

10 12 Mass. 556.

11 Jeremy's Equity Jurisdiction, book 1, p. 19.

for charitable purposes within the 43 Eliz. ch. 4, sec. 1,[1] but in all cases in which an individual may act in that capacity.[2]

§ 168. In this country the general or common-law rule is, that corporations may be seised of lands, and hold other property in trust, for purposes not foreign to their institution.[3] Thus, a bank may receive a deed of and hold land in trust for the security of a just debt due to it; and if the deed secures also other debts, void, as for usury, the trust will fail only as to them.[4] Indeed it is said by Mr. Justice Story, in delivering the opinion of the Supreme Court of the United States, in the very important and well-considered case of Vidal *v.* The Mayor, &c. of Philadelphia,[5] that there is no positive objection, in point of law, to a corporation taking property upon a trust not strictly within the scope of the direct purposes of its institution, but collateral to them, nay, for the benefit of a stranger or of another corporation. In the case of Trustees of Phillips Academy *v.* King,[6] which was an action of debt brought for the recovery of a large legacy, given to an incorporated academy, in trust for the benefit of a theological institution connected with it, but with a separate board of visitors, the above general rule was maintained by the Supreme Court of Massachusetts. Mr. Justice Thacher, in delivering the opinion of the court, very naturally expresses his surprise, that the question, whether corporations are capable of taking and holding property as trustees, should be one of *general* inquiry, — since

---

[1] 1 Ves. 536; 2 Vern. 412, 454; Hob. 136; Att'y-Gen. *v.* Mayor of Stamford, 2 Swanst. 594.

[2] Green *v.* Rutherforth, 1 Ves. 468; Mayor of Coventry *v.* Att'y-Gen. 2 Bro. P. C. 235; 2 Ves. 46.

[3] 2 Kent, Com. 226. See First Parish in Sutton *v.* Cole, 3 Pick. 237, 238, 239, 240; M'Girr *v.* Aaron, 1 Penn. 49; Green *v.* Dennis, 6 Conn. 304; Theological Seminary of Auburn *v.* Cole, 18 Barb. 360. This general rule is, however, in nine of the States, adopted or modified by statutes. In New York there is an act concerning money corporations which decides that no conveyance, assignment, or transfer of any effects for the benefit, use, or security of any such corporation shall be valid, unless made directly to the corporation. This refers to moneyed corporations chartered by the legislature of that State, and has no application to foreign corporations. And if land be conveyed in trust for the benefit of a foreign corporation, the corporation, under the provisions of another act, will only incur the penalty of not being able to maintain an action on the deed; but the conveyance, for all other purposes, will be good. Wright *v.* Douglass, 10 Barb. 97.

[4] Morris *v.* Way, 16 Ohio, 478, 479.

[5] 2 How. 128. And see authorities above, and McIntyre Poor School *v.* Zanesville Canal Co. 8 Ohio, 217.

[6] 12 Mass. 546.

these bodies are the mere creatures of the legislature, which can invest them with powers more or less enlarged, according to its own good pleasure. "I can only account for the *general* inquiry," says he, "by supposing that the oldest corporations were of prescriptive origin, and that immemorial usage did not permit them to take property in trust for third persons; and that, instead of reasoning from the abstract nature of corporations, or the power of the crown or parliament to create new ones, lawyers drew too strict a conclusion, in the nature of a maxim, from those in existence, and applied it as a principle of construction to all of a more modern date, as they were beginning to exercise powers in trust."[1] In the matter of Howe,[2] where it appeared that one had given a legacy to a church corporation, in trust, to pay the income to his housekeeper for life, and after her death, to apply it to the purchase of a church library, the support of a sabbath school in the church, and other church purposes, agreeably to the canons of episcopacy, it was held by the Court of Chancery, in New York, that the corporation might well execute the trust. "It is a general rule," says the Chancellor, "that corporations cannot exercise any powers not given to them by their charters or acts of incorporation; and for that reason they cannot act as trustees in relation to any matters in which the corporation has no interest. But wherever property is devised or granted to a corporation, partly for its own use and partly for the use of others, the power of the corporation to take and hold the property for its own use, carries with it, as a necessary incident, the power to execute that part of the trust which relates to others."[3] The supervisors of a county in New York, who were a corporation for certain special purposes, were, on the other hand, held incapable to take and hold lands as trustees for the use of an individual, or of the inhabitants of a village, or, indeed, for any other use or purpose than that of the county which they represented;[4] and, in New Hampshire, a corporation empowered "to establish an institution in the town of Newmarket, for the instruction of youth," was deemed unauthorized, as a trustee, to hold funds, and pay over the income thereof for the support of missionaries.[5] If the trust be repugnant to, or inconsistent with the proper purposes for which the

---

1 Trustees of Phillips Academy *v.* King, 2 Mass. 552, 554.

2 1 Paige, Ch. 214.

3 1 Paige, Ch. 214, 215.

4 Jackson *v.* Hartwell, 8 Johns. 422.

5 Trustees, &c. *v.* Peaslee, 15 N. H. 317.

corporation was created, it furnishes a ground why the corporation may not be compellable to execute the trust; but it will furnish no ground to declare the trust itself void, if otherwise unexceptionable. It will simply require a new trustee to be substituted by the proper court, possessing equity jurisdiction, to enforce and perfect the objects of the trust.[1] In fine, if the trusts are in themselves valid in point of law, it is now pretty well settled that neither the heirs of the testator, where the trust is created by will, nor any other private person, can have right to inquire into or contest the right of the corporation; it can only be done by the State.[2]

§ 169. A grant of lands, &c., may be made to a corporation by the same charter by which it is created;[3] the law giving a priority of operation among things in the same grant, wherever it is necessary to effectuate the objects of the grant. But the mere incorporation of tenants in common, for a particular intent, for example, for manufacturing purposes, to enable them to carry on more conveniently a common business, does not vest in the corporation a title to land, which had been previously used by the tenants for the same purpose. The title must be conveyed by proper deeds from the individuals to the corporation.[4] And if an association become incorporated, and the corporation accept a transfer of all the property of the association, for the purpose of carrying out the object of the association, the corporation will become primarily liable, in equity, to the debts of the association;[5] and the same result follows if one corporation succeed to the property of another which has been dissolved.[6] That a legislative act, passed with the assent of all interested, is *competent* to effect the same purpose, cannot

---

[1] Per Mr. Justice Story, Vidal *v.* Mayor, &c. of Philadelphia, 2 How. 128. And see Souley *v.* The Clockmaker's Company, 1 Bro. 81.

[2] Per Story, J., Vidal *v.* Mayor, &c. Philadelphia, 2 How. 128; Wade *v.* American Colonization Society, 7 Smedes & M. 697, 698.

[3] 2 Ed. 6; Bro. Corp. 89; Case of Sutton's Hospital, 10 Co. 23, 74 b; Jackson *d.* Trustees of the Parish of Newburg *v.* Nestles, 3 Johns. 115; Dartmouth College *v.* Woodward, 4 Wheat. 690, 691; The People of the State of Vermont *v.* The Soc. for Propagation of the Gospel in Foreign Parts, 1 Paine, C. C. 652.

[4] Leffingwell *v.* Elliot, 8 Pick. 455; Sec. Cong. Soc. *v.* Waring, 24 Pick. 308; Holland *v.* Cruft, 3 Gray, 162. Upon the incorporation of a parish into a town, the real estate of the parish will become vested in the new corporation. Lakin *v.* Ames, 10 Cush. 198.

[5] Haslett *v.* Witherspoon, 2 Strob. 209. And see Wesley *v.* Moore, 10 Barr, 273; Attorney-General *v.* Corporation of Leicester, 9 Beav. 546.

[6] Cushman *v.* Shepard, 4 Barb. 114; Johnson *v.* Marine Hospital, 2 Calif. 319.

be doubted; and in a case, in which it appeared that several tenants in common of a lot of land, were, on their petition, incorporated for the purpose of building a public house thereon, and the house was nearly completed, and assessments had been laid and paid by all, the Supreme Court of Maine construed the particular act of incorporation before them, as changing the interest of one of those who joined in procuring the act, and assented to all the subsequent expenditures and proceedings under it, from that of a tenant in common entitled to partition, to that of a mere owner of the corporate stock.[1] If a religious corporation be incorporated anew, under another name, the legislature, by the new act, may vest the property of the old corporation in the new one.[2] But where the minority of a neighborhood, for whose benefit a school-house and land were vested in trustees, formed an association, and procured a charter which vested the property belonging to the association in the corporation, it was held, that they could not, by virtue of an article thrown into their charter, appropriate to the corporation lands, &c., which never belonged to the association.[3] The State may undoubtedly vest its own property in a corporation by legislative act. And where a legislative act vested in an academic corporation, "all such property as hath heretofore, *or hereafter may*, accrue to the State," in a certain district, which, by the act to regulate escheats, "*hath escheated to the State*," the title to property which escheated in the district *after* the passage of the act was adjudged to be vested in the corporation.[4]

§ 170. To avoid the difficulties frequently arising from the neglect of the association or its trustees to convey its property to the corporation created to succeed it, the New York statute relative to religious societies, provides that the trustees of a church or society, when legally incorporated, shall be authorized to take possession of all the property

---

[1] Bangor House *v.* Hinkley, 3 Fairf. 385. And see London Dock Co. *v.* Knebell, 2 Moody & R. 66; see Fox *v.* Union Academy, 6 Watts & S. 353, where a doubt is expressed as to the constitutionality of an act, vesting land, conveyed to trustees in trust for an academy, in the corporation afterwards created by incorporating the trustees. In this case, however, it was decided that one who contracts with the corporation to pay for land thus obtained by them, and conveyed to him, there being no adverse claimant for the money, cannot set up such an objection in defence to an action brought by the corporation to recover the agreed price of the land.

[2] Methodist Episcopal Church *v.* Wood, 5 Ohio, 283.

[3] Commonwealth *v.* Jarrett, 7 S. & R. 460; Fox *v.* Union Academy, 6 Watts & S. 356.

[4] Brown *v.* Chesterville Academy Society, 3 Rich. Eq. 362.

of the society, whether the same be given directly to the society, or to any person for its use ; and the trustees are to hold the property as fully and amply as if the right or title thereto had been originally vested in the trustees.[1] The construction of this statute is, that, as soon as the trustees are legally competent to take the property in a corporate character, the legal estate of the property held in trust for the church or society passes to the corporation,[2] though it seems, that a bill will lie against the nominal grantee for a conveyance.[3] In some cases long possession, and in others dedication, have been adjudged to pass the legal title to the corporation, where the common law has not been aided by any such statute as the above.[4] In Massachusetts, also, proprietors of a lot of land, bought by them for the purpose of erecting a meeting-house thereon, when organized as a corporation under the provisions of the act of 1783, ch. 39, are construed by force of the statute to cede their rights in the land to the corporation.[5]

§ 171. The charter of a corporation sometimes declares, "that the lands, tenements, stock, property, and estate of the company, is, and shall be, held as real estate, and shall descend, &c., as such, when not otherwise disposed of," or more commonly, that it shall be held as personal estate, and be transferred, distributed, &c., as such. Usually there is something in such clauses indicating that they are intended to operate only as between the stockholders, and not between the corporation and third persons or strangers ; though it would certainly be competent for the legislature, by a clause in the charter, to change the legal character of the most perishable article to real estate, or of real estate into personal property.[6] The common clause declaring *the stock* of a corporation personal property, relates merely to the legal character of the property which the stockholders, as individuals, have in their shares, and not to the legal character of the property held by the corporation in its corporate character.[7]

---

1 3 Rev. St. 295, § 4.

2 Baptist Church in Hartford *v.* Witherell, 3 Paige, Ch. 299, 300 ; Trustees of the South Baptist Church *v.* Yates, 1 Hoffm. Ch. 143 ; Cammeyer *v.* United German Lutheran Churches, 2 Sandf. Ch. 221.

3 Trustees of South Baptist Church *v.* Yates, 1 Hoffm. Ch. 142.

4 City of Cincinnati *v.* White, 6 Pet. 431 ; Beaty *v.* Kurtz, 2 id. 566 ; Potter *v.* Chapin, 6 Paige, Ch. 639 ; Trustees of Watertown *v.* Cowen, id. 4, 510.

5 Second Cong. Soc. *v.* Waring, 24 Pick. 308, 309 ; Howard *v.* Hayward, 10 Met. 420, 421.

6 Cape Sable Company's case, 3 Bland, Ch. 670 ; Binney's case, 2 Bland, Ch. 146.

7 Mohawk & Hudson Railroad Co. *v.* Clute, 4 Paige, Ch. 384.

§ 172. It seems never to have been disputed, that corporations aggregate might, like natural persons, take lands, &c., by every species of conveyance by deed known to the law. In grants of lands to these bodies, the word "*successors*," though usually inserted, is not necessary to convey a fee-simple; for, admitting that such a simple grant be strictly only an estate for life, yet, as the corporation, unless of limited duration, never dies, such estate for life is perpetual, or equivalent to a fee-simple, and therefore the law allows it to be one.[1] Nor is the consideration, that a grant to a corporation, without the use of the word "successors," conveys a fee-simple, without weight in determining a court of equity to hold, that an arrangement in writing, between two railway companies, for the use of part of the property and line of one by the other, was intended to be a permanent arrangement instead of a license revocable by the company contracting to give the easement; the word "successors" being omitted in the agreement.[2] In this respect, as well as in many others, a corporation aggregate differs from a corporation sole; a grant of lands to the latter, without the word "successors," conveying only a life estate.[3] If a corporation be created for a term of years only, a grant purporting to convey a fee will not be construed to convey a term for years corresponding in duration with the corporation.[4]

§ 173. As the same presumptions are raised in favor of a corporation as of a natural person, its assent to, and acceptance of grants and deeds beneficial to it may be implied, as in case of an individual.[5] "Suppose," says Mr. Justice Story, in his very full and learned opinion in the case of Bank of the United States *v.* Dandridge, "a deed poll, granting lands to a corporation; can it be necessary to show that there was an acceptance by the corporation by an assent under seal, if it be

---

[1] 2 Bl. Com. 109; 1 Kyd on Corp. 74, 104, 105; Co. Lit. 9 b, 94 b; Butler's and Harg. notes; Union Canal Co. *v.* Young, 1 Whart. 425; Overseers of the Poor of Boston *v.* Sears, 22 Pick. 122.

[2] Great Northern Railway Co. *v.* Manchester &c. Railway Co. 5 De G. & S. 138, 10 Eng. L. & Eq. 11, 15, 16.

[3] See Overseers of the Poor of Boston *v.* Sears, 22 Pick. 122, in which the legal characteristics of the two kinds of corporations are very luminously set forth by Shaw, C. J.

[4] Nicoll *v.* The New York & Erie Railroad Co. 12 Barb. 460.

[5] Bank of United States *v.* Dandridge, 12 Wheat. 64; Dedham Bank *v.* Chickering, 3 Pick. 335; Charles River Bridge *v.* Warren Bridge, 7 Pick. 344; Union Bank of Maryland *v.* Ridgeley, 1 Harris & G. 324; Apthorp *v.* North, 14 Mass. 167; Smith *v.* Bank of Scotland, 1 Dow, P. C. 272; see Chap. VIII.

a corporation at the common law; or by a written vote, if the corporation may signify its assent in that manner? Why may not its occupation and improvement, and the demise of the land by its agents, be justly admitted by implication to establish the fact in favor and for the benefit of the corporation? Why should the omission to record the assent, if actually given, deprive the corporation of the property which it gained in virtue of such actual assent? The validity of such a grant depends upon the acceptance, not upon the mode by which it is proved. It is no implied condition, that the corporation shall perpetuate the evidence of its assent in a particular way."[1]

§ 174. Where a grant of lands is made to a corporation on condition, the breach of the condition is equally a cause of forfeiture as it would be had the grant on condition been made to a natural person. The King of Great Britain granted a township in shares to certain individuals, and one share to the Society for the Propagation of the Gospel in Foreign Parts, upon condition that the grantees, their heirs and assigns should pay rent, and cultivate a certain portion of the land; and it was decided that no reasons of public policy exempted the corporation from the performance of these conditions; but that the lands granted to it were as much subject to the burden, as the lands of individual grantees.[2] The breach of a condition to pay an ear of Indian corn for each share, for the first ten years, if lawfully demanded, was considered no ground of forfeiture; as the rent was merely nominal.[3] It was held, also, in this case, that the performance of a condition that each grantee should pay to the king in his council chamber at Portsmouth, or to such officer as should be appointed to receive the same, a rent of one shilling for every hundred acres during the first ten years, was rendered impossible by the Revolution, and the consequent separation of Great Britain from this country: and that the State in which the land was, if it had succeeded to the rights of the king as grantor, should have averred and proved that it had appointed another place of payment, or an officer to receive the same, and had given notice thereof to the corporation.[4] Where land was devised to a town for the purpose of building a school-house, and

---

[1] Bank of the United States *v.* Dandridge, 12 Wheat. 60, 72, 73. See the Proprietors of the Monumoi Great Beach *v.* Rogers, 1 Mass. 159.

[2] The People of the State of Vermont *v.* The Society for the Propagation of the Gospel in Foreign Parts, 1 Paine, C. C. 652; King's Chapel *v.* Pelham, 9 Mass. 501.

[3] 1 Paine, C. C. 658, 659.

[4] Ibid.

the town neglected for twenty years to comply with the condition, and in the mean time, applied part of the rents and profits "for the use of schooling," the residuary devisee recovered the land from the town, as forfeited by breach of the condition.[1]

§ 175. It is laid down by Mr. Kyd, as a general rule, that where a corporation aggregate has by its constitution a head, a grant to that corporation in the vacancy of the headship is void; as if a corporation consist of mayor and commonalty, and a grant be made to it while there is no mayor, or a grant be made to a corporation of dean and chapter when there is no dean, in either case the grant is void; and the reason is, that without the head the corporation is incomplete, and the only act it can do during the vacancy, is to elect another.[2] Littleton[3] puts the case of a monastery, whose abbot is dead, and says, that in time of vacation, a grant unto them is void, because the convent is but a dead body without a head. This is true of such a body, consisting of persons dead in the law. Coke, however, in his commentary on this passage,[4] remarks, that "though the rest of the corporation be no mort persons, as the chapter, in case of dean and chapter, or the commonaltie, in case of mayor and commonaltie, yet cannot they, when there is no dean or mayor, make claim, *because they have neither abilitie nor capacitie to take or sue any action*, as our author here saith." The rule seems to have originated in very early times, when that spirit prevailed which produced the statutes of mortmain, and when probably the courts viewed with great strictness grants to bodies corporate. In the case of Sutton's Hospital,[5] the corporation, if immediately incorporated by the letters patent, is said by the court to *exist*, previous to the naming of a master by the founder, and previous to the building of the hospital; "for when a corporation is created by letters-patent, by the same patent power is given to the body to choose a mayor, alderman, or bailiffs, governors, or the like, and yet they are immediately incorporated by the same letters-patent.[6] And it is true, it is immediately by the letters-patent, a corporation *in abstracto*, but not *in concreto* till the naming of a master."

---

1 Hayden *v.* Stoughton, 5 Pick. 528.

2 1 Kyd on Corp. 106; 13 Ed. 4, 8; 18 Ed. 4, 8; Bro. Corp. 58, 59; Dalison, 31.

3 1 Inst. 264.

4 Co. Lit. 264.

5 10 Co. R. 31 a, 31 b.

6 Plow. Com. 592 b; Cook's case, 21 E. 4, 59 b; 3 H. 7, Grant 36; 32 E. 3, Aid 39; 13 E. 4, 8 b, and 16 E. 3, Grant 65.

The *continued* existence of the corporation, notwithstanding the death of its members or officers, is as expressly stated in the same case; "for a corporation aggregate of many is invisible, immortal, and rests only in intendment and consideration of law; and therefore in 39 H. 6, 13 and 14, a dean and chapter cannot have predecessor or successor."[1] The grant was not held void, therefore, because it was thought that the corporation did not exist in the vacancy of its headship, but because, as is stated by Mr. Kyd, "without the head, the corporation is incomplete, and the only *act* it can do during the vacancy is to elect another."[2] Some *act* was to be done by the corporation in order to the acceptance of the grant; and we find that Littleton[3] and Sir Edward Coke[4] place the taking of a grant by a corporation upon the same footing with the making of a claim, and the suing of an action, which require something positive to be done. The incapacity of a corporation, therefore, to take a grant of lands in the vacancy of its headship, probably grew out of the well-established doctrine of early times with regard to common-law corporations, that they could not signify their assent, as, accept a deed, but by writing under their common seal. This act they could not do, any more than any other, until the body was duly organized according to its constitution, by the election of a new head; and hence, as a freehold cannot be granted to commence *in futuro*, the grant was inoperative at its inception, and therefore void.

§ 176. At this day in England,[5] and certainly in this country, as we have before shown, the acceptance by a corporation of a grant or devise, beneficial to it, may as well be *presumed*, as in favor of an individual. As no act is now necessary to be done, in order to the acceptance of a deed or devise by a body corporate, and the existence of a corporation is clear, notwithstanding the vacancy of its headship, we see no good reason why a benefaction, perhaps highly meritorious, should be defeated by an accidental death. We find no recent decision in England, and none in this country, directly upon this point;[6] but may be allowed to doubt, whether the general rule above laid down, however proper to

---

[1] Case of Sutton's Hospital, 10 Co. R. 32 b.

[2] 1 Kyd on Corp. 106; Co. Lit. 264.

[3] 1 Inst. § 443.

[4] Co. Lit. 264.

[5] Smith *v.* Bank of Scotland, 1 Dow, P. C. 272, Lord Redesdale.

[6] See Rathbone *v.* Tioga Navigation Co. 2 Watts & S. 74; Selma & Tennessee Railroad Company *v.* Tipton, 5 Ala. 787.

the old corporations of the common law, would be applied in this country to our commercial, religious, and literary corporations created by statute. Our view of this subject is, we think, greatly supported by the fact that it was always held that where a particular tenant for life, or in tail, was created by the grant, who might accept the deed and estate in privity with the corporation, a remainder to the corporation was good, notwithstanding the vacancy of its headship, provided that, during the continuance of the particular estate, a new head was chosen. If, during the vacation of the abbacy of Dale, a lease for life, or a gift in tail, had been made, the remainder to the abbot of Dale and his successors, this remainder would have been good, if an abbot had been chosen during the continuance of the particular estate. And if there be mayor and commonalty of D., and the mayor die, a grant made to the mayor and commonalty of D. is void; but if a lease for life be made, with remainder to the mayor and commonalty of D., the remainder will be good, if during the continuance of the particular estate a new mayor be elected.[1] King Edward III. newly founded a priory, and granted to the monks that they might choose a prior, and before a prior was chosen, W. made a lease to one A. for life, the remainder to the prior and convent; and in *scire facias* against A., he pleaded that W. was seised in fee, and leased to A., the remainder to the prior and convent, who were newly founded by the king, and because there was not yet a prior, he prayed aid of the king, in whom the right was, until a prior was chosen; the aid by award was granted, and a writ of *procedendo* came; then A., the defendant, showed, that after the aid granted, a prior was chosen, in whom the remainder vested, and prayed aid of the prior, but was ousted of the aid *because he had aid before*, " which proves," says Lord Coke, " that the remainder in such case is good." [2] A grant, however, in remainder to a corporation, *when no such corporation exists*, is void, though such a corporation be erected before the expiration of the particular estate.[3]

§ 177. The common-law right of taking *personal* property by *bequest* was, we believe, always enjoyed by corporations equally with individuals,[4] and a bequest to a corporation of its own stock, is as valid

---

[1] Co. Lit. 264 a.

[2] Case of Sutton's Hospital, 10 Co. R. 31 b.

[3] Hob. 33.

[4] 2 Atk. R 37; 2 Bro. 58; Trustees of Phillips Academy *v.* King, 12 Mass. 546; In

as a bequest of any thing else.[1] The want of capacity, however, to transfer and receive the freehold, though not deduced from the principles of the ancient common law of England, was, by feudal policy, engrafted upon the system of jurisprudence prevailing in that country at the time of the conquest; and the disability of aliening by devise, was not removed until long after the power of alienation by deed had been fully established, nor until long after the doctrine of uses had been introduced. We may collect, indeed, from the recitals and provisions of ancient acts of parliament, and the language of early reports, that devises of lands had grown into use anterior to the statutes of wills; but until the time of Henry VIII. no trace of any statute authority is discovered for the practice. The statutes 32 H. 8, c. 1, and 34 H. 8, c. 5, commonly called the statutes of Wills, gave liberty to every person having a sole estate in fee-simple of any manors, &c., "To give, dispose, will, or devise, to any person or persons, *except to bodies politic and corporate*, by his last will and testament in writing, or otherwise, by any acts lawfully executed in his lifetime, all his manors, &c., at his own will and pleasure, any law, statute, custom, or other thing, theretofore had, made, or used, to the contrary notwithstanding." By the express exception in these statutes, corporations were not enabled in England to take lands, &c. directly by devise, — and we find the same exception in the N. Y. Statute of Wills, with the same effect of course following upon it.[2] The exception was unquestionably made to prevent the extension of gifts in mortmain;[3] but in England, by construction of the statute 43 Eliz. c. 4, commonly called the Statute of Charitable Uses, it is held that a devise to a corporation for a charitable use is valid, as operating in the nature of an *appointment*, rather than of a *devise;* and the Court of Chancery will support and enforce the charitable donation.[4] Where the Statute of Wills excepts bodies politic as competent devisees, the usual power given to corporations by charter, or act of incorporation to *purchase* lands, &c. has been construed not to qualify them to take by devise; the word "*purchase*," being understood in its ordinary, and

---

the matter of Howe, 1 Paige, Ch. 214; McCartee *v.* Orphan Asylum Society, 9 Cowen, 437.

[1] Rivanna Navigation Co. *v.* Dawson, 3 Gratt. 19.

[2] 1 Greenleaf's ed. Laws N. Y. 387; Jackson *v.* Hammond, 2 Caines, Cas. 337; McCartee *v.* Orphan Asylum Society, 9 Cowen, 437; 2 Kent, Com. 283.

[3] 2 Bl. Com. 375; McCartee *v.* Orph. As. So. 2 Cowen, 461, per Jones, Ch.

[4] 2 Bl. Com. 375, 376; 2 Kent, Com. 285; Baptist Association *v.* Hart, 4 Wheat. 31, per Marshall, C. J.

not in its general and technical sense.[1] But where a corporation was created for the express purpose of taking certain property devised, and enabled by the act of incorporation for that purpose, the act of course operated as a repeal of the Statute of Wills *pro tanto*.[2] In those States whose statutes of wills do not contain the exception above, we need hardly add that corporations are capacitated to take by devise under the words "*person or persons*," and the like; and this view is confirmed by the words of the English statutes of wills, which empower every person having a sole estate in fee-simple to give his manors, &c., "to any *person or persons* except to *bodies politic and corporate*."

§ 178. In those States whose statutes of wills except bodies politic and corporate, as competent devisees, a very important and difficult question may arise, whether (there being no statutes of mortmain) though corporations cannot take lands directly as devisees, they may not take a use, the lands being devised to trustees for their benefit, in such a manner as not to be affected by the Statute of Uses. The use or trust of lands as distinct from the land itself may be devised; and it was upon this property of a use, that long anterior to the Statute of Wills, the general power of devising was indirectly acquired.[3] And this indirect method of disposing of lands by devise was recognized and sanctioned by the statutes 7 H. 7, ch. 3, and 16 H. 8, ch. 14. One mode was to convey the lands to feoffees to the use of the will, and then to declare the uses of the feoffment by the will. It may be observed, however, that in this mode of disposition, the estate took effect by force of the feoffment, and the use was merely declared and directed by the will;[4] whereas in the question we are considering, the whole disposition, both of the land and the use, is by force of the will. It is nevertheless true, that supposing no statutes of mortmain, and no incapacity on the part of the corporation to take lands, the only difficulty is in taking them *in a particular mode*, to wit, by devise, in consequence of the exception in the statute. The trustees, being natural persons, may of course take the legal estate in this way, and the question appears to be narrowed down to this, whether, previous to the statute of wills, and now independent of

---

1 Jackson *v.* Hammond, 2 Caines, Cas. 337; McCartee *v.* Orph. Asylum So. 9 Cowen, 507, 508; Canal Co. *v.* Railroad Co. 4 Gill & J. 1.

2 Inglis *v.* Trustees of the Sailors Snug Harbor, 3 Pet. 119, per Thompson, J.

3 1 Saunders's Uses, 72.

4 Co. Lit. 272, sects. 462, 463; Sir Edward Clerc's case, 6 Co. R. 18.

it, a corporation can take a use by devise and by *the mere force* of the devise. The practice of devising copyhold estates, which are not affected by the Statute of Wills, is supposed to be a practical illustration of the right of a corporation, to take a use by devise. It may be objected here, too, that the will operates merely as a declaration of the uses of the surrender; and that it is the surrender, and not the will, which *passes* the use. In McCartee *v.* Orphan Asylum Society,[1] this question was considered by Chancellor Jones, and in a very learned and elaborate opinion, he concluded, that in the case stated, a corporation might take a use by devise. The decree in this case was afterwards reversed by the Court of Errors in New York, but upon the ground, that by the devise before them the lands were given *directly* to the corporation, and not to trustees for its use.[2] The question may still, perhaps, be considered as open to discussion and decision. In New York it has been settled by legislation; it being provided in the Revised Statutes, that a devise of real property in trust for a corporation is void unless such corporation is expressly authorized to take in this manner by statute or charter.[3] Whether under the provisions of these statutes a pecuniary legacy to a corporation, payable out of the proceeds of real estate which the executors are directed to sell, is valid, is perhaps a question. Previous to the revision such a legacy was considered good, although the corporation was not authorized to take real estate by devise.[4] In Delaware, where, by act of assembly, passed in 1787,[5] all devises of land to *religious* corporations are declared void, a devise of the net proceeds of the sale of the testator's land to the trustees of a Methodist Episcopal Church, to be by them applied to the purpose of educating poor children, was held to be void, the court applying to the case the ordinary principle that the proceeds of the realty are to be subject to the same rules as the realty itself.[6]

---

[1] 9 Cowen, 437; and see Sheppard's Touchstone, tit. Devise; Porter's case, 1 Coke, R. 22; Chudleigh's case, 1 Coke, R. 121; Griffith Flood's case, Hob. 136; Attorney-General *v.* The Master of Brentford School, 1 Mylne & K. 376, reporting the case of Sir Anthony Brown's will, decided previous to the statute of Eliz. and after the Statute of Wills.

[2] McCartee *v.* Orphan As. Soc. 9 Cowen, 504, Woodworth, J.

[3] Theological Seminary of Auburn *v.* Childs, 4 Paige, 419; Lorillard *v.* Coster, 5 Paige, 174; 14 Wend. 266; Wright *v.* Trustees of Meth. Episc. Ch., 1 Hoffm. Ch. 217, 218. In this last case the reader will find several questions under the New York statutes, in relation to devises in trust for corporations, and especially charitable corporations, canvassed and decided.

[4] Ibid.

[5] Digest of Laws of Del. 459.

[6] The State *v.* Wiltbank, 2 Harring. Del. 22.

§ 179. The statute of 43 Eliz. ch. 4, of charitable uses, is in force in North Carolina,[1] and Kentucky,[2] and by virtue of it, the Courts of Equity in those States have jurisdiction over charities; although they do not carry out the English doctrine of *cy-pres*.[3] In Virginia it was repealed in 1792;[4] and we know of no other States in the Union in which it is in force, except the two above mentioned.[5] In both Maryland and Virginia, bequests have been adjudged void, as indefinite, upon the ground that this statute was not in force in those States.[6] Its doctrines, however, are, by the third section of the declaration of rights, prefixed to the constitution of Maryland, so far recognized as to render valid a dedication of a lot of land to public and pious uses, even though there be no specific trustee or grantee; the lot having upon the faith of the dedication having built upon and used as a burial-ground.[7] In Pennsylvania,[8] Massachusetts,[9] and Georgia,[10] the principles which the English Court of Chancery has adopted respecting charitable uses, under the statute of Elizabeth, obtain, not indeed by force of the statute, but as part of their common law; and where the object is defined, and in Pennsylvania at least, even if the object be indefinite, provided a discretionary power be vested anywhere by the testator to define it,[11] and they are not

---

1 Griffin *v.* Graham, 1 Hawks, 96; White *v.* Attorney-General, 4 Ired. Eq. 19.

2 Gass *v.* Wilhite, 2 Dana, 170.

3 McAuley *v.* Wilson, 1 Dev. Ch. 276; Bridges *v.* Pleasants, 4 Ired. Eq. 26; White *v.* Attorney-General, id. 19; Moore *v.* Moore, 4 Dana, 357; Attorney-General *v.* Wallace, 7 B. Mon. 611.

4 Gallego *v.* Attorney-General, 3 Leigh, 450; Taney *v.* Latane, 4 id. 327.

5 2 Kent, Com. 285; Union Baptist Soc. *v.* Candia, 2 N. H. 21; Baptist Soc. *v.* Wilton, 2 N. H. 510; Green *v.* Allen, 5 Humph. 170. It is not in force in New York. Owens *v.* Missionary Society, 14 N. Y. 380; Boyce *v.* City of St. Louis, 29 Barb. 650.

6 Dashiell *v.* Attorney-General, 5 Harris & J. 392; 6 Harris & J. 1; Gallego *v.* Attorney-General, 3 Leigh, 450; Taney *v.* Latane, 4 id. 327.

7 Beatty *v.* Kurtz, 2 Pet. 566.

8 Witman *v.* Lex, 17 S. & R. 88; Mayor, &c., of Philadelphia *v.* Elliott, 3 Rawle, 170; McGirr *v.* Aaron, 1 Penn. 49. See Browers *v.* Fromm, Addison, 362; Zimmerman *v.* Anders, 6 Watts & S. 218. By an act of the Assembly of Pennsylvania, April 26th, 1855, all bequests to religious and charitable uses are void, except the same be done by deed or will, at least one calendar month before the decease of the testator or alienor. Price *v.* Maxwell, 28 Penn. State, 23.

9 Going *v.* Emery, 16 Pick. 107; Sanderson *v.* White, 18 Pick. 333; 4 Dane, Abr. 6; Bartlett *v.* King, 12 Mass. 537; Milton *v.* First Parish in Milton, 10 Pick. 447; Rice *v.* Osgood, 9 Mass. 38; Shapley *v.* Pilsbury, 1 Greenl. 271; Sohier *v.* Wardens and Vestry of St. Paul's Church, 12 Met. 250; Brown *v.* Kelsey, 2 Cush. 243.

10 Beall *v.* Fox, 4 Ga. 404.

11 Beaver *v.* Filson, 8 Barr, 335; Pickering *v.* Shotwell, 10 Barr, 23; Thomas *v.* Ellmaber, 1 Parsons, Sel. Cas. 109; Pepper's Estate, id. 436. The principles of the statute of

restrained by the inadequacy of the common-law forms, which they are compelled to employ, their courts give relief nearly to the extent that chancery does in England. The broad discretion exercised by the English Chancellor, under the doctrine of *cy pres*, would not, and indeed could not, be exercised by common-law courts.[1] In those States in which the statute of Elizabeth is in force, or its doctrines have been adopted as part of their common law, there would probably be no difficulty in sustaining a direct devise, and *a fortiori* a devise of a use to a corporation for charitable purposes, notwithstanding corporations were excepted out of their statutes of wills.

§ 180. A question of more difficult solution is, whether wholly independent of the statute of charitable uses, and of the doctrines which have grown up under it, and admitting corporations *in general* cannot take as *cestuis que trust* under a devise, courts of equity may not sustain and enforce a devise to or for the use of a corporation, *provided the object be a charity in itself lawful and commendable*, notwithstanding an exception of bodies politic and corporate as competent devisees in the statute of wills. Previous to the statute of Elizabeth, the history of the law of charitable bequests is extremely obscure; and so few traces remain of the exercise by chancery of a jurisdiction over them, that Lord Loughborough informs us, that, "prior to the time of Lord Ellesmere (who presided in the Court of Chancery very shortly after the statute of Elizabeth went into operation), there was no information in the Court in which he was sitting; but they made out the case as well as they could by law." [2] This was the course in Porter's case,[3] decided in the 34th and 35th years of Elizabeth. We have, however, the testimony of some of the most able jurists and equity judges in England, that the Court of Chancery in that country, from times of very high antiquity, and long before the statute of Elizabeth, had cognizance of informations filed by the Attorney-General for the establishment of charities; and that the equity powers of the court were applied, though not so beneficially as in after times, to cases of charitable uses. Sir Joseph Jekyll, Master of the Rolls, sitting as

---

Eliz. with one or two exceptions, are also adopted in Indiana. McCord *v.* Ochiltree, 8 Blackf. 15; Sweeney *v.* Sampson, 5 Ind. 465.

[1] Witman *v.* Lex, 17 S. & R. 93. See Sanderson *v.* White, 18 Pick. 333, opinion of Shaw, C. J.

[2] Attorney-General *v.* Bowyer, 3 Ves. 714, 726.

[3] 1 Co. R. 22 b.

commissioner, informs us, that in case of a charity, the king, *pro bono publico*, has an original right to superintend the care thereof, so that, abstracted from the statute of Elizabeth relating to charitable uses, *and antecedent to it*, as well as since, it has been every day's practice to file informations in Chancery, in the Attorney-General's name, for the establishment of charities.[1] Lord Somers takes notice, too, that several things are under the care and superintendency of the king as *parens patriæ*, and instances *charities*, idiots, lunatics, and infants;[2] and in several cases, Lord Hardwicke also refers to the original jurisdiction of Chancery over the subject of charities, previous to the statute.[3] Henley, keeper, afterwards Lord Chancellor Northington, is decisive and strong in his opinion on this point; "I take," says he, "the uniform rule of this court, before and after the statute of Elizabeth, to have been, that where the uses are charitable, and the person has in himself full power to convey, the court will aid a defective conveyance to such uses;" and he illustrates his meaning by the example of a devise to a body corporate to charitable uses; thus, he observes, "though devises to corporations were void under the statutes of Henry VIII., yet they were always considered as good in equity, if given to charitable uses."[4] In the case of Attorney-General *v.* Mayor of Dublin,[5] Lord Redesdale affirms that the statute created no new law on the subject, but only a new and ancillary jurisdiction in the commissioners. The opinion of Lord Eldon evidently was, that previous to the statute the Court of Chancery had the power to render effective an imperfect conveyance for charitable uses.[6] In the case of Attorney-General *v.* The Master of Brentford School,[7] we learn that a decree was made in chancery, in the 12th year of the reign of Elizabeth, before the statutes of charitable uses, at the suit of the inhabitants of the parish of Southweald against the heir at law that he should execute a conveyance for the purpose of providing for the maintenance

---

[1] Eyre *v.* Countess of Shaftsbury, 2 P. Wms. 119.

[2] Lord Falkland *v.* Bertie, 2 Vern. 333.

[3] Bailiffs, &c. of Burford *v.* Lenthall, 2 Atk. 551; Attorney-General *v.* Middleton, 2 Ves. 327; Attorney-General *v.* Tancred, 1 W. Bl. 90, Ambler, 351, 1 Eden, 10.

[4] Attorney-General *v.* Tancred, 1 Eden, 10; 1 W. Bl. 90; and see Wilmot's Opinions, 24, 33; White *v.* White, 1 Bro. Ch. 15; Moggridge *v.* Thackwell, 7 Ves. 69; Weleden *v.* Elkinton, Plowd. 523; Duke on Charitable Uses, 154, and Moore's Readings.

[5] 1 Bligh, 347, 348.

[6] Moggridge *v.* Thackwell, 7 Ves. 69; Attorney-General *v.* Skinners Company, 2 Russ 407. See Ld. Chan. Sugden's opinion to same effect, Incorporated Society *v.* Richards 1 Drury & W. Ch. 258.

[7] 1 Mylne & K. 376.

of the master of a grammar-school, and "five poor folks," according to the intent of Sir Anthony Brown, as expressed in his will. The Master of the Rolls, Sir John Leach, expresses himself very decidedly on the subject of that decree: "That at that time no *legal* devise could be made to a corporation for a charitable use, yet lands so devised were in equity bound by a trust, which a court of equity would then execute." It seems to be placed beyond question by the Readings of Sir Francis Moore, who penned the statute, and the few cases before the statute, contained in Duke on Charitable Uses,[1] not only that the Chancellor had the jurisdiction contended for, but exercised it upon the same principles, which have been incorrectly attributed to the act of Elizabeth. It would appear, too, from the preamble to the statute of Elizabeth, that the only object of it was not to give new validity to charitable donations, but rather to provide a new and more effectual remedy for breaches of those trusts;[2] and this view of the subject is confirmed by the reports of the early adjudications under the statute.[3] Indeed, the elements of the doctrine of the English Chancery, in relation to charitable uses, do not seem to have originated with the statute of Elizabeth, but are traceable to the civil law;[4] and in White *v.* White, Lord Thurlow expressly says, "the cases had proceeded on notions derived from the Roman or civil law."[5]

§ 181. In the case of Baptist Association *v.* Hart,[6] where it appeared that a bequest had been made to an unincorporated association, for the purpose of educating youth of the Baptist denomination, for the ministry, it was the opinion of the Supreme Court of the United States, as delivered by Mr. Chief Justice Marshall, that charitable bequests, *where no legal interest was vested*, and which are too vague to be claimed by those for whom the beneficial interest was intended, cannot be established by a Court of Equity, exercising its ordinary jurisdiction, inde-

---

[1] Duke on Charitable Uses, 141, 154, 155, 163; Case of Sir Anthony Brown's Will, found in Attorney-General *v.* The Master of Brentford School, 1 Mylne & K. 376.

[2] 2 Kent, Com. 288; McCartee *v.* Orphan Asylum Society, 9 Cowen, 477, per Jones, Ch.

[3] Griffith Flood's Case, Hob. 136; see, however, 1 Chan. Cas. 134, 237; 6 Dow, 136.

[4] Code, lib. 1, t. 2, §§ 19, 26, tit. 3, § 38; Dig. 38, 2, 16; Strahan's note to Domat, b. 1, tit. 1, § 16; Swinburne, part 6, § 1; 2 Domat, b. 3, tit. 1, § 6; b. 4, tit. 2, §§ 2, 6; b. 3, tit. 1, § 16; 2 Kent, Com. 287.

[5] 1 Bro. Ch. Cas. 15.

[6] 4 Wheat. 1; s. c. 1 Hen. & M. 471 to 476.

pendent of the statute of Elizabeth. Mr. Justice Story, in a very learned and elaborate opinion in this case, subsequently published, after a very full and critical investigation of all the authorities bearing upon the point, came to the conclusion, "that the jurisdiction of the Court of Chancery over charities, *where no trust is interposed, or there is no person in esse capable of taking, or where the charity is of an indefinite nature,* is not to be referred to the general jurisdiction of that court, but sprung up after the statute of Elizabeth, and rests mainly on its provisions."[1] The Supreme Court of Connecticut decided, that a devise of a farm to the "yearly meeting of people called Quakers, in aid of the charitable fund of the boarding-school established by the Friends in Providence," which was not incorporated, could not be sustained as a charity.[2] The two last quoted cases do not, it is true, bear directly upon the question we are considering; as they seem to have been decided upon the special ground that as the objects of the testator's bounty, not being incorporated, were incapable of taking, and the words of the gifts were *in presenti, and no trusts interposed to save them,* in common-law phrase, they must fall to the ground.[3] The high authority, which the learning of the Supreme Court of the United States gave to their opinion, has thrown a doubt over the subject of equity jurisdiction in case of charitable uses, without the aid of the statute of Elizabeth, which, in a matter so interesting to the benevolence of the country, cannot but be lamented. In a subsequent case of great importance,[4] the court seems to have receded, in fact, from the ground taken in the case alluded to; and upon that account the decree was not concurred in by the venerable Chief Justice and Mr. Justice Story. Later decisions[5] by the same court seem to have been thought to give evidence of a still further recession;[6] though they are clearly defensible upon the familiar principle of dedications of lands to public uses, always supported, even though made without deed, where the intent to dedicate is clearly manifested by the owner, especially if others, upon the faith of the dedica-

---

[1] 3 Pet. Appendix, 481.

[2] Greene *v.* Dennis, 6 Conn. 292.

[3] Com. Dig. Devise K; 1 Roll. Abr. 909; Com. Dig. Chancery, 2, N. 1; Widmore *v.* Woodroffe, Ambl. 636, 640.

[4] Inglis *v.* Sailors Snug Harbor, 3 Pet. 153.

[5] Beatty *v.* Kurtz, 2 Pet. 566; City of Cincinnati *v.* White, 6 Pet. 631; Barclay *v.* Howell, 6 Pet. 498; New Orleans *v.* United States, 10 Pet. 498; and see M'Conne *v.* Trustees of Lexington, 12 Wheat. 582.

[6] Burr *v.* Smith, 7 Vt. 302, 303, 304, Williams, Ch.

tion, have been led to act in a manner prejudicial to them, if a resumption of the grant were permitted. Strong dissatisfaction with the decision in Baptist Association *v.* Hart,[1] upon the grounds taken by the court, seems to have been manifested by jurists and courts in this country. In a case of great importance, the question came directly before the Supreme Court of Vermont, in Chancery; and after several arguments, and great research on the part of both court and counsel, it was decided, that Courts of Chancery had jurisdiction of bequests to charitable uses, before the statute of Elizabeth, by virtue of their ordinary equity jurisdiction; that the law now established in relation to donations to charitable uses, is not derived from that statute, but existed anterior; and that such donations to an unincorporated society — as, to the Treasurer, for the time being, of the American Bible Society, will, by general law, be upheld.[2]

§ 182. Chancellor Walworth asserts "that it is generally admitted that the decision, in Baptist Association *v.* Hart, is wrong; and that it may now be considered as an established principle of American Law, that a Court of Chancery will sustain and protect such a gift, bequest, or dedication of property to public or charitable uses, provided the same is consistent with local laws and public policy; where the object of the gift or dedication is specific, and capable of being carried into effect, according to the intention of the donor."[3] In McCartee *v.* The Orphan Asylum Society,[4] Chancellor Jones, waiving the questions, whether a Court of

---

[1] 4 Wheat. 1.

[2] Burr *v.* Smith, 7 Vt. 241, where the reader will find in the arguments of counsel and the opinion of Williams, Chancellor, a very learned and laborious discussion of all the cases and considerations bearing upon the point. See also, Coggeshall *v.* Pelton, 7 Johns. Ch. 292; 2 Kent, Com. 287; Inglis *v.* Trustees of Sailors Snug Harbor, 3 Pet. 153; Griffin *v.* Graham, 1 Hawks, 96; Witman *v.* Lex, 17 S. & R. 88; Mayor and Corporation of Philadelphia *v.* Elliott, 3 Rawle, 170; Going *v.* Emery, 16 Pick. 107; Milton *v.* First Parish in Milton, 10 Pick. 447; Rice *v.* Osgood, 9 Mass. 38; Hadley *v.* Hopkins Academy, 14 Pick. 253; Sanderson *v.* White, 18 Pick. 333; Stone *v.* Griffin, 3 Vt. 400; Lockport *v.* Weed, 2 Conn. 287; Shapleigh *v.* Pilsbury, 1 Greenl. 271; Baptist Church *v.* Witherell, 3 Paige, Ch. 296; Wright *v.* Trustees of Meth. Episcopal Church, 1 Hoffm. Ch. 202; Shotwell *v.* Mott, 2 Sandf. Ch. 45; Hornbeck *v.* The American Bible Society, id. 133.

[3] Potter *v.* Chapin, 6 Paige, 649; and see Dutch Church in Garden Street *v.* Mott, 7 Paige, 77; and Moore *v.* Moore, 4 Dana, 357, in which case the equity jurisdiction over charitable bequests and trusts was ably discussed by Robertson, C. J., in delivering the opinion of the court.

[4] 9 Cowen, 437. And see Wright *v.* Trustees of Meth. Episc. Ch., 1 Hoffm. Ch. 202; Kinskern *v.* The Lutheran Churches, 1 Sandf. Ch. 439.

Chancery, independent of the statute of Elizabeth, would support a devise to charitable uses, where no legal interest was vested, on account of the too vague description of those who were to take, and whether an information in the name of the attorney-general of the State would be necessary in such case, if the devise could be supported, as was intimated by the Supreme Court of the United States,[1] decided, that a Court of Chancery, may, independently of the statute of Elizabeth, support a devise to trustees for the use of a charitable corporation, notwithstanding an exception of bodies politic and corporate as competent devisees, in the statute of wills. In the opinion of the Chancellor, delivered in this case, a very full view and elaborate discussion was had of all the cases bearing upon the point; and the power of Chancery over charitable donations, abstracted from the statute of Elizabeth, was very learnedly and critically considered. The decree, as we before stated, was afterwards reversed in the Court of Errors, but the reversal proceeded upon the ground, that the devise was made *directly* to the corporation, and not to trustees for its benefit.

§ 183. The recent publications of the Commissioners on the Public Records in England, establish in the most satisfactory and conclusive manner, that cases of charities, where there were trustees appointed for general and indefinite charities, as well as for specific charities, were familiarly known to and acted upon and enforced in Chancery, long before the statute of 43 Elizabeth. In some of these cases the charities were not only of an uncertain and indefinite nature, but as far as we can gather from the imperfect statement in the printed records, they were also cases, where either no trustees were appointed, or the trustees were not competent to take.[2] Accordingly, in the important case of Vidal *v.* Mayor, &c. of Philadelphia,[3] the Supreme Court of the United States reviewed their opinion in Baptist Association *v.* Hart, and admitted that whatever doubts were in that opinion expressed upon the subject, had been entirely removed by the latter and more satisfactory sources of information above alluded to. It may therefore be considered as settled that Chancery has an original and necessary jurisdiction in respect to bequests and devises in trust to persons competent to take for charitable

---

[1] Baptist Association *v.* Hart, 4 Wheat. 50; 3 Pet. Appendix, 498, opinion of Story, J.

[2] Per Story, J., Vidal *v.* Mayor, &c., Philadelphia, 2 How. 128.

[3] Ibid.; and the very learned and able argument of Mr. Binney, of counsel for the city of Philadelphia.

purposes, when the general object of the charity is specific and certain, and not contrary to any positive rule of law.[1] The object of such a trust, however, must, to be supported at common law, be definite and certain; and therefore, a bequest in Virginia, in which State the statute of 43 Eliz., concerning charitable uses, has been repealed, "to some disposition thereof which my executors may consider as promising most to benefit the town and trade of Alexandria," was recently decided by the Supreme Court of the United States, following the course of decisions in Virginia, to be void.[2]

§ 184. A devise to a corporation, *to be created* by the legislature, is held good as an executory devise, a distinction being taken between a devise *in presenti* to persons incapable, and a devise *in futuro* to an artificial being, to be created and enabled to take.[3]

§ 185. In instruments granting, devising, or bequeathing lands and other property to corporations, and in grants by them, a misnomer of the corporation does not vitiate, provided the identity of the corporation with that intended by the parties to the instrument is apparent.[4] A corporation aggregate cannot hold lands in joint-tenancy with a natural person, because, as the corporation never dies, the natural person would be subject to, without being able to take advantage of, the incident of

---

[1] 2 Kent, Com. 287, 288, 4th ed.; and see Gibson *v.* McCall, 1 Rich. 174; Attorney-General *v.* Jolly, id. 176, n.; Sohier *v.* Wardens and Vestry of St. Paul's Church, 12 Met. 250; Beall *v.* Fox, 4 Ga. 404; Miller *v.* Chittenden, 2 Iowa, 315; Williams *v.* Williams, 4 Seld. 525.

[2] Wheeler *v.* Smith, 9 How. 55; and see, to same effect, Wade *v.* American Colonization Society, 7 Smedes & M. 663; Green *v.* Allen, 5 Humph. 170; Fontain *v.* Ravenel, 17 How. 369.

[3] Porter's case, 1 Co. R. 24; Case of Sutton's Hospital, 10 Co. 32; Attorney-General *v.* Bowyer, 3 Ves. 714; Inglis *v.* Sailors Snug Harbor, 3 Pet. 115 to 120, 144; McGirr *v.* Aaron, 1 Penn. 49; Sanderson *v.* White, 18 Pick. 356, 357; Miller *v.* Chittenden, *supra.* It is not within the range of our subject, to treat particularly of the effect of the statute of Elizabeth upon grants and devises to individuals and corporations for charitable uses; but we would refer the inquirer to Duke's valuable treatise on this subject, to 2 Fonbl. Eq. 209 to 226, and notes, and to 4 Wheat. Appendix, 3 to 23, where the principles and decisions under the statute of Elizabeth are very faithfully brought together by the learned reporter.

[4] See Chap. VIII. and cases, Chancellor, &c. of Oxford, 10 Co. R. 59; Cowden *v.* Clerk, Hob. 32; Owen, 35; Foster *v.* Walter, Cro. E. 106; First Parish in Sutton *v.* Cole, 3 Pick. 236; Vansant *v.* Roberts, 3 Md. Ch. Dec. 119; Kentucky Seminary *v.* Wallace, 15 B. Mon. 35; N. Y. Annual Conference M. M. A. Soc. *v.* Clarkson, 4 Halst. Ch. 541. See also, as to *name* of corporation, Ch. III.

survivorship; nor with another corporation, since both are perpetual, or one or both of fixed limited duration. A corporation may, however, hold lands in common with a natural person, survivorship not being an incident to lands so holden.[1] The American Colonization Society was by its charter authorized to receive property by bequest or otherwise, and to use and dispose of it at its discretion, "for the purpose of colonizing, with their own consent, in Africa, the *free people of color*, residing in the United States, and for no other purpose whatever." A person bequeathed to the society all of his "*slaves*," for the purpose of sending them to Liberia in Africa. It was held that under the charter of the company, the Society could not take the slaves.[2]

§ 186. There is a *dictum* of Mr. Chief Justice Parsons, "that a corporation cannot acquire a freehold by a disseisin committed by itself." [3] No authority is cited by the learned judge; but from some very early cases, we should infer that, as a general doctrine, this could never have been true. Thus, it is laid down,[4] that a corporation cannot be aiding to a trespass, nor give a warrant to do a trespass, without writing; and it appears from the case cited,[5] that a corporation cannot give a command to enter into land, without deed, nor do any thing which vests or devests a freehold, *nor accept a disseisin made to their use, without deed.* It is said, too, by Fitzjames, Justice,[6] that *a corporation cannot do a tort but by their writing under their seal;* which imports that *by their writing* they may. *Quare impedit* lies against the corporation, though the hinderance is an act of tort.[7] The statute 9 Hen. IV. c. 5, recites the practice in assizes of novel "disseisin and other pleas of land, of naming the mayor and bailiffs and commonalty of a franchise as disseisors, in order to oust them of holding plea thereof; and directs the inquiry before the judges of assize, whether they be disseisors or tenants, or named by fraud," which plainly proves

---

1 Pl. Com. 239; 2 Lev. 12; 2 Bl. Com. 184; 1 Kyd on Corp. 72; Telfair *v.* Howe, 3 Rich. Eq. 235.

2 American Colonization Society *v.* Gartrell, 23 Ga. 448. See also, Lusk *v.* Lewis, 32 Missis. 297.

3 Weston *v.* Hunt, 2 Mass. 502.

4 Bro. Corporations, pl. 48.

5 4 H. 7, 9; 4 H. 7, 16.

6 14 H. 8, 2, 29; Bro. Corporations, pl. 34.

7 Butler *v.* Bishop of Hereford, and the University of Cambridge, Barnes, C. P. 350; and see Rast. 497; Ast. 378; 2 Mod. Ent. 291; Winch. 625; 700, 721, 733; 2 Lut. 1109; 3 Lev. 332.

that they may be considered as disseisors. Brooke also puts the case, "if the mayor and commonalty disseise me, and I release to twenty, or two hundred of the commonalty, this will not serve the mayor and commonalty;" and the reason is, because the disseisin is in their *corporate* character, and the release is to the individuals.[1] Indeed, no principle with regard to corporations, seems to have been earlier or more fully established, than that they might acquire a freehold by disseisin; though, in conformity with the strictness of the old law in relation to them, it was also considered, that if a disseisin be made to their use, they could not agree to, or accept it, without deed, or, in other words, without writing under their common seal.[2] From the ancient decisions with regard to the corporations of the common law, it would seem that the prevalent opinion was, that they could authorize no agent, do no act, give no assent, except in matters of the most trifling importance, but by deed. This notion, even with regard to the old corporations, and in England, has been greatly relaxed; and in regard to the corporations of modern times created by statute, has, in our own country at least, never been entertained. We have endeavored elsewhere fully to discuss this subject, and would refer the reader to the authorities there collected.[3] From the current of modern decisions, there can be no doubt that a corporation, equally with an individual, may gain a freehold by a disseisin committed by its agent whether authorized by deed or vote, — and that the authority of the agent, and the acceptance of his act by the corporation, may be proved by the acts and conduct of the corporation, whether manifested by it collectively, or through its officers, agents, tenants, &c.[4] In Magill *v.* Kauffman, which was an ejectment for land claimed by a Presbyterian congregation, before incorporation, under a purchase by their trustees, and after incorporation claimed in their right as a corporation, the Supreme Court of Pennsylvania held, that evidence of the acts and declarations of the trustees and agents of the corporation, both before and after the incorporation, while transacting the business of the corporation, and also evidence by witnesses of what passed at the meetings of the congregation when assembled on business, were admissible to show their possession of the land, and the extent of their

---

1 Bro. Corporations, pl. 24; and see 44 Edw. 2; 2 pl. 5; 8 H. 6, 1, 14; 4 H. 7, 13; 14 H. 8, 2; Yarborough *v.* Bank of England, 16 East, 8, 9, per Ellenborough, C. J.

2 Yarborough *v.* Bank of England, 16 East, 8, 9; 1 Kyd on Corp. 263, 264.

3 See Chap. VIII. and Chap. IX.

4 Ibid.

claim of its boundaries.[1] And where an act of the legislature authorized the trustees of a corporation to take possession of land, and the trustees accordingly entered upon it and disseised the owner, the authority thus derived was deemed equivalent to an authority from the corporation under its common seal.[2] The Supreme Court of Massachusetts fully recognize the doctrine, that a corporation may acquire a title to land by disseisin and exclusive adverse possession, although such disseisin was not authorized by deed; and in this respect is bound by, and entitled to, the same implications from its corporate acts, as an individual.[3]

§ 187. Corporations aggregate have at common law an incidental right to aliene or dispose of their lands and chattels, unless specially restrained by their charters or by statute.[4] Independent of positive law, all corporations have the absolute *jus disponendi* neither limited as to objects, nor circumscribed as to quantity.[5] The circumstance that the State holds some of the stock of the corporation, does not at all affect the right of alienating its property; the stock of the State being as much subject to the exercise of this right as the stock of an individual.[6] In England, this common-law right of disposition has been greatly restrained, on the part of religious corporations, by numerous statutes from the statute of Westminster the second, 13 Ed. I. ch. 41, to 5 Geo. III. ch. 17; and particularly by several statutes passed in the reign of Elizabeth.[7] These disabling statutes have not, we believe, been reënacted in this country; though Kent informs us, that "the better opinion upon the construction of the statute of New York, *for the incorporation of religious societies*,[8] is that no religious corporation can sell any real

---

1 4 S. & R. 317; and see Wood *v.* Tate, 5 B. & P. 246; Doe *v.* Woodman, 8 East, 228; Bank of the United States *v.* Dandridge, 12 Wheat. 64; Opinion of Story, J., Harpending *v.* Dutch Church, 16 Pet. 455.

2 Second Precinct in Rehoboth *v.* Carpenter, 23 Pick. 131; Same *v.* Catholic Congregational Church and Society in Rehoboth, 23 Pick. 139; Milton *v.* First Parish in Milton, 10 Pick. 447.

3 Ibid. Lakin *v.* Ames, 10 Cush. 198.

4 Co. Lit. 44 a, 300 b; 1 Sid. 161, note at the end of the case. The case of Sutton's Hospital, 10 Co. 30 b; 1 Kyd on Corp. 108; Com. Dig. tit. Franchise F. 11, 18; 2 Kent, Com. 280.

5 2 Kent, Com. 280; The Mayor and Commonalty of Colchester *v.* Lowten, 1 Ves. & B. 226, 237, 240, 244; Binney's case, 2 Bland, Ch. 142.

6 Binney's case, 2 Bland, Ch. 142.

7 1 Kyd on Corp. 116 to 162; 2 Kent, Com. 280, 281.

8 1 Laws of N. Y. vol. 2, 212; 3 Rev. Stat. N. Y. 298.

estate without the Chancellor's order."[1] It would seem, however, that this statute applies only to *absolute* sales; and that the Chancellor's order is not necessary to warrant the sale of *pews* in a church, in which the interest granted is merely limited and usufructuary.[2]

§ 188. A restraint upon the right of a corporation to alienate its property may be derived from the form of the instrument of alienation prescribed by its charter or by-law. And where a railway company were empowered to borrow money upon mortgage of their property, and the form of the instrument was given by which the company were to charge and assign "*the said undertaking, and all and singular the said rates, tolls, and other sums arising,*" *&c.* and by the act the mortgagees were to be entitled, one with another, to their proportions of the rates, and tolls, sums, and premises, according to the sums advanced, without preference by reason of priority of date of mortgage, and were not to be deemed shareholders by reason of their mortgages, a mortgage executed in the form prescribed was held not to convey a title to the land of the corporation, so that ejectment could be maintained, and possession of the property had. By such possession, it was said, the mortgagees might put an end to the undertaking, since the tolls would cease, the corporation alone having power to levy them.[3] But where the instrument prescribed by way of mortgage to secure a loan, imports on its face a covenant for repayment — and the corporation has power to borrow money and to sue and be sued, they may bind themselves by a covenant to repay the loan in such form that an action may be maintained thereon.[4] If the act incorporating a coal company require the assent of three fourths of the stockholders to make a mortgage, a mortgage executed without such an assent will be void, and a judgment, binding the land confessed to secure a debt, is an incumbrance, requiring such assent within the provisions of the charter.[5] A purchaser of

---

[1] 2 Kent, Com. 281. Since the adoption of the constitution of 1846, however, application for leave to sell must be made to the Supreme Court, or (N. Y. Code, § 33), to the County Court. Wyatt *v.* Benson, 23 Barb. 327.

[2] Freligh *v.* Platt, 5 Cowen, 494. A corporation, purchasing lands, may execute a mortgage for the purchase-money without the Chancellor's order. South Baptist Soc. &c. *v.* Clapp, 18 Barb. 35.

[3] Myatt *v.* St. Helen's Railway Co. 2 Q. B. 364; see, however, *ante*, §§ 190, 191.

[4] Hart *v.* Eastern Union Railway Co. 7 Exch. 246, 8 Eng. L. & Eq. 544; s. c. in error, 8 Exch. 116, 14 Eng. L. & Eq. 535.

[5] The Cape Sable Company's Case, 3 Bland, 166.

lands from an incorporated company is chargeable with notice of all the restrictions upon its power to hold and convey lands, contained in its charter.[1]

§ 189. Sometimes the charter of a corporation provides as to the *place* where it shall dispose of some kinds of property which it is permitted to acquire, and in such case a sale in any other place would in general be invalid. A charter of a fire insurance and loan company, gave the company power to take mortgages, but provided that all sales in virtue of them should be made in the county where the property was situated; yet a decree of foreclosure describing the property as situated in one county and directing a sale there, whereas it was in fact situated in another county, was not allowed to be impeached collaterally; and a title acquired under a sale in pursuance of it, was held good; such a clause, if applicable at all to a foreclosure by the Court of Chancery, being deemed merely directory to the court.[2]

§ 190. How far, under what circumstances, and upon what application a court of equity would restrain a corporation from an improper alienation of its property, must depend upon those general principles which guide it in the exercise of its powers; but there is little doubt that, in a proper case made, it would interfere to prevent a disposition of its property for other than corporate puposes.[3]

§ 191. A corporation authorized to dispose of its property may in general dispose of any interest in the same it may deem expedient, having the same power in this respect as an individual.[4] Thus it may lease, grant in fee, in tail, or for term of life,[5] mortgage,[6] and though

---

[1] Merritt *v.* Lambert, 1 Hoffm. Ch. 166.

[2] Fuller *v.* Van Geesen, 4 Hill, 171.

[3] Binney's case, 3 Bland, Ch. 142; Kean *v.* Johnson, 1 Stockt. 401.

[4] Reynolds *v.* Commissioners of Stark's County, 5 Ohio, 205.

[5] Co. Lit. 44 a, 300, 301, 325 b, 341 b, 342 a, 346 a, b; Plowd. 199; Dyer, 40, pl. 1, 97, pl. 45; Godbolt, 211; 1 Kyd on Corp. 108, 109, 110, 114, 115, 116.

[6] Jackson *v.* Brown, 5 Wend. 590; Gordon *v.* Preston, 1 Watts, 385; Collins *v.* Central Bank, 1 Kelly, 455; and see Allen *v.* Montgomery Railroad Co. 11 Ala. 437; and Mobile & Cedar Point Railroad Co. *v.* Talman, 15 Ala. 472; that a power given by charter to mortgage for a particular purpose, does not abridge the general power to mortgage for the security of creditors. At common law a mortgage of property not actually or potentially in the possession of the mortgagor would be void, even though it professed to convey property to be afterwards acquired. Jones *v.* Richardson, 10 Met. 488. In equity

insolvent, assign its property in trust for the payment of its debts,[1] defeating by preferences, where the law allows it, even the priority of the State,[2] and where there is no actual fraud, preferring, it would seem, the debts of its own stockholders.[3] The right of alienation or assignment is not affected by a provision in the charter, that the stockholders shall be individually liable for the corporate debts,[4] nor by the mere fact that the assignment was made pending a writ of *quo warranto*, against the corporation for the forfeiture of its charter,[5] or that the alienation was made just before the expiration of the charter of the corporation.[6] A

however, such mortgages have been sustained; Mitchell *v.* Winslow, 2 Story, 630, but not uniformly. Moody *v.* Wright, 13 Met. 17. Where however a corporation is authorized either by its charter or by a special act of the legislature, to sell or pledge its real and personal estate, and all rights, franchises, powers and privileges for any loans, liabilities or contracts which it has made or should make, after acquired property will pass. Phillips *v.* Winslow, 18 B. Mon. 431; Pierce *v.* Emery, 32 N. H. 484; Willink *v.* Morris Canal & Banking Co. 3 Green, Ch. 377; Farmers Loan & Trust Co. *v.* Hendrickson, 25 Barb. 484. See Howe *v.* Freeman, Sup. Jud. Ct. Mass. 1859, 23 Law Reporter, 461. In Pierce *v.* Emery, 32 N. H. 484, a mortgage made to trustees by a railroad corporation, in pursuance of an act of the legislature, to secure a loan, was held, on a proper construction of the act and of the deed, to convey to such trustees the whole road as an entirety, with all its rights and interests, and thereby to include as well subsequently acquired property as property belonging to the road at the date of the mortgage.

[1] State *v.* Bank of Maryland, 6 Gill & J. 205; Union Bank of Tennessee *v.* Elliott, 6 Gill & J. 363; Warner *v.* Mower, 11 Vt. 385; Pope *v.* Stewart, 2 Stewart, 401; Bank Commissioners *v.* Bank of Brest, Harring. Mich. Ch. 106; *Ex parte* Conway, 4 Pike, 302; Flint *v.* Clinton Company, 12 N. H. 430; Binney's case, 2 Bland, Ch. 142; Robins *v.* Embry, 1 Smedes & M. Ch. 207; Arthur *v.* Commercial & Railroad Bank of Vicksburgh, 9 Smedes & M. 394; Sargent *v.* Webster, 13 Met. 497; Catline *v.* Eagle Bank, 6 Conn. 233; Savings Bank *v.* Bates, 8 Conn. 512; Hopkins *v.* Gallatin Turnpike Co. 4 Humph. 403; Dana *v.* Bank of the United States, 5 Watts & S. 247; Lenox *v.* Roberts, 2 Wheat. 373; De Ruyter *v.* Trustees of St. Peter's Church, 3 Barb. Ch. 119, 3 Comst. 238; Town *v.* Bank of River Raisin, 2 Doug. Mich. 530; Hurlbut *v.* Carter, 21 Barb. 221. The power of assignment in contemplation of insolvency for payment of debts is taken away from certain corporations in New York by statute. 1 R. S. 695, 1st part, 18th chap. 4 tit. sec. 4. Under this statute, such assignments, though they distribute the property ratably amongst all the creditors of corporations, are wholly void. Harris *v.* Thompson, 15 Barb. 62. The 18th section of the act incorporating the N. Y. & Erie R. R. Co. is not to be construed as exempting the company from the provisions of this statute. Bowen *v.* Lease, 5 Hill, 221.

[2] State *v.* Bank of Maryland, 9 Gill & J. 205; Town *v.* Bank of River Raisin, 2 Doug. Mich. 530. And see *Ex parte* Conway, 4 Pike, 302. See, however, Opinion of Chan. Buckner, in Robins *v.* Embry, 1 Smedes & M. Ch. 258, 265.

[3] Whitwell *v.* Warner, 20 Vt. 444, 445.

[4] Pope *v.* Brandon, 2 Stew. 401.

[5] State *v.* Commercial Bank of Manchester, 13 Smedes & M. 569; The People *v.* Mauran, 5 Denio, 400, 401.

[6] Ibid.; Cooper *v.* Curtis, 30 Maine, 488.

conveyance by the trustees and stockholders of a corporation of the charter and capital stock, intending to enable the purchasers to carry on business under the act of incorporation, was holden to be a conveyance of the equitable interest in the real estate of the corporation, the corporation being the legal owner of the same.[1] It would seem to be no objection to the validity of an assignment of a railway corporation, that it transferred to assignees the power of managing and controlling the road; since the corporation may appoint any persons to be its agents, and is not necessarily limited to the directors or other officers of the corporation. The assignment cannot indeed convey the franchise, which is not in its nature assignable, but the receipts and profits may be transferred by it to assignees, who would manage the business of the corporation merely as its agents.[2] At all events, such an assignment cannot be called in question by a third person; but is wholly a matter between the directors and stockholders, and between the stockholders

---

[1] Wilde *v.* Jenkins, 4 Paige, 481.

[2] The power of a corporation to mortgage its franchise, and the right of the mortgagees to foreclose, have been much questioned, and the law on the subject cannot be said to be yet settled. The leading cases are Pierce *v.* Emery, 32 N. H. 486; Hall *v.* Sullivan R. Co., U. S. C. C., New Hamp. 1857, 21 Law Reporter, 138; Howe *v.* Freeman, Sup. Jud. Ct. Mass. 1859, 23 Law Reporter, 461; Shaw *v.* Norfolk County R. Co. 5 Gray, 162. In the first of these cases the mortgage was expressly authorized; in the second and third they were subsequently recognized by a statute; and in the fourth it was expressly confirmed. A distinction exists between the franchise of being a body politic, with rights of succession of members, and of acquiring, holding, and conveying property, and suing and being sued by a certain name, and the franchise of using the corporate property and enjoying the profits thereof. Thus Mr. Justice *Curtis*, in the case of Hall *v.* Sullivan R. Co. above mentioned, says, — speaking of the former description of franchise, "Such an artificial being, only the law can create, and when created it cannot transfer its own existence into another body, nor can it enable natural persons to act in its name, save as its agents, or as members of the corporation, acting in conformity with the modes required or allowed by its charter. The franchise to be a corporation is, therefore, not a subject of sale and transfer unless the law by some positive provision has made it so, and pointed out the modes in which such sale and transfer may be effected. But the franchise to build, own, and manage a railroad, and to take tolls thereon, are not necessarily corporate rights; they are capable of existing in and being enjoyed by natural persons, and there is nothing in their nature inconsistent with their being assignable. Whether when they have been granted to a corporation created for the purpose of holding and using them, they may legally be mortgaged by such corporation, in order to obtain means to carry out the purpose of its existence, must depend upon the terms in which they are granted, or in the absence of any thing special in the grant itself, upon the intention of the legislature, to be deduced from the general purposes it had in view, the means it intended to have employed to execute those purposes, and the course of legislation on the same or similar subjects; or, as it is sometimes compendiously expressed, upon the public policy of the State."

and the government.[1] If, however, the particular mode in which the affairs of a certain class of corporations shall be wound up, in case of insolvency, be prescribed by statute, an assignment made manifestly with a view to evade the provisions of the statute cannot be sustained.[2] And upon general principles, where the deed of assignment of a banking and railroad corporation showed upon its face an intention to postpone the creditors of the corporation, to use the effects of the bank for the completion of the railroad, pay the trustees enormous salaries, and make no dividend among the creditors of the bank until these objects were accomplished, it was held void, as fraudulent against creditors who had not become parties to it.[3] A mortgage on the real estate and works of a dock company, executed by the president of the corporation, under a vote of the directors, to secure a loan effected to complete their works, was held valid, though not expressly assented to by the stockholders; the objection in a bill to foreclose, coming not from them but from general creditors of the company.[4]

§ 192. As all or any of the property of a citizen may, upon just compensation made, be taken, and applied to the use of the public, so all property belonging to a corporation must in like manner be held liable to the same *eminent domain*, or peculiar power of the government. The only plausible ground upon which any portion of the territory of a State, or property within a State, could be claimed to be exempted from liability to be taken by virtue of this right of the government, would be, that it had been previously applied to some greater or equally beneficial public use.[5] Such an objection must yield when the power to take lands, thus

---

[1] Robins *v.* Embry, 1 Smedes & M. Ch. 268, 269, 270; Arthur *v.* Commercial & Railroad Bank of Vicksburgh, 9 Smedes & M. 394; De Ruyter *v.* St. Peter's Church, 3 Comst. 238; but see Myatt *v.* St. Helen's Railway Co. 2 Q. B. 364. The assignment by a railroad corporation of the right to use and control its road, will not exempt it from liability for the infraction by its assignees of a patent right respecting cars. Y. & Md. L. R. R. Co. *v.* Winans, 17 How. 30. As to the power of a majority of the stockholders of a corporation, whose affairs are in a prosperous condition, to sell out the whole source of their emolument and to invest the capital in another enterprise, in opposition to the wishes of the minority, see Kean *v.* Johnson, 1 Stockt. 401.

[2] Bank Commissioners *v.* Bank of Brest, Harring. Mich. Ch. 106, 112.

[3] Bodley *v.* Goodrich, 7 How. 277; Arthur *v.* Commercial & Railroad Bank of Vicksburgh, 9 Smedes & M. 394; Fellows *v.* Commercial & Railroad Bank of Vicksburgh, 6 Rob. La. 246.

[4] Enders *v.* Board of Public Works, 1 Gratt. 364.

[5] Canal Co. *v.* Railroad Co. 4 Gill & J. 1; Boston Water Power Co. *v.* Boston & Wor-

previously devoted to public use, is plainly given; because public uses are of different degrees of importance, and it is for the sovereign to say, which, as least important, must give way.[1] It applies, however, with full force where the power is not plainly given; and it cannot be implied from the authority conferred upon a railway company to take, by compulsory purchase, lands in general to make its line, that it has power thus to take lands which form a point of the actual line of another authorized railway. The defect of power in such case would be double, on the part of the one to buy, and of the other to sell, land thus devoted.[2] This ground cannot, however, apply in favor of a company chartered for the manufacture of gunpowder, who, under a clause in their charter enabling them to purchase and hold land not exceeding one thousand acres, and erect thereon all needful buildings, had purchased and erected, conformably to their charter, so as to prevent a railroad company, subsequently chartered, from locating their road over the land of the gunpowder company, and removing one of their buildings; since the land, &c. is held as private property by its incorporated owners, and the tenure by which it is held forming no part of the essence of their act of incorporation.[3]

§ 193. In general, corporations must take and convey their lands and other property, in the same manner as individuals; the laws relating to the transfer of property being equally applicable to both. In all statutes of this character, corporations, unless excepted, are included in the word "persons," and as such may transfer or *enter* lands.[4] As we shall consider in the next chapter but one[5] the kinds of deeds by which they may convey their lands, and how they are executed, we refer the reader thither for these heads. It is, however, perfectly competent to the legislative power, to confer upon corporations the privilege of taking and conveying lands or other property, in such manner as may be thought most expedient;[6] and a class of corporations, or *quasi* cor-

---

cester Railroad Corp. 16 Pick. 512. See Piscataqua Bridge *v.* N. H. Bridge, 7 N. H. 35; Barber *v.* Andover, 8 id. 398; Pierce *v.* Somersworth, 10 id. 369; Backus *v.* Lebanon, 11 id. 20; Canal Trustees *v.* City of Chicago, 12 Ill. 403.

[1] Same authorities.

[2] Ibid., and Regina *v.* South Wales Railway Co., 14 Q. B. 902.

[3] The Bellona Co.'s case, 3 Bland, Ch. 442, 446, 447, 448, 449.

[4] State *v.* Nashville University, 4 Humph. 157.

[5] Chap. VII.

[6] See Ross *v.* State Bank, 3 Strobh. Eq. 245, in which it appears that a special clause in the charter of the State Bank of South Carolina made mortgages, given to it to secure certain debts, stand recorded from their date.

porations, has grown up in New England out of the circumstances attending the settlement of the country, called Proprietors of common and undivided lands, which had, and in early times ordinarily exercised, the power of dividing amongst their members, and conveying to others their lands by *vote*. As these corporations are somewhat peculiar, and as through them this portion of the country was chiefly divided and settled, and upon their proceedings almost all our land titles ultimately rest, it may not be inappropriate for us to bring their origin, organization, and the legal effect in their doings into one view instead of scattering our remarks upon them through the whole volume. We have, therefore, made them the subject of a separate chapter, to which we would refer the reader.[1]

§ 194. If any portion of the members of a corporation secede, and are even erected into a new corporation, the corporate property will not be transferred or distributed in consequence of the separation, but will remain with the old corporation, unless indeed there be an agreement made for the partition of it.[2] And if a religious society purchase lands, a majority of them have a right to control their use and occupation, notwithstanding any supposed error in doctrine shown to be a departure from the belief of the majority at the time of the purchase.[3]

§ 195. At common law, upon the dissolution, or civil death of a corporation, all its real estate remaining unsold, reverts back to the original grantor or his heirs;[4] for, says Coke, " in case of a body politique

---

[1] Chap. VI.

[2] Dartmouth College *v.* Woodward, 4 Wheat. 518; Brown *v.* Porter, 10 Mass. 93; Baker *v.* Fales, 16 Mass. 488; North Hempstead *v.* Hempstead, 2 Wend. 135, per Savage, Ch. J.; and see The Inh. of Harrison *v.* The Inh. of Bridgeton, 16 Mass. 16; The Inh. of County of Hampshire *v.* The Inh. of County of Franklin, 16 Mass. 76; Presbyterian Church *v.* Dannon, 1 Dessaus. Ch. 154; Smith *v.* Smith, 3 Dessaus. Ch. 557; Harmon *v.* Dreher, 1 Speers, Eq. 87; Associate Reformed Church *v.* Theological Seminary of Princeton, 3 Green, N. J. Ch. 77; Gable *v.* Miller, 10 Paige, 627; Cammayer *v.* United German Lutheran Churches, 2 Sandf. Ch. 186; Smith *v.* Swormstedt, 16 How. 288.

[3] Keyser *v.* Stanisfer, 6 Ohio, 363. See Miller *v.* Gable, 2 Denio, 492; that courts will interpose to prevent the diversion of funds *appropriated* to promote the teaching of particular religious doctrines, notwithstanding such diversion is sanctioned by a majority of the church or congregation. See also, People *v.* Steele, 2 Barb. 397; Kinskern *v.* The Lutheran Churches, 1 Sandf. Ch. 439.

[4] Co. Lit. 13 b; Edmunds *v.* Brown, 1 Lev. 237; Pollexfen, Arg. Quo. War. 112; Attorney-General *v.* Ld. Gower, 9 Mod. 226; Colchester *v.* Seaber, 3 Burr. 1868, Arg.; Rex *v.* Passmore, 3 T. R. 199; 1 Bl. Com. 484; 2 Kyd on Corp. 516; Hooker *v.*

or incorporate, the fee-simple is vested in their politique or incorporate capacity created by the policy of man, and therefore the law doth annex the condition in law to every such gift or grant, that if such body politique or incorporate be dissolved, that the donor or grantor shall reënter, for that the cause of the gift or grant faileth."[1] The grant is indeed only during the life of the corporation, which may endure forever; but when the life is determined by the dissolution of the body politic, the grantor takes it back by reversion, as in the case of any other grant for life.[2] This rule by its terms applies only to such estate as remains in the corporation at the moment of its dissolution, and not to such as by the act of the corporation or the act of law has been previously alienated;[3] and where a railroad company had an estate, and not a mere easement in land condemned to the uses of their road, and their road was in part sold upon execution, to satisfy a debt, it was held that the purchaser under the execution, taking the interest in the land which the company had at the time of the sale, would not be divested of his title by the dissolution of the corporation, but would hold the same until by lapse of time the charter of the corporation had expired and the term had been completed for which the land had been taken for the use of the road.[4] A grant in fee to a corporation, created for a term of years, will not be construed to convey the property for the term of years only. The corporation in such case would have a fee-simple for the purposes of alienation, but a determinable fee only for the purposes of enjoyment.[5] In case of dissolution the personal property of a corporation, in England, vests in the king,[6] and in this country in the people, as succeeding to his right and prerogative,[7] and the debts due to and from the corporation are extinguished.[8] Every creditor of a corporation con-

---

Utica Turnp. Company, 12 Wend. 371; State Bank *v.* State, 1 Blackf. 277; 2 Kent, Com. 307; Folger *v.* Chase, 18 Pick. 66; Fox *v.* Horah, 1 Ired. Eq. 358; Commercial Bank *v.* Lockwood, 2 Harring. Del. 8.

1 Co. Lit. 13 B.

2 Bl. Com. 484.

3 State *v.* Rives, 5 Ired. 305, 309; Nicoll *v.* N. Y. & Erie Railroad Co. 12 Barb. 460; and see Fish *v.* Potter, 4 Halst. Ch. 277, 292, 293.

4 Ibid.

5 Nicoll *v.* N. Y. & Erie Railroad Co. 12 Barb. 460, 2 Kern. 121.

6 Authorities above.

7 2 Kent, Com. 307, and see above.

8 Ibid.; McLaren *v.* Pennington, 1 Paige, 111; Bank of Mississippi *v.* Wrenn, 3 Smedes & M. 791. It is held in Missouri that legal proceedings regularly commenced against a corporation are not affected by the expiration of the charter before the determi-

tracts with reference to this contingency, and the existence of a private contract cannot force a perpetual existence upon such a body, contrary to public policy.[1] If a corporation become extinct by expiration of its charter, or by decree of forfeiture pending a suit at law for a corporate demand, and that fact be brought regularly before the court, the action must terminate;[2] and an attachment made in such suit is of course dissolved, and if even after judgment in favor of the corporation the corporation become extinct, no execution can issue regularly in the name of the corporation, and if one be sued out, it may be quashed on showing that the corporation had become extinct before it was sued out.[3] The necessary intendment from a judgment in favor of a corporation is, that it was proved or admitted that the corporation was in existence at the time of judgment; and if execution be sued out, the defendant in execution will be estopped from proving that the charter had expired previous to the judgment.[4] Where, however, a corporation had assigned its rights during its existence, so that the controversy was pending on appeal, when the charter expired, in the name of the corporation for the benefit of the assignees, the court permitted the cause to proceed in the name of the corporation without noticing on the record its dissolution.[5] But if a note was made payable to the cashier of a bank, by which it was discounted as trustee for the bank, and the bank charter afterwards expired, though the cashier might sue and recover at law, yet as the bank had the sole right to the money when collected, and the right was extinguished by the dissolution of the corporation, a court of equity would, it seems, enjoin perpetually against the collection of the judgment.[6] A merger, by act of the legislature, of the rights of an old corporation in a new one, is not such a dissolution of a corporation, as that the real estate of the old corporation reverts to

---

nation of such proceedings. Lindell *v.* Benton, 6 Misso. 365, 366. But see Read *v.* Frankfort Bank, 24 Maine, 318; Farmers & Mechanics Bank *v.* Little, 7 Watts & S. 207. Also, Moultrie *v.* Smiley, 16 Ga. 289.

[1] Authorities above, and Mumma *v.* Potomac Co. 8 Pet. 281. But at the petition of creditors and stockholders, equity may relieve against the inequitable consequences of a dissolution. Bacon *v.* Robertson, 18 How. 480.

[2] May *v.* State Bank of North Carolina, 2 Rob. Va. 56; and see Farmers & Mechanics Bank *v.* Little, 7 Watts & S. 207. *Contra,* Lindell *v.* Benton, 6 Misso. 365, 366; N. Y. Marbled Iron Works *v.* Smith, 4 Duer, 362.

[3] May *v.* State Bank of North Carolina, 2 Rob. Va. 56.

[4] Ibid.

[5] Bank of Alexandria *v.* Patton, 1 Rob. Va. 499.

[6] Fox *v.* Horah, 1 Ired. Eq. 358.

the grantees.[1] After dissolution, a corporation has a prolongation of its existence in the nature of an administration of its estate. All rights under the defunct corporation are fixed at its dissolution; but it has a nominal existence for the purpose of closing its concerns in the most convenient manner, and especially of compelling it to execute its contracts and discharge its obligations and liabilities.[2]

§ 196. The consequences of dissolution upon the property of a corporation are usually averted by some provision in the charter, or by statutes general or special;[3] but an act of the legislature renewing a charter, passed after the corporation has been dissolved by expiration of its charter term of existence, will not revive its debts.[4] When the legislature proceeds under a general statute to wind up the concerns of a bank, those provisions, calculated to apprise all interested of the fundamental changes going on in the institution, must be complied with, in order to give legal efficacy to the acts done under such a statute; and if they are not complied with, the corporation will not be divested of its property, and the existence of its charter will not be thereby terminated.[5] The winding up act of Massachusetts of 1852, has been held not to take away the common-law right of a corporation to sell its property and close its business, the statute being permissive in its terms, and not restrictive.[6] That clause of the Constitution of Indiana, which provides "that no man's property shall be taken for public use without the consent of his representatives," does not prohibit a judgment of seizure of corporate franchises in *quo warranto*, nor prevent the common-law consequences, upon such a dissolution of a corporation, as to its property.[7]

---

1 Union Canal Co. *v.* Young, 1 Whart. 410; Bellows *v.* Hallowell & Augusta Bank, 2 Mason, 31; State Bank of Indiana *v.* State, 1 Blackf. 273.

2 Crease *v.* Babcock, 23 Pick. 334, 346.

3 2 Kent, Com. 307, 308; McLaren *v.* Pennington, 1 Paige, 111. Stat. Mass. 1819, ch. 43, which entitles all corporations of that State to three years from the day of their dissolution to wind up their affairs and divide their stock. Under this statute, it was held that a bank was authorized, just before the expiration of the three years, to indorse a note to trustees appointed to wind up the affairs of the bank. Folger *v.* Chase, 18 Pick. 66.

4 Comm. Bank *v.* Lockwood, 2 Harring. Del. 8. Foster *v.* Essex Bank, 16 Mass. 245.

5 Farmers Bank of Delaware *v.* Beaston, 7 Gill & J. 422.

6 Treadwell *v.* Salisbury Manuf. Co. 7 Gray, 393.

7 State Bank of Indiana *v.* State, 1 Blackf. 278.

CHAPTER VI.

OF PROPRIETORS OF COMMON AND UNDIVIDED LANDS.

§ 197. When our ancestors first came to America, it was usual in some of the New England States, for the legislatures to grant a township of land to a certain number of proprietors, as grantees in fee, to hold as tenants in common; and a great proportion of the lands of Massachusetts and Plymouth colonies were originally granted by the colonial legislatures in this way.[1] Much larger tracts in Massachusetts under grants from the Council at Plymouth, in England, from the General Courts of the colonies of Massachusetts and Plymouth, and from the Indians, were claimed by proprietors; the Kennebeck proprietors claiming about three millions of acres; the Pejepscot proprietors about as many more; the Waldo proprietors about a million of acres; the Pemaquid proprietors about ninety thousand acres; and upon settlement of rights and boundaries with the State, these proprietors retained nearly one half of what they thus claimed and held.[2] Other large tracts were also held and claimed under Indian titles recognized by the legislatures.[3] In Rhode Island, which was originally settled by persons persecuted from other colonies, and who had at first no charter of government, the proprietors acquired their lands wholly by purchases from the Indians, subsequently confirmed by the General Assembly organized under the charter of Charles II.[4] Thus, in almost every town in New England,

---

[1] 2 Dane, Abr. 698.

[2] 4 Dane, Abr. 70; Sullivan on Land Titles, 39, 40, 44 to 48.

[3] Sullivan on Land Titles, 40 to 46. The letter of Governor Winslow, of the Plymouth Colony, of the 1st of May, 1676, states, that before King Philip's war, the English did not possess one foot of Land in that colony, but what was fairly obtained, by honest purchase, from the Indian proprietors, with the knowledge and allowance of the General Court. Hazard's Collection of State Papers, vol. 2, p. 531 to 534; Holmes's Annals, vol. 1, p. 383; 3 Kent, Com. 391.

[4] See Preamble and Act of 1682; R. Island Laws, Dig. 1730, p. 30, 31. In speaking of Rhode Island, in this connection, we exclude those portions of the State over which the Massachusetts and Plymouth Colonies, and when united, the province of Massachusetts Bay, once exercised jurisdiction. Upon settlement of the boundary line of Rhode Island on the

there was a body of proprietors, distinguished from those inhabitants who had no interests in the grants and purchases referred to. As, in early times, the lands were of little money value, this latter class of inhabitants formed a very insignificant number; so that a town and proprietors' meeting would be composed of nearly the same individuals. Hence, it is by no means uncommon, in the earlier records, to find the doings of the towns and proprietors confounded; the same clerk usually acting for both, and attributing to the one body the appropriate transactions of the other.[1] It was early found that the proprietors, in many cases, were too numerous and dispersed to manage their lands as individuals; since without incorporation, they could never, as a body, legally act even by majorities, so as to bind their dissenting associates; nor make a lease or sale of their lands, without the concurrence of every proprietor in the execution of the deed.[2] Accordingly, in the old di-

---

east, and by concession on the part of Massachusetts on the north, the former State became possessed, and for the first time, of much of the territory included within her chartered limits; whereupon, by act of the General Assembly of Rhode Island, in 1746, the grants made by the late Colonies of New Plymouth and Massachusetts, or the Province of Massachusetts Bay were confirmed. The title to the Providence Purchase originated in a deed from Canonicus and Miantinomo, uncle and nephew, Narraganset sachems, to Roger Williams, of "all the lands and meadows on the two fresh rivers, the Moshasuck and the Woonasquetucket;" the same lands being more definitely bounded in a subsequent deed from the same sachems, to the Founder of Rhode Island. Between 1636 and 1638, Roger Williams, by a deed which has been lost, communicated his title thus acquired to his twelve associates, thereby giving "equal right and power of enjoying and disposing of the same grounds and lands" to his friends, the said associates, "and such others as the major of us shall admit into the same fellowship of vote with us." This was the commencement of the Proprietors of the Providence Purchase, whose very title contemplates, that it was to be shared with those who might settle in the colony, and who, from that time forward, always acted as if incorporated, disposing of their lands in the same way they transacted their town business, by mere vote. The evidence of the original "*twelve men's deed*," as it is commonly called, is found in a subsequent deed from Roger Williams to the same effect (though very much, and very interestingly expanded by a complete history of the circumstances attending the settlement and purchase), and in a memorandum concerning the lost deed left by him. All the land titles in the Providence Purchase rest on this foundation, supported by the Charter of Charles II., and the act of 1682.

[1] 2 Dane, Abr. 698. This confusion is found in the early records of Providence, R. I.; the records of both town and proprietors being kept in the same book until 1717-18.

[2] In Rhode Island, and not improbably in some of the other States, before any act was passed enabling them so to do, and in fact whilst the settlements themselves were acting under a voluntary compact of government merely, the proprietors were accustomed to assemble and pass votes and orders relative to their common property, in the same manner as if incorporated; admitting members into the propriety, upon payment of a certain sum towards the common stock, by mere vote; and in the same simple way, from time to time, dividing their lands amongst those entitled, according to their rights. As all the colonists

gests of all the New England colonies, acts are found prescribing the mode in which their meetings shall be called, and empowering them to choose officers, — pass orders relative to the management, division, and disposal of their common lands, — and in some of the colonies, to assess and collect taxes from their members; in short, communicating to them all the incidents of a corporation aggregate, without giving them that name.[1] In some of the colonies these powers were granted to others, one by one, in successive statutes; and in others, at once, by a single act of legislation. As the proprietors sold and set off their lands in severalty, they remained proprietors in common only of the residue; until at last, in some of the towns of the earlier settled States, there is a small portion only of such lands left, and in most of them, none at all. In some of the States, they have therefore become obsolete for want of something to act upon; their lands being all sold or divided, and settled; and their former existence is known only by tradition, and by their records to be found in the public offices, or in the hands of some "Proprietor's Secretary" of antiquarian taste, who, since his appointment, has never been troubled with any proceedings on the part of his constituents. In other States, they remain in the exercise of their powers to the present day, — some newly organized and almost all having yet something to do; but it requires not prophecy to foretell, that the fast and far-spreading settlements of our country, will soon gather in the last of this early growth of corporations in the soil of New England.

§ 198. By the acts before referred to, it will be found, that proprietors' meetings were called by warrant or order, issued at the request of some, or a specified number of the proprietors, by a magistrate, as a justice of the peace; the warrant, we believe, in all the colonies, being required to set forth the occasion of the meeting. When met, the pro-

---

were alike interested in the validity of such proceedings, there was then probably as little danger of their being impeached, as there would be at the present day of interference with *a squatter* in the western country, when bidding at a public sale for government lands which he had occupied without title. A similar course was taken in the colony of New Plymouth while under their famous compact. See Laws of the Col. of New Plymouth, 29 and onwards.

[1] 4 Dane, Abr. 70, 71, 72, and Sullivan on Land Titles, 122, 123, for Mass. Acts, being Acts of 1636, 1692, 1712, 1735, 1741, 1753, 1783. Laws of the Colony of New Plymouth, 197, 198, 223; Inhab. of Springfield *v.* Miller, 12 Mass. 415; Thorndike *v.* Barrett, 3 Greenl. 380; Thorndike *v.* Richards, 13 Me. 430; Coburn *v.* Ellenwood, 4 N. H. 99; Farrar *v.* Perley, 7 Greenl. 404; Woodbridge *v.* Proprietors of Addison, 6 Vt. 204, 206; Stiles *v.* Curtis, 4 Day, 328; Laws, R. I. Dig. 1730, p. 30, 31.

prietors were also empowered to choose a clerk, surveyors, and other officers, who, in some of the colonies, were required to be sworn. They could not legally act upon the business of the propriety, unless at a meeting warned according to the statute enabling them to assemble in a corporate character.[1] But, though the vote of proprietors appointing an agent for a special purpose may not, for such a cause, be legal when passed; yet, if the proprietors acquiesce in the appointment, receive the benefit of his transactions, knowing that he acted for them, and take no measures to show their dissent to his proceedings, they so far ratify his doings, that they will be as binding upon them, as if he had been legally appointed.[2] In a suit brought by the proprietors themselves, they were required to prove the warrant of the justice calling a meeting only *twenty* years before, for the purpose of reorganizing the propriety;[3] but not to prove a warrant for calling a first meeting held *seventy* years before.[4] And after the lapse of forty years, and long exercise of corporate rights, a regular warrant, calling the first meeting, may well be presumed.[5] Thus, where persons assumed to act as a propriety more than forty years ago, and having accomplished the purpose of their association, had ceased for more than thirty years to act in that character, it was held, that a stranger, as one claiming under a residuary devisee of a proprietor, could not dispute their capacity thus to associate, nor controvert rights derived from and held under them.[6]

§ 199. Copies of ancient proprietary grants are admissible in evidence, without proof that the meetings at which they were made, were legally assembled.[7] If the records of a proprietors' meeting state that it was legally warned and held, this has been deemed *primâ facie* evidence of the fact,[8] and that the articles of business acted upon at such meeting were inserted in the warrant.[9] In Maine, it has been decided that a first meeting of a propriety of that State will not be treated as illegal and void, because called by the magistrate to be held in New

---

1 Woodbridge *v.* Proprietors of Addison, 6 Vt. 204, 206.
2 Woodbridge *v.* Proprietors of Addison, 6 Vt. 204; Abbot *v.* Mills, 3 Vt. 528.
3 Proprietors of Monumoi Great Beach *v.* Rogers, 1 Mass. 159.
4 Ibid.
5 Copp *v.* Lamb, 3 Fairf. 312; Pitts *v.* Temple, 2 Mass. 538.
6 Copp *v.* Lamb, 3 Fairf. 312; Woods *v.* Banks, 14 N. H. 101.
7 Pitts *v.* Temple, 2 Mass. 538, and Ibid.; Little *v.* Downing, 37 N. H. 355.
8 Stedman *v.* Putney, N. Chip. 11; Codman *v.* Winslow, 10 Mass. 150, 151.
9 Doe *d.* Britton *v.* Lawrence, 1 D. Chip. 103.

Hampshire, in which State the proprietors resided, no place of meeting being prescribed in the statute.[1] The records and certificates of the records of proprietors, with regard to the partition and transfer of their common lands, must be, and are continually received as evidence; and their practice for a number of years is in itself proof of their agreement and consent, in a particular mode of conducting their business, which, if not illegal, or so uncertain as to be utterly void, must be considered as settled by the will of all concerned.[2] As we have before remarked, in ancient times the affairs of the towns and of the proprieties within them, were not always kept distinct. Where this has been shown to be the case, a proprietary grant, voted by the town and attested by the proprietary clerk, and also very ancient grants voted by the proprietors in their own name, and even in the name of the town, and attested by the town clerk, have been admitted in evidence.[3] But it is held that the records of meetings held forty years ago upon the petition of a proprietor, through whom the petitioners in this case claim, reciting that he was owner of one sixteenth part of the proprietary property, are not evidence of such property against a stranger.[4]

§ 200. A book of proprietors' records, which had been in the possession of the grandfather of the witness who produced it, and for thirty years in the hands of the grandfather's executor, from whom it came to the witness, was admitted in evidence, there being no proof that the propriety was still in existence with a clerk to keep their records, and no place appointed by law for the deposit of them.[5] In Vermont, the records of the proprietors' clerk, of deeds made and recorded prior to the statute of 1783, authorizing such clerks to record deeds, are not evidence of title to the lands therein described.[6] If a record in the proprietors' book be a distinct record of a vote at a regular meeting, granting to one of their number a parcel of the common land to be held in severalty, and locating and describing it by definite and intelligible terms, the plain import of such a vote cannot be controverted by parol evi-

---

[1] Copp *v.* Lamb, 3 Fairf. 312.

[2] Codman *v.* Winslow, 10 Mass. 150, 151, per Sewall, J.; Atkinson *v.* Bemis, 11 N. H. 44; Woods *v.* Banks, 14 N. H. 101.

[3] 2 Dane, Abr. 695.

[4] Goulding *v.* Clark, 34 N. H. 148.

[5] Tolman *v.* Emerson, 4 Pick. 160.

[6] Hart *v.* Gage, 6 Vt. 170.

dence.[1] But if the entry be not a record of the *vote* of the proprietors, but may be the act of the proprietors, or of the clerk or other officer, the book being ambiguous in this respect, parol evidence is admissible to show with what intent the entry was made.[2] Thus, a proprietor's clerk was admitted to testify, from his knowledge of the mode in which the records of the propriety were kept, and in which the propriety conducted its business, whether an ancient vote appearing in the records was intended as a definitive grant, or whether something further, as the action of a locating committee, and their report locating and confirming the grant and recorded in the book of locations, ought not to appear before the records could be said to afford evidence of a complete title.[3] If a book is produced, which is admitted to contain the ancient records of a proprietary corporation, the recent entries in it are not admissible in evidence without proof that the supposed clerk by whom they were made, was elected, or *de facto*, acted as clerk on other occasions.[4]

§ 201. In some of the earlier colonial statutes, the provisions enabling the proprietors to act in a corporate character in relation to their common lands, are very general. One of them, after reciting in the preamble, "that no order hath bine yett made for their orderly meeting together to devide the said lands, or to make orders for the settlement of the same," empowers them "*to come together att the same certain time and place to transact such matters as may concern them, and what shall be lawfully acted att such meeting by the proprietors, or the major pte of them, shall be vallid and binding.*"[5] Another, after reciting that "there is considerable of lands lying yet *un*common and undivided," "for the more orderly way and manner of the several proprietors, their managing the prudential affairs thereof, and for the more effectual making of just and equal division or divisions of the same, so that each and every of the proprietors may have their true and equal part or proportion of land, according to his or their proportion of right, and that the exact boundaries of each and every man's allotments, when laid to him may be held *in perpetuam*," provides for the calling of meetings and the election of officers, "*for the orderly carrying on and man-*

---

1 Williams *v.* Ingell, 21 Pick. 288.

2 Ibid.

3 Ibid.

4 Goulding *v.* Clark, 34 N. H. 148.

5 Laws of the Colony of Plymouth, 198, Brigham's edit.

agement of the whole affairs of such community."[1] In other statutes, the language used is more precise, the proprietors being empowered "*to order, manage, improve, divide, and dispose of their common lands in such* way and manner as shall be agreed on by the major part of the interested, present at a legal meeting, the votes to be collected and counted according to interest."[2]

§ 202. There is certainly nothing in the above language, taken by itself, which, at the present day would be construed to authorize a corporation to divide or convey its real estate, in a manner different from that established by the general law. On the contrary, the Plymouth statute expressly, and the rest by natural implication, recognize those acts of the proprietors only to be valid which are *lawfully* done. It should be recollected, however, that some of these statutes were undoubtedly passed in reference to, and with a view to legalize, the doings of proprietors already in the practice of assembling and acting as if incorporated, in the management and disposition of their common lands; the proprietors or settlers having in Plymouth and Rhode Island at least, without legal warrant, under voluntary compacts, and from the very necessity of their condition, assumed the power of self-government, and of disposing of their land, in the same manner as they transacted their other common business, by vote, as if in the exercise of sovereign power. In the other colonies, as we have before noticed, from the fact that the same individuals composed both the inhabitants of the towns and the members of the propriety, the doings of these different bodies were frequently confounded; and at all events, it was natural that the mode of transacting their town business, which was by vote, should be adopted in those simple times with regard to the disposition of their lands; especially when we consider the great extent and little value of their possessions, and the frequent divisions to settlers which were to be made, rendering formal conveyances on each occasion inconvenient and expensive. Construing these statutes therefore in reference to the condition and well-known practices of the proprietors, they would seem fairly to authorize the modes of conveyance and division adopted by those bodies. These varied in the different, and even in the same, proprieties.

---

[1] Laws of R. I. Dig. 1730, pages 30, 31.

[2] 4 Dane, Abr. 70, 71, 72; Inhab. of Springfield *v.* Miller, 12 Mass. 415; Thorndike *v.* Barrett, 3 Greenl. 380; Thorndike *v.* Richards, 13 Me. 430; Coburn *v.* Ellenwood, 4 N. H. 99; Woodbridge *v.* Proprietors of Addison, 6 Vt. 204.

§ 203. Without doubt, a proprietary conveyance by vote alone, definitely describing the lot sold or set off, is sufficient.[1] A common mode of partition was for the proprietors to vote that there should be a new division of their common lands, so many acres to each full right, and in the same proportion to each part right; to be taken up after a specified time. Each proprietor was thereupon entitled to call upon the surveyor to make for him a survey of so much of the common land selected at the pleasure of the proprietors, to which the vote of partition applied, as his right entitled him to; the survey was then, to avoid all collision, taken to a standing committee of proprietors for allowance, and if by them allowed, was by the clerk recorded, and thus the title in severalty became complete. Another mode was for a committee appointed for the purpose, to bound out the tract intended to be divided, and to divide the same into as many equal parcels, having regard both to quantity and quality, as there were proprietors, and to return a plat of the same to the proprietors, on which each lot was marked out and numbered. At their meeting, the proprietors, after considering the plat and accepting it, if there was no objection to it sustainable, would vote that they proceed to draw for the lots thus marked and numbered. The draft was then made, and the number drawn by each was recorded, and the name of each proprietor written on that lot on the plat, which answered to the number he had drawn, and this finished the operation.

§ 204. The practice of making partition of their lands amongst the proprietors, by vote merely, prevailed in all the proprieties; an immense amount of property eventually depended upon the validity of these proceedings, and they have always been sustained by the courts of every one of the New England States.[2] After the proprietors have made a division of certain lots by drafts, they cannot rescind such a partition, and vote lots thus set off to persons claiming the different rights in lieu of their drafts.[3] But where the proprietors, after having laid out a parcel of land to one of their number, and neither he nor his heirs having

---

[1] Williams *v.* Ingell, 21 Pick. 288; Williams *v.* Ingell, 2 Met. 83.

[2] Adams *v.* Frothingham, 3 Mass. 360; Codman *v.* Winslow, 10 Mass. 146; Baker *v.* Fales, 16 Mass. 497; Inhab. of Springfield *v.* Miller, 12 Mass. 415; Folger *v.* Mitchell, 3 Pick. 396; Coburn *v.* Ellenwood, 4 N. H. 99; Atkinson *v.* Bemis, 11 N. H. 44; Abbott *v.* Mills, 3 Vt. 280; Woodbridge *v.* Proprietors of Addison, 6 Vt. 206; Thorndike *v.* Barrett, 3 Greenl. 380; Same *v.* Richards, 13 Me. 430; Pike *v.* Dyke, 2 Greenl. 213; Stiles *v.* Curtis, 4 Day, 328.

[3] Smith *v.* Meacham, 1 D. Chip. 424.

entered, voted, that the location should be void, and that his heirs should take a new survey, and laid out the same land to another, it was held, that a stranger could not contest the validity of this rescission and relay.[1] And where the plaintiff and defendant in ejectment both claim under the same proprietary division, the defendant cannot dispute the legality of the proprietary proceedings in making the division.[2] Proprietors may arrange themselves in classes, and divide their lands by lot, an equal parcel to each class, to be held by the individuals of that class in common, to the exclusion of the rest; and if preparatory to a partition they appoint a committee to survey a tract of land, and lay it out in lots, they may either assent to the doings of such a committee, or make partition without regard to them; so that if a part only of the committee act, and the proprietors ratify their acts, and make partition accordingly, the proceedings are valid.[3]

§ 205. The power of the propriety, to make partition of the common lands amongst the proprietors, does not exclude the right of the proprietors, as tenants in common, to have partition by process of law against their associates; but the proprietors are under no obligation to suspend their proceedings in dividing their lands, to enable one of their number to obtain partition by process of law; and notwithstanding the pendency of such a suit, their voluntary partition will be valid and binding, provided the suit does not go to judgment.[4]

§ 206. It was no uncommon thing for proprietors to set apart by vote a lot or tract of land for public or pious uses, as for a training-field, a public square or common, for public buildings or a meeting-house.[5] Where land is thus dedicated for a public square or common, and individuals purchase lots bordering thereon, under an expectation, excited by the proprietors, that it shall so remain, the proprietors cannot resume the land thus dedicated, and appropriate it to another use;[6] nor can the town reclaim land thus set apart and used by the public for a number

---

[1] Davis *v.* Mason, 4 Pick. 156.

[2] Bown *v.* Bean, 1 D. Chip. 177; Bush *v.* Whitney, 1 D. Chip. 369.

[3] Folger *v.* Mitchell, 3 Pick. 396.

[4] Mitchell *v.* Starbuck, 10 Mass. 20; Oxnard *v.* Kennebec Proprietors, 10 Mass. 179; Chamberlain *v.* Bussey, 5 Greenl. 171; Folger *v.* Mitchell, 3 Pick. 396; Williams College *v.* Mallett, 3 Fairf. 401.

[5] Wellington *v.* Petitioners, 16 Pick. 98; Gould *v.* Whitman, 3 R. I. 67.

[6] Abbott *v.* Mills, 3 Vt. 521; Emerson *v.* Wiley, 10 Pick. 310.

of years, or convey a right to the exclusive possession of any part of it.[1] The public in such a case, have only an easement in the land, and any *proprietor* of the undivided lands in the town, may, it seems, maintain ejectment against one who is in the exclusive possession of land thus set apart.[2] But where the proprietors of a town, having set apart a piece of land as a common for public uses, made a division of lands consisting of one acre lots about the common, which were distributed to the proprietors, one to each right; it was held that *a purchaser* of one of these lots had no right to the fee of the common in front of it, and could not maintain trespass against one who had erected a building thereon near his lot.[3] The proprietors of a township appropriated land for a meeting-house, which was subsequently built thereon; the town was afterwards incorporated, and assumed the charge of all parochial matters, and the land around the meeting-house was called "the common, &c.," and was always open, was intersected by roads and used for the site of horse-sheds, and for all the ordinary purposes incident to a place of worship, and also for a training-field, and the first parish in the town, as the successor of the town in its parochial character, and in actual possession, maintained trespass against a mere stranger for ploughing up a portion of the land thus appropriated, though after the appropriation the proprietors had voted to sell a part of it, and had exercised other acts of ownership over other portions of it.[4]

§ 207. There never was a question but that proprietors were authorized to sell portions of their common lands, as a corporation, to one not a member of the propriety, and *a fortiori* to one who was, for the purpose of defraying their incidental expenses, and bringing forward, settling, and improving their other lands.[5] In some of the proprieties it was usual, when a half or a quarter-right-man, as he was called, in distinction from a proprietor entitled to a full right, had, in a division by drafts, drawn a particular lot, to a part of which only he was entitled according to right, to give him a right of preëmption to the remainder of the lot, the proceeds of the sale going into the common stock.[6] Neither

---

[1] Pomeroy *v.* Mills, 3 Vt. 279; State *v.* Trask, 6 Vt. 355; Stiles *v.* Curtis, 4 Day, 328; Mayo *v.* Murchie, 3 Munf. 358.

[2] Pomeroy *v.* Mills, 3 Vt. 279.

[3] Ferre *v.* Doty, 2 Vt. 378.

[4] First Parish in Shrewsbury *v.* Smith, 14 Pick. 297.

[5] 4 Dane, Abr. 120.

[6] This was the custom amongst the Proprietors of the Providence Purchase in Rhode Island.

can there be any doubt but that a deed, signed and acknowledged on behalf of the corporation, by the clerk or other agent duly authorized by vote, with the corporate seal attached, would be a competent and very proper mode of conveying lands, on the part of the propriety in case of a sale, and in modern times, this mode is frequently, if not usually adopted.[1] A vote of proprietors, authorizing a committee to sell the common lands, empowers them also to make deeds in the name of the propriety; and in executing such deeds, one seal is sufficient, though the committee may consist of several persons.[2] But where proprietors authorized their clerk, as clerk, to make a deed of a piece of their land to an individual in their name, it was decided that the grantee took no title.[3] In Maine, however, a similar deed, executed by the clerk, under a vote directing him to convey "agreeably to the usual forms in like cases practised," was sustained, on the ground, that by a general order of the proprietors, the form of the proprietary deeds was to be such "as the standing committee should judge necessary," for the purpose of granting and conveying the lands of the company, "to be approved of by at least two of the committee, and expressed on the same in writing under their hands;" and that, as the deed in question was thus approved, and conformed "to the usual forms, in like cases practised," it was good; proprietors being empowered to prescribe the forms of their conveyances.[4] It is not necessary that deeds, made by proprietors' committees, should contain recitals of their authority and proceedings in the sale; such recitals not being evidence of the facts.[5]

§ 208. It was long a question, whether proprietors could sell their common lands, merely for the purpose of turning them into money. It being found, however, that the practice had been general, and that large estates were held under such sales, the courts affirmed this practical construction of the statutes, enabling proprietors "to manage, divide, and dispose of their lands in such way and manner as hath been or shall be concluded and agreed on by the major part of the interested;" and decided in favor of such sales.[6]

---

[1] Coburn *v.* Ellenwood, 4 N. H. 99; Atkinson *v.* Bemis, 11 N. H. 44.

[2] Decker *v.* Freeman, 3 Greenl. 338.

[3] Coburn *v.* Ellenwood, 4 N. H. 99.

[4] Thorndike *v.* Barrett, 3 Greenl. 380.

[5] Innman *v.* Jackson, 4 Greenl. 237; Powell *v.* Brown, 1 Tyler, 286.

[6] 4 Dane, Abr. 12; Rogers *v.* Goodwin, 2 Mass. 475; Commonwealth *v.* Pejepscot Proprietors, 7 Mass. 399.

§ 209. A much more serious doubt once entertained was, whether proprieties could by mere vote, without deed or even location, convey their lands to one not a member of the propriety; and it was remarked by an American writer on Land Titles, in the beginning of this century, that such a grant "of any part of them by the voice of the majority, to the disinherison of the proprietor of such part, or a grant by the vote of all the proprietors to convey the whole, *without deeds in legal form*, cannot, from any precedent yet established, be justified."[1] There were, however, some instances previous to that time, where, without objection and solemn argument, the Supreme Court of Massachusetts allowed such votes of land to strangers to have the same effect against co-tenants, as deeds of bargain and sale from one individual to another would have had.[2] When, however, the question came directly before the courts for decision, so many and so large estates were found to depend upon the validity of this mode of conveyance, and so long had been the period during which it had been used, that the use was regarded as a practical construction of that portion of the statutes which empowers proprietors to manage and "dispose of their lands *in such a way and manner* as shall be agreed by the major part, &c.;" and such conveyances were held good.[3] It will be found that the earlier cases speak as if possession must accompany such a grant, and though they affirm the ancient doings of the proprietors of this sort, express doubts whether such a proprietary conveyance made at the present day would be supported.[4] We do not well see, however, with what consistency a different construction can be given to the same words in a statute, according as the transaction to which they are applied is new or old; the statute itself intimating no such difference. As proprietors could in this way convey a definite portion of their land, so they could convey an undivided interest in their common lands in the same way. In early times this was very common, upon payment of so much money into the common stock, and was sometimes done in recompense of important services.[5] A grant of land made by vote of proprietors can no more be

---

1 Sullivan on Land Titles, 123.

2 Ibid. 123.

3 Adams *v.* Frothingham, 3 Mass. 360; Codman *v.* Winslow, 10 Mass. 150, 151; Inhab. of Springfield *v.* Miller, 12 Mass. 415; Baker *v.* Fales, 16 Mass. 497; Inhab. of Rehoboth *v.* Hunt, 18 Mass. 224; Green *v.* Putnam, 8 Cush. 24, 25; Thorndike *v.* Barrett, 3 Greenl. 430; Thorndike *v.* Richards, 13 Me. 430; Kidder *v.* Blaisdell, 45 Me. 461; Coburn *v.* Ellenwood, 4 N. H. 99.

4 Same authorities.

5 Dr. John Clarke, of Newport, R. I., is said to have been voted in a proprietor of the

rescinded by a subsequent vote, even at an adjournment of the meeting at which such vote was passed, than if made by deed;[1] and the exhibition of the first vote, as the ground of his title, by no means precludes the grantee from objecting to the subsequent proceedings of the proprietors in vacating it.[2]

§ 210. The form of proprietary votes intended to operate as grants, and the ceremonies attending them in order to their completeness, vary in the different proprieties; each, as we have seen, by the construction put upon the enabling acts, being entitled to adopt its own mode of disposing of its common lands.[3] In some it was by mere vote; in others by a vote, followed up by a location and survey allowed by a committee, and recorded upon such allowance by the clerk.[4] In the great Kennebec Purchase, the mode of conveyance is for the proprietors "to vote, grant, and assign," the land specified in the vote to A. B., &c.; whereupon the clerk gives the purchaser an instrument in the nature of a certificate of the vote, and in some degree resembling a deed; being under the seal of the corporation, signed by the clerk, and by him acknowledged before a justice of the peace.[5]

§ 211. The most liberal construction has always been given to ancient proprietary grants, in order to carry into effect the intent of the parties; the courts taking into view the customs, usages, and probably the want of legal learning amongst the early settlers. Technical rules of conveyancing are not strictly applied to votes and grants of this character; and estates in fee-simple have passed without any words of limitation in the vote, because it was apparent that the corporation meant to part with all their interest in the granted premises.[6] A vote, merely author-

---

Providence Purchase for his distinguished services in procuring the charter of the colony of Rhode Island from King Charles II.

1 Rehoboth v. Hunt, 1 Pick. 224; Shapleigh v. Pilsbury, 1 Greenl. 271; Pike v. Dyke, 2 Greenl. 213.

2 Pike v. Dyke, 2 Greenl. 213.

3 Thorndike v. Barrett, 3 Greenl. 385, 386, per Mellen, C. J.

4 Adams v. Frothingham, 3 Mass. 360; Williams v. Ingell, 21 Pick. 288.

5 Thorndike v. Barrett, 3 Greenl. 385, 386.

6 Baker v. Fales, 16 Mass. 497; Inhab. of Worcester v. Green, 2 Pick. 428, 429; Stoughton v. Bates, 4 Mass. 528; Feoffees of Grammar School in Ipswich v. Andrews, 8 Met. 584. And see Goff v. Inhabitants of Rehoboth, 12 Met. 26, where the court construed a deed from proprietors to a parish of land for a meeting-house, to reserve to the inhabitants of the town the privilege of occasionally holding town meetings in the meet-

izing the clerk to convey, is not, however, a conveyance by vote, but in order to be effectual, must be followed up by a proper deed.[1] Where proprietors voted, that "the income" of a piece of their land should be devoted to the support of a school in the town where it lay, the land to be leased from time to time by the selectmen of the town; this was considered to be a grant, so that the proprietors could not rescind it.[2] A vote granting merely "the herbage or feeding of land" does not pass the soil, so that the grantee can maintain a writ of entry against the grantor, or those claiming under a subsequent grant of the soil.[3] Nor does a vote, "that a hundred acres of the poorest land, &c., be left common for the use of the town for building-stones," convey the land to the town, but merely the particular use named,[4] for the benefit of the present and future inhabitants of the town exclusively, in all modes, and for all purposes for which, in the progress of time and the arts, the material named in the vote might become useful.[5] And where proprietors voted, that "at the request of A. B. is granted to the right of C. D. half an acre in the ten acre division," and it appeared from the proprietors' book of locations, that no location had been made to A. B., and he was aided by no occupancy or possession, the court considered that he could take no benefit from this vote, without proof that he derived some title from C. D.[6]

§ 212. Proprietors have usually, by express enactment, power to raise money by tax, to be assessed on their several rights, in due proportion, for the purpose of bringing forward and settling their lands, and to defray the incidental expenses of the propriety, and when such assessments were not paid after certain periods, and certain notices had been given, and advertisements published, directed by the act, a committee, or the collector of the tax, were empowered from time to time, to sell at public auction so much of the delinquent proprietor's right or share in the common lands, as would be sufficient to pay the tax, &c.[7]

---

ing-house, from the recital of the vote making such reservation in the deed, although there was no such reservation in the granting part of the deed.

1 Thorndike *v.* Richards, 13 Me. 430; Coburn *v.* Ellenwood, 4 N. H. 99.

2 Rehoboth and Seekonk *v.* Hunt, 1 Pick. 224.

3 Ibid.

4 Worcester *v.* Green, 2 Pick. 428, 429.

5 Green *v.* Putnam, 8 Cush. 21.

6 Williams *v.* Ingell, 21 Pick. 288.

7 Dane, Abr. 71, 72; Bott *v.* Perley, 11 Mass. 175; Farrar *v.* Perley, 7 Greenl. 404; Wentworth *v.* Allen, 1 Tyler, 226.

In Maine, it has been decided, that the Massachusetts Provincial Act of Geo. II. c. 2, which authorized the sale of a delinquent proprietor's lands, after *thirty* days' notice, was not repealed by the act of 26 Geo. II. c. 2, which required a delay of six and twelve months, and a subsequent notice of forty days; the former statute applying to grants made by the General Court, and being confined to sums raised on lands granted on conditions not fulfilled, and the latter relating to all lands "lying within no township or precinct, which are owned by a considerable number of proprietors," without regard to the source from which the title to such lands was derived.[1] The forty days' notice required by the latter of these statutes, and the sixty days' similar notice required by Provincial Act 2 Geo. III. to be given before the sale of such proprietor's lands, are to be computed after the expiration of the respective periods of three, six, and twelve months, mentioned in these statutes.[2] The forty days' notice, required by the statute 26 Geo. II. must be given before the collector can sell for the non-payment of taxes; and his deed, executed before the forty days had elapsed, was held to pass no title.[3] Where, as is, we believe, universally the case, it is necessary that the warrant calling the meeting should state the purposes for which it is convened, a vote to raise a certain sum, under an article in the warrant, to raise money for certain purposes, does not exhaust the efficacy of the article, but further sums may be lawfully raised at *adjournments of the same meeting*, until the objects of the proprietors are effected.[4]

§ 213. A vote of proprietors, "that the collector be empowered to give deeds of lands sold for taxes," can, of course, empower him no further than to sell the land of delinquent proprietors *in the mode provided by law*.[5] A collector's deed, in case of sale for taxes, however it may be worded, is not even *primâ facie* evidence of a legal sale; but the delinquency of the proprietor, and that the collector has pursued the authority to sell given in the statutes, must be independently proved.[6] The collector need not, in his advertisement of sale, annex to

---

1 Farrar *v.* Perley, 7 Greenl. 404.
2 Innman *v.* Jackson, 4 Greenl. 237.
3 Farrar *v.* Eastman, 1 Fairf. 191.
4 Farrar *v.* Perley, 7 Greenl. 404.
5 Farrar *v.* Eastman, 5 Greenl. 345.
6 Powell *v.* Brown, 1 Tyler, 286.

the name of each delinquent proprietor the sum assessed on his right or share, but may mention the amount of the tax on each right generally, and insert a list of the delinquents.[1] These acts enabling proprietors to tax, and sell on non-payment, apply solely to *common and undivided* lands, and never were construed to authorize a sale of lots severed and appropriated by the votes and proceedings of the corporation to individual proprietors, and much less to lots thus severed, sold by such proprietors to third persons.[2]

§ 214. As might be inferred from what has preceded in this chapter, proprietors of common and undivided lands, when duly organized, became a corporation, and held their lands as a propriety; so that in the assertion of their proprietary rights, the proceedings must be conducted in that corporate name by which they are known and called in their own records.[3] The members of the propriety, are, however, as between themselves, tenants in common, and, as we have seen, entitled to partition by legal process.[4] Each proprietor may sell and convey the whole, or any portion of his interest or right in the common and undivided lands; and his grantees become both tenants in common with the other proprietors, and members of the corporation. On the death of a proprietor, his heirs or devisees acquire the same rights.[5]

CHAPTER VII.

OF THE COMMON SEAL, AND OF THE DEEDS OF A CORPORATION.

§ 215. The practice of using seals for the purpose of giving authenticity to written instruments, is of the highest antiquity. It was known

---

[1] Wentworth *v.* Allen, 1 Tyler, 226.
[2] Bott *v.* Perley, 11 Mass. 169.
[3] Chamberlain *v.* Bussey, 5 Greenl. 170.
[4] Ibid.; Mitchell *v.* Starbuck, 10 Mass. 20.
[5] 2 Dane, Abr. 698.

among the Jews,[1] prevailed among the Romans,[2] and has been diffused through those nations which have adopted the Civil Code as the rule of their conduct.[3] In England, seals were introduced into common use by the Normans at the Conquest;[4] although they appear to have been known to the Saxons in the time of Edgar; and to have been used by Edward the Confessor, after his residence in Normandy.[5] In those early and illiterate times, the Norman practice of sealing, any more than the ordinary Saxon practice of signing with, or appending to, the instrument, impressed on gold or lead, the sign of the cross, does not appear to have arisen from any notion of the peculiar solemnity of the seal, but from an incapacity on the part of him who would concur with the tenor of an instrument, to subscribe his name to it. Caedwalla, a Saxon king, honestly avows this reason at the end of one of his charters; "*propria manu, pro ignorantia literarum, signam sanctæ crucis expressi, et subscripsi;*"[6] and it is evident from ancient French and Norman charters still extant, which, without being signed, bear waxen seals with the name, cognizance, or device, of the makers impressed upon them.[7]

§ 216. It is probable that a common seal became incident to every corporation, either from ignorance of the art of writing on the part of its officers or agents, or from the use of seals established among individuals, and originating in *their* ignorance. Blackstone, indeed, attributes this incident to the peculiar nature of a corporation aggregate. "For," says he, "a corporation, being an invisible body, cannot manifest its intentions by any personal act or oral discourse; it therefore acts and speaks only by its common seal. For, though the particular members may express their private consents to any act, by words or signing their names, yet this does not bind the corporation; it is the fixing of the seal, and that only, which unites the several assents of the individuals who compose the community, and makes one joint assent of the whole."[8]

---

[1] Genesis, ch. xxxviii. 18; Esther, ch. viii. 8; Jeremiah, ch. xxxii. 10; Heineccius, 497; 4 Kent, Com. 445, in notis.

[2] Inst. 2, 3, 10; Heineccius, 497; and see the learned opinion of Mr. C. J. Kent, in Warren *v.* Lynch, 5 Johns. 247.

[3] Heineccius, 497; 2 Bl. Com. 305, 306.

[4] Mad. Form. Int. 27.

[5] Co. Litt. 7 *a*; Seld. Off. Chan. 3, dubitante; Mad. Form. Int. 27; 2 Bl. Com. 305.

[6] 2 Bl. Com. 305, n. d.

[7] 2 Bl. Com. 306.

[8] 1 Bl. Com. 475.

It was, however, never true, that corporations aggregate could express a corporate assent, only by their common seals. From the earliest times, their assent to by-laws, and in the election of their officers, was expressed by vote. In the same way, it appears to us, they might have chosen special agents, for the purpose of binding them by particular contracts; and these being capable "of personal act and oral discourse," were, in the nature of things, no more necessitated to use the corporate seal for the purpose of binding their constituents, within the scope of the authority conferred upon them by vote, than the agent of a natural person would be to use the private seal of his employer for the same purpose. This, we think, is rendered more clear by a comparative view of the Civil Law, in the same particular. The Civil Law, in the shape in which we have it, was instituted amongst a people more literate than that which gave origin to the common law. From the *nature* of the corporations or communities existing under it, the same incapability, literally speaking, of personal act, or of oral discourse, was attached to *them*, as to corporations aggregate at the common law; yet we find that not only did they appoint officers, capable of contracting without seal, but themselves contracted directly by vote, without the intervention of any officers whatever.[1] The truth is, that, though in its decay, the Roman empire was won back to ignorance by its barbarous invaders,[2] in its better days, neither individuals nor corporations existing within it were, in general compelled to use seals, by way of signature, from an ignorance of the art of writing. A common seal, was not, therefore, necessary to a corporation at the Civil Law, to enable it to make a written contract; and, accordingly, Wood tells us of such a corporation, that, "it may have a common chest, and *sometimes* a common seal."[3] As the art of writing became more common in England, the practice of concurring with the tenor of *every* written instrument by seal on account of its inconvenience, grew into disuse with individuals, and was confined to those writings of a peculiarly high and solemn kind, which were employed in the transfer of lands, and acts of the like nature. The practice, however, still continued with the old corporations of the common law, perhaps from the natural inflexibility of *bodies* of men, where many wills must concur to a change, and because, owing to the comparative paucity of their contracts, and the number of their agents, the incon-

---

[1] Ayliffe, Civil Law, B. 2, tit. 35, p. 198.

[2] 2 Bl. Com. 305, n. d.

[3] Wood, Civil Law, ch. 2, p. 136; and see Browne, Civil Law, b. 1st, 104.

venience of this mode of contracting would be less sensibly felt by them than by individuals. It is probable that in this way grew up the old rule, so long and so well established in England, that, excepting in the administration of its internal affairs, as the election of officers and the like, corporations aggregate could signify their assent only by their common seal, and of course could act and contract only by deed.

§ 217. This being the rule, it became incident to every corporation of this kind to have a common or corporate seal,[1] as the means necessary to enable it to appoint any special agent, except of the most inferior kind, or to make any contract whatever.[2] And not only is it incident to every corporation to have a common seal, without any clause in the charter or act of incorporation expressly empowering it to use one, but it may make or use what seal it will.[3] Accordingly, it was decided, in the reign of Edward III., that if an abbot and convent sealed a writing with the seal of a layman, and it was said in the deed, "in testimony whereof our common seal is affixed," it was sufficient; for they might change their common seal when they would.[4] It should be observed, however, that to bind a corporation by deed, the instrument must be sealed with a seal which is theirs, either originally, or by adoption; and hence, that an instrument under the private seals of their authorized agents, does not bind the body as a deed, although they may be liable in implied assumpsit for benefits conferred under it.[5] Where, by an act of the legislature, the trustees of a gospel lot were declared to be a body corporate, and the act provided, that the "said trustees" should have authority to sell the lot, a deed executed by the trustees, as such, and not in the name of the corporation, nor under the corporate seal, was

---

1 Davies, 44, 48; 1 Bl. Com. 475; 1 Kyd on Corporations, 268; 2 Kent, Com. 224.

2 The case of the Deane and Chapter of Fernes, Davies, 121.

3 The case of Sutton's Hospital, 10 Co. 30 b; and see Goddard's case, 2 Co. R. 5, and Mill Dam Foundery *v.* Hovey, 21 Pick. 417; Porter *v.* Androscoggin and Kennebec R. R. Co. 37 Me. 349; South Baptist Soc. of Albany *v.* Clapp, 18 Barb. 35. The presumption that the seal accompanying the signature of an authorized agent, is the seal of the corporation, is not overcome by showing that on several other occasions a different seal had been used by the company. Stebbins *v.* Merritt, 10 Cush. 27.

4 Ibid. and Perkins' sects. 130, 134.

5 Bank of Columbia *v.* Patterson, 7 Cranch, 304; Randall *v.* Van Vechten, 19 Johns. 65; Haight *v.* Sahler, 30 Barb. 218; Tippetts *v.* Walker, 4 Mass. 597; Brinley *v.* Mann, 2 Cush. 337; Hatch *v.* Barr, 1 Ohio, 390; Savings Bank *v.* Davis, 8 Conn. 191; Kinzie *v.* Chicago, 2 Scam. 187; Bank of Metropolis *v.* Guttschlieck, 14 Pet. 19; Ellnall *v.* Shaw, 16 Mass. 42; Stinchfield *v.* Little, 1 Greenl. 231; Decker *v.* Freeman, 3 Greenl. 838; Bank *v.* Rose, 2 Strobh. 257. See Chap. IX.

adjudged to be a valid execution of the power, and to vest the title in the grantee.[1] A deed of proprietary lands, reciting the votes authorizing the clerk of the proprietors to execute the same, approved by a written indorsement signed by three of a standing committee, two of whom were empowered to approve such deeds as they judged necessary, was, though sealed with the seal of the clerk, held to transfer the title of the proprietors *after thirty years' possession of the land by the grantee.*[2]

§ 218. At common law, the corporate seal cannot be impressed directly upon the paper, but must be upon wax, wafer, or some other tenacious substance, or the instrument, to which it is attached will not operate as a sealed instrument.[3] In a recent case in New Jersey, however, a distinctive impression of the paper without the intervention of wax or wafer, was held to be a lawful corporate seal.[4] In the Southern and Western parts of the United States, from New Jersey inclusive, a *flourish with a pen*, at the end of a name, or a circle of ink, or a scroll, has been allowed to be a valid substitute for a seal;[5] and in the States of Delaware, Virginia, Illinois, Missouri, and Tennessee, this substitute has, we believe, been introduced by acts of their legislatures. Though we know no decision upon the subject, yet we see no reason, unless, indeed, the act of incorporation expressly provides what the common seal shall be, why the substitute allowed for the private seal of an individual should not also be allowed for the seal of a corporation.[6] And it has been held that another seal than the corporate one, is valid, if used with the assent of the directors.[7]

§ 219. The old rule of the common law undoubtedly was, that corporations aggregate could contract, or appoint special agents for that pur-

---

[1] De Zeng *v.* Beekman, 2 Hill, 489.

[2] Thorndike *v.* Barrett, 3 Greenl. 380.

[3] Bank of Rochester *v.* Gray, 2 Hill, 228, 229; Farmers and Manufacturers Bank *v.* Haight, 3 Hill, 494, 495; Mitchell *v.* Union L. Ins. Co. 45 Me. 104.

[4] Corrigan *v.* Trenton Delaware Falls Co. 1 Halst. Ch. 52; and see, to same effect, Sudg. on Vend. 6th ed.; Reg. *v.* St. Paul's, 7 Q. B. 231; Davidson *v.* Cooper, 11 M. & W. 778, affirmed in error, 13 M. & W. 343; Lightfoot & Butler's case, 2 Leon. 21; Shep. Touchst. 57; Allen *v.* Sullivan R. R. Co. 32 N. H. 446; Curtis *v.* Leavitt, 15 N. Y. 9.

[5] 4 Kent, Com. 445.

[6] See Cowen & Hill's Notes to Phillips's Evidence, 1277 to 1281; Bank of Rochester *v.* Gray, 2 Hill, 228, 229.

[7] Bank of Middlebury *v.* Rutland & B. R. Co. 30 Vt. 159.

pose, or any other, except for services of the most inferior and ordinary nature, only by deed. In England, this rule has, in modern times, been greatly, though gradually, relaxed; and in our own country, where private corporations of this kind, for every laudable object, have been multiplied beyond any former example, on account of the inconvenience and injustice which must, in practice, result from its technical strictness, the rule has, as a general proposition, been completely done away.[1] The course of modern decisions seems to place corporations, with regard to their mode of appointing agents and making contracts in general, upon the same footing with natural persons. They may appoint all their agents, or make all their contracts, by deed; but are no more compelled so to do than individuals. Like these, they are subject to the rules established by the common and statute law, and cannot, therefore, take or grant lands, or any interest therein, otherwise than by deed.[2] The Statute of Frauds does not require the note or memorandum in writing of contracts for the sale of lands to be sealed; and accordingly the common seal to such a contract, when made by a corporation, is no more necessary to a recovery upon it at law, or a specific performance of it in equity, than the seal of an individual would be, if the contract had been made by him.[3] That this is the American doctrine there can be no doubt; but in England, it seems that a court of equity will not compel a public corporation to execute a legal assurance of corporate property, in pursuance of a contract not under the corporate seal, unless valuable consideration for the contract be expressly proved, or evidence be given of acts done or omitted by the other contracting party on the faith of the promised legal assurance.[4] It is almost unnecessary to remark, that the speciality of a corporation merges its simple contract, as in case of natural persons.[5]

---

[1] See Chap. VIII. and Chap. IX.

[2] Com. Dig. Franchises, F. 11; Bac. Abr. Corporations, E. 3; 1 Kyd on Corporations, 263; Harper *v.* Charlesworth, 4 B. & C. 575, per Bayley, J.; Union Bank of Maryland *v.* Ridgely, 1 Harris & G. 419, 420; Bank of United States *v.* Dandridge, 12 Wheat. 105, per Marshall, C. J.; and see Wood *v.* Tate, 5 B. & P. 246; The King *v.* Inhabitants of Chipping Norton, 5 East, 240; Doe *v.* Woodman, 8 East, 228, and *supra.*

[3] Maxwell *v.* Dulwich College, 1 Fonbl. Eq. 296, n. o. (Phil. ed. 305, n. o.); Marshall *v.* Corporation of Queensborough, 1 Simons & S. 520; Legrand *v.* Hampden-Sydney College, 4 Munf. 324; The Banks *v.* Poitiaux, 3 Rand. 143; London and Birmingham Railway Co. *v.* Winter, 1 Craig. & Ph. Ch. 63; Mayor of Stafford *v.* Till, 4 Bing. 75; Stoddert *v.* Vestry of Port Tobacco Parish, 2 Gill & J. 227.

[4] Wilmot *v.* Corporation of Coventry, 1 Younge & C., Exch. 518; where see a criticism on preceding English cases.

[5] Van Vlieden *v.* Welles, 6 Johns. 85.

§ 220. We think it may safely be laid down as a rule without exception, that corporations at this day are capable of making every species of deed.[1] It was once thought that a corporation could not stand seised to a use; and hence as a deed of bargain and sale merely passes the use, and the bargainor must stand seised of the land for a moment, that the Statute of Uses, if we may be allowed the expression, may have time to execute the use, it was thought that a corporation could not make a deed of bargain and sale. Lord Chief Baron Comyn indeed says, that a corporation may bargain and sell, for they may give a use, though they cannot stand seised to one;[2] and founds himself upon a case, where it appeared that the prioress of Hallowell conveyed certain lands, by the words *dedi et concessi pro certa pecuniæ summa*, to Lord Chancellor Audley and his heirs. It was objected, that a bargain and sale by a corporation was not good, for it could not be seised to another's use. But the court rejected the objection as dangerous; for that such were the conveyances of the greater part of the possessions of monasteries. And it was said, that although such a corporation could not take an estate to another's use, yet they might charge their possessions with a use to another.[3] The only principle, however, upon which this case can be supported, that lands may be charged with a use as with a rent or common, was rejected as an absurdity in Chudleigh's case;[4] and Mr. Cruise, in his learned and valuable Digest, informs us that in England, "it is now generally admitted that a corporation cannot stand seised to a use," with a view to prove that it was incapable of making a deed of bargain and sale.[5] In this country, however, the better opinion is, that any corporation may stand seised to a use, or trust, as it is called in modern times, for purposes not foreign to the object of its institution; and this is surely most conformable to principle, and convenient in practice.[6] If this be true, there can be no doubt of the power of a corporation to convey by deed of bargain and sale, as well as an individual. In those States in which livery of seisin is unnecessary to the complete execution of a deed of feoffment or those in which the old common-law deed of grant is made competent to all its purposes, we apprehend that

---

[1] Mobile and Cedar Point Railroad Co. *v.* Talman, 15 Ala. 472.

[2] Com. Dig. Bargain and Sale, B. 3.

[3] Holland *v.* Bonis, 3 Leon. 175.

[4] 1 Co. R. 127 a.

[5] 4 Cruise's Dig. tit. 32, Deed, c. 9, §§ 12, 13, 14, 15, 16.

[6] 2 Kent, Com. 226. See Chap. VIII.

the question we have been considering, is one of very little practical importance; for *ut res magis valeat quam pereat*, no rule of law is better settled, than if it be necessary to effectuate the intention of the parties, that one species of deed shall be construed as another.[1] "I exceedingly commend," says Lord Hobart, "the judges that are curious and almost subtile, *astuti*, to invent reasons and means to make acts, according to the just *intent* of the parties, and to avoid wrong and injury which, by rigid rules, might be wrought out of the act;"[2] and Lord Hale cites and approves this passage.[3] It has never, we believe, been doubted that a corporation might *take* by deed of bargain and sale, as well as any other species of conveyance.

§ 221. In private corporations aggregate, for the sake of convenience, the whole management of their affairs is usually vested by charter in certain officers and boards; the body of the members having no voice except in their election.[4] When this is the case, the power of making deeds, like every other power, rests with *them;* and courts will not interfere upon a petition even of a majority of the *members*, to compel that body, contrary to their own judgment, to affix the common seal to any instrument,[5] and still less can the stockholders by their vote, authorize the making of a deed, as a lease of the corporate property.[6] Sometimes the charter or act of incorporation requires a certain number of a special body, or board existing within the corporation, to be present at the doing of any corporate act, or at the making of particular species of contracts, as deeds; and in such a case, the number must be present at the making of the deed, in order to its validity as a corporate act.[7]

---

[1] Crossing *v.* Scudamore, 1 Mod. 175, 2 Lev. 9, 1 Vent. 137; Walker *v.* Hall, 2 Lev. 213; Coultman *v.* Senhouse, T. Jones, 105; Harrison *v.* Austin, Carth. 38; Roe *v.* Tranmer, 2 Wils. 75; Doe *v.* Simpson, 2 Wils. 22; Sheppard's Touchstone, 87; Wallis *v.* Wallis, 4 Mass. 135; Pray *v.* Pierce, 7 Mass. 381.

[2] Hob. 277.

[3] Crossing *v.* Scudamore, 1 Vent. 141.

[4] Bank of U. S. *v.* Dandridge, 12 Wheat. 113, per Marshall, C. J.; Union Turnpike Corporation *v.* Jenkins, 1 Caines, 381; Commonwealth *v.* The Trustees of St. Mary's Church, 6 S. & R. 508. See Chap. VIII.

[5] Commonwealth *v.* The Trustees of St. Mary's Church, 6 S. & R. 508; and see Bank of U. S. *v.* Dandridge, 12 Wheat. 113, per Marshall, C. J.; Union Turnpike Corporation *v.* Jenkins, 1 Caines, 381; McDonough *v.* Templeman, 1 Harris & J. 156; Clark *v.* Woollen Manuf. Co. of Benton, 15 Wend. 256; Leggett *v.* New Jersey Banking Co. Saxton, Ch. 541.

[6] Conro *v.* Port Henry Iron Co. 12 Barb. 27.

[7] The President, &c. of the Berks & Dauphin Turnpike Road *v.* Myers, 6 S. & R.

But though by charter, a certain number of a board are required to concur in entering into a special contract, or making a deed, it does not follow that the affixing of the seal, which is merely a ministerial act, may not be done by a less number than were at first competent to enter into the contract, provided it were done by the direction of a legal quorum.[1] Sometimes a general law provides as to the mode in which a deed of a corporation, conveying its real estate, shall be executed, as by the president reciting the vote of the corporation authorizing him to convey; and in such a case, a deed of the real estate, executed by all the shareholders, in their private capacity, or a deed by them of all the shares, will not convey the real estate of the corporation.[2]

§ 222. At the common law, the master, fellows, and scholars of a college, the master or warden, brethren and sisters of a hospital, an abbot or prior and his convent, and a dean and chapter in their aggregate capacity, had unlimited control over the property of their respective houses, and might therefore have made any grant whatever.[3] In case of an alienation by dean and chapter, the consent of the bishop in his character of ordinary was necessary, in order that the grant or lease should be good beyond the life of the dean who granted or demised.[4] The case of an abbot or prior differed from that of a dean, and of a master of a hospital or college; for with respect to the possessions of the house, the whole estate, to certain purposes, was supposed to be vested in him; whereas, in the cases of the master of a hospital, or of a college and dean, the seisin of the joint possessions of the house was jointly in the master and his brethren and sisters, the master, fellows, and scholars, and in the dean and chapter respectively.[5] There was, therefore, a difference in the manner in which conveyances were made of the possessions of these several houses; a grant or lease of the possessions of an abbey or priory was regularly made by the abbot or prior,

---

12; Case of St. Mary's Church, 7 S. & R. 530, per Tilghman, C. J.; Hill *v.* Manchester and Salford Water Works Company, 5 B. & Ad. 866, 2 Nev. & M. 573.

1 The President, &c. of the Berks & Dauphin Turnpike Road *v.* Myers, 6 S. & R. 12; Hill *v.* Manchester & Salford Water Works Company, 5 B. & Ad. 866, 2 Nev. & M. 573.

2 Wheelock *v.* Moulton, 15 Vt. 521, 522; Roberts *v.* Batten, 14 Vt. 195; Isham *v.* Bennington Iron Co. 19 Vt. 230; Hill *v.* Manchester & Salford Water Works Company, 5 B. & Ad. 865, 2 Nev. & M. 573.

3 Co. Lit. 44 a, 300, 301; 1 Burr. 221; Madox Firma Burgi, c. 1, § 4; 1 Kyd on Corporations, 108.

4 1 Kyd on Corporations, 109, 110.

5 Co. Lit. 347 a, Lit. §§ 655, 656, 657; 1 Kyd on Corporations, 114.

with the *assent* of the convent, because the convent, being composed of persons dead in law, could not with propriety be said to make a lease or grant; though if it had been said that the abbot and convent made the lease or grant, that would not have been a material objection.[1] In case of an alienation, grant, or demise, by the head of a corporation aggregate of many persons capable without the consent of the proper parties, the deed was void against the successor, and he might enter; whereas, in case of an alienation in fee, tail, or for term of life, by an abbot or prior without the consent of the convent, inasmuch as the fee was vested in him in right of his house, and not in the house jointly with him, the alienation operated as a discontinuance, and the successor was put to his writ of entry, *sine assensu capituli*.[2] The common-law restraints being found insufficient to prevent a defalcation of the revenues of these corporations, many statutes have been passed in England limiting the common-law right of alienation; but as they are wholly inapplicable to this country, it will be unnecessary for us to notice them.[3] Indeed, we have referred to these rules concerning the old corporations aggregate of the common law, rather to illustrate the general principle, that in an alienation of lands, or making of a deed, in order to its validity, they must concur who have an interest in the subject passed, than because we thought them strictly applicable to our institutions. In private incorporated companies existing in this country, the power to make special contracts, alienate lands belonging to the corporation, and the consequent power to make deeds, unless by charter vested in a special board or body, as is most common, rests, of course, like every other power, in the members, as a body at large, to be exercised by them through their agents.[4]

§ 223. The corporate seal affixed to a contract or conveyance, does not render the instrument a corporate act, unless it is affixed by an officer or agent duly authorized.[5] It must be affixed by the officer to whose custody it is confided, or some person specially authorized; the officer or

---

1 1 Plowd. 199; Dyer, 40, pl. 1 to 97, pl. 45; Godb. 211; 1 Kyd on Corporations, 114.

2 Co. Lit. 325 b, 341 b, 342 a, 346 a, b.; F. N. B. 194 k.; 1 Kyd on Corporations, 115, 116.

3 1 Kyd on Corporations, from 116 to 162.

4 See Chap. IX.

5 Jackson *v.* Campbell, 5 Wend. 572; Damon *v.* Granby, 2 Pick. 345, 353; Bank of Ireland *v.* Evan, 5 H. L. Cas. 389, 32 Eng. L. & Eq. 23.

special agent acting in consequence of the directory vote of the body, or managing board of the corporation, as the case may be.[1] The president and cashier of a bank cannot use the common seal without the authority of the board of directors.[2] A vote of proprietors, authorizing a committee to sell lands, empowers them also to make the necessary deeds in the name of the proprietors; and if a committee of several be appointed, who all sign, yet one seal is enough.[3] The effect of affixing the corporate seal to a contract is the same as when an individual affixes his seal; it makes the instrument a speciality.[4] But where the terms of a contract proposed to the committee of a corporation were contained in a letter directed to them, and the committee wrote at the bottom of the letter, that the terms proposed were accepted, and thereto affixed the corporate seal, by way of showing the corporate assent, such mode of accepting the terms of the contract was not deemed to constitute the contract a speciality.[5] There seems to be no reason why the authority to affix a corporate seal may not be established, by a vote ratifying the act, as well as by a previous vote, or even by the subsequent acts of the corporation.[6]

§ 224. The common-law rule with regard to natural persons, that an agent, to bind his principal by deed, must be empowered by deed himself, cannot in the nature of things be applied to corporations aggregate. These beings of mere legal existence, and their *boards*, as such, are, literally speaking, incapable of *personal* act. They *direct* or *assent* by vote; but their most immediate mode of *action* must be by agents. If the principal, the corporation, or its representative, the board, can assent primarily by *vote* alone, to say that it could constitute an agent to make a deed only by deed, would be to say that it could constitute no such agent, whatever; for, after all, who could seal the power of attorney, but one empowered by *vote?*[7] When the common seal of a corpo-

---

[1] Derby Canal Co. *v.* Wilmot, 9 East, 360; Bank of U. S. *v.* Dandridge, 12 Wheat. 68, per Story, J.; President, &c. of the Berks & Dauphin Turnpike Road *v.* Myers, 6 S. & R. 12; Clarke *v.* Imperial Gas Co.; 4 B. & Ad. 315, 1 Nev. & M. 206.

[2] Hoyt *v.* Thompson, 1 Seld. 320.

[3] Decker *v.* Freeman, 3 Greenl. 338; and see Burrill *v.* Nahant Bank, 2 Met. 167.

[4] Clark *v.* Woollen Manuf. Co. of Benton, 15 Wend. 256; Benoist *v.* Inhab. of Carondelet, 8 Misso. 250; Porter *v.* Androscoggin & Kennebec R. Co. 37 Me. 349.

[5] Levering *v.* Mayor, &c. of Memphis, 7 Humph. 553.

[6] Howe *v.* Keeler, 27 Conn. 538.

[7] Hopkins *v.* Gallatin Turnpike Co. 4 Humph. 403; Beckwith *v.* Windsor Manufacturing Company, 14 Conn. 594; Howe *v.* Keeler, 27 Conn. 538; Burr *v.* McDonald, 3 Gratt. 215.

ration appears to be affixed to an instrument, and the signatures of the proper officers are proved, courts are to presume that the officers did not exceed their authority, and the seal itself is *primâ facie* evidence that it was affixed by proper authority.[1] The contrary must be shown by the objecting party.[2] The presumption of authority to affix the common seal, from the fact that it is affixed to the instrument, will not be overcome, in the case of a cashier of a bank, by the mere fact that it is proved that there is no vote of the directors on the subject; since it often happens that the cashier or other officer of a bank exercises a large range of powers, with the tacit approval of his principals, although the nature and extent of his authority have never been defined by any direct act of the corporation.[3]

§ 225. The technical mode of executing the deed of a corporation is to conclude the instrument, which should be signed by some officer or agent in the name of the corporation, with, "In testimony whereof, the common seal of said corporation is hereunto affixed;" and then to affix the seal.[4] Where, however, two trustees of a parish, who were a corporation, signed their individual names to a lease, executed by them in their corporate capacity, and sealed with the common seal opposite to each name, though the signatures and *double* sealing were unnecessary, it was held that the lease was not vitiated thereby.[5] And a lease, run-

---

[1] Skin. 2; 1 Kyd on Corporations, 268; The President, &c. of the Berks and Dauphin Turnpike Road *v.* Myers, 6 S. & R. 12; The Baptist Church *v.* Mulford, 3 Halst. 183, per Ewing, C. J.; Leggett *v.* New Jersey Banking Co. Saxton, Ch. 541; Adams *v.* His Creditors, 14 La. 455; Darwell *v.* Dickens, 4 Yerg. 7; Burrill *v.* Nahant Bank, 2 Met. 166; Commercial Bank *v.* Kortright, 22 Wend. 348; Lovett *v.* Steam Saw-Mill Ass. 6 Paige, 54; Johnson *v.* Bush, 3 Barb. Ch. 207; Hopkins *v.* Gallatin Turnpike Company, 4 Humph. 403; Levering *v.* Mayor, &c. of Memphis, 7 Humph. 553; Susquehannah Bridge & Banking Co. *v.* General Ins. Co. 3 Md. Ch. Dec. 305; Reed *v.* Bradley, 17 Ill. 321.

[2] Ibid. and case of St. Mary's Church, 7 S. & R. 530, per Tilghman, C. J.; Mayor and Commonalty of Colchester *v.* Lowten, 1 Ves. & B. 226; Lovett *v.* Steam Saw-Mill Association, 6 Paige, 54; Flint *v.* Clinton Company, 12 N. H. 434; Benedict *v.* Denton, 1 Walker, Ch. 336; but see Miller *v.* Ewer, 27 Me. 509.

[3] Bank of Vergennes *v.* Wilson, 7 Hill, 95. This doctrine does not hold true of corporations falling within the provisions of a statute forbidding them to transfer property exceeding in value $1,000, without a previous vote of the directors, where such a transfer is in question; but in such case, the presumption of authority from the seal may be rebutted by showing that there was no such vote. Johnson *v.* Bush, 3 Barb. 207.

[4] Flint *v.* Clinton Company, 12 N. H. 433.

[5] Jackson *v.* Walsh, 3 Johns. 225. See too, Clark *v.* The Woollen Manuf. Co. of Benton, 15 Wend. 256.

ning in the names of certain persons, as the master and governors of a hospital, witnessing that the said master and governors have demised, with the covenants on the part of the lessee, to them and *their successors*, concluding with, "In witness whereof, the said master and governors have hereunto affixed their common seal," &c., but not *signed* by them, or either of them, was decided to be the lease of the corporation, and not of the individuals named in it as master and governors.[1] Neither is it *necessary* to the validity of a deed by a corporation, that it should say, "Sealed with our common seal," or the like, if the fact otherwise appears.[2] A mortgage executed and acknowledged by the members of a board of directors who were present, the seal of the corporation being duly affixed, was held to be well executed and acknowledged.[3] The officer or agent of a corporation, who executes a deed in the name of the corporation, by affixing thereto the impression of the common or corporate seal, intrusted to his care, is "the party executing the deed," within the meaning of the statutes requiring deeds to be acknowledged by such party,[4] or in case of an assignment, for the benefit of creditors, the party required to swear that he has assigned all his property, except what is exempted from process.[5]

§ 226. It is prudent to have witnesses to the sealing; for the common seal is not evidence of its own authenticity, but must be proved, not indeed necessarily by one who saw it affixed or adopted, but by one who, from the motto, device, &c. knows it to be the seal of the corporation, as whose it is produced.[6] The signature of the agent of the cor-

---

1 Cooch *v.* Goodman, 2 Q. B. 580, 600. In Vermont, by force of a statute passed in 1815, it would seem that the deed of a corporation must, to be valid, be signed with the name, as well as sealed with the seal of the corporation. Isham *v.* Bennington Iron Co. 19 Vt. 251, 252.

2 2 Rol. 21, l. 45; Goddard's case, 5 Co. R. 5; Com. Dig. Fait. a. 2; Mill Dam Foundery *v.* Hovey, 21 Pick. 417.

3 Gordon *v.* Preston, 1 Watts, 385.

4 Lovett *v.* The Steam Saw-Mill Association, 6 Paige, 60.

5 Flint *v.* Clinton Company, 12 N. H. 436.

6 Moises *v.* Thornton, 8 T. R. 303, 304; Peake, Law of Evidence, 48, n.; Starkie on Evidence, Part 2d, 300, n. 1; Jackson *v.* Pratt, 10 Johns. 381; Mann *v.* Pentz, 2 Sandf. Ch. 271, 272; Foster *v.* Shaw, 7 S. & R. 156; Leazure *v.* Hillegas, id. 313; Den *v.* Vreelandt, 2 Halst. 352; Darwell *v.* Dickens, 4 Yerg. 7; City Council of Charleston *v.* Moorhead, 3 Rich. 450; Farmers & Mechanics Turnpike Co. *v.* McCullough, 25 Penn. State, 303. See Doe d. Woodmas *v.* Mason, 1 Esp. 53, where Lord Kenyon held, as an exception to the general rule, that the common seal *of the City of London* proved itself. See Moises *v.* Thornton, 8 T. R. 304, per Lord Kenyon.

poration, executing the instrument in its behalf, however, being proved, the seal, though mere paper and wafer stamped with the common desk seal of a merchant, will be presumed to be intended as the seal of the corporation, until the presumption is rebutted by competent evidence.[1] A seal of a foreign corporation, as that of the City of London, cannot be admitted to be such seal without proof that it is the official seal it purports to be; nor can it be proved by comparison with a similar seal already given in evidence without objection.[2] Where a corporation, by a resolution, authorized its president to execute a deed of the corporate lands, and he executed the deed in the name of the corporation, but attested it in this form, "In witness whereof I, ——, President, have hereunto set *my hand and seal*, &c.," and signed his own name as president, opposite to a seal upon which there was no distinct impression, the deed was held inoperative, it being the individual deed of the president, who had personally no interest in the subject of the instrument.[3] It is unnecessary that deeds made by proprietors' committees should contain recitals of their authority and proceedings in the sale; as their certificates of such proceedings are not in themselves evidence of the facts they recite, and such facts may always be proved *aliunde*, and in proper cases will be presumed.[4]

§ 227. The deed of a natural person takes effect only by, and from, its delivery. This ceremony, however, is unnecessary to the complete execution of the deed of a corporation, since it is said to be perfected by the mere affixing of the common seal. Lord Hale, in a note to Coke Littleton, remarks, that, "if a dean and chapter seal a deed, it is their deed immediately."[5] This rule is to be taken with the important qualification, that, by the affixing of the seal, the complete execution of the deed was *intended;* "for if," adds Lord Hale to the above remark,

---

[1] Mill Dam Foundery *v.* Hovey, 21 Pick. 428, Putnam, J.; Flint *v.* Clinton Company, 12 N. H. 433, 434; City Council of Charleston, 2 Rich. 450; Susquehannah Bridge & Banking Co. *v.* General Ins. Co. 3 Md. Ch. Dec. 305; Phillips *v.* Coffee, 17 Ill. 154; see, however, Mann *v.* Pentz, 3 Sandf. Ch. 271, 272.

[2] Chew *v.* Keck, 4 Rawle, 163.

[3] Hatch *v.* Barr, 1 Ohio, 390; Brinley *v.* Mann, 2 Cush. 337. See Bank of the Metropolis *v.* Guttschlieck, 14 Pet. 19.

[4] Farrar *v.* Eastman, 5 Greenl. 345; Inman *v.* Jackson, 4 id. 237.

[5] Co. Lit. lib. 1, §§ 5, 36 a, n. 222, Hargrave & Butler's ed.; and see acc. Case of the Dean and Chapter of Fernes, Dav. 44; 2 Leon. 97; 1 Vent. 257; 1 Lev. 46; 1 Sid. 8; Carth. 260; 3 Keb. 307; 1 Kyd on Corp. 268; *Contra*, 2 Leon. 98, Gawdy, J.

"they (the dean and chapter) at the same time make letter of attorney to deliver it, this is not their deed till delivery."[1] In the Derby Canal Company *v.* Wilmot,[2] it appearing that the order of the managing committee to the clerk, to affix the seal, was accompanied with a direction to retain the conveyance in his hands until accounts were adjusted with the purchaser, it was held by the Court of King's Bench, that, notwithstanding the affixing of the common seal, the deed was incomplete; Lord Ellenborough, as the organ of the court, observing, "that, in order to give it (the deed) effect, the affixing of the seal must be done with an intent to pass the estate; otherwise it operates no more than a feoffment would do without livery of seisin."

CHAPTER VIII.

OF THE MODE IN WHICH A CORPORATION MAY CONTRACT, AND WHAT CONTRACTS IT MAY MAKE.

§ 228. In accordance with the notion that corporations aggregate could express their assent only by their common seals, the ancient doctrine of the common law, as has been considered, was, that they could bind themselves only by deeds, or special contracts. However well established this may have been as a rule of the courts, its extreme inconvenience must always have effectually denied it currency, as a rule of practice. It can hardly be believed that in their daily commerce for the necessaries and elegancies of life, for the decorations of their chapels and churches, for the building and repairing of their houses, and the tillage and improvement of their lands, the various religious communities, anciently so numerous and well endowed in England, contracted only by deed. Of necessity, their superiors and authorized agents must have bought and sold, bargained and contracted for them, without the delaying intervention of sealed instruments. Municipal corporations, too,

---

[1] Co. Lit. lib. 1, §§ 5, 36 a, n. 222, Harg. & Butler's ed.; and see Willis *v.* Jermin, Cro. E. 167; W. Jones, 170; Palm. 504.

[2] 9 East, 360.

whose bargains and purchases must have been numerous in the most ancient times, for the improvement and defence of their towns, for articles of civic pomp and display, can hardly be supposed to have contracted for them in all their details by deed. The inconsistency of the professed principle or reason of this doctrine with fact, is apparent, also, at a glance; for it was always the practice of corporations aggregate to express their assent in the elections of their officers by *vote;* and it appears to have been early settled, that this was a legal mode of appointing servants or agents of inferior and ordinary service.[1] Owing to this inconsistency, and the obvious injustice which might sometimes result from a rigid enforcement of the old rule, it has in modern times been somewhat relaxed even in England. In our own country, where private corporations for literary, religious, and commercial purposes, have been multiplied beyond any former example, their facility in acting and contracting is involved with public prosperity itself; and after mature consideration, the old technical rule has been condemned as impolitic, and essentially discarded.[2] Indeed, it seems to result from the very structure of these artificial beings that inasmuch as there are two general modes in which they may express their assent, there are two general modes in which they may expressly contract, first by *vote* and secondly by their duly authorized agents.[3] We propose, accordingly, in this chapter, after treating of the general modes in which private corporations aggregate may contract, with whom, and in what name, to consider what *kind* of contracts, and *what* contracts, in general, they may make.

§ 229. The course of modern decisions and particularly in our own country, seems to have assimilated in some degree the mode in which corporations may contract with us, with that usual in bodies of this kind, existing under the Roman Civil Law. Mr. Ayliffe, who cites the Digest and Castrensis, tells us, that "a corporation may, *in its own person*, whenever it pleases, do any extrajudicial act, as make contracts, and the like, and shall not be compelled to constitute a syndic (as in judicial acts) for the despatch of any public business of this kind; for a corporation may celebrate contracts by its own proper *decree*, without constituting a syndic."[4] Again, he says, "Corporations are bound by their

---

[1] See Chap. IX.

[2] 2 Kent, Com. 233.

[3] See Chap. IX.

[4] Ayliffe, Civil Law, tit. 35, b. 2, p. 198; Castrensis, in l. 1, d. 3, 4.

contracts in the same manner as individual persons; for though the members of a corporation cannot separately and individually give their consent in such manner as to oblige themselves as a collective body; yet, being lawfully assembled, it represents but one person, and may consequently make contracts, and by their collective consent, oblige themselves thereunto. And thus a corporation may consent, though not with the same readiness and facility as particular persons."[1] Indeed, it would be strange, if, when it was settled, that a corporation might by vote or decree appoint an agent whose contracts would be binding upon it,[2] it could not by vote or decree make the same contracts itself. Accordingly, although in Taylor *v.* Dullidge Hospital,[3] Lord Chancellor Parker refused to compel the specific performance of an agreement for a lease signed by the master, warden, and fellows of the corporation, on the ground, that to bind that (or indeed any corporation, *as to its revenue*) the contract must be under its common seal; yet sixty-three years afterwards it appears to have been decreed in the case of Maxwell *v.* Dullidge Hospital,[4] that the specific performance of an agreement of the major part of a corporation, entered in the corporation books, though not under the corporate seal, should be enforced; and this decision has been cited and relied on by the highest authority in this country.[5] In the Andover and Medford Turnpike Corporation *v.* Hay,[6] it is said by the learned Chief Justice Parsons, speaking as the organ of the Supreme Court of Massachusetts, that "we cannot admit that a corporation can make a parol contract, unless by the intervention of some agent or attorney, duly authorized to contract on their part." This language, we apprehend, is to be limited in its application to the facts before the court. That was an action on the case against the defendant, as the proprietor of four shares in a turnpike road, for not paying sundry assessments duly made by the directors of the corporation; and a loose declaration by him in an open meeting of the corporation, "that if one thousand dollars were not enough to make the turnpike, he would spend two thousand dollars, and if that was not enough, he would spend half his estate," was held insufficient evidence of a contract on the part of the defendant

---

[1] Ayliffe, Civil Law, sup. d. 12, 1, 22.

[2] See Chap. IX.

[3] 1 P. Wms. 655.

[4] 1 Fonbl. Eq. 296, n. o. (Phil. ed. 305, n. o.)

[5] Bank of United States *v.* Dandridge, 12 Wheat. 95, per Marshall, C. J.; and see Union Bank of Maryland *v.* Ridgely, 1 Harris & G. 425, per Buchanan, C. J.

[6] 7 Mass. 107.

with the corporation, to pay such assessments as should be made by the directors upon his shares. It needs hardly be added, that whether we consider the nature of the language used by the defendant in this case, or the fact, that there was by vote no acceptance of, or in conduct no reliance upon, his proposition on the part of the corporation, this, without the principle laid down by the learned chief justice, could not be held a serious contract. We apprehend, that a corporation may as well immediately by vote express its assent and contract, as mediately through an agent authorized by vote.[1] It may as well express by vote its assent to a proposition, as to the appointment of an agent, or the acceptance of a charter; and we know no case in which the power to act by an agent is greater than the power to act in person. A distinct proposal made in a corporate meeting, and accepted by corporate vote, would unquestionably constitute a contract binding upon the corporation; and where the agreement was entered upon the corporation books, this seems to have been held even in England.[2] In the Essex Turnpike Corporation *v.* Collins,[3] Sedgwick, Justice, in delivering the opinion of the court, tells us, that "aggregate corporations cannot contract without *vote*, because there is no other way in which they can express their assent." He adds, however, that such corporations may contract by authorized agents.

§ 230. In an English chancery case, it appeared that the bill filed charged a municipal corporation with having given a license to the complainant to fill up a part of a creek, and make a wharf and erect buildings thereon, adjoining a piece of land he held under lease from them, in consequence of which license, he had with their knowledge taken possession and erected the wharf and buildings at his expense, and prayed that they might be decreed to grant him a lease. The counsel of the complainant, on the hearing, contended that the corporation, acting by a majority of its members, and at a regular meeting, and giving a license to the complainant to do an act by which he had incurred expense, was bound thereby. For the corporation it was insisted, that a contract, to be binding on it, must be under the common

---

1 Trustees of St. Mary's Church *v.* Cagger, 6 Barb. 576; contra, Garvey *v.* Colcock, 1 Nott & McC. 231.

2 Maxwell *v.* Dullidge Hospital, 1 Fonbl. Eq. 296, n. o. (Phil. ed. 305, n. o.) See Magill *v.* Kauffman, 4 S. & R. 317; Brady *v.* The Mayor, &c. of Brooklyn, 1 Barb. 584.

3 8 Mass. 298, 299.

seal, and that no such contract was shown. The case stated in the bill not being proved, the bill was dismissed. The vice-chancellor, Sir John Leach, said, however, that if a regular corporate resolution passed for granting an interest in a part of the corporate property, and upon the faith of that resolution expenditure was incurred, he inclined to think that both principle and authority would be found, for compelling the corporation to make a legal grant in pursuance of that resolution.[1] It seems from a still more recent case,[2] in England, that a court of equity there will not compel a corporation to execute a legal assurance of corporate property, in pursuance of a contract not under seal, unless valuable consideration for the contract be expressly proved, or evidence be given of acts done or omitted by the party contracting with the corporation on faith of the promised legal assurance. In this country, it is very clear, that no such equities would be necessary in general to sustain the contract made by a committee or agent duly authorized, though not under the corporate seal.[3] Such equities are however, sometimes called in, in this country, to aid a contract legal in itself but defectively executed under the provisions of a general law or a particular charter. Thus, where an act creating and regulating banking associations provided " that contracts made by any such association, and all notes and bills by them issued and put in circulation as money, shall be signed by the president or vice-president *and cashier* thereof," and an agreement under which such an association received a loan of money was signed by the president only, the bank was held liable to repay the money on the ground of the advance made and the implied promise to repay it, though the agreement might be considered as a nullity.[4]

§ 231. The great number of the members of which corporations aggregate usually consist, renders their undoubted right of contracting by vote, in general, extremely inconvenient; and accordingly their mode of contracting is through the intervention of agents, duly author-

---

[1] Marshall *v.* The Corporation of Queensborough, 1 Simons & S. 520; and see London and Birmingh. Railroad Co. *v.* Winter, 1 Craig. & Ph. 63; Stanley *v.* Chester & Birkenhead Railway Co. 9 Simons, 264; Great Northern Railway Co. *v.* Manchester, &c. Railway Co. 5 De G. & S. 138, 10 Eng. L. & Eq. 11, 15.

[2] Wilmot *v.* Corporation of Coventry, 1 Younge & C., Exch. 518.

[3] Stanley *v.* Hotel Corporation, 13 Maine, 51; Stoddert *v.* Port Tobacco Parish, 2 Gill & J. 227; The Banks *v.* Poiteaux, 3 Rand. 136; Legrand *v.* Sidney College, 5 Munf. 324.

[4] Boisgerard *v.* The New York Banking Company, 2 Sandf. Ch. 25, 26.

ized for that purpose. These are either persons specially appointed and authorized for the occasion, or, as is more common, the general officers and boards, as directors, managers, &c., existing within the corporation, — elected, it is true, by the members, but usually deriving their ordinary powers from the charter or act of incorporation. This instrument frequently prescribes, too, their mode of action; and we need hardly add, that, where this is the case, its injunctions must be rigidly pursued. In modern corporations created by statute, the charter ordinarily contemplates the business of the corporation to be transacted exclusively by a special body or board of directors;[1] and the acts of such body or board, evidenced by a legal vote, are as completely binding upon the corporation, and as complete authority to their agents, as the most solemn acts done under the corporate seal. If these boards are appointed, and act, in the mode prescribed by the statute creating the corporation, to suppose that they were not the agents of the corporation for any purpose within the range of their duties, because not appointed under the corporate seal, or that their contracts were invalid because not solemnized by it, would be, in the language of the learned Mr. Justice Story, "to suppose, that the common law is superior to the legislative authority; and that the legislature cannot dispense with forms, or confer authorities, which the common law attaches to general corporations."[2] As we propose to treat of corporate agents in the succeeding chapter, we beg leave to refer to that chapter, for the mode in which corporations aggregate of a private nature may contract by agents.[3] Indeed, as these bodies have, either by the particular laws of their incorporation, or by the general laws of the land, power to regulate and order their affairs, no rule applicable to all corporations can be laid down, with regard to their mode of contracting. This must differ with their rules and course of doing business; and if they have practically, or upon system, neglected or dispensed with any precautions, which, at

---

[1] Union Turnpike Company *v.* Jenkins, 1 Caines, 381.

[2] Fleckner *v.* U. S. Bank, 8 Wheat. 357, 358. And see Andover, &c. Turnpike Corporation *v.* Hay, 7 Mass. 102; Hayden *v.* Middlesex Turnpike Corporation, 10 Mass. 397; Essex Turnpike Corporation *v.* Collins, 8 Mass. 292; Dana *v.* St. Andrews Church, 14 Johns. 118; Union Bank *v.* Ridgely, 1 Harris & G. 324; Kennedy *v.* Baltimore Ins. Co. 3 Harris & J. 367; Garrison *v.* Combs, 7 J. J. Marsh. 85; Savings Bank *v.* Davis, 8 Conn. 191; Legrand *v.* Hampden-Sidney College, 5 Munf. 324; Stanley *v.* Hotel Corporation, 13 Maine, 51; Stoddert *v.* Port Tobacco Parish, 2 Gill & J. 227; Andrews *v.* Estes, 2 Fairf. 267.

[3] See Chap. IX.

common law, were deemed essential to their security, still, if there is sufficient evidence of a common consent, of a joint and corporate act, they must be considered as liable; especially where individuals, who have trusted to the good faith of the corporation, would be injured and deprived of their remedy, if any other construction of the doings of the corporation was adopted.[1] Though a payment be made irregularly by the president of a corporation, yet, when it is justly due, and there is no reason for withholding it, it cannot be recovered back on the ground that the president had verbal directions only from the directors to make it.[2]

§ 232. The members of a corporation aggregate cannot separately and individually give their consent in such a manner as to oblige themselves as a collective body; for in such case it is not the *body* that acts; and this is no less the doctrine of the common, than of the Roman Civil Law. "Being *lawfully assembled*," says Ayliffe, "they represent but one person, and may consequently make contracts, and by their collective consent, oblige themselves thereunto."[3] And though all the members of a corporation covenanted on behalf of it under their private seals, binding themselves and their heirs, that the corporation should do certain acts, it was decided that they were *personally* bound.[4]

§ 233. By the Common Law, and by the Civil Code, too, as a corporation aggregate may contract with persons who are not members, so it may contract with persons who are members of it; and the contract is not on this account invalid;[5] a member of a corporation contracting

---

[1] Hayden *v.* Middlesex Turnpike Corporation, 10 Mass. 401, per Sewall, J.; Trustees of St. Mary's Church *v.* Cagger, 6 Barb. 576. Where a company acted upon and so ratified a parol agreement entered into by their chairman, they were held bound by it, though their deed of settlement required that such contracts should be signed by three directors. Reuter *v.* Electric Telegraph Co. 6 Ellis & B. 341, 37 Eng. L. & Eq. 189. See too, Bargate *v.* Shortridge, 5 H. L. Cas. 297, 31 Eng. L. & Eq. 44.

[2] New Orleans Building Co. *v.* Lawson, 11 La. 34.

[3] Ayliffe, Civil Law, tit. 35, B. 2, p. 198; 1 Bl. Com. 475; Hayden *v.* Middlesex Turnpike Corporation, 10 Mass. 403, per Sewall, J.; The Proprietors of the Canal Bridge *v.* Gordon, 1 Pick. 304; Hartford Bank *v.* Hart, 3 Day, 491; Waterbury *v.* Clark, 4 id. 198; Society of Practical Knowledge *v.* Abbott, 2 Beav. 559; Ruby *v.* Abyssinian Soc. 15 Maine, 306; Wheelock *v.* Moulton, 15 Vt. 519; Isham *v.* Bennington Iron Co. 19 Vt. 249, 250.

[4] Tileston *v.* Newell, 13 Mass. 406; Harris *v.* The Muskingum Manuf. Co. 4 Blackf. 267; Roberts *v.* Button, 14 Vt. 195; Wheelock *v.* Moulton, 15 Vt. 521, 522.

[5] Ayliffe, Civil Law, tit. 35, B. 2, p. 198; Worcester Turnpike *v.* Willard, 5 Mass. 85,

with it being regarded, as to that contract, a stranger.[1] Hence, a vote of the corporation affecting a contract between it and a member, cannot bind the member without his assent to it;[2] and a contract by a member of a corporation to pay a debt due from it, where no personal liability is imposed by the charter or general law, must be in writing, in conformity to the Statute of Frauds, the debt being the debt of another.[3] And though the member of the corporation be also one of the trustees of the corporation, it would seem that this would not incapacitate him from contracting with it; but he may recover against the corporation for his services rendered under a contract with the other trustees, in a case where there is no evidence of such gross partiality in the contract as amounts to fraud.[4] Though the 85th sect. of the Companies Clauses Consolidation Act of England, 8 & 9 Vict. ch. 16, enacts, that "no person interested in any contract with the company shall be capable of being a director, and no director shall be capable of being interested in any contract with the company during the time he shall be a director;" and the 86th sect. enacts, that, "if any director, at any time subsequent to his election be directly or indirectly concerned in any contract with the company, then the office of such director shall become vacant, and he shall cease from voting or acting as director;" yet a contract entered into with the company by a director after his election, is not rendered void thereby, but the office only of the director is vacated.[5] And where the members of three distinct corporations were the same, yet in The Proprietors of the Canal Bridge *v.* Gordon,[6] it was held, by the Supreme Court of Massachusetts, that contracts between the several corporations were valid and might even be implied from corporate acts.

---

per Parsons, Ch. J.; Gilmore *v.* Pope, id. 491; The President, &c. of the Berks & Dauphin Turnpike Road *v.* Myers, 6 S. & R. 12; Gordon *v.* Preston, 1 Watts, 385; Central Railroad & Banking Co. of Georgia *v.* Claghorn, 1 Speers, Eq. 545; Ely *v.* Sprague, 1 Clarke, Ch. N. Y. 351.

[1] Hill *v.* Manchester Water Works Company, 2 Nev. & M. 82, 5 B. & Ad. 866; Rogers *v.* Danby Universalist Society, 19 Vt. 191; Culbertson *v.* Wabash Nav. Co. 4 McLean, C. C. 544; City and County of St. Louis *v.* Alexander, 23 Misso. 483, 528.

[2] American Bank *v.* Baker, 4 Met. 176; Longley *v.* Longley Stage Co. 23 Maine, 39.

[3] Trustees of Free Schools in Andover *v.* Flint, 13 Met. 543.

[4] Rogers *v.* Danby Universalist Society, 19 Vt. 191; and see Geer *v.* School District No. 10, in Richmond, 6 Vt. 76; Sawyer *v.* Methodist Episcopal Society in Royalton, 18 Vt. 409.

[5] Foster *v.* Oxford, Worcester & Wolverhampton Railway Company, 13 C. B. 200, 14 Eng. L. & Eq. 306.

[6] 1 Pick. 297.

The banking associations of New York, under the general bank law of 1838, are to be regarded for the purpose of contract as bodies corporate; and hence, in a suit at law, by such an association against one of its members for debt, the fact of membership presents no objection to recovery.[1]

§ 234. A corporation may be known by several names as well as a natural person;[2] and will be bound by obligations of any sort assumed by it in its adopted name, as that of a firm, or of an agent. It was early held, that the misnomer of a corporation in a grant, obligation, or other written contract, does not prevent a recovery thereon either by or against the corporation in its true name, provided its identity with that intended by the parties to the instrument be averred in pleading, and apparent in proof. Lord Coke notes a just distinction in this particular between writs and grants; "for if," said he, "a writ abates, one might of common right have a new writ; but he cannot of common right have a new bond or a new lease."[3] In illustration and support of the rule above laid down, a special verdict found that the defendant's testator made, sealed, and as his deed, delivered, a writing obligatory to the plaintiffs, whose true style was, the Mayor and Burgesses of the borough of the Lord the King of Lynne Regis, commonly called, King's Lynne in the county of Norfolk, by the name of the Mayor and Burgesses of King's Lynn in the county of Norfolk; and judgment was given to the plaintiffs.[4] The learned reporter of the above case, cited with many others the case of the Abbot of York, who was incorporated by the name of "The Abbot of the Monastery of the Blessed Mary of York;" and a bond was made to the abbot by the name, "The Abbot of the Monastery of the Blessed Mary, without *the walls* of the City of York." The Abbot brought his action of debt by his true name, which implies an averment, that the abbey was within York; and although the abbey was without *the walls*, yet, because it was in truth within the *city* of York, the bond and writ were adjudged good by the opinion of the whole court.[5] In our own country, this rule has been repeatedly recog-

---

[1] Willoughby *v.* Comstock, 3 Hill, 391; The People *v.* The Assessors of Watertown, 1 Hill, 616; Ely *v.* Sprague, 1 Clarke, Ch. N. Y. 351.

[2] Minot *v.* Curtis, 7 Mass. 444, per cur.; Medway Cotton Manufacturing Co. *v.* Adams, 10 Mass. 360; Melledge *v.* Boston Iron Co. 5 Cush. 176, 177; Conro *v.* Port Henry Iron Co. 12 Barb. 27; *ante*, Chap. III.

[3] The case of the Mayor and Burgesses of Lynne Regis, 10 Co. R. 125.

[4] Ibid. 123.

[5] Ibid., where, see cited, also, the case of the Hospital of Savoy; the case of Eton Col-

nized. An action by "*The Medway Cotton Manufactory*," on a note given to "Richardson, Metcalf & Co.;"[1] also, one on a bond, by "The New York African Society for Mutual Relief," given to the Standing Committee of "The New York, &c.," *solvendum* to the corporation, by its true name,[2] has been supported on demurrer, there being proper averments in the pleadings. With proper averments and proof, recoveries have been had, too, on bonds given to a corporation, with an erroneous omission of the county[3] or addition of the State[4] in which it was located, in a corporate name. In the President, &c. *v.* Myers,[5] the declaration set forth a covenant with "The President, Managers, and Company of the Berks and Dauphin Turnpike Road," and the instrument produced on trial contained a covenant with "The Berks and Dauphin Turnpike Company." Gibson, J., in delivering the opinion of the court, said: "In pleading, the style, or corporate name must be strictly used; and while the law was, that a corporation could speak only by its seal, the same strictness in the use of the style was also necessary in contracting. But when the courts began to allow these artificial beings, most, if not all, the attributes of natural existence, and to permit them to contract pretty much in the ordinary manner of natural persons, a correspondent relaxation in the use of the exact corporate name for the purposes designated, necessarily followed. I take the law of the present day to be, that a departure from the strict style of the corporation will not avoid its contracts, if it substantially appear that the particular corporation was intended, and that a latent ambiguity may, under proper averments, be explained by parol evidence in this, as in other cases, to show the intention." With deference, however, to the learned justice we have quoted, we apprehend, that the rule he notes as a relaxation from the strictness prevailing, when corporations aggregate

---

lege, Dyer, 150; case of Dean and Chapter of Carlisle; case of Dean and Canons of Windsor; case of Merton College, in Oxford.

[1] Medway Cotton Manufactory *v.* Adams, 10 Mass. 360.

[2] African Society *v.* Varick, 13 Johns. 38; and see Trustees of McMinn Academy, 2 Swan, 94, 99.

[3] Woolwich *v.* Forrest, 1 Penning. 115; The Inhabitants of Middletown *v.* McCormick, 2 Penning. 500.

[4] The Inhabitants of Upper Alloways Creek *v.* String, 5 Halst. 323.

[5] 6 S. & R. 12; and see the Culpepper Agricultural & Manufacturing Society *v.* Digges, 6 Rand. 165; The Hagerstown Turnpike Road Co. *v.* Cruger, 15 Harris & J. 122; Pendleton *v.* Bank of Kentucky, 1 T. B. Mon. 175; Society, &c. *v.* Young, 2 N. H. 310; Clarke *v.* Potter County, 1 Barr, 162, 163; Boisgerard *v.* The New York Banking Company, 2 Sandf. Ch. 25.

could contract only by seal, was the true doctrine of the common law, even in those ancient days. For Lord Coke, in Sir Moyle Finch's case,[1] says, "It was observed, that till this generation of late times, it was never read in any of our books, that any body, politic or corporate, endeavored or attempted, by any suit, to avoid any of their leases, grants, conveyances, or other of their own deeds, for the misnomer of their true name of corporation; but after that a window was opened to give them light to avoid their own grants for the misnomer of themselves, what suits and troubles (to avoid grants, &c. as well made to them as by them) have followed thereupon, everybody knows; but it was said, for every curious or nice misnomer, God forbid that their leases or grants, &c. should be defeated; for there will be found a difference between writs and grants; and in all cases this is true, *quod apices juris non sunt jura*."

§ 235. Having, in the preceding chapter,[2] considered the special contracts of corporations, we proceed now to the inquiry, whether they are competent to make contracts of any other kind. The ancient rule of the common law was, undoubtedly, that they were not; and this, with the probable reason of it, we have before endeavored to explain.[3] It is certain that this rule has been relaxed somewhat in England; as in the case of Maxwell *v.* Dullidge Hospital,[4] before cited, and in Parbury and another *v.* The Governor and Company of the Bank of England,[5] in which, by the suggestion of Lord Mansfield,[6] a special action of assumpsit was brought against the bank, and tried before him, without objection to the form of the remedy. In Broughton *v.* The Manchester Water Works Company,[7] Lord Chief Justice Abbott declined entering "into the general question, whether an action of assumpsit will, in any case, lie against a body corporate;" as though this might be considered as open to discussion even in England; and in Harper *v.* Charlesworth,[8]

---

[1] 6 Co. R. 65; the case of the Mayor & Burgesses of Lynne Regis, 10 Co. R. 125, 146; and see Commercial Bank *v.* French, 21 Pick. 490; Charitable Association in Middle Granville *v.* Baldwin, 1 Met. 365; City of Lowell *v.* Morse, id. 473; Milford and Chillicothe Turnpike Co. *v.* Brush, 10 Ohio, 476; Bower *v.* The Bank of the State, 5 Ark. 234; Kentucky Seminary *v.* Wallace, 15 B. Mon. 35.

[2] See Chap. VII.

[3] Ibid.

[4] 1 Fonbl. Eq. 296, n. o.

[5] Doug. 526, n. 1.

[6] The King *v.* The Bank of England, Doug. 526.

[7] 3 B. & Ald. 7.

[8] 4 B. & C. 575.

it was said by Mr. Justice Bayley, that "a corporation can only *grant* by deed; yet there are many things which a corporation has power to do otherwise than by deed. It may appoint a bailiff and do other things of a like nature." The authorities recognize the power even of a municipal corporation to make simple contracts about trivial matters, frequently occurring, and essential to the business of the corporation.[1]

§ 236. The general rule in England seems, however, still to be, that a corporation aggregate cannot expressly bind itself except by deed, unless the act establishing it authorizes it to contract in another mode, or obviously contemplates that it shall so do, as make promissory notes, in order to attain the object, or do the business, for which it was created.[2] Where "a company, like the Bank of England, or the East India Company, are incorporated for the purposes of trade, it seems," says Mr. Justice Best, "to result from the very object of their being so incorporated, that they should have power to accept bills, or issue promissory notes; since without such power, it would be impossible for either of these companies to go on."[3] We find, indeed, in Edie *v.* The East India Company,[4] and from the Bank of England *v.* Moffat,[5] that actions on simple contracts have been maintained against these institutions, without the objection we are considering; and it is said, "that for all such small matters, as it would be absurd and ridiculous for the corporation to use their common seal, they may contract by parol."[6] If the contract, however, be executed, the general rule above stated does not seem to be applied;[7] and hence assumpsit for use and occupation may be main-

---

[1] Denman, C. J., Hall *v.* The Mayor, &c. of Swansea, 5 Q. B. 546; and see Mayor of Ludlow *v.* Charlton, 6 M. & W. 815; Arnold *v.* Mayor of Poole, 4 Man. & G. 860.

[2] Slark *v.* Highgate Archway Company, 5 Taunt. 792; Broughton *v.* Manchester Water Works Co. 3 B. & Ald. 1; Marshall *v.* The Corporation of Queensborough, 1 Simons & S. 520; London and Birmingham Railway Co. *v.* Winter, 1 Craig & P. 63; Mayor of Stafford *v.* Till, 4 Bing. 75; Wilmot *v.* Corporation of Coventry, 1 Younge & C., Exch. 518; Ludlow Corporation *v.* Charlton, 9 Car. &. P. 242; East London Water Works Co. *v.* Bailey, 4 Bing. 233; Dunston *v.* Imperial Gas Light Co. 3 B. & Ad. 125; Cope *v.* The Thames Haven Dock & Railway Company, 3 Exch. 841. London Dock Co. *v.* Sinnott, 8 Ellis & B. 347; Copper Miners Co. *v.* Fox, 16 Q. B. 229.

[3] Broughton *v.* Manchester Water Works Co. *supra.*

[4] 2 Burr. 1216, 1 W. Bl. 295.

[5] 3 Bro. Ch. 262.

[6] Australian Royal S. N. Co. *v.* Marzetti, 11 Exch. 228, 32 Eng. L. & Eq. 572.

[7] Fishmonger's Co. *v.* Robertson, 6 Man. & G. 192; Sanders *v.* St. Neot's Union, 8 Q. B. 810; Australian Royal Mail Steam Navigation Co. *v.* Marzetti, 11 Exch. 228, 32 Eng. L. & Eq. 572.

tained by a corporation aggregate, against a tenant who has occupied under them and paid rent.[1] In Beverly *v.* Lincoln,[2] it was held that a corporation aggregate might be sued in assumpsit on a contract by parol, express or implied, for goods sold and delivered, and in Church *v.* The Imperial Gas Company,[3] that it made no difference as to the right of a corporation to sue on a contract made by them without seal, whether the contract be executed or executory. It is said that a suit brought by a corporation upon an executory contract in England, amounts to an admission of record by them that such contract was duly entered into by them, so as to estop them from setting up in a cross action, the objection that it was not sealed with their common seal.[4] The English law on this subject is evidently in a state of slow transition.[5] A distinction is there taken between a municipal corporation and the corporations of late established by charter or act of parliament for the purpose of carrying on trading speculations; and where the nature of these latter has been such as to render the drawing of bills or the making of any other particular set of contracts necessary for the purposes of the corporation, the English courts have held that they would imply in those who are, according to the provisions of the charter or act of parliament, carrying on the corporation concerns, an authority to do those acts without which the corporation could not subsist. At the same time, they hold that a municipal corporation cannot enter into an important contract to pay a sum of money out of the corporate funds, even to make improvements in the borough, except under the common seal.[6] Indeed,

---

[1] Mayor of Stafford *v.* Till, 4 Bing. 75, 12 J. B. Moore, 260.

[2] 6 A. & E. 829, 2 Nev. & P. 35.

[3] Ibid. 846.

[4] Fishmongers' Co. *v.* Robertson, 5 Man. & G. 192. But see what is said in the Copper Miners *v.* Fox, 16 Q. B. 229, 237, 3 Eng. L. & Eq. 425.

[5] See De Grave *v.* Monmouth, 4 Car. & P. 111.

[6] Mayor of Charlton *v.* Ludlow, 6 M. & W. 815; 9 Car. & P. 242; and see Arnold *v.* Mayor of Poole, 4 Man. & G. 860; Hall *v.* Mayor, &c. of Swansea, 5 Q. B. 526; Reg. *v.* Mayor of Stamford, 6 Q. B. 433; Paine *v.* Strand Union, 8 Q. B. 340; Sanders *v.* The Guardians of St. Neot's Union, 8 Q. B. 810; Lamprell *v.* The Billericay Union, 3 Exch. 283; Reg. *v.* Council of Warwick, id. 926; Clark *v.* Guardians of Cuckfield Union, Bail Court, 1851, 11 Eng. L. & Eq. 443. In Henderson *v.* Australian Royal Mail Steam Navigation Co., 5 Ellis & B. 409, 32 Eng. L. & Eq. 167, a case arising upon a contract, not under seal, for bringing home an unseaworthy ship from a foreign port, the plaintiff maintained his action against the defendant corporation, a company incorporated for the purpose of "maintaining steam navigation and the carrying of the royal mails, passengers and cargo." See also, Reuter *v.* Electric Telegraph Co. 6 Ellis & B. 341, 37 Eng. L. & Eq. 189.

with regard to railway companies, water companies, and the like, that is, other than trading companies, the general rule in matters of moment would seem to be, that executory contracts made in their behalf by their agents, will not be binding upon them, unless under the corporate seal or made in the form prescribed by the special or general act which controls them;[1] but that whereas the purposes for which the corporation was created render it necessary that work should be done or goods supplied, to carry such purposes into effect, and such work is done or goods supplied and accepted by the corporation, and the whole consideration for payment is executed, the corporation cannot refuse to pay on the ground that the contract is not under seal.[2]

§ 237. The old rule of the English law was at first adopted in Pennsylvania; and in Breckbill *v.* Turnpike Company,[3] it was decided that implied assumpsit could not be maintained against a corporation, on the ground that such a body could contract only by deed under the corporate seal; but this case was afterwards overruled in The Chestnut Hill and Spring House Turnpike Company *v.* Rutter.[4] The same rule once prevailed in Kentucky,[5] but has now given way to the current of modern decisions.[6] In commenting upon the law, ancient and modern, on this subject, the learned Mr. Justice Story informs us that the principle that corporations aggregate could do nothing but by deed under their common seal, "must always have been understood with many qualifications, and seems inapplicable to acts and votes passed by such corporations at their corporate meetings." It was probably in its origin applied to aggregate corporations at the common law, and limited to such solemn proceedings as were usually evidenced under seal, and to be done by

---

[1] Homersham *v.* Wolverhampton Water Works Co. 6 Exch. 193, 4 Eng. L. & Eq. 426, 429; Diggle *v.* London and Blackwall Railway Co. 5 Exch. 442; Copper Miners *v.* Fox, 16 Q. B. 229, 3 Eng. L. & Eq. 420; and see Clark *v.* The Guardians of Cuckfield Union, Bail Court, 1851, 11 Eng. L. & Eq. 462; where all the English authorities on this subject are reviewed by the Court of Queen's Bench.

[2] Clark *v.* The Guardians of Cuckfield Union, Bail Court, 1851, 11 Eng. L. & Eq. 442; Doe d. Pennington *v.* Taniere, 12 Q. B. 1011, 1014.

[3] 3 Dallas, 496.

[4] 4 S. & R. 6.

[5] Frankfort Bank *v.* Anderson, 3 A. K. Marsh. 1; McBean *v.* Irvin, 4 Bibb, 17; Long *v.* Madison, Hemp & Flax Co. 1 A. K. Marsh. 105; Hughes *v.* Bank of Somersett, 5 Litt. 14.

[6] Waller *v.* Bank of Kentucky, 3 J. J. Marsh. 201; Lee *v.* Flemingsburg, 7 Dana, 28; Muir *v.* Canal Co. 8 Dana, 161; Commercial Bank of New Orleans *v.* Newport Manufacturing Company, 1 B. Mon. 14.

those persons who had the custody of the common seal, and had authority to bind the corporation thereby, as their permanent official agents. "The rule," he observes, "has been broken in upon in a vast variety of cases, in modern times, and cannot now as a general proposition be supported."[1] In general, throughout the United States, it is entirely exploded; and it is here well settled, that the acts of a corporation, evidenced by vote, written or unwritten,[2] are as completely binding upon it, and are as complete authority to its agents as the most solemn acts done under the corporate seal; that it may as well be bound by express promises through its authorized agents, as by deed; and that promises may as well be implied from its acts and the acts of its agents, as if it had been an individual.[3]

§ 238. 1. It having once been established, that corporations might contract otherwise than by their corporate seals, — that they might

---

[1] Bank of U. S. *v.* Dandridge, 12 Wheat. 68; and see Brady *v.* The Mayor, &c. of Brooklyn, 1 Barb. 584.

[2] Ibid.; St. Mary's Church *v.* Cagger, 6 Barb. 576.

[3] Bank of Columbia *v.* Patterson, 7 Cranch, 305, 306; Mechanics Bank of Alexandria *v.* Bank of Columbia, 5 Wheat. 326; Fleckner *v.* U. S. Bank, 8 Wheat. 357; Bank of U. S. *v.* Dandridge, 12 Wheat. 68; Peterson *v.* Mayor of N. Y., 17 N. Y. 449; Dunn *v.* Rector of St. Andrew's Church, 14 Johns. 118; American Insurance Company *v.* Oakley, 9 Paige, 496; Watson *v.* Bennet, 12 Barb. 196; Fister *v.* La Rue, 15 Barb. 323; Overseers of North Whitehall *v.* Overseers of South Whitehall, 3 S. & R. 117; Chestnut Hill and Spring House Turnpike Co. *v.* Rutter, 4 S. & R. 16; McGargle *v.* Hazleton Coal Co. 5 Watts & S. 436; Hamilton *v.* Lycoming Ins. Co. 5 Barr, 344, 345; Bank of Kentucky *v.* Schuylkill Bank, 1 Parsons, Sel. Cas. 251, 265; Legrand *v.* Hampden Sydney College, 5 Munf. 324; The Banks *v.* Poitiaux, 3 Rand. 143; Union Bank of Maryland *v.* Ridgely, 1 Harris & G. 413; Elysville Manufacturing Co. *v.* Okisko Co. 1 Md. Ch. Dec. 392; Ross *v.* Carter, 1 Carter, Ind. 281; Hayden *v.* Middlesex Turnpike Corporation, 10 Mass. 401; White *v.* Westport Cotton Manufacturing Company, 1 Pick. 215; Bulkely *v.* Derby Fishing Co. 2 Conn. 256; Witte *v.* The Same, id. 260; Waring *v.* Catawba Company, 2 Bay, 109; Garvey *v.* Colcock, 1 Nott & McC. 231; Petrie *v.* Wright, 6 Smedes & M. 647; Inhabitants of the Fourth School District in Rumford *v.* Wood, 13 Mass. 193; Baptist Church *v.* Mulford, 3 Halst. 182, *et infra;* and see Gray *v.* Portland Bank, 3 Mass. 364; Sanger *v.* Inhabitants of the Third Parish in Roxbury, 8 Mass. 265; Titcomb *v.* Union M. & F. Ins. Co. 8 Mass. 326; Brown *v.* Penobscot Bank, id. 445; Dorr *v.* Union Insurance Co. id. 494; Shotwell *v.* McKeown, 2 South. 828; Abbot *v.* Hermon, 7 Greenl. 118; Waller *v.* Bank of Kentucky, 3 J. J. Marsh. 201; Lee *v.* Flemingsburg, 7 Dana, 28; Muir *v.* Canal Co. 8 id. 161; Buncombe Turnp. Co. *v.* McCarson, 1 Dev. & B. 310; Bates *v.* Bank of Alabama, 2 Ala. 452; Eastman *v.* Coos Bank, 1 N. H. 26; Maine Stage Company *v.* Longley, 14 Maine, 444; Lime Rock Bank *v.* Macomber, 29 Maine, 564; Bank of Metropolis *v.* Guttschlieck, 14 Pet. 19; Poultney *v.* Wells, 1 Aikens, 180; Sheldon *v.* Fairfax, 21 Vt. 102; Gassett *v.* Andover, id. 343; San Antonio *v.* Lewis, 9 Texas, 69; Palmer *v.* Medina Ins. Co. 20 Ohio, 537.

make parol promises, either by vote, or through their authorized agents, no reason could be found in technical principle or substantial justice, why they should not be subject and entitled to the same presumptions as natural persons. Indeed, it seems early to have been settled that a charter may be presumed to have been given to persons who have long acted as a corporation; though the very case supposes that no other proof than the long-continued exercise of corporate powers could be adduced, of a charter, or of a vote of the corporators to accept it.[1] It had been held also, that the acceptance of a particular or amended charter by an existing corporation, or by corporators already in the exercise of corporate powers may be inferred from the acts of corporate officers, or facts which demonstrate that it must have been accepted; and that it is not indispensable to show a written instrument or vote of acceptance on the corporation books.[2] From the same species of evidence, the enactment,[3] and repeal[4] of by-laws have been inferred. Again, in the case of Wood *v.* Tate,[5] which was replevin upon a distress, made by the bailiff of the borough of Morpeth, for rent, it appeared in evidence, that the tenant went into possession under a lease void for not being executed under the corporate seal, even if made by proper officers; yet the court held that though the lease was void, the tenant was to be deemed tenant from year to year under the corporation; and his payment of rent from time to time to its officers, was sufficient proof of tenancy under the corporation, on which it might distrain for the rent in arrear. In Doe *v.* Woodman[6] also, where certain premises had been demised by the plaintiff to the corporation, as tenant from year to year at an annual rent, though it does not appear in what manner the demise had been accepted, except by the payment of rent by the bailiff, as such, it seems to have been taken for granted that this was proper evidence of a holding by the corporation. The English doctrine of the present day, seems to be, that where a corporation has

---

[1] Bank of United States *v.* Dandridge, 12 Wheat. 71. See Chap. II.

[2] Ibid., and The King *v.* Amery, 1 T. R. 575, 2 T. R. 515; Newling *v.* Francis, 3 T. R. 189. See Middlesex Husbandmen *v.* Davis, 3 Met. 133; Wetumpka and Coosa Rail-Railroad Company *v.* Bingham, 5 Ala. 657.

[3] Union Bank of Maryland *v.* Ridgely, 1 Harris & G. 413.

[4] Attorney-General *v.* Middleton, 2 Ves. Sen. 328.

[5] 5 B. & P. 246; and see 1 Roll. R. 82, 2 Lev. 174, 1 Vent. 298, 2 Lev. 252; Dean and Chapter of Rochester *v.* Pierce, 1 Camp. 466; Mayor, &c. of Stafford *v.* Till, 4 Bing. 75.

[6] 8 East, 228.

actually enjoyed and occupied land with the consent of the owner, an action of assumpsit will lie against it for use and occupation on the implied assumpsit arising from the actual use; but that unless the contract be under seal, the corporation would not be liable on it beyond the period of actual use,[1] and a continuous occupation by the corporation for several years will not render them tenants from year to year. In this country it has been settled by repeated decisions, that all duties imposed on corporations aggregate by law, and all benefits conferred at their request, raise implied promises, for the enforcement of which an action may well lie.[2] In assumpsit against a bank, where it appeared that the committee of the corporation had contracted expressly under their private seals, although it was held that an action might have been maintained against the committee personally, yet inasmuch as the whole benefit of the contract resulted to the corporation, and on the faith of the transaction it had from time to time proceeded to pay money, the court were of opinion that from evidence of this, the jury might legally infer an adoption of the contract, and a vote to pay the whole sum due under it by the corporation, and an acceptance of this engagement by the plaintiff's intestate.[3] In the case, too, of Dunn *v.* St. Andrew's Church,[4] where it was in proof that the plaintiff had performed services as clerk of the church, for which he had received payments at several times, the records of the corporation containing entries thereof; but no resolution was recorded, appointing the plaintiff clerk of the church, nor was there any other proof of his appointment; the court held a vote of appointment unnecessary to be shown; as there was sufficient proof of an implied promise of the corporation to make

---

1 Ibid.; Lowe *v.* London and Northwestern Railway Co. 18 Q. B. 632, 14 Eng. L. & Eq. 18; Finlay *v.* Bristol and Exeter Railway Co. 7 Exch. 409, 9 Eng. L. & Eq. 489.

2 Salem Bank *v.* Gloucester Bank, 17 Mass. 1; Gloucester Bank *v.* Salem Bank, 17 Mass. 33; Foster *v.* The Essex Bank, 17 Mass. 479; Smith *v.* First Congregational Meeting-house in Lowell, 8 Pick. 178; Bank of Kentucky *v.* Wister, 2 Pet. 318; Trustees of Limerick Academy *v.* Davis, 11 Mass. 113; Trustees of Farmington Academy *v.* Allen, 14 Mass. 172; Amherst Academy *v.* Cowls, 6 Pick. 427; Kennedy *v.* Baltimore Insurance Co. 3 Harris & J. 367; Stone *v.* Congregational Society of Berkshire, 14 Vt. 86.

3 Bank of Columbia *v.* Patterson, 7 Cranch, 306; Randall *v.* Van Vechten, 19 Johns. 65, per Platt, J.; and see Bank of U. S. *v.* Dandridge, 12 Wheat. 72; Haight *v.* Sahler, 30 Barb. 218.

4 14 Johns. 118; and see Inhabitants of Mendham *v.* Losey, 1 Penning. 347; Inhabitants of the Township of Saddle River *v.* Colfax, 1 Halst. 115; Baptist Church *v.* Mulford, 3 Halst. 191, 192; Powell *v.* Trustees of Newburgh, 19 Johns. 284; Chestnut Hill & Spring House Turnpike Company *v.* Rutter, 4 S. & R. 6.

compensation. Not only estoppels, technically so called, but estoppels *in pais*, operate both for and against corporations.[1]

§ 239. An act of incorporation carries with it all powers necessary to accomplish the object of the act, unless it impairs vested rights.[2] It should be observed, however, that since individual members of a corporation cannot, unless authorized, bind the body by express promises, neither can any corporate engagements be implied from their unsanctioned conduct or declarations.[3] As corporations can be expressly bound only by joint and corporate acts, so it is only from such acts, done either by the corporation as a body, or by its authorized agents, that any implication can be made, binding it in law. Upon a claim of the amount of their disbursements for work done upon a turnpike road, the plaintiffs not being able to prove any request by an authorized agent of the corporation; but only that their men were seen at work upon the road by different members of the body, and by an agent who was authorized to contract on its part, *but in writing only;* the court held the evidence insufficient to raise a promise by the Turnpike Company to pay the amount of the disbursements.[4]

§ 240. Though a contract made by the minority of a purchasing committee is not binding on a corporation, the ratification of their contract by the corporation may be inferred from facts attending the transaction.[5] And generally, if persons assuming to act as agents of a corporation, but without legal authority, make a contract, and the corporation receive the benefit of it, and use the property acquired under it, such acts will ratify the contract, and render the corporation liable thereon.[6] In Magill *v.* Kauffman,[7] which was ejectment for land

---

[1] Selma & Tennessee Railway Company *v.* Tipton, 5 Ala. 808; Phil. Wilmington & Baltimore R. Co. *v.* Howard, 13 How. 307, 335; Scaggs *v.* Baltimore & Washington R. Co. 10 Md. 268, 280.

[2] Morris & Essex R. Co. *v.* Newark, 2 Stock. Ch. 352.

[3] Proprietors of the Canal Bridge *v.* Gordon, 1 Pick. 304; Ruby *v.* Abyssinian Soc. 15 Maine, 306; Regents of the University of Maryland, 9 Gill & J. 365; Soper *v.* Buffalo and Rochester R. Co. 19 Barb. 310.

[4] Hayden *v.* Middlesex Turnp. Corp. 10 Mass. 397. See Burdick *v.* Champl. Glass Co. 8 Vt. 19.

[5] Trott *v.* Warren, 2 Fairf. 225.

[6] Episcopal Charitable Society *v.* Episcopal Church in Needham, 1 Pick. 372; Bank of Columbia *v.* Patterson, 7 Cranch, 299; Randall *v.* Van Vechten, 19 Johns. 60; Gooday *v.* Colchester & Stone Valley Railway Co. 17 Beav. 132, 15 Eng. L. & Eq. 596, 598, 599.

[7] 4 S. & R. 317.

claimed by a Presbyterian congregation, before incorporation, under a purchase by their trustees, and after incorporation claimed in their right as a corporation, the Supreme Court of Pennsylvania held, that evidence of the acts and declarations of the trustees and agents of the corporation, both before and after the incorporation, while transacting the corporate business, and also evidence *of what passed at the meetings of the congregation when assembled on business*, were admissible to show their possession of the land, and the extent of their claim. And where the same individuals, being members of a dam or causeway corporation which had no right of toll, and also of a canal bridge corporation which had a right of toll, as the proprietors of the causeway, voted that the free use of it be granted to the proprietors of the bridge, provided the proprietors of the bridge give the proprietors of the causeway the free use of a certain portion of the bridge, and keep the same in repair, and provided that the proprietors of the causeway have power to fill up that part of the bridge so as to make it a solid dam, whenever they should deem it expedient; it was held, that proof that a cross-bridge was built from the causeway to the canal bridge, and no tolls for four years demanded of those passing over the causeway, cross-bridge, and canal bridge or *vice versa*, was sufficient proof that the above proposition was accepted, although no vote of acceptance could be found in the books of the Canal Bridge corporation; and as a consequence, it was held, that no toll could be demanded by the proprietors of the canal bridge of those passing over it by way of the cross-bridge or dam.[1] In a case in which the rector and wardens of a church corporation, consisting of rector, wardens, and vestry merely, being authorized by a vote of the pew proprietors who were no part of the corporation, borrowed money of a charitable society for the use of the church, and gave a note in their official capacity; and it was proved, by the payment of interest from time to time, and the settlements of accounts between the rector and the church, that the corporation had recognized the debt as due by itself; it was held, that, though the corporation might not be liable on the note, it certainly was upon the money-counts.[2] And where the officers of a bank have been in the practice of receiving money and other things to be deposited in its vaults for safe keeping, the corporation impliedly adopting the acts of its officers will be considered as the depositary, and not the cashier or other agent, through whose particular

---

[1] Proprietors of the Canal Bridge *v.* Gordon, 1 Pick. 297.

[2] Episcopal Charitable Society *v.* Episcopal Church in Dedham, 1 Pick. 372.

act the articles deposited may have been received into the bank.[1] Indeed, by the whole course of decisions in this country, corporations in their contracts are placed upon the same footing with natural persons, open to the same implications, and receiving the benefit of the same presumptions.

§ 241. Banks, or indeed any other bodies corporate, may as well make contracts of bailment of every kind, as natural persons; provided it be done in the course of business permitted or contemplated by their charters. Incorporated stage-coach companies may be liable as common carriers; and banks sue every day as lenders, and are sued as depositaries, borrowers, &c. It is not necessary that the act of incorporation should give a bank particular power to receive deposits, to enable it so to do. It is sufficient that this is in the ordinary course of banking business; and such a corporation, by the mere grant of a charter for that species of business, is empowered to do it in all its branches, unless expressly restrained. It is not bound to receive on deposit the funds of every man who offers them, but may select its dealers, and the cashier is the proper officer to make the selection.[2] And though there be no special regulation or by-law relative to deposits, or any account of them required to be kept and laid before the directors and the company, or practice of examining them; yet if it is found that the bank has been in the habit of receiving money and other valuable things in this way, and the practice was known to the directors, and might be presumed to have been known to the company; their building and vaults allowed to be used for this purpose, and their officers employed in receiving into custody the things deposited; the corporation must be considered the depositary, and not the cashier or other officer, through whose particular agency commodities may have been received into the bank.[3]

§ 242. Banks are frequently restrained by statute as to their mode of contracting; and such a statute is of course applied to a contract of deposit, as well as to any other. In Massachusetts a statute provides "that no bank shall make or issue any note, bill, check, draft, accept-

---

[1] Foster *v.* Essex Bank, 17 Mass. 479; and see Salem Bank *v.* Gloucester Bank, 17 Mass. 1.

[2] Thatcher *v.* Bank of the State of New York, 5 Sandf. Ch. 121.

[3] Foster *v.* Essex Bank, 17 Mass. 497, 498, per Parker, C. J.; Bank of Kentucky *v.* Schuylkill Bank, 1 Parsons, Sel. Cas. 235. See Barnes *v.* Ontario Bank, 19 N. Y. 152, cited *post*, § 253.

ance, certificate or contract, in any form whatever, for the payment of money, at any future day certain, or with interest, except for money borrowed of the commonwealth," &c.;[1] and where, upon the deposit of money in a bank, the depositor received a book containing the cashier's certificate, in which it was stated that the money was to remain on deposit for a time certain, the agreement was, under the statute, deemed to be illegal, as a contract by the bank for the payment of money at a future day certain; and it was held, that the depositor could maintain no action against the bank *on the contract*, though he might recover back the amount deposited in an action commenced without previous demand, before the expiration of the time for which it was to remain on deposit, the parties not being *in pari delicto*, and the action being in disaffirmance of an illegal contract.[2]

§ 243. When a deposit is made in bank, it is usual for the cashier to give a certificate to that effect, and from this may be gathered the nature of the deposit, whether it be general or special, or, in other words, whether it be generally passed to the credit of the depositor, or specially lodged for *safe keeping* merely.[3] In the former case, banks are authorized to use in discounting, &c., the money deposited, as a temporary loan, liable to be withdrawn at any moment by the depositor, the deposit being a debt due from the bank to the depositor, which raises an implied assumpsit for its repayment,[4] and in the latter it is considered that they have no such right.[5] The bank has no lien on a general deposit for the amount of a bill of exchange indorsed by such depositor, and discounted by the bank, and which has not matured.[6] It is not the practice for

---

1 Rev. Stat. Mass. c. 36, § 57.

2 White *v.* Franklin Bank, 22 Pick. 181. In Pelham *v.* Adams, 17 Barb. 384, it was held that a plaintiff, who upon making a deposit had received a certificate, promising the payment of interest, might well maintain his action upon the primary legal contract of loan, even if, as the defendant insisted, the issue of the certificate were rendered illegal by statute.

3 Foster *v.* Essex Bank, 17 Mass. 504, 505, per Parker, C. J.

4 Bank of Kentucky *v.* Wister, 2 Pet. 324; State Bank *v.* Armstrong, 3 Dev. 526; State Bank *v.* Locke, id. 533, 534; State Bank *v.* Kain, 1 Breese, 45; Albany Commercial Bank *v.* Hughes, 17 Wend. 94; Matter of Franklin Bank, 1 Paige, 249; Coffin *v.* Anderson, 4 Blackf. 403; Dawson *v.* Real Estate Bank, 5 Ark. 283; Pott *v.* Clegg, 16 M. & W. 320.

5 Foster *v.* Essex Bank, 17 Mass. 503–505; Coffin *v.* Anderson, 4 Blackf. 403; Dawson *v.* Real Estate Bank, 5 Ark. 283.

6 Beckwith *v.* Union Bank, 4 Sandf. 604.

cashiers to make any return or statement of *special* deposits to the directors of banks; and it is considered highly improper for any officer even to inspect or examine them, without the consent of the depositor. When money, not in a sealed packet, bag, box, or chest, is deposited with a bank, the law presumes it to be a general deposit, until the contrary appears; but if it be deposited in a sealed packet, bag, box, or the like, the presumption is, that it was intended to be a special deposit.[1] No control whatever of a chest, or of the gold contained in it, when specially deposited, is left with the bank or its officers; and it would be a breach of trust in them to open it, or inspect its contents.[2] No profit, therefore, can arise to a bank from special deposits, unless it be that an increased, though it is evident a fallacious, credit, is acquired with the community on their account. Indeed, they are simply gratuitous on the part of the corporation, and the practice of receiving them must have originated in a willingness to accommodate members with a place for their treasures, more secure from fire and thieves than their dwelling-houses or stores; and this is rendered more probable from the well-known fact, that not only money or bullion, but documents, obligations, certificates of public stocks, wills, and other valuable papers, are frequently, and in some banks as frequently, as money, deposited for safe keeping.[3]

§ 244. Although, as a general rule, particular errors in balanced accounts may be inquired into and rectified, when the whole accounts may not be liable to be opened; with respect to accounts kept by individuals with a bank, it was said, by the learned Mr. Justice Spencer, that there was in his mind this exception, that, "if a dealer's book *accompany* the deposit, and the credit be then given, when the deposit is made, it becomes an original entry, and would be conclusive on the bank; if, however, the book is sent *to be written up afterwards* (by copying from the bank leger), it is not an original entry, and may be examined into."[4] In the subsequent case of The Mechanics and Farmers Bank *v.* Smith,[5] it was decided by the Supreme Court of New York, that an entry by the teller, of the amount of a deposit in the bank book of the depositor was not conclusive on the latter; but that if mistake could be shown as

---

[1] Dawson *v.* Real Estate Bank, 5 Ark. 283.

[2] Foster *v.* Essex Bank, 17 Mass. 504, 506.

[3] Ibid. 506, 507.

[4] Manhattan Company *v.* Lydig, 4 Johns. 389.

[5] 19 Johns. 115.

to the amount, there was a remedy as in ordinary cases of mistake. It has been held, that a bank assumes on itself a note deposited for collection, by passing the same to the credit of the depositor.[1] Although the extension of bills of exchange deposited for collection in the books of the bank, and in the bank book of the depositor, is equivalent to payment, or actual collection of the bills, yet, if made under mutual mistake, the bank is not bound by it, and frequent settlements of the depositor's bank book, previous to the discovery of the mistake in which the bills were credited to him as paid, was held not to alter the rights of the parties.[2] A bank may retain from an insolvent depositor any debt due from him to it.[3] Where one, having made a *general* deposit in a bank, of a large amount of its bills which were depreciated to half their nominal value, received from the cashier a certificate that so many *dollars and cents* were deposited, the nominal amount of the bills, the bills of the bank being by its charter redeemable in gold and silver, it was decided by the Supreme Court of the United States, that the depositor was entitled to receive the whole amount of the certificate *in gold and silver*.[4]

§ 245. A wife was intrusted by her husband with certain sums of money, and directed by him to deposit them in some bank for safe keeping, which she did, opening an account with the bank, the officers of which were ignorant of her coverture, in her own name, and from time to time checked out the whole amount there deposited. In an action brought by the husband against the bank, to recover the amount of the deposit, he was not allowed to recover, on the ground that the wife, as his agent, might fairly be presumed to have authority to withdraw the deposit; and that if this were otherwise, as the bank had no notice of the agent's coverture, and the husband, by intrusting her with the money, had enabled her to do the wrong, the loss should fall upon him rather than upon the bank.[5] And where, by the negligence of the officers and agents of a canal corporation, the corporate funds were deposited in a bank in such a manner as to lead the officers of the bank to suppose that the deposit was made by the president of the canal com-

---

[1] Whitherell *v.* Bank of Pennsylvania, 1 Miles, 399.

[2] Mechanics Bank *v.* Earp, 4 Rawle, 384.

[3] Ford *v.* Thornton, 3 Leigh, 695; State Bank *v.* Armstrong, 3 Dev. 519; McDowell *v.* Bank, 1 Harring. Del. 369.

[4] Bank of Kentucky *v.* Wister, 2 Pet. 318; and see Wallace *v.* State Bank, 2 Eng. 61.

[5] Dacy *v.* Chemical Bank, 2 Hall, 550.

pany, who at the same time left his signature in the bank, as that upon which the money was to be drawn out, and the officers of the bank afterwards paid out the money upon his check, under the supposition that he had authority to draw for the same, the bank was adjudged not to be liable for the loss sustained by the canal company from the misapplication of the deposit by the president.[1]

§ 246. It is apparent that very numerous and important questions may arise, as to how far corporations are liable as bailees, for the loss of, or any injury to, the thing bailed, and how far for the neglects, frauds, embezzlements, and thefts of their servants, as cashiers of banks, &c. The solution of these must depend upon the general principles of the law of bailments, which apply equally to corporations as to natural persons;[2] and these it would be evidently improper to notice in detail, in a treatise upon the subject we are considering. The liability of a corporation as bailee is, like that of a natural person, to be determined by the nature of the bailment, — the degree of care required from it, and the degree of care or diligence used. In case of a *special* deposit, from which it receives no profit whatever, but which is merely for the accommodation of the bailor, a bank is liable only for *gross* neglect, equivalent in its effects upon contracts, to fraud.[3] In Foster *v.* Essex Bank,[4] a case which appears to have been very fully and learnedly argued by counsel, and examined by the court, this subject came under the consideration of the Supreme Court of Massachusetts. That was *assumpsit* brought against a bank, to recover the amount of a large special deposit in gold, which had been fraudulently or feloniously taken from the vaults of the bank by the cashier and chief clerk, and converted by them to their own uses. There being no evidence of gross neglect on the part of the bank, — the directors, who represented the company, being wholly ignorant of the nature or amount of the deposit, or of the transactions of the cashier and chief clerk, and these having no right, *in the course of their official employment*, to intermeddle with the deposit, except to close the doors of the vault upon it when banking hours were over; it was adjudged that the bank was not liable for the loss, inasmuch as it only warranted the skill and faithfulness of its offi-

---

[1] Fulton Bank *v.* N. Y. & Sharon Canal Co. 4 Paige, 127.

[2] Foster *v.* Essex Bank, 17 Mass. 496, onwards; and see Chap. IX.

[3] Foster *v.* Essex Bank, 17 Mass. 507.

[4] Ibid. 479.

cers *in their employments*, and not their *general* honesty and uprightness. It was said, "that the bank was no more liable for this act of his (the cashier's), than they would be if he had stolen the pocket-book of any person, who might have laid it upon the desk, while he was transacting some business at the bank."[1] The general rule laid down was, that fraud on property deposited, committed by the depositary or his servants, acting under his authority, express or implied, relative to the subject-matter of the fraud, is equivalent to gross negligence, and renders the depositary liable.[2]

§ 247. It should be recollected, that, because one is employed generally as the agent or servant of a bank, it does not follow that a dealer with the bank may not, by trust reposed in him in a particular transaction, make him his own agent, and be burdened with any loss which may follow his neglect or fraud in the business confided to him. In Manhattan Company *v.* Lydig,[3] it was considered, that where one who was usually employed by a bank as a bookkeeper, though occasionally as teller, was intrusted by a dealer with deposits to be lodged in bank for him, and falsely obtained for the dealer credits beyond the amount deposited, that the latter, and not the bank, was liable for the deficit of deposits; inasmuch as the fraud was committed by *his* agent in discharge of *his* trust. A bank cannot be charged with negligence in not detecting the frauds of its servants, if the examinations of books, papers, &c., are in the way usual with banks.[4] A bank is bound to exhibit its books to a depositor, on proper occasions, and the officers having charge of them are *quoad hoc* the agents of both parties.[5]

§ 248. The reasonable and established customs of banks enter into and make a part of contracts made with them, and must have due weight in expounding their contracts, when knowledge of the customs can in any way be brought home to those sought to be affected by them.[6]

---

[1] Foster *v.* Essex Bank, 17 Mass. 479.

[2] Ibid. 508.

[3] 4 Johns. 377.

[4] Ibid. 389.

[5] Union Bank *v.* Knapp, 3 Pick. 96.

[6] Jones *v.* Fales, 4 Mass. 252; Widgerey *v.* Munroe, 6 Mass. 450; Lincoln & Kennebec Bank *v.* Page, 9 Mass. 155; Same *v.* Hammatt, id. 159; Smith *v.* Whiting, 12 Mass. 8; Blanchard *v.* Hilliard, 11 Mass. 88; Weld *v.* Gorham, 10 Mass. 366; Whitwell *v.* Johnson, 17 Mass. 452; City Bank *v.* Cutter, 3 Pick. 414; Yeaton *v.* Bank of Alexandria, 5

An usage established by proof that current deposits made in a bank, and the proceeds of notes and drafts placed for collection, are to be paid to the depositor upon demand, at the counter of the bank, would prevent the running of the act of limitations against such depositor, until payment of his claim had been refused, or some act done with his knowledge dispensing with the necessity of a demand.[1] A dispensation from such notice would be furnished by an express notification of the bank that his demand would not be paid,[2] or by the suspension of specie payments, and discontinuance of banking operations by the bank, when these were known to the depositor; and from the time of such knowledge, the statute of limitations begins to run.[3] Where a note was made payable at a bank, it was held that the parties were bound to know its usages, and had impliedly agreed that those usages should become a part of their contract.[4] This doctrine was afterwards adjudged to be applicable to the parties to a bill of exchange drawn on a person at Washington, on the ground that it would probably be put into a bank there for collection.[5] It has been decided in Tennessee,[6] that the law presumes that all persons getting accommodations at a bank are cognizant of all provisions of its charter which fix the law of the contract. A custom of a bank not to correct mistakes in the receipt or payment of money, unless discovered before the person leaves the room, is, however, illegal and void.[7] A custom of a bank to pay only half of a half bank-note has also

---

Cranch, 52; Morgan *v.* Bank of North America, 8 S. & R. 73; Pearson *v.* Bank of Metropolis, 1 Pet. 93; Bank of Metropolis *v.* New England Bank, 1 How. 234; Same *v.* Same, 6 id. 213; Bank of Columbia *v.* McGruder, 6 Harris & J. 180; Bank of Columbia *v.* Fitzhugh, 1 Harris & G. 239; Hartford Bank *v.* Stedman, 3 Conn. 489; Raborg *v.* Bank of Columbia, 1 Harris & G. 231; Union Bank of Georgetown *v.* Planters Bank, 9 Gill & J. 439; Pierce *v.* Butler, 14 Mass. 303; Renner *v.* Bank of Columbia, 9 Wheat. 585; Warren Bank *v.* Suffolk Bank, 10 Cush. 582.

1 Planters Bank *v.* Farmers and Mechanics Bank, 8 Gill & J. 449; Union Bank of Georgetown *v.* Planters Bank, 9 Gill & J. 489; Same *v.* Same, 10 id. 422.

2 Ibid.

3 Ibid.

4 Mills *v.* Bank of the United States, 11 Wheat. 431; Cohen *v.* Hunt, 2 Smedes & M. 227. But see Adams *v.* Otterback, 15 How. 545, that a usage to bind must be a usage of all the banks of the place rather than of a particular bank.

5 Bank of Washington *v.* Triplett, 1 Pet. 25. See also Whitwell *v.* Johnson, 17 Mass. 452.

6 Hays *v.* State Bank, Martin & Y. 179. A bank regulation, sufficiently published and authorized by the charter, which required every depositor to produce his pass-book when demanding payment of any deposit, was held to be a reasonable regulation, and binding upon the depositor. Warhus *v.* Bowery Savings Bank, 5 Duer, 67.

7 Gallatin *v.* Bradford, 1 Bibb, 209.

been held to be bad, as unsupported by law.[1] Usages of banks will not be judicially noticed, but must be proved, or must have been heretofore proved, and established by courts of justice, before they will be recognized and applied.[2] To give them the force of law, requires an acquiescence and notoriety, from which an inference may be drawn that they are known to the public, and especially to those who do business at the bank.[3]

§ 249. A very large portion of the business of banking corporations consists in the collection by them, as agents, of debts in the shape of notes and drafts; and a clause in a bank charter authorizing the bank "*to deal in bills of exchange*," was construed as authority to the bank to take bills of exchange, payable elsewhere, for collection merely.[4] And where a bank was chartered with power "to have, possess, receive, retain, and enjoy to themselves and their successors, lands, rents, tenements, hereditaments, goods, chattels, and effects of what kind soever, nature and quality, and the same to grant, demise, aliene, or dispose of, for the good of the bank," and also "to receive money on deposit and pay away the same free of expense, discount bills of exchange and notes, and to make loans &c.," and in the course of business under this charter, the bank discounted and held promissory notes, and then the legislature of the State passed a law declaring that "it shall not be lawful for any bank in the State to transfer by indorsement or otherwise, any note, bill receivable, or other evidence of debt; and if it shall appear in evidence, on the trial of any action upon such note, bill receivable, or other evidence of debt, that the same was transferred, the same shall abate upon the plea of the defendant;" this statute was decided by the Supreme Court of the United States, to be void under the Federal Constitution, as conflicting with the above clauses of the previously granted charter.[5]

§ 250. We need hardly say, that the law applicable to agents for collection in general, applies equally to banks. Where a bank, in which a

---

[1] Allen *v.* State Bank, 1 Dev. & B. 3.

[2] Planters Bank *v.* Farmers and Mechanics Bank, 8 Gill & J. 449.

[3] Adams *v.* Otterback, 15 How. 545, per McLean, J.

[4] Bank *v.* Knox, 1 Ala. 118; Bates *v.* Bank of the State of Alabama, 2 Ala. 466.

[5] Planters Bank *v.* Sharp, 6 How. 301, reversing s. c. 4 Smedes & M. 27; and see Montgomery *v.* Galbraith, 11 Smedes & M. 555, in which the court reverses its opinion given in Payne *v.* Baldwin, 3 Smedes & M. 661.

note is deposited for collection, places it in a notary's hands on the party's failure to pay, and the notary omits to give notice to the indorser, so that he is discharged, the bank is not liable to the holder, although the maker is unable to pay;[1] unless, indeed, it should be proved that the bank placed the note in the hands of a notary known to them, from being drunk at the time the note was given to him, or from other sufficient cause, to be incompetent, or whose habits were so universally intemperate as to disqualify him for the discharge of an official act.[2] But if the bank, contrary to custom, does not employ a *notary* in such a case, but employs some other person as agent, and such person omits to give notice, the bank is liable.[3] By failing to demand a note or bill left with it for collection, the bank makes the note or bill its own, and becomes liable to the owner for the amount.[4] In such case the debtor's insolvency may be shown in mitigation of damages.[5] A bank, in which bills of exchange are deposited for transmission only, fulfils its duty by sending them to the bank to which they are to be transmitted for collection, and is not responsible for any laches of that bank.[6] Bills of exchange payable at distant places, and left with a bank for collection, are presumed to be intended to be transmitted to and collected by suitable sub-agents at the places where payable; since it cannot be expected that a bank will employ one of its own officers to journey about and collect such bills. In such case, therefore, as in case of bills expressly left with a bank for transmission only, if the bank in good faith employ suitable sub-agents for collection, it is not liable for their neglect or default.[7] The bank receiving from another bank a bill or note for

---

[1] Bellemire *v.* Bank of United States, 1 Miles, 173. And see Bank of Owego *v.* Babcock, 5 Hill, 152; Frazier *v.* New Orleans Gas Light & Banking Co. 2 Rob. La. 294; Agricultural Bank *v.* Commercial Bank of Manchester, 7 Smedes & M. 592; Warren Bank *v.* Suffolk Bank, 10 Cush. 582; Citizens Bank of Baltimore *v.* Howell, 8 Md. 530.

[2] Agricultural Bank *v.* Commercial Bank of Manchester, 7 Smedes & M. 592.

[3] Ibid. and see Frazier *v.* New Orleans Gas Light & Banking Co. 2 Rob. La. 294; Bellemire *v.* Bank of United States, 1 Miles, 173.

[4] Bank of Washington *v.* Triplett, 1 Pet. 25; McKinster *v.* Bank of Utica, 9 Wend. 46; Tyson *v.* State Bank, 6 Blackf. 225.

[5] Stone *v.* Bank, 2 Dev. 408.

[6] Mechanics Bank *v.* Earp, 4 Rawle, 384; Wingate *v.* Mechanics Bank, 10 Barr, 109.

[7] Fabens *v.* Mercantile Bank, 23 Pick. 330; Dorchester and Milton Bank *v.* New England Bank, 1 Cush. 177; Wingate *v.* Mechanics Bank, 10 Barr, 109. See, however, Allen *v.* Merchants Bank, 15 Wend. 482, 22 Wend. 215. A bank receiving paper for collection from another bank which has a special interest in it by indorsement from the owner, is the agent not of the owner, but of the bank, and is liable to it alone for its own default or that of its agents. Montgomery County Bank *v.* Albany City Bank, 3 Seld.

collection, is bound to present the same for payment, and if the same is not paid at maturity, to give due notice of the dishonor *to the bank from which the note was received;* but it is not required by the law-merchant, at least as known and practised in Massachusetts, to give notice to any other party to the note unless there is a special agreement to give such notice.[1]

§ 251. It has been held that a bank that collects a bill of exchange, on its being transmitted by the cashier of another bank, where it was lodged for collection, is liable to the owner, and cannot set off a claim against the bank from which the bill was received.[2] In such a case, the bank transmitting, and the bank collecting, have been both regarded as the agents of the holder of the note, and the liability of either bank to the holder, and of the holder to either of the banks paying him by mistake, to be direct.[3] The true doctrine with regard to the right of a collecting bank to retain the proceeds of collection against the transmitting banks, seems to be, that if it have notice that the transmitting bank is a mere agent for collection, or does not give credit to it on account of the securities received, it cannot retain for the balance of its account; but if it have no such notice and trust, and give credit on such securities, as the property of the transmitting bank, it may retain.[4] In Maryland, the exemption in the statute limitations of that State of such accounts as concern the trade or merchandise between merchant and merchant, does not apply to accounts between two banking institutions, growing out of mutual deposits and collections made by each, with and for the other; the interest of banking institutions, as well as public policy, requiring that the liquidation of balances between banks should be regular and fre-

---

459, reversing the decision in 8 Barb. 396; Commercial Bank of Pennsylvania *v.* Union Bank of New York, 1 Kern. 203, 19 Barb. 391.

[1] Phipps *v.* Millbury Bank, 8 Met. 79; and see Colt *v.* Noble, 5 Mass. 167; Eagle Bank *v.* Chapin, 3 Pick. 180; Mead *v.* Engs, 5 Cowen, 303; Howard *v.* Ives, 1 Hill, 263; Bank of United States *v.* Davis, 2 id. 451; Bank of United States *v.* Goddard, 5 Mason, 366; Haynes *v.* Birks, 3 B. & P. 599, contra; Smedes *v.* Bank of Utica, 20 Johns. 372.

[2] Lawrence *v.* Stonington Bank, 6 Conn. 521; McBride *v.* Farmers Bank of Salem, 25 Barb. 657. And see Van Amee *v.* Pres. &c. of the Bank of Troy, 8 Barb. 312, that in such case, both banks are jointly liable to the principal for negligence.

[3] Bank of Orleans *v.* Smith, 3 Hill, 560; where see case, Allen *v.* Merchants Bank of City of New York, 22 Wend. 215, commented on and explained.

[4] Bank of the Metropolis *v.* New England Bank, 6 How. 212; Van Amee *v.* Pres. &c. of Bank of Troy, 8 Barb. 312; Case *v.* Mechanics Banking Association, 4 Comst. 166.

quent.[1] Not only may one bank act as a collecting agent for another, but may, unless prohibited by its charter, act as the agent of another bank in the transfer of its stock; and where such agency has been assumed by a bank through its officers and agents, the bank will be liable for their faithful discharge of the duties of the agency.[2]

§ 252. A very important class of cases, in which the doctrine of presumed assent has been applied to corporations aggregate, is in the acceptance of official bonds, grants, &c. In case of an individual, there has never been a question but that a paper intended for his benefit and found in his possession, would be considered as accepted by him, his assent thereto being presumed. A different rule was thought applicable to corporations, or their managing boards; and that, inasmuch as they ordinarily express their assent by vote, a vote entered on the corporation books was the only mode by which it could be proved. In the Bank of the United States *v.* Dandridge,[3] this subject was brought under the consideration of the Supreme Court of the United States; and upon great deliberation, and a full review of all the authorities, it was there decided, that a bond with sureties given by the cashier of a bank for the faithful performance of his duties, and found in the possession of the bank, the cashier having acted in his office, might, as in case of natural persons, be presumed to be accepted by the bank, although no vote of acceptance by the directors could be found on the records of the corporation. It is indeed the well-settled doctrine of the present day, that the same presumptions are applicable to a corporation as to a natural person. There is no reason why its assent to, and acceptance of, grants and deeds beneficial to it should not be inferred from its acts, as well as that the same inference should be drawn from the acts of individuals. "Suppose," says Mr. Justice Story, in the very full and learned opinion delivered by him in the case just mentioned, "a deed poll granting lands to a corporation; can it be necessary to show that there was an acceptance by the corporation by an assent under seal, if it be a corporation at the common law; or by a written vote, if the corporation may signify

---

[1] Farmers & Mechanics Bank *v.* Planters Bank, 10 Gill & J. 422, 441.

[2] Bank of Kentucky *v.* Schuylkill Bank, 1 Parsons, Sel. Cas. 236, 237, 238, 239.

[3] 12 Wheat. 64; Dedham Bank *v.* Chickering, 3 Pick. 335; Union Bank of Maryland *v.* Ridgely, 1 Harris & G. 324; Burgess *v.* Pue, 2 Gill, 250; and see Apthorp *v.* North, 4 Mass. 167; Smith *v.* Governor and Company of the Bank of Scotland, 1 Dow, P. C. 272, Lord Redesdale.

its assent in that manner? Why may not its occupation and improvement, and the demise of the land by its agents, be justly admitted by implication, to establish the fact in favor and for the benefit of the corporation? Why should the omission to record the assent, if actually given, deprive the corporation of the property which it gained in virtue of such actual assent? The validity of such a grant depends upon the acceptance, not upon the mode by which it is proved. It is no implied condition that the corporation shall perpetuate the evidence of its assent in a particular way." [1]

§ 252 *a*. A bridge company authorized "to do and suffer all acts, matters and things, which a body corporate may do and suffer," and "generally to do and execute all and singular such acts, matters and things as to them shall or may appertain," may contract to permit water-pipes to be attached to their bridge for the purpose of conveying water from one side of a river to the other, such use not being inconsistent with, or foreign to the principal object of the bridge.[2]

§ 253. It needs no authority to establish, that if a general statute prescribe the mode or modes in which corporations must contract, a contract made in any other mode will not be binding upon the corporation or the party contracting with it, unless the statute, as it sometimes does, provides to the contrary. The Joint-Stock Companies Act, 7 & 8 Vict. ch. 110, s. 44, enacts, among other things, that every contract made in behalf of a joint-stock company registered, under that act, "shall be in writing, and signed by two, at least, of the directors of the company," "and shall be sealed with the common seal thereof, or signed by some officer of the company on its behalf, to be thereunto expressly authorized by some minute or resolution of the board of directors applying to the particular case; and that in the absence of such requisites, or any of them, any such contract shall be void and ineffectual (except as against the company on behalf of whom the same shall have been made)," &c. In an action by such a company, upon an unilateral covenant to pay money advanced by it, for the repayment of which an annuity was granted, with a condition that certain property was to be

---

1 Bank of United States *v.* Dandridge, 12 Wheat. 70, 72, 73; Proprietors of Monumoi Great Beach *v.* Rogers, 1 Mass. 159; Amherst Bank *v.* Root, 2 Met. 533, 534; Western Railroad *v.* Babcock, 6 Met. 356, 357.

2 Frankfort Bridge Co. *v.* Frankfort, 18 B. Mon. 41.

sold to pay the arrears of the annuity, it was held, that the contract, if it had the general legal requisites, need not be in the particular form required by the statute; that, being a contract on the part of the covenantor only, it was not a contract "*on behalf of the company*," within the meaning of the act; but that to bring a contract within the act, it must be one in which the company contracts to do something *in consideration* of something else to be done.[1] By the 45th section of the same act, to bind a joint-stock company by the acceptance of a bill of exchange, it must express that it was accepted by two of the directors of the company "on behalf of the company." A bill accepted thus: "Accepted, J. B. & E. N., directors of the C. Company, appointed by resolution to accept this bill," sealed with the corporate seal, with the corporate name circumscribed and countersigned by the secretary, was deemed sufficiently to express upon the face, that it was accepted on behalf of the company.[2]

§ 253 *a.* Where the charter of a corporation prescribes the particular mode in which its contracts shall be made, that mode must in general be pursued. Hence, where an act incorporating an insurance company provided that all policies and other instruments made and signed by the president or any other officer of the company should be good and effectual to bind the company, it was held that a contract to cancel a policy must be signed by the president or other officer in order to bind the corporation.[3] In a late case in Massachusetts, the charter of the company authorized it, in its name and by the signature of its president, and in such form as it might by its rules and by-laws direct, "to make contracts and underwrite policies of insurance," and "to transact and perform all the business relating to such contracts or policies of insurance as aforesaid, according to the usage and custom of merchants; and by such contracts effectually to bind and pledge the capital stock." The company were by this charter confined to insurances within the

---

1 The British Mutual Life Assurance Company *v.* Brown, 12 C. B. 723, 14 Eng. L. & Eq. 285, 291, 292.

2 Edwards *v.* Cameron's Coalbrook, &c. Railway Co. 11 Eng. L. & Eq. 565; Halford *v.* Cameron's Coalbrook, &c. Railway Co. 16 Q. B. 442, 3 Eng. L. & Eq. 309.

3 Head *v.* Providence Insurance Company, 2 Cranch, 127; 2 Johns. 199; Dawes *v.* North River Insurance Company, 7 Cowen, 462; and see Hill *v.* Manchester Water Works Co. 2 Nev. & M. 573, 5 B. & Ad. 866; Safford *v.* Wyckoff, 4 Hill, 446, 447, 448, Chan. Walworth. An act which is an attempt to evade the provisions of a charter, confers no right on him who attempts it. Union Bank *v.* McDonough, 5 La. 63.

city and harbor of Charleston. A subsequent act empowered the company "to make contracts and underwrite policies of insurance and indemnity on property in other States." It was held that under these charters the company could make a parol contract to insure.[1] But though the charter of an insurance company require that all policies shall be signed by the president, yet it is not necessary that the assent of the company to an assignment of a policy should be signed by the president in order to bind the company.[2] The signature of the secretary to such assignment is *primâ facie* evidence of an agreement by the company; and the company, by accepting the assignee's guaranty of the premium note, adopts the act of the secretary, assenting in their behalf to the assignment.[3] It seems to have been held in Connecticut, that a corporation authorized to contract in a prescribed mode, may nevertheless by practice render itself liable on instruments executed in a different mode, the charter being held, of course, directory only.[4] And though the charter of a bank enacted "that all bills, bonds, notes, and every other contract or engagement, on behalf of the corporation, should be signed by the president and countersigned by the cashier; and that the funds of the corporation should in no case be liable for any contract or engagement, unless the same should be signed and countersigned as aforesaid," it was held that this section did not extend to contracts and undertakings implied in law; so that a recovery was had against the bank for money advanced upon a check made in the course of business, and signed by the cashier only.[5] In a recent case in New York, the defendants were organized under the general banking law of the State, a section of which provides that "contracts made by any association, and all notes and bills by them issued and put in circulation as money, shall be signed by the president or vice-president and cashier thereof." A certificate of deposit was signed by the cashier alone. Two of the judges were of the opinion that it was not a contract within the meaning of the above clause, one judge considered it a contract, but was of the opinion that the statute did not preclude the association from appointing other agents to sign contracts, or from establishing by usage

---

[1] Sanborn *v.* Fireman's Ins. Co., Sup. Jud. Ct. Mass. 1861. See also, Baptist Church *v.* Brooklyn, F. Ins. Co. 18 Barb. 69, 19 N. Y. 305.

[2] New England Marine Insurance Company *v.* D'Wolf, 8 Pick. 56.

[3] Ibid.

[4] Bulkley *v.* The Derby Fishing Company, 2 Conn. 254; Witte *v.* Same, id. 260; and see Safford *v.* Wyckoff, 4 Hill, 446, Chancellor Walworth.

[5] Mechanics Bank of Alexandria *v.* Bank of Columbia, 5 Wheat. 326.

another mode of signing. Two other judges dissented.[1] An act establishing a State bank made it the duty of the board of directors to protest notes in cases of non-payment; the clause was considered to be inserted merely for the safety and direction of the bank, and the debtors of the bank were not allowed to avail themselves of a non-compliance with the provision on the part of the board in defence to notes on which they were liable as principal debtors.[2] The same construction was put upon a clause in the charter of a similar institution directing that loans on long time should be secured by mortgage; and a bond with sureties for such a loan not secured by mortgage was adjudged binding upon the parties executing it.[3] And where the charter of a municipal corporation provided that all moneys should be drawn from the treasury in pursuance of an order of the common council, signed by the mayor, &c., a negotiable draft on the treasury, signed in the manner directed, but issued on the basis of a mere note or memorandum in the corporation minutes, without a formal order being entered, was deemed a sufficient compliance with the charter; it appearing that this was the accustomed mode of drawing moneys.[4]

§ 254. It is not unusual for the charter to prescribe what species of security shall be taken by a corporation of its officers or agents for their skill and faithfulness in the performance of their duties, as a bond with *two* sureties; and the question has been frequently agitated, whether if a different species of security is taken, as a bond with *one* surety, or none, it can be enforced by the corporation. In this particular, the well settled doctrine is, that charters or acts of incorporation are merely directory, unless they expressly avoid all security taken, other than that prescribed; and that, although neglect of this kind may be culpable on the part of the directors of the company, the security taken may be enforced against him who gave it.[5]

---

[1] Barnes *v.* Ontario Bank, 19 N. Y. 152.

[2] Moreland *v.* The State Bank, 1 Breese, 203.

[3] Bank of the State of South Carolina *v.* Hammond, 1 Rich. 281. Where the charter of a savings institution required that its funds should be invested in, or loaned on public stocks or private mortgages, and that when so loaned a sufficient bond or other personal security should be required of the borrower, it was held that a promissory note, taken without other security, was not for that reason invalid. Mott *v.* U. S. Trust Co. 19 Barb. 568; United States Trust Co. *v.* Brady, 20 Barb. 119. And see Union Mut. Fire Ins. Co. *v.* Keyser, 32 N. H. 313.

[4] Kelley *v.* Mayor, &c. of the City of Brooklyn, 4 Hill, 263.

[5] Bank of the Northern Liberties *v.* Cresson, 12 S. & R. 306; and see Posterne *v.*

§ 255. It is of the very essence of a contract, that it be mutual, and of course that there be parties to it; to be valid, it must also be founded on consideration; and this may be either an advantage to the promisor, or a disadvantage to the promisee, growing out of the transaction in pursuance of which the contract is made. In an action by an academic corporation for the amount of a subscription which the defendant with others, though not mutually, had agreed to pay, without stating to whom, for the erection of an academy (the paper having been signed before the corporation was created), although the academy had been built according to the terms of the subscription, it was adjudged by the Supreme Court of Massachusetts, that no recovery could be had, inasmuch as the corporation was not a party to the contract, there was no mutuality among the subscribers, and no consideration was passed, or had been received. "It is," says Mr. Chief Justice Sewall, "a promise to give, connected with a similar promise by others to give, to the same appropriation and purpose; but these promises are not mutual among the subscribers. At most it was a donation to come into operation at the will of each subscriber, which *has not been confirmed by any act of the party charged*."[1] It was considered, however, in this case, that if a subscriber had been named or descriptively included in the grant of incorporation, had been concerned in the subsequent proceedings, and enjoyed the advantages of a member of the corporation, that body would have been entitled to the benefit of his subscription, and the subscriber liable upon an implied promise.[2] And where, in addition to his subscription before incorporation for the building of an academy (the amount to be paid, by the terms of the paper, to any persons who should be appointed trustees by the legislature), the defendant, after the incorporation and the appointment of the trustees, delivered, on account of the sum he had subscribed, some shingles to be

---

Hanson, 2 Saund. 60 a, n. 3; Maleverer *v.* Redshaw, 1 Mod. 35; Rex *v.* Loxdale, 1 Burr, 447; Peppin *v.* Cooper, 2 B. & Ald. 431; Austen *v.* Howard, 1 J. B. Moore, 7 Taunt. 28, 379.

[1] Trustees of Phillips Limerick Academy *v.* Davis, 11 Mass. 113; and see Boutell *v.* Cowdin, 9 Mass. 254, commented upon and explained in Amherst Academy *v.* Cowls, 6 Pick. 434–436, per Parker, C. J.; also, Scots' Charitable Society *v.* Shaw, 8 Mass. 532; Trustees of Bridgewater Academy *v.* Gilbert, 2 Pick. 579; Bluehill Academy *v.* Witham, 13 Maine, 403; Trustees of Hamilton College *v.* Stewart, 1 Comst. 581; Troy & Boston R. Co. *v.* Tibbits, 18 Barb. 297, 305; Poughkeepsie Plank R. Co. *v.* Griffin, 21 Barb. 454. But see Cowle *v.* Gibson, 3 Barr, 416.

[2] Trustees of Phillips Limerick Academy *v.* Davis, 11 Mass. 118, 119, per Sewall, C. J.

used in the building; this was adjudged a sufficient recognition of the promise; and the corporation recovered on the money counts to the extent of the subscription.[1] The seconding a resolution to assess, passed before incorporation, and the payment of part of the assessments after incorporation, by an original subscriber, was held sufficient evidence of recognition to subject him in a suit brought by the corporation for subsequent assessments.[2] It is evident, too, that if one subscribes to a charitable fund after the incorporation of the body who are its trustees, and the purposes for which the subscription is made are in the process of execution, the funds being needed for and applied to the faithful application of the trust, he has no defence, either upon the ground of want of mutuality or of consideration,[3] whether the corporation has been organized or not.[4] The interest acquired by subscription to the stock of a corporation for profit is a sufficient consideration to enable the corporation to enforce the subscription.[5]

§ 256. Having treated of *the mode* in which incorporated companies may contract, with whom, and in what name, we come now to consider what contracts in general they may make. And here we would observe, that a corporation and an individual stand upon very different footing. The latter, existing for the *general* good of society, may do all acts and make all contracts which are not, in the eye of the law, inconsistent with this great purpose of his creation; whereas, the former, having been created for a *specific* purpose, not only can make no contract forbidden by its charter, which is, as it were the law of its nature, but in general can make no contract which is not necessary, either directly or incidentally, to enable it to answer that purpose. Thus, a note

---

1 Trustees of Farmington Academy *v.* Allen, 14 Mass. 172; and see Homes *v.* Dana, 12 Mass. 190; Kennebec & Portland Railroad Co. *v.* Palmer, 34 Maine, 366. Fort Edward Plank R. Co. *v.* Payne, 17 Barb. 567.

2 Vestry of Christ Church *v.* Simons, 2 Rich. 368.

3 Amherst Academy *v.* Cowls, 6 Pick. 427; First Religious Society in Whitestown *v.* Stone, 7 Johns. 112; Instone *v.* The F. & B. Co. 2 Bibb, 576. Barnes *v.* Perine, 2 Kern. 18. That a defendant subscriber had been active in inducing subscriptions and in persuading the undertaking; that he had presided at a meeting where a building contract had been accepted; and that the meeting-house was subsequently commenced and completed on the faith of the several subscriptions, were regarded as cogent arguments of consideration. Watkins *v.* Eames, 9 Cush. 537; see too, Gittings *v.* Mayhew, 6 Md. 113; Eastern Plank R. Co. *v.* Vaughan, 20 Barb. 155.

4 Selma and Tennessee Railroad Company *v.* Tipton, 5 Ala. 787.

5 Stokes *v.* Lebanon and Sparta Turnpike Co. 6 Humph. 241; Kennebec & Portland Railroad Co. *v.* Jarvis, 34 Maine, 260; and see *post*, Chap. XV.

issued by a bank, in contravention of its charter, or of a public law, is said to be void *ab initio*, and no action is maintainable upon it by the indorsee against the indorser.[1] And where a company was incorporated "for the purpose of establishing and conducting a line or lines of steamboats, vessels, and stages, or other carriages for the conveyance of passengers" *between certain places*, a contract by such a company for the breaking of ice and towing of vessels through the track broken, to another place, is invalid, and cannot be enforced against them.[2] A railway company who are promoting in parliament a bill for the extension of their line, which, if made, will pass through certain lands, cannot make an absolute contract for the purchase of such lands, until the bill is passed. Such a contract would be *ultra vires* and void.[3] Nor is a corporation, in such case, when an action is brought against them on contract, estopped, by the consideration they have received, from denying their competency to make the contract; for if so, the estoppel would apply equally to the other contracting party, and the limitation upon the power of the corporation would be of no avail.[4] The same doctrine is applied in England to contracts of railway companies to apply their funds to the payment of costs and expenses of soliciting bills pending in parliament for the extension of other lines, with a view to their own benefit. The courts of equity had before held such application of the funds of a railway company a breach of trust on the part of the directors — and to be enjoined against as beyond their authority, and illegal.[5] The courts of law hold such contracts, as contrary to the intent of the acts of parliament creating such companies, to be void and

---

[1] Rust *v.* Wallace, 4 McLean, C. C. 8; Davis *v.* Bank of River Raisin, id. 387.

[2] Pennsylvania, &c. Company *v.* Dandridge, 8 Gill & J. 248; Abbott *v.* Balt. & Rapp. Steam Packet Co. 1 Md. Ch. Dec. 442. A corporation, organized to do a general insurance agency, commission and brokerage business, cannot, in order to effect a loan, though it be in the usual course of its business, subscribe to the stock of a savings bank and building association. Mechanics, &c. Bank *v.* Meriden Agency Co. 24 Conn. 159; and see Berry *v.* Yates, 24 Barb. 199.

[3] Gage *v.* New Market Railway Co. 18 Q. B. 457, 14 Eng. L. & Eq. 57; Preston *v.* Liverpool, &c. Railway, 5 H. L. Cas. 605, 622.

[4] Ibid.; Albert *v.* Savings Bank of Baltimore, 1 Md. Ch. Dec. 407; Ohio Life Ins. & Trust Co. *v.* Merchants Ins. & Trust Co. 11 Humph. 1.

[5] Colman *v.* Eastern Counties Railway Co. 10 Beav. 15; Talemary *v.* Laing, 12 Beav. 352; Bagshaw *v.* Eastern Union Railway Co. 2 Macn. & G. 389, 7 Hare, 114; Beman *v.* Rufford, 1 Sim. N. S. 550, 6 Eng. L. & Eq. 106; Munt *v.* Shrewsbury & Chester Railway Company, 13 Beav. 1, 3 Eng. L. & Eq. 144; and see Stevens *v.* South Devon Railway Company, 13 Beav. 48, 2 Eng. L. & Eq. 138; Parker *v.* River Dannhac Company, 1 De Gex & S. 192.

incapable of enforcement against the corporation, even though all the shareholders assent to them; railway acts in England being public acts, of which all are bound to take notice.[1] So a corporation cannot make a contract to pay a certain sum to a person, on condition that he will not oppose the passage of a bill of theirs in parliament.[2] And it would clearly seem to be against sound policy, to hold a corporation liable for all the contracts entered into by the promoters of the company, before the act of incorporation.[3] An agreement that one railway company shall work a particular line of railway, and that the property and plant shall be handed over for that purpose, implies a delegation of powers which cannot be made or accepted without authority from parliament, and will be enjoined against as illegal; but equity will not excuse a company from putting its seal to an agreement to apply to parliament for the requisite powers to make such an agreement.[4] And a contract by the directors of a company, to purchase the trade and good will of another company, is not binding unless authorized by the charter or deed of settlement of each company, and made according to its provisions.[5] But where a railroad company is authorized to purchase lands for certain purposes, a person who agrees to sell his land to the company is not bound to see that it is strictly required for such purposes.[6] By the general law of Ohio, an individual may contract for, and receive any rate of interest, but can coerce payment of it only at the rate of six per cent. per annum; and a corporation, unless expressly restricted or privileged by its charter, stands, in this particular, upon the same footing with an individual. A clause in the charter of an insurance com-

---

[1] East Anglian Railway Co. *v.* Eastern Counties Railway Co. 11 C. B. 775, 7 Eng. L. & Eq. 505; McGregor *v.* The Official Manager of the Deal & Dover, &c. Railway Co. 18 Q. B. 618, 16 Eng. L. & Eq. 180. For comment on the first case cited, see cases cited at end of this section.

[2] Preston *v.* Liverpool, &c. Railway, 5 H. L. Cas. 605, 622.

[3] That a corporation is not liable in such a case if the contract is not included within the terms or scope of the charter, is decided in Caledonian, &c. Railway Co. *v.* Hellensburgh Harbor Trustees, 2 Macq. H. L. Cas. 391, 39 Eng. L. & Eq. 28. And very strong reasons for so holding in case the contract is within the scope, but not the terms of the charter, are given in this case, and in Eastern Counties Railway Co. *v.* Hawkes, 5 H. L. Cas. 331; and in Preston *v.* Liverpool, &c. Railway, 5 H. L. Cas. 605. The point was not, however, decided.

[4] Winch *v.* Birkenhead, Lancashire, &c. Railway Co. 5 De G. & S. 562, 13 Eng. L. & Eq. 506; Great Northern Railway Co. *v.* Eastern Counties Railway Co. 9 Hare, 306, 12 Eng. L. & Eq. 224.

[5] Ernest *v.* Nicholls, 6 H. L. Cas. 401.

[6] Eastern Counties Railway *v.* Hawkes, 5 H. L. Cas. 331.

pany in that State, expressly authorizing the loan of its funds, "for such period of time, *and upon such terms*, and under such restrictions" as the directors might deem expedient, was construed to confer upon the corporation the power to exact and coerce payment of any rate of interest the directors might stipulate for with the borrower.[1] But if the charter of a bank forbid it to take more than legal interest, or require "its discounts to be made upon banking principles and usages," a bill of exchange discounted at a higher rate than legal interest, is held, in Ohio, to be totally void.[2] Such, too, is the law in Michigan.[3] In Mississippi, on the other hand, such a case is held to fall under the general law against usury; and the bank would recover the principal of the note without interest; in other words, notwithstanding the charter provision, suffer no more than the ordinary penalty for usury provided by the law of that State.[4] In deciding whether a corporation can make a particular contract, we are to consider, in the first place, whether its charter, or some statute binding upon it, forbids or permits it to make such a contract; and if the charter and valid statutory law are silent upon the subject, in the second place, whether a power to make such a contract may not be implied on the part of the corporation, as directly or incidentally necessary to enable it to fulfil the purpose of its existence, or whether the contract is entirely foreign to that purpose. These principles are very obvious; the difficulty, if any, lies in the application of them.[5]

The present doctrine in England seems to be that, generally speaking, corporations are bound by their contracts when under seal as much as

---

1 State *v.* Urbana & Champaign Mutual Ins. Co. 14 Ohio, 6.

2 Chillicothe Bank *v.* Swayne, 8 Ohio, 257; Creed *v.* Commercial Bank of Cincinnati, 11 Ohio, 489; Same *v.* Reed, id. 498; Spalding *v.* The Bank of Muskingum, 12 Ohio, 544; Miami Exporting Company *v.* Clark, 13 Ohio, 1.

3 Orr *v.* Lacey, 2 Doug. Mich. 230.

4 Planters Bank *v.* Sharp, 4 Smedes & M. 75; Grand Gulf Bank *v.* Archer, 8 Smedes & M. 151. If a bank, prohibited by its charter from taking more than six per cent. in advance upon its loans and discounts, receive, in payment of a *bonâ fide* debt, the promissory note of a third party, though at a higher rate of discount than six per cent., the note being a marketable commodity, usury cannot be predicated of its sale. Dunkle *v.* Renick, 6 Ohio, State, 527; American Life Ins. & Trust Co. *v.* Dobbin, Hill & Denio, 252.

A prohibition in a charter restraining the corporation from "making any contract which by existing laws amounts to usury," does not extend to contracts made and to be performed in another State. The corporation may stipulate there for any rate of interest not forbidden by the laws of the State. Bard *v.* Poole, 2 Kern. 495; Knox *v.* Bank of U. S. 26 Missis. 655.

5 See *ante*, § 111.

individuals, but that where a corporation is created for particular purposes, with special powers, the contract does not bind it, if it appear from the express provisions of the statute creating the corporation, or by necessary and reasonable inference from its enactment, that the contract was *ultra vires*, that is, that the legislature meant that such a contract should not be made. And it is said that if it is not made out that the act prohibits the contract, it must be enforced.[1] If the contract is not under seal, no such implication it would seem arises, but the contract must be shown to be within the scope of the powers of the company.[2]

§ 257. In general, an express authority is not indispensable to confer upon a corporation the right to borrow money, to deal on credit, or become drawer, indorser, or acceptor of a bill of exchange, or to become a party to any other negotiable paper.[3] It is sufficient if it be implied as the usual and proper means to accomplish the purposes of the charter.[4] Corporations are expressly mentioned in the Statute of Anne, respecting promissory notes, as persons who make and indorse negotiable notes, and to whom such notes may be made payable; and as corporations and others have by the statute a like remedy upon notes as upon inland bills of exchange, it implies, that, by the custom of merchants they may, in some cases, at least, draw, indorse, accept, or sue upon bills of exchange.[5] Where, however, the drawing, indorsing, or accept-

---

[1] South Yorkshire R. Co. *v.* Great Northern R. Co. 9 Exch. 55, 85; Bateman *v.* Mayor, &c. 3 H. & N. 323; Mayor of Norwich *v.* Norfolk R. Co. 4 Ellis & B. 397.

[2] Ridley *v.* Plymouth, &c. Co. 2 Exch. 711; Kingsbridge Flour Mill Co. *v.* Same, id. 718; Ernest *v.* Nicholls, 6 H. L. Cas. 401, 420.

[3] Chitty on Bills (5th ed.), 17 to 21; Bayley on Bills, ch. 2, § 7, pp. 69, 70 (5th ed.); Story on Bills of Exchange, § 79, p. 94; McMasters *v.* Reed, 1 Grant, 36.

[4] Broughton *v.* Manchester Water Works Company, 3 B. & Ald. 1 to 12; Munn *v.* Commission Co. 15 Johns. 44; Pitman *v.* Kintner, 5 Blackf. 250; McIntyre *v.* Preston, 5 Gilman, 48; Bank of Chillicothe *v.* Town of Chillicothe, 7 Ohio, 31; Commercial Bank of New Orleans *v.* Newport Manufacturing Co. 1 B. Mon. 14; Attorney-General *v.* Life and Fire Ins. Co. 9 Paige, 470; Moss *v.* Oakley, 2 Hill, 265; Kelley *v.* The Mayor, &c. of the City of Brooklyn, 4 Hill, 263, per Cowen, J.; Barry *v.* Merchants Exchange Company, 1 Sandf. Ch. 280; Berry *v.* Phœnix Glass Co. 14 Barb. 358; Union Bank *v.* Jacobs, 6 Humph. 515; Burr *v.* McDonald, 3 Gratt. 215; Curtis *v.* Leavitt, 15 N. Y. 9; Leavitt *v.* Blatchford, 17 N. Y. 521; Barnes *v.* Ontario Bank, 19 N. Y. 152; Partridge *v.* Badger, 25 Bart. 146; Ketchum *v.* Buffalo, 4 Kern. 356; Magee *v.* Mokelumne Hill Canal Co. 5 Calif. 258; Hamilton *v.* Newcastle, &c. R. Co. 9 Ind. 359; Lucas *v.* Pitney, 3 Dutch. 221; Mead *v.* Keeler, 24 Barb. 20; Wright *v.* Scott, H. L. 1855, 34 Eng. L. & Eq. 1.

[5] Bayley on Bills, § 2, l. 9, pp. 60, 68 (5th ed.); Kyd on Bills, pp. 19, 20; Story on

ing such bills, is obviously foreign to the purposes of the charter, or repugnant thereto, there the act becomes a nullity, and not binding upon the corporation.[1]

§ 258. In Worthington *v.* The Savage Manufacturing Company,[2] it seems to be taken for granted that a manufacturing corporation cannot become surety upon a note unless expressly authorized by the terms of its charter. Although the decision in that case was right upon the ground of a clear misapplication by the agent of the corporate credit in favor of one who must have been cognizant of the misapplication, yet we apprehend that the general ground for the decision above assumed cannot be supported. On the contrary, the result of all the authorities is, that a corporation may, by virtue of its implied powers, unless expressly or by necessary implication prohibited, make any contract either as principal or surety proper as the usual and ordinary means of carrying on its business, under the circumstances in which it may be placed. The difficulty in such a case is to decide whether the particular contract of suretyship or guaranty is within or without the scope of the implied powers of the corporation. In New York it is held, that a banking or other corporation is not authorized to make an accommodation indorsement, or to become a surety on a note, and the corporation is not liable in such a case, unless the note has been discounted in good faith, in consequence of representations made by the proper officers that it was the note of the corporation, or unless the note has passed into the hands of a *bonâ fide* holder without notice, who has paid a valuable consideration for it.[3] And an insurance company cannot buy the notes of one who is insured

---

Bills of Exchange, § 79, p. 95. Where a railroad was authorized by charter to contract with connecting roads, for their use, &c., it was held that it might accept bills drawn by a connecting road as a consideration for a change of gauge of that road. Smead *v.* Indianapolis, &c. R. Co. 11 Ind. 104.

[1] Bacon *v.* Mississippi Ins. Co. 31 Missis. 116; Broughton *v.* Manchester Water Works Co. 3 B. & Ald. 1 to 12; Attorney-General *v.* Life & Fire Insurance Co. 9 Paige, 470; Chitty on Bills, p. 17; Story on Bills of Exchange, § 79, p. 95, *ante*, § 111. A bank may guarantee the payment of securities assigned immediately by its debtor to a party who makes advances upon them, in order to enable the debtor to discharge his obligations to the bank. The substantial interest of the bank in the securities supports the contract of guaranty. Talman *v.* Rochester City Bank, 18 Barb. 123.

[2] 1 Gill, 201, 202.

[3] Bridgeport City Bank *v.* Empire Stone Dressing Co. 30 Barb. 421; Morford *v.* Farmers Bank, 26 Barb. 568; Bank of Genesee *v.* Patchin Bank, 3 Kern. 309; Central Bank *v.* Empire Stone Dressing Co. 26 Barb. 23.

by them, for the purpose of using the notes as offsets in case of a claim made by the insured under the policy, although the charter authorizes the company to invest all or any part of the capital stock as the directors may deem best for the safety of the capital, &c.[1] In England, it has been recently decided that the directors of a railway company have no power to guarantee the profits and secure the capital of an intended Steam Packet Company, which was to run in connection with their railway, though the purpose was to increase the traffic on their railway.[2]

§ 259. The right of a corporation to become a party to negotiable paper, as the means necessary to enable it to accomplish the purposes of its charter, is not to be supposed to confer upon it *banking* powers, nor the power to issue its credits for the purchase of a majority of the stock of a bank for the purpose of engaging in the business of banking, or, by thus obtaining the control of a bank, to be able to borrow money from it.[3] Such powers, to be exercised, must be expressly granted; nor can they be inferred from such a general grant of power in the charter, as "to hold any estate, real or personal, and the same to sell, grant, dispose of, or bind by mortgage, or in such other manner as they shall deem most proper for the best interest of the corporation."[4] And a grant of a *portion* of the ordinary banking powers, as to a life insurance and trust company of a power "to buy and sell drafts and bills of exchange," by no means confers the power to issue paper designed to circulate as money.[5] The right to make loans by way of discount, and to lend upon bills, bonds, notes, and mortgages, is conveyed to a savings institution, by a clause in the charter conferring the power to invest deposits, made with it, in public stocks or other securities.[6] Such investments, and the receiving of money on deposit, do not violate a clause of the charter prohibiting to the corporation the exercise of banking powers; the restraint imposed by such a clause being limited, in Ohio, at

[1] Strauss *v.* Eagle Ins. Co. 5 Ohio, State, 59.

[2] Coleman *v.* Eastern Counties Railway, 10 Beav. 1. See *post,* § 271.

[3] Sumner *v.* Marcy, 3 Woodb. & M. 112, 113.

[4] State of Ohio *v.* Granville Alexandrian Society, 11 Ohio, 1; Same *v.* Washington Social Library Co. id. 96; Blair *v.* Perpetual Ins. Co. 10 Misso. 561.

[5] In the matter of the Ohio Life Ins. and Trust Company, 9 Ohio, 291; Duncan *v.* Maryland Savings Institution, 10 Gill & J. 299.

[6] Duncan *v.* Maryland Savings Institution, 10 Gill & J. 299; and see Gee *v.* Alabama Life Ins. and Trust Co. 13 Ala. 579.

least, to the issuing of the notes of the corporation for circulation as money.[1] Nor is such a clause prohibiting the corporation "to issue for circulation as money" any of its own notes in the nature of bank-notes, or certificates of deposit payable to bearer, violated by the issue of a certificate of deposit payable to bearer, but not adopted or intended for circulation as money.[2] A company incorporated for the purpose of effecting a communication by a plank road between designated points, with the privilege of taking tolls, is not authorized to establish a stage line on their road, nor to contract for carrying the United States mail.[3] A plank road company is not generally authorized to loan money, unless there is a clause in the charter to that effect, but if it is necessary it can loan a sum of money to one of its contractors, to enable him to build a section of the road.[4] A railroad company has a right to issue bonds to carry out the ends of its creation, and such bonds are binding on the company.[5]

§ 260. In New York, where an insurance company had power by their act of incorporation to insure buildings and personal property against fire, "to make all kinds of marine insurance, and to loan money on bottomry, respondentia, or mortgage of real estate or chattels real," provided that nothing in the act contained should in any way be construed into a grant of *banking powers;* in an action by the company as indorsee of a promissory note, which it had *discounted*, it was held, that the note was void, as received by the corporation in the course of a transaction impliedly forbidden, as a banking transaction, by its charter, and also as contrary to the *restraining act* of the State.[6] It was provided in the charter of a corporation established for loaning money, that "nothing therein contained should be construed to authorize the company to discount notes, or exercise any banking privileges whatever," and the taking of a note for the sum loaned, and receiving the interest in advance, was held to be thereby prohibited, and that there could be no recovery on the note thus discounted.[7] And where such a corpora-

---

1 State *v.* Urbana & Champaign Mutual Ins. Co. 14 Ohio, 6.

2 Mumford *v.* American Life and Trust Co. 4 Comst. 463.

3 Wiswall *v.* Greenville & Raleigh Plank Road Co. 3 Jones, Eq. 183.

4 Madison, &c. Plank Road Co. *v.* Watertown Plank Road Co. 5 Wis. 173.

5 Philadelphia & Sunbury R. Co. *v.* Lewis, 33 Penn. State, 33.

6 N. Y. Firem. Ins. Co. *v.* Sturges, 2 Cowen, 664; and see New York Firemen Insurance Co. *v.* Ely, 5 Conn. 569; Lane *v.* Bennett, 5 Conn. 574.

7 Philadelphia Loan Company *v.* Towner, 13 Conn. 249.

tion received goods of the defendant as security for money loaned, which goods were not pledged or disposed of in the manner required by charter, it was decided that, in an action for the money loaned, the defendant could not set off the value of such goods as goods sold and delivered.[1] The taking of a note as security in contravention of the provisions of the charter, did not, it seems, prevent a recovery by the corporation of the amount loaned, on the money counts.[2] If a bank, prohibited by its charter from loaning its funds to its directors, make such loan and receive a transfer of stock as collateral security for it, the bank acquires no title to the stock transferred, and if an injury accrues to a third party from its acts, it is responsible to such third party.[3] The president of a railroad company, duly authorized to sell and negotiate the bonds of the company, cannot make a valid transfer of them, as collateral security for a preëxisting debt, due by himself to another, where no new consideration passed at the time of transfer.[4] The bonds of a railroad company are not rendered void in consequence of being secured by a mortgage, which the company may have had no authority to execute. And it is no defence to an action on the bonds of a company, by a *bonâ fide* purchaser, that the defendants' books do not show that any value had been paid for them.[5]

§ 261. An insurance company of Alexandria was by its act of incorporation limited in the performance of its functions *to the bounds of the State of Virginia;* upon the separation of Alexandria from the State of Virginia, it seems that the company could make no *new contracts* of insurance until it had received additional powers,[6] although it was held by the Supreme Court of the United States that such separation could have no effect upon the existing contracts of individuals.[7] A clause in a banking charter, however, providing that its operations of discount and deposit should be carried on in a particular village or place, and *not elsewhere*, is regarded as referring to the *customary* business operations of the bank, and not to an isolated loan made by the cashier

---

1 Philadelphia Loan Company *v.* Towner, 13 Conn. 249.

2 Ibid.; and see Life and Fire Insurance Co. *v.* Mechanic Fire Insurance Co. 7 Wend. 34.

3 Albert *v.* Savings Bank, 2 Md. 159.

4 Pittsburgh & Connelsville R. Co. *v.* Barker, 29 Penn. State, 160.

5 Philadelphia, &c. R. Co. *v.* Lewis, 33 Penn. State, 33.

6 Korn *v.* Mut. Ass. So. 6 Cranch, 199, per Johnson, J.

7 Ibid.

abroad, in the course of a negotiation, the purpose of which was to secure a debt due to the bank.[1] A bank whose place of business is in one town or city in a State, and has power by its charter to deal in exchange, without restrictions as to place, may carry on that business through an agent, in another town or city in the same State.[2]

§ 262. It may well be questioned, since a corporation can make such contracts only as are allowed by its act of incorporation, whether it has power to make a contract which should so operate as to bind its legislative capacities forever thereafter, and disable it from making a by-law, which the legislature enables it to enact.[3] Upon this principle it was held, where a statute authorized a city corporation to make by-laws "regulating," or, if found necessary, "*preventing*, the interment of the dead" within the limits of the city, though it had granted lands for the purpose of interment, and had covenanted that they should be quietly enjoyed for that purpose, yet that the corporation was not estopped by its contract from passing a by-law forbidding such interment under a penalty.[4] It should be remarked, however, that both the cases last cited were concerning municipal corporations, empowered for direct public benefit.

§ 263. In Little *v.* O'Brien,[5] it was objected to the recovery on a note given for a balance of instalments due from the defendant, as one of the stockholders in an insurance company, that the act incorporating the company required that the capital stock should, within six months after payment, be invested in certain designated stocks; whereas, instead of such investment, it appeared that the company received of the several stockholders their respective promissory notes, with collateral security for the payment thereof, one of which this was. It was here said by the court, that whether for this misbehavior of the corporation

---

[1] Potter *v.* Bank of Ithica, 5 Hill, 490, 7 Hill, 530; and see Suydam *v.* Morris Canal and Banking Co. 5 Hill, 491, n. a., 6 Hill, 217, that such loan is not a violation of 1 R. S. (N. Y.), 712, § 6, prohibiting a foreign banking corporation from *keeping an office of discount and deposit* for the transaction of business.

[2] City Bank of Columbus *v.* Beach, 1 Blatchf. C. C. 425.

[3] Gozzler *v.* Corp. of Georgetown, 6 Wheat. 593, per Marshall, C. J.

[4] Presbyterian Church *v.* City of New York, 5 Cowen, 538; Coates *v.* Mayor, &c. of New York, 7 Cowen, 604.

[5] 9 Mass. 423; Selma & Tennessee Railroad Co. *v.* Tipton, 5 Ala. 787; Ely *v.* Sprague, 1 Clarke, Ch. N. Y. 351; First Municipality of New Orleans *v.* Orleans Theatre Co. 2 Rob. La. 209.

the government might not seize their franchises, upon due process, was a question not before them; but that it did not "lie in the mouth of a stockholder for this cause to avoid his contract, which, as between him and the company, was made on sufficient consideration." And, in general, it may be laid down, that in an action by a bank upon a promissory note payable to itself, it is not competent for the court, at the instance of the defendant, to inquire into the organization of the bank, or as to fraud in the taking or investing of its stock.[1]

§ 264. A clause in a bank charter that "it shall not be lawful for the president and directors of said bank to purchase or discount any draft or bill of exchange for a larger sum than five thousand dollars, and on every draft or bill of exchange purchased or discounted by said bank, there shall be at least two responsible indorsers, each of which shall be considered good for the amount of such draft or bill," was adjudged to be directory merely; and could furnish no protection to one who had borrowed money from the bank to a larger amount than the charter permitted, against the claim of the bank for the amount so borrowed.[2] The splitting of a large sum borrowed by the same person into notes of five thousand dollars and less, was held to be a clear evasion and violation of the provision.[3] To discount notes payable in a certain species of paper money, and upon renewal to take a premium of one per cent., as the difference between that and other money;[4] or to discount notes at the usual percentage, with an agreement on the part of the borrower to redeem with specie the identical bank-notes received by him on the loan, if they should be returned to the bank during the continuance of the loan, and also to purchase of the company, with specie during the loan, a certain amount of other bank-notes not current at par,[5] was held not inconsistent with a clause in a banking charter, prohibiting the company from using their moneys, &c., in trade or commerce. So a contract by which a bank lent a large sum of money, taking bills of exchange at nine months for the payment thereof, and received at the time, and as one of the conditions of the loan, a quantity

---

[1] Smith *v.* Missisippi & Alabama Railroad Co. 6 Smedes & M. 179.

[2] Bates *v.* Bank of the State of Alabama, 2 Ala. 462, 463, 464, 465; Bond *v.* Central Bank of Georgia, 2 Ga. 92.

[3] Ibid.

[4] Portland Bank *v.* Storer, 7 Mass. 433.

[5] Northampton Bank *v.* Allen, 10 Mass. 284; and see Fleckner *v.* United States Bank, 8 Wheat. 338.

of cotton, with authority to ship it to a foreign port, and sell it for the account and at the risk and expense of the owner, and to credit his bill with the amount of the net proceeds, adding the difference of exchange, is not "*a dealing in goods, wares, and merchandise,*" within the prohibition of a fundamental law of the bank forbidding such dealing, "unless it be to secure a debt due the said bank, incurred by the regular transactions of the same." [1] The word "deal," in such a clause, was construed to mean, "to buy and sell for the purpose of gain." [2] The sale by a bank of a quantity of butter which it had taken in settlement of a debt, was deemed no violation of a similar clause in its charter; and the purchase by another bank of the same butter, though under like charter restriction, the transaction being an isolated one, was sustained as a lawful transaction.[3] And where a corporation was forbidden by its charter to take and hold land, it was held that the clause would not prevent the corporation from recovering back money advanced by it upon a purchase of land at auction from one who, upon discovery by the corporation of its want of power, agreed to take the bid off its hands; the purpose of the transaction with him being not *to deal in land*, but to correct a mistake.[4]

§ 264 *a*. The objection that a contract is illegal, and that no judgment can therefore be rendered upon it, is not allowed, it is said, from from any consideration of favor to those who allege it. The courts, from public considerations, refuse their aid to enforce obligations which contravene the laws or policy of the State. But when the legislature by a subsequent act relieves a contract from the imputation of illegality, neither of the parties to the contract can insist upon this objection.[5]

§ 265. And although it is well settled that legislative acts, divesting a corporation of any rights with which it is clothed by charter, as a right to make particular contracts, are void under the constitution of

---

1 Bates *v.* State Bank of Alabama, 2 Ala. 465 to 475.

2 Ibid. A statute, which prohibited banks from purchasing and holding real estate, contained a proviso that the act should not prevent any bank from taking mortgages or other liens on lands to secure existing debts. It was held, in construction of this provision, that a bank, which had obtained such a lien, might make its security available by purchasing the property. Ingraham *v.* Speed, 30 Missis. 410.

3 Sacket's Harbor Bank *v.* President, &c. of Lewis County Bank, 11 Barb. 213.

4 Crutcher *v.* Nashville Bridge Co. 8 Humph. 403.

5 White Water Valley Canal Co. *v.* Vallette, 21 How. 414.

the United States, as impairing the obligation of the charter;[1] yet it is evident that, except so far as privileged by the instrument of their creation, corporations, like individuals, are subject to legislative action, and *a fortiori* to constitutional provision; and hence all contracts made by them in contravention of either, of constitutional provision, or the general laws of the land, are voidable, or absolutely void.[2] The question has arisen more than once in this country, whether the bills of a State bank, which has corporate property, and may be sued for its debts, are not bills of credit within the meaning of the prohibition of the constitution of the United States, when the State is the only stockholder, and pledges its faith for the ultimate redemption of the bills. The law seems to be well settled by the highest authority that they are not; but are mere bills of the bank, which, as distinguished from the State, is primarily liable for them, has funds applicable to the payment of them under the control of the directors, and that such bills will support a judicial process at the suit of creditors, over which the State can exert no higher control than any other stockholder.[3]

Persons out of a State, as well as within it, are bound to take notice of public laws limiting the powers of corporations.[4] Neither is it necessary that *corporations eo nomine* should be embraced within the terms of an act, to subject them to its prohibitions, since it is well settled that the words *inhabitants*, *occupiers*, or *persons*, may include incorporated companies.[5] In Virginia, it was decided that no recovery could be had upon notes there issued by a banking corporation of another State, through an agency established in Virginia, inasmuch as such banking

---

[1] Case of Dartmouth College, 4 Wheat. 518; Allen *v.* McKeen, 1 Sumner, 276.

[2] Paine *v.* Baldwin, 3 Smedes & M. 661; Blair *v.* Perpetual Ins. Co. 10 Misso. 561; Weed *v.* Snow, 3 McLean, 265; Hayden *v.* Davis, id. 276.

[3] Darlington *v.* State Bank of Alabama, 13 How. 12; Briscoe *v.* Bank of Kentucky, 11 Pet. 331; and see Owen *v.* Branch Bank of Mobile, 3 Ala. 258.

[4] Root *v.* Goddard, 3 McLean, 102. In New York it has been said that a citizen of one State, who purchases property, the title to which is derived from a conveyance or assignment of a corporation in another State, is presumed, it seems, to take knowledge of the powers contained in the charter of such corporation, but it is held that he is not bound to know the laws of a State other than his own, which are of a general character, although such laws may abridge the powers of all corporations within that State. Hoyt *v.* Thompson, 19 N. Y. 207.

[5] Inst. 703; Rex *v.* Gardner, Cowp. 79; Clinton Woollen and Cotton Manuf. Co. *v.* Morse (Oct. 7, 1817), cited in and see The People *v.* Utica Ins. Co. 15 Johns. 382; Mott *v.* Hicks, 1 Cow. 513; United States *v.* Johns, 1 Wash. C. C. 364; City of St. Louis *v.* Rogers, 7 Misso. 19; State of Indiana *v.* Warren, 6 Hill, 83; State *v.* Nashville University, 4 Humph. 157; McIntyre *v.* Preston, 5 Gilman, 48.

operations were contrary to the policy of the statute against unincorporated banking companies; though it was admitted that notes, originally issued by a bank in the State of its incorporation, might well be negotiated and enforced in Virginia; and that contracts ancillary to banking operations might legally be made there by such a corporation.[1] It was by virtue of this last distinction, that the Court of Chancery in New York, notwithstanding the restraining act, enforced a mortgage given to a Pennsylvanian banking corporation upon lands in New York, for the security of a loan made in Pennsylvania,[2] although banks of other States are within the restraining acts of New York, and cannot recover the amount of a check discounted by them in violation of those statutes.[3] On an information in the nature of a *quo warranto*, judgment of ouster was rendered against an insurance company in the State of New York for contracting as a bank, contrary to an act of that State, passed to restrain unincorporated banking associations.[4] The same company having, as indorsee, brought an action against an indorser of a promissory note *discounted* by the corporation, the note was adjudged void, under that section of the above restraining act which declares, "that all notes and securities for the payment of money or the delivery of property, made or given to any such association, institution, or company, not authorized for banking purposes, shall be null and void."[5] It need hardly be added, that such an act cannot be evaded by making the note payable to individuals, the corporation claiming as indorsee.[6] But though, in the above case of Utica Insurance Company *v.* Scott, the note by force of the restraining act was adjudged void, and in analogy to the statute of gaming, it was held that it would be so, into whatever hands it might pass; yet, say the court, "there is a material distinction between the security and contract of lending. The lending of money is not declared void, and therefore, wherever money has been lent, it may

---

1 Bank of Marietta *v.* Pindall, 2 Rand. 465; Rees *v.* Conococheague Bank, 5 Rand. 329.

2 Silver Lake Bank *v.* North, 4 Johns. Ch. 370.

3 Pennington *v.* Townsend, 7 Wend. 276; and see New Hope Delaware Bridge Company *v.* Poughkeepsie Silk Company, 25 Wend. 648.

4 People *v.* Utica Insurance Co. 15 Johns. 358.

5 Utica Ins. Co. *v.* Scott, 19 Johns. 1; Same *v.* Hunt and Brooks, 1 Wend. 56; Same *v.* Cadwell, 3 Wend. 296; see too, N. Y. Firemen Ins. Co. *v.* Ely, 2 Cowen, 678; Same *v.* Sturges, 2 Cowen, 664; and see Johnson *v.* Bentley, 16 Ohio, 97, as to the construction of 23d section of a statute of Ohio, passed in 1824, on the same subject, and of the repeal of the section.

6 New York Firemen Ins. Company *v.* Ely, *sup.* per Savage, C. J.

be recovered, although the *security* itself is void."[1] This distinction between the security and the contract in cases falling under the restraining acts, seems to be much shaken in New York, by the later authorities; and the contract, as well as the security, would probably now be adjudged void.[2]

§ 266. These cases by no means decide that an insurance company cannot receive a promissory note, but only that notes or securities of any kind, received by the corporation in the course of banking transactions, as the discounting of notes for the deducted interest, are void by force of the express provision of a statute. On the contrary, an insurance company has power to take notes for premiums as incidental to its proper business of insurance; and in the case of the New York Firemen Insurance Company *v.* Sturges,[3] which was an action by the corporation as indorsee against an indorser of a promissory note, given in renewal of one discounted by the corporation, the proceeds to be, and in fact, applied to the payment of a debt due by note to it for premiums; though it appeared that twenty dollars, the excess of the note discounted over the premium note taken up, was paid to the promisors, yet it was held that the corporation might recover, notwithstanding the restraining act; inasmuch as it was a transaction in the course of its proper business of insurance; the small amount urged as a discount on the funds of the institution, which might be accidental, forbidding the conclusion that it was a business transaction of borrowing and lending. The restraining acts of New York are not, it seems, violated by a foreign Life and Trust Company, which, having power to make contracts and do lawful business within that State, keeps an office in the city of New York, receives deposits of money in trust, and issues certificates therefor, payable with interest, at a specified time; nor is it a violation of those stat-

---

[1] Utica Ins. Co. *v.* Scott, *sup.*; Same *v.* Kip, 8 Cowen, 20; Philadelphia Loan Company *v.* Towner, 13 Conn. 249; and see Hussey *v.* Jacob, 1 Comyns, 4; Bowyer *v.* Bampton, 2 Stra. 1155; Barjeau *v.* Walmsley, 2 Stra. 1249; Robinson *v.* Bland, 2 Burr. 1080.

[2] Beach *v.* Fulton Bank, 3 Wend. 573; North River Ins. Co. *v.* Lawrence, 3 Wend. 482; Story *v.* Barrell, 2 Conn. 678; Life and Fire Ins. Co. *v.* Mechanic Fire Ins. Co. 7 Wend. 31; New Hope Delaware Bridge Company *v.* Poughkeepsie Silk Company, 25 Wend. 648, where we find old authorities doubted. But see Leavitt *v.* Blatchford, 5 Barb. 9, 17 N. Y. 521; and Parmley *v.* Tenth Ward Bank, 3 Edw. Ch. 395, in which the doctrine was applied to notes payable in a different manner than provided by the general banking law, though not intended to circulate as money.

[3] 2 Cowen, 664; see too, People *v.* Brewster, 4 Wend. 498.

utes, to issue such certificates in exchange for bonds and mortgages, received by the corporation.[1]

§ 267. If a corporation be authorized to raise money on promissory notes for a particular purpose, or if, as is frequently the case with other than banking institutions, it may receive notes in the course of its proper business, evidence may be admitted in the one case in favor,[2] and in the other against the corporation,[3] to impeach the notes, by showing that they were issued for another purpose, or received in the course of business improper or forbidden to it. Thus, where a bank in another State discounted indorsed notes, paying therefor bills beneath the denomination of five dollars, with a knowledge that such bills were to be circulated in New York, in violation of the statute, evidence of the knowledge of this purpose would be admitted to defeat the action of the bank, on the note discounted, against the indorser, with whom the agreement for discount was made.[4] As in ordinary cases, *ut res magis valeat, quam pereat*, the presumption is always in favor of the validity of the contract; or, in other words, it will be presumed that the debt was due, or the note or other security given, in the lawful course of business, until the contrary be shown.[5] Where the objection is that the note was issued as currency, the form and appearance of the instrument may be such, bearing devices usual on bank-notes, and resembling those used as the circulating medium of the country, as to put a holder upon his guard, and render it incumbent on him to show that he received it in the ordinary course of business, and paid a valuable consideration therefor, without notice of the illegal purpose for which it was issued, to entitle him to recover thereon.[6] In courts of law, the question of knowledge of, or participation in, the illegal intent, in such cases, is properly a question for the jury.[7] Bonds, issued by an Exchange Company, for the purpose of raising

[1] Mumford *v.* American Life Ins. & Trust Co. 4 Comst. 463.

[2] Slark *v.* Highgate Archway Co. 5 Taunt. 792.

[3] New York Firemen Ins. Co. *v.* Sturges; and Same *v.* Ely, 2 Cowen, 664 and 678.

[4] Pratt *v.* Adams, 7 Paige, 615.

[5] New York Firemen Ins. Co. *v.* Sturges; and Same *v.* Ely, *sup.*; Barker *v.* Mechanic Fire Ins. Co. 3 Wend. 94; Cuyler *v.* Sandford, 8 Barb. 225; Safford *v.* Wyckoff, 4 Hill, 444, 445, 446, Chan. Walworth; Leavitt *v.* Yates, 4 Edw. Ch. 134; Dockery *v.* Miller, 9 Humph. 731.

[6] Attorney-General *v.* Life and Fire Ins. Co. 9 Paige, 470; Smith *v.* Alabama Life Ins. and Trust Co. 4 Ala. 567; Hazleton Coal Co. *v.* Megazel, 4 Barr, 328; and see Farmers Loan and Trust Co. *v.* Caroll, 5 Barb. 613; Leavitt *v.* Yates, 4 Edw. Ch. 134, 171.

[7] Branch Bank of Montgomery *v.* Crockeron, 5 Ala. 250.

money to enable them to complete their building, printed or engraved in the form of a single bill under the seal of the corporation, payable ten years after date, with interest payable half-yearly, coupons for the interest being annexed to each bond payable to bearer, and secured by mortgages of real estate executed to a trustee, have been adjudged in New York not to be within the prohibitions of the restraining law of that State.[1]

§ 268. In general, illegality of consideration does not avoid a note in the hands of a *bonâ fide* holder without notice; and, accordingly, where the directors of a bank, for the purpose of controlling the election of its officers, entered into an arrangement to purchase on account of the bank a large amount of its stock, at a premium of seven per cent. above its par value, and to effect this object, paid for the stock to the amount of its par value, with the funds of the bank, transferring the stock in trust for the bank, and, for the purpose of paying the premium, each director borrowed money of the bank by causing his own note indorsed to be discounted at the bank; in an action brought by the bank, upon one of these notes against the indorsers, they were not allowed to set up the illegality of the original transaction as a defence, upon the ground that the bank was to be considered as an innocent third party.[2] The rule seems to be, that if the corporation have the power to make or take a note for any purpose, a note originally given by or to them would be valid in the hands of a *bonâ fide* holder or their *bonâ fide* indorsee without notice, though the corporation might not have had the power to make or take the particular note.[3]

§ 269. In the case of the Utica Insurance Company *v.* Scott,[4] we have seen that it was said by the Supreme Court of the State of New York, that notes or other securities made or given to an association,

---

[1] Barry *v.* Merchants Exchange Co. 1 Sandf. Ch. 312, 313.

[2] President, &c. of the City Bank of New York *v.* Barnard, 1 Hall, 70; and see Seneca County Bank *v.* Neass, 5 Denio, 330; Leavitt *v.* Yates, 4 Edw. Ch. 167.

[3] McIntyre *v.* Preston, 5 Gilman, 48; Stoney *v.* American Life Ins. Co. 11 Paige, 635; Leavitt *v.* Yates, 4 Edw. Ch. 134; White *v.* How, 3 McLean, 291; Ohio Life Insurance & Trust Co. *v* Merchants Insurance & Trust Co. 11 Humph. 1. But see Pearce *v.* Madison & Indianapolis R. Co. 21 How. 441.

[4] 19 Johns. 6. See, however, Branch Bank at Montgomery *v.* Crockeron, 5 Ala. 250; and remarks of Chan. Walworth, in Safford *v.* Wyckoff, 4 Hill, 444, 445, 446; Attorney-General *v.* Life and Fire Insurance Company, 9 Paige, 470.

institution, or company, in the course of unauthorized banking transactions, are void by the terms of their restraining act, even in the hands of an innocent holder; and that the only remedy is an action for the consideration. In England, the statute 15 Geo. II. c. 13, prohibited any body corporate, or any other persons in partnership, exceeding six, from borrowing, owing, or taking up any money on their bills or notes payable at demand, at any less period than six months from the borrowing; but did not expressly avoid securities made in contravention of the act. In the case of Wigan *v.* Fowler,[1] which was an action by an indorsee against seven persons as acceptors of a bill of exchange, the fact that the partnership of the acceptors consisted of more than six persons not appearing on the face of the bill, and at the time of taking the note the plaintiff not being privy to that fact, or that the note was within the prohibition of the statute, it was held that he might recover upon it. In Broughton *v.* Manchester Water Works Company,[2] Holroyd, Justice, in commenting upon this case, observes that the statute of Geo. II. does not expressly avoid the security; "if it did, the bill would (as in case of usury or gaming) be void in the hands of an innocent holder, although the defect did not appear on the face of the instrument." That[3] was an action by the plaintiffs as indorsees of a bill of exchange accepted by the defendants, and payable at three months from date. The Court of King's Bench distinguished this case from Wigan *v.* Fowler, above cited, and held that the plaintiffs could not recover on a bill prohibited by the statute of Geo. II.; inasmuch as they were not innocent indorsees, being bound to take notice of the public act of parliament by which the defendants were incorporated, and being bound to know, therefore, when they received the paper, that it was the acceptance of a corporation prohibited from owing money on such a bill. It seems, however, to be now considered in England, that, taking all the bank acts together, the object of the legislature was to give protection to the Bank of England against rival Banks only; and that they do not prevent merchants from issuing bills short of six months' date, though there were more than six partners in the firm, if really not bankers, and the bills were issued only for the purposes of commerce.[4]

---

[1] 1 Starkie, 459.

[2] 3 B. & Ald. 10, Per Holroyd, J.

[3] Broughton *v.* Manchester Water Works Company, 3 B. & Ald. 1; see, however, Slark *v.* Highgate Archway Co. 5 Taunt. 792, Gibbs, J.

[4] Wigan *v.* Fowler, 2 Chitty, 128; Perring *v.* Dunston, Ryan & M. 426.

§ 270. By a statute in New York, passed in 1840, in amendment of the general banking law, banking associations are forbidden to issue notes unless made payable on demand and without interest; and in construction of the statute it has been held that a note issued by such an association, payable on time and with interest, is void, so that no person, by any act, can give validity to it as commercial paper anywhere.[1] A guaranty of such a note by a third person, as partaking of the character of the principal contract, and intended to reinforce and secure it, is equally illegal and void.[2] Upon the same ground, an assignment of securities made by a banking association to trustees, as a collateral security for the payment of post-notes issued by it, was also adjudged void, so that no title passed to the assignee.[3]

§ 271. When the charter or act of incorporation, and valid statutory law are silent as to what contracts a corporation may make, as a general rule, it has power to make all such contracts as are necessary and usual in the course of business, as means to enable it to attain the object for which it was created, and none other.[4] The creation of a corporation, for a specified purpose, implies a power to use the necessary and usual means to effect that purpose; and though their charters were entirely silent on the subject, banks would necessarily be empowered to issue and discount promissory notes and bills of exchange, and insurance companies to make contracts of indemnity against losses by fire or marine accident, or both, as the case might be. "When," says Mr. Justice Best, "a company like the Bank of England or East India Company are incorporated for the purposes of trade, it seems to result from the very object of their being so incorporated, that they should have power to accept bills, or issue promissory notes; it would be impossible for

---

1 Bank of Chillicothe *v.* Dodge, 8 Barb. 233.

2 Swift *v.* Beers, 3 Denio, 70; Tyler *v.* Yates, 3 Barb. 222; and see White *v.* Franklin Bank, 22 Pick. 181, construing a similar statute in Massachusetts.

3 Tyler *v.* Yates, 3 Barb. 222; Leavitt *v.* Palmer, 3 Comst. 19; and see Green *v.* Seymour, 3 Sandf. Ch. 292, where the same doctrine is applied to avoid a mortgage given to the corporation to secure a debt created in violation of its charter.

4 Broughton *v.* Manch. Water Works Co. 3 B. & Ald. 12, per Best, J.; People *v.* Utica Ins. Co. 15 Johns. 383, per Thompson, J.; N. Y. Firemen Ins. Co. *v.* Ely, 2 Cowen, 699, per Sutherland, J.; N. Y. Firemen Ins. Co. *v.* Ely, 5 Conn. 568, per Hosmer, C. J.; Knowles *v.* Beaty, 1 McLean, 43. Where the proprietors of a toll-bridge were authorized by law to commute toll with any person or corporation, this was held to extend only to such corporations as had a legal capacity to enter into such a contract. Bussey *v.* Gilmore, 3 Greenl. 191.

either of the companies to go on without accepting bills." [1] And if a bank have power to issue paper for circulation, and there be no limitation in the charter or general law as to the kind of paper to be issued, it may issue post-notes, and when issued they may circulate as currency.[2] But where a company was incorporated, not for the purposes of trade, but merely for carrying on the business of supplying the inhabitants of a particular place with water, it was considered that they could not become the makers of promissory notes or the acceptors of bills of exchange, without express authority; since the nature of the business in which they were engaged did not raise a necessary implication of such a power.[3] In an action by an insurance company as indorsees against the indorsers of a promissory note, given to the company in renewal of one discounted by them in a mere transaction of borrowing and lending, it was held, upon general principles, by the Supreme Court of Errors of the State of Connecticut, that the note was void in the hands of the corporation, as received by it in the prosecution of a business unauthorized by its charter.[4] When, however, such a company sues upon a note or bond, and there is no proof of the consideration upon which it is given, it will not be presumed to have been taken in any illegal transaction, but in the course of investment of its funds, or in some other legitimate business.[5] A life insurance and trust company was incorporated with a capital of one million of dollars to be paid in cash, and such other money as it might receive in trust, and by its charter was required to invest one half of its capital of one million in bonds or notes secured by mortgage, and the remaining half, together with its premiums, profits, and moneys received in trust, might, in the discretion of the company, be invested in stocks loaned to any city, county, or company, or be invested in such *real or personal securities* as it might deem proper. It was held that the company could not lend its *credit*, by making bonds to fall due in future, and exchange such bonds for the bonds of an individual for the same amount, and that a bond so taken was void.[6] On the other hand, where a glass company, not empowered

---

[1] Broughton *v.* Manch. Water Works Co. 3 B. & Ald. 11, 12; see too, Edie *v.* East India Co. 2 Burr. 1216; Yarborough *v.* Bank of England, 16 East, 6; Murray *v.* East India Company, 5 B. & Ald. 204.

[2] Campbell *v.* Mississippi Union Bank, 6 How. Miss. 625.

[3] Broughton *v.* Manch. Water Works Company, *supra*, per Bailey and Best, JJ.

[4] N. Y. Firemen Ins. Co. *v.* Ely, 5 Conn. 560.

[5] M'Farlan *v.* The Triton Ins. Co. 4 Denio, 392; Farmers Loan and Trust Company *v.* Perry, 3 Sandf. Ch. 339; Mitchell *v.* Rome R. Co. 17 Ga. 574.

[6] Smith *v.* Alabama Life Ins. and Trust Co. 4 Ala. 558.

to sell goods generally, sold them to one in their service, upon its being objected that the company was not authorized to keep a store of goods and sell them in the manner they did, and could not, therefore, recover on a count for goods sold and delivered, it was held that the legislature did not intend to prohibit a supply of goods to those employed in the manufactory, and that the corporation might recover for them. "Besides," say the court, "the defendant cannot refuse payment on this ground; but the legislature may enforce the prohibition, by causing the charter to be revoked, when they shall determine that it has been abused."[1] And though a corporation has no banking powers, and is prohibited from issuing notes and checks under a penalty, it is bound to pay for labor and expenses in engraving a steel plate for notes and checks, and in printing therefrom under an order from its officers and agents, even though it should be presumed that they were intended to be used for an unlawful purpose.[2] A promise by a company incorporated "for the purpose of engaging in the whale fishery, and in the manufacture of spermaceti candles" to pay at a future day for State bonds by them purchased, was decided to be *primâ facie* valid and binding.[3] And where the president of a glass company executed a promissory note in the name of the company, in payment for wood furnished them to use in the manufacture of glass, a recovery was had against the company thereon; it being adjudged that a corporation could, without express authority in its charter, give a negotiable promissory note in the course of its legitimate business, as included in the word "*person*,"

---

[1] Chester Glass Co. *v.* Dewey, 16 Mass. 102; and see Moss *v.* Rossie Lead Mining Company, 5 Hill, 137; Safford *v.* Wyckoff, 4 Hill, 444, 445, 446, Chan. Walworth; Proprietors of Quincy Canal *v.* Newcomb, 7 Met. 275; Farmers and Mechanics Bank *v.* Champlain Transportation Co. 18 Vt. 131; Grand Gulf Bank *v.* Archer, 8 Smedes & M. 151. But see McCollough *v.* Ross, 5 Denio, 567, in which the Court of Errors, in New York, seem to insist upon the strict doctrine, that it must appear affirmatively that a promissory note, executed by the corporation, was made in the course of its legitimate business, and that the signature of the president and secretary is not sufficient, without proof of their authority to sign it.

[2] Underwood *v.* Newport Lyceum, 5 B. Mon. 130. A case in Pennsylvania goes the length of holding, that a municipal corporation was liable on scrip, under the denomination of five dollars, issued by its corporate officers, in contravention of the small notes act of that State, on the ground that the scrip was issued with the knowledge of the corporators, who acquiesced in and received the benefit of the issue. It should be added, that the act concerning the issue of such notes did not avoid them, but expressly provided, that recovery might be had upon them with twenty per cent. interest. Alleghany City *v.* McClarkan, 14 Penn. State, 81.

[3] State of Indiana *v.* Wiram, 6 Hill, 33.

used in the statute, 3 and 4 Ann.[1] Upon the same principle, where an incorporated commission company was empowered to employ its stock solely in advancing money, when requested on goods, and in the sale of such goods on commission, it was held that a company might agree to pay or advance money at a future day, and that, though not expressly authorized, they might engage to do this by the acceptance of a bill. It was also considered that it was not necessary that the goods should be delivered to the company prior to their advancing on them; but that they might advance money or accept a bill, *upon an agreement* to deposit or consign goods.[2] An exchange company created with power to purchase, hold, and convey such, and so much real estate, and to erect such buildings as it may deem necessary or proper for the purposes of an Exchange, has incidental authority to borrow money on its bonds secured by mortgage for that purpose.[3] Generally a railroad corporation may make all contracts that are necessary and useful to enable it to carry on the business, or accomplish the objects of its incorporation.[4] A railroad company which is incorporated for the purposes of building and constructing a railroad between two given points, cannot buy a steamboat to run from one of these points in connection with their road.[5] But it may, if authorized to transport passengers beyond its termini.[6]

§ 272. Two or more corporations cannot consolidate their funds, or enter into a copartnership, unless authorized by express grant or necessary implication.[7] And where two corporations are created by adjacent States with the same name, for the construction of a canal in both States, and are afterwards united by the legislative acts of both States, this does not merge the separate corporate existence of such corporations, but only

---

[1] Mott *v.* Hicks, 1 Cowen, 513; and see State of Indiana *v.* Wiram, 6 Hill, 33; State *v.* Nashville University, 4 Humph. 157.

[2] Munn *v.* Commission Comp. 15 Johns. 44.

[3] Barry *v.* Merchants Exchange Company, 1 Sandf. Ch. 280.

[4] See Old Colony R. Co. *v.* Evans, 6 Gray, 25, cited ante, § 153.

[5] Pearce *v.* Madison & Indianapolis R. Co. 21 How. 441; Colman *v.* Eastern Counties R. Co. 10 Beav. 1.

[6] Shawmut Bank *v.* P. & M. R. Co. 31 Vt. 491.

[7] Sharon Canal Company *v.* Fulton Bank, 7 Wend. 412; Smith *v.* Smith, 3 Desaus. Ch. 557; Pearce *v.* Madison & Indianapolis R. Co. 21 How. 441. But a corporation may contract with an individual in furtherance of the object of its creation, though the effect of the contract be to impose upon the company the liabilities of a partner. Catskill Bank *v.* Gray, 14 Barb. 471.

creates a unity of stock and interest.[1] In Massachusetts, it has been held that it is not illegal, either at common law or under the statute of that State of 1786, ch. 11, sec. 3, for two religious corporations, though one of them be in an adjoining State, to unite in the settlement of a minister, if they agree to worship together.[2] In the trustees of Amherst Academy *v.* Cowls,[3] an academy incorporated "to promote morality, piety, and religion, and for the instruction of youth in the learned languages, and in such arts and sciences as are usually taught in other academies," — with power to apply property already given, or which might thereafter be given, to the above purposes, the income thereof not to exceed five thousand dollars, — was held capable of procuring subscriptions and taking promissory notes to constitute a fund for the purpose of founding an institution "for the classical or academical and collegiate education of indigent young men, with the sole view to the Christian ministry," to be incorporated with the academy. It was further decided in this case, that an assignment by the trustees of the academy of such promissory notes, to a college incorporated distinct from the academy, but by its charter authorized to receive, and required to appropriate the fund in question according to the will of the donors, was valid; and that an action upon a negotiable note given as above, and assigned by deed to the college, but not indorsed, was rightly brought in the name of the trustees of the academy.

§ 273. We have before seen that corporations, as banks, of one State, cannot issue notes or bills, or exercise banking privileges, in another State, in violation of its restraining acts, or settled law, prohibitory of such contracts or acts. In the important case of the Bank of Augusta *v.* Earle,[4] the very important question of the general right of a corporation to make contracts in another State than that of its creation, underwent a thorough examination by the highest judicial tribunal of the country, and the result was declared in the very able and satisfactory opinion delivered by the chief justice of the Supreme Court of the United States. That was an action brought by the plaintiffs, a banking corporation incorporated by the legislature of the State of Georgia, and empowered, amongst other things, to purchase bills of

---

1 Farnum *v.* Blackstone Canal Corporation, 1 Sumner, 47.

2 Peckham *v.* North Parish in Haverhill, 16 Pick. 287, 288.

3 6 Pick. 427.

4 13 Pet. 521.

exchange, against the defendant, a citizen of the State of Alabama, on a bill of exchange drawn and indorsed in Mobile, Alabama. The bill was drawn for the purpose of being discounted by the agent of the bank, who had funds of the bank for the purpose of purchasing bills, derived from bills and notes discounted in Georgia by the bank, and payable in Mobile, with which funds the agent of the bank did discount and purchase the bill sued on, at Mobile, for the bank. It was contended that the contract was void, and did not bind the defendant to the payment of the bill, on the general ground, that a bank incorporated by the laws of Georgia could not lawfully exercise the power of discounting bills in the State of Alabama; and this ground was sustained by the decision of the Circuit Court, before whom the case was first tried. The Supreme Court of the United States reversed the decision in this and two similar cases,[1] decided in the same way by the Circuit Court; and the chief justice in delivering the opinion of the Court thus treats the question: "It is very true that a corporation can have no legal existence out of the boundaries of the sovereignty by which it is created. It exists only in contemplation of law and by force of the law; and where that law ceases to operate, and is no longer obligatory, the corporation can have no existence. It must dwell in the place of its creation, and cannot migrate to another sovereignty. But although it must live and have its being in that State only, yet it does not by any means follow that its existence there will not be recognized in other places; and its residence in one State creates no insuperable objection to its power of contracting in another. It is indeed a mere artificial being, invisible and intangible; yet it is a person, for certain purposes in contemplation of law, and has been recognized as such by the decisions of this court. It was so held in the case of The United States *v.* Amedy,[2] and in Beaston *v.* The Farmers Bank of Delaware.[3] Now, natural persons, through the intervention of agents, are continually making contracts in countries in which they do not reside; and where they are not person-

---

[1] Bank of United States *v.* Primrose, and New Orleans & Carrolton Railroad Company *v.* Earle, 13 Pet. 521; and see the Commercial and Railroad Bank of Vicksburg *v.* Slocumb, 14 Pet. 60; Irvine *v.* Lowry, 14 Pet. 293; Runyan *v.* Coster, 14 Pet. 122; Stoney *v.* American Life Ins. Co. 11 Paige 635; Day *v.* Newark India Rubber Manufactory Co. 1 Blatchf. C. C. 628, 632, 633; Mumford *v.* American Life Ins. & Trust Co. 4 Comst. 463; Ohio Life Ins. & Trust Co. *v.* Merchants Ins. and Trust Co. 11 Humph. 1; Kennebec Co. *v.* Augusta Ins. & Banking Co. 6 Gray, 204.

[2] 11 Wheat. 412.

[3] 12 Pet. 135.

ally present when the contract is made; and nobody has ever doubted the validity of these agreements. And what greater objection can there be to the capacity of an artificial person, by its agents, to make a contract within the scope of its limited powers, in a sovereignty in which it does not reside; provided such contracts are permitted to be made by them by the laws of the place? The corporation must no doubt show that the laws of its creation gave it authority to make such contracts, through such agents.[1] Yet, as in the case of a natural person, it is not necessary that it should actually exist in the sovereignty in which the contract is made. It is sufficient that its existence as an artificial person, in the State of its creation, is acknowledged and recognized by the law of the nation where the dealing takes place; and that it is permitted by the laws of that place to exercise there the powers with which it is endowed. Every power, however, of the description of which we are speaking, which a corporation exercises in another State, depends for its validity upon the laws of the sovereignty in which it is exercised; and a corporation can make no valid contract without their sanction, express or implied. And this brings us to the question which has been so elaborately discussed: whether, by the comity of nations and between these States, the corporations of one State are permitted to make contracts in another. It is needless to enumerate here the instances in which, by the general practice of civilized countries, the laws of the one will, by the comity of nations, be recognized and executed in another, where the rights of individuals are concerned. The cases of contracts made in a foreign country are familiar examples; and courts of justice have always expounded and executed them according to the laws of the place in which they were made; provided that law was not repugnant to the laws or policy of their own country. The comity thus extended to other nations is no impeachment of sovereignty. It is the voluntary act of the nation by which it is offered; and is inadmissible when contrary to its policy or prejudicial to its interests. But it contributes so largely to promote justice between individuals, and to produce a friendly intercourse between the sovereignties to which they belong, that courts of justice have continually acted upon it, as a part of the voluntary law of nations. It is truly said, in Story's Conflict of Laws, 37, that 'In the silence of

---

[1] That it is not necessary to set forth this right in the pleadings, but that it is sufficient to show it upon the hearing of a cause, see Bank of Michigan *v.* Williams, 5 Wend. 478; Marine & F. Ins. Bank of Georgia *v.* Jauncey, 1 Barb. 489.

any positive rule, affirming, or denying, or restraining the operation of foreign laws, courts of justice presume the tacit adoption of them by their own government; unless they are repugnant to its policy, or prejudicial to its interests. It is not the comity of the courts, but the comity of the nation which is administered, and ascertained in the same way, and guided by the same reasoning, by which all other principles of municipal law are ascertained and guided.' Adopting, as we do, the principle here stated, we proceed to inquire whether, by the comity of nations, foreign corporations are permitted to make contracts within their jurisdiction; and we can perceive no sufficient reason for excluding them, when they are not contrary to the known policy of the State, or injurious to its interests. It is nothing more than the admission of the existence of an artificial person, created by the law of another State, and clothed with the power of making certain contracts. It is but the usual comity of recognizing the law of another State. In England, from which we have received our general principles of jurisprudence, no doubt appears to have been entertained of the right of a foreign corporation to sue in its courts, since the case of Henriquez *v.* The Dutch West India Company, decided in 1729.[1] And it is a matter of history, which this court are bound to notice, that corporations, created in this country, have been in the open practice, for many years past, of making contracts in England, of various kinds and to very large amounts; and we have never seen a doubt suggested there of the validity of these contracts, by any court or any jurist. It is impossible to imagine that any court in the *United States would refuse to execute a contract by which an American corporation had borrowed money in England; yet if the contracts of corporations, made out of the State by which they were created, are void, even contracts of that description could not be enforced. It has, however, been supposed that the rules of comity between foreign nations do not apply to the States of this Union; that they extend to one another no other rights than those which are given by the Constitution of the United States; and that the courts of the general government are not at liberty to presume, in the absence of all legislation on the subject, that a State has adopted the comity of nations towards the other States, as a part of its jurisprudence; or that it acknowledges any rights but those which are secured by the Constitution of the United States. The court think otherwise. The intimate

[1] 2 Ld. Raym. 1532.

union of these States, as members of the same great political family; the deep and vital interests which bind them so closely together, should lead us, in the absence of proof to the contrary, to presume a greater degree of comity, and friendship, and kindness towards one another, than we should be authorized to presume between foreign nations. And when (as without doubt must occasionally happen) the interest or policy of any State requires it to restrict the rule, it has but to declare its will, and the legal presumption is at once at an end. But until this is done, upon what grounds could this court refuse to administer the law of international comity between these States? They are sovereign States; and the history of the past, and the events which are daily occurring, furnish the strongest evidence that they have adopted towards each other the laws of comity in their fullest extent. Money is frequently borrowed in one State, by a corporation created in another. The numerous banks established in different States, are in the constant habit of contracting and dealing with one another. Agencies for corporations engaged in the business of insurance and of banking, have been established in other States, and suffered to make contracts without any objection on the part of the State authorities. These usages of commerce and trade have been so general and public, and have been practised for so long a period of time, and so generally acquiesced in by the States, that the court cannot overlook them, when a question like the one before us is under consideration. The silence of the State authorities, while these events are passing before them, shows their assent to the ordinary laws of comity which permit a corporation to make contracts in another State. But we are not left to infer it merely from the general usages of trade, and the silent acquiescence of the States. It appears from the cases cited in the argument, which it is unnecessary to recapitulate in this opinion, that it has been decided in many of the State courts, we believe in all of them where the question has arisen, that a corporation of one State may sue in the courts of another. If it may sue, why may it not make a contract? The right to sue is one of the powers which it derives from its charter. If the courts of another country take notice of its existence as a corporation, so far as to allow it to maintain a suit, and permit it to exercise that power, why should not its existence be recognized for other purposes, and the corporation permitted to exercise another power, which is given to it by the same law and the same sovereignty, where the last-mentioned power does not come in conflict with the interest or policy of the State? There is certainly nothing in the nature and character of a corporation which could justly lead to such a distinction; and which should extend to it the comity of suit, and refuse to it the comity of contract. If it is allowed to sue, it would of course be permitted to compromise, if it thought proper, with its debtor; to give him time; to accept something else in satisfaction; to give him a release; and to employ an attorney for itself to conduct its suit. These are all matters of contract, and yet are so intimately connected with the right to sue, that the latter could not be effectually exercised if the former were denied." [1] The court, finding that the State of Alabama had not merely acquiesced by silence, but that her judicial tribunals had recognized the comity of suit in favor of corporations of other States, and there being no law prohibiting the contract in question, held, that it was valid, and obliged the party to pay according to its tenor and effect. The doctrines of this case had been declared in several of the States, and may now be considered as the law of the land.[2]

§ 274. It by no means follows, however, that because a corporation may, by its corporate agents, general or special, act and contract without the limits of the State which created it, that *the corporation itself* may meet out of the limits of the State, and *there* create and authorize its agents. On the contrary, in a late case in Maine,[3] it was expressly decided that such an extra-territorial meeting, unless authorized by the charter or general law, was absolutely void; that the vote of the directors, passed at a meeting also extra-territorial, authorizing their president and secretary to execute a mortgage of real property, conferred no authority, and that the mortgage executed gave no title, at least, to a

---

[1] Bank of Augusta *v.* Earle, 13 Pet. 519; Tombigbee Railroad Co. *v.* Kneeland, 4 How. 16. So a corporation may hold lands in another State, which have been conveyed to it as security for, or in payment of a debt. New York Dry Dock *v.* Hicks, 5 McLean, 111; Farmers Loan & Trust Company *v.* McKinney, 6 McLean, 7.

[2] Portsmouth Livery Company *v.* Watson, 10 Mass. 91; N. Y. Fire Insurance Company *v.* Ely, 5 Conn. 560; Bank of Marietta *v.* Pindall, 2 Rand. 465; Taylor *v.* Bank of Alexandria, 5 Rand. 471; Williamson *v.* Smoot, 7 Mart. La. 31; Lathrop *v.* Bank of Scioto, 8 Dana, 114; Bank of Edwardsville *v.* Simpson, 1 Misso. 184; Guaga Iron Company *v.* Dawson, 4 Blackf. 202; Bank of Kentucky *v.* Schuylkill Bank, 1 Parsons, Sel. Cas. 225; and see Henriquez *v.* Dutch W. India Co. 2 Ld. Raym. 1532, 1 Stra. 612, 2 id. 807; King of Spain *v.* Hullet, 1 Clark & F. 333, 1 Dow & C. 169, 3 Simons, 338; St. Charles Bank *v.* De Bernales, 1 C. & P. 569, Ryan & M. 190; Brown *v.* Minis, 1 McCord, 80; Silver Lake Bank *v.* North, 4 Johns. Ch. 370; Atterbury *v.* Knox, 4 B. Mon. 92; Blair *v.* Perpetual Ins. Co. 10 Misso. 561.

[3] Miller *v.* Ewer, 27 Me. 509; and see cases, McCall *v.* Byram Manufacturing Co. 6 Conn. 428, and Copp *v.* Lamb, 3 Fairf. 314, there commented on; see also, *ante*, Ch. III.

claimant, who, as a stockholder, at the time, had knowledge of, and actually participated in the unlawful proceedings of the corporation, or to a claimant deriving title from such a stockholder, and possessing no higher equities. In New York it is held, that the sixth section of the act prohibiting unauthorized banking,[1] relates merely to the *keeping of an office* for the purpose of receiving deposits or discounting notes or bills, &c., and not to a single isolated act of loaning money; and hence, that a foreign banking corporation might recover on a check taken by its cashier in New York for money there loaned by him.[2]

§ 275. We will close this chapter by observing, that a corporation, keeping within the scope of its general powers, may contract or bind itself to do any act *at any place;* and wherever the engagement may be broken, it will be equally liable.[3]

CHAPTER IX.

OF AGENTS OF CORPORATIONS, THEIR MODE OF APPOINTMENT AND POWER.

§ 276. IN general, the only mode in which a corporation aggregate can act or contract is through the intervention of agents, either specially designated by the act of incorporation, or appointed and authorized by the corporation in pursuance of it.[4] It is an old rule of the common law, that such a corporation cannot lay a fine, acknowledge a deed, or appear in a suit, except by attorney or agent;[5] and corporations, with power to sue and be sued, perform necessary services, incident to such

---

[1] R. S. 712, sect. 6.

[2] Suydam *v.* Morris Canal & Banking Co. Superior Court of City of New York, July Term, 1843, MS., for which see 5 Hill, 491, n.; Pennington *v.* Townsend, 7 Wend. 276, 279; New Hope Delaware Bridge Company *v.* Poughkeepsie Silk Company, 25 Wend. 648.

[3] Bank of Utica *v.* Smedes, 3 Cowen, 684; M'Call *v.* Byram Man. Co. 6 Conn. 420.

[4] Co. Lit. 66 b.

[5] Com. Dig. Attorney, C. 2.

business, by agents.[1] At the civil law, it was one of the privileges of a corporation (*universitas*) to act by an attorney or agent, who was known by the name of actor, or procurator, or more familiarly, by the name of syndic. *Quibus autem, permissum est corpus habere collegii, &c. et actorem, sive syndicum, per quem, tanquam in republica, quod communiter agi fierique oporteat, agatur, fiat.*[2]

§ 277. The power to appoint officers and agents rests, of course, like every other power, in the body of the corporators, unless some particular board or body, created or existing within the corporation, is legally vested with it; and courts cannot judicially notice that a particular board or body of the corporation is authorized by the charter and by-laws to appoint agents, where the evidence of the charter and by-laws is not introduced.[3] Where the charter or act of incorporation speaks upon this subject, it must be strictly pursued, or the appointment may be avoided. The directors of a corporation, specially empowered by the charter to contract on its behalf, have no power to appoint subagents to contract for the corporation, unless such power is expressly given them; and accordingly contracts made by such subagents will not be binding on the corporation. Canal commissioners cannot delegate the authority vested in them to enter upon and take possession of lands for canal purposes; but this must be done by themselves, or under their *express* directions, as in other cases of personal confidence and trust, where judgment and discretion are required or relied on.[4] And where, by a bank charter, the power of discounting notes and bills was vested in the board of directors, it was held, in Louisiana, that they could not delegate this trust to an agent or agents of the board.[5] In such case, indeed, it would be a violation of the charter for which the corporation would be held responsible, for the board of directors to authorize their president, or cashier, or any other officer of the bank, to make loans and discounts, without having the same formally passed upon by the board.[6] Neither can an

---

1 Planters & Merchants Bank *v.* Andrews, 8 Port. Ala. 404.

2 Dig. Lib. 3, tit. 4, l. 1, § 1; Pothier, Pand. Lib. 3, tit. 4, n. 39; Vicat. Vocabul. Syndicus; Heinecc. ad Pand. P. 1, lib. 3, tit. 3, § 419; id. tit. 4, § 439; Pothier on Oblig. art. 49.

3 Haven *v.* New Hampshire Asylum for the Insane, 13 N. H. 532.

4 Lyon *v.* Jerome, 26 Wend. 485; and see Rex *v.* Gravesend, 4 Dowl. & R. 117, 2 B. & C. 602; York & Cumberland R. R. Co. *v.* Ritchie, 40 Me. 425.

5 Percy *v.* Millauden, 3 La. 568.

6 Commissioners *v.* Bank of Buffalo, 6 Paige, 497.

agent, appointed by the corporation, and authorized to make a particular contract, or to do a certain piece of business, delegate his trust, unless specially empowered so to do; the personal confidence of the principal in the agent being the supposed motive of the selection and appointment of the latter. Accordingly, where the directors of a turnpike corporation were empowered by the corporation to contract for the making of the turnpike road, and they, without authority so to do, appointed subagents, who covenanted on behalf of the directors to pay certain sums for the making of the road, it was decided by the Supreme Court of Massachusetts, that the corporation was not bound by the contract, since it had given the directors, its immediate agents, no power to substitute agents under them.[1] And if three persons are appointed by a corporation for a particular purpose, all must act, and no contract can be made by two of the three which will be binding upon the corporation.[2] In Massachusetts, a board of *bank* directors is a body recognized by the laws; and does not exercise a *delegated* authority in the sense of the rule which forbids an agent, without express power so to do, to delegate his authority. By the by-laws of banking corporations, and by a usage so general and uniform as to be regarded as part of the law of that State, bank directors have the general superintendence and active management of all the concerns of the bank, and constitute, to all purposes of dealing with others, the corporation. It was accordingly held, that not only might the directors of a bank mortgage its real estate to secure a debt due from the bank, but might delegate such an authority to a committee of their own number.[3]

§ 278. Generally speaking, any persons may, by due appointment, be the agents of corporations, as well as of natural persons; and it is a

---

[1] Tippetts *v.* Walker, 4 Mass. 595; Emerson *v.* Providence Hat Manufacturing Co. 12 Mass. 237; Gillis *v.* Bailey, 1 Foster, 149. See Manchester & Lawrence R. R. *v.* Fisk, 33 N. H. 297.

[2] Corn Exchange Bank *v.* Cumberland Coal Co. 1 Bosw. 436.

[3] Burrill *v.* Nahant Bank, 2 Met. 166, 167. The Central Board of the Real Estate Bank of the State of Arkansas were not considered trustees in the sense of the rule forbidding trustees to delegate their trust, but rather as the representative of the corporation empowered to declare its will, and hence might appoint trustees to pay the debts of the corporation, without, legally speaking, a delegation of power. Conway, *Exparte,* 4 Pike, 359. The same rule was held by the Supreme Court of Pennsylvania, with regard to the directors of the Bank of the United States. Dana *v.* Bank of U. S. 5 Watts & S. 223. So in New York under the general banking law of that State. Palmer *v.* Yates, 3 Sandf. 175.

well-established principle, that they even who are disqualified to act for themselves, as infants and feme coverts, may yet act as the agents of others.[1] A corporation may employ one of its own members as an agent to act as auctioneer at the sale of its pews, who may make the memorandum of sale, required under the Statute of Frauds, to bind the purchaser.[2]

§ 279. It is not unusual, however, for the charters of banking, insurance, and turnpike companies, to prescribe who, and who alone, shall be the agents of the company for particular purposes; and in such cases, the boards or persons specified, and they alone, for those purposes are, or can be, the agents of the corporation.[3] Such being created agents by the charter or act of incorporation, the power of appointing others in their stead, by the very law of its nature, never existed in the corporation. These boards, it is true, are elected by the stockholders, but are constituted *agents* of the corporation, and derive all their authority from the charter.[4] Accordingly, where a member of a turnpike company agreed to pay the instalments on his stock, in such manner and proportion as the president, directors, and company of the corporation should direct, it was decided that he bound himself to pay according to the order of the president and directors, since they were the representatives of the corporation, and were by the charter alone authorized to manage its concerns.[5] A statute incorporating an insurance company enacted, that no losses should be paid without the approbation of at least *four* of the *directors*, with the president and his assistants; an attempt was made to charge the company with a total loss, upon a verbal agreement to accept an abandonment, and pay a total loss, made by the *president* and *assistants* merely, at a meeting, when it did not appear that a single *director* was present; the Supreme Court of the State of New York decided, that the acceptance, not having been made by the *agents* constituted by the act of incorporation, was not binding on the company.[6] If

---

[1] Co. Lit. 52 a; Emerson *v.* Blouden, 1 Esp. 142; Palethorp *v.* Furnace, 2 Esp. 511; Anderson *v.* Sanderson, 2 Stark. N. P. 204.

[2] Stoddert *v.* Port Tobacco Parish, 2 Gill & J. 227.

[3] Washington & Pittsburg Turnpike Company *v.* Crane, 8 S. & R. 521, 522.

[4] Bank of the United States *v.* Dandridge, 12 Wheat. 113, per Marshall, C. J.; Royalton *v.* R. & W. Turnpike Co. 14 Vt. 311.

[5] Union Turnpike Co. *v.* Jenkins, 1 Caines, 391.

[6] Beatty *v.* Marine Ins. Co. 2 Johns. 109. But see Barnes *v.* Ontario Bank, 19 N. Y. 152, cited *ante*, § 253.

the charter has invested a particular board, or select body, with power to manage the concerns of the corporation, the body at large have no right to interfere with the doings of these, their charter agents, and courts will not, even upon a petition of a majority of the members, compel the board to do any act contrary to their own judgment.[1] The directors of a bank are the sole judges of what portion of the profits of the bank they ought from time to time to divide; and their judgment in such matters will not be controlled by the courts, even though they may deem it honestly erroneous.[2]

§ 280. Boards of directors, managers, &c., are agents of the corporation, only so far as authorized directly or impliedly by the charter; and the general authority given by the act incorporating a manufacturing corporation to the directors, to manage the stock, property, and affairs of the corporation, does not enable them to apply to the legislature for an enlargement of the corporate powers; and a legislative resolve passed upon such an application without authority from the company is void.[3] Neither has a board of bank directors any right to pass a resolution excluding one of its number from an inspection of the bank books, upon the ground that he was hostile to the interests of the bank; and a mandamus will lie, directed to the cashier, commanding that the books be submitted to the inspection of a director thus excluded.[4] The directors have, in general, power to control all the property of the bank; and may authorize one of their number to assign any securities belonging to it;[5] whether they have, in general, power to assign all the estate, real and personal, of the corporation, to a trustee, for the purpose of winding up and closing its concerns, without the assent of the stockholders, may be doubted.[6] The Supreme Court of Pennsylvania have, however, held, that such a power was vested in the directors of the Bank of

[1] Commonwealth *v.* Trustees of St. Mary's Church, 6 S. & R. 508; Dana *v.* Bank of the United States, 5 Watts & S. 247; Conro *v.* Port Henry Iron Co. 12 Barb. 27.

[2] State of Louisiana *v.* Bank of Louisiana, 6 La. 745. See, however, Scott *v.* Eagle Insurance Co. 7 Paige, 198; Ely *v.* Sprague, 1 Clarke, Ch. 351.

[3] Marlborough Manufacturing Company *v.* Smith, 2 Conn. 579.

[4] People *v.* Throop, 12 Wend. 183.

[5] Spear *v.* Ladd, 11 Mass. 94; Northampton Bank *v.* Pepoon, 11 Mass. 288; Bank Com. *v.* Bank of Brest, Harring. Ch. 106.

[6] Bank Com. *v.* Bank of Brest, Harring. Ch. 106, 111. Directors have no power to alienate corporate property, essentially necessary for the transaction of the business of the corporation. Rollins *v.* Clay, 33 Me. 132.

the United States.[1] The directors of a bank may authorize the president and cashier to borrow money or obtain discounts for the use of the bank;[2] and the power of making discounts, and of fixing the conditions of them, is in general solely with them.[3] The board of directors of a banking corporation having passed a resolution authorizing the stockholders to transfer their stock to the bank in payment of their debts to it, several of the stockholders availed themselves of the authority of the resolution, and discharged their debts to the bank in this way. It was decided that the directors had power to pass the resolution, and that the stockholders were legally authorized by it thus to pay their debts to the bank; and that notwithstanding the bank had since stopped payment, equity would not compel a resumption of the stock by the stockholders, or compel them to pay their debts with other means.[4] Where the trustees of a religious corporation purchased lands with the corporate funds, and took the deeds in their individual names, it was considered that they held the lands as trustees for the corporation, and that if they subsequently sold the lands, the proceeds belonged to the corporation, and were to be held for its use.[5]

§ 281. According to the doctrine of some of the ancient judges, a corporation aggregate could manifest its assent only by affixing its common seal, and hence could act only by deed.[6] Some went so far as to assert not only that no servant of a corporation could be appointed without deed, but that without it no command to a servant to do a particular act was valid; while others admitted that no servant could be appointed without deed, yet held, that when once appointed, he might do every thing incident to the nature of his service, not only without commandment by deed, but without any commandment whatever.[7] It was early established, that a corporation might appoint officers of little importance and ordinary service, as a cook, a butler, a bailiff to take a distress, or

---

[1] Dana *v.* Bank of the United States, 5 Watts & S. 247; and see Union Bank of Tennessee *v.* Ellicott, 6 Gill & J. 363.

[2] Ridgway *v.* Farmers Bank, 12 S. & R. 256; Leavitt *v.* Yates, 4 Sandf. Ch. 134.

[3] Bank of United States *v.* Dana, 6 Pet. 51; Bank of Metropolis *v.* Jones, 8 Pet. 16; Percy *v.* Millauden, 3 La. 568; Bank of Pennsylvania *v.* Reed, 1 Watts & S. 101.

[4] Taylor *v.* Miami Exporting Company, 6 Ohio, 218. See also, City Bank of Columbus *v.* Bruce, 17 N. Y. 507.

[5] Methodist Episcopal Church of Cincinnati *v.* Wood, 5 Ohio, 286.

[6] Davies, R. 121, case of the Dean and Chapter of Fernes.

[7] 4 H. 6, 7, 13, 17; 7 H. 7, 9; 13 H. 8, 12.

that a commonalty might make an assignment of auditors, without deed.[1] In the case of Horn *v.* Ivy,[2] it is laid down, that the appointment of a bailiff to make distresses for a corporation must be under seal; and Mr. C. J. Best seems to have considered that the case of Manly *v.* Long[3] did not establish a different rule, but was to be distinguished as a case of necessity, owing to the hurry of the proceeding.[4] In matters of consequence, or in the employment of one to perform on their behalf any but ordinary services, it was still held, that corporations aggregate could not be bound without deed.[5] Thus, in trespass for taking away a ship, the defendant justified as a servant to the *Canary Company*, by whose charter it was declared, "that none but such and such persons should trade to the Canaries, on pain of forfeiting their ships, goods, &c." It was objected that he ought to have shown his deed, whereby he was authorized to seize, on behalf of the company, ships, goods, &c.; and Twisden, Justice, says, "I think they cannot seize without deed, any more than they can enter for condition broken without deed." [6] Though by no means free from doubt, it seems in early times to have been the better opinion that a corporation aggregate could not appoint a person to do any act in which its *real* property was concerned, or by which its rights thereto were to be asserted, without deed, as an attorney to make or take livery of seisin,[7] an agent or servant to enter into land on its behalf for condition broken,[8] or to revest it with an estate of which it had been disseised.[9] In the time of Elizabeth, it was, however, agreed by all the judges of the King's Bench, that if a sheriff make a warrant of arrest to a corporation which has return of writs, they may make a bailiff to execute it without writing.[10] In the first year of Queen Anne,

---

[1] See same authorities, and Plowd. 91 b.; 12 Ed. 4, 10 a.; H. 7, 15, 26; Bro. Corp. 51; 26 H. 8, 8 b.; Bro. 182 b.; Anon. 1 Salk. 191; Manby *v.* Long, 3 Lev. 107; 2 Saund. 305; and see Smith *v.* Birmingham and Staffordshire Gas Light Company, 3 Nev. & M. 771, 1 A. & E. 526.

[2] 1 Vent. 47.

[3] 3 Lev. 107.

[4] East London Water Works *v.* Baily, 4 Bing. 283.

[5] Horn *v.* Ivy, 1 Vent. 47, 1 Mod. 18, 2 Keble, 567.

[6] Ibid.

[7] 12 H. 7, 25, 26; Bro. Corp. 51; See Bailiffs, &c. Ipswich *v.* Martin, Cro. Jac. 411.

[8] 10 Ed. 4; 7 Ed. 4, 14; Bro. Corp. 54; 18 Ed. 4, 8; Bro. Corp. 59; 16 H. 7, 2; Bro. Corp. 96; 1 Rolle, 514; Dyer, 102, pl. 83; but see 12 Ed. 4, per Littleton; Bro. Corp. 56, Dyer, sup.

[9] Jenk. 131.

[10] Moore, 512.

a distinction seems to have been taken by the Court of King's Bench, between acts by a corporation upon record, and *in pais;* the former of which they might, and the latter they could not do, without their common seal. In the Mayor of Thetford's case,[1] where a mandamus was returned without the common seal, and without the hand of the mayor, it was held a good return; and Lord Holt, Chief Justice, to whom the court agreed, said, that a corporation may do an act of record without their common seal, because they are estopped by the record to say, that it is not their act; but not an act *in pais;* and he instanced the case of the City of London, who make an attorney yearly in the Court of King's Bench without signing or sealing. In commissions of bankruptcy, corporations usually appoint their clerk or treasurer to prove debts due to them; but it is said that he must produce the appointment under seal to the commissioners.[2] It is also laid down by Mr. Kyd, as a general rule, that the person who appears on behalf of a corporation in a court of justice, must be authorized by warrant under the common seal;[3] and such appears, though until recently not without question, to be the doctrine of the English courts with regard to municipal corporations,[4] as between the attorney and the corporation. As to third persons, and especially the other party to the cause, such an objection would avail nothing, at least if the corporation had notice of the appearance; and in a recent case it has been determined that an attorney of a railway corporation, appearing without seal, might refer the cause to arbitration so as to bind the company to the award.[5] Notwithstanding the general rule, however, it seems early to have been held, in accordance with the intimation of Lord Chief Justice Holt, above quoted, that a corporation might make an attorney in a court of record without other writing than the record itself;[6] and the City of London may, and do, make an attorney in the King's Bench,[7] and present their mayor in the Exchequer every year, without either sealing or signing, the record operating as an estoppel.[8] In Rex *v.* Bigg,[9] which was an indictment for razing out an

---

1 1 Salk. 191; 3 Salk. 103.

2 Cooke's Bankrupt Laws (2d ed.), 175.

3 1 Kyd on Corporations, 265.

4 Arnold *v.* The Mayor of Poole, 4 Man. & G. 893, 894, 895; Plowd. 91; 2 Show, 366; but see 1 Skin. 154.

5 Farwell *v.* Eastern Counties Railway, 2 Exch. 343.

6 13 H. 8, 12; Bro. Corp. 83.

7 Mayor of Thetford's case, 1 Salk. 192; 3 Salk. 103; Comb. 41, 422; Arnold *v.* The Mayor of Poole, 4 Man. & G. 893, 894, 895.

8 1 Kyd on Corp. 267, cites Madox, Firma, Burgi, c. 7, passim.

9 3 P. Wms. 419; 1 Stra. 18.

indorsement of part payment on a Bank of England note, it seems to have been established, that a person employed by the Governor and Company of the Bank of England, to sign notes on their behalf, was competently authorized for that purpose, though intrusted and employed by mere vote, or other corporate act not under the common seal; and in Yarborough *v.* The Bank of England,[1] it was considered that a corporation might be bound by the acts of its servants, though not authorized under seal, if done within the scope of their employment. The present doctrine upon this subject, in England, seems to be, that an agent of a municipal corporation need not be appointed under the corporate seal for acts of an ordinary nature, and which do not affect the interests of the corporation; but for acts which do affect the interests of the corporation, they must be authorized by the corporate seal. Thus, they must appoint a bailiff for entering lands for condition broken, by deed, in order to revest the estate; but they need not do so where the bailiff is only to distrain for rent.[2] Where, however, an incorporated railway company filed a bill for the specific performance of a contract for the purchase of land entered into by their agent, and it was objected that it did not appear that the agent was authorized under the corporate seal, the objection was overruled on the ground that the company had, before the bill filed, not only acted on the contract by entering into possession of the land, but actually made a railroad over it.[3] And with regard to private corporations aggregate, it would seem that at this day, in England, the jury are permitted to infer the authority of an agent of a corporation to demise land by parol, there being no direct evidence of appointment under seal.[4]

§ 282. In this country, where private corporations for every purpose are so multiplied, that their facility of action has become a matter of public importance, in the language of Kent,[5] "the old technical rule has been condemned as impolitic, and essentially discarded." A cor-

---

[1] 16 East, 6.

[2] Smith *v.* Birmingham & Staffordshire Gas Light Company, 3 Nev. & M. 771, 1 A. & E. 526; and see East London Water Works Co. *v.* Bailey, 4 Bing. 283; Edwards *v.* Grand Junction Canal Co. 1 Mylne & C. 659, 672; Murray *v.* East India Company, 5 B. & Ald. 204, 209, 210; Arnold *v.* The Mayor of Poole, 4 Man. & G. 893, 894, 895; Smith *v.* Cartwright, 6 Exch. 927, 6 Eng. L. & Eq. 528; Story on Agency, 54, n. 3.

[3] London and Birmingham Railway Co. *v.* Winter, 1 Craig & Ph. 57.

[4] Doe, dem. Birmingham Canal Co. *v.* Bold, 11 Q. B. 129.

[5] 2 Kent, Com. 289.

poration may express its assent by its seal, by vote, or through its agents; and in the case of Bank of Columbia *v.* Patterson,[1] the Supreme Court of the United States, after a full review of all the authorities, considered it as established law, that such a body might, by *mere vote*, or other corporate act not under the corporate seal, appoint an agent, whose acts and contracts, within the scope of his authority, would be binding on the corporation. In the subsequent case of Fleckner *v.* U. S. Bank,[2] where the ancient doctrine, that a corporation can act only through the instrumentality of its seal, was objected to the validity of an indorsement made by the cashier of a bank, who was authorized merely by a resolution passed by the board of president and directors, Mr. Justice Story, in delivering the opinion of the court, observes: "Whatever may be the original correctness of this doctrine, as applied to corporations existing by the common law, in respect to which it has been certainly broken in upon in modern times, it has no application to corporations created by statute whose charters contemplate the business of the corporation to be transacted exclusively by a special body or board of directors. And the acts of such body or board, evidenced by a written vote, are as completely binding upon the corporation, and as complete authority to their agents, as the most solemn acts done under the corporate seal." It was further decided in this case, that there was nothing in the civil code of Louisiana which in the slightest degree points to the necessity of using a corporate seal in appointing agents of corporations, or authorizing corporate acts; and that the fair inference deducible from the silence of the code is, that it does not contemplate any such formality as essential to the validity of any official acts done by the officers of the corporation, and gives such acts a binding authority, if evidenced by a vote.[3] In Osborn *v.* U. S. Bank,[4] upon its being objected that no authority was shown in the record from the bank, authorizing the institution or prosecution of the suit, although it was admitted by the Supreme Court of the United States that a corporation can only appear by attorney, and that the attorney must receive the authority of the corporation to enable him to represent it, yet it was

---

[1] 7 Cranch, 305; and see Bank of U. S. *v.* Norwood, 1 Harris & J. 426, per Chase, J.

[2] 8 Wheat. 357.

[3] Ibid. 360. See Civil Code of Louisiana.

[4] 9 Wheat. 738; and see McMecken *v.* The Mayor, &c. of Baltimore, 2 Harris & J. 41; Gaines *v.* Tombigbee Bank, Minor, 50; Bank of Montgomery *v.* Harrison, 2 Port. Ala. 540; Carry *v.* Bank of Mobile, 8 Port. Ala. 374; Legwood *v.* Planters, &c. Bank, Minor, 23 (overruled); Vance *v.* Bank of Indiana, 1 Blackf. 80.

held, that this authority need not be under seal. It was also decided, upon principle and invariable practice, that the power of the attorney need not appear on the record; the court perceiving in this particular no distinction between a corporation and a natural person.[1] Indeed, to prove authority from a corporation either to prosecute or withdraw a suit brought in its name, even a vote of the corporation is not necessary. If the act be done by one as its agent or attorney, no other proof of authority will be required.[2]

§ 283. It is now the well-settled doctrine in America, that as, from their very structure, corporations aggregate are made capable of acting and are supposed to act by vote, it can make no difference whether their agents are appointed under the corporate seal, or by resolution, or vote; that the appointment may be legally made in either mode, and that, too, although the agent be appointed to convey the real estate of the corporation, or whatever may be the purpose of the agency.[3] The ordinary and proper proof of the appointment and authority of an agent of a corporation is made by the production of the records or books of the corporation, containing the entry or resolution of appointment, the records being proved to be the records of the corporation;[4] and the sec-

---

1 Osborn *v.* Bank of United States, 9 Wheat. 738, per Marshall, C. J.; and see Union Manufacturing Company *v.* Pitkin, 14 Conn. 174; Farmers & Mechanics Bank *v.* Troy City Bank, 1 Doug. Mich. 457.

2 Union Manufacturing Company *v.* Pitkin, 14 Conn. 174; State Bank *v.* Bell, 5 Blackf. 127; Brookville Insurance Company *v.* Records, id. 170; Bridgton *v.* Bennett, 23 Maine, 422.

3 Randall *v.* Van Vechten, 19 Johns. 65; Baptist Church *v.* Mulford, 3 Halst. 182, 184; Perkins *v.* Washington Insurance Company, 4 Cowen, 645; Lathrop *v.* Bank of Scioto, 8 Dana, 115; Savings Bank *v.* Davis, 8 Conn. 191; Buncombe Turnpike Company *v.* McCarson, 1 Dev. & B. 306; Bank of Columbia *v.* Patterson, 7 Cranch, 299; Andover &c. Turnpike Corporation *v.* Hay, 7 Mass. 602; Hayden *v.* Middlesex Turnpike Corporation, 10 Mass. 397; Essex Turnpike Corporation *v.* Collins, 8 Mass. 292; Wright *v.* Lanckton, 19 Pick. 290; Dana *v.* St. Andrews' Church, 14 Johns. 118; Union Bank of Maryland *v.* Ridgely, 1 Harris & G. 424; Kennedy *v.* Baltimore Insurance Company, 3 Harris & J. 367; Garrison *v.* Combs, 7 J. J. Marsh. 85; Legrand *v.* Hampden Sidney College, 5 Munf. 324; Bates *v.* Bank of the State of Alabama, 2 Ala. 461, 462; Stamford Bank *v.* Benedict, 15 Conn. 445; City of Detroit *v.* Jackson, 1 Doug. Mich. 106; St. Andrews' Bay Land Co. *v.* Mitchell, 4 Fla. 192.

4 Buncombe Turnpike Company *v.* McCarson, 1 Dev. & B. 306; Owings *v.* Speed, 5 Wheat. 424; Thayer *v.* Middlesex Mutual Insurance Company, 10 Pick. 326; Narraganset Bank *v.* Atlantic Silk Company, 3 Met. 282; Clark *v.* Benton Manufacturing Company, 15 Wend. 256; Methodist Chapel Corporation *v.* Herrick, 25 Me. 354; Haven *v.* The New Hampshire Asylum, 13 N. H. 532.

retary of the corporation is obviously the proper person to have possession of, and to prove the books of the company.[1] But where, in a suit against a corporation on a bill of exchange accepted by one, in behalf of the corporation, as its treasurer, notice was given by the plaintiff to the corporation to produce its records for the purpose of proving the appointment or election of the treasurer, and the production of the records was refused, the testimony of a witness was admitted that he had seen the records, and that it appeared therein that the person accepting the bill was duly elected treasurer, as competent proof of his appointment and authority.[2] So it has been held that if one has the actual charge of the business of a corporation with the knowledge of the members and directors, this is evidence of his authority without showing a vote or other corporate act constituting him an agent.[3] And the authority of an agent to bind a corporation need not be shown by a resolution or other written evidence, but may be implied from facts and circumstances.[4]

§ 284. We have seen that, in order to the acceptance of an official bond by a corporation, so that the instrument should bind the sureties, the recording of the vote of acceptance or approval is not essential to its validity, unless the charter, statute, or by-laws expressly make it so; even though an officer of the corporation be required to keep a fair and regular record of all its proceedings; this provision usually being merely directory.[5] Neither is it indispensable to show a written instrument or vote of acceptance of a charter, or a written enactment, or repeal of by-laws on the corporation books; all which may be inferred from the acts of the corporation, through its officers or otherwise.[6] Upon the same principle, it seems clear that a vote or resolution appointing an agent need not be entered on the minutes or records of the corporation, in order to his due appointment; unless the charter, statute, or by-laws, are not merely directory in this particular, but render it absolutely essential. The vote of appointment may, therefore, as an appointment

---

1 Smith *v.* Natchez Steamboat Company, 1 How. Miss. 478.

2 Narraganset Bank *v.* Atlantic Silk Company, 3 Met. 282; and see Thayer *v.* Middlesex Mutual Insurance Company, 10 Pick. 326; Clark *v.* Benton Manufacturing Company, 15 Wend. 256.

3 Goodwin *v.* Union Screw Co. 34 N. H. 378.

4 Northern Central R. Co. *v.* Bastian, 15 Md. 494.

5 See Chap. VIII.

6 See Chap. X.

of an agent by a natural person, be implied from the permission or acceptance of his services, from the recognition or confirmation of his acts, or, in general, from his being held out as an authorized agent of the corporation. "A board," says Mr. Justice Story,[1] "may accept a contract or approve a security by vote, or by a tacit and implied assent. The vote or assent may be more difficult of proof by parol evidence, than if it were reduced to writing. But, surely, this is not a sufficient reason for declaring that the vote or assent is inoperative." The same reason applies as fully to the appointment of an agent by a corporation, or a board acting for it. And, again, the same learned judge, speaking of a cashier of an office of discount and deposit created by the Bank of the U. S. says, "If he was held out as an authorized cashier, that character was equally applicable to all who dealt with the bank, in transactions *beneficial* as well as onerous to the bank." If a person be employed for a corporation by one who professes to act for it, and renders services under the agreement with the knowledge of the corporate officers, without notice from them of the employer's want of authority, payment for the services cannot be evaded by the corporation. If, however, the contract be wholly executory, and a suit be brought against the corporation for non-performance of it on their part, they may defend on the ground that the employer had no power to bind the corporation, the burden of proving the agency resting on the plaintiff.[2] In the case of Dunn *v.* Andrew's Church,[3] it appeared that the plaintiff had performed services as clerk of the church, for which he had received some payment. The records of the corporation contained entries of the payment of money at several times to the plaintiff for his services, but no resolution was entered on the minutes or records of the corporation, appointing the plaintiff clerk of the church. The court held such vote unnecessary to be shown; and that there was sufficient evidence of an implied promise of the corporation to make the compensation. We need hardly add, that if, in such case, the agent is held duly appointed as between the corporation and himself, *a fortiori* he would be as between the corporation and third persons; though precisely the same principle seems to apply *in favor*, as against the corporation.[4] Indeed,

---

1 Bank of the United States *v.* Dandridge, 12 Wheat. 83; Johnson *v.* Pue, 2 Gill, 254, and authorities above. See also, Elysville Manuf. Co. *v* Okisko Co. 1 Md. Ch. Dec. 392; Bank of Lyons *v.* Demmon, Hill & Denio, 398.

2 Foster *v.* La Rue, 15 Barb. 323.

3 14 Johns. 118.

4 Bank of the United States *v.* Dandridge, 12 Wheat. 89, per Story, J.

it seems that the same presumptions are applicable to corporations, as to natural persons. Persons acting publicly as officers of a corporation are presumed to be rightfully in office; acts done by a corporation which presuppose the existence of other acts to make them legally operative, are presumptive proofs of the latter. If a person acts notoriously as cashier of a bank, and is recognized by the directors, or by the corporation, as an existing officer, a regular appointment will be presumed; and his acts as cashier will bind the corporation, although no written proof is or *can be* adduced of his appointment;[1] for the law will not sanction the fraud of a corporation sooner than that of an individual." And, in general, it may be laid down, that not only the appointment, but the authority of the agent of a corporation may be implied from the adoption or recognition of his acts by the corporation or its directors.[2] A proprietors' committee having in their behalf entered into a submission of demands to referees under the statute, representing themselves as duly authorized so to do, and the proprietors having been heard upon the merits before the referees, and making no objection to the submission, upon error brought to reverse a judgment rendered on the award, the court presumed that the committee had due authority, though the want of authority was assigned for error.[3]

§ 285. It is usually the case, that the charters or incorporating acts of corporations require that officers of great trust, as the cashiers of

---

[1] Ibid. 12 Wheat. 70, per Story, J.; and see Union Bank of Maryland *v.* Ridgely, 1 Harris & G. 392; Barrington *v.* Bank of Washington, 14 S. & R. 421, per Duncan, J.; Wild *v.* Bank of Passamaquoddy, 3 Mason, 505; Smith *v.* Governor & Co. of Bank of Scotland, 1 Dow, P. C. 27; Perkins *v.* Washington Insurance Company, 4 Cowen, 645; Troy Turnpike & Railroad Company *v.* McChesney, 21 Wend. 296; Doremus *v.* Dutch Reformed Church, 2 Green, N. J. 332; Warren *v.* Ocean Insurance Company, 16 Maine, 439; Badger *v.* Bank of Cumberland, 26 Maine, 428; Davidson *v.* Borough of Bridgeport, 8 Conn. 472; Selma & Tennessee Railroad Co. *v.* Tipton, 5 Ala. 787; City of Detroit *v.* Jackson, 1 Doug. Mich. 106; Farmers & Mechanics Bank *v.* Chester, 6 Humph. 458; Hall *v.* Carey, 5 Ga. 239. Mere general reputation is, however, inadmissible to prove who are the officers or agents of a corporation. Litchfield Iron Company, *v.* Bennett, 7 Cowen, 234. It must be coupled with acts of charge and management of the property and concerns of the corporation. Clark *v.* Benton Manufacturing Company, 15 Wend. 256.

[2] Ibid. and see Conover *v.* Insurance Co. of Albany, 1 Comst. 290; Lohman *v.* N. Y. & Erie Railroad Co. 2 Sandf. 39; Beers *v.* Phœnix Glass Co. 14 Barb. 358; City of Detroit *v.* Jackson, 1 Doug. Mich. 106; Bank of the State of Alabama *v.* Comegys, 12 Ala. 772; Mead *v.* Keeler, 24 Barb. 20. See also, *post*, § 302.

[3] Fryburg *v.* Frye, 5 Greenl. 38.

banks, or the clerks of insurance companies, should give bond with sureties for the faithful performance of their duties; and the question immediately arises, whether the giving of the bond with sureties, in such cases, is necessary to their complete appointment as corporate officers and agents. This must depend, in each particular case, upon whether the language of the charter or act of incorporation makes the giving of the bond a condition precedent to the complete appointment and due authorization of the agent, or whether it is in this respect merely directory. And it seems, that where the act of incorporation, charter, or general statute, binding upon a corporation, empowers a board of directors, vested with power to appoint certain officers, to require security of them, that this is merely an affirmance of the common law; and though a by-law requires a certain species of security to be taken by the directors of certain officers on entering on the duties of their office, if a different species of security than that required by the by-law is taken by the directors, and any loss is sustained in consequence, this is a matter entirely between the directors and stockholders, for the failure of duty in the former; and in such a case there seems to have been no question of the due appointment of the officer.[1] And in the case of the Bank of the United States *v.* Dandridge,[2] where it appeared that the directors of the parent bank, empowered to establish offices of discount and deposit, subject to such rules and regulations as they should deem proper, passed a by-law directing "that the cashier of each office shall give bond to the president, directors, and company of the Bank of the United States, with two or more *approved* securities, with condition for his good behavior and faithful performance of his duties to the corporation;" and a fundamental article of the constitution of the bank directed "that each cashier or treasurer, before he enters upon the duties of his office, shall be required to give bond, &c.; it was held, that a cashier appointed and permitted to act in his office, without giving any such bond, or any bond whatever, was a legal agent of the corporation; that his acts and contracts within the scope of his authority were valid, whether in favor of the bank, or against it in favor of third persons; that the charter and by-laws were directory in this particular, and the taking of the bond not made by them a condition precedent;

---

1 Bank of Northern Liberties *v.* Cresson, 12 S. & R. 306.

2 12 Wheat. 64, Marshall, C. J. dissentiente. And see analagous cases. United States *v.* Kirkpatrick, 9 Wheat. 720; United States *v.* Van Zandt, 11 Wheat. 184; Peppin *v.* Cooper, 2 B. & Ald. 436, 437.

and that, though the directors might be responsible for their neglect of duty, it was a matter wholly between themselves and the stockholders, and between the latter and the government, as a violation of the charter and by-laws. It was admitted, however, that if the statute had prescribed that the cashier should not be deemed for any purpose in his office, until an approval of his official bond by the proper board, his acts would have been utterly void, unless his bond had been given and approved.[1] And where an act, "to establish a State Bank," prescribed that the cashier should take an oath to perform the duties of his appointment, the fact that he did not take the oath was held not to prevent a recovery upon his official bond, which admitted that he was cashier, but rather to be a breach of the bond, which stipulated that he should perform all his duties as cashier.[2] So, too, where by a by-law a corporation required, for their own security, their clerk to be sworn, it was adjudged that they could not avail themselves of his omission to take the oath in defence to an action against them, by one claiming to be a stockholder under a deed recorded by the clerk in his capacity of recording officer of the corporation.[3]

§ 286. Though the charter or act of incorporation prescribe the mode in which the officers of a corporation aggregate shall be elected, and an election contrary to it would unquestionably be voidable, yet if the officer has come in under *color* of right, and not in open contempt of all right whatever, he is an officer *de facto*, — within his sphere, an agent of the corporation, — and his acts and contracts will be binding upon it.[4] Where an action has been commenced by the officers *de facto* of a corporation, no other persons claiming a right to act as the officers of the corporation, the defendant cannot be permitted to show, for the purpose of defeating the action, that the officers were illegally elected.[5] On the

---

[1] Bank of United States *v.* Dandridge, 12 Wheat. 878, per Story, J.

[2] State Bank at Elizabeth *v.* Chetwood, 3 Halst. 1; and see Hastings *v.* Bluehill Turnpike Company, 9 Pick. 80; Panton Turnpike Company *v.* Bishop, 11 Vt. 198.

[3] Hastings *v.* Bluehill Turnpike Corporation, 9 Pick. 80.

[4] The King *v.* Lisle, Andrews, 163, 2 Stra. 1090; Vestry of St. Luke's Church *v.* Matthews, 4 Des. 578, 586; Vernon Society *v.* Hills, 6 Cowen, 23; All Saints Church *v.* Lovett, 1 Hall, 191; Lovett *v.* German Reformed Church, 12 Barb. 67; Riddle *v.* County of Bedford, 7 S. & R. 392; York County *v.* Small, 9 Watts & S. 320; Kingsbury *v.* Ledyard, 2 Watts & S. 41; McGargell *v.* Hazleton Coal Co. 4 Watts & S. 425; Despatch Line of Packets *v.* Bellamy Manufacturing Co. 12 N. H. 205; Smith *v.* Erb, 4 Gill, 437; Burr *v.* McDonald, 3 Gratt. 215.

[5] Charitable Association *v.* Baldwin, 1 Met. 359; and see Green *v.* Cady, 9 Wend. 414; Elizabeth City Academy *v.* Lindsey, 6 Ired. 476.

other hand, the service of process upon the secretary *de facto* of a manufacturing corporation, for the purpose of attaching the stock of the company, was held good under a statute regulating such process.[1] Where an abbot or parson, erroneously *inducted*, made a deed or obligation, though he be afterwards deprived of his benefice, yet this shall bind; but the deed of one who usurps *before* installation or induction, or who enters and occupies in time of vacation, *without* election or presentation, is void. So, if one occupies as abbot *of his own head*, without installation or induction, his deed shall not bind the house.[2] In a case where it appeared that the queen's auditor and surveyor of a county had appointed a steward of a manor without any right so to do, it was moved by the counsel and conceded by the court, that a copy granted by the steward *de facto* in court, he having admitted the tenant, and the fine being answered to the queen, was good; "for," say they, "the law favors the acts of one in a reputed authority; and the inferior shall never inquire if his authority be lawful;" and in 2 Edw. VI., Br. Copy, 26, it was held, "that grant by copy by one in court, who hath no authority to hold court, is good." The case, it is true, went off on the special ground that the grant in question was void, not being a thing of necessity, but a *new* grant in prejudice to the queen, as a lady of the manor by escheat for felony.[3]

§ 287. A person, *by color of election*, may be an officer *de facto*, though indisputably *ineligible;*[4] or though the office was not *vacant*, but there was an existing officer *de jure* at the time.[5] Indeed, it seems to be clear law, that the act of an officer *de facto* is good, wherever it concerns a third person, *who had a previous right* to the act, or *had paid a valuable consideration for it;* and this, whether the act concerns the preservation of the corporation or not.[6] In a case in Pennsylvania, it appearing that a bank was governed by thirteen directors, five of whom were competent to the business of ordinary discounts, but nothing

---

1 McCall *v.* Byram Manufacturing Company, 6 Conn. 428.

2 Vin. Abr. Officer and Offices, G. 4, pl. 1.

3 Harris *v.* Jays, 2 Cro. E. 699.

4 Knight *v.* Corporation of Wells, Lutw. 508.

5 O'Brien *v.* Knivan, Cro. Jac. 552; Harris *v.* Jays, Cro. E. 699.

6 The King *v.* Lisle, Andrews, 163; Riddle *v.* County of Bedford, 7 S. & R. 392; Lathrop *v.* Bank of Scioto, 8 Dana, 115; Cooper *v.* Curtis, 30 Me. 488; Delaware & Hudson Canal Co. *v.* Penn. Coal Co. 21 Penn. State, 131; Bank of St. Mary's *v.* St. John, 25 Ala. 566; *Ante*, § 139.

less than a majority of the whole number constituted a quorum for transacting any other business; and *a director was elected* at a meeting at which *five* only of the board were present; it was held, that, having color of election, he was a director *de facto;* and that, as an agent of the corporation, his acts were valid, at least as between the bank and third persons.[1] The best definition we have seen of an officer *de facto* is that given by Lord Ellenborough in The King *v.* The Corporation of Bedford Level.[2] "*An officer de facto*," says he, "*is one who has the reputation of being the officer he assumes to be, and yet is not a good officer in point of law.*" He instances the case of an under-steward when the head-steward, his principal, is dead; who having color to assemble the tenants, if they do their service, the acts which *he* does, in consideration of it, are good.[3] "This," says Lord Ellenborough, "must be understood of acts of the under-steward after the death of his principal, *and before his death is known;* for if that were known to the tenants, what color could he have to act? It is said that the acts of a steward *de facto* are good, because the suitors cannot examine his title; but when his authority has notoriously ceased, no such reason obtains."[4] The cases usually found in the books concerning officers *de facto* are cases in which the form of election, though imperfectly, seems to have been observed; or those in which the officer came rightfully into office, though he improperly *continues* to exercise its functions, as in the instance of the under-steward above quoted.[5] A person in office without even the form of election, might, within the terms of Lord Ellenborough's definition, have the reputation of being the officer he assumes to be; and in such case, unless the act of incorporation or general statute law expressly avoid them, if the corporation held him out to the world as its officer, his acts would be binding on it as the acts of its agent, whether he was technically an officer *de facto* or not, upon the ground of estoppel.[6]

---

[1] Baird *v.* Bank of Washington, 11 S. & R. 411. See *Ex parte* Rogers, 7 Cowen, 530, n.

[2] 6 East, 368, 369; and see Parker *v.* Kett, 1 Ld. Raym. 658.

[3] Knowles *v.* Luce, F. Moore, 112.

[4] The King *v.* Corporation of Bedford Level, 6 East, 369.

[5] Johnson *v.* Pue, 2 Gill, 254; Smith *v.* Erb, 4 Gill, 437.

[6] Bank of United States *v.* Dandridge, 12 Wheat. 70; Union Bank of Maryland *v.* Ridgely, 1 Harris & G. 421, 422, &c.; Wild *v.* Bank of Passamaquoddy, 3 Mason, 505; Barrington *v.* Bank of Washington, 14 S. & R. 405; Minor *v.* Mech. Bank of Alexandria, 1 Pet. 46; Cahill *v.* Kalamazoo Ins. Co. 2 Doug. Mich. 124; Lovett *v.* German Reformed Church, 12 Barb. 67.

§ 288. Where the term for which a particular officer or agent of a corporation shall hold his office or agency, by virtue of an election or appointment, is prescribed by charter, act of incorporation, or general law, as a general rule, his power of course ceases with the expiration of that term;[1] though unquestionably the corporation may be liable for his acts and contracts in favor of third persons, if they still continue to hold him out as their servant.[2] With the agent of a corporation, as with an agent of a natural person, if he is appointed for a special purpose, his power determines when that purpose is answered.[3] Where, on the other hand, the act of incorporation does not limit the term of his agency, this must depend upon the term of his appointment; and where no term is prescribed at the time of his creation, whether his agency continues until his powers are specially revoked or not, must depend, as in ordinary cases, upon its nature. If the agency be general, and unlimited as to term, it lasts, of course, until the powers given are revoked.

§ 289. As the death of a natural person revokes all authority given to his agents, so must, so to speak, the *death* of a corporation, whether it takes place by limitation of law, or forfeiture of chartered rights; for there is then no master to serve.[4] The death, however, of the particular officers of a corporation, or of the members of a particular board, who may be vested with the power of appointing its agents, does not determine their agency, or revoke their power; for the principal, the corporation, still subsists.[5] Accordingly, if any corporation aggregate, as a mayor and commonalty, or dean and chapter, make a feoffment and letter of attorney to deliver seisin, this authority does not determine by the death of the mayor or dean; but the attorney may well execute the power after their death; because the letter of attorney is an authority from the body aggregate, which subsists after the death of the mayor or dean, and therefore may be represented by an attorney of their appointment; but if the dean or mayor be named by their own private name, and die before livery, or be removed, livery after seems not good.[6] The rule is different with regard to the *deputy* of an officer or agent; for though

---

1 Curling *v.* Chalklen, 3 M. & S. 510, 511; Peppin *v.* Cooper, 2 B. & Ald. 431.

2 *Ante,* § 283.

3 Seton *v.* Slade, 7 Ves. Jr. 276.

4 Union Bank of Maryland *v.* Ridgely, 1 Harris & G. 433, 434.

5 Bac. Abr. Authority, E. 14, H. VIII. 3; 11 H. VII. 19; Co. Lit. 52; 2 Roll. Abr. 12.

6 2 Roll. Abr. 12.

in Knowles *v.* Luce[1] it seems to have been held generally, that the acts of an under-steward were good, though the head-steward be dead, the Court of King's Bench, in King *v.* The Corporation of Bedford Level,[2] declare, that this must be understood of the acts of the under-steward after the death of his principal, *and before his death is known*, on the ground of his color of right. In this last case, where it appeared that a corporation had, at the request of their registrar, appointed a deputy registrar to assist him, it was considered that the authority of the latter was determined by the death of the former, upon the general principle.[3]

§ 290. Though the power of appointing a particular officer or agent of a corporation be vested in a body, as the directors, managers, &c. existing within it, it does not follow that the authority of the agent is determined by the removal of the board which appointed him; or that because they are appointed but for a year, his agency expires with that period.[4] Thus where a letter of attorney was given by the directors of a bank, it was held, that the attorney might execute his power under it, after the term for which the directors were appointed had expired, since the constituent, to wit, the corporation, still continued in existence.[5] And where the charter of a bank empowered the directors for the time being, to appoint a cashier and such other officers and servants under them as should be necessary for executing the business of the corporation, it was decided by the Supreme Court of Maryland, that the office and power of the cashier did not cease with the office and power of the directors who appointed him, nor was of annual duration only because theirs was; but that the duration of the cashier's office was limited only by the duration of the charter of the bank, subject always to be terminated by the directors, as occasion might require.[6] The mere fact that an agent is, *in some respects*, the deputy of annual officers, by no means proves

---

1 Moore, 112; Parker *v.* Kett, 1 Ld. Raym. 661; and see 1 Watkins on Copyh. 257.

2 6 East, 369.

3 Ibid.

4 Anderson *v.* Longden, 1 Wheat. 85; Brown *v.* The Inhabitants of the County of Somerset, 11 Mass. 221; Northampton Bank *v.* Pepoon, 11 Mass. 288; Dedham Bank *v.* Chickering, 3 Pick. 335.

5 Northampton Bank *v.* Pepoon, 11 Mass. 294.

6 Union Bank of Maryland *v.* Ridgely, 1 Harris & G. 431, 432, 433; Exeter Bank *v.* Rogers, 7 N. H. 33; Thompson *v.* Young, 2 Ohio, 334; Dedham Bank *v.* Chickering, 3 Pick. 34.

that he is an annual officer himself; for it may be that his appointment was made to remedy the inconvenience of annual officers, and the deficiency of service which may result from the casual interruption of an annual election.[1]

§ 291. If the charter or act of incorporation prescribe the mode in which the officers or agents of a corporation must act or contract, to render their acts or contracts obligatory on the corporation, that mode must be strictly pursued. The act of incorporation is an *enabling* act; it gives the body corporate all the power it possesses; it enables it to contract, and when it prescribes the mode of contracting, that mode must be observed, or the instrument no more creates a contract than if the body had never been incorporated. Persons dealing with a company of this sort should always bear in mind that it is a corporation, a body essentially different from an ordinary partnership or firm, for all purposes of contract; and should insist upon the contract being executed in the manner prescribed by charter or law.[2] Besides, when its agents do not clothe their proceedings with those solemnities which are required by the incorporating act to enable them to bind the company, the informality of the transaction is itself conducive to the opinion that such act was rather considered as manifesting the terms on which they were willing to bind the company, as negotiations preparatory to a conclusive agreement, than as a contract obligatory on both parties.[3] In illustration of this, where an act incorporating an insurance company enacted, "that all policies of assurance and *other instruments* made and *signed* by the president of the said company, or any other officer

---

1 Curling *v.* Chalklen, 3 M. & S. 509 to 511.

2 Williams *v.* Chester and Holyhead Railway Co. Exch. 1851, 5 Eng. L. & Eq. 503. Where, however, the deed of settlement of a joint-stock company required the directors to use certain formalities in the transfer of shares, which for ten years they had in no instance observed, it was held that, after such long-continued and universal violations of their deed, the company could not set them up to the prejudice of third parties. Bargate *v.* Shortridge, 5 H. L. Cas. 297, 31 Eng. L. & Eq. 44. The doctrine of this case is approved in Zabriskie *v.* Cleveland, &c. R. Co. 23 How. 381, 398, where it is said: "This principle does not impugn the doctrine that a corporation cannot vary from the act of its creation, and that persons dealing with a company must take notice of whatever is contained in the law of its organization. . . . . But the principle includes those cases in which a corporation acts within the range of its general authority, but fails to comply with some formality or regulation which it should not have neglected, but which it has chosen to disregard."

3 Per Marshall, C. J. in Head *v.* Providence Ins. Co. 2 Cranch, 166 to 169; and see The Cape Sable Company's case, 3 Bland, Ch. 606.

thereof, according to the ordinances, by-laws, and regulations of the said company, or of their board of directors, shall be good and effectual in law, to bind and oblige the said company to the performance thereof;" it was held that a contract to cancel a policy is as solemn an act as a contract to make one; and to become the act of the company, must be executed according to the forms in which by law they are enabled to do it; and hence, that an *unsigned* note, containing an assent to a cancellation by the directors of the company, was not a corporate act obligatory upon it.[1] In a late case in Massachusetts, a foreign insurance company was doing business in that State by an agent duly authorized for that purpose, by a power of attorney, a duly authenticated copy whereof is required to be filled in the Secretary of State's office. This power authorized the agent to effect fire insurance upon buildings, &c., "and for this purpose to survey risks, fix the rate of premium, and issue policies of insurance signed by the president, attested by the secretary of the said company, and countersigned by the said agent, and to assent to the transfer and assignment of the same, which policies so issued and assigned shall have full force and effect to bind the said company." It was held that the agent had the power to bind the company by a parol contract of insurance.[2] And where the charter of an insurance company required that all *policies* should be signed by the president, it was not considered necessary that the assent of the company to an *assignment* of the policy should be signed by the president, in order to bind the company.[3] The signature of the secretary to such an assignment is *primâ facie* evidence of an agreement by the company; and the company, by accepting the assignee's guaranty of the premium note, adopts the act of the secretary, in assenting to the assignment.[4] When by charter a board are constituted the agents of a corporation for particular purposes, and the number necessary to be present at the doing of an act is therein specified, as we have seen, an act done or a contract made by less than, or others than those specified, will not bind the company.[5] If the charter specify no particular number of the board of

---

1 Head *v.* Providence Insurance Co. 2 Cranch, 166 to 169; Ducarry *v.* Gill, 4 Car. & P. 121. But see Sanborn *v.* Fireman's Ins. Co. cited *ante* § 253.

2 Sanborn *v.* Fireman's Ins. Co., Sup. Jud. Ct. Mass. 1861.

3 New England Marine Insurance Co. *v.* D'Wolf, 8 Pick. 56.

4 Ibid.

5 Beatty *v.* Marine Insurance Company, 2 Johns. 109; and see Kupfer *v.* South Parish in Augusta, 12 Mass. 185; *Ex parte* Rogers, 7 Cowen, 529, 530; Holcomb *v.* Managers N. H. D. B. Co. 1 Stock. 457; Manderson *v.* Commercial Bank, 28 Penn. State, 379.

directors as requisite to bind the corporation, that power resides either in the number specified in a by-law [1] or in a majority,[2] as a quorum, a majority of which have authority to decide any question upon which they can act; [3] and it is very clear that a contract made by a minority of a committee appointed for the purpose of making it, not assented to by a majority, nor by the corporation, does not bind the latter.[4] A majority of a committee authorized to sell lands by legislative resolve, or to do business of a public nature, have power to execute the commission; [5] but in case of quasi corporations, where a certain number, as three persons, are appointed or authorized to do a particular act, as to choose a chaplain, or to contract for the building of a meeting-house, in general they must concur in the act or contract to render it binding; though perhaps direct proof that all assented would not be required. This, in England, it has been held, may be varied by ancient usage.[6] A bank charter provided, "that all bills, bonds, notes, and every other contract or engagement on behalf of the corporation, should be signed by the president, and countersigned by the cashier; and that the funds of the corporation should in no case be liable for any contract or engagement, unless the same be signed and countersigned as aforesaid;" the clause was held to apply only to *express* contracts, and not to extend to contracts and undertakings implied in law; and accordingly the bank was made liable under money counts, on a check signed only by the cashier.[7] In such case, however, a court will never assume that an act was done or a contract made by less than the number legally authorized: but the fact must be strictly proved. The deed of a joint-stock banking company required that the directors should not be less in number than *five* nor more than *seven;* that three or more should constitute a quorum for the transaction of *ordinary business*, and that the directors should have power to compromise debts, &c. Four directors, being the whole number then existing, executed a deed compromising a large debt

---

1 See Hoyt *v.* Sheldon, 3 Bosw. 267, affirmed by the Court of Appeals.

2 Cram *v.* Bangor House, 3 Fairf. 354.

3 Sargent *v.* Webster, 13 Met. 497.

4 Trott *v.* Warren, 2 Fairf. 257; Adams *v.* Hill, 16 Maine, 215; and see Van Hook *v.* Somerville Manufacturing Co. 1 Halst. Ch. 169. The contract of a minority of a town committee, ratified by a majority, will be as binding upon the town, as though originally made by a majority. Hanson *v.* Dexter, 36 Me. 516.

5 Pejepscot Proprietors *v.* Cushman, 2 Greenl. 94; and see Grindley *v.* Barker, 1 Bos. & P. 229; Curtis *v.* Kent Water Works Co. 7 B. & C. 332.

6 Attorney-General *v.* Davy, cited 1 Ves. Sen. 419; Kupfer *v.* South Parish in Augusta, 12 Mass. 189.

7 Mechanics Bank of Alexandria *v.* Bank of Columbia, 5 Wheat. 326.

due to the bank, taking from the debtor a large mining concern, and covenanting with him in behalf of the company to indemnify him against certain bills of exchange. In an action of covenant by the debtor for not indemnifying him, the court decided that the covenant did not bind the company; inasmuch as this was not *ordinary business*, and no smaller number than *five* directors were competent under the deed to transact it.[1] But where the act of incorporation required the number of *five* managers to constitute a *quorum*, with power to *enter* into contracts, a contract to which the seal of the corporation was affixed was held valid, though *signed* by only *three* managers; there being no proof that the seal, which was itself held *primâ facie* evidence of the legal execution of the contract, was not affixed by the direction of a legal quorum.[2] A clause in an act of parliament, authorizing a company, at any general or special meeting, to order and dispose of their common seal and the use and application thereof, empowers them to make rules and regulations for its custody, but does not require their concurrence in each particular act of sealing; and a bond to which the seal had been affixed by the company's clerk, under a general authority from the directors, was held valid.[3] And where a board of bank directors authorized the president and cashier to "borrow money," though it was considered necessary that both should *assent* to the plan of borrowing, yet it was held unnecessary that both should sign the draft, or indorse the note upon which money was raised, to bind the bank by the drawing or indorsement.[4] Where a freight agent on a railroad is authorized by the by-laws to negotiate contracts for the transportation of freight, with the approval of the president of the company, the restriction is construed to mean, subject to the approval of the president, if at any time he deems it proper to interpose.[5]

§ 291 *a*. The agents of private persons, are not in the habit of keeping regular minutes of all their joint proceedings, neither does the law requirê such a verification of their joint acts. It seems never to have been contended, either that the acts of a *board* of agents, constituted

---

[1] Kirk *v*. Bell, 16 Q. B. 290, 12 Eng. L. &. Eq. 385.

[2] President, Managers, and Co. of the Berks & Dauphin Turnpike Road *v*. Myers, 6 S. & R. 12; Van Hook *v*. Somerville Manufacturing Co. 1 Halst. Ch. 137.

[3] Hill *v*. Manchester & Salford Water Works Co. 5 B. & Ad. 806, 2 Nev. & M. 573.

[4] Ridgway *v*. Farmers Bank of Bucks County, 12 S. & R. 260; Fleckner *v*. Bank of United States, 8 Wheat. 338.

[5] Medbury *v*. N. Y. & Erie R. Co. 26 Barb. 564.

by an unincorporated company, or by a single person, must, of necessity, be reduced to writing, before they would bind the principal; and it is a matter of daily experience, that the acts of a *single* duly authorized agent of a corporation, within the scope of his authority, bind the corporation, although he keeps no minutes of such acts. It being usual, however, with the *boards* of directors or *agents* created within incorporated companies for the due management of their concerns, to keep a regular record of their proceedings, the charter or by-laws commonly directing it to be done, it has been by no means an uncommon opinion, that such a record was essential either to the validity or proof of their acts and contracts, whether in favor of or against the corporation. As a general rule, however, this opinion is by no means correct. If, indeed, the charter or creating and enabling act of a corporation expressly make the recording of the acts of its board of directors essential to their validity, or a condition precedent thereto; or if it make a record taken by a prescribed officer the only mode by which such acts can be legally proven; it is very obvious that to render the acts of the board obligatory, whether for or against the corporation, the charter requisite must be complied with in the one case, and that the charter mode of proof is the only one that can be resorted to in the other. The books, however, furnish us with no such provision, in the charter of any corporation; and without it, there seems to be nothing in principle or authority, to distinguish in this particular the acts of a board of agents existing within a corporation, from the acts of agents constituted by natural persons. It is usual, indeed, by way of notice, and to facilitate proof, for the charter and by-laws to provide that a fair and regular record of the proceedings of the managing board of a corporation should be made by some designated officer, as the cashier of a bank, or the clerk or secretary of an insurance company. Such provisions are, in common, merely *directory* to the corporation, its officers or agents; and the breach or neglect of them, though it may render the directors or their scribe responsible in case of consequential damage for violation of duty, is a matter wholly between themselves and the stockholders, and between the latter and the government, as a violation of the charter and by-laws, and by no means affects the validity of the unrecorded acts.[1] As a rule

---

[1] Bank of the United States *v.* Dandridge, 12 Wheat. 75 to 89, per Story, J., Marshall, C. J. dissentiente; Bank of the Northern Liberties *v.* Cresson, 12 S. & R. 306; Bank of Kentucky *v.* Schuylkill Bank, 1 Parsons, Sel. Cas. 251, 263; Scott *v.* Warren, 2 Fairf. 227; Cram *v.* Bangor House, 3 Fairf. 354; Russell *v.* McLellan, 14 Pick. 63; Middlesex

of evidence, indeed, where the record exists, it should be produced, as being the best proof; but if there be no record, or if the suit be against the corporation, and, upon notice, the corporation neglects or refuses to produce its books, other evidence is admitted.[1]

§ 292. Unless the act of incorporation expressly prescribe the contrary, as has been before considered, the duly authorized agents of corporations, as of natural persons, may, within the scope of their authority, bind them by simple as well as by sealed contracts; and that, too, in both cases, whether authorized by deed or vote; and from their acts or conduct, as well as from the acts or conduct of the agents of natural persons, implications may be made, either for or against their constituents.[2] It may hence be readily inferred that in case of a deed poll to a corporation, made through the intervention of a duly authorized agent, in order to bind the corporation by the stipulations of the deed, it is not necessary to show that it has been formally accepted by them, but a delivery to and an acceptance of the deed by the agent, is a delivery to and acceptance by the corporation.[3] The place where an agent of a corporation enters into a contract is, in general, immaterial, and a contract may be made out of the State where the corporation is situated.[4]

§ 293. When the agent of a corporation would bind by a contract he makes in its behalf the corporation only, his *proper* mode is, in the body of the contract, to name the corporation, as the contracting party, and to sign as its agent or officer; and this is the mode in which bank-bills and policies of insurance are ordinarily executed. The secretary of a bridge company signed his name to a lottery ticket as the secretary of the corporation, expressly contracting on its behalf, and it was held, that he was not personally responsible.[5] And on a note in which the president and directors of a glass company promise to pay, and which was signed by one as president, it was held that he was not liable.[6] And though the

---

Husbandmen, &c. *v.* Davis, 3 Met. 133; Davidson *v.* Borough of Bridgeport, 8 Conn. 472; Burgess *v.* Pue, 2 Gill, 254. See too, United States *v.* Kirkpatrick, 9 Wheat. 720; Same *v.* Van Zandt, 11 Wheat. 184; 1 Phillips, Evid. ch. 5, §§ 2, 326; Bassett *v.* Marshall, 9 Mass. 312; Goodwin *v.* U. S. Annuity & L. Ins. Co. 24 Conn. 591.

[1] See in this chap. *supra.*

[2] Chap. VIII.

[3] Western Railroad *v.* Babcock, 6 Met. 356, 357.

[4] Wright *v.* Bundy, 11 Ind. 398.

[5] Passmore *v.* Mott, 2 Binney, 201; and see McHenry *v.* Duffield, 7 Blackf. 41.

[6] Mott *v.* Hicks, 1 Cowen, 513; see too, Shotwell *v.* McKeown, 2 South. 828; Bowen

words of the note were, "I promise," yet it being signed by the agent for the company, it was held to be the note of the company, and not of the agent.[1] A bill of exchange directed to "A B, cashier of F. & M. Bank," and accepted by writing across the face thereof, "Accepted, A B, cashier," is drawn upon and accepted by the bank, and not upon and by the cashier in his individual capacity.[2] An indorsement of a note made payable to an insurance company, thus, "Without recourse, J. S., secretary," was decided to pass the legal interest of the note to the indorsee;[3] and bills of exchange drawn in favor of the cashier of a bank, and discounted by it, are in law drawn in favor of the bank, so that it may sue thereon in its own name.[4] So a promise to a company or their treasurer for the time being, is not a promise to two distinct parties in the alternative, but a promise to the company.[5] Where, too, a note was made payable to one without naming his capacity, who indorsed his name thereon as *agent*, he was considered not liable *in favor of one who knew that the indorser acted as* agent, and that the note was given by the company for their proper debt, though it was said he might be, in favor of a third person; such an indorsement being regarded as made for the purpose of transferring the interest in the note merely, and equivalent to a declaration that the indorser would not be personally responsible.[6] Again, where the rector and wardens of a church, pursuant to a vote of the proprietors, borrowed money for the use of the proprietors, and subscribed in their capacity a note for it, and the old act being repealed, a new corporation of the same name was created, which assumed the debts of the old one, it was decided that the new corporation was answerable on the note, or at least on the money counts.[7] And the proceedings of the vestry of a church pledging the corporate funds to persons who might perform work or furnish materials for it, can impose no personal liability

---

v. Norris, 2 Taunt. 374; Shelton *v.* Darling, 2 Conn. 435; Brockway *v.* Allen, 17 Wend. 40; Pitman *v.* Kintner, 5 Blackf. 250.

1 Emerson *v.* Providence Hat Company, 12 Mass. 237; Long *v.* Coburn, 11 Mass. 97; Despatch Line of Packets *v.* Bellamy Manuf. Co. 12 N. H. 205.

2 Farmers & Mechanics Bank *v.* Troy City Bank, 1 Doug. Mich. 457; Watervliet Bank *v.* White, 1 Denio, 608; Jenkins *v.* Morris, 16 M. & W. 880.

3 McIntyre *v.* Preston, 5 Gilman, 48; Nicholas *v.* Oliver, 36 N. H. 218; and see Davis *v.* Branch Bank of Mobile, 12 Ala. 463, for construction of a statute of Alabama, declaring that notes payable to the cashier may be sued on as notes payable to the bank.

4 Wright *v.* Boyd, 3 Barb. 523.

5 Atlantic Mut. F. Ins. Co. *v.* Young, 38 N. H. 451.

6 Despatch Line of Packets *v.* Bellamy Manuf. Co. 12 N. H. 205.

7 Episcopal Charitable Society *v.* Episcopal Church in Dedham, 1 Pick. 372.

upon the members of the vestry, even though the members have subsequently manifested an impression that they had assumed a personal responsibility.[1] Where one describing himself in the body of a note as treasurer of a corporation, signed it as treasurer, the note being given for a debt due the payee by the corporation, an action against him personally was not maintained.[2] In Sterling *v.* Marietta and Susquehannah Trading Company,[3] it was also decided, that a receipt, signed by the president of a bank, without the addition of his capacity, for money "to be deposited in the bank to the credit of Ostehank" (the person to whom the receipt was given), was evidence, though not conclusive, from which the jury might presume that the money went to the use of the bank. And where, on a sale of real property by a corporation, a memorandum of the sale was signed by the parties, in which it was stated that the sale was made to the purchaser, and that he and C. D., "Mayor of the corporation on behalf of himself, and of the rest of the burgesses and commonalty of the borough of Caermathen," do mutually agree to perform and fulfil on each of their parts, respectively, the conditions of sale, which was signed by the purchaser, and by "C. D., mayor," it was held, that the agreement was that of the corporation, and not of the mayor personally; and that consequently the mayor, as such, could sue thereon.[4]

§ 294. Indeed, it would seem that the acts and contracts of agents do not derive their validity from professing, on the face of them, to have been done in the exercise of their agency. In the more solemn exercise of derivative powers, as applied to the execution of instruments known to the common law, rules of form have been prescribed. But in the diversified exercise of the duties of a general agent, the liability of the principal depends upon the facts, that the act was done in the exercise, and within the limits, of the powers delegated, and especially that it was the intent of the parties that the principal, and not the agent, should be bound.[5] In ascertaining these facts, as connected with the

---

[1] Vincent *v.* Chapman, 10 Gill & J. 280, 282.

[2] Mann *v.* Chandler, 9 Mass. 335; and see McLaren *v.* Pennington, 1 Paige, 102; *Contra*, Seaver *v.* Coburn, 10 Cush. 324.

[3] 11 S. & R. 177. See State Bank *v.* Kain, 1 Breese, 45.

[4] Bowen *v.* Norris, 2 Taunt. 374. See Kennedy *v.* Gouveia, 3 Dowl. & R. 503; Hopkins *v.* McLaffey, 11 S. & R. 129; Mayor *v.* Barker, 6 Binn. 228, 234; Many *v.* Beekman Iron Company, 9 Paige, 188.

[5] Sawyer *v.* Winnegance Mill Co. 26 Maine, 127, 128; McLaren *v.* Pennington, 1

execution of a written instrument, it has been held, that parol testimony is admissible. Accordingly, where a check was signed by the cashier of a bank, without the addition of the word "Cashier" to his name, dated at the bank, and made payable to its teller, it appearing doubtful upon the face of the instrument whether it was a private or an official act, parol evidence was admitted to show that it was an *official* act, though the check was credited on the books of the bank to the cashier's private account.[1] The question in these cases seems to be, as to whom the credit is given.[2] Where, however, the president of an insurance company, in transacting the business of the company, gave a note in which he described himself as president of the company, the note was considered the note of the president, and not of the company, the addition to his name being regarded as *descriptio personæ*.[3] It would be extremely difficult to reconcile this decision either with principle or authority.[4] However this may be, it seems that a draft drawn by the agent of a manufacturing corporation, payable to "G. S., Treasurer," may be indorsed by him as treasurer, either in person or *by attorney;* since being payable to him, his power to indorse is an original and not a delegated power, and may be well exercised by an attorney lawfully authorized.[5] At this time, there can be but little doubt, that if an agent, within the scope of his authority, contracts for a corporation in his own name, without disclosing his principal, the corporation would, according to and with the limitations of the law of agency applicable to such cases, be bound by the contract.[6]

Paige, 102; Boisgerard *v.* New York Banking Company, 2 Sandf. Ch. 23; Merchants Bank *v.* Central Bank, 1 Kelly, Ga. 428; Jenkins *v.* Morris, 16 M. & W. 880; Russel *v.* Reece, 2 Car. & K. 669.

[1] Mechanics Bank *v.* Bank of Columbia, 5 Wheat. 326; Northampton Bank *v.* Pepoon, 11 Mass. 282; and see Farmers & Manufacturers Bank *v.* Haight, 3 Hill, 494, 495; McWhorter *v.* Lewis, 4 Ala. 198; Cahill *v.* Kalamazoo Mutual Insurance Company, 2 Doug. Mich. 124; Kean *v.* Davis, 1 N. J. 683; Merchants Bank *v.* Central Bank, 1 Kelly, 428; Ghent *v.* Adams, 2 Kelly 214. The agent of a company who is authorized to become a party to a bill or note, will be personally liable upon it, unless by the terms of the instrument he unequivocally disclaims personal responsibility. Mare *v.* Charles, 5 Ellis & B. 978, 34 Eng. L. & Eq. 138; Dewitt *v.* Walton, 5 Seld. 571. See also, Hicks *v.* Hinde, 9 Barb. 528; Babcock *v.* Beman, 1 Kern. 200.

[2] McWhorter *v.* Lewis, 4 Ala. 198; Mott *v.* Hicks, 1 Cowen, 536, per Woodworth, J.

[3] Barker *v.* Mechanics Insurance Co. 3 Wend. 98.

[4] Authorities above, and Hills *v.* Banister, 8 Cowen, 31; Brockway *v.* Allen, 17 Wend. 40; Story on Agency, pp. 143, 144, § 154, and note 1.

[5] Shaw *v.* Stone, 1 Cush. 253, 254.

[6] Conro *v.* Port Henry Iron Co. 12 Barb. 27.

§ 295. To bind a corporation by *specialty*, it is necessary that its corporate seal should be affixed to the instrument.[1] But a lease to which the corporate seal was affixed, signed by certain persons who were incorporated by the style of "the trustees of the parish of Newburg," with their several names, was held not vitiated as a corporate act by the several signatures.[2] The corporate seal is the only *organ* by which a body politic can oblige itself by *deed;* and though its agents affix their *private* seals to a contract binding upon it; yet these not being *seals* as regards the corporation, it is in such case bound only by simple contract.[3]

§ 296. In the Bank of Columbia *v.* Patterson,[4] which was indebitatus assumpsit for work and labor done by the intestate of the defendant in error for the bank, by virtue of an agreement made with him by the duly authorized agents of the corporation under their private seals; the contract being made for the exclusive benefit of the corporation, which had on the faith of it paid money from time to time to the intestate, the Supreme Court of the United States held the action well brought, though Mr. Justice Story, in delivering the opinion of the court, intimates that an action might have lain against the contracting committee personally, upon their express obligation. In Randall *v.* Van Vechten and others,[5] a case in its facts similar to that just mentioned, the question, whether the contracting committee were under such circumstances personally liable on their sealed covenant, came directly before the Supreme Court of the State of New York; and it being proved that the covenantee had recognized the contract as that of the corporation, the court held the committee not liable, upon the express ground that the corporation was suable in assumpsit. These cases are to be carefully distinguished from Taft *v.* Brewster,[6] and Tippets *v.* Walker;[7] for it was a matter of *evi-*

---

1 See Chap. VII.

2 Jackson *v.* Walsh, 3 Johns. 225; and see President, &c. of the Berks & Dauphin Turnpike Road *v.* Myers, 6 S. & R. 12; Clark *v.* Benton Manufacturing Company, 15 Wend. 256; McDonough *v.* Templeman, 1 Harris & J. 156.

3 Randall *v.* Van Vechten, 19 Johns. 65, per Platt, J.; Haight *v.* Sahler, 30 Barb. 218; Tippets *v.* Walker, 4 Mass. 597, per Parsons, C. J.; Bank of Columbia *v.* Patterson, 7 Cranch, 304, per Story, J.; Dubois *v.* Delaware & Hudson Canal Co. 4 Wend. 285; Mitchell *v.* St. Andrews Bay Land Co. 4 Fla. 200; and see Chap. VII.

4 7 Cranch, 299.

5 19 Johns. 60; and see McDonough *v.* Templeman, 1 Harris & J. 156.

6 9 Johns. 334; and see Skinner *v.* White, 13 Johns. 307.

7 4 Mass. 595.

dence, that the committee were duly authorized to contract on behalf of the corporation, and that credit was given to it; whereas in Taft *v.* Brewster, which came up on demurrer to the declaration, no evidence could be given upon these points, and the court held, as they well might, that the words, "trustees, &c.," appended by the obligors to their names in the contract, were mere *descriptio personarum;* and in Tippets *v.* Walker, it expressly appeared in evidence, that the committee were not authorized to make the contract in question, and of course, like the agents of natural persons, under such circumstances, were personally liable upon it.[1] To conclude, therefore, as to the *form* in which the agents of corporations must execute contracts, whether special or simple, in order to avoid personal liability, and to bind their constituents, the general principle will be found the same as with the agents of natural persons; that in general, if from the contract itself, or from this, coupled with the conduct of the parties thereto, it appears that credit was given not to the agent, but to the *corporation*, and that it was the intent of the parties that the corporation should be bound, whatever may be the particular form of the contract, the corporation is alone liable upon it.[2]

§ 297. Corporations, like natural persons, are bound only by the acts and contracts of their agents done and made within the scope of their authority.[3] This was the doctrine of the Roman law; and Wood, who cites the Digest, says, that "corporations may borrow money by their syndic; but if he borrow more than he had authority for, the community

---

[1] See Mann *v.* Chandler, 9 Mass. 336; Randall *v.* Van Vechten, 19 Johns. 64, per Platt, J.; Mott *v.* Hicks, 1 Cowen, 531, per Woodworth, J.; McDonough *v.* Templeman, 1 Harris & J. 156; Clark *v.* Benton Woollen Manufacturing Co. 15 Wend. 256.

[2] See Haight *v.* Sahler, 30 Barb. 218, where this question is fully considered.

[3] Essex Turnpike Corporation *v.* Collins, 8 Mass. 299; Mechanics Bank *v.* Bank of Columbia, 5 Wheat. 337, per Johnson, J.; Clark *v.* Corporation of Washington, 12 Wheat. 40; Bank of United States *v.* Dandridge, 12 Wheat. 83, per Story, J.; Hartford Bank *v.* Hart, 3 Day, 493; National Bank *v.* Norton, 1 Hill, 572; Seibrecht *v.* New Orleans, 12 La. Ann. 496; State Bank of Indiana *v.* State, 1 Blackf. 273; Underhill *v.* Gibson, 2 N. H. 352; Lee *v.* Flemingsborough, 7 Dana, 28; Washington Bank *v.* Lewis, 22 Pick. 24; Hayward *v.* Pilgrim Society, 21 Pick. 270; Stewart *v.* Huntington Bank, 11 S. & R. 267, 269; Cox *v* Midland Counties Railway Co. 3 Exch. 268; Kelly *v.* Troy Ins. Co. 3 Wisc. 254; Exchange Bank *v.* Monteath, 17 Barb. 171; Stephenson *v.* New York & Harlem R. R. Co. 2 Duer, 341. An insurance agent, though authorized generally to bind the company by making and receiving applications for policies, cannot receive an application from himself. Bentley *v.* Columbia Ins. Co. 19 Barb. 595; New York Central Ins. Co. *v.* National Prot. Ins. Co. 20 id. 468.

is not answerable for it, unless the money came to their use."[1] It is obvious, that the powers of officers, of the same name, are so different, in corporations created for different purposes, or in different countries and states for the same purpose, not only by the force of different statutes, charters, and by-laws, but also of a different general course and habit of dealing, that the decisions upon this subject, made in one state or country, are to be taken with many grains of allowance, when sought to be applied in another; and are to be viewed in minute reference to these differences. The duties of officers of the same name in different classes of corporations, and in the same classes in different countries and states, require and receive for their performance such difference of powers, and these again are so varied by the custom and usage of different political and commercial communities, that care must be taken not to be misled by names, but to look upon every decision upon this subject as, in a greater or less degree, individual and local, and in its general principles only, applicable in other cases and places. A much stricter rule of construction with regard to the power of a corporation or of its directors to borrow money, seems to prevail with the courts in England than that adopted in this country, growing, partly perhaps, out of a difference in the habit and usage of carrying on business. And where the deed of settlement, under which a mining company was carried on, provided a capital of 50,000*l.*, and gave power to create new shares, and to alter the provisions of the deed, by a vote of a special general meeting, although it contained a clause "that the affairs and business of the company shall be under the sole and entire control of the directors, &c.," it was held, that the directors had no implied authority to borrow money on the credit of the company, for the purpose of carrying on the mines, however useful or necessary such power might be to the objects for which the company was formed.[2] The court seemed to think that under such a deed, the borrowing of money would require the consent of all the stockholders — the deed contemplating that the mines were to be worked solely by means of the large capital provided in it for that purpose.[3] But where directors are empowered,

---

[1] Wood's Civil Law, B. 1, ch. 2, p. 135; Dig. 12, 1, 27.

[2] Burmester *v.* Norris, 6 Exch. 796, 8 Eng. L. & Eq. 487, 490, 491. Upon the decision of this case in favor of the company, the directors repaid the money which they had borrowed, and brought their action against the company for reimbursement. Held, that the directors were not only agents, but also quasi trustees, and, in the latter character, were entitled to be repaid advances, made, *bonâ fide*, for the purpose of executing their trusts. *In re* German Mining Co. 4 De G. M. & G. 19, 27 Eng. L. & Eq. 158.

[3] Burmester *v.* Norris, 6 Exch. 796, 8 Eng. L. & Eq. 487, 490, 491.

for a certain purpose, to issue *a note*, or accept *a bill of exchange*, to a certain amount, they are deemed authorized to give security for the sum, *with its legal accretions*, by *several* notes or bills, instead of a single note or bill.[1] In England the powers of agents of corporations are construed strictly, and persons seeking to render a corporation liable for the acts of the directors even, must show their authority to bind the company either by the charter or registered deed of settlement, or by proof that the body of shareholders authorized particular individuals to make contracts binding on the company.[2]

A manufacturing corporation in New Hampshire was adjudged not liable for money borrowed by one of its clerks, without authority, in the name of the corporation, and applied to his own use; though it was in evidence that he had, in two or three instances previous, borrowed money of other persons in the name of the corporation, of which the plaintiff had no knowledge, which was repaid by another clerk, the money in those cases having been applied to the use of the company.[3] But where the treasurer of a corporation was authorized by vote to hire money, on such terms and conditions as he might think most conducive to the interests of the company, for the purpose of meeting certain acceptances of the defendant, a director, of drafts of the company on him, the vote was held to authorize the treasurer to raise money by indorsing, on behalf of the company, drafts drawn by himself for that purpose; and that the acceptance of such drafts by the defendant, who was present at the meeting at which such vote was passed, and who was benefited thereby, precluded him from disputing the authority of the corporation to pass the vote.[4] The trustees of a society established for the purpose of erecting a monument and suitable buildings for their meetings, were authorized by vote to appropriate the funds of the society to the erection of a suitable edifice, and were required by the by-laws to manage the finances and property of the society; and the trustees thereupon entered into a contract for the building, and, having exhausted the funds of the society, and there remaining a debt for which they were personally responsible, voted that the treasurer should give a note to one of their number who had paid the debt, without limiting in the

---

[1] Thompson *v.* Wesleyan Newspaper Association, 8 C. B. 849.

[2] Ridley *v.* Plymouth &c. Co., 2 Exch. 711. See also, Ernest *v.* Nicholls, 6 H. L. Cas. 401.

[3] Martin *v.* Great Falls Manufacturing Company, 9 N. H. 51.

[4] Belknap *v.* Davis, 19 Maine, 455.

vote the time within which the note was to be given; it was held, that, by virtue of their authority to manage the finances, they had power to authorize the note, creating one debt to pay another, and that under their vote the treasurer might make the note several years afterwards, the claim not being then barred by lapse of time.[1] Though the charter of a manufacturing corporation, in Massachusetts, confer the power of management upon "the President and Directors," this is construed as a mere mode of designating the board of directors, in its aggregate capacity, and not as rendering the presence of the president necessary to the transaction of business by the board, unless otherwise required by the charter or by-laws.[2] And where the directors of a manufacturing corporation of that State, under a general statute authority to manage its concerns, authorized its agent to raise money for his own use, on the credit of the corporation, and to give therefor "the company note;" the words of the vote were held to authorize a bill of exchange drawn by the agent in the name of the company, the dishonor of which would not subject them to damages.[3] An agent authorized by vote of the directors "to sell and convey" its real estate, may, by reasonable construction, be held authorized to make a contract binding on the corporation to convey at a future day; upon the ground that the power to sell implies authority to negotiate and make a bargain with the purchaser, prior to the conveyance.[4] If a restricted authority be given to a special agent, a contract made by him without its limits will impose no obligation on his constituent. In accordance with this, where one was appointed the agent of a turnpike corporation to contract for the making of a certain portion of the road, with the restriction that one third of the payment on such contracts was to be made in shares in the road, it was considered that a contract made by him without this stipulation, would not charge the corporation.[5] If the officers, whose appropriate business it is to make loans for a corporation, make unlawful loans, the corporation is not bound by their acts.[6] In general, one who undertakes to

---

[1] Hayward v. Pilgrim Society, 21 Pick. 270.

[2] Sargent v. Webster, 13 Met. 504.

[3] Tripp v. Swanzey Paper Company, 13 Pick. 291.

[4] Augusta Bank v. Hamblet, 35 Maine, 491, 495.

[5] Hayden v. Middlesex Turnpike Corporation, 10 Mass. 403. So the issue of certificates of stock by a mere transfer agent is void; Mechanics Bank v. New York & New Haven R. R. Co. 3 Kern. 599; N. Y. & N. H. R. Co. v. Schuyler, 17 N. Y. 592.

[6] Life & Fire Insurance Company v. Mechanics Fire Insurance Company, 7 Wend. 31.

bind a corporation by promissory note, must show that he has authority for that purpose.[1] As, however, the appointment of an agent may be implied from the recognition of his acts, or the permission of his services, so may the extent of his authority from the powers usually given to one in his station. Upon this principle it was held, that the general agent of a commission company, who was in the habit of accepting bills which were afterwards paid by the company, had power to accept bills on an expected delivery of goods, though the by-laws of the corporation conferred no such power in express terms upon him.[2] Indeed, as the verbal instructions of managers or directors to an officer of the company can rarely be proved by third persons, if his acts, as of borrowing money or purchasing goods for the corporation, are publicly performed at the office of the company, and are numerous, it may reasonably be inferred that they conform to the instructions of the managers; and if, from inattention, they suffer him to continue in a line of conduct for a length of time which may reasonably lead others to infer authority, the corporation is as much bound by his act, in favor of an innocent dealer, as if he were expressly authorized.[3] If the officer borrow money in his capacity, it will be implied, in the absence of proof to the contrary, that he borrowed it for the uses of the corporation: and the *onus* of proving the contrary rests on the corporation.[4] Implied authority, in such cases, is, however, clearly limited to business of the company connected with, or relating to the object or design for which the company was created.[5]

§ 298. The agent of a manufacturing corporation was empowered by its by-laws to manage the affairs of the corporation committed to his care, and to exercise the power intrusted to him according to his best ability and discretion, and promptly to collect all assessments and other sums that should become due to the corporation, and to disburse them according to the order of the board of directors, who were made a

---

1 Harwood *v.* Humes, 9 Ala. 659.

2 Munn *v.* Commission Co. 15 Johns. 44.

3 Beers *v.* Phœnix Glass Co. 14 Barb. 358; Smith *v.* Hull Glass Co. 11 C. B. 897, 9 Eng. L. & Eq. 442.

4 Beers *v.* Phœnix Glass Co. 14 Barb. 358; Smith *v.* Hull Glass Co. 11 C. B. 897, 9 Eng. L. & Eq. 442. Mere excess of authority on the part of the directors of a joint-stock company, is a matter between them and the shareholders, and will not avoid a contract under seal as against innocent third parties. Royal British Bank *v.* Turquand, 5 Ellis & B. 248, 32 Eng. L. & Eq. 273; s. c. 6 Ellis & B. 327, 36 Eng. L. & Eq. 142.

5 The Pennsylvania, &c. Co. *v.* Dandridge, 8 Gill & J. 248.

board of control over him; it was held, *that, if the board of directors did not interpose to control his proceedings*, the agent had authority to employ workmen to carry on the business of the corporation, and to pay them with its funds, or, not being in funds, to give the notes of the corporation in payment.[1] But, in a case in which it appeared that the note of a manufacturing company was issued by the agent, nearly a year after the company had entirely failed, some proof of the continuance of the agency, and of the authority of the agent to bind the corporation by note, was required.[2] And where a company which had existed as a voluntary association was afterwards incorporated, it was decided that their general agent, who was authorized to sign notes on behalf of the corporation, for debts due from the voluntary company, for stock or money lent them, had no power to sign notes for the corporation given for the purchase-money of a farm, the title of which was in the voluntary association; there being members of the former who were not members of the latter body.[3] The president of a corporation is not *ex officio* an agent to sell its property, and his representations as to property to be sold are not binding on the company, unless he be specially authorized.[4] In general, the president of a bank is not, by virtue of his office, authorized to draw checks for the moneys of the corporation deposited in a bank, unless, by the established usage of the place where the operations of the company are carried on, the presidents of banks are in the practice of drawing such checks without special authority for that purpose.[5] Indeed, it seems that the president of a bank, as such, cannot make any agreement binding upon the corporation, unless it is shown to be within the scope of his authority; nor can he, unless authorized by the charter, without permission of the directors, stay the collection of an execution against the estate of a debtor of the bank.[6] The president of an insurance company, in New York, was held to be the proper officer to transfer a note of the company, to indorse it, and to convert it into money.[7] The president of a mutual insurance com-

---

[1] Bates *v.* Keith Iron Co. 7 Met. 224.

[2] Benedict *v.* Lansing, 5 Denio, 284.

[3] White *v.* Westport Cotton Manufacturing Co. 1 Pick. 215.

[4] Crump *v.* United States Mining Co. 7 Gratt. 352.

[5] Fulton Bank *v.* N. Y. and Sharon Canal Co. 4 Paige, Ch. 127; Reed *v.* Bank of Newburgh, 6 Paige, 337.

[6] Farmers Bank *v.* McKee, 2 Barr, 318; Spyker *v.* Spence, 8 Ala. 333; Bacon *v.* Mississippi Ins. Co. 31 Missis. 116.

[7] Caryl *v.* McElrath, 3 Sandf. 176, 179. See Baker *v.* Cotter, 45 Me. 236.

pany, in receiving a note for premiums in advance, for the security of dealers, cannot, however, make a valid agreement that the note shall be given up to the maker, either before or after it has matured.[1] The general agent of a manufacturing corporation is not authorized to sell or convey the real estate, or to mortgage or pledge as security for a loan the machinery of the company, or to make a general assignment of the property of the corporation for the benefit of its creditors, or to create a lien on the entire property of the corporation for the security of certain of its debts, at least, where there is a board of directors, without specific authority; though it may be incidental to his power as agent, to borrow money, give promissory notes, and do many other acts in the ordinary course of the business of the company.[2] And the treasurer of a manufacturing corporation has no authority to release a claim for a loss under a policy of insurance obtained by him in behalf of the corporation.[3] The general agent or treasurer of a corporation or joint-stock company, has undoubtedly the right to negotiate notes or bills taken in the name of his office,[4] and may receive payment for them, in cash or its equivalent, in the ordinary course of business; but he cannot, unless specially authorized, execute a technical release, in the name of the corporation, under an assignment, discharging the assignor from the debt in consideration of the dividends, or partial payment, secured by the assignment.[5] The act of the president of a coal company, in issuing an engagement of credit, in the nature of a bank-note, contrary to an act prohibiting such issue, will not subject the corporation to the penalty of the act, in the absence of proof of authority from the corporation to the president to issue such certificate of credit.[6] The vice-president of a manufacturing corporation, after it had become insolvent, gave a note to his clerk, under the seal of the corporation, for an alleged debt due from the corporation to himself, for the purpose of charging the stockholders of the company personally for the payment of the note. This note was

---

1 Brouwer *v.* Appleby, 1 Sandf. 159.

2 Stow *v.* Wyse, 7 Conn. 219; Despatch Line of Packets *v.* Bellamy Manufacturing Co. 12 N. H. 205; Whitwell *v.* Warner, 20 Vt. 446, 447.

3 E. Carver Co. *v.* Manuf. Ins. Co. 6 Gray, 214; Dedham Inst. for Savings *v.* Slack, 6 Cush. 408.

4 Perkins *v.* Bradley, 24 Vt. 66.

5 Dedham Institution for Savings *v.* Slack, 6 Cush. 408. Nor can the treasurer of a corporation, by virtue of his office, compromise nor set off against each other claims due to and from the company. Brown *v.* Weymouth, 36 Me. 414.

6 Hazelton Coal Co. *v.* Megarel, 4 Barr, 324.

not deemed evidence of a debt due from the company to the vice-president, the officer who had affixed the seal of the corporation thereto; and the person to whom he had assigned the note could not recover the amount thereof, after the dissolution of the corporation, without proving that it was given for a debt actually due.[1] But though a payment be made irregularly by the president of a corporation, yet, if it be justly due, and there be no reason for withholding it, it cannot be recovered back on the ground that he had *verbal* directions merely from the directors to pay it.[2] If the president of a corporation authorize an attorney or solicitor to appear for the corporation, the corporation will be bound by his acts, as their attorney or solicitor; and if the president exceed his authority, in retaining such attorney or solicitor, the corporation must look to him for any damages sustained in consequence of such unauthorized act.[3] In Vermont it is held, that the president of a railroad cannot, without the concurrence of the directors, bind the road to pay a compensation additional to that fixed by the board.[4]

§ 299. Bank charters usually confer on boards of directors full power to manage or conduct the affairs of the company.[5] The directors are, however, but the agents of the corporation, and, where their authority is limited by the act of incorporation, have clearly no power to bind their principal beyond it.[6] If the general power of making by-laws regulating the transactions of the corporation remain in the body at large, the power of the directors may be circumscribed by them.[7] A

---

[1] Bonaffe *v.* Fowler, 7 Paige, 576.

[2] New Orleans Building Company *v.* Lawson, 11 La. 34.

[3] American Insurance Company *v.* Oakley, 9 Paige, 496; Mumford *v.* Hawkins, 5 Denio, 355; Alexandria Canal Co. *v.* Swann, 5 How. 83. In Massachusetts, however, it seems to be decided, that the president of a manufacturing corporation has no power to bind the corporation by commencing an action in its name, unless specially authorized; and an action commenced by him without such authority being proved, was ordered to be dismissed. Ashuelot Manufacturing Co. *v.* Marsh, 1 Cush. 507. In Missouri, the president is the proper person on whom process against the corporation should be served, and is competent to confess judgment against it. Chamberlin *v.* Mammoth Mining Co. 20 Misso. 96.

[4] Hodges *v.* Rut. & B. R. Co. 29 Vt. 220.

[5] Fleckner *v.* United States Bank, 8 Wheat. 356, 357; Ridgway *v.* Farmers Bank of Bucks County, 12 S. & R. 265.

[6] Salem Bank *v.* Gloucester Bank, 17 Mass. 29, 30; Lincoln and Kennebec Bank *v.* Richardson, 1 Greenl. 81; Bank of Kentucky *v.* Schuylkill Bank, 1 Parsons, Sel. Cas. 227.

[7] Ibid.

distinction has been taken in Massachusetts between acts of an agent for his principal, in common cases, and similar acts done by the servants or officers of a corporation. In the first case, it is said the extent of the authority is known only between the principal and agent; whereas, in the latter the authority is created by statute, or is matter of record in the books of the corporation, to which all may have access who have occasion to deal with the officers.[1] The restrictions upon the power of the agents or officers of a corporation contained in the act of incorporation, we can readily conceive, every person dealing with the company is bound to notice; but whether this be true of every restriction made by a by-law upon the power of the *general* agents of the corporation, may, we think, admit of great doubt.[2] The directors of a bank alone have power to make discounts and fix the conditions of them.[3] They have, in general, authority to control all the property of a bank, and may authorize the president, or one of their number, to assign any of the securities belonging to the bank;[4] or may assign the property of the bank for the payment of its debts, without consulting the stockholders;[5] and, indeed, are vested with plenary power to regulate the concerns of the bank, according to their best judgment and discretion, within the limits of the authority conferred upon them by the charter.[6] They may make general arrangements with other banks for the collection of their notes and dividends on stock, — the redemption of their bills, — the transfer of their stock, or the doing of any other business of banking agency usual or proper for one bank to transact for another.[7] Where a charter gives to

---

1 Wyman *v.* Hallowell and Augusta Bank, 14 Mass. 58; Salem Bank *v.* Gloucester Bank, 17 Mass. 29.

2 Wild *v.* Bank of Passamaquoddy, 3 Mason, 506; and see Smith *v.* Hull Glass Co. 8 C. B. 667, 675, 677; Kingsley *v.* New England Mut. Fire Ins. Co. 8 Cush. 403; see, however, State *v.* Commercial Bank of Manchester, 6 Smedes & M. 237.

3 Bank of United States *v.* Dana, 6 Pet. 51; Bank of Metropolis *v.* Jones, 8 Pet. 16; Bank Commissioners *v.* Banks of Buffalo, 6 Paige, 497; see the Highland Bank *v.* Dubois, 5 Denio, 563; Johnson *v.* Bush, 3 Barb. Ch. 207; Barrick *v.* Austin, 21 Barb. 241; Gillet *v.* Phillips, 3 Kern. 114; — decisions under a statute of N. Y. (1 R. S. 591, sec. 8) forbidding any conveyance, assignment, or transfer of its real estate or effects, exceeding the value of $1,000, to be made by a banking corporation, unless authorized by a previous resolution of the board of directors.

4 Spear *v.* Ladd, 11 Mass. 94; Northampton Bank *v.* Pepoon, 11 Mass. 288; Stevens *v.* Hill, 29 Maine, 133.

5 Merrick *v.* Trustees, 8 Gill, 59. Contra, Gibson *v.* Goldthwaite, 7 Ala. 281.

6 Dana *v.* Bank of United States, 5 Watts & S. 246; Bank of Kentucky *v.* Schuylkill Bank, 1 Parsons, Sel. Cas. 236.

7 Bank of Kentucky *v.* Schuylkill Bank, sup.

a board of directors the management of the affairs of the corporation, the president and cashier cannot, without authority from the board, assign *choses in action*, except when due in the usual course of business.[1] The directors of a bank are not authorized to pay money for a bank which it does not owe; and, therefore, no acts of theirs, tending to create an obligation to that effect, can be operative. It was accordingly held, that if a banking company incorporated by the same name as a former one, appoint the same president and cashier, and the officers receive and issue the notes of the former company, and declare that there is no difference between the notes thus issued and those of the new company, the new company never having authorized these proceedings, are not liable to pay such notes.[2] They may, however, on behalf of the corporation, release the interest of a witness whom the corporation propose to call.[3] A board of directors, authorized to conduct the affairs of the company, may empower the president, or the president and cashier, to borrow money, indorse its notes, or to obtain a discount for the use of the bank;[4] or a banking association may authorize the president and cashier to borrow money to redeem its circulation, and they may, for that purpose, buy State stocks, on the credit of the bank, and if the president personally redeem the credit, he will stand as a good creditor against the funds of the bank in the hands of a receiver, to the amount of his payments;[5] but the president alone cannot derive authority from a resolve authorizing *him and the cashier* to borrow money.[6] If, however, both agree on the plan of borrowing, it is unnecessary that both should sign the papers, to carry it into effect.[7] In Massachusetts it has been held, that neither a president nor a cashier of a bank has *ex officio* authority to transfer the property or securities of the company; but must have an express authority to that effect from the corporation at large, or the directors, as the case might be.[8] Neither, it is said, can

---

1 Hoyt *v.* Thompson, 1 Seld. 320; and see Fulton Bank *v.* N. Y. & Sharon Canal Co. 4 Paige, 127.

2 Wyman *v.* Hallowell & Augusta Bank, 14 Mass. 58. See also, Salem Bank *v.* Gloucester Bank, 17 Mass. 29; Lincoln & Kennebec Bank *v.* Richardson, 1 Greenl. 81.

3 Lewis *v.* Eastern Bank, 32 Maine, 90.

4 Ridgway *v.* Farmers Bank of Bucks County, 12 S. & R. 56; Fleckner *v.* United States Bank, 8 Wheat. 355, 356, 357; Merrick *v.* Trustees, &c. 8 Gill, 59.

5 Bank Commissioners *v.* St. Lawrence Bank, 8 Barb. 436.

6 Ridgway *v.* Farmers Bank of Bucks County, 12 S. & R. 256.

7 Life & Fire Insurance Company *v.* Mechanic Fire Insurance Company, 7 Wend. 31.

8 Hallowell & Augusta Bank *v.* Hamlin, 14 Mass. 180; Hartford Bank *v.* Barry, 17 Mass. 97.

the president or cashier charge a bank with any special liability for a deposit, contrary to its usage, without the previous authority or subsequent assent of the corporation.[1] In Massachusetts, however, it is admitted that a cashier has authority *ex officio* to indorse a note, the property of the bank, as a measure preliminary to a suit, and to authorize a demand upon the maker, and notice to the indorser,[2] and to give new certificates of stock to a purchaser of shares sold in a tax warrant, on its face good, and issued by lawful authority, though the tax might have been improperly assessed.[3] These narrow limits on a cashier's *ex officio* power are, however, by no means generally acknowledged. On the contrary, it is said that a cashier is usually intrusted with all the funds of a bank, in cash, notes, bills, &c., to be used from time to time, for the ordinary and extraordinary exigencies of the bank. He receives directly, or through the subordinate officers, all moneys and notes. He delivers up all discounted notes and other property, when payments have been made. He draws checks, from time to time, for moneys, whenever the bank has deposits. He acts as the arm of the bank in carrying out the business arrangements and agencies assumed by the bank through the directors. In short, he is considered the executive officer, through whom and by whom the whole moneyed operations of the bank, *in paying or receiving debts, or discharging or transferring securities*, are to be conducted. It does not seem too much then to infer, *in the absence of all positive restrictions*, that it is his duty as well to apply the negotiable funds as the moneyed capital of the bank, to discharge its debts and obligations.[4] The inducement to the transfer need not appear; but the courts will presume the transfer to have been properly made by the cashier, in the absence of proof to the contrary.[5] This presumption is not, however, conclusive; and the transaction may be impeached by showing that it was not in the ordinary course of business,

---

[1] Foster *v.* Essex Bank, 17 Mass. 505.

[2] Hartford Bank *v.* Barry, 17 Mass. 97. The cashier of the Bank of Kentucky has no authority *ex officio* to accept bills of exchange. Pendleton *v.* Bank, 1 T. B. Mon. 179.

[3] Smith *v.* Northampton Bank, 4 Cush. 1.

[4] Fleckner *v.* United States Bank, 8 Wheat. 360, 361, per Story, J.; Lafayette Bank *v.* State Bank of Illinois, 4 McLean, C. C. 208; Ridgway *v.* Farmers Bank of Bucks County, 12 S. & R. 265; Bank of Kentucky *v.* Schuylkill Bank, 1 Parsons, Sel. Cas. 243; Everett *v.* United States, 6 Port. Ala. 166; Stamford Bank *v.* Benedict, 15 Conn. 445; Crockett *v.* Young, 1 Smedes & M. 241; State *v.* Commercial Bank of Manchester, 6 Smedes & M. 237; Carey *v.* Giles, 10 Ga. 9; Ryan *v.* Dunlap, 17 Ill. 40.

[5] Everett *v.* United States, 6 Port. Ala. 166.

and in prejudice of the rights and interests of the bank.[1] A transfer of a deposit belonging to a bank, however, though made in bad faith, by the cashier, will be good against the bank in favor of a *bonâ fide* holder, for value and without notice.[2] If the cashier of a bank should pay to a *bonâ fide* holder a forged check drawn on the bank, or forged bank-bills, the payment cannot be recalled; because he is intrusted by the bank with an implied authority to decide on the genuineness of the handwriting of the drawer of the check, and of the paper of the bank. The act of payment is to be distinguished, in this respect, from a mere admission.[3]

§ 300. Again, we are told that the cashier of a bank is, *virtute officii*, generally intrusted with the notes, securities, and other funds of the bank, and is held out to the world by the bank as its general agent, in the negotiation, management, and disposal of them. *Primâ facie*, therefore, he must be deemed to have authority to transfer and indorse negotiable securities held by the bank, for its use, and in its behalf; and no special authority for this purpose is necessary to be proved. If any bank chooses to depart from this general course of business, it is certainly at liberty so to do; but in such case it is incumbent on the bank to show that it has interposed a restriction, and that such restriction is known to those with whom it is in the habit of doing business.[4] A clause in a bank charter requiring the signature of the president, and the counter signature of the cashier, to any contract or engagement whatever, before the funds of the bank should be liable therefor, was construed not to apply to or restrict the power of the cashier to draw and indorse bills of exchange, drafts, and checks, in the ordinary discharge of his duty as cashier.[5] The receipt of the cashier is evidence of a deposit, so as to charge the bank,[6] and in general his acts within

---

[1] Ibid.; and see Eliot *v.* Abbot, 12 N. H. 549.

[2] Perpetual Ins. Co. *v.* Cohen, 9 Misso. 421.

[3] Levy *v.* Bank of United States, 1 Binn. 27; Bank of United States *v.* Bank of Georgia, 10 Wheat. 333; Salem Bank *v.* Gloucester Bank, 17 Mass. 1; Merchants Bank *v.* Marine Bank, 3 Gill, 96; Story on Agency, § 115, pp. 104, 105.

[4] Wild *v.* Bank of Passamaquoddy, 3 Mason, 506, per Story, J.; and see Burnham *v.* Webster, 19 Maine, 234; Eliot *v.* Abbot, 12 N. H. 556, 557; Bank of Vergennes *v.* Warren, 7 Hill, 91; Lloyd *v.* West Branch Bank, 15 Penn. State, 172.

[5] Merchants Bank *v.* Central Bank, 1 Kelly, 430; Carey *v.* McDougald, 7 Ga. 84.

[6] State Bank *v.* Kain, 1 Breese, 45; State Bank *v.* Locke, 4 Dev. 533; and see Moreland *v.* State Bank, 1 Breese, 205; that the cashier of the State Bank of Illinois may take an appeal. An agent of a corporation, who is neither president, chief officer, cashier, treas-

the scope of his duties are the acts of the bank.[1] But the act of a State, relative to banks, being construed not to authorize the receiving, as a special deposit, of a sealed package of small notes, issued contrary to law, it was held, that the receipt of the package, on special deposit, by the cashier, without the knowledge of the directors, raised no implied promise on the part of the bank for the safe-keeping of it, and that, in the absence of gross negligence or fraud, the bank was not liable therefor.[2]

§ 301. The cashier of a bank has a general authority to superintend the collection of notes under protest, and to make such arrangements as may facilitate that object, and to do any thing in relation thereto that an attorney might lawfully do. His authority does not, however, extend so far as to justify him in altering the nature of the debt, or in changing the relation of the bank from that of a creditor to that of an agent of its debtor; although a subsequent acquiescence of the bank in such an exercise of power may ratify and confirm it.[3] Nor has the cashier of a bank power to accept bills of exchange on behalf of the bank, for the accommodation of the drawers; and the holder of such a draft, with notice, cannot recover against the bank.[4] An agreement by the president and cashier of a bank, that an indorser shall not be liable on his indorsement, is not binding on the bank.[5] The power of a cashier, acting in consultation with two or more of the directors, to make an agreement, which, if carried out, would have the effect to discharge sureties on a note held by the bank, may, however, be implied from the usual course of the bank in such particulars.[6] The directors alone have

---

urer, nor secretary, cannot, under the Pennsylvania statute of March 22, 1817, enter an appeal from an award of arbitrators, though authorized so to do by the directors. Washington Company *v.* Cullen, 8 S. & R. 517.

[1] Badger *v.* Bank of Cumberland, 26 Maine, 428; and see Bank of Kentucky *v.* Schuylkill Bank, 1 Parsons, Sel. Cas. 243.

[2] Lloyd *v.* West Branch Bank, 15 Penn. State, 172.

[3] Bank of Pennsylvania *v.* Reed, 1 Watts & S. 101; Harrisburg Bank *v.* Tyler, 3 Watts & S. 376; Payne *v.* Commercial Bank of Manchester, 6 Smedes & M. 24. In Louisiana, the authority given by law to cashiers of banks to execute acts of pledge, confers on those officers only the powers of notaries-public in relation to such a contract; and they can dispense with none of the essential forms of the contract. Robinson *v.* Shelton, 2 Rob. La. 277.

[4] Farmers & Mechanics Bank *v.* Troy City Bank, 1 Doug, Mich. 457.

[5] Bank of United States *v.* Dana, 6 Pet. 51; Bank of Metropolis *v.* Jones, 8 Pet. 16.

[6] Payne *v.* Commercial Bank of Natchez, 6 Smedes & M. 24.

power to make discounts and fix the conditions of them; and the cashier can only bind the bank in the discharge of his ordinary duties.[1] Nor can a president and cashier of a bank, nor a "*finance committee*" of the board of directors, as such merely, execute a mortgage of the lands of the corporation, without the concurrence of the board of directors.[2] And where the cashier of a bank wrote to the Secretary of the Treasury, saying that the bearer of a letter was authorized to contract for the transfer of money from New York to New Orleans, it was held that such an act was not within the scope of the powers of the cashier, and, not being authorized by the directors, the bank was not bound to reimburse the money advanced in pursuance of such letter.[3]

§ 302. Independently of any *resolution* of the directors, their sanction to a draft made on the bank by the president may be inferred from circumstances.[4] And where the president of a bank, who was authorized to raise money by drawing bills on its behalf, to be applied to its use, by fraud and collusion between himself and the payee of a bill drawn on the bank, raised money on it to be applied to the payee's use; it was considered that a *bonâ fide* indorsee, who had received it in the usual course of business, might recover thereon from the bank.[5] The receiving teller of a bank, where there is one, is the only proper officer to receive deposits; and if the paying teller receive the funds of a stranger, and promise to apply them to the payment of a bill or note, he acts as the agent of the stranger and not of the bank, which is not liable for any neglect or breach of his promise.[6] In Massachusetts it has been decided, that the teller of a bank as such has no authority to certify that a check upon the bank is "good," so as to bind the bank to pay the amount thereof to any person who may afterwards present it; and a usage for him so to certify a check to enable the holder to use it at his pleasure, is bad.[7] But in New York it is held, that if it is shown

---

1 Bank of United States *v.* Dana, 6 Pet. 51; Bank of Metropolis *v.* Jones, 8 Pet. 16.

2 Leggett *v.* N. Jersey Banking Co. Saxton, Ch. 541.

3 United States *v.* City Bank of Columbus, 21 How. 356.

4 Ridgway *v.* Farmers Bank of Bucks County, 12 S. & R. 256; and see Gillett *v.* Campbell, 1 Denio, 520, 523, as to the power of the president and cashier of a banking association in New York to transfer a mortgage, belonging to the association, under the statutes of that State.

5 Ridgway *v.* Farmers Bank of Bucks County, 12 S. & R. 256; see, however, Leavitt *v.* Yates, 4 Edw. Ch. 134.

6 Thatcher *v.* Bank of the State of New York, 5 Sandf. 121; Mussey *v.* Eagle Bank, 9 Met. 306.

7 Mussey *v.* Eagle Bank, 9 Met. 306. A teller, who illegally takes in payment a for-

that the teller has been in the habit of certifying checks, and the officers of the bank have a book in which it is the duty of the teller to enter all checks certified by him, the bank is liable, although he neglects to enter the check, and the bank has no funds belonging to the drawer of the check, to a person who has *bonâ fide* received a check certified by the teller.[1] So also the authority of a treasurer of a corporation to accept drafts may be proved by showing that it was the practice of that officer, with the assent of the board of directors, to accept, and that the acceptances were recognized and treated as those of the company.[2]

§ 303. If the agent of a corporation make a contract beyond the limits of his authority, he is bound himself, in the same manner as the agent of a natural person would be.[3]

§ 304. If a corporation ratify the unauthorized act of its agent, the ratification is equal to a previous authority, as in case of natural persons; no maxim being better settled in reason and law, than "*omnis ratihabitio retro trahitur, et mandato priori æquiparatur;*" at all events, where it does not prejudice the rights of strangers.[4] Where two officers

---

eign bank-note, does not thereby render the bank liable to the penalty provided for the offence. Clark *v.* Metropolitan Bank, 3 Duer, 241.

[1] Mechanics Bank *v.* Butchers and Drovers Bank, 16 N. Y. 125.

[2] Partridge *v.* Badger, 25 Barb. 146. See also, Mead *v.* Keeler, 24 Barb. 20; and *ante*, § 284.

[3] Salem Bank *v.* Gloucester Bank, 17 Mass. 29, 30; Thayer *v.* Boston, 19 Pick. 516, 517; Stowe *v.* Wise, 7 Conn. 219; Lee *v.* Flemingsbourgh, 7 Dana, 28; Underhill *v.* Gibson, 2 N. H. 352; McClure *v.* Bennett, 1 Blackf. 190; and see Johnson *v.* Bentley, 16 Ohio, 97; Wilson *v.* Goodman, 4 Hare, 54, 61, 62; Nicholls *v.* Diamond, 9 Exch. 154, 24 Eng. L. & Eq. 403. The doctrine that the contract of an agent, which does not bind his principal, binds himself, is confined to cases where the agent had *in fact* no authority to act for his principal, per Selden, J. in Walker *v.* Bank of the State of New York, 5 Seld. 582. And he is liable in such a case, although he purports to act in his representative capacity. Haynes *v.* Hunnewell, 42 Me. 276.

[4] Fleckner *v.* United States Bank, 8 Wheat. 363, per Story J.; Essex Turnpike Corporation *v.* Collins, 8 Mass. 299; Hayden *v.* Middlesex Turnpike Corporation, 10 Mass. 403; Salem Bank *v.* Gloucester Bank, 17 Mass. 28, 29; White *v.* Westport Cotton Manuf. Co. 1 Pick. 220; Bulkley *v.* Derby Fishing Co. 2 Conn. 252; Witte *v.* Same, id. 260; Hoyt *v.* Thompson, 19 N. Y. 207; Peterson *v.* Mayor of N. Y. 17 N. Y. 449; Baker *v.* Cotter, 45 Me. 236; Church *v.* Sterling, 16 Conn. 388; Bank of Pennsylvania *v.* Reed, 1 Watts & S. 101; Hayward *v.* Pilgrim Society, 21 Pick. 270; Despatch Line of Packets *v.* Bellamy Manuf. Co. 12 N. H. 205; Planters Bank *v.* Sharp, 4 Smedes & M. 75; Burrill *v.* Nahant Bank, 2 Met. 167; Fox *v.* Northern Liberties, 3 Watts & S. 103; Bank of Kentucky *v.* Schuylkill Bank, 1 Parsons, Sel. Cas. 267, 268; New Hope & Delaware Bridge Co. *v.* Phœnix Bank, 3 Comst. 156; Everett *v.* United States,

of a lead mining corporation purchased property for the corporation, and gave several notes in the corporate name for the purchase-money, and afterwards the property was claimed by the corporation and converted to its own use, and judgment on one of the notes had already been suffered by the corporation to pass against it by default; these facts were deemed a ratification of what the officers had done, and it was decided that, even if the notes were originally given without authority, the corporation was liable upon them.[1] And on the other hand, where the president and treasurer of a railroad corporation, having, as the corporate agents, purchased a piece of land with a view to obtain a supply of gravel for the road, took a deed of it to themselves, but paid a small portion of the purchase-money out of the funds of the corporation, and gave their own note for the balance, secured by a mortgage on the land, and it was proved that the company had taken gravel from the land, and had paid the interest on the note up to a certain time, when, by direction of the company the land was sold, and the proceeds as far as needed applied to the payment of the note; it was held, that although these officers could not *ex officio* bind the corporation for the purchase of land, yet the facts amounted to a ratification of their act by the corporation, and that the agents must account in equity as trustees to the corporation for the balance of the purchase-money and land in their hands.[2] A railway company, not authorized to make a particular contract, having, in contemplation of an extension of their powers, authorized an agent to contract for them, may, upon obtaining the requisite powers, ratify, by taking advantage of, or acting upon his contract, even though at the time the contract was made, it was illegal and void.[3] If, however, the ratification by the corporation of the unauthorized contract

6 Port. Ala. 166; Medomak Bank *v.* Curtis, 24 Me. 38; Whitwell *v.* Warner, 20 Vt. 425; City of Detroit *v.* Jackson, 1 Doug. Mich. 106; Merchants Bank *v.* Central Bank, 1 Kelley, 428; Hoyt *v.* Bridgewater Copper Mining Co. 2 Halst. Ch. 253; Stuart *v.* London & Northwestern Railway Co. 15 Beav. 513, 10 Eng. Law & Eq. 57; Maclae *v.* Sutherland, 3 Ellis & B. 1, 25 Eng. L. & Eq. 92; Reuter *v.* Electric Telegraph Co. 6 Ellis & B. 341, 37 Eng. L. & Eq. 189; Durar *v.* Ins. Co. 4 N. J. 171; Emmet *v.* Reed, 4 Seld. 312.

[1] Moss *v.* Rossie Lead Mining Company, 5 Hill, 137; see contra, McCollough *v.* Moss, 5 Denio, 567; and see Alleghany City *v.* McClurkan, 14 Penn. State, 81.

[2] Church *v.* Sterling, 16 Conn. 388; Dedham Institution for Savings *v.* Slack, 6 Cush. 408.

[3] Gooday *v.* Colchester and Stour Valley Railway Co. 17 Beav. 132, 15 Eng. L. & Eq. 596, 598, 599; and see Edwards *v.* The Grand Junction Railway Co. 1 Mylne & C. 650; Preston *v.* Liverpool, Manchester, and New-Castle-upon-Tyne Grand Junction Railway Co. 1 Sim. N. S. 586, 7 Eng. L. & Eq. 124.

of their agent, consist in their having received the consideration of the contract, it must be proved that the corporation, through its proper officer or officers, knew the terms of the contract, and on what account the money was by them received.[1] And though a ratification by a corporation of the commission of a tort, by one of their agents or servants, will render them liable in trespass, equally as if they had previously authorized it; yet it must be proved by showing that the managing officer or officers, in such matters, knew and sanctioned it. The mere attendance of the company's solicitor, at the hearing before the magistrate, to conduct proceedings in behalf of the servant when arrested,[2] or the writing of a letter by the secretary of the company, for the purpose of effecting a compromise,[3] is no evidence of ratification of the authority of the servant by the corporation. The directors of a corporation act as trustees for the stockholders. If they do an unauthorized act, the stockholders may ratify it, if they have full knowledge of all the circumstances of the case, but not otherwise. For some purposes a majority of the stockholders may ratify such an act, but in others, as where a director in a company sells land belonging to it, and purchases the same himself, the majority have no right or power to bind the minority by a ratification.[4] Nor is the presence in an unofficial capacity of two directors, at an interview between a contractor for the corporation and its agent for a particular purpose, any evidence of their assent, or of the assent of the corporation, to an arrangement then made in behalf of the corporation by such agent, with the contractor, the agent having exceeded his power.[5]

§ 305. It is also well established, both in law and equity, that notice to an agent in the transactions for which he is employed, is notice to the principal; for otherwise, where notice is necessary, it might be avoided in every case by employing an agent. The rule applies equally to a corporation as to a natural person.[6]

---

[1] The Pennsylvania, &c. Co. *v.* Dandridge, 8 Gill & J. 248. See Hilliard *v.* Goold, 34 N. H. 230.

[2] Eastern Counties Railway *v.* Broom, 6 Exch. 314, 2 Eng. L. & Eq. 406.

[3] Roe *v.* Birkenhead, Lancashire, & Cheshire Junction Railway Co. 7 Exch. 36, 7 Eng. L. & Eq. 546.

[4] Cumberland Coal Co. *v.* Sherman, 30 Barb. 553, 577.

[5] Barcus *v.* H. Co. & Paris Plank Road Co. 26 Misso. 102.

[6] Lawrence *v.* Tucker, 7 Greenl. 195; Bank *v.* Whitehead, 10 Watts, 397; Boggs *v.* Lancaster Bank, 7 Watts & S. 336; Danville Bridge Co. *v.* Pomroy, 15 Penn. State, 151; McEwen *v.* Montgomery County Mutual Ins. Co. 5 Hill, 101; Conro *v.* Port Henry Iron

§ 306. In case of a joint agency, as of directors of a bank, knowledge of a material fact, imparted by a director to the board at a regular meeting, is notice to the bank.[1] Notice to either of the directors, *whilst engaged in the business of the bank*, is notice to the principal, the bank. Thus, where a bill of exchange was sent to one of the directors of a bank, to be discounted for the benefit of the drawer, and the director, who was a member of the board which ordered the discount, received the avails, alleging the discount to have been made for his benefit, the bank was held chargeable with knowledge of the fraud, and could not recover on the bill against the drawer.[2] And in Vermont, it would seem that notice to the president of a banking corporation, that stock standing upon the books in the name of one person was, in fact, held by him in trust for another, was sufficient to affect the corporation with notice of the trust, the communication, too, being not full, but only sufficient to put the president upon inquiry as to the facts.[3]

§ 307. Where, however, a director is not engaged in the business of the bank, notice to him will not be deemed notice to the bank. Thus, when one of the directors of a bank, who were authorized, *when money was abundant*, to solicit and procure notes for discount, obtained a note, under pretence of getting it discounted for the maker, *at a time when money was scarce*, and pledged it to the bank for a loan to himself, and the maker knew that the director was authorized by the bank to procure notes for discount only when money was abundant, it was held that the director had exceeded his authority in the transaction, and that the bank was not bound by his fraudulent conduct; and that, as he did not act in his capacity of director in procuring the discount, the bank was not affected by his knowledge of the circumstances under which he received the note, and might recover of the maker.[4] Indeed, it seems

---

Co. 12 Barb. 27; Cumberland Coal Co. *v.* Sherman, 30 Barb. 553, 560; Trenton Banking Company *v.* Woodruff, 1 Green, N. J. 117; Wing *v.* Harvey, 5 DeG., M. & G. 265, 27 Eng. L. & Eq. 140.

[1] Bank *v.* Whitehead, 10 Watts, 397; *Ex parte* Holmes, 5 Cowen, 426; Fulton Bank *v.* N. Y. & Sharon Canal Co. 4 Paige, 136.

[2] Bank of United States *v.* Davis, 2 Hill, 451; and see Fulton Bank *v.* Benedict, 1 Hill, 480; Washington Bank *v.* Lewis, 22 Pick. 24, 31; Fulton Bank *v.* N. Y. & Sharon Canal Company, 4 Paige, 136.

[3] Porter *v.* Bank of Rutland, 19 Vt. 410.

[4] Washington Bank *v.* Lewis, 22 Pick. 24; Bank of Pittsburg *v.* Whitehead, 10 Watts, 397; Custer *v.* Tompkins County Bank, 9 Barr, 27; Farrell Foundry *v.* Dart, 26 Conn. 376; Farmers & Citizens Pank *v.* Payne, 25 Conn. 544; General Ins. Co. *v.* U. S. Ins. Co. 10 Md. 517.

recently to have been held, in Pennsylvania, that notice to the director of a bank will not be deemed notice to the bank, unless the director be constituted an organ of communication between the bank and those who deal with it.[1] Mere conversation with a clerk of an insurance company is not notice to the office;[2] and knowledge on the part of a clerk of a bank, of the residence of a party to negotiable paper, lodged with the bank for collection, and protested by the bank, will not prevent the holder of the paper, in a suit against this party to it, from availing himself of the ignorance of the proper officer of the bank of the residence of the party.[3]

§ 308. Notice of a dissolution of copartnership published in a newspaper, and thus accidentally reaching a bank director, is not equivalent to actual notice to the bank; though, perhaps, if notice of such a dissolution had been given to him for the express purpose of being by him communicated to the bank, it would have been sufficient notice to the bank.[4] It seems that where actual notice of a dissolution of copartnership is necessary, proof that the party, as a bank sought to be charged with it, took a newspaper in which the notice was published, is a fact from which the jury are authorized to infer actual notice,[5] but is not *per se* equivalent to actual notice.[6] A private communication of a fact to a director, or his knowledge of it from rumor, is clearly no notice to the board, unless he communicate the fact to the board.[7] The circumstance, that the indorser of a note was a director in the bank in which it was discounted, will not be deemed constructive notice to the bank that the note was made for his accommodation.[8] A subsequent board of directors is to be considered as knowing all the circumstances

---

[1] Custer *v.* Tompkins County Bank, 9 Barr 27.

[2] *Ex parte* Charbis, cited 1 Mont. & A. 693. See also, *Ex parte* Ord, 2 Mont. & A. 724; Schenck *v.* Mercer Co. Mut. F. Ins. Co. 4 N. J. 447.

[3] Goodloe *v.* Godley, 13 Smedes & M. 233.

[4] National Bank *v.* Norton, 1 Hill, 578, 579, 580; and see Fulton Bank *v.* N. Y. and Sharon Canal Company, 4 Paige, 136; U. S. Ins. Co. *v.* Shriever, 3 Md. Ch. Dec. 381.

[5] Bank of South Carolina *v.* Humphreys, 1 McCord, 388; Martin *v.* Walton, id. 16; and see Greene *v.* Merchants Insurance Company, 10 Pick. 402, 406, 407.

[6] Vernon *v.* Manhattan Company, 17 Wend. 524, 527; s. c. in Error, 22 id. 183, 191, 192; and see Rowley *v.* Horne, 3 Bing. 2; National Bank *v.* Norton, 1 Hill, 578, n. a.

[7] U. S. Ins. Co. *v.* Shriever, 3 Md. Ch. Dec. 381; General Ins. Co. *v.* U. S. Ins. Co. 10 Md. 517.

[8] Commercial Bank *v.* Cunningham, 24 Pick. 270; but see North River Bank *v.* Aymar, 3 Hill, 274, 275.

communicated or known to a previous board. Thus, upon a transfer of bank stock to one, notice to the board of directors, that he held it as trustee only, was deemed to be notice to the bank; and no subsequent change of directors could render necessary new notice of the fact.[1] Knowledge of facts by a mere stockholder in an incorporated manufacturing company, turnpike, canal company, or bank, is not notice to the corporation of the existence of those facts;[2] nor is notice to a corporator notice to the corporation, unless he be constituted, by the charter or by-laws, an organ of communication between the corporation and those who deal with it.[3] And even the private knowledge of one of the directors and actuary of a company, that certain shares have been assigned or incumbered, will not be deemed notice of the fact to the company, provided the apparent ownership of the shares remain in the assignor, and he be recognized by the company as the owner.[4] But knowledge of *the cashier* of a bank, of matters occurring in the course of its ordinary business, or notice to him, is notice to the bank, or, what is the same thing, to the directors or managers of the bank;[5] but this rule does not hold as to transactions in which the cashier is acting not for the bank, but for himself.[6] And where the president of a corporation executed to some of its directors, in trust for it, a mortgage of land to which his wife had an equitable title by unrecorded deed, the same having been paid for out of her separate estate, the mortgagor's knowledge of his wife's equities will not, on account of his official position, be considered as knowledge of the corporation, and cannot affect its rights unless communicated to its managing agents. Neither the acts nor knowledge of the officer of a corporation will bind it in a matter in which he acts for himself, and deals with the corporation as if he had no official relations with it.[7]

---

1 Mechanics Bank of Alexandria *v.* Seton, 1 Pet. 299; Fulton Bank *v.* New York and Sharon Canal Co. 4 Paige, 136.

2 Housatonic and Lee Banks *v.* Martin, 1 Met. 294; Fairfield Turnpike Company *v.* Thorp, 13 Conn. 182; Union Canal *v.* Lloyd, 4 Watts & S. 393; Bank of Pittsburg *v.* Whitehead, 10 Watts, 402.

3 Bank of Pittsburg *v.* Whitehead, 10 Watts, 402.

4 *Ex parte* Watkins, 2 Mont. & A. 348; and see Terrell *v.* Branch Bank at Mobile, 12 Ala. 502.

5 New Hope & Delaware Bridge Co. *v.* Phœnix Bank, 3 Comst. 156; Bank of St. Mary's *v.* Mumford, 6 Ga. 44; Branch Bank of Huntsville *v.* Steele, 10 Ala. 915.

6 Seneca County Bank *v.* Neass, 5 Denio, 337.

7 Winchester *v.* Baltimore and Susquehannah Railroad Co. 4 Md. 231.

§ 309. The representations, declarations, and admissions of the agent of a corporation stand upon the same footing with those of the agent of an individual. To bind the principal, they must be within the scope of the authority confided to the agent, and must accompany the act or contract which he is authorized to do or make.[1] The cashier of a bank possesses no incidental power to make any declarations binding upon the bank, not within the scope of his ordinary duties. He has no authority, upon a note being offered for discount, to bind the bank by his declaration to a person about to become an indorser on it, that he will incur no risk or responsibility by his becoming an indorser upon such discount.[2] His promise to pay a debt which the corporation did not owe, or his admission that the forged bills of the bank were genuine, would not bind the bank, unless it had authorized or adopted his act.[3] The mere admissions of a director or stockholder of a corporation are not, it seems, evidence against the corporation, even though they cannot be compelled to testify on account of their interest.[4] Still less will the representations of an agent of a corporation bind the stockholders personally, since he is not *their* agent, because agent of the corporation. Hence the fraudulent representations of such an agent, concerning the value of the corporate stock, will not vitiate the sale of the stock, by a stockholder, who had no notice of the fraud.[5]

§ 310. As natural persons are liable for the wrongful acts and neg-

---

[1] Fairfield County Turnpike Company *v.* Thorp, 13 Conn. 173; Stewart *v.* Huntington Bank, 11 S. & R. 267, 269; Hayward *v.* Pilgrim Society, 21 Pick. 270; Sterling *v.* Marietta Company, 11 S. & R. 179; Westmoreland Bank *v.* Klingsmith, 7 Watts, 523; Harrisburg Bank *v.* Tyler, 3 Watts & S. 377; Bank of Northern Liberties *v.* Davis, 6 Watts & S. 285; Farmers Bank *v.* McKee, 2 Barr, 321; Hackney *v.* Alleghany Mut. Ins. Co. 4 Barr, 185; Spalding *v.* Bank of Susquehannah County, 9 Barr, 28; Crump *v.* U. S. Mining Co. 7 Gratt. 352; First Baptist Church *v.* Brooklyn F. Ins. Co. 18 Barb. 69; Devendorf *v.* Beardsley, 23 id. 656; Troy F. Ins. Co. *v.* Carpenter, 4 Wis. 20.

[2] Bank of United States *v.* Dana, 6 Pet. 51; Bank of Metropolis *v.* Jones, 8 Pet. 12; Harrisburg Bank *v.* Tyler, 3 Watts & S. 377; Merchants Bank *v.* Marine Bank, 3 Gill, 96.

[3] Salem Bank *v.* Gloucester Bank, 17 Mass. 1; Farmers and Mechanics Bank *v.* Troy City Bank, 1 Doug. Mich. 457; Story on Agency, §§ 114, 115, pp. 103, 104, 105.

[4] Fairfield County Turnpike Company *v.* Thorp, 13 Conn. 173; Hartford Bank *v.* Hart, 3 Day, 494; Osgood *v.* Manhattan Bank, 3 Cowen, 623; Polleys *v.* Ocean Insurance Company, 14 Maine, 141; Ruby *v.* Abyssinian Society, 15 Maine, 306; Bank of Oldtown *v.* Houlton, 21 Maine, 507, Shepley, J.; National Bank *v.* Norton, 1 Hill, 579; Holman *v.* Bank of Norfolk, 12 Ala. 369; Soper *v.* Buffalo and Rochester R. R. Co. 19 Barb. 310; Mitchell *v.* Rome R. R. Co. 17 Ga. 574; and see authorities above. See also, Chap. XVIII.

[5] Moffatt *v.* Winslow, 7 Paige, 124.

lects of their servants and agents, done in the course and within the scope of their employment, so are corporations, upon the same grounds, in the same manner, and to the same extent.[1] In its relations to the government, and when the acts or neglects of a corporation, in violation of its charter or of the general law, become the subject of public inquiry, with a view to the forfeiture of its charter, the wilful acts and neglects of its officers are regarded as the acts and neglects of the corporation, and render the corporation liable to a judgment or decree of dissolution.[2] But though *the directors* of a bank may, through the cashier, violate the charter, unless they can show that he departed from his duties as prescribed by them; yet it is believed to be a clear and indisputable principle, that the *cashier* cannot cause a forfeiture of the charter by a direct and palpable violation of his authority or instructions.[3]

§ 311. A bank is liable for the fraud or mistakes of its cashier or clerk, in the entries in its books, and in the false accounts of deposits,[4] and for improperly refusing, *by its directors*, to permit an individual to subscribe for,[5] or to transfer stock;[6] nor can it enforce any contract, or retain any security for its liabilities, procured for it by the fraud of its agent.[7] A railroad company is held responsible, under precisely the

---

[1] Albert *v.* Savings Bank of Baltimore, 1 Md. Ch. Dec. 407; Thatcher *v.* Bank of the State of New York, 5 Sandf. 121; Thompson *v.* Bell, 10 Exch. 10, 26 Eng. L. & Eq. 536; Bargate *v.* Shortridge, 5 H. L. Cas. 297, 31 Eng. L. & Eq. 44; National Exchange Co. *v.* Drew, H. L. 1855, 32 Eng. L. & Eq. 1; Stevens *v.* Boston & Maine R. R. 1 Gray, 277; Blackstock *v.* N. Y. & Erie R. Co. 1 Bosw. 77. A municipal corporation is not responsible for injuries caused by the failure of its officers to repress a mob. Prather *v.* Lexington, 13 B. Mon. 559. But a city is liable for injuries caused by want of care or of skill on the part of its agents in the construction of public works. City of Dayton *v.* Pease, 4 Ohio, N. S. 80.

[2] Life & Fire Ins. Co. *v.* Mechanics Fire Ins. Co. 7 Wend. 35; Bank Commissioners *v.* Bank of Buffalo, 6 Paige, 497; Ward *v.* Sea Insurance Company, 7 Paige, 294.

[3] State of Mississippi *v.* Commercial Bank of Manchester, 6 Smedes & M. 237, per Sharkey, C. J.

[4] Salem Bank *v.* Gloucester Bank, 17 Mass. 1; Gloucester Bank *v.* Salem Bank, id. 33; Foster *v.* Essex Bank, id. 479; Manhattan Company *v.* Lydig, 4 Johns. 377; Bank of Kentucky *v.* Schuylkill Bank, 1 Parsons, Sel. Cas. 248; and see Chap. VIII. of Contracts, and Chap. XI. of Capacity of a Corporation to sue, and its liability to be sued.

[5] Union Bank *v.* McDonough, 5 La. 63; and see Ware *v.* Barrataria & Lafourche Canal Company, 15 La. 168.

[6] Chap. X.

[7] Johnston *v.* S. W. R. R. Bank, 3 Strob. Eq. 263; Crump *v.* U. S. Mining Co. 7 Gratt. 352. A bank, employed for consideration to collect a bill or note, is responsible for any misconduct or neglect on the part of the agents to whom the bill or note is committed.

same circumstances, and for precisely the same degree of care on the part of its agents having the direction of vehicles upon the road, that any master is for a servant having the direction of his vehicle on an ordinary highway.[1] And where, by contract, made through its president or agent, a corporation, established for the purpose of pressing cotton, agreed to unload a boat, and the company's slaves took possession of it for that purpose, and carelessly sunk it, the corporation was held responsible for the damages.[2] And generally a corporation is civilly responsible for damages occasioned by an act, as a trespass or a tort, done at its command, by its agent, in relation to a matter within the scope of the purposes for which it was incorporated.[3] It is not, however, responsible for unauthorized and unlawful acts, even of its officers, though done *colore officii.* To fix the liability, it must either appear that the officers were expressly authorized to do the act, or that it was done *bonâ fide* in pursuance of a general authority, in relation to the subject of it, or that the act was adopted or ratified by the corporation.[4]

Commercial Bank of Penn. *v.* Union Bank of New York, 1 Kern. 203. See, however, Citizens Bank *v.* Howell, 8 Md. 530.

[1] Beers *v.* Housatonic Railroad Co. 19 Conn. 566; Bradley *v.* Boston & Maine Railroad, 2 Cush. 539; Baltimore & Susquehannah Railroad Co. *v.* Woodruff, 4 Md. 242; Sharrod *v.* London & Northwestern Railway Co. 4 Exch. 585, 586; Gillenwater *v.* Madison & Indianapolis R. R. Co. 5 Ind. 339.

[2] Marlatt *v.* Levee Steam Cotton Press Company, 10 La. 583; and see Mayor, &c. Memphis *v.* Lasser, 9 Humph. 757.

[3] Duncan *v.* Surry Canal Proprietors, 3 Starkie, 50; Smith *v.* Birmingham Gas Company, 1 A. & E. 526, 3 Nev. & M. 771; Rex *v.* Medley, 6 C. & P. 292, per Denman, C. J.; Maund *v.* Monmouthshire Canal Company, 1 Car. & M. 606, 4 Man. & G. 452, 455; Regina *v.* Birmingham & Gloucester Railway Company, 2 Gale & D. 236, 9 C. & P. 469; Eastern Counties Railway *v.* Broom, 6 Exch. 314, 2 Eng. L. & Eq. 406; Hawkins *v.* Dutchess and Orange Steamboat Company, 2 Wend. 452; Beach *v.* Fulton Bank, 7 Cowen, 485; Mayor, &c. New York *v.* Bailey, 2 Denio, 433; Hay *v.* Cohoes Co. 3 Barb. 42; Watson *v.* Bennett, 12 Barb. 196; Kneass *v.* Schuylkill Bank, 4 Wash. C. C. 106; Lyman *v.* White River Bridge Company, 2 Aik. 255; Rabassa *v.* Orleans Navigation Company, 3 La. 461; Goodloe *v.* City of Cincinnati, 4 Ohio, 513; Smith *v.* Same, id. 414; McCready *v.* Guardians, &c. 9 S. & R. 94; McKim *v.* Odom, 3 Bland, Ch. 421; Humes *v.* Mayor, &c. of Knoxville, 1 Humph. 403; Edwards *v.* Union Bank of Fla. 1 Fla. 136; Bank of Kentucky *v.* Schuylkill Bank, 1 Parsons, Sel. Cas. 251; Whiteman *v.* Wil. & Susque. Railroad Co. 2 Harring. Del. 514; Ten Eyck *v.* Del. & Rar. Canal Co. 3 Harrison, 200; Underwood *v.* Newport Lyceum, 5 B. Mon. 130; Hamilton County *v.* Cincinnati and Wooster Turnpike Company, Wright, 603; Town of Akron *v.* McComb, 18 Ohio, 229; Riddle *v.* Proprietors, &c. 7 Mass. 187; Thayer *v.* Boston, 19 Pick. 516, 517; Carman *v.* S. & I. R. R. Co. 4 Ohio, State, 399; Moore *v.* Fitchburg R. R. Corporation, 4 Gray, 465; McDougald *v.* Bellamy, 18 Ga. 411.

[4] Thayer *v.* Boston, 19 Pick. 516, 517, per Shaw, C. J.; Mitchell *v.* Rockland, 41 Me. 363; Davis *v.* Bangor, 42 Me. 522; Dodgson's case, *In re* North of England Joint-Stock

§ 312. On the other hand, the officer or agent of a corporation is liable to the corporation for all damages occasioned by his violation of the duties and obligations he owes to his principal, whether it consists in positive misconduct, or neglect, or omissions. The general rule is, that a suit, brought for the purpose of compelling the ministerial officers of a private corporation to account for breach of official duty, or misapplication of corporate funds, should be brought in the name of the corporation, and cannot be brought in the name of the stockholders, or some of them.[1] Nor is the treasurer of a corporation liable, in his individual capacity, to a stockholder, for refusing to pay him a dividend, though there were funds in the hands of the treasurer sufficient for the payment thereof at the time of his refusal; the remedy of the stockholder in such case being against the corporation.[2] Indeed, the general rule is, where third persons are injured by the neglect of a known agent to discharge the duties of his agency, *respondeat superior*, and the action must be brought against the principal. An action brought against the register of a foreign banking corporation, which had a transfer office in New York, for not permitting a transfer of stock to be made on the books of the corporation, cannot be maintained; but the suit must be brought against the corporation.[3] The directors of a moneyed institution are responsible to it, at law, in an action on the case, for improperly obtaining and disposing of the funds or property of the company.[4] They are liable, however, only *individually*, and severally, and not jointly as directors, unless the act complained of be done by a

---

Banking Co. 3 De Gex & S. 85; Roe *v.* Birkenhead, Lancashire & Cheshire Junction Railway Co. 7 Exch. 36, 7 Eng. L. & Eq. 546; Eastern Counties Railway Co. *v.* Broom, 6 Exch. 314, 2 Eng. L. & Eq. 406; Hazleton Canal Co. *v.* Megargel, 4 Barr, 324; Vanderbilt *v.* Richmond Turnpike Co. 2 Comst. 479; Watson *v.* Bennett, 12 Barb. 196.

1 Bayless *v.* Orne, 1 Freem. Missis. Ch. 175, Buckner, Ch.; Hersey *v.* Veazie, 24 Me. 12; Hodges *v.* New England Screw Co. 1 R. I. 312; Smith *v.* Hurd, 12 Met. 371; Abbott *v.* Merriam, 8 Cush. 588, 590; Austin *v.* Daniels, 4 Denio, 301; Mozley *v.* Alston, 1 Phillips, 790; Brown *v.* Vandyke, 4 Halst. Ch. 795, 799, 800; Smith *v.* Poor, 40 Me. 415.

2 French *v.* Fuller, 23 Pick. 108.

3 Denny *v.* Manhattan Co. 2 Denio, 115; s. c. 5 Denio, 639.

4 Franklin Insurance Company *v.* Jenkins, 3 Wend. 130; Austin *v.* Daniels, 4 Denio, 301; whether liable *at law* to *creditors* for mismanagement of the funds of the corporation, in improperly declaring dividends, and paying them to stockholders, when there were no profits to divide, query? See Lexington Railroad Co. *v.* Bridges, 7 B. Mon. 559. *In equity*, they certainly are, as well as stockholders for unpaid subscriptions for stock. Gratz *v.* Redd, 4 B. Mon. 178; Lexington Railroad Co. *v.* Bridges, 7 id. 559; Henry *v.* Vermillion & Ashland Railroad Co. 17 Ohio, 187.

majority of the board of directors, when, by the act of incorporation, a majority only is competent to transact the business of the company.[1] And generally, where there has been a waste or misapplication of the corporate funds, by the officers or agents of the company, a suit in equity may be brought by and in the name of the corporation, to compel them to account for such waste or misapplication,[2] directors being regarded as trustees of the stockholders, and subject to the obligations and disabilities incidental to that relation.[3] But as a court of equity never permits a wrong to go unredressed merely for the sake of form, if it appear that the directors of a corporation refuse in such case to prosecute, by collusion with those who had made themselves answerable by their negligence or fraud, or if the corporation is still under the control of those who must be the defendants in the suit, the stockholders, who are the real parties in interest, will be permitted to file a bill in their own names, making the corporation a party defendant.[4] And if the stockholders are so numerous as to render it impossible, or very inconvenient, to bring them all before the court, a part may file a bill, in behalf of themselves and all others standing in the same situation.[5] The jurisdiction of chancery, in such cases, proceeds, in case of joint-stock corporations, upon the same principles as are applied to charitable corporations in England. The directors are the trustees or managing partners, and the stockholders are the *cestuis que trust*, and have a joint interest in all the property and effects of the corporation; and no injury that the stockholders may sustain by a fraudulent breach of trust can, upon the general principles of equity, be suffered to pass without a remedy.[6] But where an incorporated company had engaged in unau-

---

[1] Franklin Insurance Company *v.* Jenkins, 3 Wend. 130.

[2] Robinson *v.* Smith, 3 Paige, 233, per Walworth, Ch.; Bayless *v.* Orne, 1 Freem. Missis. Ch. 173; Bagshaw *v.* Eastern Counties Railway Co. 7 Hare, 114; Hodges *v.* New England Screw Company, 1 R. I. 312; Hersey *v.* Veazie, 24 Me. 12, 13.

[3] Cumberland Coal Co. *v.* Sherman, 30 Barb. 553, 571.

[4] Robinson *v.* Smith, 3 Paige, 233, per Walworth, Ch.; Bayless *v.* Orne, 1 Freem. Missis. Ch. 173; Brown *v.* Vandyke, 4 Halst. Ch. 795, 799, 800; Dodge *v.* Woolsey, 18 How. 331.

[5] Ibid.; and see Hichens *v.* Congreve, 4 Russ. 562; Putnam *v.* Sweet, 1 Chandl. 286; Wood *v.* Draper, 24 Barb. 187.

[6] Robinson *v.* Smith, 3 Paige, 232, per Walworth, Ch.; and see Wood's Inst. B. 1, ch. 8, p 110; 11 Co. R. 98 b; and Verplanck *v.* Mercantile Insurance Company, 1 Edw. Ch. 34; Scott *v.* Depeyster, 1 Edw. Ch. 513; Bayless *v.* Orne, 1 Freem. Missis. Ch. 174; Hodges *v.* New England Screw Co. 1 R. I. 312; Attorney-General *v.* Wilson, 1 Craig & Ph. 1; Charitable Corporation *v.* Sutton, 2 Atk. 400; Mayor & Commonalty of Colchester *v.* Lowten, 1 Ves. & B. 226; York and North Midland Railway Co. *v.* Hudson, 16 Beav. 495, 19 Eng. L. & Eq. 361.

thorized and illegal transactions, a stockholder who has acquiesced therein, by knowingly participating in the profits of such transactions, will not be allowed to charge the directors personally for an eventual loss arising therefrom.[1] A shareholder in an incorporated company may file a bill on the behalf of himself and all the other shareholders, to restrain the directors from committing a breach of trust; as by making a contract of guaranty on behalf of the corporation, which they were not empowered by the charter to make; or committing other clear excess of chartered powers.[2] A court of equity will not, however, in such cases, interfere by injunction, in matters relating merely to the internal government of the corporation, as to restrain directors *de facto* from acting as such on the sole ground of the alleged invalidity of their title to their offices;[3] nor in cases where there is no fraud or clear excess of charter authority, and where the acts are done or sanctioned by the vote of the stockholders;[4] nor where the bill is filed on behalf of any stockholders who have sanctioned or acquiesced in the acts complained of.[5] Nor can a person holding stock in a corporation as trustee, maintain a bill in equity to obtain the instruction of the court as to what his powers and duties will be in case the corporation shall carry out a contemplated sale of all their property to a new corporation.[6] The managers or directors of a bank are not, it seems, considered in equity as trustees of the corporation, in such sense that they cannot purchase and retain stock of the bank by them purchased of it, the stock having been in the first place bought up by the bank as a mode of employing its capital.[7] Whether this would be so or not, depends, we should suppose, upon the relation which they held to the particular subject of sale; since no principle in equity is better settled than that a person who is placed in a situation of trust or confidence in reference to the subject of sale, cannot be a purchaser of the property sold on his own account. Accordingly, where a bank was bound to pay off and

---

1 Scott *v.* Depeyster, 1 Edw. Ch. 513.

2 Coleman *v.* Eastern Counties Railway, 10 Beav. 1; Cohen *v.* Wilkinson, 12 Beav. 125, 138; Bagshaw *v.* Eastern Counties Railway Co. 7 Hare, 114; Manderson *v.* Commercial Bank, 28 Penn. State, 379.

3 Mozley *v.* Alston, 1 Phillips, 790.

4 Ibid. and Foss *v.* Harbottle, 2 Hare, 492; Lord *v.* Governor and Co. of Copper Miners, 2 Phillips, 740.

5 Ffooks *v.* London Railway Co. 1 Smale & G. 142, 19 Eng. L. & Eq. 7.

6 Treadwell *v.* Salisbury Manuf. Co. 7 Gray, 393.

7 Hartridge *v.* Rockwell, R. M. Charlt. 260.

discharge a mortgage, so as to relieve the property of a third person from sale under a decree of foreclosure, and the cashier attended the sale as the agent of the bank, and bid off the property on his own account, he was regarded in equity as having purchased for the benefit of the bank.[1]

§ 313. The relation of *cestuis que trust* and trustees does not exist between the stockholders of an incorporated company and *the corporation;* nor are they in the relative situation of partners; nor are the stockholders creditors of the company.[2] The company is the mere creature of the law, a politic, and not a natural body, made up by the compact entered into by the stockholders, each of whom becomes a corporator identified with, and forming a constituent part of the corporate body.[3] Hence, when there is a fraudulent purchasing of the stock of a company, by its officers, with the company funds, the remedy is not against the latter in its corporate character, but against the directors, by whom the fraud may have been committed, or through whose management the loss has been sustained.[4]

§ 314. The officers and agents of a corporation are liable for losses and defalcations occasioned by their neglects, as well as by their positive misconduct,[5] nor does the assent of a president of a bank, who was its financial officer, protect the cashier from liability for using its funds in dealing in State stocks, or other unauthorized business.[6] It should

---

[1] Torrey *v.* Bank of Orleans, 9 Paige, 650, 7 Hill, 260; Conro *v.* Port Henry Iron Co. 12 Barb. 27; and see Mickles *v.* Rochester City Bank, 11 Paige, 118; that a stockholder of a corporation, upon a sale of the corporate property by the sheriff, upon execution, may become the purchaser thereof for his own benefit. Also, Barton *v.* Port Jackson & Union Falls P. R. Co. 17 Barb. 397; that the directors and stockholders of a Plank Road Company cannot waive the provisions of a statute, forbidding the directors to be concerned, directly or indirectly, in the building of the road. Bartlett *v.* Athenæum L. Ass. Soc., Q. B. 1856, 37 Eng. L. & Eq. 187.

[2] Verplanck *v.* Mercantile Insurance Company, 1 Edw. Ch. 87, per McCoun, Vice-Chancellor; Bayless *v.* Orne, 1 Freem. Missis. Ch. 174, 175; Hodges *v.* New England Screw Co. 1 R. I. 312.

[3] Verplanck *v.* Mercantile Insurance Company, 1 Edw. Ch. 87, per McCoun, Vice-Chancellor; Bayless *v.* Orne, 1 Freem. Missis. Ch. 174, 175; Hodges *v.* New England Screw Co. 1 R. I. 312.

[4] Ibid.

[5] Percy *v.* Millauden, 3 La. 568; Pontchartrain Railroad Company *v.* Paulding, 11 La. 41; Commercial Bank of Penn. *v.* Union Bank of New York, 1 Kern. 203.

[6] Austin *v.* Daniels, 4 Denio, 299.

be observed, however, that though loss accrue to the funds of an incorporated company, through a mere error on the part of the directors, though it be in a matter of law, they are not personally liable, unless there has been negligence or fraud. The remedy in case of loss by misjudgment merely, is to be found not in the courts, but in the corporation itself; in its power by new elections to confide its interests to other managers.[1] No man who takes upon himself an office of trust or confidence for another, or for the public, contracts for any thing more than a diligent attention to its concerns, and a faithful discharge of its duties. He is not supposed to have attained infallibility, and does not therefore stipulate that he is free from error.[2] In order to subject him, the error must be so gross as to warrant the imputation of fraud, or, at least, must indicate a want of the usual and necessary knowledge for the performance of the duty assumed by him in accepting the office or agency.[3] The directors of an incorporated company must take the same care, and use the same diligence, as factors or agents. They are answerable not only for their own fraud and gross negligence, but as they are usually interested in the stock, and act in relation to a bailment of the corporate funds to them, beneficial to both parties, they must answer for "ordinary neglect," or the omission of that care which every man of ordinary prudence takes of his own concerns.[4] Upon these principles, it is evident that in the appointment of officers and agents for the company, as a secretary, they do not become sureties for their fidelity and good behavior. If they select persons to fill subordinate situations, who are known to them to be unworthy of trust, or of notoriously bad character, and a loss by fraud or embezzlement ensues, a personal liability rests upon them. But if this be not the case, they have a right to repose confidence in their secretary in every thing within the scope of his duties.[5] Accordingly, where the secretary of an insurance company embezzled its funds, by altering checks and keeping back money received to be deposited; and whenever information was required,

---

[1] Vestry and Wardens of Christ Church *v.* Barksdale, 1 Strob. Eq. 197.

[2] Scott *v.* Depeyster, 1 Edw. Ch. 513; Vestry and Wardens of Christ Church *v.* Barksdale, 1 Strob. Eq. 197; Godbold *v.* Bank at Mobile, 11 Ala. 191; Hodges *v.* New England Screw Co. 1 R. I. 312, 3 R. I. 9.

[3] Godbold *v.* Bank at Mobile, 11 Ala. 191; Hodges *v.* New England Screw Co. 1 R. I. 312, 3 R. I. 9.

[4] Ibid.; Gratz *v.* Redd, 4 B. Mon. 178; Lexington Railroad Co. *v.* Bridges, 7 id. 559; Williams *v.* Gregg, 2 Strob. Eq. 316.

[5] Scott *v.* Depeyster, 1 Edw. Ch. 513.

produced forged bank books, the entries in the books of the company being regularly made, as if he had actually made the deposits, and had thus, from time to time, passed his accounts with committees appointed to examine them; and it appeared that the general conduct and investigation of the directors were the same pursued in other companies by prudent men; on a bill filed by a stockholder against the directors personally, it was held, that they were not liable on account of such fraud and embezzlement.[1] The rule would certainly be otherwise, however, if the directors had in any way sanctioned the breach of trust, or even by their neglect duly to examine into the doings of the agent, had enabled him to divert the funds of the corporation.[2] And where it was the duty of the president of a railroad company to take a bond for the security of the company from the secretary, which he neglected to do, he was held liable for the defalcations of the secretary to the amount of the bond, which it was his duty to take.[3]

§ 315. Indeed, whether we consider their mode of appointment or of action, their powers, rights, and liabilities, or the liabilities and rights of their constituents, by virtue of their acts or contracts, we can perceive no difference in principle or precedent, between the agents of corporations, and those of natural persons, unless expressly made by the act of incorporation or by-laws.

§ 316. With regard to the general right of a factor or agent of a corporation to maintain an action in his own name, on contracts made directly with him, or for injuries done to the property of the corporation in his possession, we can perceive no reason in principle for a distinction in this particular between him and the factor or agent of a natural person. Such a factor or agent, equally with the factor or agent of a natural person, could avail himself, in a case to which they apply, of the principles of commercial law applicable to merchants and their factors in this respect.[4] In general, however, where a contract is made through an agent with a corporation, the action must be brought in the name of the corporation,[5] and this will especially hold, as a matter of policy, in

---

[1] Scott *v.* Depeyster, 1 Edw. Ch. 513.

[2] Attorney-General *v.* Corporation of Leicester, 7 Beav. 176.

[3] Pontchartrain Railroad Company *v.* Paulding, 11 La. 41.

[4] Clay *v.* Southern, 7 Exch. 717, 14 Eng. L. & Eq. 533; see Goodall *v.* New England F. Ins. Co. 5 Fost. 169; Prot. Ins. Co. *v.* Wilson, 6 Ohio, State, 553.

[5] Binney *v.* Plumley, 5 Vt. 500; Commercial Bank *v.* French, 21 Pick. 486; Trustees

case of the agent of that greatest of all corporations, a State.[1] And where certain members of a turnpike corporation agreed in writing to pay to the agent of the corporation, or order, all assessments made by the corporation on their shares, it was held by the Supreme Court of Massachusetts, that no action could be maintained upon this undertaking in the name of the agent, but that it must be brought in the name of the corporation.[2]

§ 317. The agents of a corporation, like the agents of a natural person, are entitled, in legal presumption, to be paid for their services by the principal, the corporation, what they are reasonably worth. The officers of a corporation, who are to receive any compensation, are usually provided for by regular salaries. If there be no salary, and no particular contract, much must depend, as in other cases, upon the custom with regard to compensation for the particular services, and the expectation of the parties growing out of it. And even when an incorporated insurance company passed a vote, fixing the salary of its president at a certain sum per annum, and another president was subsequently elected, who claimed the salary fixed by that vote, as standing upon the ground of a written or record agreement with him, the court held the vote as only presumptive evidence of the amount of the president's salary, and that the presumption might be rebutted by proof that such was not the intention of the parties, but that when he was elected president, the active business of the corporation had been brought to a close, the services of a president had almost terminated, and that the purpose of his election was little more than to keep up a corporate organization.[3] Where the law required a bank to appoint a clerk, and the records showed his appointment, but did not show any fixed salary provided for him, it was held that he might recover for his services in assumpsit *quantum valebant*.[4] A railway company is not legally justified in dis-

---

v. Parks, 10 Maine, 441; Garland *v.* Reynolds, 20 Maine, 45; Alston *v.* Heartman, 2 Ala. 699. In case of a note made payable to "A. A., cashier," it was held, that the bank could sue in its own name thereon, by averring that the note was made to the corporation by the name and description of "A. A., cashier." McWalker *v.* Branch Bank of Mobile, 3 Ala. 153; Smith *v.* Branch at Mobile, 5 Ala. 28; Southern Life Insurance and Trust Co. *v.* Gray, 3 Fla. 262.

[1] Irish *v.* Webster, 5 Greenl. 172, 173.

[2] Worcester Turnpike Corporation *v.* Willard, 5 Mass. 80; Gilmore *v.* Pope, 5 Mass. 491; Taunton & South Boston Turnpike *v.* Whiting, 10 Mass. 336.

[3] Commonwealth Ins. Co. *v.* Crane, 6 Met. 64.

[4] Waller *v.* Bank of Kentucky, 3 J. J. Marsh. 206. And see Elmes *v.* Ogle, Exch.

missing a clerk without notice and without payment of his salary, because a letter was written by him, accusing the company of shuffling conduct; and the clerk was held entitled to set off his quarter's salary against a claim of the company for money received to its use.[1] Directors of corporations, and even of companies incorporated for the purpose of making profit, as banks, insurance, gas companies, and the like, are not usually compensated for their ordinary services as directors.[2] Thus, the directors of a gas company, in England, were not considered servants of the company, in such a sense as to be entitled to remuneration for their labor as directors, according to its value; and a resolution of the company, not valid under the act of incorporation, as a by-law, to allow them a stated compensation, was not considered a contract for compensation, even if, as a contract, it would have been available.[3] It was held, in Illinois, that the director of a bank, who received no compensation for his services, could not recover of the bank a reward offered by it for the recovery of money of which it was robbed, or the detection of the robber, on the ground that in affording such information to the bank, he performed nothing more than his duty, and so was entitled to no reward. One of the judges, however, with some reason, dissented.[4] The charters of banks sometimes provide expressly, "that no directors shall be entitled to any emolument, unless the same shall have been allowed by the stockholders at a general meeting."[5] Such a clause, however, is not construed to deprive directors of compensation for services rendered to the bank while they are directors, if they are not rendered in their capacity as such.[6] But where a director renders extra services to the

---

1850, 2 Eng. L. & Eq. 379, as to secondary evidence of the minute book, showing the resolution employing the clerk of a joint-stock distillery company, who brought his action against a director for his salary, the company having ceased working. The secretary of a railway company may maintain an action against it for work and labor done, although the amount of his remuneration has not, in accordance with statute provisions, been determined upon at a general meeting of the company. Bill *v.* Darenth Valley R. R. Co. 1 H. & N. 305, 37 Eng. L. & Eq. 539.

[1] East Anglian Railway Company *v.* Lythgoe, 10 C. B. 726, 2 Eng. L. & Eq. 331.

[2] New York & N. H. R. Co. *v.* Ketchum, 27 Conn. 170; Loan Association *v.* Stonemetz, 29 Penn. State, 534; Hodges *v.* Rut. & B. R. Co. 29 Vt. 220.

[3] Dunston *v.* Imperial Gas Company, 3 B. & Ad. 125.

[4] Stacy *v.* State Bank of Illinois, 4 Scam. 94, 95.

[5] Chandler *v.* Monmouth Bank, 1 Green, N. J. 255. The act of the State of Alabama of 1839, in prescribing the salary of the attorneys of the State Bank and its branches, applies only to the regular attorney in the different banks, elected by the directors, and does not inhibit the bank from engaging such other professional assistance as their interest may require. Bank of State of Alabama *v.* Martin, 4 Ala. 615.

[6] Chandler *v.* Monmouth Bank, 1 Green, N. J. 255; Henry *v.* R. & B. R. Co. 27 Vt. 435.

corporation, and presents no account, and makes no claim for compensation during eight years thereafter, and continues director during that time, he cannot recover on an implied promise to pay.[1] Sometimes, again, the charter fixes the amount of the salaries of its officers; and in such a case, where the charter fixes the salaries of *some* of its officers, *such* salaries cannot be changed by the corporation, although it is expressly empowered by charter to fix the salaries of its officers; this authority being construed to apply only to salaries not fixed by the charter.[2]

§ 318. A cashier of an insolvent bank has no lien, in New York, on the funds of the bank, for his salary, but must come in as an ordinary creditor.[3] A clergyman entered into a contract with a vestry, who were not legally elected, but were yet a vestry *de facto*, for a year's service, in ignorance of the illegality of the election, and without collusion, and having performed the service, was held entitled to recover of the church upon his contract.[4] In the ensuing year, the same clergyman entered into a contract with the same vestry, after he was apprised of the illegality of the election, and the court, upon the ground of collusion, decreed a perpetual injunction against any suit for services for that year.[5] A manufacturing corporation, whose duration was not limited by its charter, agreed with a stockholder, that, during the time for which the corporation was established, he should devote his whole time and skill to its service, in carrying on the business of the company, and be paid a yearly salary so long as he should perform such service; and that on his death, or refusal to perform the service, the corporation should be discharged from its obligation to employ him. The agent commenced his services under this agreement, but the business proving unprofitable, a majority of the stockholders, after the lapse of more than four years, voted to dissolve the corporation. The agent was accordingly dismissed,

[1] Utica Insurance Company *v.* Bloodgood, 3 Wend. 652. In Alabama it was held, that though the allowance to a bank director of compensation for extra services as an agent of the bank was unlawful, yet that it was not such an act of gross ignorance or breach of duty, as to expose the directors, who made the allowance in good faith, and with the honest intent of benefiting the bank, to personal liability. Godbold *v.* Bank at Mobile, 11 Ala. 191. The secretary of a private corporation, at a fixed salary, cannot recover extra pay for services in that capacity. Carr *v.* Chartiers Coal Co. 25 Penn. State, 337.

[2] Carr *v.* City of St. Louis, 9 Misso. 191.

[3] Bruyn *v.* Receiver, &c. 9 Cowen, 413, note.

[4] The Vestry of St. Luke's Church *v.* Matthews, 4 Des. Ch. 578.

[5] Ibid.

and the corporate property transferred to trustees, who were authorized to pay debts, and distribute the surplus amongst the stockholders, and notice was given to the governor, under the statute, that no further interest was claimed in the charter. Upon this state of facts, the court held that the agent was released from his obligation to serve the company, but that he was entitled to an indemnity for the loss sustained by its refusal to employ him.[1] Services rendered before the organization of a company, do not form a valid consideration for a vote of the directors, after the complete organization, to pay for them.[2]

§ 319. When a corporation has sustained loss by the fraud, embezzlement, or other misconduct of a corporate officer or agent of trust, it frequently becomes a question of great moment to it, whether the sureties on the bond, usually required as an indemnity against losses of this nature, are liable thereon. We have already briefly considered what species of security may in general be taken,[3] that its acceptance by the corporation may in proper cases be presumed,[4] and that the taking of such a bond is not, in general, necessary to the complete appointment of the officer required to give it;[5] and it now remains for us to present such further decisions upon this subject as its interesting nature demands. Where an act incorporating certain banks authorized the directors to make by-laws for the government of the banks, and made it the duty of the directors to take such security for the good behavior of the officers as the by-laws should prescribe; and a by-law of the directors declared that the cashier should give bond to the bank in a certain sum, with one or more sureties, to be approved by the board, and "the first book-keeper in six thousand dollars;" a bond given by two sureties, for the first book-keeper, and accepted by the board, was held binding upon the sureties, *although the book-keeper himself was not joined in the bond.*[6] Nor is a cashier's bond void, as against the policy of the law, because three of the directors, whose duty it was to examine and approve the cashier's bond, were themselves his sureties.[7] A bank was incorporated with power to appoint all necessary officers, to take bonds from them, and to

---

[1] Revere v. Boston Copper Company, 15 Pick. 351.

[2] New York & N. H. R. Co. v. Ketchum, 27 Conn. 170.

[3] See chap. on Contracts, supra, § 254.

[4] Ibid. § 252.

[5] See this chap. supra.

[6] Bank of Northern Liberties v. Cresson, 12 S. & R. 306; and see Greenfield v. Yeates, 2 Rawle, 158; Commonwealth v. Lamkin, 1 Watts & S. 263.

[7] Amherst Bank v. Root, 2 Met. 534, 535.

make all necessary by-laws, rules, and regulations. By one of the by-laws it was provided that it should be the duty of every other officer of the bank to perform such services as might be required of them by the president and cashier. In an action against the principal and sureties of a bond given by a book-keeper of a bank, conditioned for the faithful performance of the duties of his office, "*and of all other duties required of him in said bank*," the bond was adjudged to have been taken in conformity with the charter; and the book-keeper having, whilst in discharge "of the other duties required of him," taken large sums of money, the sureties were rendered liable on his bond.[1] A condition in a cashier's bond, "to account for, settle, and pay over, all money," &c., is equivalent to a condition "for good behavior;" and if it were not, a clause in the charter prescribing the latter condition is only enabling, and does not preclude the insertion of the former condition.[2] Where it is a cashier's duty to be sworn before entering on the performance of his official business, his bond is not avoided in favor of the sureties, by his omission to be sworn; but such omission is rather a breach of the condition of the bond, "to perform all the duties of cashier."[3] A bank, authorized to make by-laws, and to take bond from the cashier for the "faithful discharge of the duties of his office," may take a bond with condition that he shall perform the duties of his office according to law and the by-laws of the institution, and that he shall not make known any secrets, or the state of the funds, &c., to any person except the directors, &c.; and as these terms may be required of the cashier by the by-laws, they may be inserted in the bond.[4] A bond "well and truly to execute the duties of cashier or teller," or words tantamount, includes and secures not only honesty, but reasonable skill and diligence, on the part of such an officer. If, therefore, he perform the duties of his office negligently and unskilfully, or if he violate them for want of capacity, the condition of his bond is broken, and his sureties are liable for his misdoings.[5] In Union Bank *v.* Clossey,[6] the condition of a bond that a clerk in the bank "should well and faithfully perform the

---

1 Planters Bank *v.* Lamkin, R. M. Charlt. 29.

2 State Bank *v.* Locke, 4 Dev. 529. See Jones *v.* Wollam, 1 D. & R. 393, 5 B. & Ald. 769, 2 Chit. 322.

3 State Bank *v.* Chetwood, 3 Halst. 1.

4 Bank of Carlisle *v.* Hopkins, 1 T. B. Mon. 245.

5 Minor *v.* Mechanics Bank, 1 Pet. 46; State Bank *v.* Chetwood, 3 Halst. 25; Barrington *v.* Bank of Washington, 14 S. & R. 405; American Bank *v.* Adams, 12 Pick. 303; State Bank *v.* Trotter, 3 Dev. 535, 536; State Bank *v.* Locke, 4 Dev. 529.

6 10 Johns. 271.

duties assigned to, and the trust reposed in him, as first teller," was held to apply to his honesty, and not to his ability; and his sureties were declared not to be responsible for a loss arising from his mistake in paying a check. This decision is doubted in State Bank *v.* Trotter,[1] unless all that is meant is, that such a bond does not guaranty against *all* mistakes, or imply the utmost, and perfect, but only reasonable skill and diligence. It is agreed in such a case, that if the teller conceal deficiencies that at first arose from mistake, and make false entries in the books for the purpose of concealment, it is a breach of the bond, and that the sureties are liable for the loss sustained in consequence of such fraudulent conduct.[2] Such words clearly include, too, the omission of the plain duty of entering in the books of the bank a credit to a customer's account, by means of which omission the cashier escaped being charged for the sum, and retained the amount to his own use, until long afterwards found out.[3] A bond for the faithful performance of the duties of the office of teller or cashier, covers all defaults in the duties of such office annexed from time to time by those who are authorized to control the affairs of the bank; and the sureties enter into the contract in reference to the rights and authority of the president and directors, under the charter and by-laws.[4] Where a cashier exceeded his powers by changing the securities of the bank, his sureties were held liable; but the measure of damages, in a suit on the bond, was not the absolute amount of the securities, but the probable amount that would have accrued from them had they not been changed.[5] Where a statute prohibited any bank from issuing bills payable at any place except at the bank, and a cashier, upon receiving bills not proved to have been issued after the statute was passed, the bills having been paid and taken up by another bank at which they were made payable, put them again in circulation for his own use; this was held a breach of his bond for the faithful performance of his duties, for which his sureties were liable.[6] If a cashier permit a transfer of stock to be made to the bank beyond the amount permitted by the charter, he and his sureties are answerable to the stockholders on his bond for any loss caused thereby, although

[1] 3 Dev. 535, 536.
[2] Union Bank *v.* Clossey, 11 Johns. 182.
[3] State Bank *v.* Locke, 4 Dev. 529.
[4] Minor *v.* Mechanics Bank, 1 Pet. 46; Planters Bank *v.* Lamkin, R. M. Charlt. 29.
[5] Barrington *v.* Bank of Washington, 14 S. & R. 405.
[6] Dedham Bank *v.* Chickering, 4 Pick. 314.

such transfer was authorized by a resolution of the directors,[1] and so if he permit overdrafts without special excuse.[2] Indeed, no act or vote of the directors of a bank, contrary to their duties, and in fraud of stockholders' rights and interests, will excuse the cashier or his sureties from a violation of the stipulation in his bond, well and truly to execute the duties of his office.[3] Where it was the duty of a cashier to forward to the State treasurer the duties on dividends declared by the bank, he and his sureties were held answerable on his bond for his omission so to do, to the amount of the injury thereby necessarily sustained by the bank.[4] A cashier who receives money for deposit out of the bank, and not in banking hours, or receives its funds at places distant from the bank, and does not account for them, is, together with his sureties, liable therefor on his official bond.[5] And when he applies the notes of the bank to his own use, he is liable for the full nominal amount, and cannot avail himself of their depreciation.[6] The surety on the bond of a clerk of a banking house was held liable for carelessly losing money sent by him, specially deputed to receive it, from a customer to the banker, although the jury found that the transaction was out of the ordinary course of banking business in the part of the country in which the transaction occurred.[7] Where a cashier, before his reappointment to office, had misapplied the funds of the bank, and after his reappointment borrowed money, as cashier, and placed it in the bank, to conceal his delinquency, and afterwards repaid the money so borrowed out of the funds of the bank, and was dismissed as a defaulter, the sureties on his last bond were held answerable; as the money that he so placed in bank became the property of the bank, and his subsequent conduct, in using its funds, was a breach of the condition of his bond.[8] Where the landlord of a public house had given a bond to deliver to the committee of a Friendly Society its club box, at all times, when required by a majority of the society, at one of their annual or quarterly meetings, "or by their committee for the time being," and likewise to render a just and true account,

---

1 Bank of Washington v. Barrington, 2 Penn. 27.

2 Bank of St. Mary's v. Calder, 3 Strobh. Law, 408.

3 Minor v. Mechanics Bank, 1 Pet. 46.

4 Bank of Washington v. Barrington, 2 Penn. 27.

5 Pendleton v. Bank of Kentucky, 1 T. B. Mon. 177; Melville v. Doidge, 6 C. B. 454.

6 Pendleton v. Bank of Kentucky, 1 T. B. Mon. 177.

7 Melville v. Doidge, 6 C. B. 450.

8 Ingraham v. Maine Bank, 13 Mass. 208.

"according to the rules, orders, and regulations of the society, and of the said act of parliament, and of the said bond," the latter words were held not to qualify the power of the committee to demand the box, &c., and a refusal to comply with their request to do so was deemed a breach of the condition of the bond, it having been shown that the committee had been duly elected by a majority of the society at their annual meeting.[1]

§ 320. A cashier's bond, with condition "safely to keep all moneys," &c., does not render the obligor responsible for money violently robbed from him while in the discharge of his duty.[2] Where a bond was given by an assistant of a bank, for the faithful discharge of the duties of his office, the sureties on the bond were not held responsible for moneys taken by their principal, and from the teller's drawer, without his consent or knowledge, the accountant not being intrusted with any moneys of the bank, nor put in possession of them as accountant; or, in other words, were not held responsible for his thefts.[3] Neither were the sureties held responsible for the cashier's embezzlements of new bills, made by consent of the directors, and intended to be privately kept and and surreptitiously issued by him, in direct violation of law; such bills not being intended to make a part of the ostensible funds of the bank, nor entered on the books, nor noticed in the half-yearly returns to the governor and council;[4] nor were the sureties for the fidelity of an agent of an insurance company held liable for an embezzlement by the agent, of the funds of the corporation intrusted to his care whilst engaged in the unlawful business of banking for the corporation.[5] Nor are a cashier's sureties liable on his bond, for his not accounting to the bank for their money collected by him as an attorney at law;[6] nor for faults in the collecting department given in charge by the directors to another officer;[7] nor for his surreptitiously conveying his shares in the bank to a third person, by means of blank certificates signed by the president, and deposited in the cashier's hands, though he had previously pledged

---

1 Wybergh *v.* Ainley, McClel. 669.

2 Huntsville Bank *v.* Hill, 1 Stew. Ala. 201.

3 Alison *v.* Farmers Bank, 6 Rand. 204.

4 Dedham Bank *v.* Chickering, 4 Pick. 314.

5 Blair *v.* Perpetual Insurance Co. 10 Misso. 561.

6 Dedham Bank *v.* Chickering, 4 Pick. 314.

7 Bank of State of Alabama *v.* Comegys, 12 Ala. 772.

the shares to the bank as security for the payment of his note.[1] In such case, however, it was held that the bank might apply, towards the payment of the cashier's notes, a balance standing on its books in his favor, instead of applying it for the sureties' benefit, in reducing damages for breach of the bond.[2]

§ 321. The culpable neglect of the directors and agents of a bank to make frequent examinations of the affairs of the bank, to count the money, and generally to watch over its concerns, according to the direction of the by-laws, is no defence to the sureties in a suit on an official bond. The negligence of one agent, or set of agents, cannot deprive the corporation of its remedy for the default of another agent.[3] In order to charge a cashier's sureties it is not necessary to give them notice of his defaults; and retaining him in office after knowledge of his defalcation, does not excuse his sureties from liability for *previous* defaults.[4] But if the law require his removal for ascertained delinquency, and the managers of the bank retain him in service after knowing such cause of removal, and connive at his misconduct, his sureties are not liable for any breach of his bond which took place subsequent to the discovery of his misdoings.[5] Knowledge of the cashier's delinquency, and connivance at it on the part of the directors of the branch at which he is cashier, will not, it seems, avail in defence against a suit on his bond by the principal bank; as it is not a legal presumption that what is known to the branches, is communicated to the principal bank.[6]

§ 322. Where the bond itself limits the period of the liability of the

---

[1] Dedham Bank *v.* Chickering, 4 Pick. 314.

[2] Ibid.

[3] Amherst Bank *v.* Root, 2 Met. 541, questioning the view taken by Sup. Court of N. Y. in People *v.* Jansen, 7 Johns. 332.

[4] State Bank *v.* Chetwood, 3 Halst. 28. Where the bond of a cashier is given to secure a bank against previous delinquencies, the fact that he is already a defaulter, known to the president and directors, but not communicated to the surety, will discharge the surety. Fraudulently procuring to such a bond the name of one surety will not excuse his co-surety, unless the signature of the former were a condition of that of the latter. Franklin Bank *v.* Stevens, 39 Me. 532; Franklin Bank *v.* Cooper, id. 542. Failure to communicate to the surety on an official bond the existence of a balance on account against his principal, will not affect the surety's liability, if such indebtedness does not necessarily imply any default or misconduct of the principal. Guardians of the Stokesley Union *v.* Strother, Q. B. 1854, 24 Eng. L. & Eq. 183.

[5] Taylor *v.* Bank of Kentucky, 2 J. J. Marsh, 568.

[6] Ibid.

sureties, there can be no question concerning it. And though the bond contain no express limitation of this kind, if it recite the duration of the principal's agency or office, such recital showing that the parties must have contracted with a view to that period, it was long since settled, and upon the maturest consideration, that the sureties are not responsible for the conduct of the principal beyond it, as upon a new appointment; even though the bond stipulate for "all the time the principal shall continue" in his office or agency.[1] Again, though the bond do not recite the term of the office or agency, if it be one of limited duration, by general statute, charter, by-law, or terms of appointment, the parties are still supposed to contract with a reference to the limited term, and the sureties will not be held answerable for the misconduct of the principal beyond that term, upon a new appointment, even though the *words* of the bond are that they shall be responsible for the principal, "*at all times*, or any time hereafter."[2] If, on the other hand, the office or agency be not of limited duration, but at pleasure, or until removal, unless the bond otherwise stipulate, the sureties are bound while the principal continues in office, even though there may have been unnecessary reëlections.[3] And where a statute provided that

---

[1] Lord Arlington *v.* Merricke, 2 Saund. 404; Liverpool Water Works Co. *v.* Atkinson, 6 East, 507. A change in the salary or mode of remuneration of an officer will discharge the sureties on his bond. Northwestern Railway Co. *v.* Whinray, 10 Exch. 77, 26 Eng. L. & Eq. 488.

[2] The Wardens of St. Saviour's Southwark *v.* Bostock, 2 New R. 174; Hasel *v.* Long, 2 M. & S. 363; Peppin *v.* Cooper, 2 B. & Ald. 431; Barker *v.* Parker, 1 T. R. 295; Anderson *v.* Longden, 1 Wheat. 91; United States *v.* Kirkpatrick, 9 Wheat. 720; Union Bank of Maryland *v.* Ridgely, 1 Harris & G. 413, 420; Dedham Bank *v.* Chickering, 3 Pick. 341; Bigelow *v.* Bridge, 8 Mass. 275; Exeter Bank *v.* Rogers, 7 N. H. 33; Bamford *v.* Iles, 3 Exch. 380; Kitson *v.* Julian, 4 Ellis & B. 854, 30 Eng. L. & Eq. 326. In the Mayor, &c. of Berwick-upon-Tweed *v.* Oswald, 1 Ellis & B. 295, 16 Eng. L. & Eq. 236, s. c. 3 Ellis & B. 653, 26 Eng. L. & Eq. 85, it appeared that one Murray had been elected by the council treasurer of the borough of Berwick-upon-Tweed. The condition of his official bond was that he and his sureties should be bound for the due payment, &c., "during the whole time of his continuing in the said office, in consequence of the said election, or under any annual or other future election of the said council to the said office." Murray became a defaulter, but not till after a reëlection under the provisions of a statute changing his office from an annual one to one holden during pleasure. Held, that this change in the tenure of the office was contemplated and provided for in the terms of the bond, and did not therefore exempt the sureties from liability. In Chelmsford Co. *v.* Demarest, 7 Gray, 1, the statute, after directing that the clerk and treasurer should be chosen annually, added, that they should hold their offices until others were chosen, and qualified in their stead. It was held, that a surety on a bond of an officer so chosen, was not liable for the acts of the officer committed after the next annual election, although no successor was then elected.

[3] Curling *v.* Chalklen, 3 M. & S. 502; Anderson *v.* Longden, 1 Wheat. 85; Dedham

a cashier should retain his place until removed therefrom, or another should be appointed in his stead, the Supreme Court of Massachusetts held the sureties liable on an official bond of the cashier, the terms of which were general, for his defaults in the years 1836 and 1837, though the bond was given on his appointment in the year 1831, as it appeared from the corporate records, "for the year ensuing," the cashier continuing to hold over.[1] The giving and acceptance of a new bond, upon a reappointment, discharges the sureties on the old bond from liability for unfaithfulness in office after the reappointment and the giving and accepting of the new bond.[2] Where a bank charter limits the duration of a bank to a certain period, and a bond is given to secure the cashier's good conduct, the bond must have the same limitation; and the surety is not liable for a breach of it by the cashier after that period, though the charter be extended by the legislature beyond the first limitation.[3] In Exeter Bank *v.* Rogers,[4] however, the same question arose, and was decided against the sureties; the learned and ingenious counsel for the bank, amongst other points, taking a distinction between cases where the charter had expired before renewal, and those where the charter was renewed before expiry, which was the case before him. The court do not, however, advert to this distinction in their opinion; but profess to go on the general ground, that, where the office is held at the will of those who appoint to it, if nothing appear to the contrary, the bond is presumed to be intended to cover all the time the person appointed shall continue in office under his appointment, and that the extension of the charter by the proper authorities may fairly be presumed to enter into the contemplation of the parties, at the time of giving a bond of continuing, and, in point of time, unlimited obligation.[5] It would be difficult to reconcile this decision with the cases in Maryland

---

Bank *v.* Chickering, 3 Pick. 335; Union Bank *v.* Ridgely, 1 Harris & G. 413, 429; Exeter Bank *v.* Rogers, 7 N. H. 33.

[1] Amherst Bank *v.* Root, 2 Met. 535, 540, Dewey, J., dissenting on the ground that it was competent for the directors to limit the office to one year, and that they had done so by their votes, and therefore that the office was annual.

[2] Frankfort Bank *v.* Johnson, 23 Maine, 322. See Bruce *v.* United States, 17 How. 437; that upon an agent's reappointment to office, the sureties on his last bond are liable for his misappropriation of funds, received by him during his first term of office.

[3] Union Bank of Maryland *v.* Ridgely, 1 Harris & G. 413, 429; Thompson *v.* Young, 2 Ham. 334; and see Barker *v.* Parker, 1 T. R. 295.

[4] 7 N. H. 33.

[5] Ibid. per Richardson, C. J.

and Ohio,[1] either upon the distinction above adverted to, or any other, or with the general current of authorities respecting the obligations of sureties. Where a charter was forfeited by a cashier's omission to forward to the State treasurer the duties on dividends declared by the bank, as required by law, and, by a subsequent statute, the charter "was revived, and continued in as full force and ample a manner as if no forfeiture had taken place," it was adjudged that his sureties were not liable for his defaults which occurred after the passing of that statute.[2] Where a bank, pursuant to its by-laws, required the cashier to renew his bond, and the order requiring the renewal provided that the previous bond should not be impaired, until given up to be cancelled, the first bond, remaining uncancelled, was held to be in force as security to the bank, until the second was executed.[3] In a suit against the principal of the bond, at least, such a bond is not affected by an increase of the capital of the bank merely; since the cashier's duties are no more altered or increased by such augmentation of the capital, than by an increase of the deposits.[4] Indeed, it was held in a recent case in England, that neither the responsibility of the principal or sureties on the bond of the chief clerk of a railway company, was discharged by the consolidation of the railway company of which he was clerk with another railway company, under an act for that purpose, notwithstanding the new company formed by the consolidation possessed additional lines of road.[5] A cashier's sureties were held liable, until the time of his being discharged from office, though the order for his discharge (which was given upon the discovery of his breach of trust) was received on Sunday morning, and was not executed until the afternoon of the next day.[6] When the time of limitation of a suit on a cashier's bond is two years after the cause of action accrued, the time, it seems, begins to run not from the time of actual deficit, but from the time the officer failed to pay over, according to his bond, on his quitting office.[7]

§ 323. A misnomer of the corporation in the official bond of a

---

1 Union Bank *v.* Ridgely, 1 Harris & G. 413, 429; Thompson *v.* Young, 2 Ham. 334.

2 Bank of Washington *v.* Barrington, 2 Penn. 27.

3 Pendleton *v.* Bank of Kentucky, 1 T. B. Mon. 175.

4 Bank of Wilmington & Brandywine *v.* Wollaston, 3 Harring. Del. 90.

5 London, &c. R. Co. *v.* Goodwin, 3 Exch. 320; Eastern Union Railway Co. *v.* Cochrane, 9 Exch. 197, 24 Eng. L. & Eq. 495.

6 M'Gill *v.* Bank of United States, 12 Wheat. 511, 1 Paine, C. C. 661.

7 Bank of Wilmington *v.* Wollaston, 3 Harring. Del. 90.

cashier, by the omission of the words "and company," does not vitiate the bond.[1] Where, in debt on such a bond, the defendant, on oyer, set forth a bond which recited, that "C. is cashier," he was estopped from denying the fact of C.'s being cashier, properly appointed and qualified for all the purposes of the suit.[2] In assigning a breach of such a bond, it is sufficient to allege that the principal obligor has received money for which he has not accounted.[3]

§ 324. In a suit against an officer of a corporation on his official bond, the by-laws of the corporation are evidence against him to show that he knew what his duties were as prescribed by the by-laws.[4] An error against the bank, in the addition of a column of figures by the cashier, is *prima facie* evidence of a loss to the bank to the amount of such error; and the cashier and his sureties are liable therefor, unless they show that the loss did not in fact accrue.[5] The admissions of a cashier, made while in office, that he had misapplied the funds of the bank, are, it seems, evidence of the fact against his sureties.[6] As a cashier has not, *ex officio*, authority to accept a draft on a bank, unless the drawer have funds there, evidence is not admissible, in a suit against a surety on his bond, that the cashier, in his individual capacity, drew a draft on the bank, and having accepted it as cashier for the bank, and sold it, that the purchaser transmitted it to him to be passed, to the purchaser's credit.[7] Where it was assigned as a breach of a cashier's bond, that the cashier had received money for which he had not accounted, evidence that he had the character of an honest, careful, and vigilant officer, and that similar losses by bank officers are frequent, and that the directors have expressed their belief that the loss in question was caused by accidental overpayments, and that after the loss they continued to employ him, is not sufficient to sustain a rejoinder averring that the loss was by accidental overpayments.[8] It would seem that such a rejoinder, if proved, would be insufficient.[9] In debt on a cash-

---

1 Pendleton *v.* Bank of Kentucky, 1 T. B. Mon. 175; and see chap. on Contracts, § 324.

2 State Bank *v.* Chetwood, 3 Halst. 1.

3 American Bank *v.* Adams, 12 Pick. 303.

4 Bank of Wilmington *v.* Wollaston, 3 Harring. Del. 90.

5 Bank of Washington *v.* Barrington, 2 Penn. 27.

6 Pendleton *v.* Bank of Kentucky, 1 T. B. Mon. 177.

7 Ibid.

8 American Bank *v.* Adams, 12 Pick. 303.

9 Minor *v.* Mechanics Bank, 1 Pet. 46; State Bank *v.* Chetwood, 3 Halst. 1; Barring-

ier's bond, which stipulated that he should "account for all moneys received by him," the plaintiffs replied to a general plea of performance, that he had received divers sums of money, at divers times, to a certain amount, for which he had not accounted; and the rejoinder alleged that he had accounted for all the moneys by him received. In this state of the pleadings, it was held that the defendant was bound to show that the cashier had accounted for the sum mentioned in the replication.[1] Where, in a suit on such a bond, issue was taken on the averment that certain false and deceptive entries were made by the clerks in the books of the bank, with the connivance of the cashier, such books, on proof that they were kept by the clerks, and that the entries were in their handwriting, are evidence for the purpose of laying a foundation for other testimony by which to show the cashier's fraud.[2]

CHAPTER X.

OF THE BY-LAWS OF CORPORATIONS.

§ 325. WHEN a corporation is duly erected, the law tacitly annexes to it the power of making by-laws, or private statutes, for its government and support.[3] This power is included in the very act of incorporation;[4] for, as is quaintly observed by Blackstone, "as natural reason is given to the natural body for governing of it, so by-laws or statutes are a sort of political reason to govern the body politic."[5] Though the power to make by-laws is unquestionably an incident to the very existence of a corporation, it is rarely left to implication; but is usually conferred by the express terms of the charter. And where the charter

---

ton *v.* Bank of Washington, 14 S. & R. 405; State Bank *v.* Locke, 4 Dev. 529; State Bank *v.* Trotter, 3 Dev. 535, 536; but see Union Bank *v.* Clossey, 10 Johns. 271.

[1] Exeter Bank *v.* Rogers, 6 N. H. 142.

[2] Union Bank *v.* Ridgely, 1 Harris & G. 327.

[3] Norris *v.* Staps, Hob. 211; By-laws, 3 Salk. 76; City of London *v.* Vanacre, 1 Ld. Raym. 496; The case of Sutton's Hospital, 10 Co. R. 31 a.

[4] Norris *v.* Staps, Hob. 211.

[5] 1 Bl. Com. 476.

enables a company to make by-laws in certain cases and for certain purposes, its power of legislation is limited to the cases and objects specified, all others being excluded by implication.[1] But when so made, they are equally as binding on all their members and others acquainted with their method of doing business as any public law of the State.[2]

§ 326. This principle is undoubtedly correct; but the case in reference to which it was advanced was that of the Hudson's Bay Company, who were empowered by charter to make by-laws for the better government of the company, and for the management and direction of their business to Hudson's Bay; "which," it was said, "implied a negative that they should not make any *other* by-laws; much less could they make by-laws in relation to projects of insurance, which by acts of parliament were declared to be illegal."[3] It is apprehended, however, that if this company had not been thus *impliedly* forbidden to make by-laws on any subject which did not relate to their trade to Hudson's Bay, unless the power of legislating on other matters had been expressly conferred upon them, their legislation would be confined to the object of their incorporation.[4] The *incidental* power of a corporation to make by-laws results from the necessity of such a power, to enable the body politic to answer the purposes for which it was created, and can be applied to nothing else; and though the power is conferred by the express terms of the charter, yet the reasonable construction of this particular grant is to consider it as a means to the company for the accomplishment of the purposes of the principal grant of incorporation, and of course to be limited in its exercise to those purposes.[5]

§ 327. Unless by the charter, or some general statute to which the charter is made subject, or by immemorial usage, this power is delegated to particular officers or members of the corporation, like every other incidental power, it resides in the members of the corporation at large, to be exercised by them in the same manner in which the charter may direct them to exercise other powers or transact their general business; and if the charter contain no such direction, to be exercised according

---

1 Per Ld. Macclesfield, Ch., Child *v.* Hudson's Bay Co. 2 P. Wms. 207. See 2 Kyd on Corp. 102.

2 Cummings *v.* Webster, 43 Me. 192.

3 Child *v.* Hudson's Bay Co. 2 P. Wms. 209.

4 Rex *v.* Spencer, 3 Burr. 1837; 2 Kyd on Corp. 102.

5 Kearney *v.* Andrews, 2 Stock. 70.

to the rules of the common law.[1] The power of making by-laws is, however, frequently reposed in a select body, as the directors; in which case a majority of that body, at least, is necessary, and is sufficient to constitute a quorum for the purpose of passing a by-law.[2] And where the general power of making by-laws is vested by charter in a select body, a by-law made by that select body, in conjunction with persons of another select description, is void. Thus, where the inhabitants of a town were incorporated by the name of the bailiffs and burgesses, and there were twelve capital burgesses, and twelve common burgesses, besides common freemen, but the power of making by-laws was vested in the bailiffs and *capital* burgesses only; and the bailiffs and *all* the burgesses, including *capital* and *common* burgesses, made a by-law; this was one reason given for holding the law void.[3] So where by charter the power of making by-laws was *expressly* given to the mayor and aldermen of a city; and they, *with the assent of the commonalty*, made a by-law, which altered the constitution of the corporation, Lord Mansfield said, *the body at large* had no power to make by-laws, because that power was given by the charter to a *select* body.[4] This holds true, unless certain rights, as those of electing officers and members, remain in the body at large; in which case, as incident to the right of election, they have the power of making by-laws for regulating the manner in which that right shall be exercised;[5] and especially if the power of the select body is derived from a new charter, in derogation of the ancient right of the body at large, to make by-laws in all cases.[6] Where the power of making by-laws is confided to a select body, as mayor and aldermen, if a by-law, purporting to be made by mayor, aldermen, *and burgesses*, be found by the verdict "to be in due manner made," it will not be assumed that the burgesses joined in making this by-law, which would avoid it; but that the mayor and aldermen alone, acting in pursuance of their authority, made it in the name of the mayor, aldermen, and burgesses.[7] There are sometimes found, in the ancient municipal

---

[1] Union Bank of Maryland *v.* Ridgely, 1 Harris & G. 324; Rex *v.* Westwood, 2 Dow & C. 21.

[2] *Ex parte* Willcocks, 7 Cowen, 402; Cahill *v.* Kalamazoo Ins. Co. 2 Doug. Mich. 124.

[3] Parry *v.* Berry, Comyns, 269.

[4] Rex *v.* Head, 4 Burr. 2515, 2521; and see Hoblyn *v.* Regem, 6 Bro. P. C. 519; Rex *v.* Westwood, 4 B. & C. 799, 818; Bedford *v.* Fox, 1 Lutw. 564.

[5] Ibid.

[6] Rex *v.* Westwood, 4 B. & C. 800, 813, 7 D. & R. 273, 2 Dow & C. 21, 4 Bligh, N. S. 213, 7 Bing. 1.

[7] Greene *v.* Durham, 1 Burr. 131.

corporations of England, bodies of servants or deputies of the corporation, possessed, by immemorial usage, of exclusive rights, and, from the same source of power, a right to pass regulations binding upon the members of the body, in the exercise of them. The deputy day oyster meters of the city of London, having the exclusive right, by usage, of shovelling, unloading, and delivering oysters, are such a body; and, by usage, possess the power of making by-laws to regulate the rights and duties of their members. A by-law of this body, proved to exist by immemorial usage, that the moneys received for the shovelling, unloading, and delivering of oysters, should be equally divided amongst all the members, was enforced against two of their number, in equity, by a bill for an account, notwithstanding the committee of appointment of the city of London made the non-observance by them of this by-law the condition of the appointment to office of the two defendant members.[1]

§ 328. If the charter prescribe the mode in which the by-laws shall be made and adopted, in order to their validity, that mode must be strictly pursued. Thus, where a gas-light company was empowered to make by-laws *under seal* for its government, and for regulating the proceedings of the directors, officers, and servants, and at a meeting of the company a resolution was passed, *not under seal*, allowing each director for his attendance on courts, committees, &c., one guinea for each time of attendance, it was decided not to be a by-law within the statute.[2] But where the charter is silent upon this point, since it is now well settled that a corporation aggregate may act without seal or writing, and is open to the same implications as an individual, it may adopt by-laws as well by its own acts and conduct, and the acts and conduct of its officers, as by an express vote, or an adoption manifested by writing. In the case of Union Bank of Maryland *v.* Ridgely,[3] where it appeared that, by charter, the president and directors of the bank were authorized to make all such by-laws and regulations for the government of the corporation, its officers and members, as they or a majority of them should from time to time think fit; upon a certain writing being given in evidence, headed "By-Laws," and which purported to have been

---

[1] Thompson *v.* Daniel, 10 Hare, 296, 21 Eng. L. & Eq. 93, 99, 100, 101.

[2] Dunston *v.* Imperial Gas Company, 3 B. & Ad. 125.

[3] 1 Harris & G. 324; and see Taylor *v.* Griswold, 2 Green, N. J. 223; and Fairfield Turnpike Co. *v.* Thorp, 13 Conn. 173.

the by-laws of the bank, while its business was transacted under articles of association, and before the act incorporating it was passed, it was objected that there was no evidence that the writing produced had been adopted as the by-laws of the corporation, there being no entry or memorandum of such adoption among the minutes of its proceedings. The Court of Appeals in Maryland, however, decided, that the authority to make by-laws being specially delegated to the president and directors, without the mode of exercising it being prescribed by the charter, it was no more necessary that their adoption should be in writing, than the acts or contracts of any other duly authorized agents; and it being proved by the cashier, that the by-laws in question were always reputed to be the by-laws of the corporation, and, with the exception of two articles, were so observed by him; and by a director, that they were delivered to him as such upon his election, and that decisions by the board of directors were made agreeably to them in any question upon their conduct; this was held a sufficient adoption of the by-laws by the president and directors, and sufficient proof of the same, there being no record or minute of the fact. In the case of The King *v.* Ashwell,[1] in a plea to an information in the nature of a *quo warranto*, it was stated, among other things, that, on the 5th of May, 1577, the mayor and burgesses of Nottingham duly made a certain reasonable *by-law not now extant in writing* (and, after reciting the by-law), to which by-law the mayor and burgesses for the time being, from the time of making thereof hitherto, have consented and conformed themselves, and the same is now in force and unrepealed. The replication took, among other issues, one "that the mayor and burgesses did not make such a by-law;" yet a verdict was found for the defendant, although the only evidence of the making and terms of the by-law must have been in the long-continued and invariable usage of the corporation.

§ 329. It need hardly be mentioned, that the same body in a corporation which has a power to make, has the power to repeal, by-laws; it being of the very nature of legislative power, that by timely changes in the rule it prescribes, it should be enabled to meet the exigencies of the occasion.[2] As a court will direct a jury to find a by-law, its terms, and

---

[1] 12 East, 22; and see Rex *v.* Westwood, 4 B. & C. 786, 7 D. & R. 273.

[2] King *v.* Ashwell, 12 East, 22; Rex *v.* Westwood, 4 B. & C. 806. In the absence of any precedent, the court refused a rule *nisi* for a mandamus calling on the mayor of a town to propose a resolution to the burgesses in guild assembled, for repealing certain by-

adoption, from the usage and conduct of the corporation and its officers, so, from non-observance of one, will it presume a subsequent by-law to repeal and alter it. Thus, on an information before Lord Chancellor Hardwicke, against the master and governors of a school, in which the first and principal relief prayed was to remove the master, as not qualified by the statutes of the foundation; it not appearing that the statutes had been observed in any one instance, his lordship said, "that he must presume a repeal of them."[1]

§ 330. Eleemosynary corporations are distinguished from others in this, that they have no incidental power of legislation. They are the mere creatures of their founder, and he alone has a right to prescribe the regulations, according to which his charity shall be applied. His statutes are accordingly their laws, which they have no power to alter, modify, or amend.[2] A delay to make them for a few years after the foundation, does not affect the right or power to make them.[3] He cannot, however, by his statutes, alter the constitution of the charity as fixed in the charter granted to him; but may do what is necessary, by regulation, for the maintenance of the charity he has founded. And where a charter provided that the corporation shall consist of one master, one warden, and four fellows, but no mode of electing them was prescribed by it, statutes creating a body of six assistants, "touching the ordering of the college and the rents, revenues, and profits thereof," and giving them a vote in the election of master, were not deemed in derogation of the charter, especially as the right of the assistants to vote was aided by usage in the construction of it.[4] And after a body of statutes has been given by the founder, it is held that neither he, nor his successor as visitor, can add to or alter them, without an express reservation of power to that effect.[5] Where the college has consented

---

laws, though it was alleged that by-laws and ordinances might by charter be made, and had formerly been made, at such guilds. Garrett *v.* Newcastle, 3 B. & Ad. 252.

[1] Attorney-General *v.* Middleton, 2 Ves. Sen. 328; see too, Berwick-upon-Tweed *v.* Johnson, Lofft. 338.

[2] Phillips *v.* Bury, 1 Ld. Raym. 8, per Holt, C. J., Comb. 265, Holt. 715, 1 Show. 360, 4 Mod. 106, Skin. 447, 2 T. R. 352; Bentley *v.* Bishop of Ely, Fitzgib. 305, Stra. 912; St. John's College, Cambridge, *v.* Todington, 1 Burr. 201; Green *v.* Rutherforth, 1 Ves. Sen. 462; Trustees of Phillips Academy *v.* King, 12 Mass. 546; Dartmouth College *v.* Woodward, 4 Wheat. 660.

[3] Regina *v.* The Master, &c. of God's Gift in Dulwich, 17 Q. B. 600, 8 Eng. L. & Eq. 398.

[4] Ibid. 385, 398.

[5] Bentley *v.* Bishop of Ely, Stra. 913; Phillips *v.* Bury, Skin. 513; Green *v.* Ruther-

to receive a set of new statutes, given by *the founder*, we see, with Mr. Kyd,[1] no good reason why they should not be bound by them, even though there be no such reservation; but the practice of a college acting under a set of new statutes given by the *successor* of the founder or visitor, unless he be authorized to give them, has always been disapproved by the courts;[2] and upon sound policy; since one of the great inducements to his donation on the part of the founder, may have been the hope that his charity would always flow in the channel, and according to the rules, which he should prescribe. Where a new donation is made to, or a new fellowship ingrafted on an existing eleemosynary corporation, it is subject to the statutes or rules of the old foundation, unless the new founder prescribe rules of his own.[3] The power of making new statutes, and of altering and amending the old, may be, however, and frequently is, given to the governors, trustees, &c. of the corporation.[4] Where the words "*shall and may*" are used in a general act, or in the constitution of a private charity, they are to be construed imperatively, in the same manner as the word "*must;*" as, if the founder's constitution of the charity declare, that if certain officers are found guilty of immorality, drunkenness, or any debauchery, the governors and visitors "*shall and may* remove them;" an obligation to remove for these causes is imposed.[5]

§ 331. From the total non-observance of the statutes of a private foundation, a repeal of them has been presumed.[6]

§ 332. The law of the country, being as well a rule for the proceed-

---

forth, 1 Ves. Sen. 472, 473, 474, per Ld. Hardwicke; Attorney-General *v.* Earl of Clarendon, 17 Ves. 500; St. John's College, Cambridge, *v.* Todington, 1 Burr. 201, per Ld. Mansfield. See also, Dartmouth College *v.* Woodward, 4 Wheat. 676, opinion of Story, J.; 2 Kent, Com. 302.

[1] Kyd on Corp. 103.

[2] Bentley *v.* Bishop of Ely, Stra. 913; Green *v.* Rutherford, 1 Ves. 472; Phillips *v.* Bury, Skin. 513; St. John's College, Cambridge, *v.* Todington, 1 Burr. 201.

[3] Case of University of Oxford, cited 1 Burr. 203; Attorney-General *v.* Talbot, 1 Ves. 79, 3 Atk. 674; Green *v.* Rutherford, 1 Ves. 467, 468, 472; St. John's College, Cambridge, *v.* Todington, 1 Burr. 202, 203, 204.

[4] Eden *v.* Foster, 2 P. Wms. 325; Green *v.* Rutherforth, 1 Ves. Sen. 472, per Ld. Hardwicke; Attorney-General *v.* Locke, case of Morden College, 3 Atk. 164; Attorney-General *v.* Earl of Clarendon, 17 Ves. 491; Trustees of Phillips Academy *v.* King, 12 Mass. 547.

[5] Attorney-General *v.* Locke, case of Morden College, 3 Atk. 166, per Ld. Hardwicke.

[6] Attorney-General *v.* Middleton, 2 Ves. 330.

ings of corporations, as for the conduct of natural persons, all by-laws of a corporation contrary to the Constitution of the United States, and the Acts of Congress in pursuance of it, to the Constitution and valid statutes of the State in which it is established, and to the common law as it is accepted there, are consequently void.

§ 333. As neither a State, nor the general government, can transcend the powers conferred upon them by their constitutions, so a corporation, acting by the grant of either, must of course be bound by that supreme law which limits even the power that created it a corporation. In England, if a by-law be contrary to the general laws of the kingdom, it is void, though justified by the terms of the charter; for all by-laws, says Hobart, must ever be subject to the general law of the realm, and subordinate to it; and if the king, in his letters-patent of incorporation, make ordinances himself, they are subject to the same rule of law.[1] So neither a State, nor the general government, can grant legislative powers larger than they possess themselves; and hence, however unlimited in this particular may be the terms of its charter, all by-laws of a corporation contrary to the constitutional law of the land, must be void. For this reason, a by-law "impairing the obligation of contracts," or taking "private property for public use, without just compensation," is void.[2] But where a statute authorized the corporation of a city to make by-laws "regulating," or, if necessary, "*preventing*, the interment of the dead," within the limits of the city, it was held, that though that corporation had granted lands for the purpose of interment, and had covenanted that they should be quietly enjoyed for that purpose, yet, that it was not thereby estopped from passing a by-law forbidding such interment under a penalty. This case was decided on the ground, that the legislative power of the corporation over this subject was delegated to it for the good of the city, and that the law passed was to be regarded as if passed by the legislature; that no citizen was entitled to use his property so as to injure another, and that no covenant could give him power so to do, even though made with the corporation; since, as tending to control and embarrass the exercise of its important powers as a local legislature, the covenant, when it came in competition with them, must give way, or was repealed.[3]

---

[1] Norris *v.* Staps, Hob. 210.

[2] Stuyvesant *v.* Mayor, &c. of New York, 7 Cowen, 585. See State of New York *v.* Mayor, &c. of New York, 3 Duer, 119.

[3] Presbyterian Church *v.* City of New York, 5 Cowen, 538; Coates *v.* Mayor, &c. of

§ 334. Again, by-laws infringing the laws of Congress, made in pursuance of the constitution,[1] the general statutes of a State, or particular statutes relating to the corporation (provided these do not impair the obligation of the charter), are void.[2] Where by statute the trustees of academies were empowered "to appoint teachers or other officers, and remove or displace them at pleasure," it was held, that by no resolution of the trustees could they abridge the power of removal vested in them and their successors.[3] So where by statute a power to enforce the payment of assessments by sale of the shares exclusively existed, a *by-law*, giving an action against a stockholder for any deficiency after the sale, was held repugnant to the statute, and void.[4] A *promise* to pay assessments in a case where the charter provided for their collection only by sale, would, on the other hand, be binding.[5]

§ 335. The legislative power of a corporation is not only restricted by the constitutional and statute law of the State in which it is established, but by the general principles and policy of the common law, as it is accepted there.[6] Indeed, whenever a by-law seeks to alter a well-settled and fundamental principle of the common law, or to establish a rule interfering with the rights, or endangering the security, of individuals or the public, a statute or other special authority, emanating from the creating power, must be shown to legalize it, either expressly or by implication.[7] Thus, a bridge corporation has not incidentally, nor by

---

New York, 7 Cowen, 604. The ordinance by which, in 1780, the corporation of Georgetown first exercised the power of graduating their streets, was not in the nature of a compact, but might be repealed by the corporation. Gozzler *v.* Corporation of Georgetown, 6 Wheat. 593. See State of New York *v.* Mayor, &c. of New York, 3 Duer, 119; that the municipal corporation of the city of New York has no power to pass an ordinance, granting to an association the exclusive and perpetual right, on certain conditions, of building and running a railroad in Broadway.

[1] United States *v.* Hart, 1 Pet. C. C. 390.

[2] Norris *v.* Staps, Hob. 211; 5 Co. R. 63, Clark's case. See by-laws, 3 Salk. 76; Rex *v.* Barber Surgeons, 1 Ld. Raym. 585; Rex *v.* Miller, 6 T. R. 277; Rex *v.* Haythorne, 5 B. & C. 425; Williams *v.* Great Western Railway Co. 10 Exch. 15, 28 Eng. L. & Eq. 439; The Butchers Ben. Association, 35 Penn. State, 151.

[3] Auburn Academy *v.* Strong, 1 Hopk. Ch. 278.

[4] Jay Bridge Co. *v.* Woodman, 31 Maine, 570.

[5] Connecticut & Passumpsic Railroad Co. *v.* Bailey, 24 Vt. 465.

[6] Norris *v.* Staps, Hob. 210; Lee *v.* Wallis, 1 Kenyon, 292; Sayer, 262; The People *v.* Kip, 4 Cowen, 382, n.; Kennebec & Portland Railroad Co. *v.* Kendall, 31 Maine, 470.

[7] Taylor *v.* Griswold, 2 Green, N. J. 223; Phillips *v.* Wickham, 1 Paige, 598; but see State *v.* Tudor, 5 Day, 329.

virtue of a general clause in its charter, authorizing it to make proper by-laws for its government, not repugnant to the act of incorporation or the constitution and laws of the State, power to make a by-law conferring the right of voting by proxy, or imposing, as a test or qualification for office or admission, the ownership of a certain number of shares, or giving a vote for every share of the stock, where the charter, either by express terms, or reasonable implication, confers no such right.[1] It is upon the same principle, that though many by-laws passed by the ancient municipal corporations and trade companies in England, for the *regulation* of trade,[2] and the prevention of monopoly,[3] have been adjudged good; yet many have been adjudged void, as *in restraint* of trade, and to the oppression of the subject.[4] These corporations being very ancient, many of their by-laws, which would otherwise be void as in restraint of trade, are supported by special customs, which suppose a former grant of a monopoly.[5] Some by-laws are so oppressive, that even a special custom will not support them;[6] and in all cases, a custom, to support a by-law in restraint of trade, must be strictly proved,[7] without a material variance between the custom and the by-law.[8] It seems, how-

---

[1] Taylor *v.* Griswold, 2 Green, N. J. 223; 2 Kent, Com. 295, n. b.

[2] Chamberlain of London's case, 5 Co. R. 63; London *v.* Vanacre, 12 Mod. 371; 1 Rol. R. 5; 2 Rol. Abr. 365 to 369; 3 Salk. 76; Player *v.* Jenkins, 1 Sid. 284; Bosworth *v.* Herne, Cas. *temp.* Hardw. 408, March, 15; Butchers *v.* Morey, 1 H. Bl. 370; Peirce *v.* Bartrum, Cowp. 270; Shaw *v.* Pope, 2 B. & Ad. 465.

[3] Freemantle *v.* Silkthrowsters, 1 Lev. 229; doubted in Willcock on Municipal Corporations, 142; Davenant *v.* Hurdis, F. Moore, 576.

[4] Bedford *v.* Fox, 1 Lutw. 563; Norris *v.* Staps, Hob. 211, Hutton, 5 F. Moore, 869, Bac. Abr. 438; 3 Salk. 76; Tailors of Ipswich, 11 Co. R. 53, 1 Rol. R. 4, 5; Clothworkers of Ipswich, Godb. 253; Parry *v.* Berry, Comyns, 269; Chamberlain of London *v.* Compton, 7 D. & R. 601; The King *v.* The Cooper's Co. 7 T. R. 543; Clark *v.* Le Cren, 9 B. & C. 52.

[5] Bosworth *v.* Bugden, 7 Mod. 459; Colchester *v.* Goodwin, Carter, 117, 120; Bricklayers and Plasterers, Palm. 395, Hardres, 56; Player *v.* Jones, 1 Vent. 21; Broadnax Ca. 1 Vent. 196; Bosworth *v.* Herne, Andr. 97, 2 Stra. 1085, Cas. *temp.* Hardw. 408; Player *v.* Vere, T. Raym. 288, 328; Bowdie *v.* Fennell, 1 Wils. 233; Tailors of Bath *v.* Glazby, 2 Wils. 266; Harrison *v.* Godman, 1 Burr. 16; Hesketh *v.* Braddock, 3 Burr. 1858; Wooly *v.* Idle, 4 Burr. 1952; The King *v.* The Coopers' Co. 7 T. R. 543; The King *v.* Tappenden, 3 East, 186; Chamberlain of London *v.* Compton, 7 D. & R. 601; Clark *v.* Denton, 1 B. & Ad. 92; Clark *v.* Le Cren, 9 B. & C. 52.

[6] Davenant *v.* Hurdis, F. Moore, 576; Wood *v.* Searl, J. Bridg. 141; Davis *v.* Morgan, 1 Cromp. & J. 587, 1 Tyrw. 457, 1 Price, P. C. 77.

[7] Hesketh *v.* Braddock, 3 Burr. 1858.

[8] Colchester *v.* Goodwin, Carter, 117, 120. Where the variance is immaterial, see Hesketh *v.* Braddock, 3 Burr. 1858; Wooly *v.* Idle, 4 Burr. 1952; Tailors of Bath *v.* Glazby, 2 Wils. 266; Bosworth *v.* Bugden, 7 Mod. 459. See also, Fazakerley *v.* Wiltshire, 1 Stra.

ever, that though there be such customs as to prescriptive companies, they cannot be applied to new companies incorporated in the municipality.[1]

§ 336. In New York, where the trustees of a village corporation were authorized to make such prudential by-laws, rules, and regulations, as they from time to time should deem meet, relative "to huckster shops in said village," provided they were not inconsistent with the laws of the State or the United States, it was held that a by-law passed by the trustees, that hucksterers should take and pay for a license from the trustees under a penalty, especially where it did not expressly appear that prudence required such a by-law, was in restraint of trade, and void, as contrary to the general principles and policy of the laws of the State.[2] There are, however, numerous municipal ordinances and by-laws affecting the property of the citizen, such as ordinances requiring the owners of lots fronting on certain streets to fix curb-stones, and make a brick way in front of their lots,[3] or assessing the owners of buildings for similar purposes,[4] affecting and regulating certain occupations, and modes of using and exhibiting certain animals, such as by-laws prohibiting unlicensed persons from removing house dirt and offal from the city,[5] prohibiting vendors of the produce of their own farms, &c., from occupying stands for the purpose of vending, in certain streets constituted by the by-law a part of the market,[6] prohibiting the keeping of bowling-alleys for gain,[7] prohibiting the driving or riding of horses on the trot or gallop, in the streets of a city,[8] or the public exhibition of stud-horses,[9] or

466, 467, that a by-law, good at common law, is not vitiated by the variance or excess of the custom.

[1] Chamberlain of London *v.* Compton, 7 D. & R. 601; Bolton *v.* Throgmorton, Skin. 55, semb. *contra*. See Willcock on Municipal Corporations, 146, § 348.

[2] Dunham *v.* Trustees of Rochester, 5 Cowen, 462; and see Freeholders *v.* Barber, 2 Halst. 64.

[3] Paxton *v.* Sweet, 1 Greenl. 196; or requiring hoistways in stores, &c. to be inclosed by a railing, and closed by a trap-door upon the completion of the business of each day. Mayor, &c. of New York *v.* Williams, 15 N. Y. 502.

[4] City of Lowell *v.* Hadley, 8 Met. 180.

[5] Vandine's case, 6 Pick. 187.

[6] Nightingale's case, 11 Pick. 168; Buffalo *v.* Webster, 10 Wend. 99; and see Bush *v.* Seabury, 8 Johns. 418.

[7] Tanner *v.* Trustees of the Village of Albion, 5 Hill, 121.

[8] Commonwealth *v.* Worcester, 3 Pick. 462. In such case it is not necessary to prove that any one was endangered by the fast driving. 3 Pick. 462; City Council *v.* Dunn, 1 McCord, 333.

[9] Nolen *v.* Mayor, &c. Franklin, 4 Yerg. 163.

requiring coal to be weighed,[1] which are held reasonable and valid, as no more than a proper exercise of that general legislative power usually vested in municipalities, for the due police and government of their crowded thoroughfares.[2]

§ 337. A by-law by a company of free fishers and dredgers, that no member should carry on a separate trade in oysters on his own account, from the same shore on which the company oyster grounds were situated, under a penalty, has been adjudged good, on the ground "that the company were partners; that there was nothing illegal in partners agreeing to prevent any one partner from carrying on a separate trade elsewhere, on his own account; and that there was no reason why the same thing might not be prevented by a by-law, in the case of a company like the present."[3] A by-law, however, made by the freemen of a company of oyster fishermen, prohibiting any freeman from being engaged in the trade of sending oysters to market from any other ground on the Kentish shore than the oyster ground of the company, under a penalty of £10, and, in case of refusal to pay the same, that such freeman shall thenceforth, and until the fine be paid, be excluded from all share of profits to be made thereafter by the joint trade of the company, is void; there being no usage stated to that extent, but only an usage for the freemen to make orders for regulating the company and fishery, with fines and penalties for the breach of such orders, and for prohibiting freemen from being engaged on other oyster grounds, under penalties to be stopped out of the money arising by the sale of the stint of oysters of such freemen.[4]

§ 338. A by-law of a town, prohibiting all persons except its own inhabitants from taking shell-fish in a navigable river within its limits, is void, as against common right;[5] unless, indeed, the town has, by

---

1 Stokes *v.* New York, 14 Wend. 87.

2 State *v.* Merrill, 37 Me. 329. A by-law of a municipal corporation, imposing penalties for particular offences, does not seem to be void merely because a general law of the State imposes penalties for the same offences. Rogers *v.* Jones, 1 Wend. 237; Zylstra *v.* Corporation of Charleston, 1 Bay, 382. See, however, Southport *v.* Ogden, 23 Conn. 128.

3 Per Lord Kenyon, The King *v.* The Company of Fishermen of Faversham, 8 T. R. 352; Adley *v.* Reeves, 2 M. & S. 53. See, however, Adley *v.* Whitstable Company, 17 Ves. 323.

4 Adley *v.* Reeves, 2 M. & S. 53; s. c. called Adley *v.* Whitstable Company, 17 Ves. 304.

5 Hayden *v.* Noyes, 5 Conn. 391.

grant, &c., the exclusive right of fishing in the waters within its boundaries.[1]

§ 339. Retrospective and *ex post facto* by-laws are void at common law;[2] and certainly the latter are in this country, under the Constitution of the United States, since no State could grant to a corporation power to do that which it could not constitutionally do itself.

§ 340. In England, a by-law made by a corporation, created by letters-patent, imposing the forfeiture of goods, is void, even if the letters-patent authorized such a by-law.[3] In a case in the time of Elizabeth, where it appeared that King Henry VI. had, by letters-patent, granted to a corporation of dyers power to search, &c., and if they found any cloth dyed with logwood, to seize it as forfeited, the grant of power was adjudged void, as contrary to the 29th chapter of *magna charta;* goods and chattels being by construction included in the prohibition that "no man shall be disseised of his freehold."[4] Neither can a corporation, created by act of parliament in that country, make and enforce such a law, unless the power so to do be expressly given by the act.[5] Such by-laws as these, however, imposing the forfeiture of the goods of a stranger, are to be distinguished from those authorizing the corporation to seize and detain the stock of a member,[6] for the debts, calls, or taxes which he might owe the corporation; these last being adjudged valid by consent. A by-law levying money on the subject or citizen in general is void, since by the general law, no taxes can be imposed but by act of parliament or of the legislature.[7] This rule does not of course interfere with the right of a corporation to assess taxes *upon its members* for the purpose of defraying its general charges, or discharging a burden to which it is subject,[8] or to exact a certain

---

1 Rogers *v.* Jones, 1 Wend. 237.

2 1 Keble, 733; Howard *v.* Savannah, T. Charlt. 173.

3 Kyd on Corp. 109.

4 Waltham *v.* Austin, 8 Co. R. 125 a, 127 b; 2 Inst. 47; 1 Bulstr. 11, 12; Kirk *v.* Nowill, 1 T. R. 118.

5 Kirk *v.* Nowill, 1 T. R. 118, per Lord Mansfield; Player *v.* Archer, 2 Sid. 121; Clark *v.* Tucker, 2 Vent. 183.

6 Child *v.* Hudson's Bay Company, 2 P. Wms. 207; Mussey *v.* Bulfinch St. Society, 1 Cush. 184.

7 Case of *Quo Warranto,* Treby's Arg. 29; Sawyer's Arg. 42; Player *v.* Vere, T. Raym. 328.

8 Jeffrey's case, 5 Co. R. 66 a; Clark's case, 5 Co. R. 64 a, F. Moore, 411; Snow *v.* Dillingham, 5 Mass. 547; Mussey *v.* Bulfinch St. Society, 1 Cush. 148.

sum of a member upon his election to an office, on or before his admission.[1]

§ 341. Again, by-laws prohibiting the members from pursuing their legal remedies beyond the jurisdiction of the corporation are void; since no power less than that of the legislature can exclude the subject or citizen from his right to legal redress.[2]

§ 342. It should be observed, that what may be bad as a *by-law*, as against common right, may be good as a *contract;* since a man may part with a common right voluntarily, of which it would be impolitic and unjust to deprive him by a by-law passed without his assent, or perhaps knowledge, by those who might not know or would not consult his individual interests. Hence it will be found that a by-law may be void as against strangers, or members who do not assent to it, and yet good as a contract between members of the corporation who do assent to it.[3] An agreement, for instance, between the citizens of London, who have as extensive a power of making by-laws as any corporation, that they will not sell, except in the markets of London, would be good; but it has been declared by the legislature, in England, that a by-law to that effect is bad,[4] being in restraint of trade. Where the members of a corporation were by statute individually liable for the payment of the debts, a by-law allowing the stockholders, on paying thirty per cent. on their shares, to forfeit their stock, and thus avoid payment of the company debts, is void and inoperative as to creditors, inasmuch as it is contrary to the fundamental principles of law and equity.[5] A prior resolution of the same corporation, however, enacting that every member upon paying fifty per cent. on his shares should be discharged from all future calls on his subscription, except by forfeiture, was held binding on a creditor who was both a member and trustee of the corporation, and present at the passing of the resolution, and consenting to the same; the by-law being regarded, in this case, as a contract between the creditor and the other members of the corporation.[6] But where a

---

1 T. Raym. 446; Vintners Co. *v.* Passey, 1 Burr. 235.

2 Player *v.* Archer, 2 Sid. 121; London *v.* Bernardiston, 1 Lev. 16; Ballard *v.* Bennett, 2 Burr. 778; Middleton's case, Dyer, 333 a.

3 Stetson *v.* Kempton, 13 Mass. 282; Davis *v.* Proprietors of Meeting-house in Lowell, 8 Met. 321; Adley *v.* Whitstable Company, 17 Ves. 323, per Ld. Eldon, Ch.

4 Adley *v.* Whitstable Company, 17 Ves. 323, per Ld. Eldon, Ch.

5 Slee *v.* Bloom, 19 Johns. 456.

6 Ibid.; and see Cooper *v.* Frederick, 9 Ala. 738.

creditor, who was also a member and a trustee at the time the resolution was passed, openly protested against it, though he afterwards accepted, in part payment of his debt, money raised under it, and was present at a subsequent meeting, when the application of the money thus raised was directed, and assented to the application, it was held that this was no ratification by him of the by-law.[1] In such cases, a constructive assent to the by-law, urged from the common principle that all the corporators are presumed to assent to what is done at a regular meeting, will not be admitted to deprive one of his right; for the presumption is, that corporations will pass none but legal votes; and to all such, and such only, the assent of those who are absent may be presumed.[2] The unanimity of the vote of those present cannot affect the rights of those absent, where the vote is itself unauthorized.[3] And, indeed, so far as a member's rights, duties, and obligations as a corporator are concerned, he is bound by the acts of the majority; but the corporation has, of course, no right by by-law or resolution, without his consent, to dispense with a contract, in which he is one party, and the corporation the other.[4] Still less can it impose upon him a liability, as for the debts of the corporation, not contemplated by the charter; and his obligation to pay such debts must be proved in conformity to the Statute of Frauds — they being the debts of another.[5]

§ 343. The by-laws of a corporation must not be inconsistent with its charter;[6] for this instrument creates it an artificial being, imparts to it its power, designates its object, and usually prescribes its mode of operation. It is, in short, the fundamental law of the corporation; and in

---

[1] Slee *v.* Bloom, 19 Johns. 456.

[2] See Stetson *v.* Kempton, 13 Mass. 282, Chief Justice Parker's opinion; Ins. Co. *v.* Connor, 17 Penn. State, 136.

[3] Ibid.

[4] Revere *v.* Boston Copper Co. 15 Pick. 363; American Bank *v.* Baker, 4 Met. 176; Ins. Co. *v.* Connor, 17 Penn. State, 136.

[5] Trustees of Free Schools in Andover *v.* Flint, 13 Met. 543.

[6] In Hoyt *v.* Shelden, 3 Bosw. 267, the charter provided that the corporate powers of the company should be exercised by a board of directors to consist of twenty-three persons, who should elect a president and "possess the other privileges and powers conferred by law;" and among other powers especially enumerated was the power to adopt, establish, and carry into execution such by-laws as should by its president and directors be judged necessary and convenient for the corporation. Nothing was said in the charter respecting the number of directors which should constitute a quorum, and it was held that a by-law prescribing the number was valid. This case was affirmed by the Court of Appeals. See Hoyt *v.* Thompson, 19 N. Y. 207.

its terms and spirit, as a constitution to the petty legislature of the body, acting by and under it. Hence all by-laws in contravention of it are void. "The true test of all by-laws," says Mr. Justice Wilmot, "is the intention of the crown in granting the charter, and the apparent good of the corporation."[1] In the same case, it is said by Mr. Justice Yates, that "corporations cannot make by-laws contrary to their constitution. If they do, they act without authority."[2] With relation to the important power of electing officers by municipal corporations, this very obvious rule was, however, directly violated in the celebrated Case of Corporations,[3] decided in the time of Elizabeth. In this case it appears that, "*when divers attempts were made in divers corporations contrary to the common usage, to make popular elections*, the lords of Elizabeth's council demanded of her chief and other justices, whether, when the charters of divers municipal corporations prescribed that the mayor, bailiffs, aldermen, provosts, &c., shall be chosen by the *commonalty or burgesses*, &c., elections of these officers *by a certain selected number of the principal of the commonalty or burgesses, called the common council, or the like*, according to ancient usage, were good in law; forasmuch as, by the words of the charters, the election should be indefinitely by the commonalty or burgesses, which is to say, by *all* the commonalty or all the burgesses," &c. The justices, "upon great deliberation and conference had among themselves," as we are told, resolved that such ancient and usual elections were warranted both by law and the charters of the corporations. The reason they gave was, that by their charters these corporations were empowered to make laws, ordinances, and constitutions for the better government and order of their cities and boroughs, by force of which, and "*for avoiding of popular confusion*," they might, by their common consent, ordain that the officers should be chosen by a selected number of the principal of the commonalty, which by law, "*for the avoiding of popular disorder and confusion*," they adjudged would be good. And even if the by-law could not be shown, they decided that they would presume it from ancient and continual usage, though it began within time of memory. Lord Coke closes his

---

[1] Rex *v.* Spencer, 3 Burr. 1838; and see Rex *v.* Cutbush, 4 Burr. 2204; Rex *v.* Gravesend, 4 D. & R. 117; 2 B. & C. 602; Carr *v.* City of St. Louis, 9 Misso. 191.

[2] Rex *v.* Spencer, 3 Burr. 1839; and see The King *v.* Ginever, 6 T. R. 735, 736; Hoblyn *v.* Regem, 2 Bro. P. C. 329. And a by-law cannot explain a doubtful charter. If there be any ambiguity on the face of the charter, it is the province of the court to expound it. 2 Selw. N. P. 1144.

[3] 4 Co. R. 77, 78.

report of this decision with, "God forbid that they (the usages established by the decision) should be now innovated or altered; for many and great inconveniences will thereupon arise, all which the law has well prevented, as appears by this resolution."[1] Though Lord Kenyon intimated, and in one case very sarcastically,[2] his opinion against by-laws limiting the number of electors appointed by the charter, even when made by the whole corporation;[3] yet the Case of Corporations, settled as it was upon great deliberation, has, in England, been generally followed;[4] and its principle even extended to the election of *burgesses*, as standing upon the same footing, in this respect, with the higher orders of the corporation.[5] Such a by-law, in order to restrain the right of the commonalty, must be made by "common assent,"[6] or, in other words, by the commonalty themselves; and if made by a select body, though the power of making by-laws is reposed in them, it is void; for they do not represent the commonalty.[7] And it seems as though the *number* of electors specified in the charter may be restrained by a by-law, yet that a by-law cannot strike out *an integral part* of the electors, nor narrow nor extend the number of the eligible, or those out of whom the election is to be made.[8] But though the by-law would be void, if it lessened the number of persons eligible to office, yet this feature of a by-law, presumed from ancient usage, will not be inferred from the circumstance of the election by the limited body having almost uniformly fallen upon members of the limited body.[9] It is evident, however, that the Case of Corporations, though established as law in England, is wholly indefensible on principle. The charters prescribed

---

1 The Case of Corporations, 4 Co. 77, 78.

2 The King *v.* Ginever, 6 T. R. 735.

3 Ibid. The King *v.* Holland, 2 East, 74.

4 Colchester Case, 3 Bulst. 71; Rex *v.* Grosvenor, 7 Mod. 198; Rex *v.* Tomlyn, Cas. *temp.* Hardw. 316; Rex *v.* Castle, Andr. 124; Rex *v.* Tucker, 1 Barnard. 27; Rex *v.* Spencer, 3 Burr. 1837; Rex *v.* Cutbush, 4 Burr. 2207; Rex *v.* Head, 4 Burr. 2515; Hoblyn *v.* Regem, 6 Bro. P. C. 519; Newling *v.* Francis, 3 T. R. 189; Rex *v.* Ashwell, 12 East, 22; Rex *v.* Atwood, 7 Nev. & M. 286.

5 Rex *v.* Bird, 13 East, 384; Rex *v.* Westwood, 4 B. & C. 782, 7 D. & R. 269, 2 Dow. & C. 21, 4 Bligh, N. S. 213, 7 Bing. 1.

6 Case of Corporations, 4 Co. 77, 78.

7 Colchester Case, 3 Bulst. 71; Rex *v.* Spencer, 3 Burr. 1837; Rex *v.* Cutbush, 4 Burr. 2204.

8 Rex *v.* Atwood, 1 Nev. & M. 286; Rex *v.* Bumstead, 2 B. & Ad. 699; Rex *v.* Spencer, 3 Burr. 1838; The Carmarthen Case, there cited by Wilmot, J. See, however, Rex *v.* Westwood, 4 B. & C. 801, 802, 7 D. & R. 304, 305.

9 Rex *v.* Atwood, 1 Nev. & M. 286, 4 B. & Ad. 699.

that the elections should be by the commonalty; and we do not perceive by what right the commonalty, though unanimous, could delegate to others, or to a selected number of their own body, a right which, by the instrument that enabled them to act at all, was to be exercised by themselves. Though they had power to make laws, ordinances, and constitutions, for the better government and order of their cities, boroughs, &c., as it seems to us, this power given by their charters was clearly limited by the clause which prescribed the mode of election. Indeed, admitting that "the avoiding of the disorder and confusion of popular elections" was worth striving for, and that the by-law supposed was ever passed, the assumption by the commonalty amounts, as Lord Kenyon remarked of a similar assumption in a case before him, to this, that "the crown having, in the estimation of the corporation, made a defective instrument, the latter wish to cure that defect."[1] The truth is, probably, that no such by-law was ever passed by the commonalty. The justices *presumed* the by-law from the usage; but it is well known that even the right of returning members to parliament was regarded, in early times, rather as an inconvenience than a privilege; and the fair presumption is, that it was the mere supineness of the commonalty in general, that permitted the administration of corporate affairs, and amongst other things the election of officers, to devolve upon the select classes.[2] When we consider the arbitrary times in which this decision was made, the little attention then paid to popular rights, the well-known subserviency of the courts of justice to the ruling powers, and the fact that the resolution was made upon a reference from the lords of the council[3] to the justices, "because divers attempts were made in divers corporations, contrary to ancient usage, *to make popular elections*," we see reason enough for the decision, without recurring to the principles of the common law.[4]

§ 344. We very much doubt whether the principle introduced into England by the "Case of Corporations," with regard to the old municipal corporations of that country, will be generally applied in the United

---

[1] The King *v.* Ginever, 6 T. R. 735.

[2] Hallam's Constitutional History of England, vol. iii. pp. 54, 61 to 65.

[3] "It was perceived, however, by the assertors of the popular cause, under James I., that by this narrowing of the electoral franchise, *many boroughs were subject to the influence of the privy council,* which, by restoring the householders to their legitimate rights, would strengthen the interests of the country." Hallam's Constitutional History of England, vol. iii. pp. 62, 63.

[4] Willcock on Mun. Corp. 122 to 125.

States, at least to private corporations created by statute; and we have dwelt thus long upon it, because it seems to have been thought susceptible of such an application by the Supreme Court of Pennsylvania, in a case which, as it appears to us, might well have been decided, as it was without reference to such a principle. This was the case of Commonwealth *v.* Cain,[1] where it appeared that the charter of a church corporation authorized the minister, churchwardens, and vestrymen, to make rules, by-laws, and ordinances, and transact every thing requisite for the good government and support of the church; and directed, also, that the election of ministers, &c. should be conducted according to certain rules, one of which was, that no persons were to vote except those who had been regularly admitted, and had been members of the church twelve months previous to the election. A by-law, enacting that no member whose pew-rent was in arrear for a longer time than two years, should be entitled to vote for officers, was held valid; inasmuch as it was reasonable for the good government and support of the church, *and not contradictory to the charter of incorporation.* The punctual payment of pew-rent was a duty of each pew-owner, which the corporation, unless expressly or impliedly forbidden by their charter, might enforce by penalties; and we see no reason why the penalty should not as well be the loss of a vote as the seizure and detention of stock. The charter contemplated that each pew-owner would perform the obvious duty of supporting the church; without which, his voting for officers would be nugatory; and there was no occasion for a reference to those English cases which support the doctrine, that "by-laws for the good of the corporation are valid, although they reduced the number of *electors* to narrower bounds than were marked out by the charter." And where a church corporation was authorized to hold property to a certain amount, and to divide their whole capital stock into shares, with a provision that each share was not to be assessed in a greater sum than twenty-five dollars, and that when the dividends upon the shares should have paid all assessments thereon, with interest, the income of the property of the corporation should be applied exclusively to parochial purposes; and the corporation passed a by-law that the price of each share should be twenty-five dollars, and that if any person should elect to pay into the treasury, in addition to this sum, the further sum of three dollars, he should be entitled to a certificate, with the word "redeemable" written thereon,

---

[1] 5 S. & R. 510.

which certificate should not be assignable, but should entitle the holder to have the same redeemable out of the corporation funds, whenever he should leave the town in which the meeting-house of the corporation was situated, and take up his permanent residence elsewhere; the by-law was held to be valid, as providing a mode of raising funds, which was one of the objects necessarily embraced in the objects of the corporation.[1]

§ 345. As transcending the charter, by-laws creating a new office,[2] imposing an oath of office where none is provided by the constitution,[3] giving a vote to a person[4] or a casting vote to an officer[5] who is not entitled to it by the charter, restricting the right of an officer to vote to a mere casting vote in case of a tie,[6] restricting[7] or extending[8] the right of admission or eligibility to office, or restricting the discretionary power of removing a master or usher of a grammar school vested in the governors,[9] as given by the charter; altering the prescribed mode of election, or imposing new or additional tests or qualifications on members or voters; delegating the power of laying assessments to the directors when the charter or general law vests it exclusively in the corporation;[10] or changing the salaries of officers,[11] or imposing a personal liability for the debts of the corporation,[12] or for calls or assessments due from the stockholders to the corporation[13] not contemplated by the charter or general

---

1 Davis *v.* Proprietors of Meeting-house in Lowell, 8 Met. 321.

2 Rex *v.* Ginever, 6 T. R. 735.

3 Rex *v.* Dean and Chapter of Dublin, 1 Stra. 539. And in England, if an oath be appointed by the constitution, and no one provided to administer it, the corporation cannot empower an officer for that purpose; but application must be made to chancery, and a *dedimus* obtained to confer on some person authority to administer the oath. Ibid.

4 Rex *v.* Bird, 13 East, 384.

5 Rex *v.* Ginever, 6 T. R. 736.

6 McCollough *v.* Annapolis and Elkridge Railroad Co. 4 Gill, 58.

7 Rex *v.* Coopers of Newcastle, 7 T. R. 548; Rex *v.* Cambridge, 2 Selw. N. P. 1144; Rex *v.* Tappenden, 3 East, 191; Lee *v.* Wallis, 1 Keny. 292, Sayer, 263; Rex *v.* Atwood, 1 Nev. & M. 286.

8 Powell *v.* Regem, 3 Bro. P. C. 436; Rex *v.* Weymouth, 7 Mod. 374; 4 Bro. P. C. 464; Rex *v.* Bumstead, 2 B. & Ad. 699.

9 Reg. *v.* Governors of Darlington School, 6 Q. B. 682.

10 *Ex parte* Winsor, 3 Story, 411. In this case it was held, that a by-law authorizing the directors "to take care of the interests and manage the concerns of the corporation," did not in fact impart such a delegation of power.

11 Carr *v.* City of St. Louis, 9 Misso. 191.

12 Trustees of Free School in Andover *v.* Flint. 13 Met. 539.

13 Kennebec & Portland Railroad Co. 31 Maine, 470.

law, are void.[1] And where a by-law confers the right of voting by proxy,[2] or imposes the ownership of a certain number of shares as a qualification for office, or admission,[3] there being nothing in the charter expressed or implied specially authorizing such by-law, or where, in cases of a "Savings Institution," a by-law is passed, prescribing that persons owning one share of the capital, required to be invested for the purpose of security to the depositors, should be members, and should cease to be members upon its transfer, the by-law is held void, as invading the spirit and meaning of the charter.[4] So where the act incorporating an insurance company gave a vote for each share of stock, but provided that no share should entitle the holder to a vote unless the stock should have been held by him at least sixty days next and immediately preceding an election, and provided that the major part of the directors should constitute a board, with power to pass such by-laws as to them should appear needful and proper respecting elections, and they passed a by-law requiring a transfer of stock to be registered in order to be effectual, it was held that a by-law requiring the inspectors of elections, whenever they should or might suspect that stock voted on had been sold or bargained for within the sixty days, but not transferred on the books, to oblige the person proposing to vote on such stock to adduce satisfactory proof, either by his own oath or affirmation or otherwise, that the stock had not been sold, or the beneficial interest parted with by any bargain or contract within the sixty days, and in default of such proof to reject the vote, was void; and that the vendor might vote, notwithstanding the transfer within sixty days, *the same being unregistered;* the inspectors having no right to require other tests of a voter than those provided in the act of incorporation, and it not being competent to the directors to pass any by-law at variance with the provisions of the same.[5] An act incorporating a church provided, that the vestry should

---

1 Rex *v.* Spencer, 3 Burr. 1833; Rex *v.* Tappenden, 3 East, 191; Taylor *v.* Griswold, 2 Green, N. J. 223; Rex *v.* Bumstead, 2 B. & Ad. 699, per Parke, J.; The People *v.* Tibbetts, 4 Cowen, 358.

2 Taylor *v.* Griswold, 2 Green, N. J. 223; Phillips *v.* Wickham, 1 Paige, 598; but see State *v.* Tudor, 5 Day, 329.

3 Taylor *v.* Griswold, 2 Green, N. J. 223.

4 Commonwealth *v.* Gill, 3 Whart. 228; Philadelphia Savings Institution case, 1 Whart. 461. An insurance company, authorized by its charter to insure against loss by fire simply, has no power to pass a by-law "that the company will be liable for losses on property burned or *damaged* by lightning." Andrews *v.* Union Mut. F. Ins. Co. 37 Me. 256.

5 The People *v.* Tibbetts, 4 Cowen, 358; The People *v.* Kip, 4 Cowen, 382, n. A

be elected "in the manner accustomed," which was, at a certain time and place, by the inhabitants of the parish, being of the religion of the Church of England, and possessing certain other enumerated qualifications. It was held that a by-law made by the vestry, enacting that no person should be admitted a member of the church, or be entitled to the privilege of a vote in the election of the vestry, unless he should pay the sum of fifty dollars, a qualification not named in the charter, was void; inasmuch as "it required a new qualification to entitle persons otherwise qualified to vote, was therefore an attempt to transcend the powers given, and to alter the qualifications of the voters, and was a violation of the charter."[1] And, generally, where the charter vests the admission of members in the body at large, a power vested in the directors, to provide for the admission of members, gives them only a right to prescribe in their by-laws, the *time*, *place*, and *manner* of holding the election of members, and not the right to pass a by-law imposing a test of membership not contemplated by the charter, as the ownership of a share in the capital stock of a "Savings Institution."[2] In a recent case in England, it was decided that a by-law of a navigation company, that the navigation should be closed on Sundays, except for works of necessity and for the purpose of going to and returning from any place of divine worship, was not authorized by a charter empowering the company to make by-laws for the good government of the company and for the good and orderly using the navigation, and also for the well governing of the bargemen, watermen, and boatmen, who should carry goods on any part of the navigation; on the ground, that the power of making by-laws was vested in them solely for the orderly use of the navigation, and not for the purpose of controlling the moral or religious conduct of carriers along the navigation, which is to be left to the general law of the land, and to the laws of God.[3]

§ 346. A corporation may *renounce* by a by-law a privilege conferred

---

by-law of a mutual insurance company, giving to a mortgagee of the property insured all the rights and privileges conferred by the charter upon an absolute purchaser, is a valid by-law under a clause of the incorporating act, granting the power to make all necessary and convenient by-laws for managing the business of the corporation. Rollins *v.* Columbian F. Ins. Co. 5 Fost. 200.

[1] Per Desausure, Chan., Vestry of St. Luke's Church *v.* Mathews, 4 Des. Ch. 578. See Rex *v.* Breton, 4 Burr. 2260.

[2] Commonwealth *v.* Gill, 3 Whart. 228.

[3] Calder Navigation Co. *v.* Pilling, 14 M. & W. 75.

by charter or statute; and from a constant omission to enforce a privilege against common right, where the privilege has been continually violated, such a renunciation has been presumed.[1]

§ 347. The power of making by-laws binding upon all the members of a corporation, whether it reside in the majority of the body at large, or of those present at a corporate meeting, or be confided by charter to a select class, is in trust for the benefit of the whole, and must therefore be exercised with discretion. Hence, by-laws must be reasonable; and all which are nugatory, and vexatious, unequal, oppressive, or manifestly detrimental to the interests of the corporation, are void.[2] Thus, a by-law, or rule of a bank, that all payments made and received must be examined at the time, does not prevent a party dealing with the bank from showing afterwards that there was a mistake in the accounts of deposits and receipts.[3]

§ 348. A by-law compelling the stewards of a corporation, under a penalty, to make a dinner for the master, wardens, and assistants, was adjudged void; since it was unreasonable to compel a man to make a dinner for the luxury of others merely, without benefit to himself or the corporation.[4] It was said, however, by the judges, that if the by-law had been to make a dinner, to the end that the *company* might assemble and choose officers, or do any thing for the benefit of the corporation, *it had been well enough;*[5] and in case of old corporations by prescription, an ancient custom, or by-law, compelling the stewards of the corporation to give a customary feast, has been held good.[6] And, though the by-law, after enacting that the stewards shall provide the dinner at their own proper costs and charges, contains the clause, "with such allowance out of the stock of said company, or otherwise, as the master, wardens, and assistants of said company, for the time being, or the major part of them, should think fit and convenient to be allowed in that behalf," it nevertheless is bad.[7]

---

[1] Colchester *v.* Goodwin, Carter, 118; Berwick-upon-Tweed *v.* Johnson, Lofft, 338; and see Canal Company *v.* Sansom, 1 Binney, 70.

[2] Gosling *v.* Veley, 12 Q. B. 347.

[3] Farmers & Mechanics Bank *v.* Smith, 19 Johns. 115; and see Gallatin *v.* Bradford, 1 Bibb, 209.

[4] Master and Co. of the Framework Knitters *v.* Green, 1 Ld. Raym. 113; Carter *v.* Sanderson, 5 Bing. 79, 2 M. & P. 164; Scrivener's Company *v.* Brooking, 3 Q. B. 95.

[5] Ibid.; Carter *v.* Sanderson, 5 Bing. 79, 2 M. & P. 164.

[6] Ibid.; Lutw. 1324; Wallis's case, Cro. Jac. 555.

[7] Carter *v.* Sanderson, 5 Bing. 79, per Best, C. J., Burrough & Gaselee, Jus. dub.; Scrivener's Company *v.* Brooking, 3 Q. B. 95.

§ 349. In a recent English case, it seems to have been considered that a by-law of a railway company authorized to make orders for regulating the travelling upon and use of their railway, requiring a passenger not producing or delivering up his ticket on leaving the company's premises, to pay fare from the place where the train originally started, was a reasonable by-law.[1] In a late case in New York, it was held that the reasonableness of a regulation requiring way passengers on a railroad to surrender their tickets before reaching the station nearest to that of their destination, without receiving any check or other evidence of the payment of fare, was a question of law, and not one of fact for the jury.[2]

§ 350. A by-law by a college of physicians, that no person should be admitted into the class of candidates before admission into the college, unless he had taken a degree of M. D. at Oxford, Cambridge, or Dublin, except in certain specified cases, was considered reasonable, as "tending to insure a proper education, and competence in learning."[3] A similar by-law, by a company of surgeons, that no member should take an apprentice who did not understand the Latin language, his ability therein to be tried in a specified manner;[4] or by a company of tradesmen, as masons, carpenters, &c., that no one should be free of their company until examined and found qualified according to the directions of the by-law, has been adjudged good.[5] Again, a by-law of a beneficial society, that no soldier of a *standing army*, seaman, or mariner, shall be capable of admission; and any member who shall voluntarily enlist as a soldier, or enter on board any vessel as

---

[1] Chilton *v.* London & Croydon R. Co. 16 M. & W. 212, 230, 231. So also, the regulation of a telegraph company, requiring messages of consequence to be repeated. MacAndrew *v.* Electric Telegraph Co. 17 C. B. 3, 33 Eng. L. & Eq. 180.

[2] Vedder *v.* Fellows, 20 N. Y. 126. Some of the judges were of the opinion that such a regulation was reasonable, but the court did not pass upon that question. In this case *Strong*, J., said: "There was, it is true, no positive proof that it (the regulation) had been made by the directors of the company or their general superintendent, nor was it absolutely necessary that there should have been. The conductors, in the absence of any directions from their superior officers, have a right, and indeed it is obligatory upon them, to adopt some rule relative to the surrender of the tickets of the passengers."

[3] Rex *v.* College of Physicians, 7 T. R. 282; Willcock on Municipal Corporations, 135. Regulations of a medical society, establishing a certain tariff of fees for medical service, and subjecting its members to expulsion for non-compliance therewith, are void, as unreasonable and contrary to law and to public policy. People *v.* Medical Society, 24 Barb. 570.

[4] Rex *v.* Masters, &c. of Surgeons Company, 2 Burr. 892.

[5] Lofft, 556; Green's case, 1 Burr. 127; and see Rex *v.* Marshall, 2 T. R. 2.

a seaman or mariner, shall thenceforth lose his membership, "is not forbidden by any principle of public policy;" but a volunteer in the late war with Mexico was not deemed to be "an enlisted soldier of a standing army," within the meaning of the by-law.[1] And where a legal by-law is made for regulating admissions, it may impose a penalty on any corporate officer, who has power to admit, for making admissions contrary to such by-law.[2]

§ 351. Where the mode of electing to corporate offices is not prescribed by charter, or immemorial usage, it may be wholly ordained by by-laws.[3] A by-law creating inspectors of votes at elections, and vesting the appointment of them in the president of the corporation, was held to be good, as tending to prevent disorder on the day of election; although it was contended that the right of electing the vestrymen and church-wardens belonging by charter to the congregation, the appointment of inspectors, as an incident to that right, must be exercised also by them.[4] There would seem to be much force in this objection;[5] but the other resolution in the same case is less doubtful. It having been found that at elections of officers, tickets were inscribed with witticisms, the names of lewd women, &c., a by-law prohibiting the counting of tickets which had on them other things besides the names of the voters, was held reasonable; and an eagle printed on the tickets, as a party badge, was adjudged a violation of this by-law; since it deprived a voter of that secrecy to which he was entitled in the exercise of his franchise, so as to avoid the odium and violence of party prejudice.[6] A by-law, disfranchising a member for vilifying another member of the corporation, has been held void, as unnecessary to the good government of the corporation.[7] A by-law, however, giving power of amotion for just cause, is a

---

1 Franklin *v.* Commonwealth, 10 Barr, 359, 360.

2 Green's case, 1 Burr. 131.

3 Newling *v.* Francis, 3 T. R. 189; Rex *v.* Passmore, 3 T. R. 199.

4 Commonwealth *v.* Woelper, 3 S. & R. 29.

5 Rex *v.* Westwood, 4 B. & C. 786, 7 D. & R. 273, per Littledale and Holroyd, Justices.

6 Commonwealth *v.* Woelper, 3 S. & R. 29.

7 Commonwealth *v.* St. Patrick Benevolent Society, 2 Binney, 441. The charter of a private corporation provided, that if any member should break the rules of the society, he should be served with a notice to attend at the next stated meeting, after which a decision should be made by ballot, and if two thirds considered him guilty, he should be dealt with according to the by-laws. The by-laws provided, that no member should be entitled to receive any benefit from the society, which was a friendly or relief society, whose com-

good by-law, though the corporation that made it had no power of amotion, expressly given by charter, or claimed by prescription.[1]

§ 352. A corporation has a right to the service of all its members, and may make by-laws to enforce it. It may thus impose a penalty on members eligible[2] to an office, who refuse to accept it;[3] or who refuse to take the oath appointed by law, as a necessary qualification for holding it;[4] and on members who refuse to attend the corporate meetings.[5] Nor, it would seem, is a by-law of this nature less valid, though it require that the person accepting the office shall pay a fee on his admission; and the court will not scrutinize the reasonableness of the fee, since the members of the corporation have assented to the amount; which raises a presumption that under their peculiar circumstances it is reasonable, or at least, that they deem it so.[6] And where a municipal corporation passed a by-law imposing a penalty on a member who should refuse the office of sheriff, an office requiring a substantial man on account of its dignity and expense, "unless the person elected shall swear he is not worth £10,000, and bring six compurgators, approved by the court of the corporation, to swear that they believe the truth of his assertion;" the by-law was held reasonable and good. It did not impose an oath, but allowed a favor to the person liable, by permitting him to exonerate himself by a form more indulgent than that prescribed by the old common law, in an action of debt; where, in order to relieve himself from the claim, the defendant was not only required to swear that it was not owing, but to produce *twelve* compurgators, to affirm on

---

plaints were the result of intoxication. A member, having been expelled by the requisite majority, after due notice, brought his action to recover the allowance of a disabled member; and it was held that the regularity of the proceeding could not be inquired into in that way, but the remedy must be by mandamus. Black and White-Smiths Society *v.* Vandyke, 2 Whart. 312.

[1] Rex *v.* Richardson, 1 Burr. 519; 2 Kenyon's Ca. 85.

[2] Rex *v.* Weymouth, 7 Mod. 374, 4 Bro. P. C. 464.

[3] Ibid.; Barber Surgeons *v.* Pelson, 2 Lev. 252; Rex *v.* Grosvener, 1 Wils. 18; Bodwic *v.* Fennell, 1 Wils. 233; London *v.* Vanacre, 1 Ld. Raym. 496; Vintners *v.* Passey, 1 Burr. 239, Kenyon's Ca. 500; Rex *v.* Bower, 1 B. & C. 587, 2 D. & R. 843; Graves *v.* Colby, 1 Perry & D. 235; Tobacco-Pipe Makers *v.* Woodroffe, 7 B. & C. 838, 5 D. & R. 530.

[4] 2 Show. 159.

[5] Tobacco-Pipe Makers *v.* Woodroffe, 7 B. & C. 838, 5 D. & R. 530.

[6] Barber Surgeons *v.* Pelson, 2 Lev. 252; Taverner's case, T. Raym. 446; Stationers *v.* Salisbury, Comb. 221, 222; Vintners *v.* Passey, 1 Kenyon's Ca. 500, 1 Burr. 339.

oath their confidence in his veracity.[1] In Carter *v.* Sanderson,[2] however, Mr. Chief Justice Best was of opinion that a by-law imposing a penalty on the steward of a company who did not provide a dinner on Lord Mayor's day, unless he excused himself by swearing he was not worth £300, was void, as tending to the multiplication of unnecessary oaths; and the learned judge distinguished the case before him from that just alluded to, inasmuch as there the oath excusing the sheriff was necessary to the purposes of justice. It is not necessary to the validity of a by-law enforcing by a penalty the acceptance of an office, that it provide for notice to the corporator of his election; since he is presumed to be always present at the corporate meetings, and acquainted with its proceedings, according to his duty.[3] It is held, however, that even an old English municipal corporation cannot enforce the acceptance of an office by the imprisonment of the person elected, unless there be a special custom to that effect.[4] And a company of London cannot imprison a member for refusing the livery, though it may impose a penalty.[5] A by-law, however, imposing a penalty "on *any person* who shall refuse to undertake an office within the corporation, has been adjudged void; for it includes strangers who are not within the corporate jurisdiction.[6] Although by-laws, imposing a penalty for the refusal of an office, usually contain a provision that the party elected shall be liable only, if he be "without reasonable excuse," yet this is unnecessary; for in an action to recover the penalty, the defendant may show any reasonable excuse, although there be no such provision.[7] The laying down of an office, without permission from the corporation, or the discontinuance of official service, may as well be punished by a by-law as the first refusal.[8] A by-law requiring every other officer of a bank to perform such duties as may be required of them by the president and cashier, was held to be authorized by a general power to make by-laws, and to be reasonable.[9]

---

[1] London *v.* Vanacre, 1 Ld. Raym. 497, 5 Mod. 442, 12 Mod. 272, 1 Salk. 142, Carth. 482.

[2] 5 Bing. 79, per Best, C. J., Burroughs, J., *dubitante.*

[3] London *v.* Vanacre, 12 Mod. 273, 1 Ld. Raym. 499.

[4] Grafton's case, 1 Mod. 10; Willcock on Mun. Corpor. 132, § 305; Rex *v.* Grosvener, 1 Wils. 18.

[5] Grafton's Case, 1 Mod. 10; Poulterer's Company *v.* Phillips, 7 Bing. N. C. 314; Tobacco-Pipe Makers Company *v.* Woodroffe, 7 B. & C. 738.

[6] Mayor of Oxford *v.* Wildgoose, 3 Lev. 293.

[7] Stationers *v.* Salisbury, Comb. 222; London *v.* Vanacre, 1 Ld. Raym. 500, 5 Mod. 442, 12 Mod. 273.

[8] Cambridge *v.* Herring, 1 Lutw. 405.

[9] Planters Bank *v.* Lamkin, R. M. Charlt. 34.

A corporation may also, for their own security, make a by-law requiring their clerk to be sworn; but cannot avail themselves of his omission to take the oath for the purpose of setting aside the title of a *bonâ fide* purchaser, on the ground that his deed had not been recorded by their duly qualified clerk.[1]

§ 353. A very important subject, upon which companies incorporated for the purpose of profit are accustomed to legislate, is the transfer of their stock; and very interesting questions have arisen with regard to the effect of their by-laws regulating such transfers. The charter and by-laws frequently provide that the stock of the company shall be transferable on the books of the company only, or that, to be valid and effectual, the transfer must be registered, by the clerk or treasurer of the corporation, on the company books; and where the charter required the transfer to *be made* on the books, the requisition was considered satisfied by a by-law, requiring the transfer *to be registered* on the books of the company.[2] A very literal construction has been given in Connecticut to such clauses, either in the charter or by-laws of a corporation; the scope and object of such provisions being, in the view of the Supreme Court of that State, "to render the purchase of the stock secure to any person, if at the *moment* of his purchase the company books did not furnish evidence that it had been previously transferred."[3] The settled law of Connecticut is, that where such clauses are found in the charter and by-laws,[4] or either,[5] the transfer is invalid and of no effect for any purpose, unless made or registered on the books of the company. The registry is there deemed the originating act in the change of title; and an entry by the clerk on the deed, "received for record," is not considered equivalent to a registry.[6]

§ 354. A more liberal construction, and one far more in accordance with their spirit and meaning, has been given to such clauses in charters and by-laws of corporations, by the courts of other States, and by the

---

[1] Hastings *v.* Bluehill Turnpike, 9 Pick. 80.

[2] Northrop *v.* Newtown, 3 Conn. 544, Hosmer, C. J.

[3] Marlborough Manufacturing Co. *v.* Smith, 2 Conn. 544; Same *v.* Same, 5 Conn. 246; Northrop *v.* Newtown, 3 Conn. 544; Oxford Turnpike Co. *v.* Bunnel, 6 Conn. 552.

[4] Ibid.

[5] Oxford, &c. *v.* Bunnel, 6 Conn. 552.

[6] Northrop *v.* Newtown, 3 Conn. 544.

Supreme Court of the United States. As they are intended merely for the protection of the interests of the corporation, no effect is given to them further than is necessary to effect that purpose. It is necessary that an incorporated company should have the means of knowing who are stockholders and members, in order that they may know to whom dividends are to be paid, and who are entitled to vote upon the stock; and where the company has a lien upon the stock for debts due to it from a stockholder, that it should have the means of preventing a transfer in derogation of its own rights. To secure this knowledge, and to enable corporations to avail themselves of their lien upon the stock of the company, without danger to the rights of purchasers, these clauses are usually inserted in their charters, or form a part of their by-laws. Accordingly, where transfers of stock are made without conforming to the requisitions of the charter or by-laws in making them, or having them registered on the books of the company, the better opinion decidedly is, that the transfer passes to the purchaser all the right that the seller had; that such provisions were not intended to, and do not, incapacitate the owner of the stock from transferring it at his pleasure, by way of equitable assignment of his interest in it, subject to the charter rights of the corporation, which all must notice,[1] or compel him to own it, unless the corporation allow him to sell, against his will; and the only effect allowed to them seems to be, that the purchaser cannot claim a certificate of, or a dividend upon the shares, unless he first applies for a transfer according to the charter and by-laws. Any other proper transfer is equally valid, as between vendor and vendee, and even as against a creditor of the vendor, who attached the shares before he or the corporation, through its officers, had notice of the transfer. In other words, such provisions, whether by charter or by-law, apply solely to the relation between the corporation and its stockholders, — to the questions, who shall vote, to whom dividends shall be paid; and enable the corporation to protect any lien it may have upon the stock, or equity in it, as between itself and the stockholder transferring it.[2] They constitute a privilege of the cor-

---

1 Farmers Bank of Maryland *v.* Iglehart, 6 Gill, 50; Stebbins *v.* Phœnix Fire Ins. Co. 3 Paige, 350.

2 Union Bank *v.* Laird, 2 Wheat. 390; Black *v.* Zacharie, 3 How. 513; Arnold *v.* Suffolk Bank, 27 Barb. 34; Bank of Utica *v.* Smalley, 2 Cowen, 770; Gilbert *v.* Manchester Iron Manufacturing Co. 11 Wend. 627; Stebbins *v.* Phœnix Fire Ins. Co. 3 Paige, 350; Sargent *v.* Essex M. Railway Co. 9 Pick. 202; Sargent *v.* Franklin Insurance Co. 8 Pick. 90; Nesmith *v.* Washington Bank, 6 Pick. 324; Quiner *v.* Marblehead Social Insurance Co. 10 Mass. 476; Grant *v.* Mechanics Bank, 15 S. & R. 143; Bank of Kentucky *v.*

poration which may be waived or asserted at the pleasure of the president and directors.[1] With this construction of the effect of such a by-law, there seems to be no good reason why a corporation should not have an incidental power to pass it, as a reasonable and proper exercise of its legislative power, although the charter does not specially speak upon the subject. Interpreted, however, as they are in Connecticut, such by-laws might reasonably be regarded, unless expressly sanctioned by charter, as an infringement of the general law respecting the transfer of personal property, and on that account void.[2] It seems, however, that such is not the opinion of the courts in that State, as the same rigid effect is there given to a by-law of this sort, whether expressly authorized by charter, or only passed under a general authority to pass "such by-laws as should appear necessary or expedient for the government of the corporation, or the regulation of its concerns, not contrary to law.[3]

§ 355. Another and very important species of by-laws to moneyed and trading corporations, and to which those which we have just been considering are to some degree only ancillary, are by-laws securing to the corporation a lien upon the shares of a stockholder for debts due from him to the corporation. Such a lien does not, it is clear, exist at common law, in favor of an incorporated company.[4] It is, however, usually given by statute or act of incorporation to incorporated banking companies, so that all must take notice of it;[5] and where the clause of the statute or act of incorporation provides that "no stockholder, *indebted* to a bank, shall be authorized to make a transfer, or receive a dividend, until such debt shall have been discharged," it includes notes discounted by the bank for the stockholder, as well as debts due for an original subscrip-

---

Schuylkill Bank, 1 Parsons, Sel. Cas. 247; Duke *v.* Cahawba Navigation Co. 14 Ala. 82; Farmers Bank of Maryland *v.* Iglehart, 6 Gill, 50; and see Hodges *v.* Planters Bank, 7 Gill & J. 366; Chouteau Spring Co. *v.* Harris, 20 Misso. 382; Fisher *v.* Essex Bank, 5 Gray, 373.

[1] Hall *v.* U. S. Ins. Co. 5 Gill, 484; and see *In re* The Northern Coal Mining Co. 13 Beav. 162, 4 Eng. L. & Eq. 72, 78, 79.

[2] Sargent *v.* Franklin Insurance Co. 8 Pick. 90, Putnam, J.

[3] Oxford Turnpike Co. *v.* Bunnel, 6 Conn. 552.

[4] Mass. Iron Co. *v.* Hooper, 7 Cush. 183; Heart *v.* State Bank, 2 Dev. Eq. 111; Frankfort & Shelbyville Turnp. Co. *v.* Churchill, 6 T. B. Mon. 427; Dana *v.* Brown, 1 J. J. Marsh. 306.

[5] Union Bank *v.* Laird, 2 Wheat. 390; Utica Bank *v.* Smalley, 2 Cowen, 770; Rogers *v.* Huntington Bank, 12 S. & R. 77; Grant *v.* Mechanics Bank 15 id. 140; Sewall *v.* Lancaster Bank, 17 id. 285; Downer *v.* Bank of Zanesville, Wright, 477; Farmers Bank of Maryland *v.* Iglehart, 6 Gill, 50.

tion,[1] and that, too, whether such notes have come to maturity at the time the transfer is applied for, or not,[2] and whether the stockholder is liable on the same as principal or indorser.[3] The lien extends, too, to dividends as well as to shares, though only "shares and stock" be specifically named,[4] and continues, though all other remedy for the debt be barred by the Statute of Limitations.[5] It is not defeated or prevented from attaching by a transfer to a fictitious holder, and subsequently by a person represented by the indebted stockholder to be that holder, to one who pays no consideration for it;[6] nor does it yield to a claim of priority on the part of the general government.[7] Such lien being intended solely as a protection to the bank for debts due to it, equity will not compel the bank to enforce it in favor of the sureties on such debts, on the ground that it was intended for the benefit of the sureties, and giving precedence to debts prior in date; although, upon general principles, it might interpose at the suit of the sureties, to prevent an abuse by the directors of the power conferred upon them by the clause giving the lien.[8] And where the charter of a corporation, authorized to lend money, enacts that the stock shall be assignable on the books of the corporation, under such regulations as the board of trustees shall establish, it is competent for the trustees to enact a by-law, that "no stockholder shall be permitted to transfer his stock while he is in default."[9] If a stockholder borrow money of a bank, with full knowledge of a *usage* not to permit a transfer of his stock while he is indebted to the bank, he is bound by such usage; and neither he nor his assignee, under a voluntary general assignment, can maintain an action against the bank for refusing to permit his stock to be transferred.[10] A *by-law* of a bank, giving to the institution a lien upon the shares of a stockholder for debts

---

1 Rogers *v.* Huntington Bank, 12 S. & R. 77.

2 Brent *v.* Bank of Washington, 10 Pet. 596; Grant *v.* Mechanics Bank, 15 S. & R. 140; Sewall *v.* Lancaster Bank, 17 id. 285; Downer *v.* Bank of Zanesville, Wright, 477; St. Louis Perpetual Ins. Co. *v.* Goodfellow, 9 Misso. 149.

3 Brent *v.* Bank of Washington, 10 Pet. 596; McDowell *v.* Bank of Wilmington, 1 Harring. Del. 27; St. Louis Perpetual Ins. Co. *v.* Goodfellow, 9 Misso. 149.

4 Hague *v.* Dandeson, 2 Exch. 741.

5 Farmers Bank of Maryland *v.* Iglehart, 6 Gill, 50.

6 Stebbins *v.* Phœnix Fire Ins. Co. 3 Paige, 350.

7 Brent *v.* Bank of Washington, 10 Pet. 596.

8 Cross *v.* Phœnix Bank, 1 R. I. 39.

9 Cunningham *v.* Alabama Life Insurance & Trust Co. 4 Ala. 652; St. Louis Perpetual Ins. Co. *v.* Goodfellow, 9 Misso. 149.

10 Morgan *v.* Bank of North America, 8 S. & R. 73.

due from him to the bank, is a reasonable and valid by-law; and under it, a bank may defend against a suit brought by a stockholder for a refusal to permit him to transfer his stock on its books, without first paying the debts he owes to it.[1] Whether, however, a by-law of a corporation, merely as such, can create a general lien on the shares of a stockholder to the amount of the debts due from him to the bank, so as to affect the rights of creditors, or of a special assignee for value, without notice of the restriction, has been considered questionable.[2] In a late case in Georgia, in which the whole subject seems to have been very ably and elaborately examined by the Court, the majority of the judges came to the conclusion that such a lien would be good against a purchaser of the stock at a sheriff's sale, *with notice of the lien*, as to all liability of the stockholder to the bank prior in time to the lien acquired under the judgment; and that such a purchaser was not entitled to a transfer of the stock so purchased, without first discharging the lien created by the by-law.[3] In New York, the general banking act invests stockholders of banks formed under it with the unconditional right of transferring their stock, except as they may agree to limit it by their articles of association. It has been held that a delegation by the articles to the board of directors of the general powers of the association and the management of its stock, does not authorize a by-law subjecting the stock to a lien in favor of the bank for the indebtedness of the stockholder.[4] An early case in the law of incorporated trading companies, bears somewhat upon the general question.

§ 356. The Hudson's Bay Company, being empowered by charter to make by-laws for the better government of the company, and for the management and direction of their trade to Hudson's Bay, made a by-law, that if any of their members should be indebted to the company, his company stock should in the first place be liable for the payment of

---

[1] McDowell *v.* Bank of Wilmington, 1 Harring. Del. 27; Tuttle *v.* Walton, 1 Ga. 43; St. Louis Perpetual Ins. Co. *v.* Goodfellow, 9 Misso. 149.

[2] McDowell *v.* Bank of Wilmington, 1 Harring. Del. 27; Morgan *v.* Bank of North America, 8 S. & R. 73; Nesmith *v.* Bank of Washington, 6 Pick. 329; Plymouth Bank *v.* Bank of Norfolk, 10 Pick. 454.

[3] Tuttle *v.* Walton, 1 Ga. 43.

[4] Bank of Attica *v.* Manufacturers & Traders Bank, 20 N. Y. 501. In this case, a stockholder of a bank which had such a by-law sold his stock, without notice of the by-law, and the bank gave him credit before a transfer of the stock in its books and without notice of his assignment. It was held that the purchaser had an equitable title to the stock, free from any lien on the part of the bank.

such debts as he might owe the company, who might seize and detain the stock for the same. This by-law, *in a contest between the assignees in bankruptcy of the shareholder and the company*, was adjudged good, upon the ground that the legal interest in all the stock was in the company, who were trustees for the several members, and might order that the dividends to be made should be under certain restrictions or terms; and that, upon the same reason that this by-law was objected to, the common by-laws of companies, to deduct the calls out of the stock of the members refusing to pay them, might be said to be void.[1] That part of the by-law, which empowered the company to seize and detain the stock, was held also good; though it was said that there ought to be some act of the company, to order or declare that the stock of such member is seized for the debt due to them.[2] The whole by-law being, however, to the prejudice of other creditors, it was said, must be construed strictly, "and not extended to such debts as the members do not owe *in law*, but only in equity;" so that under it, the stock of a member was not held liable for a debt due by him to one as *trustee* for the company.[3] It is very clear that a corporation has no power to make a by-law, imposing upon a stockholder *a forfeiture* of his shares for non-payment of instalments due thereon, unless the power to make such a by-law is expressly conferred upon it, by statute or act of incorporation,[4] as it sometimes is.[5]

§ 357. Whether a by-law is reasonable or not, is a question for the court solely; and evidence to the jury on the subject, showing the effects of the law, was held inadmissible.[6] To set as idea by-law, however, for unreasonableness, there should be no equipoise of opinion upon the matter, but its unreasonableness should be demonstrably shown.[7] Courts, in construing by-laws, will interpret them *reasonably;* not scru-

---

1 Child *v.* Hudson's Bay Company, 2 P. Wms. 207; and see Utica Bank *v.* Smalley, 2 Cowen, 770; Cunningham *v.* Alabama Life Ins. & Trust Co. 4 Ala. 652.

2 Child *v.* Hudson's Bay Company, 2 P. Wms. 207.

3 Ibid.

4 In the matter of the Long Island Railroad Co. 19 Wend. 37. Perrin *v.* Granger, 30 Vt. 595.

5 Herkimer Manuf. & Hydraulic Company *v.* Small, 21 Wend. 273; Troy Turnpike and Railroad Company *v.* McChesney, id. 296.

6 Commonwealth *v.* Worcester, 3 Pick. 462. The regulations which railroad companies adopt to secure the safety of travellers, and to protect their own rights and privileges, are not, properly speaking, by-laws. Their validity depends upon their reasonableness, and is a question of fact for the jury. State *v.* Overton, 4 N. J. 435.

7 Paxson *v.* Sweet, 1 Green, N. J. 196.

tinizing their terms for the purpose of making them void, nor holding them invalid if every particular reason for them does not appear.[1] Thus, a by-law of a poulterers' company, enabling the master, &c., to call and admit into livery all such freemen as they shall think meet, and imposing a fine upon such persons called who shall refuse to be of the same livery without cause, was reasonably construed to imply that the freemen called to livery must be such only as were eligible by law.[2] Where a charter or statute empowers a corporation to pass such by-laws as are *necessary*, the by-law, to be valid, need not recite that it was necessary; but the "*necessity*" will be implied from the act of passing it, being, in fact, synonymous with "*expediency*."[3] Where a by-law merely *empowers* a select body to do a particular act, it is to be construed as a *license*, and not as a *command*, to them; nor does it communicate to those for whose benefit the power might be exercised, a right to compel the exercise of it in their favor; as, if the by-law declare that it "shall be lawful," for the select body to admit certain classes of persons, members, at appointed times.[4] And where the statutes of the founders of a divinity school authorize the trustees to remove a professor for "gross neglect of duty, scandalous immorality, mental incapacity, or any other just and sufficient cause;" they cannot remove a professor upon grounds of mere expediency and convenience, nor unless he has forfeited his office for some of the causes mentioned in the statutes.[5] In such a case, a charge of jealousy of other members of the faculty, of want of confidence in his colleagues and in the trustees, unaccompanied with an allegation of actually existing mischief caused thereby, is not sufficient ground for removal.[6] Nor is a charge, that there is a settled difference of opinion between a professor and the trustees respecting the arrangement of his department, in such case, of itself, a sufficient cause for removal; nor that he has unfavorably represented to another

---

[1] Vinters *v.* Passey, 1 Burr. 235, 239, Dennison, J.; Workingham *v.* Johnson, Cas. *temp.* Hardw. 285; Colchester *v.* Goodwin, Carter, 119, 120.

[2] Poulterers Company *v.* Phillips, 7 Bing. N. C. 314; Tobacco Pipe Makers Company *v.* Woodruffe, 7 B. & C. 738.

[3] Stuyvesant *v.* Mayor, &c. of New York, 7 Cowen, 606. Whether a by-law requiring all meetings to be notified by the clerk in a particular manner, in a clause relating to special meetings, relates to annual or stated meetings, and whether a failure to comply with the formal part of the notice renders the business transacted at the meeting void, see Warner *v.* Mower, 11 Vt. 385.

[4] Rex *v.* Eye, 4 B. & Ald. 272, 2 D. & R. 174, 1 B. & C. 85.

[5] Murdock *v.* Phillips Academy, 12 Pick. 244.

[6] Murdock's Appeal, 7 Pick. 303.

professor the character of a third; nor that he has disclosed the proceedings and differences of the faculty in their official meetings; nor that he has conversed freely with the students, as to the character and conduct of other professors, and expressed to them his opinion that certain laws of the institution were unreasonable and unjust; nor that he has discussed with the students subjects belonging to the departments of his colleagues, impugning their arguments.[1]

§ 358. The words "*shall and may*," when used together, are, however, as we have seen, construed to mean "*must*," whether employed in an act of parliament or public statute, or in the statute of a private foundation.[2] And if a select body be empowered by a by-law to examine and approve candidates for admission, their examination and approval does not confer a right to be admitted, but the company is as free to refuse admission as before examination.[3] The by-law of a beneficial society provided for the relief of diseased members on application to the stewards of the society; and under it a member was adjudged entitled to relief only from the date of his application, and not from that of his disability or sickness.[4] If a by-law be entire, so that the part which is void influences the whole, the entire by-law is void; as if in its terms it embrace strangers, not subject to the legislative power of the corporation as well as members.[5] For the same reason, if the by-law empower the levy of the penalty to be by distress and sale, where there is a custom to warrant the distress, but not the sale, it is void in toto, for the distress as well as the sale.[6] On the other hand, if the by-law consist of several distinct and independent parts, although one or more of them may be void, the rest are equally valid as if the void clauses had been omitted; for where it consists of several particulars, it is to all purposes as several by-laws, though the provisions are thrown together under the form of one.[7]

---

1 Murdock's Appeal, 7 Pick. 303.

2 Attorney-General *v.* Lock, case of Morden College, 3 Atk. 166; but see Rex *v.* Flockwood Inclosure, 2 Chit. 251.

3 Rex *v.* Askew, 4 Burr. 2190.

4 Breneman *v.* Franklin Beneficial Association, 3 Watts & S. 218.

5 Dodwell *v.* Oxford, 2 Vent. 34; Guilford *v.* Clarke, 2 Vent. 248; Oxford *v.* Wildgoose, 2 Lev. 293.

6 Clarke *v.* Tucker, 3 Lev. 282; Lee *v.* Wallis, 1 Kenyon, Ca. 295; and see Rex *v.* Feversham, 8 T. R. 356; Player *v.* Vere, T. Raym. 328; Rex *v.* Spencer, 3 Burr. 1839.

7 Fazakerly *v.* Wiltshire, 1 Stra. 469, per Pratt, C. J.; 11 Mod. 353; Harris *v.* Wakeman, Sayer, 256; Lee *v.* Wallis, 1 Kenyon, Ca. 295; Rex *v.* Coopers Co. 7 T. R. 549, per Lawrence, J.; Rex *v.* Feversham, 8 T. R. 356; Rogers *v.* Jones, 1 Wend. 237.

§ 359. Though a corporate company may, by prescription or statute, be vested with a local jurisdiction, so that its by-laws will bind those within its jurisdiction, whether strangers or members of the corporation;[1] yet unless this be the case, a corporation has jurisdiction over its own internal concerns only, and its by-laws are binding upon none but its members[2] or officers.[3] These, the by-laws obligate, upon the ground of their express or implied consent to them;[4] nor is it an objection to a corporator's being bound by a by-law, that he had no notice of it, or that he was not a member of the corporation at the time the by-law was passed.[5] Where, however, a railway company had power by statute to bind its passengers by by-laws painted on a board and hung up at the stations, it seems that a by-law regulating the responsibility of the company for luggage, does not obviate the company's liability at common law, unless knowledge of the by-law be brought home to the passenger.[6]

§ 360. 1. The power to make by-laws necessarily supposes the power to enforce them by pecuniary penalties, competent and proportionable to

---

[1] Kirk *v.* Nowell, 1 T. R. 118; Rex *v.* College of Physicians, 4 Burr. 2186; 5 Burr. 2740; Vandine's case, 6 Pick. 187; Marietta *v.* Fearing, 5 Ohio, 427. In Massachusetts, a statute of that State which forbids innkeepers, &c., to give credit to any undergraduate of a college, without consent of the president thereof, or of such other officer as may be authorized by the government of the college, *or in violation of any rules and regulations of the college,* has been held to be constitutional. But no penalty is incurred by an innkeeper, &c., under this statute, unless some rules have been made by the college on the subject of giving credit, nor unless some officer has been authorized to give or withhold his consent; and in action for the penalty imposed by the statute, the declaration is fatally defective, if it do not allege that rules have been established, and an officer authorized, &c. Soper *v.* Harvard College, 1 Pick. 177.

[2] Butchers Company of London, 1 Bulst. 11, 12; Com. Dig. By-Law, C. 2; Dodwell *v.* University of Oxford, 2 Vent. 33, 34; Masters, &c. of Trinity House *v.* Crispin, T. Jones, 144; Company of Horners *v.* Barlow, 3 Mod. 159. See 1 Rol. Abr. 366; Carth. 170; 1 Salk. 193; Mayor of Oxford *v.* Wildgoose, 3 Lev. 293; Mechanics Bank *v.* Smith, 19 Johns. 115; Susquehannah Insurance Company *v.* Perrine, 7 Watts &. S. 348; Palmyra *v.* Morton, 25 Misso. 593; Worcester *v.* Essex, &c. Bridge Co. 7 Gray, 457.

[3] Bank of Wilmington and Brandywine *v.* Wollaston, 3 Harring. Del. 90.

[4] Masters of Trinity House *v.* Crispin, T. Jones, 145; Adley *v.* Reeves, 2 M. & S. 60; Stetson *v.* Kempton, 13 Mass. 282; Corporation of Columbia *v.* Harrison, 4 Const. R. 213; Susquehannah Insurance *v.* Perrine, 7 Watts & S. 348.

[5] Lutw. 405; Cudden *v.* Estwick, 6 Mod. 124; Prigge *v.* Adams, Skin. 350; London *v.* Vanacre, 12 Mod. 273; 1 Ld. Raym. 499; Pierce *v.* Bartrum, Cowp. 270; Susquehannah Insurance Co. *v.* Perrine, 7 Watts & S. 348.

[6] Great Western Railway Company *v.* Goodman, 12 C. B. 313, 11 Eng. L. & Eq. 546.

the offence;[1] and a penalty incurred may be enforced after the expiration of the period it was intended to regulate.[2] It is impossible to lay down any rule as to what is a reasonable penalty; but this must be determined by the nature of the offence.[3] The penalty must be a sum certain, and not left to the arbitrary assessment of the governing part of the company upon the circumstances of the particular case, even though the utmost limit of the sum be fixed; for this would be allowing a party to assess his own damages.[4] A by-law, however, with a penalty of £5 or less, at the discretion and pleasure of the master and wardens, so that it be not less than 40*s.* was held not bad for uncertainty in the amount of the penalty.[5] And where the amount of the penalty to be inflicted by a corporation, on the breach of one of its by-laws, is expressly or impliedly fixed by the charter, a by-law, the penalty of which exceeds that amount, is void; as a by-law of a city corporation inflicting a penalty beyond what can be recovered in its court of wardens.[6] When a corporation is empowered to enforce its by-laws by fine and amercement, they are by implication precluded from adopting any other method of enforcing them.[7] Neither can obedience to a by-law be enforced by the imprisonment of the offender,[8] or of the forfeiture of his goods, unless power be expressly given by statute — both these being against magna charta.[9] If either of these modes are adopted, an action of false imprisonment in the one case, and trespass for taking away the goods in the other, may be maintained by the injured party against the officer.[10]

---

[1] Chamberlain of London's case, 5 Co. 63, b; The City of London's case, 8 Co. 253; 3 Leon. 265; Mayor & Aldermen of Mobile *v.* Yuille, 3 Ala. 137; 2 Kyd on Corp. 156; Willcock on Mun. Corporations, 154, § 368.

[2] Stevens *v.* Dimond, 6 N. H. 330.

[3] 2 Kyd on Corp. 156; Willcock on Mun. Corp. 154, § 368.

[4] Wood *v.* Searl, J. Bridg. 141; 3 Leon. 8; Rex *v.* Newdigate, Comb. 10; Mayor & Aldermen of Mobile *v.* Yuille, 3 Ala. 137; 2 Kyd on Corp. 157; Willcock on Mun. Corp. 154, § 368.

[5] Piper *v.* Chappell, 14 M. & W. 624, where see case Wood *v.* Searl, commented on and explained; Mayor, &c. of Huntsville *v.* Phelps, 27 Ala. 55.

[6] McMullen *v.* City Council of Charleston, 1 Bay. 382.

[7] Kirk *v.* Nowill, 1 T. R. 125, Buller, J.

[8] Clark's case, 5 Co. 64; Chamberlain of London's case, 5 Co. 63; City of London's case, 8 Co. 253; Bab *v.* Clerke, F. Moore, 411; London *v.* Wood, 12 Mod. 686; 3 Salk. 76; Barter *v.* Commonwealth, 3 Pen. & W. 253; Hart *v.* Mayor, &c. Albany, 9 Wend. 571.

[9] Player *v.* Archer, 2 Sid. 121; Clark *v.* Tucker, 2 Vent. 183; City of London's case, 8 Co. 253; 1 Bulstr. 11, 12; 2 Inst. 47; Kirk *v.* Nowill, 1 T. R. 118; Cotter *v.* Doty, 5 Ohio, 395; Mayor & Aldermen of Mobile *v.* Yuille, 3 Ala. 144.

[10] Strode *v.* Deering, Show. 168; Lamb *v.* Mills, Skin. 587; Wood *v.* Searl, J. Bridg. 139; Clark's case, 5 Co. 64; Kirk *v.* Nowill, 1 T. R. 118.

Nor can obedience to a by-law relating to the payment of instalments due on shares of the stock of an incorporated company be compelled, without express authority given by statute or act of incorporation, by forfeiture of such shares;[1] nor can the directors of a corporation declare a forfeiture of the stock of a stockholder in any case, except when and in the mode prescribed by charter.[2] A power reserved by by-law to the directors of a mutual insurance company, in case of non-payment of a call on a premium note given by a member to the corporation, to require payment of the whole amount of the note, to be held for the payment of assessments due and thereafter made, the balance, if any, to be returned to the member after the expiration of his policy, is not a power to impose a forfeiture, and requires no express authorization by charter.[3] Where, as is sometimes the case, the remedy by forfeiture of the stock is given, it is cumulative, and does not deprive the company of the right to proceed by action for the recovery of the calls, or instalments of their subscriptions.[4] And even after such suit brought, the company may declare a forfeiture of the stock, which cannot be pleaded in bar of the further maintenance of the suit, where the value of the stock forfeited is not equal to the money due to the company.[5] In such case, however, the stockholder is entitled, on assessment of damages, to insist that the value of the stock forfeited shall be allowed in diminution

---

1 In the matter of the Long Island Railroad Company, 19 Wend. 37. The forfeiture of the policy, in case of non-payment of assessments on the premium note, was held good as a condition of the policy of a mutual insurance company, on the ground of contract. Beadle *v.* Chenango County Mutual Insurance Company, 3 Hill, 161, 162; and see Cahill *v.* Kalamazoo Mutual Insurance Company, 2 Doug. Mich. 139.

2 State *v.* Morris & Essex Railroad Company, 3 N. J. 360.

3 Cahill *v.* Kalamazoo Mutual Insurance Company, 2 Doug. Mich. 138, 139.

4 Herkimer Manufacturing & Hydraulic Co. *v.* Small, 21 Wend. 273; Troy Turnpike & Railroad Co. *v.* McChesney, 21 Wend. 296; Northern Railroad Co. *v.* Miller, 10 Barb. 260; Hightower *v.* Thornton, 8 Ga. 486; Klein *v.* Alton & Sangamon Railroad Co. 13 Ill. 516; Instone *v.* Frankfort Bridge Co. 2 Bibb, 576; Gratz *v.* Redd, 4 B. Mon. 193, 194; Tar River Nav. Co. *v.* Neal, 3 Hawks, 520; Grays *v.* Turnpike Co. 4 Rand. 578; Stokes *v.* Lebanon & Sparta Turnpike Co. 6 Humph. 241; Beene *v.* C. & M. R. R. Co. 3 Ala. 660; Selma & Tennessee R. R. Co. *v.* Tipton, 5 Ala. 787; Fort Edward & Fort Miller P. R. Co. *v.* Payne, 17 Barb. 567; Ogdensburgh, Rome & Clayton R. R. Co. *v.* Frost, 21 id. 541; N. Albany & Salem R. R. Co. *v.* Pickens, 5 Ind. 247; Peoria & Oquawka R. R. Co. *v.* Elting, 17 Ill. 429. The same construction is put in England upon the provisions of the Companies Clauses Consolidation Act, which gives the two remedies to railway companies for the enforcement of payment of calls. Great Northern Railway Co. *v* Kennedy, 4 Exch. 417; Inglis *v.* Great Northern Railway Co. 1 Macq. H. L. 1112, 16 Eng. L. & Eq. 55, 60.

5 Ibid.

of the sum which the company would otherwise be entitled to recover.[1] But where the stock forfeited is equal in value to the amount due to the company, the forfeiture may be pleaded in bar, and the plea will be good, provided it avers that the value of the stock is equal to the amount due.[2]

§ 361. In an action against a mutual fire insurance company, on a policy which, in terms, was to become void if assigned *without the consent of the company in writing*, it appeared that one of the by-laws of the company was as follows: "When any buildings are mortgaged at the time they are insured, the mortgagee may have the policy assigned to him on his signing the premium note, or giving security for the payment of the same;" and on his so doing, any agent, &c., "shall be authorized to give the assent of the company to said assignment." It appeared that the buildings covered by the policy being under mortgage, the plaintiff stated the fact in his written application, adding that he *wished an assignment to the mortgagee*. The court held that the act of issuing the policy could not be deemed a consent in writing to the assignment, though the policy contained an express reference to the application, and that the policy was therefore void. Neither was the policy revived by the fact that the company, with a knowledge that the policy had been forfeited by assignment, had assessed the assured on account of losses occurring before the assignment, and had collected the assessments; the assured being held liable to contribute to all losses which happened while the policy was in force, though the assessment was not made until afterwards.[3]

§ 362. A by-law cannot be enforced by avoiding any bond or covenant made in contravention of it;[4] nor by disfranchising the offender.[5]

---

[1] Herkimer Manufacturing & Hydraulic Company *v.* Small, 21 Wend. 273.

[2] Ibid.

[3] Smith *v.* Saratoga County Mutual Fire Insurance Company, 3 Hill, 508. The by-laws of mutual insurance companies, of which the persons insured are the members, usually provide that misrepresentation of his interest by the assured, neglect to give notice of increase of risk, &c., shall invalidate the policy. Such by-laws are commonly incorporated by reference into the policy, as conditions and limitations of the contract, and are strictly enforced by the courts, unless the company has expressly or impliedly waived them. Wellcome *v.* People's Eq. Mut. Fire Ins. Co. 2 Gray, 480; Bowditch Mut. Fire Ins. Co. *v.* Winslow, 3 id. 415; Philbrook *v.* New England Mut. Fire Ins. Co. 37 Me. 137; Gardiner *v.* Piscataquis Mut. Fire Ins. Co. 38 id. 439; Union Mut. Fire Ins. Co. *v.* Keyser, 32 N. H. 313; Hale *v.* U. M. Fire Ins. Co. id. 295.

[4] Harscot's case, Comb. 203; Doggerell *v.* Pokes, F. Moore, 411.

[5] Rex *v.* London, 2 Lev. 201; Clark's case, 1 Vent. 327; Bab *v.* Clerke, F. Moore, 411, contra.

But it has been held, in Pennsylvania, that a by-law of a church corporation, enforcing the payment of pew-rent by suspending one in arrear for a longer time than two years of his right to vote for officers, was valid.[1]

§ 363. 2. The general mode of enforcing the penalty of a by-law is by bringing an action of debt or assumpsit to recover it.[2] In England, it is held, that the penalty of a by-law is recoverable by distress and detention until payment, according to the forms of the common law.[3] But when a by-law gives power to distrain upon due proof before the master and wardens, there can be no distress before verdict for the penalty; for there is no legal proof other than the finding of a jury.[4] And unless there be a special custom or legislative authority for it, the penalty of a by-law cannot be enforced by distress and *sale;*[5] or by detaining the offender's share of the profits of the company, until the amount shall be sufficient to liquidate the penalty.[6] And a by-law founded on a custom to exclude foreigners, and authorizing a distress for the penalty in case of a breach of the by-law, *without a previous demand and refusal of such penalty*, is bad; and the defendant, justifying the taking of goods as a distress for a penalty incurred by breach of a by-law, must aver a previous demand and refusal of payment, and must prove that averment, although the by-laws do not exact any such preliminary.[7] A by-law cannot compel the payment of a penalty, by excluding the offender from all participation in the profits of the com-

---

1 Commonwealth *v.* Cain, 5 S. & R. 510.

2 Barber Surgeons *v.* Pelson, 2 Lev. 252; Clift, 901, 902, cited Com. Dig. By-law, D. 1; Tidd, Prac. 3, 4; Lee *v.* Wallis, 1 Kenyon, Cas. 295; Wooly *v.* Idle, 4 Burr. 1952; Feltmakers *v.* Davis, 1 Bos. & P. 98; Adley *v.* Reeves, 2 M. & S. 60; Mayor of London *v.* Goree, Carth. 92; Mayor of Exeter *v.* Tumlet, 2 Wils. 95; Corporation of Columbia *v.* Harrison, 4 Const. R. 213.

3 Clark *v.* Tucker, 3 Lev. 281, 2 Vent. 183; Bodwic *v.* Fennell, 1 Wils. 237; Clark's case, 5 Co. 64 a; City of London's case, 8 Co. 253; Lee *v.* Wallis, Sayer, 263, 1 Kenyon, Cas. 295; City of London *v.* Wood, 12 Mod. 686.

4 Wood *v.* Searl, J. Bridg. 142.

5 Clark *v.* Tucker, 3 Lev. 281, 2 Vent. 183; Lee *v.* Wallis, 1 Kenyon, Cas. 295, Sayer, 263; Adley *v.* Reeves, 2 M. & S. 60. The corporation of Albany cannot pass a by-law subjecting a vessel, lying in any basin, dock, &c., to seizure and sale, in case of refusal by the owner, after notice, to remove her; the remedy for enforcing their by-laws being specified, and the right to make by-laws creating a forfeiture, not being given. Hart *v.* Mayor, &c. of Albany, 9 Wend. 571.

6 Adley *v.* Reeves, 2 M. & S. 60, called Adley *v.* Whitstable Co. 17 Ves. 304.

7 Davis *v.* Morgan, 1 Cromp. & J. 587, 1 Tyrw. 557, 1 Price, P. C. 77.

pany until payment;[1] or by making a stop of his gun proof, which would prevent him from carrying on his trade with equal advantage;[2] or by committing him to prison until payment; though he has assented to the by-law;[3] unless there be a special custom, or power granted by statute. In these cases there is penalty upon penalty.[4]

§ 364. 3. The penalty of a by-law can in general be given only to the corporation injured by the offence against its regulations.[5] And where the penalty is given in general terms, without specifying to whose use it is to be applied, it is to be understood to the use of the corporation.[6] The form of reserving the penalty, however, is equally good, whether it be to the company, or to the masters, &c., for the use of the company.[7] The penalty cannot be given to a mere stranger, as, "*to any who shall sue for the same;*" for this would be like assigning a chose in action, which the policy of the law will not endure.[8] Upon this principle it has been held in England, that if the injury be to a particular company, as where a custom excludes foreigners from the practice of a particular trade, or from the practice of the trade of a particular company, as well freemen as foreigners, unless free of that company, the penalty of the by-law founded upon it ought not to be given to the municipal corporation, or their officer, but to the company injured, or their treasurer in trust for them.[9] But where a by-law gave a penalty for trading against a custom excluding foreigners, to be recovered by the chamberlain, one third of it for the benefit of the prisoners of the

---

[1] Adley *v.* Reeves, 2 M. & S. 60.

[2] Gunmakers *v.* Fell, Willes, 390.

[3] 1 Rol. Abr. 363 to 365; Wood *v.* Searl, J. Bridg. 141; Clark's case, 5 Co. 64 a; City of London's case, 8 Co. 253; Bab *v.* Clerke, F. Moore, 411; Rex *v.* Clerke, 1 Salk. 349; Rex *v.* Boston, W. Jones, 162; Rex *v.* Merchant Tailors, and Rex *v.* London, 2 Lev. 200; London *v.* Wood, 12 Mod. 686, 1 Salk. 397; Barter *v.* Commonwealth, 3 Penr. & W. 253.

[4] Adley *v.* Reeves, 2 M. & S. 53.

[5] Hollings *v.* Hungerford, cited in Bodwic *v.* Fennell, 1 Wils. 235; London *v.* Wood, 12 Mod. 686.

[6] 2 Kyd on Corp. 157.

[7] Graves *v.* Colby, 1 Perry & D. 235.

[8] Bodwic *v.* Fennell, 1 Wils. 233, 236, 237; Hollings *v.* Hungerford, and Ellington *v.* Cheney, there cited; Totterdell *v.* Glazby, 2 Wils. 266.

[9] Wilton *v.* Wilks, 2 Ld. Raym. 1133, 6 Mod. 21; Weavers of London *v.* Brown, Cro. E. 803; Bodwic *v.* Fennell, 1 Wils. 235; Hesketh *v.* Braddock, 3 Burr. 1847; Wooly *v.* Idle, 4 Burr. 1951; York *v.* Wellbank, 4 B. & Ald. 440. But see Tailors of Bath *v.* Glazby, 2 Wils. 266.

jail, another third part for the informer, and the other third part remaining undisposed of, for the use of the corporation; no exception was taken to this distribution of the penalty;[1] and it appears, says Mr. Willcock, to be unexceptionable, for the division is subsequent to the recovery, and no injury to the defendant.[2]

§ 365. 4. If the by-law does not specify in whose name the action for the penalty is to be brought, it must be brought in the name of the corporation.[3] And where the penalty is given to the master and wardens of a company, to the use of the master, wardens, and company, the action cannot be maintained in the name of the master, wardens, and company, but must be brought in the name of the master and wardens alone, who would probably declare both in their natural and official capacities.[4] But where the action for the penalty was brought by the master and wardens, who were such at the time the fine was incurred, but had ceased to be so at the time the action was commenced, a plea, that the plaintiffs were not master and wardens, was held good.[5] If the by-law, as it may, limit the penalty to be recovered by the chamberlain or treasurer of the corporation, for the use of the corporation, the action must be brought in the name of the chamberlain or treasurer.[6]

§ 366. If the chamberlain or treasurer sue for the penalty, it is sufficient for him to allege that he is chamberlain or treasurer; and it is not

---

[1] Hesketh *v.* Braddock, 3 Burr. 1848; Player *v.* Archer, 2 Sid. 121; Harris *v.* Wakeman, Sayer, 254. When the penalty of a town by-law is to be paid, one half to the informer, and the other half into the treasury of the town, a *qui tam* action therefor may, it seems, be sustained in the name of the informer and the town treasurer. Bradley *v.* Baldwin, 5 Conn. 288.

[2] Willcock on Mun. Corpor. 156, § 373.

[3] 2 Kyd on Corp. 157; Vintners *v.* Passey, 1 Burr. 235.

[4] Feltmakers *v.* Davis, 1 B. & P. 101; Wood *v.* Mayor and Commonalty of London, 1 Salk. 399; Graves *v.* Colby, 9 A. & E. 356, 1 Perry & D. 225; Piper *v.* Chappell, 14 M. & W. 643.

[5] Graves *v.* Colby, 1 Perry & D. 235. And *it seems* that the right of action did not pass to the succeeding master and wardens. But qu. id.

[6] Chamberlain of London's case, 5 Co. 63 b; Harris *v.* Wakeman, Sayer, 254; Hollings *v.* Hungerford, cited, 1 Wils. 235; Bodwic *v.* Fennell, 1 Wils. 235, 236, 237; Hesketh *v.* Braddock, 3 Burr. 1847, 1854; Feltmakers *v.* Davis, 1 B. & P. 101, 102. The statute of 1802, regulating the town of Hillsborough (N. C.), enables the treasurer of the town to sue in his own name for penalties incurred under the by-laws authorized thereby, as well as for those incurred under the statute itself. Watts *v.* Scott, 1 Dev. 291.

necessary for him to set forth or show in what manner he was elected or appointed.[1] He must, however, set forth and show that the penalty was made payable to and recoverable by him.[2] Where the by-law is made by virtue of the incidental power in the body at large, it is not necessary to set forth the authority of the corporation to make it. But if it be made by virtue of a special power of making by-laws, the special authority must be set out in the pleadings, and proved, and also that it was made by the select body in whom such power was vested, and at what time it was made.[3] In an action of debt for the penalty of a by-law, the by-law itself must be fully set out, and not by way of mere recital; and it is not sufficient to aver that the defendant incurred the penalty by the breach of a certain by-law.[4] In an action of assumpsit founded upon a by-law, it would seem that this averment was sufficient, the same strictness of pleading not being required in this form of action; since, after all, it comes to a question on the evidence, what legal consideration there is to raise and support the promise.[5] It must appear by proper averments in the proceeding, that the defendant was subject to the by-law; though, if this be once shown, it is not necessary to aver formally that he was so at the time the offence was committed; for it having been stated that he became a member of the corporation, it will be presumed that he continued one until the contrary appear.[6] It is, however, never necessary to aver that the defendant had notice of the by-law; for every one subject to the action of a law is presumed to know its import, as is his duty.[7] If the by-law except certain classes of persons from its oper-

---

[1] Harris v. Wakeman, Sayer, 256; Hollings v. Hungerford, there cited by Rider, C. J.

[2] Exon v. Starre, 2 Show, 159.

[3] Rex v. Lyme Regis. 1 Doug. 157, 158, 159; Feltmakers v. Davis, 1 B. & P. 100, 101; Rex v. Decan' et Capitul' Dublin, 1 Stra. 539; Dunham v. Trustees of Rochester, 5 Cowen, 462.

[4] Com. Dig. Pl. 2, W. 11; 2 Vent. 243; 1 Bro. Ent. 170; Gerrish v. Rodman, 3 Wils. 155, 164; Feltmakers v. Davis, 1 B. & P. 102. For form of declaration in debt on by-law, see Stuyvesant v. Mayor, &c. of New York, 7 Cowen, 606. A statute which renders it unnecessary, in prosecutions on the by-laws of the city of Boston, to set forth the by-law at large, does not conflict with the constitution of Massachusetts. Commonwealth v. Worcester, 3 Pick. 462. A complaint for the breach of a by-law of the city of Boston, concluding, "against the form of the by-law, in such case made and provided," is not sufficient, unless it conclude, also, "against the form of the statute, &c." Commonwealth v. Gay, 5 Pick. 44; see also, Commonwealth v. Worcester, 3 Pick. 475; Stevens v. Dimond, 6 N. H. 331.

[5] Barber Surgeons v. Pelson, 2 Lev. 252; 1 B. & P. 101, n. b; Willcock on Mun. Corp. 173, § 426. But see Feltmakers v. Davis, 1 B. & P. 101, 102, Eyre, C. J. For pleadings in Replevin on Distress, see Gerrish v. Rodman, 3 Wils. 171.

[6] Colchester v. Goodwin, Carter, 119; Gunmakers v. Fell, Willes, 390; *Ex parte* Eden, 2 M. & S. 229.

[7] London v. Bernardiston, 1 Lev. 16; James v. Tutney, Cro. Car. 498.

ation, and the exception be material, it is necessary to aver that the defendant is not within the exception, in a return to a writ of *habeas corpus cum causâ;*[1] and it is necessary to state in such a return every thing necessary to be stated in an action of debt in a superior court, and no more.[2] But when in a by-law, making certain regulations, for breach of which parties are liable to be sued for a penalty, there is a separate proviso, making certain exceptions, a party suing for breach of the by-law need not aver in the declaration that the case was not within the exception in the proviso; but such fact, if it exist, must be shown by the defendant by way of excuse.[3] If a by-law, imposing a duty on a member, contain a condition precedent to his liability thereto, the declaration must aver a performance of the condition, or it will be bad.[4] Where the by-law, after imposing the penalty, declares that if the offender "deny, refuse, or neglect," to pay the penalty, it shall be recoverable in an action of debt, it is not necessary to aver a demand; though, had the word "neglect" been omitted, perhaps it might have been presumed that an indulgence was intended, and a demand necessary before an action could be maintained.[5]

§ 367. In an action by a society of innholders for the penalty of a by-law imposed upon those who, being elected, refused to accept the livery and clothing of the company, it was held that it was necessary to state in the declaration that the company of innholders has a livery, since the court will not notice what companies have, and what have not, a livery.[6] And in an action to recover a penalty for refusing an office, it is not necessary to aver that the defendant had notice of his election, nor when, nor where, the meeting at which he was elected, was held; for these he is presumed to know.[7] To such an action the defendant may either plead specially a reasonable excuse, or give it in evidence under the general issue.[8]

---

1 Rex *v.* Abington, Salk. 432; Rex *v.* Coopers of Newcastle, 7 T. R. 547.

2 Watson *v.* Clerke, Carth. 75; 2 Kyd on Corp. 170; Willcock on Mun. Corp. 174, rule laid down generally.

3 Carmarthen Mayor, &c. *v.* Lewis, 6 C. & P. 608.

4 Carter *v.* Sanderson, 5 Bing. 79.

5 Butchers *v.* Bullock, 3 B. & P. 434, 437.

6 Innholders *v.* Gledhill, Sayer, 275; Rex *v.* Clerke, 1 Salk. 349; see Piper *v.* Chappell, 14 M. & W. 648, in which it was held that the declaration was not bad for not showing that the company had a livery when the declaration set forth the charter, which mentioned that the company had a livery.

7 London *v.* Vanacre, 5 Mod. 442, 1 Ld. Raym. 500; Vintners *v.* Passey, 1 Burr. 239.

8 Ibid.; Rex *v.* Leyland, 3 M. & S. 188.

§ 368. Although, as we have seen, the adoption of a code of by-laws may sometimes be proved by implication,[1] yet in general, in order to prove what they are, it is necessary that they should be produced; and parol proof of their contents, as in case of the by-laws of a bank, by the cashier, is insufficient.[2] When the books of the corporation, in which it is proved that the by-laws of the corporation are registered, are produced, they are evidence of the by-laws even against strangers to the corporation.[3] To prove private statutes and by-laws it is not necessary to set out their provisions in the pleadings, and they may be proved by the instrument to which they are attached, if this has been received by the party bound by them.[4] In England, it is held that where a by-law is pleaded to have been made and lost, the jury may, from ancient and unvaried usage, though within time of memory, in conformity to it, find the facts of its having been made in the terms set forth, and since lost; particularly if the usage be traced to a period when an alteration, like that contained in the by-law, was suddenly introduced; and this, too, whether the corporation be by prescription or charter.[5] Sixty years' usage has been considered evidence of a by-law.[6] If the jury only find, however, that such a usage has prevailed from a time within memory, without finding a by-law, the alteration supposed to have been made by the by-law cannot be sustained, whether the corporation be ancient or modern; it cannot as a by-law, since no by-law is found; nor as a custom; for though in an ancient corporation, usage within time of memory may be *evidence of a custom*, yet if a period be shown at which the contrary prevailed, that evidence is rebutted.[7] Corporators are not competent witnesses to prove a custom of excluding strangers from exercising trades within a town, where a moiety of the penalty, imposed by a by-law for the breach of that custom, goes to the corporation; nor even, it seems, though that moiety be granted away by them, by the by-law, to a company.[8] It has been decided in Massachusetts, that the

---

[1] Union Bank *v.* Ridgely, 1 Harris & G. 324; *Supra*, § 1.

[2] Lumbard *v.* Aldrich, 8 N. H. 35.

[3] Case of Thetford, 12 Vin. Abr. 90.

[4] Atlantic F. Ins. Co. *v.* Sanders, 36 N. H. 252.

[5] Case of Corporations, 4 Co. 78; Rex *v.* Tomlyn, Cas. *temp.* Hardw. 316; Rex *v.* Miller, 6 T. R. 280; Rex *v.* Westwood, 4 B. & C. 786. And see Taylor *v.* Griswold, 2 Green, N. J. 223; Rex *v.* Atwood, 1 Nev. & M. 286, 4 B. & Ad. 699.

[6] Perkins *v.* Cutler's Company, 1 Selw. N. P. 1144, Mansfield, C. J.

[7] Rex *v.* Westwood, 4 B. & C. 786.

[8] Davis *v.* Morgan, 1 Cromp. & J. 587; 1 Tyrw. 457, 1 Price, P. C. 77.

legislature of that State may constitutionally enact, that the interest which an inhabitant of a city may have in a penalty for the breach of a by-law thereof, shall not disqualify him to act as judge, juror, or witness, in a prosecution to recover the penalty; and that such prosecution may be in the name of the Commonwealth.[1]

CHAPTER XI.

OF THE POWER TO SUE AND THE LIABILITY TO BE SUED.

§ 369. FIRST, *of the power to sue.* It is very obvious, that a corporation would be entirely incapacitated to manage its concerns and to carry into effect the objects for which it is constituted, if it had not the capacity of protecting its rights and of enforcing the just claims in its favor, by ordinary judicial process. The power, therefore, of a corporation to sue is, as has already been stated, one of its *incidental* powers, although it is most generally expressly given in charters to private corporations. The construction of acts respecting foreign attachment which would preclude a private corporation from suing out a writ of attachment, on the ground of the insufficiency of an affidavit made by its *attorney*, would be entirely inconsistent with the act of incorporation and the meaning and intent of the legislature. If an affidavit from the corporation itself were required, or the use of the writ denied without such affidavit, the law then which gives existence to the corporation, and which necessarily confers upon it an authority to perform by its agents, by whom it alone can act,[2] incidental services, like the one in question, would be defeated.[3] As a general rule the consent of a majority of the directors or trustees of a corporation is necessary to entitle the corporation to sue.[4]

§ 370. It is indeed now, as it has ever been, perfectly well estab-

---

1 Commonwealth *v.* Worcester, 3 Pick. 462.

2 See *ante*, Chap. IX.

3 Trenton Bank *v.* Haverstick, 6 Halst. 171.

4 Dart *v.* Houston, 22 Geo. 506.

lished, that corporations, whether public or private, may commence and prosecute all actions, upon all promises and obligations, implied as well as expressed, made to them, which fall within the scope of their design, and the authority conferred upon them.[1] The suit must generally be brought or defended in the corporate name.[2] Where the question was, whether a corporation could sue for use and occupation, where the tenant had occupied land belonging to the corporation without deed, it was held, that it could, as otherwise, or if a promise could not be implied, an action for use and occupation could never be brought by a corporation.[3] It is equally well settled, that corporations may sustain actions for all injuries done to the body corporate, as if an injury is done to one of the members, by which the body at large is put to any damage, it may sue on that account.[4] Thus a corporation owning a toll bridge may maintain a bill in equity, as for a nuisance to restrain a city from unlawfully laying out the bridge as a highway.[5] A private corporation (an insurance company for instance) may maintain an action for a libel for words published of them concerning their trade or business, by which they have suffered special damage.[6] A corporation may also have a writ of right as any tenant in fee-simple may;[7] and may prosecute all such real and possessory actions as are applicable to the case.[8] Moreover, where the charter of a corporation does not in terms give the power to refer to arbitration, the power to sue includes a power of reference; that being

---

[1] See McKim *v.* Odom, 3 Bland, Ch. 417; Gordon *v.* Mayor, &c. of Baltimore, 5 Gill, 231. In Ohio, by statute, claims accruing to a corporation during its existence may be prosecuted in the name of the corporation after its dissolution. Stetson *v.* City Bank of N. O. 2 Ohio, State, 167.

[2] Bradley *v.* Richardson, 2 Blatchf. C. C. 343.

[3] Mayor of Stafford *v.* Till, 4 Bing. 54. In Rutland & B. R. Co. *v.* Proctor, 29 Vt. 93, it was held that where a Railroad company bought property which by its charter it was perhaps not authorized to do, and sold part of it, the want of authority was no defence to an action for the price of the part sold. Where a special remedy is given by statute, assumpsit by a corporation will not lie, on an implied promise; otherwise, if there be an express contract. Kidder *v.* Boom Co. 24 Penn. State, 193. And see *ante*, Chaps. VIII., IX.

[4] 1 Kyd, 190, who cites Brian, C. J., 21 Ed. 4; Bro. Corp. 63. It has been held, in Connecticut, by a majority of the court, that an action on the case may be sustained for a vexatious suit against a corporation. Goodspeed *v.* East Haddam Bank, 22 Conn. 530. See South Royalton Bank *v.* Suffolk Bank, 27 Vt. 505.

[5] Central Bridge *v.* Lowell, 4 Gray, 474.

[6] Trenton Mutual Life and Fire Ins. Co. *v.* Perrine, 3 N. J. 402.

[7] 1 Kyd, 185.

[8] Chitty, Pl. 102; Com. Dig. tit. Franchise; Gospel Society *v.* Wheeler, 3 Gallis. 105.

one of the modes of prosecuting a suit to judgment.[1] A corporation aggregate may, in England, be the petitioning creditor, and sue out a commission of bankruptcy.[2]

§ 371. Two incorporated companies may unite in an action of assumpsit to recover a sum of money deposited in a bank in their joint names. Not being partners, they are tenants in common, and in that character there is no objection to their joining in a suit.[3] It cannot be necessary for this purpose, to decide whether it be in the power of the two corporations, who are plaintiffs, to consolidate their stock, or to form a partnership. General principles are against the power of corporations to do such acts.[4]

§ 372. A company claiming to be incorporated has only to show that it has been regularly and effectually made a corporate body, to enable it to sustain a suit beyond the jurisdiction within which it is constituted. Thus, in the case of the Dutch West India Company, it was long since decided in England, both in the King's Bench and Common Pleas, that a Dutch corporation might sue in England, though the objection was made, that it could not maintain a suit on account of its foreign character.[5] And it has been more recently held that a foreign corporation may maintain an action of assumpsit in England by their corporate name.[6] In the case of the National Bank of St. Charles, in the kingdom of Spain, which sued in England in its corporate capacity, letters of the defendant were put in and read, in which he admitted that he held in his hands a very large sum of money, the property of the bank. A witness produced a copy of the charter of the king of Spain, incorporating this bank. He at the same time stated that he procured this copy from the office of the council of Castile, which is the proper place for charters of this kind to be kept, and that he examined this copy with the original charter. The jury on being asked by the court whether the bank in question was the one incorporated by the king of Spain, having answered in the affirmative, the verdict was for the plain-

---

1 Alexandria Canal Co. *v.* Swann, 5 How. 83; Sawyer *v.* Winnegance Mill Co. 26 Me. 122; Day *v.* Essex Co. Bank, 13 Vt. 97.

2 *Ex parte* Bank of Ireland, 1 Molloy, Ch. 261.

3 New York and Sharon Canal Co. *v.* Fulton Bank, 7 Wend. 412.

4 Ibid.

5 Dutch West India Company *v.* Van Moyses, 2 Ld. Raym. 1535; 1 Stra. 612.

6 Chitty on Contracts, 86, who cites 1 Ryan & M. 190.

tiff.[1] Indeed, it may in England be deemed well settled, that after it has been proved, like any other matter of fact, that an association of persons, who bring a suit in any foreign court by a corporate name, have been incorporated, there is no more reason why their suit should not be sustained, than there is why the suit of a natural individual, who is a foreigner, should not be. A corporation established by a statute of Great Britain, may bring an action in one of the State courts in this country.[2]

§ 373. But every argument in favor of entertaining, in American courts, suits by corporations created by the laws of a country, not forming part of the American confederacy, applies with still greater force to corporations of the States composing the confederacy. It was with much truth said by Judge Cabell, of Virginia, in a case before him respecting the power of a foreign corporation to sue abroad, "It is rendered doubly necessary by the intimacy of our political union, and by the freedom and frequency of our commercial intercourse."[3] In an action where the defendants pleaded in abatement, that the "Portsmouth Livery Company" was not a body incorporated by the legislature of Massachusetts; and where it was said that the damages should have been demanded in the name of *all the persons constituting the said company, suing in their private and individual capacities;* the court said that the principle suggested by the plea had no foundation in any maxim, or in any argument of public policy; that the legislature of the State recognized in many instances, and to many purposes, corporations existing by foreign laws; and that the power of a corporation to sue a personal action, within the State of Massachusetts, was not restricted to corporations created by the laws of that State, as was supposed by the plea in abatement. The plea accordingly was held to be insufficient.[4] Nothing is, indeed, better settled, than that corporations may institute suits in the courts of States other than those under whose laws they have been established.[5] Trustees of a foreign corporation, appointed by

---

[1] National Bank of St. Charles *v.* De Bernales, 1 Car. & P. 569; and see Beverly *v.* Lincoln Gas-Light Co. 6 A. & E. 829.

[2] British American Land Co. *v.* Ames, 6 Met. 391.

[3] Bank of Marietta *v.* Pindalf, 2 Rand, 465.

[4] Portsmouth Livery Co. *v.* Watson, 10 Mass. 91.

[5] Holcomb *v.* Illinois, &c. Canal Co. 2 Scam. 236. See also, Bank of Washtenaw *v.* Montgomery, 2 id. 428; British American Land Co. *v.* Ames, 6 Met. 391; Frazier *v.* Wilcox, 4 Rob. La. 518; Bank of Edwardsville *v.* Simpson, 1 Misso. 5; Lewis *v.* Bank of Kentucky, 12 Ohio, 132; New York Fire Insurance Co. *v.* Ely, 5 Conn. 605; Corpo-

a court of equity, may maintain an action in their own names upon a negotiable note, which came to their hands with other assets of the institution.[1]

§ 374. The legislature undoubtedly has power to prohibit foreign corporations from contracting in the State; but until it does so, contracts so made will be enforced.[2] In Bank of Marietta *v.* Pindalf,[3] the court (though as a general rule they allowed that a corporation created by the laws of one State might sue in another), yet they said that it would not be permitted to a bank in Ohio to establish an agency in Virginia for discounting notes; or for carrying on any other banking operations; nor could they sustain an action on any note thus acquired by them. But they said there was nothing in the policy of the laws of Virginia which restrained its citizens from promoting their accommodation and interest by borrowing money from a bank in Ohio; nor was it the policy of its laws to restrain one citizen in Virginia from executing to another citizen or to a foreigner a note payable at a banking house legally constituted in Ohio; nor to prevent such bank from taking an assignment of such note by discounting it in Ohio; and a debt thus contracted, the court said, might be recovered by the bank by suit in Virginia. It was held by the Supreme Court of the State of New York, that a foreign corporation, keeping an office in that State for receiving deposits and discounting notes, without being expressly authorized by the laws of that State to do so, cannot maintain an action for the money loaned, either on a note or other security taken on such loan, or on the count for money lent. This decision was made in reference

---

rations of other States may sue in Louisiana. Christy's Digest, 91, who cites Williamson *v.* Smoot, 7 Mart. La. 31; and also see President, &c. of Lombard Bank *v.* Thorp, 6 Cowen, 46; Hartford Bank *v.* Barry, 17 Mass. 97; Marine & Fire Insurance Bank of Georgia *v.* Jauncey, 1 Barb. 486; Tombigbee Railroad Co. *v.* Kneeland, 4 How. 16; Guager Iron Co. *v.* Dawson, 4 Blackf. 202; Savage Mann. Co. *v.* Armstrong, 17 Me. 34; New York Dry Dock *v.* Hicks, 5 McLean, 111.

[1] Stewart *v.* Insurance Co. 9 Watts, 126.

[2] Frazier *v.* Wilcox, 4 Rob. La. 518; Atterbury *v.* Knox, 4 B. Mon. 92. A foreign corporation, although prohibited by its charter within the State of its creation, to take more than six per cent. per annum, on its loans or discounts, is not affected by such prohibition in another State, by whose comity it is permitted to make contracts. Hitchcock *v.* United States Bank of Pennsylvania, 7 Ala. 387; Bard *v.* Poole, 2 Kern. 495; Knox *v.* Bank of United States, 26 Missis. 655. And see Bank of Augusta *v.* Earle, 13 Pet. 584; and *ante*, Ch. VIII. in relation to contracts by corporations.

[3] Bank of Marietta *v.* Pindalf, 2 Rand, 465. See Slaughter *v.* Commonwealth, 13 Gratt. 767.

to a provision in the revised laws of that State, that where, by the laws of the State, any act is forbidden to be done by a corporation, without express authority of law, and such act be done by a foreign corporation, it shall not be authorized to maintain any action founded upon such act, or upon any liability or obligation, express or implied, arising out of, or made or entered into, in consideration of such act.[1]

§ 375. It was on one occasion made a ground of defence to a bill in equity, that the plaintiffs were a corporation created by a law of another State. "But," said Chancellor Kent, "the Court of Chancery should be as freely open to such suitors as a court of law; and it would be most unreasonable and unjust to deny them that privilege." "They might well," he said, "exclaim,

> Quod genus hoc hominum?
> ———— hospitio prohibemur arenæ."[2]

§ 376. As to the question raised in the case of the Bank of United States *v.* Devaux,[3] whether the old United States Bank, by virtue of its act of incorporation, was empowered to sue in the federal courts of the Union, the opinion, as given by Marshall, C. J., is as follows: "The judicial power of the United States, as defined in the constitution, is dependent, — 1st. On the nature of the case, and, 2d. On the characters of the parties. By the judicial act, the jurisdiction of the circuit courts is extended to cases where the constitutional right to plead and be impleaded, in the courts of the Union, depends on the character of the parties; but the circuit courts derive no jurisdiction from that act, except in the single case of a controversy between citizens of the same State, claiming land under grant from different States.

---

[1] New Hope, &c. Co. *v.* Pough. Silk Co. 25 Wend. 648. The cases in the same court avoiding the note, but allowing a recovery on the count for *money lent*, were questioned. Those cases were Utica Insurance Co. *v.* Kip, 8 Cowen, 20; Id. *v.* Caldwell, 3 Wend. 296. A foreign corporation may sue, in Pennsylvania, in its own name, or in that of its trustees. But *quære*, whether an agreement between a foreign banking institution and a citizen of Pennsylvania, by which the bank-notes of the institution were to be kept in circulation, by means of lending or discounting negotiable paper with them, is such an establishment of an office of discount in that State, as to be a violation of the act of the 28th of March, 1808. Stewart *v.* Ins. Company, 9 Watts, 126.

[2] Silverlake Bank *v.* North, 4 Johns. Ch. 370.

[3] Bank of United States *v.* Devaux, 5 Cranch, 84.

Unless, then, jurisdiction over this cause has been given to the Circuit Court, by some other than the judicial act, the Bank of the United States had not a right to sue in that court, upon the principle that the case arises under the law of the United States. The plaintiffs contend that the incorporating act confers this jurisdiction. That act creates the corporation, gives it a capacity to make contracts, and to acquire property, and enables it 'to sue and be sued, plead and be impleaded, answer and be answered, defend and be defended, in courts of record, or any other place whatsoever.' This power, if not incident to a corporation, is conferred by every incorporating act, and is not understood to enlarge the jurisdiction of any particular court, but to give a capacity to the corporation to appear, as a corporation, in any court, which would, by law, have cognizance of the cause, if brought by individuals. If jurisdiction is given by this clause to the federal courts, it is equally given to all courts having original jurisdiction, and for all sums, however small they may be. But the 9th article of the 7th section of the act furnishes a conclusive argument against the construction for which the plaintiffs contend. That section subjects the president and directors, in their individual capacity, to the suit of any person aggrieved, by their putting into circulation more notes than is permitted by law, and expressly authorizes the bringing of that action in the federal or State courts. This evinces the opinion of Congress, that the right to sue does not imply a right to sue in the courts of the Union, unless it be expressed. This idea is strengthened also by the law respecting patent rights. That law expressly recognizes the right of the patentee to sue in the circuit courts of the United States. The court, then, is of opinion that no right is conferred on the bank, by the act of incorporation, to sue in the federal courts." But it was held in this case, of Bank of United States *v.* Devaux, that a foreign corporation *in the character of its members*, *as aliens*, may sue in the federal courts of the United States; but these courts will not now (as will be shown in a subsequent section) go behind the corporate residence, so to speak, as to see *who the persons* really interested are.

§ 377. The right of a foreign corporation to sue, as such, in the courts of the United States, though it is generally acknowledged, may be suspended. Mr. J. Story, in the year 1814, in a suit instituted in the Circuit Court for the District of New Hampshire, during the war with England, by a religious corporation, constituted in England, by the name of The Society for the Propagation of the Gospel in Foreign

Parts,[1] considered that there were two objections to the rendition of judgment for the demandants. First, the corporation itself, being established in the enemy's country, acquired the enemy's character from its domicile; secondly, that the members of the company were subjects of the enemy, and therefore personally affected with the disability of hostile alienage. As to the first objection, the judge observed, "In general, an aggregate corporation in law is not deemed to have any commorancy, although the corporators have;[2] yet there are exceptions to this principle; and where a corporation is established in a foreign country, by a foreign government, it is undoubtedly an alien corporation, be its members who they may; and if the country become hostile, it may, for some purposes at least, be clothed with the same character. Even in respect to mere municipal rights and duties, an aggregate corporation has been deemed to have a local residence. It has been held to be an 'inhabitant' under the statute for the reparation of bridges;[3] and an 'inhabitant and occupier,' liable to pay poor rates, under the statute, 43 Eliz. ch. 2.[4] It may therefore acquire rights, and be subject to disabilities, arising from the country, if I may so express myself, of its domicil. And indeed, upon principle or authority, it seems to me difficult to maintain that an aggregate corporation, as, for instance, an insurance company, a bank, or a privateering company, established in the enemy's country, could, merely from its being an invisible, intangible thing, a mere incorporeal and legal entity, be entitled to maintain actions, to enforce rights, acquire property, or redress wrongs, when its own property on the ocean would be good prize of war. If the reason of the rule of the disability of an alien enemy be, as is sometimes supposed, that the party may not recover effects, which, by being carried hence, may enrich his country, that reason applies as well to the case of a corporation, as of an individual, in the hostile country. If the reason be, as Lord Chief Justice Eyre, in Sparenburgh *v.* Bannatyne,[5] asserts it to be, that a man, professing himself hostile to our country, and in a state of war with it, cannot be heard, if he sue for the benefit and protection of our laws in the courts of our country, that reason is not less significant in the case of a foreign corporation than of a foreign individual,

---

1 Society for the Propagation of the Gospel, &c. *v.* Wheeler, 2 Gallis. 105.

2 Inhabitants of Lincoln County *v.* Prince, 2 Mass. 544.

3 22 H. ch. 5; 2 Inst. 697, 703.

4 Rex *v.* Gardner, Cowp. 83.

5 1 B. & P. 163.

taking advantage of the protection, resources, and benefits of the enemy's country. In point of law, they stand upon the same footing. It has been argued that the court will look to the purposes for which the corporation was instituted, and to the conduct which it observes; if these be innocent or meritorious, they afford an exception from the general rule. But it is not the private character or conduct of an individual which gives him the hostile or neutral character. It is the character of the nation to which he belongs and where he resides. He may be retired from all business, devoted to mere spiritual affairs, or engaged in works of charity, religion and humanity, and yet his domicil will prevail over the innocence and purity of his life. Nay, more, he may disapprove of the war, and endeavor by all lawful means to assuage or extinguish it; and yet, while he continues in the country, he is known but as an enemy. The same principle must apply, in the same manner, to a corporation. The objects, indeed, of the present corporation, are highly meritorious, and worthy of public favor; but upon the doctrines of law, it must be deemed a British alien corporation, and as such, liable to the imputation of being an enemy's corporation, unless it can be protected upon other principles."

§ 378. But although the opinion of the court in the above case was that the corporation itself and the members also were alien enemies, yet for aught that appeared on the face of the record, every member of the corporation might then be domiciled in the United States, under the license of government. And in respect to the corporation itself, although established in Great Britain, it might have had the safe conduct or license of the United States government, for its property and corporate rights. This was one reason why the court sustained the power to sue, notwithstanding their opinion upon the abstract question of right. And another consideration which the court thought would weigh in the case, was, that the suit was commenced during peace, and on the declaration of war it was competent for the tenants to plead the hostile alienage of the demandants, if it existed in bar to the further prosecution of the suit, in the nature of a *puis darrein continuance.* And as they did not so plead, they thereby affirmed the ability of the demandants to prosecute to judgment.[1] As the right of a foreign corporation to

---

[1] Le Bret *v.* Papillon, 4 East, 502; and also West *v.* Sutton, 2 Ld. Raym. 853, were cited by the court. Another consideration which the court mentioned, as one which was in favor of their overruling the motion in arrest of judgment, was thus stated by Judge

sue depends upon the comity of the country or State where the suit is brought, the government of the country may decline to exercise this comity and refuse to allow suit to be brought; so, too, it would seem that a court might decline to take cognizance of the action if the corporation was instituted for a purpose hostile to the interests of the State.[1]

§ 379. Secondly, of *the liability to be sued.* Having thus considered the subject of the corporate right to sue, we are next to treat of the corporate liability to be sued. The ancient doctrine was, that the action of assumpsit could not be supported against a corporation, unless in the case of promissory notes, and other contracts sanctioned by particular legislative provisions.[2] And as late as 1799, in a case in the Supreme

---

Story: "Another consideration, derived from the express provision of the 9th article of the British Treaty of 1794, ought not to be omitted. That article stipulates that British subjects, who then held land in the territories of the *United States*, and American citizens, who then held land in the dominions of his Majesty, shall continue to hold them, according to the nature and tenure of their respective estates and titles therein, and may grant, sell, and devise the same, to whom they please, in like manner as if they were natives; and that neither they, nor their heirs or assigns, shall, so far as respects the said lands and the legal remedies incident thereto, be regarded *as aliens.* This article has never been annulled, and therefore remains in full force. It deserves, and ought to receive, a liberal and enlarged construction. There can be no doubt that corporations, as well as individuals, are within its purview; and the present claim not only may be, but in fact is, one which it completely embraces. The title of the demandants, as has been already stated, accrued before the Revolutionary war. It was obviously the design of the contracting parties to remove the disability of alienage, as to persons within the purview of the article, and to procure to them a perfect enjoyment and disposal of their estates and titles. If, during war, their right to grant, sell, or devise such estates and titles were suspended, it would materially impair their value. If the remedies incident to such estates, for trespasses, disseisin, and other tortious acts, were during war suspended, not only would the security of the property be endangered, but if war should last for many years, the Statute of Limitations of the various States would, by lapse of time, bar the party of his remedy, and in some cases of his estate. This seems against the spirit and intent of the article, and puts the party upon the footing of an alien enemy, while the language concedes to him all the benefits of a native. Looking to the general moderation with which the rights of war are exercised in modern times, under the policy, if not the law, of nations, perhaps it would not seem (for I mean not to give any absolute opinion) an undue indulgence to hold that, as to all titles and estates within the article, an alien enemy may well maintain all the legal remedies, as in a time of peace. At least, it cannot be presumed that in this favored class of cases, the party has not received the license or safe conduct of the government to pursue his rights and remedies during the war. And unless such presumption can be made, when there are no facts on the record to warrant it, the plaintiffs must be entitled to judgment."

[1] See Am. Colonization Society *v.* Gartrell, 23 Ga. 448.

[2] 1 Chit. on Pleading, 102; 6 Vin. 317, pl. 49; 16 East, 611. Where the power of a

Court of Pennsylvania, the question arose upon a special verdict, whether an action of *indebitatus assumpsit*, upon an implied promise, could be maintained against an incorporated turnpike company, as a corporation could only contract by deed under the corporate seal; and the court held that, on the ground stated, the company was not liable to be sued in that form of action.[1] But it having since become well settled, by the more recent decisions of the courts of the United States, that corporations may act by parol,[2] it has resulted, as a matter of course, that assumpsit will lie against a corporation; and such is now the established doctrine in this country. The Supreme Court of Massachusetts, a number of years since, decided that assumpsit would lie against a corporation, where there is an express promise by an agent of the corporation, or a duty arising from some act or request of such agent, within the authority of the corporation.[3] And in a very late case in the same State, it was held, that either an action of debt or of assumpsit may be maintained upon an implied promise, for labor done and materials found, under a special contract, which has not been performed on the part of a corporation.[4] In a case in the Supreme Court of the United States, an attempt was made to distinguish between express and implied promises, as to the liability of corporations to be sued in assumpsit;[5] but the distinction was disregarded, and the court went the whole length of giving the same remedies against incorporated companies, in matters of contract, as against individuals. The old cases are there reviewed, showing that the law has been progressively altering, with respect to the validity of acts done by corporations not under their seal. The court observe, upon the English authorities referred to, that, as soon as it was settled that a regularly appointed agent of a corporation could contract in its name without a seal, it was impossible to maintain any longer that a corporation was not liable upon promises; otherwise there would be no remedy against the corporation; and the court concluded by saying, that it is a

---

trading or other corporation to draw and accept bills is recognized by statute, assumpsit lies against it; although, in England, says Mr. Chitty, an action of debt is generally the only remedy against a corporation. Chitty on Contracts, 86; and see Murray *v.* East India Co. 5 B. & Ald. 204; 5 East, 239.

[1] Breckbill *v.* Turnpike Co. 3 Dallas, 496; and see Marine Ins. Co. *v.* Young, 1 Cranch, 332.

[2] See *ante*, Chap. VII. and VIII. as to power and mode of contracting.

[3] Hayden *v.* Middlesex Turn. Co. 10 Mass. 39; State *v.* Morris, 3 N. J. 360; and see *ante*, Ch. IX.

[4] Smith *v.* Congregational Meeting-house, 8 Pick. 178.

[5] Bank of Columbia *v.* Patterson, 7 Cranch, 299.

sound rule of law, that whenever a corporation is acting within the scope of the legitimate purposes of the corporation, all parol contracts made by its authorized agents are express promises of the corporation, and all duties imposed upon them by law, and all benefits conferred at their request, raise implied promises, for the enforcement of which an action will lie. In the Supreme Court of New York, also, Mr. Chief Justice Thompson held expressly that assumpsit will lie against a corporation on an implied promise. In this case, a turnpike company covenanted to pay money, and a part had been paid; assumpsit, the court held, would lie on the implied promise to pay the balance.[1] And in another case in New York it was held, that assumpsit would lie against the corporation, on the implied promise to pay the amount of damages assessed by a jury, for the land of the plaintiff taken by the corporation.[2] The same is the general rule in Pennsylvania,[3] and in New Jersey,[4] and, we believe, throughout the country.[5] And in an action of assumpsit against a corporation, it makes no difference whether the agent who makes the contract in behalf of the corporation was appointed under seal or by vote.[6]

§ 380. By the Revised Statutes of New York,[7] whenever a receiver of an insolvent corporation "shall by his own oath, or other competent proof," show that any person is indebted to the corporation, the officer to whom the application is made shall issue a warrant to bring such person before him for examination. Under this enactment a person having in his custody, as *administrator* of a deceased person, effects of the corporation, or being indebted as such administrator, is liable to be proceeded against.[8]

---

[1] Danforth *v.* President, &c. of S. & D. Turnpike Road, 12 Johns. 227.

[2] Stafford *v.* Corporation of Albany, 6 Johns. 1, 7 Johns. 541.

[3] Chestnut Hill Turnpike Co. *v.* Rutter, 4 S. & R. 16; Overseers of N. Whitehall *v.* Overseers of S. Whitehall, 3 S. & R. 117.

[4] Baptist Church *v.* Mulford, 3 Halst. 182.

[5] See also Worcester Turnpike Corporation *v.* Willard, 5 Mass. 80; Gilmore *v.* Pope, 5 Mass. 491; Andover and Medford Turnpike Co. *v.* Gould, 6 Mass. 40; Dun *v.* Rector, &c. of St. Andrew's Church, 14 Johns. 118; Randall *v.* Van Vechten, 19 Johns. 60; Haight *v.* Sahler, 30 Barb. 218; Quin *v.* Hartford, 1 Hill, 82. In Vermont, Essex Bridge Co. *v.* Tuttle, 2 Vt. 393; Proctor *v.* Webber, D. Chip. 371; Stone *v.* Congregational Soc. 14 Vt. 86; Mutual Ins. Co. *v.* Cummings, 11 Vt. 503; Jesograrly *v.* Alton, 13 Ill. 366.

[6] Bank of the Metropolis *v.* Guttschlieck, 14 Pet. 19; and see *ante*, Chapters VIII. and IX.; Finlay *v.* Bristol and Exeter Railway Co. 7 Exch. 409, 9 Eng. L. & Eq. 483.

[7] 2 R. S. 464, §§ 41, 42; id. 469, §§ 67, 68, 72; id. 43, § 12.

[8] Noble *v.* Halliday, 1 Comst. 330.

§ 381. It has been held, in England, that a special *action on the case* will lie against a corporation, for improperly refusing to make a transfer of stock; and a special action of assumpsit was afterwards maintained against the Bank of England for this cause.[1] In a case in New York, where a motion was made for a *mandamus*, to be directed to the president, directors, and company of the Mechanics Bank, commanding them to permit M. S. to transfer eight shares of the capital stock of the bank standing on the books of the bank; the court refused to allow that remedy, and said there was an adequate remedy by a special action on the case, to recover the value of the stock, if the bank unduly refused to transfer it.[2] So, in Gray *v.* The Portland Bank,[3] it was held by the Supreme Court of Massachusetts, that a special action on the case lies against an incorporated bank, for refusing to permit an original stockholder to subscribe and hold the new stock created by the corporation. So, too, in an action of assumpsit against the Franklin Insurance Company, it was held that the company was liable in damages, to persons to whom shares had been conveyed by a stockholder, for refusing to enter upon the books the transfer which the stockholder had made.[4]

§ 382. Though it has been supposed that a corporation cannot be sued in that character, for torts, and that the action must be brought against each person who committed the tort, by name;[5] yet at this time it is clear that incorporated companies may be sued in their corporate character for damages arising from neglect of duty, and for trover.[6] The Supreme Court of Pennsylvania considered that if any injury was done by the agents of corporations, in the course of their employment,

---

[1] Rex *v.* Bank of England, Doug. 524, cited in Danforth *v.* President, &c. of S. & D. Turnpike Co. 12 Johns. 227. Where the act of incorporation provided for a register of proprietors, and prescribed certain formalities to be observed upon the absolute conveyance of shares or upon their involuntary transmission by death, &c., it was held that the company could not be compelled to register a mortgage to a mortgagee, to whom shares had been transferred by a deed not executed in the specified form. Regina *v.* General Cemetery Co. 6 Ellis & B. 415, 36 Eng. L. & Eq. 126.

[2] Shipley, &c. *v.* Mechanics Bank, 10 Johns. 484; and see Rex *v.* Bank of England, Doug. 524.

[3] 3 Mass. 364.

[4] Sargent *v.* Franklin Ins. Co. 8 Pick. 90; and see also, Bates *v.* New York Ins. Co. 3 Johns. Cas. 238, and the authorities cited *post*, Chapter XVI., relating to the transfer of shares.

[5] 1 Kyd, 225; Bac. Abr. Corp. E. 2, 5.

[6] Chitty on Plead. 68; Fowle *v.* Common Canal of Alexandria, 3 Pet. 409; Bushel *v.* Commonwealth Insurance Co. 15 S. & R. 173.

the corporation should be responsible, in the same manner that an individual is responsible for the actions of his servants, touching his business; that the act of the agent was the act of the principal; and that there was no solid ground for a distinction between contracts and torts. Indeed, say the court, with respect to torts, the opinion of the courts seems to have been more uniform than with respect to contracts; for it might be shown, that, from the earliest times to the present day, corporations have been liable for torts;[1] and it is clear that Lord Ellenborough entertained the same opinion.[2] It has moreover been held, in England, that a corporation is liable in tort for the tortious act of its agent, though the appointment of the agent be not under seal, if the act be done in the ordinary service; and that a jury may infer the agency from an adoption of the act by the corporation.[3]

§ 383. An action on the case will lie against a corporation for a neglect of a corporate duty, as for not repairing a creek which they were bound to repair.[4] So, in an action against the Susquehannah Turnpike Company, for the value of a horse killed by the fall of a bridge on the road, it was held, that the defendants were liable in an action on the case, as they had not used ordinary care and diligence in the construction of their bridges.[5] So, also, an action was maintained in Massachusetts against a canal company for damage suffered by the plaintiff, in consequence of the locks not being kept in repair.[6] So, also, in Pennsylvania, in an action of trespass on the case for stopping a watercourse, where the defendants were incorporated as a turnpike company, and

---

1 Chestnut Hill, &c. Turnp. Co., in error, *v.* Rutter, 4 S. & R. 6. In this case much learning will be found on the subject, and many references to the Year Books, and other ancient as well as modern authorities. First Baptist Church *v.* Schenectady, &c. R. Co. 5 Barb. 79. See also, N. Y. & Wash. P. Tel. Co. *v.* Dryburg, 35 Penn. State, 298.

2 Yarborough *v.* Bank of England, 16 East, 6.

3 Smith *v.* Birmingham Gas Light Co. 1 A. & E. 526.

4 Mayor of Lynn *v.* Turner, Cowp. 86. So, against a railway corporation, for losses caused by misrepresentation in their published time-tables. Denton *v.* Great Northern Railway Co. 5 Ellis & B. 860, 34 Eng. L. & Eq. 154. See also, Conger *v.* Chicago & Rock Island R. R. Co. 15 Ill. 366; Keegan *v.* Western R. R. Co. 4 Seld. 175.

5 Townsend *v.* Susquehannah Turnp. Co. 6 Johns. 90. But it must be a clear case of negligence; and if it is only for a breach of public duty, an indictment is the proper remedy. Harris *v.* Baker, 4 M. & S. 27. See Pittsburgh City *v.* Grier, 22 Penn. State, 54. Smoot *v.* Mayor, &c. of Wetumpka, 24 Ala. 112. And an action on the case will not lie against the *inspectors of an election*, for refusing the vote of a person legally qualified to vote, without proving malice, express or implied. Jenkins *v.* Waldran, 11 Johns. 114.

6 Riddle *v.* The Proprietors of Locks, &c. 7 Mass. 169.

who caused the water of a rivulet to overflow the plaintiff's tanyard; it was held that the action would lie, and that the defendants were guilty of a wrong.[1] In this case, it was strongly objected, that a corporation could not be guilty of a tort; but Tilghman, C. J., said that this doctrine was fallacious in principle and mischievous in its consequences, as it tends to introduce actual wrongs and ideal remedies; for a turnpike company might do great injury, by means of laborers having no property to answer the damages recovered against them.[2]

§ 384. It was established, in the case where the Bank of England was the defendant, that *trover* will lie against a corporation. In this case, the bank was declared against in an action of trover, for three promissory notes of the bank, payable on demand, for £100 each, describing them by their dates and numbers. After a verdict for the plaintiff, before Lord Ellenborough, C. J., at Guildhall, it was moved to arrest the judgment, on the ground that the action, being founded in tort, did not lie against a corporation. But his lordship was of opinion, that, wherever a corporate body can competently do or order any act to be done on their behalf, they are liable to the consequences of such act, if it be of a tortious nature, and to the prejudice of others, and the action was sustained in this case.[3] Consequently, if A. puts a note into the bank,

---

[1] Chestnut Hill, &c. Turnp. Co. *v.* Rutter, 4 S. & R. 6.

[2] A corporation having the return of writs, or to which any writ, on a mandamus, for instance, is directed, is liable eventually to an action for a false return. The case of Argent *v.* Dean and Chapter of St. Paul's (the case was referred to by Buller, J., in 2 T. R. 16), was an action for a false return to a mandamus respecting an election to a verger's place in that cathedral; and no objection was made that the action would not lie. See also, the cases cited in Yarborough *v.* Bank of England, 16 East, 6; and that actions on the case lie against corporations for nonfeasance and misfeasance; see Burdick *v.* Champlain Glass Co. 11 Vt. 19; Ward *v.* Newark Turnp. Co. Spencer, 323; Hamilton County *v.* Cincinnati, &c. Turnp. Co. 6 Wright, 603; Fletcher *v.* Auburn Railroad Co. 25 Wend. 482; Savage Man. Co. *v.* Armstrong, 17 Me. 34; Rector of, &c. *v.* Buckhart, 3 Hill, 193; Rhodes *v.* Cleveland, 10 Ohio, 159; Smoot *v.* Mayor, &c. of Wetumpka, 24 Ala. 112; Mayor of New York *v.* Bailey, 2 Denio, 433, and the cases therein cited. The defendants, as a corporation, dug a canal upon their own land, for the purpose authorized by the charter, and in so doing it was necessary to blast rocks with gunpowder, and the fragments were thrown against and injured the plaintiff's house; it was held, that the defendants were liable for the injury, although no negligence or want of skill in executing the work was alleged or proved; but the court in their decision relied upon the maxim, *sic utere tuo*, &c. Hay *v.* Cohoes Company, 2 Comst. 159, 3 Barb. 42; see Carman *v.* Steu. & Ind. R. R. Co. 4 Ohio, State, 399.

[3] Yarborough *v.* Bank of England, 16 East, 6. And the decision is confirmed by the case of Duncan *v.* Surrey Canal, 3 Stark. 50.

and wishes to get it out, and the bank refuse to deliver it, the bank may be sued in an action of trover. In another case, in which an action of trover was maintained against a corporation, the court held, that the corporation were liable to the action, although the agent who committed the tortious act of conversion was not appointed by seal; and that the jury might infer the agency from an adoption of the act of conversion, as from their having received the proceeds of the conversion.[1]

§ 385. It has been laid down as the general rule, that an action of *trespass* cannot be maintained against a corporation aggregate, and the technical reason given is, that a *capias* and *exigent* do not lie against a body corporate, which is the proper process in an action of trespass; and that if any of the members or servants of the corporation commit a trespass in asserting the right of the corporation, the action must be brought against *them* individually, and they may justify in right of the corporation.[2] Now, both by the civil and canon law, corporations might be proceeded against and punished for offences, as well as natural individuals, if the offence was committed *communicato consilio.* That is to say, a corporation might be punished for any wrong done by any member, if the wrong was suffered or ratified by the corporate body; and the instance given is, if a member of a corporation ousts a man of his castle, and the corporation retains the possession of such castle to its own use;[3] for that which is done by the member, is deemed to be the act of the whole, when the whole body is apprized of it and permits it; provided it is not a high public misdemeanor.[4] The subject seems to have been viewed very much in the same light in ancient times in England; and there are several cases in the Year Books, of actions of trespass brought against a mayor and commonalty, in which, though many objections were taken on other points, none appears to have been taken to the action itself. Thus in an action of trespass against a mayor and commonalty, and a private person (a member of the corporation) jointly; in which the plaintiff declared on a right of exemption from toll, and alleged that the mayor and bailiffs and the individual had distrained certain beasts for the toll; much was said on the impropriety of joining

---

[1] Smith *v.* Birmingham and Staffordshire Canal Company, 1 A. & E. 526; Mayor, &c. of Baltimore *v.* Norman, 4 Md. 352.

[2] Bro. Corp. 43; 1 Kyd, 223.

[3] Code, b. 4, t. 28, § 7; Dig. b. 17, t. 1.

[4] Ayliffe, Civil Law, 200.

the individual in an action against the corporation; but no question was made whether such an action could be maintained or not against the corporation simply.[1] So, also, in an action of trespass against the mayor and commonalty of York, when it was pleaded that all the inhabitants had a right of common in the land where the trespass was supposed to have been committed, the plea was held not good, because the action was against the *corporation*, and the plea was a justification as to *individuals*. In a subsequent part of this case, it is said that a corporation cannot give a warrant to commit a trespass *without writing*, which shows that it was considered that a warrant might be given in writing, which would have been sufficient for the plaintiff's purpose. So, also, where the archbishop of York brought an action of trespass against the mayor, &c. of Kingston-upon-Hull and a private person, in which he alleged that he and all his predecessors, from time immemorial, had enjoyed the franchise of having all deodands and other profits in the water of Hull, and that the defendants had disturbed him in taking the said profits; the private person pleaded in abatement of the writ, that he was named with the mayor and commonalty; in support of which it was contended that there ought to have been several actions, because the process was several, being *capias* and *exigent* against the individual, and *distringas* against the mayor and commonalty. The mayor and commonalty alleged that they held the town at farm of the king, by a charter which they produced, and said that the water was parcel of the town, and that they had so held it immemorially, &c.; but it was not objected that such an action would lie against the corporation.[2] Mr. J. Patteson, in giving judgment in a case of an indictment against a corporation aggregate, took occasion to say as follows: "It was not contended, on the part of the company, that an action of trespass might not be maintained against a corporation; for, notwithstanding some *dicta* to the contrary in the older cases, it may be taken for settled law, since the case of Yarborough *v.* The Bank of England, that both trover and trespass are maintainable." [3]

§ 386. Yet it is somewhat remarkable that the question, whether an action of trespass would lie against a corporation, should not, until with-

---

[1] 9 Hen. 6, 1; 9 Hen. 6, 36.

[2] 45 Ed. 3, 23; see these cases cited in the opinion of the court in Yarborough *v.* Bank of England, 16 East, 6; Chestnut Hill Turn. Co. *v.* Rutter, 4 S. & R. 16.

[3] Regina *v.* Birmingham & Gloucester Railway Co. 3 Q. B. 223.

in a very late period, have been the subject of express judicial decision. In the case of Maud *v.* Monmouthshire Canal Company,[1] it was expressly decided by the English Court of Common Pleas, in 1842, that trespass will lie against a corporation. The action was brought for breaking and entering locks on a canal, and seizing and carrying away barges and coal. The trespasses, it was proved, had been committed by an agent of the company, which was incorporated by act of parliament; and the barges and coal, it appeared, had been seized for tolls claimed to be due them. The only question being, whether trespass would lie against a corporation aggregate for an act done by their agent within the scope of their authority; the court held that when it is established that trover will lie against a corporation, there could be no reason why trespass should not also lie against them; that it was impossible to see any distinction between the two actions.

§ 387. In Edwards *v.* Union Bank of Florida, the declaration charged, that the said bank, by its servants, officers, and agents, with force and arms broke and entered certain closes of the plaintiff, and seized and carried away certain negro slaves; and the court held that this declaration in trespass could be maintained.[2] In Whiteman *v.* Wilmington and Susquehannah Railroad Company,[3] the action was trespass *quare clausum fregit*, against the company, for entering upon the plaintiffs' land, for the purpose of making their road through the same; and it was held that there was no settled rule of law exempting corporations from the action of trespass. Numerous as corporations have become, and constantly multiplying as they are, it would be unjust to society, as well as unreasonable in itself, to permit them to escape the consequences of direct injuries inflicted upon citizens by

---

[1] Maud *v.* Monmouthshire Canal Co. 4 Man. & G. 452, 5 Scott, N. R. 457. That trespass will lie against a corporation for acts done by its agents in the course of their employment as such, or by the direction of the corporation, — Hay *v.* Cohoes Co. 3 Barb. 42; Barnard *v.* Stevens, 2 Aikens, 429; Lyman *v.* Bridge Co. 2 id. 255; Underwood *v.* Newport Lyceum, 5 B. Mon. 130; Humes *v.* Mayor, &c. of Knoxville, 1 Humph. 403; President, &c. of Crawfordsville & W. R. R. Co. *v.* Wright, 5 Ind. 252; Hazen *v.* Boston & Maine R. R. 2 Gray, 574. Chicago & Rock Island R. Co. *v.* Fell, 22 Ill. 333; Same *v.* Whipple, id. 105. Trespass on the case, and not trespass *vi et armis*, is the proper action to be brought against a corporation for the negligence of its servants. Illinois Central R. R. Co. *v.* Reedy, 17 Ill. 580.

[2] Edwards *v.* Union Bank of Florida, 1 Fla. 136.

[3] Whiteman *v.* Wilmington & Susquehannah Railroad Company, 2 Harring. Del. 514.

their agents, *in the course of their business.*[1] And it is now held that a railroad company is liable for the publication of a libel.[2] So it is said that although a corporation itself cannot, strictly speaking, be guilty of a fraud, yet, if it can accomplish the objects for which it was formed only through the agency of individuals, and these act fraudulently, the corporation is liable for the fraud.[3]

§ 388. It is of importance, however, to be observed that an action of trespass cannot be sustained against a private corporation for an act done by one of its agents, unless done *communicato consilio;* or, in other words, unless the act has been directed, suffered, or ratified by the corporation.[4] A corporation is liable for an injury done by one of its servants, in the same manner, and to the same extent only, as a natural individual would be liable under like circumstances.[5] An incorporated district is not liable in trespass for the illegal seizure of the plaintiff's horse by one of the officers of the district, for an alleged violation of its ordinances, when in fact no such violation took place, unless the corporation previously authorized or subsequently ratified the seizure.[6] It has been expressly held, too, that trespass would not lie for an injury done to the plaintiff by their locomotive steam engine, whether such injury be wilful or accidental on the part of the servants of the company, if it do not appear that the particular injury was done by the command or with the assent of the company.[7] The well-known rule of law is, that if the cause of an injury to a person be immediate, though it happen accidentally, the author of it is answerable in trespass as well as in case; but a master, whether a natural individual or an artificial one, is not liable for a *wilful* act of trespass of his servant.[8] That is, when a servant quits sight of the object for which he is employed, and, without having in view his regular duties, pursues a course suggested by malice,

---

1 Bloodgood *v.* Mohawk & Hudson Railroad Company, 10 Wend. 9.

2 Philadelphia, &c. R. Co. *v.* Quigley, 21 How. 202; Whitfield *v.* South Eastern R. Co. 1 Ellis, B. & E. 115.

3 Ranger *v.* Great Western Railway Co. 5 H. L. Cas. 72, 87.

4 See *ante;* Underwood *v.* Newport Lyceum, 5 B. Mon. 129; Van Brundt *v.* Schenk, 13 Johns. 414.

5 First Baptist Church *v.* Schenectady & Troy Railroad Co. 5 Barb. 80.

6 Fox *v.* Northern Liberties, 3 Watts & S. 103.

7 Philadelphia, Germantown, and Norristown Railroad Company *v.* Wilts, 4 Whart. 143.

8 Ibid.; Illinois Central R. Co. *v.* Downey, 18 Ill. 259.

he no longer acts in pursuance of the authority given him.[1] The dividing line is the wilfulness of the act; and there is no case where the principal has been made liable for a wilful trespass committed by a servant, because commanded and approved by a general agent.[2] The injury of which the plaintiff complained, in an action on the case in Vanderbilt *v.* Richmond Turnpike Company,[3] was occasioned by the wilful act of the captain who had charge of the defendants' steamboat. It was proved that before the injury complained of was done, the captain of the boat told the president of the company that the plaintiff's boat had crowded him out of his course a few days before, and had said she was a much smarter boat than that of the defendants; that the president told the captain, "if she ever does that again, run into her, sink her." She was run into, but the corporation was held not liable for the collision. In Orr *v.* Bank of the United States, in Ohio,[4] the action was for an assault and battery and false imprisonment, the declaration being in the common form, charging the defendants jointly with the commission of the trespass, as though they were all natural persons. It was expressly held, that a corporation could not be sued in an action of assault and battery, nor can it be joined in such action with other defendants. A distinction exists as to the liability of a corporation for the wilful tort of its servant towards one to whom the corporation owes no duty except such as each citizen owes to every other, and that towards one who has entered into some peculiar contract with the corporation, by which this duty is increased. Thus it has been held that a railroad corporation is liable for the wilful tort of its servants whereby a passenger on the train is injured.[5]

§ 389. Lord Ellenborough thought that the statute 9 Hen. IV. c. 5, reciting the practice, in assizes of novel disseisin and other pleas of land, of naming the mayor and commonalty, as disseisors, plainly proves that corporations may be considered as disseisors.[6] In Massachusetts, a

---

1 Macmanus *v.* Cricket, 1 East, 106; 2 Stark. Ev. 1111 (London ed. 1842). See also St. Louis, &c. R. Co. *v.* Dalby, 19 Ill. 353.

2 Wright *v.* Wilcox, 19 Wend. 343; Fox *v.* Northern Liberties, 3 Watts & S. 103; Croft *v.* Allison, 4 B. & Ald. 590.

3 Vanderbilt *v.* Richmond Turnp. Co. 2 Comst. 479, 1 Hill, 480.

4 Orr *v.* Bank of United States, 1 Hamm. 25.

5 Weed *v.* Panama R. Co. 5 Duer, 193, affirmed 17 N. Y. 362; Philadelphia & Reading R. Co. *v.* Derby, 14 How. 468.

6 Yarborough *v.* Bank of England, 16 East, 8.

writ of entry *sur disseisin* was brought against an incorporated company, and no exception was taken that the defendants were incorporated.[1] It is clear enough, that an action of ejectment will lie against a corporation.

§ 390. A private corporation may be sued by one of its own members. This point came directly before the court in the State of South Carolina, in an action of assumpsit against the Catawba Company. The plea in abatement was that the plaintiff was himself a member of that company, and therefore could maintain no action against it in his individual capacity. The court, after hearing the argument, overruled the plea, as containing principles subversive of justice; and they moreover said that the point had been settled by two former cases, wherein certain officers were allowed to maintain actions for their salaries due from the company.[2] In this respect, the cases of incorporated companies are entirely dissimilar to those of ordinary copartnerships, or unincorporated joint-stock companies. In the former, the individual members of the company are entirely distinct from the artificial body endowed with corporate powers. A member of a corporation who is a creditor, has the same right as any other creditor to secure the payment of his demands, by attachment or levy on the property of the corporation, although he may be personally liable by statute to satisfy other judgments against the corporation.[3] An action was maintained against a corporation on a bond securing a certain sum to the plaintiff, a member of the corporation, the member being deemed by the court, for the purpose of the suit, to be a stranger.[4] So of notes and book accounts,[5] and right to dividends.[6] In the case of an incorporated *beneficial* society, where the charter provided that sick members should be entitled to a certain allowance, whilst so much remained in the funds; it was held that an action

---

[1] Doane *v.* Broad Street Association, 6 Mass. 332. Doe *d.* Parr *v.* Roe, 1 Q. B. 700; Dexter *v.* Troy T. & R. R. Co. 2 Hill, 629; Bloodgood *v.* M. & H. R. R. Co. 18 Wend. 9. In this last case, the action went through the Supreme Court and Court of Errors of the State, without the objection being thought of. And see, also, Carmichael, &c. *v.* Trustees, &c. 3 How. Miss. 84.

[2] Waring *v.* Catawba Co. 2 Bay, 109; and see Culberton *v.* Hubush Nav. Co. 4 McLean, 544.

[3] Pierce *v.* Partridge, 3 Met. 44.

[4] Hill *v.* Manchester & Salford Water Works, 5 A. & E. 866; and see also, Dunston *v.* Imperial Gas Co. 3 B. & Ad. 125.

[5] Gerr *v.* School District, 6 Vt. 187; Sawyer *v.* Methodist Episcopal Society, 18 id. 405; Rogers *v.* Danby Universalist Society, 19 id. 187.

[6] Marine Bank of Baltimore *v.* Biays, 4 Harris & J. 338.

would not lie by a member to recover the allowance, as it must be presumed the proper authorities had determined the corporation was not in funds, and the member is concluded by the forum of his own selection.[1]

§ 391. That in cases where the legal remedy against a corporation is inadequate, a Court of Equity will interfere, is well settled; and there are cases in which a bill in equity will lie against a corporation by one of its members. It is a breach of trust towards a shareholder in a joint-stock incorporated company, established for a certain definite purpose prescribed by its charter, if the funds or credit of the company are, without his consent, diverted from such purpose, though the misapplication be sanctioned by the votes of a majority; and, therefore, he may file a bill in equity against the company in his own behalf to restrain the company by injunction from any such diversion or misapplication.[2] The language of Lord Brougham, in the case of a bill filed by a member of a water company against the company, was, "It is said that this is an attempt on the part of the company to do acts which they are not empowered to do by the acts of parliament. So far I restrain them by injunction."[3] Indeed, an investment in the stock of any corporation must, by every one, be considered a wild speculation, if it exposed the owners of the stock to all sorts of risks in support of plausible projects not set forth and authorized by the act of incorporation, and which may possibly lead to extraordinary losses. In Bagshaw *v.* Eastern Counties Railway Company,[4] the objection was expressly taken on the part of the

---

[1] Toram *v.* Howard Beneficial Society, 4 Barr, 519.

[2] Cunliff *v.* Manchester & Bolton Canal Company, 2 Russ. & M. 480, *note.* Dodge *v.* Woolsey, 18 How. 331; Manderson *v.* Commercial Bank, 28 Penn. State, 379; Balt. & Ohio R. R. Co. *v.* City of Wheeling, 13 Gratt. 40. As to whether such a bill of a single corporator against the corporation should aver that it is filed on behalf of himself and of all others similarly situated, see Wood *v.* Draper, 24 Barb. 187.

[3] Ware *v.* Grand Junction Water Company, 2 Russ. & M. 486. Lord Brougham founded himself upon the case of Natusch *v.* Irving (Gow on Part. App. 2). The question there was, whether an incorporated company could, by a major vote of the company, make a fundamental change in the objects for which they were associated under their articles of agreement. The plaintiff was a member of the British Alliance, British & Foreign Life and Fire Assurance Company. Without the consent of the plaintiff, the business of the company was changed from life and fire assurance to *marine* assurance. Lord Eldon was of opinion that the plaintiff could not thus be engaged in a new enterprise without his consent, and granted the *festinum remedium,* an injunction to restrain the company from carrying on the business of marine assurance.

[4] Bagshaw *v.* Eastern Counties Railway Co. 7 Hare, 114, 1 Beav. 1.

corporation, that the corporation ought not to be a party to the suit. But the vice-chancellor, Sir James Wigram, said, that he had no hesitation in overruling that objection; that the acts of the directors (in diverting the corporate moneys for a purpose different from what was originally contemplated, against the will of a single shareholder) were the acts of the directors as the representatives of the company, and as such were the acts of the company itself, and that the company would not be bound, unless it were a party in its corporate character. Again, in Colman *v.* Eastern Counties Railway Company,[1] it appeared that the directors of the company, for the purpose of increasing their traffic, proposed to guarantee certain profits, and to secure the capital of an intended Steam Packet Company, who were to act in connection with the railway; and it was held that, in the first place, such a transaction was not within the scope of their powers, and they were restrained by injunction; and in the second place, that, in such a case, one of the shareholders in the railway company was entitled to sue on behalf of himself and all the other shareholders except the directors, who were defendants, although some of the shareholders had taken shares in the Steam Packet Company. It was contended in this case, that the corporation might pledge, without limit, the funds of the company for the encouragement of other transactions, however various and extensive, provided the object of that liability was to increase the traffic upon the railway, and thereby to increase the traffic to the shareholders. But the Master of the Rolls, Lord Langdale, said, "there was no authority for any thing of that kind."

§ 392. It is not only illegal for a corporation to apply its *capital* to objects not contemplated by its charter, but also so to apply its *profits;* and therefore a shareholder may maintain a bill in equity against the directors and the company, to *have refunded* to them any of the profits thus improperly applied. It is an improper application for a railway company to invest the profits of the company in the purchase of shares in another company; and it cannot be authorized by legislative sanction. "The *dividend,*" says Lord Langdale,[2] Master of the Rolls, "which belongs to the shareholders, and is divisible among them, may be applied by them severally as their *own* property, but the company

---

1 Colman *v.* Eastern Counties Railway Co. 10 Beav. 1.

2 Salomons *v.* Laing, 12 Beav. 339, 377.

itself, or the directors, or any number of shareholders assembled at a meeting or otherwise, have no right to dispose of the shares of the general dividends which belong to the particular shareholder, in any manner contrary to the will, or without the consent or authority, of that particular shareholder."

§ 393. Therefore, although the result of the authorities clearly is, that in a corporation, acting within the scope of, and in obedience to, the provisions of its constitution, the will of the *majority*, duly expressed at a legally constituted meeting, must govern;[1] yet *beyond the limits of the act of incorporation*, the will of the majority cannot make an act valid; and the powers of a Court of Equity may be put in motion, at the instance of a single shareholder, if he can show that the corporation are employing their statutory powers for the accomplishment of purposes not within the scope of their institution.[2] Yet it is to be observed, that there is an important distinction between this class of cases and those in which there is no breach of trust, but only error and misapprehension, or simple negligence on the part of the directors.[3] And a suit at law cannot be maintained by an individual stockholder against the directors of a corporation for mismanaging its affairs, for the purpose of defrauding the corporation.[4]

---

1 See *ante*, § 380.

2 See also, Foss *v.* Harbottle, 2 Hare, 461; Preston *v.* Grand Collier Dock Company, 1 Simons, 327; Salmon *v.* Randall, 3 Mylne & C. 444. See also, 1 Mylne & K. 154; Dodge *v.* Woolsey, 18 How. 331; Sears *v.* Hotchkiss, 25 Conn. 171; Gifford *v.* New Jersey R. Co. 2 Stock. 171; Kean *v.* Johnson, 1 Stock. 401. In Ward *v.* Society of Attorneys, on a motion made in behalf of the minority for an injunction to restrain the majority of the members of the corporation from surrendering their charter with a view to obtain a new charter, for an object different from that for which the original charter was granted; the court granted the injunction. 1 Collyer, 370. A bill in equity can not only be maintained in these cases by a shareholder, against the company of which he is a member, but one may be maintained also, against another distinct company to which the former has united itself by the application of its moneys for the purposes of the latter. The latter company are supposed to have full notice of the only legal purpose for which the moneys of the former could be appropriated, and having such notice, and avowedly thus receiving money for the purpose of applying it to an illegal purpose for which it is expressly paid to them, it is guilty of a fraud. Both companies are guilty of a fraud against the legislature, which incorporated them for different purposes, and guilty of collusion also, in uniting and combining for the purpose of completing that fraud. It is enough, also, to say, that they were parties to the same breach of trust, one in paying and the other in receiving the moneys for a known illegal purpose; and both, therefore, may be made parties to a bill in equity, in a suit by a shareholder in the former company. Salomons *v.* Laing, 12 Beav. 339, 377.

3 Smith *v.* Hurd, 12 Met. 371; Hodgson *v.* Copeland, 16 Me. 314.

4 Allen *v.* Curtis, 26 Conn. 456.

§ 394. As to the liability of a corporation to *indictment*, it is said by Kyd, that it seems that where a corporation has been used, from time immemorial, to repair a creek, highway, or bridge, an indictment will lie against it for not repairing. It is indeed, he says, reported to have been said by Lord Chief Justice Holt,[1] that "a corporation is not indictable, but the particular members are." This, in the apprehension of Kyd, can apply only to the case of a crime or misdemeanor, and that an indictment may lie against a corporation in the cases mentioned, as well as against a county or a parish.[2] In an indictment in the Supreme Court of Maine, charging a mill and manufacturing corporation with a nuisance, in the erection of a dam across the river Penobscot; the counsel for the defendant contended, that an indictment could not be sustained against a corporation, in cases like this, though he admitted that towns and parishes might be indicted for not removing nuisances; but even those quasi corporations, he maintained, could not be indicted for the erection of nuisances, but only the individuals erecting them. In this view he was sustained by the court, which considered that a corporation was incapable of committing any crime or misdemeanor, by any positive or affirmative act, or of inciting others to do so, as a corporation; and suggested that, were it otherwise, the innocent dissenting minority would become equally amenable to punishment with the guilty majority, and that such only as take part in the measure should be prosecuted as individuals, either as principals, or as aiders and abettors. Therefore, the court decided that, when a crime or misdemeanor is committed under the color of corporate authority, the individuals acting in the business, and not the corporation, should be indicted.[3] Wherever a corporation owes a duty to the public, and neglects to perform it, there is clearly a remedy by presentment.[4] Thus an indictment was sustained, in a case at the Worcester Assizes in England, against a railway company, for disobeying an order of justices, for constructing a bridge over a road, which was regarded by the court as coming within the general rule of the liability of corporations to indictment for neglect of duty.[5] The Manchester and Leeds Railway Company were empowered by statute to make obstructions in public or private roads, for the

---

[1] 1 Mod. 559.

[2] Kyd on Corp. 225, 226.

[3] State *v.* Great Mill & Man. Co. 20 Maine, 41.

[4] Freeholders, &c. *v.* Strader, 3 Harrison, 108.

[5] Regina *v.* Birmingham & G. Railway Co. 9 Car. & P. 469.

purposes of their undertaking, doing as little damage as might be; and a subsequent section enacted, that wherever it was found necessary to use that power, they should, before any such road should be cut through, &c., make a good and sufficient road thereof, as convenient for passengers as the road to be cut through, or as near thereto as may be. The company, having obstructed a public road, *without making a new one*, equally convenient, or as nearly so as might be, it was held they were indictable for a nuisance on the old highway.[1] A turnpike road company is liable to an indictment at common law for suffering their road to be out of repair, notwithstanding that by the terms of the charter, a specific penalty is provided; if the charter contain no negative words, nor any thing from which it can be inferred that the legislature intended to take away the common-law remedy.[2] Where, by an act of incorporation of a turnpike road company, it was made the duty of the president and directors to keep the road in repair, and the neglect to do so was declared to be a *misdemeanor* in the president and *individual* directors, for the time being, it was held, that an individual director might be indicted for such neglect, either separately or jointly with his co-directors, and on conviction might be punished separately. It was thus held, although the board of directors consisted of seven members, and the concurrence of a majority was necessary to the *doing* of a corporate act.[3]

§ 395. But the assumption that for a *wrongful act* a corporation is not amenable to indictment, was treated by Lord Denman, C. J., in giving the judgment of the court of Queen's Bench, as entirely unfounded. The question directly presented for the determination of the

---

[1] Regina *v.* Scott, 3 A. & E. 543; Commonwealth *v.* Vermont and Mass. R. R. 4 Gray, 22.

[2] Susquehannah & Bath Turn. Co. *v.* People, 15 Wend. 267.

[3] Kane *v.* People in Error, 8 Wend. 203, and id. 363. And see Ferguson *v.* Earl of Kinnoul, 9 Clark & F. 251. A corporation aggregate (e. g. a railway company) may be indicted by their corporate name for disobedience to an order of justices requiring such corporation to execute works pursuant to a statute. Regina *v.* Birmingham & Gloucester Railway Co. 3 Q. B. 223. The proper mode of proceeding against a corporation to enforce the remedy by indictment, is by distress infinite to compel appearance. Ibid. A corporation is not liable to the penalty imposed by the Act in Massachusetts, on the owners, agent, or superintendent of a manufacturing establishment, for employing children under a certain age. The fact of knowledge of such employment could not, in ordinary cases, be brought home to the corporation as such. Benson *v.* Monson & Brimfield Manuf. Co. 9 Met. 562.

court was, whether an indictment will lie at common law against a corporation for a *misfeasance*, it being admitted, in conformity to undisputed decisions, that an indictment may be maintained against a corporation for *nonfeasance*. In giving judgment, Lord Denman said, "Many occurrences may be easily conceived, full of annoyance and danger to the public, and involving blame in some individual or corporation, of which the most acute person could not clearly define the cause, or ascribe them with more correctness to mere negligence in providing safeguards, or to an act rendered improper by nothing but the want of safeguards. If A. is authorized to make a bridge with parapets, but makes it without them, does the offence consist in the construction of the unsecured bridge, or in the neglect to secure it? But, if the distinction were always easily discoverable, why should a corporation be liable for one species of offence, and not for the other? The startling incongruity of allowing the exemption is one strong argument against it. The law is often entangled in technical embarrassments; but there is none here. It is as easy to charge one person, or a body corporate, with erecting a bar across a public road as with the non-repair of it; and they may as well be compelled to pay a fine for the act as for the omission.[1]

§ 396. It was said by the court in the case of The State *v.* Great Mill & Manufacturing Co. in Maine, before cited,[2] in which they recognize in these cases, a distinction between misfeasance and nonfeasance, that at a corporate meeting a majority might authorize an agent to commit a battery, and then the defendant plead the corporate authority in his defence, unless the distinction in question was recognized. But a battery derives its character from the corrupted mind of the person committing it; and is a violation of the social duties that belong to men and subjects. A corporation, which, as such, has no such duties, cannot be guilty in these cases;[3] though they may be guilty as com-

[1] Regina *v.* Great North of England Railway Co. 9 Q. B. 314. The learned judge cited Regina *v.* Birmingham & Gloucester Railway Co. 3 Q. B. 223, which he said, was confined to the state of things then before the court, which amounted to nonfeasance only; but was by no means intended to deny the liability of a corporation for a misfeasance. State *v.* Morris & Essex Railroad Co. 3 N. J. 360; Commonwealth *v.* New Bedford Bridge, 2 Gray, 339; State *v.* Vermont Cent. R. Co. 27 Vt. 103; B. C. & M. R. R. *v.* State, 32 N. H. 215.

[2] See *ante*, § 394.

[3] Kyd on Corp.; 21 Edw. 4, 7, 12, 27, 67; Orr *v.* Bank of United States, 1 Ham. 25. See, however, Moore *v.* Fitchburg R. R. 4 Gray, 465.

manding acts to be done to the nuisance of the community at large. Admitting that a corporation cannot be guilty of offences against the person, nor of perjury, nor of treason or felony;[1] still, for that which is analogous to a mere trespass on land, an indictment may lie against it.

§ 397. It was expressly decided, in the year 1806, in Massachusetts, that an aggregate corporation cannot be summoned as trustee under the statute of February 28, 1795.[2] The action was *assumpsit*, in which the plaintiffs set forth their charter of incorporation from the State of New York, sundry assessments made in pursuance of the charter upon the stockholders, of which the defendant was one, and his undertaking and promise to pay the amount of those assessments. The New England Marine Insurance Company were summoned as *trustees* of the defendant, by a service on their president. The question made was, whether the property attached in the hands of the New England Insurance Company can be held to respond to the judgment which the plaintiffs may obtain, or, in other words, whether a corporation aggregate may be summoned as trustee, under the statute of this commonwealth, passed February 28, 1795, entitled, "An act to enable creditors to receive their just demands out of the goods, effects, and credits of their debtors, when the same cannot be attached by the ordinary process of law." For the plaintiffs it was argued that the great and leading object of this statute was to prevent debtors from concealing their effects, or putting them out of the reach of legal process. That this object, so desirable, would be in a great measure defeated, if it was once settled that credits in the hands of corporate bodies were safe from attachment. That, as the officers of every corporation of this kind have the sole management of their affairs, keep all their accounts, and are perfectly acquainted with all the facts respecting the debts and credits of those with whom the company transact business, the useful and salutary purposes of the statute would be fulfilled by permitting those officers to come in and make answer upon their oaths, in behalf of the company to the interrogatories. That this has, in fact, been frequently practised without opposition; and two or three cases were named wherein it had been done. The court, without hearing the defendant's counsel, were unanimously of opinion (but gave no reasons for it), that an aggregate corporation cannot be summoned as trustee, and that effects and credits in the hands of such a corporation cannot be attached under the statute.

---

[1] Kyd on Corp.; 21 Edw. 4, 7, 12, 27, 67; Orr *v.* Bank of United States, 1 Ham. 25.

[2] Union Turnpike Road *v.* New England Marine Insurance Co. 2 Mass. 37.

§ 398. In Holland *v.* Leslie, in Delaware,[1] which was a case of foreign attachment against a railroad corporation, there was a rule to show cause why the service of the attachment on the president of the company should not be set aside. "The difficulty," said the court, "is how to enforce the attachment of the company, should they refuse to answer. We could not appoint a person to answer, or direct them to appoint some one to do it, as a court of equity might possibly do. The act of assembly contemplates only individuals; it gives no power to this court in relation to corporations. The legislature have not gone so far as to make them liable to being summoned as garnishees, and to provide the means of compelling them to answer."

§ 399. In Massachusetts, by the act of 1832, ch. 164, corporations are expressly made liable to the process of foreign attachment.[2] In Missouri, a corporation may be summoned as garnishee, and its answer verified as in chancery. The revised statutes of that State enact, that when any party or person is described or referred to, by words importing the singular number or masculine gender, bodies corporate, as well as individuals, shall be deemed to be included. To the objection that a corporation could not answer under oath, the court replied, that the same objection might be made in a suit in equity; and the case was to be governed by the general principles of law in order to ascertain how the answer of the corporation is to be verified.[3]

§ 400. But, wherever a foreign attachment will lie against a corpo-

---

[1] Holland *v.* Leslie, 2 Harring. Del. 306.

[2] But the statute does not extend to foreign corporations, though lessees of property within the State. Gold *v.* Housatonic R. R. Co. 1 Gray, 424. So in Rhode Island, the property of a debtor in the possession of a foreign corporation doing business out of the State, cannot be attached by process of foreign attachment served upon the treasurer, although the treasurer is a resident of Rhode Island. Taft *v.* Mills, 5 R. I. 393.

[3] St. Louis Perpetual Insurance Co. *v.* Cohen, 9 Misso. 421. The Supreme Court of Alabama, without undertaking to inquire whether a private corporation is subject to the process of garnishment, were satisfied that the answer on which the court below acted, did not warrant its judgment; and held, that it was not within the scope of the powers ordinarily conferred upon the cashier of a bank to appear and defend suit against the corporation; that duty pertained to the directors, to whom the management of its affairs are intrusted, and must be exercised under seal; the seal should appear to have been used either by the express authority of the directors, or should actually have been used by the president of the bank, who thus far is the executive officer of the board. Branch Bank at Mobile *v.* Poe, 1 Ala. 396. Under the statutes of Missouri and of Alabama, municipal corporations are not subject to the process of garnishment. Fortune *v.* City of St. Louis, 23 Misso. 239; Mayor, &c. of Mobile *v.* Rowland, 26 Ala. 498.

ration as defendant, the civil death before judgment against it, produced by a decree of forfeiture of its charter by a judicial tribunal, dissolves the attachment. The primary intent being to procure an appearance, a foreign attachment is dissolved the instant the defendant has appeared, or lost his capacity to appear.[1] It has been expressly held, also, in Connecticut, that a corporation, like a natural person, is subject to the process of foreign attachment, though the words of the act in relation to it are, "When debts due from any *person*." Such construction, the court maintained, ought to be given to the act as would effectuate the intentions of the legislature, and promote the object and prevent the evil in view. "Could the legislature," say the court, "have intended that a debtor might deposit his money or effects in a bank, and then abscond beyond the reach of process, and thus draw from the bank from time to time, and yet the bank not to be subject to garnishment?"[2] It has been likewise so held in New Hampshire.[3] In Pennsylvania, it has, in two instances, been expressly adjudged, that a loss incurred on a fire insurance policy, the amount of which has been fixed by the award of persons mutually chosen by the insured and insurer, may be attached by garnishment, as a debt due from the corporation to the insured.[4]

§ 401. In Alabama, the debtor of a corporation may be garnished under the general law of garnishment of that State. But no proceeding can be had under the act of 1841, to subject the debts of stockholders for stock due the company on process of garnishment, issuing previous to the passage of the act.[5] The act of 1841 requires the debtor to state in what he is indebted to the corporation as stockholder or otherwise. The answer of a garnishee, that he had been informed and believed that the corporation ceased to have "any legal existence," previous to the issuing of the garnishment, is equivalent to the assertion that it was dissolved; and if not negatived in the manner prescribed by the statute, will be taken to be true.[6] The design of the act appears to

---

1 Farmers & Mechanics Bank *v.* Little, 8 Watts & S. 207.

2 Knox *v.* Protection Insurance Co. 9 Conn. 430. Held, in this case, that an unadjusted claim for a loss on a policy of insurance, is subject to the process of foreign attachment.

3 Libby *v.* Hogdon, 9 N. H. 394. So also in Virginia. Balt. & Ohio R. R. Co. *v.* Gallahue, 12 Gratt. 655.

4 Boyle *v.* Franklin Fire Insurance Co. 7 Watts & S. 76; Franklin Fire Insurance Co. *v.* West, 8 id. 350.

5 De Mony *v.* Johnston, 7 Ala. 51.

6 Paschall *v.* Whitsett, 11 Ala. 473.

have been to reach the stockholder, as a debtor of the corporation through his stock, and without any call of the company.[1] Before the act, stock held by an individual in a corporation, being a mere chose in action, could not be subjected to the payment of his debts by process of garnishment.[2] A ticket agent cannot be made a garnishee in a suit against a railroad corporation for which he sells.[3] In a late case in New York it is held, that although a foreign corporation may generally be sued by the process of foreign attachment, yet its bonds, in the hands of an agent for the purpose of sale, are not property subject to seizure under an attachment against such corporation.[4]

§ 402. It has been thought that as a corporation can sue within a foreign jurisdiction, there is no reason why it should not be liable to be sued without its jurisdiction, in the same manner, and under the same regulations, as domestic corporations.[5] The technical difficulty which is said to stand in the way is, that the process against a corporation must, by the common law, be served on its head or principal officer, within the jurisdiction of the sovereignty where this artificial body exists. But if a foreign corporation (for instance, an insurance company in Boston) should establish its president in New York, for the express purpose of making contracts there, and should also have property there, it might seem strange if the president could not be summoned there to answer to a debt contracted by him in the corporate name; and that a *distringas* could not be allowed to issue against the corporate property. And Rogers, J., who gave the opinion of the court in the case just referred to, in the Supreme Court of Pennsylvania, very strongly intimates that, under such circumstances, a corporation created by the laws of one State might be sued in the manner just mentioned, in another.[6] Perhaps there is no substantial and satisfactory reason why the technical

---

[1] Cooper *v.* Frederick, 9 Ala. 738.

[2] Planters Bank *v.* Leavens, 4 Ala. 753; and see Bingham *v.* Rushing, 5 id. 403.

[3] Fowler *v.* Pittsburg &c. R. Co. 35 Penn. State, 22.

[4] Coddington *v.* Gilbert, 17 N. Y. 489.

[5] Bushel *v.* Commonwealth Insurance Company, 15 S. & R. 176.

[6] Ibid. Mr. Tidd says: "In proceeding against a corporation, the process should be served on the mayor or other head officer, and if the defendants do not appear before or on the *quarto die post*, of the return of the original, the next process is a *distringas*, which should go against them in their public capacity; and under this process may be distrained the lands and goods which constitute the common stock of the corporation." 1 Tidd's Practice, 116. See *post*, Chap. XVIII., of Process, Pleadings, &c. in Suits by and against Corporations, at Law and in Equity.

rules of the common law respecting suits against corporations, should not, like many other rules respecting them, be so far made to yield as to correspond with the present state of things, and to accomplish the ends of justice, by making the property of an absent corporation liable to be attached in the same manner as the property of any other absent debtor. This view of the subject is supported by the case in question, in the Supreme Court of Pennsylvania, wherein it was held expressly, by a majority of the court, that the property of a Massachusetts corporation might be attached under the foreign attachment law of Pennsylvania, as the property of an absent *person*.[1] This case turned upon the construction of that section of the act of Pennsylvania respecting foreign attachment, which grants the writ of attachment against the effects of any *person* or *persons* who are not residing within the State, &c.

§ 403. From the opinion in the above case, Duncan, J., dissented,[2] and in giving his reasons for so doing, he placed much stress upon the case of M'Queen *v.* Middletown Manufacturing Company in the State of New York;[3] a case in which it was held, that the attachment law of New York only contemplated the case of a liability to arrest. There is an intimation to the same effect by Tilghman, C. J., in Pittsburg Turn-

---

[1] Bushel *v.* Commonwealth Insurance Company, *supra.* See also Ocean Ins. Co. *v.* Portsmouth Railway Co. 3 Met. 420.

[2] He did not view the question as one of so much magnitude as had been represented, or consider that such serious mischiefs would arise from deciding that the effects of a corporation created by a sister State cannot be attached. As to the argument, *ab inconvenienti*, he remarked, "Inconvenient it may be to the party entering into a contract with a foreign corporation, to be obliged to apply to the forum of another State for justice; but the man who contracts with a foreign corporation takes his risk of that, and judges for himself whether that inconvenience is, or is not counterbalanced by the lesser premium, and contracts accordingly, as in his judgment the scales of advantage or inconvenience preponderate." But he mentioned this, "not because he thought courts ought to be governed by considerations of this kind, where a law is plain, and the uniform construction has prevailed for more than a century." As to whether a corporation was a "person," within the meaning of the act relative to foreign attachment, he observed, that, in his humble judgment, there was a demonstration in the act itself, that natural persons were alone intended and alone comprehended; that the legislature, he said, intended to give to all debtors, whom they subjected to foreign attachment, the right to dissolve it on entering *special bail*, which corporations could not give, because it would not be taken; that the debtor corporation was not such an entity as could enter special bail; that it could not be arrested, because invisible; that it could not be delivered in bail, because it could not be in custody, or surrendered.

[3] M'Queen *v.* Middletown Manuf. Company, 16 Johns. 5.

pike Co. *v.* Cullen;[1] and in subsequent cases, in Pennsylvania, it has been expressly held, that a foreign corporation cannot be summoned by a service on its head or chief officer, who at the time of service may be within the territorial jurisdiction of the State; and that such service is bad at common law, as well as under the act of Pennsylvania of 1817.[2] In the above-mentioned case of the Middletown Manufacturing Company, it appears that an attachment had issued against the estate of a corporation established in Connecticut; and the attachment, it was contended, might issue in such a case, under the 23d section of the act of the State, which section enacts that the real and personal estate of every debtor who resides out of the State, and is indebted within it, shall be liable to be attached, and sold for the payment of his debts, in like manner, in all respects, as the estates of debtors residing within the State. The construction the court gave to this clause, from a view of the whole act, was, that the legislature intended to authorize proceedings under it against natural persons only. Spencer, J., who gave the opinion of the court, observed: "We think, a foreign corporation never could be sued here. The process against a corporation must be served on its head, or principal officer, within the jurisdiction of the sovereignty where this artificial body exists. If the president of a bank of another State were to come within this State, he would not represent the corporation here; his functions and his character would not accompany him, when he moved beyond the jurisdiction of the government under whose laws he derived this character; and though, possibly, it would be competent for a foreign corporation to constitute an attorney to appear, and plead to an action instituted under another jurisdiction, we are clearly of the opinion that the legislature contemplated the case of liability to arrest, but for the circumstance, that the debtor was without the jurisdiction of the process of the courts of this State; and that the act, in all its provisions, meant, that attachments should go against natural, not artificial, or mere legal entities. The first section speaks of persons; and throughout the act, natural persons only were intended to be subjected to its provisions. It is true, that there are cases in which corporate property has been held liable to be taxed, under acts which subject the property of *inhabitants* to taxation; but in all such cases the tax operated *in rem* on the estate; and it has been held, that whoever

[1] Pittsburg Turn. Co. *v.* Cullen, 8 S. & R. 517.

[2] Nash *v.* Rector, &c. 1 Miles, 78; Dawson *v.* Campbell, 2 id. 171.

resided on the property represented, in that respect, the corporation, and, in the view of the act, were inhabitants; but it would not be correct to say, abstractly, that a corporation or mere legal entity was an inhabitant." In this opinion of Mr. J. Spencer, the Supreme Court of Massachusetts, in Peckham *v.* North Parish of Haverhill, fully concurred, in a case by which it seems that, in an action upon a joint contract, made by the defendant, and a corporation not within the State, and not liable to be sued, it is not necessary that such corporation should be named in the writ as a co-defendant.[1] After the property of a foreign corporation has been transferred to a receiver, for the benefit of the creditors of the corporation, and the title thereto has become vested in the receiver, under an order of the Court of Chancery of the State where the corporation is situated, such property cannot be reached by an attachment in another State, as the property of the corporation.[2]

§ 404. The case of Libby *v.* Hogdon, in New Hampshire,[3] in which the Portland Stage Company was trustee, involved the inquiry whether a foreign corporation could be sued in that State. It is there provided by statute "That when any body politic or corporate was sued in this State, who have no clerk or member residing therein on whom service can be made, an attested copy of the writ shall be delivered to the agent, overseer, or person having the care or control of the corporate property, or part thereof, in this State." It was objected, that one section of the act directing proceedings against trustees of debtors did not extend to foreign corporations; that section providing that "when any corporation or body politic *within this State* shall be possessed of any money," &c. The court were, however of opinion, that this clause of the statute was not confined to corporations created by the laws of New Hampshire; but that any corporation having property there, or being suable there, was, within the meaning of the statute, "a body politic within the State." Though the court doubted whether the casual presence of the principal officer of a foreign corporation, and service upon him, would be sufficient, yet they held, that if such a corporation have estate there, or if it send its officer, upon whom, by the law of New Hampshire, process is to be served, to reside in the State and transact business on account of the corporation, there was no reason why an

[1] Peckham *v.* North Par. of Haverhill, 16 Pick. 286.

[2] Thomas *v.* Merchants Bank, 9 Paige, 215.

[3] Libby *v.* Hogdon, 9 N. H. 394.

attachment of such estate, or service upon such officer, might not be sufficient.[1]

§ 405. It has been held in Vermont, that there was no ground to doubt whether a private corporation of another State could be held to answer to an action in the courts of Vermont; the court, in the case referred to, being unable to perceive any substantial reason why *artificial* persons should not be liable to suits in the courts of another State, as well as natural persons.[2] The law, as it has been laid down in Missouri, is, that a foreign corporation is liable to be sued in any State where service of process can be made upon its property according to the laws of such State.[3] A foreign corporation, having appeared and pleaded to an action, cannot afterwards object to the jurisdiction; it not being requisite, in such case, to inquire whether an appearance could be compelled, that is, if the court has jurisdiction over the subject-matter.[4]

§ 406. The principal point in controversy in Clark *v.* New Jersey Steam Navigation Company was, whether the respondents, being a corporation created by, and having its corporate existence and organization in, the State of New Jersey, is, as a foreign corporation, liable to a suit *in personam*, in the *admiralty*, in the District of Rhode Island, not directly, but indirectly, through its attachable property in that district, so as to compel the appearance of the corporation to answer the suit, or at all events to subject the property attached to the final judgment and decree of the District Court. It was held by Mr. J. Story, that though by the Common Law foreign corporations and non-resident foreigners cannot be served with process by any of the Courts of Common Law, nor their property be attached to compel their appearance, the District Courts of the United States (as Courts of Admiralty) may award attachments against the property of foreign corporations found within their local jurisdiction. In all proceedings *in rem* (the court having jurisdiction over the property itself), it was wholly unimportant, the learned

---

[1] See, to the same effect, Moulin *v.* Insurance Co. 4 N. J. 222.

[2] Day *v.* Essex County Bank, 13 Vt. 97.

[3] St. Louis Perpetual Insurance Company *v.* Cohen, 9 Misso. 422.

[4] Cook *v.* Champlain Transportation Company, 1 Denio, 91. See also, South Carolina Railroad Company *v.* McDonald, 5 Ga. 531; Martin *v.* Branch Bank of Alabama, 14 La. 415; United States Bank *v.* Merchants Bank, 1 Rob. Va. 573. As to the parties being bound by the face of the record, — Society for the Propagation of the Gospel in Foreign Parts *v.* Wheeler, 2 Gallis. 105.

judge asserted, whether the property belongs to a private person or to a corporation. But if this case had been one exclusively dependent on the local law of Rhode Island, the jurisdiction of the District Court would have been equally clear, as by an act of the legislature of the State, the personal and real estate of an incorporated company established without the State is made liable to attachment upon any just demand.[1]

§ 407. A late decision of the Supreme Court of the United States, in Louisville Railroad Company *v.* Letson,[2] on the construction of that clause of the constitution which extends the judicial power to controversies between "citizens of different States," which by former decisions was viewed in reference to the *citizenship* of the members of a corporation, and required them to be citizens of a different State from the opposite party, has overruled those decisions, and declared that a "corporation created by and doing business in a particular State is to be deemed, to all intents and purposes, as a person, and an inhabitant of the same State, for the purposes of its incorporation, capable of being treated as a citizen of that State, as much as a natural person."[3] The rule laid down in Strawbridge *v.* Curtis,[4] that if there be two or more joint plaintiffs, and two or more joint defendants, each of the plaintiffs must be capable of suing each of the defendants in the Courts of the United States, in order to give to those courts jurisdiction of the case on the ground of the citizenship of the parties; coupled with the decision in the case of Bank of the United States *v.* Devaux,[5] that a corporation could not, for the purpose of jurisdiction, be a citizen, but its right to sue and liability to be sued in the Federal Courts, so far as dependent upon the citizenship of the parties to the case, must depend upon the citizenship of its stockholders or members, seemed to bar the jurisdiction of these courts in classes of cases which specially called for it. At the January term of the Supreme Court of the United States, in 1844, in

---

1 Clark *v.* New Jersey Steam Navigation Co. 1 Story, 531.

2 Louisville Railroad Co. *v.* Letson, 2 How. 558. And see Commonwealth *v.* Milton, 12 B. Mon. 212. Stockholders, who are citizens of other States than that under whose laws the corporation is chartered, may file a bill in equity against it in the courts of the United States. Paine *v.* Indianapolis R. R. Co. 6 McLean, 395; Dodge *v.* Woolsey, 18 How. 331.

3 See 4 Am. Law Mag. 256; and *ante,* § 376.

4 3 Cranch, 267.

5 Bank of United States *v.* Devaux, 5 id. 61. See also, Hope Ins. Co. *v.* Boardman, 5 Cranch, 57; Kirkpatrick *v.* Lehigh Coal & Nav. Co. 4 Wash. C. C. 595; Flanders *v.* Etna Ins. Co. 3 Mason, 158.

the above case of the Louisville Railroad, the court declared that, after mature deliberation, they felt free to say, that those cases were carried too far, and that consequences and inferences had been argumentatively drawn from the reasoning employed in the latter of them, which ought not to be followed. And it was moreover stated by the court, that by no one was the correctness of the decisions in those two cases more questioned than by C. J. Marshall, who gave the opinions; and that it was within the knowledge of several of the court, that that late learned judge had repeatedly expressed regret that these decisions had been made; the court also adding, whenever the subject was mentioned, that if the point of jurisdiction was an original one, the conclusion would be different. "We may safely assert," said the court, "that a majority of the members of this court have at all times partaken of the same regret, and that, whenever a case has occurred on the circuit, involving the application of the case of The Bank *v.* Deveaux, it was yielded to because the decision had been made, and not because it was thought to be right." Mr. J. Wayne, who gave the opinion of the court, then proceeded to consider the act of February, 1839, enlarging the jurisdiction of the courts, as follows: "The first section of that act provides 'that, where in any suit at law or in equity, commenced in any court of the United States, there shall be several defendants, only one or more of whom shall not be inhabitants of or found within the district where the suit is brought, or shall not voluntarily appear thereto, it shall be lawful for the court to entertain jurisdiction, and proceed to the trial and adjudication of such suit between the parties who may be properly before it; but the judgment or decree rendered therein shall not conclude or prejudice other parties, not regularly served with process, or not voluntarily appearing to answer.'" We think, as was said in the case of Commercial Bank of Vicksburg *v.* Slocomb,[1] that this act was intended to remove the difficulties which occurred in practice, in cases both in law and equity, under that clause in the 11th section of the judiciary act, which declares, "that no civil suit shall be brought before either of said courts against an inhabitant of the United States, by any original process, in any other district than that whereof he is an inhabitant, or in which he shall be found at the time of serving the writ;" but a reëxamination of the entire section will not permit us to reaffirm what was said in that case, that the act did not contemplate a change in

---

[1] Commercial Bank of Vicksburg *v.* Slocomb, 14 Pet. 60.

the jurisdiction of the courts as it regards the character of the parties. If the act, in fact, did no more than to make a change, by empowering the courts to take cognizance of cases other than such as were permitted in that clause of the 11th section which we have just cited, it would be an enlargement of jurisdiction as to the character of parties. The clause that the judgment or decree rendered shall not conclude or prejudice other parties, who have not been regularly served with process, or who have not voluntarily appeared to answer, is an exception, exempting parties so situated from the enactment, and must be so strictly applied. It is definite as to the persons of whom it speaks, and contains no particular words, as a subsequent clause, by which the general words of the statute can be restrained. The general words embrace every suit at law or in equity, in which there shall be several defendants, "any one or more of whom shall not be inhabitants of or found within the district where the suit is brought, or who shall not voluntarily appear thereto." The words "shall not be inhabitants of," applies as well to corporators as to persons who are not so; and if, as corporators, they are not suable individually, and cannot be served with process, or voluntarily appear in an action against the corporation of which they are members, the conclusion should be that they are not included in the exception, but are within the general terms of the statute. Or, if they are viewed as defendants in the suit, then, as corporators, they are regularly served with process in the only way the law permits them to be, when the corporation is sued by its name. The case before us might be safely put upon the foregoing reasoning and upon the statute; but hitherto we have reasoned upon this case upon the supposition that, in order to found the jurisdiction in cases of corporations, it is necessary there should be an averment, which, if contested, was to be supported by proof, that some of the corporators are citizens of the State by which the corporation was created, where it does its business, or where it may be sued. But this has been done in deference to the doctrines of former cases in this court, upon which we have been commenting. But there is a broader ground upon which we desire to be understood, upon which we altogether rest our present judgment, although it might be maintained upon the narrower ground already suggested. It is, that a corporation created by and doing business in a particular State, is to be deemed, to all intents and purposes, as a person, although an artificial person, an inhabitant of the same State, for the purposes of its incorporation, capable of being treated as a citizen of that State, as much as a natural person. Like a citizen it makes contracts; and though in regard to what it may do in some particulars it differs from a natural person, and in this especially, the manner in which it can sue and be sued, it is substantially, within the meaning of the law, a citizen of the State which created it, and where its business is done, for all the purposes of suing and being sued."

If a foreign corporation, sued in a State court, appears there and removes the suit to the United States court, under the 12th section of the Judiciary Act of 1789, it is too late to object to the jurisdiction of the State court, or to take any exception to the process by which the corporation was brought in, and it is not a valid objection, that not being an inhabitant or found within the district, the suit could not have been commenced in the United States court.[1]

§ 407 *a*. A foreign corporation as well as one within the State where the suit is brought may plead the statute of limitations to a suit on a contract. And it has been held that the general exceptions in the statutes of limitations of cases where the debtor shall be out of the State when the cause of action accrues, or shall afterwards depart from and reside out of the State, apply only to natural persons, and do not embrace corporations.[2]

CHAPTER XII.

OF DISFRANCHISEMENT AND AMOTION OF MEMBERS AND OFFICERS.

§ 408. A DISTINCTION has been pointed out (and one which has not been always regarded) by Willcock, in his treatise on Municipal Corporations,[3] between disfranchisement and amotion. Disfranchisement is applicable only to the rights of a member of a corporation, as such; for

---

[1] Sayles *v*. North-Western Ins. Co. 2 Curtis, C. C. 212.

[2] Faulkner *v*. Delaware & Raritan Canal Co. 1 Denio, 441; Olcott *v*. Tioga Railroad Co. 26 Barb. 147.

[3] Willcock on Mun. Corp. 270.

every member of a corporation, as it has been asserted by Blackstone,[1] is understood to have "a franchise, or freedom;" and therefore when a member is deprived of this franchise, by being expelled, it may aptly be said, that he has been disfranchised. The term applies to *members*, but the term "amotion" only to such members as are *officers;* and, consequently, if an officer be removed for good cause, he may still continue to be a member. Misconduct in a corporate office warrants only an amotion from that particular office, and, as is obvious, may not always warrant an exclusion from the franchise, or the incidental rights of membership.

§ 409. It was resolved in Bagg's case,[2] that no freeman of any corporation could be disfranchised by the corporation, unless they had authority, either by the express words of the charter, or by prescription. Although the arguments in that case were more applicable to disfranchisement, the particular case was of amotion from office. The position just mentioned, however, as to the power of a corporation to disfranchise a member, has never been (though by many supposed to have been) expressly overruled in England; and in the cases of Lord Bruce,[3] Rex *v.* Richardson,[4] and others, the questions were questions of amotion. Mr. Willcock considers that some of the remarks of Sir E. Coke on this subject, in Bagg's case, are worthy of considerable attention.[5]

---

1 See *ante*, Introd. § 4.

2 Bagg's case, 11 Co. R. 99.

3 Lord Bruce's case, 2 Stra. 820.

4 Rex *v.* Richardson, 1 Burr. 525.

5 Willcock on Mun. Corp. 271. At the time when James Bagg's case was before the court, their attention had been rarely attracted to the consideration of corporate causes, and the distinction between the right to the offices and the right to the freedom of a municipality had been little considered. The particular case was of amotion from office; the arguments were in general more applicable to disfranchisement. But there is a material difference in principle. The enjoyment of office is not for the private benefit of the corporator, but an honorable distinction, which he holds for the welfare of the corporation, and therefore, although it be an office of a freehold nature, it is entirely conditional; in the first place, depending on the particular regulations of the constitution, such as residence, &c.; secondly, upon his discharge of those duties which belong to the office, neglect of which is cause of amotion; thirdly, on his being such a person as ought to be permitted to hold office, and therefore defeated by commission of any infamous offence, although not relating to the corporation. But the franchise of a freeman is wholly for his own benefit, and a private right; a right in the municipality similar to that of a natural subject in the State, of which he ought not to be deprived for any minor offence against his corporate fealty, than that for which, as a subject, he ought to be deprived of his franchise as a liegeman. For this reason all minor corporate offences, such as improper behavior to his

§ 410. With regard to what are called joint-stock incorporated companies, or indeed any corporations owning property, it cannot be pretended that a member can be expelled, and thus deprived of his interest in the stock or general fund, in any case, by a majority of the corporators, unless such power has been expressly conferred by the charter. And if an owner of stock could be excluded, without any provision in the charter, from participating in the election of officers, and in the other affairs of the company, he would still be entitled to the amount of his stock, and could recover it in an action against the corporation. It will be shown, in a subsequent chapter, that transferable shares in the stock of any company cannot be divested out of the proprietor by any act of the company, without the authority of the stockholder.[1]

§ 411. In the case of the Bank of England, the court say, "The legislature, so far from allowing an act of the bank to deprive the stockholder of his interest, has taken care to direct in what manner the interest he has shall be conveyed away."[2] As in banks, insurance, canal, turnpike companies, &c., a person is made a member by the purchase of stock,[3] so he of course ceases to be a member by making a transfer of his stock; for by such transfer he disqualifies himself to be a member. It would certainly seem to be a reasonable rule, with regard to the expulsion or removal of members of corporations generally, that when a member disqualifies himself to assist in promoting the object and purposes of corporation, he forfeits his corporate franchise, and may thus justify a vote of expulsion. For example, if a member of a corporation, created for the advancement of religion, should conduct himself in such a manner as to counteract the efforts of the other members in effecting that object, the corporation might be authorized to disfranchise or expel him. It is, no doubt, a tacit condition annexed to the franchise of a member, that he will not oppose or injure the interests of the corporate body; and consequently, if he breaks this condition, he may be disfranchised.[4] In Bagg's case it was resolved, that the cause of disfran-

---

fellow-corporators, where not punishable by the general law of the land, as well as violations of his corporate duties, ought to be punished by penalties imposed by the ordinances. of the municipality, and not by disfranchisement. Ibid. 271, 272.

1 See *post*, Chapter XVI. relating to transfer of stock.

2 Davis *v.* Bank of England, 2 Bing. 393; State *v.* Tudor, 5 Day, 329; Delacy *v.* Neuse River Nav. Co. 1 Hawks, 520; Ebaugh *v.* Herdel, 5 Watts, 43.

3 See *ante*, Ch. IV.

4 Commonwealth *v.* St. Patrick Society, 2 Binn. 448.

chisement should be grounded upon an act, which is against the duty of a citizen or burgess, and to the prejudice of the public good, of the city or borough, and against his oath which he took when he was sworn a freeman; for it is a condition of law tacitly annexed to his freedom or liberty. A mere attempt, however, to do such an act, unattended with an eventual injury, is not a sufficient cause; for a freeman has a freehold in the franchise for his life.

§ 412. The law, as it has been laid down by the Supreme Court of Pennsylvania, is, that a corporation possesses inherently the power of expelling members in *certain cases*, as such power is necessary to the good order and government of corporate bodies; and that the cases in which this inherent power may be exercised, are of three kinds: 1. When an offence is committed which has no immediate relation to a member's corporate duty, but is of so infamous a nature as renders him unfit for the society of honest men; such are the offences of perjury, forgery, &c. But before an expulsion is made for a cause of this kind, it is necessary that there should be a previous conviction, by a jury, according to the law of the land. 2. When the offence is against his *duty as a corporator;* in which case he may be expelled on trial and conviction by the corporation. 3. The third is an offence of a mixed nature, against the member's duty as a corporator, and also indictable by the law of the land.[1] But these principles, as before suggested, of course cannot be considered applicable to corporations, the members of which are stockholders. And where the visitatorial power is vested in trustees, in virtue of their incorporation, there can be no removal of them; though they are subject, as managers of the revenues of the corporation, to the superintending power of chancery, which (without comprehending a visitatorial authority, or a right to control the charity) includes a general jurisdiction in all cases of an abuse of trusts, to redress grievances and suppress frauds. Indeed, where a corporation is a mere trustee of a charity, a Court of Equity will go yet further; and though it cannot appoint or amove a corporator, it will, in a case of gross fraud or abuse of trust, take the trust from the corporation, and vest it in other hands.[2] In the American books there are very few

---

[1] Commonwealth *v.* St. Patrick Society, 2 Binn. 448; and see the opinion of Lord Mansfield, in Rex *v.* Richardson, 2 Burr. 536.

[2] Dartmouth College *v.* Woodward, 6 Wheat. 676, 688; Society for the Propagation

cases to be found on this subject of disfranchisement; and the cases in the English books which we have met with, relating to the causes that are sufficient to justify a vote of disfranchisement, are confined to municipal corporations. We will proceed, however, in endeavoring to show, by such cases directly in point as we are able to find, the limits of the power of disfranchisement, when the charter is silent.

§ 413. As Mr. Willcock observes, few cases have ascertained what is sufficient cause of disfranchisement; those which have been decided on this point are almost all of the negative kind, which only show what causes, being relied upon, were considered insufficient to warrant a disfranchisement.[1] A corporate assembly, being apprehensive of a riot from the violence of the different parties, was dissolved, and some of the members remained, saying, that the assembly was not dissolved, and thereupon made divers orders, and caused them to be entered in the books. This conduct was held to be sufficient cause for disfranchising those who remained and concurred in such acts; for the irregular entry of such orders was very prejudicial to the corporation, &c.[2] Being so poor as to be incapable of paying his scot and lot, was held insufficient to disfranchise a member of a municipal corporation in England; and so was the conviction of an assault, or saying of an alderman that he was a knave. The first is a misfortune, and not an injury to the corporation, as such; and the others are offences punishable at common law, upon conviction by a jury, and not fit subjects for the investigation of a corporate body.[3] Even a usage, in a prescriptive corporation, to disfranchise or suspend a freeman for insulting words to a principal officer of the corporation, was, in England, held void, though the corporate customs were in general terms confirmed by statute.[4] In the case of the Plainfield Academy, where the return, by the members of the corpora-

---

of the Gospel *v.* New Haven, 8 Wheat. 464; Fuller *v* Plainfield Academic School, 6 Conn. 532.

[1] Willcock on Mun. Corp. 273.

[2] The Protector *v.* Kingston, Style, 478, 480.

[3] Rex *v.* Andover, 3 Salk. 229; Jay's case, 1 Vent. 302; Earle's case, Carth. 174, b; Rex *v.* Oxford, Palm. 455; Rex *v.* London, 2 Lev. 201; Rex *v.* Lane, 2 Mod. 270. It was said by Twisden, C. J., that a freeman may be disfranchised for saying of the mayor, that he had burnt the charters of the corporation; but the observation was immaterial to the decision. Jay's case, 1 Vent. 302.

[4] Rex *v.* London, 2 Lev. 201; Rex *v.* Rogers, 2 Ld. Raym. 777; Rex *v.* Guilford, 1 Lev. 162.

tion, to a writ of mandamus, complaining of the removal of a member, and seeking his restoration, alleged, as the grounds of removal, first, disrespectful language towards his associates; secondly, neglect of official duty in not acting on committees; it was held, that these charges were insufficient to justify a removal. The place of a trustee in an eleemosynary corporation, though no emoluments are attached to it, it was also held, is a franchise of such a nature that a person improperly dispossessed of it is entitled to redress by writ of mandamus.[1] The mere misemployment of corporate funds is no cause for amotion; but charging the corporation with money which the member never paid, is sufficient cause for amotion.[2]

§ 414. A case was decided in Pennsylvania, in the year 1810, which arose on the return of a mandamus directed to the St. Patrick Benevolent Society, an incorporated body, commanding them to restore John Binns to the rights of a member of said society. The question was, whether the by-law under which the expulsion was made was valid, the by-law providing for the dismissal of members for vilifying a corporator. In determining the question, the court considered it necessary to regard the nature of the corporation, which was an association having for its object the raising of a fund to be applied to the relief of its members, in case of sickness and misfortune, and to the assistance of distressed Irishmen emigrating to the United States. Each member paid a certain sum, on admittance to the society, and likewise an annual contribution; and each member was entitled, in case of sickness, or distress occasioned by unavoidable accident, to pecuniary assistance from the funds of the society. The corporation had power to make by-laws for the good order and support of the affairs of the corporation, provided the said by-laws were not repugnant to the instrument of incorporation; and by the charter any member who was guilty of insulting or disrespectful behavior to any of the society, was to be fined for the first offence, in the sum of one dollar, double that sum for the second offence, and for the third be expelled the society. Tilghman, C. J., in giving the opinion of the court, after stating that the case provided for in the charter was, from its nature, confined to disrespectful behavior in the *presence* of the party offended, observed as follows: "My opinion will be founded on the great and single point on which the cause turns: Is

---

[1] Fuller *v.* Plainfield Academic School, 6 Conn. 532.

[2] Commonwealth *v.* Guardians of the Poor, 6 S. & R. 469.

this by-law necessary for the good government and support of the affairs of the corporation? I cannot think that it is. I have considered the case with a mind strongly disposed to give a liberal construction to the power of making by-laws. It is my wish to give all necessary powers for carrying into effect the benevolent purposes of this society, and many others which have lately been incorporated on similar principles. But these powers must not be constrained, or the societies, instead of being protected, will be dissolved. The right of membership is valuable, and not to be taken away without an authority fairly derived from the charter, or *the nature of corporate bodies*. Every man who becomes a member looks to the charter; in that he puts his faith, and not in the uncertain will of a majority of the members. The offence of vilifying a member or a private quarrel, is totally unconnected with the affairs of the society, and therefore its punishment cannot be necessary for the good government of the corporation. So far from it, that it appears to me that taking cognizance of such offences will have the pernicious effect of introducing private feuds into the bosom of the society, and interrupting the transaction of business." The chief justice concluded by saying: "On mature reflection, it appears to me that, without an express power in the charter, no man can be disfranchised, unless he has been guilty of some offence, which either affects the interests or good government of the corporation, or is indictable by the law of the land. I am therefore of opinion that the cause returned by the president of the St. Patrick Benevolent Society for not restoring John Binns to the rights of a member is insufficient."[1]

§ 415. When the charter expressly authorizes the expulsion of members in certain specific cases, it does not follow that the power of expulsion may not be exercised in other cases, when the good government of the corporation requires it, unless it is positively confined to particular offences.[2] In a case where the articles of a corporation authorized the expulsion of a member for being concerned in scandalous or improper proceedings, which might injure the reputation of the society, it was held to be sufficient cause of expulsion, that a member claiming relief from the society had altered the amount of a physician's bill from four dollars to forty, and had presented the bill to the president as the basis of his claim.[3]

---

1 Commonwealth *v.* St. Patrick Society, 2 Binn. 441.

2 Ibid. 4 Binn. 448.

3 Commonwealth *v.* Philanthropic Society, 5 Binn. 486.

§ 416. Where the rules of a religious society inflicted the penalty of expulsion on any member who should commence a suit at law against another member, "except the case were of such a nature as to require and justify a process at law," a return to a mandamus to restore a member to his standing, which set forth the rule, and also that the expelled member had commenced a suit against another (without averring that the case was not of such a nature as to require and justify a process at law), was held to be insufficient.[1]

§ 417. A by-law of an incorporated beneficial institution provided that "no soldier of a standing army, seaman, or mariner, shall be capable of admission; and any member who shall voluntarily enlist as a soldier, or enter on board of any vessel as a seaman or mariner, shall henceforth lose his membership." A member of this association joined a volunteer corps raised in another State who tendered their services to the United States, under the act of 1846, and who were accepted and mustered into service. The member continued in such service in Mexico until the expiration of his term; and it was held that this act did not authorize his expulsion from the association. The member became a soldier, but not a regular one; in other words, he did not embrace the profession of arms as a business, and was but a citizen soldier. The words "standing army," in connection with the word "enlist," the court were of opinion, meant no more than the regular army, in contradistinction to a force composed of volunteers.[2]

§ 418. Where the charter of an association provides for an offence, directs the mode of proceeding, and authorizes the society, on conviction of a member, to expel him, an expulsion, if the proceedings have been regular, is conclusive, and cannot be inquired into collaterally by mandamus, or by any other mode. The sentence is like an award made by a tribunal of the party's own choosing; for he became a member under, and subject to, the articles and conditions of the charter, and of course, to the provisions in relation to this subject, as well as in relation to others. The society being empowered by its charter to act *judicially*, its sentence is just as conclusive as that of any other judicial tribunal.[3]

---

[1] Green *v.* African Methodist Episcopal Society, 1 S. & R. 254.

[2] Franklin Beneficial Association *v.* Commonwealth, 10 Barr, 357.

[3] Commonwealth *v.* Pike Beneficial Society, 8 Watts & S. 247. A corporator may, undoubtedly, surrender, by consent, a matter of common right, which he could not be de-

The charter of a private corporation provided, that if any member should be found breaking the rules of the society, he should be served with a notice to attend to answer at the next stated meeting; after which a decision should be made by ballot, and if two thirds considered him guilty, should be dealt with conformably to the by-laws. The by-laws provided that no member should be entitled to receive any benefit from the society whose complaints were the results of habitual intoxication, &c. A member was expelled, by the required majority, after due notice, and brought an action to recover the allowance granted to disabled members. It was held, that the regularity of the proceedings to expel him could not be investigated in such action, and that the court had no jurisdiction, by action, to compel payment of the allowance.[1]

§ 419. Where, under the charter of incorporation, none but the members of "The Reformed German Reformed Church of Heidelburg, citizens of the commonwealth," were corporators; it was held, that as a person excommunicated ceased to be a member, he lost his rights as a corporator. In this case, it seems that, under the articles for the discipline of that church, the consistory only had the power of excluding a member from the communion; and that an act of excommunication or expulsion from the church, required the consent of the congregation, either expressly or tacitly given. If the consistory, however, should proceed to disfranchise or excommunicate a member, without the consent of the congregation, his remedy would be by appeal to a *higher tribunal* of the church, the *judicatories* of which consisted of the classis and the synod; and the member who thought himself aggrieved by the decision of a low tribunal, had the right to appeal to a higher one. The decision of ecclesiastical courts, to the extent of the power derived from an act of the legislature (as has been already laid down), are, like those of any other supreme judicial tribunal, final; they are, indeed, the best judges of what constitutes an offence against the discipline of the church.[2]

§ 420. In none of the above cases, wherein it is considered that there

---

prived of by a by-law that had not received his assent. Astley *v.* Whitstable Co. 17 Ves. 323. See *post,* Chap. XX. on the Writ of Mandamus.

[1] Black & White Smith's Society *v.* Vandyke, 2 Whart. 309. See also, Anacosta Tribe *v.* Murbach, 13 Md. 91.

[2] German Reformed Church *v.* Seibert, 3 Barr, 282.

is just and sufficient cause for amotion, can the party be expelled, unless he has been *duly notified* to appear.[1] And where a corporation strikes off one of its members, without giving previous notice, and affording an opportunity to be heard, a *mandamus* to restore him will be granted.[2] J. H., a member of the Pennsylvania Beneficial Institution, having been expelled from the society, and having applied to the Supreme Court for a *mandamus* to restore him, the officers of the corporation made a return, showing cause why the said J. H. should not be restored to the rights of a member. It appeared by the return, that by the articles of incorporation, each member was to pay fifty cents in specie, as a monthly contribution, and that should any member neglect to pay his contribution for three months, he was to be expelled. J. H., it was stated, was three months in arrear, as was reported by a committee appointed for the purpose of making inquiry on that subject; whereupon he, together with others who were found to be in the like situation, were struck off the roll, as having forfeited their rights of membership in the society. There was no vote of expulsion, because, in the opinion of the officers who made the return to the mandamus, the non-payment of contributions for three months, was, *ipso facto*, a forfeiture of membership. But the court were clear that there must be some act of the society, declaring the expulsion; and that this could not be done without a vote of expulsion *after notice* to the member supposed to be in default. For it was possible that the member might either prove that he was not in arrears, or give such reason for his default as the society might think sufficient.[3] And the notice must be served upon the accused a reasonable time before the amotion; and where an amotion is shown, the notice must be particularly and positively averred; if it be under a recital, as *licet summonitus fuit*, it is insufficient.[4]

---

[1] Willcock on Mun. Corp. 264; Fuller *v.* Plainfield Academic School, 6 Conn. 532. That it is irregular to expel a member on a report of a committee of investigation, and that the return to a *mandamus* must show that the relator had notice to appear and defend himself, was held, in Pennsylvania, in Commonwealth *v.* German Society, 15 Penn. State, 251.

[2] Delacey *v.* Neuse Navigation Co. 1 Hawks, 274.

[3] Commonwealth *v.* Pennsylvania Beneficial Institution, 2 S. & R. 141. And where under the constitution and by-laws of a society, a member was entitled to twenty-four hours' notice before his expulsion, and such notice was not given, nor waived by him, and the expulsion took place in the absence of the member, he was held entitled to recover damages to the extent of the injury. Washington Ben. Society *v.* Bacher, 20 Penn. State, 425. See also, Southern Plank Road Co. *v.* Hixon, 5 Ind. 166; State *v.* Trustees of Vincennes University, id. 77.

[4] Rex *v.* Richardson, 1 Burr. 540; Rex *v.* Liverpool, 2 Burr. 731; Bagg's case, 11 Co.

§ 421. This notice may of course be dispensed with, when the party has appeared at the meeting, and either defended himself, or answered or confessed the charge against him; for this is a waiver of his right to notice.[1] If the accused member is present, say the Supreme Court of Pennsylvania, when the subject is taken up, and is willing to enter into the inquiry immediately, there is no occasion for further notice.[2]

§ 422. It does not appear necessary that the summons or notice should particularize the charges; though some intimation should be given of them, that the accused may have an opportunity of vindicating himself.[3] In one case it was said that there should be a notice of the charge, and that a general summons was not sufficient, when particular offences were alleged, which the accused might not be prepared to answer.[4] And although, if a notice set forth one charge, and a different one is preferred, the accused may decline answering the new matter, yet in the allegation of the charge technical precision is not required.[5] That the member must have an opportunity of answering the charges preferred against him, and making a full defence, fully appears by the case before cited, of The Commonwealth *v.* Pennsylvania Beneficial Institution, and the authorities therein cited. If the member remain silent and do not deny the charge, it must be examined and proved, and all proceedings must be conducted as though he had denied it; for an amotion, on pretence that silence amounts to a confession, is void; though

---

99. Any society may make any rules by which the admission and expulsion of its members are to be regulated, and the members must conform to these rules; but where there is not any property in which all the members of the society have a joint interest, and where there is no rule as to expulsion, the majority may by resolution remove any member; but before that is done, *notice must be given to him* to answer the charge made against him, and an opportunity given to him for making his defence. Where, therefore, a member of such a society has used menacing language towards another member of the society, and for this a majority of a general meeting of the society voted that he should no longer be considered a member of the society, but did not give him notice of the intention to take his conduct into consideration, or any opportunity of making his defence, it was held, that the expulsion was void, and that he was still a member. Innes *v.* Wylie, 1 Car. & K. 257. But where the rules required a summons before expulsion, — it was held that want of summons was not a sufficient objection after the matter had been submitted to arbitrators, who had heard and decided upon the objection. *Ex parte* Long, Q. B. 1854, 29 Eng. L. & Eq. 194.

1 Willcock on Mun. Corp. 265.

2 Commonwealth *v.* Pennsylvania Beneficial Institution, 2 S. & R. 141.

3 Rex *v.* Liverpool, 2 Burr. 734.

4 Exeter *v.* Glide, 4 Mod. 37.

5 Rex *v.* Lyme Regis, Doug. 174.

it does not afford sufficient ground for an action against those who disfranchise him, unless malice be shown.[1] We have mentioned, as one of the causes of disfranchisement, the conviction of a member, by a jury of his country, of an infamous crime. In such case it is apprehended a vote of expulsion would be legal, without any notice or preferment of charges; however proper and necessary those ceremonies may be, when the offence has a particular reference to the corporate interests.

§ 423. If private corporations have an incidental power of disfranchising a member in certain cases, they would seem *a fortiori* to have the power of amoving, when the interests and good government of the corporate body require it, their official agents from the stations assigned to them, and before the expiration of the term for which they were appointed.[2] "Suppose," says Lord Mansfield, in the case of a municipal corporation, "a by-law made 'to give power of amotion for just cause,' such a by-law would be good." "And if so," he adds, "a corporation, by virtue of an *incidental* power, may raise to themselves authority to amove for just cause, though not expressly given by charter." [3] So the court, in Lord Bruce's case, say, "The modern opinion has been, that a power of amotion is *incident* to the corporation." [4] Lord Mansfield, in Rex *v.* Richardson, specified three sorts of offences for which an officer might be discharged. First, such as have no immediate relation to the office, but are in themselves of so infamous a nature as to render the offender unfit to execute any public franchise. Secondly, such as are only against his oath, and the duty of his office as a corporator, and amount to breaches of the *tacit* condition annexed to his office. Thirdly, the third offence is of a mixed nature, as being an offence not only against the duty of his office, but also a matter indictable at common law. And Lord Mansfield considered the law as settled, that though a corporation has *express* power of amotion, yet for the first sort of offences there must be a previous indictment and conviction; and that there was no authority since Bagg's case,[5] which says that the power of *trial*, as well as amotion, for the second sort of offences is not incident to *every* corporation. He also observed, "We think that from the

---

1 Rex *v.* Feversham, 8 T. R. 356; Harman *v.* Tappenden, 1 East, 562; and see Fuller *v.* Plainfield Academic School, 6 Conn. 532.

2 People *ex rel.* Stevenson *v.* Higgins, 15 Ill. 110.

3 Rex *v.* Richardson, 1 Burr. 539.

4 Lord Bruce's case, 2 Stra. 819.

5 11 Co. 99.

reason of the thing, from the nature of the corporation, and for the sake of order and government, this power is *incident*, as much as the power of making by-laws." [1]

§ 424. Ministers, elders, or deacons, of an incorporated church society, who are *virtute officii* trustees, though they afterwards secede and renounce the authority of the classes and general synod, and unite with another ecclesiastical body, do not thereby divest themselves of their offices, and there must be an amotion by a competent power, to determine an office. When the original title to an office is unquestionable, though good cause of amotion be shown, even in a case where a charter declares that for such cause of amotion the officer shall vacate his office, the office is not determined until there be an amotion.[2]

§ 425. The English books, it may be said, afford a very considerable number of adjudged cases, relating to the causes that are sufficient for the removal of officers in *municipal* corporations. A summary of these cases it is our duty to lay before the reader, as they have at least a strong, if not a direct bearing upon the kind of corporations to which our treatise is more particularly confined.

§ 426. It is to be observed, in the first place, that a distinction is made between such persons as hold a *ministerial* office and such as hold an office *of the essence of the corporation*. A mere ministerial officer, appointed *durante bene placito*, may be removed without any other cause than that the pleasure of those who appointed him is determined; and a formal amotion for the appointment of another to the office is sufficient, without resorting to notice. In these cases, says Mr. Willcock, the right to amove is, of course incidental to the right of appointment.[3] And a ministerial officer may be so amoved, when appointed *durante bene placito*, where the power of appointment is "for life," or "during pleasure." [4] Of this class is a town clerk or recorder; that is, it seems, where the recorder is a mere counsel to advise, and not one who has a corporate office and voice in the common council.[5] But there cannot be

---

[1] And see Rex *v.* Lyme Regis, Doug. 149.

[2] Doremus *v.* Dutch Reformed Church, 2 Green, N. J. 332.

[3] Willcock on Mun. Corpor. 253.

[4] Ibid. 254.

[5] Dighton's case, T. Raym. 188, 1 Vent. 77, 82; Rex *v.* Cambridge, 2 Show. 70; Rex *v.* Canterbury, 11 Mod. 403, 1 Stra. 674.

a custom to amove at pleasure from an office of the essence of the corporation; such, for example, as an alderman; for he has a franchise in his office.[1] In the case of a private corporation (a religious society) it has been held, in New York, that it being the established usage of the society that no question whatever arising at any of its meetings, for consideration, is decided by a majority of voices, but is determined by the presiding officer for the time being, a majority have not the power to displace their presiding officer, whose term has not expired, and appoint another in his stead. In case of the absence of such presiding officer, or of his incompetency to perform the duties of his office, such new appointment may be made, but not otherwise.[2]

§ 427. The following is a summary of the cases it was proposed to offer, in which it was held that there were sufficient causes for discharging such officers of a municipal corporation (as are not amovable at pleasure), on account of a dereliction of their corporate duty: Non-residence, having deserted the borough and resided at a considerable distance for the last four years continually, by reason of which he has neglected to attend the business of the corporation, although it does not appear that any special damage has arisen to the body from his absence, or that the charter required residence.[3] Having deserted his habitation in the city for the space of three years, and been forty times absent from the corporate meetings after general notice, although his presence was not absolutely necessary, is sufficient cause for amoving an alderman; for it is incident to his duty and place to be resident where he is chosen, and such absence renders him incapable of doing his duty where he ought.[4] Non-residence which has caused a neglect of duty, by

---

[1] Dighton's case, 1 Vent. 77, 82, 1 Sid. 461; Warren's case, Dyer, 332, b. n. And it is wholly unimportant that there be a custom to elect such officers "during pleasure," or to elect them "during life, if it appear to them expedient," and that it is alleged that they deemed it expedient to amove them. If such a clause be contained in a charter it is absolutely void. Willcock on Mun. Corpor. 254, 255. But a custom was alleged for the mayor and major part of the corporation to turn out whom they pleased; on which Holt, C. J., observed, that there was no remedy for it, the constitution being so. Rex *v.* Andover, 12 Mod. 665. But see Primm *v.* City of Carondelet, 23 Misso. 22, where it was held that a city counsellor has no such vested right in his office, during the term for which he is elected, as to render an ordinance abolishing the office void, as interfering with the obligation of a contract.

[2] Field *v.* Field, 9 Wend. 394.

[3] Rex *v.* Doncaster, Say. 39; Rex *v.* Trueboy, 11 Mod. 75, 2 Ld. Raym. 1275; Rex *v.* Lyme Regis, Doug. 153.

[4] Exeter *v.* Glide, 4 Mod. 36, Comb. 197; Vaughn *v.* Lewis, Carth. 229.

which some person is injured in his corporate franchise, is cause for amoving an alderman; but unless residence be required by the charter, it is sufficient that the corporator at reasonable times attend to the corporate business, although he reside at some distance from the town. Non-attendance at several corporate meetings, after having received proper notice, if, by reason of his neglect, the business of the corporation has been impeded, was held sufficient cause for amoving a recorder;[1] and so is the temporary and less frequent non-attendance of an officer, whose duty calls upon him to be constantly present, such as mayor.[2] So is non-attendance at one corporate meeting appointed by himself, where his presence is proper, though not absolutely necessary, he being in the neighborhood and able to attend, although he did not receive notice at the time of the meeting.[3] Not accounting for rents by him received in his official capacity, and charging for payments never made, was held a sufficient cause for amoving a chamberlain; provided it appears that he had been called upon to account.[4] Razing of genuine and true entries in the corporation books, to falsify them and injure the corporation, is a sufficient cause; but a general allegation that he razed and altered the books is insufficient; for the razure or alteration may have been to correct an entry originally erroneous.[5] Being so poor that he was not able to pay the taxes for which he was liable in the municipality, was adjudged to be sufficient cause for the amoving an alderman.[6] Habitual drunkenness was cause for amoving an alderman, on account of his consequent insufficiency to discharge his peculiar duties.[7] Disturbing the election of mayor, or preventing the corporators from assembling in their business in the corporate assembly is also sufficient; and the amotion may be before a conviction for riot.[8]

---

[1] Rex *v.* Portsmouth, 3 B. & C. 56, 4 D. & R. 775; Rex *v.* Trueboy, 11 Mod. 75.

[2] Rex *v.* Wells, 4 Burr. 2004; Lord Bruce's case, 2 Stra. 819, and notes; Rex *v.* Ipswich, 2 Ld. Raym. 1233, Salk. 443.

[3] Atk. 184, case 456; Bul. N. P. 206, 207. Continued absence of about five years, and general neglect of attending when courts were to be held, was sufficient for amoving a recorder, though no particular mischief had arisen to the corporation from his neglect. Semb. Lord Hawley's case, 1 Vent. 115. But it may be observed that other charges were brought against this recorder. Rex *v.* Ipswich, 2 Ld. Raym. 1237; and see 2 Burr. 2004.

[4] Rex *v.* Doncaster, 2 Ld. Raym. 1566; but see Rex *v.* Chalke, 1 Ld. Raym. 226.

[5] Rex *v.* Chalke, 5 Mod. 257, 1 Ld. Raym. 226.

[6] Rex *v.* Andover, 3 Salk. 229.

[7] Rex *v.* Taylor, 3 Salk. 231; Taylor *v.* Gloucester, 1 Rol. 409, 3 Bulst. 190.

[8] Haddock's case, T. Raym. 339; Rex *v.* Derby, Cas. *temp.* Hard. 155.

Bribing a corporator to vote for a particular candidate to fill an office in the corporation, such as that of mayor, or to vote for a candidate at the election of members of parliament is good cause for amotion; but in this case there should be a previous conviction by a jury.[1]

§ 428. We will next proceed to enumerate the causes that have been relied upon in returns of an amotion, and which were held to be *insufficient*, in cases of municipal bodies corporate. That which only disqualified the person to be elected, although it made the election voidable *ab initio*, is insufficient; for one so disqualified is not in law a corporate officer, and therefore cannot be amoved by the corporation, but must be ousted by proceedings in *quo warranto*. Of this nature is non-residence, when required only as a qualification before election, or any irregularity in the election or admission. And if a corporator so disqualified, or illegally coming into office, has held it undisturbed for six years, being protected by the statute against an ouster in *quo warranto*, he cannot be amoved by the corporation declaring his office originally void on this account, for he has acquired an indisputable title.[2] Non-residence is not a sufficient cause of amotion, unless residence be required by the charter, or the non-residence be attended with some special injury to the corporation.[3] Departure from the borough and its liberties, about five months before, with his family, and not having returned at the time of the amotion, is not sufficient to warrant it unless a special damage has been caused to the borough by such absence.[4] Residing two or three miles from the borough, and non-attendance at a meeting of the common council, is not of itself a sufficient cause; for it is not the imperative duty of a common councilman to attend every assembly, and his general attendance is sufficient.[5] Absence of a portman from four occasional great meetings, one of which was on the charter-day, he having received ordinary but no particular notice, when it did not appear that any business was by that means impeded, is not sufficient cause.[6] Nor is absence of a recorder from the corporate meeting, not having received a special notice that his appearance was necessary, and the

---

[1] Rex *v.* Tiverton, 8 Mod. 186.

[2] Rex *v.* Doncaster, Say. 40; Rex *v.* Miles, Buller, N. P. 203; Rex *v.* Lyme Regis, Doug. 85; Symmers *v.* Regem, Cowp. 502.

[3] Unless a penalty is imposed for not residing. Rex *v.* Williams, 2 M. & S. 144.

[4] Rex *v.* Leicester, 4 Burr. 2087.

[5] Rex *v.* Doncaster, Say. 39.

[6] Rex *v.* Richardson, 1 Burr. 540.

corporation having received no inconvenience from his absence.[1] Razing entries in the corporation books, unless it be shown that they were originally correct, and that the razure was mischievous or to falsify them, is an insufficient cause. It has been held to be insufficient cause for amoving an alderman, that he used insulting words to the mayor in common council, as saying that he was a base fellow, &c.; or for amoving a common councilman, for saying of an alderman that he was a knave; for personal offences from one member to another are to be punished according to law, and not by the corporation.[2] Refusal to deliver over the corporation books intrusted to his custody, as the proper officer, to persons applying for them with an order from the corporation, is insufficient, for the books may be consulted in his hands.[3] Refusing to pay the usual fee on admission to the livery, or his share towards the expense of the renewing charter, are not causes of amotion, but the proper subjects of a by-law, which the body has power to make for enforcing such payments when reasonable.[4] Misemployment of funds in his custody, when it is the proper subject of an action, is not sufficient generally, though it may be a good cause of suspension from a financial office.[5] Casual intoxication, it was held, was not sufficient cause for amoving an alderman, for this is likely to happen to the best of them.[6]

§ 429. It is of course necessary, in the removal of an officer, that there should be a meeting of the corporation, or of such part of it as has been designated and empowered for that purpose. And it is also necessary, that the proceedings should be conducted in such a manner, that the officer may have a fair opportunity of defending himself.[7] As to the form required in amoving a *ministerial* officer, elected during pleasure,[8] very little formality is requisite. Such an officer is not entitled to any

---

[1] Rex *v.* Wells, 4 Burr. 2003; and see also, Rex *v.* Pomfret, 10 Mod. 108, and Rex *v.* Exeter, Comb. 197.

[2] Rex *v.* Chalke, 1 Ld. Raym. 236, 5 Mod. 259; Rex *v.* Oxford, Palm. 466; Jay's case, Vent. 302; Earle's case, Carth. 174; Rex *v.* Lare, Fort. 275.

[3] Or detinue will lie for them, if the corporation have a right to compel the delivery; or a mandamus, Anon. 1 Barnard. 402; Rex *v.* Ipswich, 2 Ld. Raym. 1238; Rex *v.* Ingram, 1 W. Bl. 50.

[4] Taverner's case, T. Raym. 446; Rippon's case, Sid. 282.

[5] Rex *v.* Chalke, 1 Ld. Raym. 226; Rex *v.* Mayor of London, 2 T. R. 182.

[6] Rex *v.* Taylor, 3 Salk. 231.

[7] As to the form of notice, preferment of charges, &c. see *ante*, 420, 422.

[8] See *ante*, 426.

notice; and a summons to those who have the power of amotion and the authority to elect another, is sufficient without a summons to convene to amove him from office. And if those who have the power of amotion elect a new officer, this act is of itself an amotion of the former officer, without a declaration of his amotion. It would, therefore, have no weight, if those who voted for the new officer were under the impression that they were electing him to a vacancy, and would not have voted for the amotion of his predecessor.[1]

§ 430. An amotion from one office, does not, of course, in the least impair the title of the person amoved to another office; and much less is it a disfranchisement from his right, as a mere member of the corporation.[2] If the amotion is legal, it will not invalidate any act which the corporator may have previously done, or in which he may have concurred; but from the moment of amotion his official authority *ipso facto* ceases, and another may be elected into the vacant place. Should the person amoved continue to act, he is a mere usurper without color of title, unless it be acquired by length of time; he may be ousted in *quo warranto*, and punished for the usurpation; and all corporate acts in which he has concurred are equally void as though he had never been elected.[3]

§ 431. When a corporator has been excluded from participating in corporate business, in which he has a right to act, under pretence of amotion or suspension (the latter being a temporary amotion), he is entitled to a writ of restoration, to which the court will compel obedience, unless it be shown that the amotion relied upon was legal.[4] But if the amotion is irregular, and there appear to have been good cause for removal, a mandamus will not lie to compel his restoration.[5] A restoration is merely an abstaining, on the part of the amoving body, from opposing the right of the corporator to transact the duties and enjoy the franchises appertaining to his office. As the effect of the restoration is not to create the person an officer *de novo* and give him a new title, and as it replaces him exactly in the same situation in which he stood before

---

[1] Rex *v.* Canterbury, 11 Mod. 403; Rex *v.* Thame, 1 Stra. 115; Rex *v.* Taunton, Cowp. 413; Rex *v.* Pateman, 2 T. R. 777.

[2] Willcock on Mun. Corpor. 268.

[3] Jay's case, 1 Vent. 302; Symmers *v.* Regem, Cowp. 503.

[4] Willcock on Mun. Corpor. 269; Fuller *v.* Plainfield Academic School, 6 Conn. 532; Howard *v.* Gage, 6 Mass. 462; see *post*, chapter treating of Mandamus.

[5] People *v.* Rankin, 9 Johns. 147.

the attempted amotion, all corporate acts, in which he has concurred between the moment of his amoval and restitution, are of equal validity as if he had never been amoved. If he were before a legal officer, such acts are legal; if he were only an officer *de facto*,[1] his acts before his amoval, during the amotion and subsequently to the restoration, are equally voidable, and he may be ousted in *quo warranto* for any defect in his original title. If he were originally a legal officer, and amoved for sufficient cause, but restored on account of informality in the amotion, all his corporate acts, both before and since the amotion, are valid; but he may again be amoved in a more formal manner, which vacates his office from the time of the second amotion, but has no retrospective effect upon the former irregular amotion. Indeed, if the amotion were voidable on account of an insufficient cause, or insufficiency, in the form in which it was effected, the person has not been ousted; and if he continues to be treated as an officer, and acts as such, there is no need of a writ of restoration.[2]

§ 432. The power of disfranchisement and amotion, unless it has been expressly confided to a particular person or class, is to be exercised by the corporation at large, and not by the person or class in whom the right of appointing or admitting is vested. For this reason, when an amotion is pleaded, if the authority by which it has been transferred to a select class be not shown, it will be construed to be in the body at large, and must be proved to have been exercised by the whole corporation.[3] If the power of amoving certain officers be antecedently in a select body, and the corporation accept a new charter, silent upon that head, but making other alterations and recognizing or confirming such body, although under a different name, and in general terms confirming the corporation in all cases where no alterations are introduced, the right of amotion still continues in this select body.[4] It has not been

---

[1] To constitute even an officer *de facto*, there must be, at least, the forms of election, though these may, upon legal objections, be afterwards found defective. Willcock on Mun. Corpor. 280.

[2] The principles we have just stated are laid down by Mr Willcock, who cites in support of them Taylor *v.* Gloucester, Cowp. 503; Rex *v.* Ipswich, 2 Ld. Raym. 1283, Salk. 448; Symmers *v.* Regem, Cowp. 503; and see Mr. Willcock's Treatise, p. 260 to 270.

[3] Willcock on Mun. Corpor. 245, 246; Lord Bruce's case, 2 Stra. 819; Rex *v.* Lyme Regis, Doug. 153; Rex *v.* Doncaster, Say. 38, 249; Rex *v.* Richardson, 1 Burr. 530; Rex *v.* Ponsonby, 1 Kenyon, 29; Rex *v.* Feversham, 8 T. R. 536; Bagg's case, 11 Co. 29; Rex *v.* Sadler, Styles, 477; Rex *v.* Oxford, Palm. 452.

[4] Willcock on Mun. Corpor. 246; Haddock's case, T. Raym. 239; Rex *v.* Knight, 4 T. R. 429.

directly determined, says Mr. Willcock, though it was assumed by Lord Mansfield, that the power of amotion may be transferred to a select body, by a by-law in the same manner as the right of election.[1] It was said that when a common council had the sole right of election and making by-laws, there is some foundation for thinking that they possess the power of amoving those whom they elect, though claiming it neither incidentally nor by grant of the charter.[2] Mr. Willcock apprehends that, when the corporation is prescriptive, this is evidence for a jury to presume a custom, if nothing contradictory appear; but in a corporation by charter, such a power, he is confident, must be shown to have been expressly granted by the charter, or a subsequent by-law, or at the utmost these facts should be left to a jury as evidence of a lost by-law.[3]

§ 433. It is said that an office may be resigned in two ways; either by an express agreement between the officer and the corporation, or by such an agreement implied from his being elected to another office incompatible with it.[4] Where neither the charter nor by-laws prescribe any particular form in which the members may resign their rights of membership, and their resignation be accepted, such resignation and acceptance may be implied from the acts of the parties.[5] And some of the acts and delinquencies, such as removing and residing at a distance, which have been mentioned as causes of amotion, may be properly regarded as an *implied* resignation.[6] To complete a resignation, it is necessary that the corporation manifest their acceptance of the offer to resign, which may be done by an entry in the public books, or electing another person to fill the place, and thereby treating it as vacant.[7] Every corporation has an incidental power of accepting the resignation of its officers; and, therefore, when it is averred generally that the resignation was made to a corporate assembly, if the right to receive it be in a select body, *that* should appear on the pleading, and how it was acquired by them.[8] It is presumed that the right to accept a resignation

---

1 Willcock, *ut supra;* Rex *v.* Richardson, 1 Burr. 539; Cowp. 502.

2 Rex *v.* Doncaster, 1 Barnard. 265.

3 Willcock, *ut supra*, 247, 248.

4 Willcock on Mun. Corpor. 238.

5 State *v.* Ancker, 2 Rich. 245.

6 Willcock on Mun. Corpor. 238.

7 Ibid. 239; Rex *v.* Lane, 2 Ld. Raym. 1304, 11 Mod. 270; Rex *v.* Rippon, 1 Ld. Raym. 563; Jenning's case, 12 Mod. 402; Hazard's case, 2 Rol. 11.

8 Rex *v.* Tidderly, 1 Sid. 14.

passes incidentally with the right to elect; for it is not a power to be compared with that of amotion, and it seems that an office should be relinquished by the consent of those in whose authority it originated.[1]

§ 434. A resignation by *implication* may not only take place by an abandonment of the official duties, as before mentioned, but also by being appointed to and accepting a new office incompatible with the former one. It was supposed at one time that such a resignation could only be where the second office is superior to the former. It has, however, been determined to be unimportant, and that if one holding a superior office accept a subordinate one that is incompatible, the appointment to the second operates to vacate the former.[2] But the election of an officer to an incompatible office does not vacate the former, before acceptance by the officer; for although the corporation has a right to the service of all its qualified members, in any office to which they are elected, yet they having been already appointed to one, that is a temporary disqualification, which renders them ineligible to the other; and the corporation having chosen to elect them, must be presumed to have been aware of that circumstance, and to have precluded themselves from calling again upon their services.[3] Where the offices are not in fact incompatible, acceptance of a second may be a resignation of the first, on account of the form of the constitution; for it is not to be presumed that when the government constitutes a certain number of distinct offices, it means that the corporation may consolidate two or more of them in one person.[4] A corporator is not bound to elect between resigning his corporate franchise and submitting to persons who have illegally seized upon the corporate authority.[5]

---

[1] See Willcock, *ut sup.* and Rex *v.* Tidderly, *ut sup.*

[2] This is an absolute determination of the original office, and leaves no shadow of title to the possessor; so that neither *quo warranto* nor amotion is necessary before any other may be elected. Willcock on Mun. Corp. 240; Gabriel *v.* Clarke, Cro. Car. 138; Verrior *v.* Sandwich, 1 Sid. 305; Rex *v.* Godwin, Doug. 383, n. 22; Milward *v.* Thatcher, 2 T. R. 87; Rex *v.* Pateman, 2 T. R. 779. The offices of mayor and aldermen, being judicial offices, are incompatible with that of recorder, who is an adviser to them. Rex *v.* Marshall, cited in Rex *v.* Trevenen, 2 B. & Ald. 340.

[3] Willcock, *ut sup.* Barton's case, Popham, 176; Milward *v.* Thatcher, *ut sup.*; Rex *v.* Pateman, *ut sup.*

[4] Milward *v.* Thatcher, *ut sup.* If the corporation consist of mayor, recorder, town clerk, and twelve aldermen, the recorder or town clerk cannot be an alderman, though there be no inconsistency in the duties of the two officers, for such a method of electing would reduce the corporation to a mayor and twelve or thirteen other officers, instead of fourteen, of which it ought invariably to consist. Ibid.; and Willcock, *ut sup.* 243.

[5] Ebaugh *v.* Kendell, 5 Watts, 43.

CHAPTER XIII.

OF THE BURDENS TO WHICH THE BODY CORPORATE IS SUBJECT, AND OF ITS LIABILITY TO BE TAXED.

§ 435. TAXES are burdens or charges imposed upon property or persons to raise money for public purposes, when the income of public property is insufficient for the public exigencies and welfare.[1] It is too evident to be reaffirmed, that the legislative prerogative of taxation is one of vital importance, and essential to the very existence of government; and in this country it is one which is conferred in virtue of the general designation of, and is incidental to "legislative power."

§ 436. "The things to be aimed at," says Blackstone, when speaking of the fiscal prerogative of taxation, "are wisdom and moderation, not only in granting, but also in the method of raising the necessary supplies; by contriving to do both in such a manner as may be most conducive to the national welfare, and at the same time most consistent

---

[1] Tax, Lat. *Taxa* from Gr. *ταξις*, from tassein, to set in order, to arrange, or adjust. A rate or sum of money assessed on the person or property of a citizen by the government, for the use of a nation or State. Webster's Dict. In a general sense, any contribution imposed by government upon individuals for the use and service of the State; whether under the name of toll, tribute, tallage, gabel, impost, duty, custom, excise, subsidy, aid, supply, or other name. In a stricter sense, a rate or sum imposed upon individuals (polls), lands, houses, horses, cattle, possessions, and occupations, as distinguished from customs, duties, and excises; and this is the ordinary sense of the word. Webster; Story on the Constit. 14; The Federalist, Nos. 21, 36; 2 Bouvier, Law Dict. tit. "Taxes," and also 2 Burrill Law Dict. tit. "Tax." The latter adds the following: "Literally, or according to its derivation, an imposition laid by government upon individuals, *according* to a certain *order* and proportion (*tributum* certo ordine constitutum); Spelman, voc. *Taxa.* Webster observes, that taxes, in free governments, are usually laid upon the property of citizens, *according to their income,* or the *value* of their estates. 'To Tax,' from Latin, *taxare,* to lay, impose, or assess, upon the citizens or subjects of a government, a certain sum of money, or amount of property, to be paid to the public treasury, to defray the expenses of the government. — Webster. According to Lord Coke, the word 'taxes' means burdens, charges, or impositions, put or set upon persons or property, for public use, — 2 Inst. 532; and Lord Holt gives, in substance, the same definition, in Carth. 438. In *practice,* to assess, fix, or determine *judicially,* as to tax costs in a suit."

with economy, and *the liberty of the subject;* who, when properly taxed, contributes only some part of his property in order to enjoy the rest."[1] This sentiment should most unquestionably be the controlling sentiment of every legislature. In this country, though the right to impose taxes is inherent in the legislature and extends to subordinate communities, as counties, cities, towns, &c., yet it is not admitted to be omnipotent; it being limited and controlled by certain principles that lie at the very foundation of our civil and political institutions.[2] The principle that the right cannot properly exist without representation, was a fundamental ground of the American Revolution. But it is not sufficient that no tax or imposition can be imposed upon the citizens of the United States, unless by their representatives in the legislature, or by their representatives which constitute the government of a county, town, &c., but every person, natural and corporate, is entitled to require of the lawgivers that taxation be *fair* and *equal* in proportion to the value of his or their property; and no one class of individuals should be unjustly assessed. One of the avowed objects of the Constitution of the United States, was to establish justice; and checks have been put upon local legislation by some of the State constitutions in the west, which prohibit taxation of the land of non-resident proprietors thereof, at a higher rate than those of residents. It is nevertheless true, that this duty of protecting every man's property by means of just laws uniformly and impartially administered, while it is one of the strongest and most interesting obligations on the part of the government, is frequently found to be the most difficult in the performance.[3] A just and a perfect system of taxation is considered to be still a desideratum in civil government, in order to protect every owner of property in the enjoyment of it, from unequal and undue assessments thereon by government.[4] The Constitution of the State of Arkansas declares a sound principle in taxation, in saying that all prop-

---

[1] 1 Bl. Com. 307, 308. Edward I. secured the property of the subject by abolishing all arbitrary taxes and talages, levied without consent of the national council. 4 id. 426. It is the ancient and indisputable right of the British House of Commons that all grants of subsidies or parliamentary aids do begin in their house. The supplies being raised upon the body of the people, it is proper that they alone should have the right of taxation. 1 id. 169.

[2] See the opinion of the court, in People *v.* Mayor of Brooklyn, 6 Barb. 209.

[3] See 2 Kent, Com. 250; Vattel, §§ 240–244. And see numerous authorities cited in West River Co. *v.* Dix, 6 How. 507. A tax levied by a city may be declared void by the judiciary for oppression. Mayor of Columbia *v.* Beaseley, 1 Humph. 232; Claurent *v.* Commissioners, 3 Md. 259.

[4] 2 Kent, Com. 250; Attorney-General *v.* Bank of Newburn, 1 Dev. & B. Eq. 216.

erty subject to taxation shall be taxed according to its value, and the value to be ascertained by laws making the same *equal* and *uniform;* that no one species of property shall be taxed higher than another species of property of equal value.[1]

§ 437. But the right to impose a tax being inherent in every government, and essential to its existence, it may be taken to be generally true, that whatever appertains to the persons of the citizens over whom, or over whose property the supreme authority has control, is a legitimate subject of taxation, unless it be expressly, or by implication, exempted by such supreme authority. Thus, houses and lands, as well as articles of personal property, and stock owned in moneyed institutions, have been among the most common subjects of taxation.[2] United States stock is not, however, liable to be taxed.[3]

§ 438. There is no reason why private corporations should not be subject (in the absence of any express or implied exemption in the charter or act of incorporation) to the same burdens, in the character of *owners and occupiers of lands and houses*, to which natural individuals in the same character are subject. In this country, it is always supposed that the legislature of a State has the power to tax the real property of the citizens for the purpose of raising additional revenue, to be applied towards the payment of interest, and the extinguishment of the debts of the State, created by internal improvements; and every owner, whether a corporation or not, of real estate, is bound to pay such part of the State tax as is assessed on such estate for such uses.[4]

§ 439. An individual banker doing business under the general banking law of a State, who assumes a special name by which his business as banker is characterized and known, may be assessed by that name, and the warrant for the collection of the tax, issued against such name, may be levied upon the money or property used in the business of such banker.[5]

---

[1] See 2 Kent, Com. 331, note.

[2] Bulow *v.* City Council of Charleston, 1 Nott & McC. 527; Berney *v.* Tax Collector, 2 Bailey, 654; People *v.* Mayor, &c. of Brooklyn, 4 Comst. 419; Mayor, &c. of Troy *v.* Mutual Bank, 20 N. Y. 387.

[3] International Life Ass. Co. *v.* Comm'rs of Taxes, 28 Barb. 318; Weston *v.* City Council of Charleston, 2 Pet. 449.

[4] Shitz *v.* Berks County, 6 Barr, 80; Dunnell Manuf. Co. *v.* Pawtucket, 7 Gray, 277.

[5] Patchin *v.* Ritter, 27 Barb. 34.

§ 440. Lord Coke, in commenting on the word "inhabitant," as used in the statute of Henry VIII., for the repair of bridges, says, that every corporation, residing in any county, riding, city, or town-corporate, or having tenements in any shire, riding, city, or town-corporate, *quæ manibus et sumptibus possident et habent*, are "inhabitants," within the purview of the statute.[1] Corporate bodies have ever been considered, in England, ratable to the repairs of a church, in respect of their corporate lands;[2] and when seised in fee of lands for their own profit, they are in respect thereof held to be liable in their corporate capacity (within the meaning of the statute of 43 Eliz.) to be rated to the poor.[3] The statute of 47 Geo. III. c. 111, has been held to be a statute *in pari materia* with the statute just referred to, of 43 Eliz. In Curtis *v.* Kent Waterworks Company,[4] the first objection to the plaintiff's right of action was, that a body corporate did not come within the meaning of the sixteenth section of the statute above mentioned, of 47 Geo. III. The title to that act plainly showed that one of the purposes which the legislature had in view, was the better relief of the poor; and it did not appear that there was any intention to exonerate any person who before that time was liable to contribute to the poor-rate. By the sixteenth section, the commissioners were to make rates upon all and every *person* or *persons*, who shall hold, occupy, possess, &c., any land within the parish. The court held, that, by virtue of this act a corporation was liable to be rated. "If," said Bayley, J., "by reason of the provisions of this act, corporations be not liable to contribute, then all property belonging to a corporation, which was before liable to contribute to the poor-rate, will be exempt; and that without any express words in the act to show that such was the intention of the legislature." It was argued, that, as one of the sections of the act gave an appeal to any *person* or *persons* aggrieved by any rate, upon such appellant giving the notice therein mentioned, and entering into a recognizance with sureties, and that as a corporation could not enter into a recognizance, this provision clearly showed that a corporation was not intended to be included by the legislature; because it could not be intended to compel a corporation to an act which is impossible. But the court held, that assuming that a corporation cannot of itself enter into a recognizance, still its sureties

---

[1] Kyd on Corp. 317; Ironmonger's Co. *v.* Nalor, 2 Mod. 185.

[2] 2 Inst. 703.

[3] Rex *v.* Gardiner, Cowp. 79.

[4] Curtis *v.* Kent Waterworks, 7 B. & C. 314.

might;[1] and that a corporation might satisfy the clause in question, by procuring sureties to enter into such recognizance.

§ 441. In the State of New York, although in the act for the assessment and collection of taxes, *corporations* are not named as liable to be taxed, and the act speaks only of *persons* liable to be assessed, corporations are held liable to be assessed for property owned by them.[2] But where an act of the legislature directs a thing to be done, which it is impossible for a corporation to do, but which natural persons may do, the corporation is of course excused;[3] and it has been held in New York, that moneyed corporations are not liable to be assessed to work on the public highway, they not being within the purview of the act prescribing such assessments.[4]

§ 442. In England, the party rated must either be an inhabitant of the parish, or he must be an occupier of one or other of the descriptions of real property mentioned in the statute of 43 Eliz.; and an occupier is considered as an *inhabitant* of the township, within the extended definition of that word by the before-mentioned construction of Lord Coke of the statute in relation to bridges, as comprehending all who have lands and tenements in possession, though living in a foreign country.[5]

---

[1] See *ante*, Chap. VIII. in relation to Contracts by Corporations, and Chap. IX. in relation to the Agents of Corporations.

[2] Per Thompson, C. J., in People *v.* Utica Ins. Co. 15 Johns. 382, who cites Clinton Woollen & Cotton Man. Co. *v.* Morse, Oct. Term, 1817. So under another act where the phrase is "persons or associations." International Life Ass. Co. *v.* Commr's of Taxes, 28 Barb. 318. So in Maine, where the term used is *inhabitants*. Baldwin *v.* Trustees of Ministerial Fund, 37 Me. 369.

[3] Curtis *v.* Kent, *ut sup.*

[4] Bank of Ithaca *v.* King, 12 Wend. 390. When the question was, whether, when village taxes are directed to be assessed upon the *freeholders* and *inhabitants* of the village according to law, a joint-stock corporation, having its banking house in the village, could be taxed, the court held, that there could be no doubt the term "inhabitant" includes a corporation occupying an office or building in a town, ward, or village, in conducting the business of the corporation, for many purposes, and especially with reference to the burden of taxation for public purposes. Ontario Bank *v.* Bunnell, 10 Wend. 186. The associations formed under the general banking laws of New York are corporations, and as such, are liable to be taxed by a town both upon real and personal property. Bank of Watertown *v.* Assessors, 25 Wend. 686. But it has been held, in Connecticut, that bank stock of a corporation required by its charter to keep, and actually keeping its office in Hartford, is not taxable in that city; such corporation not being an *inhabitant*. Hartford Fire Insurance Co. *v.* Hartford, 3 Conn. 15.

[5] Rex *v.* Nicholson, 12 East, 330.

An act of parliament having empowered the Duke of Bridgewater to erect a lock upon the Rochdale Canal, and to receive at such lock certain tolls, as a compensation for the profits of certain wharves, which were sacrificed for the public benefit, it was held, that a poor rate on his trustees, occupiers of the canal lock (the tolls upon which were only other names for the *lock* rated therewith), is good, though the trustees were found not to be *inhabitants* of the township for which the rate was made.[1] In this country, whatever difference of opinion there may be as to whether a corporation created by the laws of one State can be sued in another State,[2] when the attachment laws of such other State speaks only of "persons," still it is liable to be taxed under other acts which subject the property of "inhabitants" to taxation; the tax operating *in rem* on the estate.[3] In Massachusetts, real estate belonging to a manufacturing company, within a parish, is liable to be assessed in the taxes of such parish; and the liability to taxation extends to lands of citizens of other States, and to foreigners.[4]

§ 443. The English authorities go to establish, that the tolls of canal companies, &c., though not ratable *per se*, become so where they spring from or are connected with land. The oldest case on the subject is Rex *v.* Wickham Market;[5] there the market-place was the thing ratable, and the tolls were the measure of its value. In Rex *v.* Cardigan,[6] the rate was also imposed upon the tolls, although the sluice where they were received, was the property ratable; and the objects of a charitable foundation, in the actual occupation of the almshouse and lands for their own benefit in the manner prescribed by the rules of the institution, it is held, in England, are ratable, in respect of such occupation. The question was not whether it were wise or meritorious to rate these poor subjects; but the overseers have a right to insist that they come within the description of persons liable to be rated under the statute of 43 Eliz.; that is, that they are *beneficial occupiers* of lands and houses; and if so,

---

[1] Rex *v.* Mc Donald, 12 East, 324.

[2] See *ante*, Ch. XI. in relation to Suits by and against corporations.

[3] Per Spencer, J., in McQueen *v.* Middletown Man. Co. 16 Johns. 5.

[4] Goodell Man. Co. *v.* Trask, 11 Pick. 513. Property in a manufacturing corporation is held, in New Hampshire, liable to be taxed in the town where it is situated. Smith *v.* Burley, 9 N. H. 423. Real estate is taxable wherever it is situated, and without regard to who is the owner. Water-Power Co. *v.* City of Boston, 9 Met. 199.

[5] Rex *v.* Wickham Market, 3 Keble, 540.

[6] Rex *v.* Cardigan, Cowp. 581.

it cannot be said they are not ratable. "Wherever," said Lawrence, J., "persons have been found in possession of property *from whence they derived benefit to themselves*, they have been holden ratable as occupiers. However poor the persons rated might have been at the time when they were selected as objects of the charity, yet, after their appointment to be members of the foundation, they ceased to be of that description of persons, and, therefore (under the stat. 43 Eliz.), became ratable in proportion to the property so acquired."[1] The Hull Dock Company was held ratable in respect of the tonnage duties received, although it appeared that the expenditure in repairs during the period for which the rate was made, exceeded the amount of the duties received,[2] and the trustees of the Duke of Bridgewater were held liable to be rated for the sum at which his canal would let, and not for the gross receipts of it, minus the expenses.[3] But in these cases, the interest in the soil, in order to be rated, must be of such a nature as to enable a company to maintain trespass for any injury done to the soil.[4] Where, by a *canal act*, in England, it was provided, that lands, &c. belonging to the company, should be ratable to the maintenance of the poor in the several parishes where they were respectively situated; it was held, that land of the company, used by them for the purpose of the canal, was ratable

---

[1] Rex *v.* Munday, 1 East, 584. In England, a local act for lighting a hamlet, enacted that rates should be laid upon all persons who should inhabit, or be in possession of, or enjoy any messuages, warehouses, or other buildings, &c. as should from time to time be lighted by virtue of the act. It was held, that the general words, "tenements and hereditaments," included only things *ejusdem generis*, with those before. Regina *v.* East London Waterworks, 17 Q. B. 512, 9 Eng. L. & Eq. 271. Under a local act, which enabled trustees to lay rates upon persons holding or enjoying any tenements, &c., &c., in the district, a steamboat company were rated in respect of their floating pier, by the description of "tenement, land, landing-place, &c., and the easements, &c., enjoyed therewith." The pier consisted of three floating barges. Passengers embarking by the steamboats passed through the ground-floor of the building, where a fare is paid, and then proceeded over the platform, bridges, and barges, to the steamboats. The ground-floor, as well as the said pier and landing-places, were in the exclusive occupation of the steamboat company. It was held, by the Court of Queen's Bench, that the rate was laid not on the barges, &c., as distinguished from the land, but upon the landing-place and premises, together with the floating barges, &c., by which the occupation of the land was rendered more profitable, and the rate was, therefore, valid. Regina *v.* Leith, 1 Ellis & B. 121, 10 Eng. L. & Eq. 370.

[2] Rex *v.* Hull Dock Co. 5 M. & S. 394; and see Rex *v.* Birmingham Canal Co. 2 B. & Ald. 570.

[3] Rex *v.* Trustees of the Duke of Bridgewater, 9 B. & C. 68; and see Rex *v.* Proprietors of Mersey, &c. Navigation Co. id. 95.

[4] Williams *v.* Jones, 12 East, 346; Rex *v.* Thomas, 9 B. & C. 114; Rex *v.* Calder & Heble Navigation Co. 1 B. & Ald. 263.

as land, not in respect of its improved value, but in respect of that which would have been its value, if it had not been used for the purposes of a canal; because the act stated, that the making of the canal would be *of great public utility.*[1]

§ 444. A *railroad* or *railway* company in England, viewed as owners or occupiers of the line of railway, are liable to all rates, charges, and other burdens ordinarily incidental to the ownership or occupation of *realty*, that is, so far *as is not otherwise provided by their act of incorporation;* and, accordingly, a railway company, in the occupation of their own line of railway, are liable to be rated for the same for the relief of the poor.[2] As to the general principles of rating in England in the cases of railways, a railway company is, in the first place, ratable upon the net annual value of the railway; or, in other words, to such an amount as a tenant from year to year might fairly be expected to pay for the railway, by way of net rent, assuming him to have the same power of using the railway, and the like privileges and advantages as the company.[3] Supposing, therefore, that the land and buildings of the company became themselves more valuable, and capable of commanding a higher rent in consequence of the facility afforded by the occupation of them to the carrying on a lucrative trade, and earning the profits on the fares, in whatever proportion this is the case, the rate ought to be raised accordingly.[4] Hence, it would seem a proper way for calculating the ratable value of railway property, first, to take the gross receipts of the company, and then to deduct therefrom a percentage (the amount of which it belongs to the sessions to determine), first, for the interest of capital actually invested by the company in movable carrying stock; secondly, for tenant's profits and the fair profits of trade; thirdly, for the depreciation of stock beyond ordinary annual repairs, &c.; fourthly, for the annual cost of conducting the business, maintenance of way, &c. and other disbursements of the company, as railway owners and carriers; and, lastly, a mileage for the renewal and

---

[1] Rex *v.* Regent's Canal Co. 6 B. & C. 720.

[2] Walf. on the Law of Railways, 755.

[3] Regina *v.* London & Southwestern Railway Co. 2 Rail. Cas. 629, 1 Q. B. 558; Regina *v.* Grand Junction Railway Co. 4 Q. B. 16, 4 Rail. Cas. 1.

[4] Ibid. And the profits on a main line derived by occupation of a branch, may be taken into account in estimating the ratable value of the branch, and not the local profits only. Regina *v.* Southeastern Railway Co., Q. B. 1854, 25 Eng. L. & Eq. 176.

reproduction of those portions of the subject-matter of the rate which are of a perishable nature, such as chairs, sleepers, &c.[1] As these deductions, taken together, seem to exhaust whatever is properly referable to the trade, as distinguished from the increased value which that trade imparts to the land, the residue may fairly be taken to represent the value of the occupation, which we have seen constitutes the proper subject of the rate.[2]

§ 445. Secondly, as to the principle on which it is held, in England *the rate is to be distributed among the different portions of the line lying in dffierent parishes.*[3] As a general rule, the subject-matter of the rate in any particular parish is the *beneficial occupation* of the land *there;* and there cannot be drawn into the rate the value of the occupation of buildings, &c. elsewhere; still, as it is on the value in the parish, however occasioned, that the rate is to be imposed, it cannot be allowed to strike off any portion of such value, because it would not have existed but for the occupation of buildings, &c. elsewhere, and in another parish; and, therefore, cannot escape the rate there.[4] The value of the occupation in the particular parish being the proper subject of the rate in such parish, it follows, that, as a general rule, the proper mode of apportioning the rate among the various parishes along the line of railway is not by a mileage division, which assumes the profits to arise equally throughout the whole line, but according to the actual earnings in each parish.[5] But if, in a particular case, both parties agree on adopting the former principle, it is open to them to do so.[6] But, instead of leaving a railway company under the operation of the general law, the legislature may provide that it may be rated upon a principle of its own.[7]

§ 446. In the State of New York, a railroad corporation is not liable to taxation upon its capital, as *personal estate*, for that part thereof

---

[1] Regina *v.* Grand Junction Railway Co. *ubi sup.* Regina *v.* Gr. Western Railway Co. 15 Q. B. 1085; Regina *v.* Midland Railway Co. 6 Rail. & Can. Cas. 464, 469.

[2] Walf. *ubi sup.*

[3] Regina *v.* London & Southwestern Railway Co. *ubi sup.*

[4] Judgment of Lord Denman, C. J., in Regina *v.* London & Southwestern Railway Co. *ubi sup.*

[5] Ibid.

[6] Regina *v.* Grand Junction Railway Co. 4 Q. B. 18, 4 Rail. Cas. 1.

[7] Walf. *ubi sup.*

which is vested in the lands over which the road runs, and in the railways and other fixtures connected therewith; but *that part* of the corporate property is to be taxed in the several towns and wards in which the same is situated, as *real estate*, and at its actual value at the time of the assessment thereof. In the first title of the chapter of the Revised Statutes of the State relative to the assessment and collection of taxes, it is declared that the term "real estate," wherever it occurs in that chapter, shall be construed to include land and all buildings and other fixtures erected upon, or affixed to the same; and the term "personal estate" is to be construed to include such portion of the capital of incorporated companies, liable to taxation in their capital, as is not invested in real estate. By the sixth section of the second title, real estate of all incorporated companies liable to taxation, is to be assessed in the town or ward in which it lies, in the same manner as the real estate of individuals; and the personal estate of such companies is to be assessed in the town or ward where the principal office, or place for transacting the financial concerns of the company, is situated. By the provisions of the fourth title of the same chapter, the assessors, in making up the assessment rolls, are directed to enter, in the column of the valuations of lands or real estate, the actual value of the real estate of the company situate within their town or ward; and in the column containing the valuations of the taxable personal property of individuals, they are to enter the amount of the capital of the company paid in or secured, after deducting from such capital the amount paid out for all the real estate then owned by the company, wherever such estate may be situated, and also making certain other deductions on account of stock not liable to taxation. To enable the assessors to ascertain what part of the capital stock of the company is taxable as personal estate, the president, or other proper officer of the company, is required to deliver to them a statement, on oath, showing the amount of capital paid in or secured, and of the stock which is exempt from taxation; and containing a particular specification of all the real estate owned by the company. When this chapter of the Revised Statutes of New York was passed, and when it went into effect, no railway had been constructed in that State, and only one charter for one had been granted. Therefore, no *special* provision in regard to railway companies, was found in the tax laws; so that those companies had to be governed by the general provisions relative to the taxation *of the real and personal estates of corporations.* Taking the several provisions referred to together, the construction has been, that such companies whose stock, or the principal part thereof, is vested in the land necessary for their roads, and in their rails and other fixtures connected therewith, are taxable on that portion of their capital, as real estate (as before mentioned), in the several towns or wards in which such real estate is situated; and such estate is to be taxed upon its actual value at the time of the assessment, whether that value is more or less than the original cost thereof. Such companies, of course, are not taxable upon their capital, as personal estate, except upon so much thereof, if any, as remains after deducting all their real estate at cost, including the railway itself. Such was held by Chancellor Walworth to be unquestionably the *most equitable* mode of taxing such property, inasmuch as it gives to each town and ward through which the railway runs, its fair proportion of the tax imposed upon the property of the company. He considered that very little inconvenience could result to the corporation from this mode of assessment; as it would be only necessary for its officers to make a fair estimate of the cost of the railway, fixtures, and other real estate in each town or ward, to enable them to furnish their annual statement to the comptroller, and to the assessors of the town in which the company is liable to be taxed on its capital. From such estimates, likewise, the assessors of the other towns and wards may generally ascertain the fair value of those portions of the railway which they are to assess, by comparing the original cost thereof with the value of the stock of the company, at the time of such assessment.[1]

§ 447. In the case of the Philadelphia, Wilmington, and Baltimore Railroad Company, the act of the legislature of Maryland declares the stock personal estate, exempts it from taxation, and reserves the right to tax the fixed and permanent works of the corporation, upon the section of it within that State, and provides, that any tax which should thereafter be levied upon said section should not exceed the rate of any general tax which might at the same time be imposed upon similar real or personal property of the State, for State purposes.[2] Taxing the buildings, and steamboats, and rails, as of the value they bear, irrespective of their being portions of a railroad, and taxing the land as land, and not as of increased value by reason of its being used as a railroad, is held to be the principle of valuation proper to be adopted.[3] A ques-

[1] Mohawk & Hudson Railroad Co. *v.* Chute, 4 Paige, 384. See also opinion of Bronson, J., in People *v.* Supervisors of Niagara, 4 Hill, 20.

[2] Tax Cases, 12 Gill & J. 117.

[3] Ibid.

tion was raised whether that portion of the permanent and fixed works of that company, lying within the limits of Hartford county, was subject to the county levies. The opinion of the court was as follows: "That they are so, in common with all other property in the county, is conceded, unless exempted therefrom by some legislative enactment upon the subject; and such enactment, it is insisted, is to be found in the latter part of the 19th section of the act of the General Assembly of Maryland passed at December session, 1831, chap. 296, entitled 'An act to incorporate the Delaware and Maryland Railroad Company,' which declares, 'that the said road or roads, with all their works, improvements, and profits, and all the machinery of transportation used on said road, are hereby vested in said company, incorporated by this act, and their successors, forever; and the shares of the capital stock of said company shall be deemed and considered personal estate, and shall be exempt from the imposition of any tax or burden, by the States assenting to this law, except upon that portion of the permanent and fixed works of said company which may be within the State of Maryland; and that any tax which shall hereafter be levied upon said section shall not exceed the rate of any general tax which may, at the same time, be imposed upon similar real or personal property of this State, for State purposes.' According to the true construction of this provision of the act of Assembly, we think that, by the first part of it, the shares of the capital stock of the company thereby created, its works, improvements, profits, and machinery of transportation, except its permanent and fixed works, which lay within the State of Maryland, were exempted from all taxation or levies, whether for County or State purposes; and that, as far as regards the said first part of said recited provision, such permanent and fixed works which lay within the State of Maryland remained subjects of taxation or assessment, either for County or State purposes, or for both, in the same manner as if no such exemption had been inserted in the act of Assembly. That, as to the succeeding part of the said provision, it has no reference to taxes or assessments, or levies for County purposes; and, therefore, in no wise impairs the rights asserted by the appellee in the present action. That it relates exclusively to taxes laid for State purposes, and is to be construed in the same manner as if the words 'for State purposes,' which now stand at the end of the section, had been inserted after the words 'any tax;' when it would read, and that any tax for State purposes, which shall hereafter be levied upon said section, shall not exceed the rate of any general tax, which may, at the same time, be imposed upon similar real or personal property of this State. But, suppose we are wrong in the construction we have given to the portion of the act of Assembly referred to, what has that to do with the question now before us? The act of Assembly related to the Delaware and Maryland Railroad Company, the southern terminus of which road was at the river Susquehannah. The powers and exemptions given by its charter to that company, as regards matters of the character of those now in controversy, apply to *Cecil*, not *Hartford* County. To determine the question now before us, we must look to the act of 1831, ch. 288, entitled 'an act to incorporate the Baltimore and Port Deposite Railroad Company;' not to the act of Assembly for the incorporation of the Delaware and Maryland Railroad Company. Under the first of these laws you will look in vain for any such exemption as that now claimed by the Philadelphia, Wilmington, and Baltimore Railroad Company. The acts of Assembly of 1835, ch. 93, and 1837, ch. 30, by which the Wilmington and Susquehannah Railroad Company, and the Delaware and Maryland Railroad Company, and the Baltimore and Port Deposite Railroad Company, were united into one company, by the name of the Philadelphia, Wilmington, and Baltimore Railroad Company, confer no such exemption."[1]

§ 448. The act incorporating the Bangor & Piscataqua Railroad Company, among other things, authorized them "to procure, purchase, and hold in fee-simple, improve and use for all purposes of business, to be transacted on or by means of said railroad, lands, or other real estate, and to manage and dispose thereof as they may see fit;" and provided that the capital stock be divided into shares, to be holden and considered *as personal estate*. It was held that the real estate owned and used by the company, either as a railroad or as a depot, was not subject to taxation, otherwise than as personal estate; that each shareholder was taxable for the amount of his interest in it in the town where he resided, and not elsewhere; and that to allow the inhabitants of the towns through which the road might pass, to tax it, would be subjecting it to a *double* taxation, "which could be tolerated neither by the policy nor justice of the law; and the legislature could have designed no such thing."[2]

§ 449. The question in the case of the Inhabitants of Worcester *v.*

---

1 Philadelphia, Wilmington, & Balt. R. Co. *v.* Bayless, 2 Gill, 355.

2 Bangor & Piscataqua Railroad Co. *v.* Harris, 21 Me. 533.

Western Railroad Corporation,[1] was in respect to the exemption of the road from taxation. The corporation were authorized to lay out their road, not exceeding five rods wide; and it was held that the road so laid out, and the buildings and structures thereon erected by them (such buildings and structures being reasonably incident to the support of the road, or to its convenient and advantageous use), were not liable to be taxed; that whenever the corporation had occasion to use any part of such strip of five rods in width, for any of the purposes intended by their act of incorporation, it was within the *franchise*, and being so used to promote the purposes contemplated it was exempted from taxation, as *property appropriated to public use.* "It is true," say the court, "that the real and personal estate necessary to the establishment and management of the road is vested in the corporation; but it is in trust for the public. The company have not the general power of disposal incident to the absolute right of property; they are obliged to use it in a particular manner, and for the accomplishment of a well-defined public object; they are required to render frequent accounts of their management of this property to the agents of the public; and they are bound ultimately to surrender it to the public, at a price and upon terms established. Treating the railroad then as a public easement, the works erected by the corporation as public works intended for public use, we consider it well established, that, to some extent at least, the works necessarily incident to such public easement are public works, and as such exempted from taxation. Such, we believe, has been the uniform practice in regard to bridges, turnpikes, and highways, and their incidents; and also in regard to other public buildings and structures of a like kind."[2] On the other hand, the rails, sleepers, bridges, &c. of a railway corporation, together with its easement in land within the located limits of the road, are held in Rhode Island to be taxable as real estate, in the towns in which they are situated; the tax act, under which the decision was made, expressly providing that "no property whatsoever, of any description, not ceded or belonging to the United States or to this State, except as aforesaid, shall, on any pretence whatever, be

---

[1] Inhabitants of Worcester *v.* Western Railroad Corporation, 4 Met. 564. In R. & G. Railroad Company *v.* Davis, in North Carolina, it was held, that although the company was a private corporation, the road they constructed was a public highway. 2 Dev. & B. 451. See Rex *v.* Pease, 4 B. & Ad. 31.

[2] See Proprietors of Meeting-house *v.* City of Lowell, 1 Met. 538.

deemed to be exempted from taxes; any law or act, public or private, to the contrary notwithstanding."[1]

§ 450. It was contended, in Boston Water-Power Co. *v.* City of Boston,[2] that the property of the plaintiffs was exempted from taxation on the ground upon which the decision cited in the preceding section was made, that their property was appropriated to public use. The plaintiffs, by virtue of their act of incorporation, were proprietors of a large water-power created by the dams erected by the Boston and Roxbury Mill Corporation; and the distinction between this case and the one before cited is thus explained by Shaw, C. J., who delivered the judgment of the court: "If it be true that public ways, namely, railroads, turnpikes, and bridges, are so exempted, and the incorporated proprietors are liable only for their shares, we think it does not apply to estates used for purposes not directly incident to the public accommodation contemplated. What was granted to the corporation was simply a right to use a portion of the public land covered with navigable water; but the avowed purpose was to erect mills, and employ or let them. We think there is no analogy between the cases." Where an assessment was made in Pennsylvania upon a railroad company, by the county of Berks, it was held, that it is only such property belonging to a railroad corporation as is appurtenant and indispensable to the construction and preparation of the road for use, that can claim to be exempt from taxation. The court say: "It would no doubt be desirable and convenient to the company to own extensive warehouses, coal-yards, board-yards, coal-shutes, and extensive machine-shops, at many points and places on the road; but these erections and conveniences form no part of the road."[3]

§ 451. Water-power for mill purposes, not used, being only a capacity of land for a certain mode of improvement, cannot be taxed independently of the land; as where a dam is extended across a river — the thread of which is the dividing line between two towns — and the water created by the dam is applied exclusively to mills situated in one of the

---

1 Providence & Worcester Railroad Co. *v.* Wright, 2 R. I. 459.

2 Boston Water-Power Co. *v.* City of Boston, 9 Met. 199.

3 Berks County *v.* Railroad, 6 Barr, 70. See also, State *v.* Powers, 4 N. J. 406; State *v.* Newark, 1 Dutcher, 315, 2 Dutch. 519; State *v.* Commissioners of Mansfield, 3 N. J. 510.

two towns, the water-power is not subject to taxation in the town opposite.[1]

§ 452. In Pennsylvania, the bed, berme-bank, tow-paths, toll-houses, and collectors' offices, being constituent parts of an incorporated canal, and incident thereto, cannot be assessed as real estate under the acts of the 15th April, 1834, and the 29th April, 1844.[2] This was decided, a short time after the passage of the latter act, in a case in which the court say, "The lands, houses, and lots of ground, according to the true meaning of the acts, intended to be made taxable by the legislature, were such as formed the principal part of that which was designed to be charged and taxed, and not merely such things as were accessory to something else which everybody regarded as the principal. It must be admitted that a canal is a species of property, and that it may also be very valuable, and as such may be made taxable; but few, if any, would consider it as property designated by either of the terms, 'lands,' 'houses,' or 'lots of ground,' or even by all these terms put together. Canals and every species of improvement facilitate the trade and commerce of the State, have ever been considered a matter of public interest and concern, and instead of being made the subjects of taxation, have on the contrary been patronized by the legislature in lending the aid of the State to their construction and subsequent preservation."[3] In this view of the subject, it was held, in the case of The Company for erecting a Permanent Bridge over the Schuylkill *v.* Frailey,[4] that the bridge, or the land necessarily connected with it, was not taxable under the act of 1799, which was similar in its enumeration of the taxable property to that of the above-mentioned act of 1834. Likewise a toll-house erected under the charter of a turnpike company, within the limits obtained by the company for constructing the road, was considered necessary to the proper use and management of their road, and, therefore, warranted by the act of incorporation, which authorized them to construct a turnpike road, and to receive the tolls from those who should travel upon it; and the owner of the land upon which the road was constructed, where the toll-house was erected, could maintain no action against the company for

---

[1] Boston Man. Co. *v.* Inhabitants of Newton, 22 Pick. 22.

[2] Schuylkill Navigation Company *v.* Commissioners of Berks County, 11 Penn. State, 202.

[3] Lehigh Coal and Navigation Co. *v.* Northampton County, 8 Watts & S. 334.

[4] Bridge Co. *v.* Frailey, 13 S. & R. 442.

such occupation and use of the land, because the house was a necessary appendant to the road.[1]

§ 453. By an act of the Pennsylvania legislature, it is provided, that in estimating the value of any real estate subject to the payment of any dower, *ground-rent*, or mortgage, the principal of said dower, ground-rent, or mortgage, shall first be deducted, and the tax assessed on the remainder of the estimated value of said real estate. This act has been considered as free from all ambiguity, and was observed as the rule until by a subsequent act it was repealed, and the legislature declared, that such real estate shall be hereafter estimated at its full value, and taxed accordingly. The question arose, could a tax on the full value of real estate, subject to ground-rent, be legally assessed on the tenant, as in the case of fee-simple property, and at the same time a tax on the principal of the ground-rent, or the ground-rent landlord? and the court held the affirmative, saying that all considerations of hardship or inequality must be referred to the legislature.[2]

§ 454. The moneyed corporations of the State of New York, deriving income and profit, are liable to taxation on their capital, and it is held that in ascertaining the sum to be inserted in the assessment roll, no regard is to be had either to accumulations or losses; but only to the amount of capital stock paid in and secured to be paid; and that the word *income* means that which is received from the investment of capital, without reference to out-going expenses; and the term *profits* means gain made upon any investment when both receipts and payments are taken into account. A moneyed corporation liable to be assessed on its capital, is to be assessed on the whole *nominal amount* paid in and secured to be paid, after deducting expenditures for real estate, and such of the stock as the statute exempts; no deduction is to be made for losses of capital, nor for debts due.[3] By the Revised Statutes of

---

[1] Ridge Turnpike Co. *v.* Stoever, 6 Watts & S. 378. It is observable that the lands, houses, and lots mentioned in the act of Assembly, are placed under the head of real estate, but from the 4th section of the act incorporating the Lehigh Coal and Navigation Company, their whole capital stock is denominated and made *personal* estate, by declaring, in express terms, that "the shares of the stock of said company shall be considered and taken as personal property."

[2] Robinson *v.* County of Alleghany, 7 Barr, 161.

[3] People *v.* Supervisors of Niagara, 4 Hill, 20; People *v.* Assessors of Watertown, 1 id. 616; Farmers Loan & Trust Co. *v.* Mayor, &c. of New York, 7 id. 261.

New York, it was provided that if any incorporated company was not in receipt of any profits or income, the name of such company should be stricken out of the assessment roll, and no tax imposed upon it. By an act passed in 1853,[1] this was altered, and it was provided that if any such company "has not been, during the preceding year, in the receipt of net annual profits, or clear income equal to five per cent. of the capital stock of any such company, paid in or secured to be paid in, after deducting from the amount of their capital stock the assessed value of their real estate, such companies shall be entitled to commute for their taxes or such capital stock, by paying directly to the treasurer of the county in which the business of such company is transacted a sum equal to five per cent. on such net annual profits, or clear income, and also such further sum as shall have been assessed on such roll as the taxes on their real estate." It has been held that these laws do not apply to taxation by municipalities, unless they are expressly or impliedly adopted by the charters or other laws regulating taxation for municipal objects.[2] Under the act of the State of New Jersey, of 1810, to tax bank stock, it was held, that although the capital of the bank might have been diminished by losses, yet the tax must be paid on the whole amount of the capital stock subscribed and paid in; and that neither the treasurer or the court could look into the losses of the bank and make allowances proportioned to the tax to be paid; but that where the legislature reduces the shares of the stock to two fifths, it was in effect declaring, that the capital is reduced two fifths, and the bank is only subject to pay tax upon the remaining three fifths.[3] Under the act of Ohio to tax banks, &c., the State is entitled to five per cent. upon dividends, regardless of the time when the profit so divided accrued; the tax is to be paid by the bank out of the corporate property, and not by the several stockholders, after the profits shall have been divided.[4]

§ 455. In Waltham Bank *v.* Inhabitants of Waltham, in Massachusetts,[5] the question was, whether one joint-stock incorporated company might be legally taxed by the defendant town for stock *pledged* to such

---

[1] Laws of 1853, c. 654, 1240.

[2] American Transp. Co. *v.* City of Buffalo, cited 20 N. Y. 388; Mayor, &c. of Troy *v.* Mutual Bank, 20 N. Y. 387.

[3] Gordon *v.* New Brunswick Bank, 1 Halst. 100.

[4] State of Ohio *v.* Franklin Bank, 10 Ohio, 91.

[5] Waltham Bank *v.* Waltham, 10 Met. 334.

corporation as collateral security for a debt, which stock was owned in another joint-stock incorporated company; whether the tax in question was legally assessed on the corporation, or whether it ought to have been assessed on the debtor or pledger. It was held, that, for such collateral security, the corporation could not legally be taxed; that, although the corporation (a bank) had a special property in the shares pledged, that is, as collateral security for the payment of the debtor's note, the debtor was nevertheless the owner; the general property (by the well-settled law in relation to mortgages) remained in him. It is on this principle, that, in a clear case of hypothecation of stock, the pledger may vote at a corporate election, the possession continuing in him, consistently with the nature of the contract.[1]

§ 456. An act of the State of New Hampshire enumerates among the objects of taxation, after bank stock, marine and fire insurance stock in any corporation or company, on which an income is received or dividend made. This was held to be broad enough to include a bridge corporation. According to the usual method of taxation, the court said, shares in a corporation are to be taxed where the owner lives, if in the State; whereas, toll bridges, by a special provision of the act referred to, are to be invoiced and assessed in the towns where the same are located. A question in the case was suggested, whether bridges on Connecticut River were within the statute, because such bridges were partly within the State of Vermont; but the court considered, that, though a portion of the western abutment of the bridge was within the limits of Vermont, and the toll-house actually there situate, it was not the intention of the legislature of New Hampshire to exclude such a bridge from taxation on that account, while others were taxed.[2]

§ 457. A question was made whether an act of the State of New York, which expressly exempted from taxation the property of manufacturing corporations, was repealed by a subsequent act, which was intended as a repeal of all the laws upon the subject of taxation, and which provided that all incorporated companies, receiving a regular income, &c., shall be considered *persons* within the meaning of the

---

[1] See *ante*, Chap. IV. § 132.

[2] Cornish Bridge Co. *v.* Richardson, 8 N. H. 207. The property of a bridge corporation chartered in two States, is held taxable in each. Easton Bridge Company *v.* The County, 9 Barr, 415.

act; and whether assessments shall be made, and taxes imposed and levied upon them, and collected, in the same manner as upon and from individuals. The court held, that the terms of the act of 1823 were sufficiently broad and comprehensive to render the real and personal estates of manufacturing corporations liable to taxation; and that it repealed the act of 1817, as it fell within the general principle, that *leges posteriores priores contrarias abrogant.*[1] But an implied repeal of a legislative act is not favored by law. A general law taxing the dividends of banks was passed by the State of Pennsylvania on the *first* of April; and afterwards on the *seventh* of that month, an act was passed extending the charter of an existing bank from a future period, when the former charter would expire. The act of the seventh contained a provision for taxation similar to that of the first, but taxes were not to be levied under it until the new charter went into operation. The latter act, it was held, did not repeal the former.[2]

§ 458. The general rule appears clearly to be, that in regard to public taxes, every person is liable to be assessed for his *personal* property in the State of which he is an inhabitant; and stock owned in incorporated banks, &c., by non-resident holders thereof, is not subject to the taxing power of the State. Indeed, the stock is not a thing in itself capable of being taxed on account of its locality; and any tax imposed upon it must be in the nature of a tax upon income, and of necessity confined to the person of the owner, who, if he be a non-resident, is beyond the jurisdiction of the State, and not subject to its laws.[3] In New York, an act was passed, in 1855, which provided that all persons or associations doing business in the State and non-residents thereof, shall be assessed and taxed on all sums invested in any manner in said business, the same as if they were residents. It has been held, that this statute applies to corporations, and that a foreign insurance company is liable to be taxed on securities deposited by law with the comptroller of the State for the security of policy holders.[4]

§ 459. In Salem Iron Factory Company *v.* Danvers, in Massachu-

---

[1] Columbia Man. Co. *v.* Vanderpool, 4 Cowen, 556; Ontario Bank *v.* Bunnel, 10 Wend. 185.

[2] Commonwealth *v.* Easton Bank, 10 Barr, 442.

[3] Union Bank of Tennessee *v.* State, 9 Yerg. 490.

[4] International Life Ass. Co. *v.* Comm'rs of Taxes, 28 Barb. 318.

setts,[1] where the question was in respect to the liability of the company to be taxed, it was decided, that it was taxable for its real estate in the town in which it was situated, but was not to be assessed for its personal estate in and about the manufactory, the individual corporators being liable to be taxed for their several shares in such property; and that that was the form in which the personal estate was to be taxed. In a subsequent case in the same State a question arose under a later tax act, which act, it was contended, had so far changed *the place* for the assessment of such personal estate, as to authorize and require its assessment in the town in which the manufactory was situated, or without reference to the inhabitancy of the individual holders of the stock. No question was made as to the right to tax the corporate property, but the inquiry was as to the place where such property should be taxed; and the court held, that the later tax act had made no change in respect to the manner of taxing the personal estate of corporations.[2] Thus the new tax act, and the decision under it, sanctioned the decision of the court in the case preceding.[3] In New York, all personal estates of an incorporated company, liable to taxation on its capital, is required to be assessed in the town or ward "where the principal office or place for transacting the financial concerns of the company shall be." It is also provided by statute that persons organizing under the general act, may file a certificate in the office of the clerk of the county in which the principal office for the management of the business of the company shall be situated. This certificate must state the name of the city or town and county in which the principal office is to be situated. This certificate has been held to be conclusive of the fact therein stated, and evidence is not admissible to show that the principal office was elsewhere.[4]

§ 460. The cases cited in the preceding section are of importance, as recognizing the rule that the property of a corporation is not to be *twice* taxed. In Boston Water-Power Company *v.* City of Boston,[5] the court were of opinion that the corporation was not liable to be taxed

---

1 Salem Iron Factory *v.* Inhabitants of Danvers, 10 Mass. 514.

2 Amesbury Woollen and Cotton Man. Co. *v.* Inhabitants of Amesbury, 17 Mass. 461.

3 So considered and held by the court, under the Rev. St. of Massachusetts, in Boston and Sandwich Glass Co. *v.* Boston, 4 Met. 184. See likewise, Gardiner *v.* Cotton and Woollen Factory Co. 3 Greenl. 133.

4 Western Transp. Co. *v.* Schew, 19 N. Y. 408.

5 Boston Water-Power Co. *v.* City of Boston, 9 Met. 199.

for personal estate, or income, inasmuch as the whole value of its personal property was included in the *shares* of the stock, and, as such, was liable to be taxed to the holders of the shares, *eo nomine.* On the other hand, by the tax laws of New Hampshire, the property of corporations is made taxable to the corporations, in the town where the property is situated, and accordingly no authority exists to tax the stock in corporations to the owners of the shares, though living in a different town. A taxation of the shares, at their appraised value, it was therefore held, "would in fact be a *double taxation*, once to the corporation itself, and again to the corporators, which would be unjust, oppressive, and unconstitutional."[1]

§ 461. It appears, then, that the capital stock of a corporation may, in the discretion of the legislature, be taxed as an aggregate, to the corporation, according to its value, or to the stockholders, on account of their separate ownership of it; but cannot be taxed at the same time in both modes.[2] In Rex *v.* Vandewall,[3] quitrents and other casual profits of a manor were not considered as the objects of the poor rates in England, and that was because they arose out of the profits of land for which the occupiers were ratable in another shape; and, as Lord Kenyon said, in Rex *v.* Churchwardens and Overseers,[4] "The case of quitrents goes upon the objection of doubly rating the same property, in the hands of the landlord, as well as the tenant." And again, says he, "Landlords who derive a certain profit in the nature of rent, could not have been rated, because that would be to rate the subject-matter *twice*."

§ 462. If the stock of a corporation is subjected to a general assessment, whether the assessment is made upon the corporation at large or upon the individual corporators, every extra imposition of a tax is of course a *specific* tax, like one imposed upon the business of selling goods at auction. The principle recognized by the Supreme Court of Pennsylvania,[5] that all trades and avocations by which people acquire a

---

1 Smith *v.* Burley, 9 N. H. 423. But see State *v.* Newark, 1 Dutcher, 315.

2 Bank of Cape Fear *v.* Edwards, 5 Ired. 516; Gordon *v.* Mayor, &c. of Baltimore, 5 Gill, 231; Cases of Taxation, 12 Gill & J. 117.

3 Rex *v.* Vandewall, 2 Burr. 991.

4 Rex *v.* Churchwardens and Overseers of, &c. 1 East, 534. Quitrent, a yearly rent, by the payment of which the tenant goes *quit* and free of all other services.

5 Riddle *v.* Commonwealth, 13 S. & R. 409; and see Sun Mutual Insurance Co. *v.* Mayor, &c. of New York, 8 Barb. 450.

livelihood, may be taxed, it is believed has never been in many instances seriously impugned. But an important question is presented; whether, when a power has been conferred and a license granted to prosecute any trade or occupation, having in view the public benefit, as well as private emolument, by an *unconditional* charter of incorporation, the charter, after its acceptance by the persons incorporated, and their corporate organization by virtue of it, does not amount to a contract which would be impaired by a tax like the one above mentioned; or, in other words, a tax upon the *corporate franchise.* Clearly, the franchise, under such a charter, could not be taken away without just cause of forfeiture, and clearly a power to tax *ad libitum* is, to all intents and purposes, a power to *destroy.*[1]

§ 463. The first case in this country, in which a question partaking of the character of the above met with a judicial determination, was in 1812, in the case of Brown *v.* Penobscot Bank.[2] It was there decided, that the act which imposed two per cent. per month, on the amount of bills of any bank *of which payment is by such bank refused*, militated with no principle of the Constitution, either of the United States or of the State of Massachusetts. The tax in this case, it must be observed, was inflicted as a *penalty*, for the violation of an important corporate duty; and, therefore, it affords no authority for the infliction of a similar penalty, in cases where no negligence or misconduct appears. On the contrary, the court say, respecting the penalty, "As it had no *retrospective* effect, there was no ground of complaint on the part of the banks." We are led to understand that the court meant to imply, by this expression, that if the tax had not been imposed as a penalty for *future* misconduct, or want of punctuality and promptitude in the performance of duty, it would *not* have been constitutional. The court apparently, in this case, justified the tax, as being a proper punishment for a breach of *trust;* and upon the ground that the corporation had substantially varied from the purposes for which it had an existence. They seemed to have taken the view which Mr. Burke took in his speech on the East India Bill, that every commercial privilege for the

---

[1] McCullough *v.* State of Maryland, 4 Wheat. 316.

[2] Brown *v.* Penobscot Bank, 8 Mass. 445. In Harrisburg Bank *v.* Commonwealth, 26 Penn. State, 451, it was held, that a statutory forfeiture, of a certain percentage on its circulation, imposed on a bank if it failed to keep its notes at par, was a *penalty* and not a tax.

mere private benefit of the holders, was a *trust*, and that it was the very nature of a trustee to be *accountable*, and the trust even totally to *cease*, when it was perverted from its purpose.[1] And if the Bank of England, he said, should be oppressed with demands it could not answer, or engagements which it could not perform, no charter should protect the management from correction.[2]

§ 464. But the American books afford us precedents for the infliction of a penalty like the one above mentioned, in the shape of a specific tax upon a corporation, which has not been guilty of any omission of duty or mismanagement. In the year 1812, in the case of the Portland Bank *v.* Apthorpe, in Massachusetts,[3] it was decided by the Supreme Court, that an act levying a tax on the stock of an incorporated banking company, whose charter existed prior to the passing of the act, was within the constitutional authority of the legislature. The question was taken up by the court, not in reference to the Constitution of the United States; and the prohibition therein contained, as to the *impairing the obligation of contracts*, is not noticed. It was considered wholly in reference to the Constitution of Massachusetts, and to the words of that constitution, which authorize the legislature "to impose and levy proportionate and reasonable assessments, rates, and taxes upon all the inhabitants of, and persons resident, and estates lying within, the Commonwealth; and also to impose and levy reasonable duties and excises upon any produce, goods, wares, merchandise, and commodities whatsoever, brought into, produced, manufactured, or being within the same." The court admitted, at once, that the tax could not be justified under the *first* branch of the before-mentioned power, namely, that which required taxes to be *proportionate;* the exercise of which required, they said, an estimate or valuation of all the property in the commonwealth; and

---

1 "To whom, then, would I make the East India Company accountable? Why, to parliament, to be sure; to parliament, from whom their trust was derived; to parliament, which is alone capable of comprehending the magnitude of its object and its abuse, and alone capable of an effectual legislative remedy. The very charter, which is held out to exclude parliament from correcting malversation with regard to the high trust vested in the company, is the very thing which at once gives a title and imposes a duty on us to interfere with effect, *wherever power and authority originally derived from ourselves are perverted from their purpose, and become instruments of wrong and violence.*" Burke's Speech on East India Bill.

2 Ibid.

3 Portland Bank *v.* Apthorpe, 12 Mass. 252.

then an assessment upon each individual, according to his *proportion* of that property. And the court say expressly, "to select any individual or *company*, or any specific article of property, and assess them by themselves, would be a violation of this provision of the constitution." Then they refer to the *second* branch of the before-mentioned power, relating to reasonable duties and excises, upon goods, merchandise, and *commodities*. This last word, the court consider, will embrace every thing which may be a subject of taxation; and that it had always been applied by the *Massachusetts* legislature to the *privilege of using particular branches of business or employment*, as the business of an auctioneer, tavern-keeper, retailer of spirits, &c. The court in fact considered, that under the general term "commodity," the legislature, in subjecting an *incorporated* bank to a *specific* tax, were authorized so to do, because they might exact sums of money from vendue-masters, retailers, and other persons, who have a *natural* right to exercise certain employments until forbidden by the government; and because the legislature, when they granted the charter, did not expressly relinquish the right of levying a tax upon the business the corporation should transact during the continuance of its charter. They give this hypothetical case: "Suppose that heretofore the legislature should have enacted that no person should keep a public-house, or retail spirituous liquors, without a license from some authority by them designated, but without exacting any tax or duty therefor; could it be contended that afterwards they were precluded from establishing a tax or excise upon the business thus permitted to be exercised?" It is believed to have been never the general understanding, that where an individual, whether he has paid a certain sum in *money* or not, if he has made a contract with the government, or any of its authorized agents, by which he has been licensed to prosecute any kind of business or trade, can be called on to pay for the privilege, before the expiration of the license.

§ 465. By an act of the legislature of Rhode Island, it was directed that all the banks in the State should annually pay to the State a tax, at the rate of twelve and a half cents upon every one hundred dollars of the capital stock actually paid in. This tax, it will be observed, was a specific tax upon the corporation, and was in addition to the general taxes. The charters of several of the Rhode Island banks, among which was the Providence Bank, are unlike those which are granted at this day; that is, they are free and unconditional, and were granted without any limit as to time. The Providence Bank refused to pay the tax as above exacted, on the ground that it was a burden upon its corporate franchises, the power to impose which was not expressly reserved in the charter. Its property was accordingly seized by the sheriff, upon the warrant of the State treasurer, to the amount required by the act. The sheriff and treasurer were thereupon both sued in an action of trespass, and it was thus that the question of the constitutionality of the above law was finally brought before the Supreme Court of the United States.[1] Now it is to be observed that the question presented by the above statement of facts was not whether the *capital* of the bank was exempted from taxation, but the point in controversy was, virtually, whether the grant of the charter opened to the State any *new* source of revenue. The right of the State to tax the property, both real and personal, of the bank, appears to have been admitted; that is to say, were there a general State tax upon real or personal property, the property of the bank was liable thereby to contribute its proportion. In the opinion of the court, however, it appears to be assumed that the bank was contending against any such liability. Thus, say the court, "The charter contains *no stipulation promising an exemption from taxation.*" Again, "No words have been found in the charter which, in themselves, would justify the opinion that the power of taxation was in the view of either of the parties, and *that an exemption from it was intended, though not expressed.*" It appears by this language, certainly, that the court took the ground that the bank claimed an entire exemption from the general and ordinary imposition of a State tax; and the opinion of the court, from almost the beginning to the conclusion, is bottomed upon that basis.

§ 466. We much doubt if there is any man who would refuse to accede to the proposition laid down by the court, that "the taxing power is of vital importance, and that it is essential to the existence of a government;" or who would hesitate in admitting that "the relinquishment of such a power is never to be assumed." But the claim of the Providence Bank was not for any *relinquishment* of the taxing power of the State. On the contrary, the ground upon which the bank proceeded was not in the least in derogation of any prerogative the State might have exercised, if it had never given such a charter. Before the franchise which was guaranteed by the charter existed, it would be nonsense to say the franchise could be taxed; and when the franchise was ushered

---

[1] Providence Bank *v.* Billings, 4 Pet. 514.

into being, the question was, whether the power to tax it *did attach.* We are unable to view the real question in this case in any other light than the following: Did the right to tax the franchise conferred by the State EVER EXIST? and not whether it has been *impliedly exempted* from the right. It would seem, however, to have been the view of the court, that the bank had arrogated to itself an entire freedom from the power which the State had, before the establishment of the bank, to tax the property composing its capital, in common with all other property. Thus, say the court, "The plaintiffs would give to this charter the same construction *as if it contained a clause exempting the bank from taxation on its stock in trade.*"

§ 467. The court say again, that "*Land* has in many, perhaps in all, the States, been granted by the government since the adoption of the constitution. This grant is a contract, the object of which is, that the profits issuing from it shall enure to the benefit of the grantee; yet the power of taxation may be carried so far as to absorb those profits. Does this impair the obligation of the contract? The idea is refuted by all, and the proposition appears so extravagant, that it is difficult to admit any resemblance in the cases aforesaid. *Yet if the proposition for which the plaintiffs contended be true, it carries us to this point.*" Now, with the most profound respect for the opinion of the Judges of the Supreme Court, we are compelled to say that we cannot agree that the proposition really contended for by the plaintiffs goes to the extent here pronounced. We do not wish for a better example, by the way, than that given by the court (of land) to illustrate the precise principle which, as we conceive, was contended for by the Providence Bank. The bank put their case upon the principle which admits that every man who receives a grant of land from the State, is liable to be taxed for it; but which denies the power of the State, after having taxed the land, to exact the payment of any *additional* impost. The bank acquiesces in the claim of the legislature to tax the whole of its property to the same extent that all other property is taxed, but resists the claim to all extra pecuniary burdens. But, it is asked, "If the policy of the State should lead to the imposition of a tax upon *un*incorporated companies, could those which might be incorporated *claim an exemption?*" We apprehend that no one would say there was any distinction between unincorporated companies and those incorporated, where a general tax is imposed upon real or upon personal property. In one point of view, however, there is an important distinction between them (and one which we believe has never been denied), which is, if the legislature should enact that in future no association should prosecute the business of banking, unincorporated companies established for that purpose would be reached by it, whereas companies unconditionally *licensed* for that purpose would not be. The existence of the former is always at the mercy of the legislature; but the existence of the other is put, by solemn stipulation, completely beyond the legislative power to destroy it, without cause of forfeiture.

§ 468. Again, say the court, "Any privileges, which may exempt it (the corporation) from the burdens common to individuals, do not necessarily flow from the charter, but must be expressed in it, or they do not exist." We inquire of every person who has attentively examined the case of the Providence Bank, whether that bank has demanded an exemption from the *burdens common to individuals?* And whether the point at issue was not that all *exactions* upon the *privilege* conferred by the charter "must be expressed in it, or they do not exist." The bank say, that while they are subject to the same *burdens* they have the same *rights* as individuals. What, in fact, it appears the bank wished to have decided was, 1st. If an individual, upon a good consideration, is unconditionally licensed to pursue a particular occupation, can he be called upon by a specific tax to pay, at a future period, any thing more than what was stipulated in the contract? and, if not, 2d. Whether a corporate body which has been thus licensed can be called upon for that purpose; and, 3d. Has not the Providence Bank, by the free, unconditional, and unqualified terms of its charter, been established and *licensed* to pursue the trade of banking? In the celebrated case of Dartmouth College, the trustees of that institution were divested, by a law of New Hampshire, of the property which they held from the founder, and which was transferred to other trustees for the support of a different institution called "Dartmouth University." The law in this case was held to be unconstitutional. Now, would it not have been equally unconstitutional if the funds had been drawn away by a *specific tax?*[1]

---

[1] And yet the Supreme Court of Pennsylvania have placed much reliance upon the judgment of the court in the case of the Providence Bank, in deciding, in the case of the Commonwealth *v.* Easton Bank, 10 Barr, 442, that a bank chartered under an act which prescribes the payment of a certain tax on dividends declared, is subject to a subsequent general law which increases the rate of taxation, although its charter had not then expired.

§ 469. It is very plain, that, should the State of Rhode Island withdraw the tax upon the franchise of the Providence Bank, it would not deprive itself of any resources it originally possessed. If it intended to create a new source of revenue, it should have been so stipulated in the charter, and what amount was to be paid for the franchise defined. Suppose that the State, for example, had imposed an annual tax of one per cent. on its capital, and had made no reservation to impose any greater tax; the tax, being inserted in the charter, becomes a part of the contract, and is a consideration in addition to that of having the public provided with such an institution,[1] for the privilege of incorporation. The very nature and terms of such a contract, it must be obvious to every one, carry with it a pledge that no innovations are to be made, nor new taxes imposed. What stockholders of a bank would propose to pay a tax or *bonus* for a charter of incorporation, with a conviction that the legislature might exercise an unlimited power to alter and increase it at pleasure? That the State have not such a power, after having prescribed the amount of tax to be collected, or after having received a *bonus*, has been put beyond all doubt, as we shall proceed to show.

§ 470. By the very same high court which decided the case of the Providence Bank, it was subsequently held that the charter of a bank is a *franchise*, which, as such, is not taxable if a price has been paid for it, which the legislature accepted, and that the *corporate property* is separable from the *franchise*, and may be taxed, unless there is a special agreement to the contrary. The legislature of Maryland, in 1821, continued the charters of several banks to 1845, upon condition that they would make a road and pay a school-tax; this, the court held, would have exempted their *franchise*, but not their *property*, from taxation. But another clause in the law provided, that upon any of the aforesaid banks accepting of, and complying with the terms and conditions of the act, the faith of the State was pledged not to impose any further tax or burden upon them during the continuance of their charters, under the act. This, the court held, was a contract relating to something *beyond* the *franchise*, and exempted the *stockholders* from a tax levied upon them as individuals, according to the amount of their stock. In giving their opinion, the court said, "A franchise for banking is, in every State of the Union, recognized as property. The banking capital attached to the franchise, is another property owned in its parts by

---

[1] See *ante*, §§ 13, 31, 40, 53.

persons, corporate or natural, for which they are liable to be taxed, as they are for all other property, for the support of government."[1]

§ 471. In the case of Gordon *v.* Mayor, &c. of Baltimore, in the Court of Appeals of Maryland,[2] it was contended that, as the *State* was disabled by the decision in the above case from taxing the banks, no tax could be imposed upon the stock of the *City of Baltimore.* But to this proposition that court refused to assent, on the ground that the act incorporating the city granted the taxing power in the most comprehensive terms, and without any limitation as to the objects on which the power was to operate.[3] The court yet further decided (what is of much importance in the discussion of the particular subject in question), that the stock of a bank is the representative of its whole property; and that when a tax has been imposed on the stock in the hands of the shareholders, the real and personal estate of the corporation becomes exempt from taxation. "*To tax,*" say the court, "*the real and personal property and the stock, would be a double tax, and is, therefore, illegal.*" Five or six years prior to the decision of this important principle in this case, the same court had decided that when a tax is imposed by the *State* on the stock in the hands of shareholders, the property of the bank, real or personal, cannot be taxed.[4]

§ 472. In the case of the Bank of Cape Fear *v.* Edwards, in North

---

[1] Gordon *v.* Appeal Tax Court, 3 How. 133. In the Court of Appeals in the State of Maryland, in the case of Mayor, &c. of Baltimore, 6 Gill, 288, Dorsey, J., who delivered the opinion of the court, held, that the decision in this case of Gordon *v.* &c., meant a *special legislative charge or imposition upon the franchise.* "The correctness of the principle," said the learned judge, "could not be denied; and if it meant a special tax, *technically speaking,* levied for the support of the government of Maryland, it would be void, as repugnant to 13th Art. of the *Declaration of Rights of Maryland.*" The decision of the court was, in fact, that a franchise, as property, is, according to its value, liable to taxation for the support of government, whether paid for by a *bonus* or not. It appeared in this case, that the charter of the Baltimore and Ohio Railroad Company — Act of 1826 — declares, that the capital stock of that company shall be considered *personal* estate, and exempt from the imposition of any tax; hence, the State's right to tax that stock is excluded by the comprehensive terms of the exemption.

[2] Gordon *v.* Mayor, &c. of Baltimore, 5 Gill, 231.

[3] In this decision the court do not seem to have recognized the distinction which appears to exist between a public and a private corporation. See *ante,* § 11 *et seq.*; 31 *et seq.*; and, also, Regents of the University of Maryland *v.* Williams, 9 Gill & J. 365.

[4] Cases of Taxation, 12 Gill & J. 117. And see State *v.* Powers, 4 N. J. 400.

Carolina,[1] it appeared that by the act of incorporation, it was provided that a tax of twenty-five cents on each share of the stock owned by individuals, in the bank, should annually be paid in to the State treasurer, by the president or cashier of the corporation, and that the bank should not be liable for any further tax; that there was demanded of the bank by the sheriff the amount of the State and county taxes, under the general State revenue law, the amount of taxes assessed upon *the house* occupied by the bank, and upon *the lot* on which the house stood. The plaintiffs paid the amount claimed under protestation, and brought the action to recover it back. The judgment of the court was delivered by Nash, J., who said: "The legislature, about to incorporate a company with banking privileges, to induce individuals to invest their private funds in its stock, engage, in so many words, that the bank shall not be liable for any tax, but one of twenty-five cents on each share; and it is now contended, that, in violation of this express declaration, the property of the bank, that is, of the individual stockholders, shall, in addition to the twenty-five cents payable on each share of the stock owned by them, be subjected to the operation of the general revenue law, and to the payment of taxes imposed for county purposes. This cannot be. It would be in direct violation of the plighted faith of the State."

§ 473. By the charter of the Union Bank of Tennessee, it is stipulated that the bank agrees to pay to the State annually one half of one per cent. on the amount of capital stock paid in by the stockholders. It was held, by the Supreme Court of that State, that by this clause the State contracted that the bank should enjoy the privileges conferred, one of which was to use its capital for all legitimate banking purposes; and that a law imposing an additional tax upon the capital stock of a corporation, impaired the contract, and was unconstitutional. The court, in giving judgment in this case, said, in answer to the argument, that if the capital stock of the institution be necessary to an enjoyment of the privilege granted, so is a banking house: "A banking house has no immediate connection with the privileges granted by the State to the bank, and is only incidentally necessary to their enjoyment, and, therefore, cannot be assimilated to the capital stock, the use of which, accord

---

1 Bank of Cape Fear *v.* Edwards, 5 Ired. 516. The case of the Bank of Cape Fear *v.* Deming, 7 Ired. 516, came within that of the same plaintiff *v.* Edwards.

ing to the powers granted by the charter, is, in our opinion, the substance of the contract with the State." [1]

§ 474. Again, in the State of New Jersey, a charter from the legislature of that State, to the Paterson and Hudson River Railroad Company, provided for the payment of certain taxes to the State, and then enacted that no further tax or impost should be levied on the company; and the Supreme Court of that State held, that this not only exempted from taxation the franchise, but the company generally, and its property, for county, township, and all purposes except those stated in the charter.[2] At a subsequent period, it became a matter of dispute in the Court of Appeals in New Jersey, between Jersey City and the Paterson and Hudson Railroad Company, whether the real estate of that company, in that city, was subject to taxation; and it was contended, that the exemption contained in the act incorporating the company, that no further tax shall be assessed upon the company, only extended to the tax to be levied by the State upon the franchise of the company. The court, however, expressly decided that the tax of one quarter of one per cent. stipulated by the act of incorporation, to be paid yearly, was a commutation for all taxes on such property as might necessarily be held for purposes reasonably incident to the enjoyment of the *franchise;* that the charter exempted the company and *its property* held for such purposes from all other taxes, *whether assessed for State, or for city, or township purposes.*[3]

§ 475. So in other States. The act incorporating the Northern Bank of Kentucky, required payment from that corporation to the State, of a tax of twenty-five cents per annum, on each share of the stock. This was held to be a contract between the State and the stockholders, which exempted the stock from any further taxation.[4] The provision in the charter of the State Bank of Illinois, exempting its property from taxation, beyond the extent stipulated, was held to be a contract binding on the legislature.[5]

§ 476. Thus it appears, beyond dispute, that not only the *franchise,*

---

1 Union Bank of Tennessee *v.* The State, 9 Yerg. 490.
2 State of New Jersey *v.* Burry, 2 Harrison, 84.
3 Gardner *v.* The State, 1 N. J. 527.
4 Johnson *v.* The Commonwealth, 7 Dana, 342.
5 Bank of Illinois *v.* The People, 4 Scam. 304.

but the *property* of a corporation may be exempted from taxation by an express contract. The privilege of banking of the Providence Bank, was by an executed contract *purchased*, though no money was paid for it, or none stipulated to be paid; and its charter of incorporation, being unconditional, according to the determination of the Supreme Court of the United States, in the case of Dartmouth College,[1] carried with it an *implied* valuable consideration; and Chief Justice Marshall, in delivering the opinion of the court in that case, says: "The objects for which a corporation" (meaning a private corporation) "is created, are universally such as the government wishes to promote; they are deemed beneficial to the country; and this benefit constitutes the consideration, and in most cases the *sole* consideration of the grant." In the case of the Regents University of Maryland *v.* Williams, the doctrine is expressly asserted, by the Court of Appeals of that State, that "the objects for which almost if not all corporations are created, are such as the government deems it expedient to promote, upon the supposition that they will be beneficial to the public; *and these expected benefits constitute the chief and usually the only consideration of the grants.*[2] In the case of an incorporated *banking institution*, the object in creating it is no less than the public good, and the profit to stockholders is incidental merely.[3] Now, it is a familiar maxim, that when a privilege is granted, ever thing necessary to its undisturbed enjoyment is also granted; every thing purchased carries with it what is necessary for the unmolested enjoyment of all that is purchased. There can be shown to be no difference in principle between an act of the legislature which in terms impairs the obligation of a contract, and one which produces the same effect in the construction and practical execution of it; both are repugnant to the Constitution of the United States, and void.[4]

§ 477. But what is conclusive on the subject of the remarks which have been offered upon the decision of the court, in the case of the Providence Bank, is the decision by the same court, in the case of the West River Bridge Company *v.* Dix,[5] in which a corporate franchise is treated like all other property; that is, it cannot be condemned, by

---

1 Dartmouth College *v.* Woodward, 4 Wheat. 518.

2 Regents University of Maryland *v.* Williams, 9 Gill & J. 365.

3 Williams *v.* Union Bank of Tennessee, 2 Humph. 339.

4 Chesapeake and Ohio Canal Co. *v.* Railroad Co. 4 Gill & J. 6.

5 West River Bridge Co. *v.* Dix, 6 How. 507.

virtue of the law of eminent domain, without compensation, and unless for the public good. A provision for compensation, it was held by the court, was as requisite to render the condemnation of a corporate franchise constitutional, as it is in the case of any other property; and, in this respect, the franchise is not to be distinguished from other property; every kind of property being equally protected by the constitution.[1] When a State grants a tract of land, an estate in fee passes as much as if a private individual grants it; but, in each case, it is subject to the power of being retaken for public use on compensation being made. The right rests upon the principle, that individual interests must be subservient so far to the public; but those interests never yield except when public exigency requires; and even then but upon ample compensation; and this doctrine holds in respect to a corporate franchise.[2] Now the power of a State to tax *ad libitum* a corporate franchise which it has, from motives of policy, unconditionally granted to a certain number of individuals and their successors, it has been asserted and decided by the Supreme Court of the United States, "would involve a power to *destroy*."[3]

§ 478. It was, it is believed for the first time, considered, in Brewster *v.* Hough, in New Hampshire,[4] that the legislature had not the power to contract the obligation, that any property liable to be assessed should be in future exempt from taxation. The Assembly and Council of that State, under the form of government existing in 1780, appointed a committee to take into consideration what was requisite to be done concerning the lands which were granted and conveyed to Dartmouth College; and the committee reported, that no lands belonging to the institution be sold for taxes, provided the trustees gave notice seasonably to the selectmen of each town respectively, of what lands they had in such towns; and that the taxes for the present should be charged to the State. The report was accepted; and it was resolved, that all persons take notice, and govern themselves accordingly. It was held, that

---

1 And see Boston & Lowell R. R. Corp. *v.* Salem & Lowell R. R. Co. 2 Gray, 1; Central Bridge *v.* Lowell, 4 Gray, 474; Richmond, &c. R. Co. *v.* Louisa R. 13 How. 71; Crosby *v.* Hanover, 36 N. H. 404.

2 Enfield Bridge Co. *v.* Hartford & New Haven Railroad Co. 17 Conn. 40. And see Skinners Co. *v.* Irish Society, 1 Mylne & C. 162.

3 McCulloch *v.* State of Maryland, 4 Wheat. 316; and see, also, Weston *v.* City Council of Charleston, 2 Pet. 449.

4 Brewster *v.* Hough, 10 N. H. 138.

this was but a *temporary* provision, or that it created no permanent exemption from taxation; that the general right of a legislature to surrender the power of taxing a portion of the property within the State, by a contract with some of its own citizens in such a manner as to deprive a future legislature of the right to subject such property to the taxing power, might be denied.[1]

§ 479. The above case of Brewster *v.* Hough, in which was denied the power of government to contract the obligation, that any property liable to be assessed should be in future exempt from taxation, was decided in 1839. The same court, in 1834, in the case of the Piscataqua Bridge Company *v.* New Hampshire Bridge Company,[2] decided that the legislature might grant an exclusive right to build a bridge, within certain limits, and to take tolls, and the grant was considered as a contract, which the legislature could not annul. It is, indeed (as it has been by others considered),[3] difficult to comprehend any distinction, in principle, between these two cases. In the last named case, the grant

---

[1] The Supreme Court of Ohio has taken strong ground in support of this doctrine. In several recent cases that court maintains: That the taxing power, being of vital importance to the existence of every government, cannot be abridged by the General Assembly. That this power is not the subject of contract, barter, or sale by the legislature, and if the legislature make such a contract, it is a fraud upon the government, and of necessity void. That an ordinary charter is not a contract within the meaning of the 10th section of the first article of the Constitution of the United States.

The Supreme Court of Pennsylvania also upholds the first of these propositions, and in a very recent case decided, that an act of the legislature, providing "That if the Pennsylvania Railroad Company shall become the purchaser of the main line of the public improvements of that State, they shall pay in addition to the purchase-money $1,500,000, and that in consideration thereof the said Railroad company, and the Harrisburg Railroad Company, shall be discharged by the commonwealth *forever* from the payment of all taxes whatever, except for school, city, county, borough, and township purposes," was unconstitutional and void, and an injunction was granted to prevent the same from forming terms of the sale. Mott *v.* Penn. R. R. Co. 30 Penn. State, 9.

The Supreme Court of the United States, however, and a majority of the State courts, hold a different opinion on both the above propositions. See Bank of Toledo *v.* Bond, 1 Ohio, State, 622; Mechanics & Traders Bank *v.* Deboldt, id. 591, reversed in the Supreme Court of the United States, 18 How. 380; State Bank *v.* Knoup, 1 Ohio, State, 603, reversed in 16 How. 369; Woolsey *v.* Dodge, 6 McLean, 142, affirmed in 18 How. 331; Milan Plank Road Co. *v.* Husted, 3 Ohio, State, 578; Norwalk Plank Road Co. *v.* Same, id. 586. See also, Illinois Central R. R. *v.* County of McLean, 17 Ill. 291; O'Donnell *v.* Bailey, 24 Missis. 386; Seymour *v.* Hartford, 21 Conn. 481, 486, and cases there cited.

[2] Piscataqua Bridge Co. *v.* New Hampshire Bridge Co. 7 N. H. 35.

[3] See Am. Law Mag. vol. 6, p. 296.

to the former company to build the bridge, conferred the exclusive right within certain limits, and was, in effect, a covenant on the part of the State, that no other bridge should be erected within those limits. The court, whilst in one case they gave effect to the exclusive grant, and allowed an injunction against the defendants, who were proceeding to erect a bridge within the limits of the franchise, maintain in the other, that the State cannot, for what the law deems a valuable consideration, relinquish its prerogative of taxing *certain* property, without relinquishing its right of sovereignty. The right of sovereignty is retained; and the State only becomes obligated not to exercise that right in derogation of vested rights which it has created, for the promotion of the public good.[1]

§ 480. A provision to exempt certain individuals from the government prerogative of taxation was, at an early period in the judicial history of the United States, decided by the Federal Supreme Court, to be a *contract*, and one not to be rescinded by any subsequent legislative act. The colonial legislature of New Jersey, in 1758, passed an act to give effect to an agreement made by it with a remnant of the tribe of Delaware Indians. Among other provisions of this act, authority was given to purchase land for those Indians, and it was expressly enacted, "that the land to be purchased for the Indians aforesaid, shall not hereafter be subject to any tax." The agreement with the Indians was executed; but in October, 1804, the legislature passed an act *repealing* that section of the act of 1758, which exempted the lands in question from the imposition of taxes. The Supreme Court of the United States, on a writ of error, decided, that the provision of the constitution, that no State shall pass any law impairing the obligation of contracts, which extended to contracts to which a State was a party, as well as to contracts between citizens,[2] was violated by the act above mentioned, of 1804. The privilege, though for the benefit of the Indians, it was held, was annexed by the terms which created it, to the land itself.[3]

§ 481. A statute of the colony of Connecticut, passed in 1702, provided, that all such lands, &c., that formerly have been, or hereafter shall be, given and granted, either by the general assembly, or any

---

[1] See Am. Law Mag. vol. 6, p. 296.
[2] See Fletcher *v.* Peck, 6 Cranch, 88.
[3] New Jersey *v.* Wilson, 7 Cranch, 164.

town, village, or particular person, for the maintenance of the ministry of the gospel, or school of learning, or for the relief of the poor, shall forever remain to such uses, and be also exempted out of the general list of estates, and free from the payment of rates. The lands in question, in the case of Osborne *v.* Humphrey, in that State, had been leased for nine hundred and ninety-nine years, and buildings had been erected on them. The court held that this provision was repealed at the revision of the statutes in 1821; but relying upon the above decision, in New Jersey *v.* Wilson, they were of opinion that the repeal was inoperative, as to the rights already acquired by virtue of that act, inasmuch as it impaired the obligation of a contract, and that the land continued to be exempt from taxation.[1]

§ 482. By the colonial act of Massachusetts, of 1650, all lands and tenements, or revenues of Harvard College, not exceeding the value of £500 per annum, are exempted from taxation; and it has been held, under this act, that the lands first acquired by the college, before their annual income amounted to that sum, would never be taxable so long as they were owned by the college; and that they were equally exempt from taxation in the hands of a lessee, as if in the immediate possession of the college.[2]

§ 483. It has been said, that, "in a government so complicated as our own, in its various relations to the citizens of the States and the States themselves, it may well be that there is more difficulty in keeping the taxing powers of the *United States* and a *State* within clear constitutional limits, than would at first appear."[3] By declaring the powers of the general government supreme, the constitution is a shield to its action in the exercise of its powers, from any restraining or controlling action of the local governments;[4] and congress has created no inconsiderable class of subjects without the reach of the *taxing* power of a State. Thus, the fiscal agents of the government, the army and navy, the judicature of the United States, the public vessels, and the national institutions and property, are exempt from State taxation.[5]

---

1 Osborne *v.* Humphrey, 7 Conn. 335.

2 Hardy *v.* Waltham, 7 Pick. 108.

3 Howell *v.* The State, 3 Gill, 14.

4 1 Kent, Com. 428, 429.

5 Ibid. Howell *v.* The State, *ubi sup.* It has been held by the Supreme Court of the

The institutions of the United States, though really within the territory of a State, are constructively without the local jurisdiction, in every respect and for every purpose.[1] A State tax on stock issued for loans made to the United States, has been held to be unconstitutional, inasmuch as it is a tax on the power given to congress to borrow money on the credit of the United States, and thereby diminishes the means of the United States used in the exercise of its powers.[2]

§ 484. There is little difficulty in applying the above interpretation of the Constitution of the United States to a corporation created by congress within its authority to create.[3] The claim of a State to tax the Bank of the United States, was denied in the case of McCulloch *v.* the State of Maryland,[4] there being a manifest repugnancy between the power of the State to tax, and the power of congress to preserve the institution of the Branch Bank; and a tax on the operations of the bank, being a tax on the operations of an instrument employed by congress to carry its powers into execution. In this case the State of Maryland had imposed a tax on the Branch Bank of the United States established within that State; and in adjudging that State governments have no right to tax such an institution, the inability of the States to impede or control, by taxation or otherwise, the lawful institutions and measures of the national government, was largely discussed.[5]

§ 485. The decision in the above case against the validity of a State

---

United States, that an officer of the United States was not liable to be rated and assessed *for his office*, by State rates and levies, for this would be to diminish the recompense secured by law to the officer. Dobbins *v.* Commissioners of Erie County, 16 Pet. 435. In a case in the Supreme Court of Massachusetts, it was stated as a question undecided, whether a tax assessed upon the *income* of an officer of the United States would not be lawful and not within the case just cited; but it was decided in the Massachusetts case, that a clerk *in the post-office* was not an officer exempted from taxation of his income. Melcher *v.* City of Boston, 9 Met. 73. It is not every employment in the United States service that constitutes the person thus employed an officer, as, for instance, a *mail contractor*. Whitehouse *v.* Langdon, 10 N. H. 331.

[1] Howell *v.* The State, *ubi sup.*

[2] Weston *v.* City Council of Charleston, 2 Pet. 449.

[3] See *ante*, § 72.

[4] McCulloch *v.* State of Maryland, 4 Wheat. 316.

[5] "A case," says Chancellor Kent, "could not be selected from the decisions of the Supreme Court of the United States, superior to this one, of McCulloch *v.* State of Maryland, for the clear and satisfactory manner in which the supremacy of the laws of the Union have been maintained by the Court, and an undue assertion of State power overruled and denied." 1 Kent, Com. 427.

tax on a bank of the United States, was made on the 7th of March, 1819; and it was on the 7th of February preceding, that the legislature of the State of Ohio imposed a similar tax, to the amount of fifty thousand dollars annually, on the Branch Bank of the United States established in that State. It was attempted to withdraw this case from the authority of the other, by the suggestion that the Bank of the United States was a mere private corporation,[1] engaged in its own business, with its own views, and that its principal end and object were private trade and private profit. But it was considered by the court, that the business of lending and dealing in money for private purposes, was an *incidental circumstance*, and not the *primary object;* and the institution was endowed with this faculty, in order to enable it to effect the great public ends of the institution; and without such faculty and business, the institution would be without a capacity to perform its intended public functions.[2]

§ 486. The rule established by the decision in the above important case of McCulloch *v.* State of Maryland, that the United States Bank was not liable to be taxed by the States, is made by the learned Chief Justice, in his opinion therein, subject to the exception, that the rule does not deprive the States of any resources which they originally possessed; it does not extend to a tax paid by the real property of the bank, in common with other real property within the State; *nor to a tax imposed on the interest which the citizens of Maryland may hold in the institution*, in common with other property of the same description throughout the State. The Court of Appeals of South Carolina considered themselves warranted (relying in a measure upon this conclusion of the great judge and constitutional lawyer) in deciding, that the tax of one per cent. on dividends arising from stock, owned by the citizens of South Carolina, which was imposed by the act of December, 1830, was not incompatible with the Constitution of the United States.[3]

---

[1] See *ante,* § 31, *et seq.*

[2] Osborne *v.* Bank of the United States, 9 Wheat. 738.

[3] Berney *v.* Tax Collector, 2 Bailey, 654. It had been before held, by the Constitutional Court of South Carolina, that the ordinance of the City Council of Charleston, laying a tax on all bank stock within the city not exempted from taxation by the acts of the legislature, which exception did not include United States Bank Stock, was neither repugnant to nor inconsistent with the law of the land; and the stock of the United States Bank, in the hands of an *individual,* was a legitimate subject of taxation. Bulow *v.* City Council of Charleston, 1 Nott & McC. 527. The power of State taxation is to be meas-

§ 486 *a*. Corporations created by one State have no right to exercise corporate power within the limits of other States, without consent; so that the States are empowered to impose upon corporations chartered by other States, a tax for the privilege of transacting the business in such State, although no such burden be imposed upon like corporations chartered by its own legislature; and this right of taxing a foreign corporation may be conferred upon a city.[1]

CHAPTER XIV.

OF THE CORPORATE MEETINGS, AND OF THE CONCURRENCE NECESSARY TO DO CORPORATE ACTS.

§ 487. THE principal points which present themselves under the above title, are in respect to the mode of convening a corporate meeting, the place of meeting, and the number of members, or of certain officers required to be present, in order to render the acts, done at the meeting of the assembly, valid.

§ 488. The rule applicable to municipal corporations, namely, that all corporate affairs must be transacted at an assembly convened upon due notice, at a proper time and place, consisting of the proper number of persons, the proper officers, classes, &c.,[2] will in general apply to private corporations; though as we have seen, in some private corporations, the body may be bound by the acts of officers and authorized agents in

---

ured by the extent of State sovereignty, and this leaves to a State the command of all its resources. To render a State law unconstitutional, on the ground that it is repugnant to powers vested in Congress, the repugnancy must be clear, immediate, and direct, and not merely speculative, indirect, and contingent. By an act of the legislature of Maryland, the interest or proportion in all ships or other vessels, whether in port or out of port, owned by persons resident of that State, are directed to be valued as other property is directed, and charged according to such valuation, with the public assessment of a certain sum on every one hundred dollars of assessed value. It was held, that the tax was constitutional, not being incompatible with commerce and navigation, the right to regulate which, by Congress, is supreme and paramount. Howell *v.* State, 3 Gill, 14.

[1] Commonwealth *v.* Milton, 12 B. Mon. 212.

[2] Willcock on Mun. Corpor. 42.

affairs relating to its ordinary business.[1] The presumption is, that every member knows what days and times are appointed by the charter, by-laws, or by usage for the transaction of particular business; and, therefore, no special notice is requisite for assembling to transact the business specially allotted for such days. In most private corporations, there is a particular day appointed for the election of officers; and when the day is thus appointed for an election, no particular notice may be required.[2] Neither, as we apprehend, if a particular day is appointed in each year (as is often the case in charters to private corporations in the United States) for the transaction of all business, is a notice required of the particular business which is to be done.[3] Notice of a special meeting, it has been held, need not state the object of the meeting, when it is for the transaction of ordinary business.[4] And in a recent case in New Hampshire it is held to be immaterial in what manner the days of regular meetings of directors are fixed, provided they are regularly held on stated days.[5]

§ 489. Although, when a day certain is appointed for a particular business, no notice may be necessary when that alone is to be transacted, or the mere ordinary affairs of the corporation are to be acted upon; yet when the intention is to do other acts of importance, a notice of it is required. The election or amotion of an officer, the making of a by-law, or any act of similar importance, on any day not expressly set apart for that particular transaction, is illegal and void.[6] A vote of a corporation, which affects the liability of those of its members who are *its debtors*, cannot be regarded as assented to by them, if they were not

---

1 *Ante*, chapters relating to Common Seal, Contracts, and Agents.

2 Willcock, *ut sup.* Rex *v.* Hill, 4 B. & C. 441, 443; Rex *v.* Carmarthen, 1 M. & S. 702.

3 Warren *v.* Mower, 11 Vt. 385; Sampson *v.* Bowdoinham Steam Mill Corp. 36 Me. 78.

4 Savings Bank *v.* Davis, 8 Conn. 191.

5 Atlantic F. Ins. Co. *v.* Sanders, 36 N. H. 252.

6 Willcock, *ut sup.*; Rex *v.* Liverpool, 2 Burr. 734; Rex *v.* Doncaster, 2 Burr. 744; Rex *v.* Theodorick, 8 East, 545. And see Atlantic De Laine Co. *v.* Mason, 5 R. I. 463; Bank of Chester *v.* Allen, 11 Vt. 302; *Ex parte* Holmes, 5 Cowen, 426; Hardenburg *v.* Farmers and Mechanics Bank, 2 Green, N. J. 68; Smith *v.* Erb, 4 Gill, 437; Burgess *v.* Pue, 2 id. 251; Currie *v.* Mutual Insurance Co. 5 Hen. & M. 315. It has been said (see Rex *v.* Theodorick, 8 East, 546), that when an amotion is intended, the notice should not only mention the purpose of the meeting, but state the name of the person to be proceeded against, and his offence; but Mr. Willcock apprehends that a more general statement, if it answers the purposes of justice, will be sufficient. Willcock on Mun. Corp. 46. See *ante*, Chap XII. in relation to Amotion of Members, &c.

present at the meeting at which the vote passed, although they had legal notice of the meeting.[1]

§ 490. In New York, where a charter declares that the election of electors shall be had in the manner prescribed in the by-laws of the company, and the by-laws fix a time and place for the election of directors, and require notice of the same, but omit to specify the length of notice and the mode of giving it, notice must be given for the time and in the manner prescribed by the general statute law in relation to corporations.[2] But an election of trustees of a church has been held good in that State, although the requirements of the statute in respect to the notice of such election have not been complied with; *provided* that the election was fairly conducted and there be no complaint of want of notice.[3]

§ 491. The summons must be issued by order of some one who has authority to assemble the corporation; though the want of authority in such case may be waived by the presence and consent of all who have a right to vote.[4] In Massachusetts, where an incorporated religious society, that owns a meeting-house, neither makes any by-laws nor passes any vote providing for the warning of its meetings, and has no assessors nor committee authorized to issue a warrant for meetings, it can legally call and warn a meeting only as provided by the Revised Statutes of that State; and where a meeting of such religious society was called by its clerk, on the application of less than five of the proprietors of the meeting-house, it was held, that a vote passed at such meeting appointing an agent to *convey the real estate* of the society, was invalid, and that a conveyance of the estate by him was void against a creditor of the society who subsequently attached the estate, and levied his execution upon it.[5]

---

[1] American Bank *v.* Baker, 4 Met. 164; *Ex parte* Johnson, Ch. 1854, 31 Eng. L. & Eq. 430.

[2] Long Island, &c. Railroad Co. 10 Wend. 37.

[3] People *v.* Peck, 11 Wend. 694. In this case the time was well understood, and there was no pretence that every voter was not present. No fraud was imputed, and no evil could result from want of notice. All parties attended and thereby admitted notice. Per *Savage*, C. J. But where the charter specified the place of meeting, a meeting at another place was held illegal, although all members had been notified. Den d. American Prim. Society *v.* Pilling, 4 N. J. 653.

[4] Rex *v.* Gaborian, 11 East, 86, n.; Rex *v.* Hill, 4 B. & C. 441; Jones *v.* Milton & Rush. Turnp. Co. 7 Ind. 547.

[5] Wiggin *v.* Free Will Baptist Church, 8 Met. 301.

§ 492. The meetings of a joint-stock corporation must be called by a *personal* notice to all the members unless some other provision is made in the charter or in a by-law; and a vote passed at a meeting not so called, is not binding.[1] In the Supreme Court of Connecticut, in a case in which it was insisted that a meeting of the Middletown Manufacturing Company was illegal, Daggett, J., who gave the opinion of the court, observed, "It is very clear that a meeting of the stockholders, constituted as this was, could do no acts binding on the company. Though a meeting regularly warned would be competent to do any act within their chartered powers, by a bare majority; yet if not thus warned, the act must be void. *If no particular mode of notifying the stockholders be provided, either in the charter or in any by-law, yet personal notice might be given; and this, in such a case, would be indispensable.*"[2] In case of his temporary absence, the notice must be left with the member's family, or at his last place of abode. It is no sufficient reason for omitting to summon a member, that it was supposed that he was without the reach of summons; for to support the validity of corporate acts, each member must be actually summoned. Hence a mere order to summon all the members is not sufficient, for if it were, corporators under this pretence might be taken by surprise.[3] But a summons by the proper officer may, by virtue of a by-law, be given so as to warn a meeting by posting up a written notice.[4] Notice to an individual corporator is not of course notice to the corporation.[5]

§ 493. The rules just stated may not in every particular be equally applicable to all private corporations. In moneyed institutions, for instance, the mere owning of shares in the stock of the corporation gives a right of voting; and it would be singular if, when members of such

---

[1] Wiggin *v.* Free Will Baptist Society, 8 Met. 301. According to a dictum of Lord Kenyon, special notice must be given to every member of an "indefinite" body who has a right to vote. Rex *v.* Feversham, 8 T. R. 356; and see Rex *v.* May, 5 Burr. 2682; Rex *v.* Langhorne, 6 Nev. & M. 203; Smyth *v.* Darley, 2 H. L. Cas. 803.

[2] Stow *v.* Wise, 7 Conn. 219; Savings Bank *v.* Davis, 8 id. 191; Bethany *v.* Sperry, 10 id. 200.

[3] Willcock on Mun. Corp. 445; Kynaston *v.* Shrewsbury, 2 Stra. 1051.

[4] Stevens *v.* Eden Meeting-house Society, 12 Vt. 688; Taylor *v.* Griswold, 2 Green, N. J. 222. See *ante*, Chap. X. on By-Laws. Mr. Willcock, in reference to municipal corporations, says, that it is unnecessary that the notice should be in writing, and that if the members are fully informed, by a parol warning, that there is to be a meeting, it is sufficient. Willcock on Mun. Corp. 46. And see Rex *v.* Hill, 4 B. & C. 442.

[5] Pittsburg *v.* Whitehead, 10 Watts, 402.

institutions are absent, the attorney, whom they may have appointed to attend to the management of their property and concerns generally, could not represent them at a meeting of the corporation. In such cases, therefore, it seems proper that the authorized agents and attorneys of absent members should be summoned.[1]

§ 494. In order to guard against and prevent surprise, the notice must be given a reasonable time before the hour of meeting; and what is a reasonable time, of course depends upon the circumstances of the case. If it has been usual to give the notice a certain time before the hour of assembling, that interval will at least be required; but if it does not afford a sufficient opportunity to those who wish to attend, usage will not justify a practice thus unreasonable.[2]

§ 495. If the members be duly assembled, they may unanimously agree to waive the necessity of notice, and proceed to business; but if any one person having a right to vote is absent or refuses his consent, all extraordinary proceedings are illegal;[3] and if the charter requires a special notice, it cannot be dispensed with even by unanimous consent.[4] When some of those who have a right to vote are assembled upon due notice, and all the others who have a right to notice attend without it, and agree to enter upon the proceedings, it is a legal waiver of the notice and the act of the assembly cannot be impeached for the omission of it.[5]

§ 496. If there is no proper *place* established for the transaction of the regular business of the corporation, some place in particular should be appointed in the notice. All acts done at an unusual place by a

---

1 See State *v.* Tudor, 5 Day, 229. And see also, what has been said respecting the right of voting by proxy, *ante*, §§ 128–131. See Campbell *v.* Pultney, 6 Gill & J. 94; and the matter of the Mohawk Railroad, &c. Co. 19 Wend. 135; *Ex parte* Barker, 6 Wend. 509.

2 Rex *v.* Hill, 4 B. & C. 442; Rex *v.* May, 5 Burr. 2682. Where the customary summons is sufficient for the residents, as if it require a notice of twenty-four hours, for the election of a capital burgess, in granting a mandamus, the court will not, on the application of the defendant, appoint a particular time for executing the writ, nor require a notice of six days to be given contrary to the constitution of the place and for the conveniency of one party. Ibid. and Willcock, *ubi sup.*

3 Rex *v.* Theodorick, 8 East, 543; Rex *v.* Gaborian, 11 East, 86 n., 87 n.

4 Rex *v.* Theodorick, *ubi sup.*

5 Rex *v.* Oxford, Palm. 453; Jones *v.* Milton & Rush. Turnp. Co. 7 Ind. 547.

municipal corporation carry the appearance of contrivance, secrecy, and fraud. A meeting of a municipal corporation held at an inn, instead of the town hall, particularly when partaking of an entertainment, has been deemed not a proper corporate assembly, though all the members were present.[1] But this was probably on the ground that the conduct of the members at such a place and under such circumstances, would have little of the deliberation which should attend the discharge of offices of confidence and authority. It is certainly essential in all corporations, that whenever the meeting is held at an unusual place, intimation of that circumstance should be contained in the notice; otherwise much fraud may be practised and great injustice committed.[2]

§ 497. Where, according to the laws and usages of a society, their meetings for the transaction of business are opened by a presiding officer, who holds his office for a fixed term, and no meeting is considered duly organized unless opened by him, and such officer is prevented by the violence of members of the association from discharging his duty at the accustomed place of meeting, he and such of the society as think proper to accompany him, may retire to some convenient place adjacent, and there open the meeting; and their acts and doings will be obligatory upon the society, although those who thus withdraw are a minority of the members of the society; it being a principle of the *common law*, that where a society is composed of an indefinite number of persons, a majority of those who appear at a regular meeting of the society constitute a body to transact business.[3] So a corporation may transact any business at an adjourned meeting, which they might have transacted at the original meeting.[4]

§ 498. All votes and proceedings of persons professing to act in the capacity of corporations, when assembled beyond the bounds of the State granting the charter of the corporation, are wholly void.[5]

§ 499. Corporations are subject to the emphatically republican principle (supposing the charter to be silent), that the whole are bound by the acts of the *majority*, when those acts are conformable to the arti-

---

1 Rex *v.* May, 5 Burr. 2682.

2 See Willcock on Mun. Corpor. 51; Miller *v.* English, 1 N. J. 317.

3 Field *v.* Field, 9 Wend. 394.

4 Warner *v.* Mower, 11 Vt. 385.

5 Miller *v.* Ewer, 27 Me. 509. And see Freeman *v.* Machias Water Power & Mill Co. 38 Me. 343.

cles of the constitution. The general rule upon this subject has been thus very correctly laid down by Gibson, J., of the Supreme Court of Pennsylvania: "The fundamental principle of every association for the purposes of self-government is, that no one shall be bound except with his own consent, expressed by himself or his representatives; but actual assent is immaterial, the assent of the majority being the assent of all; and this is not only constructively but actually true; for that the will of the majority shall in all cases be taken for the will of the whole, is an implied but essential stipulation in every compact of the sort; so that the individual who becomes a member, assents, beforehand, to all measures that shall be sanctioned by a majority of the voices."[1] "It seems," says Mr. Kyd, "to be the first suggestion of reason, that an act done by a simple majority of a collective body of men, which concerns the common interest, should be binding on the whole;" and this, he adds, "is the principle of the rule adopted by the Common Law of England, with respect to aggregate corporations."[2] Notwithstanding that a by-law or rule of a corporation requires that certain corporate acts shall be in a prescribed form, and that no alteration of such law or rule shall be made, except by a vote of two thirds of the members, yet the same body by which the by-law or rule was made, may repeal it by a majority; and may without such repeal pass the corporate act by a

---

1 St. Mary's Church, in Philadelphia, 7 S. & R. 517. And see the doctrine recognized in Presbyterian Congregation *v.* Johnston, 1 Watts & S. 9; New Orleans, Jackson, & Gr. N. R. R. Co. *v.* Harris, 27 Missis. 517; Gifford *v.* N. Jersey R. R. & Trans. Co. 2 Stock. 171; Sprague *v.* Illinois River R. Co. 19 Ill. 174; East Tenn. &c. R. Co. *v.* Gammon, 5 Sneed, 567.

2 1 Kyd, 422; and see 2 Kent, Com. 236. In general it would be the understanding of a plain man, that when a body of persons is to do an act, a majority of that body would bind the rest. Per Lawrence, J., in Withnell *v.* Gartham, 6 T. R. 388; and see case of Wadham College, Cowp. 377; Rex *v.* Beeston, 3 T. R. 593. See Field *v.* Field, 9 Wend. 394; Currie *v.* Mutual Assurance Co. 4 Hen. & M. 315; Hardenburgh *v.* Farmers and Mechanics Bank, 2 Green, N. J. Ch. 68. The Attorney-General (Legare), in Louisville Railroad Company *v.* Lester, 2 How. 522, contends, very justly, that the rule is founded in the law of nature, inasmuch, as if unanimity were demanded, it would be impossible for any corporation to will or act. He, also, in confirmation of the rule, cites Savigny's System of the Roman Law, as it now is, vol. 2, p. 329, sect. 97; cites L. 160, 1, reg. jur. Dig. 50, 17. *Refertur ad universos quod publice fit per majorem partem.* The powers given to fish committees, by the legislature of Maine, cannot be exercised by an individual member; they are confided to a majority of the committee. Stephenson *v.* Gooch, 7 Greenl. Me. 152. In corporations aggregate, where the principle of election is not specified in the charter, it requires a majority of the corporators, contrary in this respect to the plurality principle, which may govern in State elections. State *v.* Wilmington City Council, 3 Harring. Del. 294.

majority, not in the prescribed form.[1] The rule has been so far applied, that if a religious society purchase lands, a majority of them have a right to control their use and occupation, notwithstanding a supposed error in doctrine shown to be a departure from the belief of a majority at the time of the purchase.[2] The presumption is, that all the members present who observe silence when a question is put, concur with the majority of those who actually vote; that is, if the question be put audibly and explicitly.[3] The rule that the majority shall govern applies only to corporate acts. And if the corporation is dissolved by the act of the legislature allowing all the property of the company to be sold to a new company, a stockholder cannot be compelled to take payment for the shares in the old company in shares of the new, nor have a majority of the members a right to transfer all the corporate property to the other corporation and take payment in the shares of the new; thus divesting the interests of the dissenting stockholder, without first giving him security for his interest.[4]

§ 500. But the rule, that the acts and proceedings of a majority, at a meeting properly convened, are binding on the minority, is confined to temporal affairs; matters of faith, in the case of a religious corporation, being governed by a different rule.[5] And the members of a corporation for temporal purposes are not bound by the acts of a majority when they are such as are inconsistent with the object and purpose for which the body corporate was organized. Thus, where a company is authorized by an act of parliament to raise money for a specific purpose only, it is not competent to any majority of the shareholders of the company to divert such money to another purpose against the will of a *single* shareholder; nor, indeed, would unanimity among the shareholders make such a diversion lawful.[6]

§ 501. There is this distinction between a corporate act to be done by a definite number of persons, and one to be performed by an indefi-

---

1 Commonwealth *v.* Mayor of Lancaster, 5 Watts, 152.

2 Keyser *v.* Stanisber, 6 Ohio, 363.

3 Commonwealth *v.* Green, 4 Whart. 531.

4 Lauman *v.* Lebanon Valley R. Co. 30 Penn. State, 42.

5 See *ante*, § 38; Miller *v.* English, 1 N. J. 317; Smith *v.* Erb, 4 Gill, 437.

6 Bagshaw *v.* Eastern Counties Railway Co. 7 Hare, 114; New Orleans, Jackson, & Gr. N. R. R. Co. *v.* Harris, 27 Missis. 517; Kean *v.* Johnson, 1 Stock. 401. See *ante*, § 391, *et seq.*

nite number. In the first case, it is to be observed that a majority is necessary to constitute a quorum, and that no act can be done unless a majority be present; in the latter, a majority of any number of those who appear may act. Thus, the act of incorporating the Utica Insurance Company, provided that the affairs and concerns of the corporation should be managed by *nine directors*. At a meeting purporting to be a meeting of the president and directors of the company, but at which no one was present besides the president and one of the directors, the president being also a director, they appointed themselves and another of the directors to act as inspectors of elections. The question was, whether those three were thus authorized to preside at an election. It was said by the court, "Whether we are to regard this as an electing power, or as part of the business of the directors in their regulations of the election; and (among other regulations) a designation of the persons who shall receive and canvass the votes; in either view, we think there must be at least a *majority of the directors* present, to constitute a board. We do not understand the words, 'a majority of the directors present shall be competent,' &c., as amounting to a declaration that a minority, however small, may decide. It leaves the number competent to a quorum, to be determined by the rules of the common law, which in no case of *this kind* is satisfied with less than a *majority*." [1]

---

[1] *Ex parte* Willcocks, 7 Cowen, 402. The following English authorities may be deemed to have a bearing upon this point; Rex *v.* Whitaker, 9 B. & C. 648. In this case three assessors were appointed under the act for draining, but only two signed the appointment, though the third was present at all their meetings. Held, that the concurrence and signature of the majority was sufficient. Lord Tenterden, after consulting with the other judges, added, "Perhaps it may not be necessary that all should meet, certainly a majority must meet. In this case all the three had met. Where it is granted by charter, that a corporation shall have so many aldermen and so many capital burgesses, and that when one of the latter shall die, depart, or be removed, another shall be elected in his place by the 'mayor and aldermen and other capital burgesses then surviving or remaining, or the greater part of them,' the election must be made by a majority of the full numbers of aldermen and of capital burgesses; a mere majority of members of both bodies who happened to survive, is not sufficient." Rex *v.* May, 4 B. & Ad. 853, per Lord Denman. "There may be distinctions drawn between this case and Rex *v.* Devonshire, but they are the same in principle." Where a hospital for the relief of poor people is duly incorporated, and consists of a master and twelve poor brethren, and the advowson of a living is conveyed to them to hold up to the use of the master and brethren, and their successors forever, the right to nominate to the living, belongs to the majority of the entire body of master and brethren; and the master's concurrence in the act of the majority is not necessary. Regina *v.* Kendall, 1 A. & E. 364. An act of parliament directed that the commissioners, under a paving act, or the major part of them, assembled at any meeting, not being less than thirteen, might, by writing under their hands, appoint a treasurer; and it was

§ 502. It is very clearly the opinion of the court, in the above case, as appears by the quotation just offered, that where a corporate act is to be done by a *definite* number of persons, a majority at least must be present; and the court distinguished such a case from the case of an *indefinite* number. In the latter case the court admit that a majority of those present are competent to act, however few in number. The distinction certainly seems to be warranted by the authorities, though according to Mr. Kyd's construction it is not. That author lays down the following proposition: "At common law, independently of any specific constitution, when the power of acting is intrusted to any specific number, *whether definite* or *indefinite*, any number of the whole body, however minute, is sufficient to form a legal assembly, if all be properly summoned to attend." He instances the House of Commons, composed of 558 members, and says 40 form a house; and he then adds, "any number less than 40 would do so too, *were there not a standing order that no business shall be agitated unless that number be present.*" Now we are inclined to think, that if there were no such standing order, it would be necessary that a majority of the 558 should convene.[1] In this opinion we are certainly sustained by the before-mentioned con-

decided, that an appointment of a treasurer, signed by a majority of the seventeen commissioners present at a meeting, was valid, and that it need not be signed by thirteen. Treasurer to the Commissioners, &c. *v.* Town of Woolwich, 7 B. & C. 346.

[1] In a late case in England, where commissioners for building and enlarging churches, appointed, pursuant to statute, twenty-six persons, to be a select vestry, for the care and management of a church, it was held, that in order to constitute a good assembly of the select vestry so appointed, there must be present a majority of the members (namely, fourteen) named in the appointment; and, therefore, that a rate for the repair of the church, made at a meeting where there was not such a majority, was illegal. Blacket *v.* Blizard, 9 B. & C. 851. Where an authority is confided to several persons for a *private* purpose, *all* must join in the act. A controversy between G. & M. was submitted to five arbitrators; and the submission did not provide that a less number than the whole might make an award. All the arbitrators met, and heard the proofs and allegations of the parties, but four only agreed on the award made. Whether the award was binding, was the question before the court. No case was cited where the question had been directly decided. The court were, however, satisfied, that as a submission to arbitrators is a delegation of power, *for a mere private purpose*, it is necessary that all the arbitrators should concur in the award, unless otherwise provided by the parties. Thompson, J., who gave the opinion, said: "In matters of public concern, a different rule seems to prevail; there the voice of the majority shall govern." Green *v.* Miller, 6 Johns. 38. In the case of Grindley *v.* Baker, 1 B. & P. 236, Chief J. Eyre says, "It is now pretty well established, that where a number of persons are intrusted with power, *not of mere private confidence*, but in some respects of a general nature, and all of them are regularly assembled, the majority will conclude the minority, and their act will be the act of the whole." See Orvis *v.* Thompson, 1 Johns. 500; Rex *v.* Courtenay, 9 East, 246.

struction of the Supreme Court of New York; and we are also sustained in the opinion, by the authorities in relation to corporations composed of several classes, or integral parts, which we shall next consider. If a vote is passed at a meeting of the directors to do a certain thing, and this is void because of there not being a sufficient number of directors present, the vote may nevertheless be afterwards ratified. Thus, if less than a quorum of directors of an insurance company vote to allow certain losses, this may be ratified by a vote of a quorum to lay an assessment to pay the losses.[1]

§ 503. We have beforo stated that aggregate corporations are sometimes composed of several distinct parts or classes of persons, which are called integral parts;[2] neither of which is a distinct corporation. According to the authorities afforded by the English books relating to municipal corporations, there must be present at a corporate assembly (besides the president), a majority of each integral part, if composed of a *definite* number, and not merely a majority of the surviving or existing members of each class. Indeed, if there be not a surviving majority of the constitutional numbers, no corporate assembly, say those authorities, can be formed, and the functions of every meeting in which that class ought to participate are suspended; and, according to some authorities, the corporation is even dissolved.[3] The rule, that a majority of every integral part of a corporation consisting of a definite number, must be present, was recognized in the case of *St. Mary's Church* in Pennsylvania, wherein it was decided, that in corporations, where there are different classes, the majority of each class must consent before the charter can be altered, unless there is a provision in the charter respecting alterations. In this case, Duncan, J., lays down the law as follows: "When legally assembled, the majority of voices govern; but every integral part must be present at a corporate assembly by *a majority at least* of its proper members, though the major part of all present, when assembled, are competent to do a corporate act."[4] In a case where a

1 Atlantic F. Ins. Co. *v.* Sanders, 36 N. H. 252.

2 *Ante*, §§ 75, 76.

3 Rex *v.* Lathorp, 1 W. Bl. 471; Rex *v.* Bellringer, 4 T. R. 823; Rex *v.* Miller, 6 T. R. 278; Rex *v.* Morris, 4 East, 26; Rex *v.* Thornton, 4 East, 307; Rex *v.* Devonshire, 1 B. & C. 614; Rex *v.* Hill, 4 B. & C. 441; Willcock on Mun. Corpor. 62. And see Mr. Cowen's note to *Ex parte* Willcocks, 7 Cowen, 410. And see *post*, Chap. XXII., on the Dissolution of Corporations.

4 St. Mary's Church, in Philadelphia, 7 S. & R. 517; Booker *v.* Young, 12 Grat. 303; Beck *v.* Hanscom, 9 Foster, 213.

charter of a bank required seven directors to make a *quorum*, and declared the president to be entitled to the powers of a director, a meeting composed of the president and six directors, was treated as a sufficient board for the transaction of business.[1]

§ 504. It was held, in an early case, that where the power to make a by-law was in the mayor and aldermen, a by-law made by the mayor, aldermen, and *commonalty*, was void.[2] So the trustees of a religious incorporated society could alone bind the corporation, the action of the vestry having no such force; and where the act relied upon was adopted at a meeting of the conference or council, which consisted of the minister, elders, deacons, and trustees, convened in mass, the corporation was not bound, although a majority of the trustees were present.[3] Suppose, in the case of a bank, that, at a general meeting of the stockholders, certain resolutions should be adopted to do any corporate act, and it should be made to appear that all the directors of the bank were present and assenting to what was done; the corporation could not be bound, unless the directors, *at a meeting of the board*, should concur in the resolutions. The separate action, individually, without consultation, although a majority in number should agree upon a certain act, would not be the act of the constituted body of men clothed with the corporate powers. Nor would their action in a meeting of the whole body of corporators, of another and larger class of which they are a component part, be a valid corporate act. In thus acting, they are not distinguishable from their associates, and their action is united with that of others, who have no proper or legal right to join with them in its exercise.[4]

§ 505. When a corporation consists of several integral parts, one of which is *indefinite*, if any number of persons composing the latter, however small, are present after having been duly summoned, it is sufficient. The distinction is between a definite and an indefinite number. In the former case a majority must be present; whereas in the latter a majority of those present may act, whether a majority of the whole body or not.[5]

---

1 Bank of Maryland, &c. *v.* Ruff, 7 Harris & G. 448.

2 10 Co. R. 77 b.

3 Cammeyer *v.* United German Lutheran Churches, 2 Sandf. Ch. 186.

4 Ibid.

5 Willcock on Mun. Corpor. 66; Rex *v.* Whitaker, 9 B. & C. 648.

§ 506. What we have said respecting the number required to be present in different corporations in order to do corporate acts, is confined to corporations whose charter or constitution is silent upon the subject. The rules of the common law may be, and frequently are, superseded by the express provisions of the charter; and there have been provisions of this nature introduced into charters, that have been the source of much discussion and controversy.[1] It was considered in England at one time, that the phrase "for the time being," referred to the state of the corporation from time to time, and that when an act was to be done by a definite class, or the majority of them for "the time being," it required only the presence of the majority of the surviving members at that time, although less than the constitutional number. The effect of this would be, that if the corporation ought to consist of twelve aldermen and twelve burgesses, an act required to be done by a majority of each class for "the time being," might be done by two aldermen and two burgesses, if the number happened to be reduced to three members of each class. The law on this point is now, however, well settled in England; and the words "for the time being" are construed (rightly, says Mr. Willcock) to apply to the persons who shall from time to time be the members of such classes; so that such an act cannot be done by less than seven aldermen and seven burgesses, although at that time they are all who survive.[2] And it is immaterial into what combination of words this phrase is introduced, for a majority of the constitutional number of each definite class is requisite, if the charter direct the act to be done by the mayor, aldermen, bailiffs, capital, and other burgesses, and inhabitants, "for the time being," assembled, or the greater part of them, by the majority of voices "of them so assembled."[3]

§ 507. The words "surviving and remaining," might, says Mr. Willcock, be imagined to refer to the existing number of members in a definite class, and to derive greater force from the presence of a majority of those surviving and remaining being required at elections to supply vacancies in the same class, when from necessity it must consist of at

---

1 See note to *Ex parte* Rogers, 7 Cowen, 530.

2 Willcock on Mun. Corp. 63; and see Rex *v.* May, 4 B. & Ad. 843; Rex *v.* Morris, 4 East, 26; Rex *v.* Bellringer, 4 T. R. 823; Rex *v.* Bower, 2 D. & R. 770; Rex *v.* Williams, 3 D. & R. 81, 1 B. & C. 614.

3 Rex *v.* Bower, 2 D. & R. 770, 1 B. & C. 498.

least one less than the constitutional number. But the implication from this, even, is not so strong as to induce the courts to admit a violation of the rule; and therefore, if there ought to be twelve capital burgesses, and the charter directs that when a capital burgess is dead or removed, the other capital burgesses, "at that time surviving and remaining," or the greater part "of the same," shall elect another to be a capital burgess, the election is void, unless seven capital burgesses be present.[1]

§ 508. The construction of a charter may sometimes require the assembly to consist of more than a simple majority of the select class; for it was held that when the corporation consisted of a mayor and eleven aldermen, and the charter directed that two aldermen should be nominated, of whom one should be elected by "the *then residue* of the aldermen or the major part of them," there must at least be present five aldermen (the majority of nine, the residue of the constitutional number after two had been nominated), besides the mayor and the two nominees, making altogether seven aldermen instead of a simple majority of six.[2] But, perhaps, says Mr. Willcock, it is not necessary that the nominees should be present, and the mayor and five, or at least six, aldermen may proceed to an election if they nominate two of those who are absent.[3] But if the charter plainly and explicitly empower a less number to make an election, the court cannot assume to alter the constitution;[4] and so if the charter require a greater number than the majority.[5]

§ 509. The words, "a majority of the directors present shall be competent," &c., in the 15th section of the act incorporating the Utica Insurance Company, were considered by the Supreme Court of the State of New York as not amounting to a declaration that a minority, however small, might decide; and that it left the number competent to form a quorum, to be determined by the rules of the Common Law.[6] In Rex *v.* Beeston,[7] a statute had authorized the church-wardens and overseers of the poor to make certain contracts; they had all joined, with the ex-

---

1 Rex *v.* Devonshire, 1 B. & C. 617, 3 D. & R. 81.

2 Rex *v.* Smith, 2 M. & S. 579.

3 Willcock on Mun. Corpor. 65.

4 Rex *v.* Hoyte, 6 T. R. 432; Rex *v.* Richardson, 1 Burr. 541.

5 Palmer *v.* Doney, 2 Johns. Cas. 346.

6 *Ex parte* Willcocks, 7 Cowen, 409.

7 3 T. R. 492.

ception of the defendant, one of the overseers, who refused to join, and made a contract, and the money was in the defendant's hands to be paid upon it. On a motion for a mandamus to compel him to pay, he insisted that he was not bound, inasmuch as the *statute* required the contract to be made by the church-wardens and overseers, without saying, "*or a majority;*" and that, therefore, they should all concur; and that he having dissented, the contract was void. But the motion was granted. It has been decided in New York, that when the charter of an insurance company prescribes that every act of the corporation shall be done by the president and *at least four directors*, the president alone could not legally accept an abandonment.[1] The agents of a corporation can never bind it, if they do not act pursuant to the requisites of the charter or incorporating act.[2]

§ 510. In the case of King *v.* Norris,[3] at one of the assemblies of the corporation of Newcastle (where the *presence* of the mayor was necessary), as soon as the lists of certain persons were given in as candidates for freemen, and before they were admitted to their freedom, the mayor dissolved the assembly, who, notwithstanding, proceeded to admit them. The court said, "It is very true, that no new business can be proposed in the absence of such officer; but the assembly has always the right to proceed in the business *begun* when he was present." This case was cited (and apparently with approbation), in the Supreme Court of Pennsylvania, by Duncan, J., in a case where the trustees of a corporation consisted of three *clerical* and eight *lay* members. The decision was, that if one of the clerical members be *excluded* from the board by a resolution of the lay members, *without authority*, the proceedings in the absence of such member were unlawful. But the opinion of the court in some degree implies, that if the member had *voluntarily* absented himself, after the business of the meeting had commenced, no such conclusion could be drawn.[4] The English authorities, however, since the case of King *v.* Norris, have been strict in requiring the *actual* presence of all the integral parts of a

---

[1] Beatty *v.* Marine Insurance Company, 2 Johns. 109.

[2] Head *v.* Providence Insurance Company, 2 Cranch, 266 and see *ante*, Chapter VIII., relating to the Power of Agents to make Contracts.

[3] 1 Barnard. 385.

[4] Case of the Corporation of St. Mary's Church, in Philadelphia, 7 S. & R. 517; see also, Cowen's note to the case of *Ex parte* Rogers, 7 Cowen, 533.

corporation. So strict have they been, that in several instances where a mayor has deserted his post, after business had begun, when he perceived that the corporation were disposed to act against him, they have adjudged the proceedings, in his absence, void. Thus, it appeared by the charter, that the mayor, aldermen, and burgesses, of the borough of S., or the major part of them, were, on the charter day, to assemble in the Guildhall; when the *mayor and aldermen*, or the major part of them, were to nominate and put in election for mayor, two of the aldermen; and they were there to continue together, or in due manner adjourn, until the mayor and the other integral parts should have elected one of the two aldermen nominated for a year. Being thus convened, B., the mayor, and two aldermen, nominated the two latter for mayor; but the other aldermen, a majority, nominating two out of their number, the mayor and his two nominees quitted the Guildhall. The other aldermen, with the burgesses, proceeded to an election of those nominated by the four. On a rule to show cause against B., the mayor, why a mandamus should not issue, commanding him to swear his successor into office, the above case of King *v.* Norris was, at first, overlooked. On examination, afterwards, its authority appeared to the court somewhat questionable; and the election passed as irregular, for want of the actual presence of the old mayor. The decision of the court was upon the ground that the mayor was an *integral part* of the corporation.[1] In a still later case, the mayor, burgesses, and commonalty of C. were to elect a mayor annually. They being assembled at a quarter before 1, P. M., the mayor, contrary to the advice of the recorder, and the sense of the burgesses, proposed to adjourn till 3, P. M. He did not do so, however; and in his presence, one E. was suddenly proposed and seconded as a candidate, before the mayor left the place; but he departed before E. was declared duly elected, though this was done immediately after his departure, by the burgesses and commonalty. The King's Bench held, that the election was void for the absence of the presiding officer, an *integral part* of the corporation.[2]

§ 511. It was held in *Ex parte* Rogers, in New York, that where a *statute* or *charter* requires that a certain number of persons shall be present at the consummation of any act, they must all be so present;

---

1 King *v.* Buller, 8 East, 388. See also, note to this case.

2 King *v.* Williams, 2 M. & S. 141; Dampier, J., relied on the case of King *v.* Buller, *supra.*

and the act is not good, though it be begun while all are present, if one of them depart, though wrongfully, before its consummation.[1] The learned reporter, in a note to the case just cited, observes, "Where a public act is to be done, by three or more commissioners appointed in a statute, and a competent number have met and conferred, though they separate, and then a majority do the act, without the presence of the others, the act seems good in consideration of law; though it is otherwise where there is a positive statute or charter, requiring that a full board shall be present at the consummation."[2]

§ 512. Acts purporting to be done by corporations, which relate to the constitution and the rules of government of the body corporate, are not to be considered as having received a legal concurrence, merely because they appear under the corporate seal; and the court have authority to inquire, in such cases, by what authority the seal was affixed. Thus it was held, in the case of St. Mary's Church in Philadelphia, that proposed amendments of the charter, though authenticated by the seal, were not regarded as conclusive evidence that the proposition was the legal act of the corporation. The C. J. in this case (Tilghman), in delivering his opinion, remarked as follows: "Is the court bound to consider the proposal for alteration of the charter as the act of the corporation, because it is presented under the corporate seal; or may it look beyond the seal and inquire in what manner and by what authority

---

[1] *Ex parte* Rogers, 7 Cowen, 526.

[2] The reporter then cites the following case: "The statute of March 1, 1778 (2 Greenleaf, 116, § 11, ch. 48, s. 2), declared that no permit should be granted to retail spirituous liquor, unless three commissioners (a full board) should be *present at the granting thereof.*" This provision came under consideration in Palmer *v.* Doney, 2 Johns. Cas. 346, which was an action of debt, for several penalties alleged to have been incurred by the defendant under the 10th section of the act for selling without a permit. The main question was, whether the permit was granted by a competent board. The supervisor and two justices (a full board) being met, the defendant applied to them for license. The supervisor decided against granting it, whereupon the two justices retired into another room, and gave the license required. In this case it is evident, from the language of Lewis, C. J., who delivered the opinion of the court, that they considered the statute as substantially satisfied in its equity and spirit; but they yielded to its strong letter, expressly putting themselves on the positive *proviso,* that three commissioners *should be present.* This is a case which stands almost alone in our statute book; and is evidently founded on the extreme jealousy of the legislature against the heedless multiplication of taverns. The provision is continued to this day, with the addition, that the supervisor of the town shall be one of the three who shall be present; and that unless they are all actually present, the license shall be void. (1 R. L. 177, § 3.)

it was affixed? Undoubtedly it may and it ought. Suppose amendments should be voted at a meeting of the corporation, not lawfully convened, and some of the members who were absent should dissent. Suppose a meeting lawfully convened, and then the majority should force the minority to retire, after which they should pass a resolution for amendments. Suppose, by the constitution of the corporation, a certain quorum should be required to do business, and a number less than the quorum should pass resolutions for amendment, and affix the seal. Or suppose the constitution provided, that the assent of certain members should be necessary, and the others proceeded to act without their assent. In all these cases, it is too clear to admit of argument, that the court would do flagrant injustice, if it suffered the seal to preclude an examination of the truth."[1] As the affixing the corporate seal is a mere ministerial act, the seal may be affixed to a contract by a less number than was competent to enter into the contract, provided it is done by the direction of a legal quorum. Thus, where the charter required a certain number of managers to constitute a quorum for the purpose of entering into contracts, a contract to which the seal of the corporation was affixed by a less number than were competent to make the contract, was holden to be valid, provided it was done by the order of a legal quorum. If the seal, the court say, were in fact affixed by persons having no authority, it was matter for subsequent consideration by the jury.[2]

§ 513. The *books* and *minutes* of a corporation, if there is nothing to raise a suspicion that the corporate proceedings have been irregular, will of course be treated and referred to as evidence of the legality of the proceedings. Thus, the books are admissible to prove the organization and existence of the corporation;[3] and it has been held, that where the charter requires two thirds to form a quorum, and it is stated on the minutes, that on due invitation the corporators met, and it is not usual to mention on the minutes the names or number of those present, it is *primâ facie* evidence that two thirds did assemble.[4]

---

[1] Case of St. Mary's Church, 7 S. & R. 530. But the seal is *primâ facie* evidence of the assent of the corporation. Reed *v.* Bradley, 17 Ill. 321.

[2] President, &c. of B. & D. Turn. Road *v.* Myers, 6 S. & R. 12.

[3] Grays *v.* Lynchburg and Salem Turnpike Co. 4 Rand. 578; Buncombe Turn. Co. *v.* McCarson, 1 Dev. & B. 306. See also, Penobscot and Kennebec R. R. Co. *v.* Dunn, 39 Me. 578; and *ante*, Chap. II. § 7.

[4] Commonwealth *v.* Woelper, 3 S. & R. 29.

§ 514. In the case of Grays *v.* Lynchburg and Salem Turnpike Co., in Virginia, it was objected, that the entry in the book did not show that the meeting consisted of "a number of persons, entitled to a majority of all the votes which could be given on all the shares subscribed," which the law requires. The court said, "The entry certainly has not followed the words of the law; and if it intended to express the same idea, it has done it a little awkwardly; yet that it did so intend, we are strongly inclined to think. It must have been apparent to every member, that the law required a majority of the stock to be represented in the first meeting; and to that end, directed that those who first met should adjourn from time to time, until such majority should attend. We can conceive no motive for the departing from the law. The meeting consisted of partners in the firm, all interested in putting the institution legally into operation. They did organize it, and it has gone on ever since, without objection, that we hear of. Under these circumstances, may we not fairly conclude that the meeting was a legal one? That by the words 'majority of the stockholders,' the clerk meant such a majority as the law required, to wit, *holders of a majority of the stock?* We think this by no means a strained inference."[1]

§ 515. The recording officer of a corporation may make and verify copies of its records, and of the verity of such copies his certificates are evidence; but it is no part of the duty of such officer to certify facts, nor can his certificate be received as evidence of such facts.[2] But the secretary of a banking corporation, it was held, is not a certifying officer; and copies certified by him must be sworn to before they can be given in evidence.[3]

§ 516. As against the corporation, it is to be presumed that the forms required by the charter have been complied with, and, therefore, it lies upon it, where it seeks to avail itself of any default in this respect, to give strict proof thereof.[4]

---

[1] Grays *v.* Lynchburg and Salem Turn. Co. 4 Rand. 578.

[2] Oakes *v.* Hill, 14 Pick. 442.

[3] Hallowell and Augusta Bank *v.* Hamlin, 14 Mass. 178; and see *post,* Chapter on Writ of Mandamus.

[4] Hill *v.* Manchester Waterworks Co. 5 B. & Ad. 874; Clarke *v.* Imperial Gas Light Co. 4 id. 324.

CHAPTER XV.

OF SUBSCRIPTIONS FOR, AND ASSESSMENTS UPON, SHARES IN JOINT-STOCK CORPORATIONS.

§ 517. A SUBSCRIPTION for shares in the stock of a joint-stock incorporated company, is a contract; and the interest thereby acquired is a sufficient consideration to enable the company to support an action against the subscriber for a recovery of the amount subscribed.[1] With the view of facilitating the formation of these companies, it is usual to have the capital subscribed for, payable in instalments, or in small sums payable from time to time; and an engagement so to pay at stipulated periods, is one which causes the Statute of Limitations to attach to each instalment as it becomes due.[2] A subscription to the stock of a company in the name of a third person, without authority, is not of course binding on such person; but such an act may be ratified, and a letter of attorney, executed by the person in whose name the subscription was made, constituting the attorney his proxy to vote at a meeting of the company, is evidence of such ratification.[3] To give validity to a ratification, a full knowledge of all the material facts and circumstances attending the transaction is necessary, and it has been held that the party must know that he would not be bound without such ratification.[4]

---

[1] Wordsworth on Joint-Stock Companies, 317; Birmingham & Bristol Railway Co. *v.* White, 1 Q. B. 541; Pendergast *v.* Turton, 1 Younge & C. Ch. 97; Baltimore, &c. Turnp. Co. *v.* Barnes, 6 Harris & J. 57; Hall *v.* United States Insurance Co. 5 Gill, 784; Small *v.* Herkimer Man. Co. 2 Comst. 330; Mann *v.* Pentz, 2 Sandf. Ch. 258; Corning *v.* McCullough, 1 Comst. 47; Trumbull *v.* Mutual Fire Insurance Co. 17 Ohio, 407; Gayle *v.* Cahawba & Marion Railroad Co. 8 Ala. 586; Stokes *v.* Lebanon Turnp. Co. 6 Humph. 241; Hartford & New Haven Railroad Co. *v.* Kennedy, 12 Conn. 499; Harlaem Canal Co. *v.* Seixas, 2 Hall, 504; Essex Bridge Co. *v.* Tuttle, 2 Vt. 393; Union Locks and Canal Co. *v.* Towne, 1 N. H. 44; Tonica & Petersburg R. Co. *v.* McNeely, 21 Ill. 71.

[2] Baltimore Turnp. Co. *v.* Barnes, 6 Harris & J. 57; Corning *v.* McCullough, 1 Comst. 47.

[3] McCully *v.* Pittsburgh, &c. R. Co. 32 Penn. State, 25. See also, Mobile &c. R. Co. *v.* Tandal, 5 Sneed, 294.

[4] Pittsburgh &c. R. Co. *v.* Gazzam, 32 Penn. State, 340.

If the charter of a corporation does not require a written notice of calls for stock, a verbal notice by the secretary, by order of the president, in pursuance of a resolution of the board of directors, is sufficient.[1]

§ 518. The case of the Goshen Turnpike Co. *v.* Hurtin,[2] was an action of assumpsit, on a promissory note made by the defendant, by which he promised to pay the plaintiffs a certain sum for five shares of the capital stock of the corporation, in such manner and proportion, and at such time and place as the plaintiffs should from time to time require. The question which the parties had principally in view in this case, was, whether an action would lie on a promise by a subscriber for turnpike stock to pay his instalments; and it was held in the affirmative. In the case of the Dutchess Manufacturing Company *v.* Davis,[3] the court (referring, as authority, to the decision in the case just cited, and also to the one in the case of Union Turnpike Company *v.* Jenkins[4]) held, that the defendant, having undertaken to enter into a contract with the plaintiffs in their corporate name, thus admitted them to be a body politic; and that, by his subscription for a certain number of shares, at a certain sum, he became liable for the amount of his subscription, on the same principle that the maker of a promissory note renders himself liable.[5]

§ 519. The consideration which is necessary to sustain such a promise, is raised by inference of law from the subscription itself, and the privileges thereby conferred; and, from the same circumstance, the law will infer a duty to pay for the stock, and an implied obligation of equal force with an express contract, where nothing appears repugnant to such a construction.[6] As was said by Mr. Justice Sutherland, in deliv-

---

[1] Smith *v.* Plank Road Co. 30 Ala. 650.

[2] Goshen Turnp. Co. *v.* Hurtin, 9 Johns. 217.

[3] Dutchess Man. Co. *v.* Davis, 14 Johns. 238.

[4] Union Turnp. Co. *v.* Jenkins, 1 Caines, 86.

[5] And see, likewise, Sagory *v.* Dubois, 3 Sandf. Ch. 466; Hibernia Turnp. Co. *v.* Henderson, 8 S. & R. 219, opinion of Duncan, J.; Ogle *v.* Somerset, &c. Co. 13 S. & R. 256; Commonwealth *v.* Gill, 3 Whart. 228; Vermont Central Railroad Co. *v.* Clayes, 21 Vt. 30; Beere *v.* Cahawba Railroad Co. 3 Ala. 660. A note given to an incorporated company, for stock, is valid in the hands of an *indorsee,* without notice, notwithstanding the statutory provision forbidding directors to receive a note, or other evidence of debt, in payment of any instalment actually called in and required to be paid, where it is not affirmatively shown that the note was given for stock called in and required to be paid. Willmarth *v.* Crawford, 10 Wend. 341.

[6] Sagory *v.* Dubois, 3 Sandf. Ch. 466; Herkimer *v.* Man. Co. *v.* Small, 2 Hill, 127, and 21 Wend. 273; Troy & Boston R. R. Co. *v.* Tibbits, 18 Barb. 297.

ering the judgment of the court, in Spear *v.* Crawford,[1] "The promise of the defendant and the other subscribers, although it is in form to take the shares subscribed by them respectively, is undoubtedly (when taken in connection with what precedes it, and with the act of incorporation which is there referred to, and in part recited) a promise not only to take the shares, but to pay for them; to take them upon the terms and conditions set forth in the subscription paper."[2]

§ 520. One of the banking associations of New York had made several calls upon its stockholders for payment on their shares. It declared dividends on the stock paid in, and applied the same to meet some of such calls, the last of which dividends was unauthorized by the situation of the company, and was contrary to the general banking law. After the calls on the shares had amounted to half their nominal amount, the directors resolved that no further calls should ever be made, and forthwith discontinued the business of the company, which soon after became insolvent; and on the application of a creditor, the Court of Chancery appointed a receiver of its property and effects; and, on a bill filed by the receiver, to compel a stockholder to pay the balance of the nominal amount of his shares, it was held, that the defendant having become liable by his subscription *to pay up his shares in full*, as called for by the directors, might be compelled to pay the same by the receiver representing the creditors of the company. It was insisted, on

---

1 Spear *v.* Crawford, 14 Wend. 20.

2 By the court, Duer, J. "The law must now be considered as settled, that the obligation of actual payment is created in all cases by a subscription to a capital stock, unless the terms of the subscription are such as plainly to exclude it." Palmer *v.* Lawrence, 3 Sandf. 161; Elysville *v.* Okisko Co. 5 Md. 152; Greenville & Columbia Railroad Co. *v.* Smith, 6 Rich. 91, referring to 3 Strob. 245; Klein *v.* Alton & Sangamon Railroad Co. 13 Ill. 514; Cubbertson *v.* Wabash Nav. Co. 4 McLean, 544; Northern Railway Co *v.* Miller, 10 Barb. 11, 260; Barret *v.* Alton, 13 Ill. 504, 514. The provision in a charter of a corporation, for the forfeiture of stock, is for the benefit of the corporation and not of the stockholder, and does not take away the right to compel payment of subscriptions by action. Hightower *v.* Thurston, 8 Ga. 486. See too, *In re* Shrewsbury & Leicester Railway Co. 1 Sim., N. S. 281, 7 Eng. L. & Eq. 28; Birmingham, &c. Rail. Co. 1 Sim., N. S. 394, 7 Eng. L. & Eq. 64; *Ex parte* Dale, 1 De G., M. & S. 513, 9 Eng. L. & Eq. 255. Where an ecclesiastical society had subscribed for shares in a bank, by virtue of a provision for such subscription in the charter of the bank, the bank afterwards became insolvent; and thereupon the society gave due notice of its intention to withdraw the shares so subscribed. It was held, that the society, by virtue of its subscription, became a stockholder in the bank, and part of the corporation; and, consequently, after the insolvency of the bank, was incapable of withdrawing its shares, or of recovering the amount as a debt against the bank. United Society *v.* Eagle Bank, 7 Conn. 456.

the part of the defendant, that the banking law exempted him from personal liability. That, said the court, was very true, but that the provision was not applicable, inasmuch as the suit was brought to compel the defendant to pay his own debt *to* the association; that it was not an attempt to subject him to the debts due from the company, any further than it required him to make good his *subscription*, on the faith of which the company acquired a corporate existence, and the credit to contract obligations.[1]

§ 521. In the State of New York, persons wishing to institute an association under the act to authorize the business of banking,[2] after subscribing articles of association, proceeded to elect a president and the directors. The *latter* signed and recorded a certificate of its organization, made in the form prescribed, and proceeded to the transaction of business. This certificate not being signed by the stockholders, was not in compliance with the law, and, therefore, the association had no legal existence. Subsequently, a certificate, signed by stockholders owning the amount of capital originally designated in the articles, was filed in pursuance of the act, and the bank became legally organized. C. subscribed the articles for twenty shares of stock, intermediate the recording of the first certificate and the making the second; and he and his wife gave their bond and mortgage for the par value of the shares, payable to the president of the bank; but he did not sign the second certificate, though he paid interest on the bond and mortgage half-yearly for two years ensuing. It was held, that until the second certificate was filed, the bond and mortgage were in effect payable to a fictitious person; they were *without consideration*, and no person could make an available title to the same; that after the bank became a legitimate association, the stock formed a consideration, and C. recognized its existence, and so acted in regard to it, that his redelivery of the bond and mortgage ought to be inferred; that a bond and mortgage given for stock subscribed to organize a bank under the act in question, are valid, when the articles provide for that mode of securing the stock.[3]

§ 522. Less strictness is required (as there has before been occasion

---

1 Sagory *v.* Dubois, 3 Sandf. Ch. 466.

2 See *ante*, §§ 64, 88.

3 Valk *v.* Crandall, 1 Sandf. Ch. 179; and see Danbury & Norwalk R. R. Co. *v.* Wilson, 22 Conn. 435.

to observe),[1] in contracts with corporations, than in actions by or against them; and so, therefore, where the form prescribed by the charter of a turnpike company, was, "We, whose names are hereunto subscribed, do promise to pay to the *President*, Managers, and Company of the Hagerstown Turnpike Road Company, the sum of —— dollars, for every share of the stock in said company set opposite to our respective names," it was held, that if the form used by the subscriber omitted the word "President," it was sufficient and binding.[2]

§ 523. A person subscribing *before the organization* of a proposed incorporated joint-stock company, raises a mutuality in his contract which will render him liable to the company after incorporation. A subscriber or partner in an intended undertaking, subscribing an agreement to take measures to carry out the same, cannot discharge himself of liability, or repudiate the concern to which he may have thus pledged himself; and if an act of the legislature has been passed for effectuating the purpose of the undertaking, by which certain obligations are created, such original subscriber is not exonerated from the liabilities imposed by the act, by having, during the progress of the bill, renounced all further connection with the undertaking, and desired that his name might be in consequence omitted from the act; nor can the circumstance of his name being so omitted, have the effect of disengaging him. Such was the decision, in the case of the Kidwelly Canal Co. *v.* Raby,[3] and such is also the doctrine maintained by the Supreme Court of Alabama.[4] Nor is the insolvency of a corporation any ground for restraining the enforcement of subscriptions to its stock.[5]

---

[1] See *ante*, § 101.

[2] Hagerstown Turnp. Corp. *v.* Creeger, 5 Harris & J. 22.

[3] Kidwelly Canal Co. *v.* Raby, 2 Price, 93. "If Raby," said Baron Richards, "had not endeavored to withdraw, there would have been no doubt of his liability; then the question becomes, whether he has in fact withdrawn; and I think he has not, inasmuch as he *could not do so* without the consent of all those with whom he had become engaged in the undertaking."

[4] Selma *v.* Tennessee Railroad Company, 5 Ala. 786, in which the court cited the above case of Kidwelly Canal Co. It is not to be intended, that the legislature meant to dispose of the subscriptions of those who became parties to the contract between themselves, made before they became incorporated. Turnpike Co. *v.* Phillips, 2 Pen. & W. 184. And see Eastern P. R. Co. *v.* Vaughan, 20 Barb. 155; Poughkeepsie & S. Point P. R. Co. *v.* Griffin, 21 Barb. 454; Danbury & Norwalk R. R. Co. *v.* Wilson, 22 Conn. 435.

[5] Dill *v.* Wabash Valley R. Co. 21 Ill. 91. See also, West Chester & Ph. R. Co. *v.* Thomas, 2 Wall. Phil. 344.

§ 524. The objection was taken in one case, that the written paper signed by the defendant was made before the company was incorporated, and was, therefore, a contract only with the individuals. But the answer given, and which the court thought sufficient, was, that the act incorporated all who might afterwards associate, as well as those who had then been associated. The defendant, the court said, signed the paper after the act of incorporation had passed; but that he must be taken to have signed it on the day it bore date. It was besides objected, that the corporation had never been duly authorized under the statute, and that, therefore, no contract had been made with them, and that they had no right to maintain assumpsit to recover the amount of the subscription. The statute referred to, required that the first meeting should be called by a major part of the persons incorporated; and it appeared that one King and one Leister, who were partners in trade, were named in the act of incorporation, and that to the advertisement for calling the meeting, the name of the firm was signed. The court said, that, considering this as one signature, there was not a majority; though taking the names separately, there was. At any rate, they thought the objection could not be made by one of the company, after they had in fact been organized, and for several years transacted business, as a corporation; and that it would be right to consider the advertisement as signed by each of the partners, the one who actually signed acting as agent for the others.[1]

§ 525. In the case of Farmington Academy *v.* Flint, in Massachusetts, the trustees of that institution, after being incorporated, and becoming seised in trust of the land which the legislature had granted on the faith of the private funds raised by subscription, proceeded to erect a building for the use of the institution. Flint being one of the trustees, *never having dissented* from any of their acts, and having, when called upon for payment, sent a man, who was a debtor of his, to work out a part of his subscription; it was thought that the recognition of his promise, accompanied by a knowledge on his part that the expense was going on, authorized a recovery against him to the amount of his subscription, on the ground of *money paid, laid out*, &c., to his use, and at his request. The court also thought it to be like the case of a

---

[1] Chester Glass Co. *v.* Dewey, 16 Mass. 94; and see Instone *v.* H. Bridge Co. 2 Bibb, 570.

man working upon the house of another, who had knowledge of his proceedings; in which case, though he could prove no express promise, he would undoubtedly recover for his labor.[1] The case of Farmington Academy *v.* Allen,[2] differs from the case we have just cited, only in the circumstance that the defendant, who subscribed for the establishment of an academy, was not a trustee; but he was an inhabitant of the town, and knew of the erection of the building; and he, moreover, actually advanced some part of the materials, excusing himself from paying the whole subscription only on the ground of his inability at the time. This was held sufficient to justify the trustees in proceeding to incur expense on the faith of the defendant's subscription; and having so done, they have expended money for him, as the court said, on his *implied* request. The defendant was, therefore, held liable to the trustees for the remainder of his subscription, on the ground of money laid out by them for his use. But if the corporation had brought *assumpsit* on an *express promise.* for the money subscribed, it could not, in that mode of suing, have been recovered.[3] Where the members of an incorporated religious society subscribed a written agreement with the trustees of the society, by which they individually engaged to pay to the trustees the sums set opposite their respective names, for raising a salary for the minister; it was held, that this was a valid contract in law, and binding on the subscribers, and that it could not be dissolved but by mutual consent, nor cease to be obligatory until the minister ceased to render the service stipulated.[4]

§ 526. But it is plain, that, to render a subscription for stock a contract, a due consideration must appear; for *voluntary* agreements and promises, however reasonable the expectation from them of gifts and disbursements to public uses, are not to be enforced as contracts.[5] Sundry

---

[1] This case is not reported; we have given it as stated by Parker, C. J., in Farmington Academy *v.* Allen, 14 Mass. 175. See also, Watkins *v.* Eames, 9 Cush. 537; Barnes *v.* Perine, 2 Kern. 18.

[2] Ibid.

[3] Ibid. and Phillips Limerick Academy *v.* Davis, 11 Mass. 113.

[4] Religious Society *v.* Stone, 7 Johns. 112. It seems that if a number of subscribers promise to contribute money on the faith of the common engagement, for the accomplishment of an object of interest to all, and which cannot be accomplished save by their common performance, the mutual promises constitute a reciprocal obligation in law. Watkins *v.* Eames, 9 Cush. 537; Eastern P. R. Co. *v.* Vaughan, 20 Barb. 155.

[5] See *ante*, § 255.

persons having subscribed an agreement to pay certain sums, respectively, for the erection of an academy, and the legislature having afterwards incorporated certain trustees of such academy; and in the act of incorporation provided, that all the moneys subscribed should be received and held by said trustees in trust for the academy, it was held, that the corporation could not maintain assumpsit against a subscriber, for the money by him subscribed.[1]

§ 527. It seems that the criterion of the liability of a subscriber to stock in a corporation, is, whether any act has been done by which the corporation has been forced to receive the subscriber.[2] The case of Union Turnpike Company *v.* Jenkins[3] was an action of assumpsit brought by the president, directors, and the company, against the defendant, on two several subscriptions, for certain payments called for pursuant to the act of incorporation, by the said president and directors. The declaration contained three counts. The first set forth the act of incorporation, the formation of the company pursuant thereto, the subscription of the defendant, the call for certain payments of seven dollars on each share, and his refusal to pay, whereby he became liable. The two remaining counts were on the several subscriptions of the defendant, as on his promissory notes. The principal ground of the motion in arrest of judgment was the alleged want of a consideration to support the promise, without which, it was insisted, the action was not sustainable. No consideration was stated on the record, and no loss or gain to either party; and one of the judges observed, that, testing the conduct of the commissioners by the provisions of the act, none was to be found in the contract itself. The act required, that, to constitute a stockholder, he should subscribe an engagement in the words following: "We whose names are hereunto subscribed, do for ourselves and our legal representatives, promise to pay to the president, directors and company of the Union Turnpike Road, the sum of twenty-five dollars for every share of stock in the said company set opposite to our respective names, in such manner and proportion as shall be determined by the said president, directors, and company." It is also further required, that every subscriber should, at time of subscribing, *pay unto either of the commissioners the*

[1] Phillips Limerick Academy *v.* Davis, 11 Mass. 113.

[2] Essex Turnp. Co. *v.* Collins, 8 Mass. 299; Religious Society *v.* Stone, 7 Johns. 112; Selma *v.* Tennessee Railroad Co. 5 Ala. 787.

[3] Union Turnp. Co. *v.* Jenkins, 1 Caines, 381; and *ante*, § 517.

sum of ten dollars for each share so subscribed. It was observed by the court, that the subscription and payment were *both* essential to the consummation of the contract. The declaration stated the subscription merely, without averring any payment or demand of the ten dollars on each share; and it was in fact admitted on the argument, that they were neither demanded nor paid. The court were at a loss, under the circumstances, to see any consideration for the promise; and observed, that the legislature appear to have been apprised of the inconvenience that might arise from this source, and had provided for it in some measure, by the last clause in the statute, which gave power to the directors, "to call for and demand of and from the stockholders respectively, all such sums of money by them subscribed, or to be subscribed, at such times and in such proportions as they shall see fit, under pain of forfeiture of their shares, and of all previous payments made thereon." Lewis, C. J., in concluding his opinion in the case, observed, "Suppose the speculation had been an advantageous one, and before the first call of the president and directors, the stock had risen considerably in value, could not the directors with propriety have refused to consider Mr. Jenkins as a stockholder, on account of his not having made the payment required by the act on his subscribing? I think they could. No positive benefit, then, arising from the future emoluments of the company transactions, can be considered as a consideration for the promise; and if it could, none such is stated on the record. Notwithstanding the motion to amend, it was insisted the suit was maintainable on the second and third counts. I think not. For a promise to pay on a contingency, which may or may not happen, cannot be declared on as a note of hand. The instrument must be *payable at all events*."

§ 528. In the case of the Highland Turnpike Co. *v.* McKean, in New York,[1] which was an action brought by the corporation against a subscriber, to recover the amount of the shares subscribed by him, the ground urged by the defendant's counsel in support of the motion in arrest of judgment, was the want of an averment in the declaration, that the defendant, at the time of subscribing, paid the sum of five dollars on each share subscribed by him, as directed by the act of incorporation; and the court held (and citing as authority the above case of Jenkins *v.* Union Turnpike Company), that the averment was neces-

---

[1] Highland Turnp. Co. *v.* McKean, 11 Johns. 8, cited in Sagory *v.* Dubois, 3 Sandf. Ch. 494.

sary. Yet the court were of opinion that where an act incorporating a company required every subscriber to the stock to pay, at the time of subscribing, to one of the commissioners, five dollars, and one of the commissioners subscribed for a certain number of shares, this was equivalent to the payment of the five dollars on each share; as it would be a useless ceremony for him to pay himself the money required to be advanced on the subscription.[1]

§ 529. In the case of Hibernia Turnpike Company *v.* Henderson, in Pennsylvania,[2] the defendant signed a positive promise to pay fifty dollars "in such manner and proportions and at such times as shall be determined by the president and managers, in pursuance of said act of assembly." At the time of subscription, there were no president and managers in existence, and no body corporate; but when fifty persons, or more, should have subscribed two hundred shares of the stock, the commissioners were to certify the names of the subscribers, and the number of shares subscribed by each, to the governor, and thereupon the governor was authorized to erect the subscribers, and those who should afterwards subscribe, into a body corporate. It was held that the commissioners could not dispense with the *previous* payment of five dollars; and that if they permitted a subscription to be made without such payment, the contract was void, and the company could not, after their incorporation, recover the amount which ought to have been paid. The majority of the court assumed that it was the intent of the law, that no subscription should be received, without a previous payment of five dollars a share, and considered that a contract could not be enforced in a court of justice, which was made in violation of an act of the legislature.[3] But from the opinion of the majority of the court, Duncan J., dissented, and he considered that, in the cases in New York, in which the question had arisen in subscriptions for stock in corporations, the only objection was the want of consideration, and not an imputed fraud on the law. "It would ill comport," said he, "with the honor and dignity of the State, and it would be manifestly unjust, under such circumstances, that the title of the plaintiffs should be deemed invalid and their charter void, on the ground of a supposed illegality in the bare omission, or actual misconduct of the commissioners, in which the other subscri-

---

1 See also, Ryder *v.* Alton & Sang. R. R. Co. 13 Ill. 516.

2 Hibernia Turnp. Co. *v.* Henderson, 8 S. & R. 219.

3 See also, Ogle *v.* Somerset, &c. Turnp. Co. 13 S. & R. 256.

bers could not, by possibility, have either agency or control." With regard to want of consideration, the learned judge said, "If this defendant had obtained the receipt of the commissioners, and had given his note to the company for the money to be paid in advance, it could be recovered. Has he not done this? for the subscription includes this, and is a note for five dollars, payable on demand; and the company could have recovered, though no note had been given for it." It has been held, by the Supreme Court of Alabama, that where the charter of a corporation requires the payment of five per cent. on the amount subscribed, at the time of subscription, if the subscriber, instead of making the cash payment, gives his note therefor, participates in the organization of the company, becomes one of the directors, and pays his note, he cannot afterwards insist, as a defence to an action to recover an instalment, that he did not pay the five per cent. at the time of subscribing.[1]

§ 530. Though the Supreme Court held, in the above case of Union Turnpike Company *v.* Jenkins,[2] that the non-payment of the first instalment did not affect the validity of the subscription, yet the decision was reversed by the Court of Errors, and it has been questioned which was the better opinion.[3] By one of the sections incorporating the Vermont Central Railroad Company, certain persons were constituted commissioners for receiving subscriptions to the capital stock of the company; and it was enacted thus: "And every person, at the time of subscribing, shall pay to the commissioners five dollars on each share for which he may subscribe, and each subscriber shall be a member of said company;" and it was further enacted, that when one thousand shares should be subscribed for, the commissioners might issue a notice for the stockholders to meet and elect directors. An individual, after some other shares (but less than one thousand) had been subscribed for, subscribed for fifty shares, and instead of paying to the commissioners, in money, five dollars upon each share at the time of subscribing, he gave them his promissory note for that amount, being two hundred and fifty dollars, which was made payable to "The Commissioners of the Vermont Central Railroad Company," on demand, for value received. This note was received by the corporation from the commissioners, upon

---

1 Selma *v.* Tennessee Railroad Co. 5 Ala. 787. And see McRae *v.* Russel, 12 Ired. 224; Everhart *v.* W. Chester & Phil. R. R. Co. 28 Penn. State, 339.

2 *Ante*, § 527.

3 Vermont Central Railroad Co. *v.* Clayes, 21 Vt. 30.

its organization; and it was held, that the note was given upon sufficient consideration, and was a valid note in the hands of the corporation, upon which an action could be sustained; though it was claimed that the note was without consideration.[1] In a late case in New Hampshire, where an article in the by-laws of a corporation provided that "ten per cent. shall be payable upon subscription, or the subscription shall be void," the court held, that a subscription made without paying any thing was not void, but voidable only, at the election of the corporation.[2]

§ 531. Where a charter has been obtained by means of fictitious subscriptions for part of the stock, and a fraud has been committed on a *bonâ fide* subscriber, by which he has either sustained, or might sustain, injury, no action can be maintained against him by the corporation for the amount of his subscription; unless such subscriber has accepted the charter, and by his *own acts* has assisted in putting it in operation; in that case, he cannot avail himself of the fact that part of the stock was fictitious.[3] And if a stock company lets off a part of its subscribers, and returns them their money, other subscribers not consenting thereto are discharged from all liability growing out of their original subscriptions.[4] If a person is induced to subscribe for stock by means of representations which are not fulfilled, it has been held that he is not bound to take the stock.[5] But generally parol representations or agreements made at the time of subscribing for stock, and inconsistent with the written terms of subscription, are inadmissible and void, unless fraud is shown.[6] And it has been held that a contract of subscription must be in writing, and cannot be established by parol evidence.[7]

---

1 Vermont Central Railroad Co. *v.* Clayes, 21 Vt. 30.

2 Piscataqua Ferry Co. *v.* Jones, 39 N. H. 491. See also, Smith *v.* Plank Road Co. 30 Ala. 650. But see Erie & Wat. P. R. Co. *v.* Brown, 25 Penn. State, 156, 160; Mitchell *v.* Rome R. R. Co. 17 Ga. 574; Wight *v.* Shelby R. R. Co. 16 B. Mon. 4.

3 Centre & Kish Turnp. Co. *v.* McConaby, 16 S. & R. 142; see Thorp *v.* Hughes, 3 Mylne & C. 742; Crump *v.* U. S. Mining Co. 7 Gratt. 352; Brockwell's case, 29 Law Times, 375; Southern P. R. Co. *v.* Hixon, 5 Ind. 166. But when he discovers the fraud, he ought to renounce the shares and all benefit to be derived under them, else he will still be held as a shareholder. Deposit & Gen. Life Ass. Co. *v.* Ayscough, 6 Ellis & B. 761.

4 McCully *v.* Pittsburgh & C. R. Co. 32 Penn. State, 25; County of Crawford *v.* Pittsburgh & Erie R. Co. 32 Penn. State, 141. But see Dorman *v.* Jacksonville, &c. Plank Road Co. 7 Fla. 265.

5 Rives *v.* Plank Road Co. 30 Ala. 92. See Smith *v.* Plank Road Co. 30 Ala. 650; Hester *v.* Memphis & Ch. R. Co. 32 Missis. 378; Keller *v.* Johnson, 11 Ind. 337; East Tenn. &c. R. Co. *v.* Gammon, 5 Sneed, 567.

6 Smith *v.* Plank Road Co. 30 Ala. 650, 667; Johnson *v.* Crawfordsville R. Co. 11 Ind. 280; Piscataqua Ferry Co. *v.* Jones, 39 N. H. 491. See also, cases cited *post*, § 540, note.

7 Pittsburgh, &c. R. Co. *v.* Gazzam, 32 Penn. State, 340.

§ 532. The meaning of the word "subscriber," under an act of incorporation, received attention in the English Court of King's Bench, in the case of the Thames Tunnel Company. The act provided, that the persons who had subscribed, or who should thereafter subscribe or advance money towards making the tunnel, should pay the money by them subscribed, at the time and place, and in the manner directed by the company; and in case any such subscribers should neglect, the company are empowered to sue for and recover the money. By sec. 91, reciting that the probable expenses would amount to £160,000, and that more than four-fifths part had already been subscribed, by several persons, binding them and their heirs, &c. for payment of the sums so subscribed by them, it was enacted, that the whole £160,000 should be subscribed in the like manner, before the act should be put in force. The word "subscribers," in the act, was held to mean only those who had stipulated to pay, and not those who had paid money; and, therefore, a person whose name was inserted in the act, and who paid a deposit on shares, *but who had not signed the contract*, was not a subscriber within the act, nor liable to be sued by the company.[1] But it will not be necessary to show the execution of any contract, if, from the conduct of the party sued, he shall be estopped from questioning the validity of the act.[2]

§ 533. Where, by the act of incorporation, shares are to be forfeited in case of non-payment of instalments, and no suit can be resorted to for their recovery, and the shares become of no value, an *adminitsrator* is not at liberty to take money from the assets of the estates of a deceased member to pay instalments; though, where the shares are valuable, it may be his duty to pay them, and redeem the shares for the benefit of the estate.[3] The question, whether an administrator of a subscriber to a projected canal corporation, deceased before the act of incorporation passed, could be sued as a subscriber to the undertaking, or proprietor of the shares, was one which arose under the words of the act of incorporation. The act indemnified executors and administrators against their *cestui que trust*, if they should pay calls upon the shares of deceased persons out of their effects, and enabled the company, if the executors had not assets, or refused to pay, to transfer the shares to others, who

---

[1] Thames Tunnel Co. *v.* Shelden, 6 B. & C. 341.

[2] Crawford & Highpeak Railway Co. *v.* Lacey, 3 Younge & J. 80.

[3] Ripley *v.* Sampson, 10 Pick. 373.

would repay to the administrators the calls paid on the shares, and pay the future calls. The act also provided, that if no persons would take the shares, the shares might be declared forfeited to the company. The court seemed to have held, that no action could be maintained against an administrator, though he has paid one call, for not paying subsequent calls.[1]

§ 534. When an original subscriber to the stock of an incorporated company, who is bound to pay the instalments on his subscription, from time to time as they are called in by the company, *transfers* his stock to another person, such other person is substituted not only to the rights, but to the obligations of the original subscriber; and *he* is bound to pay up the instalments called for after the transfer to him. The liability to pay up instalments is shifted from the outgoing to the incoming shareholder. A privity is created between the two, by the assignment of the one and the acceptance of the other; and also between them and the corporation, for it would be absurd to say, upon general reasoning, that if the original subscribers have the power of assigning their shares, they should, after disposing of them, be liable to the burdens which are thrown upon the owners of the stock.[2] Where a subscriber to the capi-

---

[1] Weald of Kent Canal Co. *v.* Robinson, 5 Taunt. 801.

[2] Huddersfield Canal Co. *v.* Buckley, 7 T. R. 36; Aylesbury Railway Co. *v.* Mount, 5 Scott, N. R. 127; West Philadelphia Canal Co. *v.* Innes, 3 Whart. 198; Mann *v.* Currie, 2 Barb. 294; Cowles *v.* Cromwell, 25 Barb. 413; Hall *v.* United States Ins. Co. 5 Gill, 484; Bend *v.* Susquehannah Bridge Co. 6 Harris & J. 123; Mann *v.* Pentz, 2 Sandf. Ch. 258; Hartford & New Haven Railroad Co. *v.* Boorman, 12 Conn. 539. Acts of parliament, in England, establishing joint-stock companies as corporations, generally give not only a power to declare shares forfeited where calls are not paid, but also to bring an action for the amount of the calls. The latter course of procedure can, however, only be taken whilst the party remains a shareholder; and if he assigns the shares before the call is made, he is not liable to be sued for it. Woodsworth on Joint-stock Companies, 321. "It would be ridiculous," says Lord Kenyon, Ch. J., "to determine that a person, after he has sold his shares, in respect to which only he became a proprietor, should still continue to be a proprietor." Huddersfield Canal Co. *ubi sup.* But a subscriber for stock cannot subrogate another person to his obligation without a substitution of his name on the books of the company or some other equivalent act, required by charter or by-laws. Ryder *v.* Alton & Sang. R. R. Co. 13 Ill. 516. The registry book of shareholders is *primâ facie* evidence against those whose names appear upon it. Mann *v.* Cooke, 20 Conn. 178. Nor can a shareholder divest himself from his liability by paying the directors a sum of money for his discharge, even though the shares be transferred in consequence. *Ex parte* Bennett, 18 Beav. 339, 5 De G., M. & G. 284, 27 Eng. L. & Eq. 572. Nor by transferring his stock, it would seem, if it is done for the purpose of escaping liability upon it, and without the assent of the company. Everhart *v.* Chester & Phil. R. R. Co. 28 Penn. State, 339; Graff *v.* Pittsburgh & Steubenville R. Co. 31 Penn. State, 489.

tal stock of a banking company transfers to a purchaser the shares allotted to him, without having paid the amount of his subscription, and the purchaser thereupon executes a bond and mortgage to the company to secure the payment of the nominal amount or par value of the shares, and the company accepts the same in satisfaction of the subscription, the transaction is a *novation* — the substitution of one debt for another.[1]

§ 535. But a solvent stockholder, who has given a *stock note* to the corporation for the purchase-money of his stock, cannot, upon the insolvency of the company, or in contemplation of that event, even with the consent of the directors, transfer his stock to an irresponsible person, and be discharged from his liability upon substituting the note of such person for his own. Such an arrangement has the effect of a withdrawal of so much of the capital of the corporation. Those who have paid for their stock have a right to insist that the receiver, who has been appointed to close up the affairs of the corporation, shall collect the stock notes, or so much thereof as is necessary to equalize the losses among all the stockholders ratably. A note given to a corporation for stock, is valid in the hands of an indorsee without notice, though a statute forbids the receiving of a note in payment of any instalment actually called in and required to be paid, if it be shown, affirmatively, that the note was given for stock called in.[2]

§ 536. We next proceed to treat of how, and under what circumstances, both a subscriber and the assignee of stock of an incorporated company will be absolved from the liability to pay instalments of which we have been treating. It is presumed to be very well known, that in the case of private unincorporated associations, where the articles of partnership entered into and subscribed by the members, are regarded as the fundamental law of the society, no powers not consistent with such fundamental law can be exercised by the society over those who have become partners without their agreement or consent.[3] "It is not, I apprehend," says Lord Eldon, "competent to any number of persons in a partnership (unless they show a contract rendering it competent to them) formed for *specified purposes*, if they propose to form a partner-

---

[1] Palmer *v.* Lawrence, 3 Sandf. 151. "Novation," a term from the civil law.

[2] Nathan *v.* Whitlock, 9 Paige, 152. The decision in this case, the reporter says, was affirmed on appeal to the Court of Errors, in December, 1842.

[3] See Livingston *v.* Lynch, 4 Johns. Ch. 673.

ship *for very different purposes*, to effect that formation by calling upon some of the partners to receive the subscribed capital and interest and quit the concern." "And again," says he, "those who seek to embark a partner in a business not originally part of the partnership concern, *must make out clearly* that he did expressly or tacitly acquiesce.[1]

§ 537. Such, precisely, is the law with regard to partnership associations which are *incorporated*, and no point of law is more clearly and firmly settled, than that if a corporation procure an alteration to be made in its charter, by which a new and different business is superadded to that originally contemplated, such of the stockholders as do not assent to the alteration, will be absolved from liability on their subscriptions to the capital stock; and *a fortiori*, if the alteration be one plainly prejudicial to their interests.[2] Nothing is plainer than that an alteration of a charter by the legislature may be so extensive and radical as to work an entire dissolution of the contract entered into by a subscriber to the stock, as by procuring an amendment of the charter, by which is superadded to the original undertaking an entirely new enterprise. The correct doctrine upon this subject is very clearly stated by Mr. Justice Woodbury, in giving the judgment of the Supreme Court of New Hampshire,[3] in a case in which the matter in dispute was between an incorporated company and one of its members. "A recurrence," says he, "to the nature of the liabilities of members to their own corporation will, we apprehend, divest the case of many of its difficulties. Every individual owner of shares, whether a petitioner, or associate, or purchaser, expects, and indeed stipulates with the other owners, as a corporate body, to pay them his proportion of the expense which a majority may please to incur *in the promotion of the particular objects of the corporation*. By acquiring an interest in the corporation, therefore, he enters into an obligation with it in the nature of a special contract, the terms of which contract are limited by the specific provisions, rights, and liabilities detailed in the act of incorporation. To make a valid change in this private contract, as in any other, the assent of both parties is indispensable. The corporation, on one part, can assent by a vote of the majority; the individual, on the other part, by his

---

1 Natusch *v.* Irving, App'x to Gow on Partn. 576 (Am. ed. 1830).

2 So laid down by Nelson, C. J., in New Haven & Hartford Railroad Company *v.* Croswell, 5 Hill, 383.

3 Union Locks & Canal Co. *v.* Towne, 1 N. H. 44.

own personal act. However the corporation, then, may be bound by the assent to the additional acts, this defendant, in his individual capacity, having never assented to either of them, is under no obligation to the plaintiffs, except what he incurred by becoming a member under the first act. Consequently, the assessment sued for, *if raised to advance objects essentially different, or the same objects in methods essentially different from those originally contemplated, are not made in conformity to the defendant's special contract with the corporation.*" [1]

§ 538. Where the directors of a turnpike corporation, with the assent of the corporation, procured an act of the legislature altering the course of the turnpike road, an individual, who, before such alteration, had subscribed for a share, and had expressly promised to pay all assessments, was held not to be answerable in an action for the assessments. The court, in giving judgment, said: "The plaintiffs rely on an express contract, and they are bound to prove it as they allege it. Here, the proof is of an engagement to pay assessments for making a turnpike in a certain specified direction, and of the making a turnpike in a different direction. The defendant may truly say, *Non hæc in fœdera veni.* He was not bound by the application of the directors to the legislature for the alteration of the course of the road, nor by the consent of the corporation thereto. *Much fraud might be put in practice under a contrary decision.*" [2]

§ 539. Where an individual had contracted to take a share in a cor-

---

[1] The learned judge approved of the decisions in the cases in Massachusetts, of Middlesex Turnp. Co. *v.* Locke, 8 Mass. 268, and the Same *v.* Swan, 10 Mass. 384; Hamilton & Deanville Plankroad Co. *v.* Rice, 7 Barb. 157; Commonwealth *v.* Claghorne, 13 Penn. 133; Sumner *v.* Marcy, 3 Wooodb. & M. 105; Charlotte & South Carolina Railroad Co. *v.* Blakely, 3 Strob. 245; Hodgson *v.* Earl of Powis, 1 De G., M. & G. 6, 8 Eng. L. & Eq. 257; Kean *v.* Johnson, 1 Stock. 401; New Orleans, Jackson, & Gr. N. R. R. Co. *v.* Harris, 27 Missis. 517; Hamilton Mut. Ins. Co. *v.* Hobart, 2 Gray, 543; *Ex parte* Johnson, Ch. 1855, 31 Eng. L. & Eq. 430.

[2] Middlesex Turnp. Corp. *v.* Locke, 8 Mass. 268, and see also, Same *v.* Swan, 10 Mass. 385. Carlisle *v.* T. H. & Richm. Railroad Co. 6 Ind. 316; Winter *v.* Muscogee Railroad Co. 11 Ga. 438; Macedon & Bristol Pl. R. Co. *v.* Lapham, 18 Barb. 312; Buff. Corn. & N. York Railroad Co. *v.* Pottle, 23 Barb. 21. But where the charter provides for modifications, the subscribers are bound by all such as come fairly within the power. Cork & Youghal Railroad Co *v.* Paterson, 18 C. B. 414, 37 Eng. L. & Eq. 398; and so they remain bound if the legislature after incorporation alter the charter, they having power so to do by the general laws of the State as to all corporations. South Bay M. D. Co. *v.* Gray, 30 Me. 547. See *ante*, § 391, *et seq.*

poration created for the purpose of making a river navigable, and which was empowered to hold real estate, not to exceed *six* acres, and to collect a toll, for forty years, not exceeding twelve per cent. on the amount of money expended, and afterwards the legislature, upon the petition of the corporation, *but without the consent of the individual member*, authorized them to hold real estate to the amount of *one hundred* acres, and to collect toll, unlimited as to its amount and duration, it was held, that the individual was discharged from his contract, and not liable to any subsequent assessments on the share.[1] In a late case, a subscription was made to a certain institution "for the purpose of building a medical college for said institution," the last instalment to be paid "when the building shall be completed, the building to be such an one as is referred to in the plan and specification to be made by E. B." After the payment of all the instalments but the last, and after the building had been occupied for three years as a medical college, it was conveyed, not being completed, to an institution for the education of females, who completed it according to the plan and specification, but occupied it for their own use. It was held that an action would not lie for the last instalment.[2] So the change of one of the termini of a plank road, by authority of the legislature, releases previous subscribers.[3]

§ 540. But, as in all legal questions, there have been some cases which exemplify the difficulty attending the question as to what will amount to a radical deviation from the original act of incorporation. The defence pleaded in an action for calls by a turnpike company, was, amongst other things, that there had been a deviation from the original line, and that the money called for was in respect of such deviation. The court said, the effect of allowing such an answer as this would be, that if there is any deviation to the extent of two or three yards, with the consent of the person whose land immediately adjoins, and at the wish of the

---

[1] Union Locks & Canal Co. *v.* Towne, 1 N. H. 44. See Supervisors &c. *v.* Miss. & W. R. Co. 21 Ill. 338. But a misstatement of the length of a railroad, in the articles of association, if there be no fraud, or the lease or sale of the franchises of the corporation to another company, which is void, or the neglect to make the whole road, will not exonerate a subscriber from paying calls. Troy & Rutland Railroad Co. *v.* Kerr, 17 Barb. 581. See also Del. & Atl. Railroad Co. *v.* Irick, 3 N. J. 321; Everhardt *v.* W. Chest. & Phil. Railroad Co. 28 Penn. State, 339; Banet *v.* All. & Sang. Railroad Co. 13 Ill. 504; Danbury & Norw. Railroad Co. *v.* Wilson, 22 Conn. 435.

[2] Worcester Med. Inst. *v.* Bigelow, 6 Gray, 498.

[3] Manheim, &c. Plank Road Co. *v.* Arndt, 31 Penn. State, 317.

directors and the company generally, every individual subscriber, from the moment that deviation is made, may stay his hand, and refuse his call, and the whole concern be broken up altogether; and, accordingly, the plea was disallowed.[1] And it has been held, that a change in a railroad charter allowing the company to purchase stock in another connecting road, whereby to control it and virtually extend their road twenty-five miles, does not release a subscriber.[2]

To an action on a subscription for the purpose of building a hotel, it was held to be no defence, that a large and valuable portion of the building erected, was constructed and occupied for shops.[3] In Pennsylvania it has been held, that a subscription to railroad stock, under the act of 1849, made to the commissioners before the organization of the company, is absolute, notwithstanding a condition, that a certain route should be followed, is contained in it, but not complied with, on the ground that the commissioners had no power to take a conditional subscription, and the condition was void as a fraud upon the commonwealth and the other subscribers.[4]

§ 541. A benefit which results to the property of a subscriber to stock in a turnpike company, does not, it has been held, in contemplation of law, enter into the contract of subscription; and hence the subscriber was bound, notwithstanding there was some change in the location of the road; though the court were not unanimous in this decision.[5] Additional privileges granted to a corporation, in aid of carrying out the avowed object of the act of incorporation, and of the petitioners for it, is clearly no violation of the contract between the corporation and a subscriber to the stock.[6] But, in these cases, the great

---

[1] London & Brighton Railway Co. *v.* Wilson, 6 Bing. N. R. 135, 8 Dowl. 40; Piscataqua Ferry Co. *v.* Jones, 39 N. H. 491; Rice *v.* Rock Island & Alton R. Co. 21 Ill. 93. But see *contra*, Stevens *v.* Rutland, &c. R. Co. 29 Vt. 545. The subscription of stock, like other contracts, ought to receive such a construction as to carry into effect the probable intention of the parties. McMillan *v.* Maysv. & Lex. Railroad Co. 15 B. Mon. 218. But parol evidence is not admissible to show what that intention was, if it varies the written terms of the subscription. N. Car. Railroad Co. *v.* Leach, 4 Jones, N. C. 340; Madison & Ind. Railroad Co. *v.* Stevens, 6 Ind. 379; Wight *v.* Shelby Railroad Co. 16 B. Mon. 4.

[2] Terre Haute & Alton R. Co. *v.* Earp, 21 Ill. 291.

[3] City Hotel *v.* Dickinson, 6 Gray, 586.

[4] Pittsburg, &c. R. Co. *v.* Biggar, 34 Penn. State, 455.

[5] Irvin *v.* Turnp. Co. 2 Penn. 466.

[6] Gray *v.* Monongahela Nav. Co. 2 Watts & S. 156; Poughkeepsie & S. P. Pl. R. Co. *v.* Griffin, 21 Barb. 454; Peor. & Oquawka Railroad Co. *v.* Elting, 17 Ill. 429.

general principle is recognized, that an essential alteration by the legislature works a dissolution of the contract; while it is admitted that a modification and regulation of the application of the principle, so as to admit of improvements in the charter, useful to the public, and beneficial to the company, and in accordance with what was the understanding of the subscribers to stock, as to the real object to be effected, is without this consequence. If a person subscribes for the purpose of building a railroad between two given points, and this project is abandoned, the person is not liable to another company who are authorized by an act of the legislature to enforce such subscription for another purpose; such act not being in the power of the legislature to grant.[1]

§ 542. Where the amount of subscription for stock for a particular object is deemed inadequate to the purposes of it, a delay in action, in organizing the corporation, and in applying the funds to the object of the charter, may be so long continued that such of the subscribers as, on the faith of abandonment of the project, had so changed their circumstances as to be no longer interested therein, will not be liable upon their subscription.[2] It is true, it has been made a point, whether a canal company, after the lapse of considerable time, without completing the object for which the act of incorporation was granted (and no precise time limited by the act), could then claim the easement of the right of passage over land to which the act entitled them; and it was held that no limitation as to time could be assigned to the powers conferred in this respect, by an intendment that they were to be exercised in a *reasonable* time; and, consequently, that the works might be resumed at any period.[3] But this is evidently different from the case of a contract between a subscriber to the stock of a corporation and the corporation, it being implied that the object contemplated in the proposed corporate organization should be entered upon without unreasonable delay, and the presumption being that the subscriber so understood it; indeed he certainly could not suppose that he was to be bound for an unlimited period of delay in the action contemplated. In late cases in Pennsylvania it is held, that if no call is made for subscriptions to stock in a

---

1 Pittsburg, &c. R. Co. *v.* Gazzam, 32 Penn. State, 340.

2 Fountain Ferry Co. *v.* Jewell, 8 B. Mon. 142. But subscribers for stock in a Railroad Corporation will not be released by the suspension of the work. Funds may be necessary to pay debts incurred. McMillan *v.* Maysv. & Lex. Railroad Co. 15 B. Mon. 218.

3 Hicknesse *v.* Lancaster Canal Co. 4 M. & W. 471.

railroad company, until more than six years from the time of subscription, the law will presume that the company meant to abandon the enterprise, and will not enforce the subscription.[1] And if the undertaking for which the company is incorporated is not commenced *boná fide* within the period prescribed by the charter, no action can be maintained for the subscription.[2] If, however, the delay is assented to by the subscriber as a matter of corporate policy, he will be estopped from setting this up as a defence.[3] But after he has been released by the neglect of the company, he is not again rendered liable by giving an incomplete letter of attorney, to vote on a question of accepting a supplement to the charter, and subscription that might be tendered for stock.[4]

§ 543. In the case of Salem Mill Dam Corporation *v.* Ropes,[5] it appeared that, in the act creating the corporation, it was provided that the capital stock should be divided into five thousand shares, not exceeding $100 each, and that after one thousand shares should be subscribed for, a meeting of the proprietors might be called, at which any acts might be done for the purpose of organizing the corporation, and arranging its affairs. It was held, that no call could be made for the general objects of the act of incorporation until *all* the shares should have been subscribed for; but that a call to defray preliminary expenses incurred in obtaining the act of incorporation, and in ascertaining the utility of the enterprise, would be valid. In a subsequent case between the same parties,[6] the like position was reaffirmed by the court, and also in the case of Central Turnpike Company *v.* Valentine.[7] A statute in England, establishing a joint-stock corporation, provided that "the whole of said sum of £100,000, shall be subscribed before any of the powers and provisions given by this act shall be put in force; and it was held that the completion of the subscription list was necessary to enable the company to make a call upon the shares.[8] An act of incorporation, in

---

1 Pittsburgh, &c. R. Co. *v.* Byers, 32 Penn. State, 22; McCully *v.* Pittsburgh, &c. R. Co. id. 25.

2 McCully *v.* Pittsburgh, &c. R. Co. 32 Penn. State, 25.

3 Ibid.

4 Ibid.

5 Salem Mill Dam Corp. *v.* Ropes, 6 Pick. 23.

6 9 Pick. 187.

7 Central Turnp. Co. *v.* Valentine, 10 Pick. 142; Worcester & Nashua Railroad Co. *v.* Hinds, 8 Cush. 110; Atlantic De Laine Co. *v.* Mason, 5 R. I. 463; Somerset, &c. R. Co. *v.* Cushing, 45 Me. 524.

8 Norwich & Lowestoft Co. *v.* Theobald, 1 Moody & M. 151.

New Hampshire, provided that the members of the body incorporated might divide the capital stock into as many shares as they might think proper ; and, by a written agreement, the subscribers fixed the capital stock at fifty thousand dollars, divided into five hundred shares of one hundred dollars each; but only one hundred and thirty-eight shares were subscribed for; and it was held that no call for the general purposes of the corporation could legally be made until all the shares were taken. It did not appear in this case, that the calls were laid for the purpose of defraying the preliminary expenses of the corporation, in which case they might (according to the above case of the Salem Mill Dam Corporation) have been recovered by virtue of the promise contained in the written agreement; nothing was said about preliminary expenses, and it appeared that the company went into operation, and built a factory, and called on the defendant to pay his calls. The calls, it was held, were not "duly made," agreeably to the charter, because the stock was not all subscribed.[1] But if a corporation is organized in good faith, their proceedings will not be invalid, though part of the subscribers are not responsible persons, and therefore the amount of stock required by the charter is not really taken.[2] And the validity of an assessment does not depend upon the use afterwards made of the money.[3] In a late case in Pennsylvania, a commissioner appointed to receive subscriptions for railroad stock, subscribed for shares in his own name. He then united with other commissioners in making a return to the governor, which stated that the subscriptions were in all respects made and taken in good faith and agreeably to the provisions and requirements of the laws of the State, and that he had subscribed for twenty shares. On the strength of this return the charter was granted. It was held that, in an action for assessments upon the subscription, he was estopped from showing that it was made upon a condition which had not been complied with. It was also decided, that proof of an authorized fourth call was proof that the third call was authorized.[4]

§ 544. In the case of turnpike, canal, bridge, and other incorporated

---

1 Littleton Man. Co. *v.* Parker, 14 N. H. 543; Cont. Valley R. R. *v.* Barker, 32 N. H. 363; Oldtown & Linc. R. R. Co. *v.* Veazie, 39 Me. 571; N. H. Central R. R. *v.* Johnson, 10 Foster, 390; Stoneham Branch R. R. Co. *v.* Gould, 2 Gray, 277.

2 Penobscot R. Co. *v.* White, 41 Me. 512.

3 Same case.

4 Bavington *v.* Pittsburg, &c. R. Co. 34 Penn. State, 358.

companies, it will sometimes happen that the amount originally subscribed and the amount of tolls received, are not sufficient fully to complete the work; in such a case the directors, if authorized so to do, sometimes issue new shares, giving the old stockholders the preference; and it is no defence to an action on a note given by a stockholder for a part of the new stock, that all the shares contemplated to be issued were not sold, nor can he recover back money paid for said shares.[1] Or instead of issuing new shares, the old are sometimes assessed; and the power of the corporation in such case to *assess* the shares, depends upon the extent of the subscriber's engagement. The value of shares in such corporations will always depend on the expenses of making the turnpike, &c., compared with the expected profits from the toll; and although, when the act of incorporation has been obtained, the presumption is that the toll will be an indemnity, yet as this presumption may fail, it may be very reasonable for the corporation not to trust to a sale of the shares for a reimbursement of the expenses; but before any expense be incurred, to require an express undertaking from the corporation that they will pay the several assessments on their shares. Where such an express agreement has been made, it may be enforced by action, there being a legal consideration for the contract. Very clearly, a corporation has not power *as incident to it, to assess* for its own use a sum of money on the corporators, and compel them by action at law to the payment of it. The power must be derived from an express promise, or from statute;[2] as where the owner of a pew was sued by a religious corporation *in personam*, to recover an assessment, he was held not liable upon any implied promise to pay it, in consequence of the occupation of the pew.[3] The extent of liability to pay future assessment, of course, is measured by the extent of the engagement. The engagement may be only to pay assessments upon the shares originally subscribed; or it may be to pay upon all shares he may at any period own. It may be to pay assessments on all shares then owned, so long as the promisor belongs to the corporation; or it may be to pay upon those shares when he shall have ceased to be a member.[4]

---

[1] Nutter *v.* Lexington & West Cambridge R. Co. 6 Gray, 85.

[2] Tippetts *v.* Walker, 4 Mass. 595; Worcester Turnp. Co. *v.* Willard, 5 id. 80; Andover & Medford Turnp. Corp. *v.* Gould, 6 id. 40; Knowles *v.* Beatty, 1 McLean, 41; Small *v.* Herkimer Man. Co. 2 Comst. 330; Littleton Manuf. Co. *v.* Parker, 14 N. H. 543; Atlantic De Laine Co. *v.* Mason, 5 R. I. 463; Odd Fellows Hall Co. *v.* Glazier, 5 Harring. Del. 172; Palmer *v.* Ridge Mining Co. 34 Penn. State, 288.

[3] First Presbyterian Congregation *v.* Quackenbush, 10 Johns. 217.

[4] Franklin Glass Co. *v.* Alexander, 2 N. H. 380; Mayor, &c. *v.* McKee, 2 Yerg. 167;

§ 545. In an action by the New Bedford and Bridgewater Turnpike Corporation *v.* Adams,[1] the plaintiffs claimed to recover the amount of certain assessments for the expenses incurred in making the turnpike. The writing by which it was contended the defendant was liable, was one which was subscribed by him and others, and was as follows: "We, the subscribers, desirous to promote the building of a turnpike and bridges from New Bedford to Weymouth, comprehended in a petition signed by W. Roach, Jr., and others, granted by the honorable legislature in their present session, have divided the expense of building said turnpike and bridges from Thompson's Pond, in Middleborough, to communicate with the Braintree and Weymouth Turnpike, in the town of Weymouth, into five hundred shares, and engage to take the number of shares affixed to our names." The court considered that the defendant, by signing this agreement, simply engaged to become the proprietor of a certain number of shares, and that the only remedy which the corporation had for non-payment of assessments, was to sell the shares.

§ 546. The case of Franklin Glass Co. *v.* White,[2] is a still stronger case against the right of incorporated companies to recover from the stockholders the amount assessed upon their shares, when the act of incorporation authorizes a sale of the shares in case of a neglect to pay the assessment. In this case, the defendant became owner of one share of the capital stock, by purchase. The company, at three several times, made assessments upon the shares, and at each time *the defendant was present* at the meetings, and acted as a stockholder; and often before *expressed his desire* to have money assessed, to pay the debts of the company; and he, moreover, afterwards expressed *his satisfaction* with what had been done. It was held, notwithstanding, that the sale of the shares, pursuant to the act, was the only remedy of the company. The counsel for the plaintiff contended that there was a distinction between this case and a *turnpike* company; that the making and maintaining a turnpike

---

Portland, &c. Railroad Co. *v.* Graham, 13 Met. 311; Kennebec & Portland Railroad Co. *v.* Kendall, 31 Maine, 470. An agreement to *pay and fill* shares in a R. R. Co. has been held an agreement to pay all assessments legally made. Buckf. Br. R. R. Co. *v.* Irish, 39 Me. 44; Penobscot & Kenn. R. R. Co. *v.* Dunn, id. 587; Penobscot R. R. Co. *v.* Dummer, 40 id. 172.

[1] 8 Mass. 138.

[2] 14 Mass. 286. See also, Fort Edw. & Fort Miller Pl. R. Co. *v.* Payne, 17 Barb. 567, 574, and cases there cited.

road was an affair of public concern and convenience, seldom entered upon or prosecuted for the sake of the profit the undertakers would realize; and that they could not lawfully effect their object without authority from the legislature; whereas a company of *manufacturers* could not be presumed to have any object in view but their private or personal gain; they might carry on their business without legislative interference; and they asked for an incorporation merely for greater convenience in managing their affairs. The court were not able, however, to perceive a sufficient distinction between the case before them and the cases above mentioned, to justify them in giving a different decision; as the legislative provisions relative to manufacturing corporations, for the sale of the shares of those proprietors who are delinquent in paying their assessments, were nearly in the same words as those used in the general act respecting turnpike corporations. In a case where one expressly engaged to take certain shares in a turnpike road, and to pay all assessments thereon, and afterwards the course of the road was altered by law; it was held that he was not bound by his engagement to pay the assessments, notwithstanding he had acted in several offices of the corporation, and had, as one of the directors thereof, petitioned the legislature for such alteration.[1]

§ 547. Under an act of the legislature of Massachusetts, the power to lay assessments is vested exclusively in the corporation, and cannot be delegated to the directors. Where the powers and privileges of the Norfolk Manufacturing Company were by virtue of its charter made subject to the provisions of the act above mentioned, and a by-law was passed authorizing the directors "to take care of the interests and manage the concerns of the corporation;" it was held, that the corporation had no power to delegate an authority to the directors to lay assessments, and that the by-law did not, in fact, import an intention to delegate it. The corporation in question having made a dividend, and, before payment thereof, laid an assessment of the exact amount of such dividend, payable on the same day, the corporation, it was held, was not entitled to take the dividend of any stockholder, without an order from him, in payment of, or as a set-off to, the assessment.[2]

---

[1] Middlesex Turnpike Corporation *v.* Swan, 10 Mass. 384; and see Middlesex Turnp. Corp. *v.* Locke, 8 Mass. 268; Union Locks and Canals *v.* Towne, 1 N. H. 44.

[2] Winsor, *ex parte*, 3 Story, 411.

§ 547 *a*. In New Hampshire it has been held that, where the charter of a company provides that all assessments shall be determined by the directors, and lays down the rules by which the amount to be raised, and the manner in which it is to be apportioned, are fixed, all that is necessary is, that the directors determine by vote that an assessment be made, and such vote is a sufficient requirement of payment agreeably to their charter and by-laws.[1]

§ 548. In the case of Worcester Turnpike Corporation *v*. Willard,[2] the court decided that the defendant, having subscribed a contract by which he engaged to take one share, and *to pay all legal assessments*, it was a personal engagement to pay assessments, which gave to the corporation a cumulative remedy against Willard, in addition to the remedy provided by the statute, to enforce the payment of assessments by a sale of shares. In the case of Taunton and South Boston Turnpike Company *v*. Whiting,[3] the case was where one subscribed an engagement to pay on demand to J. G., or order, "*all assessments that may at any time be made by said corporation*, for the purpose of laying out said road, making and keeping the same in repair, and for damages to individuals for land," &c. It was holden, agreeably to the above case of Worcester Turnpike Corporation *v*. Willard, that the defendant having expressly promised to pay all assessments, he was liable in an action of assumpsit brought by the corporation for the assessments. Where one subscribed for certain shares in a turnpike, and promised to pay A. B., agent of the proprietors, all assessments, &c., it was held, that though the agent could maintain no action for the unpaid assessments, yet that the promise would support an action by the proprietors in their corporate capacity.[4]

§ 549. It is well settled that a power conferred by the legislature on a corporation, to sell the stock for default of payment of an instalment by a subscriber, does not exclude the common-law remedy to recover it, and he is still liable on an action of assumpsit. The penalty of forfeiture is cumulative, so that the company may waive it and proceed *in personam* on the promise.[5]

---

1 Atlantic F. Ins. Co. *v*. Sanders, 36 N. H. 252.

2 5 Mass. 80.

3 10 Mass. 327.

4 Gilmore *v*. Pope, 5 Mass. 491, per Parsons, C. J. See also, N. E. R. R. Co. *v*. Rodrigues, 10 Rich. 278.

5 London Grand Junction Railway Co. *v*. Graham, 1 A. & E. 270; Bristol & Thames

§ 550. When it is said that remedies by action or forfeiture are *cumulative*, nothing more is to be understood, than that the company has a right to sue, or the right to forfeit, at their election; or that they may proceed to judgment upon the subscription, and then forfeit the stock for the same delinquency. But the converse of the proposition, that they may exercise the right of forfeiture, and *then* maintain or enforce a judgment, is not maintainable. A forfeiture is more than a means of satisfaction, and is of itself a satisfaction. It has, therefore, been held that after a corporation, pursuant to a provision in its charter, has forfeited the stock of a subscriber, for non-payment of an instalment due upon his subscription, it cannot maintain an action to recover any part of such subscription. And where an action had been commenced to recover certain instalments of the subscription, which had been duly called for, and then a further call was made, and the stock forfeited for non-payment thereof, it was held that the subscriber might plead such forfeiture in bar of the further maintenance of the suit.[1] In Giles *v.* Hutt,[2] the language was in the disjunctive; namely, that the company might sue *or* declare a forfeiture of the shares; and it was held that the remedy being in the alternative, the company could not adopt one, and then resort to another.[3]

Railway Co. *v.* Locke, id. 25; Goshen Turnp. Co. *v.* Hurtin, 9 Johns. 217; Herkimer Man. Co. *v.* Small, 2 Wend. 273, 2 Comst. 330; Harlaem Canal Co. *v.* Seixas, 2 Hall, 504; Spear *v.* Crawford, 14 Wend. 20; Sagory *v.* Dubois, 3 Sandf. Ch. 466; Delaware & Schuylkill Canal Co. *v.* Sansom, 1 Binn. 70; Tar River Navigation Co. *v.* Neal, 3 Hawks, 520; Highland Turnp. Co. *v.* McKean, 11 Johns. 89; Dutchess Cotton Man. Co. *v.* Davis, 14 id. 233; Troy Turnp. & Railroad Co. *v.* McChesney, id. 296; Beene *v.* Cahawba Railroad Co. 3 Ala. 660; Gratz *v.* Redd, 4 B. Mon. 193; White Mts. R. R. *v.* Eastman, 34 N. H. 124, 147; Piscataqua Ferry Co. *v.* Jones, 39 N. H. 491; City Hotel *v.* Dickinson, 6 Gray, 586; Troy & Rutl. R. R. Co *v.* Kerr, 17 Barb. 581; Troy & Boston R. R. Co. *v.* Tibbits, 18 Barb. 297; Ogd., Rome, & Clayton R. R. Co. *v.* Frost, 21 Barb. 541; Mann *v.* Cooke, 20 Conn. 178; Peoria & Oquawka R. R. Co. *v.* Elting, 17 Ill. 429. In some cases both the power to sell, and sue the shareholder for the balance, are expressly conferred in the act of incorporation or the general laws of the State. Brockenbrough *v.* James Riv. & K. Co. 1 Patton & H. 94.

[1] Small *v.* Herkimer Man. Co. 2 Comst. 330; N. Y. Court of Appeals, 1849. By the general railroad act of Connecticut, corporations may sue for overdue assessments, even after the forfeiture of the shares, if such shares do not sell for a sum sufficient to pay the assessments. Danbury & Norw. R. R. Co. *v.* Wilson, 22 Conn. 435.

[2] Giles *v.* Hutt, cited in 4 Exch. 417; Great Northern Railway Co. *v.* Kennedy, 4 Exch. 417.

[3] See also Edinburgh, &c. Railway Co. *v.* Hebblethwaite, 6 M. & W. 707; London & Brighton Railway Co. *v.* Fairclough, 2 Man. & G. 674. But it is not incumbent on the company to make their election before suit brought, and to notify the stockholder thereof. New Alb. & Salem R. R. Co. *v.* Pickens, 5 Ind. 247.

§ 551. It was held by the Supreme Court of New York, that the stock of a subscriber in a corporation is a security, in the nature of a mortgage, for the payment of a debt incurred by the subscription, and that a forfeiture for non-payment is, in effect, nothing more than a strict foreclosure.[1] But this case was overruled by the Court of Appeals of that State in 1849.[2] The truth is, upon a foreclosure and sale of mortgaged property, if it bring more than the debt, the mortgagor is entitled to the surplus; but in the other case, no provision is made for the company's refunding the surplus; and if the company, after forfeiture, should sell the stock for a sum beyond the amount unpaid thereon at the time of forfeiture, the subscriber cannot recover such surplus. Moreover, in all cases of a mortgage, the mortgagor has in equity a right of redemption until a strict foreclosure, or a foreclosure and sale of the mortgaged property. But no such remedy exists for the redemption of stock forfeited under the usual acts of incorporation. Courts of equity, in cases of non-compliance by stockholders with the terms of payment of their instalments of stock at the times prescribed, by which a forfeiture of their shares is incurrred, have refused to interfere by granting relief against such forfeiture.[3] Such has been the ruling of the Court of Chancery in England.[4] When a penalty or forfeiture is imposed by statute, upon the doing or omission of a certain act, courts of equity will not interfere to mitigate the penalty or forfeiture incurred, inasmuch as it would be in contravention of the direct expression of legislative will.[5]

§ 552. In the case of Grays *v.* Turnpike Company,[6] in the Court of Appeals of Virginia, the question as to liability to pay assessments depended upon the *sixth* section of the general turnpike law, which enacted, that if a stockholder shall fail to pay the sum required of him, the president and directors may sell his stock at auction, and, retaining the sum due, pay the overplus to the owner. But if the sale shall not produce the sum required to be advanced, with the incidental charges, then the president and directors may recover the balance of the stock-

---

1 Herkimer Man. Co. *v.* Small, 21 Wend. 273, 2 Hill, 127.

2 Small *v.* Herkimer Man. Co. 2 Comst. 330.

3 Story, Eq. Jurisp. § 1325.

4 Sparks *v.* Liverpool Water Works Co. 13 Ves. 428.

5 Story, Eq. Jurisp. § 1326, and authorities cited in Small *v.* Herkimer Man. Co. *ubi sup.*

6 4 Rand. 578.

holder by motion and ten days' notice. The plaintiffs failing to pay the requisitions, the stock was advertised, but not sold, for want of bidders; and the question was, whether they were liable to a recovery, by motion, for the amount of the requisitions. There were other questions in the case, but this was considered by Judge Carr, who gave the opinion of the court, as the most difficult. He, however, gave the following opinion, in which all the judges concurred. "The power to sell the stock of delinquents was given to the company for their benefit. It was thought no doubt, that this power would coerce the stockholders to punctuality in paying the calls; and if not, would secure to the company the speedy receipt of the money by sale of the stock. But, in case this sale should not raise the whole sum, a motion is given for the balance. Now ought we to turn this power of sale, given for the safety of the company, to their ruin? If the stock had sold for a single *cent*, there can be no doubt that this motion would have been sustained for the whole sum required, even for more than is now required; for the sum given would not have paid the costs of sale, and the motion would have been for the sum required, with the addition of such costs. In such case, then, the stockholder would have lost his stock entirely, and been subject, by motion, for the sum demanded; whereas, in the case before us, he is left in possession of his stock, and is only held to pay the sum required, which was certainly the meaning of the law. For it seems clear that the intention was to give the motion to supply all deficiencies which could not be answered by a sale of the stock."

§ 553. In an action to recover calls, it is not necessary to insert in the declaration a count for interest; nor ought the amount of interest to be added by the company to the calls, and declared for as part of the calls. The proper course is for the company to declare for the bare amount of the calls, and for the jury to add the interest. It was so held in a case where the act empowered the company to declare for calls and to allege that the defendant, being a proprietor of so many shares, was indebted to the company in such sum of money as the calls in arrear amounted to, for so many calls of such sums of money upon so many shares belonging to the defendant, whereby an action had accrued to the company, by virtue of the act, without setting forth the special matters; and that on the trial of such action, it should only be necessary to prove that the defendant, at the time of the making of such respective calls, was a proprietor of such shares as such action was brought in respect of, and that such calls were in fact made, and that notice thereof was given as directed by the act, without proving the appointment of the directors who made such call, or any other matter whatsoever, and that the company should thereupon be entitled to recover what should appear due including interest at five per cent.[1]

§ 554. If a part of the authorized capital stock of a corporation remains untaken at the time of its incorporation, the right to issue the remainder of it is a corporate franchise, held by the corporation in trust for the corporators, and it is to be disposed of for the benefit of all; and the directors have no right to distribute such share of stock among those of the stockholders merely who are not in arrear on the shares already taken by them, and exclude those who are in arrear.[2] And a share in the stock of a corporation, when only the least sum mentioned in the charter has been paid in, is a share in the power of increasing it, when the trustee (the corporation) determines, or rather when the original shareholders (the *cestui que trusts*) agree upon employing the greater sum mentioned in the charter. The augmentation of the capital to the larger sum, is supposed to be intended for the profit of the joint concern; the capacity under the charter to augment it, is in virtue of their joint interest. If a corporation, in other words, is created with the privilege of raising a stock not less than one sum, nor exceeding a certain greater sum, and commence business with the smaller capital, and it is afterwards decided by a vote to augment it to the greater, an original subscriber has, as a stockholder, a right to subscribe for and hold the new stock, in proportion to his interest in the old stock; and should he be denied the exercise of this right, he may have a special action of assumpsit against the corporation for the injury. In case of such action, the measure of damages would be the excess of the market value of the stock, above the par value at the time of the payment of the last instalment, with interest on such excess.[3]

---

1 Southampton Dock Co. *v.* Richards, 1 Man. & G. 448.

2 Reese *v.* Bank of Montgomery Co. 31 Penn. State, 78.

3 Gray *v.* Portland Bank, 3 Mass. 364. "Viewing," said Sewall, J., "a corporation of this kind as a copartnership, a power of increasing their stock, reserved in their original agreement, is a beneficial interest vested in each partner, to which no stranger can be made a party, but by the consent of each subsisting partner; and it is plainly a power which the subsisting partners must exercise proportionably, and according to their interest in the original stock. Or, considering the incorporation to be a trust, as it undeniably is, created for certain limited purposes, in which the corporation is the trustee for the management of the property, and each stockholder a *cestui que trust,* according to his interest and

§ 555. Still an original subscriber is not compelled to take the new stock. The shares originally taken might be the property of infants, or they might be owned by persons in a foreign country; and no compulsion could be used in the case. Besides, the maxim *volenti non fit injuria* will with as much reason apply in such cases, as in any instance that may be mentioned. The rights of the original stockholders might be forfeited; and "taking," said Sedgwick, J., "into consideration the nature of the corporation, and the purposes for which an augmentation of the capital was designed, the stockholders, when they determined to augment their capital, ought to have given a reasonable time to all their partners to have claimed this right of subscribing to the new stock; that all who were partners must be presumed, by themselves or their lawful agents, to have notice of the legal acts and votes of the corporation; and that if any neglected, in this case, to subscribe, after a reasonable time, strangers or other stockholders might lawfully be admitted to the shares so relinquished." [1]

CHAPTER XVI.

OF THE NATURE AND TRANSFER OF STOCK IN JOINT-STOCK INCORPORATED COMPANIES.

§ 556. ONE of the principal points of view, as it has been already stated,[2] in which a joint-stock corporation may be regarded, is in relation to its *stock*. By the term "joint-stock" corporation, we would be understood to mean such a corporation as has for its object a dividend of profits among its stockholders. A corporation of this sort is invaria-

---

shares, then a limitation of the capital to be employed in the trust, that it shall not be less than one, and not exceeding a certain greater sum, is not a power granted to the trustee, to create another interest for the benefit of other persons than those concerned in the original trust, or for their benefit in any other proportions than those determined by their subsisting shares."

[1] Ibid. See this point discussed in Miller *v.* Ill. Central R. R. Co. 24 Barb. 312.

[2] *Ante,* § 110.

bly empowered to raise a certain amount of capital, by the mutual subscriptions of its members;[1] and this capital is divided into *shares*, which are made to vest in the subscribers according to their respective contributions; and they entitle the holders of them to a corresponding proportionate part of the profits of the undertaking.[2] Generally the number of shares is fixed by the charter, but sometimes it is provided that there shall be not less than a certain number nor more than another number. In such a case it is left for the company to determine the number within the limits prescribed.[3]

§ 557. A share in one of these companies may be defined to be a right to partake, according to the amount of the party's subscription, of the surplus profits obtained from the use and disposal of the capital stock of the company to those purposes for which the company is constituted.[4] It is believed to be not unusual for the act of incorporation to provide that this interest shall be *personal* property, though it must be so regarded independently of any enactment to that effect; and this, notwithstanding it arises, in a measure, out of *realty;* it being the surplus profit only that is divisible among the individual shareholders. The land, buildings, &c., of canal, turnpike, and railroad companies, are the mere instruments whereby the joint-stock of the company is made to produce that profit; and, moreover, belong exclusively to the corporate body, which is altogether a separate person from the individual members.[5] In the case of Bligh *v.* Brent,[6] which was in relation to the Chelsea waterworks, Baron Alderson explains at some length the nature of the interest of shares holden in the stock of these sorts of companies. "In the first place," says he, "there is a corporation, to whose man-

---

[1] See preceding chapter.

[2] Walf. on Railways, 252.

[3] Somerset, &c. R. Co. *v.* Cushing, 45 Me. 524. See *ante,* § 528.

[4] See Jones *v.* Terre Haute & Richmond R. Co. 29 Barb. 353, where the right of directors to discriminate between the stockholders at different periods, is doubted, and where their power to declare a dividend payable to holders of stock on a previous day, is questioned, so far as such order affects the rights of persons who have bought stock between the periods mentioned. See also, Phelps *v.* Farmers & Mech. Bank, 26 Conn. 269.

[5] See *ante,* § 443, *et seq.;* Bradley *v.* Holdsworth, 3 M. & W. 334; Bank of Waltham *v.* Waltham, 10 Met. 595. The property of every member of a turnpike company is a right to receive a proportionate part of the toll, which is considered as personal estate. Tippetts *v.* Walker, 4 Mass. 595. But *contra,* in Welles *v.* Cowles, 2 Conn. 597.

[6] Bligh *v.* Brent, 2 Younge & C., Exch. 268, 294.

agement the joint-stock of money subscribed by its individual corporators is intrusted. They have power, at their pleasure, of vesting it in real estate, or in personal estate, limited only as to amount, and of altering from time to time the species of property they may choose to hold; and in order to give them greater facilities and advantages, certain powers are intrusted to the undertakers by the legislature, and that even before they were constituted a body corporate, of laying down pipes, and thereby occupying land for the purposes of their undertaking. These powers render the use of joint-stock by the body corporate more profitable, but they form no part of the joint-stock itself; and one decided test is this, that they belong inalienably to the corporation; whereas, all the joint-stock is capable expressly of being sold, exchanged, varied, or disposed of, at the pleasure of the corporate body." The learned judge went on further to say, that the property was *money*, the subscriptions of individual corporators; and, in order to make that profitable, it was intrusted to a corporation who have an unlimited power of converting a part of it into land, part into goods, and of changing and disposing of each from time to time. The purpose of all this is the obtaining a clear surplus profit, from the use and disposal of the capital, for the individual contributors.

§ 558. In the case of Rex *v.* Hull Dock Company,[1] it was decided that lands purchased by the company, and converted into dock, were ratable to the poor, notwithstanding a clause in the act of parliament, that the shares of the proprietors should be personal estate; the rate was upon the property in the hands of the company, and not on the share of any individual proprietor. A corporation may be seised of real property, as well as a great deal of personal property, but, as has been stated by Lord Abinger, "the interest of each individual shareholder is a share of the net produce of both, when brought into one fund." [2]

---

[1] Rex *v.* Hull Dock Co. 1 T. R. 219.

[2] Bradley *v.* Holdsworth, *ubi sup.* A stockholder in a moneyed corporation has a perfect ownership over his own stock, and may sell and transfer it to whom he pleases, and from doing which the bank has no power to restrain him; and such stock entitles the owner to his proportion of the dividends, which may be from time to time declared. Brightwell *v.* Mallory, 10 Yerg. 196; State *v.* Franklin Bank, 10 Ohio, 90, 97. And a devise of the dividends, without limitation as to time, or other qualification, will carry the stocks themselves. Collier *v.* Collier, 3 Ohio, State, 374. In modern practice, shares in corporate stock, of whatever nature, are usually declared by statute to be personal property. See 1 Greenl. Cr. 39, 40.

§ 559. Where lands are vested in the individual shareholders, and the management is only in the corporation, the shares are real estate; for the company has no power of converting it into any other sort of property, and indeed is not seised, as a corporation, of the land.[1] If a company purchase property, each individual shareholder has an interest in it; but the moment the company becomes a corporation, the corporation, if invested with the legal title, has the property in trust for the individuals.[2]

---

[1] Drybutter *v.* Bartholomew, 2 P. Wms. 127; Stafford *v.* Buckley, 2 Ves. Sen. 182; Weekley *v.* Weekley, 2 Younge & C., Exch. 281; Buckeridge *v.* Ingran, 2 Ves. Jr. 652; and see cases cited in Bligh *v.* Brent, *ubi sup.*

[2] Wordsworth on Joint-stock Companies, 288. The legal nature and incidents of stock in the public funds in England, have been fixed by various acts of parliament, by which these funds have been created. The provisions of these acts are generally similar, and one of the earliest of them (stat. 1 Geo. 1, c. 19, s. 9) provided, that all persons who shall be entitled to any of the annuities thereby created, and all persons lawfully claiming under them, shall be possessed thereby *as of a personal estate, and the same shall not be descendible to the heir.* Williams on the Law of Personal Property, 151. The nature and incidents of shares in the joint-stock companies incorporated by letters-patent or act of parliament, have generally been determined by their respective charters or acts of incorporation; and, in all the modern charters and acts of incorporation, the shares are declared to be personal estate and transmissible as such. In a few of the older companies, the New River Co. 2 P. Wms. 127, is an instance, the shares are real estate, in the nature of incorporeal hereditaments. For the future, however, all the provisions contained in special acts for the incorporation of joint-stock companies, will, as far as possible, be the same; for an act of parliament has recently passed "for consolidating in one act certain provisions usually inserted in acts with respect to the constitution of companies incorporated for carrying on undertakings of a public nature." Ibid. 159. The act of assembly of Maryland, by which the Cape Sable Company was incorporated, declares, that "the lands, tenements, and hereditaments, stock, property, and estate of that company, shall be held as real estate, and shall descend as such, agreeably to the acts of assembly in such cases made and provided, when not otherwise disposed of." By Chancellor Bland: "It would seem to be perfectly clear, that this mere perishable personalty is as much a part of that stock, property, and estate of the Cape Sable Company, which it is declared shall be held as real estate, as their lands and tenements; and that it must be so treated, as far as practicable, whatever inconveniences may ensue. But it is added, that the estate shall descend as such when not otherwise disposed of; thereby indicating it to have been the intention of the act, that it should only be so held as regarded the interests of the stockholders themselves, and as real estate to descend accordingly from them; not that the actual legal character of the perishable movables should be changed, as well in regard to the rights and interests of all other persons as the stockholders themselves." Cape Sable Company's case, 3 Bland, Ch. 670; and see Binney's case, 2 id. 99. Shares in incorporated companies holding land for the purposes of their business, will not fall under the prohibition of the *mortmain* act, as an estate or interest in land, notwithstanding there is no clause in their charter declaring the shares to be personal property, and a bequest of such shares for the endowment of churches and chapels is valid. Edwards *v.* Hall, 6 De G., M. & G. 74, 35 Eng. L. & Eq. 433.

§ 560. Shares in joint-stock companies are not, however, strictly speaking, *chattels;* and it has been considered that they bear a greater resemblance to *choses in action;* or, in other words, they are merely evidence of property.[1] They are, it is held, mere demands for dividends, as they become due, and differ from movable property, which is capable of possession and manual apprehension.[2] "If," says C. J. Shaw, "a share in a bank is not a chose in action, it is in the nature of a chose in action, and what is more to the purpose, it is personal property."[3] By bank-stock, say the Supreme Court of Tennessee, is meant individual interest in the dividends as they are declared, and a right to

---

[1] Chattels personal are things tangible and movable, as money, jewels, corn, &c. Personal rights not reduced to possession, but recoverable by suit at law, are *choses in action,* as money due on bond, or note, or other contract, damages due for breach of covenant, for the detention of chattels, or for wrongs. Indeed, by far the greater part of the questions arising in the intercourse of social life, or which are litigated in the courts of justice, are to be referred to this head of *personal rights in action.* 2 Kent, Com. 285; Long on Sales, 2. In Palmer *v.* Merrill, 6 Cush. 282, a case of life insurance, Shaw, C. J., says,—"According to the modern decisions, courts of law recognize the assignment of a *chose in action,* so far as to vest an equitable interest in the assignee, and authorize him to bring an action in the name of the assignor, and recover a judgment for his own benefit. But, in order to constitute such an assignment, two things must concur: first, the party holding the *chose in action* must, by some significant act, express his intention that the assignee shall have the debt or right in question, and, according to the nature and circumstances of the case, deliver to the assignee, or to some person for his use, the security, if there be one, bond, deed, note, or written agreement, upon which the debt or *chose in action* arises; and, secondly, the transfer shall be of the whole and entire debt or obligation, in which the *chose in action* consists, and, as far as practicable, place the assignee in the condition of the assignor, so as to enable the assignee to recover the full debt due, and to give a good and valid discharge to the party liable. The transfer of a *chose in action* bears an analogy, in some respect, to the transfer of personal property; there can be no actual manual tradition of a *chose in action,* as there must be of personal property, to constitute a lien; but there must be that which is similar, a delivery of the note, certificate, or other document, if there is any, which constitutes the *chose in action,* to the assignee, with full power to exercise every species of dominion over it, and a renunciation of any power over it, on the part of the assignor. The intention is, as far as the nature of the case will admit, to substitute the assignee in place of the assignor as owner." "Certificates of stock," says Judge Comstock, in Mechanics Bank *v.* N. York & N. Haven R. R. Co., "are not securities for money in any sense, much less are they negotiable securities. They are simply the muniments and evidence of the holder's title to a given share in the property and franchises of the corporation of which he is a member." 3 Kern. 627. He concludes, that as certificates do not partake of the properties of negotiable paper, even a *bonâ fide* assignee will take them, subject to all the equities which existed against the assignor. Ibid.; also, New York & N. H. R. Co. *v.* Schuyler, 17 N. Y. 592. And see *ante,* § 211.

[2] Wildman *v.* Wildman, 9 Ves. 177; Kirby *v.* Potter, 4 id. 751; Planters Bank *v.* Merchants Bank, 4 Ala. 753; Denton *v.* Livingston, 9 Johns. 96.

[3] Hutchins *v.* State Bank, 12 Met. 421.

a *pro rata* distribution of the effects of the bank on hand at the expiration of the charter; and the capital stock of the bank is the whole undivided fund paid in by the stockholders, the legal right to which is vested in the corporation, to be used and managed in trust for the benefit of the members.[1] The value of the stock will of course depend on the condition of the corporation, but the corporation, so far as its own property is concerned, is not affected by that value.[2]

§ 561. The interesting question in Slaymaker *v.* Gettysburg Bank, in Pennsylvania,[3] was whether a bequest of bank-stock to a wife was *her husband's* personal estate, or a chose in action; and it was held, that bank-stock held by the wife before marriage, or bequeathed to her afterwards, will not pass by an assignment by the husband, and that unpaid dividends were subject to the same rule. Rogers, J., who gave the opinion of the court, said, "Money, due on bond or note, or other contract, for detention of chattels, or for torts, is included under the head of title to things in action. Bank shares would seem to be included in that class, as they merely entitle the holder to receive on demand a proportion of the profits or earnings of the bank, and never in this country have been considered as other than chattels, giving no such interest to the holder as that of a partner in a partnership transaction. I know of no case in which the point has been directly adjudged, but in Gilpin *v.* Howell,[4] such would seem to be the opinion of the court. In that case, so far from treating stock as real estate, or as personal property in possession (as a horse, for example), it is ruled, that when one purchases stock for another, and takes a transfer on the books of the bank in his own name, it is sufficient if he retain so much of the same stock as will enable him to transfer to his principal on demand the whole amount purchased for him, and that it is not necessary he should retain the identical scrip or shares. Although bank shares may be said to indicate or represent the proportion of interest which the shareholder

---

[1] Union Bank of Tennessee *v.* State, 9 Yerg. 490. Where personal property belongs to the members of a *voluntary unincorporated* association, *especially for public,* and *not for private* purposes, if a member abandons the association, he thereby abandons his interest in such property, and those who remain are entitled to such interest. Curtis *v.* Hoyt, 19 Conn. 154.

[2] Hart *v.* State Bank, 2 Dev. Eq. 111; Brightwell *v.* Mallory, 10 Yerg. 196; State *v.* Franklin Bank, 10 Ohio, 90, 97.

[3] Slaymaker *v.* Gettysburg Bank, 10 Barr, 373.

[4] Gilpin *v.* Howell, 5 Barr, 57.

has in the property of every kind belonging to the company, yet it cannot be said, with any propriety, that he is in the actual possession of the common property of the bank, any more than the owner of a bond or note is in possession of the money of which it is the representative. The only possession the holder has is the certificate, which is merely the evidence of his interest, as title deeds are of *title* to land, but not of the possession. That stock cannot be considered in the light of a thing in possession and personal estate, as distinguished from a chose in action, would also appear from this, that, at common law, it could not be taken in execution and sold for debts." The learned judge added, that there was no difference as to the rights of the wife, whether the bequest be before or after marriage, except as respects the joinder of the wife to receive the legacy; but that did not affect her right of survivorship, where the husband refuses or neglects to reduce her choses into possessions.[1] It was also ruled, that *dividends* unpaid, and in bank, depended on the same principle.

§ 562. Where by a judgment in partition certain shares in the stock of a corporation were set off to the husband and wife, in her right, the shares having come to the wife by devise previous to marriage, it was held, by the Supreme Court of Rhode Island, that the judgment only suspended her power over them, during her husband's life, by recognizing his marital rights; and that, to have made the property absolute in himself, he should have transferred them in his own name. "A share" (said Mr. C. J. Durfee, in delivering the opinion of the court in this case) "is a *mere ideal thing* — it is no portion of matter, it is no portion of space, it is not susceptible of tangible and visible possession, actual or constructive. It is not, therefore, a chattel personal, susceptible of possession actual or constructive." . . . "If a right be an ideal thing merely, or something existing but in law or contract, the possession must be ideal, subsisting from law or contract."[2]

§ 563. It was for some time a matter of doubt in England, whether shares in an incorporated company were of the nature of *goods*, *wares*, and *merchandise*, within the Statute of Frauds, so as to require *an*

---

[1] A legacy to a wife will not pass by an assignment of the husband of his personal property, for the benefit of his creditors. Skinner's Appeal, 5 Barr, 262; and see Dennison *v.* Nigh, 2 Watts, 90; Robinson *v.* Woelper, 1 Whart. 179.

[2] Arnold *v.* Ruggles, 1 R. I. 165.

agreement for a transfer of them to be in writing, &c. Upon one occasion, the question in England was directly and fully argued, before the twelve judges, who were equally divided in opinion on the question;[1] but in later years it has become well settled in England, that shares in joint-stock corporations are not goods, wares, or merchandise, within the Statute of Frauds, and that, therefore, a contract relating to a sale and transfer of them, need not be in writing.[2] In Duncuft *v.* Albrecht[3] it was held, that a parol agreement for the sale of railway shares is valid, for they are neither an interest in land, nor goods, wares, or merchandise.[4] The Supreme Court of Massachusetts have expressed a different opinion, and have deliberately held, that contracts for the sale of stocks and shares in incorporated companies, were within the Statute of Frauds, and were not valid unless there has been a note or memorandum in writing, or earnest or part payment. They considered that there is nothing in the *nature of stocks* which, in reason or sound policy, should exempt contracts in respect to them from those restrictions designed by that statute to prevent frauds in the sale of other commodities; but that, on the contrary, joint-stock incorporated companies had become so numerous, so large an amount of the property of the community had

---

[1] Pickering *v.* Appleby, Comyns, 354; 2 P. Wms. 308; and see Colt *v.* Netterville, 2 P. Wms. 304, and Stark on Ev. (Am. ed.), vol. 2, p. 608; Long on Sales, 56.

[2] Humble *v.* Mitchell, 11 A. & E. 205. In this case, a purchaser of shares in the Northern and Central Bank of England, brought an action of assumpsit against the vendor for refusing to sign a notice of transfer tendered to him for signature, and to deliver the certificates of shares, without which the shares could not be transferred. The defence was, first, that the contract mentioned in the declaration was an entire contract for the sale of goods, wares, and merchandise, for a price exceeding 10*l.*, and that the plaintiff had not accepted or received the said goods, &c., and did not give any thing in earnest to bind the bargain, or in part payment, and that no note or memorandum in writing of the bargain was made and signed by the defendant, or his agent thereto lawfully authorized; and, secondly, that the contract was a contract for the sale of, and relating to an interest in and concerning lands. In regard to the first point the court held, that shares in a joint-stock company, like the one under consideration, are mere choses in action, incapable of delivery, and not within the scope of the Statute of Frauds; and that, therefore, a contract in writing was unnecessary. In regard to the second point, Lord Denman, C. J., who gave the judgment of the court, said: "You should have proved, that the company was entitled to real property, and that the shareholders had an interest in it. That stock in an incorporated company is, in England, deemed to be neither goods, wares, and merchandise, nor an interest in land." Duncuft *v.* Albrecht, 12 Simons, 189; Hargreaves *v.* Parsons, 13 M. & W. 561; Lancaster Canal Co. *ex parte*, 1 Deacon & Ch. 300.

[3] Duncuft *v.* Albrecht, 12 Simons, 189.

[4] This case cited and approved in Johns *v.* Johns, 1 Ohio, State, 350.

become invested in them, and as the ordinary *indicia* of property arising from delivery of possession cannot take place, there was peculiar reason for extending the statute to them. Accordingly, that court held, that a contract for the sale of shares in a manufacturing corporation, is a contract for the sale of goods, wares, and merchandise, and, in the absence of the other requisites of the statute, must be proved by some note or memorandum in writing, signed by the party to be charged, or his agent.[1] Again, it was subsequently held in Massachusetts (the court adopting the reasoning of the court in the preceding case), that a contract for the sale of a promissory note was within the Statute of Frauds.[2]

§ 564. A contract for the sale of stock becomes executed by a delivery to the purchaser of certificates of the shares, such delivery being analogous to the delivery of chattels, and so rendering the transfer complete.[3] Though, to be sure, it is a symbolical delivery, yet it is one which should, and which does have the same operation as the delivery of the documentary proofs of title to a ship at sea, which, being as complete a delivery as the subject-matter admits of, will convey the property in the ship. The well-established general rule, that there may be a symbolical delivery when the subject-matter does not admit of an actual delivery, has been recognized by the Court of Appeals of New York, as applicable to shares in a joint-stock incorporated company;[4] and a certificate of stock is transferable by a blank indorsement, which may

---

[1] Tisdale *v.* Harris, 9 Pick. 9.

[2] Baldwin *v.* Williams, 3 Met. 365. In this case, there was offered, to the contrary, the decision in the English case of Humble *v.* Mitchell, *ub. sup.*, as authority; but the court rejected it as such, and sanctioned the decision in Tisdale *v.* Harris, *ub. sup.*

[3] See opinion of Parker, C. J., in Howe *v.* Starkweather, 17 Mass. 243; Sargent *v.* Franklin Ins. Co. 8 Pick. 98; United States *v.* Vaughn, 3 Binn. 394. And a tender of certificates of stock, with a power of attorney to transfer the same, is a valid tender under a contract for the sale of stock at a future day, and if the vendee refuses to take and pay for them, without objection for want of transfer, the vendor may recover the contract price. Munn *v.* Barnum, 24 Barb. 283; Noyes *v.* Spaulding, 27 Vt. 420; Orr *v.* Bigelow, 20 Barb. 21; *Ante*, § 556, *et seq.*

[4] Wilson *v.* Little, 2 Comst. 443. There is a marked distinction, in the Civil Code of Louisiana, between the transfer of corporeal things movable, and things incorporeal. In the former, a manual delivery of the thing is ordinarily, but not universally, required to perfect the title. In the case of incorporeal things, no such delivery can be made, and, therefore, such a delivery as the thing admits of, a *symbolical* delivery, is admitted by the Code as a substitute. See Civil Code of Louisiana, Art. 2612 and 2456, also 16 Mart. La. 56, and 19 id. 137.

be filled up by the holder by writing an assignment and power of attorney over the signature indorsed.[1] If a person sells stock and receives consideration therefor, and gives a power of attorney to transfer it, he will not be permitted in equity to defeat the rights acquired under the transfer by alleging the insufficiency of the instrument by which the transfer was made.[2] But generally where a transfer is made under a power of attorney, the corporation allowing it are bound by it, and if the power is forged, or is made by an infant, a married woman, or a lunatic, or other person not competent to contract, the corporation is liable, if such person receives no benefit from the transfer.[3]

§ 565. But a person to whom shares have been *bonâ fide* transferred will hold them without any certificate.[4] In a case in Massachusetts, in which the objection was made, that the plaintiff had no certificate of his ownership of shares (though he had an instrument of transfer), the court said, "We think that cannot prejudice his claim, as it is not in his power to obtain one without the consent of the corporation."[5] It was strongly insisted, in another case, that the defendant could not be a member of the Chester Glass Company without a certificate of his share; it being provided by the act respecting manufacturing corporations, that the stock shall be divided into shares, and that certificates shall issue to the stockholders; and the court held, that it was not essential that certificates should have issued, and that the corporation might be compelled, if there were a court of chancery, to give certificates; and for the want of them a stockholder would not lose his rights.[6] An action on the case will lie for a refusal to have stock transferred on the books of the company,[7] or an action of assumpsit to recover damages or dividends.[8] In Kortright *v.* Buffalo Commercial Bank,[9] in an action of assumpsit brought for the refusal of a bank to permit a transfer to be made on its books of a certain number of bank shares, it was contended, that the action should

---

[1] Kortright *v.* Buffalo Commercial Bank, 20 Wend. 91. See also, Ellis *v.* Proprietors of Essex Merrimac Bridge, 2 Pick. 243.

[2] Chew *v.* Bank of Baltimore, 14 Md. 299.

[3] Ibid.

[4] Agricultural Bank *v.* Burr, 24 Me. 256; Same *v.* Wilson, id. 273.

[5] Ellis *v.* Proprietors of Essex Merrimac Bridge Co. 2 Pick. 243.

[6] Chester Glass Co. *v.* Dewey, 16 Mass. 94.

[7] Presbyterian Church *v.* Carlisle Bank, 5 Barr, 345.

[8] Ellis *v.* Proprietors, &c. *ub. sup.*; Sargent *v.* Franklin Ins. Co. 8 Pick. 98.

[9] Kortright *v.* Buffalo Commercial Bank, 20 Wend. 91.

have been case instead of assumpsit. The court, however, held, that case might, perhaps, have been the most appropriate, but assumpsit was warranted by sufficient authority.[1] But an action for money had and received will not lie against a corporation by one who has subscribed for a certain number of shares and paid for the same, merely on the ground that the corporation refuses to deliver the certificates of such stock.[2] In the case of the Bank of England *v.* Moffatt,[3] it appeared, that the executors of the will of Moffatt, and certain trustees named therein, to whom the residue of his personal estate, consisting of certain bank-stock, and other various kinds of public stocks, was specifically devised, had applied to the bank for permission to transfer in a particular manner, which was refused by the bank; and thereupon the executors commenced an action against the bank in the King's Bench. This gave occasion to a bill in chancery, brought by the bank, praying an injunction to restrain the defendants from proceeding at law, and insisting upon a *certain custom* of the bank, opposed to the claim of the executors. They answered, and admitted the custom of the bank, but insisted on their right; which, being determined in their favor, the chancellor decreed, that the bank ought to permit the transfer as requested, and he dissolved the injunction. The plaintiff, in such case, is entitled to recover the full value of the stock at its highest price, between the time of the refusal to permit a transfer, and the time of the commencement of the suit.[4]

§ 566. A stockholder is rendered a competent witness for the corporation by a transfer of his stock;[5] and it has been held, that a *bonâ fide* sale and transfer of a bank stockholder *to the bank*, will divest him of all interest arising from his having been owner of such stock, and that hence he becomes a competent witness for the bank.[6]

---

1 And the court cited Rex *v.* Bank of England, Doug. 523; 3 Mass. 381; 10 id. 397; 17 id. 503; 2 Kent, Com. 289, 291. This case was affirmed. Commercial Bank *v.* Kortright, 22 Wend. 348. See also, Mechanics Bank *v.* N. Y. & N. H. R. Co. 3 Kern. 624. Bank of Attica *v.* Manufacturers and Traders Bank, 20 N. Y. 501. But a *mandamus* will be refused, to compel a corporation to enter a transfer of stock on its books, on the ground that an action will lie for a complete satisfaction, equivalent to specific relief. Rex *v.* Bank of England, *ub. sup.;* and see *post,* Chap. XX. on the Writ of Mandamus.

2 Arnold *v.* Suffolk Bank, 27 Barb. 424.

3 Bank of England *v.* Moffatt, 3 Brown, Ch. 262; and see *ante,* § 236.

4 Kortright *v.* Buffalo Commercial Bank, 20 Wend. 91, affirmed, Commercial Bank *v.* Kortright, 22 Wend. 348; Sargent *v.* Franklin Ins. Co. 8 Pick. 90.

5 Bank of Utica *v.* Smalley, 2 Cowen, 770; Gilbert *v.* Manchester Iron Manuf. Co. 11 Wend. 627.

6 Farmers & Mechanics Bank *v.* Champlain Transp. Co. 18 Vt. 131; Manchester Bank

§ 567. A provision is often contained in an act or charter of incorporation, empowering the company to regulate transfers by a by-law, to be passed by the company, leaving the general principles of the common law and of equity applicable to the sales of the shares.[1] But a by-law requiring any unreasonable formality, or imposing any extraordinary impediment in the transfer of stock, unless the power to make it has been expressly conferred by the legislature, would be void.[2] Thus, it has been held, that a by-law which limits the transfer of stock in an assurance company to be made at the office, personally, or by attorney, and *with the assent of the president*, would be in restraint of trade, and contrary to the general law which permits the right to personal property to be transferred in various other ways.[3] The purchaser or other person entitled, in such a case, has only to make his right known to the corporation, that it may be entered upon the books; and this is all that can be required.[4] Under a statute enacting that any share of the property of a particular corporation may be transferred by the proprietor, by deed acknowledged, and subsequently recorded by the clerk of the corporation, a transfer by deed not recorded is so far effectual as to render the vendee personally liable in equity to a creditor of the corporation.[5]

---

v. White, 10 Foster, 456. Nor will the circumstance make any difference, that the stockholder assigned his interest after suit brought, and is personally liable in case of the insolvency of the bank, this liability being an interest of too contingent a nature to disqualify him. Meighen *v.* The Bank, 25 Penn. State, 288.

1 United States *v.* Vaughn, 3 Binn. 394.

2 See *ante*, § 355, *et seq.*

3 Sargent *v.* Franklin Ins. Co. 8 Pick. 90; Quiner *v.* Marblehead Ins. Co. 10 Mass. 476; 2 Kyd, 122.

4 Sargent *v.* Franklin Ins. Co. *ub. sup.* And see *ante*, § 113; United States *v.* Vaughn, *ub. sup.* Where a by-law required the consent of electors to a transfer of stock by a stockholder indebted to the company, but in practice the company in such cases were never brought before the board, a transfer by such a stockholder, made without that consent, but according to the *usage* of the company, was held good against the company. Chambersburg Ins. Co. *v.* Smith, 11 Penn. State, 120. And see Choteau Spring Co. *v.* Harris, 20 Misso. 382; Bargate *v.* Shortridge, 5 H. L. Cas. 297, 31 Eng. L. & Eq. 44.

5 Eames *v.* Wheeler, 19 Pick. 442; and as to personal liability, in equity, for members of a joint-stock corporation, for the debts of the company, see *post*, Chap. XVII. The better opinion, sustained by numerous decisions, seems to be, that clauses in an act of incorporation, providing that its stock shall only be transferred in the books of the company, is for the security of the corporation, and does not prevent the title from passing as between vendor and vendee; therefore, one is a competent witness who has sold his stock, and transferred it, although not in the manner prescribed by the act. Per Goldthwaite, J., in Duke *v.* Cahawba Nav. Co. 10 Ala. 82.

§ 568. A subscriber to the capital stock of a corporation, under the general laws of New York,[1] to whom shares were awarded by the commissioners, on its being filled up, secured the payment of the par value by a bond and mortgage; and thereupon, the shares were placed in his name in the books of the corporation, and entered to his credit. Subsequently, the corporation, without any valid ground, refused to issue to him scrip for the stock, or to permit him to transfer the stock upon the books of the institution. It was held that this proceeding did not render the bond and mortgage invalid, or entitle the mortgagor to have them delivered up for want, or failure of consideration; but that his remedy was by an action at law. By the entry of stock in his name, and to his credit, in the books of the corporation, the mortgagor became entitled to all the rights and privileges of a stockholder, and thereby received the stipulated consideration for his bond and mortgage.[2]

§ 569. A joint-stock incorporated company has no implied *lien* upon the stock of a shareholder, which has been transferred by him as security for any demand against him; and the company is under obligation, notwithstanding they may have any such demand, to enter on their books the transfer of such stock, in pursuance of the assignment of the same, and becomes liable in damages to the assignees for a refusal so to do. That is, the holder of stock in a bank, for example, borrows money from the institution upon giving security for the payment of it, as any other person does who is not a stockholder; and the money is loaned upon the strength of such security, and not upon any supposed liability of the stock; unless otherwise provided by charter or by-law.[3] In Bates *v.* The New York Insurance Company,[4] there was a refusal on the part of the company to transfer, unless the assignee would pay the debts due from the assignor; and the assignee, who accordingly did so pay, was permitted to recover back the money, on the ground that the corporation were not authorized to require such payment. A different rule was, however, adopted with regard to the dividends which

---

[1] See *ante*, §§ 88, 89.

[2] Thorp *v.* Woodhull, 1 Sandf. Ch. 411. But where one gives his note, payable at a future day, for a certain number of shares, and no certificate is issued to him until the note has matured and is paid, he becomes a shareholder only from that time. Tracy *v.* Yates, 18 Barb. 521.

[3] Sargent *v.* Franklin Ins. Co. 8 Pick. 90; Heart *v.* State Bank, 2 Dev. Eq. 111; Mass. Iron Co. *v.* Hooper, 7 Cush. 183.

[4] Bates *v.* New York Ins. Co. 3 Johns. Cas. 238.

were due when the corporation had notice of the assignment. The money, then being in the hands of the company, was considered appropriated to the debt which was then actually due; but the company were held to be obliged to make the transfer on the day when the last instalment was made, and the assignee was held to be entitled to the dividends thereafter to be made.[1] In a late case, a certificate of stock declared that the holder was entitled to a certain number of shares in a bank, "transferable at said bank only by him or his attorney on surrender of this certificate, subject, nevertheless, to his indebtedness and liability at the bank, according to the charter and by-laws of said bank." It was held, that this last clause referred to the mode of transfer, and did not mean that the lien must be one provided for by the charter and by-laws; and that the bank had a lien on the stock, although none was expressly given by any by-law, and the charter provided that the stockholders might establish by-laws and regulations for the well ordering of the concerns of the bank, and made the stock transferable according to rules to be so prescribed.[2]

§ 570. The rule that an assignor of stock may convey a title without paying what he owes the company, will not of course hold, if by the charter of the company it is provided, that all debts due the company from a stockholder must be satisfied before any transfer of his stock shall be made.[3] In the case of the Union Bank of Georgetown *v.* Laird,[4] it appeared, that by the act of incorporation, the shares of a stockholder were transferable only on the books of the bank, according to the rule established by the president and directors, and that all debts due and payable to the bank, by a stockholder, must be satisfied before the transfer shall be made, unless the president and directors should direct to the contrary. It was held by the Supreme Court of the United

---

1 See Rogers *v.* Huntingdon Bank, 12 S. & R. 77.

2 Vansands *v.* Middlesex County Bank, 26 Conn. 144.

3 See *ante*, § 355. The English Stat. of 1845, called "The Companies Clauses Consolidation Act," requires all calls to be paid before any valid transfer can be made. Under this statute, and similar provisions in special charters, it has often been made a question, when a call may be said to be made; and it seems finally to be settled, that the company are not obliged to regard any transfer, made after the resolution of the directors making the assessment, which need not specify the time of payment, but that may be determined by a subsequent act of the board. Redfield on Railw. pp. 63, 64. And see Regina *v.* Wing, Q. B. 1855, 33 Eng. L. & Eq. 80; Copeland *v.* N. East. R. R. Co. 6 Ellis & B. 277, 37 Eng. L. & Eq. 118, 120, and note 2.

4 Union Bank of Georgetown *v.* Laird, 2 Wheat. 390.

States that no person could acquire a legal title to any shares, except under a regular transfer according to the rules of the bank; and that if any person took an equitable assignment, it must be subject to the rights of the bank, under the act of incorporation, of which he was bound to take notice. The president and directors, in this case, expressly denied that they had waived, or ever intended to waive the right of the bank to the lien, for debts due to the bank, by the form of the certificate, and that they ever directed any transfer to be made which should stipulate to the contrary. As a creditor may take and hold several securities for the same debt from his joint debtors, and cannot be compelled to yield up either until the debt is paid, it was, therefore, further held, that the bank had a right to take security from one of the parties to a bill or note discounted by it, and also to hold the shares of another party as security for the same.[1]

§ 571. In the case of the Huntingdon Bank, in Pennsylvania, it appeared that, by the act of the legislature, *no stockholder indebted to the bank, shall be authorized to make a transfer, or receive a dividend, till such debt shall have been discharged*, or security to the satisfaction of the directors given for the same. A stockholder, who was indebted to the bank on a note discounted, and also for an *instalment* due on the capital stock, gave a power of attorney to receive the dividends in his own name, and, at the same time, another power of attorney to transfer his stock to the plaintiffs, who placed in the hands of an attorney a sum of money to pay the instalment. The attorney, after depositing the money to his own credit, drew a check in favor of the stockholder, and the money was applied to the payment of the instalment, no notice having been given to the bank of the power to transfer the stock until some months afterwards. The court held, that the plaintiff was not entitled to a transfer of the stock, nor to a return of the money which had been applied to the payment of the instalment. Tilghman, C. J., in giving the opinion of the court, said, "The words (of the act) embrace *all* debts, and there is good reason for their extending to *all*. When the directors discount a note of a stockholder, they know that his stock is liable, and, therefore, may be less attentive to the sufficiency of the indorsers. The indorsers, too, have an interest in the lien of the bank, and it may be presumed that many persons

---

1 And see Conant, &c. *v.* Seneca County Bank, 1 Ohio, State, 298.

have been induced to indorse, on the strength of this lien."[1] But where the charter of a corporation declares, that no stockholder indebted to the company shall be permitted to transfer his stock until his debt be paid or secured to the satisfaction of the directors, it is a privilege which may be waived or asserted, at the pleasure of the directors; the provision is not imperative.[2]

§ 572. The lien which a bank has on stock attaches to the stock of a depositor who has overdrawn his account by checks.[3] Under a general act of the State of Pennsylvania of 1814, banks, it seems, have a lien on stock, although levied on by a judgment creditor, for notes drawn before, but falling due after, the levy, even though renewed. The question in Grant *v.* The Mechanics Bank of Philadelphia,[4] was as to what was meant by the use of the word "indebted." It was held, that a note given by a stockholder to the bank was a debt due from him to the bank, before, as well as after, it became due. The court considered that the restraint on the transfer of stock would fail of the intended benefit, if a stockholder had an unrestrained right to transfer at any time before his note fell due; though to be sure, if it were clearly ascertained that by "indebted" the law meant nothing but a debt *actually due*, the bank directors would have no right to complain, inasmuch as they would know that the stock was no security.[5] And in a recent case, where the articles of association provided that no share of stock should be transferred unless the shareholder should previously discharge all debts *due* by him to the association, it was held, that the lien did not extend to a promissory note, made by the stockholder, and discounted by the bank, which had not yet reached maturity, the word *due* being construed to mean due at time of the proposed transfer.[6] Where a transfer is demanded accompanied by a refusal to pay the debts due,

---

[1] Rogers *v.* Huntingdon Bank, 12 S. & R. 77. See also, Morgan *v.* Bank of North America, 8 S. & R. 12, 73.

[2] Hall *v.* United States Ins. Co. 5 Gill, 484. And by waiving this privilege the company will not discharge a surety of such shareholder, unless the surety gave notice to the company not to transfer the stock or pay the dividends. Perrine *v.* Firemen Ins. Co. of Mobile, 22 Ala. 575.

[3] Reese *v.* Bank of Commerce, 14 Md. 271.

[4] Grant *v.* Mechanics Bank of Philadelphia, 15 S. & R. 140.

[5] The same construction was given to a similar act of Missouri, by the Supreme Court of that State, in St. Louis Perpetual Insurance Co. *v.* Goodfellow, 9 Misso. 149.

[6] Leggett *v.* Bank of Sing Sing, 25 Barb. 326.

and afterwards another demand is made, when other debts have become due, the person making the demand is not entitled to a transfer without offering to pay all the debts then due.[1]

§ 573. In the act of Pennsylvania of 1824, entitled "an act to re-charter certain banks," the words are strikingly different from the act of 1814. Instead of saying no stockholder "indebted to the institution," the expressions are, "no stockholder indebted to the bank, *for a debt actually due and unpaid*, shall be authorized to make a transfer." This was not intended as an *explanation* of the first law, but as an *alteration*, in consequence of a change of policy.[2] It was held, under the act of 1824, that where W., being the owner of forty shares of bank-stock, bequeathed them to his four sons, and during the minority of one of the legatees, the bank, with notice of the will, permitted the transfer of thirty shares of the stock, by the consent of all the legatees, to a stranger; the bank could not, under the above act of 1824, refuse to permit a transfer of the ten remaining shares, on the ground of a debt being due by two of the sons, who were of full age when the transfer of the thirty shares was permitted. The suit brought was not on the *chose*, but an action on the case for wrongfully preventing the equitable owner obtaining the legal evidence of title.[3]

§ 574. In the case of the assignees of Evans, a bankrupt, against the Hudson Bay Company,[4] the company had made a *by-law* subjecting the stock of any of its members in the first place to debts which they might owe the company. Chancellor King thought the by-law was not a good one, but Raymond, C. J., and Price, B., thought otherwise; and they were all of opinion, that without a by-law, or some other law subjecting the stock to the company's debts, they had no lien upon it. In a case where it appeared that the plaintiffs went with the sheriff to attach (under the statute) shares of a stockholder in a bank, and were informed by the cashier that, by virtue of a by-law of the bank, the shares of the stockholder were pledged to the bank for their full value, as security for a loan made to him, and likewise that he had assigned

---

[1] Reese v. Bank of Commerce, 14 Md. 271.

[2] Tilghman, C. J., in Grant v. Mechanics Bank, *ubi sup.*

[3] Presbyterian Congregation v. Carlisle Bank, 5 Barr, 345.

[4] Evans v. Hudson Bay Co. 7 Vin. Abr. 125, pl. 2; the same case, perhaps, under another name, may be found in 1 Stra. 645, and 2 P. Wms. 207. See, on this subject, *ante*, § 355, 356.

the shares to another creditor, who had exhibited the assignment, with a certificate of the stock, and a power of attorney to transfer the same, and had demanded to have the shares transferred on the books of the bank, and that the bank had refused, on the ground that the shares were pledged to them, and the plaintiffs, nevertheless, obtained execution, and bought the shares at a sheriff's sale under it; in an action for the plaintiffs against the bank for refusing to transfer the shares to them, it was held, that either the pledge to the bank, or the assignment to the other creditor, was valid; and that the plaintiffs, therefore, had no cause of action against the corporation.[1]

§ 575. The lien of a bank on stock for debts due to it from the stockholders, is not waived by the certificate of stock, which states that the stockholder is entitled to ——— shares in the capital stock of the company.[2] The rules and by-laws of a corporation which prohibit any transfer, except upon the books of the company, and upon notice, have reference either to the right of voting, or to the security of the company by way of lien on the stock for any indebtedness of the stockholder. They do not incapacitate a stockholder from selling his stock, but the purchaser only acquires the right of property, which the seller had; so that, if the stock is under incumbrance, it remains so.[3] So, where it is provided that no transfer of any share in the capital stock shall be valid until *the whole be paid in*, if a stockholder assign his interest before that time, it is conveyed to the assignee. Thus, in Massachusetts, in the Marblehead Social Insurance Company case, the action was assumpsit for money had and received; second count, for that, D. B. and W. S. were indebted to B. R., and to recover his demand, &c., he caused to be attached 150 shares of the capital stock subscribed by them in the said company, and sold the same to satisfy his execution, and, thereupon, the plaintiff purchased them, and notice thereof being given to defendants, they became obliged to admit him, &c. The statute incorporating the company provided, that no transfer of any share in it should be valid, *until the whole capital stock should be paid in*. D. B., for himself and partner, previously to the attachment

---

1 Plymouth Bank *v.* Bank of Norfolk, 10 Pick. 454.

2 Reese *v.* Bank of Commerce, 14 Md. 271.

3 Bank of Utica *v.* Smalley, 2 Cowen, 770; Gilbert *v.* Manchester Man. Co. 11 Wend. 627; Commercial Bank of Buffalo *v.* Kortright, 22 Wend. 348, 362; *Ex parte* Mayhew, 5 De G., M. & G. 837, 31 Eng. L. & Eq. 331; and see authorities cited *ante*, §§ 355, 356.

and *before all the stock was paid in*, transferred the 150 shares to J. S., who was their creditor, in satisfaction of his demand. It was held, that they transferred to him the equitable interest, so far as to justify the corporation in issuing the certificate of shares to him, and to consider him the true owner when all the stock was paid in. The court went on the ground, that the intent of the legislature, in the prohibition, was only to prevent speculations in the scrip, &c., and *not to prevent a debtor's bonâ fide transfer to his creditor;* [1] and that the creditor might be substituted for the debtor, and might acquire the right, by payment of the residue of the subscription, to have the transfer entered upon the books, and to have a certificate of his shares.[2]

§ 576. The Supreme Court of Connecticut have, however, considered, that where it is required that a sale of shares shall be registered, the registry operates, not merely to perfect a conveyance previously begun, or to give notice of a conveyance previously perfected, but is of itself *the originating act in the change of title*. Thus, the shares of the Marlborough Manufacturing Company were made, by the charter of the company, transferable only on their books, in such form as the directors should prescribe. A by-law was duly established, which required, "that all transfers of stock should be made by assignment on the treasurer's book, either in person, or by authorized attorney, on surrender of the certificate granted for the stock, and a new certificate being granted by the treasurer." No assignment was made on the book; no certificates of ownership were surrendered, or new ones received; and nothing was done, but the giving of the credit of the amount of the share, on the treasurer's book, to the successive holders. The court was of opinion, that the stock had not been legally transferred. "Though the form of the assignment is not pointed out," said C. J. Swift, "yet the by-law, on its fair construction, requires, that there must be a *written assignment on the treasurer's book, subscribed by the assignor, or his authorized attorney, to constitute a transfer of the stock*." [3]

§ 577. And a sale or pledge of stock, accompanied by a letter of

---

[1] Quiner *v.* Marblehead Social Ins. Co. 10 Mass. 476; 1 Dane's Abr. 466.

[2] And see Sargent *v.* Essex Mar. Railway Corp. 9 Pick. 202; Orr *v.* Bigelow, 20 Barb. 21.

[3] Marlborough Man. Co. *v.* Smith, 2 Conn. 579; and see the Newton and Bridgeport Turn. Co. 3 Conn. 544; Fisher *v.* Essex Bank, 5 Gray, 373.

attorney to make the transfer, where the regulation is that no transfer shall be valid until received for record, is of no avail, in Connecticut, to convey a title, until the transfer is received for record; for in all transfers subject to such regulation, the change of title takes place when the instrument of transfer is received for record by the clerk; and the transfer bears date from that time. Therefore, where A., the holder of certain shares of stock, agreed with B. to transfer them to him, as security for acceptances and advancements made by B. for A.; and for that purpose A., on the 20th October, at 9 o'clock, A. M., executed and delivered to B. a letter of attorney to the clerk of the company, authorizing him to transfer such shares to B., which was sent by mail to the clerk, and was received by him, on the 8th of November following, in pursuance of which he made a regular transfer of the shares to B. on the books of the company; C., a creditor of A., attached the same shares, on the 20th of October, at 10 o'clock, A. M., in a suit against A., in which he recovered judgment, more than two years afterwards, and had his execution levied on the shares, which were sold, and C. became the purchaser; it was held, that C. obtained thereby a legal title, and B. had no title, to the shares. Daggett, J., who gave the opinion, said, that the case must be governed by the decision in the case of the Marlborough Manufacturing Company, and the Newton and Bridgeport Turnpike Company;[1] and that, in the last of those cases, the judgment proceeded upon the precise point raised in the case before him.[2] And in a late case in Massachusetts it is held, that the delivery of a certificate of stock in a manufacturing corporation, indorsed with a printed transfer signed in blank, with the intention of transferring the stock as security for a debt due from the holder to the person to whom it is delivered, passes no title as against attaching creditors.[3]

§ 578. In Connecticut, a written assignment of stock, if made *in pais*, according to the prescribed form, and seasonably registered on the books of the company, *is a transfer on the books of the company*, within

---

[1] *Supra.*

[2] Oxford Turn. Co. *v.* Bunnell, 6 Conn. 552. See also, Fisher *v.* Essex Bank, 5 Gray, 373. In the case of the Newton and Bridgeport Turn. Co. it was held, that the registry operates not merely to perfect a conveyance previously begun, or to give notice of a conveyance previously perfected, but is of itself *the originating act in the change of title.* 3 Conn. 544.

[3] Boyd *v.* Rockport Steam Cotton Mills, 1 Gray, 406.

the meaning of the charter requiring it. Thus, in Northup *v.* Curtis,[1] the sole question was, whether, when stock in a turnpike had been attached, the stock had not been previously and in a legal manner transferred to one H. The act incorporating the company provided that the shares of the stock should be transferable only on the books of the company, in such manner as the company should by their by-laws direct; and a by-law of the company provided that the board of directors should prescribe the form of transfer to be registered by the clerk, on the books of the company, and that no transfer should be valid unless so made and registered. In 1803, before any transfer of the shares, the directors prescribed the following form of transfer: "I, B. D. of N., in the county of F., do, by these presents assign, make over, and transfer to G. H. of W., full original shares in the capital stock of the Bridgeport and Newton Turnpike Company, with all the privileges, and subject to all the burdens thereunto appertaining, value received of him, the said G. H. Witness my hand," &c. In 1814, B. Hine held two shares of the stock, for which he was an original subscriber, and was the assignee of one hundred and sixty and a half shares, under bills of sale from sundry persons, made *in pais*, in the form prescribed by the by-law, and afterwards registered on the books of the company. The plaintiff claimed, that, on the twenty-seventh of December, 1814, Hine, in payment of debts due from him to them respectively, assigned to E. Graves, and J. Graves, sixty-two and an half shares, and to the plaintiff one hundred shares, by bill of sale, in the form prescribed by the by-law; and that afterwards, namely, on the 28th of December, 1814, such assignments were registered at full length, on the books of the company, by the clerk. The plaintiff had since acquired the title of E. and J. Graves. The defendants claimed, and introduced evidence to prove, that after the bills of sale had been executed by Hine, they were delivered by him to one Masters, to be carried to be registered; and that Masters then had in his hands five writs of attachment against Hine; and it was agreed by Hine, that these writs would be carried with the bills of sale to the clerk's office, and should be served first on Hine's stock, and that the bills of sale should then be delivered to the clerk to be registered; and that accordingly the writs were served, and the bills of sale delivered, in that order. The defendants also claimed, that S. Noble attached the stock of Hine, on the same day, before the

---

[1] Northup *v.* Curtis, 5 Conn. 246.

bills of sale were received for record; and that after the service of the other attachments, and after the receipt of the bills of sale by the clerk, but before they were recorded at length, namely, at two o'clock in the morning of the 28th of December, J. Nichols attached the same stock; and that in all these attachments judgments were regularly recovered, and executions issued thereon levied on the stock in question, the whole of which was sold according to law. And the defendants offered in evidence such attachments, judgments, and executions, and sales thereon, to show that the plaintiff had no title to any part of the stock. The plaintiff admitted that the two shares, for which Hine was an original subscriber, might legally be taken by attachment and execution; but objected to the evidence offered by the defendants for the purpose of disproving the plaintiff's title to any of the other shares claimed by him, on the ground, that Hine had no title at law to them. The defendants insisted, that the transfers to Hine, having been made and registered on the books of the company, in pursuance of the by-law, and in the form prescribed by the directors, were made on the books of the company pursuant to the charter; so that Hine thereby had a legal title to all the shares; and that, as all the attachments were made before the transfers from Hine to E. and J. Graves, and to the plaintiff, were recorded at full length on the books of the company, they had priority thereto, and took all the shares, so that the plaintiff acquired no title whatsoever, in law or equity, to any part of the stock in question. The court were of this opinion, and admitted the evidence offered by the defendants, and thereupon decreed, that the plaintiff should take nothing by his bill; and upon a motion for a new trial it was held by all the judges, that it could not be granted.[1]

§ 579. How far merely formal transfers on the books of a banking corporation, for the purpose of defeating the proper objects of the charter, are to be regarded as of any force, as to those who are instrumental in bringing them about, was the question in Sabin *v.* Bank of Woodstock, in Vermont.[2] By a provision in the charter of that institution, no transfer in its stock was to be valid unless recorded in a book to be kept by the bank for that purpose, and unless the person making the same should have previously discharged all debts due from him to the

---

[1] See, as to transfer of stock in reference to regulations established by by-laws, *ante*, Chap. X.

[2] Sabin *v.* Bank of Woodstock, 21 Vt. 353.

bank. In October, 1835, one S., who was the owner of nearly two hundred shares in the capital stock of the bank, and who was not then indebted to the bank, transferred his stock, in due form, upon the book of the bank, to forty-five different persons, without consideration, and for the purpose of increasing the vote upon his stock at an approaching election of bank officers; and, by this transfer, four shares were conveyed to the plaintiff. Nearly all of these shares (but not those conveyed to the plaintiff) were reconveyed to S., by the persons to whom they had been transferred; and on the 9th of October, 1837, he made a similar distribution of his stock, by transfer in due form upon the book of the bank, for a similar purpose, and at this time transferred to the plaintiff two shares. S. was at this time indebted to the bank to an amount exceeding the value of all the stock owned by him. The plaintiff had no interest in the six shares which stood in his name until October 25, 1837, when he purchased them of S. in payment of pre-existing debts. On the 16th day of November, 1839, the bank attached these six shares, as the property of S., upon a debt which accrued January 6, 1837, and caused them to be sold on execution, to satisfy the said debt, on December 19, 1840. From the time the transfers were made upon the book to the plaintiff, until the time of the attachment, S. controlled these six shares, as well as the other shares transferred by him, as his own property, and he received all the dividends upon them which were paid previous to the attachment; and the plaintiff made no claim upon the bank until 1841, when he demanded the dividends; and one dividend, which became due previous to the sale on execution, was paid to him; and payment of those which accrued after the sale was refused. It was held by the court, that the plaintiff (having suffered S. for so long a period to treat the shares as his own) was bound to inquire of the bank as to the state of the title, before purchasing, and to give notice to the bank of his having become the beneficial owner; that his title, as between him and the bank, could only be regarded as accruing from the time such notice was given; and that the bank, having attached the shares previous to receiving such notice, was entitled to hold their avails, as against the plaintiff. It was moreover held, that it made no difference in the case, that a majority of those who were the directors of the bank, advised or procured the transfers to be made by S. upon the books of the bank; that, as directors, they could have no right to make or advise such operation; though *bonâ fide* purchasers of stock, without notice, were at liberty to act upon the faith of the title being where, upon the books of the bank, it appears to be. "The great question," said the court, "here is, whether the plaintiff was at liberty to purchase these shares upon the faith of the formal title merely being in himself; or whether, having for years suffered the former nominal owner, and in fact the real owner, to treat the stock, to all intents and purposes, as his own, he was not bound to make inquiries as to the state of the title, before he purchased, and after he purchased, to give notice to the bank of his having become the beneficial owner, before he could compel the court to protect him as such? It seems to us that such was his duty."

§ 580. As stock may be sold, so it may be *pledged;*[1] but the possession may still continue in the pledgor consistently with the nature of the contract, till the title is made absolute in the pledgee.[2] The transfer of the legal title to stock is not inconsistent with a pledge of it. A stockholder transferred on the books of the company, shares in the New York and Erie Railroad Company, and the transfer was absolute in its terms; but, at the same time, the stockholder gave his note for a certain amount of borrowed money, and in the note it was stated that the stock was deposited as collateral security; and it was held, that the transaction was a pledge, and not a mortgage of the stock.[3]

§ 581. Where shares of stock have been pledged, and the debtor has offered to pay the debt, and requested a return of the stock, and the pledgee, who has already sold it, promises to return the shares or others of the same kind, and the debtor waits from time to time for him to do so, and in the mean time the stock rises in value, the pledgor is entitled to the enhanced value.[4] There is a breach of trust when a stockholder transfers shares in a corporation and covenants that they were free from incumbrance, if the shares of the stockholders were by statute pledged and made liable for the debts of the corporation, and if, at the time of the transfer, the assets of the corporation are not equal to its liabilities.[5] And where a repealing act makes the directors then in office trustees of the creditors and the stockholders, the stock cannot be

---

[1] Marine Bank *v.* Biays, 4 Harris & J. 338.

[2] *Ante,* § 132.

[3] Wilson *v.* Little, 2 Comst. 443.

[4] Wilson *v.* Little, *ubi sup.*

[5] Clark *v.* Perry, 30 Me. 148. See *post,* Chap. XVII. as to the personal liability, in equity, of members for debts of the company.

transferred so as to pass a legal title after the dissolution; for after such dissolution, the interests of the several stockholders become equitable rights to a proportionate share of the assets, after payment of the debts. If stock is purchased after the dissolution, by a debtor of the corporation, such purchaser is in the same situation as though he had been a stockholder when the corporation was dissolved, and must, therefore, submit to have the debt which he owes deducted from his share of the assets; and one who purchases the stock from him takes it subject to the like deduction.[1]

§ 581 *a*. The mere fact that a bank permits stock which stood in the name of a testator, to be transferred by the executor, furnishes no ground of complaint against the bank, although it is made to appear that the executor was, by the act of transfer, converting the money to his own use; for a party dealing with an executor, is not bound to inquire into his object, nor is at all liable for the executor's misapplication of the money. The party dealing with an executor must have *reasonable ground* for believing that he (the executor) intended to misapply the money.[2]

§ 582. It is an incumbent duty on the part of the bank or other joint-stock corporation, not to permit a transfer of stock until they are satisfied of a party's authority to transfer. If stock be transferred under a *forged* power of attorney, the real proprietor is entitled to have it replaced by the company, and also to the dividends due thereon. This point was determined in a case in which the Bank of England was defendant, and one which was twice argued.[3] It was an action on the case; and it appeared that the plaintiff, in the month of May, 1819, had standing in his own name, on the books of the bank, £10,000 3 per cent. consolidated bank annuities, £178 10 per cent. long annuities, and £800 navy 5 per cent. annuities. In October, 1819, by virtue of certain instruments purporting to be powers of attorney executed by the plaintiff to the Messrs. Drummonds, they sold out two several sums of £5,000 of the 3 per cent. consolidated bank annuities, and afterwards £75 bank long annuities, part of the said stock then standing in the name

---

[1] James *v.* Woodruff, 10 Paige, 541, and s. c. in Error, 2 Denio, 574.

[2] Albert *v.* Savings Bank, 2 Md. 159. And see *Ex parte* Northern Coal Mining Co. 3 Macn. & G. 726, 10 Eng. L. & Eq. R. 171.

[3] Davis *v.* Bank of England, 2 Bing. 393; and also fully reported in 3 Petersdorf's Abr. 410.

of the plaintiff. The signatures to these powers of attorney proved to be forgeries; and the question the court were called upon to decide was, whether the stocks which stood in the plaintiff's name on the books of the bank had been transferred out of that name. Their opinion was, that the plaintiff's property in the funds had not been transferred; that he was still the legal holder of those funds, and entitled to the dividends payable on account of them. They considered it clear, that a transfer in writing not made by the party transferring, or some agent duly authorized, could have no effect; and they thought that the rule, that a forged indorsement on a bill of exchange conveys no interest in such bill, was applicable to the question before them. They laid down the broad principle, that transferable shares of the stock of any company could not be divested out of the proprietor by *any* act of the company, without the authority of the stockholder; and maintained, that the Bank of England had no more authority to affect the interest of any stockholder, than the most insignificant chartered company had to dispose of the shares of the members of such a company.[1]

§ 583. In the opinion given by the court in the above case, the court observed: "We are not called on to decide whether those who purchase the stocks transferred to them under the forged powers, might require the bank to confirm that purchase to them and to pay them the dividends on such stocks, or whether their neglect to inquire into the authenticity of the power of attorney might not throw on them the loss that has been occasioned by the forgeries. But, to prevent, as far as we can, the alarm which one argument urged on behalf of the bank is likely to excite, we will say, that the bank cannot refuse to pay the dividends to subsequent purchasers of these stocks. If the bank should say to such subsequent purchasers, the persons from whom you bought were not legally possessed of the stocks they sold to you, the answer.

---

[1] Where a company have registered a transfer, which is alleged to be a forgery, and are threatened with a suit from both the transferrer and transferree, the court will not grant an interpleader. Dalton *v.* Midl. Railway Co. 12 C. B. 458, 22 Eng. L. & Eq. 452. But where shares were fraudulently transferred, and the owner treated the transaction as being valid, as against the transferree, but filed a bill against the company for damages, it was held that he could not recover. Duncan *v.* Lintley, 2 McN. & G. 30. It was held, by the New York Court of Appeals, 3 Seld. 274, that a bank which has permitted a transfer of stock owned by a stockholder, upon a *forged power* of attorney, and has cancelled the original certificates, may be compelled to give new certificates, and if it has no shares which it can so issue, to pay him the value thereof. Pollock *v.* National Bank, 3 Seld. 274; Cohen *v.* Gwinn, 4 Md. Ch. Dec. 357.

would be, that the bank, in the books which the law requires them to keep, and for the keeping of which they receive a remuneration from the public, have registered these persons as the owners of these stocks, and the bank cannot be permitted to say that such persons were not the owners. If this be not the law, who will purchase stock, or who can be certain that the stock which he holds belongs to him? It has ever been an object of the legislature to give facility to the transfer of shares in the public funds. This facility of transfer is one of the advantages belonging to this species of property; and this advantage would be entirely destroyed if a purchaser should be required to look to the regularity of the transfers to all the various persons through whom such stock had passed. Indeed, from the manner in which the stock passes from man to man, from the union of stock bought of different persons under the same name, and the impossibility of distinguishing what was regularly transferred from what was not, it is impossible to trace the title of stock as we can that of an estate. We cannot look further, nor is it the practice ever to attempt to look further, than the bank books, for the title of the persons who propose to transfer to the persons therein named." The court having decided that the stocks remained the property of the plaintiff, he of course was also entitled to the dividends; and, therefore, the whole consequences of the forgery would fall upon the bank.[1]

§ 584. In the case last cited, it appears that the plaintiff knew of the forgeries, and concealed them, though they did not come to his knowledge until several months *after they were committed*. And when he was informed by the person who committed them (his brother) that he had done so, he did not communicate such information either to the bank or to any magistrate, until after the brother had escaped from the prison in which he was confined, and was probably out of the kingdom. This conduct of the plaintiff, the court thought, under circumstances, might amount to a misdemeanor; and they said that in this case the plaintiff could only receive such dividends as he had required the bank to pay him, and which they, having been so required, had refused to

---

[1] Bridgeman, in his Chancery Digest, says: "Where stock was transferred under a forged power, the transfer is void, and the right owner shall not be hurt; but the dividends received under the false power, together with the stock, shall be taken from the assignees, and restored to the right owner;" and the case of Hildyard *v.* South Sea Co. 2 P. Wms. 76, is cited. But this decision, Bridgeman adds, does not appear to have been followed; for Ashby *v.* Blackwell, Amb. 503, is *contra*.

pay, and that the dividends demanded were those which became due on the long annuities on the 5th April, 1820, and those on the consols which became due in the month of July in the same year. These dividends, it was contended, the plaintiff was barred from receiving, because the bank (the plaintiff not having given information of the forgeries) might have paid them to other persons. The opinion of the court was as follows: "We agree with the counsel for the bank, that if it had appeared that the bank had paid these dividends to persons to whom (if the plaintiff had informed them of the forgeries, as he ought to have done, on the 25th March, 1820) they could have refused to pay, then he cannot recover such dividends in this action. We say, in the language of Lord Mansfield, in Bird *v.* Randall, that whatever will in equity and conscience, according to the circumstances of the case, bar the plaintiff's recovery, may be given in evidence by the defendant, because the plaintiff must recover upon the justice and conscience of his own case, and on that only; but we say, that it does not appear in this case that any thing was given in evidence by the defendants that did in equity and conscience bar the plaintiff. It is not enough for the defendants to say, that they might have paid these dividends to other persons. To defend the action, on the principle laid down by Lord Mansfield, they must prove, that they have paid them to persons to whom they could have refused to pay them, had they been informed of the forgeries. But no evidence of any such payment appears in this case. It has been insisted at the bar, that upon principles of public policy, we ought not to permit the plaintiff to prevail in his action. Public policy is a doctrine on which judges should proceed with caution, otherwise the rights of the subjects of this country would depend on their discretion. There are many things which most of us think against good policy, for which actions are brought; for instance, wagers. We ought not to trust ourselves with so dangerous a power, as that of acting judicially on disputable policy.

"Can we say, that indisputable policy requires that a man should lose his all for a misprision of felony? Policy prevents the assertion of a civil right, in cases of this nature, where actions are brought for doing something directly injurious to the public, or declared to be so by positive law.

"Thus, if the law has forbidden the doing of an act, it has recognized the impolicy of doing it, or if it has commanded an act to be done, it has recognized the impolicy of not doing it; and the courts would not allow an action to be maintained for doing the act prohibited, or abstaining from doing the act commanded. Therefore, if the plaintiff's action had been founded on the concealment of the forgeries, it could not have been supported. But the action is founded on the refusal of the bank to pay on demand the dividends of the plaintiff, due on stocks belonging to him. The misprision of felony, of which he has been guilty, forms no part of this case. If misprision of felony is to be opposed to the action, it must be on the ground that the plaintiff, having had a good cause of action, on account of the bank's refusing to do their public duty by paying his dividends, has forfeited his right to maintain such action by being guilty of misprision of felony. We know nothing of forfeitures on notions of public policy; for forfeitures we must have positive law. Misprision of felony is but a misdemeanor, and punished not by any forfeiture, but by fine and imprisonment, at the discretion of the court before which the offender is convicted. The defendants cannot have attempted to apply to this case the rule, that civil actions are merged in a felony. If the plaintiff was seeking to recover what had been obtained by means of these forgeries, either from the forger or any person who had received the property from him, the defendants might protect themselves under this rule.

"But it has never been held, that the owner cannot, before prosecution of the felon, proceed for redress against the persons through whose negligence the thief committed the felony. If goods are stolen from a carrier or innkeeper, the owner may bring his action against them without instituting any prosecution against the felon. The bank stands in the situation of the carrier or innkeeper. It has never been decided that a concealment of felony from the carrier or innkeeper, by the owner of the goods, was an answer to such an action. Concealment can be no answer, except the jury were to infer from it, that the owner was privy to the robbery, or the defendant could show that such concealment had prevented him from recovering the goods. This case was put to us in argument; A., knowing that B. has forged A.'s name to a draft on his banker, sees B. come out of the banker's shop with the money obtained by the forgery, and neither arrests B., or gives any information to the banker. Could A. recover this money again from the banker? A jury in such a case must find that A. was privy to the forgery at the time it was committed, and they would, I think, infer, that A. assented to it, and such finding would prevent his recovering in an action against the banker. But in the present case, the jury have expressly negatived all knowledge by the plaintiff, until three months after the forgeries. They have also negatived assent, saying, they have no instance of assent, except the concealment of what came to the defendant's knowledge in three months after the forgeries, from which they have not inferred assent, nor can we."[1]

§ 585. There is a case in the old reports of Barnardiston, where a man of the name of Edward Harrison got the South Sea stock belonging to another Edward Harrison, put to his account in the books of the company, and then transferred this stock to his broker to sell, which stock the broker sold. A bill in chancery was filed by the executors of Edward Harrison, the owner of the stock, against the executors of Edward Harrison, who so fraudulently procured it to be put in his name; and the chancellor said, that the plaintiff should have a quantity of stock equal to that transferred bought for him, or else have satisfaction for the stock, equal to what it was worth at the time it was sold out; and his lordship added, there is another more difficult question, and that is, how far the company may be liable to make satisfaction, in case there are not sufficient assets left by the Harrison who improperly possessed himself of this stock. It was assumed, in this case,[2] that the stock had passed out of the name of the owner, by this transfer, under a fraudulent assumption of his name, although he never assented to such transfer; but whether it had so passed or not, was not considered. But it has been thought that this case was not correctly reported by

---

[1] The judgment in this case was reversed in the Court of K. B., 5 B. & C. 185, and although the reversal took place on the ground of a defect in the pleadings, the guarded manner which was used in delivering the judgment, so as to avoid giving any sanction to the decision in the Common Pleas, gives reason to suspect, says a late English writer, that the latter is not to be considered as an unimpeachable authority. Woolrych on Com. & Mer. Law, 282. In Coles *v.* Bank of England, 10 A. & E. 449, it was held, that where the negligence of the stockholder misled the bank to believe that the transfer, which was in fact fraudulent, had been made with the assent of the stockholder, and on the faith of that they paid dividends to the transferree, the executors of such stockholder could not recover the dividends from the bank. The soundness of this opinion, however, has been questioned in Bank of Ireland *v.* Evans, 5 H. L. Cas. 389, 32 Eng. L. & Eq. 23, a case which came up from the Court of Exchequer Chamber in Ireland, and was fully argued before the House of Lords. The unanimous opinion of all the judges, delivered by Parke, B., was, that the negligence of the stockholder, in order to give a valid defence to the bank, must be in, or immediately connected with the transfer itself, and that the negligence of the plaintiffs below, allowing their secretary to keep in his exclusive possession their corporate seal, by which he was enabled, by means of forged powers of attorney, to transfer their stock on the books of the bank, was too remote to affect the transfer itself, — and the judgment of the court below to the same affect was confirmed accordingly. Ibid. 39–45.

[2] Such was the construction of the court in Davis *v.* Bank of England, 2 Bing. 393, *ub. supra.*

Barnardiston.[1] The same case is to be found in 2 Atkyns, in the name of Harrison *v.* Harrison. It appears, by the latter report, that the stock was transferred by a trustee; and if so, the question, whether a transfer unauthorized by the stockholder would alter the property in the stock, could not have arisen, the trustee having a legal authority to transfer, though he might be guilty of a breach of trust by exercising that authority.

§ 586. From the nature of corporate stock, which is created by, and under the authority of, a State, it is necessarily, like every other attribute of the corporation, governed by the local law of that State, and not by the local law of any foreign State. The legal title to stock held in a corporation, in Louisiana, does not pass under a general assignment of property, until the transfer is completed in the mode pointed out by the laws of Louisiana regulating those corporations. But the equitable title will pass, if the assignment be sufficient to transfer it by the laws of the State in which the assignor resides; and if the laws of the State where the corporations exist do not prohibit the assignment of equitable interests in stock. Such an assignment will bind all persons who have notice of it.[2]

§ 587. In Hutchins *v.* State Bank, in Massachusetts,[3] the question was, whether, in permitting a transfer of shares in that bank, made by an executrix of the will of a shareholder, proved in *another State*, accompanied by a surrender of the certificate, the bank was so negligent, or acted so much in their own wrong, that they were afterwards obliged,

---

[1] Davis *v.* Bank of England, 2 Bing. 393, *ub. sup.*

[2] Black *v.* Zacharie, 3 How. 483. See *ante*, § 108, *et seq.* It was laid down by C. J. Tilghman, that "every country has the right of regulating the transfer of all personal property within its territory; but when no positive regulation exists, the owner transfers it at pleasure." Morton *v.* Milne, 6 Binn. 361. Lord Mansfield has mentioned, that the local nature of contracts respecting the public funds or stocks, requires them to be carried into execution according to the local law. Robinson *v.* Bland, 2 Burr. 1079. The same rule, says Story, in his Conflict of Laws, may properly apply to all other local stock, although of a personal nature, such as bank-stock, insurance stock, turnpike, canal, and bridge shares, and other incorporeal property, owing its existence to, or regulated by, local laws. Story on Conflict of Laws, 315. Again, says the same learned writer, contracts to transfer such property would be valid if made according to the *lex domicilii* of the owner, or the *lex rei contractus*, unless such contracts were specially prohibited by the *lex rei sitæ;* and the property will be treated as personal or as real, in the course of administration, according to local law. Ibid. 316.

[3] Hutchins *v.* State Bank, 12 Met. 421.

without any equivalent or advantage to themselves, to stand responsible for the value of those shares. A testator in New Hampshire, who owned shares in a bank in Boston, made the following bequest to his wife: — "All the property, both real and personal, that I am possessed of during her life, except my farm in the town of W. No part of the bank-stock is to be disposed of, unless her comfort should require it; but it is to be apportioned to my relations according to her discretion, to be enjoyed by them after her decease." She caused the will to be proved in New Hampshire, and gave bond as executrix, but never caused the will to be allowed and recorded in Massachusetts, according to the provisions of the statute. She also gave a power of attorney to a citizen of Boston, authorizing him to sell the shares in the bank there, which were accordingly sold by him, and a transfer thereof was made to the purchaser, in due form, on the books of the bank. After the death of the executrix, the will was duly allowed and recorded in Massachusetts, and administration, with the will annexed, was granted to H., who brought an action against the bank to recover the dividends on the shares, from the time of the said sale and transfer. It was held, that the executrix (as such) had the legal power to convert the shares into money, without the aid of the Probate Court in Massachusetts, *if she could do it without legal process;* that the bank was not bound to see to the application of the proceeds, nor to decide whether her comfort required the sale; that if she had no authority to appropriate the proceeds to her own use, or if she sold the shares when she ought to have retained them, she was guilty of a violation of official duty, for which her sureties were responsible on the probate bond. But had the bank declined voluntarily making the transfer, and it had become necessary for the executrix to institute legal process, in her representative character, she must then have clothed herself with the necessary authority, by an act of a Probate Court in Massachusetts.

§ 588. Where property is of so *intangible* a nature, as shares in the stock of a corporation,[1] that there can be no change of possession, and it cannot be known whether they are attached or not, the sale of them on execution is a mode of transfer not authorized by the Common Law.[2] Thus, in an action brought against a sheriff, in the State of New York,

---

[1] See *ante*, § 557, *et seq.*

[2] Howe *v.* Starkweather, 17 Mass. 240; Denny *v.* Hamilton, 16 id. 402.

it appeared that the sheriff had sold, among other property, one share in the Bank of Columbia, and three shares in the Hudson Library; Kent, C. J., said: "The bank and library shares were levied on by mistake; for these were mere *choses in action*, and not the subject of a levy and sale by a *fieri facias* any more than bonds and notes."[1] In Connecticut, it seems that shares in a *turnpike* company are held to be real estate; and the decision to this effect would as properly apply to a *canal* company, it being founded upon the supposition, that the company had an incorporeal right or easement in the land upon which the road is constructed.[2] But in Massachusetts, in the case of Howe *v.* Starkweather,[3] Parker, C. J., who gave the opinion of the court, expressly says: "Shares in a *turnpike* or *other* incorporated company, have more resemblance to choses in action, being merely evidence of property; the sale of them upon execution not being justifiable at common law." When the stockholder of a corporation is garnisheed as a debtor of the company, and answers that he has paid all the calls made by the company upon him, he cannot be made responsible upon the residue of his stock, upon which no calls have been made.[4] So stock owned by an individual cannot be subjected to the payment of his debts by garnisheeing the corporation.[5]

§ 589. Shares in incorporated companies being not thus at *common law* liable to execution, they have been expressly made so in Massachusetts and in some other States, by *statute*. The statute in these cases generally directs the mode of attachment by mesne process, the course to be pursued when they are attached, and when they are sold on execution. But under such provisions, where the charter, or a general act of the legislature, requires that no stockholder, who is indebted to a bank, shall make a transfer of his stock until his debt is discharged, the judgment creditor cannot levy. Or, perhaps, it might be more proper

---

[1] Denton *v.* Livingston, 9 Johns. 96; and see Com. Dig. tit. *Execution*, c. 4. In Louisiana, the creditors of a stockholder cannot sell his share in the property of a corporation. Williamson *v.* Smoot, 7 Mart. La. 31. See *ante*, § 560.

[2] Swift's Digest, and 2 Conn. 567. But see Amment *v.* New Alexandria, &c. Turnp. Co. 13 S. & R. 173, in which it was held, that a turnpike road could not be levied upon under a judgment against the company, because they had no tangible interest, nothing but a right to receive tolls. And see *ante*, § 556, *et seq.*

[3] Howe *v.* Starkweather, 17 Mass. 243. See *post*, § 611, *et seq.*

[4] Bingham *v.* Rashing, 5 Ala. 403. See *ante*, § 397, *et seq.*

[5] Planters & Merchants Bank of Mobile *v.* Leavens, 4 Ala. 753.

to say, that if the judgment creditor does levy, the lien of the bank will be preserved; and this lien will extend to notes *drawn* before, and *falling due* after the levy. So much respect is in fact paid to this lien given by statute, that a bank is not bound to appropriate part of the debtor's shares to pay their demands, and transfer the balance to the judgment creditor, even though the stock is sufficient to pay it, and leave a balance.[1] In the case just referred to, it was observed by the court: "It is long settled, and not disputed, that a lien is a good bar to an action of trover; the bank had a lien, and were justified in refusing to permit a transfer of the stock until the lien was discharged." Where an act of incorporation prescribes the particular manner in which the shares of members in the stock are to be attached and sold on execution, such provision supersedes the general provision of a statute on the same subject.[2]

§ 590. By the act of 1796, establishing the Third Massachusetts Turnpike Corporation, it was provided, that the shares therein "may be attached, and may be sold on execution, in the same manner as is or may by law be provided for the sale of personal property by execution;" *a copy of the execution and of the officer's return being left with the clerk of the corporation within ten days after the sale.* It was afterwards decided, that the general act of 1804, directing the mode of attaching and selling by execution shares of debtors in incorporated companies, repealed the provision for the same objects contained in the act of incorporation.[3]

---

[1] Sewall *v.* Lancaster Bank, 17 S. & R. 285. It had been before settled in Pennsylvania, that the word "indebted" extended to notes given to the bank which had not fallen due. Rogers *v.* Huntingdon Bank, 2 S. & R. 77; Grant *v.* Mechanics Bank, 15 id. 140. See *ante*, §§ 572, 573.

[2] Titcomb *v.* Un. Marine & Fire Ins. Co. 8 Mass. 326.

[3] Howe *v.* Starkweather, 17 Mass. 240. The same general act respecting the sale, &c., of shares in corporations, provides, also, for the sale, &c., of an equity of redemption; and it has been held, that an officer, who had sold an equity of redemption on execution, was bound to pay over the surplus money arising from the sale, to another officer having an execution against the same debtor. Denney *v.* Hamilton, 16 Mass. 402. By the Rev. Stat. of Massachusetts, ch. 90, § 36, any share of a stockholder, in any joint-stock company, that is or may be incorporated, may be attached by leaving an attested copy of the writ (without the declaration), and of the return of the attachment, with the clerk, treasurer, or cashier of the company, if there be any such officer; otherwise, with any officer or person who has at the time the custody of the books and papers of the corporation. Any share or interest so attached, shall be held as security to satisfy the final judgment in the suit, in like manner as any other personal estate is held. Ibid. § 37.

§ 590 *a.* An agreement is often made by railroads to pay the persons building them a certain proportion of the contract price in stock. Under such a contract, the contractor is entitled to the proportion in stock at its current market value, at the time payment should have been made. And if the stock depreciate so that it has no market value, the amount agreed to be paid in stock, must be paid in money.[1]

CHAPTER XVII.

OF THE PERSONAL LIABILITY OF THE MEMBERS OF JOINT-STOCK INCORPORATED COMPANIES, FOR THE DEBTS OF THE CORPORATION.

§ 591. THERE has already been occasion, in treating of the nature and meaning of civil corporations established for the purposes of trade and commercial adventure, to distinguish them from the common association of partnership, in respect to the personal liability of the members for the company debts. No such personal liability, it was shown, attached to the individuals united under the sanction of the government, and invested by charter, or other act of legislation, with the full powers and immunities of a corporate body; while it was, on the other hand, shown, that each and every individual of a common partnership association is personally responsible for every debt of the firm.[2] There is the same distinction between incorporated and unincorporated *joint-stock* companies; the latter, in fact, being but partnerships, though established upon a large scale, and consisting of an indefinite, or of a very large number, of joint undertakers. Whatever name they may assume and use, in the transaction of their business, it is but a *partnership*, and not a corporate designation; and every suit upon a contract with the company, must be brought in the names of the several persons composing the firm.[3] Still, the object of their institution is to prosecute some

---

[1] Hart *v.* Lauman, 29 Barb. 410.

[2] See *ante*, § 41, *et seq.*

[3] Williams *v.* Bank of Michigan, 7 Wend. 542; Wells *v.* Gates, 18 Barb. 554.

important undertaking, for which the capital and exertions of a few individuals would be inadequate; like most of the English fire and life insurance companies, which have no charter, nor any corporate functions or immunities conferred upon them by the government.[1] They differ, it is true, from ordinary partnerships, in their formation; and a variety of acts are to be done before the partnership is actually commenced,[2] which is either under what is called "a deed of settlement," or under what is called a "provisional agreement."[3] The first is a covenant between a few of the shareholders chosen as *trustees* for the purpose, and the others, by which each of the latter covenants with the rest of the shareholders for the due performance of a series of articles which are set forth; and this deed is the only instrument of regulation, and, as between the shareholders themselves, contains the law affecting them. Upon points, however, which are not comprehended in the deed, the general law of partnership prevails; and even as to the provisions of the deed itself, effect would be given to, or taken away from it by courts of law and equity. But, as to the transactions between the company and the world, the deed of regulation is wholly inoperative, and the shareholders stand upon the same footing as ordinary partners in respect to the rights and remedies of the persons with whom they deal.[4] It is well known, says Chancellor Walworth, that there are, and have been, many joint-stock, and even banking companies, which are mere partnerships, as to every person except their own stockholders; they never having been legally incorporated.[5] A *provisional agreement* may

---

[1] Gow on Part. 10.

[2] Collyer on Part.; Smith on Mer. Law, Chaps. III. & IV.

[3] Wordsworth on Joint-stock Companies.

[4] Ibid. Whether companies so formed are legal or not, depends upon the common law, unless so far as they are subject to some special statute. The principal act which has been designed to prohibit them is the "Bubble Act," or, as the Master of the Rolls, in Stent *v.* Bailis, 2 P. Wms. 219, termed it, the *moonshine* act. It was passed in the year 1719, in the sixth year of the reign of George I., and during the excitement occasioned by the noted South Sea Company; and it originated in an intention to restrain the extraordinary spirit of speculation which prevailed at that period, and which had its commencement in the preceding reign of Queen Anne. It having been the source of much litigation, from time to time, both in the courts of law and equity, it was at length repealed by the act of 6 Geo. IV. Notwithstanding its repeal, the common law, in respect to all schemes of hazard, is expressly reserved by the repealing statute, and if it can be shown (as it may, if the fact be so) that such schemes are *fraudulently* designed, and are injurious to the public welfare, it is an offence indictable. See Duvergier *v.* Fellows, 5 Bing. 248; Blunden *v.* Winsor, 8 Simons, 601.

[5] Williams *v.* Bank of Michigan, 7 Wend. 542.

be defined as containing the heads of certain stipulations which it is intended should thereafter be comprised within a deed of settlement, where such an instrument is in the contemplation of the parties. It is sometimes nothing more than a prospectus, and frequently so publicly advertised. In like manner as a deed of settlement, it contains the conditions which regulate the proceedings of the shareholders *among themselves*.[1]

§ 592. Where an association, which has existed as a mere copartnership, becomes incorporated, and the corporation then accepts an assignment of all the property of such association, for the purpose of carrying out their objects, they are primarily, and jointly and severally liable for all the debts incurred before the act of incorporation.[2] The incorporation of a joint-stock company in Pennsylvania, which had united under articles, one of which provided for an application to the legislature for a charter, does not substitute the responsibility of the corporation for contracts previously made with the associates, and exempt the members from liability beyond the joint funds. And the action of the legislature declaring the corporation solely responsible on such contracts, without the assent of all parties, is in direct contravention of the provision of the federal constitution which interdicts the impairing of the obligation of contracts.[3] In Goddard *v.* Pratt, in Massachusetts,[4] the members of an iron manufacturing company, which had been in operation for some time, obtained an act of incorporation, by the name of the "Wareham Iron Company," but continued to carry

---

[1] Wordsworth on Joint-stock Companies. The principles which govern a common-law partnership are in general applicable to a joint-stock company, whether incorporated or not, except so far as modified by statute or special rules of law. Ketchum *v.* Bank of Commerce, New York Superior Co., Special Term, November, 1854, 3 Am. Law Reg. 145. In England, contracts entered into on behalf of companies which are not provisionally *registered*, are illegal and void. Abbot *v.* Rogers, 16 C. B. 277, 30 Eng. L. & Eq. 446. But the company, after complete registration, is liable upon contracts entered into during the period of their provisional registration, if such contracts are within the powers conferred by stat. 7 & 8 Vict. Taylor *v.* Crowland Gas & Coke Co. 10 Exch. 293, 26 Eng. L. & Eq. 460. Where they are not within the powers conferred by statute, the agreements must be incorporated into the act of parliament incorporating the company, in order to be binding on the latter. Caledonian, &c. R. Co. *v.* Helensburgh Harbor Trustees, H. L. 1856, 39 Eng. L. & Eq. 28.

[2] Haslett *v.* Wotherspoon, 1 Strob. Eq. 209.

[3] Witmer *v.* Schlatter, 2 Rawle, 259.

[4] Goddard *v.* Pratt, 16 Pick. 412. But otherwise if there is notice of dissolution, and the creation of a corporate body. Whitwell *v.* Warner, 2 Vt. 425.

on their business in the name of the old firm. The court refused, in a suit against the company, to admit evidence to show a general reputation, that, in using the name of the firm, the name of the corporation was meant; and held, that although the act of incorporation might operate as a dissolution of the company, yet the members were liable as partners when dealing with persons having no notice of the dissolution. The doctrine proceeds on the principle, that if a retiring partner neglects to give notice, or suffers his name to be used, he will be liable to the debts of the new concern. In a late case, it was held that the incorporation, pursuant to a general statute, of an unincorporated loan fund association, did not affect the right of the trustees to maintain an action in their own names on a bond previously given to them by one of the members.[1]

§ 593. An attempt was once made, in Pennsylvania, to evade the rule as to the unlimited personal liability of partners, and beyond the amount of the shares for which they subscribed. The association, under the name of "Farmers and Mechanics Bank of Fayette County Pennsylvania," engaged to pay, by the terms of their notes, "out of their *joint funds*, according to their articles of association;" and it was made a part of the case of the partners who were sued, that they had no joint funds. The question thus being, whether they were liable in their *separate estates*, the court gave their opinion, that every partner was liable, on the general principle that partners are as much liable for partnership debts as they are for debts contracted personally; and that it was not merely their stock which was hazarded, but their individual fortunes.[2] In another case, in the same State, the "Farmers Bank of Lancaster" claimed to be virtually incorporated by a general "Act relating to the association of individuals for the purpose of banking." The act provided, that no association should thereafter be formed for the purpose of banking, unless every member thereof should be individually and personally liable for the company debts. The court held, that this provision could not be viewed as impliedly incorporating that bank, or any other company; it was merely an acknowledgment that such associations were lawful. The intent of it was to prevent associations that were about to be formed, the members whereof were to shield themselves from personal responsibility, by a publication to the world

[1] Merrill *v.* McIntire, 13 Gray, 157.
[2] Werts *v.* Hess, 4 S. & R. 356.

that they were exempt from such responsibility; it was never the intention to incorporate an unlimited number of associations, free from all restraint and liability, without special restriction, as to the amount of capital, the nature of the business, and the length of duration of the association.[1]

§ 594. Whatever, then, may be the stipulations voluntarily entered into between the parties to a copartnership, they cannot arrogate to themselves the functions of a corporation; and without an express sanction of the legislature, amounting, at least, to the creation of a *quasi* body corporate, they cannot form an association capable of acting independently of the rules and principles which govern a simple partnership.[2] Stipulations, says Lord Brougham, for the purpose of restricting the liability of partners, would plainly be of no avail; and "whoever," he adds, "becomes a subscriber upon the faith of the restricting clause, or of the limited responsibility which that holds out, would have himself to blame, and be the victim of his ignorance of the known law of the land."[3] A very serious practical result of the inflexibility of the rule of the personal liability of the members of a commercial firm, according to Bell, the author of the Commentaries on the Law of Scotland, occurred in that country, in the case of the *Douglas Bank.* That bank, says he, was formed for the generous but short-sighted purpose of relieving the distresses of the country, occasioned by the excessive use of bills of exchange, and the stop in the usual discounts to which the regular banks were forced to have recourse. After the bank had been established a little more than two years, it failed, with a loss of £430,000. Many of the stockholders were eminent lawyers, and they raised every possible point, in order to shield themselves and their families from the *personal responsibility* of the members of a company so circumstanced. But it was never for a moment imagined that the partners were not responsible for the last fraction of the debts.[4] But an eminent jurist[5] has suggested that it may well deserve inquiry,

---

[1] Myers *v.* Irwin, 2 S. & R. 368; Dauchy *v.* Brown, 24 Vt. 197.

[2] And see Collyer on Partnership, b. 3, ch. 3; Story on Partnership, ch. 8; Smith, Mer. Law, chaps. 3 and 4. Wells *v.* Gates, 18 Barb. 554; Dennis *v.* Kennedy, 19 Barb. 517.

[3] Walburn *v.* Ingilby, 1 Mylne & K. 51.

[4] 2 Bell's Com. 263.

[5] Story on Partnership, ch. 8, pp. 255–257.

how far stipulations in articles of copartnership, which limit the responsibility of the members to the mere joint funds, or to a qualified extent, will be binding upon their creditors, *who have due notice* of such a stipulation.

§ 595. This personal liability of the members of unincorporated joint-stock companies has already been shown[1] to be inconsistent with one fully endowed with a corporate character, as in the case of the latter, the law recognizes only the creature of the charter, and knows not the individuals. Thus it is, that the proceedings of a vestry of a church, pledging its corporate funds to persons who might perform work, or furnish materials for it, can impose no personal liability upon the members of the vestry; and an impression, moreover, subsequently manifested by them, that they had assumed a personal responsibility, cannot vary the legal interpretation of the act upon which the question of responsibility depends.[2]

§ 596. Indeed, the stockholders in a company endowed with full corporate functions and privileges are exempted in their estates and persons from their liability to an *action at law*, even when it appears that a portion of the corporate property has been assigned to them in exclusion of *bonâ fide* creditors. In the case of Vose *v.* Grant,[3] it appeared that the stockholders of the Hallowell and Augusta Bank, after the expiration of their charter, made dividends of their capital stock among themselves, so that there were not corporate funds left sufficient to redeem their outstanding bills. It was admitted that the stockholders, in making those dividends, had been guilty of no fraud, for at the time they were made, the debts due to the bank, with twenty-five per cent. of the capital stock undivided, would be sufficient to pay all the debts due from the bank. But it happened that the president and one of the directors, both apparently in good circumstances and in good credit, and

---

[1] *Ante*, § 41, *et seq.*

[2] Vincent *v.* Chapman, 10 Gill & J. 279. See also, Matthews *v.* Stanford, 17 Ga. 543. A stockholder in a bank is not liable personally to a judgment obtained against the corporation, in the absence of any statute or legislative provision making it otherwise. Whitman *v.* Cox, 26 Me. 335; Slee *v.* Bloom, 19 Johns. 456. The treasurer of a corporation is not liable, in his individual capacity, to a stockholder, for refusing the payment of a dividend, although there are funds in the hands of the treasurer sufficient for the payment at the time of such refusal. French *v.* Fuller, 23 Pick. 168.

[3] 15 Mass. 505.

largely indebted to the bank when the dividends were voted, afterwards failed. The plaintiff was a holder of the bills of the bank, and brought an action on the case for the neglect, carelessness, and default of the defendant, who was a stockholder, in order to recover the amount. The opinion of the court, which had been prepared with great deliberation by Judge Jackson, was, first, if any right of action accrued, it was to those who held the bills at the time of the misconduct complained of; and that such a right could not be assigned to the plaintiff. That alone, it was considered, would have been decisive of the action; but as the general question presented in the case was a very important one, it was deemed proper to investigate and decide it. In investigating the question, the learned judge alluded to the fact, that there was no evidence of fraudulent or dishonest intentions on the part of the defendant and the other stockholders; and said, if the present action could be maintained, as for a tort, several consequences would follow, which, all would admit, were highly unreasonable and unjust. He then proceeded to state what the consequences would be: "In the first place, any of the stockholders might be sued alone, because, in an action founded on tort, it is not necessary to join all the wrongdoers; and the defendant cannot, in such a case, plead the omission of the others in abatement. Secondly, the individual who was sued would be liable to the whole extent of the injury complained of, without regard to the amount which he had received on the division of the stock. If a man has done me an injury, for which I bring an action of this kind, it is no defence for him to say that he has not been enriched by it. The same stockholder would, therefore, be liable to successive actions of the same kind, by all the different holders of the bank-notes; and the defendant in the case at bar, although he received less than 1,200 dollars on the division of the capital stock, might be compelled, if he has estate sufficient, to pay the whole of the notes for 90,000 dollars and upwards, which are said to be still unpaid. Thirdly, if any thing could make this more strikingly unjust, it is the circumstance, that the defendant, after paying all that money, could have no remedy for contribution against the other stockholders. No such action will lie by one trespasser or wrongdoer against his companions; but either one may, at the election of the injured party, be made liable for the whole." [1] The decision accordingly was, that the plaintiff could not recover.

---

[1] Black, C. J., in Hill *v.* Frazier, 22 Penn. State, 323.

§ 597. In the case of Spear *v.* Grant,[1] the defendant, a stockholder in the Hallowell and Augusta Bank, withdrew from the bank his proportion of stock, when the bank was indebted on bills which had previously issued. Some of those bills came into the hands of the plaintiff; and as the bank was broken up and dissolved, he contended that the members of the company were individually liable, on the principle that copartners are individually liable, after the dissolution of the firm. But Mr. Chief Justice Parker, who gave the opinion of the court, thought that no such inference could be drawn from the relation of a stockholder to the bank or its creditors. A claim like the one instituted by the defendant, he considered, would be liable to the effect of the statute of frauds and perjuries; as, most clearly, the debt was not originally the debt of the individual stockholders, but of the company; and that if any engagement existed against the defendant, or the other stockholders, it must have been collateral, and so within the principles that had been applied in the construction and application of the statute just mentioned. But he referred to other less technical difficulties, which he deemed insuperable: "If a promise," said he, "can be supposed to have been made by the defendant, or created by law, what party is the promisee? Can it be that each stockholder has promised each holder of the notes to pay his demand, if the bank should become unable or unwilling? This would be to encounter a hazard limited only by the amount of the whole number of notes which the bank may issue. This certainly cannot be imagined to be the nature of the liability. Shall the responsibility be limited to the amount of interest which the stockholder has in the bank? If so, which creditor shall have it? He who is the sharpest and has made the first demand? Or he who has been more modest and perhaps more meritorious? Shall the original holder, who paid the value to the bank, be indemnified? Or he also who, when the credit of the bank has run down, may have bought the notes for a trifle? These questions would certainly be very difficult to settle, if the stockholder was liable to the amount of his share of the stock only; and if he were equally liable to each holder of the notes (which he must be if he be liable at all; for if the facts agreed create a promise to one, they create a promise to all), then the most palpable injustice would take place. For a stockholder, wholly innocent and ignorant of the mismanagement which has brought the bank into discredit, might be ruined by reason of owning a single share in the stock of the corporation. There is no view of the subject, in which we can give effect to the claim of the plaintiff."

---

[1] 16 Mass. 9.

§ 598. In the above case, the action (which was an action on the case) was considered by the plaintiff's counsel, as in the nature of a *bill in equity*, to recover no more than the amount of the stock of the corporation which had been assigned to the defendant on its dissolution. And the principle contended for was, that the stock actually vested was, by force of the act of incorporation, pledged for the payment of all the debts of the institution; and that it ought not to be withdrawn until all such debts are paid. But the court observed, that even this would give actual security but for one half of the possible amount of the debt; as all banks had the privilege of creating debts to double the amount of their capital. The stock, the court admitted, should be considered a pledge, as far as it would go; and if it was withdrawn before the debts were discharged, they seem to think there was an *equitable* obligation, on the part of the stockholders, to account for so much as they originally consented to pledge. But they were unable to discover any mode, at *common law*, by which one creditor could compel any stockholder to pay him the amount of his stock; and were clear if any remedy did exist to this effect, it was before a tribunal which was empowered to act upon the whole subject-matter in an *equitable* point of view. At common law, they could conceive of no case in which an action would lie, without evidence of a fraudulent contrivance on the part of the person sued, to withdraw his share of the capital stock, and to cheat the creditors of the bank. What would be proper evidence of such fraud, the court did not, however, decide; but they said, the present action suggested no fraud, and the facts led to the suspicion of none, against the defendant.

§ 599. We will next proceed to show the circumstances under which the creditors of a joint-stock corporation have an adequate remedy in a court of equity, against the individuals composing it. In the case of Vose *v.* Grant, before citėd, the learned judge (Jackson) said: "In the case of this bank, a court of chancery would probably sustain a bill by one or more of the creditors of the bank in behalf of all who should choose to come in, against all the stockholders. In such a process, new plaintiffs and new defendants might be added after the commencement of the suit, as might be found necessary; and the rights of all concerned, on both sides, might be considered at once. It could then be ascertained how much was due in the whole, to all who should choose to adopt this remedy, and what had been received by each stockholder. The latter might then be compelled to pay each one his proportion of the whole debt, provided it did not exceed the amount of his dividend; and the money thus paid might be divided among the plaintiffs in proportion to their respective claims. If any of the stockholders had become insolvent, it would be determined, upon the same principles as in a like case in a court of common law, whether the loss arising from that circumstance should be borne by the stockholders or the creditors; and this point being settled, the court of chancery would proceed to apportion the loss accordingly among the respective parties. It might also be ascertained, whether any of the present holders of the bills had purchased them at a great discount, and at a late period; and if this circumstance ought to have any influence in estimating the amount of the debt, or in distributing the money to be paid by the defendants, that court would be competent to make the distribution accordingly."

§ 600. The case of Wood *v.* Dummer,[1] which also grew out of the insolvency and dissolution of the Hallowell and Augusta Bank, has fully recognized the jurisdiction of a court of equity under the circumstances above mentioned. That case was a bill in equity, brought by the plaintiff in the Circuit Court of the United States, before Mr. Justice Story, in Maine, at the May Term, 1824. The plaintiff brought the bill, as holder of the notes of the bank aforesaid, against certain stockholders in the same bank. It was held by the court, that, upon general principles, as well as according to the legislative intention, the capital stock of banks was to be deemed a *pledge*, or *trust fund*, for the payment of the debts contracted by the bank; that the public, as well as the legislature, had always supposed this to be a fund appropriated for such purpose. That the charter relieved the individual stockholders from personal responsibility, and substituted the capital stock in its stead; and that to this fund credit was universally given by the public, as the only means of repayment. During the existence of the corporation, he said, it was the sole property of the corporation, and could be applied only according to its charter, that is, as a fund for payment of its debts, upon the security of which it might discount and circulate notes. If the stock, he continued, might, the next day after it was paid in, be withdrawn by the stockholders without payment of the debts of the corporation, why is its amount so studiously provided for, and its payment by the stockholders so diligently required? The point appeared to the learned judge so plain upon principles of law, as well as common sense, that he could not doubt that the charters of our banks made the capital

---

[1] Wood *v.* Dummer, 3 Mason, 308.

stock a trust fund for the payment of all the debts of the corporation. The bill-holders and other creditors, he considered, had the first claims upon it; and the stockholders had no right, until all the other creditors were satisfied. He viewed the stockholders as having the full benefit of all the profits made by the establishment, and as being unable to take any portion of the fund, until all the other claims on it were extinguished; and that their rights were not to the capital stock, but to the *residuum*, after all demands on it were paid. He admitted that, upon the dissolution of the corporation, both the bill-holders and the stockholders had each equitable claims; *but those of the bill-holders possessed*, as he conceived, *a prior exclusive equity*. On the principle, then, that the capital stock was a *trust fund*, it was clear that it might be followed by the creditors into the hands of *any* persons having notice of the trust attached to it; and that, as to the stockholders themselves, there could be no pretence to say, that, both in law and fact, they were not affected with the *most ample* notice. The learned judge then referred to the well-settled doctrine of following trust funds into the hands of any persons, who were not innocent purchasers, and did not otherwise possess superior equities; though he considered, upon the plain *import of the charter*, "the capital stock was a trust fund for creditors, and that the stockholders, upon the division, took it subject to all equities attached to it." [1]

---

[1] The judge referred to the following case, in Skinner, 84, as one which was very like the one before him, in many of its circumstances. It was the case of Curson *v.* African Company, which is also reported in 1 Vern. 121. The plaintiff, in that case, was a creditor on bond of the old African Company, which became insolvent, but did not surrender its charter, and a new company was incorporated, consisting, for the most part, of the old members, to which the old company assigned its effects for payment of its debts. The suit was against the new company, for payment of the plaintiff's debt out of these effects, as a *trust fund*. The difficulty was, that the old company was not made a party to the bill. Lord Keeper North had some hesitation about the necessity of issuing process against the old company, because they had no property on which a *distringas* could issue to compel them to appear. But he seems to have had no doubt of proceeding, if the company was dissolved, nor of operating on the fund itself. The doctrine laid down in the above case of Wood *v.* Dummer, is in accordance with the views of courts in the United States, as expressed in cases subsequently decided. Cooper *v.* Frederick, 9 Ala. 742; Dudley *v.* Price, 10 B. Mon. 84; Bank of Natchez *v.* Chambers, 8 Smedes & M. 49; State *v.* La Grange & Memphis Railroad Co. 2 Humph. 488; Bank of St. Mary's *v.* St John, 25 Ala. 566; and see Johnson *v.* Trustees of State Marine Hosp. 2 Calif. 319. In New York, it has been held, that when an incorporated company becomes insolvent, before its surplus fund have been apportioned as dividends among the stockholders, such surplus funds, as well as the capital stock of the company, must, if necessary, be applied to satisfy its debts, to the exclusion of any prior claim of stockholders on such surplus. And the unearned

§ 601. Another important question considered by Mr. J. Story, in the above-mentioned case, was, whether the plaintiffs were entitled to a decree, to the *full amount* of the dividends received by the defendants respectively, toward payment of the debts due from the bank to them, or whether they were entitled only to a *pro rata* payment out of that dividend, in the proportion which the stock, held by the defendants, bore to the whole capital stock. In considering this question, he alluded to the defective manner in which the bill was drawn, and that it contained no averment of the insolvency of the other stockholders, or of other circumstances denoting a peculiar equity. He also alluded to the long delay in instituting the suit, which was not accounted for in any averments framed for that purpose. It was possible, and probable, he said, that there had been intermediate insolvencies of some of the stockholders, and that injustice might arise to other creditors not before the court, unless it was guarded against by the decree. His conclusion accordingly was, that the duty of the court "was best performed by holding the plaintiffs entitled to a decree, that the defendants pay out of the dividends of the capital stock, received by them, so much of the debts due to the plaintiff, as the number of shares held by them in the same capital stock (namely, 320 shares) bears to the whole number of shares in the capital stock (namely, 2,000)." In Vermont, not only the corporation, but the members composing it, are individually liable in chancery if they do not appropriate their money to payment of their debts, or if they permit their property to be wasted.[1]

§ 602. Though the court, in the above case of Wood *v.* Dummer, proceeded upon the principle that the stock was a trust fund, and that the stockholders, both in law and fact, were affected with notice of the trust, it has been viewed, that the foundation of the decree was the

---

premiums, received by an insurance company, in advance, upon policies of insurance, are not surplus profits which the directors are authorized to distribute as dividends, among the stockholders of the company, but are the ordinary means or primary fund out of which the losses upon such policies should be paid. Scott *v.* Eagle Fire Company, 7 Paige, 198. The capital stock of an insurance company is not the primary or natural fund for the payment of losses which may happen by the destruction of the property insured. The charter of the company contemplates the interest upon the capital stock, and the premiums received for insurance, as the ordinary fund out of which losses are to be paid. De Peyster *v.* American Ins. Co. 6 id. 486.

[1] Bigelow *v.* Con. Society, 11 Vt. 283. A stockholder may maintain an action to restrain the directors from misapplying the funds of the corporation in paying dividends when there is no money earned for that purpose. Carpenter *v.* N. Y. & New Haven R. R. Co. 5 Abbott, Pr. 277; South Car. Man. Co. *v.* Bank of S. Car. 6 Rich. 227.

agreement of the stockholders to pay the sums they had respectively subscribed to the capital stock. That the agreement was with the corporation, which was liable in the first instance, and the creditors had a right to claim that, as against the corporators, their equities should be worked out through the corporation.[1] It has been held, that where the trustees, or other proper agents for that purpose, neglect to call in the debts due by the stockholders of a corporation, for stock, so as to enable the company to pay its debts, a creditor, by a bill in chancery, can compel such agents to enforce contribution from the stockholders according to their subscription.[2] The same principle was acted upon in Slee *v.* Bloom,[3] in which the stockholders were required in the first instance to pay up the amount of their subscriptions, for the benefit of the creditors. An act of the State of Connecticut incorporating a manufacturing company, provided that the capital stock of the corporation should not exceed $50,000; that a share of the stock should be $100; that the directors might call in the subscriptions to the capital stock by instalments, in such proportions, and at such times and places as they should think proper. After the stockholders had paid in forty per cent. on their subscriptions, the corporation became insolvent, having no visible property. On a bill in chancery, brought by certain creditors, praying that they might be compelled to pay in the remaining sixty per cent. (or so much thereof as should be necessary), to be applied in payment of the debts of the corporation, it was held, that the obligation which the stockholders assumed, by their subscription to the capital stock of the corporation, was to pay the sum of $100 on each share, in such instalments and at such times as should be required by the directors; that the amount of the shares subscribed, and not the sum actually paid in, constituted the capital stock of the corporation; that it was the duty of the directors to call in such instalments as were necessary to meet the debts of the corporation, and that this duty might be enforced by a decree in chancery.[4] It was held, in South Carolina, by

---

[1] See 1 Am. Law Mag. 102; but see contra, 4th vol. of the same work, 363.

[2] Briggs *v.* Penniman, 8 Cow. 387. See also, Society of Practical Knowledge *v.* Abbott, 2 Beav. 559, and cases there cited; Wallworth *v.* Holt, 4 Mylne, & C. 619.

[3] Slee *v.* Bloom, 19 Johns. 474; and see Fowler *v.* Robinson, 31 Me. 789.

[4] Ward *v.* Griswoldville Man. Co. 16 Conn. 593. In Ohio, the principle has been recognized, by the Supreme Court of the State, that a creditor's bill will lie against a stockholder of an incorporated company, to compel him to pay over to a judgment creditor the amount of his subscription, which had not before been paid to the company. Henry *v.* Vermillion & Ashland Railroad Co. 17 Ohio, 187, and see 11 Ohio, 273, and 13 id. 197.

Chancellor Desaussure, that, where the funds of a corporation are not whole and tangible, but consist in the liability of members to be assessed, a court of equity will lend it aid in favor of a creditor of the company, to assist it in enforcing the payment of instalments required by the members, and will apply the fund so raised to discharge the debt. It is, as it were, he said, a *subrogation* of the complainant to the rights of the company.[1] The Chancellor, in this case, relied upon the case of Salmon *v.* Hamburg Company.[2]

§ 603. The ground of the equitable liability of the members is the *credit* which the company has gained as a corporation, on the promise of the individual members, to raise a fund which should enable the corporation to fulfil its engagements. And it has been considered, that if the doctrine of Chancellor Desaussure is founded upon a just view of the undertaking and liabilities of individual corporators, they would be liable in equity for debts contracted beyond the amount of their capital stock, *with their consent*, on the same principle that they are bound for their subscriptions to the capital.[3] In New York, upon an appeal by the defendant from the Vice-Chancellor, the case was, the directors of an insurance company agreed among themselves to take a majority of the stock, and to give their stock notes for the same, secured by an hypothecation of the stock, and after the company had became greatly embarrassed, one of the directors agreed with the president to give him $6,000, if he would take his stock and substitute his own note in lieu of the stock note of such director, which was accordingly done. It was held to be a fraud upon the creditors of the company, and the other stockholders who had paid for their stock; and that the receiver who

---

See also, Atwood *v.* R. Island Agricultural Bank, 1 R. I. 376. It was held, by the Supreme Court of Georgia, in the case of a bill in equity filed by the creditors of the Habersham Iron Works Co., and seeking to make the stockholders personally liable for the debts of the corporation, that a sale of stock by a portion of the shareholders to the rest, is not such a sale by the corporation as will make the purchasers liable to the creditors of the company. Berry *v.* Matthews, 1 Kelly, 519.

[1] Per Chan. Desaussure in Hume *v.* Winyaw, &c. Canal Co., originally published in Carolina Law Journ. vol. i. p. 217, and afterwards in 1 Am. Law Mag. 92; and see S. Carol. Man. Co. *v.* Bank of S. Car. 6 Rich. 227.

[2] 1 Cases in Chan. 204; and reported in 1 Kyd on Corp. 273; and the same case was cited by Spencer, J., in Briggs *v.* Penniman, *ub sup.* See Society, &c. *v.* Abbott, 2 Beav. 559; Robinson *v.* Smith, 3 Paige, 222; Haslett *v.* Wotherspoon, 1 Strob. Eq. 209.

[3] 1 Am. Law Mag. 103. But see the doctrine controverted by a writer in 4 Am. Law Mag. 363.

had been appointed to wind up the affairs of the company, was entitled to recover the amount of the stock note of the director thus given up, with the exception of the sum which had actually been paid by the president to the company, out of the $6,000 received by him as a premium upon his purchase.[1]

§ 604. In New York, under the general banking law of that State, the receiver of a banking corporation represents both the creditors and stockholders, and he may assert the rights of each.[2] And upon the granting of an order of sequestration, and for the appointment of a receiver of an insolvent corporation, in an action brought in behalf of all its creditors, the right of action against its stockholders, for the amount of their unpaid subscriptions to its capital, vests in the receiver, and a judgment creditor of the corporation will be restrained from prosecuting an action against the stockholder, commenced by him after the making of such order, but before the appointment of the receiver under it was perfected.[3] The remedy provided by the thirty-sixth section of the Revised Statutes of New York, relative to proceedings against corporations in equity, is limited to creditors who have proceeded to an execution against property without effect; and it may be exercised, although no call has ever been made for the sums remaining unpaid on the shares; and it is concurrent, and may be enforced at law or in equity; a suit for that purpose in equity being maintainable against each stockholder severally.[4]

§ 605. It has been the legislative policy, in several of the States, to provide, in acts of incorporation of companies who have for their object

---

[1] Nathan *v.* Whitwell, 9 Paige, 152; see also, *Ex parte* Bennett, 18 Beav. 339, 5 De G., M. & G. 284, 27 Eng. L. & Eq. 572; *Ex parte* Walker, Ch. 1856, 39 Eng. L. & Eq. 576.

[2] Gillet *v.* Moody, 3 Comst. 479.

[3] Rankine *v.* Elliott, 16 N. Y. 377.

[4] Mann *v.* Pentz, 2 Sandf. Ch. 257. As to the appointment and duty of a receiver in New York, in the case of an insolvent corporation, see Jackson Marine Insurance Co. 4 Sandf. Ch. 559; Pentz *v.* Hawley, 1 Barb. Ch. 122; Halliday *v.* Noble, 1 Barb. 137; Morgan *v.* New York & Albany Railroad Co. 10 Paige, 290; City Bank of Buffalo, id. 378; Mickles *v.* Rochester Bank, 11 Paige, 118. It was held, by the New York Court of Appeals, 3 Comst. 415, that when the return of an execution at law unsatisfied is the ground of proceeding against a corporation, and the effects of the corporation are not sufficient to pay the debts, the creditor may resort to equity to recover the unpaid subscriptions of the capital stock, by making the delinquent stockholders parties to the bill against the corporation.

a dividend of profits among the stockholders, that each stockholder shall be personally liable in his *private estate* for the company debts.[1] It appears, also, that the same material alteration in the common law has been introduced, in relation to corporations of this description to be in future created. There is certainly nothing which could more conclusively show the understanding in the community at large, that the individuals composing the body corporate were not liable for the corporate engagements at common law, than the adoption of this course of legislative policy.[2] Some persons have disapproved of this policy, while others have entertained the opinion that a legislative body acts wisely in allowing the principle of a simple copartnership to be continued in operation. The latter argue, that, considering the multitude of joint-stock corporations in the United States,[3] which the increasing spirit of

---

1 Middletown Bank *v.* Magill, 5 Conn. 28, and Southmayd *v.* Russ, 3 id. 52. To create any individual liability for the debt of a corporation, a body politic created by law, and regarded as a legal being, distinct from that of all the members composing it, and capable of contracting and being contracted with as a person, is a wide departure from established rules of law, founded in considerations of public policy, and depending solely on provisions of positive law. It is therefore to be construed strictly, and not extended beyond the limits to which it is plainly carried by such provisions of statute. Per Shaw, C. J., in Gray *v.* Coffin, 9 Cush. 199. In Cable *v.* McCune, 26 Misso. 371, it is held that a claim for damages against a corporation arising from the negligence or misfeasance of its servants, is not a " debt " of the corporation within the meaning of the statute imposing a personal liability. In England, shareholders have been made personally liable for the debts of the corporation, to a great extent by several recent statutes. For decisions under the same, extent of liability, and mode of proceeding, see Hitchins *v.* Kilk. & Gr. S. & W. Railway Co. 15 C. B. 459, 29 Eng. L. & Eq. 341; Mackenzie *v.* Sligo & Sh. Railway Co. 4 Ellis & B. 119, 28 Eng. L. & Eq. 217; Moss *v.* Steam Gond. Co. 17 C. B. 186, 33 Eng. L. & Eq. 198; Addison *v.* Tate, 11 Exch. 250, 33 Eng. L. & Eq. 343; King *v.* Parental End. Ass. Co. 11 Exch. 443, 33 Eng. L. & Eq. 408; Russell *v.* Croysdill, 11 Exch. 123, 32 Eng. L. & Eq. 584; Morisse *v.* Royal Br. Bk., C. B. 1856, 37 Eng. L. & Eq. 447; Ridgway *v.* Sec. Mut. Life Ass. Co. 18 C. B. 686, 37 Eng. L. & Eq. 269; Baily *v.* Univ. Prov. Life Ass., C. B. 1856, 38 Eng. L. & Eq. 246; Edwards *v.* Kilk. & Gr. S. & W. Railway Co., C. B. 1856, 38 Eng. L. & Eq. 226; Hill *v.* London & Co. Ass. Co. 1 H. & N. 390, 38 Eng. L. & Eq. 407; Nixon *v.* Brownlow, 1 H. & N. 405, 38 Eng. L. & Eq. 323. And it has been repeatedly held there, that a shareholder whose name appears on the last delivered memorial on an application of a judgment creditor of the company for leave to issue execution against him, cannot divest himself of his liability by showing that he was induced to become a shareholder by the fraudulent misrepresentations of the directors, and that as soon as he became aware of the fraud he repudiated the contract. Powis *v.* Harding, 1 C. B., N. S., 533, 37 Eng. L. & Eq. 451; Henderson *v.* Off. Man. of Royal Br. Bk. 7 Ellis & B. 356, 38 Eng. L. & Eq. 86; Daniell *v.* Royal Brit. Bk. 1 H. & N. 681, 38 Eng. L. & Eq. 559.

2 See Spear *v.* Grant, 16 Mass. 9.

3 See *ante*, § 63-66.

enterprise gives rise to, a regard for the interests of the community requires that the individuals whose property (thus put into a common mass) enables them to obtain credit, universally, should not shelter themselves from a responsibility to which they would, as members of an unincorporated copartnership, be subjected to.[1]

§ 606. It has been the policy of the legislature of Massachusetts, from the year 1809, to increase the liability of the individual stockholders[2] in manufacturing corporations, for the debts of the corporation. The earliest general legislative regulation to this effect in that State was made in 1809; though previously, one or two acts of incorporation contained a similar provision. By this general act it is provided, that, "when any action shall be commenced against any corporation that may hereafter be created, or whenever any execution may issue against such corporations on any judgment rendered in any civil action, and the said corporation shall not, within fourteen days after demand thereof made upon the president, treasurer, or clerk of such corporation, by the officer to whom the writ or execution against such corporation has been committed to be served, show to the same officer sufficient real or personal property, or estate, to satisfy any judgment that may be rendered upon such writ, or to satisfy and pay the creditor the sums due upon such execution, then, and upon such neglect and default, the officer to whom such writ and execution may have been committed for service, shall serve and levy the same writ or execution upon the body or bodies, and real and personal estate of any member or members of such corporation."

§ 607. The above act, we are told,[3] did not satisfy the Massachusetts legislature; and, in 1818,[4] a new statute was passed, which provides, "that whenever any action shall be commenced against any manufacturing corporation, that may hereafter be created, or whenever any execution may issue against such corporation on any judgment rendered

---

[1] See opinion of Parker, C. J., in Marcy *v.* Clark, 17 Mass. 334, and 2 Am. Jurist, p. 95, and 4 id. 307.

[2] A holder of shares in a corporation, the certificate of which is absolute, is liable for the debts of the company, in the same manner as any other member, although he has agreed to retransfer the shares upon the performance of certain conditions, and although the transfer was intended to be collateral. Holyoke Bank *v.* Burnham, 11 Cush. 183.

[3] See Am. Jurist, vol. 2, p. 102, and 4 id. p. 307.

[4] Mass. St. 1818, c. 183.

in any civil action, and the said corporation shall not, before the day on which the said execution is returnable, after demand thereof made upon the president, treasurer, or clerk of such corporation, by the officer to whom the writ or execution against such company has been committed to be served, show to the same officer sufficient personal estate to satisfy any judgment that may be rendered upon such writ, or to satisfy and pay the creditor the sums due upon such execution, then, upon such neglect and default, upon the issuing of an *alias* execution, the officer, to whom such execution may be committed for service, may serve and levy the same writ and execution upon the body or bodies, and real and personal estate or estates of any member or members of such corporation, or upon the body or bodies, and upon the real and personal estate of any person or persons, who were members of said corporation, at the time when the debt or debts accrued, upon which such writs or executions may have issued."[1]

§ 608. By a subsequent statute of Massachusetts, it is enacted, "that every person who shall become a member of any manufacturing corporation which may hereafter be established within this commonwealth, shall be liable in his individual capacity, for all debts contracted during the time of his continuing a member of such corporation."[2] Such was the state of the laws of Massachusetts, respecting what is called "personal responsibility" of members of corporations, until 1827, when the legislature, by a statute,[3] changed in some measure the nature and du-

---

1 "We cannot forbear noticing," says a writer in the American Jurist (vol. 2, p. 97), "the very slovenly manner in which this statute is drawn. It would seem, from the words of the statute, which speaks, in the beginning of an action being commenced, and couples the words '*writ* and execution' together several times, that it proposed to give some power on the original writ, yet no power is given; and though the demand is made on the original writ, yet no authority to do any thing is still given, till an *alias* execution. And persons who are members of the corporation at the time when the debt accrued, but who are not members when the suit is brought, appear, as we at first thought, to be only liable on an *alias* execution, not on the writ, nor on the first execution, nor on a *pluries*. If the propriety of making such persons liable at all be admitted, no reason can be perceived why their liability should be confined to an *alias* execution. On looking more closely at the words of the statute, although no power is given until the issuing of the *alias*, it seems to be left uncertain whether the *alias* itself is to be served on the individual members, or whether the original writ or the prior execution, on which the demand was made, and which would be defunct in the common course, are not to be revived for the purpose of serving them on the individual members."

2 Mass. St. 1821, c. 38.

3 Mass. St. 1826, c. 137.

ration of this responsibility. The statute referred to enacts as follows: —

"Sec. 1. That no member of any manufacturing corporation, and no person who shall have been such member at the time when any debt may have been contracted by such corporation, or at the time when any debt so contracted may have accrued, shall hereafter be liable in his individual capacity for any such debt, unless a suit shall have commenced therefor, and prosecuted against such corporation, within one year after such debt shall have become due, and unless a suit therefor shall be commenced against such person, having been a member as aforesaid, within one year after he shall have ceased to be a member.

"Sec. 2. Any person whose real or personal estate shall have been levied on for payment of the debt of such corporation, or who shall have paid any such debt on execution, shall have an action at law or in equity in the Supreme Court, for contribution against the other members of such corporation, and persons having been members as aforesaid; or he may, at his election, have an action at law against the corporation.

"Sec. 3. Any corporation already established may adopt this law by vote, publishing the vote and the act in one or more Boston papers, in which the laws of the commonwealth are published, and in one or more of the newpapers of the county where the corporation has its manufacturing establishment; or if no newspaper in the county, in one of the nearest county; and provided this adoption shall not affect any liabilities existing at the time of the adoption.

"Sec. 4. The provisions of this and former acts on the same subject, shall not be construed to render personally liable for the debts of such corporation persons holding stock as *executors*, *administrators*, *guardians*, *or trustees*, *nor any persons holding stock as collateral security*. But the persons pledging the stock are to be liable as members, and to be considered as members for the purpose of voting and transacting business.

"Sec. 5 repeals all acts as far as inconsistent with this, except with regard to such existing corporations as do not adopt this."[1]

---

[1] This statute is commented on by the writer to whom we have before referred, in the American Jurist, as follows: "The first section provides, that no person shall be liable for a corporate debt, unless a suit therefor shall be commenced against such person, having been a member as aforesaid, within one year after he shall have ceased to be a member. None of the previous acts provide for such a suit; they all specify the cases in

§ 609. It has been believed, that the effect of imposing an unlimited responsibility upon the members of manufacturing corporations in Massachusetts, has been to drive millions of capital into the neighboring States for investment.[1] The legislature, at a later period, have set themselves about alleviating this supposed public injury, and at the same time affording an adequate security to creditors. We refer to the

---

which the bodies or property of individual members may be taken; but it is always on a suit against the corporation, not against the individual. Nor does this statute give any action against the individual members, unless it is given by implication in this clause. The question then arises, whether any action against the individual stockholders be in fact given, and if so, what is the form of the action? Is it debt, or the same action which could be maintained against the corporation; is it a suit in equity, or at common law; is it a several action against every person liable, or a joint action against more than one; must all the persons liable be joined in one action or not; when may the suit be brought; can it be brought simultaneously with a suit against the corporation, or not until after judgment has been rendered against the corporation? If an action is not thus given by an implication, the condition of the liability, that is, the suit against the individual, being precedent and impossible, is any individual responsibility created?

The second section of the statute gives the person who pays the corporate debts a right of action against the corporators individually, *or* the corporation, *at his election.* It seems to us that his remedies ought to be cumulative, both against the corporation and the individual members also.

With regard to the third section, it appears to us that if any publication of assent was necessary, in order to entitle corporations to the benefit of the act, it could hardly be necessary to require every one of them to publish the whole act at length.

The propriety of exempting executors, administrators, guardians, and trustees, from any personal responsibility, is obvious. A further effect of this act is perhaps to exempt the estates of deceased persons, as well as their executors and administrators, from any liability for the debts of corporations contracted subsequently to the death of the testators and intestates; and it seems also that *cestui que trusts,* as well as their trustees, are not subject to any personal responsibility. It would be perhaps a great hardship to those who are beneficially interested in the estates of deceased stockholders, to make these estates liable for the debts of the corporations over which they have no control, where the debts are contracted subsequently to the death of the stockholders. But notwithstanding this hardship, which we acknowledge, we do not see why the estate of a deceased stockholder should not be as liable as that of a living one. The law continuing the partnership after death, and thus entitling the estate of the deceased to share in the profits, if any are realized, ought, one would think, to make it liable to share in the losses. Exempting trustees and their *cestui que trusts* both from responsibility, appears liable to some exception, as it affords a very convenient mode of evading the whole operation of the statutes on the subject, and of one of which, we believe, advantage has already been taken. Indeed, we do not see why the estate of the *cestui que trust,* who is beneficially interested in the corporation, should not be liable in the same manner as that of any stockholder."

[1] American Jurist, vol. 4, p. 307. For the course of legislation in Massachusetts as to *banks,* and which render the stockholders liable personally, see Crease *v.* Babcock, 10 Met. 547, *et seq.*

Massachusetts act of 1830, entitled, "An act defining the general powers and duties of manufacturing corporations." The substance of this act is, that each and every member shall be jointly and severally liable for all the debts, until the whole amount of the capital stock shall have been actually paid in, and not afterwards; or not after a certificate, signed and sworn to by certain of the officers of the company, that a member has contributed his full share of the stock, has been recorded in the registry of deeds in the county wherein the manufactory shall be established. The act also provides, that, if such certificate be wilfully false in any material representation, then all the officers who have signed the same shall be liable personally for all claims and demands against the corporation, which were created while they were members. And if the president and directors of any such corporation shall declare and pay, or cause to be declared and paid, any dividend, such corporation being at the time insolvent, or if payment of such dividend would render it insolvent, they are all (with the exception of those who protest against it) made personally liable for the full amount of such dividend so declared and paid. Under the Revised Statutes of Massachusetts, a member of a manufacturing company may be liable for the debts of the company contracted while he was a member, although he ceases to be such before the debts become payable; but he is not liable for debts contracted before he became a member, if his membership expires before the debts become payable, and action brought.[1]

§ 610. The liability of stockholders of joint-stock incorporated companies, has been the subject of frequent attention in the State of New York. In that State, an act relative to manufacturing corporations, passed in 1811, declares, "that for all debts which shall be due and owing by the company, at the time of its dissolution, the persons then composing such company shall be individually responsible, to the extent of their respective shares of stock in the said company, and no further."[2] Some of the charters of companies, since incorporated in that State, contain a provision, that the stockholders "shall be holden, in their

---

[1] Holyoke Bank *v.* Burnham, 11 Cush. 183.

[2] In Rosevelt *v.* Brown, 1 Kern. 148, it was held, that by the words "the persons composing such company," the owners of stock are meant; and that B., who held stock at the time of the dissolution of the company as a collateral security, the transfer to him on the books of the company being absolute, was individually responsible to a creditor of the company, to the amount of the stock so held by him.

individual capacities, responsible jointly and severally for the payment of all debts contracted by the said company, to the nominal amount of the stock held by such stockholders respectively; and any person having any demand against the said company may sue any stockholder singly, or any two or more stockholders thereof jointly, and recover in any court having cognizance thereof; *provided*, such suit shall not be maintained without proof that such demand had been presented to the proper officer of said company for payment thereof, and the payment thereof neglected or refused. The revised laws of New York, in the regulations respecting moneyed corporations, provide, that each stockholder shall be liable ratably for corporate debts, but not to an amount exceeding the nominal amount of his shares.[1] And if an action is

---

[1] Extracts from Revised Statutes, vol. 1, ch. 18, pp. 592, 593. "Of Incorporations." Title 2d, Article 1st.

"§ 14. Every insolvency of a moneyed corporation shall be deemed fraudulent, unless its affairs shall appear, upon investigation, to have been fairly and legally administered, and, generally, with the same care and diligence, that agents, receiving compensation for their services, are bound by law to observe; and it shall be incumbent on the directors and stockholders of every such insolvent corporation, to repel by proof the presumption of fraud.

"§ 15. In every case of a fraudulent insolvency, the directors of the insolvent company, by whose acts or omissions the insolvency was wholly or in part occasioned, and whether then in office or not, shall each be liable to the stockholders and creditors of the company, for his proportional share of their respective losses; the proportion to be ascertained by dividing the whole loss among the whole number of directors liable for reimbursement; but this section shall not be construed to diminish the liability of directors, as before declared, who shall have violated or have been concerned in violating the provisions of this article.

"§ 16. If the moneys, remaining due to the creditors of a corporation whose insolvency shall be adjudged fraudulent, after the distribution of its effects, shall not be collected, in whole or in part, from the directors liable for their reimbursement, the deficiency shall be made good, by the contribution of the stockholders of the company; the whole amount of the deficiency shall be assessed on the whole number of shares of the capital stock, and the sum necessary to be paid on each share shall be then ascertained, and each stockholder shall be liable for the sum assessed on the number of shares held by him, not exceeding the nominal amount of such shares, in addition to the sums paid, or which he may be liable to pay, on account of those shares.

"§ 17. If the amount assessed on the shares of any stockholder, under the provision of the last section, shall not be collected from such stockholder, by reason of his insolvency, or his absence from this State, the sum remaining due on such assessment shall be recoverable against the person, from whom the delinquent stockholder, at any time within six months previous to the insolvency of the company, shall have received a transfer of the shares, or any portion of the shares held by him; and every person having made such transfer shall be liable in the same manner, and for the same proportion, that he would have been liable, had he continued to hold the shares so transferred."

The later enactments on this subject are: The act of 1838, ch. 98. By the first section

brought to enforce the individual liability of a stockholder for debts incurred before the capital stock was paid up, it may be defeated by showing that the defendant has already paid, on account of the debts of the corporation, a sum equal to the amount of his stock.[1] Married women are also liable in New York to the amount of the stock owned by them;[2] and an apportionment of the debts of a corporation among the stockholders may be ordered, notwithstanding there is a large amount of assets in the receiver's hands not disposed of.[3] In Rhode Island, it is provided, in the latest bank charters, that in case of default and mismanagement on the part of the directors, and of want of corpo-

---

of which, persons holding stock as executors, administrators, guardians, or trustees, are exempted from any personal liability, but the estates and funds in their hands are made liable to the same extent, as if the testator, &c., would have been living or competent to act. By the second section, executors, &c., are made competent to vote at all meetings of the corporation as representatives of such stock. By the third section, the pledgor of stock is alone made liable as a stockholder, but the certificate issued to the pledgee must state, that such stock is holden by him merely as a security. The fourth section makes it the duty of the officer in custody of the records of the corporation, to exhibit the records upon a written request of the creditor of the owner of the stock so pledged, and if he neglects to do so, and a loss ensues in consequence to such creditor, the company is made liable therefor.

The act of 1851, ch. 252. By which stockholders are made liable, jointly and severally, for debts of the corporation that may be due to their laborers, servants, an dapprentices, their wives and minor children, that may be hereafter performed by them, as operatives of such corporation. This statute merely relates to corporations created for manufacturing, mechanical, mining or quarrying purposes.

The act of 1851, ch. 315, which relates merely to the mode of proceeding upon execution against stockholders of manufacturing corporations.

The 6th section of the general act of 1852, ch. 228, provides that the stockholders shall be severally individually liable to the creditors of the corporation, to an amount equal to the amount of stock held by them respectively, for all debts and contracts made by such corporation until the amount of its capital stock shall have been paid in and a certificate made and recorded. Under this statute it has been held, that each stockholder is individually liable. Abbott *v.* Aspinwall, 26 Barb. 202.

The act of 1855, ch. 290, which enacts, "That any manufacturing company may issue two kinds of stock, *general* stock and *special* stock. The *special* stock shall at no time exceed two fifths of the actual capital of the corporation, and shall be subject to redemption at par after a fixed time, to be expressed in the certificate. Holders of such *special* stock shall in no event be liable for the debts of the corporation beyond their stock. Holders of *general* stock shall be jointly and severally individually liable for all the debts of the corporation until such *special* stock shall be redeemed in full: provided, always, that no corporation shall issue such *special* stock, except by a vote of three fourths of the general stockholders at a meeting duly called for that purpose."

[1] Garrison *v.* Howe, 17 N. Y. 458.

[2] In the matter of the Reciprocity Bank, 29 Barb. 369.

[3] Ibid.

rate property to pay the corporate debts, the members of the company shall be individually responsible for such debts.

§ 611. We now proceed to consider the new and peculiar class of cases that owe their origin to the particular acts of incorporation and to the general statutes of the kind we have referred to, imposing a responsibility upon the members of a private corporation, in case of the neglect of the corporate body to pay the demands which it has incurred. The responsibility so imposed, it has been observed, may not extend beyond the doctrine recognized and enforced by a court of equity, which is, that the capital stock of a corporation is a *trust fund*, and that it may as such be followed by the creditors of the corporation into the hands of the stockholders.[1] But where each of the stockholders is made personally responsible in his private estate, the stockholders are then subject to the same liabilities they would have been had they been associated for prosecuting their enterprise without a charter of incorporation.[2] In Allen *v.* Sewall,[3] the words of the statute were, that "the members of the company shall be liable individually," and Savage, C. J., said, "It was the intention of the legislature to put the defendants (stockholders) upon the same footing as to liability, as *if they had not been incorporated.*" "*Individual* liability in the act must be understood in contradistinction to *corporate* liability; and the defendants must, therefore, be held responsible to the same extent, and in the same manner, as if there was no act of incorporation." And judgment was rendered in accordance with this opinion.[4] In one respect, the personal liability may be full as onerous as that of a common copartner, as it is when a statute makes the stockholders *severally*, as well as jointly, personally liable.[5]

---

[1] See *ante*, § 599, *et seq.;* Langley *v.* Little, 26 Me. 162, 10 id. 234.

[2] Middletown Bank *v.* Magill, 15 Conn. 28; Clark *v.* Terry, 30 Me. 148.

[3] Allen *v.* Sewall, 2 Wend. 327.

[4] Although that judgment was afterwards reversed, 6 Wend. 335, it was upon a ground which did not touch the doctrine in question.

[5] Moss *v.* Oakley, 2 Hill, 269. Dealers contract with the corporation on the faith of that security for the performance of what is contracted, and they trust as well to the personal liability of the stockholders, as to the responsibility of the corporation for the fulfilment of the engagements of the corporation. A provision in the act of incorporation, that creditors must first obtain a judgment against the corporation, does not affect their right to the personal liability of the stockholder; nor does it prevent the liability of the stockholder to the creditor from attaching and becoming perfect, on the consummation of the contract of the creditor with the corporation. It simply defers the remedy by action upon that responsibility until the remedy at law against the corporation shall be exhausted, or

A defect in the proceedings to organize a corporation is no defence to a stockholder sued to enforce his individual liability, if he has participated in the acts of user of the corporation *de facto*.[1]

§ 612. There can be no question as to the constitutional authority of the legislature to pass such statutes, though that question was raised in Massachusetts. The authority of the legislature was objected to as infringing some of the principles of the constitution, and particularly two of the articles of the declaration of rights of that State; the first of which is intended to secure the liberty and property of the citizen, and the second to establish the right of trial by jury. If the fact were so, said Mr. C. J. Parker, the laws would undoubtedly be void. But all who are members of the corporation are virtually defendants in the action, and have an opportunity to be heard, in the form they have chosen by joining the company. As to those who have become members, after judgment against a corporation, or after a debt has accrued, they voluntarily subject themselves to the inconvenience, having the means to satisfy themselves of the solvency of the company, if they choose to make the inquiry.[2]

§ 613. Where it is provided, in an act creating such a corporation, that the individuals composing it shall be liable, at the time of the *dissolution* of the company, for the debts *then* due, any inability of the company, by reason of a total want of funds, to exercise its corporate powers, will be deemed a dissolution. That is to say, it is not necessary, in such a case, that the corporate rights should be regularly adjudged

---

the corporation shall have been dissolved. Corning *v.* McCullough, 1 Comst. 47; and 2 Denio, 77; Morgan *v.* New York & Albany Railroad Co. 10 Paige, 290; Fiske *v.* Keesville Man. Co. id. 592. The stockholders are the principal debtors of, and not *sureties* for, the corporation. Harger *v.* McCullough, 2 Denio, 119; *Ex parte* Van Riper, 20 Wend. 614. See also, Wright *v.* Field, 7 Ind. 376.

[1] Eaton *v.* Aspinwall, 19 N. Y. 119.

[2] Per Parker, C. J., in Marcy *v.* Clark, 17 Mass. 335; see also, Child *v.* Coffin, 17 Mass. 64; U. S. Trust Co. *v.* U. S. Fire Ins. Co. 18 N. Y. 199. As the act of incorporation of a Woollen Manufacturing Corporation, in Maine, was passed in 1833, it was contended, that it was not competent for the legislature afterwards to enact that the individual stockholders in it should be made liable for its debts. But it was held that the legislature had the constitutional power, as by the statute of 1839, to make the stockholders of a corporation personally liable *to the amount of their stock* for the debts of the corporation, contracted while they were stockholders, after the last act went into operation. Stanley *v.* Stanley, 26 Me. 191.

forfeited by any tribunal, before a creditor can maintain a suit against a stockholder. The government has no interest in dissolving a manufacturing or trading corporation, and it is not within the control of the creditors of the company to proceed by *scire facias*, or information in the nature of a writ of *quo warranto*, in order to obtain a judgment, that a corporation has forfeited its franchises. The case of Penniman *v.* Briggs, in the Court of Chancery of the State of New York,[1] fully supports these positions. In that case it was decided, that a corporation for manufacturing purposes, formed under the act of 22d March, 1811, having ceased to act as a manufacturing company, and being without funds and indebted, was dissolved, within the intent of the act, so as to give a remedy to creditors against the individual stockholders. And it was further held, that an election of trustees, made apparently for no purpose but to keep the company in existence, did not prevent such dissolution. The true question, as the Chancellor considered, was, whether the company was not dissolved, in the sense of the statute authorizing its creation. The statute, he said, contemplated the dissolution of the company, as an event which might occur, within the time prescribed for its existence; and the remedy given to creditors against stockholders was evidently intended for every mode of dissolution, which might deprive a creditor of an effectual remedy against the corporate body.

§ 614. In Kentucky, a judgment, execution, and return of no property, is sufficient ground for proceeding against the stockholders;[2] and so in Maine.[3] The judgment is at least *primâ facie* evidence of the

---

[1] Hopk. Ch. 300; and in error, 8 Cow. 387; also Bank of Poughkeepsie *v.* Ibbotson, 24 Wend. 473. For a limitation of this rule, see Brinkerhoff *v.* Brown, 7 Johns. Ch. 217; Bradt *v.* Benedict, 17 N. Y. 93, cited *post*, § 773.

[2] Castleman *v.* Holmes, 4 J. J. Marsh. 1.

[3] Drinkwater *v.* Portland Marine Railway, 18 Me. 35; Grose *v.* Hilt, 36 Me. 22; Chaffin *v.* Cummings, 37 Me. 76; Came *v.* Brigham, 39 Me. 35. See Whitney *v.* Hammond, 44 Me. 305. But in an action against a stockholder under the Maine statute, it is necessary to establish the existence and organization of the corporation, and a judgment obtained against the corporation is not conclusive of such existence in an action to which he is a stranger. Hudson *v.* Carman, 41 Me. 84. In Coffin *v.* Rich, 45 Me. 507, it was held that the repeal of a statute making stockholders personally liable for debts of the corporation is not a law impairing the obligation of contracts, even as to debts contracted before the repeal. In Georgia it has been held, that a return of no property on an execution against the assignee of a bank was not to be taken as conclusive against a stockholder, unless he had previously due notice that a *fi. fa.* had been placed in the officer's hand, with instructions to levy. Lane *v.* Harris, 16 Ga. 217.

validity of the debt.[1] Under the Revised Statutes of Massachusetts, though a creditor who has two demands against a manufacturing company, one only of which the stockholders are liable to pay, recovers a single judgment on all the demands, yet he may levy his execution on the personal property of a stockholder, to the amount of the demand which the stockholders are liable to pay.[2] And if a person holds stock in a manufacturing corporation as trustee, and also holds other property on the same trust, such other property may be taken for the debts of such company, if the stockholders of the company are liable to pay its debts.[3]

§ 615. A debt contracted by the agents or trustees of the company, renders the stockholders personally liable to the extent imposed by the statute. In the case of Slee *v.* Bloom, in the Court of Errors of the State of New York,[4] it appeared, that the respondents associated together for establishing a cotton manufactory, and became a corporation for twenty years, according to the provisions of an act passed in March, 1811, the seventh section of which declared "that for debt which shall be due and owing by the company *at the time of its dissolution*,[5] the persons *then* composing such company shall be individually responsible, *to the extent of their respective shares of stock* in said company. The corporation, in November, 1816, executed a bond to the appellant, under their corporate seal, on which a judgment was obtained in May, 1817. The corporation having been dissolved in February, 1818, it was held, that the judgment debt of the corporation was binding and conclusive on the respondents individually, to the extent of their respective shares. The Chancellor had, however, previously decided, that the judgment was not conclusive upon the respondents in their individual capacities, on the ground, *that the acts of trustees, while the corporation subsisted, however binding on the corporation and its property, were not binding upon the individual stockholders.* The Court of Errors, on the other hand, could perceive no escape from the conclusion, that the respondents were individually liable, to the same extent that the company itself was liable. And it was said, by Chief Justice Spencer,

---

1 Moss *v.* Oakley, 2 Hill, 265.

2 Stedman *v.* Eveleth, 6 Met. 114.

3 Ibid.

4 20 Johns. 669. The original case in Chancery will be found in 5 Johns. Ch. 366; and proceedings on appeal, also, in 19 Johns. 456.

5 As to what is a dissolution see *post*, ch. XXII.

that "whatever was a debt against the company, is now, by force of the statute, a debt against them; and if the company itself was concluded, the respondents are equally concluded. As an abstract proposition, he said, it was undoubtedly true, that the trustees of the company were not the trustees or agents of the individual stockholders. The trustees could not bind the individual members beyond the funds of the company, with this qualification, that they could bind the individual stockholders in the event of the dissolution of the corporation, to the extent of their respective shares, and no further."

§ 616. In an action under the New Hampshire statute against a stockholder for a debt of the corporation, it is necessary to allege specially and in a traversable form, that the defendant had notice before suit that the debt was demanded of the corporation and not paid, nor property exposed to attachment within sixty days afterwards.[1] By an act of the State of New Hampshire establishing the Hillsborough Bank, it was enacted, that if the corporation should neglect or refuse to pay any of their bills, when presented for payment, "the original stockholders, their successors or assigns, and the members of the said corporation," should be jointly and severally holden for the payment of them; and that the members compelled to pay should be authorized to recover of the remaining members of said corporation their proportion of the sum paid. The Supreme Court of Massachusetts, in expounding this law, in the case of Bond *v.* Appleton,[2] said, that the words of the law were very extensive, but that it was the reasonable construction of them, that *such* of the original stockholders, their successors and assigns, as should be members *when the payment of the bills should be refused*, were bound to make satisfaction. This construction, the court thought, was warranted by the remedy furnished to the members against the *remaining* members. In the State of New York, it has been held, that, if a charter provides generally, that the stockholders shall be personally liable for the payment of the corporate debts, and that persons having demands against the company, who have obtained judgment against the corporation, may sue any stockholder, the suit can only be brought against such as were stockholders when the debt was contracted, and not those who became so afterwards.[3] By an act of the legislature of

[1] Hicks *v.* Burns, 38 N. H. 141. See Haynes *v.* Brown, 36 N. H. 545.

[2] 8 Mass. 472. And see McDougald *v.* Bellamy, 18 Ga. 44.

[3] Moss *v.* Oakley, 2 Hill, 265; and see Judson *v.* Galena Co. 9 Paige, 548. In the

Connecticut, incorporating a manufacturing company, it was provided, that the persons and property of the members of the corporation should at all times be liable for all debts due by the corporation. This clause, it was held, did not include those who were members at the time the debt was contracted, but who had transferred their stock before the commencement of the suit.[1]

§ 617. In Massachusetts, it was enacted by the statute of 1808 that, "whenever any execution shall issue against any manufacturing corporation thereafter created, and such corporation shall not, within fourteen days after demand made upon the president, treasurer, or clerk of such corporation, by the officer holding the execution, show to him sufficient real or personal estate, to satisfy and pay the sums due on such execution, the officer shall serve and levy the same upon the body or bodies, and real and personal estate, of any member or members of such corporation." Although the statute made the estate of *any member or members* liable, yet, in the opinion of the Supreme Court, the statute applied to such as were members *at the time of the commencement of the action*, and to them only.[2] As that statute did not by it-

---

Court of Errors of New York, in 1846, it was held, that the provision in the act incorporating the Rossie Lead Mining Company, rendering the stockholders liable for its debts, is applicable to persons owning stock when the suit is brought, and not to those who were stockholders when the debt was contracted. Loft, Senator, in giving his opinion, said, that he was "aware that this construction is not in accordance with the decisions in Massachusetts and Connecticut on statutes of an analogous character." The opinion in Moss *v.* Oakley, *ub. sup.* and Moss *v.* Galena Co. 5 Hill, 137, disapproved. McCullough *v.* Moss, 5 Denio, 567.

[1] Middletown Bank *v.* Magill, 5 Conn. 28; Hosmer, C. J., and Brainard, J., dissenting. The case is not in accordance with Southmayd *v.* Russ, 8 Conn. 54; as per the court in Moss *v.* Oakley, *sup.* The act establishing the Pawlet Manufacturing Company, in Vermont, contained the following provision: "The persons and property of said corporation shall be holden to pay their debts, and when any execution shall issue against said corporation, the same may be levied on the persons or property of any individual thereof." It was held, that this provision imposed upon the corporation a primary liability, and upon the stockholders a liability subordinate to, and depending upon, the liability of the corporation, and is a liability carved out and existing by statute; and can have no existence independent of its provisions. Dauchy *v.* Brown, 24 Vt. 197. The 36th section of the Comp. Clauses Cons. Act, 8 & 9 Vict. ch. 16, which enacts that "if any execution, &c., shall have issued against the property or effects of the company, and there cannot be found sufficient whereon to levy such execution, then such execution may be issued against any of the shareholders, to the extent of their shares, not then paid up," has been held to mean shareholders at the sheriff's return of *nulla bona*. Nixon *v.* Green, 11 Exch. 550, 33 Eng. L. & Eq. 522.

[2] Child *v.* Coffin, 17 Mass. 64.

self render the estate of a deceased member liable for the corporate debts, his administrator cannot be allowed, in a probate account, for money paid to make up a deficit, where the corporate funds, on closing the concerns of the corporation, are found insufficient.[1] Under this act, no action can be maintained against a stockholder or his administrator, to recover assessments.[2] By the Massachusetts statute of 1817, c. 183, the legislature provided, that the bodies and estates of those who were members at the time any debt accrued, as well as those who were members when the execution issued, should be liable.[3]

§ 618. Under the statute of Massachusetts of 1829, c. 53, one who was a member of a manufacturing corporation, which had neglected to publish an annual statement of the amount of its capital stock, at the time a debt was contracted by the corporation, was held to be individually liable for such debt, though not a member at the time of the trial of the action.[4] Under the same statute, it was also held, that an unliquidated claim for damages, against a manufacturing corporation, is a debt making individual members liable. It appearing, in this case, that the annual notice published by the corporation, next before the debt was contracted, did not certify the amount both of their debts and of their capital stock, as required by the statute, but of their debts only, it was held, that one who was a member of the corporation at the time the debt was contracted, but who had ceased to be such when the action was tried, was individually liable for the debt, and consequently not a competent witness in behalf of the corporation. The certificate of the officers of a manufacturing company prescribed by the *Rev. Stat.* of Massachusetts, stating the amount of the capital fixed and paid in, sworn to and recorded, within the time prescribed in the registry of deeds, is conclusive evidence, for the stockholders, of the facts therein stated, so as to exempt them from personal liability for the subsequent debts of the company.[5] Under the Massachusetts statute of 1851, it

---

[1] Ripley *v.* Sampson, 10 Pick. 371.

[2] Cutler *v.* Middlesex Factory Co. 14 Pick. 483.

[3] Per Parker, C. J., in Marcy *v.* Clark, 17 Mass. 335.

[4] Mill-Dam Foundery *v.* Hovey, 21 Pick. 417. The decision in this case is approved by Mr. J. Story in Carver *v.* Braintree Man. Co. 2 Story, 431; Gray *v.* Bennett, 3 Met. 522, 530.

[5] Stedman *v.* Eveleth, 6 Met. 114. The provision of the Revised Statutes of Massachusetts, that all the members of an incorporated manufacturing company shall be jointly and severally liable in certain cases for the debts of the company, has been held to extend

has been determined that a person duly summoned as a stockholder and defaulted, cannot afterwards deny the existence of the corporation or his liability to be arrested as a stockholder in the execution against the corporation. It may also be shown, in an action against a sheriff by a stockholder for arresting him on an execution against the corporation, that he was a stockholder, although the return of the sheriff merely stated that he was arrested as "now or formerly an officer of the within-named corporation." And an execution against a corporation, which merely contains a command to take their property, authorizes the officer to take the body of a stockholder who is duly summoned in the action. The directions of the creditor, and not those of the precept merely, are to be followed.[1] A creditor of a corporation, who is also a stockholder individually liable for its debts, cannot take, upon attachment or execution against the corporation, the property of other stockholders equally so liable, but resort should be had to a bill in equity against them for a contribution.[2] And the property of stockholders cannot be taken on an execution against the corporation, if there are officers liable, upon whose property the execution may be levied.[3]

§ 619. The liability of members under these statutes, unless otherwise provided, is several, and not joint, or in the nature of a guaranty;[4] and a member who voluntarily pays a company debt for which all are liable, has no claim upon the other members for contribution.[5] But where the members voluntarily agree to reimburse to each other such sums as they may respectively be obliged to pay, in consequence of indorsing the notes of the corporation, they have a remedy for contribution on such agreement.[6] If they are declared to be jointly liable, they

---

to those who are members when the liability of the company is sought to be enforced, and is not confined to those who were members when the debt was contracted. The term "members," the court thought, must be held to include all the actual stockholders; and with their membership they take all the benefits and all the responsibilities which attach to that relation. Nor can this liability be a surprise upon them, if they exercise due diligence in examining the public records of the county. Curtis *v.* Harlow, 12 Met. 3.

[1] Richmond *v.* Willis, 13 Gray, 182.

[2] Thayer *v.* Union Tool Co. 4 Gray, 75.

[3] Denny *v.* Richardson, 4 Gray, 274.

[4] Bank of Poughkeepsie *v.* Ibbotson, 24 Wend. 473.

[5] Pratt *v.* Bacon, 10 Pick. 127; Andrews *v.* Callender, 13 Pick. 484. The stockholders of a manufacturing company created under the act of New York, of March 22, 1811, are severally and not jointly liable for debts due from the company at the time of its dissolution. Bank of Poughkeepsie *v.* Ibbotson, 5 Hill, 461.

[6] Andrews *v.* Callender, 13 Pick. 484.

are like copartners. The charter of an incorporated company, after declaring that the stockholders should be jointly and severally personally liable for the payment of all debts contracted by the company, and that any person having a demand against the company, might sue any stockholder and recover the same, provided that, before such suit upon any demand, judgment must be obtained thereon against the company, execution issued and returned unsatisfied, &c. It was held, that the charter placed the stockholders upon the same footing as if they had not been incorporated, making them answerable for demands against the company like partners; and consequently one stockholder, though a creditor of the company, could not maintain an action for his demand against the others or either of them. The remedy is in equity.[1] But if a member is a creditor of the corporation, he has the same right as any other creditor, to secure his demand by attachment or levy on the corporate property, although he may be personally liable, by statute, to satisfy other judgments against the corporation.[2]

§ 620. Where corporators are made personally responsible by charter for debts contracted "during the time they hold stock," those who are members at the date of a note given for a preëxisting debt, are liable, and not those who may have been liable when the original debt was contracted.[3] Under the statute of Massachusetts, of 1826, c. 137, § 1, where land was leased to a corporation, the stockholders of which were liable by the statute, after ceasing to be such, for any debt contracted by the corporation, while they were such, it was held, that no action could be maintained against a stockholder for the rent of a quarter which commenced after he had sold out his shares, although the lease was executed before such sale, inasmuch as rent does not accrue to the lessor as a debt, until the lessee has enjoyed the use of the land.[4]

§ 621. Where, by the terms of the charter of a joint-stock company,

---

[1] Bailey *v.* Bancker, 3 Hill, 188. The case of Simpson *v.* Spencer, 15 Wend. 548, considered, certain *dicta* overruled.

[2] Pierce *v.* Partridge, 3 Met. 44.

[3] Castleman *v.* Holmes, 4 J. J. Marsh. 1.

[4] Boardman *v.* Osborn, 23 Pick. 295. The provision of the Rev. St. of Massachusetts, c. 38, § 16, that all the members of an incorporated company shall be jointly and severally liable, in certain cases, for the debts of the company, extends to those who are members when the liability of the company is sought to be enforced, and is not confined to those who were members when the debts were contracted. Curtis *v.* Harlow, 12 Met. 3. And see Holyoke Bk. *v.* Burnham, 11 Cush. 183.

the stockholders are individually liable for the corporate debts to the nominal amount of their stock, a party who subscribes for a certain number of shares of the stock, is liable for the debts of the company to the nominal amount of the stock subscribed by him, although he has not paid in any part of his subscription, or done any act whatever as a stockholder of the company.[1] And under such a provision in the charter, it is no defence, that the creditors have paid in the full price of their stock; and they are liable individually to pay as much more, if necessary to discharge the debts due at the time of the dissolution.[2]

§ 622. It was held, in New York, that in a proceeding by attachment against a non-resident debtor, who is sought to be charged as a director of a foreign bank, the president and directors of which are by charter declared to be individually liable for all notes, &c., issued by the bank, it is not necessary, for the purpose of showing personal liability, that the charter should be produced as part of the preliminary proofs on application for the process.[3] On motion to set aside the attachment, the court will inquire into his liability, and will hold him personally liable if the charter declares him so.[4] It is no objection to the remedy by attachment, that the charter gives another remedy. A party to whom an action is thus given, is not confined thereto, but may resort to any remedy known to the law in any place in which the debtor or his property may be found.[5]

§ 623. But, however strictly the personal responsibility imposed upon the members of an incorporated company may be construed against creditors, there is one point which is very clear, and that is, no member can exonerate himself from his liability, and defeat the claims of creditors, by transferring his interest to a *bankrupt*. This was expressly admitted by the court in the case just cited, who said, that no principle was better settled, than that a conveyance, made with an intention to defeat a creditor, is void. The members of a corporation, therefore, who would be liable, if they continued members, to the creditors of the corporation, may still be treated as members, if they have disposed of their interest

---

1 Spear *v.* Crawford, 14 Wend. 20.

2 Briggs *v.* Penniman, 8 Cowen, 387.

3 *Ex parte* Van Riper, 20 Wend. 614.

4 Ibid.

5 Ibid.

with the view merely of exonerating themselves from their personal responsibility. In the case of Marcy *v.* Clark, in Massachusetts,[1] the question arose as to whether M. was a *member* of the company *at the time* the goods were taken. It appeared that, before the execution was levied, he had made a bill of sale of his share to one E., without adequate consideration, and for the express purpose, as found by the jury, of avoiding his liability to the execution as a member of the corporation. It was contended that he had a right thus to shift the burden from himself, and to give away his shares, if he chose. But Parker, C. J., said: "It is very true, every man may dispose of his own property as he pleases; but always subject to the equitable principle, that he is not to injure another by his gift." And he entertained no doubt that a transfer of an interest in the stock of a corporation, for the debts of which the members were personally liable, for the purpose of defeating the creditors of the corporation, was fraudulent and void. If it were otherwise, he said, the wholesome provision of the statute for the security of creditors of the company, would be unavailing at the very time, and under the very circumstances, in which it was intended to operate. The same has been held in New York.[2] And it had been held, in Kentucky, that if one subscribes for stock, in the name of minors, for the purpose of avoiding personal responsibility in case the corporation becomes insolvent, and receives the benefit of the stock, he will be liable for the corporate debts.[3] But it is also held in Massachusetts, that a retransfer of shares of stock by B. to A., in pursuance of an agreement to do so made contemporaneous with the original transfer by A. to B., terminates B's liability as a stockholder, although the retransfer is made for that very purpose.[4]

§ 624. It may be proper to refer to the remedies which the creditors of an insolvent incorporated company have against the members of the

---

[1] 17 Mass. 330. Under the Massachusetts statute of 1817, even a *bonâ fide* transfer of shares will not relieve the member from any debt which occurred while he was a member of the corporation. Ibid. 335.

[2] Moss *v.* Oakley, 2 Hill, 265. In Clark *v.* Perry, 30 Me. 148, it was held, that there is a breach of covenant, when a stockholder sells shares in a manufacturing corporation, and covenants that they were free from all incumbrances, if the shares of the stockholders were by statute made liable for the debts of the corporation; and if, at the time of the sale, the assets of the corporation are not equal to its liabilities.

[3] Roman *v.* Fry, 5 J. J. Marsh. 634.

[4] Holyoke Bank *v.* Burnham, 11 Cush. 183.

company, where a personal responsibility has been imposed by an express act of the legislature. The members in such a case, if their obligation is joint, it has appeared, stand in the same relation to creditors as the individuals who compose a simple copartnership. The creditors of the latter, although they have a remedy at law, yet if that remedy is defective, may call in aid the interference of a court of equity.[1]

§ 625. The principal question sought to be presented in Bank of Poughkeepsie *v.* Ibbotson,[2] was, whether an action at law would lie to charge the stockholder personally liable. The statute imposing the liability provided, that for all the debts due and owing by the company at the time of its dissolution, the persons then composing it shall be *individually* liable to the extent of their respective shares in the stock. The dissolution *sub modo*, or resulting from the fact of insolvency, being proved, and the liability of the stockholder, as declared by the act, becoming absolute, the court saw no valid objection to the enforcement of it in a court of law. The ground and the extent of the liability were distinctly given; and although it is true that the stockholder may be subjected to several suits, yet he can be charged only to the extent of his stock. An action of debt lies in favor of the creditor against the stockholder, as by the holder of a dishonored bank-bill, in a case where the members of an incorporated bank are made personally liable for the amount of their stock.[3]

---

1 See *ante*, § 609; Wood *v.* Dummer, 3 Mason, 308; Bailey *v.* Bancker, 3 Hill, 188; Atwood *v.* Rhode Island Agricultural Bank, 1 R. I. 376. Where the charter of a corporation permits its creditors to sue the stockholders in any court having cognizance thereof, a suit may be commenced in equity. Masters *v.* Rossie Lead Mining Co. 2 Sandf. Ch. 301. The common law, though it professes to adopt the *lex mercatoria,* has not adopted it throughout, in what relates to partnerships in trade. It holds, indeed, that although partners are in the nature of joint tenants, there shall be no survivorship between them in point of interest; yet, with regard to partnership contracts, it applies its own peculiar rule; and because they are in form joint, holds them only to produce a joint obligation, which consequently attaches exclusively upon the survivors. By the general mercantile law, however, a partnership contract is *several* as well as *joint,* and courts of equity, adopting, to its full extent, that law for their guidance, have considered joint contracts, which are in the nature of partnerships, as standing upon a different footing from *ordinary* joint contracts; and have ascribed to them a several as well as a joint operation. Gow on Partn. 232.

2 Bank of Poughkeepsie *v.* Ibbotson, 24 Wend. 473.

3 Ballard *v.* Bell, 1 Mason, 243. The creditor may proceed either in equity or law where the charter is silent, and if at law, may elect any appropriate action. Adkins *v.* Thornton, 19 Ga. 325.

§ 626. The same rule as to an election of legal and equitable remedies, will apply where the members are individually liable, that is applied where they are made jointly liable. That is, although a creditor may enforce a contribution at law, yet, as he may not be able to do it without numerous suits, his case is one of equitable jurisdiction. The creditors, if more than one, may also, if they apprehend a deficiency in the funds, enforce in equity a *pro rata* distribution, but this must be at their election. Any difficulty that may exist on the part of a stockholder in protecting himself at law beyond the statute liability, has never been suggested as a ground for proceeding in equity.[1]

§ 627. Under the Revised Statutes of Massachusetts, which provide that "holders of stock in any bank, at the time when the charter shall expire, shall be liable in their individual capacities for the payment and redemption of all bills which may have been issued by said bank, and which shall remain unpaid, in proportion to the stock" they may respectively hold at the dissolution of the charter; in a bill in equity against numerous stockholders in the Chelsea Bank, it was held, that the bill-holders could not severally maintain a bill in equity against the stockholders, to compel payment and redemption of the unpaid bills held by them respectively, but that all of them must join in one bill, or one or more of them must file a bill for the benefit of all, against all the stockholders; that those who own stock in a bank, as collateral security, are within the meaning of the said section; also, that when any part of the stock is owned by the bank itself, the individual stockholders are not, for that reason, liable to any further extent than they would have been if none of the stock had been so owned; also, that holders of stock are not jointly responsible for each other, but that each is severally liable in such a sum, not exceeding the par value of his shares, as the amount of unpaid bills may require; and that the liability of solvent holders cannot be extended by reason of the insolvency of other holders; also, that the holders of the stock are not liable to pay notes, called "post-notes," issued by the bank, payable on time, and with interest; nor to pay interest on unpaid bank-bills, either from the time when payment was demanded of the bank, or the time of filing a bill in equity to compel payment; also, that the remedy against the individual stock-

---

[1] Bank of Poughkeepsie *v.* Ibbotson, *sup.*; Briggs *v.* Penniman, 8 Cowen, 392. See also, Slee *v.* Bloom, 19 Johns. 456; Garrison *v.* Howe, 17 N. Y. 458; Wood *v.* Dummer, 3 Mason, 308. But see Harris *v.* First Parish in Dorchester, 23 Pick. 112.

holders, is not confined to those who held the bills of the bank at the time when the charter expired, but extends to those who, after the charter expired, took the bills in the ordinary course of business, or otherwise acquired a good title to them; also, that the terms, "bills which shall remain unpaid," mean bills that shall be ultimately unpaid after the application of the assets of the bank towards payment thereof, and that the holders of unpaid bills are not entitled to a decree for payment against the individual stockholders, until after the assets of the bank have been so applied.[1] In a subsequent case, at the same term of the court, several questions were raised at the argument, upon points similar to those in the case just cited, which had not then been decided. The principal question considered in the last-mentioned case was, whether the plaintiff, at the time of the commencement of his suit in equity, had such an interest as a bill-holder of the Nahant Bank, at the time of its dissolution, that he could maintain a suit in equity on the statute, to recover of the stockholders, in proportion to the amount respectively held by them at the time of the dissolution, the balance due to him as a holder of its bills, after receiving his dividend, in proportion with other creditors, of the assets of the bank. The first objection was, that he was not a holder of the bills in his own right, but only as a trustee for others, and that, as such trustee, he could not maintain such suit, or that if he could, he could not do so without joining those who stood in the relation of *cestuis que trust*, as parties. The court held, that a holder of bank-bills purchased by him as trustee, is enabled to maintain a bill in equity in his own name, without joining the *cestuis que trust*, against the stockholders, for himself and for all other holders of unpaid bills. Another ground of objection, on the part of the defendants, was, that they were not answerable, because these and many bills of the Nahant Bank were disposed of clandestinely, by fraud and collusion with the directors and officers of the bank, to the injury of the stockholders; that the plaintiff and other holders did not receive them in good faith, as money or currency, but with the knowledge that they were clandestinely issued. But it was held, that a person who buys bank-bills of a broker, at a discount, under an agreement to keep them from circulation for a certain time, is entitled to the statute remedy against the stockholders, for the full amount of the bills, unless he has notice, when he buys them, that they are improperly issued by the officers of the bank; but that

---

[1] Crease *v.* Babcock, 10 Met. 525. See also, Adkins *v.* Thornton, 19 Ga. 325.

such a sale to him by a broker, is not evidence of such notice. It was held, also, that when bills of a bank are sold by its officers, on a usurious contract, a subsequent *bonâ fide* purchaser of them is entitled to recover of the stockholders the full nominal value thereof, without any deduction on account of the usury in the sale by the officers of the bank. It was held, also, that an agreement by a bank, with a holder of its bills, to convey property to him in payment thereof, which agreement is not executed, by reason of an injunction on the bank and the placing of its assets in the hands of receivers, does not impair the bill-holder's remedy against the stockholders. When the assets of the bank are placed in the hands of receivers, it is held that the holders of its bills who do not present their claims to the receivers, cannot recover of the stockholders the full amount thereof, but only the balance which they would have been entitled to recover, if they had proved their claims before the receivers, and obtained part payment.[1]

§ 628. An insurance company, that owned stock in a bank, was made party to a bill in equity, under the Revised Statutes of Massachusetts, which renders the holders of stock in a bank, when its charter expires, liable for the payment of all its bills, and was ordered, by a decree of the court, to pay a certain sum for the benefit of the holders of unpaid bills; and an execution was issued against the company, which was returned unsatisfied. The plaintiffs in this bill afterwards filed another bill, alleging therein that the only property of said company was a promissory note for a large amount, payable to its own order; that the company had placed said note in the hands of S. and B. for safe keeping, to remain the property of the company until the suit by the above-mentioned first bill should be determined; that the plaintiffs were remediless, inasmuch as the company had no property on which an execution could be levied; that the company refused to indorse the note to the plaintiffs, and that S. and B. refused to do what was equitable and just towards the plaintiffs, and to enforce payment of the note by the makers; and praying, that the aforesaid decree against the company might be enforced, and that the maker of the note might be decreed to pay to the plaintiffs the amount due from said company on said decree. It was held, on demurrer, that the second bill was maintainable.[2]

---

[1] Grew *v.* Breed, 10 Met. 569.

[2] Grew *v.* Breed, 12 Met. 363.

§ 628 *a.* Officers and trustees of corporations are often personally liable by statute for neglect in the performance of their duties to creditors of the corporations. Thus, under the 12th section of the general manufacturing law of New York (1848, c. 40), if a company fails to make and publish a report of its condition annually, within twenty days from the 1st of January, all the trustees are jointly and severally liable for all the debts of the company then existing, and for all contracted before the report is made. Under this statute, it has been held that trustees who are elected subsequent to the neglect to publish, are not liable for such neglect.[1] Such debt must also have been contracted during a default, or have existed at the time of a subsequent default.[2] In New Jersey, it is provided that, if the certificate of the state of the company is false in any material representation, the officers signing it shall be personally liable. A certificate set forth that the capital stock had been paid in in cash, whereas in fact it had been paid in in property of an uncertain value, and it was held that this was a material misrepresentation, and that the officers were liable.[3] In Massachusetts, officers of a corporation are liable in several specified cases, but no provision is made for summoning them in a writ issued against the corporation.[4]

§ 629. Before we conclude the present chapter, it may be proper to refer to the distinction that exists between the personal liability, by the Common Law, of members of private corporations, and the members of public *quasi* corporations.[5] With respect to the former, we have already shown that, by the Common Law, no individual responsibility attaches to the members for the corporate debts, though the corporation may be sued for the recovery of them. A very different rule prevails with regard to the inhabitants of any districts, as counties or towns, incorporated by statute, which come under the head of *quasi* corporations; for against them no private action will lie, unless given by statute; and if a power to sue them is given by statute, each inhabitant is liable to satisfy the judgment.[6]

---

[1] Boughton *v.* Otis, 29 Barb. 196.

[2] Garrison *v.* Howe, 17 N. Y. 458.

[3] Waters *v.* Quimby, 3 Dutch. 198.

[4] Thayer *v.* Union Tool Co. 4 Gray, 75; Denny *v.* Richardson, 4 Gray, 274.

[5] As to the meaning of *quasi* corporations, see Introduction, §§ 23, 24.

[6] 2 Kent, Com. 221; Merchants Bank *v.* Cook, 4 Pick. 414. Though *quasi* corpora-

§ 630. In a case which came before the Court of Errors of the State of New York, it was said by Tallmadge, President, "that *overseers of the poor* must be made liable in their official or corporate capacity, or be charged as individuals. The action must be shaped accordingly, and be supported by sufficient proof. For official neglect or misconduct they may be indicted; but they never can be prosecuted for official liabilities, and be rendered individually responsible for the judgment, in their property and persons. This distinction between individual and official liability must be regarded; and will regulate the form of the proceedings, and the proof necessary to sustain the action. The judgment in the one case is against them as individuals, and becomes a lien on their property; and in the other, it is against them as a corporation, and binds only the corporate property.[1]

§ 630 *a*. After a corporation has been recognized as a corporation, and has claimed to be, and acted as such for over twenty years, and an individual has recognized its corporate existence by becoming the owner of a portion of its stock, and continuing to hold it, until the dissolution of the company, he will not be permitted, when sought to be made liable for a debt of the company, to allege that the corporation has never been legally incorporated.[2]

---

tions are liable to information or indictment for a neglect of a public duty imposed on them by law, yet it is settled, in the case of Russell *v.* Inhabitants of the County of Devon, 2 T. R. 667, that no private action can be maintained against them for a breach of their corporate duty, unless such action be given by statute. Per Parsons, C. J., in Riddle *v.* Proprietors of Locks, &c. on Merrimack River, 7 Mass. 187; and see also, Hawks *v.* Inhabitants of Kennebec, id. 462; Mower *v.* Leicester, 9 Mass. 247; Inhabitants of Brewer *v.* Inhabitants of New Gloucester, 14 Mass. 216; Adams *v.* Wiscasset Bank, 1 Greenl. 361; and see *ante*, §§ 23, 24.

[1] Flower *v.* Allen, 5 Cowen, 670, and see note to the case of Todd *v.* Birdsall, 1 id. 260.

[2] Mead *v.* Keeler, 24 Barb. 20.

CHAPTER XVIII.

OF THE PROCESS, PLEADINGS, AND EVIDENCE, IN SUITS, BY AND AGAINST CORPORATIONS, AT LAW AND IN EQUITY.

§ 631. In treating, in this chapter, of the process, pleadings, and evidence, in actions and suits by and against corporations, we shall confine ourselves to actions at law and suits in equity, in ordinary cases, as separate chapters are devoted to the proceedings in *mandamus*, and informations in the nature of *quo warranto*. It may be premised, that it has been shown, in a preceding chapter, that corporations may bring, both at home and abroad, the same actions for the recovery of their debts and property, and for redress for injuries, as natural persons.[1] Even in ejectment, they may now proceed in the ordinary way, without executing a power of attorney, authorizing a third person to enter and make a lease on the land, as was formerly the practice.[2] A stockholder in a corporation is a party to a suit brought against a corporation, to some extent and for some purposes. Thus if the judge before whom the case is tried could not sit if it were against a stockholder personally, he cannot hear the suit although the corporation alone is sued.[3]

§ 632. In England, and in some States of this country, the rule is, that when a body corporate institutes legal proceedings either on a contract, or to recover real property, it must, at the trial, under the general issue, prove the fact of incorporation,[4] unless, indeed, the act of incorpo-

---

[1] See *ante*, Chap. XI. Springfield *v.* Connecticut River Railroad Co. 4 Cush. 63.

[2] Adams on Eject. 193; St. George's Church *v.* Nestles, 3 Johns. 115. The president of a trading corporation has no right to commence an action in the name of the corporation. Ashuelot Man. Co. *v.* Marsh, 1 Cush. 507.

[3] Place *v.* Butternuts Woollen & Cotton Manf. Co. 28 Barb. 503.

[4] Norris *v.* Staps, Hob. 210 *b;* Henriquez *v.* Dutch West India Co. 2 Ld. Raym. 1535; 1 Kyd, 292, 293; Peters *v.* Mills, Buller, N. P. 107; Jackson *v.* Plumbe, 8 Johns. 295; Dutchess Cotton Manufactory *v.* Davis, 14 Johns. 245; Bank of Auburn *v.* Weed, 19 Johns. 303; Bill *v.* Fourth Western Turnp. Co. 14 Johns. 414; Ernest *v.* Bartle, 1 Johns. Cas. 319; Utica Bank *v.* Smalley, 2 Cowen, 778; Vernon Society *v.* Hills, 6 Cowen, 25;

ration be a public act which the courts are bound to notice *ex officio*.[1] It is, however, generally admitted, that a corporation may declare in its corporate name, without setting forth in the declaration the act of incorporation, or averring that it is a corporation, if the act be private.[2] The proof of incorporation seems to have been held equally necessary in case of motions made by corporations, as in suits brought by them.[3] But though, in an action by a corporation, it must be prepared to show its evidence of incorporation, yet it is not so when the action is to recover lands, the legal title to which is in trustees for the use of the corporation, and the suit is in their name.[4]

§ 633. In many of the States, on the other hand, the rule is well established, that if in a suit brought by a corporation the defendant plead the general issue, it is an admission of the corporate existence of the plaintiffs, which dispenses with all proof on their part to that point.[5]

Wood *v.* Jefferson Co. Bank, 9 Cowen, 205; Williams *v.* Bank of Michigan, 7 Wend. 540; United States *v.* Stearns, 15 Wend. 314; Wolf *v.* Goddard, 9 Watts, 544; Agnew *v.* Bank of Gettysburgh, 2 Harris & G. 478; Rees *v.* Conocheaque Bank, 5 Rand. 326; Hargrave *v.* Bank of Illinois, 1 Breese, 84, 86; Central Manuf. Co. *v.* Hartshorne, 3 Conn. 199; Middletown Bank *v.* Russ, id. 135; Jackson *v.* Bank of Marietta, 9 Leigh, 240; and that it has uniformly been held, in Virginia, that under the general issue the fact of incorporation must be proved, see 5 Rand. 326; 5 Leigh, 471; Farmers Bank *v.* Troy City Bank, 1 Doug. Mich. 457.

1 Agnew *v.* Bank of Gettysburgh, 2 Harris & G. 478; Dntchess Cotton Manufactory *v.* Davis, 14 Johns. 245; Rees *v.* Conocheaque Bank, 5 Rand. 326; Vance *v.* Bank of Indiana, 1 Blackf. 80; Carmichael *v.* Trustees, &c. 3 How. Miss. 84; Hays *v.* N. Western Bank of Va. 9 Gratt. 127; Durham *v.* Daniels, 2 Greene, Iowa, 518.

2 Lafayette Ins. Co. *v.* Rogers, 30 Barb. 491; Kennedy *v.* Cotton, 28 Barb. 59; Union Mut. Ins. Co. *v.* Osgood, 1 Duer, 707; United States Bank *v.* Haskins, 1 Johns. Cas. 132; Utica Bank *v.* Smalley, 2 Cowen, 770; Dutchess Cotton Manufactory *v.* Davis, 14 Johns. 245; Bank of Michigan *v.* Williams, 5 Wend. 482; Grays *v.* Turnp. Co. 4 Rand. 578. But see Rees *v.* Conocheaque Bank, 5 Rand. 326; Central Manuf. Co. *v.* Hartshorne, 3 Conn. 199; Lithgow *v.* Commonwealth, 2 Va. Cas. 297; Zion Church *v.* St. Peter's Church, 5 Watts & S. 215; Bank of Waterville & W. W. Bk. *v.* Beltser, 13 How. Pr. 270.

3 Grays *v.* Turnpike Co. 4 Rand. 578.

4 Wolf *v.* Goddard, 9 Watts, 544. And see Binney *v.* Plumley, 5 Vt. 500. Where a charter provided that each should pay to the trustees for the time being of a certain corporation, his proportion of certain expenses, and empowered the trustees to sue for the same, the action should be in the name of the trustees who might declare both in their natural and official capacities. Comfort *v.* Leland, 3 Whart. 81.

5 Proprietors of Monumoi Great Beach, 1 Mass. 159; Christian Society in Plymouth *v.* Macomber, 3 Met. 235; School District *v.* Blaisdell, 6 N. H. 197; Concord *v.* McIntire, 6 N. H. 527; Brown *v.* Illias, 27 Conn. 84; West Winsted Sav. Bk. *v.* Ford, 27 Conn. 282; Whittington *v.* Farmers Bank, 5 Harris & J. 489; Taylor *v.* Bank of Illinois, 7 T. B. Mon. 584; Methodist Church *v.* City of Cincinnati, 5 Ohio, 286; Prince *v.* Com. Bank

There is no rule of pleading, it has been said, more universal than that, by pleading to the merits, the defendant admits the capacity of the plaintiff to sue; and no reason can be shown why a corporation should be placed on a different footing, in this particular, from a natural person.[1] But a plea in abatement or in bar compels a corporation plaintiff to prove its existence.[2] In those States in which the courts hold, that under the general issue it is not necessary to prove the corporate existence of the plaintiffs, an exception is made in case of foreign corporations.[3] The United States Bank has been held to be a foreign corporation, so that an exemplification of its charter must be produced to prove its corporate character; for, of the acts of Congress creating corporations, a State court has no judicial knowledge.[4] In New York, an action against a foreign corporation can be brought by a resident of the State, for any cause of action, but a non-resident can only proceed against a foreign corporation when the cause of action has arisen, or the subject of the action is situated in the State.[5] When a foreign corporation has appeared in an action, it is as much within and subject to the jurisdiction of the court, as if it were a corporation under the laws of the State.[6] If a corporation is incorporated by the laws of the State where action is brought, it is regarded as a domestic corporation, although it may also be incorporated by another State.[7]

---

of Columbus, 1 Ala. 241. In a suit by a corporation, the declaration need not contain a *profert* or averment of charter. The want of a charter may be pleaded in abatement or perhaps in bar; but the defendant, by pleading the general issue and going to trial, waives the objection. Zion Church *v.* St Peter's Church, 5 Watts & S. 215; Woodson *v.* Bank of Gallipolis, 4 B. Mon. 203; Jones *v.* Bank of Tennessee, 8 id. 122; Duke *v.* Cahawba Navigation Co. 10 Ala. 82; McIntire *v.* Preston, 5 Gilman, 48; Roxbury *v.* Huston, 37 Me. 42; and see Oldt. & Linc. R. R. Co. *v.* Veazie, 39 Me. 571; Penobs. & Ken. R. R. Co. *v.* Dunn, id. 587; Orono *v.* Wedgewood, 44 Me. 49.

[1] Prince *v.* Com. Bank of Columbus, 1 Ala. 241.

[2] Ins. Co. *v.* Peck, 28 Vt. 93; Rheem *v.* Naugatuck Wheel Co. 33 Penn. State, 356.

[3] Society, &c. *v.* Young, 2 N. H. 310; School District *v.* Blaisdell, 6 N. H. 198; Lord *v.* Bigelow, 8 Vt. 445. In the case of a *foreign* corporation, under a plea of the general issue, the defendant may call in question the corporate character of the plaintiff. Lewis *v.* Bank of Kentucky, 12 Ohio, 132.

[4] United States Bank *v.* Stearns, 15 Wend. 314. Where a foreign corporation appears in court, it must establish its right to bring the suit, and to make the contract it seeks to enforce. But it is sufficient if this is shown upon the hearing of the cause. It is not necessary to set forth, in the pleadings, the authority upon which it relies to sustain its right to sue or enforce the contract. Marine & Fire Insurance Co. *v.* Jauncey, 1 Barb. 436; Bank of Michigan *v.* Williams, 5 Wend. 478.

[5] House *v.* Cooper, 30 Barb. 157; Cumberland Coal & Iron Co. *v.* Hoffman Steam Coal Co. id. 159.

[6] Dart *v.* Farmers Bk. of Bridgeport, 27 Barb. 337.

[7] Sprague *v.* Hartford, &c. Railroad Co. 5 R. I. 233.

§ 634. Although, from an old precedent,[1] and from a note of Sergeant Williams,[2] it appears, that the plea of *nul tiel corporation* was once a good plea in bar to an action by a corporation, yet, in England and in those States of our own country in which a corporation plaintiff is bound to prove incorporation under the general issue, upon the principles of good pleading, it would, upon the ground that it amounts to the general issue, be bad on special demurrer.[3] The rule holds with regard to foreign as well as domestic corporations.[4] In those States, on the other hand, where, under the general issue, a corporation plaintiff is not bound to prove their incorporation, the plea is good;[5] and in such States, if special pleading be dispensed with by statute, and notices of grounds of defence substituted, the defendant, if he would avail himself of an objection to the corporate existence or character of the plaintiff, must give notice of his objection, or he cannot avail himself of it.[6] Though the fact of incorporation is to be proved, yet, after a verdict in favor of plaintiffs, who sue as a corporation, the court will presume, that the fact of their being a corporation, and capable of suing in their aggregate capacity, was conceded or proved at the trial.[7]

§ 634 *a*. If a contract is made with a corporation to pay in such por-

---

[1] Year Book, 2 Edw. 4, 34.

[2] Saund. R. 340 a, b, n. 2.

[3] Bank of Auburn *v.* Weed, 19 Johns. 300; Farmers & Mechanics Bank *v.* Rayner, 2 Hall, 195; and see Kennedy *v.* Strong, 10 Johns. 291; 1 Tidd. Prac. 559, 560; 1 Chitty, Pleading, 467, 497. But any ground of defence which admits the facts alleged in the declaration, but avoids the action by matter which the plaintiff would not be bound to prove in the first instance, on the general issue, may be specially pleaded. Bank of Auburn *v.* Weed, 19 Johns. 300. Corporations are sometimes created *ipso facto, et eo instanti*, by the mere passage of a statute; but more frequently the statute declares, and points out the mode in which the legal body may thereafter be brought into existence. It is to corporations of the latter class, and to actions in which the plea of *nul tiel corporation* may be pleaded, that the statute of New York applies, which declares, that, in suits brought by a corporation created by or under any statute of this State, it shall not be necessary to prove, on the trial of the cause, the existence of such corporation, unless the defendant shall have pleaded, in abatement or in bar, that the plaintiffs are not a corporation. Propr. &c. of Southhold *v.* Horton, 6 Hill, 501; and 2 N. York R. St. 458, § 3.

[4] Farmers & Mechanics Bank *v.* Rayner, 2 Hall, 195; School District *v.* Aldrich, 13 N. H. 139.

[5] Proprietors of Monumoi Great Beach *v.* Rogers, 1 Mass. 159; Proprietors of Sunapee *v.* Eastman, 32 N. H. 470.

[6] Christian Society in Plymouth *v.* Macomber, 3 Met. 235.

[7] British America Land Co. *v.* Ames, 6 Met. 391; Williams *v.* Bank of Michigan, 7 Wend. 539.

tions and at such times as the directors of the corporation, agreeably to their act of incorporation and by-laws, require, it is not sufficient in a suit on such a contract to aver that the directors required and ordered that the defendant pay an assessment of, &c. Conformity to the charter and by-laws should be alleged.[1]

§ 635. The existence of a corporation, incorporated by a private act, may be proved either by an exemplified copy of the act, authenticated by affixing thereto the seal of the State, without other proof,[2] — by a sworn copy of the same, or by admission;[3] all such proof being accompanied by proof of acts of *user* under the act or charter; such as, that shortly after the passage of the act, the company had an office or place of business, where the business, to carry on which they were incorporated, was carried on, and that the affairs of the company had been managed by directors from time to time chosen;[4] and the acts and admissions of a party, acting as the president of the corporation, and giving a note to it in its corporate name, is *primâ facie* evidence of *user*.[5] The degree of proof required on the subject of user, is said to depend to some extent upon the nature of the incorporation and the law under which it is organized. "Where no provision is made for any permanent evidence of the fact of organization, more proof of user is necessary than where the essential steps, by which the organization is accomplished, are required to be made a matter of record. In such cases, if

---

[1] Atlantic Mut. F. Ins. Co. *v.* Young, 38 N. H. 451.

[2] British America Land Co. *v.* Ames, 6 Met. 391; Williams *v.* Bank of Michigan, 7 Wend. 539; Wood *v.* Jefferson County Bank, 9 Cowen, 194; Utica Insurance Company *v.* Tillman, 1 Wend. 555; Bank of Michigan *v.* Williams, 5 Wend. 478; Williams *v.* Bank of Michigan, 7 Wend. 540; Utica Ins. Co. *v.* Cadwell, 3 Wend. 296; State *v.* Carr, 5 N. H. 367; United States *v.* Johns, 4 Dallas, 416; Searsburgh Turnp. Co. *v.* Cutler, 6 Vt. 315; United States *v.* Johns, 1 Wash. C. C. 363; Came *v.* Brigham, 39 Me. 35. Acts incorporating banks, turnpike companies, &c., in Delaware, though not strictly *public* laws, yet, being published as such, are evidenced by the statute book. Bank of Wilmington *v.* Woolaston, 3 Harring. Del. 90. They may be so evidenced in Massachusetts, Worcester Med. Inst. *v.* Harding, 11 Cush. 288; and in Iowa, Durham *v.* Daniels, 2 Greene, Iowa, 518.

[3] Gospel Society *v.* Young, 2 N. H. 310. In a suit by a foreign corporation, the complaint need not state the act of incorporation or charter at large. Holyoke *v.* Banks, 4 Sandf. 675.

[4] Utica Ins. Co. *v.* Tillman, 1 Wend. 556; United States Bank *v.* Stearns, 15 Wend. 314; Method. Episc. Union Church *v.* Picket, 23 Barb. 436, 19 N. Y. 482; Sampson *v.* Bowd. Steam Mill Corp. 36 Me. 78.

[5] Bank of Michigan *v.* Williams, 5 Wend. 478; Williams *v.* Bank of Michigan, 7 Wend. 540; Searsburgh Turnp. Co. *v.* Cutler, 6 Vt. 315; State *v.* Carr, 5 N. H. 367.

the record is perfect, then, perhaps, nothing else need be shown; but if imperfect, it may still stand in place of, and be equivalent to, a very considerable degree of evidence of user. The imperfection of the record cannot be taken advantage of by a private individual, who has entered into engagements with the corporation. The rightfulness of its existence not being in issue, of course evidence of any irregularities or defects in its organization, short of such as would show a want of good faith on the part of those concerned in the proceedings, would be wholly irrelevant. If the law exists, and the record exhibits a *bona fide* attempt to organize it, a very slight evidence of user beyond this is all that can be required."[1] Where the corporation was a domestic corporation, the printed statute book, as printed by the printer of the State, has been admitted as evidence of the act of incorporation;[2] but in case of a turnpike company, the appointment of inspectors by the governor, and the certificate of the inspectors that the road was completed, and that the gates were erected, are not sufficient evidence of the existence of the corporation.[3] But the evidence of *user* seems to be necessary to accompany the evidence of the act of incorporation, only when something is required by the act to be done *in futuro*, to entitle it to corporate powers; though not where the corporation is declared to be such by statute, and nothing is required to be performed to give effect to the act incorporating it.[4] To prove the acts of a corporation necessary to be done in order to their corporate existence, the books of the corporation, proved by the clerk or secretary, are competent evidence.

Producing the books showing the election of the officers, together with the affidavit required by the act of incorporation, has been held sufficient *primâ facie* evidence to prove that all the previous steps required were taken.[5] It would be a very dangerous doctrine to the numerous corporations every day created, that, at any distant day, at which a controversy might arise with them, they should be obliged to produce the advertisement calling the meeting which organized them.[6]

---

[1] Methodist Episc. Church *v.* Pickett, 19 N. Y. 482.

[2] Wood *v.* Jefferson County Bank, 9 Cowen, 205, 206, and the case of Chenango Bank *v.* Noyes there cited.

[3] Bill *v.* Fourth Western Turnp. Co. 14 Johns. 416.

[4] Fire Department *v.* Kip, 10 Wend. 269; Bank of Auburn *v.* Aiken, 18 Johns. 137; Onondaga Co. Bank *v.* Carr, 17 Wend. 443.

[5] Wood *v.* Jefferson County Bank, 9 Cowen, 194. Penobs. & Ken. R. R. Co. *v.* Dunn, 39 Me. 587; Wellersburg & W. N. Plankroad Co. *v.* Bruce, 6 Md. 457. And see Jameson *v.* The People, 16 Ill. 257.

[6] Grays *v.* Turnp. Co. 4 Rand. 578; King *v.* Mothersell, 1 Stra. 93; 12 Vin. Abr. tit.

If charter commissioners are directed to ascertain the performance of a condition precedent to incorporation, and they declare it, though falsely, to have been performed, it shall be deemed true until the sovereign power interposes. A wrongdoer, sued by the corporation, cannot show the falsity of such declaration, for the purpose of defeating the suit of the corporation.[1] And, indeed, when a corporation has gone into operation, and rights have been acquired under it, every presumption should be made in favor of its legal existence.[2] Where a cognizance,[3] mortgage,[4] note,[5] or other instrument, is given to a corporation, as such, the party giving it is thereby estopped from denying the corporate existence of the corporation, and no further proof thereof is necessary until such proof is rebutted.[6] The mere indorsement of a bill of exchange to a bank does not, however, in Illinois, admit that the bank is a corporation;[7] and in New York, by the course of recent decisions, it would seem that the mere fact that, in a contract with a joint-stock company, a party has designated it by a name which is appropriate to a corporate body, does not dispense with proof of incorporation, unless it be distinctly stated in the contract that the company is an incorporated company.[8]

Evid. 90, pl. 16; 2 Camp. 101; Turnp. Co. *v.* M'Kean, 10 Johns. 167; Owings *v.* Speed, 5 Wheat. 424; Hagerstown Turnp. Road Co. *v.* Creeger, 5 Harris & J. 122; Bank of Michigan *v.* Williams, 5 Wend. 478, authorities cited by the counsel.

[1] Tar River Nav. Co. *v.* Neal, 3 Hawks, 520; and see Hamtranck *v.* Bank of Edwardsville, 2 Misso. 169; Hughes *v.* Bank of Somerset, 5 Litt. 47; Searsburgh Turnp. Co. *v.* Cutler, 6 Vt. 315; and see *post*, Ch. XXI.

[2] Hagerstown Turnp. Road Co. *v.* Creeger, 5 Harris & J. 122; Farmers & Mechanics Bank *v.* Jenks, 7 Met. 592; and see this matter considered, *ante*, Chap. II.

[3] Henriques *v.* Dutch West India Co. 2 Ld. Raym. 1535.

[4] Den *v.* Van Hauten, 5 Halst. 270.

[5] Congregational Society *v.* Perry, 6 N. H. 164. All Saints Church *v.* Lovett, 1 Hall, 191; John *v.* Farmers & Mechanics Bank, 2 Blackf. 367; Ryan *v.* Vanlandingham, 7 Ind. 416.

[6] Dutchess Cotton Manuf. Co. *v.* Davis, 14 Johns. 245, Thompson, C. J.; Hamtranck *v.* Bank of Edwardsville, 2 Misso. 169; Hughes *v.* Bank of Somerset, 5 Litt. 47; Searsburgh Turnp. Co. *v.* Cutler, 6 Vt. 315; Tar River Nav. Co. *v.* Neal, 3 Hawks, 520; Worcester Med. Inst. *v.* Harding, 11 Cush. 285, 289; Brook. & Greens. T. Co. *v.* M'Carty, 8 Ind. 392.

[7] Hargrave & Jones *v.* Bank of Illinois, 1 Breese, 84, 86.

[8] Williams *v.* Bank of Michigan, 7 Wend. 540; Welland Canal Co. *v.* Hathway, 8 Wend. 480; denying the dictum of Thompson, J., in Dutchess Cotton Manuf. Co. *v.* Davis, 14 Johns. 245; and see United States *v.* Stearns, 15 Wend. 316. But suing a corporation by its corporate name, admits its corporate existence, and allegations that it has failed to perform conditions precedent to its existence, will be disregarded as irrelevant and impertinent. People *v.* Ravenswood, &c. T. & Br. Co. 20 Barb. 518.

A judgment in favor of such company will, however, estop the defendant from denying its corporate existence, in an action on such judgment, or in a suit on the recognizance of bail, either in the original action or in error.[1] Evidence of the incorporation of a company under and pursuant to a statute of one State which such statute declares, shall be deemed sufficient, will be held sufficient in the courts of another State, to prove the fact of such incorporation.[2]

§ 636. It cannot be shown, in defence to the suit of a corporation, that the plaintiff's charter was obtained by fraud;[3] nor especially by a subscriber who accepted the charter, and assisted in putting it into operation.[4] Neither can it be shown in defence that the plaintiffs have forfeited their corporate rights by misuser or nonuser. Advantage can be taken of such forfeiture only on process on behalf of the State, instituted directly against the corporation for the purpose of avoiding the charter or act of incorporation; and individuals cannot avail themselves of it in collateral suits, until it be judicially declared.[5] And where a company was incorporated for the purpose of removing from a river all obstructions to the free passage of logs, &c., and were authorized to demand tolls of the owners of logs, &c., for freely passing down the river, in an action to recover tolls for logs that passed the river freely, it was held, that the defendant could not show that the corporation had not removed the obstructions, even though the act of incorporation was to be void if

[1] Williams *v.* Bank of Michigan, 7 Wend. 540.

[2] Eagle Works *v.* Churchill, 2 Bosw. 166.

[3] Charles River Bridge *v.* Warren Bridge, 7 Pick. 371; All Saints Church *v.* Lovett, 1 Hall, 198; Bear Camp River Co. *v.* Woodman, 2 Greenl. 404.

[4] Centre, &c. Turnp. Road Co. *v.* M'Conaby, 16 S. & R. 140.

[5] Vernon Society *v.* Hills, 6 Cowen, 23; All Saints Church *v.* Lovett, 1 Hall, 198; Eagle Works *v.* Churchill, 2 Bosw. 166; Centre, &c. Turnp. Road Co. *v.* McConaby, 16 S. & R. 140, 1 Penn. 426; Lehigh Bridge Co. *v.* Lehigh Coal Co. 4 Rawle, 9; Chester Glass Co. *v.* Dewey, 16 Mass. 102; State of Vermont *v.* Society, &c. 1 Paine, C. C. 652; Bear Camp River Co. *v.* Woodman, 2 Greenl. 404; Day *v.* Stetson, 8 Greenl. 372; State *v.* Carr, 5 N. H. 367; John *v.* Farmers & Mechanics Bank of Indiana, 2 Blackf. 367; Canal Co. *v.* Railroad Co. 4 Gill & J. 121; Webb *v.* Moler, 8 Ham. 552; Buncombe Turnp. Co. *v.* McCarson, 1 Dev. & B. 306; Tar River Nav. Co. *v.* Neal, 3 Hawks, 520; Hughes *v.* Bank of Somerset, 5 Litt. 47; Searsburgh Turnp. Co. *v.* Cutler, 6 Vt. 315; Hamtranck *v.* Bank of Edwardsville, 2 Misso. 169; Union Branch R. R. Co. *v.* East Tennessee and Georgia R. R. Co. 14 Ga. 327; Cleveland P. & Asht. R. R. Co. *v.* City of Erie, 27 Penn. State, 380; Wright *v.* Shelby R. R. Co. 16 B. Mon. 7; Brookville and Greensb. Turnp. Co. *v.* McCarty, 8 Ind. 392; and see *post*, Ch. XXI.

they should not be removed within a year, and more than a year had elapsed before the action was brought.[1]

§ 637. In proceeding against a corporation, says Tidd, the process should be served on the mayor, or other head officer; and if the defendants do not appear before or on the *quarto die post* at the return of the original, by an attorney appointed under their common seal (for they cannot appear in person), the next process is a *distringas*, which should go against them in their public capacity; and under this process, the sheriff may distrain the lands and goods which constitute the common stock of the corporation. If they have neither lands nor goods, there is no way to compel them to appear, at law or in equity, but only in parliament; for it is a rule, that, for a public concern, the sheriff cannot distrain any private person who is a member of the corporation.[2]

---

[1] Bear Camp River Co. *v.* Woodman, 2 Greenl. 404. Where a corporation brings a bill in equity, and alleges therein, that certain acts were done by committees thereof, whereby a resulting trust in certain land, conveyed to a third party, was raised in favor of the corporation, it cannot prove the authority of the committees to act therefor by parol evidence; their power to act can only be shown by its records. Methodist Chapel Corp. *v.* Herrick, 25 Me. 354.

[2] 1 Tidd's Practice, 116. By the common law there is no process which can be served, either upon natural persons, not inhabitants of or within the realm, or upon foreign corporations, by which their appearance can be compelled in any court; for the reason that the former are not found within the realm, and the latter has no corporate existence within it, nor could either be compelled to appear by an attachment on their property. Middlebrooks *v.* Springfield Fire Ins. Co. 14 Conn. 301 (citing Com. Dig. Attachment, B. D., 1 Tidd, Pract. 116). If, therefore, they can be brought into court, it must be by virtue of some *statutory* provisions. In Connecticut, all judicial process, and the mode of its service, are regulated by statute; and to those regulations it is necessary to refer, in order to ascertain whether jurisdiction is conferred. Middlebrooks, &c. *ubi sup.* In this case, on p. 303, of 14 Conn. is the following note: —

"Cornelius V. S. Kane *v.* The Morris Canal and Banking Company. The opinion of the court was delivered by Jones, C. J. This was an application to set aside proceedings for commencing an action in this court, against the defendants, by summons. The defendants are a foreign corporation, holding a charter under the laws of the State of New Jersey, and having a banking-house at Jersey City. The summons was served on a teller of the bank, at an office kept by the company, in the City of New York.

"In the Revised Statutes, vol. 2, p. 373, title 4, act 1, entitled, 'Of proceedings by and against corporations in courts of law,' are found the provisions on the subject. Section 1st provides, that a foreign corporation created by the laws of any other State or country, may, upon giving security for the payment of the costs of suit, prosecute in the courts of this State, in the same manner as corporations created under the laws of this State. The 4th section provides, that the first process for the commencement of a suit against a corporation, shall be a summons, except in cases where a *scire facias,* or other process is allowed by law; and that such process, and all other writs and processes against corporations, may

Serving a summons on any private individual of a corporation is not sufficient notice to hold the corporation to trial; and the individual sum-

---

be issued, tested, and made returnable in the same manner as process issued against individuals; and section 5th authorizes the service of the process on the presiding officer, cashier, secretary, or treasurer, or, if no such officer can be found, on such other officer or member, or in such other manner as the court may direct. And the 15th and 16th sections provide that suits brought in the Supreme Court, by a resident of this State, against any corporation created by or under the laws of any other State, government, or country, for the recovery of any debt or damages, may be commenced by attachment, to be issued, on the application of the plaintiff, to the sheriff of the county in which any property of such corporation may be, commanding him to attach and safely keep all the estate, real and personal, of such corporation.

"By other sections of the statute the application is to be founded on an *affidavit* of the debt or demand, as bond is to be given for the costs, and the property seized, or the proceeds of it, if sold, are to be kept to answer any judgment to be obtained in the suit; and sureties are given for the prosecution of the suit and the application of the property to the satisfaction of the judgment therein.

"The corporation is permitted to appear in the suit, and defend the same; and upon the application for that purpose, and bond with sureties given to the plaintiff for the payment on demand, of the amount of the judgment that may be recovered against the corporation, the attachment may be discharged, and the property given up; and in case of more than one attachment against a foreign corporation, at the same term, or during the same vacation of a term, and judgment rendered in favor of the plaintiffs, the court is to apportion the proceeds arising from the sale of the defendant's property, among the plaintiffs, in proportion to the amount of their respective judgments.

"The plaintiff has taken his proceedings under the 4th and 5th sections, as embracing in the general term corporations, which it uses, foreign as well as domestic corporations, and as authorizing the commencement of suits against the latter, as well as the former, by summons. In this we think he erred; those sections apply to domestic corporations solely. They are wholly inapplicable to a foreign corporation. Suits against them must be by attachment, under the provisions of the 15th and 16th sections of the statute. Domestic corporations exist and have their location within the State, and actions lie against them equally with natural persons residing or found within the State. But foreign corporations have their legal existence, and are located within the territory, the State, or government that creates them, and can in no legal sense, be said to be within this State. No suit can be brought, in this court, directly against a corporation which is out of the State, any more than against an individual debtor who is absent therefrom. The foreign corporation is equally an absent debtor with the person who resides abroad, and must in like manner be reached, and payment of the debt be enforced against them by attachment against the property, and not by the personal process of summons. The proceeding is against the property of the corporation within the State; and to the extent that corporate property can be found within the reach of the attachment, and made applicable to the payment of the demands against them, and no further, will such proceeding of itself be available and effectual to the creditor. It does not become, and cannot be made, a personal action against the corporation, in its corporate capacity, unless the corporation voluntarily appears, and makes itself a party; in which case the attachment is discharged, and the property attached by the sheriff is given up, and bond with sureties given for the payment of the amount of the judgment to be recovered against the corporation; and the proceed-

moned may plead the want of notice to the corporation.[1] Members of a corporation aggregate, not being liable to a *capias*, cannot be holden to bail for any thing done by them in their corporate capacity.[2] No precedent of an original writ against a corporation has been known; and in all the elementary writers, and in all books of practice which treat of the proceedings against corporations, it is laid down as the universal rule, that the process must be by summons, and not by attachment.[3] In 1816, several suits were brought against certain banks in New York, on notes issued by those banks, which they had refused to pay in gold or silver, that had been demanded of them; the banks generally having suspended their payments in *specie*. The suits were commenced by original writs. The court held, that the original writ, in

---

ing then takes the form of a regular suit, and proceeds to judgment according to the course and practice of the court. The proceeding by summons was, consequently, irregular, and unauthorized by law, and must be set aside." By the Rev. Stat. of Massachusetts, ch. 44, § 11, the franchise of any turnpike or other corporations authorized to receive toll, and all the rights and privileges thereof, shall be liable to attachment, or other service of mesne process shall be made on any such corporation. The officer serving the same shall leave an attested copy, &c. Members of corporations aggregate cannot be sued for any thing done in their corporate capacity. Id. 193. The process against a corporation must be served on its head, or principal officer; per Spencer, J., in M'Queen *v.* Middletown Man. Co. 16 Johns. 5. And see *ante*, § 379, *et seq.* It was contended for the plaintiffs in error, in the Supreme Court of New York, that the act for the recovery of debts to the value of twenty-five dollars, did not authorize any proceedings against a corporation; and the court held, that the provisions of the act, both as to the first process and the execution, precluded the construction that a corporation could be sued before a justice of the peace. Ministers, &c., of Reformed Church *v.* Adams, 5 Johns. 346. But a corporation, in New York, may sue in a Justice's Court. Among the difficulties in the way of a suit against a corporation, is, that the justice has no process provided by the act, to compel a corporation to appear. But when they are plaintiffs, they can constitute an attorney to appear for them. Hotchkiss *v.* Religious Society, 7 Johns. 356. Proceedings against aggregate corporations must be by original summons, and *distringas.* 2 Archb. Practice, 98. In England, by 2 Will. 4, ch. 39, every writ of summons against a corporation aggregate may be served on the mayor, or other head officer, or on the town secretary of such corporation. Har. Dig. Addenda, 2402. A corporation may be sued in their corporate capacity, and need not be named individually; but in a suit against the trustees of a town, they must be severally named. Trustees of Lexington *v.* M'Connell, 3 A. K. Marsh. 224.

[1] Rand *v.* Proprietors of Locks on Connecticut River, 3 Day, 441.

[2] Bro. Corpor. pl. 43; and see *ante*, Chap. XVII. § 1. Proceedings against aggregate corporations are very much the same as against peers of the realm. 2 Archb. Practice, 98; 1 Tidd's Practice, 115.

[3] Per Curiam, in Lynch *v.* Mechanics Bank, 13 Johns. 137; and see also, 1 Kyd, 271; 2 Impey, C. B. Pr. 675, n.; 6 Mod. 183; Com. Dig. Plead. (2 B. 2); 1 Bac. Abr. 507, tit. Corp.; 2 Sellon, 148. Suits against foreign corporations by residents of the State may be commenced by attachment in New York. Rev. St. 1829, vol. 2, p. 459, § 4.

assumpsit, against a corporation, must be in the nature of a *summons*, and not by *pone* or *attachment*.[1] In Pennsylvania, it is provided by statute, that a suit may be commenced against a corporation by a summons served on its president, or other head officer; but the statute is held to be inapplicable to such an officer of a foreign corporation, merely because he is found within the jurisdiction of the State.[2] It is held in that State to be necessary, in an action against a corporation, to serve the summons at the place where the corporation is located within the State; and an action against the Bank of Pennsylvania, which is located in Philadelphia, cannot be instituted in the county of Berks, by a service of the process upon the cashier of the bank located in that county.[3] In an action of trespass against a corporation,[4] Tindal, C. J., said: "The process is the same, both in case and trespass, namely, by attachment, distress, capias, and outlawry."[5] The proper mode of proceeding against a corporation by *indictment*,[6] is by distress infinite to compel appearance.[7] In England a foreign corporation cannot be sued, there being no mode of serving it with process provided by statute.[8]

§ 638. Where, during the pendency of a suit, a corporation surren-

---

[1] Lynch *v.* Mechanics Bank, 13 Johns. 147; *contra*, Styles, 367, cited in Cowp. 85.

[2] Nash *v.* Rector, &c. 1 Miles, 78, and see *ante*, §§ 402, 403. See also, Moulin *v.* Trenton Mut. Fire & Life Ins. Co. 4 N. J. 222. But if a statute enacts that process in a suit against a foreign corporation, may be served on its agent residing in the State, a judgment obtained on such process is binding on the corporation, and entitled to the same credit in the State where the corporation exists as in the State where rendered. Lafayette Ins. Co. *v.* French, 5 McLean, C. C. 461, 18 How. 404.

[3] Brobst *v.* Bank of Penn. 5 Watts & S. 379; aliter in Indiana Mut. Fire Ins. Co. *v.* Routledge, 7 Ind. 25. Where a railroad passes over parts of two counties, the railroad corporation may maintain an action of assumpsit in that county wherein they have an office which is "made the depository of the books and records of the company by a vote of the directors, and a place where a large share of the business is transacted," although the company may at the same time have another office in the other county where the residue of their business is transacted, and in which the clerk and treasurer reside. Androscoggin Railroad Co. *v.* Stevens, 28 Me. 434. And it may be sued in the county where its principal office is, although no part of the road runs through that county. Bristol *v.* Chicago & Aurora R. R. Co. 15 Ill. 436. And see *ante*, §§ 103–110.

[4] See *ante*, § 386.

[5] Maund *v.* Monmouthshire Canal Co. 4 Man. & G. 452, 5 Scott, N. R. 457.

[6] See *ante*, § 395.

[7] Regina *v.* Birmingham & Gloucester Railway Co. 3 Q. B. 223. *Distress infinite* is a process commanding the sheriff to distrain a person from time to time, by taking his goods by way of pledge to enforce the performance of something due from the party distrained upon. 3 Bl. Com. 231.

[8] Ingate *v.* Lloyd Austriaco, 1 C. B., N. S., 704.

ders its charter, which is accepted by the legislature, it becomes defunct, and the suit abates, unless the legislature, by some act, saves the right of action against the corporation. The case of a corporation, in other words, is not to be distinguished from the case of a private person dying *pendente lite*. In the latter case, the suit is abated at law, though capable of being revived by the enactment of some statute.[1] But that the corporation has become extinct since judgment obtained upon proceedings regularly commenced, and where there has been a levy of execution, cannot affect the right of the plaintiff.[2]

§ 639. No exception can be taken to the service of a writ in favor of a corporation, for the reason that it was made by an officer who is a member. In an action brought by the Merchants Bank in Massachusetts, the writ was served by a deputy sheriff who was a member of the corporation; and the court held, that he was not a party to the writ within the meaning of St. 1783, ch. 43. The court observed, that it was true, a sheriff or his deputy, in serving process by or against corporations of which he is a member, has an opportunity to commit frauds in his own favor, which it may be difficult to guard against or detect; but that the sheriff was an officer in whom great confidence is necessarily reposed. It was well deserving of attention, the court remarked, whether a slight pecuniary interest is a greater cause for taking from him the power of serving a writ, than his standing in the relation of father, or son, or expectant heir, or devisee, would be, and yet neither of these relations prevented his serving process.[3] In a case in Maine, the writ was served by a deputy sheriff who was a stockholder in the Wiscasset Bank, and this was pleaded in abatement, on the ground that he was party to the suit; but the plea was overruled.[4]

§ 640. The suit against a corporation, like a suit against an individual, proceeds to judgment and execution.[5] Thus, in Pierce *v.* Par-

---

[1] Greeley *v.* Exchange Bank, 3 Story, 657. For an able discussion of the subject, how far this will operate in abating suits brought against officers of a corporation as such, see Moultrey *v.* Smiley, 16 Ga. 289. Provisions to prevent the abatement of suits by or against corporations, in such cases, are made in several States by statute. Woolsey *v.* Judd, 4 Duer, 379; Stetson *v.* City Bank of N. Orl. 2 Ohio, State, 167.

[2] Linden *v.* Benton, 6 Misso. 361.

[3] Merchants Bank *v.* Cook, 4 Pick. 405.

[4] Adams *v.* Wiscasset Bank, 1 Greenl. 361.

[5] See 4 Am. Law Mag. 256. The tangible property and estate of a corporation are no

tridge,[1] it was held, that a member of a manufacturing corporation, who is a creditor thereof, has the same right as any other creditor to secure his demand by attachment or levy on the corporate property, although personally liable by statute to satisfy other judgments against the corporation. Another instance of a levy and sale under execution against a corporation, in Massachusetts, is the case of Perry *v.* Adams.[2] According to Buchanan, C. J., the property of a corporation may be seized and sold under an execution, for the payment of its debts, as in the case of an individual; and a corporation is bound to provide for its just debts, whether the payment is made by sale of property for that purpose, or with money from its vaults.[3] In Slee *v.* Bloom,[4] all the estate, real and personal, of the corporation, was sold on execution, and it was in consequence that the corporation ceased from acting. In a late case in England, the plaintiff, after establishing his demand against the company, by the judgment of a court of law, applied to the secretary for payment, and received for answer that the company had no funds unless the shareholders would pay up calls, which were in arrear to a considerable amount. Upon this he obtained a rule for a mandamus, to be directed to the company, commanding them to pay the money recovered by the judgment, and to make calls for that purpose, if necessary, on the shareholders. After judgment, the court discharged the rule, Lord Denman, C. J., observing, "the judgment which had been entered against the company formed a decisive answer to the first part, at least, of the application, because the plaintiff *has the ordinary legal remedy of an execution.*" If, said he, the plaintiff seeks only the payment of the debt and costs, an execution by *fi. fa.* is a perfect remedy in its nature.[5]

§ 641. The Supreme Court of Pennsylvania have held, that a turnpike road could not be levied upon by an execution, upon a judgment against the company, because the defendants had no tangible interest, nothing but a right to receive tolls. But Tilghman, C. J., in delivering the opinion, observed: "If a turnpike company has a right to *land*, or

---

more exempt from execution than those of an individual. State *v.* Rives, 5 Ired. 307; Arthur *v.* Commercial & Railroad Bank, 9 Missis. 394.

[1] Pierce *v.* Partridge, 3 Met. 44.

[2] Perry *v.* Adams, id. 51.

[3] State of Maryland *v.* Bank of Maryland, 6 Gill & J. 219.

[4] Slee *v.* Bloom, 19 Johns. 475. See Martins *v.* Bank of Alabama, 14 La. 415; U. States Bank *v.* Merchants Bank, 1 Rob. Va. 573.

[5] Regina *v.* Victoria Park Co. 1 Q. B. 289.

other property not on the road, there is no reason why it should not be subject to an execution."[1] In North Carolina, it has been decided that a railroad company has an estate in the land, and not a mere easement, and that the estate is subject to sale under execution. The estate, it is there held, results not only from the express provisions of the charter, but from the necessity of the case; and it is not the franchise which is sold, but the property and estate of the corporation.[2] In a case in the High Court of Appeals of Mississippi,[3] the charter of a corporation authorized it to purchase the lands necessary for the site of a railroad, and the requisite depôts, stations and buildings, and to possess and hold the same in fee-simple. The court could not perceive, if the estate was one in fee, why it was not subject to sale on execution.

§ 642. With regard to *money*, the Supreme Court of the United States have adopted, after a careful investigation of the authorities, the rule expressly laid down in Dalton's Sheriff,[4] that money may be taken by virtue of a *fieri facias*. They can perceive, they say, no reason why an execution should not be levied on money; that the one given in the books, that money could not be sold, was not a good one; that the reason of a sale is, that money only will satisfy an execution; that if any thing else be taken, it must be turned into money; but this could be no good reason for refusing to take these very articles to produce

---

[1] Ammant *v.* New Alexandria, &c. Turn. Road Co. 13 S. & R. 210; see Bushell *v.* Commonwealth Ins. Co. 15 S. & R. 173. A railroad is different from a turnpike, as in the one the company seek not the right of passage to the *public*, but to the *company*, who have the exclusive right of using the track of the road in their own peculiar manner. Trustees of Presb. Society *v.* Auburn and Rochester Railroad Co. 3 Hill, 567.

[2] State *v.* Rives, 5 Ired. 307.

[3] Arthur *v.* Commercial & Railroad Bank, 9 Smedes & M. 394. In Tennessee, the judgment creditors of a turnpike company, in which the State is a stockholder, by virtue of the act of 1837, have the right to seize *slaves, mules,* and other property owned and used by the company in the repair of the road, and such company cannot interfere and set up in chancery the lien of the State to protect such property against the execution of such creditors. F. & C. Turnpike Co. *v.* Young, 8 Humph. 103; and see State *v.* Lagrange, &c. Railroad Co. 4 id. 448. Under the act of Pennsylvania, of 1836, an attachment execution did not lie against a corporation. By that act, the property of an insolvent corporation could not be seized for the benefit of a particular creditor; and the test of insolvency is the absence of tangible property. On the return of an unsatisfied execution, the plaintiff should proceed no further than to sue out a *writ of sequestration,* for a *pro rata* payment of all the debts. Ridge Turnpike Co. *v.* Peddle, 4 Barr, 490.

[4] Dalton's Sheriff, 145.

which is the sole object of the execution.[1] That money, or *bank-bills*, may be taken on execution, has been expressly decided in New York,[2] and subsequently adhered to.[3] And a corporation, as has already been mentioned, is bound for its just debts on execution, whether the payment is made by a sale of property, or with money from its vaults.[4]

§ 643. As a corporation must take and grant by its corporate name,[5] so by that name it must sue and be sued.[6] It has not been deemed necessary, however, to repeat the full name of the corporation at every recurrence in the declaration; reference in a clear manner to the name already given, being sufficient. Thus, it was held, in New Jersey, that where the name of the corporation is correctly stated at the commencement of the declaration, as, "The Trustees of the A. B. C. of," &c., and in the subsequent part of the declaration it is alleged, that, "being indebted, they, the said trustees undertook and promised," it is a sufficient allegation that the promise was made by the corporation, and not by the trustees individually.[7]

§ 644. If a corporation changes its name, it must sue by its new

---

1 Turner *v.* Fendall, 1 Cranch, 117.

2 Hardy *v.* Dobbin, 12 Johns. 220.

3 Holmes *v.* Nuncaster, id. 395; and see also, Williams *v.* Rogers, 5 id. 167; Orr *v.* McBride, 2 N. Car. Law Repos. 257; Spencer *v.* Blaisdell, 4 N. H. 198.

4 State of Maryland, &c. See *ante,* § 640.

5 *Ante,* Ch. III. § 99, *et seq.*

6 1 Kyd, 253; Berks & Dauphin Turn. R. *v.* Myers, 6 S. & R. 17; Porter *v.* Nekervis, 5 Rand. 359; Minot *v.* Curtis, 7 Mass. 444; First Parish in Sutton *v.* Cole, 3 Pick. 236; 2 Salk. 451. A mayor of a corporation cannot sue on a contract made by him on behalf of the corporation. Bowen *v.* Morris, 2 Taunt. 374. A corporation may sue in their name of creation, though express power be given to them to sue by another name. College of Physicians *v.* Talbois, 1 Ld. Raym. 153.

7 Trustees of Antipædo Baptist Society *v.* Mulford, 3 Halst. 182. The case of Woolwych *v.* Forrest, 1 Penn. 115, cited at the bar, the court considered did not bear upon the question before them. That case proves, that in a suit by or against a corporation, it should be correctly named; and that if there be a variance between the real name and the name given in an obligation or other instrument, on which the suit is founded, the declaration should contain proper averments of identity; but it did not prove that, if, in the writ and in the commencement of the declaration, the proper corporate name is used, the same full name must throughout be repeated. And see Mayor and Burgesses of Lyme Regis, 10 Co. 120; London *v.* Lynn, H. Bl. 260; Mayor, &c. of Stafford *v.* Bolton, 1 Bos. & P. 40. In these cases the full name of the corporation was not on every occasion repeated. See also Precedents in 1 Wentworth, 181; 5 id. 163, 176, 182, 201, 255.

name. This was decided in debt on a bond given about thirty years before to a corporation, that was said to be "dissolved by being rendered incapable of exercising any of its functions" most of that time, and that it received a new charter in 1763, and a new name. The bond was given to a corporation named "mayor, aldermen, and commonalty;" for many years before 1763, no mayor or aldermen had been elected. The bond was declared on as made to the new corporation.[1] The mere change of the name of the corporation by the legislature does not, however, abate, nor can it under any circumstances be used for the purpose of abating, a suit brought by the corporation in its old name before the change was made.[2] Where the name of a corporation was changed by an amendatory act, and a suit was brought by it in its first name, it was not necessary, it was held, that the corporation should show the amendatory act had been rejected by the stockholders.[3]

§ 645. It is said, that if a corporation be *known* by a name, it is sufficient to sue them by that name;[4] but this seems to be confined to the case of a corporation by *prescription;* for it is said on another occasion,[5] that when a corporation is created by the king, and the commencement of it appears by record, it can have no other name by use, nor be named otherwise than as the king by his letters-patent has appointed, and the court will not permit it to be sued by any other name. Mr. Kyd, in adverting to these authorities, says, he is unable to perceive any reason why, in the case of a corporation by charter, which has acquired, by long usage, a name of reputation different from its real name of foundation, it may not be sued by that name of reputation, as well as a man may be sued by a name of reputation different from his name of baptism; or why, if the corporation plead a misnomer, the plaintiff may not reply, that it is known by the one name as well as by the other.[6] In the case of Minot *v.* Curtis, it was intimated by the court, that a corporation may be known by several names. But the observation was applied to a parish, which may be by prescription.[7] An individual banker doing

---

1 Mayor and Commonalty of Colchester, 3 Burr. 1866, and 5 Dane, Abr. 151; and see Mayor of Scarborough *v.* Butler, 3 Lev. 237. But see Proprietors of Sunapee *v.* Eastman, 32 N. H. 470, 474.

2 Thomas *v.* Visitors, &c. 7 Gill & J. 369.

3 Beene *v.* Cahawba & Marion Railroad Co. 3 Ala. 660.

4 Bro. Corpor. 40; 8 Ass. pl. 24. See *ante,* § 99, *et seq.*

5 1 Anders. 223.

6 1 Kyd, 254; and see *ante,* Chap. III. § 4.

7 Minot *v.* Curtis, 7 Mass. 444.

business under the general banking law of the State, who assumes a special name by which his business as banker is known, may be taxed by that name.[1]

§ 646. A declaration in the corporate name, it has been adjudged, is good, without mentioning the name of the head of the corporation.[2] It is in fact said to be more safe to omit the name of the head, for if his name be mentioned, and he die pending the action, it will abate.[3] And the trustees of a college, being incorporated, should sue by their corporate title, and need not set out their individual names.[4] The trustees of a town in Kentucky must, when sued, be individually named.[5]

§ 647. Where a corporation is designated by a name, with which the description in the charter does not exactly correspond, but it appears that there is a body politic substantially answering the appellation, the declaration is holden good.[6] The rule is well settled, that if the name given sufficiently designates the corporation, the contract, whether sealed or not, cannot be avoided for the misnomer.[7] Where a promissory note was given to the "president, directors and company of the Newport Mechanics Manufacturing Company," instead of the "Newport Mechanics Manufacturing Company," which was the true name of the corporation to which the note was designed to be given, it was held that the variance was not such as to preclude recovery in the name of the corporation.[8] Upon a promise to pay the "president, directors, and company of the Milford and Chilicothe Turnpike Company," a suit may be maintained by the "Milford and Chilicothe Turnpike Company," the latter being the true name of the corporation.[9] If the undertaking

---

1 Patchin *v.* Ritter, 27 Barb. 34.

2 Newton *v.* Travers, 3 Salk. 103; S. P., Rex *v.* Rippon, 1 Comyns, 86; s. c. 2 Salk. 433. Formerly the point was somewhat doubted. 1 Kyd, 281.

3 6 Peterdorf's Abr. (Am. ed.), 446 (note); and see 1 Kyd, 291.

4 Legrand *v.* Hampden Sidney College, 5 Munf. 324.

5 Trustees of Lexington *v.* McConnel's Heirs, 3 A. K. Marsh. 224.

6 Mayor, &c. of Malden *v.* Miller, 1 B. & Ald. 699; Kentucky Seminary *v.* Wallace, 15 B. Mon. 45.

7 African Society *v.* Varick, 13 Johns. 38; Middletown *v.* McCormack, 2 Penning. 500; 1 id. 115; Inhabitants of Alloways Creek *v.* String, 5 Halst. 323; Medway Cotton Manuf. Co. *v.* Adams, 10 Mass. 360; Berks & Dauphin Turn. Co. *v.* Myers, 6 S. & R. 16; Hagerstown Turnpike *v.* Creeger, 5 Harris & J. 122; see *ante*, Chap. III. § 99, *et seq.*, and Chap. VIII. § 234.

8 Newport Mechanics Manuf. Co. *v.* Starbird, 10 N. H. 123. And see Forbes *v.* Marshall, 11 Exch. 166, 32 Eng. L. & Eq. 589; Lafayette Ins. Co. *v.* French, 18 How. 409.

9 Milford & Chilicothe Turn. Corp. *v.* Brush, 10 Ohio, 111.

be to the corporation, whether a right or wrong name be used, or that of some of its officers, it should be declared on and treated as a promise to the corporation. Thus, where a promissory note was made payable "to the cashier of the Commercial Bank, or his order," and the consideration proceeded from the bank, an action on the note was maintained in the name of the bank as the promisee.[1] A declaration upon a promissory note to the Medway Cotton Manufactory, by the name of R. M. & Co., was holden good upon demurrer in Massachusetts. The declaration charged the defendants upon a note made by them; with an averment, that it was made to the corporation, by the name of R. M. & Co. The court said, "Upon the *demurrer*, we have only to determine, whether the declaration is in itself absurd and repugnant, and incapable of proof. We think it is not, upon the authorities respecting *misnomers* of corporations, or upon the reason of the thing."[2] In debt on bond to the *committee* or trustees of a corporation, *solvendum* to the corporation by its true name, the corporation may declare in their own name, and may allege that the bond was made to them by the description of the *committee*, &c.[3]

§ 648. Kyd lays it down, that, where a deed is made to a corporation, by a name varying from the true name, the plaintiffs may sue in their true name, and in their declaration aver, that the defendant made the deed to them by the name mentioned in the deed;[4] or, if the plaintiffs in the declaration, take no notice of the variance, and the defendant trusts to the advantage he may have of it at the trial; then, if a special verdict be found, "that the defendant made and sealed the writing in question, and delivered it to the corporation (describing them by their true name), by the name mentioned in the deed, this will entitle the plaintiff to judgment."[5] So, if a deed be made *by* a corporation, by a name different from the true name, the plaintiff may sue them by their true name, and aver, that, "by the name mentioned in the deed," they made such a deed to him; or, if he take no notice of the variance in his declaration, he may have the same advantage from a

---

[1] Commercial Bank *v.* French, 21 Pick. 486.

[2] Medway Cotton Man. Co. *v.* Adams, 10 Mass. 360; and see Dyer, 279; Dance *v.* Girdler, 4 B. & P. 40; 1 Chitty, Pl. 252.

[3] New York African Society *v.* Varick, 13 Johns. 38.

[4] 1 Kyd, 287, who cites 10 Co. 125 b. See also, Trustees of McMinn Academy *v.* Reneau, 2 Swan, 94.

[5] 1 Kyd, 287, who cites 10 Co. 125 b.

special verdict as the corporation may have when they are plaintiffs.[1] Kyd, it seems, feels no hesitation in saying, that in *all* cases, where, by express averment, or by the finding of the jury, it is made apparent, that the corporation *sued* is the same that made the deed, whether the name in the deed be the same in *effect* or not, with the name of incorporation, or whether the difference between them be *seeming* or *real*, that judgment *ought* to be given in favor of the deed.[2]

§ 649. In a suit *against* "the president and trustees of the Savings Bank in the county of Strafford," to recover payment for serving a writ of execution for them, a copy thereof in the name of the "Savings Bank of the County of Strafford," was held to be inadmissible in evidence.[3] In another case, in an action against an incorporated bank, the writ described the defendants by their corporate name of the president and directors of the Marine Bank of Baltimore. The declaration was against "the said Marine Bank;" and the plea was, that the Marine Bank did not assume, and the verdict and judgment used the corporate name. It was held, on objections made to the declaration, that it was sufficient.[4] A corporation may be declared against by the name by which it is known, without alleging it to be chartered or incorporated; if the description impliedly amounts to an allegation that the defendants are a corporate body.[5]

§ 650. If a corporation sue or be sued by a wrong name, or one not sufficiently certain, to take advantage of the misnomer, it should be pleaded in abatement, and not in bar.[6] In a suit by a corporation it

---

[1] 1 Kyd, 288.

[2] 1 Kyd, 287, who cites 10 Co. 125 b. Ibid. 288.

[3] Burnham *v.* President, Trustees, &c. 5 N. H. 466.

[4] Marine Bank of Baltimore *v.* Blays, 4 Harris & J. 338.

[5] Wolf *v.* City Steamboat Co. 7 C. B. 103.

[6] 26 H. 8, 1 b; 1 Kyd, 283. It was once doubted if a mistake of the *plaintiff's* Christian name or surname were not ground of nonsuit; but it is now settled that the mistake must be pleaded in abatement, even in the case of a corporation. 1 Chitty, Pl. 440; Bank of Utica *v.* Smalley, 2 Cowen, 778; Medway Cotton Man. Co. *v.* Adams, 10 Mass. 360; Burnham *v.* President, Trustees, &c. 5 N. H. 449; and see 7 id. 309; Bank of Metropolis *v.* Orrine, 3 Gill, 443; Proprietors of Sunapee *v.* Eastman, 32 N. H. 470. To make the mistake of the name of a corporation pleadable in bar, it should appear that there is no such corporation. Debts due to a corporation in N. Carolina must be sued for in the name of the body corporate, and cannot be recovered in the name of A. B., president, &c., and directors of such company. Britain *v.* Newman, 2 Dev. & B. 363. See *ante*, § 99, *et seq.* § 234.

was objected, that the charter given in evidence varied the name of the plaintiff so much from the declaration, as to form good ground of nonsuit, and the plaintiffs were nonsuited; but on a rule to set it aside, the court said, the objection taken would operate in bar, if the plaintiff had declared so that they could not be identified with the persons entitled to the tolls claimed; but the objection taken only abates the suit, being a mere formal variance; the plaintiffs were therefore improperly nonsuited.[1] A corporation defendant cannot take advantage of a misnomer, in arrest of judgment, but must plead it in abatement.[2]

§ 651. Where a bank issued notes by a wrong corporate name, and was sued on its notes by such name, the plaintiff was permitted to amend without costs, as he was led into the mistake by the fault of the defendants.[3] A plaintiff brought an action by the name of "The Proprietors of a Bridge over Connecticut River between Montague and Greenfield, late in the county of Hampshire, and now in the county of Franklin." On motion to the court, the plaintiff was permitted to amend his writ by altering the name of the defendants to that of "The Proprietors of Connecticut River Bridge." The defendants objecting to said amendment, the question was reserved for the consideration of the court. The court said, "that the first corporation was dead, and the new one was created for the same purpose and object." The writ was served on the clerk of the existing corporation, by which regular notice was given to the real proprietors of the bridge. This is then the common case of a *misnomer*.

---

[1] Mayor, &c. of Stafford *v.* Bolton, 1 B. & P. 40.

[2] Gilbert and another *v.* Nantucket Bank, 5 Mass. 97. It is said, where a mayor and commonalty, or other corporation aggregate, are sued by a wrong name, they may make an attorney by special warrant, by their true corporate name, who may plead the misnomer. 22 Ed. 4, 13 b, Bro. Corpor. 65. But this, it seems, must be by special application to the court. 1 Ld. Raym. 118. Mr. Kyd says, "It is true, indeed, that in most of the cases where the question of misnomer of a corporation has been agitated, it has arisen on special verdict;" but, he apprehends, "that where a corporation have taken no advantage of a variance from their name, either by plea or at the trial, they cannot arrest the judgment, or reverse it on that account." 1 Kyd, 285. If, however, there be a variance in the name apparent in the entry of the judgment, that *may* be error; a judgment in the common pleas was thus: "That the mayor and commonalty and citizens of London should recover the debt for which they sued, and £6 costs to the same *mayor* and *commonalty* adjudged; and it was held, that this was error, there being no such corporation as the mayor and commonalty, without citizens; but it appearing on the docket roll that it was well entered, it was awarded by the Common Pleas to be amended. Cro. Car. 574.

[3] Bullard *v.* Nantucket Bank, 5 Mass. 99.

The amendment may be made, on the common rule of an election by the defendants of the costs of the action to this time, or a continuance.[1] In an action against a corporation as indorser of a promissory note, if the declaration alleges that the note was indorsed by the defendants, that is enough, as it implies that the note was lawfully indorsed by them, and the burden is thrown on the defendants to show that it was not lawfully done.[2]

§ 652. By the civil law, a member could not be a witness in a cause where a corporation is a party, if the particular members may have any advantage. But if the profit redounds to the community in general, a member of the body may be admitted a witness.[3] In a case in the Court of Chancery, in the State of New York, Chancellor Walworth said, that he believed it was now the practice of all the courts to admit corporators to testify in behalf of the corporation, where they have no personal interest in the controversy; and against the corporation, where the witness does not object; but that corporators were excluded from testifying where they have a direct personal interest in favor of the party calling them, in virtue of the corporation or otherwise.[4] This, as a general rule of law, is so well established that it is merely necessary to refer to it.[5]

---

[1] Sherman *v.* Proprietors of Connecticut River Bridge, 11 Mass. 338.

[2] Mechanics' Banking Association *v.* Spring Valley, &c. Co. 25 Barb. 419.

[3] Wood's Civil Law, 308.

[4] In the matter of Kip, 1 Paige, 613. The Chancellor cited Hartford Bank *v.* Hart, 3 Day, 491; Magill *v.* Kauffman, 4 S. & R. 317. See also, Philad. & W. Chester R. R. Co. *v.* Hickman, 28 Penn. State, 318; Montg. & Wet. Pl. R. Co. *v.* Webb, 27 Ala. 618; S. Life Ins. & Trust Co. *v.* Cole, 4 Fla. 359; Stevenson *v.* Simmons, 4 Jones, 13, 14. The inhabitants of a corporate town are competent witnesses for the corporation, in a suit brought by the town, and in which the rights of the town are in controversy. Burada *v.* Carondeley, 8 Misso. 644; Mann *v.* Yazoo City, 31 Missis. 574. So the trustees of a charitable foundation may be admitted as witnesses. Wellen *v.* Governors of Foundling Hospital, Peake, Cas. 206; and a person who has only one of two qualifications, may be called as a witness to prove that certain privileges belong to such persons as have both. Stevenson *v.* Nevinson, 2 Stra. 583. See also, Society, &c. *v.* Perry, 6 N. H. 144. In many States,

[5] A person who has acted in breach of an alleged corporate custom, is not a competent witness to disprove the existence of the custom. The witness is clearly interested. If the company had failed in establishing the custom, he would have been discharged from actions to which he was liable for the breach of it. Company of Carpenters *v.* Hayward, 1 Doug. 373. A stockholder cannot be a witness for the corporation in Louisiana. Lynch *v.* Postlethwaite, 7 Mart. La. 69. An inhabitant of a place is incompetent to prove a common right of fishery in all the inhabitants. Jacobson *v.* Fountain, 2 Johns. 179; Lufkin *v.* Haskell, 3 Pick. 357.

§ 653. In a somewhat important case, in Maryland, it was made a question, among many others, whether one Payson, a stockholder in the Union Bank of Georgetown, could be admitted to prove himself to have been the depositary of the muniments of the corporation. Buchanan, C. J., who gave the opinion of the court, said, that though an interested corporator cannot be received to testify generally for the corporation, yet it did not, therefore, follow that he is competent for no purpose; but that he might be placed in a situation to render him a necessary and competent witness for some purposes. He instanced the case of The King *v.* Inhabitants of Netherthong,[1] as an appropriate example, where a rated inhabitant of that township, whose interest was admitted, was called by the respondents, and was held to be competent to give evidence as to the custody of a certificate from the township of Honley (which was produced), acknowledging the pauper's father and grandfather to belong to Honley, in accordance with a decision in another case that was mentioned by Lord Ellenborough.[2] "Payson, being a stockholder in the bank," the judge proceeded to observe, "was not a competent witness for the plaintiffs for all purposes; but he was offered to prove, among other things, that he was president of the bank from the 27th of April, 1812, until after the 27th of May, 1819; that, as such, he was the depositary of the bank; and that during the time he was president, a certain book called the by-laws was one of the books of the bank. And if an interested corporator is competent to give evidence in behalf of the corporation, as a depositary of the muniments, in relation to

---

stockholders, even in moneyed corporations, are competent witnesses for the corporation; interest in the event of the suit merely affecting the credibility and not the competency of the witness. N. C. & Richmond R. R. Co. *v.* Brumback, 5 Ind. 544; New Albany & Salem R. R. Co. *v.* Gillespy, 7 Ind. 245; Covington & Lex. R. R. Co. *v.* Ingles, 15 B. Mon. 641. Secs. 398 & 399 of the New York Code provide, that no person offered as a witness shall be excluded by reason of his interest in the event of the action, unless he is a party to the record, or the suit be prosecuted or defended for his *immediate* benefit. Stockholders, in virtue of this provision, if not parties to the record, have been held competent witnesses in behalf of the corporation. Mont. Co. Bk. *v.* Marsh, 3 Seld. 481; and, in one case, R. & A. who were the sole proprietors of an incorporated bank, have been held competent to testify in behalf of the bank, in a suit brought by the same against the acceptor of a bill of exchange of which the bank was the indorsee. N. Y. & Virginia St. Bank *v.* Gibson, 5 Duer, 574.

[1] 2 M. & S. 337.

[2] In New York, an inhabitant of a town, who pays taxes to support the poor, is a competent witness, in a suit brought by the overseers of that town against the overseers of another town, relative to the settlement of a pauper. Bloodgood *v.* Overseers of Jamaica, 12 Johns. 285; S. P., Falls *v.* Belknap, 1 Johns. 386.

his custody of a paper produced as one of the muniments, why was not Payson within the exception to the general rule, and competent to prove himself the depositary of the book called the by-laws, as a muniment of the bank? The only argument urged against his competency, as being within the exception, is, that at the time he was called as a witness he appears from the plaintiff's own offering to have ceased to be the depositary. But that, it is conceived, makes no difference: and that he was a competent witness to identify the book as a muniment of the bank, during the time that he was the depositary. Higginbotham, too, then acting as the cashier, and being a witness for that purpose, ought not to have been rejected as incompetent to prove any of the matters for which he was offered. He was not competent to prove, that it continued to be one of the books of the bank, after he had ceased to be the depositary, and when he stood only in the relation of a stockholder in the bank, any more than any other stockholder. But admitting the existence, as to depositaries, of the exception to the general rule of evidence, no reason is perceived why his having ceased to be a depositary at the time he was called as a witness, disqualified him from proving the book produced to have been a muniment of the bank while he was the depositary; the nature of his interest as a stockholder not being changed, but remaining the same as it was while he continued to be the depositary."[1]

§ 654. In the case of the United States *v.* Johns, in the Circuit Court of the United States, before Washington, J., the president of an incorporated insurance company, by whom property was assured, although a stockholder, was admitted a witness to prove the handwriting of the defendant to the manifest of the cargo; because the conviction of the defendant would not be evidence in a suit on a policy against the company.[2]

§ 655. Upon a question, in the English Court of Chancery, whether a bond belonged to the plaintiff or defendant, it was objected that all the plaintiff's witnesses were members of the corporation, and the objection was allowed. The Lord Keeper said, every corporation ought to have a town clerk, and other clerks, not freemen, that they may be competent witnesses, if necessary. But the defendant having in this case cross-

---

[1] Union Bank of Maryland *v.* Ridgely, 1 Harris & G. 408, 409.

[2] United States *v.* Johns, 1 Wash. C. C. 363.

examined some of the plaintiff's witnesses, the Lord Keeper said that a cross-examination of a witness on one side, in any matter tending to the merits, makes him a competent witness on the other, though otherwise liable to exception.[1]

§ 656. In the matter of Kip, in the Court of Chancery of New York, it appeared that the testimony of Kip was material in the prosecution of suits against the Reformed Protestant Dutch Church, and his examination was applied for before the Master, pursuant to the provisions of the act to perpetuate the testimony of witnesses. The Master made an order for the examination of Kip, who appeared before the Master, but declined testifying, on the ground that he was the treasurer, and one of the corporators of the Dutch Church; and that he was also a pew-holder in two churches which were on lands, the title whereof depended upon the same questions which arose in the case. The Master decided that Kip was bound to testify, notwithstanding his objection; and on his refusal to be sworn, the Master issued warrants for his commitment, in pursuance of the provisions of the act. It was decided, by Chancellor Walworth, that the witness was not so far a party as to excuse him from testifying.[2] The only case within the recollection of the Chancellor, precisely in point, was a case decided by the Court of Appeals, of Maryland, wherein it was adjudged that the president of a moneyed corporation, who was a stockholder therein, might be called as a witness for the adverse party, and compelled to testify against his interest.[3] An express provision to the same effect is made in the late revision of the laws of the State of New York.[4] The note to this provision in the report of the revisors is, that it is intended as declaratory of the rule believed to exist, but sometimes questioned.[5]

---

[1] Sutton Coldfield Corporation *v.* Wilson, 1 Vern. 254; and see Steward *v.* E. India Co. 2 Vern. 380; and see 1 Paige, 601, in the matter of Kip.

[2] In the matter of Kip, 1 Paige, 601.

[3] City Bank of Baltimore *v.* Bateman, 7 Harris & J. 104.

[4] 2 Rev. Stat. 405, 407.

[5] Revisor's Report, part 3, ch. 7, tit. 3, § 96. The notes of the revisors are not considered as authorities settling what the law previously was; but they may properly be referred to for the purpose of showing that a particular section was not introduced by them into the statute as containing a new principle. Per Walworth, Chancellor, in the matter of Kip, *ut supra.* A stockholder in a company may be a witness, in an action of ejectment by the company, to prove service of a notice on the defendant's agent, and the admission of such person that he was agent, and that notice was served on him. Union Canal Co. *v.* Loyd, 4 Watts & S. 394.

§ 657. As to whether the confessions of a member may be evidence against the corporation: The general rule, as to receiving the admissions of one person to the prejudice of another, is, that such a practice is warranted, if the parties have a joint interest in possession, and not a mere community of interest.[1] In a case in Great Britain, the admission of a parishioner, liable to be assessed for taxes, was received, on the ground that the parish was an *aggregate company*, of which he was a member.[2] The ground upon which this case was put, has, however, been deemed questionable in the State of New York;[3] and has been directly overruled, as to a corporation aggregate, in Connecticut.[4]

§ 658. It was decided in a case before Lord Ellenborough, that the declarations of individual members of a corporation are inadmissible in contradiction of the rights of the corporation, in an action by the corporation. In this case, in order to contravene a right claimed by the city of London to appoint a gauger without the limits of the city, the defendant's counsel, in cross-examination, inquired what the witnesses had heard a certain member of the corporation say respecting it, and contended for the validity of this evidence, as coming from one of the plaintiffs on the record. Lord Ellenborough held that the declaration of an indifferent member of the corporation could not be conclusive against the body, although he would allow the witness to speak as to any thing he might have heard from the city gauger.[5]

§ 659. Declarations and admissions of *agents* or *trustees* of a corporation, in their official capacities, both before and after the act of incorporation, are evidence against those whom they represent; though, if not made in the transaction of the business of their principal, they are not evidence.[6] The admissions and statements of the engineer of a locomotive, made after an accident, are inadmissible against the corpo-

---

[1] Gray *v.* Palmers, 1 Esp. 135; Hackley *v.* Patrick, 3 Johns. 536; Smith *v.* Ludlow, 6 id. 267; Whitney *v.* Ferriss, 10 id. 66.

[2] King *v.* Hardwick, 11 East, 578.

[3] Osgood *v.* Manhattan Company, 3 Cowen, 623.

[4] Hartford Bank *v.* Hart, 3 Day, 493.

[5] Mayor of London *v.* Long, 1 Camp. 22.

[6] Magill *v.* Kauffman, 4 S. & R. 317; Burnham *v.* Ellis, 39 Me. 319; Franklin Bank *v.* Cooper, id. 543; Cov. & Lex. R. R. Co. *v.* Ingles, 15 B. Mon. 637; Franklin Bank *v.* Steward, 37 Me. 519; Glidden *v.* Unity, 33 N. H. 577; and see *ante*, Ch. IX.

ration whose servant he was.[1] And the admissions of the treasurer of a corporation made after the termination of his service, as to his own defaults while in such service, are not admissible in evidence against a surety on the bond, in an action against the surety alone.[2]

§ 660. One mode of rendering the individual members of a corporation competent witnesses, when they are incompetent for the reasons we have mentioned, is by an assignment of their interest. To prove the truth of the return of a mandamus to restore an alderman, seven freemen were called, who had released to the corporation all advantage, &c., which they could derive, &c. On objection, they were rejected; but on motion in arrest of judgment, the court held, that by releasing all the advantage they could derive from the corporation, their competency was restored.[3] It was made an objection in New York, that a stockholder of a bank was not a competent witness in favor of the bank. The stockholder transferred his stock, and, though the transfer was not registered in a book kept for that purpose, according to a provision in the charter, he was permitted to testify.[4] Whether, if a bank has forfeited its charter, and is unable from the funds paid in to satisfy its debts, an *original subscriber*, who has transferred his stock, is a competent witness for the bank, to increase its funds, was left questionable.[5]

§ 661. Another mode is by *disfranchisement*. Upon an issue joined on a prescription for a toll, the defendant produced as a witness, a freeman, who was objected to, as being interested. Upon which the defendant produced a judgment in the Mayor's Court, where, on a *scire facias* awarded, and two *nihils* returned, there had been judgment of his disfranchisement; but it appearing that the judgment of disfranchisement was irregular, inasmuch as the man had never been summoned, Lord Chief Justice Holt rejected him.[6] It is said, in another case, if a corporation would examine one of their own members as a witness, they must disfranchise him, and the method to do so is by an

---

1 Robinson *v.* Fitchburg & Worcester R. Co. 7 Gray, 92.
2 Chelmsford Co. *v.* Demarest, 7 Gray, 1.
3 Enfield *v.* Hills, 2 Lev. 236, T. Jones, 116.
4 Bank of Utica *v.* Smalley, 2 Cowen, 777; and see *ante*, Ch. XVI. § 6.
5 Barrington *v.* Bank of Washington, 14 S. & R. 405.
6 Brown *v.* Corporation of London, 11 Mod. 225.

information, in nature of a *quo warranto* against him, who, confessing the information, judgment passes to disfranchise him.[1]

§ 662. As to *proceedings in Equity* where corporations are parties: It has already been stated, at the commencement of the present chapter, that, in England and in some of the States in this country, in an action at law by a corporation, it must, under the general issue, at the trial, prove the fact of incorporation. Where that is so, in equity, a demurrer lies to a bill, on the ground that the plaintiffs are suing as a corporation, while it does not appear that they are entitled to sue in that character.[2]

§ 663. The manner in which creditors of a corporation are to make themselves parties to a suit commenced against the corporation to wind up its affairs, it has been held, in New York, must be substantially the same as that in which creditors of a deceased individual make themselves a party to a suit for the settlement of his debts and credits, by coming in before a Master, under a decree, and proving their debts.[3] In Pennsylvania, a bill for the discovery of assets, &c., lies against a corporation; but such a bill can only be filed by a sequestrator appointed under the provisions of the act of the legislature.[4]

§ 664. When the charter of a corporation permits its creditors to sue the stockholders in "any court having cognizance thereof," a suit may be commenced in equity against the corporation and the stockholders conjointly.[5] If the corporation is sued, in the first instance, and the creditor apprehends that remedy will be ineffectual, he may seek a discovery of the parties who are made personally and primarily liable.[6] Where spurious certificates of stock in a corporation have been issued by an officer having apparent authority to do so, and which are undistinguishable on their face from the certificates of genuine stock, they are considered as clouds upon the title of the genuine stockholders,

---

[1] Colchester Corporation *v.* ———, 1 P. Wms. 595 (note).

[2] Lloyd *v.* Loaring, 6 Ves. 773. See *ante*, Chap. XI.

[3] Rossie *v.* Rossie Galena Co. 9 Paige, 598.

[4] Bevans *v.* Turnpike Co. 10 Barr, 174.

[5] Masters *v.* Rossie Galena Lead Mining Co. 2 Sandf. Ch. 301; Mann *v.* Pentz, id. 257.

[6] This course was pursued in Judson *v.* Rossie Galena Co. 9 Paige, 598. See *ante*, as to personal liability imposed by statute, § 599, *et seq.*

which a court of equity will remove by a suit in equity instituted for that purpose by the corporation, acting as the representative of the genuine stockholders, and in their behalf.[1]

§ 665. It seems that formerly it was in a degree uncertain, whether defendants, as a politic body, were to answer in a suit against them in equity, under an oath.[2] It is now, however, well settled, that a corporation aggregate makes its answer, not as in common cases under oath, but under the *common seal*.[3] In a case in the Circuit Court of the United States, before the late Judge Washington, it was made a question, whether the court could regard the statement made by the answer of a corporation, so far as it contradicted the allegations of the bill; the answer being put in, not upon oath, but under the common seal of the corporation. The question was not, whether the answer of an aggregate corporation under its common seal would avail the defendants at the hearing, in like manner as the answer of an individual under oath would; but whether such an answer, when it denies the equity of the bill, is not sufficient to prevent the granting of an injunction, and even to dissolve it after it has been granted. No cases were cited on either side, nor were any authorities relating to the question, within the learned judge's recollection; but he decided the question upon reasons *ab inconvenienti*, as follows: "I am strongly of opinion, upon principle, that such an answer is sufficient to produce either of the consequences which have been mentioned. The corporate body is called upon, and is compellable, to answer all the allegations of the bill, but can do so under no higher sanction than its common seal. A peer of the realm, in England, answers upon his honor, the oath *being dispensed with*. In like manner, the plaintiff may, in ordinary cases, dispense with the oath to an answer; and, if he do so, the court will order the answer to be taken without oath. Now, if, in these cases, the answer, denying the equity of the bill, cannot avail the defendant as an answer under oath would do, to prevent the granting of an injunction, or to dissolve it when granted, the legal impossibility to take an oath in the first case, the

---

1 New York & N. H. R. Co. *v.* Schuyler, 17 N. Y. 592.

2 Acton *v.* Dean of Ely, Toth. 7.

3 Rex *v.* Windham, Cowp. 377; 1 Grant, Chan. Prac. 120; Brumley *v.* Westchester Manufacturing Society, 1 Johns. Ch. 366; Anonymous, 1 Vern. 117; Fulton Bank *v.* N. York & Sharon Canal Co. 1 Paige, 311; Balt. & Ohio R. Co. *v.* City of Wheeling, 13 Gratt. 40.

privilege of the peer in the second, and the dispensation extended to the defendant in the last, would place each of those defendants in a situation infinitely more disadvantageous than that of the other defendants, whose answers cannot be received otherwise than upon oath. Such, then, cannot be the practice of a Court of Equity."[1] The caption of the answer of an aggregate corporation is: "The answer of the above-named defendants, the Mayor, Aldermen, &c. (or as the case may be), was taken under the common seal of the said corporation, as by the said seal affixed appears, at, &c."[2]

§ 666. In the case of The King *v.* Dr. Windham, a majority of the body obeyed the process of the Court of Chancery, as far as was within their power, and were ready to put in their answer; but Dr. Windham, the Warden, whose act was necessary to render the answer complete, refused to put the corporate seal to it. This was the first instance of the kind; and if the regular process of the Court of Chancery for the contempt had issued, it would have punished the corporation at large, when it was not in fault. The Court of Chancery, therefore, stayed its proceedings, in order that an application might be made to the King's Bench for a mandamus, to compel the defendant to affix the seal. The application was granted by the Court of King's Bench, Lord Mansfield observing, that it had been truly said, at the bar, that where there is no other legal specific remedy to attain the ends of justice, the course must be by mandamus; the very form of which writ shows that its object was to prevent a defect of justice; thus it came recommended by the Court of Chancery to have it specifically done. Dr. Windham seemed to have misconceived the consequence of his affixing the seal to the answer of the fellows, and to think it would make his corporate answer inconsistent with his private separate answer, for he was of opinion that the plaintiff's suit was just; but his putting the corporate seal did not contradict his private separate answer; and by refusing to put it, he defeated the end he wished to obtain.[3]

---

[1] Haight *v.* Proprietors of Morris Aqueduct, 4 Wash. C. C. 601; and see Callahan *v.* Hallowell, 2 Bay, 10. But see Bouldin *v.* Baltimore, 15 Md. 18. A foreign corporation cannot be compelled to file an answer; and the want of an answer, where it was not needed for purposes of discovery, was held no good objection on a motion to dissolve an injunction. Balt. & Ohio R. Co. *v.* City of Wheeling, 13 Gratt. 40.

[2] 1 Grant. Chan. Prac. 123.

[3] Rex *v.* Windham, Cowp. 377.

§ 667. The proceedings in equity against a corporation, on return of subpœna, affidavit of service, &c., is, instead of an attachment, a *distringas* directed to make distress upon their lands and chattels. An *alias* and *pluries* might issue, and, lastly, an order for sequestration, as in other cases, except that, when awarded against corporations, they could not stay it on entering appearance; and thereupon the complainant's bill might be taken *pro confesso*.[1] It was laid down by Lord Mansfield, that if a corporation be in contempt for not answering a bill in chancery, the mode of compulsion is by sequestration; that the plaintiff is to proceed to take possession of all the personal estate of the corporation; and if that will not make the members agree, he is to take possession, by sequestration, of the rents and profits of their real estate.[2]

§ 668. The *distringas*, we have said, is the first process against the corporation, after they have refused to answer the bill, having been regularly served with subpœna, or other process. This is directed to the sheriff, commanding him to distrain the lands, goods, and chattels of the corporation, so that they may not possess them till the court make other order to the contrary, and that in the mean time the sheriff is to answer to the court for what he so distrains, so that the defendants may be compelled to appear in chancery, and answer the contempt. The writ is delivered to the sheriff to execute, who is bound to make return thereof after it is returnable. When the sheriff has made his return, it is to be taken to the plaintiff's clerk in court, who makes out an *alias distringas*, to be used and acted upon in the same manner as the *distringas*. Should the defendants still stand out, then, when the sheriff has returned the writ, a *pluries distringas* is to be made out, in like manner as the former. This being also returned by the sheriff, counsel is to be instructed to move for a sequestration upon a *pluries distringas* returned against the said corporation to sequester all their lands, chattels, &c., until they appear to, or answer the plaintiff's bill, or perform the decree, and the court make other order to the contrary. The sequestration cannot be discharged until the defendants have performed all they were enjoined to do, paid all costs, and the commissioners their fees.[3]

---

[1] 1 Moulton, Chan. Practice, 230; 2 Maddock's Chan. 203; 1 Chan. Cas. 203; 1 Vent. 351; 1 Tidd, Practice, 116, and authorities there cited in *notis*. See also, Union Bank *v.* Lowe, Meigs, 225.

[2] Rex *v.* Windham, Cowp. 377.

[3] 1 Grant, Chan. Prac. 95; Thes. Brev. 144, 145; 1 Tidd, Prac. 107, 109. In Jones

§ 669. Where a *distringas* was issued against a corporation for non-performance of a decree, and afterwards a sequestration *nisi*, for want of appearance, the court ordered the proceeding to go on, notwithstanding these objections taken, and would not allow the company to enter an appearance on the *distringas*, and discharge the sequestration.[1] A rule to show cause why a *distringas* should not issue, will be awarded against a banking company for non-payment of a bill of costs.[2]

§ 670. The process of sequestration is a writ or commission under the great seal, sometimes directed to the sheriff, or most commonly to four or more persons of the plaintiff's own naming, empowering any two or more of them to enter upon, possess, and sequester the real and personal estate and effects of the defendant (or some particular part and parcel of the lands), and to take and keep the profits, or pay them as the court shall appoint, until the parties have appeared to or answered the plaintiff's bill, or performed some other matter which has been ordered by the court, and for not doing whereof he is in contempt.[3] A

---

v. Boston Mill Corporation, 4 Pick. 511, it was said by Parker, C. J., that the Supreme Court of Massachusetts as a court of equity, had authority to issue such processes against corporations as may be issued by the English chancery courts; as *distringas*, sequestration, &c. And see Holland *v.* Craft, 20 Pick. 321; Grew *v.* Breed, 12 Met. 363.

[1] Harvey *v.* E. India Co. 2 Vern. 395.

[2] Orange Co. Bank *v.* Worden, 1 Wend. 309; and see 4 Cowen, 111, n. a.

[3] Hind. Pract. 127, 136; 1 Grant, Chan. Prac. 90. As regards corporations established for private emolument, Chancellor Bland, of Maryland, in giving judgment in McKim *v.* Odom, 3 Bland, 422, says, that "evils and embarrassments must arise from a rigid adherence to the notion that such a corporation can only be forced to respond to a suit against it by *distringas* and sequestration of its property. Take the case of a turnpike road company that had refused to answer a bill in chancery. The road itself could not be taken and closed by virtue of a *distringas* or sequestration, because that, as one of the highways of the Republic, it could not, nor ought not to be obstructed by any process whatever against those whose only interest in it is the toll they are allowed to exact in consideration of keeping it in repair. Consequently, in this instance, the only method by which the court could effectually levy upon its property, as a means of enforcing an answer, would be to appoint a sequestrator or receiver to take the place of the company's toll-gatherer, at each gate along the whole line of the road." See *ante*, §§ 640, 641, as to the levy of an execution upon corporate property. In Grew *v.* Breed, 12 Met. 363, the objection was, that a chose in action was not subject to the process of sequestration. Wilde, J., in giving the opinion of the court, said, that, in examining the English authorities, the court did not find it so settled. 2 Daniell, Ch. Prac. 1262. The authorities, as the learned judge stated, are also reviewed in Johnson *v.* Chippendale, 8 Simons, 55; and it is there intimated, that choses in action may be reached by bill, for the purpose of subjecting them to sequestration. The Vice-Chancellor said: "I find no instance in which the court has compelled a third party to pay in a chose in action, without a bill, where any resistance

sequestration out of chancery is more effectual than an execution by *fieri facias* at law; for a sequestration may be awarded against the goods, though the party is in custody upon the attachment; whereas at law, if a *ca. sa.* be executed, there can no *fieri facias* issue. This writ is always obtained upon motion, *of course* (not upon petition). The sequestrators should be of sufficient substance to answer what may come to their hands.[1]

§ 671. Sequestrations, now a common process, are said to have been introduced in Lord Bacon's time;[2] but it rather seems they were first adopted in the time of his predecessor, Lord Coventry.[3] North, in his entertaining life of the Lord Keeper Guildford, says, that "Sequestrations were not heard of till the Lord Coventry's time, when Sir John Read lay in the Fleet (with £10,000 in an iron cash-chest in his chamber), for disobedience of a decree, and would not submit and pay the duty. This being represented to the Lord Keeper as a great con-

---

has been made by the holder of a chose in action." So in Francklyn *v.* Colhoun, 3 Swanst. 309, Lord Eldon said: "The true question is, whether this chose in action can be taken by this sequestration, or whether there must not be some proceeding in aid of the sequestration." In Wilson *v.* Metcalf, 1 Beavan, 269, Lord Langdale said: "A chose in action is subject to the process of sequestration; but how the sequestration is to be made effective in respect of choses in action, may be a question requiring much consideration. In a clear and simple case, it may be by order only, or a voluntary payment may be protected; in other cases, it may be necessary to resort to an action or suit, under the direction of the court." See *ante*, § 557, *et seq.* The doctrine maintained by these cases, said Judge Wilde, seemed well founded upon principle, and was sustained in the case of White *v.* Gemaert, 1 Edw. Ch. 330, and in Dovoe *v.* Ithaca & Oswego Railroad Co. 5 Paige, 521. The principle, said Judge Wilde, is the same on which a creditor's bill is sustained in favor of a judgment creditor at law, after his remedy at law has been fully exhausted. Clarkson *v.* De Peyster, 3 Paige, 320; Speiglemger *v.* Crawford, 6 Paige, 254. And Judge Wilde considered, that the court, in the case before them, were authorized, by the Revised Statutes of Massachusetts, to make and award all such judgments and decrees, and orders and injunctions, and to issue all such executions and other writs and processes, and to do all such other acts as may be necessary or proper to carry into effect the powers which are, or may be given by the laws of Massachusetts. The court, therefore, he said, had plenary power to do all such acts as might be necessary and proper to carry into effect all the powers given them by law. It was said by the counsel in Union Bank *v.* Lowe, in Tennessee, Meigs, 225, that a justice of the peace had no jurisdiction against a corporation; and the court said, "this is true in all cases where an appearance must be entered before a judgment can be taken; because a corporation can only be forced to appear by a *distringas*, which a justice of the peace cannot issue."

[1] Hind. 127; see Ammant *v.* New Alexandria & Pittsburg Turn. Co. 13 S. & R. 210.

[2] 1 Grant, Chan. Prac. 91.

[3] Earl of Kildare *v.* Sir M. Eustace, 1 Vern. 421.

tempt and affront upon the court, he authorized men to go and break up his iron chest, and pay the duty and costs, and leave the rest to him, and discharge his commitment. From thence," says North, "came sequestrations, which now are so established as to run of course after all other process fails; and is but in nature of a grand distress, the best process at common law, and after summons, such as a subpœna is, what need," he observes, "all that grievance and delay of the intervening process?"[1]

§ 672. It is doubtful whether sequestrators can seize the *books*, *papers*, &c., of a corporation;[2] though it seems they may break locks.[3] In some cases, where doors were locked, and admittance refused to sequestrators, the court has ordered a writ of assistance, in order to put them in possession.[4]

§ 673. By the New York revised laws, it is provided, that whenever a judgment at law or a decree in equity shall be obtained against any corporation, incorporated under the laws of that State, and an execution issued thereon shall have been returned unsatisfied, in part or in the whole, upon the petition of the person obtaining such judgment or decree, or his representatives, the Court of Chancery may sequestrate the stock, property, things in action, and effects of such corporation, and may appoint a receiver of the same.[5] Upon a final decree on any such petition, the court shall cause a just and fair distribution of the property of such corporation, and of the proceeds thereof, to be made among the fair and honest creditors of such corporation in proportion to their debts respectively, who shall be paid in the same order as is provided in a case of a voluntary dissolution of a corporation.[6] A creditor of a corporation whose execution has been returned unsatisfied, can proceed by bill as well as by petition, under these revised laws, to obtain a sequestration of the effects of the corporation.[7]

---

1 North's Life of Lord Keeper Guildford, vol. 2, p. 73, octavo edition.

2 Lowten *v.* Mayor of Colchester, 2 Meriv. 397.

3 Ibid.

4 See Register's Statement of the Practice, 2 Dick. 695, and the cases there cited.

5 2 N. Y. Rev. Stat. 463, § 36. See, for a discussion of this statute, Bangs *v.* McIntosh, 23 Barb. 591; Devendorf *v.* Beardsley, id. 656. See also, Curtis *v.* Leavitt, 15 N. Y. 12. No action can be maintained against a bank after its property has been placed in the hands of a receiver. Leathers *v.* Shipbuilder's Bk. 40 Me. 386.

6 2 N. Y. Rev. St. 463, § 37.

7 Judson *v.* R. Galena Co. 9 Paige, 598.

§ 674. It is the usual practice to make such of the individual members of a corporation parties, as are supposed to know any thing of the matters inquired after in the bill.[1] As it is not very likely that corporations, in answering under their common seal, will discover any thing to their prejudice, it is common to make the clerk, treasurer, directors, or some of the principal members, in their natural capacities, co-defendants with the corporation. This practice appears, it has been stated, to have commenced in the reign of Charles II., and was afterwards expressly recognized by Lord Talbot.[2] In 1623, the members of a corporation, charged as private persons, answered under oath.[3] In 1680, upon a bill against a corporation, they answered under their common seal, and so, not being sworn, would answer nothing to their prejudice; it was ordered that the clerk of the company, and such principal members as the plaintiff should think fit, should answer on oath, and that a Master settle the oath.[4] One of the officers of the East India Company was made a defendant to a bill of discovery of some entries and orders in their books; the defendant demurred, for that he might be examined as a witness, and for that his answer could not be read against the company. The court said it had been a usual thing for a plaintiff, in order to have a discovery, to make the secretary, book-keeper, or any other officers of a company defendants, who have not demurred, but answered; that there would otherwise be a failure of justice, as the company were not liable to a prosecution for perjury.[5]

§ 675. The same rule has been recognized in this country; and it was laid down by the Court of Chancery in New York, that individual members of a corporation were compelled to answer, not only with the rest under the common seal, but individually upon oath.[6] And in another case in the same court, it was held to be well settled that the officers of the Fulton Bank might be made parties to a bill of discovery, to enable the complainants to obtain a knowledge of facts, which could not be arrived at by the answer of the corporation put in without oath.

---

1 1 Grant, Chan. Prac. 28.

2 6 Bacon, Abr. tit. Cor. (E.), and authorities there cited.

3 Warren *v.* Feltmakers' Co. Toth. 7.

4 Anon. 1 Vern. 117.

5 Wych *v.* Meal, 3 P. Wms. 310. This decision has been followed in Moodalay *v.* Morton, in 1785, 1 Bro. C. C. 469; and as late as 1807, in Dummer *v.* Chippenham Corporation, 14 Ves. 245.

6 Brumley *v.* Westchester Manufacturing Society, 1 Johns. Ch. 366.

It was also held, that the corporation ought to be permitted to put in a separate answer, in order to make offers and admissions, and to deny facts which the officers may suppose to exist.[1] The receiver of a bankrupt corporation cannot be joined as a party defendant, in an action against the corporation upon a mere money demand, where no relief is prayed, or cause of action shown against the corporation.[2]

§ 676. The well-established general rule, then, we perceive, that a mere witness cannot be made defendant, has been relaxed in the case of a corporation. This relaxation is on the ground, that the answer of a corporation is not put in under oath, and that hence an answer is required from some person capable of making a full discovery, as the agents or the officers of a corporation. It was stoutly contended, in a case in the English Court of Chancery, in the year 1807, that the exception to the general rule we have referred to was applicable only to agents and officers, or to persons who stood in a confidential situation. The case stated is, in substance, that the plaintiff, being fully capable of executing the duty of a schoolmaster, was appointed and had long been continued in that character; that, at the election of members of parliament for the borough of Chippenham, certain individuals and members of the corporation wished that he should give his vote against his own judgment, in favor of a particular candidate; that, meaning to procure that vote, they gave him an intimation that if he would not vote according to their wish, he would be immediately dismissed; that he voted contrary to their wishes; and then the five individuals, in the execution of their corrupt purpose, found the means of making the corporation the means of dismissing him. The bill prayed that the bailiff and burgesses might, in their corporate capacity, answer their matters in the usual way, but that the five defendants particularly named in the bill, might answer upon oath. To this bill the five defendants demurred, insisting that the plaintiff had not shown a title to discovery against them, they being mere members of the corporate body, not standing in any official or confiden-

---

1 Vermilyea *v.* Fulton Bank and others, 1 Paige, 37. The jurisdiction of a court of equity to make the officers of a corporation parties for the purpose of discovery, is considered to be well established. Masters *v.* Rossie Galena Lead Mining Co. 2 Sandf. Ch. 301; McIntyre *v.* Trustees of Union College, 6 Paige, 229; Many *v.* Beekman Iron Co. 9 id. 188.; Glasscott *v.* Governor & Co. of the Copper Miners, 11 Sim. 305; Bevans *v.* Dingman's Turnpike, 10 Barr, 174; McKim *v.* Odom, 3 Bland, 421.

2 Arnold *v.* Suffolk Bank, 27 Barb. 424.

tial situation. The chancellor observed that the case was in many points very important, and was quite new to him; but he thought there was no sound distinction between an individual, and the town clerk or servant. There might be, he said, no officer for the time, and the individual might perhaps be the only person who could give any information. He referred to the English chancery cases which we have cited; and from those cases he was able to extract the principle, that a bill might be entertained against the individuals, and that they could be called on, under the circumstances, for an answer.[1]

§ 677. It is proper to refer to another ground of demurrer, which, in the above case, was laid before the court *ore tenus*, namely, that every charge in the bill was made with the view to the discovery of an illegal conspiracy, which was an *indictable offence*. The chancellor was perfectly satisfied, as to this demurrer, that if he allowed it, he should destroy the jurisdiction of his court, as without the ordinary words charging the parties with combining and confederating, in nine cases out of ten, from all time past, they would, upon modern doctrine, be liable to indictment; yet courts of equity have been constantly compelling the discovery.

§ 678. It appears to have been held, in the State of New York, that an injunction against a corporation cannot be dissolved on bill and answer, unless the answer is duly verified by the oath of some of the individual members, who are acquainted with the facts stated therein. On a motion to dissolve an injunction against a canal company, upon bill and answer, B. & R., two former officers of the company, were made defendants for the sake of discovery merely. The answer of the company was put in under their corporate seal; and the then secretary, who was not an officer of the company at the time of the transactions

---

[1] Dummer *v.* Corporation of Chippenham, 14 Ves. 245. The counsel for the defendants in this case relied upon Steward *v.* East India Company, 2 Vernon, 380; but Sir Samuel Romilly, counsel for the plaintiff, said it was among the many bad cases in that book; and the chancellor said he suspected a misprint. As it stood, observed the latter, that the demurrer was allowed without putting them to answer as to matters of fraud and contrivance, it was nonsense; but if it was read, that the demurrer was disallowed, with liberty to insist by their answer, that they should not answer the charges of fraud and contrivance, it was unintelligible. As it stood, he could not comprehend it, unless the argument could be maintained, that the demurrer was allowed, as otherwise they would be put to answer those charges.

which were the foundation of the injunction, swore that the matters stated in the answer relating to his acts and deeds were true, and so far as related to the acts and doings of other persons, he believed them to be true. The president, who was an officer of the company at the time of those transactions, swore to the seal of the company affixed to the answer, but said nothing as to the truth of the matters stated therein. The separate answer of B. admitted the truth of the principal allegations contained in the bill. The motion was denied, with costs, the chancellor observing, the case of a corporation defendant is an anomaly in the practice in relation to the dissolution of an injunction. In most cases, the injunction is dissolved as a matter of course, if the answer is perfect, and denies all the equity of the bill, in the points upon which the injunction rests. It is not, however, a matter of course to dissolve the injunction where the defendant acts in a representative character, and founds his denial of the equity of the bill upon information and belief only. Corporations answer under seal and without oath; and they are, therefore, at liberty to deny every thing contained in the bill, whether true or false. Neither can any discovery be compelled, except through the medium of their agents and officers, and by making them parties defendant. But no dissolution of the injunction can be obtained upon the answer of a corporation, which is not duly verified by the oath of some officer of the corporation, or other person who is acquainted with the facts contained therein. There can be no hardship in this rule as applied to corporations, as it only puts them in the same situation with other parties. Other defendants can only make a positive denial as to facts within their own knowledge. In relation to every other matter, they must answer as to information and belief. If the agents of the institution, under whose direction the answer is put in, are acquainted with the facts, so as to justify a positive denial in the answer, they can verify its truth by a positive affidavit; and if none of the officers are acquainted with the facts, their information and belief can have no greater effect than that of ordinary defendants, however positive the answer in the denial may be. In this case, the officer of the institution, who was such at the time referred to in the claimant's bill, has studiously avoided saying any thing as to the truth of the answer, leaving it to the secretary, who knows nothing of its truth or falsehood, to express his belief on this subject.[1] This view of the subject seems to differ from that

---

[1] Fulton Bank *v.* New York & Sharon Canal Company, 1 Paige. 311.

expressed by Mr. J. Washington, in the case of Haight *v.* The Morris Aqueduct.[1]

§ 679. As a general rule, *corporation books* are evidence of the acts and proceedings of the corporate body, when it appears that they are kept as such by the proper officer, or some person authorized to make entries in his necessary absence.[2] Thus, we have seen that the books and minutes of a corporation, if there is nothing to render them suspicious, may be referred to, in order to show the regularity and legality of corporate proceedings, &c.[3] But entries which are made in corporation books, of matters relative to any property or right claimed by them, can never be evidence for them,[4] unless made so by act of the legislature.[5] It is true, the following case is to be found in the English books: In an action by a corporation for non-payment of certain tolls, called "water-bailiff's dues," an entry had been made in the corporation books, as follows: "A particular note of all such duties, &c., as by the water-bailiffs, are to be received for the use of the mayor and burgesses of Kingston, according to the order prescribed and set down in a certain year, J. B. then being mayor, and continued and put in use from that

---

[1] 4 Wash. C. C. 600, and cited in this chapter (*ante*, § 665).

[2] Rex *v.* Mothersell, 1 Stra. 93; Highland Turnpike Company *v.* M'Kean, 10 Johns. 154; Penobs. & Ken. R. R. Co. *v.* Dunn, 39 Me. 587; Hudson *v.* Carman, 41 Me. 84; Penobscot R. R. Co. *v.* White, 41 Me. 512; White Mountain Railroad *v.* Eastman, 34 N. H. 124; N. A. Building Assoc. *v.* Sutton, 35 Penn. State, 463; Banks *v.* Darden, 18 Ga. 318; Goodwin *v.* U. S. Ann. & Life Ins. Co. 24 Conn. 591. Entries in corporation books, and in the books of public companies, relating to things public and general, and entries in other books, may be proved by examined copies. Whitehouse *v.* Bickford, 9 Foster, 471; 1 Stra. 93, 307. Entries in the books of the custom-house, of the Bank of the E. India Company, of the South Sea Company, and the like, may be proved in this manner. 2 Ld. Raym. 851; 2 Stra. 594, 605; Hardw. 128; 2 Doug. 593, n. 3; Peake, 30; 4 Taunt. 787. But instruments of a private nature, such as a letter found in the corporation chest (1 Stra. 401), or the like, must be proved in the ordinary way, as any other private instrument. So the books of a private company must be produced, and they cannot be proved by examined copies. 9 Petersdorf, Abr. 212, tit. Ev.

[3] *Ante*, Chap. XIV. § 513; Coffin *v.* Collins, 17 Maine, 444; Buncombe Turnp. Co. *v.* McCarson, 1 Dev. & B. 306; Mayor, &c. *v.* Wright, 2 Port. Ala. 230; Owing *v.* Speed, 5 Wheat. 420; Howard *v.* Haywood, 10 Met. 408; Duke *v.* Cahawba Nav. Co. 10 Ala. 82; McFarlan *v.* Triton Insurance Co. 4 Denio, 392.

[4] 3 B. & Ald. 142; Phil. & W. Chester R. R. Co. *v.* Hickman, 28 Penn. State, 318; New Engl. Man. Co. *v.* Vandyke, 1 Stock. 498. But a memorandum made by the bookkeeper as agent of both parties, and at their request, in the books of the company, may be given in evidence in such a case. Ibid. 500.

[5] Bristol, &c. Canal Nav. Co. *v.* Amos, 1 M. & Sel. 569.

time to the present day." This was permitted to be given in evidence.[1] This case was afterwards cited before Wilson, J., who said he was counsel in the case, and that the books were admitted by consent.[2] In the Supreme Court of New York, entries that were made by a clerk in the books of trustees, being a corporation by the direction of the trustees, were considered not evidence in a cause in which they were interested.[3] The English Court of Chancery has decided, that private entries in the books of a corporation, which are under their own control, and to which none but the corporation have access, cannot be used to establish rights of the corporation against third parties. In this case the question was, to whom the nomination of a curate belonged, — to the vicar or to the corporation. Entries in their books were not received in evidence to establish the right of the corporation, as against the vicar.[4] In suits between third parties, the records of a corporation need not be produced to prove the authority of the president, but it may be proved by other evidence.[5] And entries in the books of a corporation of private pecuniary transactions with a stockholder are not admissible against him, especially when it does not appear by whom the entries were made.[6]

§ 680. It has been decided in New York, that if a dealer with a bank send his bank-book, with money to be deposited, and the clerk enter the amount to his credit in the bank-book, at the time the deposit was made, it is conclusive on the bank; but *aliter*, if the deposit is first made, and the entry is afterwards copied from the leger into the dealer's bank-book.[7] In Massachusetts, the books of a bank are deemed evidence to prove receipts and payments of money; and if the clerk who made the entries be dead or insane, the book is admissible, proving his handwriting.[8]

§ 681. With respect to the *members of a corporation*, the *books of the*

---

[1] Mayor of Hull *v.* Horner, Cowp. 102.

[2] Mayor of London *v.* Lynn, 1 H. Bl. 214, n. The court, in this case, refused to permit the defendants to give in evidence their corporation books to prove their own rights.

[3] Jackson *v.* Pierce, 2 Johns. 226. Nor is the evidence of the clerk who made the entries of the declarations of the trustees, admissible.

[4] Attorney-General *v.* Corporation of Warwick, 4 Russ. 222.

[5] Cabot *v.* Given, 45 Me. 144.

[6] Haynes *v.* Brown, 36 N. H. 545.

[7] Manhattan Co. *v.* Lydig, 4 Johns. 377.

[8] Union Bank *v.* Knapp, 3 Pick. 196.

company are public books; they are common evidence, which must of necessity be kept in some one hand, and then each individual possessing a legal interest in them has a right to inspect, and to use them as evidence of his rights.[1] The board of directors of a bank have no authority to pass a resolution excluding one of the members of the institution from an inspection of its books, although they believe him to be hostile to the interests of the institution.[2] A stockholder in any joint-stock corporation is entitled, during the usual hours of business, not only to inspect the books in which transfers of stock are registered, and the books containing the names of the stockholders, but also to take a copy or memorandum of the names of the stockholders.[3] But with respect to a mere stranger, unconnected in interest, such books are to be considered as the books of a private individual, and no inspection can be compelled. This was decided after much consideration in the case of The Mayor of Southampton *v.* Greaves,[4] notwithstanding several modern cases, in which the granting such applications, in case of corporations, seemed to have been considered as a matter of course.[5] In that case the corporation brought an action against the defendant for tolls, and the court denied an application to inspect. A similar application had been refused in an action of trespass, where the defendant justified under the corporation of Ipswich, for distraining for a toll for repairing the quay,[6] and in many other instances.[7]

§ 682. In the case of The Utica Bank *v.* Hilliard,[8] it was held, that the defendant could not compel the cashier of the bank to produce the books and papers by a *subpœna duces tecum.* The court said, the course for proving the books or papers of a bank, when it is the adverse party, is to give notice to produce them, and on its non-compliance, to show the contents by inferior evidence in the cause. "The effect of this

---

1 2 Starkie on Evid. 734. The acts, resolutions, and proceedings of a corporation, through their directory, are evidence against the company. Gratz *v.* Redd, 4 B. Mon. 185; Haven *v.* New Hampshire Asylum for the Insane, 13 N. H. 532; Owings *v.* Speed, 5 Wheat. 424.

2 People *v.* Throop, 12 Wend. 183.

3 Brouwer *v.* Cotheal, 10 Barb. 216, affirmed, Cotheal *v.* Brouwer, 1 Seld. 562.

4 8 T. R. 590; see the opinions of Lord Hardwicke and C. J. De Gray, there cited.

5 Mayor of Lynn *v.* Denton, 1 T. R. 689; 3 T. R. 303; Mayor of London *v.* Lynn, 1 H. Bl. 511; and see Davies *v.* Humphreys, 3 M. & S. 233.

6 Per Lawrence, J., 8 T. R. 595; Hodges *v.* Atkins, 3 Wils. 398.

7 2 Starkie on Evid. 734.

8 5 Cowen, 419.

motion for a *duces tecum*," said the court, "would be to compel a party to produce evidence against himself; true, the books are ordinarily in the possession of the cashier; how? He holds them as the officer, the agent, or the servant of the bank; in the same manner as an attorney holds the papers of his client. The cases in which the production of papers may be coerced by *subpœna*, are, where they are the property of a competent witness; or at least, where they do not belong exclusively to the adverse party; when he can say, *these are my papers*."[1] A bank depositor, it has been held in Massachusetts, has a right, on proper occasions, to inspect the bank books; the bank officers having charge of them being so far agents of both parties.[2] And such are the best evidence of the authority of the officers and agents of a corporation to bind the corporation by contract.[3]

When a suspension of specie payments by banks is general, and nearly universal, the mere fact of suspension by a bank of circulation is not proof of insolvency.[4]

§ 683. In an action of debt for the penalty of a by-law, the time when it was made, the parties to whom it was made, their authority to make it, the by-law itself, and the breach of it by the defendant, must be set forth; that the court may judge both whether the by-law be good, and whether the defendant be a proper object of the action.[5]

§ 683 *a*. In New York, by an act passed in 1850, corporations are prohibited from interposing the defence of usury.[6] This act has been held to be retrospective in its operation, and to apply to foreign corporations litigating in the courts of that State.[7] But it does not apply to the accommodation indorsers of a promissory note made by a corporation.[8] A corporation cannot, under this act, recover back a usurious premium paid by it on the loan of money.[9]

---

1 See 6 Cowen, 62.

2 Union Bank *v.* Knapp, 3 Pick. 96.

3 Narragansett Bank *v.* Atlantic Silk Co. 3 Met. 282.

4 Livingston *v.* Bank of New York, 26 Barb. 304. See also, *post*, § 774.

5 Kyd, 167; Hob. 211; 1 Stra. 539; Stuyvesant *v.* Mayor, &c. of New York, 7 Cowen, 608; see Chap. X. § 8.

6 Curtis *v.* Leavitt, 15 N. Y. 9.

7 Southern Life Ins. & T. Co. *v.* Packer, 17 N. Y. 51.

8 Hungerford's Bank *v.* Dodge, 30 Barb. 626; Market Bank of Troy *v.* Smith, U. S. D. C. Wisconsin, 7 Am. Law Reg. 667; Bock *v.* Lauman, 24 Penn. State, 435.

9 Butterworth *v.* O'Brien, 28 Barb. 187.

CHAPTER XIX.

OF THE VISITATORIAL POWER.

§ 684. To render the charters or constitutions, ordinances, and by-laws of corporations of perfect obligation, and generally to maintain their peace and good government, these bodies are subject to *visitation;* or, in other words, to the inspection and control of tribunals recognized by the laws of the land. Civil corporations are visited by the government itself, through the medium of the courts of justice;[1] but the internal affairs of ecclesiastical and eleemosynary corporations are, in general, inspected and controlled by a private visitor.[2] This difference in the tribunals naturally results from a difference in the nature and objects of corporations. Civil corporations, whether public or private, being created for public use and advantage, properly fall under the superintendency of that sovereign power whose duty it is to take care of the public interest; whereas, corporations, whose object is the distribution of a private benefaction, may well find jealous guardians in the zeal or vanity of the founder, his heirs or appointees.

§ 685. Lord Mansfield, in commenting upon the convenience of the tribunal of a visitor, observes: "It is a *forum domesticum*, calculated to determine *sine strepitu* all disputes that arise within learned bodies; and the exercise of it is in no instance more convenient, than in that of elections. If the learning, morals, or proprietary qualifications of students were determinable at common law, and subject to the same

[1] 2 Kyd on Corp. 174; 2 Kent, Com. 300, 301; Amherst Academy *v.* Cowls, 6 Pick. 433, Parker, C. J.; Binney's case, 2 Bland, Ch. 141.

[2] Per Holt, C. J., 1 Show. 252; 1 Bl. Com. 480; 2 Kyd on Corp. 174; 2 Kent, Com. 300, 301; Binney's case, 2 Bland, Ch. 141. Regents of the University of Maryland *v.* Williams, 9 Gill & J. 401. In Murdock's Appeal, 7 Pick. 303, it was held, that the common law of England, as to the visitation of eleemosynary corporations, is the law of Massachusetts, except so far as it has been repealed, as to the visitors of Phillips Academy, by the statute of 1823, ch. 50, § 3, which gives a limited appeal to the Supreme Court from their decrees or sentences.

reviews as in legal actions, there would be the utmost confusion and uncertainty; while he, who has the right, may possibly be kept out of the profits, of what is in itself but a temporary subsistence. This power, therefore, being exercised properly and without parade, is of infinite use."[1] In this country, where there is no individual founder or donor, the legislature are the visitors of all corporations founded by them for public purposes, and may direct judicial proceedings against them for abuse or neglects which at common law would cause a forfeiture of their charters.[2]

§ 686. The visitatorial power, in England, of the bishop over the ecclesiastical corporations within his diocese, finds its origin and rules in the ecclesiastical polity of that country; and as this does not apply to our religious institutions, we propose in this chapter to treat of the power of visitation, in reference to eleemosynary corporations only.

§ 687. Private and particular corporations, founded and endowed by individuals for charitable purposes, are, without any special reservation of power to that effect, subject to the private government of the founder and his heirs; not from any ecclesiastical canons or constitutions, but by appointment of law, as an incidental right, arising from the property which the founder had in the land or funds assigned to support the charity.[3] The origin of such a power, says Lord Hardwicke, is the property of the donor, and the power every one has to dispose, direct, and regulate his own property; like the case of patronage, *cujus est dare, ejus est disponere;* and, therefore, if either the crown or the subject creates an eleemosynary foundation, and vests the charity in the persons who are to receive the benefit of it, since a contest might arise about the government of it, the law allows the founder, or his heirs, or the person specially appointed by him to be visitor, to

---

1 The King *v.* Bishop of Ely, 1 W. Bl. 82.

2 Amherst Academy *v.* Cowls, 6 Pick. 433, Parker, C. J.

3 Per Holt, C. J., Phillips *v.* Bury, Skin. 447, 1 Ld. Raym. 5, 2 T. R. 346; Ca. Parl. 45. To this celebrated judgment of Lord Holt we would refer our readers, as it is reported in 2 T. R. 346, from his lordship's own manuscript. Eden *v.* Foster, 2 P. Wms. 326; Attorney-General *v.* Rigby, 3 P. Wms. 145; Green *v.* Rutherforth, 1 Ves. 472; Attorney-General *v.* Gaunt, 3 Swanst. 148, n. 1; The case of Queen's Coll. Camb. 1 Jacobs, 20, 400; Dartmouth College *v.* Woodward, 4 Wheat. 673, 674, per Story, J.; Murdock, appellant, &c., 7 Pick. 322, per Parker, C. J.; Murdock *v.* Phillips Academy, 12 Pick. 244; Allen *v.* M'Keen, 1 Sumner, 276; Sanderson *v.* White, 18 Pick. 334, 335, Shaw, C. J.; Nelson *v.* Cushing, 2 Cush. 530.

determine concerning his own creature.[1] Although the rule, that in the absence of any appointment of visitors by the founder, the visitatorial power rests in his heirs, seems always to have been recognized as law in this country, yet the difference between the condition of heirs in England, where the inheritance descends to the eldest son or brother, and in this country, where it vests in all the children, male and female, indifferently, is such, as would render the rule extremely difficult of application in practice, especially after a considerable lapse of time and many descents cast. If such inconveniences are found to be numerous and formidable in practice, the remedy, it is presumed, must be sought in legislative interposition.[2] But the founder may, if he please, at the time of endowment, part with his visitatorial power, and the person to whom it is assigned will, in that case, possess it to the exclusion of the founder's heirs.[3] No technical terms are necessary to assign or vest the visitatorial power;[4] it is sufficient, if from the nature of the duties to be performed by particular persons, under the charter, it can be inferred that the founder meant to part with it in their favor. Where a testator in his will directed that vacancies in the board of trustees of an academy founded by him should be filled by nominations from themselves, subject to the approval of the selectmen of the town, and further provided that the selectmen "are always and at all times to have and exercise the right of visitation for the purpose of looking to the security of the funds, and that the interest or income of them be applied according to the bequest," it was adjudged that this language, not being controlled by any words of restriction and no visitatorial powers being reserved, conferred general visitatorial power upon the selectmen.[5] The power to interpret the statutes of the foundation, it

---

[1] Green v. Rutherforth, 1 Ves. 472, per Lord Hardwicke; Eden v. Foster, 2 P. Wms. 325; Gilv. Eq. 78; Sel. C. in Ch. 36; Attorney-General v. York, Archbishop, 2 Russ. & M. 717.

[2] Sanderson v. White, 18 Pick. 335, 336, where see the subject briefly and luminously discussed by Shaw, C. J.

[3] Eden v. Foster, 2 P. Wms. 325; Attorney-General v. Middleton, 2 Ves. 327; St. John's College v. Todington, 1 W. Bl. 84, 1 Burr. 158; Attorney-General v. Clare College, 3 Atk. 662, 1 Ves. 78; Dartmouth College v. Woodward, 4 Wheat. 674, per Story, J.; Murdock's Appeal, 7 Pick. 322, per Parker, C. J.; Nelson v. Cushing, 2 Cush. 530; The King v. Bishop of Worcester, 4 M. & S. 415.

[4] *Sit visitator*, or "Let him be a visitor," in the charter or statute, is sufficient to vest general visitatorial power in the person of whom it is said. The King v. Bishop of Ely, 1 W. Bl. 83; Attorney-General v. Middleton, 2 Ves. 327; The King v. Bishop of Worcester, 4 M. & S. 415; Sanderson v. White, 18 Pick. 338, 339, Shaw, C. J.

[5] Nelson v. Cushing, 2 Cush. 530, 531.

is said, constitutes a visitor.[1] And the founder may divide the visitatorial power among various persons, or subject it to any modifications, or control by the fundamental statutes of the corporation. But where the appointment is given in general terms, the whole power vests in the appointee."[2] A direction to a visitor to visit yearly, *et si quid reperit corrigendum*, to amend it, are sufficient words to create a general visitatorial power.[3] In the construction of charters, it is said, too, to be a general rule, that if the objects of the charity are incorporated, as the master and fellows of a college, or the master and poor of an hospital, the visitatorial power, in the absence of any special appointment, silently vests in the founder and his heirs. But where trustees or governors are incorporated to manage the charity, the visitatorial power is deemed to belong to them in their corporate character.[4] The visitatorial power over colleges, academies, and schools in this country, together with all other powers, franchises, and rights of property belonging to them, are usually vested in boards of trustees or overseers, established by charter, who have a permanent title to their offices, which can be divested only in the manner pointed out in the charter.[5] Sometimes, however, these boards are, by the will of the testator, or the statutes of his foundation, subjected to the visitation of some other board created by law, and vested with municipal authority, as the selectmen of a town. In such case the board of visitors, in the visitatorial powers to be exercised by them, are not the agents of the town; nor are they acting directly upon the interests of the town, or accountable to the town; and cannot be directed, controlled, limited or restrained, in the exercise of their powers, by the act of the town. They exercise a special authority, created by the will of the testator, and where the trustees are incorporated, conferred by the act of incorporation.[6] It is held a material objection to

---

1 Rex *v.* Bishop of Ely, 1 W. Bl. 85; but see Kirkby Ravensworth Hospital, 8 East, 221.

2 Ibid.; Green *v.* Rutherforth, 1 Ves. 473.

3 Attorney-General *v.* Talbot, 3 Atk. 674; 1 Ves. 78.

4 Phillips *v.* Bury, 1 Ld. Raym. 5, 2 T. R. 346; Green *v.* Rutherforth, 1 Ves. 472; Attorney-General *v.* Middleton, 2 Ves. 327; Case of Sutton Hospital, 10 Co. 23, 31; Dartmouth College *v.* Woodward, 4 Wheat. 674, 675, per Story, J.; Fuller *v.* Plainfield Academic School, 6 Conn. 544, 545; Sanderson *v.* White, 18 Pick. 338, 339, Shaw, C. J.; 2 Kent, Com. 302; 2 Kyd on Corp. 195.

5 Dartmouth College *v.* Woodward, 4 Wheat. 518; Allen *v.* McKeen, 1 Sumner, 276; Bracken *v.* William & Mary College, 1 Call, 161, 3 Call, 573; Sanderson *v.* White, 18 Pick. 338, Shaw, C. J.

6 Nelson *v.* Cushing, 2 Cush. 529.

the visitatorial power of the governors or trustees over the application of the revenue, that the estate and revenue of the charity is vested in them; since they might misapply the fund, and cannot visit themselves. But it has never been held, that the governors cannot be visitors, in this particular, merely because the legal estate of the charitable fund was in them, the revenue to be received and accounted for by others.[1]

§ 688. The incidental power of one appointed visitor, generally, may be inferred from his duty to inspect and regulate the affairs of the charity. He may examine into and regulate the conduct of members who partake of the charity, correct abuses, remove officers, and in case of a college, expel or admit a fellow, and generally superintend the management of the trusts.[2] The visitors of William and Mary College have power to change the schools, and put down the professorships of the college, and their statutes discontinuing a grammar school in that institution were held valid, and a professorship to be rightfully abolished by them, together with the salary of the professor.[3] But where the visitatorial power of an academic school was lodged in a body of trustees, it was held that they could not remove one of their number for misconduct, though they had power, by charter, to supply vacancies occasioned by death, or non-residence within a specified district, and might displace any officer appointed by them. This decision proceeded upon the ground, that they could not visit themselves, or each other; could not be visitors and visited.[4] The power of making new statutes, and of repealing or amending the old, may be, and frequently is, communicated to the governors, trustees, and visitors of the foundation.[5] It has even been attributed to them as incidental to their general power of visitation; but upon principle and precedent, this may well be doubted.[6] If a person is constituted visitor, in general terms, whatever

---

[1] Attorney-General *v.* Middleton, 2 Ves. 329; Sutton's Hospital, 10 Co. 21; Eden *v.* Foster, 2 P. Wms. 327; Phillips *v.* Bury, 2 T. R. 352, 353; Fuller *v.* Plainfield Academic School, 6 Conn. 545, 547.

[2] Coveney's case, Dyer, 209; Bagg's case, 11 Co. 99; Phillips *v.* Bury, 2 T. R. 353; Attorney-General *v.* Talbot, 1 Ves. 78, 79; Attorney-General *v.* Middleton, 2 Ves. 330; Dartmouth College *v.* Woodward, 4 Wheat. 676, per Story, J.; Murdock's Appeal, 7 Pick. 322; Murdock *v.* Phillips Academy, 12 Pick. 244; Sanderson *v.* White, 18 Pick. 334; 2 Kent, Com. 302; Bracken *v.* Wm. & Mar. College, 3 Call, 573; 2 Kyd on Corp. 195.

[3] Bracken *v.* William & Mary College, 1 Call, 161; 3 Call, 573.

[4] Fuller *v.* Plainfield Academic School, 6 Conn. 545.

[5] Chap. X.

[6] Ibid.

comes in derogation of his power must be expressed; otherwise he is *pleno jure*.[1] A clause of distress, given to an injured person, does not take away the party's remedy by application to the visitor.[2] In some instances the power of the visitor is regulated by statutes or ordinances imposed by the founder; and in such, it must be gathered from the whole purview of the statutes, considered together;[3] for though the founder appoint a general visitor, he may except some particular cases out of his general jurisdiction.[4] And where by the rules of the founder, the visitor must, in order to remove the rector of the college, have the consent of the four senior fellows, though he may have suspended some of the four, their consent is nevertheless essential to the removal, since, though they are suspended, their places are full.[5] Where there are particular statutes, they are the rule of the visitor; if he acts contrary to, or exceeds them, he acts without his jurisdiction; and the question being still open, whether he has acted within his jurisdiction or not, if not, his act is a nullity,[6] except under certain circumstances in England, where the king is visitor.[7] But though the tenure of a professor's office, in a theological school be, by the statutes of the foundation, during good behavior, yet it is forfeited upon the honest judgment of the proper tribunal, that he has ceased to behave well, in the sense attached to the phrase by the founders.[8] If the words "*shall and may*" are used in a general act, or in the constitution of a private charity, they are to be construed imperatively, in the same manner as the word "*must;*" as, if the founder's constitution of the charity declares, that if certain officers are found guilty of immorality, drunkenness, or any debauchery, the governors and visitors "*shall and may* remove them;" an obligation to remove for these causes is imposed.[9] An eleemosynary school established in Massachusetts by a private founder for the instruction of "youth," was adjudged to be established for the benefit of both

---

1 The King *v.* Bishop of Worcester, 4 M. & S. 415.

2 The King *v.* Bishop of Ely, 1 W. Bl. 89.

3 Ibid. 52, 71, 84.

4 Ibid. 84, per Ld. Mansfield.

5 Phillips *v.* Bury, 2 T. R. 350, 351.

6 Green *v.* Rutherforth, 1 Ves. 472, per Lord Hardwicke; Phillips *v.* Bury, 2 T. R. *supra*, per Holt, C. J.

7 Case of Queen's Coll. Cam. 1 Jacobs, 20.

8 Murdock's Appeal, 7 Pick. 303.

9 Attorney-General *v.* Locke, case of Morden College, 3 Atk. 166, per Lord Hardwicke.

sexes; as there was nothing in the will to control the general meaning of the term according to its common usage, and the same term was used in the statutes of Massachusetts providing for public education in application to both sexes.[1] In some instances, the power of the visitor is entirely uncontrolled by statutes or ordinances; when, having no guide but his own discretion,[2] with which no person has a right to interfere,[3] his power is arbitrary. Where a new donation is made to, or new fellowship ingrafted on, an existing eleemosynary corporation, it is subject to the rules and statutes, and of consequence, to the visitatorial power of the visitor of the old foundation, unless the new founder prescribe rules of his own.[4] Though the visitor of a college have a jurisdiction over matters of election, he has no right to appoint to a vacant office in default of the electors; and, if the statutes, in default of an election by the college, by express provision, give the appointment to the same person who is general visitor, he has that appointment not as a visitor, but by virtue of that express provision.[5] The tribunal of the visitor is strictly domestic; and hence he cannot act on a proceeding by a third person against the corporation, for the specific performance of an agreement. An application to the visitor in such a case would be nugatory; for he cannot compel a specific performance.[6] Upon the same principle, where an estate is vested in the corporation in trust, the visitor can give no remedy upon it, but application must be made to chancery.[7] Again, independent members of colleges in the universities, or fellow-commoners, who are mere boarders, and have no corporate rights, are not subject to the jurisdiction of the visitor, and cannot obtain redress for any grievances, by appealing to him.[8] Neither in a

---

[1] Nelson *v.* Cushing, 2 Cush. 530 to 535.

[2] Attorney-General *v.* Governors of the Foundling Hospital, 2 Ves. jr. 42, 4 Bro. C. C. 167.

[3] Ibid.; Attorney-General *v.* Talbot, 1 Ves. 78; Show. P. C. 51; 3 Atk. 675; Bedford Charity, 2 Swanst. 479; Attorney-General *v.* Middleton, 2 Ves. 328.

[4] Case of University of Oxford, cited 1 Burr. 203; Attorney-General *v.* Talbot, 1 Ves. 79, 3 Atk. 574; Green *v.* Rutherforth, 1 Ves. 467, 468, 472; St. John's College, Cambridge, *v.* Todington, 1 Burr. 202, 203, 204, 1 W. Bl. 51, 71, 82, 89.

[5] Rex *v.* Bishop of Ely, 2 T. R. 290, 345; and see Bishop of Chichester *v.* Harward, 1 T. R. 650; Rex *v.* Bishop of Chester, 1 Wils. 206.

[6] Rex *v.* Windham, Cowp. 377, 378, and see Reg. *v.* Kendall, 1 A. & E. 385.

[7] Green *v.* Rutherforth, 1 Ves. 470, 474; Attorney-General *v.* Master, &c. of St. Cross, 18 Beav. 475, 21 Eng. L. & Eq. 378, 398.

[8] Kyd, Corp. 330. *Ex parte* Davison, cited, Cowp. 319; and in 2 Kyd on Corp. 240, 241, 242, 243.

matter which concerns the discipline of the college, can an independent member have redress in a court of law.[1] A person, however, who though not yet a member of an eleemosynary corporation, claims a right to become one, may, it seems, be a proper subject of visitatorial jurisdiction, and prefer his claim to the visitor; since the question is one that concerns the constitution of the corporation.[2] A visitor cannot visit himself, or inquire into and decide upon the propriety of his own conduct, unless *expressly* empowered by the founder; for this would be to determine upon his own right.[3] Upon this ground, it was held, in case of a spiritual corporation, that where the express visitor had taken an office involving the performance of certain duties, a mandamus might go to him to compel the performance of those duties, his visitatorial power being suspended during his continuance in that office.[4] As the forum of the visitor is domestic, his power is confined to offences against the private laws of the corporation; and he has no cognizance of acts of disobedience to the general laws of the land. Thus, several fellows of a college refused to take the oaths of supremacy and allegiance imposed by a general statute, whereupon a mandamus was issued from the Court of King's Bench to the master, commanding him to remove those fellows. On the return of the writ, one principal objection was, that there was a visitor who ought to take cognizance of the matter; but the court, on the principle above stated, held, that this was not a proper subject of the visitatorial jurisdiction, and that, therefore, it was proper for the king's courts to interpose.[5] A visitor may, however, proceed upon a grievance done in the time of his predecessor.[6] In case of a private, particular, limited jurisdiction, and of courts proceeding by rules different from the general law of the land, no appearance, answering, or pleading, by the party, will give a jurisdiction to the court; but if there is a want of jurisdiction in the cause, it may be called in question at any time, even after sentence. Upon this principle, it was held

---

[1] Rex *v.* Gundon, Cowp. 315, 322.

[2] Rex *et* Reg. *v.* St. John's College, Oxford, 4 Mod. 260; Comb. 238; 2 Kyd on Corp. 248.

[3] The King *v.* Bishop of Ely, 2 T. R. 338, 339, per Buller, J.; The King *v.* Bishop of Chester, 2 Stra. 797; Green *v.* Rutherforth, 1 Ves. 471; Fuller *v.* Plainfield Academic School, 6 Conn. 544, 545.

[4] Rex *v.* Bishop of Chester, 1 Stra. 797. And see § 693 of this chapter, as to the remedy in such case.

[5] Rex *v.* St. John's College, 4 Mod. 233.

[6] Case of All-Souls, Oxford, Skin. 13; 2 Show. 170.

by Lord Hardwicke, that a party's answering to an appeal before a visitor, by no means concluded him upon the question of the visitor's jurisdiction; but that, notwithstanding such answer, he might contest the validity of the sentence upon that ground, either in a direct or collateral action or suit.[1]

§ 689. If the statutes of the foundation direct the mode in which the visitatorial power shall be exercised, that mode must be pursued, otherwise the sentence is a nullity.[2] But it should be recollected, that though a mode of visitation is prescribed in any particular case, this will not take away the general powers incident to the office of visitor.[3] Thus, though a visitor be restrained by the constitution of a college from visiting *ex officio* more than once in five years, yet as visitor, he has a standing, constant authority at all times to hear the complaints, and redress the grievances of the particular members; for visiting is one act, in which he is limited to time; but hearing appeals, and redressing grievances, is his proper office and work at all times.[4] The case is analogous to that of the bishops of England, who can visit but once in three years; but their courts are always open to hear complaints, and determine causes.[5] Accordingly, where one came, upon the commission of the visitor of a college, to examine the appeal of an expelled fellow, it was held no visitation; for it was only a commission upon a particular complaint, made by a single expelled fellow, for an injury supposed to be done to him.[6] By the constitution and statutes of a college, a visitation could last but three days. The visitor appointed a visitation to be held in the chapel on the sixteenth of June; when he found that the doors were shut, that the rector and scholars would not open them, but protested in the area against the visitation. He called over the names of the rector and scholars, and swore one to prove the summons, and went away without doing any thing more. After this, another visitation was appointed to be held in the hall on the 24th of July; at which time the visitor repaired thither, and divers protestations against the visitation were made; but he proceeded, called over the

---

1 Green *v.* Rutherforth, 1 Ves. 471.

2 Phillips *v.* Bury, 2 T. R. 348, per Holt, C. J.

3 The King *v.* Bishop of Ely, 1 W. Bl. 83, per Lord Mansfield.

4 Phillips *v.* Bury, 2 T. R. 348, per Holt, C. J.; The King *v.* Bishop of Ely, 1 W. Bl. 83, per Lord Mansfield; Attorney-General *v.* Price, 3 Atk. 103.

5 Phillips *v.* Bury, *supra.*

6 Ibid.

names, registered the act of the 16th of June, and upon several warnings to appear, the rector and divers of the fellows absenting themselves, and refusing to submit to the visitation, were pronounced contumacious, and the rector was afterwards deprived. It was objected, that, inasmuch as the visitor administered an oath in June, and made an act of it in July, this was tacking the visitation of the one time to that of the other, so that it continued much longer than it could by the constitution and statutes of the college. Lord Holt, however, held, and his decision was afterwards confirmed by the House of Lords, that "when he was hindered in June, and made an act of this at his visitation in July, that was only in order to his calling them to account for their contumacy, and to bring them in judgment at his visitation; that it was no more than taking an affidavit of the service of his citation." "If," continues he, "that which was done in June should amount to a visitation, it would be in the power of the rector and fellows, by their contumacy, at any time, to hinder the effect of a visitation, and such their contumacy would never be punished."[1] If an appeal is exhibited to a visitor he must take it;[2] and if he will not, a mandamus lies to compel him to exercise his visitatorial power, by receiving and hearing the appeal. To use an expression of Lord Kenyon's, the court will put the visitatorial power in motion.[3] It seems, however, that the court will not grant a mandamus directed to one in such case, unless it can be clearly made out that he is a visitor.[4] A visitor is certainly not bound to proceed according to the rules of the common law, nor according to any exact *forms* of proceeding;[5] but unless there be a general visitation of the college, there should be an appeal, and he should proceed upon that.[6] He must exhibit all proceedings against the appellant, until the appeal be determined;[7] direct the complaint, to which an answer is required

---

1 Phillips *v.* Bury, 2 T. R. 346 to 349; 1 Ld. Raym. 5; 4 Mod. 106; Skin. 447; Ca. Parl. 42.

2 Ayl. H. of Oxford, vol. 2, p. 81; Com. Dig. Visitor, C.; *Ex parte* Buller, Bail Court, 1855, 30 Eng. L. & Eq. 356.

3 The King *v.* Bishop of Lincoln, 2 T. R. 338, n. a; The King *v.* Bishop of Ely, 2 T. R. 338; The King *v.* Bishop of Ely, 5 T. R. 447; The King *v.* Bishop of Worcester, 4 M. & S. 415; Nelson *v.* Cushing, 2 Cush. 532.

4 Rex *v.* Episcopum Eliensis, 1 Wils. 266; 1 W. Bl. 52.

5 Bishop of Ely *v.* Bentley, 2 Bro. P. C. 220; Case of Queen's College, 1 Jacobs, 19; Murdock *v.* Phillips Academy, 12 Pick. 262, 263, Shaw, C. J.

6 The King *v.* Bishop of Ely, 2 T. R. 338, per Buller, J.

7 Com. Dig. Visitor, C.

to be put in writing, fully, plainly, substantially, and formally;[1] summon all parties concerned to appear before him;[2] and allow a convenient time for an answer, and for the examination of witnesses.[3]

§ 690. The proceeding before visitors, for the removal of a professor, is a judicial proceeding; and to render it binding on him, there must be a monition or citation to him to appear, a charge given to him, which he is to answer, a competent time assigned for proofs and answers, liberty for counsel to defend him, and to except to proofs and witnesses, and a sentence after a hearing of all the proofs and answers. It is not, indeed, to be insisted on, that in exercising the powers vested in a new jurisdiction, where no forms are prescribed, any precise course as to forms is to be followed; but these rules must in substance be pursued by every tribunal acting judicially upon the rights of others.[4]

§ 691. It is no objection to a sentence of a board of visitors, that they refused to conduct the trial with open doors, or to admit any persons within the room in which their sittings were held, but those who were engaged in the trial, and not even witnesses, except one by one as they were examined.[5] And where an officer of a theological institution, being removed by the trustees, appealed to the visitors, whose duty it was to hear the whole case anew, and they affirmed the removal, it was held, on appeal to the Supreme Court of Massachusetts, such an appeal being authorized by the incorporating act of the institution, that any irregularity or injustice in the proceedings before the trustees was immaterial, their sentence being entirely vacated by the appeal to the visitors.[6] It is said, that if the visitor proceed on a citation, professedly founded on an authority, which it afterwards appears he did not possess, his whole proceedings are void, though he might have taken cognizance of the same subjects under his general visitatorial power.[7] A visitor may

---

1 Com. Dig. Visitor, C.; Murdock's Appeal, 7 Pick. 330, per Parker, C. J.; Murdock *v.* Phillips Academy, 12 Pick. 266, Shaw, C. J.

2 Ibid.; The King *v.* Bishop of Ely, 2 T. R. 338, per Buller, J.

3 Com. Dig. Visitor, C.; Murdock *v.* Phillips Academy, 14 Pick. 266.

4 Murdock *v.* Phillips Academy, 12 Pick. 262, 263, Shaw, C. J.

5 Murdock's Appeal, 7 Pick. 329, 330; and see Garnett *v.* Ferrand, 6 B. & C. 611.

6 Murdock's Appeal, 7 Pick. 327, per Parker, C. J.

7 Bentley *v.* Bishop of Ely, Fitz. 310 to 312, 1 Barnard. 192, Fortes. 298, 2 Stra. 912, 2 Kyd on Corp. 278. In the two latter books, it is said, the judgment was afterwards reversed in the House of Lords upon a writ of error.

administer an oath, or require an answer upon oath;[1] but he is not *obliged* to hear the appellant *personally*, or to receive parol evidence; it is sufficient if he receive the grounds of the appeal, and the answer to it in writing; and this is the usual mode of proceeding.[2] Finally, he should always proceed, whether upon a general visitation, or a particular appeal, *summarie, simpliciter, et de plano sine strepitu aut figura judicii;* for herein consists the whole excellence of his tribunal.[3] A general visitor cannot have a mandamus to help him to visit his college, or to compel an inferior officer to do his duty;[4] but may suspend or deprive any for contumacy; or who may refuse to acknowledge or submit to his visitatorial power; since this is necessary to its exercise.[5]

§ 691. As the jurisdiction of the visitor is exclusive, it may, when the interposition of a court is sought in the affairs of the corporation, be extremely important to ascertain whether there be one or not. This question may sometimes be decided on affidavits; but if a mandamus has been granted, commanding the party to whom it is directed, to admit a person to a fellowship, on an affidavit of his election, the court will not supersede the writ on affidavits that there is a visitor, but will put the defendant to make a return; because where the point is determined on affidavits against the party complaining, he has no opportunity to do himself justice in an action.[6] If, in the return to a mandamus directed to a college, it be set forth, in general terms, that such a person is visitor, it is not necessary to specify his powers; for, as visitor, he has the power to determine all matters, that come as grievances before him, unless he be particularly restrained by the statutes; and such restraint will not be presumed.[7]

§ 693. But if there be one to whom the visitatorial power over a corporation is confided, it is his duty to exercise it upon all matters prop-

---

[1] Ibid.; Phillips *v.* Bury, 1 T. R. 348, 349.

[2] The King *v.* Bishop of Ely, 5 T. R. 477, per Buller, J.; 1 W. Bl. 85; Murdock's Appeal, 7 Pick. 382, per Parker, C. J.

[3] Com. Dig. Visitor, C.; The King *v.* Bishop of Ely, 1 W. Bl. 82, per Lord Mansfield.

[4] Dr. Walker's case, B. R. H. 212; Com. Dig. Visitor (Day's ed.), C.; 2 Kyd on Corp. 281 to 284.

[5] Phillips *v.* Bury, 2 T. R. 349, 357, 358.

[6] Rex *v.* Whaley, 2 Stra. 1139.

[7] Case of All-Souls, Oxford, Skin. 13; 2 Show, 170, 2 Kyd on Corp. 239, 240.

erly falling within his jurisdiction; and, as we have seen, if an appeal is exhibited to him, and he will not take it, a mandamus lies to compel him to receive and hear it.[1] He will not, however, be obliged to go into the merits of the complaint; but it is sufficient if he decide that the appeal comes too late.[2] Neither will a court grant a mandamus directed to one in such case, if it is doubtful whether he is visitor or not;[3] nor, if there be a visitor, will it interpose in a case coming within the general visitatorial power, if it appear that no application has been made to him; for no court, whether of law or equity, can anticipate the judgment of the visitor, or take away his jurisdiction.[4] When the existence of a visitor is not doubted, it frequently becomes a question, whether the person complaining, or the act of which the complaint is made, be within the visitor's jurisdiction; and the determination of such questions belongs ultimately, in England, to the king's courts, though the visitor may decide in the first instance.[5] Upon subjects within his jurisdiction, the sentence of a visitor is final and conclusive; nor, in England, can the king's court, in any form of proceeding, either directly or collaterally, review the sentence.[6] And it has been held, that where a visitor has actually executed a sentence of expulsion, though he may appear to have exceeded his jurisdiction, a mandamus will not lie to restore the party expelled; for that would be to command a visitor to reverse his own sentence.[7] But it is said, that in such case the party, against whom the

---

[1] Usher's case, 5 Mod. 452, no decision. Dr. Walker's case, B. R. H. 212; and 2 Kyd on Corp. 279; Rex *v.* Bishop of Ely, 1 Wils. 266; 1 W. Bl. 52, where it is considered doubtful. The King *v.* Bishop of Lincoln, 2 T. R. 338, n. a; The King *v.* Bishop of Ely, 2 T. R. 338; The King *v.* Bishop of Ely, 5 T. R. 477; The King *v.* Bishop of Worcester, 4 M. & S. 415.

[2] The King *v.* Bishop of Lincoln, 2 T. R. 338, n. a.

[3] Rex *v.* Episcopum Eliensis, 1 Wils. 266, 1 W. Bl. 52; 2 T. R. 290, 345.

[4] Attorney-General *v.* Talbot, 3 Atk. 674, per Lord Hardwicke; Appleford's case, 1 Mod. 82; Regina *v.* Dean of Chester, 15 Q. B. 513; 2 Kyd on Corp. 239.

[5] *Ex parte* Davison, cited Cowp. 319; 2 Kyd on Corp. 240, 241, 242, 243.

[6] Appleford's case, 1 Mod. 82; Carth. 92, 93, cites, 1 Mod. 82; 1 Lev. 23, 65; 2 Lev. 14; Raym. 56, 94, 100; Sid. 94, 152, 346; Phillips *v.* Bury, 2 T. R. 346, Skin. 447, 1 Ld. Raym. 5; Ca. Parl. 45; Rex *v.* Bishop of Ely, 2 T. R. 290; 1 W. Bl. 85; Regina *v.* Dean & Chapter of Rochester, 17 Q. B. 1, 6 Eng. L. & Eq. 269. Nor need the cause of a sentence of deprivation be disclosed in pleading. Phillips *v.* Bury, 2 T. R. 353, 354; Kean's case, 7 Co. 42; Rastal's Ent. fol. 1; Allen *v.* Nash, W. Jones, 393; Murdock's Appeal, 7 Pick. 322, per Parker, C. J.; *Ex parte* Buller, Bail Court, 1855, 30 Eng. L. & Eq. 356.

[7] Brideoak's case, H. 12, Anne, and cited in Rex *v.* Bishop of Chester, 1 Wils. 209, 1 W. Bl. 25, and in Rex *v.* Bishop of Ely, 1 W. Bl. 58; 2 Kyd on Corp. 281. But see Regina *v.* Dean and Chapter of Rochester, 17 Q. B. 1, 6 Eng. L. & Eq. 281.

sentence has been executed, may have a remedy by ejectment,[1] or an action for damages against the visitor.[2] Though at common law, no appeal lies from the sentence of a visitor, this is sometimes given by the charter, or legislative act creating the corporation. Thus, from a decree of the visitors of the theological institution in Phillips Academy, in Andover, a limited appeal lies to the Supreme Court of Massachusetts, by force of a statute, which enables that court to inquire whether the visitors have exceeded the limits of their jurisdiction, or have acted contrary to the statutes of the founder, but not to go into a hearing *de novo* of the allegations and defence, or of the evidence adduced in support of either.[3] But it was said, that if, on such an appeal, it had been proved to the court, that the visitors had been partial or corrupt, the court would have annulled their sentence, as violating the statutes of the foundation, by which they were required to administer justice impartially, and exercise the functions of their office in the fear of God, according to the said statutes, the constitution of the seminary, and the laws of the land. But in such a case, if the party arraigned before the visitors shall intend to impeach their judgment for partiality or corruption, he must seasonably demand that the evidence be reduced to writing, that it may come up authenticated by the presiding member of the board, and perhaps tender a bill of exceptions to the order or opinion of the board in matters of law to which he objects, so that from the entire want of evidence, or misapplication of it, the court might infer partiality, or, having a record of the opinion of the visitors as to a matter of law, be able to correct a palpable error in this respect.[4] Although it be a general rule that the jurisdiction of a visitor is exclusive, so that no mandamus lies to compel the execution of any thing within it; yet this rule does not apply where the visitor is himself the party to do the act required; or, in other words, where the same person, who by one office is to do an act, is, in another right, also, visitor.[5] These cases proceed upon the idea that one cannot be a judge in a matter in which he is personally interested, or, in other words, in his own cause. But where the master of a grammar-school was removed by the dean and chapter of Rochester, on the ground

---

1 Per Lee, C. J., Rex *v.* Bishop of Chester, 1 Wils. 209.

2 Green *v.* Rutherforth, 1 Ves. 470.

3 Murdock, Appellant, 7 Pick. 303.

4 Murdock, Appellant, 7 Pick. 325, 326, Parker, C. J.

5 Rex *v.* Bishop of Chester, 1 Barnard. 52; 2 Stra. 798; Green *v.* Rutherforth, 1 Ves. 471; The King *v.* Bishop of Ely, 1 W. Bl. 86, per Lord Mansfield; The King *v.* Bishop of Ely, 2 T. R. 338, 339, per Buller, J.

that he had libelled them as well as the bishop of Rochester, who was visitor of the school, and the deans and canons of other cathedral churches, it was decided, that neither the dean and chapter nor the bishop of Rochester had such an interest in the matter as would oust their jurisdiction, so as to warrant the court to interfere in the matter, upon a mandamus to restore.[1] If one who is no visitor attempt a visitation,[2] or if a visitor exceed his authority, or intermeddle with a matter out of his jurisdiction, a writ of prohibition lies against him.[3] But if no person, who claims the visitatorial power, apply to the court, except one who has long exercised it, the court will not grant a prohibition on the motion of a single fellow, who suggests that the right of visitation is in another.[4]

§ 694. In England, where no specific provision is made for the regulation and management of a charity, the Court of Chancery, by virtue of its general jurisdiction, takes cognizance of it, by information in the name of the attorney-general, and since the statute of 43 Eliz. c. 4, by commission, in all cases within the general purview of the statute, and not coming within the exception of the proviso in it. But where there is a charter, giving proper powers, the charity must be regulated in the manner which the charter has pointed out; and where there is a local visitor, the Court of Chancery has no jurisdiction over any subject within the cognizance of the visitor.[5] In New York, however, it seems

---

1 Regina *v.* Dean & Chapter of Rochester, 17 Q. B. 1, 6 Eng. L. & Eq. 269, 281, 282, 283.

2 Phillips *v.* Bury, 4 Mod. 110, cites Year Book, 6 H. 7, pl. 14; Fitz. N. B. 41, 42. See 2 Roll. 230, l. 15, 27; Com. Dig. Visitor, D. & E.

3 Bentley *v.* Bishop of Ely, Fitz G. 108, 305, 310, 311; Bishop of Ely *v.* Bentley, 2 Bro. P. C. 220; 1 Barnard. 192, Fortes. 298, 2 Stra. 912; Rex *v.* Bishop of Chester, 1 Wils. 206, 209, 1 W. Bl. 22, 25. The King *v.* Bishop of Ely, 1 W. Bl. 81, 82; Bishop of Chichester *v.* Harward, 1 T. R. 650; Com. Dig. Visitor, D.; 2 Kyd on Corp. 277. Where the court inclines to grant the motion for the prohibition, there the defendant has a sort of right to insist that the plaintiff shall declare in prohibition; but where the court inclines against granting the motion, there the plaintiff has no such right to insist upon declaring. Rex *v.* Bishop of Ely, 1 W. Bl. 81, per Lord Mansfield.

4 And. 258; Com. Dig. Visitor, E. (Day's ed.).

5 Attorney-General *v.* Price, 3 Atk. 108; Attorney-General *v.* Middleton, 2 Ves. 328, 329; Attorney-General *v.* Governors of Harrow School, 2 Ves. 551; Attorney-General *v.* Bedford, 2 Ves. 505; and see Attorney-General *v.* Dixie, 13 Ves. 519; *Ex parte* Berkhampstead School, 2 Ves. & B. 134; Nelson *v.* Cushing, 2 Cush. 530, 532; Attorney-General *v.* Magdalen College, 10 Beav. 402; Whiston *v.* Dean & Chapter of Rochester, 7 Hare, 532, 558–563; 2 Kyd on Corp. 182–187; but see Kirkby Ravensworth Hospital, 8 East, 221, 15 Ves. 305.

settled that the Court of Chancery can exercise no authority over an eleemosynary corporation, in a visitatorial character.[1] The persons entitled to execute the visitatorial functions, as the governors of schools, &c., have frequently the management of the revenues with which the charity is endowed; and in such cases, courts of chancery, by virtue of their general jurisdiction, will, in England, and would undoubtedly in this country, compel them to account for their administration in the same manner as other trustees.[2] And in New York, though the Court of Chancery decided that it could take no cognizance of an academic corporation in a visitatorial character, yet it is also held, that it might take cognizance of a cause in which the academy on one side, and the teacher on the other, were parties, upon some ground of its proper jurisdiction, as its power to cause contracts to be delivered up and cancelled.[3] In England, too, the Court of Chancery, though it exercises no control over persons intrusted merely with the regulation of the charity, carries its interference so far, that where these persons have the management of the estate, it makes the corporations themselves amenable to it for a breach of the trust.[4]

§ 695. Where no visitor has been appointed by the founder, and his heirs are extinct, it has been made a question in England, whether the visitatorial power devolves personally on the king, or belongs to the Court of King's Bench by virtue of its general superintending authority. On an application to the Court of King's Bench, in the time of

---

[1] Auburn Academy *v.* Strong, 1 Hopkins, Ch. 278. See Attorney-General *v.* Utica Ins. Co. 2 Johns. Ch. 379.

[2] Eden *v.* Foster, 2 P. Wms. 326; Attorney-General *v.* Governors of Harrow School, 2 Ves. 551; Attorney-General *v.* Governors of the Foundling Hospital, 2 Ves. jr. 42, 4 Bro. C. C. 167; *Ex parte* Berkhampstead Free School, 2 Ves. & B. 134; Attorney-General *v.* Dixie, 13 Ves. 519; Attorney-General *v.* Corp. of Bedford, 2 Ves. 505; Attorney-General *v.* Lubbock, 1 Coop. Ch. C. 15; Attorney-General *v.* York Archbishop, 2 Russ. & M. 461; Attorney-General *v.* Magdalen College, Oxford, 10 Beav. 402; Whiston *v.* Dean & Chapter of Rochester, 7 Hare, 532, 558–563; Sanderson *v.* White, 18 Pick. 339, Shaw, C. J.; Nelson *v.* Cushing, 2 Cush. 532.

[3] Auburn Academy *v.* Strong, 1 Hopkins, Ch. 278; and see Sanderson *v.* White, 18 Pick. 339.

[4] Lydiat *v.* Foach, 2 Vern. 412; Mayor of Coventry *v.* Attorney-General, 2 Bro. P. C. 235; Attorney-General *v.* Corporation of Bedford, 2 Ves. 505; *Ex parte* Greenhouse, 1 Madd. 92; Attorney-General *v.* Skinner's Company, 5 Madd. 173; Attorney-General *v.* Caius College, 2 Keene, 150; Attorney-General *v.* Fishmongers' Co. 1 Keene, 492; Attorney-General *v.* East Retford, 2 Mylne & K. 35; Chambers *v.* Baptist Education Society, 1 B. Mon. 220.

Lord Chief Justice Holt, the latter is reported to have said: "I take this to be altogether a lay corporation, and then the visitation belongs to the founder and his heirs; and if he die without heirs, I take the visitation goes to the king; and this is my private opinion;"[1] and he cites, in support of this opinion, a case from the Year Books.[2] The same question coming incidentally before Lord Mansfield, in the case of a college, his lordship considered, that, as "the foundation was not a charity, the power of superintending it did not go to the king as visitor;" but that "the right devolved to the crown to be exercised by the Court of King's Bench;"[3] and he founded himself upon the case of Rex *v.* Bishop of Chester,[4] where it was held, that during the suspension of the visitatorial power, it was the same as if there had been no visitor; and the king, in Court of King's Bench, proceeded by mandamus upon that ground. It is now, however, well settled, in England, that if there be no person who can act as visitor over a private foundation, in consequence of a failure of the founder's heirs,[5] or their incapacity, as from lunacy,[6] the duties of that office devolve upon the king; which it then becomes the task of the Court of Chancery to execute for his majesty,[7] in the same manner as if it had been a mere royal foundation.[8] The mode of proceeding, in such case, is neither by bill nor information, but by petition to the Lord Chancellor, as keeper of the great seal, in his visitatorial capacity.[9]

---

1 Anon. 12 Mod. 232.

2 Simon de Montford's case, 5 Ed. 4, Long. Quint. 123.

3 Rex *v.* Gregory, 4 T. R. 240, 241, in notes.

4 2 Stra. 797.

5 Rex *v.* Master, &c. of St. Catherine's Hall, Cambridge, 4 T. R. 233; *Ex parte* Wrangham, 2 Ves. jr. 609; Attorney-General *v.* Black, 11 Ves. 191; Attorney-General *v.* Earl of Clarendon, 17 Ves. 491.

6 Attorney-General *v.* Dixie, 13 Ves. 519.

7 Attorney-General *v.* Price, 3 Atk. 109.

8 Case of Queen's College, Camb. 1 Jacobs, 1.

9 Attorney-General *v.* Dixie, 13 Ves. 527, 534, 535; Attorney-General *v.* Earl of Clarendon, 17 Ves. 498, 499; *Ex parte* Wrangham, 2 Ves. jr. 609; Attorney-General *v.* Black, 11 Ves. 191.

CHAPTER XX.

OF THE WRIT OF MANDAMUS.

§ 696. One of the modes in which courts exercise common-law jurisdiction over civil corporations, for the purpose of compelling them to observe the ordinances of their constitution, and to respect the rights of those entitled to participate in their privileges, is, as we have remarked in the preceding chapter, by writ of mandamus. We propose, therefore, to treat of this writ, so far as it is applicable to civil corporations aggregate of a private nature; and in doing so shall be compelled to illustrate its nature, and the mode of proceeding under it, principally, by a reference to cases concerning public corporations.

§ 697. The writ of mandamus is substantially a command in the name of the sovereign power, directed to persons, corporations, or inferior courts of judicature within its jurisdiction, requiring them to do a certain specific act, as being the legal duty of their office, character, or situation; and, in the specific relief it affords, resembles a bill in chancery. In England it is termed a prerogative writ, in distinction from a writ of right; issuing exclusively from, and granted at the discretion of the Court of King's Bench.[1] From its high and controlling nature, it runs in that country into exclusive jurisdictions, as the palatinates, the city of London, the Cinque Ports, and ancient towns, notwithstanding their exclusive privileges, in the same manner as a writ of habeas corpus.[2] In our own country it is issuable, in general, by the highest courts of ordinary jurisdiction in the several States; courts of error never issuing this writ. By "*ordinary*" we do not of course mean "*original*" jurisdiction; and in Pennsylvania, though a statute of that

---

[1] Audley *v.* Joyce, Poph. 176; Rex *v.* Commissioners of Excise, 2 T. R. 385, per Ashurst, J.; Rex *v.* Winchelsea, 2 Lev. 86. It seems that anciently the Court of Chancery exercised the power of issuing writs of mandamus to inferior courts, though not to the King's Bench. The Rioter's case, 1 Vern. 175.

[2] Rex *v.* Commissioners of Excise, 2 T. R. 385; Rex *v.* Winchelsea, 2 Lev. 86.

State provides that the Supreme Court shall have no original jurisdiction in *civil cases*, this does not deprive that court of the power of issuing a mandamus.[1] Neither does an act prohibiting a court from trying issues of fact in bank, prevent it from issuing a mandamus; for, at common law, the return to a mandamus must be received as true, until it is proved to be false in an action for a false return, which may be brought in some other court.[2] The circuit courts of the United States may also issue writs of mandamus; but their power in this particular is confined exclusively to those cases in which it may be necessary to the exercise of their jurisdiction.[3] And on error to the Circuit Court for the District of Columbia, it was determined by the Supreme Court of the United States, that a writ of error would lie under the act relating to the District of Columbia, which is similar in its provisions to the judiciary act of 1789, c. 20, sec. 22, to reverse the judgment of the Circuit Court, awarding a peremptory mandamus, to admit the defendants in error to the offices of directors of the Columbian Insurance Company, where the matter in controversy amounted to one thousand dollars. The value of an office, it was held, must be ascertained by the salary.[4]

§ 698. As the writ of mandamus is not a writ of right, it is not granted, as of course, but only at the discretion of the court to whom the application for it is made;[5] and this discretion will not be exercised in favor of the applicant, unless some just or useful purpose may be answered by the writ;[6] and especially if the application be not made *bonâ fide*, but indirectly, and for an improper purpose,[7] or if gross and un-

---

[1] Commonwealth *v.* Commissioners of Lancaster, 6 Binn. 5. And the Supreme Court sitting in one of the districts, may issue writs of mandamus returnable there, to any part of the State. Penns. R. R. Co. *v.* Canal Commissioners, 21 Penn. State, 9. But see State *v.* Farwell, 4 Chand. 106; *Ex parte* White, 4 Fla. 165.

[2] Ibid. In Pennsylvania, the practice is not to issue writs of mandamus, except from the court which sits in the district in which the persons reside, to whom the mandamus is to be directed. Commonwealth *v.* Clark, 9 S. & R. 62.

[3] McIntire *v.* Wood, 7 Cranch, 504; McClung *v.* Silliman, 6 Wheat. 598; Smith *v.* Jackson, 1 Paine, C. C. 453.

[4] Columbian Ins. Co. *v.* Wheelwright, 7 Wheat. 534.

[5] Rex *v.* Chester, 1 T. R. 403; Rex *v.* London, 1 T. R. 425; Rex *v.* Ely, 2 T. R. 336; Anon. 2 Barnard. 237; Woodbury *v.* County Commissioners, 40 Me. 304, 306.

[6] Rex *v.* Commissioners of Excise, 2 T. R. 385; Corporation *v.* Paulding, 16 Mart. La. 189; Van Rensselaer *v.* Sheriff of Albany, 1 Cowen, 501; Williams *v.* County Commissioners, 35 Me. 345; People *v.* Supervisors of Westchester, 15 Barb. 607.

[7] Regina *v.* Liverpool, &c. Railway Co., Q. B. 1852, 11 Eng. L. & Eq. 408; Regina *v.* London & Northwestern Railway Co. 16 Q. B. 864, 6 Eng. L. & Eq. 220.

reasonable laches and delay have been shown by him in asserting his right,[1] or if without fault, as by unforeseen casualties, the respondent is unable to fulfil the duty to be required.[2] In a proper case, the interest of an applicant for a writ of mandamus need be no greater than that of an applicant for a *quo warranto* — the cases being analogous; and it has been frequently determined that the interest which an inhabitant, merely as such, and though no member of the corporate body, has in the good government of the borough or city which he inhabits, is sufficient to entitle him to be relator in a *quo warranto*, filed to question the election of mayor or members of the town council.[3] The motion for the writ must be founded on affidavits drawn up in so certain and formal a manner that an indictment for perjury may be sustained upon them, if the averments be wilfully false. If the corporation is by prescription, its constitution, as well as the applicant's right, must be proved by affidavit; if by charter, a copy of the charter must be produced at the time of making the motion.[4] In England, if the affidavits be sworn in court or before a judge at chambers, they need not be entitled in the King's Bench. But if sworn before a commissioner, they must be entitled of the court, unless they say, "before A. B., commissioner of the Court of King's Bench."[5] Strictly speaking, the affidavits should not be entitled with the names of any parties; for there is at the time no cause pending before the court. In the Court of King's Bench, the practice seems to have varied upon this point, until settled by a rule of court.[6] In New York, a motion for a mandamus, grounded upon affidavits thus entitled, was denied; for it was said by the court, that an

---

[1] The Queen *v.* Halifax Road Trustees, 12 Q. B. 442; Mayor, &c. of Savannah *v.* State, 4 Ga. 26. There is no special limitation, by statute, in New York, within which a writ of mandamus must be obtained, probably, because it is discretionary with the court whether to grant or refuse it. People *v.* Supervisors of Westchester, 12 Barb. 446. The applicant should be allowed the time given by statute for pursuing his remedy for similar injuries in the ordinary way. Ibid.

[2] Regina *v.* York & North Midland Railway Co. 1 Ellis & B. 178, 16 Eng. L. & Eq. 326, per Lord Campbell, Ch. J.; Regina *v.* Great Western Railway Co. 1 Ellis & B. 253, 16 Eng. L. & Eq. 345; Regina *v.* London & Northwestern Railway Co. 16 Q. B. 864, 6 Eng. L. & Eq. 220.

[3] Regina *v.* Archbishop of Canterbury, 11 Q. B. 578, 579, per Coleridge, J.

[4] Bul. N. P. 200; Selw. N. P. 1076.

[5] Rex *v.* Hare, 13 East, 189. The entitling the affidavit of the court in which it is sworn will not vitiate it. *Ex parte* La Farge, 6 Cowen, 61.

[6] Rex *v.* Lewis, 1 Stra. 704; Rex *v.* Jones, 1 Stra. 704, 705; Rex *v.* Pearson, Andr. 313; Bevan *v.* Bevan, 3 T. R. 601; Rex *v.* Harrison, 6 T. R. 60; King *qui tam v.* Cole, 6 T. R. 640; Clarke *v.* Cawthorne, 7 T. R. 317.

indictment for perjury in making such an affidavit must fail, as it could not be shown that the cause of which the affidavit was entitled, existed in the court when the affidavit was made.[1] Where, however, an affidavit was entitled "Sup. Court in the matter of J. L. *v.* The Judges, &c.," it was permitted to be read; upon the ground that it was not entitled as of a case pending in court, and did not, therefore, fall within the spirit of the rule.[2] When an application is made for a mandamus, and the question is one which the parties litigant are desirous of having tried, the court will grant the writ for that purpose, or they will direct an issue to be tried. But in such cases, a foundation must be laid before them, and they must see that there is some ground for the application. The writ will not be granted merely for asking;[3] and when a rule for a mandamus to compel a corporation to make an order has been discharged, on the ground that no demand and refusal have taken place, the court will not grant a new rule for a mandamus to the same effect, though a demand and refusal have taken place since the discharge of the former rule.[4] Before proceeding to hear the parties on a motion for a mandamus to a board of examiners, to compel them to give a certificate of election to a county commissioner, another having on a new election been elected to his place, the Supreme Court of Massachusetts ordered notice of the application first to be given to the incumbent.[5]

§ 699. Previous to the time of Lord Mansfield, the principles upon which the writ of mandamus ought to be granted, do not appear to have been well settled or understood; and from an attention to the letter of former precedents, rather than to the nature of this useful remedy, it would seem that the earlier judges sometimes denied it, where, at the present day, it would undoubtedly be granted. The great judge whom we have just mentioned, indeed, tells us, that, in his time, *within the last century*, it had been liberally interposed for the benefit of the subject, and the advancement of justice. The original nature of the writ, says he, and the end for which it was framed, direct upon what occasions it should be used. It was introduced to prevent disorder from a failure

---

[1] Haight *v.* Turner, 2 Johns. 371, 372, 373.

[2] *Ex parte* La Farge, 6 Cowen, 61.

[3] Per Lord Mansfield, 1 T. R. 333, 334; Mayor, &c. of Savannah *v.* State, 4 Ga. 26; Moody *v.* Fleming, id. 115; Commonwealth *v.* Councils of Reading, 13 Penn. State, 196.

[4] *Ex parte* Thompson, 6 Q. B. 721.

[5] Strong *v.* Petitioner, &c. 20 Pick. 484.

of justice, and a defect of police. Therefore it ought to be used upon all occasions where the law has established no specific remedy, and where in justice and good government there *ought* to be one. The value of the matter, *or the degree of its importance to the public police*, is not scrupulously weighed. If there be a legal *right*, and *no other specific* remedy, *this* should not be denied.[1]

§ 700. Accordingly, in cases of public corporations, it has been decided that a mandamus lies to compel them to proceed to the election of a new mayor, at any time after the charter day has passed without such election, where the former mayor, having power to do so, holds over, and refuses to convoke an assembly for that purpose; unless, indeed, the charter restrain the right of electing to a particular time;[2] to compel a new election of a mayor, where the reëlection of the former mayor was void;[3] to compel the corporation to proceed to an election of members to supply vacancies in a *definite* integral class, after a reasonable time has expired from the period of their occurrence, during which they have neglected to fill them up; nor is it an objection to the granting of the writ, that, at the time of application for it, an information in the nature of a *quo warranto* is pending against the mayor and corporators, to whom it is directed.[4] It will also be granted to compel the corporation to proceed to the election of one out of two persons put in nomination for an office, when the course of proceeding is for one class of the corporation to nominate two persons, of whom another class is to elect one into office.[5] And though the officers be annual ministerial officers, as mace-bearers, yet if public ministers, and necessary in the execution of the judicial functions of the corporation, and not mere servants, a mandamus lies to the corporation to compel it to elect them.[6] A mandamus, however, will not be granted to compel a corporation to

---

[1] Rex *v.* Barker, 3 Burr. 1267; The King *v.* Commissioners of the Land Tax in St. Martin in the Fields, 1 T. R. 148, 149; and see People *v.* Stevens, 5 Hill, 616. *In re* the Trustees of Williamsburgh, 1 Barb. 34; People *v.* Steele, 2 id. 337; People *v.* Judges of Branch Circuit Court, 1 Doug. Mich. 319; State *v.* Bruce, 3 Brev. 270; State *v.* Watson, 2 Speers, 105; Towle *v.* The State, 3 Fla. 202. In the matter of the White River Bank, 23 Vt. 478; Harwood *v.* Marshall, 9 Md. 83, 98.

[2] Rex *v.* Cambridge, 4 Burr. 2011; Rex *v.* Gregory, 8 Mod. 113, 127.

[3] Reg. *v.* Pembroke Corp. 8 Dowl. P. C. 302.

[4] Anon. 2 Barnard. 236; Rex *v.* Grampound, 6 T. R. 302; Rex *v.* Fowey, 2 B. & C. 596, 4 D. & R. 139.

[5] Rex *v.* Abingdon, 1 Ld. Raym. 561; Rex *v.* Ely, 2 T. R. 334.

[6] Rex *v.* St. Martin, 1 T. R. 149; Rex *v.* Liverpool, 1 Barnard. 83.

supply vacancies in an indefinite class, if sufficient remain out of whom to elect members for the definite class; since this would be lessening their chance of being elected into the definite class. In such case, the application ought first to be, to compel the corporation to fill up the vacancies in the definite body; and afterwards, to prevent a dissolution of the corporation, the court would perhaps grant a mandamus to elect a sufficient number into the indefinite class, although it may be very difficult to point out how many are to be elected, which is a strong argument against granting the writ.[1] It has also been resolved, that a mandamus would lie to compel a dean and chapter to fill up a vacancy among the canons residentiary; and that on such a mandamus the court would compel the election at the peril of those who resisted.[2] We see no reason why the same remedy should not lie against a private corporation aggregate, to enforce an obedience on the part of the members to the charter, or act of incorporation under which they act, if they neglect or refuse to elect their proper officers. In the case of Rex *v.* Bishop of Ely,[3] the Court of King's Bench awarded a mandamus against the bishop, commanding him to appoint as master one of two fellows presented to him by the fellows of a college; holding, that he enjoyed his power of the appointment not in virtue of his visitatorial capacity, but by the special appointment of the founder. And in The King *v.* Master and Fellows of St. Catharine's Hall,[4] which was an application for a mandamus to a college, commanding them to declare a fellowship vacant, and to proceed to the election of another fellow, though the Court of King's Bench disclaimed jurisdiction over the particular case as being in the King in Chancery, yet no objection was taken that mandamus could not lie, to compel an election in case of a private corporation.

§ 701. In case of a public corporation, it has been decided, that if a corporator, duly elected, refuse or neglect to take upon himself the execution of his office, a mandamus will issue to compel him to do so; though the defendant may either show for cause upon the rule, or plead to the writ, any sufficient excuse for not accepting the office.[5]

---

[1] Rex *v.* Fowey, 2 B. & C. 590, 593, 4 D. & R. 139.

[2] Bishop of Chichester *v.* Harward, 1 T. R. 650.

[3] 2 T. R. 290.

[4] 4 T. R. 233, 243, 244, 245.

[5] Rex *v.* Merchant Tailors, 2 Lev. 200; Rex *v.* Bedford, 1 East, 80; Rex *v.* Brown, and Rex *v.* Leyland, 3 M. & S. 186, 188.

§ 702. Numerous cases are found in the books, from which it appears that mandamus lies, to admit one elected to an office in a corporation, to the legal possession of his right. The writ, however, confers no title upon the person admitted, its sole operation being to put him in a situation to enforce his former title, if sufficient in law. For the sake of preserving peace in corporations, it will not be granted, unless the applicant show a *primâ facie* title. Thus, it lies to compel the proper officers to admit to the possession of his office or place one elected to be mayor, bailiff, or other officer, an alderman, jurat, capital or other burgess; one of the approved-men, or one of the eight-men, if the affidavits show that approved-men or eight-men are a class of corporate officers; a high-steward, a common-councilman, recorder, a town-clerk, a steward of a court leet, an attorney of the court of a liberty; a liveryman of a company, being a member of a municipal corporation; a sword-bearer, if an officer of justice; a sergeant, a constable, a bailiff, though a ministerial officer, or even a common freeman.[1] It will lie also to compel the proper officers to admit to the freedom of a corporation any of that class of persons who are possessed of an incorporate right according to the regulations of the constitution, such as apprentices who have served their time; and to take all such steps as may be necessary, preparatory to their admission.[2] This writ has also been granted to compel an insurance company to swear in a director, the company having been created by charter from the crown;[3] to restore directors of a banking corporation, who were refused the exercise of their rights as directors by a majority of the board,[4] or a member of a

---

[1] 2 Rol. Abr. Rest, p. 4, 8, 7; Stephens' case, T. Raym. 431; Shuttleworth *v.* Lincoln, 2 Bulst. 122; Rex *v.* Canterbury, 1 Lev. 119; Taylor's case, Poph. 133; Braithwaite's case, Vent. 19; Anon. 1 Lev. 148; Rex *v.* Wilton, 5 Mod. 257; Clerk's case, Cro. Jac. 506; Parker's case, 1 Vent. 331; Rex *v.* Tidderley, Sid. 14; Guilford's case, T. Raym. 152; Roe's case, Comb. 145; London *v.* Estwick, Style, 32; Bret's case, Comb. 214; Rex *v.* Wells, 4 Burr. 1999; Anon. Dyer, 332 b, n.; Taverner's case, T. Raym. 446; Middleton's case, 1 Sid. 169; Milward *v.* Thatcher, 2 T. R. 87; Stamp's case, T. Raym. 12; Baxter's case, Style, 355; Audley *v.* Joyce, Poph. 176, Noy, 78; Dighton's case, 1 Vent. 78, 82; Rex *v.* Campion, 1 Sid. 14; Baxter's case, Style, 457; Hurst's case, 1 Lev. 75, 1 Sid. 94, 152; Anon. & Rex *v.* Westminster, Comb. 244; Rol. Abr. 456.

[2] Townsend's case, T. Raym. 69, 1 Lev. 91, 1 Sid. 107; Green *v.* Durham, 1 Burr. 131; Clithero's case, Comb. 239; Rex *v.* Ludlam, 8 Mod. 270; Wannel *v.* London, 1 Stra. 675; Rex *v.* Harrison, 3 Burr. 1328, 1 W. Bl. 372.

[3] Anon. 1 Stra. 696. To compel the officer of a municipal corporation to administer the oath of office to a commissioner of deeds duly appointed. Achley's case, 4 Abbott, Pr. 35, 40.

[4] Prieur *v.* Commercial Bank, 7 La. 509.

navigation company who was disfranchised without notice or opportunity of defence;[1] to compel the trustees of a meeting-house to admit a dissenting minister who was duly elected;[2] and trading companies to admit as members those entitled to become such.[3] It will not, however, lie to the benchers of one of the inns of a court, to compel them to admit an individual a member of the society, with a view to his qualifying himself to be called to the bar,[4] nor will it lie to compel the benchers to call to the bar a member of the society, who has complied with all the usual requisites, such as paying the dues, and performing the exercises.[5] The original institution of the Inns of Court, says Lord Mansfield, nowhere precisely appears; but it is certain that they are not corporations, and have no constitution by charters from the crown. They are voluntary societies, which for ages have submitted to government analogous to that of other seminaries of learning. But all the power they have concerning admission to the bar is delegated to them by the judges, and in every instance, their conduct is subject to the control of the judges as visitors. The ancient and usual way of redress is by appeal to the judges.[6] Where a statute provided that any subject desiring admission to a particular company should, on request made for that purpose by himself or any other person to the governor or deputy governor of the company, be admitted a member, on payment of a certain sum for the use of the company, and taking the oath prescribed by the statute; it was held, that a mandamus lies to compel the governor or deputy governor to admit any person desiring it, and tendering the sum, and offering to take the oath.[7] Although a mandamus will not be granted to admit a deputy on the application of the *deputy* himself,[8] it will be on the application of the principal, if he be empow-

---

[1] Delacy *v.* Neuse River Nav. Co. 1 Hawks, 274.

[2] Rex *v.* Baker, 3 Burr. 1265; People *v.* Steele, 2 Barb. 397.

[3] Da Costa and the Russia Company, 2 Stra. 783; Rex *v.* March, 2 Burr. 999.

[4] The King *v.* Benchers of Lincoln's Inn, 4 B. & C. 855. The court considered that it had no authority to interfere with the society of Barnard's Inn, and refused a mandamus to compel them to admit an attorney into the society. Rex *v.* Barnard's Inn, 5 A. & E. 17.

[5] The King *v.* Gray's Inn, 1 Doug. 353; and see Style, 457; Townsend's case, T. Raym. 69; Mar. 177.

[6] The King *v.* Gray's Inn, 1 Doug. 354, 355. The Supreme Court of the United States have decided that the writ will not lie, to restore an attorney removed for official misconduct, from his place as attorney in one of the territorial courts, holding that it rests exclusively with the court to determine who is qualified to be one of its attorneys, and for what cause he ought to be removed. *Ex parte* Secombe, 19 How. 9.

[7] B. R. H. 261; 2 Kyd on Corp. 303.

[8] Rex *v.* President des Marches, 1 Lev. 306.

ered to appoint a deputy.[1] If the charter has not empowered him to appoint a deputy, but the corporation has subsequently imposed new duties upon him, to be performed in person or by deputy, the writ will not be granted to admit his deputy to the place of deputy generally, but perhaps to the discharge of those particular duties subsequently imposed. Unless, therefore, the constitution has declared the deputy to be a corporate officer, the mandamus must not be to admit and swear in the deputy as a member of the corporation, but merely to the discharge of his delegated office.[2] On an application for a mandamus to compel admission to an office, the affidavits must show the nature of the office, unless it be one judicially noticed by the court, as that of mayor, &c.; in order that the court may know that the office is of such a nature that a mandamus will lie to compel admission to it.[3] The affidavits must also show the mode of election, or the corporate regulations for admission; the preliminary conditions,[4] the applicant's title by election, or the acquisition of an inchoate right to admission; his performance of the conditions, that he has made due application to the proper officer to admit him, and been rejected.[5] It must also appear, that he has complied with any statute regulations, necessary to his admission to the office.[6] Though a mandamus to admit gives no title, yet it will not be granted, when there is an officer *de facto*, though that officer be in under a peremptory mandamus obtained by collusion, and claim under the same election with the applicant; for the remedy to try the title of the officer *de facto* is an information in the nature of a *quo warranto*, on

---

[1] Rex *v.* Clapham, 1 Vent. 111; Rex *v.* Ward, 2 Stra. 897; Rex *v.* St. Albans, 12 East, 559, n.; Rex *v.* Gravesend, 2 B. & C. 604, 4 D. & R. 117; Jones *v.* Williams, 5 D. & R. 660.

[2] Ibid.

[3] Anon. 2 Mod. 316; Rex *v.* Guilford, 1 Lev. 162, T. Raym. 152.

[4] Rex. *v.* Newling, 3 T. R. 310; Moore *v.* Hastings, Cas. temp. Hardw. 353, 362.

[5] Moore *v.* Hastings, Cas. temp. Hardw. 353, 363; Rex *v.* West Looe, 3 B. & C. 686. "If there is a fine payable, it is necessary to show a tender of it; but if it be said, that there is a reasonable *fine* payable by custom, and it has been usual to receive a certain sum, it is sufficient, without showing the amount; and it is sufficient also to allege the tender of a reasonable fine, without stating the amount; for a reasonable fine does not imply a fine uncertain, or any discretion in the officer to vary the amount or dispute the reasonableness of the usual payment; it is only necessary that the court should perceive that the officer has been previously called on to do his duty, and that the applicant is in no default." Willcock on Mun. Corp. 372, 373, part 2, tit. 85; Moore *v.* Hastings, Cas. temp. Hardw. 353, 362.

[6] Crawford *v.* Powell, 2 Burr. 1016; Rex *v.* Monday, Cowp. 530, 539, 540; Rex *v.* Hawkins, 10 East, 216; Rex *v.* Parry, 14 East, 561.

which, if judgment of ouster go against the defendant, a mandamus may be granted with less inconveniency to the corporation; nor will it be granted to admit to office the candidate therefor, on account of improper votes having been received for one who was declared elected, had accepted the office, and made the requisite declaration.[1] But though the office be full, if *quo warranto* does not lie, a mandamus will be granted; otherwise, in many cases, the applicant would be without remedy.[2] Where one has been previously admitted to a corporate office under a peremptory mandamus, the court refused the writ to another applicant who claimed to have been duly elected. The person admitted under the peremptory mandamus was considered the officer, until the matter had been tried by an action.[3] A mandamus to admit will not be granted to an applicant elected contrary to a usage, that the same person shall not be elected to the office for more than two years in succession; and though there be evidence in explanation, if there be none in contradiction of the usage, the court will summarily determine upon it without sending the question to a jury.[4] If an application be made for a writ to swear, or admit, the court will, in case the right appear plain, grant the writ upon the first motion; otherwise the rule will only be granted *nisi*.[5]

§ 703. When a public statute requires all persons in possession of corporate offices to take a particular oath, under penalty of being displaced, a mandamus may be directed to an eleemosynary corporation, commanding it to remove certain persons from their offices, for a noncompliance with the statute.[6] In this case, says Mr. Kyd, a *quo war-*

---

1 Rex *v.* Winchester, 2 Nev. & P. 274; People *v.* Corporation of New York, 3 Johns. Cas. 79; People *v.* Hillsdale & Chatham Turnpike Co. 2 Johns. 190; St. Louis County Court *v.* Sparks, 10 Misso. 117; Bonner *v.* The State, 7 Ga. 473. See also, Regina *v.* Mayor, etc. of Chester, Q. B. 1856, 34 Eng. L. & Eq. 59. In Maryland, by general incorporating act of 1828, ch. 70, for intrusion upon, usurpation, or unlawful holding of a corporate office, as of trustee of a church. Clayton *v.* Carey, 4 Md. 26.

2 Rex *v.* Barker, 3 Burr. 1265; Rex *v.* Colchester, 2 T. R. 260; Rex *v.* Thatcher, 1 D. & R. 427; People *v.* Corporation of N. Y. 3 Johns. Cas. 79. And there may be cases where even though a *quo warranto* would lie, yet the relator will be entitled to a mandamus. People *v.* Scrugham, 20 Barb. 302, 305; Harwood *v.* Marshall, 9 Md. 83, 100; People *v.* Kilduff, 15 Ill. 492, 502; Banton *v.* Wilson, 4 Texas, 400.

3 Rex *v.* Turner, T. Jones, 215.

4 Rex *v.* London, 1 T. R. 426.

5 B. N. P. 199; Rex *v.* Jotham, 3 T. R. 377.

6 Rex *v.* St. John's College, Skin. 549, 3 Salk. 230.

ranto would not have lain, because the college was an eleemosynary foundation; but it would lie in case of corporation officers who should neglect, &c., and therefore a mandamus would not be the proper remedy.[1]

§ 704. The writ of mandamus, when employed to restore officers illegally displaced, was anciently termed "a writ of restitution;" and the title "mandamus" is not found in the older abridgments. The ancient writ appears to have been confined exclusively to offices of a public nature;[2] but in modern times, the writ of mandamus, as we have before remarked, lies wherever there is a *right* and *no other* specific remedy to enforce it. In general, it will be granted to restore, wherever it would be granted to admit, a member or officer of a corporation. If a corporator has been unjustly or irregularly amoved, or suspended from his office, or disfranchised, the court will grant a mandamus to restore him.[3] The old rule appears to have been, that a mandamus will lie to compel an admission or restoration to no place or office, unless it have some relation to the public; and upon this ground, an application for a writ, to be directed to a company of gunmakers, commanding them to restore an approver of guns who had been deprived of his place, was rejected.[4] So, too, because his office was not of a public nature, the court refused a mandamus to restore a surgeon to an hospital.[5] Partly upon the same ground, a mandamus was refused, in Lord Holt's time, to restore a man to the office of clerk of a butcher's company;[6] though it was afterwards granted, upon the ground that the case was the same with that of a town clerk, in which a mandamus had often been granted.[7] In the time of Lord Mansfield, however, a more liberal doctrine was established; and the value of the matter, or the degree of its importance to the public police, was not scrupulously weighed.[8] An assize lay for a tenant of an office, in fee, in tail, or for life, against the tenant of a freehold, or against the tenant and the disseisor, where the office was one of profit, and not of mere charge.[9] Upon the ground that an assize

---

1 2 Kyd on Corp. 337, n. a.

2 2 Sel. N. P. (Wheaton's ed.), 817.

3 See cases cited, *ante*, sec. 698.

4 Vaughn *v*. Company of Gunmakers in London, 6 Mod. 82.

5 Comb. 41.

6 White's case, 6 Mod. 18, 3 Salk. 232.

7 White's case, 2 Ld. Raym. 959, 1004.

8 Per Lord Mansfield, Rex *v*. Barker, 3 Burr. 1267.

9 Webb's case, 8 Co. 47; 2 Inst. 312; Fitz. N. B. 177; Com. Dig. Assize, B. 2, 3, 4, 5, 6; B. R. H. 100.

was another specific remedy, a mandamus was formerly refused, where the assize would lie.[1] The remedy by assize, says Mr. Kyd, has now become obsolete, and therefore the question, whether it will lie, never makes any part of the consideration, whether a mandamus ought to be granted or not.[2] The nature of the interest which the possessor of a place or office has in it, seems now the principal question to be considered on an application for a mandamus, either for admission or restoration.[3] It would not lie to restore an officer at the will of the corporation, unless it is said, he is turned out by others than the corporation.[4] Mr. Willcock justly remarks upon this case, that he does not know how he could be turned out by others; for their attempt could not amount to an amotion, but a mere preclusion and disturbance in the exercise of his right.[5] In Rex *v.* Slatford,[6] it was resolved, that where a man was elected to hold at will, he may be removed at pleasure, without cause shown;[7] yet, that if it did not appear that the corporation had declared their will to remove him, the court might grant him restitution. A query is made in the case, whether a removal by the corporation is not a declaration of their will. A mandamus has been granted to restore a clerk to a butchers' company,[8] a clerk to a company of masons, a treasurer to the governors of the new water works,[9] a clerk or surveyor of the city works,[10] a town clerk, a common clerk of a vill, a parish clerk, a sexton, and a scavenger.[11] In England, it has been decided, that it lies to restore the schoolmaster of a grammar school founded by the crown,[12] or the minister of an endowed dissenting meeting-house;[13] and

---

1 White's case, 6 Mod. 18; and see Comb. 244; 1 T. R. 404; Comb. 347, 348.

2 Kyd on Corp. 320; White's case, 2 Ld. Raym. 959, 1004.

3 2 Kyd on Corp. 320.

4 Anon. 1 Barnard 195; and see 1 Sid. 15.

5 Willcock on Mun. Corp. 378.

6 Comb. 419.

7 See Dighton's case, Sid. 461, 1 Vent. 77, 82.

8 White's case, 3 Ld. Raym. 1004.

9 Rex *v.* Governors of Water Works, 1 Lev. 123, 2 Sid. 112; Middleton's case, 1 Sid. 169.

10 Rex *v.* Mayor, &c. of London, 2 T. R. 182, n.

11 1 Vent. 143, 153; Rex *v.* Slatford, Comb. 419; Sty. 458; Rex *v.* Guardianos de Thame in Com. Oxon. 1 Stra. 115; Rex *v.* Barker, 3 Burr. 1267, per Lord Mansfield; 2 Kyd on Corp. 320.

12 Rex *v.* Ballivos de Morpeth, 1 Stra. 58; Reg. *v.* Governors of Darlington School, 6 Q. B. 682.

13 Rex *v.* Barker, 3 Burr. 1265, 1 W. Bl. 300, 352; Rex *v.* Jotham, 3 T. R. 575.

in our own country to restore a trustee of a private academic corporation, though no emoluments were attached to his office.[1] Here, too, the remedy has been applied to restore a member and trustee of a religious corporation,[2] and in several cases, to restore the members of private corporations for charitable purposes,[3] illegally expelled. If, however, the charter of a society provide for an offence, direct the mode of proceeding, and authorize the society on conviction of a member to expel him, their judgment of expulsion, if the proceedings are not irregular, is conclusive, and cannot be inquired into collaterally, by mandamus, action, or any other mode.[4]

§ 705. A suspension from office warrants the granting of this writ as well as a removal; for a suspension is a temporary amotion, and otherwise, it is said, under pretence of repeated suspensions, an officer might be entirely excluded from the advantage of his situation.[5] And the writ has been granted to restore a member of a university, who has been improperly suspended of his degrees.[6] As in case of admission, so it will be granted to restore a deputy on the application of his principal, though not on the application of the deputy himself.[7] The modern decisions upon this subject seem, indeed, to be made in the spirit of Lord Mansfield's rule, that wherever there is a *right* and no other specific remedy, this will not be refused. Where it appears, from the showing of an officer, that he has been justly though irregularly removed,[8] or in case of a financial officer for life, or *quamdiu bene se gesserit*, who is suspended until he has submitted his accounts to the proper officer, and paid over the balance due, that he has refused

---

1 Fuller *v.* Plainfield Academic School, 6 Conn. 533.

2 Green *v.* African Methodist Episcopal Society, 1 S. & R. 254.

3 Commonwealth *v.* St. Patrick Benevolent Society, 2 Binn. 448; Commonwealth *v.* Philanthropic Society, 5 Binn. 486; Commonwealth *v.* Pennsylvania Beneficial Institution, 2 S. & R. 141; Franklin *v.* Commonwealth, 10 Barr, 357; Commonwealth *v.* German Society, 15 Penn. State, 251.

4 Commonwealth *v.* Pike Beneficial Society, 8 Watts & S. 247; Commonwealth *v.* German Society, 15 Penn. State, 251.

5 Rex *v.* Guilford, 1 Lev. 162, T. Ray. 152; Rex *v.* London, 2 T. R. 182; Rex *v.* Whitstable, 7 East, 355, and n.; Willcock on Mun. Corp. 379.

6 Rex *v.* University of Cambridge, T. 19, G. 3, Dr. Ewin's case, 2 Sel. N. P. (Wheat. ed.), 824.

7 Rex *v.* President des Marches, 1 Lev. 306.

8 Rex *v.* Axbridge, Cowp. 523; Rex *v.* Bristol, 1 D. & R. 389; s. c. Rex *v.* Griffiths, 5 B. & Ald. 731; Rex *v.* Bank of England, 2 B. & Ald. 620.

to do so, and been guilty of contumacy and improper conduct towards those whose officer he is, a mandamus to restore, it has been decided, will not be granted.[1] Neither will the writ be granted to restore one who has been ousted in *quo warranto*, or who has resigned his office; since judgment in *quo warranto* is conclusive against the defendant, whether on the writ or on the information; and after a resignation has been accepted, the corporator cannot resume his office.[2] And where A. was removed, and B. elected in his place, afterwards A. restored by mandamus, and subsequently his office became vacant; upon the application of B. for a mandamus without a new election, the writ was refused; for A. was a legal officer at the time of B.'s election, so that B. never acquired any title to the office.[3] It is, however, no objection to the granting of a mandamus to restore, that another has been elected to the office since the amotion of the applicant. In such case, the court will grant leave to file an information in the nature of a *quo warranto* against the person so elected, at the same time that they award the mandamus.[4] A party whose right to an office has been established by verdict, cannot have a peremptory mandamus to restore him until he has signed a judgment in the action.[5]

§ 706. In the case of Howard *v.* Gage,[6] which was an application for a mandamus to restore an annual officer, it appearing that the validity of the election was disputed upon the facts, the Supreme Court of Massachusetts refused the writ, upon the ground, that the statute of Anne not having been adopted in that State, the verdict in the action for a false return would not be found until after the expiration of the year for which the party complaining was chosen. "The cases," say the court, "in which the writ of mandamus may be an adequate remedy, in admitting or restoring to office, seem to be where the office is holden for a longer term than a year, or where the return to the writ will involve merely a question of law, so that admitting the facts to be true, a peremptory mandamus ought to go."[7] We find nowhere else a re-

---

1 Rex *v.* London, 2 T. R. 182.

2 Rex *v.* Tidderly, 1 Sid. 14; Rex *v.* Champion, id.

3 Shuttleworth *v.* Lincoln, 2 Bulst. 122.

4 Rex *v.* Bedford Level, 6 East, 360; Shuttleworth *v.* Lincoln, 2 Bulst. 122; People *v.* Steele, 2 Barb. 397. But see St. Louis County Court *v.* Sparks, 10 Misso. 117.

5 Neale *v.* Bowles, 1 Har. & W. 584.

6 6 Mass. 462.

7 Ibid. 464. A similar decision has recently been made for the same reason, in the case

fusal of the writ upon this ground. The course in England has probably been to grant the writ of mandamus, and if the facts stated in the return are false, to leave the applicant to his remedy in damages on his action for a false return. On application for a mandamus to restore, it is unnecessary for the prosecutor to state, that he was once in the office, since, if this was not the case, it may be shown by the opposite party.[1] As a mandamus to admit or swear in is merely to enable a party to assert his right, whereas a mandamus to restore, places a party in full possession of his office; a distinction is made between the two cases, in the granting of the writ. In the former, if the right appear plain, the court will grant the writ upon the first motion; whereas, in the latter, however plain the applicant's right may appear, they will first grant a rule to show cause why such a writ should not issue.[2]

§ 707. The writ of mandamus lies, too, to compel a corporation or its officers to do many other acts, which, by general law, or by virtue of official station, they are bound to do, which the party prosecuting the writ has a right to have done, and for which there is no other adequate, specific, legal remedy. Thus, though the courts cannot control the acts of a visitor done within his jurisdiction, yet a mandamus lies to compel him to exercise his visitatorial power within his jurisdiction; as to receive and hear an appeal. In the words of Lord Kenyon, the court will put the visitatorial power in motion.[3] So, it lies to the warden of a college, commanding him to affix the corporation seal to an answer of the fellows to a bill in chancery, though he disapprove of the answer, and it is contrary to his own separate answer put in;[4] to the keepers of the common seal of a university, commanding them to put it to the instrument of appointment of their high steward, pursuant to a grace passed in the senate;[5] to a master of an hospital possessed of the advowson of a living, to compel him to put the corporate seal to a presen-

---

of Woodbury *v.* County Commissioners, 40 Me. 304, the court relying on the above case of Howard *v.* Gage as authority. Ibid. 306.

[1] Rex *v.* Cutlers, Cas. temp. Hardw. 129.

[2] Bul. N. P. 199; Rex *v.* Jotham, 3 T. R. 577.

[3] The King *v.* Bishop of Lincoln, 2 T. R. 338, n. a.; The King *v.* Bishop of Ely, 2 T. R. 338; The King *v.* Bishop of Ely, 5 T. R. 477; The King *v.* Bishop of Worcester, 4 M. & S. 415; Ayl. H. of Oxford, vol. 2, p. 81; Com. Dig. Visitor, C. See Chap. XIX.

[4] Rex *v.* Windham, Cowp. 377.

[5] Rex *v.* Vice-Chancellor, &c. of Cambridge, 3 Burr. 1648.

tation where the nomination has been made by a majority of the body of the master and brethren, the right to nominate being in such body;[1] and to the mayor of a city corporation, to compel him to put the corporate seal to the certificate of an officer's election, where, by the constitution of the corporation, the mayor is bound to certify the election to the king for his approbation.[2] In the Commonwealth *v.* Trustees of St. Mary's Church,[3] which was an application for a mandamus to compel the trustees of a religious corporation to affix the common seal to certain alterations and amendments of the charter, no objection was taken by the court to the form of remedy; though, for substantial reasons of another kind, the application was rejected. A mandamus lies merely to command that to be done which ought by law to be done, and not to order the undoing of that which ought not to be done; and hence it will not lie to order a railway company to take the seal off from the register of shareholders on the suggestion that it was affixed without authority and contrary to the provisions of a statute.[4] Where the regulations of a corporation rendered it necessary for the acquisition of the freedom, that the indentures of apprenticeship should be enrolled, a mandamus was granted to compel the proper officer to enroll them; the applicant showing in his affidavits the necessity of the enrolment, and that application had been made in vain to the officer to perform his duty.[5] So a corporator may have a mandamus to compel the custos of corporate documents to allow him an inspection, and copies of them, at proper times and upon proper occasions; he showing clearly a right on his part to such inspection and copies, and refusal on the part of the custos to allow it.[6] A director of a bank may also have the writ

---

[1] Rex *v.* Kendall, 1 Q. B. 366.

[2] Rex *v.* York, 4 T. R. 699, 700; and see Strong, Petitioner, &c. 20 Pick. 484; where a mandamus was held to lie to a board of examiners to compel them to give a certificate of his election to a county commissioner, though another person, upon a new election ordered, was elected in his place, whom he might be obliged to remove by *quo warranto*.

[3] 6 S. & R. 508.

[4] *Ex parte* Nash, 15 Q. B. 92.

[5] Rex *v.* Coopers of Newcastle, 7 T. R. 545.

[6] Rex *v.* Newcastle, 2 Stra. 1223; Rex *v.* Shelley, 3 T. R. 142; Rex *v.* Babb, 3 T. R. 580, 581; Rex *v.* Lucas, 10 East, 235; Edwards *v.* Vesey, Cas. temp. Hardw. 128; Rex *v.* Tower, 4 M. & S. 162; Rogers *v.* Jones, 5 D. & R. 484; Rex *v.* Travannion, 2 Chitty, 366, n.; Rex *v.* Chester, 1 Chitty, 476, 477, n., 479; Cockburn *v.* Union Bank, 13 La. Ann. 289. When the corporator's application to inspect is founded on his general right, he has a mandamus; but when on a suit pending, he has a rule. Ibid.; and see Southampton *v.* Greaves, 8 T. R. 562; Bateman *v.* Phillips, 4 Taunt. 162; Willcock on Mun. Corp. 349. A judgment creditor of the company may have the writ to compel the production of

directed to the cashier who refuses, under a resolution of the board of directors to that effect, to permit him to see the discount book; and in such case, the writ may also be well directed to the directors themselves.[1] In such cases, however, there must be a distinct refusal on the part of those having the control of the books to permit the corporator or director to inspect them, he, it seems, stating the purpose for which he demanded the inspection at the time of demand.[2] A mandamus lies also to the *late* mayor of a city corporation, to deliver the insignia of his office to the *new* mayor,[3] to a former town clerk,[4] or clerk of a company,[5] or clerk, or treasurer of a religious society,[6] to deliver to his successor the common seal, books, papers, and records of the corporation, which belong to his custody; or to a steward who keeps the public books of a corporation, to compel him to attend with the books at the next corporate assembly.[7] Indeed, it lies to any person who happens to have the books of a corporation in his possession, and refuses to deliver them up; as to an executor, who refuses to deliver up the books of a borough, until money expended by a testator on account of it should be repaid.[8] The writ has also been directed to canal appraisers, compelling them to appraise damages done by a canal,[9] or to certify the case to the proper court of appeal;[10] to canal commissioners, enforcing a payment by them of assessments duly made under a statute, for recompensing such damages,[11] to a railway company, bound by act of parliament to set out their

---

the registry of shareholders for his inspection. Regina *v.* Derbyshire, &c. R. 3 Ellis & B. 784, 26 Eng. L. & Eq. 101.

[1] People *v.* Throope, 12 Wend. 183.

[2] Rex *v.* Wilts. & Berks. Canal Navigation, 3 A. & E. 477; Rex *v.* Trustees of North Leach & Whitney Roads, 5 B. & Ad. 978.

[3] Rex *v.* Owen, Comb. 399; Rex *v.* Dublin, 1 Stra. 539; Rex *v.* Ipswich, 2 Ld. Raym. 1238; Crawford *v.* Powell, 2 Burr. 1016; Rex *v.* Monday, Cowp. 539; People *v.* Kilduff, 15 Ill. 492.

[4] Crawford *v.* Powell, 2 Burr. 1016; Commonwealth *v.* Athearn, 3 Mass. 285; Walter *v.* Belding, 24 Vt. 658.

[5] Rex *v.* Wildman, 2 Stra. 879.

[6] Proprietors of St. Luke's Church, in Chelsea, *v.* Slack, 7 Cush. 224, 239.

[7] Case of the Borough of Calne in Wilts. 2 Stra. 949. See also, Kimball *v.* Lamprey, 19 N. H. 215.

[8] Rex *v.* Ingram, W. Bl. 50.

[9] *Ex parte* Jennings, 6 Cowen, 518; and see Reg. *v.* North Union Railroad Co. 8 Dowl. P. C. 329; Birmingham & Oxford Junction Railway Co. *v.* Regina, Exch. 1851, 4 Eng. L. & Eq. 276.

[10] Trustees of Wabash & Erie Canal, 2 Ind. 219.

[11] *Ex parte* Rogers, 7 Cowen, 526. To compel a township committee to raise funds and pay for lands taken for roads. Miller *v.* Town Com. of Bridgewater, 4 N. J. 54.

deviations, and make their compulsory purchases within stated periods, to do those acts within the times limited, so that they might complete the line of railroad, which, having undertaken, they were obliged by the act to finish;[1] or, at the suit of a landholder whose land had been taken, or will be prejudiced by the non-completion of the line chartered, or of the attorney-general, where the public interests are involved, or at the suit of a shareholder who has not assented to the neglect or abandonment complained of, fully to complete the same;[2] to a water-power company, carrying their trench across a highway so as to render a bridge necessary for passage, to compel them to erect and maintain a bridge at their own expense;[3] and to a dock company, commanding them to repair the bank of a new channel by them cut, which was broken down, to the obstruction of navigation.[4] It lies, too, to compel a mayor to perform any part of his duty, as presiding officer, after he has been guilty of a default in the performance of it.[5] It has also been granted to compel a canal company to enter upon their books the probate of a will of a deceased shareholder,[6] to register a conveyance,[7] though not to compel them to enroll a conveyance of lands to them pursuant to the provisions of an act, *after the lapse of sixty-five years, without effort during that time to compel them so to do.*[8] And where a statute made it the duty of a turnpike corporation to grant a certificate of amounts due by them for repairs, &c., attested in a certain manner, and to transmit a duplicate of

---

[1] Reg. *v.* Eastern Counties Railway Co. 2 Per. & D. 648; and see Reg. *v.* Birmingham Railroad Co. 2 Q. B. 47; Reg. *v.* Manchester & Leeds Railroad Co. 3 Q. B. 428; Regina *v.* Ambergate, &c. Railway Co. 1 Ellis & B. 372, 18 Eng. L. & Eq. 222.

[2] Regina *v.* York & North Midland Railway Co. 1 Ellis & B. 178, 16 Eng. L. & Eq. 299; Regina *v.* Lancashire & Yorkshire Railway Co. 1 Ellis & B. 228, 16 Eng. L. & Eq. 327; Attorney-General *v.* Birmingham, &c. Railway Co. 4 De G. & S. 490, 7 Eng. L. & Eq. 283; Regina *v.* York, Newcastle, &c. Railway Co. 16 Q. B. 886, 6 Eng. L. & Eq. 260; Regina *v.* Ambergate, Nottingham, &c. Railway Co. 17 Q. B. 362, 6 Eng. L. & Eq. 332, 333.

[3] *In re* Trenton Water Power Co., Spencer, 659. State *v.* Wilmington Bridge Co. 3 Harring. Del. 312. But see Lawrence *v.* Great Northern Railway Co. 16 Q. B. 643, 4 Eng. L. & Eq. 265, 270.

[4] Reg. *v.* Bristol Dock Company, 2 Q. B. 64. To compel a R. R. Company to keep road-crossings in repair. State *v.* Gorham, 37 Me. 461. And to compel the removal of an obstruction to navigation, caused by the improper manner in which the road is built, notwithstanding that an indictment would also lie for such obstruction as a nuisance. State *v.* N. E. R. R. Co. 9 Rich. 247.

[5] Rex *v.* Everet, Cas. temp. Hardw. 261; Rex *v.* Williams, 2 M. & S. 144.

[6] Rex *v.* Worcester Canal Company, 1 Man. & R. 529.

[7] Cooper *v.* Dismal Swamp Co. 2 Murphy, 195.

[8] Reg. *v.* Leeds Canal Co. 4 Per. & D. 174.

the same to the State treasurer, in order that payment might be made by the State, and deducted out of the appropriations made to the corporation; a mandamus was granted to compel them to deliver to the relator, and transmit to the treasurer, such a certificate.[1] It has been held, too, that mandamus, at the suit of the State, will lie against the proper officer of a bank, to compel him to pay a State tax on its stock, where the law provides no other mode for the recovery of the tax,[2] and against parish commissioners for payment of a salary out of the rates for which no action lies.[3] A dock company was empowered by act of parliament to make a floating harbor in the city of Bristol; and the directors of the company were authorized and *required* "to make such alterations and amendments in the sewers of said city as might or should be necessary in consequence of the floating of said harbor;" it was held, that a mandamus lay to the directors, commanding them to "make such alterations," &c., in the words of the act, and that it was neither requisite nor proper to call upon the company to make any specific alterations, the mode of remedying the evil being left to their discretion by parliament.[4] Where the act incorporating a dock company directed that all actions against the company should be brought against the treasurer, or a director for the time being, but that the body, goods, lands, &c., of such treasurer or director should not by reason thereof be made liable, and cross actions between the treasurer, as such, and another, were referred to an arbitrator, who awarded against the treasurer, it was held, that mandamus would lie to the treasurer and directors commanding them to pay the sums awarded.[5] And where a railway company was incorporated by an act, which provided, that the public should have the beneficial enjoyment of the same, it was held, that mandamus would lie, to compel them to lay down, and reinstate the railway; they having torn up the iron tram-plates for several hundred yards, in order to prevent the collieries of others from coming in competition with those of several leading members of the company.[6] In the time of Lord Holt, a mandamus was

---

1 Commonwealth *v.* President, Managers, and Company of the Anderson Ferry, Waterford and New Haven Turnpike Road, 7 S. & R. 6.

2 State *v.* Mayhew, 2 Gill, 487.

3 Bogg *v.* Pearse, 10 C. B. 534, 3 Eng. L. & Eq. 508.

4 The King *v.* Bristol Dock Company, 6 B. & C. 181; and see State *v.* Washington County, 2 Chand. 247.

5 Rex *v.* St Catherine's Dock Co. 4 B. & Ad. 360; 1 Nev. & M. 121.

6 The King *v.* Severn & Wye Railway Company, 2 B. & Ald. 646; and see Whitemarsh Township *v.* Philadelphia, Germantown, & Norristown Railroad, 8 Watts & S.

prayed to the master and wardens of a company of gun-makers, to cause them to give a proof-mark to a freeman of the company, without which, it was urged, he could not sell his guns. According to the report, his lordship rejected the application, upon the ground, that the company was "no legal establishment," and informed the applicant that his remedy was a petition to the queen for a *quo warranto*, to repeal the charter of the company.[1] It seems difficult to understand what was meant by the assertion, that the company was "no legal establishment," since it was created by charter; and it is apprehended, that a mandamus would, in such a case, be granted at the present day, without the least hesitation.[2] This writ will not, however, be granted to compel a corporation to make leases of lands, which, having been leased, have fallen into their hands; for this is their own private property.[3] In general, it should be observed, that a mandamus will not be granted, unless it is clear that there has been a direct refusal to do that which it is the object of the writ to enforce, either in terms, or by circumstances which distinctly show an intention not to do the act required.[4] Mere complaint made whilst the act is proceeding, though a proper precaution, does not excuse a specific demand to do the particular thing required.[5] When a writ of mandamus is fully executed, if it does not effectuate the purposes for which it is granted, the court will, it seems, award a second or auxiliary writ to complete the act begun, and administer ample justice.[6]

§ 708. In noticing those cases in which the writ of mandamus lies to a corporation or its officers, we have necessarily noticed many where it has been determined that this remedy does not apply. Although mandamus lies to compel a visitor to hear an appeal, and give some judg-

---

365; where it is held, that a mandamus may be applied for in Pennsylvania by the supervisors of a township, commanding a railroad company to make a road for public accommodation, required by their charter.

1 Anon. 2 Ld. Raym. 989.

2 2 Kyd on Corp. 299, 300.

3 Rex *v.* Liverpool, 1 Barnard. 83.

4 Rex *v.* Brecknock & Abergavenny Canal Co. 4 Nev. & M. 871, 3 A. & E. 217, 1 Har. & W. 279; Rex *v.* Wilts. & Berks. Canal Co. 3 A. & E. 477; Reg. *v.* Company of the Navigation of the Rivers Thames & Isis, note (b) to Reg. *v.* Select Vestrymen of St. Margaret, Leicester, 8 A. & E. 901; Reg. *v.* Eastern Counties Railway, 10 A. & E. 531, 545, n. b.; Reg. *v.* Bristol & Exeter Railway Co. 4 Q. B. 162.

5 Ibid.

6 Rex *v.* Water Eaton, 2 J. P. Smith, 55.

ment,[1] yet, as his jurisdiction is exclusive, and his power discretionary, none lies to control his sentence, or to compel the *doing* of any thing which falls within his jurisdiction.[2] And though he transcend his jurisdiction, as in executing a sentence of expulsion, yet mandamus does not lie to restore the party expelled, or to reverse the visitor's sentence; but the injured person is left to his action of ejectment, or of the case for damages.[3] It is upon the ground, that the judges of England enjoy a species of visitatorial power over the inns of court, that a mandamus will not lie to compel the benchers to admit a member, or to call one qualified to the bar.[4]

§ 709. In order to obtain a writ of mandamus, the applicant must show a specific and complete *right*, which is to be enforced; and, accordingly, the writ was refused to enforce the admission of one as a doctor of the Civil Law, and a graduate at Cambridge, to be an advocate of the Court of Arches; Lord Ellenborough observing, that the applicant had no more claim to admission than any other of his Majesty's subjects.[5] It was for want of a complete legal right to pay from the East India Company, that the writ was refused to Sir Charles Napier, when applied for by him to compel the East India Company to pay him his arrears of allowances as commander-in-chief of the queen's or of the native forces in India.[6] Upon the same ground, a mandamus was refused to a doctor of physic, who had been licensed by a college of physicians, to admit him upon examination as a fellow of the college;[7] and in Rex *v.* Jotham,[8] the court refused a mandamus to restore a minister of an endowed dissenting meeting-house, because it did not appear that he had complied with the requisites necessary to give him a *primâ facie* title. The right to be enforced, it seems, must also be a legal

---

1 Chap. XIX.; and see Anon. 2 Penn. 737; and Hall *v.* Supervisors of Oneida, 19 Johns. 295; Griffith *v.* Cochran, 5 Binn. 87, 103; Regina *v.* Archbishop of Canterbury, 11 Q. B. 483.

2 Chap. XIX.

3 Ibid.

4 The King *v.* Gray's Inn, 1 Doug. 353; The King *v.* Benchers of Lincoln's Inn, 4 B. & C. 855; Chap. XIX.

5 The King *v.* Archbishop of Canterbury, 8 East, 213, 219, 240; and see People *v.* Collins, 19 Wend. 56. A mere inchoate right is not sufficient. People *v.* Trustees of Brooklyn, 1 Wend. 381.

6 Napier, *ex parte,* 18 Q. B. 692, 12 Eng. L. & Eq. 451.

7 Rex *v.* College of Physicians, 7 T. R. 282.

8 3 T. R. 575.

right; and if it be a mere equitable right, as a trust, the party will be left to his remedy in equity.[1] In the case of the Rugby Charity, a mandamus was refused to compel the trustees to pay increased alms to claimants on the funds, although the applicants were at an advanced age, and would probably be dead before relief could be had in chancery.[2]

§ 710. Courts will not exercise their extraordinary power by writ of mandamus to effect purposes, as well effected by the ordinary remedies; and accordingly, to obtain relief by this process, the applicant must not only show a specific legal right, but there must be no other specific remedy adequate to enforce that right.[3] Upon this ground a mandamus has been refused to compel a bank to permit a transfer of stock on the books of the company, since complete satisfaction, equivalent to a specific relief, may be obtained in an action of the case;[4] and to compel a railway company to carry goods, there being nothing in the act rendering it compulsory on the company to carry, and they being liable in an action, as common-carriers.[5] It has been refused, also, to compel a bank,[6] or to compel a fishing company,[7] to produce their accounts, and divide, or pay over to the stockholders, or freemen, the profits; and for

---

[1] Ibid.; and The King *v.* Marquis of Stafford, 3 T. R. 646, 651, 652, per Buller, J.; Reg. *v.* Abrahams, 4 Q. B. 157.

[2] *Ex parte* Rugby Charity Trustees, 9 D. & R. 214.

[3] Middleton's case, 1 Sid. 169; Rex *v.* Ward, Fitzgib. 124; Rex *v.* Owen, Comb. 399; Rex *v.* Dean & Chapter of Dublin, 1 Stra. 538; Rex *v.* Barker, 1 W. Bl. 352; Rex *v.* Marquis of Stafford, 3 T. R. 651; Rex *v.* Windham, Cowp. 378; Rex *v.* Canterbury, 8 East, 219; Rex *v.* Margate Pier Company, 3 B. & Ald. 224; Rex *v.* Haythorne, 5 B. & C. 422, 429; Rex *v.* Severn & Wye Railway Comp. 2 B. & Ald. 646; Rex *v.* Dean, 2 M. & S. 80; Rex *v.* Bank of England, Doug. 526; Rex *v.* Commissioners of Customs, 1 Nev. & P. 536, 5 A. & E. 380; Commonwealth *v.* Rosseter, 2 Binn. 368; Shipley *v.* Mechanics Bank, 10 Johns. 484; People *v.* Trustees of Brooklyn, 1 Wend. 318; The King *v.* Free Fishers, &c. of Whitstable, 7 East, 356, per Lawrence, J.; Boyce *v.* Russell, 2 Cowen, 444; People *v.* Mayor of New York, 25 Wend. 680; *Ex parte* Lynch, 2 Hill, 45; State *v.* Holiday, 3 Halst. 205; Oakes *v.* Hill, 8 Pick. 47; In the matter of the White River Bank, 23 Vt. 478; Arberry *v.* Bearers, 6 Texas, 457; Cullem *v.* Latimer, 4 Texas, 329; People *v.* Sup. of Chenango Co. 1 Kern. 563.

[4] The King *v.* Bank of England, Doug. 526; Boyce *v.* Russell, 2 Cowen, 444; Shipley *v.* Mechanics Bank, 10 Johns. 484. And see Asylum, &c. *v.* Phœnix Bank, 4 Conn. 172; *Ex parte* Firemen Insurance Co. 6 Hill, 243; Wilkinson *v.* Providence Bank, 3 R. I. 22.

[5] Robins, *ex parte*, 7 Dowl. P. C. 568.

[6] The King *v.* Bank of England, 2 B. & Ald. 620, 622.

[7] The King *v.* Free Fishers, &c. of Whitstable, 7 East, 356, per Lawrence, J.

the same reason, to a turnpike company, to compel them to pay the interest on a mortgage of their tolls and toll-houses,[1] the remedy being in equity; nor will mandamus lie against a railway company, to compensate the owners of a bridge for decrease of their tolls under the act incorporating the railway company, and for which debt lies;[2] nor will it be granted to compel a company to pay a judgment, or to make calls to enable them to pay a judgment, it appearing that calls sufficient had been made, but not paid, and that the company had not now the proper officers to make such calls;[3] nor against the intruding officers of a religious corporation, to compel them to deliver up the corporate property to the lawful officers thereof.[4] Neither will a court grant a mandamus to compel the trustees of an incorporated church to restore the prosecutor to the possession of a pew to which he claims title, inasmuch as he has another complete remedy by an action on the case against the person disturbing him.[5] And in England, mandamus will not lie to a corporation, commanding it to pay a poor's rate, unless, indeed, it be shown in the applicant's affidavits, that the corporation had no effects upon which a distress could be levied.[6] It is hardly necessary to add, that a mandamus will not be granted, requiring the trustees of a savings bank to refer a dispute to arbitrators, where it is clear that the inquiry could have no result.[7]

§ 711. It is said by Mr. Justice Buller, in The King *v.* The Marquis of Stafford, that if the party applying for a mandamus "show a legal right, and there be also a remedy in equity, that is no answer to an application for a mandamus; for when the court refuse to grant a mandamus, because there is another specific remedy, they mean only a *specific remedy at law.*"[8] It is true, that the courts in

---

1 Regina *v.* Trustees of Balby & Worksop Turnpike Road, Bail Court, 1853, 16 Eng. L. & Eq. 276.

2 Rex *v.* Hull & Selby Railway Corporation, 6 Q. B. 70.

3 Reg. *v.* Victoria Park Company, 1 Q. B. 288.

4 Smith *v.* Erb, 4 Gill, 437; *Ex parte* Holloway, Q. B. 1855, 30 Eng. L. & Eq. 240.

5 Commonwealth *v.* Rosseter, 2 Binn. 360; and see Francis *v.* Levy, Cro. Jac. 366; Dawney *v.* Dee, id. 605; Kenrick *v.* Taylor, 3 Wils. 326; Stocks *v.* Booth, 1 T. R. 428.

6 The King *v.* Margate Pier Company, 3 B. & Ald. 221, 224, 225.

7 Reg. *v.* Northwich Savings Bank, 9 A. & E. 729; 1 Per. & D. 477.

8 3 T. R. 651, 652. And see People *v.* Mayor, &c. of New York, 10 Wend. 293; *Ex parte* Nelson, 1 Cowen, 423; People *v.* Supervisors of Albany, 12 Johns. 414; People *v.* Supervisors of Greene, 12 Barb. 217; Goolsby's case, 2 Gratt. 575.

laying down the rule usually say, that mandamus will not lie where there is another specific *legal* remedy; but in The King *v.* Free Fishers, &c. of Whitstable,[1] and in The King *v.* Bank of England,[2] the Court of King's Bench gave as a reason for refusing a mandamus, that there was a complete remedy in chancery: and there seems but little reason, at the present day, for a court of law refusing to notice the relief that chancery can afford.

§ 712. In order to exclude the writ of mandamus, the remedy must, however, be *adequate*, or must afford *specific*, or what in the case is equivalent to specific relief.[3] Thus, though trover or detinue would lie for the insignia of office belonging to a corporation, yet, as we have seen, mandamus lies to compel the old mayor to yield them to the new, because, as is said, the office is annual, and it is necessary that the mayor should have them immediately, in order to command the more respect.[4] It lies, too, to compel an officer to execute the duties of his office, though he be liable to penalties or an action of the case, for the neglect of them.[5] And though it was admitted, that an indictment would lie against a railway company for breaking up their railway, so as to render it impassable, the act of parliament, by which they were incorporated, providing that the public should have the beneficial enjoyment of the same, yet it was also held, that mandamus would lie to compel the company to reinstate and lay down again the railway; for, it was said, that an indictment could not compel the corporation to repair the road, and that at all events a considerable delay must take place.[6] In the case of Clark *v.* Bishop of Sarum, reported in Strange[7] and Andrews,[8] it appears that the court ordered a mandamus, where a *quare*

---

[1] 7 East, 356, per Lawrence, J.

[2] 2 B. & Ald. 622, per Bayley, J.

[3] See Rex *v.* Bank of England, Doug. 526, per Lord Mansfield.

[4] Rex *v.* Dublin, 1 Stra. 537, 538, 539, per Powys, Jus.; Rex *v.* Owen, Comb. 399; Rex *v.* Ipswich, 2 Ld. Raym. 1238; Crawford *v.* Powell, 2 Burr. 1016; Rex *v.* Monday, Cowp. 539.

[5] Rex *v.* Everett, Cas. temp. Hardw. 261; McCollough *v.* Brooklyn, 23 Wend. 458; Western *v.* Brooklyn, 23 Wend. 334.

[6] King *v.* Severn & Wye Railway Company, 2 B. & Ald. 646, 650, 651; Reg. *v.* Bristol Dock Company, 2 Q. B. 70; Reg. *v.* Manchester & Leeds Railway Co. 3 Q. B. 528; The King *v.* Commissioners of the Dean Enclosure, 2 M. & S. 80; People *v.* Mayor, &c. of New York, 10 Wend. 293. *In re* Trenton Water Power Co., Spencer, 659.

[7] 2 Stra. 1082.

[8] Andr. 20.

impedit would lie, upon the ground that the former was a more *expeditious* and *less expensive* remedy than the latter. This case is not, however, to be considered as authority; for when it was subsequently cited, Lord Mansfield remarked, that Mr. Justice Dennison had always thought that case wrong; and added as a reason, that no case was proper for a mandamus, but where there is no other specific remedy.[1] We have before seen, that as the remedy for a freehold office by assize has become obsolete, it never makes any part of the consideration whether a mandamus ought to be granted or not.

§ 713. If discretionary power is granted to a corporation or its officers over any subject, though the court may issue a mandamus to compel them to exercise their discretion, yet it will not control them in the exercise of it. This principle is illustrated by the case of a visitor, before referred to, who may be enforced to hear and decide an appeal, but whose sentence cannot be reversed.[2] And where all the powers of a religious corporation were vested in certain trustees, and a mode was prescribed by statute, in which any corporations *desirous* of altering or amending their charters might proceed, a mandamus, on the motion of several of the members of the corporation, to compel the trustees to take the necessary steps to alter the charter, was refused, on the ground that this was left to them as a matter of discretion.[3]

§ 714. In the case of The King *v.* Bristol Dock Company,[4] too, where it appeared that the directors of the company were authorized and required "to make such alterations and amendments in the sewers, as were necessary in consequence of the floating of the harbor," it was held, that a mandamus in the terms of the act was in the proper form; and that it was neither requisite nor proper to call upon the company to make any specific alteration, the mode of remedying the evil being left at their discretion by the act of parliament. Indeed, it is a general rule, that wherever there is a discretionary power vested in officers, the court will not interfere by mandamus; for they cannot, and ought not to control them in the exercise of it.[5]

---

[1] Powell *v.* Millbank, 1 T. R. 399, 400, 401, 402, in the note; Cowp. 103, n.

[2] Chap. XIX. And see Board of Police of Attala County *v.* Grant, 9 Smedes & M. 77; Towle *v.* State, 3 Fla. 202.

[3] Case of St. Mary's Church, 6 S. & R. 498.

[4] 6 B. & C. 181. And see Reg. *v.* Eastern Counties Railway Company, 2 A. & E. 569.

[5] Giles's case, Stra. 831; Rex *v.* Nottingham, Sayer, 217; Reg. *v.* Middlesex Asylum,

§ 715. If the applicant for a mandamus make out a probable case, in general, a rule is granted upon the defendant to show cause why the writ should not issue; and this rule must be directed to and served upon persons to whom the writ is to be directed, all those principally interested in the defence being included in it.[1] Where, however, full notice has been given to him or those against whom the mandamus is prayed, and their interests have been represented before the court, the rule has been dispensed with, and a mandamus granted upon motion;[2] though without due notice of the motion, a mandamus will never be granted.[3] Buller thinks there may be this difference between a mandamus to restore, and a mandamus to admit; that where it is to swear or to admit, the court will, in case the right appear plain, grant the writ upon the first motion; but where it is to restore one who has been removed, they would first grant a rule to show cause why the writ should not issue.[4] The reason is, that in the former case the writ is granted merely to enable the party to try his right; whereas, in the latter, he may try his right without the writ, by bringing an action for money had and received, for the profits.[5] Upon a party's appearing to show cause why the writ should not issue, the relator has the affirmative.[6] Where a rule is obtained, if upon it the defendant do every thing for the performance of which the *writ* is sought, the rule will be discharged, and the de-

---

2 Q. B. 433. Wilson *v.* Supervisors of Albany, 12 Johns. 414; Hall *v.* Supervisors of Oneida, 19 Johns. 259; Blunt *v.* Greenwood, 1 Cowen, 15; *Ex parte* Nelson, id. 417; *Ex parte* Bailey, 2 Cowen, 479; Matter of Gilbert, 3 id. 59; *Ex parte* Johnson, id. 371; *Ex parte* Bacon, 6 id. 392; *Ex parte* Benson, 7 id. 363; Com. *v.* Judges of Common Pleas, 3 Binn. 273; Griffith *v.* Cochran, 5 id. 87, 103, 6 id. 456; Com. *v.* County Commissioners, 5 id. 536; Respublica *v.* Clarkson, 1 Yeates, 46; Respublica *v.* Guardians of the Poor, id. 476; Anon. 2 Penn. 576; Foreman *v.* Murphy, id. 1024; People *v.* Sup. Court of the City of N. Y. 5 Wend. 144; Chase *v.* Blackstone Canal Co. 10 Pick. 244; Rice *v.* Commissioners of Middlesex, 13 Pick. 225; Gibbs *v.* Commissioners of Hampden, 19 Pick. 298; Inhabitants of Ipswich, Petitioners, &c. 24 Pick. 343; State *v.* Washington Co. 2 Chand. 247; Arberry *v.* Bearers, 6 Texas, 457; State *v.* Bonner, Busbee, 257; People *v.* Atty.-General, 13 How. Pr. 179; Sights *v.* Yarnalls, 12 Gratt. 292, 300; Hill *v.* County Commissioners, 4 Gray, 415.

1 B. N. P. 200; Rex *v.* Bankes, 1 W. Bl. 445, 3 Burr. 1453; Rex *v.* St. John's Coll. Skin. 549; People *v.* Everitt, 1 Caines, 8; *Ex parte* Bostwick, 1 Cowen, 143; Board of Police of Attala County *v.* Grant, 9 Smedes & M. 77.

2 *Ex parte* Rogers, 7 Cowen, 526, 532, 533, 534. And see Rex *v.* Justices of Berkshire, Sayer, 160; Rex *v.* Aldermen of Heydon, id. 208, 209.

3 Anon. 2 Halst. 192.

4 B. N. P. 199.

5 Rex *v.* Jotham, 3 T. R. 577, 578, per Buller, J.

6 People *v.* Throop, 12 Wend. 183, note.

fendant saved the expense of making a return.[1] But though he do all that is required of him, after the rule is made absolute, and before the issuing of the writ, yet, if in fact the writ afterwards issue, the court will not supersede it, but leave him to show his obedience to their precept in his return.[2] The defendant may show, for cause why the writ should not be granted, any of the reasons before stated why the writ will not lie, or the applicant has not a right to it,[3] or he may show that the applicant has, by his own neglect or misconduct, precluded himself from all right to the assistance of the court.[4] If the affidavits upon which cause is shown by the defendant, so positively and expressly deny the facts charged in the affidavits upon which the rule to show cause is made, that if the denial be false, an indictment will lie for the perjury, it is the course of the court to discharge the rule, and leave the party, upon whose application it was obtained, to prosecute for perjury.[5] In England, if the affidavits upon which cause is shown are sworn before a commissioner, they cannot be read unless the name of the place where they are sworn is inserted in the jurat. The object of this rule is to point out a venue for laying the perjury, if the affidavits are false, and to assist the court in ascertaining from their records the fact of the person being a commissioner.[6] In New York, the general practice, on denying motions for a mandamus, has been, not to give costs; especially where the motion is merely *ex parte*. But where notice of the motion is given to the adverse party, and the law is plain against the relator, costs will follow the denial.[7]

§ 716. If, after the parties have been heard upon the rule, the applicant still has a reasonable claim to the writ, upon a doubt either in fact or law, the rule will be made absolute; though it is said that the court

---

1 Rex *v.* Liverpool, 1 Barnard. 83; Anon. id. 362.

2 Ibid. Board of Police *v.* Attala County, 9 Smedes & M. 77.

3 Willcock on Mun. Corp. 384, 385.

4 Ibid. And see People *v.* Delaware C. P. 2 Wend. 256; People *v.* Seneca C. P. 2 Wend. 264.

5 Per Curiam, Rex *v.* Harrison, Sayer, 111.

6 Rex *v.* West Riding, 3 M. & S. 494.

7 *Ex parte* Root, 4 Cowen, 548. In Vermont, costs on a petition for a mandamus, rest in the discretion of the court, as in chancery proceedings. Myers *v.* Pownal, 16 Vt. 426, 427. As to costs on motions for a mandamus in England, see Reg. *v.* Bingham, 4 Q. B. 877; Reg. *v.* Green, id. 646, 650; Reg. *v.* Sheriff of Middlesex, 5 id. 365; West London Railway Co. *v.* Bernard, 3 id. 873; Regina *v.* East Anglian Railway Co. 2 Ellis & B. 475, 22 Eng. L. & Eq. 274.

will not readily grant applications of a novel kind, which may probably tend to the disturbance of corporations in general.[1] It is not necessary that the rule of court should specify the whole mandamus;[2] but it must give the general outline, to be filled up in the more particular phraseology of the writ.[3] In New York, where a mandamus, whether alternative or peremptory, is granted upon motion, costs are not usually given to the relator; but if he wishes to secure them, he must go to his demurrer, or issue in fact.[4]

§ 717. It is said, that writs of mandamus were originally no more than letters by which the king enjoined his officers, &c., to do their duty; and that it was not until the twelfth year of the reign of William the Third, that they were ever entered of record; when a rule was made that they should be entered of the same term they came in.[5] They have now, however, become formed writs, and, like other writs, must bear teste in term.[6] No precise form is necessary in a mandamus;[7] but it is in substance a command, in the name of the sovereign power, to persons, corporations, or inferior courts of judicature within its jurisdiction, requiring them to do a certain specific act, as being the duty of their office, character, or situation, agreeably to right and justice.[8] Though, as we are told by Mr. Willcock, the writ may enlarge in directing those things which are, as it were, incidents to a mandamus, and in drawing it up, the practice of the court is to be observed, instead of adhering to the strict letter of the rule, yet, in all material circumstances, it must follow the rule upon which it is founded.[9] Accordingly, where a motion was made for a mandamus to the mayor of a corporation, to assemble the body and to do the corporate business, and in drawing up the writ, they made it out for an assembly, and to admit all

---

[1] Rex *v.* Rye, 2 Kenyon, 468; Rex *v.* West Looe, 5 D. & R. 599; Willcock on Mun. Corp. 385.

[2] The King *v.* Willis, 7 Mod. 262, per Chapple, J.

[3] Willcock on Mun. Corp. 386. For form of a rule for a peremptory mandamus, see *Ex parte* Jennings, 6 Cowen, 529.

[4] People *v.* Supervisors of Columbia, 5 Cowen, 291.

[5] Rex *v.* Dublin, 1 Stra. 540, per Fortescue, J.

[6] Ibid.; and 2 Keble, 91.

[7] Rex *v.* Nottingham, Sayer, 37, per Lee, C. J. For form of mandamus, see Blunt *v.* Greenwood, 1 Cowen, 15, 22, note *e*, and for forms of writ, return, and demurrer to return, see Regina *v.* Dover, 11 Q. B. 260–267.

[8] 2 Sel. N. P. (Wheaton's ed.), 816.

[9] Willcock on Mun. Corp. 387.

persons having a right to the freedom, who should appear before them and demand it, the writ was superseded.[1] And where the rule for a mandamus to the clerk of a company was to deliver all the books, papers, &c., *to the new clerk*, and the writ commanded him to deliver them *to the company*, the variance was held fatal to the writ.[2]

§ 718. The party who applies for a writ of mandamus must see that it is rightly directed; for if it be directed to the wrong persons, it may be superseded on motion or argument;[3] and if it be directed to a corporation by an erroneous name, this must be relied upon in the return, and thereupon the writ is superseded as upon a plea in abatement.[4] If the act commanded must be done by the whole corporation, or if a portion of the act by the whole corporation, and another portion by the head officer, in the first case,[5] the writ *ought* to be directed, and, in the latter,[6] it is most proper to direct it to the whole corporation; and not to the different enumerated classes, or individual members, who compose it. And though the head officer, who is an integral part of the corporation, and included in the corporate name, be dead, and the writ be to compel an election to the vacant place, this does not alter the case.[7] If the act commanded is to be done by a select body, the writ may be directed to the select body,[8] or to the whole corporation,[9] since the act of the select body is the act of the corporation. But if, being directed to a select body, it include in its direction any others than those whose duty it is to obey the command, it will be superseded for misdirection.[10] The writ must be directed to the corporation or select body, not only in

---

[1] Rex *v.* Kingston, 1 Stra. 578, 8 Mod. 210, 11 Mod. 382.

[2] Rex *v.* Wildman, 2 Stra. 879, 880; Rex *v.* Water Eaton, 2 J. P. Smith, 55.

[3] Rex *v.* Norwich, 1 Stra. 55; Rex *v.* Hereford, 2 Salk. 701; Rex *v.* Abingdon, 1 Ld. Raym. 560; Rex *v.* Smith, 2 M. & S. 598.

[4] Regina *v.* Ipswich, 2 Ld. Raym. 1239, 2 Salk. 435.

[5] Rex *v.* Smith, 2 M. & S. 598; Rex *v.* Abingdon, 1 Ld. Raym. 560.

[6] Rex *v.* Tregony, 8 Mod. 112, 128.

[7] Rex *v.* Borough of Plymouth, 1 Barnard. 81; Rex *v.* Cambridge, 4 Burr. 2011; Rex *v.* Smith, 2 M. & S. 598.

[8] Taylor *v.* Gloucester, 1 Rol. 409; Rex *v.* Gloucester, Holt, 451; Pees *v.* Leeds, 1 Stra. 640, n.; Rex *v.* Smith, 2 M. & S. 598.

[9] Holt's case, Freem. 442, and n., T. Jones, 52; Rex *v.* Abingdon, 1 Ld. Raym. 560; Rex *v.* Gloucester, Holt, 451; Rex *v.* Newsham, Sayer, 212; Rex *v.* Smith, 2 M. & S. 598.

[10] Rex *v.* Smith, 2 M. & S. 598; Rex *v.* Abingdon, 2 Salk. 700, 1 Ld. Raym. 560; Rex *v.* Hereford, 2 Salk. 791; Pees *v.* Leeds, 1 Stra. 640; Rex *v.* Norwich, 1 Stra. 55; Rex *v.* Wigan, 2 Burr. 782.

their proper names, but in their proper capacity, and the application must state that capacity.[1] Though several persons may be included as prosecutors in the same writ, at the discretion of the court, and will be where they constitute but one officer, and claim in the same right;[2] they being entitled in such case only to one writ;[3] yet several distinct rights cannot be included in the same writ; as, to restore or admit several persons to their offices in the same corporation.[4] Neither can one and the same writ of mandamus be directed to the officers of several corporations, to enforce them to perform distinct duties, growing out of distinct liabilities.[5]

§ 719. The right of the applicant, and the default of the defendant, must be shown in the writ; though a defect in these particulars may be cured by a return admitting the title, and avoiding it by some other objection.[6] Where, however, from a mandamus to compel the restoration of documents, it appeared that the person to whom it was issued was merely a stranger in the possession of them, against whom the party should have proceeded by the ordinary remedies, it was held that this defect in the writ was not aided by the return in which it appeared that he claimed the documents of right, in an official character.[7] If the right to be enforced is a general right, and no particular person is interested, the general right must be shown in the writ.[8] The writ

---

[1] Papilion and Dubois's case, Skin. 64; Rex *v.* West Looe, 3 B. & C. 685; 5 D. & R. 599.

[2] Rex *v.* Montacute, 1 W. Bl. 60; Rex *v.* Kingston, 1 Stra. 578, n.; Rex *v.* Ipswich, 1 Barnard. 407.

[3] Scott *v.* Morgan, *ex parte*, 8 Dowl. P. C. 328.

[4] Rex *v.* Kingston, 1 Stra. 578; Andover case, 2 Salk. 433; Anon. 2 Salk. 436; Rex *v.* Chester, 5 Mod. 11; Rex *v.* Liverpool, 1 Barnard. 83; Rex *v.* Water Eaton, 2 J. P. Smith, 55; Smith *v.* Erb, 4 Gill, 437. See also, Heckart *v.* Roberts, 9 Md. 41.

[5] State *v.* Township Committees of Chester & Eversham, 5 Halst. 292.

[6] Rex *v.* Whiskin, Andr. 3; Rex *v.* Coopers of Newcastle, 7 T. R. 548; Peat's case, 3 Mod. 310; Rex *v.* Bristol, 1 Show. 288. In a writ to admit, however, it is not necessary to aver a tender of the fee payable on admission; though this must be stated in the application. Moore *v.* Hastings, C. T. H. 363.

[7] Rex *v.* Hopkins, 1 Q. B. 169.

[8] Rex *v.* Nottingham, Sayer, 36; s. c. Bul. N. P. 201; Rex *v.* Devizes, id. 204. In England the general interest which an inhabitant of a borough, though no member of the corporate body, has in the good government of the borough which he inhabits, is sufficient to entitle him as applicant for a mandamus in a question of the election of the mayor or members of the town council of the borough. The Queen *v.* Archbishop of Canterbury, 11 Q. B. 578, 579. In this country, however, at least, if public rights only are involved in the application, it seems that the public officers alone can apply for the

must contain convenient certainty, in setting forth the duty to be performed; but it need not particularly set forth by what authority the duty exists.[1] If the mandamus be to compel one to serve in a corporate office to which he is elected, it is not necessary to aver, that he was able and fit to serve, but only to state his liability, election, and refusal to undertake the office without reasonable cause.[2] It is said by Mr. Willcock, that the command must be to perform some definite and specific act or acts, so that a certain and conclusive return may be made, that the act is done.[3] This must be understood, however, to refer to those cases in which the officer or corporation acts merely in a ministerial capacity; and not where the mode of action, the object being specified, is left to his or their discretion. Thus, as we have seen, where the directors of the Bristol Dock Company were empowered "to make such alterations and amendments in the sewers of the city as might or should be necessary in consequence of the floating of the harbor," a mandamus to them "to make such alterations and amendments in the sewers of said city as might or should be necessary in consequence of the floating of said harbor," was held sufficient; and that it was neither requisite nor proper to call upon the company to make any specific alterations, the mode of remedying the evil being left to their discretion.[4] A writ of mandamus, ordering a corporation to command certain persons to do an act, was quashed as absurd; it should have commanded the corporation to do it.[5] If the mandamus be to compel an election, the command should not be to elect a particular person, but to proceed to the election of some one to supply the vacancy.[6]

---

writ. The fact that the applicant is a petitioner for a road in the location of which he is interested merely as one of the community, is not deemed such an interest here as will enable him to move for a mandamus to the county commissioners to locate it. Sanger *v.* County Commissioners of Kennebec, 25 Me. 295. And see Commonwealth *v.* Council of Reading, 11 Penn. State, 191; Heffner *v.* Commonwealth, 28 Penn. State, 108.

[1] Bul. N. P. 204; Rex *v.* Bettesworth, 2 Stra. 857; Rex *v.* Ward, 2 id. 897.

[2] Rex *v.* Merchant Tailors, 2 Lev. 200.

[3] Willcock on Mun. Corp. 394. And see Andover case, 2 Salk. 433; Anon. id. 436; Rex *v.* Kingston, 1 Stra. 578; Rex *v.* Water Eaton, 2 J. P. Smith, 55; Rex *v.* Liverpool, 1 Barnard. 83.

[4] The King *v.* Bristol Dock Company, 6 B. & C. 181, 9 D. & R. 309. For the same reason, where a railway company had the option to carry a highway either over their railway, or to carry their railway above the highway in crossing the latter, a mandamus commanding them to do the former was held bad by all the judges of England. Regina *v.* Southeastern Railway Co. 4 H. L. Cas. 471, 25 Eng. L. & Eq. 13.

[5] Regina *v.* Derby, 2 Salk. 436.

[6] Rex *v.* Bridgewater, 2 Chitty, 257; Shuttleworth *v.* Lincoln, 2 Bulstr. 122; 2 Rol. Abr. Restitut. 5; Anon. 2 Barnard. 237.

The term "*evidentias*" has been held sufficient to include corporate documents in a mandamus to compel their delivery;[1] but it has been made a question whether the command to deliver books in the possession of an ex-officer should be, to deliver them to the corporation, or to the officer who is to have the custody of them. Though they must be received by the new officer, it would seem most proper to command them to be delivered to the corporation.[2] In the case of The King *v.* Nottingham, however, the writ commanded the delivery to be made to the new officer.[3]

§ 720. Unless the mandamus be peremptory, the command is to do the act, or show cause to the contrary. The writ will not, however, be superseded, though the words "or show cause" are omitted; for it is the very nature of an alternative mandamus to compel the defendant to perform the act, or show good cause for his refusal.[4] In an alternative mandamus, the relator must set forth his title, or the facts upon which he relies for relief, so that they may be admitted or traversed; and this he should do clearly and distinctly, and not by reference to affidavits and papers on file; and by it, on the other hand, the defendant is required to do the particular act required, or show cause to the contrary.[5]

§ 720 *a*. Service of the writ should be made upon him who is to make the return; and, where the writ is directed to the corporation, it should be served upon the head officer.[6] In the case of Rex *v.* Fowey,[7] however, it was held, that a personal service on the town-clerk of a public corporation was sufficient to found an application for an attach-

---

[1] Rex *v.* Nottingham, 1 Sid. 31.

[2] Willcock on Mun. Cor. 395; Rex *v.* Holford, 2 Barnard. 330, 350; Rex *v.* Wildman, 2 Stra. 879.

[3] Rex *v.* Nottingham, 1 Sid. 31.

[4] Rex *v.* Owen, 5 Mod. 315, Comb. 399; Rex *v.* St. John's Coll. 1 Vent. 549. For form of alternative mandamus, see People *v.* Judges of Westchester, 4 Cowen, 73. In Kentucky, after a rule to show cause, if a proper case be made out, a peremptory mandamus issues in the first instance. Justices of Clark County Court *v.* P. W. & K. R. Turnp. Co. 11 B. Mon. 143.

[5] Commercial Bank of Albany *v.* Canal Commissioners, 10 Wend. 52; People *v.* Rawson, 2 Comst. 492; Canal Trustees *v.* People, 12 Ill. 248; People *v.* Supervisors of Westchester, 15 Barb. 607.

[6] Rex *v.* Exeter, 12 Mod. 251.

[7] 4 D. & R. 614.

ment. If the writ is informal, the party may apply to amend it at any time before the return,[1] even, it seems, in a departure from the rule; though, after a motion to quash the writ for such a departure or for insufficiency in substance, it must be superseded.[2] If, however, the objection be to the form of the writ merely, it may be amended by leave of the court.[3] After the return has been made and traversed, the court will not permit an amendment in the mandamus.[4] In Rex *v.* Mayor of York,[5] it was held by Kenyon, C. J., and Buller, J., that the defendant would not be permitted to avail himself of any exception to the writ after the return. But it would seem, that though an objection to the form of the writ may be taken before the time for making the return has expired, and that after that time the court will not supersede the writ until the return is made, unless for gross faults, or because the writ has issued erroneously,[6] yet that an objection for substantial faults may be taken after the return, although the return is bad, and indeed at any time before the peremptory mandamus has issued.[7] And although the fact, for want of which the alternative mandamus is defective be admitted in the return, the writ will not be aided by it. The reason is, that if the return be bad in law, a peremptory mandamus is always awarded, and its form *must be the same* as the form of the mandamus originally awarded, as otherwise the defendants might make a new return to it. Hence the peremptory mandamus would, on the face of it, be equally bad as the alternative, and could derive no benefit from the admission in the previous return.[8] "According to the ancient practice," says Mr. Willcock, "if a return was not made in due time to the origi-

---

[1] Rex *v.* Clitheroe, 6 Mod. 1333, per Holt, C. J.

[2] Ibid.; Rex *v.* Water Eaton, 2 J. P. Smith, 55, 56; Rex *v.* Marg. Pier Comp. 3 B. & Ald. 224; Rex *v.* Kingston, 1 Stra. 578; Rex *v.* Wildman, 2 Stra. 880.

[3] Ibid.; and see Regina *v.* Derbyshire, &c. R. 3 Ellis & B. 784, 26 Eng. L. & Eq. 101.

[4] Rex *v.* Mayor of Stafford, 4 T. R. 690.

[5] 5 T. R. 74, 75.

[6] Rex *v.* Norwich, 1 Stra. 55; Rex *v.* Tregony, 8 Mod. 112; Rex *v.* Willingford, 2 Barnard. 132; Rex *v.* Whitchurch, id. 447; Whitford *v.* Jocam, Sel. N. P. (Wheat. ed.), 829; Rex *v.* Kingston, 8 Mod. 218, 11 Mod. 382; Willcock on Mun. Corp. 397.

[7] Rex *v.* Overseers of Mallett, 5 Mod. 421; Rex *v.* Kingston, 8 Mod. 210, 11 Mod. 382; Rex *v.* Ward, 2 Stra. 897; Rex *v.* Smith, 2 M. & S. 598; Rex *v.* Margate Pier Company, 3 B. & Ald. 223; Clarke *v.* Company of Proprietors, 6 Q. B. 898; Mayor of London *v.* The Queen, 13 Q. B. 39, 40, 41; Commercial Bank *v.* Canal Commissioners, 10 Wend. 28; Canal Trustees *v.* People, 12 Ill. 248; People *v.* Supervisors of Westchester, 15 Barb. 607; Willcock on Mun. Corp. 397.

[8] Per Parke, B., Mayor of London *v.* The Queen, 13 Q. B. 39, 40, 41.

nal writ, an *alias* issued, and a *pluries* returnable immediately, and if no return was made to that, on affidavit of service, an attachment was obtained against the defendant for disobedience to the process of the court."[1] Since the 9th of Anne, ch. 20, § 1, to compel a return to mandamus, the Court of King's Bench does not drive the prosecutor to an *alias* and *pluries*, even in cases not falling within its provisions; but compels a return to the first writ.[2]

§ 721. The return must be made by the body or persons to whom the writ is directed; and if the writ is directed to a corporation, though the head officer be merely an officer *de facto*, yet he must join in the return.[3] Where a mandamus was directed to B. C. and others, as a township committee, a return made by them as a *late* township committee, was held good.[4] The same certainty is required, it has been said, in a return to a writ of mandamus as in indictments or returns to writs of habeas corpus.[5] Whether the same strictness of certainty is necessary in a return to a mandamus, as in an indictment, may well be doubted. In The King *v.* Lyme Regis,[6] Lord Mansfield (Buller, Justice, concurring), says, "There is a great difference between a *charge* as a ground of disfranchisement, and an indictment. In criminal prosecutions, technical forms are established, and ought to be followed. If, in an indictment, you say that A. forged, *and* caused to be forged, the proof of either fact, will support the indictment; but to say that he forged, *or* caused to be forged, would be bad. This, being determined, must be adhered to. But such nicety is not required in accusations against a corporator in a corporate court. *There* substantial certainty is all that is necessary." The return must, however, be certain upon a reasonable construction; and where presumption and intendment are permitted, it is said, they will be in favor of the return.[7] It must state

---

[1] Willcock on Mun. Corp. 398; and cites Anon. 2 Salk. 434; DaCosta *v.* Russia Company, 2 Stra. 783; Anon. 11 Mod. 265.

[2] Willcock on Mun. Corp. 399, 400.

[3] Manaton's case, T. Raym. 365; Stevens's case, id. 432; Knight *v.* Wells, 1 Lutw. 519; Rex *v.* Lisle, Andr. 173; Rex *v.* Clitheroe, 6 Mod. 133. So the return to a mandamus directed to justices of a county, to compel them to fulfil a contract with the relator, must be made by them as a body. McCoy *v.* Justices of Harnett Co. 4 Jones, 180.

[4] State *v.* Griscom, 3 Halst. 136.

[5] Per Buller, J. Rex *v.* Lyme Regis, Doug. 158.

[6] 1 Doug. 181.

[7] Bagg's case, 11 Co. 99 b; Rex *v.* Abingdon, 12 Mod. 401, 1 Ld. Raym. 560, 2 Salk. 432; Rex *v.* Sterling, Sayer, 175; Rex *v.* Lyme Regis, Doug. 153, 154; Willcock on Mun. Corp. 403.

facts, and not conclusions of law,[1] must not be argumentative, nor aver material facts by way of recital,[2] but must positively and expressly[3] assert, deny, or answer, all facts in their full extent, the assertion, denial, or avoidance of which may be necessary for justification or defence.[4] Thus, if the return rely upon the misdirection of the writ, it must assert positively that it is misdirected, and show in what manner.[5] If it rely upon a judgment, however, the proceedings upon which it is founded need not be set forth; for these cannot be investigated, except upon writ of error, unless for the purpose of showing fraud or collusion.[6] A return by county commissioners to an alternative mandamus, directing them to take supervision of a bridge, as a part of a highway laid out by the Court of Sessions, was held good, though the return set forth that the bridge had been dedicated to the public, without averring in what manner; the proceedings of the town, which were made part of the return, showing for what purpose the bridge was built, and the building of a bridge on a highway being *ipso facto* a dedication of it to the public.[7] A return to a writ of mandamus need not be single, but may contain several defences, or justifications; and if one of these be sufficient, the return must be allowed as to that.[8] It is sufficient, if it contain a legal reason for not obeying the writ, though certain facts of it are unsatisfactory; for these may be considered as surplusage, and the remainder tried.[9] Where, however, inconsistent causes for not

---

[1] Rex *v.* Liverpool, 2 Burr. 731; Rex *v.* York, 5 T. R. 76.

[2] Rex *v.* Winchelsea, 2 Lev. 86; Rex *v.* Hereford, 6 Mod. 309; Basse *v.* Barnstable, T. Raym. 153, 1 Sid. 286; Rex *v.* Coventry, 1 Ld. Raym. 391, 2 Salk. 430; Rex *v.* Ilchester, 4 D. & R. 330.

[3] Rex *v.* Malden, 1 Ld. Raym. 481, 2 Salk. 431; Rex *v.* Ipswich, 2 Ld. Raym. 1239, 2 Salk. 435; Commercial Bank of Albany *v.* Canal Commissioners, 10 Wend. 25. A denial may, however, be composed of several assertions. Rex *v.* King's Lynn, Andr. 105. But a denial of the matters of the writ, with a protestando, is ill. Rex *v.* Bristol Dock Co. 6 B. & C. 181, 9 D. & R. 309.

[4] Rex *v.* Clapham, 1 Vent. 111, Rex *v.* President des Marches, 2 Lev. 86; Rex *v.* Coventry, Salk. 430; Rex *v.* Ilchester, 4 D. & R. 330; Reg. *v.* Mayor of Weymeath, 7 Q. B. 46; Rex *v.* Lyme Regis, Doug. 79, 85; Gorgas *v.* Blackburn, 14 Ohio, 252; Harwood *v.* Marshall, 10 Md. 451.

[5] Rex *v.* Ipswich, 2 Ld. Raym. 1239, 2 Salk. 435.

[6] Rex *v.* West Riding, 7 T. R. 467; Rex *v.* Suddis, 1 East, 315.

[7] Springfield *v.* Commissioners of Hampden, 10 Pick. 59.

[8] Rex *v.* Norwich, 2 Ld. Raym. 1244; Wright *v.* Fawcett, 4 Burr. 2044; Rex *v.* Cambridge, 2 T. R. 261.

[9] Rex *v.* Cambridge, 2 T. R. 461; Rex *v.* York, 6 T. R. 495; Rex *v.* Bristol, 1 Show. 288; Springfield *v.* Commissioners of Hampden, 10 Pick. 59.

obeying the mandamus are stated in the return, it must be quashed; for, taken as a whole, it is false.[1] . Neither the signature of an individual, nor the seal of a corporation, is necessary to the validity of a return by them to a mandamus.[2]

§ 722. Ouster upon *quo warranto* is always a sufficient return to a mandamus to admit, where the ouster took place prior to the prosecutor's acquisition of the title to admission upon which he relies.[3] Where the writ avers generally, that the prosecutor has been elected, it is sufficient to answer generally in the return, that he has not been elected,[4] or, what is the same thing, that he has not been *duly* elected.[5] This general answer, however, is not sufficient, if the writ sets forth certain facts, and concludes with, "by reason whereof the prosecutor was elected;" but the return in such case should traverse some material fact, on the truth of which the election is founded; or, if this cannot be done, and the facts stated are nevertheless insufficient to sustain the election, it should state what is necessary to a legal election, and negative the legal nature of that set forth in the writ.[6] Where the writ avers, that the corporation was duly assembled on a certain day, and elected the prosecutor, it is not sufficient for the return to admit a corporate assembly on that day sufficient for the election of other officers, and merely to aver, that they were not duly assembled for the election of the prosecutor; but some fact must be stated, showing why the assembly was incompetent to proceed to such an election.[7] It is not sufficient to return that the prosecutor was not elected *at the time* the writ was received; for he might have been elected *before;* but if the

---

[1] Rex *v.* Chalice, 2 Ld. Raym. 848; Thetford case, 1 Salk. 192; Rex *v.* St. John's Coll. 4 Mod. 241; Powell *v.* Price, Comb. 41; Liddleston *v.* Exeter, Comb. 422, 12 Mod. 126, 1 Ld. Raym. 223; Rex *v.* Holmes, 3 Burr. 1644.

[2] Widdrington's case, T. Raym. 68.

[3] Rex *v.* Serle, 8 Mod. 332, Rex *v.* Hull, 11 Mod. 391; Rex *v.* Taylor, 7 Mod. 172.

[4] Rex *v.* Ward, Fitzg. 195; Rex *v.* Harwood, 2 Ld. Raym. 1045; Wright *v.* Fawcett, 4 Burr. 2034; Co. Litt. 381; Manaton's case, T. Raym. 365; Steven's case, T. Raym. 432; Hereford's case, 1 Sid. 209; Rex *v.* Cornwall, 11 Mod. 174; Rex *v.* Lambert, 12 Mod. 3, Carth. 170; Rex *v.* Chester, 5 Mod. 11.

[5] Rex *v.* Lyme Regis, Doug. 84; Willcock on Mun. Corp. 413.

[6] Rex *v.* York, 5 T. R. 76; Rex *v.* Malden, 1 Ld. Raym. 481, 2 Salk. 431; Rex *v.* Abingdon, 1 Ld. Raym. 560, 2 Salk. 432; Rex *v.* Ludlow, 8 Mod. 270; Rex *v.* Whiskin, Andr. 3.

[7] Rex *v.* York, 5 T. R. 74, 75.

writ states that he was elected in a certain week, a return denying his election in that week is sufficient.[1] If the corporation is entitled to judge of the fitness of the prosecutor's deputy, the return to a mandamus to admit him may state that right, and that the deputy is not a sufficient person.[2] So, if the approbation of a certain officer, or the payment of a certain fine, is necessary, to entitle the prosecutor to admission, the return may state that fact, and aver that he has not been approved,[3] or that he has not paid the fine.[4] Where certain days are appointed for admission to a corporation, and no person is admissible at any other time, the return to a mandamus to admit may show this, and if it negative the right to be admitted at any other time, it will be sufficient.[5] A return to a mandamus to admit, that the office is already full, is insufficient; for if the prosecutor has the prior title, the possessor is merely an officer *de facto;* and if the title of the possessor is good, the return should show that.[6]

§ 723. Ouster in *quo warranto*, outlawry,[7] or that the prosecutor in due manner resigned his office, are good[8] returns to a mandamus to restore; and in the latter case, though a deed is necessary to the resignation, that the resignation was by deed will be implied in the general averment as a legal requisite.[9] It is an insufficient averment of a resignation, that the prosecutor had consented to be turned out; it should be more certain, as that the prosecutor resigned.[10] Where, however, the resignation is by mere implication, as by the acceptance of an incompatible office, a general averment of resignation is insufficient; but the return must show the particulars.[11] The return need not show the authority of the whole body, or a select class, to accept a resignation; for with either, this authority is incidental to the right of appointment.[12] In every case of amotion or disfranchisement, the return should show

---

1 Rex *v*. Clapham, 1 Vent. 111; Rex *v*. Penrice, 2 Stra. 1235.
2 Rex *v*. Clapham, 1 Vent. 111.
3 Wright *v*. Fawcett, 4 Burr. 2044.
4 Taverner's case, T. Raym. 447.
5 Rex *v*. Whiskin, Andr. 3.
6 Rex *v*. Ward, Fitz. 195.
7 Rex *v*. Bristol, 1 Show. 288.
8 Rex *v*. Rippon, 1 Ld. Raym. 563, 2 Salk. 432.
9 Ibid.
10 Reg. *v*. Lane, 2 Ld. Raym. 1304, 11 Mod. 270, Fortes. 275.
11 Verrior *v*. Sandwich, 1 Sid. 305.
12 Rex *v*. Tidderley, 1 Sid. 14.

precisely the cause of the same, and the proceedings had; as, that an assembly of the proper persons was duly held, notice given to the prosecutor, a conviction of an offence, and an actual amotion, or disfranchisement thereupon, in order that the court may judge of the legality of the cause, and the regularity of the proceedings. Accordingly, if the return merely allege, that the prosecutor was duly amoved or expelled the corporation for a violation of duty, without specifying the charges upon which he was convicted, or the "manner of proceeding, it is insufficient." [1]

§ 724. If, however, the officer is an officer at the will of the corporation, the return should state that circumstance, and that he was duly removed on the determination of their pleasure, without assigning any other cause; [2] for if they allow it to appear, that he has a permanent right to his office, and set forth an insufficient cause of amotion, he will be entitled to a peremptory writ for his restoration.[3] So, too, if the case is within the jurisdiction of a visitor, that fact need only be duly shown in the return, and the cause of amotion need not be specified.[4] In general, any causes of amotion duly set forth in the return are good answers to the writ for restoration.[5] The acts, however, constituting the cause of amotion must be specifically set forth, and such general allegations as these, "for removing servants of the corporation, who ought only to be displaced by the common council," or, "that the prosecutor has been guilty of general neglect and omission of duty in his office," without stating particular instances of neglect or omission, are insufficient.[6] And where the rules of a religious society inflicted the penalty of expulsion on any member, who should commence a suit at law against another member, "except the case were of such a nature as to require and justify a process at law," a return to a mandamus to restore a mem-

---

[1] Rex v. Doncaster, Sel. N. P. 1052; Bruce's case, 2 Stra. 819; Rex v. Abingdon, 2 Salk. 432; Bagg's case, 11 Co. 99; Rex v. Liverpool, 2 Burr. 731, 736, 2 Kenyon, 431; Commonwealth v. Guardians of the Poor of Philadelphia, 6 S. & R. 469, per Duncan, J.

[2] Rex v. Thame, 1 Stra. 115; Dighton's case, 1 Vent. 77, 82.

[3] Rex v. Campion, 1 Sid. 14; Rex v. Ipswich, 2 Ld. Raym. 1240; Rex v. Oxon, 2 Salk. 428.

[4] Regina v. Dean of Chester, 15 Q. B. 512, 517, 518, 519; Appleford's case, 1 Mod. 82; Philips v. Bury, 2 T. R. 356.

[5] For causes of amotion, see Chap. XII.

[6] Rex v. Wilton, 5 Mod. 259, 12 Mod. 113; Rex v. York 2 Ld. Raym. 1566; Rex v. Doncaster, Sayer, 39.

ber to his standing, which set forth the rule, and that the expelled member had commenced a suit at law against another member, without averring that the case was not of such a nature as to require and justify a process at law, was held to be insufficient.[1] Where, however, the constitution of the corporation required the officer to be learned in the laws of the land, a general return that he was not learned in the laws of the land, was adjudged sufficient; "for," said Kelying, Chief Justice, "if he were learned in the laws of the land, he might have cause for the false return, and, if it was found for him, he should be restored."[2] It was held, that a man cannot be removed from one office for misconduct in another; and the return should show by express statement, or necessary implication, that the prosecutor had misbehaved in the office from which he was removed.[3] If the power of amotion be in the body at large, it is unnecessary to set it forth in the return, since the law implies it;[4] but a return to a mandamus to restore an expelled member or officer, that he was tried and expelled by a select body or or number, without showing by what authority this select body or number acted, is insufficient.[5] Where it was shown that the power of amotion was in the mayor and aldermen and such burgesses as had been aldermen, it was held sufficient to allege in the return, that the amotion was by the mayor and burgesses, *according to the charter*.[6]

§ 725. In The King *v.* Shrewsbury,[7] where the return stated the amotion to have been made, "at a meeting of the mayor and the major part of the aldermen and common council *duly assembled*," upon its being objected, that inasmuch as this was not the common and ordinary business of the corporation to be done by charter on a particular day, the return should state *a general summons of all the resident members*, Lord Hardwicke, with whom the court concurred, held, that the words "*duly* assembled" were sufficient, and that the special manner of sum-

---

1 Green *v.* African Methodist Episcopal Society, 1 S. & R. 254.

2 Rex *v.* Lord Hawles, 1 Vent. 145, 2 Keb. 770, 778, 796; s. c. cited Rex *v.* Coventry, 1 Ld. Raym. 391, per Holt, C. J.

3 Rex *v.* York, 2 Ld. Raym. 1566; Rex *v.* Lyme Regis, Doug. 177, 181.

4 Rex *v.* Lyme Regis, Doug. 153, 154; Braithwaite's case, 1 Vent. 19.

5 Rex *v.* York, 2 Ld. Raym. 1566; Symmers *v.* Regem, Cowp. 503; Rex *v.* Feversham, 8 T. R. 356; Rex *v.* Lyme Regis, Doug. 153; Rex *v.* Cambridge, Fort. 203, 2 Ld. Raym. 1346; Green *v.* African Methodist Episcopal Society, 1 S. & R. 254.

6 Rex *v.* Feversham, 8 T. R. 356; Braithwaite's case, 1 Vent. 19; Rex *v.* Doncaster, Sayer, 37, Buller, N. P. 205.

7 7 Mod. 202, 203.

moning, &c., would come in evidence. In Rex *v.* Liverpool,[1] however, it was subsequently adjudged by the court of King's Bench, that if a select number of the corporation have power to amove and do amove, *on a day not directed by the charter*, *all* that are within summons must be summoned; and that, in such case, it is not sufficient to allege in the return, "that they were *duly*, or *in due manner*, met and assembled;" but it should be expressly alleged, "that they were *all summoned*." Where the power of amotion was vested in "the mayor, aldermen, and common council assembled," an allegation according to the legal effect, that "the mayor *and major part* of the aldermen, &c." assembled, &c. was considered sufficient.[2] If the officer is entitled to it, the return must specifically aver notice to him to appear and defend himself, or must show that the corporation did what they could to summon him.[3] This averment of summons is sufficiently made by "we caused to be summoned, &c.;" but not by "we commanded the proper officer to summon him,"[4] nor under a recital, as "although he was summoned."[5] If the return show a total desertion of the municipality, and it does not appear that the officer subsequently returned to it,[6] or if it show that the prosecutor actually appeared and defended himself,[7] no previous summons need be alleged. The return must also state specifically the charges that were made against the prosecutor as grounds for his amotion,[8] and that they were either proved on oath, or confessed.[9] If it be necessary, that the amotion should be under the corporate seal, or be entered on the corporation books, it is not necessary to aver that it was so done; for this will be implied in the general averment, that he

---

1 2 Burr. 731, &c.

2 Rex *v.* Shrewsbury, 7 Mod. 203; Hardwicke, C. J., *dubitante.*

3 Rex *v.* King's Lynn, Cunningh. 98; Rex *v.* Cambridge, Fort. 206, 2 Ld. Raym. 1348; Rex *v.* Gaskin, 8 T. R. 209; Commonwealth *v.* Pennsylvania Beneficial Institution, 2 S. & R. 141; see Chap. XII.

4 Braithwaite's case, 1 Vent. 19.

5 Commonwealth *v.* Pennsylvania Beneficial Institution, 2 S. & R. 141. And if the return alleges a place to which the relator was summoned, and it appears that such a place was improper, the return will be quashed. Regina *v.* Archbishop of Canterbury, 6 Ellis & B. 546, 37 Eng. L. & Eq. 59.

6 Rex *v.* Exon, 1 Show. 365, Rex *v.* Glyde, 12 Mod. 28, 4 Mod. 36.

7 Rex *v.* Chalke, 1 Ld. Raym. 225; Rex *v.* Wilton, 2 Salk. 428; Rex *v.* Gaskin, 8 T. R. 209; Commonwealth *v.* Pennsylvania Beneficial Institution, 2 S. & R. 141.

8 Rex *v.* Carlisle, 8 Mod. 103, Fort. 200; Commonwealth *v.* Guardians of the Poor of Philadelphia, 6 S. & R. 469.

9 Rex *v.* Carlisle, 8 Mod. 99; Rex *v.* Wilton, 5 Mod. 258, 2 Salk. 428; Rex *v.* Feversham, 8 T. R. 356.

was amoved.[1] Where a return to a mandamus to restore a common-council man averred, "that they were chosen yearly, and that before the coming of the writ they were chosen and continued for a year, and at the end of the year were duly amoved from their offices by the election of others," it was held bad for its uncertainty; for it should have shown the time when they were elected, so that it might have appeared that they were not amoved before the expiration of their year.[2] It is held, that in case of an officer at pleasure, a new election is an actual amotion; and hence that a return to a mandamus to restore such an officer, that he was only an officer at pleasure, and that upon due summons to choose another, they did choose another, and *thereby* the former was removed, was not objectionable for argumentativeness.[3] The return, "not amoved by us," has been held sufficient.[4] It is a good return to a mandamus requiring books and papers to be delivered up, to say, "that on and since the teste of the writ, A. had not, nor has had the books, &c., or any of them, in his custody, power, or possession;" and if it is unnecessarily stated by him, that he had them not on a prior day, he is not bound to negative a possession intermediate between that day and the teste of the writ.[5]

§ 726. The granting of costs after argument upon a return is in England discretionary; but where the party succeeding has not been to blame, it is now the general rule that he recovers costs.[6]

§ 727. In England, by statute 9th of Anne, it is made lawful for persons prosecuting writs of mandamus to plead to or traverse any of the

---

1 Rex *v.* Chalke, 1 Ld. Raym. 226, 5 Mod. 258; Willcock on Mun. Corp. 423.

2 Rex *v.* Chester, 5 Mod. 11.

3 Rex *v.* Canterbury, 11 Mod. 404, 1 Stra. 674; Rex *v.* Thame, 1 Stra. 115.

4 Lucas *v.* Colchester, in Hereford's case, 1 Sid. 210.

5 Rex *v.* Round, 5 Nev. & M. 427, 1 Har. & W. 546. But see People *v.* Kilduff, 15 Ill. 492, 502.

6 Reg. *v.* Eastern Counties Railway Company, 2 Q. B. 577; Reg. *v.* Mayor, &c. of Newbury, 1 Q. B. 751, 752; Rex *v.* Commissioners of the Thames and Isis Navigation, 5 A. & E. 804; Rex *v.* Lord of Manor of Arundle, 1 A. & E. 283, 299, n. c; Rex *v.* Commissioners of the Harbor of Rye, 5 B. & Ad. 1094, n. a; Reg. *v.* Lady of Manor of Dallingham, 8 A. & E. 858, 871, n. a; Reg. *v.* Justices of the West Riding, 5 Q. B. 1; Regina *v.* Harden, Bail Court, 1854, 24 Eng. L. & Eq. 167; Regina *v.* Langridge, Bail Court, 1854, 29 Eng. L. & Eq. 177; Regina *v.* Justices of Gr. Yarmouth, Q. B. 1855, 30 Eng. L. & Eq. 261. See People *v.* Densmoore, 1 Barb. 557, that costs are entirely discretionary in New York, and if not expressly granted are presumed to be denied.

material facts contained in the return; and under this statute and similar statutes passed in some of the States of this Union, upon the coming in of the return to an alternative mandamus, the relator may traverse the return, or any material part of it by plea; or he may demur to it.[1] Before that statute, if the return was sufficient in law, but false in fact, it could not be called in question in the proceeding in which it was made, any more than the ordinary return of a sheriff; but, if the public were concerned, the remedy was by criminal information;[2] if an individual was the party more particularly interested, his only remedy was an action on the case for a false return.[3]

§ 728. In this country, unless the statute of Anne, or some similar statute, has been adopted or enacted, the only remedy for the prosecutor, if the return be false, is an action against him or those who have made the false return.[4] If the facts stated in the return necessarily imply what is false, an action lies as well as if the return stated an express falsehood. Thus, a corporation set forth in a return their charter, and, as no special power of amotion was given thereby to the whole body, or any select part, the implication was that this power was vested in the whole body. Lord Mansfield considered, that if there were another charter, or by-law restraining this power to a select class, and that were not set out, there could be no doubt that an action would lie; inasmuch as this would be misleading the court.[5] And though a return

---

[1] People v. Beebe, 1 Barb. 379. It has been held in Maryland, that upon a mandamus to admit to a *public* office, the facts stated in the return are not traversable; the return is conclusive, and if sufficient in law, the only remedy left to the relator is an action on the case for a false return. Harwood v. Marshall, 10 Md. 451.

[2] Rex v. Spotland, Cas. temp. Hardw. 185; Rex v. Surgeons, 1 Salk. 374; Rex v. Abingdon, 2 Salk. 431, 432, 12 Mod. 309, Carth. 499; Anon. 12 Mod. 559; Rex v. Pettiward, 4 Burr. 2453; Rex v. Williamson, 3 B. & Ald. 582; Rex v. Borron, 3 B. & Ald. 434; Rex v. Lancaster, 1 D. & R. 485. On the information, if judgment goes against the defendants for falsity of the return, they will be fined, and a peremptory mandamus awarded against them. Rex v. Surgeons, 1 Salk. 374; Rex v. Abingdon, 2 Salk. 431, 432, 12 Mod. 308.

[3] Manaton's case, T. Raym. 365; Turner's case, 4 Sid. 257; Bagg's case, 11 Co. 99 b; Kynaston v. Shrewsbury, 2 Stra. 1053; Rich v. Pilkington, Carth. 171; Bul. N. P. 204; Howard v. Gage, 6 Mass. 462; Board of Police of Attala County v. Grant, 9 Smedes & M. 77.

[4] Howard v. Gage, 6 Mass. 462. In New York, by statute, the person prosecuting the writ may demur, or plead to such of the facts contained in the return as he thinks proper. 1 R. L. 107, § 2; 2 R. S. 586, § 55; People v. Commissioners of Hudson, 6 Wend. 559; People v. Beebe, 1 Barb. 379.

[5] Rex v. Lyme Regis, 1 Doug. 158.

be true in words, if it be false in substance, an action lies.[1] In an action for a false return, it is said to be immaterial, whether the mandamus ought originally to have been granted or not; at least, after a plea affirming the truth of the return, says Mr. Willcock, it shall be taken *pro confesso*, that the writ was granted and the return made by the defendant.[2] In England, judgment upon the sufficiency of the return to the mandamus must be actually entered upon the record before the action for a false return can be commenced.[3] To obtain by it, too, a peremptory writ, it should be brought in the Court of King's Bench; inasmuch as that court will not take judicial notice of a judgment in the Common Pleas, and the peremptory writ commences with a statement, that the return is false, *prout constat nobis per recordum*.[4] It seems, however, that where, in an action for a false return, judgment was given for the defendant, and upon writ of error, judgment was reversed in the Exchequer Chamber, the Court of King's Bench granted a peremptory mandamus, before judgment was entered, saying, it was a mandatory writ, and not a judicial writ founded on the record.[5] Where there are several joint prosecutors of a writ of mandamus, the action for a false return must be brought by them, or the survivors of them jointly; for the peremptory mandamus, which issues on judgment that the return is false, must pursue the form of the writ in the action for the false return, and cannot be granted to one without the rest.[6] If the false return be made by several, the action may be brought against them jointly or severally, as on any other tort.[7] And though the return be made in the name of the corporation, the action may be brought against the particular person or persons who caused it to be made.[8] In such case, however, if the defendant should prove that the return was made contrary to his will, but that he was overruled by a majority, this would be good

---

1 Braithwaite's case, 1 Vent. 19; Rex *v.* Lyme Regis, 1 Doug. 159, per Buller, J.

2 Green *v.* Pope, 1 Ld. Raym. 126; Willcock on Mun. Corp. 438.

3 Enfield *v.* Hill, 2 Lev. 239, T. Jones, 116.

4 Green *v.* Pope, 1 Ld. Raym. 129, Skin. 670; Anon. 2 Salk. 428; Foot *v.* Prowse, 2 Stra. 698.

5 Bul. N. P. 202.

6 Ward *v.* Brampston, 3 Lev. 362; Green *v.* Pope, 1 Ld. Raym. 128; Rex *v.* Andover, 2 Salk. 433, 12 Mod. 332; Butler *v.* Kews, 12 Mod. 349; Rex *v.* Montacute, 1 W. Bl. 60; Willcock on Mun. Corp. 439, 440.

7 Rich *v.* Pilkington, Carth. 171, 172.

8 Enfield *v.* Hills, T. Jones, 116, 2 Lev. 239; Rex *v.* Rippon, 1 Ld. Raym. 564; Comyns, 86; Reg. *v.* Chalice, 2 Ld. Raym. 849; Rich *v.* Pilkington, Carth. 171; Vaughan *v.* Lewis, Carth. 229.

evidence under the general issue, not guilty; and the plaintiff will be non-suited.[1] The declaration in an action for a false return need not allege that it was the duty of the defendant to obey the mandamus; for this is admitted by his alleging in the return a reason for his not obeying the writ.[2] It must, however, aver, that the return was made by the defendant; and proof that the mandamus was delivered to the head officer of a corporation, and has a return made upon it, is *primâ facie* evidence that he made it.[3] Proof that the defendant was served personally with an alias mandamus, and told the person who served him with the writ, "that he should take care that a return was made to it," and further, that two rules of court were made, one, for an attachment against the defendant for not making a return, and the other, to discharge that rule upon paying the costs, and appearing, &c., was held sufficient proof that the defendant made the return.[4] The declaration sets forth the return with sufficient certainty, if it set forth that it was made, "*modo et forma sequenti.*"[5] In an action for a false return to a mandamus to admit, it was held immaterial on what day the plaintiff laid his election, so that it was before action brought; but that where there is a customary day of election, if the plaintiff does not prove his election on that day, though he has laid it right, yet he must fail.[6] The action for a false return is local, but the venue may be laid either in the county where the return was made, or that in which it appears of record.[7] Where the return to a mandamus is, that the prosecutor was not elected, the plaintiff in his action must falsify the return by showing his own title.[8]

§ 729. On application for a mandamus, the usual course is to obtain a rule upon the defendant to show cause why a mandamus should not issue; and if the cause be deemed insufficient, then a mandamus in the alternative issues, to which a return is to be made; and if good cause is not thereby shown for not doing the thing required, then a peremptory

---

[1] Rich *v.* Pilkington, Carth. 172.
[2] Mayor of Norwich's case, 12 Mod. 322.
[3] Reg. *v.* Chalice, 2 Ld. Raym. 849.
[4] Vaughan *v.* Lewis, Carth. 229.
[5] Pullen *v.* Palmer, 1 Ld. Raym. 496; Rex *v.* Powell, 2 W. Bl. 787.
[6] Vaughan *v.* Lewis, Carth. 228.
[7] Lord *v.* Francis, 12 Mod. 408; Russell *v.* Succlen, 1 Sid. 218; Rex *v.* Oxford, 2 Salk. 669; Cameron *v.* Gray, 6 T. R. 363; Rex *v.* Newcastle, 1 East, 116.
[8] Crawford *v.* Powell, 2 Burr, 1013, 1 W. Bl. 229; Willcock on Mun. Corp. 442.

mandamus issues.[1] Where both parties have been fully heard, and there is no dispute about facts, the court will, if perfectly satisfied, without going through the forms of an alternative mandamus, grant a peremptory mandamus in the first instance.[2] Where, however, a rule for a peremptory mandamus has, in such case, been obtained, the court will sometimes vacate the rule, and grant one for an alternative mandamus only, so as to bring the question more fully and solemnly before them on the return.[3] The court will not award a peremptory mandamus on a part of the record, whilst proceedings on the first mandamus are incomplete.[4] Upon the return of an alternative mandamus, if the return be disallowed as insufficient in law, or inconsistent with itself, the court will grant a peremptory writ, to which, as its name implies, the only answer is implicit obedience.[5] By moving for a peremptory mandamus upon petition and answer, the truth of the answer is admitted; and on a similar motion, on a showing against a rule to show cause why a mandamus should not issue, the truth of the showing is admitted.[6] And on motion for a peremptory mandamus, upon return to an alternative mandamus, the court do not look at the affidavits on which the

---

[1] Board of Police of Attala County *v.* Grant, 9 Smedes & M. 77.

[2] *Ex parte* Jennings, 6 Cowen, 229; *Ex parte* Rogers, 7 Cowen, 526, 533, 534; People *v.* Throop, 12 Wend. 183; Commonwealth *v.* President, &c. of the Anderson Ferry, W. & New Haven Turnpike Road, 7 S. & R. 6; Board of Police of Attala County *v.* Grant, 9 Smedes & M. 77. For form of rule for peremptory mandamus, see *Ex parte* Jennings, 6 Cowen, 529. The rule for a peremptory mandamus may, if the court please, be granted *nisi*, so as to allow them time for advisement; and if they do not alter their opinion in the course of the same term, the writ issues. Rex *v.* Tappenden, 3 East, 192. In New York, after a peremptory mandamus has been awarded at a special term, there is no power to stay proceedings upon it. People *v.* Steele, 1 Barb. 554.

[3] *Ex parte* Jennings, 6 Cowen, 529, 535, 536, where see form of rule for peremptory mandamus. In Missouri an appeal will not lie on a refusal to grant a mandamus, and in South Carolina, though an appeal lies from an order awarding a mandamus, either alternative or peremptory, it is no *supersedeas;* but the writ must be executed. Pinckney *v.* Henegan, 2 Strob. 250; Shaw *v.* Livingston County, 9 Misso. 196.

[4] Reg. *v.* Baldwin, 8 A. & E. 947, 3 Per. & D. 124.

[5] Stephens' case, T. Raym. 432; Rex *v.* Cambridge, Fort. 205; Rex *v.* Norwich, 2 Ld. Raym. 1245; Rex *v.* Ilchester, 4 D. & R. 329; People *v.* Seymour, 6 Cowen, 579. In the matter of the Trustees of Williamsburgh, 1 Barb. 34. And in England, where the return is not void on the face of it, the court will not allow its validity to be questioned by motion to take it off the file upon affidavit; it can only be discussed on a *concilium* in the regular way. Rex *v.* Payne, 3 Nev. & P. 165.

[6] Board of Police of Attala County *v.* Grant, 9 Smedes & M. 77. See also, Carroll *v.* Board of Police of T. Co. 28 Missis. 38. The relator by taking issue on the allegations set forth in the return, admits, that upon its face the return is a sufficient answer to the case made by the alternative writ. People *v.* Finger, 24 Barb. 341.

alternative writ was founded, but to the return to the alternative writ.[1] Yet, notwithstanding the insufficiency of the return, if it appear that the applicant ought not to have the writ, as if on a mandamus to restore, it seems, that though irregularly amoved, he may, upon restoration, be immediately amoved for a sufficient cause, the court will not grant the peremptory writ.[2] But if, however, they have merely the *power* to amove again, as in case of an officer at pleasure, and it be not incumbent upon them as a duty to exercise it, the peremptory writ may, it seems, be granted.[3] This writ is issued, too, upon judgment for the plaintiff in an action for a false return to an alternative mandamus, if the action be brought in the same court,[4] though it be carried up by writ of error, and judgment affirmed in the court above.[5] Neither a bill of exceptions, nor a writ of error in the action for a false return, delays the issuing of the peremptory writ;[6] though it seems that a motion for a new trial stays the writ until the motion is disposed of.[7] A return to a writ of mandamus was allowed to be amended by the Supreme Court of Massachusetts, after exceptions to it had been filed.[8] Though the direction of the alternative mandamus was erroneous, the peremptory writ founded upon, and issuing to enforce it, must be directed in the same manner; and by their return to the substance of the alternative, the defendants are precluded from objecting to the direction of the peremptory writ.[9] In case of an officer restored by peremptory writ for *irregularity* of the amotion, and inefficiency of the cause alleged, it was held, that the writ was obeyed, though the corporation summoned him to show cause why he should not be amoved, at the same time that they restored him, and in pursuance thereof amoved him for the same, or nearly the same offences.[10] If the writ is not effectually obeyed, the

---

[1] People *v.* Hudson, 7 Wend. 474.

[2] Rex *v.* Campion, 1 Sid. 14; Rex *v.* Axbridge, Cowp. 523; Rex *v.* Griffiths, 1 D. & R. 390, 5 B. & Ald. 735; Commercial Bank of Albany *v.* Canal Co. 10 Wend. 25.

[3] Protector *et* Rex *v.* Campion, 2 Sid. 97; 1 Sid. 14; Rex *v.* Oxon, 2 Salk. 429; Rex *v.* Slatford, 5 Mod. 316; Reg. *v.* Ipswich, 2 Ld. Raym. 1240.

[4] Buckley *v.* Palmer, 2 Salk. 431; Green *v.* Pope, 1 Ld. Raym. 128, Skin. 570, Anon. but s. c. 2 Salk. 428; Foot *v.* Prowse, 2 Stra. 698.

[5] Bul. N. P. 202; Foot *v.* Prowse, 2 Stra. 698. See Rex *v.* Amery, 1 Anst. 183.

[6] Wright *v.* Sharp, 11 Mod. 175; Bul. N. P. 200.

[7] Ibid.; Dublin *v.* Dowgate, 1 P. Wms. 350; *contrà*, Ruding *v.* Newel, 2 Stra. 983.

[8] Springfield *v.* Commissioners of Hampden, 10 Pick. 59.

[9] Reg. *v.* Ipswich, 2 Ld. Raym. 1240.

[10] Reg. *v.* Ipswich, 2 Ld. Raym. 1240; Bagg's case, 11 Co. 99 b.

prosecutor may object to the filing of the return.[1] Where it was proved that a peremptory mandamus was unfairly obtained, the court set it aside on motion.[2]

§ 730. If the defendant neglect to make a return to a writ of mandamus, an attachment issues against him, under which the court punish the contempt, and enforce obedience to their writ. If the defendant in such case be a corporation, the attachment issues only against the persons guilty of the contempt in their natural capacity.[3] If the mandamus is directed to several in their natural capacity, unless all join in making the return, the attachment for disobedience must issue against all, whether guilty or not, though when they are before the court, their punishment will be proportioned to their offences.[4] Where no return was made to a mandamus, because the parties to whom it was directed could not agree on a return, inasmuch as they disagreed as to certain rights under the charter, a decision upon which was involved in the return to be made, the court, instead of granting an attachment, allowed the parties to enter into a rule to try their right under a feigned issue, whether the prosecutor was or was not elected.[5] An attachment issues after a peremptory rule to return the first writ,[6] or, for a neglect to return a peremptory writ on the day assigned,[7] or for neglecting to make a return to the *pluries;*[8] but not for neglecting to make a return to the first writ on the day assigned.[9] So it is granted if a frivolous return is made, or if, when the writ is directed to the head officer, and also to the corporation, he make a return contrary to the consent of the corporation.[10] The application for an attachment is made by a motion for a rule *nisi*, founded on affidavits, upon which the defendant may show cause; unless the contempt be gross, when the rule is made abso-

---

1 Reg. *v.* Ipswich, 2 Ld. Raym. 1283.

2 People *v.* Everitt, 1 Caines, 8.

3 Mill's case, T. Raym. 152.

4 Case of the Bailiffs of Bridgenorth, 2 Stra. 808; Rex *v.* Salop, Bul. N. P. 201, 202; New Sarum, Comb. 327.

5 Rex *v.* Rye, 2 Burr. 798.

6 Coventry case, 2 Salk. 429; Anon. id. 434; Anon. Comb. 234.

7 Rex *v.* Fowey, 5 D. & R. 614.

8 Coventry case, 2 Salk. 429; Anon. 2 Salk. 434.

9 Ibid.; Anon. Comb. 234.

10 Rex *v.* Robinson, 8 Mod. 336; Rex *v.* Hoskins, Cas. temp. Hardw. 188; Rex *v.* Abingdon, 12 Mod. 308.

lute at first.[1] Where the peremptory writ was directed to a corporation, an attachment was granted upon proof of a personal service upon the town-clerk alone.[2] And in The King *v.* Tooley,[3] upon affidavit that the defendant had kept out of the way, so that personal service of a peremptory writ could not be made upon him, and that the writ had been left at his house, the court ordered him to show cause. If a mandamus is served upon all those to whom it is directed, and a motion for an attachment against all of them is made, it is sufficient to produce an affidavit of service of the writ at the time of showing cause upon the attachment; nor is even this necessary, unless required by the other side. But if the writ were served upon some of the members only, and the attachment is moved against them alone, they ought, it seems, to have an opportunity of answering the affidavit of the special service of the writ.[4] Lord Holt says, that there are "two sorts of attachments upon a mandatory writ; the one entitles the party to his action for damages, and that must be upon the *pluries;* and the other punishes the contempt, which may be upon the *alias.*"[5]

CHAPTER XXI.

OF INFORMATIONS IN THE NATURE OF QUO WARRANTO.

§ 731. As by the feudal law the king was the source of all public franchises, the method of proceeding against those who exercised them without, or inconsistently with his grant, was in his name, under the direction of his attorney-general. Anciently, this method was by the original writ of *quo warranto*, called the king's writ of right for franchises and liberties, which commanded the sheriff of the county to summon the defendant to be at such a place before the king at his next

---

1 Tidd's Prac. 484; Chaunt *v.* Smart, 1 B. & P. 477.

2 Rex *v.* Fowey, 5 D. & R. 614.

3 12 Mod. 312.

4 Rex *v.* Esham, 2 Barnard. 265.

5 Anon. 12 Mod. 348; Anon. 12 Mod. 164.

coming into the county, or before the justices itinerant at the next assize, "when they should come into those parts," to show "*quo warranto*," "by what warrant" he claimed the franchises mentioned in the writ. This writ has now become obsolete; but it is the origin of informations in the nature of *quo warranto* at the common law, filed in England by the king's attorney-general of his own authority, or by the king's coroner, commonly called the master of the crown office, *formerly* of his own authority, but since the statute of 4 and 5 of Wm. & Mary, c. 18, under sanction of the Court of King's Bench.[1]

§ 732. Informations in the nature of a *quo warranto* are, in England, of three kinds. The first is an information filed by the attorney-general of his own authority; the second an information filed by the king's coroner, or the master of the crown office, under the direction of the court, in the exercise of its common-law jurisdiction; and the third a similar information by leave of the court, in pursuance of the statute of Anne, c. 20, §§ 2, 4. This last species of information is the one usually employed, in England, in cases where corporations of a municipal character are concerned; and its object, mode of issuing, and general requisites will be best understood by a reference to the statute by which it was authorized. By this statute, it was enacted, that, "if any person or persons shall usurp or intrude into, or unlawfully hold and execute, the offices of mayors, bailiffs, portreeves, or other officers, or the franchises of burgesses or freemen in any city, town corporate, borough, or place within England or Wales, it shall be lawful for the proper officer of the Court of Queen's Bench, the Courts of Sessions of counties palatine, and the Courts of Grand Sessions in Wales, with the leave of the said courts respectively, to exhibit one or more information or informations, in the nature of a *quo warranto*, at the relation of any person or persons desirous to sue or prosecute the same, and who shall be mentioned in such information or informations to be the relator or relators, against such person or persons so usurping, intruding into, or unlawfully

[1] Stat. *quo warranto*, 6 Edw. 1, § 5; 18 Edw. 1, stats. 2, 3; Strata Marcella, 9 Co. 29; Rex *v.* Trinity House, 1 Sid. 86; Rex *v.* Trelawney, 3 Burr. 1616; 2 Kyd on Corp. 395, 403, 411; Willcock on Mun. Corp. 463; 2 Sel. N. P. (Wheat. ed.), 872, 873; State *v.* Ashley, 1 Pike, 279; State *v.* St. Louis Perpetual Mar. Fire & Life Ins. Co. 8 Misso. 330. As to remedy by *writ of quo warranto* under Civil Code of Louisiana, see Reynolds *v.* Baldwin, 1 La. Ann. 162. In Pennsylvania, remedy is given by *writ of quo warranto*, under the act of 1836, at the instance of a private relator, in which case, the writ issues at the discretion of the court. Commonwealth *v.* Jones, 12 Penn. State, 365.

holding or executing any of the said offices or franchises, and to proceed therein in such manner, as is usual in cases of information in the nature of *quo warranto*."[1]

§ 733. In our own country, writs or informations in the nature of writs of *quo warranto* are filed in the highest courts of ordinary jurisdiction in several of the States,[2] either by the attorney-general of his own authority, or by the prosecutor, who is entitled *pro forma* to use his name,[3] as the case may be. The Supreme Court of Arkansas, however, has decided that that court has no jurisdiction over an information in the nature of a *quo warranto*, under that clause of their constitution which authorizes the court to issue writs of *quo warranto*, on the ground that the former is a criminal, and the latter a civil proceeding, and that the power "to issue other remedial writs, granted by the constitution, embraces only such writs, other than those specifically enumerated, as may be properly used in the exercise of appellate powers, or of the powers of control over interior, or other courts, expressly granted by the constitution."[4] The opposite construction has been put by the Supreme Court of the State of Missouri, upon a similar provision in the constitution of that State.[5] In Tennessee, neither the writ nor information in *quo warranto* are in force; the sole remedy being, by statute, in the

---

[1] 9 Anne, c. 20, § 4. And see it in Willcock on Mun. Cor. 460, 461.

[2] 4 Cowen, 102, n. a; People *v.* Richardson, 6 Cowen, 102, n.; Commonwealth *v.* Fowler, 10 Mass. 290; Respublica *v.* Griffiths, 2 Dall. 112; State *v.* Foster, 2 Halst. 101; State *v.* City Council of Charleston, 1 Const. R. 36. In California, the Supreme Court, being by the Constitution strictly an appellate tribunal, and having no original jurisdiction except in cases of *habeas corpus*, is not empowered to issue writs of *quo warranto*, the jurisdiction conferred upon that court by the constitution, being exclusive of all other jurisdiction. People *ex rel.* Attorney-General *ex parte*, 1 Calif. 85. Nor has the Superior Court of the City of San Francisco, which is an inferior court, power to issue such a writ. People *ex rel.* Hughes *v.* Gillespie, id. 342; People *ex rel.* Hagan *v.* King, id. 345. The District Courts of that State not only possess original jurisdiction in all civil cases, but are expressly authorized to issue, amongst other writs, the writ of *quo warranto*. People *ex rel.* Hughes *v.* Gillespie, id. 342, 343, per Hastings, C. J. The Supreme Court of Wisconsin, in a recent and very important case, decided, that it had power to issue a writ of *quo warranto*, and that it may exercise this power either by issuing writs of *quo warranto* as at common law, or on the filing of an *information in the nature of quo warranto* under the statute of that State. Attorney-General *ex rel.* Bashford *v.* Barstow, 4 Wis. 567.

[3] Respublica *v.* Griffiths, 2 Dall. 112; Dambonam *v.* Empire Mill, 12 Barb. 341.

[4] State *v.* Ashley, 1 Pike, 279.

[5] State *v.* Merry, 3 Misso. 278; State *v.* McBride, 4 id. 302; State *v.* St. Louis Perpetual Mar. Fire & Life Insurance Co. 8 id. 330.

Court of Chancery.[1] At common law, strictly speaking, no such person as a relator to an information is known;[2] he being altogether a creature of statute. But the courts in this country, even where no statute similar to that of Anne prevails, allow, in their discretion, informations to be filed by private persons desirous to try their rights in the name of the attorney-general;[3] and these are commonly called relators;[4] though no judgment for costs can be rendered for or against them.[5] Though in form these informations are criminal, in their nature they are but civil proceedings;[6] and hence it was decided in Pennsylvania, that they did not fall within the prohibition of the tenth section of the ninth article of the constitution of that State, which declares, "that no person shall, for any indictable offence, be proceeded against criminally by information;" the court observing, "that the constitution refers to informations, as a form of prosecution, to punish an offender, without the intervention of a grand jury; whereas, an information in the nature of a writ of *quo warranto* is applied to the mere purposes of trying a civil right, and ousting the wrongful possessor of an office."[7] For the same reason, it was decided in Indiana, that the twelfth section of the first article of the constitution of that State, "that no person shall be put to answer any criminal charge, but by presentment or impeachment," does not prohibit a *quo warranto* information.[8] Nor is the right to proceed against a corporation by *quo warranto* taken away by a power reserved to the legislature in the charter to repeal it to a limited extent, leaving power to

---

[1] State *v.* Turk, Mart. & Y. 287; State *v.* Merchants Ins. Co. 8 Humph. 253, 254, 255; Attorney-General *v.* Leaf, 9 id. 753.

[2] Bull. N. P. 211; Sel. N. P. (Wheat. ed.), 874, n. 4; Commonwealth *v.* Woelper, 3 S. & R. 52; Commonwealth *v.* Arrison, 15 S. & R. 127, and cases there cited. The mention of a relator is, however, no more than surplusage. Rex *v.* Williams, 1 Burr. 408, per Dennison, J.

[3] Respublica *v.* Griffiths, 2 Dall. 112, 113; Commonwealth *v.* Jones, 12 Penn. State, 365; Commonwealth *v.* Union Ins. Co. 5 Mass. 231, 232. In Texas the *writ* of *quo warranto* is alone authorized by the laws, and can be issued only in the name of the State on the application of its prosecuting officer. Wright *v.* Allen, 2 Texas, 158.

[4] Commonwealth *v.* Arrison, 15 S. & R. 127.

[5] Rex *v.* Williams, 1 Burr. 407, 408, 409; Commonwealth *v.* Woelper, 3 S. & R. 52.

[6] Rex *v.* Francis, 3 T. R. 484; 2 Kyd on Corp. 439; and see Commercial Bank of Rodney *v.* State, 4 Smedes & M. 439. In Illinois an information in the nature of *quo warranto* seems to be regarded as a criminal proceeding. Donnelly *v.* People, 11 Ill. 552; People *v.* Mississippi & Atlantic Railroad Co. 13 Ill. 66.

[7] Respublica *v.* Wray, 3 Dall. 490, 491, per Shippen, J.; Commonwealth *v.* Brown, 1 S. & R. 385, per Tilghman, C. J.; and see People *v.* Cook, 4 Seld. 67.

[8] Bank of Vincennes *v.* State, 1 Blackf. 267.

the corporation to wind up its affairs; this remedy being regarded as cumulative merely to the common-law remedy.[1]

§ 734. In England, the crown has at all times a right to inquire into claims to any office, or franchise, and to remove the parties, unless they can show a complete legal title thereto.[2] In prosecution of this right, the attorney-general may, of his own authority, and without any application to the court for leave,[3] exhibit an information in the nature of a *quo warranto* in the Court of King's Bench, against those who assume to act as a corporation, to compel them to show by what prescription, statute, or charter, they make title to the franchise; or against an individual who possesses a corporate office, or any other franchise, to compel him to show his right.[4] The attorney-general may also file an information against a body corporate, in its corporate name, compelling it to show by what title it holds a franchise alleged to be usurped.[5] Informations of this kind were filed in New York by the attorney-general, in the Supreme Court of that State, against several corporations, alleging that they exercised banking privileges without authority from the legislature. The first of these cases was People *v.* Utica Insurance Company.[6] In this case it appeared that application had been previously made, by the attorney-general to chancery, for an injunction to restrain the company from usurping the franchise of bank-

---

[1] Grand Gulf Railroad & Banking Co. *v.* State of Mississippi, 10 Smedes & M. 434; Dambonan *v.* Empire Mill, 12 Barb. 341.

[2] Per Yates, J., Rex *v.* Dawes, and Rex *v.* Martin; Opinion of Mr. J. Yates, quoted in The King *v.* Clarke, 1 East, 43.

[3] Per Abbot, C. J.; The King *v.* Trevenen, 2 B. & Ald. 482. In People *v.* Trustees of Geneva College, 5 Wend. 220, it is stated by Chief Justice Savage, that "an information in the nature of a *quo warranto* may also be filed by the attorney-general, upon his own relation, *on leave granted*, against any corporate body, whenever it shall exercise any franchise or privilege not conferred upon it by law." If the leave of the court be necessary, in New York, to enable the attorney-general to file such an information, the practice of that State differs in this particular from the English practice. See, too, People *v.* Oakland County Bank, 1 Doug. Mich. 285, 286, that such leave was refused after the lapse of five years' omission to prosecute for a non-compliance with the condition of a bank charter. In South Carolina, it was also held, that application for a rule to show cause why an information in the nature of a *quo warranto* should not issue to oust one holding a public office, must be in the name of the attorney-general, and depends upon the sound discretion of the court. State *v.* Schnile, 5 Rich. 300.

[4] The King *v.* Clarke, 1 East, 43; The King *v.* Trevenen, 2 B. & Ald. 482.

[5] Rex *v.* Cusack, 2 Rol. 115.

[6] 15 Johns. 358.

ing, and violating the restraining act of the State of New York; which application was rejected by the court for want of jurisdiction, because there was a complete and adequate remedy at law, by an information in the nature of a *quo warranto*.[1] An information in the nature of a *quo warranto* was then filed by the attorney-general against the company in the Supreme Court, and judgment of ouster thereupon rendered against them.[2] In the subsequent cases of People *v.* Bank of Niagara,[3] People *v.* Washington and Warren Bank,[4] and People *v.* Bank of Hudson,[5] informations of the same kind were filed against several banks, alleging that they exercised banking powers without any warrant, grant, or charter, although the real question was, not whether banking powers had been conferred upon them by the legislature, but whether they had not forfeited their charters by misconduct. In these cases, the informations were filed against the corporations in their corporate names, charging them generally with usurpations; and on the defendants setting out their charters of incorporation, and justifying under them, the attorney-general replied the causes of forfeiture specially, and this was held to be no departure. Where, too, a college, incorporated and located in a particular place, established, as a branch of the college, a medical school in a place different from that in which the college was located, and claimed the right of granting the degree of Doctor of Medicine, and of granting and issuing diplomas of such degree, it was held, that the establishment of such school, the appointment of professors to take charge of the same, and the granting of degrees and diplomas was the usurpation of a franchise, for which an information in the nature of a *quo warranto* might be filed against the college.[6] The attorney-general may also file an information against a corporate officer, to compel him to show by what title he exercises a particular franchise, claimed

---

[1] Attorney-General *v.* Utica Ins. Co. 2 Johns. Ch. 371, 377; People *v.* Utica Ins. Co. 15 Johns. 378, 379. See, too, Mickles *v.* Rochester City Bank, 11 Paige, 118, that the Court of Chancery will not interfere to restrain persons claiming to be the rightful trustees of a corporation from acting as such upon the ground that they have not been duly elected; the remedy of the corporators in such case, in New York, is by application to the Supreme Court.

[2] Ibid. 15 Johns. 386, 395.

[3] 6 Cowen, 196, where see the forms of the information and of the pleadings thereto; and see Rex *v.* Amery, 2 T. R. 515; Case of City of London, 3 Harg. St. T. 545; 1 Bl. Com. 485; 2 Kyd on Corp. 486, 487.

[4] 6 Cowen 211.

[5] 6 Cowen, 217.

[6] People *v.* Trustees of Geneva College, 5 Wend. 211.

in his official capacity; as if the mayor of a city corporation assume a right to admit freemen, without the assent of the rest of the body corporate.[1] In all these cases, the attorney-general acts *ex officio*, of his own authority, and at his own relation;[2] though it seems, that a statement in the information by the attorney-general, that he filed it in compliance with the order of a branch of the government, as the house of representatives,[3] or at the relation of any one,[4] will be considered as surplusage, and will not vitiate the proceeding. A very important class of cases, in which the power of the courts is exercised over corporations, through informations in the nature of *quo warranto*, is that in which corporations have forfeited their charters, by non-user or mis-user.[5] An information for the purpose of dissolving a corporation, or of seizing its franchises, cannot be prosecuted but by the authority of the king, in in England, exercised through his attorney-general, and of the commonwealth in this country, exercised by the legislature, or by the attorney or solicitor-general.[6] In Commonwealth *v.* Union Fire and Marine Insurance Company in Newburyport,[7] application was made on behalf of several members of the corporation, for a rule upon it, to show cause why the solicitor-general should not be directed to file an information against it, that the company might be dissolved, and their corporate power adjudged void. The parties applying for the rule alleged, that the corporation had been guilty of malfeasance in not requiring from the members payment of fifty per cent. of their subscriptions, within a time limited by the statute of incorporation, and also in taking

---

[1] Rex *v.* Hertford, 1 Salk, 374, 1 Ld. Raym. 426.

[2] Rex *v.* Ogden, 10 B. & C. 230; State *v.* Patterson & Hamburg Turnpike Co. 1 N. J. 9.

[3] Commonwealth *v.* Fowler, 10 Mass. 290, 293, 294, 295; State *v.* Patterson & Hamburg Turnpike Co. 1 N. J. 9.

[4] People *v.* Trustees of Geneva College, 5 Wend. 220.

[5] State *v.* Mayor and Aldermen of Savannah, R. M. Charl. 342; State *v.* Essex Bank, 8 Vt. 489; People *v.* Hudson Bank, 6 Cowen, 217.

[6] Rex *v.* Ogden, 10 B. & C. 230; Dambonan *v.* Empire Mill, 12 Barb. 341; Wight *v.* People, 15 Ill. 417; Murphy *v.* Farmers Bank of Schuylkill Co. 20 Penn. State, 415.

[7] 5 Mass. 230; and see to same effect Chester Glass Company *v.* Dewey, 15 Mass. 94; Rex *v.* Carmarthen, 1 W. Bl. 187, 2 Burr. 869; President, &c. of the Kishacoquillas and Centre Turnp. Road Company *v.* M'Conaby, 16 S. & R. 144, 145, 146, per Duncan, J.; Commonwealth *v.* Burrell, 7 Barr, 34; The Banks *v.* Poitiaux, 3 Rand. 142, per Green, J.; Vernon Society *v.* Hills, 6 Cowen, 23; The Society, &c. *v.* Morris Canal & Banking Co., per Chan. Williamson (MS.), opinion, cited Halsted Dig. 93; State *v.* Patterson & Hamburg Turnpike Co. 1 N. J. 9; Commonwealth *v.* Lexington and Harrodsburgh Turnpike, 6 B. Mon. 397.

greater risks than were authorized by the terms of that statute. The court, however, refused the information; and Mr. Chief Justice Parsons, delivering the opinion of the court, observed:

"In this case, the parties applying for the rule do not complain of any illegal election or admission of any officer or member of the corporation; but the object of the application is, to obtain a judgment of forfeiture of the franchises of the corporation, and a seizure of them by the commonwealth.

"We are well satisfied that a corporation, as well when created by charter under the seal of the commonwealth, as by a statute of the legislature, may, by nonfeasance or malfeasance, forfeit its franchises, and that by judgment on an information, the commonwealth may seize them. And if the allegations stated in the motion for the rule in this case, were true, and the commonwealth had caused an information to be filed and prosecuted for the purpose of seizing the corporate franchises for such malfeasance, judgment for those causes might have been rendered for the commonwealth.

"But an information for the purpose of dissolving the corporation, or of seizing its franchises, cannot be prosecuted but by the authority of the commonwealth, to be exercised by the legislature, or by the attorney or solicitor-general, acting under its direction, or *ex officio* in its behalf.[1] For the commonwealth may waive any breaches of any condition expressed or implied, on which the corporation was created;[2] and we cannot give judgment for the seizure by the commonwealth of the franchises of any corporation, unless the commonwealth be a party in interest to the suit, and thus assenting to the judgment.

"This distinction between informations in the nature of a *quo warranto*, to impeach any election or admission of a corporate officer or member, and informations to dissolve a corporation, is well settled, and upon sound principles of law."

§ 735. In the reign of Queen Anne, a statute was passed in England introducing a new and more convenient mode of proceeding on

---

[1] See the remarks of Shaw, C. J., upon this case, in Goddard *v.* Smithett, 3 Gray, 116, 124. The solicitor of a circuit in Alabama, cannot, of his own volition, sue out a *scire facias* against a corporation to obtain a judgment of forfeiture against it, but can only act under the direction of the legislature or of the attorney-general. State *v.* Moore, 19 Ala. 514.

[2] State of Mississippi *v.* Commercial Bank of Manchester, 6 Smedes & M. 218.

informations in the nature of a *quo warranto* in cases of intrusion or usurpation into certain enumerated offices and franchises of municipal corporations.[1] It is said, however, that the power of the Court of King's Bench in granting such information is not founded upon this act; but that it was intended merely to regulate the proceedings in the cases mentioned in it.[2] In the State of New York, a similar statute has been enacted, though the words of it are much broader than the English, as to the kind of offices or franchises, for the usurpation of, or intrusion into which, the remedy is given.[3] The English statute does not seem

---

[1] 9 Anne, c. 20, § 4; Bac. Abr. Information, D.; Willcock on Mun. Corp. 460. The first words of this statute are, "If any person or persons shall usurp, or intrude, or unlawfully hold and execute the offices of mayor, bailiffs, portreeves, or other officers, or the franchises of burgesses or freemen, in any city, town, corporate borough, or place, within England or Wales, it shall be lawful for the proper officer," &c. See Willcock, *supra*. There is a similar statute in New Jersey (Rev. L. 206); and which, like the statute of Anne, is construed to allow individuals to prosecute for usurpation of an office of franchise, but not to file with leave of court informations to dissolve a corporation. State *v.* Patterson & Hamburg Turnpike Co. 1 N. J. 9.

[2] Bul. N. P. 211.

[3] 1 R. L. (N. Y.), 108, § 4; 4 Cowen, 101, n. a. The New York statute gives this proceeding against any person who shall usurp, intrude into, or unlawfully hold and execute any office, or franchise, within the State. Per Spencer, J., People *v.* Utica Ins. Co. 15 Johns. 386; and see act of that State, passed April 21, 1825; L. N. Y. 7 vol. 448, sess. 48, ch. 325; see summary of same, 4 Cowen, 122, 133. For 17 sec. see 3 Wend. 589, 590, n. The object of this act is to facilitate proceedings against incorporated companies, &c.; and by it the Supreme Court are authorized, upon the application of any person or persons, natural or corporate, aggrieved by, or who may complain of, any election or any proceedings, act, or matter, in or touching the same, to proceed in a summary way to hear the affidavits, proofs, &c., or otherwise to inquire into the cause of complaint, and to order a new election, or establish the election complained of, or declare the election complained of to be void, and to establish the election of others, &c. For decisions under this clause of the statute, see *Ex parte* Holmes, 5 Cowen, 426. *Ex parte* Desdoity, 1 Wend. 98. By the seventeenth section of this act, the attorney-general, or any creditor of an incorporated bank, which is insolvent, and unable to pay its debts, or has violated any of the provisions of its incorporating act, may apply by petition to chancery; and that court may enjoin the company from exercising any of its franchises, and appoint a receiver, and distribute its property among its fair and honest creditors. For decisions under this section, see, in the matter of the Niagara Ins. Co. 1 Paige, 258; Attorney-General *v.* Bank of Columbia, 1 id. 511; s. c. Bank of Columbia *v.* Attorney-General, 3 Wend. 588; Paxtun *v.* Bishop, 3 Wend. 13; Lawrence *v.* Greenwich Fire Ins. Co. 1 Paige, 587. The Massachusetts statute of 1852, ch. 312, § 42, enacts: That any person whose private right or interest has been injured, or is put in hazard, by the exercise, by any private corporation, or any persons claiming to be a private corporation, of a franchise or privilege not conferred by law, whether such person be a member of such corporation or not, may apply to the Supreme Judicial Court for leave to file an information in the nature of a *quo warranto*. It was held, that a religious society is not a private corporation within the meaning of this statute. Goddard *v.* Smithett, 3 Gray, 116, 120.

to apply to the offices or franchises of private corporations aggregate; and if in England there be any remedy by information in cases of intrusion into, or usurpation of, such offices or franchises, it must be, as in this country, by information in the nature of a *quo warranto* at the common law. This, as we have before observed, is filed in England by the king's coroner, commonly called the master of the crown office, under the direction of the Court of King's Bench, on application by any subject, who shows that a public injury is done by the usurpation of franchises.

§ 736. It is said by Mr. Willcock,[1] that "the court will not sanction this proceeding *either when the franchise is not of a public character*, or the applicant appears to them in the light of one intermeddling unnecessarily with the affairs of others; in these cases they will leave him to inform the attorney-general, who will use his own discretion as to filing the information." We find in the English books many cases, in which this information has been granted for intrusions into offices of municipal corporations, and offices of a public and important nature,[2] and also for usurpations of franchises by officers of municipal corporations,[3] but none in which it has been granted, where the office or franchise of a mere private corporation was concerned. In Sir William Lowther's case, a motion for leave to file an information against Sir William Lowther to show by what authority he had made and set up a warren, was denied; *because it was of a private nature*, and therefore proper to be prosecuted only in the name of the attorney-general by information, if his Majesty thought fit.[4] And in the case of Regina *v.* Mousley,[5] it was recently held, for the same reason, to be very clear that an information in the nature of a *quo warranto*, could not be issued to try the title to the mastership of a private hospital founded by the will of a private individual. In The King *v.* Hansel,[6] Lord Hardwicke informs us, that

---

[1] Willcock on Mun. Corp. 457.

[2] Clifton's case, 3 Leon. 235; Rex *v.* Medlicot, 2 Barnard. 222; Rex *v.* Hullston, 1 Stra. 621; Rex *v.* Bingham, 2 East, 312; Rex *v.* Meir, 3 T. R. 598, 599, n.; Rex *v.* Highmore, 5 B. & Ald. 771, 1 D. & R. 442; Rex *v.* McKay, 4 B. & C. 356; Rex. *v.* Boyles, 2 Ld. Raym. 1560, 2 Stra. 836, Fitzg. 82; Rex *v.* Duke of Bedford, 1 Barnard. 282; Rex *v.* Ragsden, Cunningh. 54; Anon. 1 Barnard. 279.

[3] Rex *v.* Williams, 1 Burr. 407, 2 Keny. 75; Rex *v.* Hertford, 1 Ld. Raym. 426, 1 Salk. 374; Bul. N. P. 208; Rex *v.* Breton, 4 Burr. 2261.

[4] Sir William Lowther's case, 2 Ld. Raym. 1409, Stra. 637.

[5] 8 A. & E. 957, 958.

[6] Cas. temp. Hardw. 247.

"the court, indeed, have themselves made this distinction, to grant informations for *public usurpations;* but if it is only of a *private franchise*, not concerning the government, as a *fair*, *&c.*, the court has sometimes refused them, and directed an application to the attorney-general." Lord Hardwicke, as has been observed by the learned Mr. Chief Justice Tilghman,[1] does not here deny the *right* of the court to grant the information, but affirms it. Indeed, he speaks of the above distinction, as made by the court, rather than as founded in their legal right to grant informations in cases of this kind. The franchise of maintaining a bridge across a navigable river, and exacting toll, is a franchise of a public nature; and *quo warranto*, or an information in the nature of *quo warranto*, is an appropriate remedy for any person aggrieved by a non-compliance on the part of the grantee of the franchise with the condition of the grant, and may be filed at his relation.[2] The question whether an information in the nature of a *quo warranto* would lie against one who intruded himself into an office of a private corporation, may, however, be considered as settled in this country. In Commonwealth *v.* Arrison and others,[3] it underwent a full and learned discussion before the Supreme Court of Pennsylvania. There, a rule was laid on the defendants to show cause why an information in the nature of a writ of *quo warranto* should not be filed against them for exercising the office of trustees of a church corporation. Their counsel objected, that the office exercised by the defendants was a mere private matter, in which the public had no concern, and therefore, not the subject of an information. The court, however, after a full argument, and upon a review of all the authorities, decided that the information would lie. Tilghman, C. J., in delivering the opinion of the court observed: "I find no instance of an information in the nature of a *quo warranto* in England, except in a case of a usurpation of the king's prerogative, or of one of his franchises, or where the public, or at least a considerable number of people were interested. In England, the number of corporations is very small indeed, compared with the United States of America. Consequently, the quantity of that kind of business, which may be brought into our courts, will be much greater than theirs. But that alone is not a sufficient reason for rejecting it. We are

---

1 Commonwealth *v.* Arrison, 15 S. & R. 131.

2 People *ex rel.* Taylor *v.* Thompson, 21 Wend. 235; Thompson *v.* People *ex rel.* Taylor, 23 Wend. 537.

3 15 S. & R. 127.

now to decide a general question on the *right* of the court; not on the expediency of exercising that right, either in the present or any other case. Now, to establish it as a principle, that no information can be granted in cases of what the counsel call *private corporations*, might lead to very serious consequences. Perhaps it may be said, that banks, and turnpike, canal, and bridge companies, are of a *public* nature; but yet they have no concern with the government of the country, or the administration of justice. They are no further public, than as they have to do with great numbers of people. But if numbers alone be the criterion, it will often be difficult to distinguish public from private corporations. Let us consider *churches*, for example. In some, the congregation is very numerous, in others very small. How is the court to make the line of distinction? If you say the court has the right, in both cases, to grant or deny the information, according to its opinion of the expediency, there is no difficulty as to the right. But if it be alleged, that there is a right in one case, and not in the other, the difficulty will be extreme. I strongly incline to the opinion, that in all cases where a *charter* exists, and a question arises concerning *the exercise of an office claimed under that charter*, the court may, in its discretion, grant leave to file an information. Because, in all such cases, although it cannot be strictly said that any prerogative or franchise of the commonwealth has been usurped, yet, what is much the same thing, the privilege granted by the commonwealth has been abused. The party against whom the information is prayed, has no claim but from the grant of the commonwealth, and an unfounded claim is a usurpation, under pretence of a charter of a right never granted." [1] In the same State, in the previous cases of Commonwealth *v.* Woelper,[2] and Commonwealth *v.* Cain, and others,[3] an information was granted against the defendants, who were vestrymen of church corporations, without objection. In Commonwealth *v.* Murray,[4] the point was made; but the information was refused on another ground, namely, because the party who moved for it claimed in opposition to the charter under which the defendant held. In Massachusetts, in the case of Commonwealth *v.* Union Fire and Marine Insurance Company in Newburyport,[5] Chief

---

1 15 S. & R. 131, 132.

2 3 Ibid. 2.

3 5 Ibid. 510.

4 11 Ibid. 74.

5 5 Mass. 231, 232. And see People *v.* Tibbets, 4 Cowen, 358.

Justice Parsons, in his opinion, takes it for granted, that an information would lie in case of an illegal election or admission of an officer or member of an insurance company; and in Ohio it was held to be the proper remedy to inquire by what authority a person holds the office of a bank director, to try the officer and arrest the usurper.[1] In Arkansas, also, though as we have seen, the Supreme Court of that State have disclaimed any jurisdiction over informations in the nature of *quo warranto*, yet they hold that a writ of *quo warranto* will lie, to inquire by what authority one exercises the franchise and office of president or director of the Real Estate Bank of Arkansas, which is the State bank of Arkansas.[2] The mere private officers or servants of a corporation, as the managers of a lottery granted to it, removable by it at pleasure, or, for good cause, it is held, are not liable to this process; for the only effect of judgment against them would be a removal from office, and the corporation might immediately reinstate them.[3]

§ 737. The information is said to be grantable only where the ancient writ of *quo warranto* would lie;[4] and this, as we have seen, issued against those who exercised franchises in derogation of the rights of the crown. "Franchise" is a word of extensive signification; and is defined by Finch, to be "a royal privilege in the hands of a subject."[5] The purpose and effect of the writ of *quo warranto* are either to oust the defendant of the franchise exercised, if he fails to show in himself a complete right to its exercise; or if the franchise has been once legally granted, and afterwards forfeited, to seize it into the hands of the State. The writ, however, cannot be used to prohibit or restrain a public officer, or person exercising a public franchise, pending any particular act or thing, the right of doing which is claimed by virtue of his office or franchise of which he is legally possessed, and constitutes but a portion of the rights, powers, and privileges incident thereto.[6] If in England, a privilege in the hands of a subject, which the King alone can grant, would be a franchise, — with us, a privilege or immunity of a

---

1 State *v.* Buchanan, Wright, 233.

2 State *v.* Ashley, 1 Pike, 514; State *v.* Harris, 3 Pike, 570.

3 Commonwealth *v.* Dearborn, 15 Mass. 126, 127. And see Rex *v.* Corporation of Bedford Level, 6 East, 359, per Lawrence, J.

4 Rex *v.* Dawbeny, Stra. 1196; Rex *v.* Shepherd, 4 T. R. 381. The Commonwealth *v.* Murray, 11 S. & R. 74, per Tilghman, C. J.

5 Finch, 164.

6 State *v.* Evans, 3 Pike, 585.

public nature, which cannot legally be exercised without legislative grant, would be a franchise.[1] The State or Commonwealth, stands in the place of the King, and has succeeded to all the prerogatives and franchises proper to a republican government. With us, therefore, to assume a power which cannot be exercised, without a grant from the sovereign authority, or to intrude into the office of a private corporation, contrary to the provisions of the statute which creates it, is, in a large sense, to invade the sovereign prerogative, to assume or violate a sovereign franchise.[2]

§ 738. In New York, it has been decided, that where a person is in office by color of right, the remedy is not by mandamus to admit another having lawful claim; but by information in the nature of a *quo warranto*.[3]

§ 739. Where the attorney-general files an information *ex officio*, we have seen that it is not necessary for him to obtain the leave of the court.[4] But informations at the suit of private persons, whether under the statute of Anne,[5] or the statute of New York,[6] or exhibited as at the common law, can be filed only by leave of court. The information is not granted of course, but depends upon the sound discretion of the court, upon the circumstances of the case,[7] and will not be granted, where, as in case of a turnpike company opening a road through the land of a person without making him a compensation pursuant to the

---

1 People *v.* Utica Ins. Co. 15 Johns. 387, per Spencer, J.

2 Ibid.; Commonwealth *v.* Arrison, 15 S. & R. 130, 131, per Tilghman, C. J.

3 People *v.* Corporation of New York, 3 Johns. Cas. 79; People *v.* Hillsdale & Chatham Turnp. Co. 2 Johns. 190. And see St. Louis County Court *v.* Sparks, 10 Misso. 117. For cases in which the information will lie, see 4 Cowen, 101, n. a. The same is the rule in England, and in a recent case it has been held to be an inflexible rule of law, that where a person has been *de facto* elected to a corporate office, and has accepted, and acted in the same, the validity of his election can only be tried by proceeding on a *quo warranto* information. Regina *v.* Mayor, &c. of Chester, Q. B. 1855, 34 Eng. L. & Eq. 59. Nor can the title to an office in such a case be decided in a collateral suit, it must be in a direct proceeding. Conover *v.* Devlin, 24 Barb. 587; Mayor, &c. of New York *v.* Conover, 5 Abbott, Pr. 171; Lewis *v.* Oliver, 4 Abbott, Pr. 121, 127.

4 *Ante.*

5 *Ante,* § 732.

6 1 R. L. (N. Y.), 108, § 4.

7 Bac. Abr. Informations, D.; The King *v.* Trevenen, 2 B. & Ald. 339; People *v.* Sweeting, 2 Johns. 184. People *v.* Tisdale, 1 Doug. Mich. 59; Commonwealth *v.* Jones, 12 Penn State, 365; State *v.* Lehre, 7 Rich. 234.

direction of the act, there is an adequate remedy by action.[1] It would seem, that previous to the 4 and 5 William and Mary, c. 18, all the king's subjects might make use of the name of the clerk or master of the crown office, in filing informations as at common law, without the leave of the court;[2] but that statute restrains the clerk of the crown office from exhibiting or filing informations, without the express order of the court.[3] In analogy to this statute and the statute of Anne, even in those States of our own country, where these or similar acts are not in force, it is assumed in all the cases, that an information in the nature of a *quo warranto*, to try the right to an office, &c., at the prosecution of one of the parties interested, is grantable only at discretion.

§ 740. Courts will, however, usually grant this information, where the right, or the fact on which the right depends, is disputed and doubtful;[4] where the right turns upon a point of new or doubtful law,[5] or where there is no other remedy.[6] It has been held, that an information may be granted to impeach the title to an office, though the objection to the title arises from a defect in the title of the officer's electors,[7] provided the application be made within a proper time.[8] This is done, it is said, by introducing on the record an issue respecting the title of the electors, so that their right is tried, as incidental to the principal question, though they have not been ousted on an information filed against them.[9] The usual and most proper mode is, however, to attack by information the title of the electors first; though there may be cases where the title of the electors cannot be impeached at all, unless in a proceeding against the person whom they have elected.[10] And in the

---

[1] People *v.* Hillsdale & Chatham Turnpike Co. 2 Johns. 190.

[2] Rex *v.* Trelawney, 2 Burr. 1616, per Wilmot, J.; see, however, Willcock on Corp. 465.

[3] Ibid.; Bul. N. P. 210; Sel. N. P. (Wheat's ed.), 873, where see stat. For forms of informations to try the title to offices, &c. see 6 Wentw. Plead. 28 to 234; 2 Kyd on Corp. 403; Commonwealth *v.* Fowler, 10 Mass. 291; State *v.* Tudor, 5 Day, 329; 4 Cowen, 106, &c.

[4] Rex *v.* Latham, 3 Burr. 1485, Rex *v.* Lathorp, 1 W. Bl. 468.

[5] Rex *v.* Carter, Cowp. 58; Rex *v.* Goodwin, Doug. 397; Rex *v.* Scott, 1 Barnard. 24.

[6] Cas. K. B. 225; Bul. N. P. 212.

[7] The King *v.* Corporation of Penryn, 8 Mod. 216.

[8] Symmers *v.* Regem, Cowp. 507; Rex *v.* Mein, 3 T. R. 598, per Kenyon, C. J.

[9] Rex *v.* Hebden, 2 Stra. 1109, Andr. 388; Symmers *v.* Regem, Cowp. 500, arguendo.

[10] Symmers *v.* Regem, Cowp. 500, arguendo; Rex *v.* Mein, 3 T. R. 598, per Kenyon, C. J.

case of The King *v.* Hughes,[1] it was laid down by Bailey, J., as settled law, since the case of Symmers *v.* Regem,[2] that where the electors are members of a corporation, whose titles might be impeached by *quo warranto* informations, those titles could not be investigated collaterally in order to affect the title of the elected. And where judgment of ouster has been given against electors, through whom an office is claimed, this may be a reason for granting an information to impeach the title to the office; and the judgment of ouster against his electors will be admissible evidence against the officer; though not conclusive, since it might have been obtained by collusion.[3] It was no objection to granting the writ at the instance of a private relator, that the objection by him made lies against every member of the corporation, and tends to dissolve it altogether.[4]

§ 741. If a *primâ facie* case of usurpation is made out, and there appears a fair doubt on the title of the defendant, the court will not discuss the question in the summary way of motion, but send the facts to a jury.[5] In the following cases, the court has thought proper to send the question to a jury, or leave the parties to bring it more solemnly before them, on demurrer; and therefore allowed the information. Where the eligibility of the defendant to the office of burgess was doubtful, on account of his nonage;[6] or his eligibility to the office of capital burgess was doubtful, on account of his non-residence;[7] or residence being a qualification, where the question, upon the facts, was, whether he was a resident.[8] Where the questions were, whether being a capital burgess was required by the charter as a previous qualification for being elected mayor; and whether the defendant had been duly elected into the office of capital burgess, it being admitted he was a burgess, which he contended to be the only qualification required by the charter.[9] Where A being

---

[1] 4 B. & C. 368, 377, 378.

[2] Cowp. 489.

[3] Rex *v.* Hebden, 2 Stra. 1109, Andr. 388; Symmers *v.* Regem, Cowp. 500, arguendo; Rex *v.* Grimes, 5 Burr. 2601.

[4] Rex *v.* White, 1 Nev. & P. 84; Rex *v.* Perry, 6 A. & E. 810; Reg. *v.* Parry, 2 Nev. & P. 414.

[5] Willcock on Mun. Corp. 469.

[6] Rex *v.* White, Cas. temp. Hardw. 8; Rex *v.* Carter, Cowp. 59, 226; Rex *v.* Courtenay, 9 East, 261; Claridge *v.* Evelyn, 5 B. & Ald. 86.

[7] Rex *v.* Pool, 2 Barnard. 93.

[8] Rex *v.* Lathorp, 1 W. Bl. 471, s. c. Rex *v.* Latham, 3 Burr. 1487; Rex *v.* Richmond, 6 T. R. 561.

[9] Rex *v.* Tucker, 1 Barnard. 27.

one of two nominees, notice had been given that he was ineligible, and a majority voted for A; but B, the defendant, was admitted; the question was upon the ineligibility of A under the statute of Anne; for if it was found that he was qualified, B must be ousted, and A admitted.[1] Where the direction was doubtful, the question being upon the qualification of the electors,[2] or upon an omission, in the notice, of the purpose of the corporate meeting,[3] or where the doubt upon the affidavits was, whether the bailiff was an integral part of the corporate assembly, he not having been present at the election.[4] Where the question was, whether the officer, who had a right by custom to hold over, could be put out by a new appointment, after a defective appointment made at the proper time.[5] Where there was a doubt, on the words of the charter, who were the persons who ought to admit, and, of course, whether the defendant was legally admitted.[6] Where the doubt was, whether the office, to oust the defendant from which the information was prayed, was compatible with another which he had subsequently accepted.[7]

§ 742. Although it is evident that the defendant has no right, yet, if the public has sustained no injury, the court will exercise a discretion as to granting the information on the relation of the particular applicant. It has been granted, however, to one having no interest in the affairs of the corporation, where there was a strong case against the defendant;[8] to the inhabitant of a borough, though not a freeman, the municipal government being vested in the corporation;[9] to one who was elected into the corporation previous to, but admitted during the mayoralty of the defendant, to oust whom the information was sought;[10] to a corporator so poor as not to be responsible for costs;[11] to a corporator who voted for the defendant at his election to the office, from which he seeks to oust

---

1 Anne, ch. 20, § 8; Rex *v.* Goodwin, Doug. 385.

2 Rex *v.* Whitchurch, 8 Mod. 210.

3 Rex *v.* Tucker, 1 Barnard. 27; Rex *v.* Sandys, 2 Barnard. 301, 302.

4 Rex *v.* Lathorp, 1 W. Bl. 470, s. c. Rex *v.* Latham, 3 Burr. 1485.

5 Rex *v.* Butler, 8 Mod. 350.

6 Rex *v.* Trew, 2 Barnard. 371.

7 Rex *v.* Pateman, 2 T. R. 779. And see Rex *v.* Bond, 6 D. & R. 333.

8 Rex *v.* Brown, 3 T. R. 574, n. The application was made, however, in this case for the purpose of enforcing a general act of parliament, which interested all the corporations in the kingdom.

9 Rex *v.* Hodge, 2 B. & Ald. 344, n.

10 Rex *v.* Trevenen, 2 B. & Ald. 342.

11 Rex *v.* Trevenen, 2 B. & Ald. 342.

him, he being ignorant at the time of his election, of his disqualification;[1] to a corporator who was present and voted at the defendant's election (against him), and who has since attended corporate meetings, at which the defendant presided, even though a judgment against the defendant would suspend the corporation;[2] to a corporator who applied to oust the defendant from the office of alderman, having objected to his qualification at the time of his election, though he afterwards made no objection to his election to the principal office of magistracy, which required the defendant to be an alderman as a qualification, and who attended at, and concurred in corporate meetings, where the defendant presided or attended in his official capacity;[3] to a town-clerk who had been long acquainted with a defect in the defendant's title, it not appearing that he had lain by intentionally, or been guilty of any improper conduct in the affair;[4] to an applicant friendly to the defendant, who instituted the proceeding for the purpose of enabling the latter to enter a disclaimer, where it was doubtful whether he held incompatible offices, and there was no way of resigning one of them. In such case, however, the court will impose any restrictions on the parties, which the interests of third persons may require.[5] And where the application is made on the affidavit of several persons, all of whom, but one, concurred in the election of the defendant, if that one will avow himself the relator, and render himself responsible for costs, his being joined with others, who concurred in the election, will be no reason for refusing the information to the unexceptionable applicant, provided it does not appear that he is the tool of the others.[6] The abandonment of a former information for the same cause is, of itself, no reason for refusing an information; as that may have been by collusion.[7]

§ 743. The court will refuse an information in the nature of a *quo warranto*, if the defendant can show that his right has already been determined on a writ of mandamus;[8] or been acquiesced in for a length of time.[9] The time, within which the title to a corporate office might be

---

1 Rex *v.* Smith, 3 T. R. 574.

2 Rex *v.* Morris, and Rex *v.* Stewart, 3 East, 216.

3 Rex *v.* Clarke, 1 East, 46.

4 Rex *v.* Binstead, Cowp. 77.

5 Rex *v.* Marshall, 2 Chitty, 370.

6 Rex *v.* Simmons, 4 T. R. 223; Rex *v.* Cudlipp, 6 T. R. 509.

7 Rex *v.* Bond, 2 T. R. 771.

8 2 Hawk. P. C. ch. 26, § 9.

9 Bac. Abr. Informations, D.

impeached at the common law, was indefinite, varying with the circumstances of each particular case;[1] and it was at one time thought better by Lord Mansfield, that there should be no fixed rule on the subject, but that the period of limitation should in each case be left to the discretion of the court.[2] The Court of King's Bench, at length, however, set a limit to their discretion, and in the famous Winchelsea causes, after taking due time to consider, publicly declared their resolution to be, that after twenty years' unimpeached possession of a corporate franchise, no rule should be granted against the person in possession, to show by what right he holds it, in analogy to other cases of limitation.[3] Lord Mansfield said, in the name of the court, "that twenty years was the *ne plus ultra*, beyond which the court would not disturb a peaceable possession of a franchise; but that in every case *within* twenty years, their granting the rule, or refusing to grant it, would depend upon the particular circumstances of the case that should be in question before them."[4] In Easter Term, 1791, the court, finding twenty years much too long a period of limitation, and Buller, Justice, observing, that previous to the Winchelsea causes, several cases had been decided wholly on the ground of length of time, though considerably within twenty years, of which the court were entirely unapprised at the time those causes were decided, limited their discretion, in granting application of this nature to six years, beyond which time they would not under any circumstances, suffer a party who had been so long in possession of his franchise, to be disturbed.[5] This last period of limitation was shortly afterwards confirmed by act of

---

[1] Rex *v.* Powell, 8 Mod. 165; Rex *v.* Pike, 8 Mod. 286, cited 1 T. R. 4, n. and 3 T. R. 311; Rex *v.* Williams, 1 Stra. 677; Rex *v.* Latham, 3 Burr. 1486, per Lord Mansfield; and see Rex *v.* Stacey, 1 T. R. 1, 3, n.; Rex *v.* Newling, 3 T. R. 210, 211; Rex *v.* Bond, 2 T. R. 767.

[2] Rex *v.* Latham, 3 Burr. 1486. In Michigan, where there is no statute limiting the time within which a *quo warranto,* may be brought, the court held, that an information filed by the attorney-general *ex-officio* against a bank, seven years after it had gone into operation, upon the ground that the amount required by the charter to be paid in specie within two years after its passage had been fraudulently withheld, was filed too late: and that though the attorney-general had power to file the information without leave of court, yet the court at the hearing might consider this objection, derived by them from the analogous objection to the filing of information by private individuals in England. People *v.* Oakland County Bank, 1 Doug. Mich. 285, 286.

[3] Winchelsea Causes, 4 Burr. 1962, 2022, 2121; Rex *v.* Rogers, 4 Burr. 2523; and see Rex *v.* Stephens, 1 Burr. 433; Rex *v.* Bond, 2 T. R. 767; Rex *v.* Carter, Cowp. 58; Rex *v.* Binsted, Cowp. 75.

[4] Winchelsea Causes, 4 Burr. 1963.

[5] Rex *v.* Dicken, 4 T. R. 282, 284; Rex *v.* Peacock, 4 T. R. 684.

parliament.[1] The meaning of the above rule, as subsequently explained by the court, is, that after a quiet possession of his office for six years, the officer shall be taken to be a good one, to all intents and purposes.[2] Hence, the court will not grant an information to impeach a derivative title, if the person claiming the original title has been in undisturbed possession of his office for six years; for the period of limitation would be no protection to an officer, if all his acts done previous to the expiration of that period, were after it to be treated as null.[3] In Ohio, the period of limitation in such case is, by statute, three years. After that period of time has run against a cause of ouster, the remedy of a stranger by information is lost, and the remedy against indefinite usurpation is with the corporation, by removal, affording a fresh cause of ouster.[4] The limitation in England, does not, however, apply to a case of continuing incompatibility of offices; as where a party held the offices of capital burgess and town-clerk for more than six years.[5]

§ 744. The court will not grant an information against one who has merely claimed to be admitted to an office or franchise, though his claim is founded upon an election which is not *primâ facie* void, nor against those who merely claim to be a corporation; but there must be a user and possession.[6] But an actual swearing in has been adjudged a sufficient user, though it be defective because made before an improper person, or before the corporate assembly after the president, an integral

---

[1] Stat. 32 Geo. 3, 58; and see Rex *v.* Autridge, 8 T. R. 467; Rex *v.* Trevenen, 2 B. & Ald. 482; Rex *v.* Robert Brooks, 8 B. & C. 321; 2 M. & R. 389. By 7 Will. 4, and 1 Vict. ch. 78, § 23, all applications for a *quo warranto* to question the election of corporate officers, are to be made before the end of twelve calendar months after the election or the time when the person against whom the application is made shall have become disqualified. In a case in which a continuing contract with the council had been entered into by an officer, disqualifying him, it was held that a *quo warranto*, might be applied for against him, notwithstanding more than twelve months had elapsed from the time of his election and from the time when his disqualification first attached. Regina *v.* Francis, 18 Q. B. 526, 12 Eng. L. & Eq. 419.

[2] Rex *v.* Peacock, 686, per Ashurst, J.

[3] Ibid.

[4] State *v.* Granville Alexandria Society, 11 Ohio, 9; State *v.* Beecher, 16 id. 362, 363.

[5] Rex *v.* Lawrence, 2 Chitty, 371.

[6] Rex *v.* Ponsonby, Sayer, 247, 1 Kenyon, 26; Rex *v.* Whitwell, 5 T. R. 86; People *v.* Thompson, 16 Wend. 655; Regina *v.* Armstrong, Bail Court, 1856, 34 Eng. L. & Eq. 288, and see State *v.* Lehre, 7 Rich. 234, 324. The first words of the statute of Anne are, as we have seen, "If any person or persons shall usurp, or intrude into, or unlawfully hold and execute," &c. *Ante.*

part of it, had left.[1] If a person has been recently elected into office by persons having no color of authority to elect, it is said to be unnecessary to oust him in *quo warranto*, though he has entered upon his office; for the election is a nullity, and the proper electors may choose an officer into the place as vacant. But if he has held undisturbed possession of the office, and exercised it for some time, he is to be regarded as an officer *de facto*, and an information may be granted.[2] And in New York, it has been decided, that where a person is in office by color of right, the remedy is not by mandamus to admit another having lawful claim, but by information in the nature of *quo warranto*.[3] In Rex *v.* Scott,[4] an information was, after some hesitation, granted against a mayor for holding over his year, and preventing the election of a successor, because it was said there was no other remedy. Mr. Willcock thinks, that in such case, a mandamus would now be granted to proceed to a new election, notwithstanding the right to hold over, and without a previous ouster.[5] In People *v.* Sweeting,[6] the Supreme Court of New York, and in Commonwealth *v.* Athearn,[7] the Supreme Court of Massachusetts, refused informations against officers whose time it appeared would expire before the inquiry could have any effect, leaving the parties to their common remedies. In Ohio, the writ of *quo warranto* will be made returnable forthwith, or at a short day, in such cases, in order that a trial may be had before the term of office expires.[8] And an information will not be granted after the term of office has expired, so that a judgment of ouster cannot be pronounced.[9] In England, however, it is not considered absolutely necessary that the person should continue to hold the office at the time of applying for the information against him; but it has been granted in case of an annual office, where the year had expired, and four years elapsed since, during which others had been successively elected; also where the office was perma-

---

[1] Rex *v.* Pursehouse, 2 Barnard. 264; Rex *v.* Harwood, 2 East, 180; Rex *v.* Tate, 4 East, 340; Rex *v.* Buller, 8 East, 392; see also, Rex *v.* Williams, 1 Burr. 407, 1 W. Bl. 95, 2 Kenyon, 75.

[2] Anon. 1 Barnard. 345.

[3] People *v.* Hillsdale & Chatham Turnp. Comp. 2 Johns. 190.

[4] 1 Barnard. 24.

[5] Willcock on Mun. Corp. 462, 463.

[6] 2 Johns. 184.

[7] 3 Mass. 285; and see Commonwealth *v.* Sparks, 6 Whart. 416.

[8] State *v.* Buchanan, Wright, 233; but see Commonwealth *v.* Sparks, 6 Whart. 416.

[9] State *v.* Jacobs, 17 Ohio, 143.

nent, but the usurpation had ceased by the resignation of the intruder before the application, particularly as there was a doubt of the insufficiency of the resignation, and also where one legally in office had resigned it, though without deed, and afterwards usurped it, and acted again.[1] And if the office has determined, though there can be no ouster, there may be judgment for the fine.[2] In such cases, however, although the English courts do not invariably exclude the application because it is made so late — they require good reasons to be given for the delay; and where no such reasons are given, and the office is an annual one, on which no title to any other office depends, the application is, in the discretion of the court, refused, if made at such a time that the case could not come to judgment till the year had expired.[3] When the original title of an officer is sufficient, though good cause of amotion be shown, the information will not be granted until an actual amotion has been made, even in a case where the charter declares that for such cause of amotion the officer shall vacate his office; for the office is not determined until the amotion.[4]

§ 745. In England, where the franchise no ways concerns the public, as all those franchises which relate to the government of a corporation, or the election of members of parliament,[5] to fairs and markets,[6] are said to do, but is wholly of a private nature, as a coney warren,[7] or the office of a church-warden,[8] the information will be refused. We have before seen, however, that in this country, at least, informations are granted in case of the usurpation of the offices or franchises of private corporations.[9]

---

[1] Rex *v.* Powell, Sayer, 239; Rex *v.* Williams, 1 W. Bl. 95; Rex *v.* New Radnor, 2 Kenyon, 498; Rex *v.* Warlow, 2 M. & S. 76; Rex *v.* Payne, 2 Chitty, 367.

[2] Ibid.

[3] Reg. *v.* Hodson, 4 Q. B. 648, n. b.

[4] Lord Bruce's case, 2 Stra. 819; Rex *v.* Ponsonby, Sayer, 248, 1 Kenyon, 26, 5 Bro. P. C. 298; Rex *v.* Heaven, 2 T. R. 776.

[5] Case of Borough of Horsham, 3 T. R. 599, n. a; Rex *v.* Mein, 3 T. R. 598, 599; Rex *v.* Bingham, 2 East, 208. For "an office of great trust and preëminence within the borough, touching the election and return of burgesses to serve in parliament," *quo warranto* will not lie. Rex *v.* McKay, 4 B. & C. 351, 6 D. & R. 432.

[6] 2 Hawk. P. C. 26, § 9. Qu. as to fairs and markets. Rex *v.* Marsden, 3 Burr. 1812; 1 W. Bl. 579; Ibbotson's case, Cas. temp. Hardw. 248; Hardres, 162, arguendo.

[7] Rex *v.* Lowther, 2 Ld. Raym. 1409, 1 Stra. 637; Ibbotson's case, Cas. temp. Hardw. 248; Rex *v.* Cann, Andr. 15; Rex *v.* Shepard, 4 T. R. 381.

[8] Rex *v.* Dawbeny, 2 Stra. 1196; Rex *v.* Shepard, 4 T. R. 381.

[9] *Ante.*

§ 746. The conduct and motives of relators, are always properly before the court on the rule for an information, and indeed only then, properly;[1] and on the ground of personal objection to the applicant, the court has refused the information, to the legal adviser of the defendant, who had counselled him during the exercise of his office that his election was good;[2] to a stranger who had no interest in the affairs of the corporation, where public expediency did not require the application;[3] to a corporator who appeared to be the mere tool of some other person, on whose application the court would have refused it,[4] whose own title is subject to the same defect as that which he seeks to impeach,[5] who was elected under a president whose title is subject to the same defect as the defendant's,[6] or who voted at the election sought to be impeached on the ground of an objection to the presiding officer, unless he shows that he was ignorant of the objection at the time of voting;[7] who has concurred in the act, or acquiesced in the title of the defendant, which he seeks to impeach,[8] or in the election of another officer of the same kind in the corporation, who was liable to the same objection, provided the[9] irregularity complained of was at the time a subject of notice; who has concurred in an agreement not to enforce a by-law, upon which he grounds his attempts to impugn the defendant's title,[10] or who has long known the defect, and lain by intentionally until judgment against the defendant would have the effect to dissolve the corporation,[11] or who makes the application merely for the purpose of procuring indirectly a decision upon his own case, which he does not, as he might, bring directly before the court.[12] It has been refused to

---

1 Per Williams, J., Reg v. Anderson, 2 Q. B. 743.

2 Rex v. Payne, 2 Chitty, 369.

3 Rex v. Grant, 11 Mod. 299; Rex v. Stacey, 1 T. R. 3; Miller v. English, 1 N. J. 217.

4 Rex v. Stacey, 1 T. R. 4; Rex v. Cudlipp, 6 T. R. 503; Rex v. Trevenen, 2 B. & Ald. 344, 482. When the court suspects collusion from the affidavits, it will require explanatory affidavits. Ibid.

5 Rex v. Bond, 2 T. R. 771; Rex v. Peacock, 4 T. R. 687; Rex v. Cudlipp, 6 T. R. 503; Rex v. Cowell, 6 D. & R. 336; Rex v. Bracken, 1 Alcock & N. 113. As to defendant's affidavits in such case, see Rex v. Bond, 2 T. R. 771.

6 Rex v. Cudlipp, 6 T. R. 503.

7 Rex v. Slythe, 6 B. & C. 240; 9 D. & R. 190; Reg. v. Parry, 2 Nev. & P. 414.

8 Rex v. Stacey, 1 T. R. 2; Rex v. Clarke, 1 East, 47; Rex v. Trevenen, 2 B. & Ald. 343, 482; The Queen v. Greene, 2 Q. B. 460.

9 Rex v. Parkyn, 1 B. & Ad. 690; Rex v. Benney, id. 684.

10 Rex v. Mortlock, 3 T. R. 301.

11 Rex v. Bond, 2 T. R. 771; Rex v. Trevenen, 2 B. & Ald. 482.

12 Reg v. Anderson, 3 Q. B. 740.

persons who have lain by without prosecuting within a reasonable time, though with a full knowledge of the facts;[1] to a town-clerk, who seeks to impugn the defendant's title on the ground that the defendant has not taken the oaths of government, which the town-clerk, being the proper officer to administer, did not tender, and which the defendant made affidavit he would have taken, had he known them to be necessary;[2] to a town-clerk, who, after a long acquiescence, made affidavit that he did not administer the oath of allegiance to a corporator, though he made the entry on the corporation books that he did so;[3] and it has been refused to one who founds his application upon a confession of a defect of title, which he had artfully obtained from the defendant.[4] It is no objection, however, that the relator and other persons with whom he acted were influenced by strong party spirit, and had, during two or three years, withdrawn themselves from corporation business, to the inconvenience of the borough,[5] or that the person applying is in low and indigent circumstances, and that there is strong reason to suspect that he is applying, not on his own account, but at the expense, and in collusion with a stranger; though in this last case the court required security for costs.[6]

§ 747. If the application is manifestly frivolous and vexatious, the court will discharge the rule with costs.[7] If the person, from whom the title was derived, has been some time dead,[8] or the parties have acquiesced in the title,[9] it seems that an information will not be granted to impeach it. Neither will it be granted after a long acquiescence, where the objection, if it prevailed, might go to dissolve the corporation.[10] And the court will, in their discretion, disregard a secondary and incidental ground for an information (though it might have been sufficient if brought before them in the first instance), where it is resorted to by

---

1 Rex *v.* Wardrober, 4 Burr. 2024, per Aston, J.; Reg *v.* Anderson, 2 Q. B. 740.

2 Rex *v.* Hart, 8 Mod. 56. In this case the town-clerk had long lain by and came forward at the instigation of a stranger to increase the latter's interest in an election.

3 Rex *v.* Williams, 1 Stra. 674.

4 Rex *v.* Dicken, 4 T. R. 283.

5 Rex *v.* Benney, 1 B. & Ad. 684.

6 Rex *v.* Wakelin, id. 50; and see Rex *v.* Parry, 6 Q. B. 810.

7 Rex *v.* Carpenter, 2 Stra. 1039; Rex *v.* Lewis, 2 Burr. 780; Rex *v.* Mortlock, 3 T. R. 301.

8 Rex *v.* Spearing, 4 T. R. 4, n. a.

9 Rex *v.* Stacey, 1 T. R. 4.

10 Rex *v.* Carter, Cowp. 59, per Ld. Mansfield.

way of forlorn hope, after the original and main ground has failed.[1] And where the relator has twice obtained rules *nisi* for informations in the nature of *quo warranto*, calling upon the party to show why he exercised the office of mayor of a borough, which rules have been discharged on cause shown; the court will not allow the same relator, on an application against the succeeding mayor, to raise the same questions as to the title of the former mayor to exercise the office.[2] The information has been refused to enforce a claim against a turnpike company, for damages done to a relator's property in laying out a road, though the act required the company to pay the damages;[3] and, in Pennsylvania, it was refused to impugn the title of the minister of a religious society, on the ground, that the party moving for the information, and the defendant, did not claim under the same charter of incorporation.[4]

§ 748. The motion for leave to file an information must be founded on affidavits, stating all the grounds upon which the defendant's title is impeached. These ought not to be entitled in any cause.[5] The affidavits must state facts and not legal deductions; as, not the mere acceptance of an office, but the facts which constitute the acceptance, and that, too, with so much certainty and form, that an indictment for perjury may be sustained upon them, if they are wilfully false.[6] The affidavit of a relator, "that he has been informed and believes" that the defendant exercises the office which he is charged with usurping, is, however, sufficient.[7] If affidavits are made on a motion for an information against A., they cannot be read in a similar motion against B., because, it is said, that in such case an indictment for perjury will not lie upon them if false.[8] It seems, that the prosecutor may use the affidavits of a person, whom the court would not allow to be the relator.[9] When the affida-

---

[1] Rex *v.* Osbourne, 4 East, 327, 336.

[2] Rex *v.* Langhorne, 2 Nev. & M. 618.

[3] People *v.* Hillsdale & Chatham Turnp. Co. 2 Johns. 190.

[4] Commonwealth *v.* Murray, 11 S. & R. 73.

[5] Rex *v.* Pierson, Andr. 313; Rex *v.* Cole, 6 T. R. 642; Haight *v.* Turner, 2 Johns. 371, 372.

[6] Rex *v.* Sargeant, 5 T. R. 469; Rex *v.* Scolden, 2 Barnard. 439; Rex *v.* Harwood, 2 East, 180; Rex *v.* Newling, 3 T. R. 310; Rex *v.* Lane, 5 B. & Ald. 488; Reg. *v.* Hatter, 3 Per. & D. 263. For form of affidavits, see Commonwealth *v.* Douglass, 1 Binn. 77.

[7] Rex *v.* Slythe, 6 B. & C. 240, 9 D. &. R. 226.

[8] Rex *v.* Thetford, 11 Mod. 141; Tidd's Prac. 498, &c.

[9] Rex *v.* Binstead, Cowp. 77; Rex *v.* Symmons, 4 T. R. 224; Rex *v.* Brame, 1 Nev. & P. 773; Reg. *v.* Parry, 2 Nev. & P. 415.

vits set forth a charter, they must state either its acceptance, or that an usage has prevailed in conformity to it, from which its acceptance may be inferred; and where the affidavits were ill for omitting this, the court refused leave to amend them, but put the party to a new application.[1] Affidavits in support of a *quo warranto* should also state any usage which there may be differing from what might be held to be the construction of the charter,[2] and a rule for a *quo warranto* was dismissed with costs, where the affidavits in support had suppressed several material facts.[3] If the affidavits in support of the rule omit a material fact, which is stated in an affidavit filed on the other side, the latter may be read by the prosecutor in support of his rule.[4] On a motion for an information against a corporator, on the ground of his acceptance of an incompatible office, the relator must show a legal appointment to the second office.[5] He is bound, on a rule *nisi*, by the day on which, in his affidavit, though founded on information and belief, the election is alleged to have taken place; and if that day is mistaken, the defendant is not bound to show a regular election on another day.[6]

§ 749. If the applicant make out a *primâ facie* case, the usual course is for the court to grant a rule *nisi* upon the defendant, to enable him to prove the evasiveness or insufficiency of the charge against him, or any legal reason why the information should not be granted.[7] The court have, however, a discretion, whether they will go through the formality of a rule to show cause; and where the whole case had been disclosed by the defendant's answers in chancery and the answers of others, touching the subject of the application, the court looked into the answers, and granted a rule for an information in the first instance.[8]

---

[1] Rex *v.* Barzey, 4 M. & S. 253.

[2] Rex *v.* Headley, 7 B. & C. 496; 1 M. & R. 345.

[3] Rex *v.* Hughes, 7 B. & C. 719; 1 M. & R. 625.

[4] Rex *v.* Mein, 3 T. R. 597.

[5] Rex *v.* Day, 9 B. & C. 702; 4 M. & R. 541.

[6] Rex *v.* Rolfe, 1 Nev. & M. 773.

[7] Bul. N. P. 210.

[8] People *ex rel.* Barker *v.* Kipp, 1 U. S. Law Journal, 286, cited, 4 Cowen, 106, n. In Pennsylvania, where a writ of *quo warranto* was granted, under the act of 1836, upon motion after notice, upon mere suggestion, without a rule to show cause, a motion to quash will be entertained. Commonwealth *v.* Jones, 12 Penn. State, 365, 370. But see Murphy *v.* Farmers Bank of Schuylkill Co. 20 Penn. State, 415. In New Jersey it was held, that although in the case of a corporation, or high public officer, a rule to show cause should first be granted, yet in the case of a small township office, the rule for an information may be granted in the first instance. State *v.* Gummersall, 4 N. J. 529.

Whether facts are asserted or denied by the defendant, he should always be prepared with affidavits of others, as well as with his own; for his alone will not be much respected where the facts are of such a character that they would be known to others as well as to himself.[1] These may be entitled,[2] or not,[3] at the defendant's choice. If the affidavits for the defendant so positively deny the facts asserted on the other side, as to sustain an indictment for perjury, the information will, it seems, be refused, until an indictment has been prosecuted, and the persons perjured, convicted.[4] If these affidavits, and the cause shown, do not place the matter beyond dispute, the rule will be made absolute;[5] but the Court of King's Bench, in conformity to the rule concerning criminal informations will not grant the rule for an information on the last day of the term.[6] By the English rules of practice, on applying for informations in the nature of a *quo warranto*, objections, intended to be made to the title of the defendant, must be specified in the rule to show cause; and no objection, not so specified, can be raised by the prosecutor in the pleadings, without the special leave of the court, or of some judge thereof.[7]

§ 750. By the statutes of Anne,[8] and of New York,[9] one information may be exhibited to try the right of several persons. And after rules for several informations have been made absolute, where the situation of the defendants is precisely similar, the court will direct several informations to be consolidated.[10] This, however, the court will not do, unless the office be joint; for the consolidation would deprive the defendants of the opportunity of severally disclaiming or maintaining their offices, if several.[11] Sometimes, however, where there are several informations for the trial of titles, precisely similar, one of them is tried, and the

---

1 Rex *v.* Trew, 2 Barnard. 371; Respublica *v.* Prior, 1 Yeates, 206, that the evidence must be by affidavit.

2 Rex *v.* Pierson, Andr. 313; Rex *v.* Cole, 6 T. R. 642.

3 Rex *v.* Cole, 6 T. R. 642, per Kenyon, C. J.

4 Rex *v.* Woodman, 1 Barnard. 101; Rex *v.* Trew, 2 Barnard. 371.

5 Bul. N. P. 210.

6 Rex *v.* Davies, Sayer, 241.

7 Reg. Gen. H. T. 7 & 8 Geo. 4; 9 D. & R. 247; and see Rex *v.* Thomas, 3 Nev. & P. 288.

8 9 Anne, ch. 20, § 4.

9 1 R. L. (N. Y.), 108, § 4.

10 Rex *v.* Foster, 1 Burr. 573; Symmers *v.* Regem, Cowp. 500, 501.

11 Rex *v.* Warlow, 2 M. & S. 76.

rest suspended upon an undertaking of the other parties to disclaim according to the event of the trial;[1] but in Rex *v.* Cozens, the court refused to compel the relators and defendants in several informations to submit to be bound by the result of one, although the objections, in all, were the same.[2]

§ 751. An information cannot be quashed on motion, though both parties consent that it shall be done; but the court will, upon consent, direct the recognizances on both sides to be discharged.[3] The appearance of the defendants to a rule to show cause why an information should not be filed against them, does not constitute an appearance to the information; and therefore on filing the information, the relators are not entitled to a rule to plead. The rule to show cause is intended to obtain leave to institute the proceeding; but it is *commenced* by the information.[4]

§ 752. The next step is to compel the appearance of the defendant. On the ancient writ of *quo warranto*, the process to effect this was a summons; and if the party did not appear at a certain stage, the franchise or subject of the writ might be seized, on process to the sheriff, as a distress, and the defendant was put to come in and replevy it, as he would any other distress. On an information in the nature of a *quo warranto* the first process is a *venire facias* in the nature of a summons, and if there be no appearance upon it, then a *distringas*, between the teste and return of which, in England, there must be fifteen days if the corporation be in a foreign county. But on information against a corporation, there can be no seizure of the franchise, for a default, before a *distringas* has issued.[5] In Massachusetts, the first process against the defendant appears to be a summons;[6] but in a case in Pennsylvania, it was a *venire facias*, returnable at the next term.[7] If, where the proceeding is against a corporation, there be a default, there may be a

---

1 Ibid. per Dampier, J.

2 6 Dow. P. C. 3; and 2 Nev. & P. 164.

3 Rex *v.* Edgar, and Rex *v.* Brickell, 4 Burr. 2297.

4 Commonwealth *v.* Springer, 5 Binn. 353, 354.

5 Rex *v.* Trinity House, 1 Sid. 86; Briggs' Case, 2 Roll. 46; Rex *v.* Wygorne, 2 Roll. 92; Rex *v.* Hertford, 1 Ld. Raym. 426, 1 Salk. 374, Carth. 503; Rex *v.* Yarmouth, 3 Salk. 104.

6 Commonwealth *v.* Fowler, 10 Mass. 291; Commonwealth *v.* Dearborn, 15 Mass. 126.

7 Commonwealth *v.* Springer, 5 Binn. 353, 354.

judgment of seizure of the franchise usurped, into the king's hand, or in the king's right *quousque*, that is, *until the court shall further order;* and Chief Baron Eyre said, he conceived the effect of the judgment and seizure by the sheriff to be, that it laid the king's hands on the franchise of being a corporation, and upon other franchises mentioned as usurped in the information, so that the corporation could not use its liberties; the action of its vital powers was suspended; and in this situation he had no doubt that a custos of the franchises might be appointed; and that the corporation might be restored on paying a fine to the king, or that the king might pardon the default by proclamation or charter.[1] Some of the old cases on the writ of *quo warranto* look as if, when the franchise was seized for a default, it was forfeited forever, unless replevied at a short day, in the same eyre or term. The practice on the information, in the time of Charles the Second, is said to have been similar; and if the party did not appear, there was a judgment of seizure *quousque*, and if they did not replevy and appear in the next term, there was final judgment, unless they should plead within a certain time.[2] The law seems, however, to be, that if the defendant being summoned, make default, and makes another default at the return of the *venire facias*, judgment shall be, that the franchise be seized into the king's hands, and not that it shall be forfeited; for it does not yet appear whether there be any cause of forfeiture, and no man shall finally lose his land or his franchise, on any default, if he has never appeared. The process must therefore be continued until the king may have final judgment.[3] In Rex *v.* Mayor of Hedon,[4] Lord Chief Justice Lee said, "that there never was any process to outlawry on an *information* in the nature of a *quo warranto*, this not being like a *quo warranto* by original writ, which was in use before this manner of proceeding." Mr. Kyd seems, however, to think, that if there be any distinction between the writ and information in this particular, the process of outlawry lies in the latter, and does not lie in the former proceeding.[5]

---

[1] Strata Marcella, 9 Co. 29; 2 Chester Cas. 510, per Eyre, C. B. 567, 568; The King *v.* Amery, 4 T. R. 122; 2 Kyd on Corp. 496 to 511; Co. Ent. 539, b; Willcock on Mun. Corp. 483, 484.

[2] Maidstone Cas. Poph. 180; Judgment in *quo warranto*, Comb. 19; Rex *v.* Chester, 2 Show. 366; Glos'ter Stat. 2 Ins. 282.

[3] 3 Jenkins, Cent. Ca. 91; 2 Kyd on Corp. 502; Strata Marcella, 9 Co. 29; 2 Chest. Ca. 566; Willcock on Mun. Corp. 484.

[4] 1 Wils. 245.

[5] 2 Kyd on Corp. 438, 439.

§ 753. If the defendant suffer the rule to show cause to be made absolute, or suffer judgment by default, others, whose derivative titles may be affected by the judgment, may, it seems, open the rule again, and be permitted to show cause against the information, upon undertaking to indemnify the defendant against all expenses, costs, &c.[1]

§ 754. At common law, the court may either grant or deny a second imparlance, as they see cause.[2] By the statute of Anne,[3] and also by the statute of New York,[4] such convenient time may be allowed to the prosecutor, as well as to the defendant, to plead, reply, rejoin, or demur, as the court may think reasonable.

§ 755. The defendant may disclaim the franchise mentioned in the information altogether, or he may disclaim it as to a part of the time during which he is alleged to have usurped it, and justify as to the other part.[5] And under particular circumstances, as where the defendant was a very young man, and had never acted in the office, the court will, upon making the rule absolute, direct the defendant to enter a disclaimer without paying costs.[6] In general, however, costs, upon disclaimer, must be paid by the defendant.[7]

§ 756. To a writ of *quo warranto*, or an information in the nature of one, the defendant must either disclaim, or justify, and the State is bound to show nothing.[8] In this country it seems to be not an unusual practice for the information, whether it be for an intrusion into or usurpation of an office, or for an assumption or continued exercise of corporate

---

[1] Bac. Abr. Informations, D.; Rex *v.* Newling, 3 T. R. 310, 311.

[2] For entry of an imparlance, see People *v.* Utica Ins. Co. 15 Johns. 363. As to second imparlance, Herring *v.* Brown, Comb. 11, 12.

[3] 9 Stat. Anne, ch. 20, § 6; 2 Lill. Prac. Reg. 510, B.; Willcock on Mun. Corp. 485. For rules to plead, reply, &c., in England, see Rex *v.* Ginever, 6 T. R. 695, and n.

[4] 1 R. L. 109, § 6. In New York the rules to plead, reply, &c. are the same as in ordinary cases. See People *v.* Clark, 4 Cowen, 95; id. 119, n. a.

[5] Co. Ent. 527 b; Tidd's Prac. 984; Rex *v.* Biddle, 2 Stra. 952. As to form of disclaimer, see Co. Ent. 527 to 529; 2 Kyd on Corp. 405; 4 Cowen, 113, n., 114, n.

[6] Rex *v.* Holt, 2 Chitty, 366.

[7] Reg. *v.* Morton, 4 Q. B. 146; and see in this case a comment on Rex *v.* Holt. See also, Rex *v.* Warlow, 2 M. & S. 75; Rex *v.* Marshall, 2 Chitty, 370. And see a very strong case to that effect. Regina *v.* Hartley, 3 Ellis & B. 143, 25 Eng. L. & Eq. 175.

[8] State *v.* Ashley, 1 Pike, 553; State *v.* Harris, 3 Pike, 572; People *v.* Utica Ins. Co. 15 Johns. 358.

powers without right, to set forth specially the right of the relator who claims the office, as well as the usurpation of the defendant; or the specific grounds upon which a forfeiture of the charter is claimed. Where the relator is claimant of the office, he is considered, in New York, as a co-plaintiff with the people, in whose name the information runs; and judgment, it is held, may be rendered to oust the defendant and induct the relator, or merely to oust the defendant.[1] If, therefore, the relator's title be defectively set out, but the information shows that the defendant's title is defective, a demurrer to the whole information is too broad, and judgment will be rendered on it to oust the defendant.[2] It is a sufficient allegation of the title of the claimant, that "he received a majority of all the votes given for the office;" and he need not allege "that a majority of all the votes given at the election were given for him for the office."[3] The relator need not set forth the number of votes he received, which is matter of evidence; nor that he possessed the requisite qualifications for the office, which will be presumed until the contrary is alleged and proved; nor that he has taken and filed the proper oath of office, which by statute of New York, may be done after judgment in his favor.[4] In a recent case in Massachusetts, the information, instead of pursuing the usual form, contained two counts; the first of which averred, in general terms, that the corporation (turnpike) had, for six years previously thereto, exercised, without warrant, grant, or charter, and therefore, had usurped, without right, the liberties, franchises, and privileges (enumerating them), and exercised the powers, including that of receiving tolls, usually exercised and enjoyed by turnpike corporations. The second count, admitting the grant of the charter, specified numerous omissions of duty, as grounds of its forfeiture. The respondents demurred to the whole information; and the court held, that if the second count alleged matter enough to sustain an information, judgment must be rendered for the Commonwealth.[5] The justification should be set up by plea, and not by answer.[6] The defendant cannot plead *non usurpavit;* for the object of the proceeding is to ascertain, by enforcing the defend-

---

[1] People *ex rel.* Crane *v.* Ryder, 16 Barb. 370. And see Att.-Gen. *ex rel.* Bashford *v.* Barstow, 4 Wis. 567.

[2] People *ex rel.* Crane *v.* Ryder, *ubi sup.*

[3] Ibid.

[4] Ibid.

[5] Commonwealth *v.* Tenth Massachusetts Turnp. Corp. 5 Cush. 509. See also, People *v.* Ravenswood, &c. T. & Bridge Co. 20 Barb. 518.

[6] People *v.* Purcells, 3 Gilman, 59.

ant to set forth, "by what warrant or authority" he exercises the office, or holds the franchise.[1] For the same reason it is not sufficient to show a title in another; but any defect in the plea may be helped, by treating facts, stated in the information by way of inducement, as though they formed a part of the plea.[2] The plea in bar should set out the defendant's title, at length, and conclude with a general traverse "without this, that he usurped, &c." or "by his authority, &c." [3] If the information aver an usurpation of an office, the plea of title to it need only set out the authority for holding the election, the holding of it, and that the defendant received the requisite number of votes.[4] If, however, the averment of the information is a usurpation of an office, *by a loss of the qualifications necessary to the holding of it*, the plea must set out expressly the continuance of every qualification down to the filing of the information; and it is not sufficient to state that the incumbent was qualified at the time of his appointment, and rely on the presumption of the continuance of the qualifications until the loss of them is shown.[5] A plea to such an information differs in this respect from one filed to dissolve a corporation; for a plea to an information to dissolve a corporation, setting forth the charter, is a *primâ facie* defence; the corporation being presumed to exist and to perform its duties until the contrary is alleged. If in addition it goes on to state the continued existence of the corporation down to the filing of the information, or that the State is estopped from insisting upon forfeiture of the corporate franchises for causes which arose prior to a certain period, such allegations are surplusage, and will be stricken out on motion.[6] The defendant may also plead in abatement; but he must, as in other cases of dilatory pleas, verify the plea by affidavit;[7] and if the affidavit be not entitled, the plea

---

1 Anon. 12 Mod. 225, per Holt, C. J.; Rex *v.* Blagden, 10 Mod. 299; Rex *v.* Trinity House, 1 Sid. 86; Strata Marcella, 9 Co. 28, a; Glos'ter stat. 2 Inst. 281; State *v.* Ashley, 1 Pike, 504; People *v.* Bartlett, 6 Wend. 422.

2 Chest. Ca. 548; 2 Leon. Ca. 31; Partridge's Ca. Cro. E. 125; Musgrave *v.* Nevinson, 1 Stra. 585; Rex *v.* Leigh, 4 Burr. 2145; Rex *v.* Hebden, Andr. 392; German Reformed Church *v.* Seibert, 3 Barr, 290.

3 Rex *v.* Blagden, Gilb. 145; Strata Marcella, 9 Co. 27 a. For forms of pleas, see Co. Ent. Quo Warranto; 2 Kyd on Corp. 406; 6 Went. plead. 28 to 242; State *v.* Foster, 2 Halst. 101; State *v.* Tudor, 5 Day, 330; People *v.* Utica Ins. Co. 15 Johns. 363, 365; People *v.* Kip, 1 U. S. Law Journal, 284, 4 Cowen, 114 to 117; State *v.* Harris, 3 Pike, 572, 573; Clark *v.* People *ex rel.* Crane, 15 Ill. 213.

4 People *v.* Van Cleve, 1 Mann. Mich. 362.

5 State *v.* Beecher, 15 Ohio, 723.

6 Attorney-General *v.* Michigan State Bank, 2 Doug. Mich. 350.

7 2 Kyd on Corp. 439; 1 R. L. (N. Y.), 519, § 19; Rex *v.* Jones, 2 Stra. 1161; Rex *v.* Mayor of Hedon, 1 Wils. 244; 6 Went. Plead. 51.

must be set aside.[1] The general statutes of double pleas in England,[2] and New York,[3] do not extend to informations in the nature of a *quo warranto;* and there is no instance in which the court has given leave to plead two pleas.[4] But in England, under the statutes 32 Geo. III. c. 58, the defendant may plead several pleas.[5] This statute also gives the defendant leave to plead, that he has held the office for six years previous to the filing of the information, either singly, or with other pleas.[6] To make out his title to an office, &c., the defendant, and indeed each party, must set forth in his pleadings so much of the charter or act of incorporation as he relies upon, without indeed it be set forth in the anterior pleadings,[7] or, as in case of some of our State banks, is of a public nature.[8] It would seem that the pleas need not set forth that the charter had been accepted by the stockholders, since the information admits the existence of the corporation, or that it once had a legal existence.[9] If the affidavit of the relator charge the defendant as "an incorporated bank," and the information and subpœna are against the corporation, and the subsequent pleadings conform in this respect to the affidavit and process, it is too late to question the existence of the corporation, upon the ground of its non-performance of conditions precedent to its corporate existence, the State waiving the performance of such conditions through these acts and admissions of its own officers, or being estopped from asserting their non-performance. If such conditions are to be insisted on, the proceedings should be against the usurping individuals, and should not treat them as a corporation; since this last course would be to charge them in one character, and to proceed against them

---

[1] Rex *v.* Jones, 2 Stra. 1161.

[2] 9 Anne, ch. 16, § 4.

[3] 1 R. L. (N. Y.), 519, § 9.

[4] Rex *v.* Newland, Sayer, 96; Rex *v.* Leigh, 4 Burr. 2146, Sir Fletcher Norton, and Lord Mansfield; 4 Cowen, 114, n.; People *v.* Jones, 18 Wend. 601; Rex *v.* Powell, 8 Mod. 180.

[5] 32 Geo. 3, c. 58, cited Rex *v.* Autridge, 8 T. R. 468; Rex *v.* Stokes, 2 M. & S. 71.

[6] 32 Geo. 3, c. 58, § 1; Rex *v.* Richardson, 9 East, 470; Rex *v.* Stokes, 2 M. & S. 71; Rex *v.* Lawrence, 2 Chitty, 371. But query, whether this statute enabling defendants in *quo warranto* to plead double, is confined to *corporate offices.* Rex *v.* Highmore, 5 B. & Ald. 771; 1 D. & R. 438.

[7] Chest. Cas. 549, 551; Rex *v.* Smith, 2 M. & S. 597.

[8] State *v.* Ashley, 1 Pike, 514.

[9] People *v.* Niagara Bank, 6 Cowen, 196; Bank of Auburn *v.* Aikin, 18 Johns. 137; Wood *v.* Jefferson County Bank, 9 Cowen, 194; Utica Ins. Co. *v.* Tillman, 1 Wend. 555; People *v.* Saratoga and Rensselaer Railroad Co. 15 Wend. 125. See, however, State *v.* Ashley, 1 Pike, 514; State *v.* Harris, 3 Pike, 573.

in another.[1] In a proceeding against a *corporation* the question is one of *forfeiture*, not of *existence*. The sole party defendant to the proceeding is, in such case, the corporation, though the stockholders have a pecuniary interest in the result of the proceeding. Hence, in Massachusetts, where by statute, the franchise, with all the rights and privileges of a turnpike corporation, "so far as relates to the receiving of toll," may be levied upon by a creditor of the corporation, and pass by sale on execution — the corporation to retain its powers in all other respects, and to be bound to the same duties as before the sale[2] — it was decided by the Supreme Court, that the fact, that a creditor of the corporation had levied upon the franchise and acquired, by purchase on the execution, the right to the tolls for ninety-nine years, did not make it necessary that he should be a party to the information upon the question of forfeiture.[3]

§ 757. Where a company was incorporated on the condition that it should, "within ten years from the passing of the act, furnish and continue a supply of pure and wholesome water, sufficient for the use of all such citizens dwelling in said city as shall agree to take it on the terms to be demanded by the company, in default whereof the corporation shall be dissolved," and an information in the nature of a *quo warranto* was filed against them, it was held, that the company being declared a body politic and corporate *in presenti*, and having ten years to perform the acts required of them, the proviso was a defeasance, and not a condition precedent, and that therefore they were not bound in their plea to set forth the condition and allege performance, even for the purpose of showing a present right, although at the time of plea, the period limited by the proviso had long since expired; as in judgment of law, a corporation once shown to exist is presumed to continue, until the contrary be shown.[4] In alleging a breach of this condition, the court held that the attorney-general was bound to name such citizens as were willing to agree, &c., and that the naming of one individual would have been sufficient, and that he was also bound to aver a request on the part of those citizens who wished a supply of water, or an offer to pay

---

[1] Commercial Bank of Natchez *v.* State of Mississippi, 6 Smedes & M. 614, 615. See, however, Commonwealth *v.* Tenth Massachusetts Turnp. Corp. 5 Cush. 510, Dewey, J.

[2] Rev. Sts. c. 44, §§ 12, 15, 16.

[3] Commonwealth *v.* Tenth Massachusetts Turnp. Co. 5 Cush. 509, 511, 512.

[4] People *v.* Manhattan Company, 9 Wend. 351.

for it, or that the defendants had notice of such willingness or desire.[1] A general allegation of the breach, "that the defendants have not furnished or continued a supply of water sufficient (or a supply or any other quantity of pure and wholesome water) for the use of such citizens dwelling in the city of New York, as were willing to agree for and take the same as aforesaid," was held not to be an allegation of a material fact on which issue could be taken, as it tended to an issue upon an emotion or affection of the mind, which is not traversable or susceptible of trial.[2] On the other hand, an allegation against a bank that it refused to pay its notes "on the first day of November, 1841, and on divers other days and times before and since," was held to be a sufficiently certain allegation of such a cause of forfeiture.[3]

§ 758. If the right of election or admission is in a select body of the corporation, the defendant must show how they became possessed of that right, by setting forth specially in his plea the custom or clause in the charter conferring it upon them.[4] He must with certainty set forth the custom or clause in the charter prescribing the mode of election;[5] must show a vacancy of the office to which he was elected,[6] and his own legal election and admission.[7] If the defendant's plea admit his user of the office, and is insufficient, or if he demur and fail on demurrer, judgment must pass against him, and a repleader will not be awarded, though the plea raised an immaterial issue.[8] It is no answer to an allegation against a turnpike company, alleging as ground of forfeiture, that they have not kept their road in repair, that the individuals aggrieved have their remedy by private action; or that the gates of the turnpike company may be thrown open by public officers, when the road is so much out of repair as to amount to a nuisance; or that a penalty is imposed for a particular nonfeasance, unless the remedy by information is in such case taken away by express terms, or necessary implica-

---

1 People *v.* Manhattan Company, 9 Wend. 351.

2 Ibid.

3 Commercial Bank of Natchez *v.* State of Mississippi, 6 Smedes & M. 624, 625, 626.

4 Rex *v.* Lyme Regis, Doug. 153.

5 Rex *v.* Birch, 4 T. R. 610; Rex *v.* Haythorne, 5 B. & C. 427; Rex *v.* Hill, 4 B. & C. 443; Rex *v.* Rowland, 3 B. & Ald. 134; Rex *v.* Holland, 2 East, 74.

6 Rex *v.* Smith, 2 M. & S. 597.

7 Rex *v.* Holland, 2 East, 74; Rex *v.* Lisle, Andr. 174; Rex *v.* Smith, 2 M. & S. 599, 600.

8 Rex *v.* Phillips, 1 Stra. 397; Rex *v.* Boyles, 2 Ld. Raym. 1560; Rex *v.* Patteson, 4 B. & Ad. 9, 1 Nev. & M. 612.

tion.[1] Nor does a bond given by a grantee of the franchise of keeping a toll bridge, in pursuance of a statute requirement, that he would erect and complete the bridge, take away the proceeding by information, the bond being considered but a cumulative remedy.[2]

§ 759. It seems that the prosecutor may demur to the whole plea, by which a defect in the information is reached,[3] and reply to particular parts of it;[4] or he may reply specially, and put as many new matters in issue as he pleases, provided the new matter be consistent with that contained in the plea.[5] If several things are necessary to constitute a complete title in the defendant, issue may be taken on each, and if any one of the issues, on a fact material to the title, be found against the defendant, there shall be judgment of ouster, and the defendant shall pay the costs on all the issues.[6] The replication may impeach a necessary qualification of the defendant to an office, set forth in the plea as possessed by him;[7] or allege that the corporation was not "in due manner" assembled for the election of officers at the time of the defendant's election, though the words "in due manner" are implied in the averment, that the corporation was not assembled for the purpose of electing.[8] It may impeach the title of the presiding officer of the assembly at which the defendant was elected, thus showing the illegal nature of the assembly, and that too, it seems, even though the presiding officer be dead.[9] It may impeach the title of the defendant, by impeaching the legality of the titles of those who voted for him, at least, if their titles cannot be impeached by an information directly filed against them; but, it seems, that where informations could have been obtained against the electors, as in all cases where they elect in right of

---

[1] People *v.* Bristol & Rensselaerville Turnp. Road, 23 Wend. 222; People *v.* Hillsdale & Chatham Turnp. Road, id. 254.

[2] Thompson *v.* People *ex rel.* Taylor, id. 537.

[3] People *v.* Mississippi & Atlantic Railroad Company, 13 Ill. 66.

[4] Rex *v.* Ginever, 6 T. R. 733, n.

[5] Rex *v.* Latham, 3 Burr. 1487; Rex *v.* Lathorp, 1 W. Bl. 471; Rex *v.* Knight, 4 T. R. 424.

[6] Bac. Abr. Information, D.; Rex *v.* Hearle, 1 Stra. 627; 2 Ld. Raym. 1447; Rex *v.* Downes, 1 T. R. 453.

[7] Rex *v.* Brown, 4 T. R. 277; Piper *v.* Dennis, 12 Mod. 253.

[8] Rex *v.* Hill, 4 B. & C. 443.

[9] Rex *v.* Hebden, 2 Stra. 1109, Andr. 392; Rex *v.* Spearing in Rex *v.* Stacy, 1 T. R. 4, n.; Rex *v.* Smith, 5 M. & S. 279. This right to impeach the title of the presiding officer is restricted in England by 32 Geo. 3, c. 58, § 3.

a corporate franchise, it is sufficient for the defendant that they were *de facto* in the enjoyment of their franchise.[1] Where the plea is, that the election was according to the charter, the replication should be, not duly elected; for this puts every thing in issue.[2] If the defendant and prosecutor in the pleadings both treat the former's admission as if it were an election, they cannot treat it otherwise on the trial, so as to affect the pleadings.[3] The replication must not be argumentative;[4] and where it sets forth a condition on which a duty of the corporation arises, the facts which go to make up the condition, should be averred with all the exactness of pleading required in an action for a penalty.[5]

§ 760. Where an information charges a corporation generally, with usurpation, and the defendants set forth their charter, and justify under it, it is no departure for the prosecutor to reply the causes of forfeiture.[6] But if the defendant relies upon a charter qualification in his plea, and sets out a by-law introducing a different qualification in his rejoinder, and relies on it, it is a departure.[7]

---

1 Rex *v.* Penryn, 8 Mod. 216; Rex *v.* Pyke, 8 Mod. 287; Rex *v.* Hebden, 2 Stra. 1109, Andr. 381; Symmers *v.* Regem, Cowp. 503; Rex *v.* Grimes, 5 Burr. 2601; Rex *v.* Mein, 3 T. R. 598; Rex *v.* York, 5 T. R. 72; Rex *v.* Hughes, 4 B. & C. 377, 378, 6 D. & R. 443; Rex *v.* Smith, 5 M. & S. 279.

2 Rex *v.* Hughes, 4 B. & C. 376.

3 Symmers *v.* Regem, Cowp. 501.

4 Rex *v.* Hughes, 4 B. & C. 377.

5 People *v.* Kingston & Middletown Turnp. Co. 23 Wend. 215, Cowen, J.; People *v.* Manhattan Co. 9 Wend. 373, 375, Sutherland, J.

6 People *v.* Bank of Niagara, 6 Cowen, 196; Same *v.* Wash. & War. Bank, id. 211; Same *v.* Bank of Hudson, id. 217; Rex *v.* Amery, 2 T. R. 515; Case of City of London, 3 Hargrave, St. Trials, 545; 1 Bl. Com. 485; 2 Kyd on Corp. 486, 487. See, too, Commonwealth *v.* Tenth Massachusetts Turnp. Corp. 5 Cush. 510. It is held, however, in North Carolina, that an information to have the charter of a corporation declared forfeited must set forth a substantial cause of forfeiture. Attorney-General *v.* Petersburg & Roanoke Railroad Co. 6 Ired. 450.

7 Rex *v.* Weymouth, 7 Mod. 374, 4 Bro. P. C. 464. But see Rex *v.* Hughes, 4 B. & C. 368. For forms of pleas, see 4 Cowen, 113, 117, n. a. For forms of replication, see 6 Wentw. Plead. 28–242; State *v.* Foster, 2 Halst. 101; 4 Cowen, 148, n. a; People *v.* Bank of Niagara, 6 Cowen, 196. For forms of demurrers and joinder, see 6 Wentw. Plead. 52, 62, 106, 113, 152; People *v.* Utica Ins. Co. 15 Johns. 265, 4 Cowen, 148, 149. For forms of rejoinders, see 6 Wentw. Plead. 58, &c.; State *v.* Foster, 2 Halst. 103; 4 Cowen, 119, n. a; People *v.* Bank of Niagara, 6 Cowen, 200, 201. For forms of joinders in demurrer, see People *v.* Utica Ins. Co. 14 Johns. 365; 6 Wentw. Plead. 52, 62, 114, 152, &c. For form of surrejoinder, see 6 Wentw. Plead. 58; 4 Cowen, 119, n. a.

§ 761. The admission of a party to the proceedings may be read against him; but an agreement of counsel for a rule to show cause is, like a demurrer, an admission only for the purpose for which it is made.[1] The person procuring the writ is, it seems, incompetent as a witness for the State, if he claims the office in question, and his competency can be restored only by his resignation of the office.[2]

§ 762. Where a fair trial cannot be had in the same county, on account of local prejudice, the court will, in its discretion, order a change of venue;[3] and in questions of great importance and difficulty, it will order a trial at bar.[4] In Massachusetts, according to the well-settled practice, though an information may be filed by the solicitor-general in any county where the court may be sitting, yet the respondents can be holden to answer only in their own county.[5]

§ 763. Though it was formerly doubted whether a new trial could be granted on an information, when a verdict had been rendered for the defendant, because it was then thought that this was a criminal proceeding, yet since it has been settled that it is in substance but a civil action, new trials, it is well established, may be granted, even after a trial at bar.[6] It has been held, however, in Connecticut, that a new trial will not be granted for misdirection, where it appears that the defendant's term of office had expired, and a new election of officers made.[7] Though there be verdicts and judgment on demurrer for the defendant on all of his pleas, it is good cause for arrest of judgment on motion, that by his own showing on the record he has no title to the office.[8] It is, however, no cause for motion in arrest of judgment, that from the whole record it appears that the defendant has a good title,

---

[1] State *v.* Buchanan, Wright, 233.

[2] Ibid.

[3] Rex *v.* Amery, 1 T. R. 368; Rex *v.* St. Mary, 7 T. R. 735; 3 Wood. Lect. 341.

[4] Rex *v.* Whitchurch, 8 Mod. 211; Rex *v.* Amery, 1 T. R. 364, n., 367.

[5] Commonwealth *v.* Smead, 11 Mass. 74. See Cutts *v.* Commonwealth, 2 Mass. 284.

[6] Rex *v.* Francis, 2 T. R. 484; Rex *v.* Ellames, 7 Mod. 224, Cas. temp. Hardw. 48; Rex *v.* Bennet, 1 Stra. 105; Musgrave *v.* Nevinson, 1 Stra. 584, 2 Ld. Raym. 1358; Rex *v.* Bell, 2 Stra. 995, 1105; Smith *ex dem.* Dormer *v.* Parkhurst, 2 Stra. 1105; Rex *v.* Blunt, Sayer, 102; Gay *v.* Crop, 7 Mod. 37; Bright *v.* Enyon, 1 Burr. 395; Rex *v.* Jones, 8 Mod. 208; Rex *v.* Corporation of Brecknock, 8 Mod. 208; 3 Wood. Lect. 355; 2 Kyd on Corp. 445; Commonwealth *v.* Woelper, 3 S. & R. 29.

[7] State *v.* Tudor, 5 Day, 329.

[8] Rex *v.* Nance, 7 Mod. 341.

when in his plea he has wholly relied upon another title, which he has failed to establish;[1] and judgment in such case cannot be given for him.[2] And if one material issue be found against the defendant, showing that he has no title, though several be found for him, the judgment must be for the king or people.[3]

§ 764. Under the old writ of *quo warranto*, where the franchise usurped might be repossessed and enjoyed by the crown, the judgment was a judgment of seizure into the king's hands, and is here into the State's hands;[4] and in case of an information, if it extend to seizure of the *property* of the corporation, the inquiry being concerning the forfeiture of corporate rights, that part of the judgment is erroneous.[5] The corporation may be thus dissolved; but the *judgment* of seizure, it seems, does not effect the dissolution; the corporation continues to exist until the franchises are seized on execution.[6] Hence it was held, in a very important and elaborately considered case in Mississippi, that until *the execution* of the judgment there was no extinction of the debts due to the corporation; but that these passed by legal assignment to the trustees, under the act of that State, passed in 1843, simultaneously with the judgment, and would be safe in their hands from the consequences of dissolution, even if afterwards the judgment should be executed by a seizure of the franchises of the corporation.[7] In Ohio, also, under the act of that State passed in February, 1842, the debts upon judgment of forfeiture pass to the receivers; and the receivers alone, and not the corporation, can sue for them in the name of the corporation; and their suit in the name of the corporation will be dismissed unless they set out sufficient to show the character in which they prosecute it.[8] But where the franchise cannot be possessed and enjoyed by the king or people, as in case of a corporation, or corporate office, the

---

[1] Rex *v.* Leigh, 4 Burr. 2145.

[2] Symmers *v.* Regem, Cowp. 506.

[3] Rex *v.* Leigh, 4 Burr. 2145; Rex *v.* Hebden, Andr. 391.

[4] Rex *v.* Hertford, 1 Ld. Raym. 426; Strata Marcella, 9 Co. 24, b; Rex *v.* Hearle, 1 Stra. 627; State *v.* Ashley, 1 Pike, 304, 305; and see State Bank *v.* State, 1 Blackf. 278; People *v.* Hudson Bank, 6 Cowen, 217, that this is the judgment in such cases, in informations in the nature of *quo warranto*.

[5] State Bank *v.* State, 1 Blackf. 278.

[6] Ibid.; State *v.* Bank, 1 Speers, 449; Nevitt *v.* Bank of Port Gibson, 6 Smedes & M. 568.

[7] Nevitt *v.* Bank of Port Gibson, 6 Smedes & M. 568.

[8] Miami Exporting Co. *v.* Gano, 13 Ohio, 269.

judgment on the information, whether at common law, or under the statute of Anne, must be of ouster of the person or persons usurping the franchise or office, and of fine for the misdemeanor.[1] It has been decided in Indiana, that the clause in the constitution of that State, which provides, "that no man's property shall be taken for public use without consent of his representatives," does not prohibit a judgment of seizure of the franchises of a corporation for a violation of its charter, whatever may be the effect of the judgment upon private property.[2] If the defendant's title be defective in fact, as, if being duly qualified and elected he has not been legally admitted, the judgment against him must be absolute, and cannot, as was once thought, be *quousque*, that is, until he shall be legally admitted.[3] If the defendant since his usurpation has been duly elected and admitted, or if his office has long expired, or been relinquished by him, judgment must be for the fine only.[4] And though the office has expired when judgment on the right of the parties comes to be pronounced, the court will proceed and pronounce judgment, in New York, as there the relators, if successful, are entitled to costs.[5] The fine imposed on the defendant is usually nominal; though in cases of gross misconduct a heavy penalty will be imposed.[6] As the fine is usually nominal, its omission in a judgment of seizure of franchises cannot be assigned by a corporation for error, especially as the omission is manifestly for the benefit of the corporation.[7] If the judgment be against persons presuming to act as a corporation,

---

1 Rex *v.* Cusack, 2 Rol. 115; Virginia Company, 2 Rol. 445; Rex *v.* Dublin, Palm. 1; Strata Marcella, 9 Co. 25 b; Rex *v.* Hertford, 1 Ld. Raym. 426; Smith's Ca. 4 Mod. 58, 1 Show. 278, 580; Rex *v.* Grosvenor, 7 Mod. 199; 2 Barnard. 391; Rex *v.* Hearle, 1 Stra. 627; Symmers *v.* Regem, Cowp. 510; Rex *v.* Carmarthen, 2 Burr. 869, 1 W. Bl. 187; Rex *v.* Amery, 2 T. R. 567; Rex *v.* Pasmore, 3 T. R. 244; Rex *v.* Courtenay, 9 East, 267; Commonwealth *v.* Union Ins. Co. 5 Mass. 231, 232, Per Parsons, C. J.; Commonwealth *v.* Woelper, 3 S. & R. 52; People *v.* Utica Ins. Co. 15 Johns. 386; State *v.* Ashley, 1 Pike, 305. For form of judgment, see Hoblyn *v.* Regem, 6 Bro. P. C. 517. In New York, 1 R. L. 108, § 5.

2 State Bank *v.* State, 1 Blackf. 278.

3 Rex *v.* Pindar, 8 Mod. 235; s. c. Rex *v.* Serle, 8 Mod. 332; s. c. Rex *v.* Hall, 11 Mod. 391; s. c. Rex *v.* Hearle, 1 Stra. 627; Rex *v.* Reeks, 2 Ld. Raym. 1447; Symmers *v.* Regem, Cowp. 510; Rex *v.* Clarke, 2 East, 83; Rex *v.* Courtenay, 9 East, 267.

4 Rex *v.* Biddle, 2 Stra. 952; s. c. Rex *v.* Taylor, 7 Mod. 172; s. c. 2 Barnard. 238, 281.

5 People *v.* Loomis, 8 Wend. 396.

6 Rex *v.* Cracker, 8 Mod. 286; Commonwealth *v.* Woelper, 2 S. & R. 52.

7 State Bank *v.* State, 1 Blackf. 270.

when in fact no such corporation was ever created, the judgment is, "that it shall be extinguished, and forbids the usurpers from exercising the franchise again."[1] Such a judgment was held to be conclusive not only upon the State and the defendants, but upon strangers, in a case in which the question arose collaterally.[2] Upon the writ of *quo warranto* the judgment *for the defendant*, inasmuch as it was upon the mere right, was conclusive upon the the crown; and upon writ and information judgment *for the crown* is conclusive. But even after judgment for the defendant, upon an information, another information may be granted to impeach his title.[3] A judgment of ouster may be given in evidence, without being pleaded, by parties and all others, on an issue involving the rights upon which it is passed.[4] Upon disclaimer, judgment is immediately rendered for the king or people.[5] The statutes of amendments and jeofails both in England and New York, are extended to all the proceedings on informations in the nature of *quo warranto;*[6] and in

---

[1] Smith's Ca. 4 Mod. 58, 1 Show. 278, 280; and see Corporation of Dublin, 1 Palm. 1, 9.

[2] Thompson *v.* New York & Harlem Railroad Co. 3 Sandf. Ch. 625.

[3] Strata Marcella, 9 Co. 28; Anon. 12 Mod. 225; Rex *v.* Trinity House, 1 Sid. 86; Rex *v.* Carpenter, 2 Show. 47; Utica Ins. Co. *v.* Scott, 8 Cowen, 720, 721, per Colden, Senator.

[4] Utica Ins. Co. *v.* Scott, 8 Cowen, 709.

[5] Co. Ent. 527 b; 2 Kyd on Corp. 407.

[6] 9 Anne, c. 20, § 7; 1 R. L. (N. Y.), 117, 121, § 10; People *v.* Clarke, 4 Cowen, 95; and see id. 119, n. a. For decisions under the English statute, see Rex *v.* Barzey, 4 M. & S. 255; Symmers *v.* Regem, Cowp. 506; Rex *v.* Symmons, 4 T. R. 224; Rex *v.* Wynne, 2 M. & S. 347, n.; Rex *v.* Armstrong, Andr. 109; Attorney-General *v.* Trinity House, 1 Sid. 54; Rex *v.* Ellames, 7 Mod. 224, 2 Stra. 975, Cas. temp. Hardw. 42, 50, Cunningh. 44; Rex *v.* Phillips, 1 Kenyon, 539, 1 Burr. 304; Rex *v.* Birch, 4 T. R. 610; Phillips *v.* Smith, 1 Stra. 136. For pleading *de novo*, Rex *v.* Grimes and Rex *v.* Blatchford, 4 Burr. 2147; 4 Cowen, 120. When no repleader, Rex *v.* Leigh, 4 Burr. 2145; Symmers *v.* Regem, Cowp. 506. Judgment amended, Tufton and Ashley, Cro. Car. 144; Rex *v.* Amery, 1 Anstr. 183. For New York Practice as to rule for pleading, People *v.* Richardson, 3 Cowen, 357; execution, 4 Cowen, 122, n. a; writ of error, id.; return, id.; trial and evidence, 4 Cowen, 119, n. a; bill of exceptions, 4 Cowen, 120, n. a; postea, id.; consolidation, id. 109, n. a; quashing information, id.; of the process, id. 109, 111; how defendant shall be named, id. 111, n. a.; teste and return of process, id.; of issues of distringas, id.; of seizure *nomine districtionis* for non-appearance, id.; whether defendant can be pursued to outlawry, id. 112, n. a; who may defend, id.; time to plead, id.; imparlance, id. 113, n. a; of affidavits on which motion for leave, &c., is founded, id. 105, n. a; rule thereupon, id. 106, n. a; rule to inspect books, id.; of affidavits on showing cause, id.; showing cause, id.; form of rule to appear, id. 384; special verdict allowed preference in an argument on calendar, id. 297; costs, id. 120, 122, n. a. The general rules of court in relation to pleading, amendments, &c., are ap-

Pennsylvania, whether the statute of 1806 applies or not, the court will in their discretion allow the pleadings to such informations to be amended.[1]

§ 765. On informations in the nature of a *quo warranto*, at common law, neither party could recover costs;[2] and cannot at this day, in England, in cases not within the statutes.[3] In New York, it seems, that costs are recoverable; though a defendant, against whom an information has been filed, cannot, if successful, recover double costs.[4]

CHAPTER XXII.

OF THE DISSOLUTION AND REVIVAL OF A CORPORATION.

§ 766. IN England, it has been much questioned, whether a municipal corporation could be dissolved, except by the death of all the people in the place, or, it may be, by act of parliament. There is certainly nothing in the nature of corporations of this kind which renders them incapable of dissolution; and the only substantial difficulty seems to be, the hardship of making the local government and privileges of the *many* dependent upon the acts or neglects of the *few*, who usually enjoy the principal franchises, and fill the offices, of municipal corporations.[5] It is evident that this objection applies with less force to private corpora-

---

plicable, in New York, to proceedings upon informations in the nature of *quo warranto*. People *v.* Clarke, 4 Cowen 95.

[1] Commonwealth *v.* Gill, 3 Whart. 236. Formal errors in the information itself upon which the writ is founded, are always amendable, either before or on the trial. Commonwealth *v.* Commercial Bank, 28 Penn. State, 383.

[2] Commonwealth *v.* Woelper, 3 S. & R. 52.

[3] Rex *v.* Williams, 1 Burr. 402, 1 W. Bl. 93; Rex *v.* Wallis, 5 T. R. 380; Rex *v.* Richardson, 9 East, 469; Rex *v.* Hall, 1 B. & C. 237; Rex *v.* McKay, 5 B. & C. 641; English Statutes with regard to costs, see informations, 9 Anne, ch. 20, § 5; 4 and 5 Wm. & Mary, ch. 18, § 2, 6; 32 Geo. 3, § 1.

[4] People *v.* Loomis, 8 Wend. 396; People *v.* Adams, 9 Wend. 464.

[5] Willcock on Mun. Corp. 325, 326.

tions, many of which, in our own country, are little more than limited partnerships, every member exercising through his vote an immediate control over the interests of the body. Indeed, the general force of the objection is almost done away by the fact, that even those who contend for the indissolubility of municipal corporations admit, that they may be *suspended*, or practically dissolved; that the members cannot enjoy the principal advantages of incorporation without a renovating grant from the sovereign power.[1] By far the better opinion at the present day, as we shall have occasion to consider, is, that even municipal bodies may be dissolved, and their privileges and franchises granted to a new, or to *the old set of corporators*. In England, a corporation may, at least to all practical purposes, be dissolved, first, by act of parliament; secondly, by the loss of all its members, or of an integral part, by death or otherwise; thirdly, by the surrender of its franchises; and fourthly, by forfeiture of its charter, through negligence or abuse of the privileges conferred by it.[2] To these modes of dissolution may be added, one grown to be quite common in this country; the dissolution of a corporation by expiration of the term of its duration, limited by charter or general law.

§ 767. By the theory of the British constitution, parliament is omnipotent; and hence an act of that body would undoubtedly be effectual to the dissolution of a corporation.[3] It is to the honor of the British nation, however, that this power, restrained by public opinion, rests mainly in theory; and except in the instances of the suppression of the order of Templars, in the time of Edward the Second,[4] and of the religious houses in the time of Henry the Eighth,[5] we know of no occasion on which parliament have thought proper to dissolve, or confirm the

---

1 Willcock on Mun. Corp. 327.

2 2 Kyd on Corp. 445 *et seq;* Willcock on Mun. Corp. 326 *et seq;* 1 Bl. Com. 485; 2 Kent, Com. 305. See Boston Glass Manufactory *v.* Langdon, 24 Pick. 52; McIntyre Poor School *v.* Zanesville Canal Co. 11 Ohio, 203.

3 1 Co. Lit. 176, n.; Bl. Com. 160, 485; 3 Kyd on Corp. 446, 447; Vanhorne *v.* Dorrance, 2 Dallas, 307, 308, per Patterson, J.; Dartmouth College *v.* Woodward, 4 Wheat. 643, per Marshall, C. J.; 2 Kent, Com. 305.

4 See Sawyer's Arg. Quo Warranto, 13; 2 Kyd on Corp. 446.

5 1 Hallam's Const. Hist. of England, 94 *et seq.* Some of the great foundations were held to fall, against every principle of law, by the attainder of their abbots for high treason; and these illegal forfeitures were confirmed by act of parliament. The smaller convents, whose revenues were less than £200 a year, were suppressed by act of parliament, to the number of three hundred and seventy-six, and their estates vested in the crown. Ibid. 97.

arbitrary dissolution of corporate bodies. When, in 1783, a bill was introduced for the purpose of remodelling the charter of the East India Company, it was opposed by Mr. Pitt and Lord Thurlow, not only as a dangerous violation of the charter of the company, but as a total subversion of the law and constitution of the country. In the nervous language of the latter, it was "an atrocious violation of private property, *which cut every Englishman to the bone.*" Indeed some of the greatest jurists and judges of England have not hesitated to declare, that an act of parliament against common right and natural equity is void.[1] Corporate property and franchises, important as they usually are in amount and extent, and undefended by the same strong sympathies which guard individual rights, offer a more tempting and easier spoil to misguided power, whether it reside in the prince or the people; and we find a late elegant and critical historian regarding them as upon a different footing from the property and rights of private persons, and admitting the full right of the legislature to remould and regulate them in all that does not involve existing interests (as the interests of the successors) upon far slighter reasons of convenience.[2] It is a happy feature in the constitution of our own government, that the power of the legislatures of the different States resembles in this particular the prerogative of the king of Great Britain, who may create, but cannot dissolve a corporation, or, without its consent, alter or amend its charter.[3] In the tenth section of the first article of the Constitution of the United States it is declared, that, "no State shall enter into any treaty, alliance, or confederation; grant letters of marque and reprisal; coin money; emit bills of credit; make any thing but gold and silver coin a tender in payment of debts; pass any bill of attainder, *ex posto facto* law, *or law impairing the obligation of contracts*, or grant any title of nobility."[4] Under this clause it has been settled, that the charter of a private corporation, whether civil or eleemosynary, is an executed contract between the government

---

[1] Bracton, L. 4, foll. 228; Dr. Bonham's case, 8 Co. 234, per Coke, C. J.; London *v.* Wood, 8 Mod. 687, 688, per Holt, C. J.; Day *v.* Savage, Hob. 87, per Hobart, C. J. And see Regents of the University of Maryland *v.* Williams, 9 Gill & J. 408, 409, Buchanan, C. J.

[2] 1 Hallam's Const. Hist. of England, 101, 102.

[3] Rex *v.* Amery, 2 T. R. 568, 569; Sir James Smith's case, 4 Mod. 54, 55, arg.; Rex *v.* Pasmore, 3 T. R. 205, 206, arg.; Dartmouth College *v.* Woodward, 4 Wheat. 657, 658, per Washington, J., 675, per Story, J.; 2 Kyd on Corp. 447; 2 Kent, Com. 305, 306.

[4] Constitution of the United States, Art. 1, § 10.

and the corporators, and that the legislature cannot repeal, impair, or alter it, against the consent, or without the default of the corporation judicially ascertained and declared.[1] If the charter of a college recites that a certain sum "be annually and forever hereafter given and granted, as a donation by the public to the use of the said college," the legislature cannot repeal such a grant.[2] A distinction has been, however, taken between private corporations and public, such as counties, cities, towns, and parishes, which, existing for public purposes only, the legislature have, under proper limitations, a right to change, modify, enlarge, or restrain, securing, however, the property to the use of those for whom it was purchased.[3] A State bank, in which the State is the sole stockholder, is, within the meaning of this rule, a public corporation; but an act of the State repealing or modifying the charter, so as to appropriate to itself the funds of the bank which it had pledged for the redemption of its bills, whether passed by it in the character of a creditor of the bank, or of a trustee for creditors, is in derogation of the contract between the State and the bill-holders, and void.[4] Public corporations may and often do have private rights and interests, and as to such rights and interests, they are to be regarded and dealt with in the same light

---

1 Dartmouth College *v.* Woodward, 4 Wheat. 518; Fletcher *v.* Peck, 6 Cranch, 88; State of New Jersey *v.* Wilson, 7 Cranch, 164; Terrett *v.* Taylor, 9 Cranch, 43; Town of Pawlet *v.* Clark, 9 Cranch, 292; Wales *v.* Stetson, 2 Mass. 143; Enfield Toll Bridge Co. *v.* Connecticut River Co. 7 Conn. 53, per Daggett, J.; McLaren *v.* Pennington, 1 Paige, 107, per Walworth, Chan.; 2 Kent, Com. 305, 306; Green *v.* Biddle, 8 Wheat. 1; Society for establishing Useful Manufactures *v.* Morris Canal & Banking Co. per. Chan. Williamson, cited Halst. Dig. 93; Regents of the University of Maryland *v.* Williams, 9 Gill, & J. 402, 403; Payne *v.* Baldwin, 3 Smedes & M. 661; Trustees of Aberdeen Female Academy *v.* Mayor & Aldermen of Aberdeen, 13 id. 645; Young *v.* Harrison, 6 Ga. 130; Coles *v.* County of Madison, Breese, 120; Bush *v.* Shipman, 4 Scam. 190; People *v.* Marshall, 1 Gilman, 672; State *v.* Hayward, 3 Rich. 389; Bailey *v.* Railroad Co. 4 Harring. Del. 389; Le Clercq *v.* Gallipolis, 7 Ohio, 217; State *v.* Commercial Bank of Cincinnati, 7 Ohio, 125; State *v.* Wash. Soc. Lib. 9 Ohio, 96; Michigan Bank *v.* Hastings, 1 Doug. Mich. 225; Boston & Lowell R. R. Corp. *v.* Salem & Lowell R. R. Corp. 2 Gray, 1; Commonwealth *v.* Proprietors of New Bedford Bridge, id. 339; Aurora & Lau. T. Co. *v.* Holthouse, 7 Ind. 59; City of Louisville *v.* Pres. & Trust. of University of Louisville, 15 B. Mon. 642; Yarmouth *v.* North Yarmouth, 34 Me. 411.

2 St. John's College *v.* State, 15 Md. 330.

3 Dartmouth College *v.* Woodward, 4 Wheat. 694, 695, 659-664; Hampshire *v.* Franklin, 16 Mass. 76; Marietta *v.* Fearing, 4 Ohio, 427; 2 Kent, Com. 306; Bush *v.* Shipman, 4 Scam. 190; People *v.* Urell, id. 273; County of Richland *v.* County of Lawrence, 12 Ill. 1; Trustees of Schools *v.* Tatman, 13 Ill. 27; City of St. Louis *v.* Allen, 13 Misso. 400; State *v.* Curran, 7 Eng. 321; City of Patterson *v.* Society for establishing Useful Manufactures, 4 N. J. 385; Berlin *v.* Gorham, 34 N. H. 266, 275.

4 Curran *v.* State of Arkansas, 15 How. 304; State *v.* Curran, 7 Eng. 321, *contra.*

as individuals; and grants of property and of franchises coupled with an interest, to public or political corporations, are beyond legislative control equally with the property of private corporations.[1] So the grant of a ferry franchise, which has been accepted and acted upon, partakes of the nature of a contract and cannot be taken away without making compensation.[2] Corporations created by the King of Great Britain previously to the Revolution, are equally within the protection of the constitution with those since created by the different States; for the dismemberment of empire, it is well settled, causes no destruction of the civil rights of individuals or corporate bodies.[3] It has been held, that a provision in the act of incorporation, which gave a summary process to a bank, was no part of its corporate franchises, but as the mere remedy, and not the right, might be repealed or altered at pleasure by the legislative will.[4] Upon the same ground, the change of the place of trial of suits against an insurance company, from a county prescribed in the charter, to the county where an agency of the company is established, in a matter arising out of the transactions of such agency, is no infringement of the charter.[5] In a case where the legislature divested itself by a charter, of imposing "any other or further duties, liabilities, or obligations," it was held, that it might provide a remedy more effectually to compel a performance of the duties and liabilities of such corporation, and the mode, time when, and court where such remedy should be enforced.[6] And a law raising a commission to visit a bank, examine its officers, who are compelled to testify under a penalty, and if the bank is in a condition dangerous to the public, to apply to a justice of the Supreme Court for an injunction, and the appointment of a receiver, is

---

[1] Dartmouth College *v.* Woodward, 4 Wheat. 663, 698, 699; 2 Kent, Com. 305, 306; Trustees of Aberdeen Female Academy *v.* Mayor & Aldermen of Abaen, 13 Smedes & M. 646, 647; Bailey *v.* Mayor of New York, 3 Hill, 541; City of St. Louis *v.* Russell, 9 Misso. 507; Trustees of Schools *v.* Tatman, 13 Ill. 27; City of Louisville *v.* Pres. & Trust. of University of Louisville, 15 B. Mon. 642; State *v.* Springfield, 6 Ind. 83.

[2] Benson *v.* New York, 10 Barb. 223; Aiken *v.* Western R. Co. 20 N. Y. 370, and the dissenting opinion of Strong, J.

[3] Dawson *v.* Godfrey, 4 Cranch, 323; Terrett *v.* Taylor, 9 Cranch, 43; Dartmouth College *v.* Woodward, 4 Wheat. 518, 706, 707; Society, &c. *v.* New Haven, 8 Wheat. 481; People of Vermont *v.* Society for Propagating the Gospel, 1 Paine, C. C. 653.

[4] Bank of Columbia *v.* Oakley, 4 Wheat. 245; and see Young *v.* Bank of Alexandria, 4 Cranch, 384; McLaren *v.* Pennington, 1 Paige, 107, 108, per Walworth, Ch.; Sturges *v.* Crowninshield, 4 Wheat. 122.

[5] Howard *v.* Kentucky & Louisville Ins. Co. 13 B. Mon. 286.

[6] Gowen *v.* Penobscot R. Co. 44 Me. 140. See also, Veazie *v.* Mayo, 45 Me. 560.

not unconstitutional, on the ground that a suspension of the proceedings of the bank by injunction diminishes the period for which the bank by charter is empowered to act, since this is but a process in the administration of justice.[1] In consequence of the construction that has been put upon the clause of the Constitution above quoted, it has become usual for legislatures, in acts of incorporation for private purposes, either to make the duration of the charter conditional,[2] or to reserve to themselves a power to alter, modify, or repeal the charter at their pleasure; and as the power of modification and repeal is thus made a qualifying part of the grant of franchises, the exercise of that power cannot, of course, impair the obligation of the grant.[3] Such alterations or modifications are to be made in accordance with the forms prescribed by the Constitution which is in force when the alteration is made, and not according to the forms prescribed at the time the charter was granted.[4] Sometimes this power is reserved by a general act applicable to all corporations, in which case it may be exercised upon any corporation, as a railroad company, whose charter had been granted since the passage of the general act, although no special clause containing or alluding to such reserved power be inserted in the company's charter.[5] The general statutes of a State apply to a corporation, unless they are expressly repealed by the charter of that corporation, and the incorporating of a part of a general statute in the charter does not by implication repeal the rest of the statute.[6] When such a power is reserved, a creditor of the corporation cannot interpose a valid objection to the constitutional power of the legislature to repeal the charter, on the ground that such an act would prevent the prosecution of a pending suit by him brought against the corporation, in which property had been attached.[7]

---

1 Commonwealth *v.* Farmers & Mechanics Bank, 21 Pick. 542; and see Commercial Bank of Rodney *v.* State, 4 Smedes & M. 439.

2 Crease *v.* Babcock, 23 Pick. 334.

3 Wales *v.* Stetson, 2 Mass. 146, per Parsons, C. J.; Dartmouth College *v.* Woodward, 4 Wheat. 708, Story, J.; McLaren *v.* Pennington, 1 Paige, 108, 109; Enfield Toll Bridge Co. *v.* Connecticut River Co. 7 Conn. 53, per Daggett, J.; President, Directors & Co. of the Miners Bank of Dubuque *v.* United States, 1 Morris, 482; 2 Kent, Com. 306, 307; Erie & N. E. Railroad *v.* Casey, 26 Penn. State, 287; In the matter of the Reciprocity Bank, 29 Barb. 369. But see Sage *v.* Dillard, 15 B. Mon. 340.

4 In the matter of the Reciprocity Bank, 29 Barb. 369.

5 Suydam *v.* Moore, 8 Barb. 358. See also, Mass. General Hospital *v.* State Mut. Life Ass. Co. 4 Gray, 227.

6 Pratt *v.* Atlantic & St. Lawrence R. Co. 42 Me. 579.

7 Read *v.* Frankfort Bank, 23 Me. 318.

Sometimes the power of repeal is reserved, to be exercised only in certain contingencies; as, "if the said corporation shall fail to go into operation, or shall abuse or misuse their privileges under this charter." It would seem that in such a case the corporation cannot, in defence to a *quo warranto*, impeach the repeal of the charter, on the ground that there has been no abuse or misuse of their privileges, but are forever concluded and estopped by the decision of the legislature, manifested by the act of repeal.[1] Sometimes, also, the right to amend is reserved, if the corporation desire it, and this right does not, as against a non-consenting stockholder, extend to amendments going to the essence of the charter, not asked for by the stockholders.[2] In Massachusetts it is provided by a general statute, that every act of incorporation shall at all times be subject to amendment, alteration, or repeal, at the pleasure of the legislature, provided that no act of incorporation shall be repealed, unless for some violation of its charter or other default, when such charter shall contain an express provision limiting the duration of the same. In a late case in that State, the Supreme Court, after mentioning that the power must have some limit, and stating some extreme cases, said: "Perhaps from these extreme cases, for extreme cases are allowable to test a legal principle, the rule to be extracted is this, that where under power in a charter, rights have been acquired and become vested, no amendment or alteration of the charter can take away the property or rights which have become vested under a legitimate exercise of the powers granted."[3] The reservation, in a royal charter, to the crown, of a power to avoid it for non-compliance with its directions or conditions, either absolutely or upon terms, does not limit the power of repealing the charter by *scire facias*, but was intended, though possibly without effect, to give the crown an additional power of revocation.[4] When

---

[1] Miners Bank *v.* United States, 1 Greene, Iowa, 553, 563–566; State *v.* Curran, 7 Eng. Ark. 321; and see Erie & N. E. Railroad *v.* Casey, *supra*; Crease *v.* Babcock, 23 Pick. 334.

[2] Booe *v.* Junction R. Co. 10 Ind. 93.

[3] Commonwealth *v.* Essex Co. 13 Gray, 239, 253. In this case the legislature had entered into a contract with the defendants to exempt them from the obligations of making and maintaining a suitable and sufficient fishway, by indemnifying all persons damnified in the fisheries, and the defendants had, in execution of their part of the contract, paid large sums of money for such damages. It was held, that it was not competent for the legislature without any change of circumstances, under their authority to amend and repeal the charter of the company, to pass a law requiring them to do acts from which by the terms of the contract they had been exempted. See also, Delaware R. Co. *v.* Tharp, 5 Harring. Del. 454.

[4] Eastern Archipelago Co. *v.* Regina, 2 Ellis & B. 857, 22 Eng. L. & Eq. 328.

the legislature has, under a general statute, reserved to itself power to wind up the concerns of banking corporations, those provisions of the statute calculated to apprise all interested of the fundamental change about to be wrought, should be complied with, in order to give legal efficacy to the acts done under it; otherwise the property of the corporation will not be divested, and its charter will continue in force.[1] It is obvious from the distressing consequences which ensue from the dissolution of a corporation, both to its members and creditors, that this reserved right of repeal is one, which, as a matter of policy as well as of justice, should be exercised with the greatest moderation and caution. It would seem that sometimes the courts are disposed to construe such statutes of repeal with great strictness as if they were in the nature of penal laws. It was upon this ground that the Supreme Court of Michigan refused to treat the act of the legislature of that State repealing the charter of "*the Bank of Oakland County*," as an act repealing a charter granted to and constituting a banking corporation by the name of "*The President, Directors, and Company of the Oakland County Bank*," objecting to this want of descriptive certainty in the act of repeal.[2]

§ 768. By the death of all its members a corporation aggregate is, or rather may be, dissolved.[3] And where from death or disfranchisement so few remain, that by the constitution of the corporation they cannot continue the succession, to all purposes of action at least, the corporation itself is dissolved.[4] As long, however, as the remaining corporators are sufficient in number to continue the succession, the body remains; as though all the monks of an abbey died, yet if the abbot was alive, the corporation was not determined, since the abbot might profess others.[5]

§ 769. Municipal corporations have been held to be dissolved by omitting to elect their chief officer on the charter day, where he has no

---

1 Farmers Bank of Delaware *v.* Beaston, 7 Gill & J. 422.

2 People *v.* Oakland County Bank, 1 Doug. Mich. 286, 287, 288.

3 20 H. 6, 7; Bro. Mortmain; 1 Inst. 13, b; 2 Kyd on Corp. 447, 448; Canal Co. *v.* Railroad Co. 4 Gill & J. 1; Trustees of McIntire Poor School *v.* Zanesville Canal & Manuf. Co. 9 Ohio, 203; Penobscot Boom Co. *v.* Lamson, 16 Me. 224; Hodson *v.* Copeland, id. 314; Boston Glass Manufactory *v.* Langdon, 24 Pick. 52.

4 2 Kyd on Corp. 448.

5 11 Ed. IV. 4; 2 Kyd on Corp. 448; and see State *v.* Trustees of Vin. University, 5 Ind. 77.

right to hold over, inasmuch as they had no power of afterwards electing one;[1] and it was in consequence of these decisions that the statute of 11 Geo. I. ch. 4, § 1, was enacted, which provides, that no corporation shall be dissolved or disabled to elect such officer on that account.[2] These corporations have also been considered as dissolved by the loss of all or a majority of the members of any integral part, or select body, without which they cannot transact their municipal business, unless the power of restoration is vested in the subsisting parts of the corporation.[3] In some cases, where municipal corporations in this condition have been under the consideration of the court, they have been spoken of as *suspended* rather than *dissolved*, their remaining members, as still continuing in the enjoyment of certain rights, and the crown, as being able by the appointment of a new set of officers to revive their activity, without reincorporating them.[4] In the case of The King *v.* Pasmore,[5] however, where the Court of King's Bench appear to have reviewed and considered the authorities on this point with great attention, it was held, that in such case the corporation was dissolved *to certain purposes*, that the personal privileges of its members were extinguished, and its property and franchises vested in the crown; but that the franchises created by the crown did not merge in it or become extinguished, but might be regranted to a new body of men, or be renovated in the old.

§ 770. The principle, that a corporation is extinguished by the loss of one of its integral parts, appears to have been early applied to the case of a private corporation; and it is laid down by Rolle, that if a corporation consist of so many brothers, and so many sisters, and all the sisters die, the whole is dissolved, and all acts done, and all grants afterwards made by the brothers are void; because, says he, the brothers and sisters are integral parts of the corporation, *and it cannot subsist by halves.* But, he adds, if the king make a corporation consisting

---

1 Sawyer's Arg. Quo Warranto, 21; 21 Ed. 4, 14; Banbury Ca. 10 Mod. 346; Rex *v.* Pasmore, 3 T. R. 245; Rex *v.* Tregony, 8 Mod. 129; Lea *v.* Hernandez, 10 Texas, 137.

2 See 2 Kyd on Corp. 453, 454, 455; Willcock on Mun. Corp. 328, 329.

3 Colchester *v.* Seaber, 3 Burr. 1870, 1 W. Bl. 591; Rex *v.* Pasmore, 3 T. R. 241; Rex *v.* Miller, 6 T. R. 278; Rex *v.* Morris, 3 East, 216; 4 East, 26; Mayor of Colchester *v.* Brooke, 7 Q. B. 383-386.

4 Rex *v.* London, 1 Show. 278, 280; Colchester *v.* Seaber, 3 Burr. 1870, 1 W. Bl. 591; Scarborough *v.* Butler, 3 Lev. 237.

5 3 T. R. 241, 244; and see Strata Marcella, 9 Co. 25 b; 2 Kent. Com. 308, 309.

of twelve men, to continue forever in succession, and when one of them dies, that the rest may elect another in his place; though three or four of them die, yet all acts done by the remaining members are valid, because the members deceased did not constitute a distinct integral part.[1] From a reference to the cases which have been cited, it will be seen that the dissolution of a corporation from the loss of an integral part, whether the head officer or a select body, results from the incapacity of the corporation, in its imperfect state, to act, or to restore itself by a new election. Wherever, therefore, the corporation may restore itself by a new election, though until the new election the rights of the corporators may be suspended, yet they are not extinguished. Upon this principle the Court of Chancery in New York decided, that a *quasi* corporation of the owners or proprietors of certain drowned lands was not extinguished by their neglect to elect their commissioners, who were annual officers, at the time and place fixed by the act of incorporation; but that at the period of the next annual election, they might meet and choose commissioners for the ensuing year, whether the old commissions held over in the mean time, or not.[2] "No act," says the chancellor, "is required to be done by the commissioners, except to report their proceedings for the last year to the meeting; and if there were no commissioners, there could be no proceedings to report. The commissioners are not even required to preside at the meeting. There is nothing in the nature of the duties to be performed, which necessarily requires a continued succession of commissioners."[3] The mere insolvency of a corporation neither impairs its power to manage its affairs, nor converts its property into a trust fund for the benefit of its creditors.[4]

§ 771. Private corporations aggregate, as they are constituted in this country, are to be distinguished from the municipal corporations of England, in this, that they are not in general composed of integral

---

[1] 1 Rol. Abr. 514; Com. Dig. Franchises, G. 4; and see Rex *v.* Pasmore, 3 T. R. 241, 243; Phillips *v.* Wickham, 1 Paige, 596, where the case put by Rolle is recognized as law. See also, 11 Ed. IV. 4; 2 Kyd on Corp. 448; Slee *v.* Bloom, 19 Johns. 459; Canal Co. *v.* Railroad Co. 4 Gill & J. 1; Trustees of McIntire Poor School *v.* Zanesville Canal & Manuf. Co. 9 Ohio, 203; Penobscot Boom Co. *v.* Lamson, 16 Maine, 224; Hodson *v.* Copeland, id. 314.

[2] Phillips *v.* Wickham, 1 Paige, 597.

[3] Ibid. 597.

[4] Pondville Co. *v.* Clark, 25 Conn. 97.

parts. The stockholders compose the company; and the managers, or directors and officers, are their agents, necessary for the management of the affairs of the company, but not essential to its existence as such, and not forming an integral part. The corporation exists *per se* so far as is requisite to the maintenance of perpetual succession, and the holding and preserving of its franchises. The non-existence of the managers does not suppose the non-existence of the corporation. The latter may be dormant, its functions may be suspended for want of the means of action; but the capacity to restore its functionaries by means of new elections may remain. There is no reason why the power of action may not be revived by a new election of the managers and officers, competent to carry on the affairs of the corporation, conformably to the directions of its charter. When, therefore, the election of its managers, directors, or other officers, is by charter to be conducted solely by the stockholders, the charter or act of incorporation not requiring the managers, directors, or other officers to preside at, or to do any act in relation to the election, a failure to elect such officers on the charter day will not dissolve the corporation, but the election of officers may take place on the next charter day without any new legislative aid.[1]

§ 772. Another mode in which a corporation may be dissolved is, by the surrender of its franchise of being a corporation into the hands of the government. The power of a municipal corporation to surrender its corporate existence has, however, in England, been much questioned.[2] In the cases cited by those who deny the right, the question seems, in general, to have been upon the validity of the mode of surrender, or upon the terms of the instrument,[3] rather than upon the power of a cor-

---

[1] Rose *v.* Turnp. Co. 3 Watts, 46; Wier *v.* Bush, 4 Littell, 433; Blake *v.* Hinkle, 10 Yerg. 218; Nashville Bank *v.* Petway, 3 Humph. 524, 525; Lehigh Bridge Company *v.* Lehigh Coal Company, 4 Rawle, 9; Smith *v.* Natchez Steamboat Company, 2 How. Miss. 478; Phillips *v.* Wickham, 1 Paige, 590; Russell *v.* McClellan, 14 Pick. 63; Knowlton *v.* Ackley, 8 Cush. 94, 95; Cahill *v.* Kalamazoo Mutual Ins. Co. 2 Doug. Mich. 140, 141; Evarts *v.* Killingworth Manuf. Co. 20 Conn. 447; Commonwealth *v.* Cullen, 13 Penn. State, 133. And municipal corporations by the terms of their charter may be composed of the citizens, and not the mayor, aldermen, &c., the latter being, in such cases, merely officers of the corporation. Lowber *v.* Mayor, &c. of New York, 5 Abbott, Pr. 325, 329; Clarke *v.* City of Rochester, id. 107, 115.

[2] Treby's argument, *quo warranto*, 10, 11, 12, 13, &c.; 1 Kyd on Corp. 1, 9, 10; Rex *v.* Amery, 2 T. R. 531, 532, arguendo; Rex *v.* Grey, 8 Mod. 361.

[3] Case of Dean and Chapter of Norwich, 3 Co. 73, 2 Anders. 165; Hayward & Fulcher, W. Jones, 166, Palm. 491; Butler *v.* Palmer, 1 Salk. 191; Rex *v.* Bridgewater, 11 Mod. 291.

poration to dissolve itself in this way; and by far the better opinion is, that where the surrender is duly made and accepted, it is effectual to dissolve a municipal body.[1] In this country, the power of a private corporation, to dissolve itself by its own assent, seems to be assumed by nearly all the judges who touch upon the point;[2] although it would seem that, as there are two parties to the charter compact, the assent of both would be necessary to the abrogation of it.[3] The officers of a corporation cannot dissolve it, without the assent of the great body of the society;[4] and indeed a temporary injunction was granted, in a recent English case, on a motion made on behalf of a *minority* of the *stockholders* of a corporation, to restrain a majority of the stockholders from surrendering the charter of the corporation, with the view of obtaining a new charter for an object different from that for which the original charter had been granted.[5] But it is held in Massachusetts, that corporations of a private nature, established solely for trading or manufacturing purposes, may by a vote of a majority of their members, against the protest of a minority, wind up their affairs and close their business, if in the exercise of a sound discretion they deem it expedient so to do; that they may sell the whole of their property to a new corporation, taking payment in shares of the new corporation, to be distributed among those of the old stockholders who were willing to take them.[6] Sometimes, however, the act under which the society is formed prescribes the mode in which it may be dissolved; as, by the consent, in writing, of five sixths in value of the members, or by the concurrence

---

[1] Rex *v.* Miller, 6 T. R. 277; Rex *v.* Haythorne, 5 B. & C. 412, 425; Rex *v.* Grey, 8 Mod. 361; Butler *v.* Palmer, 1 Salk. 191; Newling *v.* Francis, 3 T. R. 196, 197; Rex *v.* Holland, 2 East, 72; Rex *v.* Osborne, 4 East, 335; 2 Kyd on Corp. 465, &c.; Willcock on Mun. Corp. 231, 232; 2 Kent, Com. 310, 311.

[2] Riddle *v.* Proprietors of the Locks and Canals on Merrimack River, 7 Mass. 185, per Parsons, C. J.; Hampshire *v.* Franklin, 16 Mass. 86, 87; McLaren *v.* Pennington, 1 Paige, 107, per Walworth, Chan.; Enfield Toll Bridge Co. *v.* Connecticut River Co. 7 Conn. 45, 46, 52; Slee *v.* Bloom, 19 Johns. 456; Canal Co. *v.* Railroad Co. 4 Gill & J. 1; Trustees of McIntire Poor School *v.* Zanesville Canal & Manuf. Co. 9 Ohio, 203; Penobscot Boom Co. *v.* Lamson, 16 Me. 224; Hodson *v.* Copeland, id. 314; Mumma *v.* Potomac Co. 8 Pet. 281; 2 Kent, Com. 310, 311. See also, Savage *v.* Walshe, 26 Ala. 619, 630; Mobile & Ohio R. R. Co. *v.* State, 29 Ala. 573; Attorney-General *v.* Clergy Society, 10 Rich. 604.

[3] Town *v.* Bank of River Raisin, 2 Doug. Mich. 530.

[4] Smith *v.* Smith, 3 Des. Ch. 557.

[5] Ward *v.* Society of Attorneys, 1 Collyer, 370; Kean *v.* Johnson, 1 Stock. 401; and see N. Orl. Jackson & Gr. N. R. R. Co. *v.* Harris, 27 Missis. 517.

[6] Treadwell *v.* Salisbury Manuf. Co. 7 Gray, 393.

of three fourths of the members present at a general meeting, in which case, it is hardly necessary to add, that a dissolution in either of the modes prescribed will be effected.[1] In England, the mode of surrender is by deed to the king; and as the king can take only by matter of record, the deed of surrender must be enrolled; it being no record without enrolment.[2] It seems that if a corporation, consisting of mayor, aldermen, and burgesses, surrender by the name of mayor, aldermen, and *capital* burgesses, the deed is void.[3] It is said, that when the effect of the surrender is to destroy the end for which the corporation or the corporate capacity was instituted, the corporation or the corporate capacity is itself destroyed.[4] Thus, Lord Coke informs us, that if there be a warden of a chapel, and the chapel and all the possessions are aliened, he ceases to be a corporation, since he cannot be warden of nothing; yet, that it is otherwise with a prebendary, who has *stallum in choro et vocem in capitulo*, and is prebendary, although he have no possessions. And if an abbot, or a prior and convent sold all their possessions, the corporation remain, "*if they were the chapter to a bishop.*"[5] Where a dean and chapter surrendered by deed enrolled "their church and all their possessions" to the king, it was held, that notwithstanding, the dean and chapter remained; for they were the bishop's chapter and council as long as the bishopric remained, and may be *without* possessions.[6] Upon the same ground it was determined, that a dean and chapter were not dissolved by a surrender "of all their possessions, rights, liberties, privileges, and hereditaments, which they had in right of their corporation."[7]

§ 773. In this country, where corporations are usually created by act of the legislature, no mode of surrender is pointed out by the books as *necessary*, differing from that in England, where corporations are usually created by charter from the crown. Sometimes, however, the charter provides the mode in which the whole or a portion of the powers of the corporation may be surrendered, and in such a case after the sur-

---

[1] *In re* Eclipse Mutual Benefit Association, 1 Kay, App. XXX. 23 Eng. L. & Eq. 309.

[2] Butler *v.* Palmer, 1 Salk. 191; Rex *v.* Grey, 8 Mod. 361; 2 Kyd on Corp. 465, 466.

[3] Rex *v.* Bridgewater, 11 Mod. 292.

[4] Kyd on Corp. 445.

[5] The case of the Dean and Chapter of Norwich, 3 Co. 75 a.

[6] Ibid.; s. c. 2 Anders. 120, 165.

[7] Hayward & Fulcher, W. Jones, 166, Palm. 491; and see Rex *v.* Grey, 8 Mod. 358.

render provided for, the corporation cannot exercise the powers surrendered without the sanction of the legislature.[1] It is said that a surrender, if accepted, will be sufficient,[2] and that it is of no avail until accepted.[3] But the mode in which it shall be made is nowhere specifically pointed out. Mere *non-user* of its franchises by a corporation is not a surrender; nor are courts warranted in inferring a surrender from an abandonment of the franchises in intention only, unless there be something in the act of incorporation to justify it.[4] But where a corporation lacks the express power to dissolve itself by the consent of the majority of its guardians, such consent, and consequently the dissolution of the corporation, may be inferred from the conduct of the parties and the disposition of the corporate property to other uses than those of the corporation.[5] An act of the legislature, repealing the act of incorporation, passed with the assent of the corporation, would undoubtedly be sufficient;[6] but it is not dissolved, at least, so that it can avoid its contract to employ an agent during the whole time it was established, by a vote of the majority of the members to dissolve it and close its concerns, and by transferring all its property to trustees, and giving notice to the executive department of the government, that the corporation claims no further interest in the charter.[7] And after a surrender of its charter has been accepted by the legislature, yet if the corporate existence of a bank is continued, for a limited time to enable it to close its affairs, it was held, in Maine, that

---

[1] Green *v.* Seymour, 3 Sandf. Ch. 285.

[2] 2 Kent, Com. 311; Enfield Toll Bridge Co. *v.* Connecticut River Co. 7 Conn. 45, 46; Revere *v.* Boston Copper Co. 15 Pick. 351.

[3] Boston Glass Manufactory *v.* Langdon, 24 Pick. 49; Harris *v.* Muskingum Manuf. Co. 4 Blackf. 268; Ward *v.* Sea Insurance Company, 7 Paige, 294; Campbell *v.* Mississippi Union Bank, 6 How. Miss. 681; Town *v.* Bank of River Raisin, 2 Doug. Mich. 530. See Norris *v.* Mayor, &c. of Smithville, 1 Swan, 164, in which it is said, that not only must the surrender be accepted by the government, *but a record made thereof.*

[4] Regents of the University of Maryland *v.* Williams, 9 Gill & J. 365.

[5] Woodbridge Union *v.* Colneis, 13 A. & E. 269.

[6] Riddle *v.* Proprietors of the Locks and Canals on Merrimack River, 7 Mass. 185, Parsons, C. J.; McLaren *v.* Pennington, 1 Paige, 107; Dartmouth College *v.* Woodward, 4 Wheat. 518; Canal Co. *v.* Railroad Co. 4 Gill & J. 1; Enfield Toll Bridge Co. *v.* Connecticut River Co. 7 Conn. 45; Revere *v.* Boston Copper Co. 15 Pick. 351; President & Selectmen of Port Gibson *v.* Moore, 13 Smedes & M. 157; Cooper *v.* Curtis, 30 Me. 488; and see Dyer, 282; Treby's Argument, Quo Warranto, 11; Leon. 234; 2 Kyd on Corp. 471, 472.

[7] Revere *v.* Boston Copper Co. 15 Pick. 351; Campbell *v.* Mississippi Union Bank, 6 How. Miss. 681. And see Portland Dry Dock & Ins. Co. *v.* Trustees of Portland, 12 B. Mon. 77.

the directors might legally elect a cashier, under the general banking law of that State.[1] A corporation, by dissolving and reorganizing itself, cannot avoid a debt due even to a stockholder who consented to such dissolution and reorganization, unless it be found that thereby the stockholder intended to surrender or discharge his claim against the corporation.[2] Still less can a banking corporation discharge itself of an obligation to pay a bonus for its charter to the State, by any act of its own, in which the State did not participate, such as discontinuing its discounts and assigning a portion of its assets.[3] It does not follow, it has been said, that a corporation is dissolved by the sale of its visible and tangible property for the payment of its debts, and by the temporary suspension of its business, so long as it has the moral and legal capacity to increase its subscriptions, call in more capital, and resume its business.[4] And where a manufacturing corporation became insolvent, and assigned its property for the payment of its debts, the instrument of assignment providing that the assignees might use the name of the corporation for the collection of debts, and that the corporation would perform any further acts which might be necessary to enable the assignees to execute the trust, and the corporation omitted for several years to hold meetings or to elect officers, the by-laws, however, providing that the officers, though elected for one year, should continue in office until others should be chosen in their places, it was held, that the corporation had not been dissolved, so that a suit could not be brought and maintained in its name.[5] A railroad corporation is not dissolved by sale upon execution of a part or of the whole of their road;[6] nor by a sale to another corporation, which sale is authorized by an act of the legislature;[7] nor is a corporation dissolved by one or two individuals becoming possessed, by purchase or otherwise, of all the shares of its stock, although this be accompanied by the omission of the corporation for two or more years to elect

---

1 Cooper *v.* Curtis, 30 Me. 488.

2 Longley *v.* Longley Stage Co. 23 Me. 39.

3 Bank of the United States *v.* Commonwealth, 17 Penn. State, 400.

4 Brinkerhoff *v.* Brown, 7 Johns. Ch. 217; Bradt *v.* Benedict, 17 N. Y. 93; Mickles *v.* Rochester City Bank, 11 Paige, 118; Barclay *v.* Tatman, 4 Edw. Ch. 123; State *v.* Bank of Maryland, 6 Gill & J. 205; Rollins *v.* Clay, 33 Maine, 132.

5 Boston Glass Manufactory *v.* Langdon, 24 Pick. 49; Brandon Iron Co. *v.* Gleason, 23 Vt. 228; and see State *v.* Commercial Bank of Manchester, 13 Smedes & M. 569; Town *v.* Bank of River Raisin, 2 Doug. Mich. 530.

6 State *v.* Rives, 5 Ired. 309. See Commonwealth *v.* Tenth Massachusetts Turnp. Corp. 5 Cush. 509.

7 Lauman *v.* Lebanon Valley R. Co. 30 Penn. State, 42.

officers, or to do any other corporate act.[1] The stock, if every member should die at the same moment, would be distributed under the Statute of Distributions, or according to the testaments of the deceased. The legal representatives of the deceased members would have authority by law to manage the corporation, and no dissolution would, in such case, take place; and if the shares should all centre in one man, and the forms of proceeding under the charter should require acts to be done by two or more, the owner could make sale of shares so as to conform to the letter of the rule.[2] But if a corporation suffer acts to be done which destroy the end and objects for which it was instituted, it is equivalent to a surrender of its rights. This doctrine has been maintained and applied by the courts of New York, in the construction of a statute of that State, concerning manufacturing corporations, which provides that for all debts due and owing by the company at the time of its dissolution the persons then composing such company shall be individually responsible to the extent of their respective shares or stock, and no further.[3] Under this statute, if a corporation, being indebted, suffer all its property to be sacrificed, and the trustees actually relinquish their trust, and omit the annual election, and do no one act manifesting an intention to resume their corporate functions, the courts may, *for the sake of the remedy against the individual members, and in favor of creditors*, presume a virtual surrender of the corporate rights, and a dissolution of the corporation.[4] And an election of trustees, made after the insolvency of the company, for the mere purpose of keeping it in existence, will not prevent such dissolution.[5] In these cases, the courts of New York did not decide that the companies had lost all their rights, but, that even if they

[1] Russell *v.* McClellan, 14 Pick. 63; Oakes *v.* Hill, id. 442; Spencer *v.* Campion, 9 Cowen, 536; Wilde *v.* Jenkins, 4 Paige, 481. See, however, Bellona Company's case, 3 Bland, 446.

[2] Russell *v.* McClellan, 24 Pick. 63.

[3] R. L. (N. Y.), 247.

[4] Slee *v.* Bloom, 19 Johns. 456; commented on in 2 Kent, Com. 311, 312; Penniman *v.* Briggs, 1 Hopkins, 300, 8 Cowen, 387.

[5] Penniman *v.* Briggs, 1 Hopkins, 300, 8 Cowen, 387. Whether mere insolvency would dissolve a corporation under this statute, *query*, id. per Spencer, senator. Under the act of New York, providing for the dissolution of insurance companies, the Court of Chancery of that State exercise a discretion, as to decreeing a dissolution, in the same manner that the legislature would in such a case. It is not bound to decree a dissolution, simply because a majority of the directors and stockholders request it, though such a request would be deemed presumptive evidence that the interest of the stockholders would be promoted by a dissolution. Matter of Niagara Ins. Co. 1 Paige, 258.

had a right to reorganize themselves, the case had happened in which, with regard to their creditors, they were dissolved.[1]

§ 774. A corporation may also be dissolved, by a forfeiture of its charter judicially ascertained and declared. It was once doubted, whether the *being* of a corporation could be forfeited by a misapplication of the powers intrusted to it; but it is now well settled, that it is a tacit condition of a grant of incorporation, that the grantees shall act up to the end or design for which they were incorporated; and hence through neglect or abuse of its franchises, a corporation may forfeit its charter as for condition broken, or for a breach of trust.[2] Even a clause in the charter of a bank, that the corporation shall not be dissolved before the time specified in the charter, *unless all debts are paid*, does not protect the corporation from dissolution by *quo warranto*, for a violation of the charter; such clause being merely intended to prevent the corporation from dissolving itself before the expiration of the charter, without paying its debts.[3] A corporation cannot forfeit its charter before it has begun to exist. Fraud and collusion between the State commissioners and the original subscribers, as to opening the books of sub-

---

[1] Slee *v.* Bloom, 19 Johns. 475, 476, per Spencer, J.; Penniman *v.* Briggs, 1 Hopkins, 305, per Sandford, Ch.; 2 Kent, Com. 311, 312; and see Mickles *v.* Rochester City Bank, 11 Paige, 118; Jackson Marine Ins. Co., in the matter of, 4 Sandf. Ch. 559, as to remedy under section 38, 2 R. L. 463, against corporations, for judgment of dissolution, in case of certain acts of *non-user*.

[2] Tailors of Ipswich, 1 Roll. 5; Rex *v.* Grosvenor, 7 Mod. 199; Sir James Smith's case, 4 Mod. 55, 58, 12 Mod. 17, 18, Skin. 311, 1 Show. 278, 280; Rex *v.* Saunders, 3 East, 119; Case of City of London, cited 2 Kyd on Corp. 474, &c.; Rex *v.* Amery, 2 T. R. 515; Rex *v.* Pasmore, 3 T. R. 246, per Buller, J.; Eastern Archipelago Co. *v.* Regina, 2 Ellis & B. 857, 22 Eng. L. & Eq. 328, 337, 338; s. c. 1 Ellis & B. 310, 18 Eng. L. & Eq. 167; Terrett *v.* Taylor, 9 Cranch, 51, 52, per Story, J.; Dartmouth College *v.* Woodward, 4 Wheat. 658, 659; Commonwealth *v.* F. & M. Ins. Co. 5 Mass. 230; People *v.* Bank of Niagara, 6 Cowen, 196; People *v.* Washington & Warren Bank. id. 211; People *v.* Bank of Hudson, id. 217; Lehigh Bridge Co. *v.* Lehigh Coal Co. 4 Rawle, 9; State Bank *v.* State, 1 Blackf. 279; Canal Co. *v.* Railroad Co. 4 Gill & J. 1; Trustees of McIntire Poor School *v.* Zanesville Canal & Manufacturing Co. 9 Ohio, 203; Penobscot Boom Corporation *v.* Lamson, 16 Me. 224; Hodson *v.* Copeland, id. 314; Atchafalaya Bank *v.* Dawson, 13 La. 497; People *v.* Manhattan Co. 9 Wend. 351; Charles River Bridge *v.* Warren Bridge, 7 Pick. 371; All Saints Church *v.* Lovett, 1 Hall, 198; John *v.* Farmers & Mechanics Bank of Indiana, 2 Blackf. 367; Hamtranck *v.* Bank of Edwardsville, 2 Misso. 169; Day *v.* Stetson, 8 Greenl. 372; State *v.* New Orleans Gaslight & Banking Co. 2 Rob. La. 529; Commonwealth *v.* Commercial Bank of Pa. 28 Penn. State, 383; 1 Bl. Com. 485; 2 Kyd on Corp. 474, &c.; Willcock on Mun. Corp. 334. And see authorities below.

[3] State Bank *v.* State, 1 Blackf. 270.

scription to the capital stock of a bank, whereby the directions given by the State to its own agents in regard to subscriptions were violated, is no cause of forfeiture.[1] It is said that all franchises may be lost by non-user or neglect; and, as the strongest case of neglect, the case put is, where the parties are called upon in a court of justice to state their right, and neglect or refuse to do it.[2] It seems, that the mere omission by a corporation to exercise its powers does not, of itself, disconnected with any acts, work a forfeiture of the charter.[3] Thus, the failure of the directors of a bank to sell the stock of subscribers who have not paid their calls, as empowered to do by a provision of the charter, is no more a cause of forfeiture in itself than their omission to sue such subscribers for their unpaid calls, to which suit the charter remedy is merely cumulative.[4] *A fortiori*, an insurance company will not lose its charter, through non-user, by refusing to insure against extra-hazardous risk;[5] although it may, by discontinuing all its ordinary business for a year, except that of settling up its concerns.[6] Nor, in Ohio, does the mere suspension of specie payments by a bank, where a penalty of twelve per cent. damages therefor is given to the holder of its notes both by the general law and its charter, work a forfeiture of the charter of a bank;[7] nor does the contracting by a bank to take a higher rate of interest than six per cent. where such contract is illegal.[8] A suspension of specie payments by a bank may, however, be carried so far as to afford evidence of entire misuser of powers, and thus extinguish its chartered privileges;[9] and strictly no bank can wilfully refuse to pay specie for

---

[1] Commercial Bank of Natchez *v.* State of Mississippi, 6 Smedes & M. 613, 614; Minor *v.* Merchants Bank of Alexandria, 1 Pet. 46. And see People *v.* Oakland County Bank, 1 Doug. Mich. 285, 286.

[2] Rex *v.* Amery, 5 T. R. 567, per Ashurst, J.

[3] Attorney-General *v.* Bank of Niagara, 1 Hopkins, 316, per Sandford, Ch.; Society, &c. *v.* Morris Canal & Banking Co. per Williamson, Ch., cited Halst. Dig. 93; Regents of the University of Maryland *v.* Williams, 9 Gill & J. 365.

[4] Commercial Bank of Natchez *v.* State of Mississippi, 6 Smedes & M. 615, 616.

[5] State *v.* Urbana & Champaign Mutual Ins. Co. 14 Ohio, 6.

[6] Jackson Marine Ins. Co., In the matter of, 4 Sandf. Ch. 550.

[7] State *v.* Commercial Bank, 10 Ohio, 535. And in New York, it has been held that, where the suspension of specie payments by banks is general and nearly universal, the mere fact of suspension by a bank is not proof of insolvency. Livingston *v.* Bank of New York, 26 Barb. 304.

[8] Ibid. In Pennsylvania, however, it was held, that taking higher interest than the charter permitted, was sufficient cause to work a forfeiture. Commonwealth *v.* Commercial Bank of Penn. 28 Penn. State, 383, 391.

[9] Ibid. The penalty it should seem can make no difference. Commercial Bank of Natchez *v.* State of Mississippi, 6 Smedes & M. 617–624.

a single day without exposing its charter to forfeiture.[1] The establishment by a bank, located in one county, of an agency in another, for the purpose of receiving deposits and buying and selling exchange, is held in Michigan a cause of forfeiture; though such an agency to redeem bills, it seems, would not be.[2] Where a company which had been incorporated for the purpose of making marine insurances, and of lending money on bottomry and respondentia securities, suspended business for more than a year, under a formal resolution of the board of directors to that effect, this was held, in New York, a sufficient ground for the chancellor to decree the forfeiture of the charter and the dissolution of the corporation, at the instance of a creditor or stockholder, under the provisions of the revised statutes of that State.[3]

§ 775. The withdrawing of stock under the form of loans on private security, by a bank, with intent to reduce the effective capital of the institution below the amount required by the charter, may be good cause of forfeiture; although it is discretionary with the court, on proceedings to procure a forfeiture of the charter for such cause, whether it will declare the charter forfeited; and it will not do so, if no existing danger to the community require it.[4] The contracting of debts, or issuing of bills to a larger amount than the charter allows, or issuing with a fraudulent intention more paper than the bank can redeem, or embezzling large sums deposited for safe keeping, or making large dividends of profits, while it refuses to pay specie for its bills, all subject a bank to the forfeiture of its charter.[5] The establishment by a bank located by its charter in one county, of an agency in another county, where it receives deposits and buys and sells exchange, is a violation of its charter, and was held in Michigan, a good cause of forfeiture, although only

---

[1] State *v.* New Orleans Gas-light & Banking Co. 2 Rob. La. 529; Attorney-General *v.* Bank of Michigan, Harrington, Ch. Mich. 315; Com. Bank of Natchez *v.* State of Mississippi, 6 Smedes & M. 617–624; Planters Bank *v.* State, 7 Smedes & M. 163; State *v.* Bank of South Carolina, 1 Speers, 441.

[2] People *v.* Oakland County Bank, 1 Doug. Mich. 282.

[3] Ward *v.* Sea Insurance Company, 7 Paige, 294; Jackson Marine Ins. Co., In the matter of, 4 Sandf. Ch. 559. In Indiana if a judgment debt of any other than a banking corporation remains unpaid for one year, and the execution thereon is not stayed by appeal, or supersedeas, the circuit court of the proper county shall have power to declare the franchise forfeited. 1 R. St. p. 242; Aurora & Lau. T. Co. *v.* Holthouse, 7 Ind. 59.

[4] State *v.* Essex Bank, 8 Vt. 489.

[5] State Bank *v.* State, 1 Blackf. 270. And see Bank Commissioners *v.* Rhode Island Central Bank, 5 R. I. 12.

punished with fine and costs, under the discretion vested in the court in such cases.[1] The loaning by a bank to its directors or any of them, or upon paper upon which they are responsible, to an amount exceeding in the aggregate one third of the capital of the bank, contrary to a statute of New York, was held by the chancellor of that State sufficient to authorize him, at the instance of the bank commissioners, to grant an injunction against the bank, to appoint a receiver to wind up its affairs, and to decree its dissolution. For this purpose the acts of the officers were considered the acts of the bank, and their ignorance or neglect form no excuse for a violation of law.[2] At the same time it should be observed, that the mere act of the cashier of a bank, contrary to the express instructions of the directors, and without their knowledge and acquiescence, in receiving in payment for stock other than gold and silver and the notes of specie-paying banks, and thereby violating a law of the State, will not work a forfeiture of the charter.[3] The insolvency of a bank, and an assignment by it of so much of its property to trustees for the payment of its debts, as to prevent it from resuming banking business, the purpose for which the bank was instituted being thus defeated, though not, as we have seen, *per se* a dissolution, is good cause of forfeiture on *quo warranto*.[4] In such case, the assignment may be alleged by the attorney-general in general terms, without stating how much was assigned, or how much, or what value, was sufficient to disenable the bank from resuming its operations.[5] And where the replication in such case alleged, that the bank became insolvent by the fraud, neglect, or mismanagement of its officers or agents, or some of them, and that it stopped payment and discontinued its banking operations for several years; a rejoinder, admitting these facts, but averring that the bank resumed payment and has continued it ever since, was held to be sufficient.[6]

§ 776. In general, to work a forfeiture, there must be something

---

1 People *v.* Oakland County Bank, 1 Doug. Mich. 288–291; Attorney-General *v.* Oakland County Bank, 1 Walker, Mich. 90.

2 Bank Commissioners *v.* Banks of Buffalo, 6 Paige, 497. And see Bank Commissioners *v.* Rhode Island Central Bank, 5 R. I. 12.

3 State of Mississippi *v.* Commercial Bank of Manchester, 6 Smedes & M. 237, 238.

4 People *v.* Hudson Bank, 6 Cowen, 217; People *v.* Niagara Bank, id. 196. And see Bank Commissioners *v.* Bank of Brest, Harrington, Ch. Mich. 106, 111, 112; State *v.* Commercial Bank of Manchester, 13 Smedes & M. 569; Carey *v.* Greene, 7 Ga. 79.

5 Ibid.

6 Ibid.

wrong, arising from *wilful abuse* or improper *neglect*, something more than *accidental negligence*, *excess of power*, or *mistake* in the mode of exercising an acknowledged power. A single act of *abuser*, or *wilful non-feasance*, in a corporation, may be insisted on as a ground of total forfeiture; but a specific act of *nonfeasance*, not committed *wilfully* or *negligently*, not producing nor having a tendency to produce mischievous consequences to any one, and not being contrary to any particular requisition of the charter, will not work a forfeiture.[1] Slight deviations from the provisions of a charter would not necessarily be either an abuse or a misuser of it and ground for its annulment, although it would be competent, by apt words, to make the continuance of the charter conditional upon the strict and literal performance of them.[2] The duties assigned by an act of incorporation are conditions annexed to the grant of the franchises conferred. Hence non-compliance with the requirements of an act incorporating a turnpike company, as to the construction of the road, is, *per se*, a *misuser*, forfeiting the privileges and franchises of the company.[3] Indeed, the non-perforance of a particular act required by the charter, whether for the benefit of an individual or the State is, or may be, a cause of forfeiture, although not specially declared to be such by the charter itself.[4] The non-payment of the portion of the capital required by the charter for the beginning of business, and the sending in by the directors of a false certificate that it was paid, and thereupon commencing business, is, as a breach of the conditions of the charter, or an abuse of its franchises, cause of forfeiture.[5] A *substantial* performance of conditions, however, is all that is required, whether they be conditions *precedent* or *subsequent*.[6] If a railroad corporation should suffer their railroad to be sold on execution,

---

[1] People *v.* Bristol & Rensselaerville Turnpike Road, 23 Wend. 222, Cowen, J.; Bank Commissioners *v.* Bank of Buffalo, 6 Paige, 497; Ward *v.* Sea Insurance Company, 7 Paige, 294; Paschall *v.* Whitsett, 11 Ala. 472; State *v.* Merchants Ins. Co. 8 Humph. 235; Board of Commissioners for the Frederick Female Seminary, 9 Gill, 379; State *v.* Col. & Hampsh. Pl. Co. 2 Sneed, 254.

[2] Eastern Archipelago Co. *v.* Regina, per Martin, B., 2 Ellis & B. 857, 22 Eng. L. & Eq. 338.

[3] People *v.* Kingston & Middlesex Turnp. Road Co. 23 Wend. 193; and see Lumbard *v.* Stearns, 4 Cush. 60, 62.

[4] Attorney-General *v.* Petersburg & Roanoke Railroad Co. 6 Ired. 456.

[5] Eastern Archipelago Co. *v.* Regina, 2 Ellis & B. 857, 22 Eng. Law & Eq. 328, 18 Eng. Law & Eq. 167.

[6] People *v.* Thompson, 21 Wend. 235; s. c. in error, Thompson *v.* People, 23 id. 537; Commonwealth *v.* Allegh. Br. Co. 20 Penn. State, 185.

and broken up, in whole or in part, it would be a cause of forfeiture which might be insisted on by the State;[1] and sometimes there is express statute provision limiting a time, disuse of the corporate privileges, during which, amounts of itself to a forfeiture.[2] Long-continued and wilful neglect, on the part of a turnpike company, to repair their road, is undoubtedly cause of forfeiture;[3] but where a single instance of neglect in this respect is relied upon, *wilful* negligence must be averred and proved.[4] If a bridge, necessary to render the road passable, be carried away by a sudden flood, a bridge company must rebuild it within a reasonable time, or they will forfeit their charter.[5] The neglect of such a company to give a bond for the completion of their bridge within a limited time, as required by the charter, is not, it seems, of itself a cause of forfeiture.[6] The favorable report of commissioners to view a turnpike-road, under a general turnpike act, and the subsequent license of the governor to erect turnpike gates for the collection of tolls, are not a bar to an information in the nature of *quo warranto*, charging a non-compliance with the act of incorporation in the original construction of the road.[7] An abuse in a particular department of an entire franchise is cause of forfeiture of the whole franchise; but where a particular franchise is added to a corporation subsequently to its creation, such a franchise may be forfeited, and the residue remain.[8]

§ 777. A cause of forfeiture cannot be taken advantage of, or enforced against a corporation, collaterally or incidentally, or in any other mode than by a direct proceeding for that purpose against the corporation, so that it may have an opportunity to answer. And the government creating the corporation can alone institute such a proceeding; since it may waive a broken condition of a compact made with it, as well as an individual.[9] An act of the legislature will not be deemed

---

[1] State *v.* Rives, 5 Ired. 309.

[2] Ibid.

[3] State *v.* Royalton & Woodstock Turnp. Co. 11 Vt. 431; People *v.* Hillsdale & Chatham Turnpike Co. 23 Wend. 254.

[4] Ibid.

[5] People *v.* Hillsdale & Chatham Turnp. Co. 23 Wend. 254.

[6] Enfield Toll Bridge *v.* Connecticut River Co. 7 Conn. 28.

[7] Tar River Navigation Co. *v.* Neal, 3 Hawks, 520; People *v.* Kingston & Middlesex Turnp. Road Co. 23 Wend. 193, Cowen, dissenting.

[8] People *v.* Bristol & Rensselaerville Turnp. Road, 23 Wend. 222, Cowen, J.

[9] Rex *v.* Stevenson, Yelv. 190; Rex *v.* Carmarthen, 1 W. Bl. 187, 2 Burr. 869; Rex *v.*

a waiver of conditions, and a confirmation of the charter, unless the intent of the legislature in that respect be expressly declared, or is necessarily to be implied from the provisions of the act.[1] The appointment, by the governor and senate, of a director in a corporation, under a reserved power of appointment in the charter, made pending an information in the nature of a *quo warranto* for its dissolution, is no waiver of the forfeiture incurred by a previous misuser.[2] Where the banks of a State had suspended specie payments, and an act was passed requiring them to pay specie on their bills of a certain denomination, on or before a day named in the act, and on their bills of a certain other denomination, on or before another day named in the act, this was held in effect to amount to a waiver on the part of the State, of the right to

---

Amery, 2 T. R. 515; Rex *v.* Pasmore, 3 T. R. 244; Terrett *v.* Taylor, 9 Cranch, 51; People of Vermont *v.* Society for Propagating the Gospel, 1 Paine, C. C. 653; Silver Lake Bank *v.* North, 4 Johns. Ch. 379, 381; Slee *v.* Bloom, 5 Johns. Ch. 366, 380, 19 Johns. 456; Vernon Society *v.* Hills, 6 Cowen, 23; Thompson *v.* New York & Harlem Railroad Co. 3 Sandf. Ch. 652, 653; Caryl *v.* McElrath, 3 Sandf. 176; President, &c. of the Kishacoquillas & Centre Turnp. Road Co. *v.* M'Conaby, 16 S. & R. 145, per Duncan, J.; Commonwealth *v.* F. & M. Ins. Co. 5 Mass. 230; Chester Glass Co. *v.* Dewey, 16 Mass. 94; Boston Glass Manufactory *v.* Langdon, 24 Pick. 52, 53; Proprietors of Quincy Canal *v.* Newcomb, 7 Met. 276; Knowlton *v.* Ackley, 8 Cush. 95; Society, &c. *v.* Morris Canal & Banking Co., per Williamson, Ch., cited Halst. Dig. 93; Enfield Toll Bridge Co. *v.* Connecticut River Co. 7 Conn. 46; Pearce *v.* Olney, 20 Conn. 544; Connecticut & Passumpsic Railroad Co. *v.* Bailey, 24 Vt. 465; The Banks *v.* Poitiaux, 3 Rand. 142, per Green, J.; Crump *v.* U. S. Mining Co. 7 Gratt. 352; Canal Co. *v.* Railroad Co. 4 Gill & J. 1; Planters Bank *v.* Bank of Alexandria, 10 Gill & J. 346; Regents of the University of Maryland *v.* Williams, 9 Gill & J. 365; Hamilton *v.* Annapolis & Elkridge Railroad Co. 1 Md. Ch. Dec. 107; Atchafalaya Bank *v.* Dawson, 13 La. 497; State *v.* New Orleans Gas Light & Banking Co. 2 Rob. La. 529; Webb *v.* Moler, 8 Ohio, 548; Receivers of Bank of Cincinnati *v.* Renick, 15 id. 322; Johnson *v.* Bentley, 16 id. 97; Myers *v.* Manhattan Bank, 20 Ohio, 283; Bank of Gallipolis *v.* Trimble, 6 B. Mon. 599; Harrison *v.* Lexington & Frankfort Railroad Co. 9 B. Mon. 476; Bank of Missouri *v.* Merchants Bank of Baltimore, 10 Misso. 123; Young *v.* Harrison, 6 Ga. 130; Selma & Tennessee Railroad Company *v.* Tipton, 5 Ala. 805, 806; Duke *v.* Cahawba Nav. Co. 16 Ala. 372; State *v.* Centreville Bridge Co. 18 Ala. 678; Smith *v.* Plank Road Co. 30 Ala. 650; Bayless *v.* Orne, Freem. Miss. 173; Smith *v.* Mississippi & Alabama Railroad Co. 6 Smedes & M. 179; Grand Gulf Bank *v.* Archer, 8 Smedes & M. 151; State *v.* Mayor & Aldermen of Savannah, R. M. Charlt. 342; Buncombe Turnp. Co. *v.* McCarson, 1 Dev. & B. 306; John *v.* Farmers & Mechanics Bank, 2 Blackf. 367; Peirce *v.* Somersworth, 10 N. H. 375, Parker, C. J.; State *v.* Fourth New Hampshire Turnp. 15 N. H. 162; Cahill *v.* Kalamazoo Mutual Ins. Co. 2 Doug. Mich. 141; Wilmans *v.* Bank of Illinois, 1 Gilman, 667; Bohannon *v.* Binns, 31 Missis. 355; Clev. P. & Ashtab. R. R. Co. *v.* City of Erie, 27 Penn. State, 380, 387; Commonwealth *v.* Allegh. Br. Co. 20 Penn. State, 185, 190; 2 Kent, Com. 313.

[1] People *v.* Kingston & Middlesex Turnpike Co. 23 Wend. 193.

[2] People *v.* Phœnix Bank, 24 Wend. 431.

enforce a forfeiture for the previous suspension.[1] And though a forfeiture incurred by a corporation by non-performance of a condition in its charter may be waived by the legislature, as, by subsequent legislative acts recognizing the continued existence of the corporation, yet this doctrine does not apply, if by the terms of the charter, the estate or franchise absolutely determines on failure to perform the condition.[2] But where the terms of a charter are, that the corporation shall be dissolved on non-performance of a condition, the mere failure to perform is not *ipso facto* a dissolution, but judicial proceedings and a judgment of ouster must be had, in order to effect a dissolution.[3] The proceeding to dissolve a corporation must be instituted in the country where the corporation is located; for neither the courts nor legislatures of this country can adjudge a forfeiture of the property or franchises of a foreign corporation.[4] The forfeiture of a charter can be enforced in a court of law only; for though a court of chancery may hold trustees of a corporation accountable for abuse of trust, it cannot divest it of its corporate character and capacity;[5] unless indeed, as is the case in New York and some other States, it be specially empowered by statute.[6]

---

1 Commercial Bank of Natchez *v.* State of Mississippi, 6 Smedes & M. 622, 623; and see State *v.* Bank of Charleston, 2 McMullan, 439; Lumpkin *v.* Jones, 1 Kelly, 30; State *v.* Fourth New Hampshire Turnp. 15 N. H. 162.

2 People *v.* Manhattan Co. 9 Wend. 351; Commonwealth *v.* Union Fire & Marine Ins. Co. 5 Mass. 232; Proprietors of Quincy Canal *v.* Newcomb, 7 Met. 277. In the matter of Highway, 2 N. J. 293; see, however, People *v.* Oakland County Bank, 1 Doug. Mich. 282.

3 People *v.* Manhattan Co. 9 Wend. 351; Bank of Niagara *v.* Johnson, 8 Wend. 645; Bear Camp River Co. *v.* Woodman, 2 Greenl. 404. Under 38th sect. of Rev. Statutes of New York, although a corporation may be deemed to have surrendered its charter by mere *non-user*, yet it is not actually dissolved until its dissolution is actually declared in some proceeding instituted for that purpose. Mickles *v.* Rochester City Bank, 11 Paige, 118; and see People *v.* Hillsdale Turnpike Co. 23 Wend. 254.

4 Society, &c. *v.* New Haven, 8 Wheat. 483, 484; People of Vermont *v.* Society for Propagating the Gospel, 1 Paine, C. C. 653.

5 The King *v.* Whitwell, 5 T. R. 85; Attorney-General *v.* Reynolds, 1 Eq. Cas. Abr. 131, pl. 10; 3 Johns. 134, per Van Ness, J.; Slee *v.* Bloom, 5 Johns. Ch. 380; Attorney-General *v.* Utica Ins. Co. 2 Johns. Ch. 376, 378, 388; Attorney-General *v.* Earl of Clarendon, 17 Ves. 491; Bayless *v.* Orne, 1 Freem. Miss. 173; Fountain Ferry Turnp. Road Co. *v.* Jewell, 8 B. Mon. 142; State *v.* Merchants Ins. & Trust. Co. 8 Humph. 252.

6 L. (N. Y.), sec. 40, ch. 146, and sec. 44, ch. 148; and sec. 48, ch. 325. In Tennessee this power is given to the Court of Chancery, by stat. of 1846, ch. 55. State *v.* Merchants Ins. & Trust Co. 8 Humph. 253, 254, 255. The English winding-up acts, and the numerous statutes of the different States of this union, of the same general nature, are only incidentally noticed in this treatise. They, with the decisions under them, form a body of law of local interest merely, and illustrate rather the doctrines of equity in the distribu-

§ 778. The mode of proceeding against a corporation, to enforce a repeal of the charter or a dissolution of the body, for cause of forfeiture, is by *scire facias*, or an information in the nature of a *quo warranto*. "A *scire facias*," says Mr. Justice Ashurst, "is proper where there is a legal existing body, capable of acting, but who have been guilty of an abuse of the power intrusted to them;[1] and a *quo warranto* is necessary where there is a body corporate *de facto*, who take upon themselves to act as a body corporate, but from some defect in their constitution, cannot legally exercise the power they affect to use."[2] It would seem, however, that an information in the nature of *quo warranto* would lie against a legally existing corporation for an abuse of its franchises, as well as a writ of *scire facias*.[3] Where a charter has been granted upon an erroneous consideration, or been fraudulently obtained, or is otherwise voidable, either in whole or part, it may be repealed entirely, or as to the voidable part only, without affecting the remainder by proceedings in *scire facias*. If, however, the charter is absolutely void, this process is unnecessary; for a void charter can afford no justification to any one acting under it.[4] The process seems to be unnecessary, where the corporation is absolutely dissolved, by the loss of an integral part.[5] A charter will not be avoided merely because it refers to a preceding charter as valid, which in fact was void, unless it be founded on such charter;[6] nor if the facts stated by the grantee be true, though the king be mistaken in his inference of the law.[7] And it is said, that if a corporate election be not made as the letters-patent appoint, these may be repealed by *scire facias;* for all franchises are

---

tion of insolvent estates, as modified by statute in their application to corporations, than the general law peculiar to these bodies.

1 Rex *v*. Pasmore, 3 T. R. 244; and see Smith's case, 4 Mod. 57; Rex *v*. Wynne, 2 Barnard. 391.

2 Rex *v*. Pasmore, 3 T. R. 244, 245; Regents of the University of Maryland *v*. Williams, 9 Gill & J. 365; and see Chap. XXI.

3 1 Bl. Com. 485; and see Case of City of London, cited 2 Kyd on Corp. 474–486, 487; People *v*. Bank of Niagara, 6 Cowen, 196; People *v*. Bank of Hudson, id. 217; People *v*. Washington & Warren Bank, id. 211.

4 Sackville College cas. T. Ray. 178; Butler's case, 2 Vent. 344; Rex *v*. Pasmore, 3 T. R. 244; 2 Chest. case, 556; President, &c. of the Kishacoquillas & Centre Turnp. Road Co. *v*. M'Conaby, 16 S. & R. 145; and see Earl of Rutland's case, 8 Co. 55; Rex *v*. Kemp, 12 Mod. 78.

5 Canal Co. *v*. Railroad Co. 4 Gill & J. 1.

6 Rex *v*. Haythorne, 5 B. & C. 426.

7 Rex *v*. Pasmore, 3 T. R. 249, per Grose, J.

granted on condition that they shall be duly executed according to the grant.[1] Where a demurrer was put into a writ of *scire facias*, it was held, that its legal effect was the same as that of demurrer to the declaration; for a declaration upon a *scire facias* is no more than a copy of the writ.[2] And if one demurs to the whole writ or declaration in a *scire facias*, in which several breaches of the conditions of a grant are assigned, some sufficient, and some not, judgment must go against him; for he should have demurred only to such as are insufficient.[3] And this rule applies equally to a single count, part of which is good and part bad, when the matters are divisible in their nature.[4]

§ 778 *a*. The last mode in which a corporation may be dissolved, is, by expiry of the period of its duration, limited by its charter or by general law; upon dissolution in which mode, all the consequences of dissolution in any other mode, such as forfeiture of property, extinguishment of debts, abatement of suits,[5] &c., ensue, unless, as is usual, they are provided against.[6] Upon such a dissolution, without previous provision, it is beyond the power of the legislature, by renewing the charter, to revive the debts and liabilities owing to the corporation.[7] The corporation may, however, just before the expiration of its corporate existence, assign to a trustee, for the use of the stockholders, the corporate property, or indorse, through the cashier, its unpaid paper for such use; and the trustee may sue, in his own name, as indorsee of such paper, after the expiry of the charter.[8] Nor does the expiry of a charter, pending a bill in chancery for the collection of a debt due to it, affect the right to the debt which was previously vested in others — as in the superintendent and board of common-school commissioners of a State.[9] If a corporation be created for a term of years only, a grant to it purporting to convey a fee, will not be construed to convey only a term of years; but the corporation will have a fee-simple for the purposes of alienation,

---

1 London *v.* Vanacre, 12 Mod. 271, per Holt, C. J., 1 Ld. Raym. 499.

2 People of Vermont *v.* Society for Propagating the Gospel, 1 Paine, C. C. 660.

3 Ibid.

4 Ibid.

5 See, however, Lindell *v.* Benton, 6 Misso. 361.

6 Bank of Mississippi *v.* Wrenn, 3 Smedes & M. 791; Commercial Bank *v.* Lockwood, 2 Harring. Del. 8.

7 Bank *v.* Lockwood, 2 Harring. Del. 8.

8 Cooper *v.* Curtis, 30 Me. 488.

9 Ingraham *v.* Terry, 11 Humph. 572.

although, like all other corporations, a determinable fee only, subject upon dissolution to reverter to the grantor, or his heirs for the purposes of enjoyment.[1] If the original act of incorporation is continued in force "until" a day named, the word "until" is exclusive in its meaning unless something in the context shows that it was the intention of the legislature to give it a different and an inclusive sense.[2]

§ 779. At common law, upon the civil death of a corporation, all its real estate remaining unsold, reverts to the grantor and his heirs; for the reversion, in such an event, is a condition annexed by the law, inasmuch as the cause of the grant has failed.[3] The personal estate, in England, vests in the king; and in our own country, in the people or State, as succeeding to this right and prerogative of the crown.[4] The debts due to and from it are totally extinguished; so that neither the members nor directors of the corporation can recover, or be charged with them in their natural capacities;[5] according to that maxim of the civil law, "*si quid universitati debetur, singulis non debetur; nec, quod debet universitas, singuli debent.*"[6] Upon dissolution of a corporation in any mode, it follows therefore that all suits pending for or against it, abate,[7] and where a judgment has been recovered against a bank, after its charter had been revoked — a stockholder, whose property has been levied upon by an execution thereon, may maintain a writ of error to reverse it.[8] The

---

1 Nicoll *v.* New York & Erie Railroad Company, 12 Barb. 460.

2 People *v.* Walker, 17 N. Y. 502.

3 Co. Lit. 13 b, 102 b; Knight *v.* Wells, 1 Lut. 519; Edmunds *v.* Brown 1 Lev. 237; Attorney-General *v.* Lord Gower, 9 Mod. 226; Pollex. Arg. Quo Warrant. 112; Colchester *v.* Seaber, 3 Burr. 1868, arg.; Rex *v.* Pasmore, 3 T. R. 199; State Bank *v.* State, 1 Blackf. 267; White *v.* Campbell, 5 Humph. 38; Bingham *v.* Weiderwax, 1 Comst. 509; 4 Bl. Com. 484; 2 Kyd on Corp. 516; 2 Kent, Com. 307; see Chap. V.

4 Ibid. Held in Pennsylvania, that when a charter is constitutionally repealed, the franchises are resumed to the State, and a railroad belonging to the corporation remains what it always was, public property. Erie & N. E. R. R. *v.* Casey, 26 Penn. State, 287.

5 Edmunds *v.* Brown, 1 Lev. 237; Rex *v.* Pasmore, 3 T. R. 241, 242; Colchester *v.* Seaber, 3 Burr. 1866; Bank of Mississippi *v.* Wrenn, 3 Smedes & M. 791; Commercial Bank of Natchez *v.* Chambers, 8 Smedes & M. 9; President and Selectmen of Port Gibson *v.* Moore, 13 Smedes & M. 157; Miami Exporting Co. *v.* Gano, 13 Ohio, 269; Renick *v.* Bank of West Union, id. 298; White *v.* Campbell, 5 Humph. 38; Hightower *v.* Thornton, 8 Ga. 486; 1 Bl. Com. 484; 2 Kent, Com. 307.

6 Ff. 3, 4, 7.

7 Greely *v.* Smith, 3 Story, 657; Merrill *v.* Suffolk Bank, 31 Maine, 17, 57; Ingraham *v.* Terry, 11 Humph. 572; Saltmarsh *v.* Planters & Merchants Bank of Mobile, 17 Ala. 761; Contrà, Lindell *v.* Benton, 6 Misso. 361.

8 Rankin *v.* Sherwood, 31 Maine, 509.

common law, in this particular, is, however, usually modified by charter or statute.[1] It is a legitimate and proper exercise of legislative power to provide by law for the preservation of the property of a corporation for the benefit of its creditors, by remitting the penalties which attach to a judgment of forfeiture of its charter; and such legislation does not impair the obligation of the contracts of debtors of the bank, although they became such prior to it, and is, in all respects, constitutional.[2] Where a corporation, whose charter was declared forfeited by proclamation of the governor under an act of the legislature for not paying specie, was permitted by the act "to retain and use its corporate name for the purpose of winding up and liquidating its affairs, and for no other purpose whatever," this clause was held to continue to it all remedies for the collection of its debts.[3] Upon the repeal of the charter of a joint-stock corporation, the effects of the corporation are usually vested in trustees, for the collection of its debts and the division of its property and effects amongst the stockholders, after payment of its debts and the expenses of the trust. In such case, the right of a stockholder to pass a *legal* title to his stock ceases upon the dissolution of the corporation, and his interest is reduced to a mere equitable right to his distributive share of the funds of the corporation, which he may assign, subject to all claims which the corporation has against him. In the division, he is to be charged with all debts due from him to the corporation, and his assignee, becoming such after the dissolution, takes his interest in the corporate funds subject to this burden; and if such assignee or purchaser be a debtor of the corporation, the distributive share purchased or assigned becomes subject to *his* debts to the corporation, and remains so as against *his* assignee.[4]

§ 779 *a.* The rule of the common law, in relation to the effect of dis-

---

[1] 2 Kent, Com. 307, 308; Ingraham *v.* Terry, 11 Humph. 572.

[2] Nevitt *v.* Bank of Port Gibson, 6 Smedes & M. 513; Commercial Bank of Natchez *v.* Chambers, 8 Smedes & M. 9.

[3] Campbell *v.* Mississippi Bank, 6 How. Miss. 674. See Nevitt *v.* Bank of Port Gibson, 6 Smedes & M. 513; Commercial Bank of Natchez *v.* Chambers, 8 Smedes & M. 9; State of Mississippi *v.* Commercial and Railroad Bank, 12 Smedes & M. 276; Grand Gulf Bank *v.* Wood, id. 482; Grand Gulf Bank *v.* Jeffers, id. 486; Bacon *v.* Cohea, id. 516; Robertson *v.* Hay, id. 566; Chew *v.* Peale, id. 700; Lewis *v.* Robertson, 13 id. 558; for the effect in this and other respects of the Mississippi act of 1843; and see *supra.* Ch. XXI. and see Nashville Bank *v.* Petway, 3 Humph. 522; Ferguson *v.* Miners & Man. Bk. 3 Sneed, 609.

[4] James *v.* Woodruff, 10 Paige, 541, 2 Denio, 574.

solution upon the property and debts of a corporation, has in fact become obsolete and odious. Practically, it has never been applied, in England, to insolvent or dissolved moneyed corporations; and in this country its unjust operation upon the rights of both creditors and stockholders of this class of corporations, is almost invariably arrested by general or special statute provisions. Indeed, at this day it may well be doubted whether, in the view at least of a Court of Equity, it has any application to other than public and eleemosynary corporations, with which it had its origin. The sound doctrine of equity is, that the capital or property and debts due to banking, trading, and other moneyed corporations, constitute a trust fund, pledged to the payment of the dues of creditors and stockholders; and that a Court of Equity will lay hold of this fund, into whosoever hands it may pass, and collect and apply it to the purposes of the trust. This strong equity is emphatically declared by the Supreme Court of the United States, in an important case recently decided by that court; and, with the non-applicability of the old common-law rule to the case of dissolved joint-stock trading and moneyed corporations, forms in part the ground upon which equitable aid was given to the creditors of a State bank, against the State itself, as a stockholder, and the sole stockholder thereof. Accordingly, in the judgment of that court, a statute distributing the property of an insolvent trading or banking corporation amongst its stockholders, or giving it to a stranger, or seizing it to the use of the State, would as clearly impair the obligation of its contracts, as a law, giving to heirs the effects of a deceased natural person to the exclusion of his creditors, would impair the obligation of his contracts.[1] It is obvious that such a conclusion could not be arrived at, except upon the notion that such a statute did not administer the rule of law prevalent when the contracts of the dissolved corporation were made or its debts incurred, but created a new, and therefore, being in derogation of the obligation of such contracts, an unconstitutional rule.

In a recent case in New York, it was held, that where a company incorporated by a foreign government, had been partially dissolved by that government, but the decree of dissolution declared that the company should be considered in existence for certain specified purposes, an injunction would not be granted and a receiver appointed, the corpo-

---

[1] Curran *v.* State of Arkansas, 15 How. 312; 2 Kent, Com. 307, n. a; and see Hightower *v.* Thornton, 8 Ga. 493; Bacon *v.* Robertson, 18 How. 480.

ration holding property in New York over which the foreign government had no jurisdiction, and it appearing for the best interest of all concerned that the relief prayed for should not be granted.[1] The appointment of a receiver of an insolvent corporation takes effect from the time of granting an order of reference therefor, and from that time no act can be done affecting the property of the corporation either by the corporation or its creditors.[2] A receiver takes merely the same rights which the corporation had, and the liabilities of third parties to the corporation are not increased by the appointment of one.[3]

§ 780. Where a corporation has been dissolved, in England, the king may, either by grant,[4] or by proclamation under the great seal,[5] revive or renovate the old corporation, or by grant or charter create a new one in its place.[6] And the old corporation may be revived with the old or new set of corporators; and at the same time new powers may be superadded.[7] If the old corporation be revived, all its rights and responsibilities are of course revived with it; but if the grant operate as a new creation, the new corporation cannot be subject to the liabilities nor possess the rights of the old.[8] An authorized merger of the rights of the old corporation in the new one, by legislative act, is not such a dissolution of the corporation, as to throw back the real estate of the former upon the grantors,[9] or to free the corporation from an obligation to pay its debts.[10] It may become therefore a question of great practical importance, whether the charter be one of revival merely, or a charter of new incorporation. This is not to be determined by the collateral facts, that the name of both corporations, the new and the old,

---

1 Hamilton *v.* Accessory Transit Co. 26 Barb. 46.

2 *In re* Berry, 26 Barb. 55.

3 Lincoln *v.* Fitch, 42 Me. 456.

4 Rex *v.* Grey, 8 Mod. 361, 362; Rex *v.* Pasmore, 3 T. R. 199.

5 Newling *v.* Francis, 3 T. R. 189, 197, 198, 199.

6 Colchester *v.* Seaber, 3 Burr. 1870, 1 W. Bl. 591; Rex *v.* Pasmore, 3 T. R. 242; Rex *v.* Amery, 2 T. R. 569; Scarboro' *v.* Butler, 3 Lev. 387; Luttrel's case, 4 Co. 87; Lincoln & Kennebec Bank *v.* Richardson, 1 Greenl. 79; President and Selectmen of Port Gibson *v.* Moore, 13 Smedes & M. 157; 2 Kyd on Corp. 516.

7 Rex *v.* Pasmore, 3 T. R. 241, per Kenyon, C. J.

8 Colchester *v.* Seaber, 3 Burr. 1866; Scarboro' *v.* Butler, 3 Lev. 287; Rex *v.* Pasmore, 3 T. R. 241, 242, 246; Luttrel's case, 4 Co. 87; Bellows *v.* President, &c. of the Hallowell & Augusta Bank, 2 Mason, 43, per Story, J.; Union Canal Co. *v.* Young, 1 Whart. 410; and see Smith *v.* Morse, 2 Calif. 524, 554.

9 Union Canal Co. *v.* Young, 1 Whart. 410.

10 Hopkins *v.* Swansea Corporation, 4 M. & W. 621.

that the officers and a majority of the members, are the same, and that the business of the old corporation was for a time done, and its debts paid, by the new one. It is certainly true, says Mr. Justice Story, that a corporation may retain its personal identity, although its members are perpetually changing; for it is its artificial character, powers, and franchises, and not the natural character of its members, which constitute that identity. And for the same reason corporations may be different, although the names, the officers, and the members of each are the same. "To ascertain whether a charter creates a new corporation, or merely continues the existence of an old one, we must look to its terms, and give them a construction consistent with the legislative intent and the intent of the corporators."[1] Upon the ground of the intent of the corporators, where a religious society, incorporated under a general act, having mislaid their certificate of incorporation, elected new trustees for the purpose of incorporation, and filed a new certificate — the purpose of the new election and certificate being to preserve the old corporation, and not to change or dissolve it — this proceeding was decided to operate merely a continuance of the old corporation.[2] The distinction between the creation of a new and the continuance of an old corporation was taken by the Supreme Court of Illinois, in a very important case arising under the constitution of that State. The Bank of Illinois had been incorporated in 1816, by the territorial government, to continue for a limited number of years, and in the State constitution subsequently adopted, it was provided, "that there shall be no other banks or moneyed institutions in this State, but those already provided by law, except a State bank and its branches, which may be established and regulated by the general assembly of the State, as they may think proper." After the adoption of the constitution and previous to the expiry of the charter of the bank, the general assembly, by an act passed in 1835, extended the duration of the charter for a period of twenty years, and in 1837 increased the capital stock of the bank, and gave it authority to establish branches. The court decided, two of the judges dissenting, that the acts of 1835 and 1837 were no infringements of the above clause of the constitution of Illinois, upon the ground that the clause did not inhibit the continuance of the old banks or the

---

[1] Bellows *v.* President, &c. of the Hallowell & Augusta Bank, 2 Mason, 43, 44; Wyman *v.* Hallowell & Augusta Bank, 14 Mass. 58; and see Rex *v.* Pasmore, 3 T. R. 241, 242, 247, 248, 249.

[2] Miller *v.* English, 1 N. J. 317.

increase of their capitals; arguing, that the distinction between the creation of a new and the continuance and increase of powers of an old corporation must have been well known to the convention, and was probably kept in view in the wording of the prohibitory clause.[1] In a late case in New Hampshire it has been held, that where a corporation whose recent deed has been relied on, has become dormant by lapse of time, its reorganization must be shown, and the burden is on the party relying on it to show that all the requirements of the statutes were complied with in such reorganization, and that the proceedings were regular in every respect.[2]

---

1 People *v.* Marshall, 1 Gilman, 672.
2 Goulding *v.* Clark, 34 N. H. 148.

INDEX.

[The references are to the Sections.]

A.

B.

I.

J.

L.

M.

Q.

R.

W.

www.ingramcontent.com/pod-product-compliance
Lightning Source LLC
LaVergne TN
LVHW100021220926
848483LV00002BA/264
* 9 7 8 1 5 8 4 7 7 4 7 3 0 *